American Casebook Series
Hornbook Series and Basic Legal Texts
Black Letter Series and Nutshell Series

of

WEST PUBLISHING COMPANY
P.O. Box 64526
St. Paul, Minnesota 55164–0526

Accounting

FARIS' ACCOUNTING AND LAW IN A NUT-SHELL, 377 pages, 1984. Softcover. (Text)

FIFLIS' ACCOUNTING ISSUES FOR LAWYERS, TEACHING MATERIALS, Fourth Edition, 706 pages, 1991. Teacher's Manual available. (Casebook)

SIEGEL AND SIEGEL'S ACCOUNTING AND FINANCIAL DISCLOSURE: A GUIDE TO BASIC CONCEPTS, 259 pages, 1983. Softcover. (Text)

Administrative Law

AMAN AND MAYTON'S HORNBOOK ON ADMINISTRATIVE LAW, Approximately 750 pages, 1993. (Text)

BONFIELD AND ASIMOW'S STATE AND FEDERAL ADMINISTRATIVE LAW, 826 pages, 1989. Teacher's Manual available. (Casebook)

GELLHORN AND LEVIN'S ADMINISTRATIVE LAW AND PROCESS IN A NUTSHELL, Third Edition, 479 pages, 1990. Softcover. (Text)

MASHAW, MERRILL, AND SHANE'S CASES AND MATERIALS ON ADMINISTRATIVE LAW—THE AMERICAN PUBLIC LAW SYSTEM, Third Edition, 1187 pages, 1992. (Casebook)

ROBINSON, GELLHORN AND BRUFF'S THE ADMINISTRATIVE PROCESS, Third Edition, 978 pages, 1986. (Casebook)

Admiralty

HEALY AND SHARPE'S CASES AND MATERIALS ON ADMIRALTY, Second Edition, 876 pages, 1986. (Casebook)

MARAIST'S ADMIRALTY IN A NUTSHELL, Sec-

ond Edition, 379 pages, 1988. Softcover. (Text)

SCHOENBAUM'S HORNBOOK ON ADMIRALTY AND MARITIME LAW, Student Edition, 692 pages, 1987 with 1992 pocket part. (Text)

Agency—Partnership

DEMOTT'S FIDUCIARY OBLIGATION, AGENCY AND PARTNERSHIP: DUTIES IN ONGOING BUSINESS RELATIONSHIPS, 740 pages, 1991. Teacher's Manual available. (Casebook)

FESSLER'S ALTERNATIVES TO INCORPORATION FOR PERSONS IN QUEST OF PROFIT, Third Edition, 339 pages, 1991. Softcover. (Casebook)

HENN'S CASES AND MATERIALS ON AGENCY, PARTNERSHIP AND OTHER UNINCORPORATED BUSINESS ENTERPRISES, Second Edition, 733 pages, 1985. Teacher's Manual available. (Casebook)

REUSCHLEIN AND GREGORY'S HORNBOOK ON THE LAW OF AGENCY AND PARTNERSHIP, Second Edition, 683 pages, 1990. (Text)

SELECTED CORPORATION AND PARTNERSHIP STATUTES, RULES AND FORMS. Softcover. Revised 1991 Edition, 953 pages.

STEFFEN AND KERR'S CASES ON AGENCY-PARTNERSHIP, Fourth Edition, 859 pages, 1980. (Casebook)

STEFFEN'S AGENCY-PARTNERSHIP IN A NUTSHELL, 364 pages, 1977. Softcover. (Text)

Agricultural Law

MEYER, PEDERSEN, THORSON AND DAVIDSON'S AGRICULTURAL LAW: CASES AND MATERIALS, 931 pages, 1985. Teacher's Manual avail-

Agricultural Law—Cont'd
able. (Casebook)

Alternative Dispute Resolution
KANOWITZ' CASES AND MATERIALS ON ALTERNATIVE DISPUTE RESOLUTION, 1024 pages, 1986. Teacher's Manual available. (Casebook) 1990 Supplement.

NOLAN–HALEY'S ALTERNATIVE DISPUTE RESOLUTION IN A NUTSHELL, 298 pages, 1992. Softcover. (Text)

RISKIN AND WESTBROOK'S DISPUTE RESOLUTION AND LAWYERS, 468 pages, 1987. Teacher's Manual available. (Casebook)

RISKIN AND WESTBROOK'S DISPUTE RESOLUTION AND LAWYERS, Abridged Edition, 223 pages, 1987. Softcover. Teacher's Manual available. (Casebook)

RISKIN'S DISPUTE RESOLUTION FOR LAWYERS VIDEO TAPES, 1992. (Available for purchase by schools and libraries.)

American Indian Law
CANBY'S AMERICAN INDIAN LAW IN A NUTSHELL, Second Edition, 336 pages, 1988. Softcover. (Text)

GETCHES AND WILKINSON'S CASES AND MATERIALS ON FEDERAL INDIAN LAW, Second Edition, 880 pages, 1986. (Casebook)

Antitrust—see also Regulated Industries, Trade Regulation
BARNES AND STOUT'S ECONOMIC FOUNDATIONS OF REGULATION AND ANTITRUST LAW, 102 pages, 1992. Softcover. Teacher's Manual available. (Casebook)

FOX AND SULLIVAN'S CASES AND MATERIALS ON ANTITRUST, 935 pages, 1989. Teacher's Manual available. (Casebook) 1993 Supplement.

GELLHORN'S ANTITRUST LAW AND ECONOMICS IN A NUTSHELL, Third Edition, 472 pages, 1986. Softcover. (Text)

HOVENKAMP'S BLACK LETTER ON ANTITRUST, Second Edition approximately 325 pages, April 1993 Pub. Softcover. (Review)

HOVENKAMP'S HORNBOOK ON ECONOMICS AND FEDERAL ANTITRUST LAW, Student Edition, 414 pages, 1985. (Text)

POSNER AND EASTERBROOK'S CASES AND ECONOMIC NOTES ON ANTITRUST, Second Edi-

tion, 1077 pages, 1981. (Casebook) 1984–85 Supplement.

SULLIVAN'S HORNBOOK OF THE LAW OF ANTITRUST, 886 pages, 1977. (Text)

Appellate Advocacy—see Trial and Appellate Advocacy

Architecture and Engineering Law
SWEET'S LEGAL ASPECTS OF ARCHITECTURE, ENGINEERING AND THE CONSTRUCTION PROCESS, Fourth Edition, 889 pages, 1989. Teacher's Manual available. (Casebook)

Art Law
DUBOFF'S ART LAW IN A NUTSHELL, Second Edition, approximately 325 pages, 1993. Softcover. (Text)

Banking Law
BANKING LAW: SELECTED STATUTES AND REGULATIONS. Softcover. 263 pages, 1991.

LOVETT'S BANKING AND FINANCIAL INSTITUTIONS LAW IN A NUTSHELL, Third Edition, 470 pages, 1992. Softcover. (Text)

SYMONS AND WHITE'S BANKING LAW: TEACHING MATERIALS, Third Edition, 818 pages, 1991. Teacher's Manual available. (Casebook)

Statutory Supplement. *See Banking Law: Selected Statutes*

Bankruptcy—see Creditors' Rights

Business Planning—see also Corporate Finance
PAINTER'S PROBLEMS AND MATERIALS IN BUSINESS PLANNING, Second Edition, 1008 pages, 1984. (Casebook) 1990 Supplement.

Statutory Supplement. *See Selected Corporation and Partnership*

Civil Procedure—see also Federal Jurisdiction and Procedure
AMERICAN BAR ASSOCIATION SECTION OF LITIGATION—READINGS ON ADVERSARIAL JUSTICE: THE AMERICAN APPROACH TO ADJUDICATION, 217 pages, 1988. Softcover. (Coursebook)

CLERMONT'S BLACK LETTER ON CIVIL PROCEDURE, Third Edition, approximately 350 pages, May, 1993 Pub. Softcover. (Review)

COUND, FRIEDENTHAL, MILLER AND SEXTON'S

Civil Procedure—Cont'd

CASES AND MATERIALS ON CIVIL PROCEDURE, Fifth Edition, 1284 pages, 1989. Teacher's Manual available. (Casebook)

COUND, FRIEDENTHAL, MILLER AND SEXTON'S CIVIL PROCEDURE SUPPLEMENT. 476 pages, 1991. Softcover. (Casebook Supplement)

FEDERAL RULES OF CIVIL PROCEDURE—EDUCATIONAL EDITION. Softcover. 761 pages, 1992.

FRIEDENTHAL, KANE AND MILLER'S HORNBOOK ON CIVIL PROCEDURE, Second Edition, approximately 1000 pages, May 1993 Pub. (Text)

KANE AND LEVINE'S CIVIL PROCEDURE IN CALIFORNIA: STATE AND FEDERAL 1992 Edition, 551 pages. Softcover. (Casebook Supplement)

KANE'S CIVIL PROCEDURE IN A NUTSHELL, Third Edition, 303 pages, 1991. Softcover. (Text)

KOFFLER AND REPPY'S HORNBOOK ON COMMON LAW PLEADING, 663 pages, 1969. (Text)

LEVINE, SLOMANSON AND WINGATE'S CALIFORNIA CIVIL PROCEDURE, CASES AND MATERIALS, 546 pages, 1991. Teacher's Manual available. (Casebook)

MARCUS, REDISH AND SHERMAN'S CIVIL PROCEDURE: A MODERN APPROACH, 1027 pages, 1989. Teacher's Manual available. (Casebook) 1991 Supplement.

MARCUS AND SHERMAN'S COMPLEX LITIGATION—CASES AND MATERIALS ON ADVANCED CIVIL PROCEDURE, Second Edition, 1035 pages, 1992. Teacher's Manual available. (Casebook)

PARK AND McFARLAND'S COMPUTER-AIDED EXERCISES ON CIVIL PROCEDURE, Third Edition, 210 pages, 1991. Softcover. (Coursebook)

SIEGEL'S HORNBOOK ON NEW YORK PRACTICE, Second Edition, Student Edition, 1068 pages, 1991. Softcover. (Text) 1992 Supplemental Pamphlet.

SLOMANSON AND WINGATE'S CALIFORNIA CIVIL PROCEDURE IN A NUTSHELL, 230 pages, 1992. Softcover. (Text)

Commercial Law

BAILEY AND HAGEDORN'S SECURED TRANSACTIONS IN A NUTSHELL, Third Edition, 390 pages, 1988. Softcover. (Text)

EPSTEIN, MARTIN, HENNING AND NICKLES' BASIC UNIFORM COMMERCIAL CODE TEACHING MATERIALS, Third Edition, 704 pages, 1988. Teacher's Manual available. (Casebook)

HENSON'S HORNBOOK ON SECURED TRANSACTIONS UNDER THE U.C.C., Second Edition, 504 pages, 1979, with 1979 pocket part. (Text)

MEYER AND SPEIDEL'S BLACK LETTER ON SALES AND LEASES OF GOODS, Approximately 300 pages, 1993. Softcover. (Review)

NICKLES' BLACK LETTER ON COMMERCIAL PAPER, 450 pages, 1988. Softcover. (Review)

NICKLES, MATHESON AND DOLAN'S MATERIALS FOR UNDERSTANDING CREDIT AND PAYMENT SYSTEMS, 923 pages, 1987. Teacher's Manual available. (Casebook)

NORDSTROM, MURRAY AND CLOVIS' PROBLEMS AND MATERIALS ON SALES, 515 pages, 1982. (Casebook)

NORDSTROM, MURRAY AND CLOVIS' PROBLEMS AND MATERIALS ON SECURED TRANSACTIONS, 594 pages, 1987. (Casebook)

RUBIN AND COOTER'S THE PAYMENT SYSTEM: CASES, MATERIALS AND ISSUES, 885 pages, 1989. Teacher's Manual Available. (Casebook)

SELECTED COMMERCIAL STATUTES. Softcover. 1897 pages, 1992.

SPEIDEL, SUMMERS AND WHITE'S COMMERCIAL LAW: TEACHING MATERIALS, Fourth Edition, 1448 pages, 1987. Teacher's Manual available. (Casebook)

SPEIDEL, SUMMERS AND WHITE'S COMMERCIAL PAPER: TEACHING MATERIALS, Fourth Edition, 578 pages, 1987. Reprint from Speidel et al., Commercial Law, Fourth Edition. Teacher's Manual available. (Casebook)

SPEIDEL, SUMMERS AND WHITE'S SALES: TEACHING MATERIALS, Fourth Edition, 804 pages, 1987. Reprint from Speidel et al., Commercial Law, Fourth Edition. Teacher's Manual available. (Casebook)

SPEIDEL, SUMMERS AND WHITE'S SECURED

Commercial Law—Cont'd

TRANSACTIONS: TEACHING MATERIALS, Fourth Edition, 485 pages, 1987. Reprint from Speidel et al., Commercial Law, Fourth Edition. Teacher's Manual available. (Casebook)

STOCKTON AND MILLER'S SALES AND LEASES OF GOODS IN A NUTSHELL, Third Edition, 441 pages, 1992. Softcover. (Text)

STONE'S UNIFORM COMMERCIAL CODE IN A NUTSHELL, Third Edition, 580 pages, 1989. Softcover. (Text)

WEBER AND SPEIDEL'S COMMERCIAL PAPER IN A NUTSHELL, Third Edition, 404 pages, 1982. Softcover. (Text)

WHITE AND SUMMERS' HORNBOOK ON THE UNIFORM COMMERCIAL CODE, Third Edition, Student Edition, 1386 pages, 1988. (Text)

Community Property

MENNELL AND BOYKOFF'S COMMUNITY PROPERTY IN A NUTSHELL, Second Edition, 432 pages, 1988. Softcover. (Text)

VERRALL AND BIRD'S CASES AND MATERIALS ON CALIFORNIA COMMUNITY PROPERTY, Fifth Edition, 604 pages, 1988. (Casebook)

Comparative Law

BARTON, GIBBS, LI AND MERRYMAN'S LAW IN RADICALLY DIFFERENT CULTURES, 960 pages, 1983. (Casebook)

FOLSOM, MINAN AND OTTO'S LAW AND POLITICS IN THE PEOPLE'S REPUBLIC OF CHINA IN A NUTSHELL, 451 pages, 1992. Softcover. (Text)

GLENDON, GORDON AND OSAKWE'S COMPARATIVE LEGAL TRADITIONS: TEXT, MATERIALS AND CASES ON THE CIVIL LAW, COMMON LAW AND SOCIALIST LAW TRADITIONS, 1091 pages, 1985. (Casebook)

GLENDON, GORDON AND OSAKWE'S COMPARATIVE LEGAL TRADITIONS IN A NUTSHELL. 402 pages, 1982. Softcover. (Text)

Computers and Law

MAGGS, SOMA AND SPROWL'S COMPUTER LAW—CASES, COMMENTS, AND QUESTIONS, 731 pages, 1992. Teacher's Manual available. (Casebook)

MAGGS AND SPROWL'S COMPUTER APPLICATIONS IN THE LAW, 316 pages, 1987. (Coursebook)

MASON'S USING COMPUTERS IN THE LAW: AN INTRODUCTION AND PRACTICAL GUIDE, Second Edition, 288 pages, 1988. Softcover. (Coursebook)

Conflict of Laws

CRAMTON, CURRIE AND KAY'S CASES–COMMENTS–QUESTIONS ON CONFLICT OF LAWS, Fourth Edition, 876 pages, 1987. (Casebook)

HAY'S BLACK LETTER ON CONFLICT OF LAWS, 330 pages, 1989. Softcover. (Review)

SCOLES AND HAY'S HORNBOOK ON CONFLICT OF LAWS, Student Edition, 1160 pages, 1992. (Text)

SIEGEL'S CONFLICTS IN A NUTSHELL, 470 pages, 1982. Softcover. (Text)

Constitutional Law—Civil Rights—see also First Amendment and Foreign Relations and National Security Law

ABERNATHY'S CIVIL RIGHTS AND CONSTITUTIONAL LITIGATION, CASES AND MATERIALS, Second Edition, 753 pages, 1992. (Casebook)

BARNES AND STOUT'S THE ECONOMICS OF CONSTITUTIONAL LAW AND PUBLIC CHOICE, 127 pages, 1992. Softcover. Teacher's Manual available. (Casebook)

BARRON AND DIENES' BLACK LETTER ON CONSTITUTIONAL LAW, Third Edition, 440 pages, 1991. Softcover. (Review)

BARRON AND DIENES' CONSTITUTIONAL LAW IN A NUTSHELL, Second Edition, 483 pages, 1991. Softcover. (Text)

ENGDAHL'S CONSTITUTIONAL FEDERALISM IN A NUTSHELL, Second Edition, 411 pages, 1987. Softcover. (Text)

FARBER AND SHERRY'S HISTORY OF THE AMERICAN CONSTITUTION, 458 pages, 1990. Softcover. Teacher's Manual available. (Text)

FISHER AND DEVINS' POLITICAL DYNAMICS OF CONSTITUTIONAL LAW, 333 pages, 1992. Softcover. (Casebook Supplement)

GARVEY AND ALEINIKOFF'S MODERN CONSTITUTIONAL THEORY: A READER, Second Edition, 559 pages, 1991. Softcover. (Reader)

LOCKHART, KAMISAR, CHOPER AND SHIFFRIN'S CONSTITUTIONAL LAW: CASES–COMMENTS–QUESTIONS, Seventh Edition, 1643 pages,

Constitutional Law—Civil Rights—Cont'd
1991. (Casebook) 1992 Supplement.

LOCKHART, KAMISAR, CHOPER AND SHIFFRIN'S THE AMERICAN CONSTITUTION: CASES AND MATERIALS, Seventh Edition, 1255 pages, 1991. Abridged version of Lockhart, et al., Constitutional Law: Cases–Comments–Questions, Seventh Edition. (Casebook) 1992 Supplement.

LOCKHART, KAMISAR, CHOPER AND SHIFFRIN'S CONSTITUTIONAL RIGHTS AND LIBERTIES: CASES AND MATERIALS, Seventh Edition, 1333 pages, 1991. Reprint from Lockhart, et al., Constitutional Law: Cases–Comments–Questions, Seventh Edition. (Casebook) 1992 Supplement.

MARKS AND COOPER'S STATE CONSTITUTIONAL LAW IN A NUTSHELL, 329 pages, 1988. Softcover. (Text)

NOWAK AND ROTUNDA'S HORNBOOK ON CONSTITUTIONAL LAW, Fourth Edition, 1357 pages, 1991. (Text)

ROTUNDA'S MODERN CONSTITUTIONAL LAW: CASES AND NOTES, Fourth Edition, approximately 1100 pages, April, 1993 Pub. (Casebook)

VIEIRA'S CONSTITUTIONAL CIVIL RIGHTS IN A NUTSHELL, Second Edition, 322 pages, 1990. Softcover. (Text)

WILLIAMS' CONSTITUTIONAL ANALYSIS IN A NUTSHELL, 388 pages, 1979. Softcover. (Text)

Consumer Law—see also Commercial Law
EPSTEIN AND NICKLES' CONSUMER LAW IN A NUTSHELL, Second Edition, 418 pages, 1981. Softcover. (Text)

SELECTED COMMERCIAL STATUTES. Softcover. 1897 pages, 1992.

SPANOGLE, ROHNER, PRIDGEN AND RASOR'S CASES AND MATERIALS ON CONSUMER LAW, Second Edition, 916 pages, 1991. Teacher's Manual available. (Casebook)

Contracts
BARNES AND STOUT'S THE ECONOMICS OF CONTRACT LAW, 127 pages, 1992. Softcover. Teacher's Manual available. (Casebook)

CALAMARI AND PERILLO'S BLACK LETTER ON CONTRACTS, Second Edition, 462 pages, 1990. Softcover. (Review)

CALAMARI AND PERILLO'S HORNBOOK ON CONTRACTS, Third Edition, 1049 pages, 1987. (Text)

CALAMARI, PERILLO AND BENDER'S CASES AND PROBLEMS ON CONTRACTS, Second Edition, 905 pages, 1989. Teacher's Manual Available. (Casebook)

CORBIN'S TEXT ON CONTRACTS, One Volume Student Edition, 1224 pages, 1952. (Text)

FESSLER AND LOISEAUX'S CASES AND MATERIALS ON CONTRACTS—MORALITY, ECONOMICS AND THE MARKET PLACE, 837 pages, 1982. Teacher's Manual available. (Casebook)

FRIEDMAN'S CONTRACT REMEDIES IN A NUTSHELL, 323 pages, 1981. Softcover. (Text)

FULLER AND EISENBERG'S CASES ON BASIC CONTRACT LAW, Fifth Edition, 1037 pages, 1990. (Casebook)

HAMILTON, RAU AND WEINTRAUB'S CASES AND MATERIALS ON CONTRACTS, Second Edition, 916 pages, 1992. Teacher's Manual available. (Casebook)

KEYES' GOVERNMENT CONTRACTS IN A NUTSHELL, Second Edition, 557 pages, 1990. Softcover. (Text)

SCHABER AND ROHWER'S CONTRACTS IN A NUTSHELL, Third Edition, 457 pages, 1990. Softcover. (Text)

SUMMERS AND HILLMAN'S CONTRACT AND RELATED OBLIGATION: THEORY, DOCTRINE AND PRACTICE, Second Edition, 1037 pages, 1992. Teacher's Manual available. (Casebook)

Copyright—see Patent and Copyright Law

Corporate Finance—see also Business Planning
HAMILTON'S CASES AND MATERIALS ON CORPORATION FINANCE, Second Edition, 1221 pages, 1989. (Casebook)

OESTERLE'S THE LAW OF MERGERS, ACQUISITIONS AND REORGANIZATIONS, 1096 pages, 1991. (Casebook) 1992 Supplement.

Corporations
HAMILTON'S BLACK LETTER ON CORPORATIONS, Third Edition, 732 pages, 1992. Softcover. (Review)

HAMILTON'S CASES AND MATERIALS ON CORPORATIONS—INCLUDING PARTNERSHIPS AND

Corporations—Cont'd

LIMITED PARTNERSHIPS, Fourth Edition, 1248 pages, 1990. Teacher's Manual available. (Casebook) 1990 Statutory Supplement.

HAMILTON'S THE LAW OF CORPORATIONS IN A NUTSHELL, Third Edition, 518 pages, 1991. Softcover. (Text)

HENN'S TEACHING MATERIALS ON THE LAW OF CORPORATIONS, Second Edition, 1204 pages, 1986. Teacher's Manual available. (Casebook)

> Statutory Supplement. *See Selected Corporation and Partnership*

HENN AND ALEXANDER'S HORNBOOK ON LAWS OF CORPORATIONS, Third Edition, Student Edition, 1371 pages, 1983, with 1986 pocket part. (Text)

SELECTED CORPORATION AND PARTNERSHIP STATUTES, RULES AND FORMS. Revised 1991 Edition, 953 pages. Softcover.

SOLOMON, SCHWARTZ AND BAUMAN'S MATERIALS AND PROBLEMS ON CORPORATIONS: LAW AND POLICY, Second Edition, 1391 pages, 1988. Teacher's Manual available. (Casebook) 1992 Supplement.

> Statutory Supplement. *See Selected Corporation and Partnership*

Corrections

KRANTZ' THE LAW OF CORRECTIONS AND PRISONERS' RIGHTS IN A NUTSHELL, Third Edition, 407 pages, 1988. Softcover. (Text)

KRANTZ AND BRANHAM'S CASES AND MATERIALS ON THE LAW OF SENTENCING, CORRECTIONS AND PRISONERS' RIGHTS, Fourth Edition, 619 pages, 1991. Teacher's Manual available. (Casebook)

Creditors' Rights

BANKRUPTCY CODE, RULES AND OFFICIAL FORMS, LAW SCHOOL EDITION. 910 pages, 1992. Softcover.

EPSTEIN'S DEBTOR-CREDITOR LAW IN A NUTSHELL, Fourth Edition, 401 pages, 1991. Softcover. (Text)

EPSTEIN, LANDERS AND NICKLES' CASES AND MATERIALS ON DEBTORS AND CREDITORS, Third Edition, 1059 pages, 1987. Teacher's Manual available. (Casebook)

EPSTEIN, NICKLES AND WHITE'S HORNBOOK

ON BANKRUPTCY, Approximately 1000 pages, January, 1992 Pub. (Text)

LoPUCKI'S PLAYER'S MANUAL FOR THE DEBTOR-CREDITOR GAME, 123 pages, 1985. Softcover. (Coursebook)

NICKLES AND EPSTEIN'S BLACK LETTER ON CREDITORS' RIGHTS AND BANKRUPTCY, 576 pages, 1989. (Review)

RIESENFELD'S CASES AND MATERIALS ON CREDITORS' REMEDIES AND DEBTORS' PROTECTION, Fourth Edition, 914 pages, 1987. (Casebook) 1990 Supplement.

WHITE AND NIMMER'S CASES AND MATERIALS ON BANKRUPTCY, Second Edition, 764 pages, 1992. Teacher's Manual available. (Casebook)

Criminal Law and Criminal Procedure—see also Corrections, Juvenile Justice

ABRAMS' FEDERAL CRIMINAL LAW AND ITS ENFORCEMENT, 866 pages, 1986. (Casebook) 1988 Supplement.

BUCY'S WHITE COLLAR CRIME, CASES AND MATERIALS, 688 pages, 1992. Teacher's Manual available. (Casebook)

DIX AND SHARLOT'S CASES AND MATERIALS ON CRIMINAL LAW, Third Edition, 846 pages, 1987. (Casebook)

GRANO'S PROBLEMS IN CRIMINAL PROCEDURE, Second Edition, 176 pages, 1981. Teacher's Manual available. Softcover. (Coursebook)

HEYMANN AND KENETY'S THE MURDER TRIAL OF WILBUR JACKSON: A HOMICIDE IN THE FAMILY, Second Edition, 347 pages, 1985. (Coursebook)

ISRAEL, KAMISAR AND LaFAVE'S CRIMINAL PROCEDURE AND THE CONSTITUTION: LEADING SUPREME COURT CASES AND INTRODUCTORY TEXT. 802 pages, 1992 Edition. Softcover. (Casebook)

ISRAEL AND LaFAVE'S CRIMINAL PROCEDURE—CONSTITUTIONAL LIMITATIONS IN A NUTSHELL, Fourth Edition, 461 pages, 1988. Softcover. (Text)

JOHNSON'S CASES, MATERIALS AND TEXT ON CRIMINAL LAW, Fourth Edition, 759 pages, 1990. Teacher's Manual available. (Casebook)

JOHNSON'S CASES AND MATERIALS ON CRIMI-

Criminal Law and Criminal Procedure—Cont'd

NAL PROCEDURE, 859 pages, 1988. (Casebook) 1992 Supplement.

KAMISAR, LaFAVE AND ISRAEL'S MODERN CRIMINAL PROCEDURE: CASES, COMMENTS AND QUESTIONS, Seventh Edition, 1593 pages, 1990. (Casebook) 1992 Supplement.

KAMISAR, LaFAVE AND ISRAEL'S BASIC CRIMINAL PROCEDURE: CASES, COMMENTS AND QUESTIONS, Seventh Edition, 792 pages, 1990. Softcover reprint from Kamisar, et al., Modern Criminal Procedure: Cases, Comments and Questions, Seventh Edition. (Casebook) 1992 Supplement.

LaFAVE'S MODERN CRIMINAL LAW: CASES, COMMENTS AND QUESTIONS, Second Edition, 903 pages, 1988. (Casebook)

LaFAVE AND ISRAEL'S HORNBOOK ON CRIMINAL PROCEDURE, Second Edition, 1309 pages, 1992 with 1992 pocket part. (Text)

LaFAVE AND SCOTT'S HORNBOOK ON CRIMINAL LAW, Second Edition, 918 pages, 1986. (Text)

LOEWY'S CRIMINAL LAW IN A NUTSHELL, Second Edition, 321 pages, 1987. Softcover. (Text)

LOW'S BLACK LETTER ON CRIMINAL LAW, Revised First Edition, 443 pages, 1990. Softcover. (Review)

SALTZBURG AND CAPRA'S CASES AND COMMENTARY ON AMERICAN CRIMINAL PROCEDURE, Fourth Edition, 1341 pages, 1992. Teacher's Manual available. (Casebook) 1992 Supplement.

SUBIN, MIRSKY AND WEINSTEIN'S THE CRIMINAL PROCESS: PROSECUTION AND DEFENSE FUNCTIONS, Approximately 450 pages, February, 1993 Pub. Softcover. Teacher's Manual available. (Text)

VORENBERG'S CASES ON CRIMINAL LAW AND PROCEDURE, Second Edition, 1088 pages, 1981. Teacher's Manual available. (Casebook) 1990 Supplement.

Domestic Relations

CLARK'S HORNBOOK ON DOMESTIC RELATIONS, Second Edition, Student Edition, 1050 pages, 1988. (Text)

CLARK AND GLOWINSKY'S CASES AND PROB-

LEMS ON DOMESTIC RELATIONS, Fourth Edition. 1150 pages, 1990. Teacher's Manual available. (Casebook) 1992 Supplement.

KRAUSE'S BLACK LETTER ON FAMILY LAW, 314 pages, 1988. Softcover. (Review)

KRAUSE'S CASES, COMMENTS AND QUESTIONS ON FAMILY LAW, Third Edition, 1433 pages, 1990. (Casebook)

KRAUSE'S FAMILY LAW IN A NUTSHELL, Second Edition, 444 pages, 1986. Softcover. (Text)

KRAUSKOPF'S CASES ON PROPERTY DIVISION AT MARRIAGE DISSOLUTION, 250 pages, 1984. Softcover. (Casebook)

Economics, Law and—see also Antitrust, Regulated Industries

BARNES AND STOUT'S CASES AND MATERIALS ON LAW AND ECONOMICS, 538 pages, 1992. Teacher's Manual available. (Casebook)

GOETZ' CASES AND MATERIALS ON LAW AND ECONOMICS, 547 pages, 1984. (Casebook)

MALLOY'S LAW AND ECONOMICS: A COMPARATIVE APPROACH TO THEORY AND PRACTICE, 166 pages, 1990. Softcover. (Text)

Education Law

ALEXANDER AND ALEXANDER'S PUBLIC SCHOOL LAW, Third Edition, 880 pages, 1992. Teacher's Manual available. (Coursebook)

ALEXANDER AND ALEXANDER'S THE LAW OF SCHOOLS, STUDENTS AND TEACHERS IN A NUTSHELL, 409 pages, 1984. Softcover. (Text)

YUDOF, KIRP AND LEVIN'S EDUCATIONAL POLICY AND THE LAW, Third Edition, 860 pages, 1992. (Casebook)

Employment Discrimination—see also Gender Discrimination

ESTREICHER AND HARPER'S CASES AND MATERIALS ON THE LAW GOVERNING THE EMPLOYMENT RELATIONSHIP, Second Edition, 966 pages, 1992. (Casebook) Statutory Supplement.

JONES, MURPHY AND BELTON'S CASES AND MATERIALS ON DISCRIMINATION IN EMPLOYMENT, (The Labor Law Group). Fifth Edition, 1116 pages, 1987. (Casebook) 1990 Supplement.

PLAYER'S FEDERAL LAW OF EMPLOYMENT DIS-

Employment Discrimination—Cont'd
CRIMINATION IN A NUTSHELL, Third Edition, 338 pages, 1992. Softcover. (Text)

PLAYER'S HORNBOOK ON EMPLOYMENT DISCRIMINATION LAW, Student Edition, 708 pages, 1988. (Text)

PLAYER, SHOBEN AND LIEBERWITZ' CASES AND MATERIALS ON EMPLOYMENT DISCRIMINATION LAW, 827 pages, 1990. Teacher's Manual available. (Casebook) 1992 Supplement.

Energy and Natural Resources Law—see also Oil and Gas
LAITOS' CASES AND MATERIALS ON NATURAL RESOURCES LAW, 938 pages, 1985. Teacher's Manual available. (Casebook)

LAITOS AND TOMAIN'S ENERGY AND NATURAL RESOURCES LAW IN A NUTSHELL, 554 pages, 1992. Softcover. (Text)

SELECTED ENVIRONMENTAL LAW STATUTES—EDUCATIONAL EDITION. Softcover. 1296 pages, 1992.

Environmental Law—see also Energy and Natural Resources Law; Sea, Law of
BONINE AND MCGARITY'S THE LAW OF ENVIRONMENTAL PROTECTION: CASES—LEGISLATION—POLICIES, Second Edition, 1042 pages, 1992. (Casebook)

FINDLEY AND FARBER'S CASES AND MATERIALS ON ENVIRONMENTAL LAW, Third Edition, 763 pages, 1991. Teacher's Manual available. (Casebook)

FINDLEY AND FARBER'S ENVIRONMENTAL LAW IN A NUTSHELL, Third Edition, 355 pages, 1992. Softcover. (Text)

PLATER, ABRAMS AND GOLDFARB'S ENVIRONMENTAL LAW AND POLICY: NATURE, LAW AND SOCIETY, 1039 pages, 1992. Teacher's Manual available. (Casebook)

RODGERS' HORNBOOK ON ENVIRONMENTAL LAW, 956 pages, 1977, with 1984 pocket part. (Text)

SELECTED ENVIRONMENTAL LAW STATUTES—EDUCATIONAL EDITION. Softcover. 1296 pages, 1992.

Equity—see Remedies

Estate Planning—see also Trusts and Estates; Taxation—Estate and Gift
LYNN'S INTRODUCTION TO ESTATE PLANNING

IN A NUTSHELL, Fourth Edition, 352 pages, 1992. Softcover. (Text)

Evidence
BERGMAN'S TRANSCRIPT EXERCISES FOR LEARNING EVIDENCE, 273 pages, 1992. Teacher's Manual available. (Coursebook)

BROUN AND BLAKEY'S BLACK LETTER ON EVIDENCE, 269 pages, 1984. Softcover. (Review)

BROUN, MEISENHOLDER, STRONG AND MOSTELLER'S PROBLEMS IN EVIDENCE, Third Edition, 238 pages, 1988. Teacher's Manual available. Softcover. (Coursebook)

CLEARY, STRONG, BROUN AND MOSTELLER'S CASES AND MATERIALS ON EVIDENCE, Fourth Edition, 1060 pages, 1988. (Casebook)

FEDERAL RULES OF EVIDENCE FOR UNITED STATES COURTS AND MAGISTRATES. Softcover. 549 pages, 1992.

FRIEDMAN'S THE ELEMENTS OF EVIDENCE, 315 pages, 1991. Teacher's Manual available. (Coursebook)

GRAHAM'S FEDERAL RULES OF EVIDENCE IN A NUTSHELL, Third Edition, 486 pages, 1992. Softcover. (Text)

LEMPERT AND SALTZBURG'S A MODERN APPROACH TO EVIDENCE: TEXT, PROBLEMS, TRANSCRIPTS AND CASES, Second Edition, 1232 pages, 1983. Teacher's Manual available. (Casebook)

LILLY'S AN INTRODUCTION TO THE LAW OF EVIDENCE, Second Edition, 585 pages, 1987. (Text)

MCCORMICK, SUTTON AND WELLBORN'S CASES AND MATERIALS ON EVIDENCE, Seventh Edition, 932 pages, 1992. Teacher's Manual available. (Casebook)

MCCORMICK'S HORNBOOK ON EVIDENCE, Fourth Edition, Student Edition, 672 pages, 1992. (Text)

ROTHSTEIN'S EVIDENCE IN A NUTSHELL: STATE AND FEDERAL RULES, Second Edition, 514 pages, 1981. Softcover. (Text)

Federal Jurisdiction and Procedure
CURRIE'S CASES AND MATERIALS ON FEDERAL COURTS, Fourth Edition, 783 pages, 1990. (Casebook)

CURRIE'S FEDERAL JURISDICTION IN A NUTSHELL, Third Edition, 242 pages, 1990.

Federal Jurisdiction and Procedure—Cont'd
Softcover. (Text)

FEDERAL RULES OF CIVIL PROCEDURE—EDUCATIONAL EDITION. Softcover. 761 pages, 1992.

REDISH'S BLACK LETTER ON FEDERAL JURISDICTION, Second Edition, 234 pages, 1991. Softcover. (Review)

REDISH'S CASES, COMMENTS AND QUESTIONS ON FEDERAL COURTS, Second Edition, 1122 pages, 1989. (Casebook) 1992 Supplement.

VETRI AND MERRILL'S FEDERAL COURTS PROBLEMS AND MATERIALS, Second Edition, 232 pages, 1984. Softcover. (Coursebook)

WRIGHT'S HORNBOOK ON FEDERAL COURTS, Fourth Edition, Student Edition, 870 pages, 1983. (Text)

First Amendment

GARVEY AND SCHAUER'S THE FIRST AMENDMENT: A READER, 527 pages, 1992. Softcover. (Reader)

SHIFFRIN AND CHOPER'S FIRST AMENDMENT, CASES—COMMENTS—QUESTIONS, 759 pages, 1991. Softcover. (Casebook) 1992 Supplement.

Foreign Relations and National Security Law

FRANCK AND GLENNON'S FOREIGN RELATIONS AND NATIONAL SECURITY LAW, 941 pages, 1987. (Casebook)

Future Interests—see Trusts and Estates

Gender Discrimination—see also Employment Discrimination

KAY'S TEXT, CASES AND MATERIALS ON SEX-BASED DISCRIMINATION, Third Edition, 1001 pages, 1988. (Casebook) 1992 Supplement.

THOMAS' SEX DISCRIMINATION IN A NUTSHELL, Second Edition, 395 pages, 1991. Softcover. (Text)

Health Law—see Medicine, Law and

Human Rights—see International Law

Immigration Law

ALEINIKOFF AND MARTIN'S IMMIGRATION: PROCESS AND POLICY, Second Edition, 1056 pages, 1991. (Casebook)
  Statutory Supplement. *See Immigration and Nationality Laws*

IMMIGRATION AND NATIONALITY LAWS OF THE UNITED STATES: SELECTED STATUTES, REGULATIONS AND FORMS. Softcover. 519 pages, 1992.

WEISSBRODT'S IMMIGRATION LAW AND PROCEDURE IN A NUTSHELL, Third Edition, 497 pages, 1992. Softcover. (Text)

Indian Law—see American Indian Law

Insurance Law

DEVINE AND TERRY'S PROBLEMS IN INSURANCE LAW, 240 pages, 1989. Softcover. Teacher's Manual available. (Coursebook)

DOBBYN'S INSURANCE LAW IN A NUTSHELL, Second Edition, 316 pages, 1989. Softcover. (Text)

KEETON'S COMPUTER-AIDED AND WORKBOOK EXERCISES ON INSURANCE LAW, 255 pages, 1990. Softcover. (Coursebook)

KEETON AND WIDISS' INSURANCE LAW, Student Edition, 1359 pages, 1988. (Text)

WIDISS AND KEETON'S COURSE SUPPLEMENT TO KEETON AND WIDISS' INSURANCE LAW, 502 pages, 1988. Softcover. Teacher's Manual available. (Casebook)

WIDISS' INSURANCE: MATERIALS ON FUNDAMENTAL PRINCIPLES, LEGAL DOCTRINES AND REGULATORY ACTS, 1186 pages, 1989. Teacher's Manual available. (Casebook)

YORK AND WHELAN'S CASES, MATERIALS AND PROBLEMS ON GENERAL PRACTICE INSURANCE LAW, Second Edition, 787 pages, 1988. Teacher's Manual available. (Casebook)

International Law—see also Sea, Law of

BERMANN, DAVEY, FOX AND GOEBEL'S CASES AND MATERIALS ON EUROPEAN COMMUNITY LAW, Approximately 1200 pages, 1993. (Casebook) Statutory Supplement. *See European Economic Community: Selected Documents*

BUERGENTHAL'S INTERNATIONAL HUMAN RIGHTS IN A NUTSHELL, 283 pages, 1988. Softcover. (Text)

BUERGENTHAL AND MAIER'S PUBLIC INTERNATIONAL LAW IN A NUTSHELL, Second Edition, 275 pages, 1990. Softcover. (Text)

EUROPEAN ECONOMIC COMMUNITY: SELECTED DOCUMENTS. Approximately 550 pages,

International Law—Cont'd

1993. Softcover

FOLSOM'S EUROPEAN COMMUNITY LAW IN A NUTSHELL, 423 pages, 1992. Softcover. (Text)

FOLSOM, GORDON AND SPANOGLE'S INTERNATIONAL BUSINESS TRANSACTIONS—A PROBLEM-ORIENTED COURSEBOOK, Second Edition, 1237 pages, 1991. Teacher's Manual available. (Casebook) 1991 Documents Supplement.

FOLSOM, GORDON AND SPANOGLE'S INTERNATIONAL BUSINESS TRANSACTIONS IN A NUTSHELL, Fourth Edition, 548 pages, 1992. Softcover. (Text)

HENKIN, PUGH, SCHACHTER AND SMIT'S CASES AND MATERIALS ON INTERNATIONAL LAW, Second Edition, 1517 pages, 1987. (Casebook) Documents Supplement.

INTERNATIONAL LITIGATION AND ARBITRATION: SELECTED TREATIES, STATUTES AND RULES. Approximately 275 pages, 1993. Softcover

INTERNATIONAL ORGANIZATIONS IN THEIR LEGAL SETTING: SELECTED DOCUMENTS. Approximately 500 pages, March, 1993 Pub. Softcover

JACKSON AND DAVEY'S CASES, MATERIALS AND TEXT ON LEGAL PROBLEMS OF INTERNATIONAL ECONOMIC RELATIONS, Second Edition, 1269 pages, 1986. (Casebook) 1989 Documents Supplement.

KIRGIS' INTERNATIONAL ORGANIZATIONS IN THEIR LEGAL SETTING, Second Edition, approximately 1150 pages, March, 1993 Pub. Teacher's Manual available. (Casebook) Statutory Supplement.

LOWENFELD'S INTERNATIONAL LITIGATION AND ARBITRATION, Approximately 875 pages, 1993. (Casebook) Statutory Supplement. *See International Litigation: Selected Documents*

WESTON, FALK AND D'AMATO'S INTERNATIONAL LAW AND WORLD ORDER—A PROBLEM-ORIENTED COURSEBOOK, Second Edition, 1335 pages, 1990. Teacher's Manual available. (Casebook) Documents Supplement.

Interviewing and Counseling

BINDER AND PRICE'S LEGAL INTERVIEWING AND COUNSELING, 232 pages, 1977. Softcover. Teacher's Manual available. (Coursebook)

BINDER, BERGMAN AND PRICE'S LAWYERS AS COUNSELORS: A CLIENT–CENTERED APPROACH, 427 pages, 1991. Softcover. (Coursebook)

SHAFFER AND ELKINS' LEGAL INTERVIEWING AND COUNSELING IN A NUTSHELL, Second Edition, 487 pages, 1987. Softcover. (Text)

Introduction to Law—see Legal Method and Legal System

Introduction to Law Study

HEGLAND'S INTRODUCTION TO THE STUDY AND PRACTICE OF LAW IN A NUTSHELL, 418 pages, 1983. Softcover. (Text)

KINYON'S INTRODUCTION TO LAW STUDY AND LAW EXAMINATIONS IN A NUTSHELL, 389 pages, 1971. Softcover. (Text)

Judicial Process—see Legal Method and Legal System

Jurisprudence

CHRISTIE'S JURISPRUDENCE—TEXT AND READINGS ON THE PHILOSOPHY OF LAW, 1056 pages, 1973. (Casebook)

SINHA'S JURISPRUDENCE (LEGAL PHILOSOPHY) IN A NUTSHELL. Approximately 350 pages, 1993. Softcover. (Text)

Juvenile Justice

FOX'S JUVENILE COURTS IN A NUTSHELL, Third Edition, 291 pages, 1984. Softcover. (Text)

Labor and Employment Law—see also Employment Discrimination, Workers' Compensation

FINKIN, GOLDMAN AND SUMMERS' LEGAL PROTECTION OF INDIVIDUAL EMPLOYEES, (The Labor Law Group). 1164 pages, 1989. (Casebook)

GORMAN'S BASIC TEXT ON LABOR LAW—UNIONIZATION AND COLLECTIVE BARGAINING, 914 pages, 1976. (Text)

LESLIE'S LABOR LAW IN A NUTSHELL, Third Edition, 388 pages, 1992. Softcover. (Text)

NOLAN'S LABOR ARBITRATION LAW AND PRAC-

Labor and Employment Law—Cont'd

TICE IN A NUTSHELL, 358 pages, 1979. Softcover. (Text)

OBERER, HANSLOWE, ANDERSEN AND HEINSZ' CASES AND MATERIALS ON LABOR LAW—COLLECTIVE BARGAINING IN A FREE SOCIETY, Third Edition, 1163 pages, 1986. Teacher's Manual available. (Casebook) Statutory Supplement. 1991 Case Supplement.

RABIN, SILVERSTEIN AND SCHATZKI'S LABOR AND EMPLOYMENT LAW: PROBLEMS, CASES AND MATERIALS IN THE LAW OF WORK, (The Labor Law Group). 1014 pages, 1988. Teacher's Manual available. (Casebook) 1988 Statutory Supplement.

WOLLETT, GRODIN AND WEISBERGER'S COLLECTIVE BARGAINING IN PUBLIC EMPLOYMENT, (The Labor Law Group). Fourth Edition, approximately 600 pages, April, 1993 Pub. (Casebook)

Land Finance—Property Security—see Real Estate Transactions

Land Use

CALLIES AND FREILICH'S CASES AND MATERIALS ON LAND USE, 1233 pages, 1986. (Casebook) 1991 Supplement.

HAGMAN AND JUERGENSMEYER'S HORNBOOK ON URBAN PLANNING AND LAND DEVELOPMENT CONTROL LAW, Second Edition, Student Edition, 680 pages, 1986. (Text)

WRIGHT AND GITELMAN'S CASES AND MATERIALS ON LAND USE, Fourth Edition, 1255 pages, 1991. Teacher's Manual available. (Casebook)

WRIGHT AND WRIGHT'S LAND USE IN A NUTSHELL, Second Edition, 356 pages, 1985. Softcover. (Text)

Legal History—see also Legal Method and Legal System

PRESSER AND ZAINALDIN'S CASES AND MATERIALS ON LAW AND JURISPRUDENCE IN AMERICAN HISTORY, Second Edition, 1092 pages, 1989. Teacher's Manual available. (Casebook)

Legal Method and Legal System—see also Legal Research, Legal Writing

ALDISERT'S READINGS, MATERIALS AND CASES IN THE JUDICIAL PROCESS, 948 pages, 1976. (Casebook)

BERCH, BERCH AND SPRITZER'S INTRODUCTION TO LEGAL METHOD AND PROCESS, Second Edition, 585 pages, 1992. Teacher's Manual available. (Casebook)

BODENHEIMER, OAKLEY AND LOVE'S READINGS AND CASES ON AN INTRODUCTION TO THE ANGLO-AMERICAN LEGAL SYSTEM, Second Edition, 166 pages, 1988. Softcover. (Casebook)

DAVIES AND LAWRY'S INSTITUTIONS AND METHODS OF THE LAW—INTRODUCTORY TEACHING MATERIALS, 547 pages, 1982. Teacher's Manual available. (Casebook)

DVORKIN, HIMMELSTEIN AND LESNICK'S BECOMING A LAWYER: A HUMANISTIC PERSPECTIVE ON LEGAL EDUCATION AND PROFESSIONALISM, 211 pages, 1981. Softcover. (Text)

KEETON'S JUDGING, 842 pages, 1990. Softcover. (Coursebook)

KELSO AND KELSO'S STUDYING LAW: AN INTRODUCTION, 587 pages, 1984. (Coursebook)

KEMPIN'S HISTORICAL INTRODUCTION TO ANGLO-AMERICAN LAW IN A NUTSHELL, Third Edition, 323 pages, 1990. Softcover. (Text)

MEADOR'S AMERICAN COURTS, 113 pages, 1991. Softcover. (Text)

REYNOLDS' JUDICIAL PROCESS IN A NUTSHELL, Second Edition, 308 pages, 1991. Softcover. (Text)

Legal Research

COHEN AND OLSON'S LEGAL RESEARCH IN A NUTSHELL, Fifth Edition, 370 pages, 1992. Softcover. (Text)

COHEN, BERRING AND OLSON'S HOW TO FIND THE LAW, Ninth Edition, 716 pages, 1989. (Text)

COHEN, BERRING AND OLSON'S FINDING THE LAW, 570 pages, 1989. Softcover reprint from Cohen, Berring and Olson's How to Find the Law, Ninth Edition. (Coursebook)

Legal Research Exercises, 4th Ed., for use with Cohen, Berring and Olson, 253 pages, 1992. Teacher's Manual available.

ROMBAUER'S LEGAL PROBLEM SOLVING—ANALYSIS, RESEARCH AND WRITING, Fifth Edition, 524 pages, 1991. Softcover. Teacher's Manual with problems availa-

Legal Research—Cont'd

ble. (Coursebook)

STATSKY'S LEGAL RESEARCH AND WRITING: SOME STARTING POINTS, Fourth Edition, approximately 270 pages, 1993. Softcover. Teacher's Manual available. (Coursebook) Student Workbook.

TEPLY'S LEGAL RESEARCH AND CITATION, Fourth Edition, 436 pages, 1992. Softcover. (Coursebook)

Student Library Exercises, Fourth Edition, 276 pages, 1992. Answer Key available.

Legal Writing and Drafting

CHILD'S DRAFTING LEGAL DOCUMENTS: PRINCIPLES AND PRACTICES, Second Edition, 425 pages, 1992. Softcover. Teacher's Manual available. (Coursebook)

DICKERSON'S MATERIALS ON LEGAL DRAFTING, 425 pages, 1981. Teacher's Manual available. (Coursebook)

FELSENFELD AND SIEGEL'S WRITING CONTRACTS IN PLAIN ENGLISH, 290 pages, 1981. Softcover. (Text)

GOPEN'S WRITING FROM A LEGAL PERSPECTIVE, 225 pages, 1981. (Text)

MARTINEAU'S DRAFTING LEGISLATION AND RULES IN PLAIN ENGLISH, 155 pages, 1991. Softcover. Teacher's Manual available. (Text)

MELLINKOFF'S DICTIONARY OF AMERICAN LEGAL USAGE, 703 pages, 1992. Softcover. (Text)

MELLINKOFF'S LEGAL WRITING—SENSE AND NONSENSE, 242 pages, 1982. Softcover. Teacher's Manual available. (Text)

PRATT'S LEGAL WRITING: A SYSTEMATIC APPROACH, Second Edition, approximately 550 pages, April, 1993 Pub. Teacher's Manual available. (Coursebook)

RAY AND COX'S BEYOND THE BASICS: A TEXT FOR ADVANCED LEGAL WRITING, 427 pages, 1991. Softcover. Teacher's Manual available. (Text)

RAY AND RAMSFIELD'S LEGAL WRITING: GETTING IT RIGHT AND GETTING IT WRITTEN, 250 pages, 1987. Softcover. (Text)

SQUIRES AND ROMBAUER'S LEGAL WRITING IN A NUTSHELL, 294 pages, 1982. Softcover.

(Text)

STATSKY AND WERNET'S CASE ANALYSIS AND FUNDAMENTALS OF LEGAL WRITING, Third Edition, 424 pages, 1989. Teacher's Manual available. (Text)

TEPLY'S LEGAL WRITING, ANALYSIS AND ORAL ARGUMENT, 576 pages, 1990. Softcover. Teacher's Manual available. (Coursebook)

WEIHOFEN'S LEGAL WRITING STYLE, Second Edition, 332 pages, 1980. (Text)

Legislation—see also Legal Writing and Drafting

DAVIES' LEGISLATIVE LAW AND PROCESS IN A NUTSHELL, Second Edition, 346 pages, 1986. Softcover. (Text)

ESKRIDGE AND FRICKEY'S CASES AND MATERIALS ON LEGISLATION: STATUTES AND THE CREATION OF PUBLIC POLICY, 937 pages, 1988. Teacher's Manual available. (Casebook) 1992 Supplement.

NUTTING AND DICKERSON'S CASES AND MATERIALS ON LEGISLATION, Fifth Edition, 744 pages, 1978. (Casebook)

STATSKY'S LEGISLATIVE ANALYSIS AND DRAFTING, Second Edition, 217 pages, 1984. Teacher's Manual available. (Text)

Local Government

FRUG'S CASES AND MATERIALS ON LOCAL GOVERNMENT LAW, 1005 pages, 1988. (Casebook) 1991 Supplement.

MCCARTHY'S LOCAL GOVERNMENT LAW IN A NUTSHELL, Third Edition, 435 pages, 1990. Softcover. (Text)

REYNOLDS' HORNBOOK ON LOCAL GOVERNMENT LAW, 860 pages, 1982 with 1990 pocket part. (Text)

VALENTE AND MCCARTHY'S CASES AND MATERIALS ON LOCAL GOVERNMENT LAW, Fourth Edition, 1158 pages, 1992. Teacher's Manual available. (Casebook)

Mass Communication Law

GILLMOR, BARRON, SIMON AND TERRY'S CASES AND COMMENT ON MASS COMMUNICATION LAW, Fifth Edition, 947 pages, 1990. (Casebook)

GINSBURG, BOTEIN AND DIRECTOR'S REGULATION OF THE ELECTRONIC MASS MEDIA: LAW

Mass Communication Law—Cont'd

AND POLICY FOR RADIO, TELEVISION, CABLE AND THE NEW VIDEO TECHNOLOGIES, Second Edition, 657 pages, 1991. (Casebook) Statutory Supplement.

ZUCKMAN, GAYNES, CARTER AND DEE'S MASS COMMUNICATIONS LAW IN A NUTSHELL, Third Edition, 538 pages, 1988. Softcover. (Text)

Medicine, Law and

FISCINA, BOUMIL, SHARPE AND HEAD'S MEDICAL LIABILITY, 487 pages, 1991. Teacher's Manual available. (Casebook)

FURROW, JOHNSON, JOST AND SCHWARTZ' HEALTH LAW: CASES, MATERIALS AND PROBLEMS, Second Edition, 1236 pages, 1991. Teacher's Manual available. (Casebook)

FURROW, JOHNSON, JOST AND SCHWARTZ' BIOETHICS: HEALTH CARE LAW AND ETHICS, Reprint from Furrow et al., Health Law, Second Edition. Softcover. Teacher's Manual available. (Casebook)

FURROW, JOHNSON, JOST AND SCHWARTZ' THE LAW OF HEALTH CARE ORGANIZATION AND FINANCE, Reprint from Furrow et al., Health Law, Second Edition. Softcover. Teacher's Manual available.

FURROW, JOHNSON, JOST AND SCHWARTZ' LIABILITY AND QUALITY ISSUES IN HEALTH CARE, Reprint from Furrow et al., Health Law, Second Edition. Softcover. Teacher's Manual available. (Casebook)

HALL AND ELLMAN'S HEALTH CARE LAW AND ETHICS IN A NUTSHELL, 401 pages, 1990. Softcover (Text)

JARVIS, CLOSEN, HERMANN AND LEONARD'S AIDS LAW IN A NUTSHELL, 349 pages, 1991. Softcover. (Text)

KING'S THE LAW OF MEDICAL MALPRACTICE IN A NUTSHELL, Second Edition, 342 pages, 1986. Softcover. (Text)

SHAPIRO AND SPECE'S CASES, MATERIALS AND PROBLEMS ON BIOETHICS AND LAW, 892 pages, 1981. (Casebook) 1991 Supplement.

Military Law

SHANOR AND TERRELL'S MILITARY LAW IN A NUTSHELL, 378 pages, 1980. Softcover. (Text)

Mining Law—see Energy and Natural Resources Law

Mortgages—see Real Estate Transactions

Natural Resources Law—see Energy and Natural Resources Law, Environmental Law

Negotiation

GIFFORD'S LEGAL NEGOTIATION: THEORY AND APPLICATIONS, 225 pages, 1989. Softcover. (Text)

TEPLY'S LEGAL NEGOTIATION IN A NUTSHELL, 282 pages, 1992. Softcover. (Text)

WILLIAMS' LEGAL NEGOTIATION AND SETTLEMENT, 207 pages, 1983. Softcover. Teacher's Manual available. (Coursebook)

Office Practice—see also Computers and Law, Interviewing and Counseling, Negotiation

HEGLAND'S TRIAL AND PRACTICE SKILLS IN A NUTSHELL, 346 pages, 1978. Softcover (Text)

MUNNEKE'S LAW PRACTICE MANAGEMENT: MATERIALS AND CASES, 634 pages, 1991. Teacher's Manual available. (Casebook)

Oil and Gas—see also Energy and Natural Resources Law

HEMINGWAY'S HORNBOOK ON THE LAW OF OIL AND GAS, Third Edition, Student Edition, 711 pages, 1992. (Text)

KUNTZ, LOWE, ANDERSON AND SMITH'S CASES AND MATERIALS ON OIL AND GAS LAW, Second Edition, approximately 1000 pages, 1993. Teacher's Manual available. (Casebook) Forms Manual. Revised.

LOWE'S OIL AND GAS LAW IN A NUTSHELL, Second Edition, 465 pages, 1988. Softcover. (Text)

Partnership—see Agency—Partnership

Patent and Copyright Law

CHOATE, FRANCIS AND COLLINS' CASES AND MATERIALS ON PATENT LAW, INCLUDING TRADE SECRETS, COPYRIGHTS, TRADEMARKS, Third Edition, 1009 pages, 1987. (Casebook)

HALPERN, SHIPLEY AND ABRAMS' CASES AND MATERIALS ON COPYRIGHT, 663 pages, 1992. (Casebook)

Patent and Copyright Law—Cont'd

MILLER AND DAVIS' INTELLECTUAL PROPERTY—PATENTS, TRADEMARKS AND COPYRIGHT IN A NUTSHELL, Second Edition, 437 pages, 1990. Softcover. (Text)

NIMMER, MARCUS, MYERS AND NIMMER'S CASES AND MATERIALS ON COPYRIGHT AND OTHER ASPECTS OF ENTERTAINMENT LITIGATION—INCLUDING UNFAIR COMPETITION, DEFAMATION, PRIVACY, ILLUSTRATED, Fourth Edition, 1177 pages, 1991. (Casebook) Statutory Supplement. See *Selected Intellectual Property Statutes*

SELECTED INTELLECTUAL PROPERTY AND UNFAIR COMPETITION STATUTES, REGULATIONS AND TREATIES. Softcover.

Products Liability

FISCHER AND POWERS' CASES AND MATERIALS ON PRODUCTS LIABILITY, 685 pages, 1988. Teacher's Manual available. (Casebook)

PHILLIPS' PRODUCTS LIABILITY IN A NUTSHELL, Third Edition, 307 pages, 1988. Softcover. (Text)

Professional Responsibility

ARONSON, DEVINE AND FISCH'S PROBLEMS, CASES AND MATERIALS IN PROFESSIONAL RESPONSIBILITY, 745 pages, 1985. Teacher's Manual available. (Casebook)

ARONSON AND WECKSTEIN'S PROFESSIONAL RESPONSIBILITY IN A NUTSHELL, Second Edition, 514 pages, 1991. Softcover. (Text)

LESNICK'S BEING A LAWYER: INDIVIDUAL CHOICE AND RESPONSIBILITY IN THE PRACTICE OF LAW, 422 pages, 1992. Softcover. Teacher's Manual available. (Coursebook)

MELLINKOFF'S THE CONSCIENCE OF A LAWYER, 304 pages, 1973. (Text)

PIRSIG AND KIRWIN'S CASES AND MATERIALS ON PROFESSIONAL RESPONSIBILITY, Fourth Edition, 603 pages, 1984. Teacher's Manual available. (Casebook)

ROTUNDA'S BLACK LETTER ON PROFESSIONAL RESPONSIBILITY, Third Edition, 492 pages, 1992. Softcover. (Review)

SCHWARTZ, WYDICK AND PERSCHBACHER'S PROBLEMS IN LEGAL ETHICS, Third Edition, approximately 400 pages, 1993. (Coursebook)

SELECTED STATUTES, RULES AND STANDARDS ON THE LEGAL PROFESSION. Softcover. 940 pages, 1992.

SMITH AND MALLEN'S PREVENTING LEGAL MALPRACTICE, 264 pages, 1989. Reprint from Mallen and Smith's Legal Malpractice, Third Edition. (Text)

SUTTON AND DZIENKOWSKI'S CASES AND MATERIALS ON PROFESSIONAL RESPONSIBILITY FOR LAWYERS, 839 pages, 1989. Teacher's Manual available. (Casebook)

WOLFRAM'S HORNBOOK ON MODERN LEGAL ETHICS, Student Edition, 1120 pages, 1986. (Text)

WYDICK AND PERSCHBACHER'S CALIFORNIA LEGAL ETHICS, 439 pages, 1992. Softcover. (Coursebook)

Property—see also Real Estate Transactions, Land Use, Trusts and Estates

BARNES AND STOUT'S THE ECONOMICS OF PROPERTY RIGHTS AND NUISANCE LAW, 87 pages, 1992. Softcover. Teacher's Manual available. (Casebook)

BERNHARDT'S BLACK LETTER ON PROPERTY, Second Edition, 388 pages, 1991. Softcover. (Review)

BERNHARDT'S REAL PROPERTY IN A NUTSHELL, Second Edition, 448 pages, 1981. Softcover. (Text)

BOYER, HOVENKAMP AND KURTZ' THE LAW OF PROPERTY, AN INTRODUCTORY SURVEY, Fourth Edition, 696 pages, 1991. (Text)

BROWDER, CUNNINGHAM, NELSON, STOEBUCK AND WHITMAN'S CASES ON BASIC PROPERTY LAW, Fifth Edition, 1386 pages, 1989. Teacher's Manual available. (Casebook)

BRUCE, ELY AND BOSTICK'S CASES AND MATERIALS ON MODERN PROPERTY LAW, Second Edition, 953 pages, 1989. Teacher's Manual available. (Casebook)

BURKE'S PERSONAL PROPERTY IN A NUTSHELL, Second Edition, approximately 400 pages, May, 1993 Pub. Softcover. (Text)

CUNNINGHAM, STOEBUCK AND WHITMAN'S HORNBOOK ON THE LAW OF PROPERTY, Second Edition, approximately 900 pages, May, 1993 Pub. (Text)

DONAHUE, KAUPER AND MARTIN'S CASES AND MATERIALS ON PROPERTY, AN INTRODUCTION TO THE CONCEPT AND THE INSTITUTION, Third

Property—Cont'd

Edition, approximately 1000 pages, 1993. Teacher's Manual available. (Casebook)

HILL'S LANDLORD AND TENANT LAW IN A NUTSHELL, Second Edition, 311 pages, 1986. Softcover. (Text)

JOHNSON, JOST, SALSICH AND SHAFFER'S PROPERTY LAW, CASES, MATERIALS AND PROBLEMS, 908 pages, 1992. Teacher's Manual available. (Casebook)

KURTZ AND HOVENKAMP'S CASES AND MATERIALS ON AMERICAN PROPERTY LAW, Second Edition, approximately 1350 pages, March, 1993 Pub. Teacher's Manual available. (Casebook)

MOYNIHAN'S INTRODUCTION TO REAL PROPERTY, Second Edition, 239 pages, 1988. (Text)

Psychiatry, Law and

REISNER AND SLOBOGIN'S LAW AND THE MENTAL HEALTH SYSTEM, CIVIL AND CRIMINAL ASPECTS, Second Edition, 1117 pages, 1990. Teacher's Manual available. (Casebook) 1992 Supplement.

Real Estate Transactions

BRUCE'S REAL ESTATE FINANCE IN A NUTSHELL, Third Edition, 287 pages, 1991. Softcover. (Text)

MAXWELL, RIESENFELD, HETLAND AND WARREN'S CASES ON CALIFORNIA SECURITY TRANSACTIONS IN LAND, Fourth Edition, 778 pages, 1992. Teacher's Manual available. (Casebook)

NELSON AND WHITMAN'S BLACK LETTER ON LAND TRANSACTIONS AND FINANCE, Second Edition, 466 pages, 1988. Softcover. (Review)

NELSON AND WHITMAN'S CASES AND MATERIALS ON REAL ESTATE TRANSFER, FINANCE AND DEVELOPMENT, Fourth Edition, 1346 pages, 1992. (Casebook)

NELSON AND WHITMAN'S HORNBOOK ON REAL ESTATE FINANCE LAW, Second Edition, 941 pages, 1985 with 1989 pocket part. (Text)

Regulated Industries—see also Mass Communication Law, Banking Law

GELLHORN AND PIERCE'S REGULATED INDUSTRIES IN A NUTSHELL, Second Edition, 389 pages, 1987. Softcover. (Text)

MORGAN, HARRISON AND VERKUIL'S CASES AND MATERIALS ON ECONOMIC REGULATION OF BUSINESS, Second Edition, 666 pages, 1985. (Casebook)

Remedies

DOBBS' HORNBOOK ON REMEDIES, Second Edition, approximately 1000 pages, April, 1993 Pub. (Text)

DOBBS' PROBLEMS IN REMEDIES. 137 pages, 1974. Teacher's Manual available. Softcover. (Coursebook)

DOBBYN'S INJUNCTIONS IN A NUTSHELL, 264 pages, 1974. Softcover. (Text)

FRIEDMAN'S CONTRACT REMEDIES IN A NUTSHELL, 323 pages, 1981. Softcover. (Text)

LEAVELL, LOVE AND NELSON'S CASES AND MATERIALS ON EQUITABLE REMEDIES, RESTITUTION AND DAMAGES, Fourth Edition, 1111 pages, 1986. Teacher's Manual available. (Casebook)

O'CONNELL'S REMEDIES IN A NUTSHELL, Second Edition, 320 pages, 1985. Softcover. (Text)

SCHOENBROD, MACBETH, LEVINE AND JUNG'S CASES AND MATERIALS ON REMEDIES: PUBLIC AND PRIVATE, 848 pages, 1990. Teacher's Manual available. (Casebook) 1992 Supplement.

YORK, BAUMAN AND RENDLEMAN'S CASES AND MATERIALS ON REMEDIES, Fifth Edition, 1270 pages, 1992. Teacher's Manual available. (Casebook)

Sea, Law of

SOHN AND GUSTAFSON'S THE LAW OF THE SEA IN A NUTSHELL, 264 pages, 1984. Softcover. (Text)

Securities Regulation

HAZEN'S HORNBOOK ON THE LAW OF SECURITIES REGULATION, Second Edition, Student Edition, 1082 pages, 1990. (Text)

RATNER'S SECURITIES REGULATION IN A NUTSHELL, Fourth Edition, 320 pages, 1992. Softcover. (Text)

RATNER AND HAZEN'S SECURITIES REGULATION: CASES AND MATERIALS, Fourth Edition, 1062 pages, 1991. Teacher's Manual available. (Casebook) Problems and Sample Documents Supplement.

Statutory Supplement. *See Securities*

Securities Regulation—Cont'd

Regulation, Selected Statutes

SECURITIES REGULATION, SELECTED STATUTES, RULES, AND FORMS. Softcover. Approximately 1375 pages, 1993.

Sports Law

CHAMPION'S SPORTS LAW IN A NUTSHELL,. Approximately 300 pages, January, 1993 Pub. Softcover. (Text)

SCHUBERT, SMITH AND TRENTADUE'S SPORTS LAW, 395 pages, 1986. (Text)

Tax Practice and Procedure

GARBIS, RUBIN AND MORGAN'S CASES AND MATERIALS ON TAX PROCEDURE AND TAX FRAUD, Third Edition, 921 pages, 1992. Teacher's Manual available. (Casebook)

MORGAN'S TAX PROCEDURE AND TAX FRAUD IN A NUTSHELL, 400 pages, 1990. Softcover. (Text)

Taxation—Corporate

KAHN AND GANN'S CORPORATE TAXATION, Third Edition, 980 pages, 1989. Teacher's Manual available. (Casebook) 1991 Supplement.

SCHWARZ AND LATHROPE'S BLACK LETTER ON CORPORATE AND PARTNERSHIP TAXATION, 537 pages, 1991. Softcover. (Review)

WEIDENBRUCH AND BURKE'S FEDERAL INCOME TAXATION OF CORPORATIONS AND STOCKHOLDERS IN A NUTSHELL, Third Edition, 309 pages, 1989. Softcover. (Text)

Taxation—Estate & Gift—see also Estate Planning, Trusts and Estates

McNULTY'S FEDERAL ESTATE AND GIFT TAXATION IN A NUTSHELL, Fourth Edition, 496 pages, 1989. Softcover. (Text)

PEAT AND WILLBANKS' FEDERAL ESTATE AND GIFT TAXATION: AN ANALYSIS AND CRITIQUE, 265 pages, 1991. Softcover. (Text)

PENNELL'S CASES AND MATERIALS ON INCOME TAXATION OF TRUSTS, ESTATES, GRANTORS AND BENEFICIARIES, 460 pages, 1987. Teacher's Manual available. (Casebook)

Taxation—Individual

DODGE'S THE LOGIC OF TAX, 343 pages, 1989. Softcover. (Text)

GUNN AND WARD'S CASES, TEXT AND PROBLEMS ON FEDERAL INCOME TAXATION, Third Edition, 817 pages, 1992. Teacher's Manual available. (Casebook)

HUDSON AND LIND'S BLACK LETTER ON FEDERAL INCOME TAXATION, Fourth Edition, 410 pages, 1992. Softcover. (Review)

McNULTY'S FEDERAL INCOME TAXATION OF INDIVIDUALS IN A NUTSHELL, Fourth Edition, 503 pages, 1988. Softcover. (Text)

POSIN'S FEDERAL INCOME TAXATION, Second Edition, approximately 650 pages, May, 1993 Pub. Softcover. (Text)

ROSE AND CHOMMIE'S HORNBOOK ON FEDERAL INCOME TAXATION, Third Edition, 923 pages, 1988, with 1991 pocket part. (Text)

SELECTED FEDERAL TAXATION STATUTES AND REGULATIONS. Softcover. 1686 pages, 1993.

Taxation—International

DOERNBERG'S INTERNATIONAL TAXATION IN A NUTSHELL, 325 pages, 1989. Softcover. (Text)

KAPLAN'S FEDERAL TAXATION OF INTERNATIONAL TRANSACTIONS: PRINCIPLES, PLANNING AND POLICY, 635 pages, 1988. (Casebook)

Taxation—Partnership

BERGER AND WIEDENBECK'S CASES AND MATERIALS ON PARTNERSHIP TAXATION, 788 pages, 1989. Teacher's Manual available. (Casebook) 1991 Supplement.

BISHOP AND BROOKS' FEDERAL PARTNERSHIP TAXATION: A GUIDE TO THE LEADING CASES, STATUTES, AND REGULATIONS, 545 pages, 1990. Softcover. (Text)

BURKE'S FEDERAL INCOME TAXATION OF PARTNERSHIPS IN A NUTSHELL, 356 pages, 1992. Softcover. (Text)

SCHWARZ AND LATHROPE'S BLACK LETTER ON CORPORATE AND PARTNERSHIP TAXATION, 537 pages, 1991. Softcover. (Review)

Taxation—State & Local

GELFAND AND SALSICH'S STATE AND LOCAL TAXATION AND FINANCE IN A NUTSHELL, 309 pages, 1986. Softcover. (Text)

HELLERSTEIN AND HELLERSTEIN'S CASES AND MATERIALS ON STATE AND LOCAL TAXATION, Fifth Edition, 1071 pages, 1988. (Case-

Taxation—State & Local—Cont'd book)

Torts—see also Products Liability

BARNES AND STOUT'S THE ECONOMIC ANALYSIS OF TORT LAW, 161 pages, 1992. Softcover. Teacher's Manual available. (Casebook)

CHRISTIE AND MEEKS' CASES AND MATERIALS ON THE LAW OF TORTS, Second Edition, 1264 pages, 1990. (Casebook)

DOBBS' TORTS AND COMPENSATION—PERSONAL ACCOUNTABILITY AND SOCIAL RESPONSIBILITY FOR INJURY, 955 pages, 1985. Teacher's Manual available. (Casebook) 1990 Supplement.

KEETON, KEETON, SARGENTICH AND STEINER'S CASES AND MATERIALS ON TORT AND ACCIDENT LAW, Second Edition, 1318 pages, 1989. (Casebook)

KIONKA'S BLACK LETTER ON TORTS, 339 pages, 1988. Softcover. (Review)

KIONKA'S TORTS IN A NUTSHELL, Second Edition, 449 pages, 1992. Softcover. (Text)

PROSSER AND KEETON'S HORNBOOK ON TORTS, Fifth Edition, Student Edition, 1286 pages, 1984 with 1988 pocket part. (Text)

ROBERTSON, POWERS AND ANDERSON'S CASES AND MATERIALS ON TORTS, 932 pages, 1989. Teacher's Manual available. (Casebook)

Trade Regulation—see also Antitrust, Regulated Industries

MCMANIS' UNFAIR TRADE PRACTICES IN A NUTSHELL, Third Edition, approximately 450 pages, 1993. Softcover. (Text)

SCHECHTER'S BLACK LETTER ON UNFAIR TRADE PRACTICES, 272 pages, 1986. Softcover. (Review)

WESTON, MAGGS AND SCHECHTER'S UNFAIR TRADE PRACTICES AND CONSUMER PROTECTION, CASES AND COMMENTS, Fifth Edition, 957 pages, 1992. Teacher's Manual available. (Casebook)

Trial and Appellate Advocacy—see also Civil Procedure

APPELLATE ADVOCACY, HANDBOOK OF, Second Edition, 182 pages, 1986. Softcover. (Text)

BERGMAN'S TRIAL ADVOCACY IN A NUTSHELL,

Second Edition, 354 pages, 1989. Softcover. (Text)

BINDER AND BERGMAN'S FACT INVESTIGATION: FROM HYPOTHESIS TO PROOF, 354 pages, 1984. Teacher's Manual available. (Coursebook)

CARLSON'S ADJUDICATION OF CRIMINAL JUSTICE: PROBLEMS AND REFERENCES, 130 pages, 1986. Softcover. (Casebook)

CARLSON AND IMWINKELRIED'S DYNAMICS OF TRIAL PRACTICE: PROBLEMS AND MATERIALS, 414 pages, 1989. Teacher's Manual available. (Coursebook) 1990 Supplement.

CLARY'S PRIMER ON THE ANALYSIS AND PRESENTATION OF LEGAL ARGUMENT, 106 pages, 1992. Softcover. (Text)

DESSEM'S PRETRIAL LITIGATION IN A NUTSHELL, 382 pages, 1992. Softcover. (Text)

DESSEM'S PRETRIAL LITIGATION: LAW, POLICY AND PRACTICE, 608 pages, 1991. Softcover. Teacher's Manual available. (Coursebook)

DEVINE'S NON-JURY CASE FILES FOR TRIAL ADVOCACY, 258 pages, 1991. (Coursebook)

GOLDBERG'S THE FIRST TRIAL (WHERE DO I SIT? WHAT DO I SAY?) IN A NUTSHELL, 396 pages, 1982. Softcover. (Text)

HAYDOCK, HERR, AND STEMPEL'S FUNDAMENTALS OF PRE-TRIAL LITIGATION, Second Edition, 786 pages, 1992. Softcover. Teacher's Manual available. (Coursebook)

HAYDOCK AND SONSTENG'S TRIAL: THEORIES, TACTICS, TECHNIQUES, 711 pages, 1991. Softcover. (Text)

HEGLAND'S TRIAL AND PRACTICE SKILLS IN A NUTSHELL, 346 pages, 1978. Softcover. (Text)

HORNSTEIN'S APPELLATE ADVOCACY IN A NUTSHELL, 325 pages, 1984. Softcover. (Text)

JEANS' HANDBOOK ON TRIAL ADVOCACY, Student Edition, 473 pages, 1975. Softcover. (Text)

LISNEK AND KAUFMAN'S DEPOSITIONS: PROCEDURE, STRATEGY AND TECHNIQUE, Law School and CLE Edition. 250 pages, 1990. Softcover. (Text)

MARTINEAU'S CASES AND MATERIALS ON APPELLATE PRACTICE AND PROCEDURE, 565 pages, 1987. (Casebook)

Trial and Appellate Advocacy—Cont'd

SONSTENG, HAYDOCK AND BOYD'S THE TRIALBOOK: A TOTAL SYSTEM FOR PREPARATION AND PRESENTATION OF A CASE, 404 pages, 1984. Softcover. (Coursebook)

WHARTON, HAYDOCK AND SONSTENG'S CALIFORNIA CIVIL TRIALBOOK, Law School and CLE Edition. 148 pages, 1990. Softcover. (Text)

Trusts and Estates

ATKINSON'S HORNBOOK ON WILLS, Second Edition, 975 pages, 1953. (Text)

AVERILL'S UNIFORM PROBATE CODE IN A NUTSHELL, Second Edition, 454 pages, 1987. Softcover. (Text)

BOGERT'S HORNBOOK ON TRUSTS, Sixth Edition, Student Edition, 794 pages, 1987. (Text)

CLARK, LUSKY AND MURPHY'S CASES AND MATERIALS ON GRATUITOUS TRANSFERS, Third Edition, 970 pages, 1985. (Casebook)

DODGE'S WILLS, TRUSTS AND ESTATE PLANNING—LAW AND TAXATION, CASES AND MATERIALS, 665 pages, 1988. (Casebook)

MCGOVERN, KURTZ AND REIN'S HORNBOOK ON WILLS, TRUSTS AND ESTATES—INCLUDING TAXATION AND FUTURE INTERESTS, 996 pages, 1988. (Text)

MENNELL'S WILLS AND TRUSTS IN A NUTSHELL, 392 pages, 1979. Softcover. (Text)

SIMES' HORNBOOK ON FUTURE INTERESTS, Second Edition, 355 pages, 1966. (Text)

TURANO AND RADIGAN'S HORNBOOK ON NEW YORK ESTATE ADMINISTRATION, 676 pages, 1986 with 1991 pocket part. (Text)

UNIFORM PROBATE CODE, OFFICIAL TEXT WITH COMMENTS. 863 pages, 1991. Softcover.

WAGGONER'S FUTURE INTERESTS IN A NUTSHELL, 361 pages, 1981. Softcover. (Text)

Water Law—see also Energy and Natural Resources Law, Environmental Law

GETCHES' WATER LAW IN A NUTSHELL, Second Edition, 459 pages, 1990. Softcover. (Text)

SAX, ABRAMS AND THOMPSON'S LEGAL CONTROL OF WATER RESOURCES: CASES AND MATERIALS, Second Edition, 987 pages, 1991. Teacher's Manual available. (Casebook)

TRELEASE AND GOULD'S CASES AND MATERIALS ON WATER LAW, Fourth Edition, 816 pages, 1986. (Casebook)

Wills—see Trusts and Estates

Workers' Compensation

HOOD, HARDY AND LEWIS' WORKERS' COMPENSATION AND EMPLOYEE PROTECTION LAWS IN A NUTSHELL, Second Edition, 361 pages, 1990. Softcover. (Text)

LITTLE, EATON AND SMITH'S CASES AND MATERIALS ON WORKERS' COMPENSATION, 537 pages, 1992. Teacher's Manual available. (Casebook)

LEGAL PROBLEMS OF
INTERNATIONAL ECONOMIC RELATIONS

CASES, MATERIALS AND TEXT ON THE NATIONAL AND INTERNATIONAL REGULATION OF TRANSNATIONAL ECONOMIC RELATIONS

Second Edition

By

John H. Jackson
Hessel E. Yntema Professor of Law,
University of Michigan

William J. Davey
Associate Professor of Law, University of Illinois

AMERICAN CASEBOOK SERIES

WEST PUBLISHING CO.
ST. PAUL, MINN., 1986

COPYRIGHT © 1986 By WEST PUBLISHING CO.
610 Opperman Drive
P.O. Box 64526
St. Paul, MN 55164–0526

Library of Congress Cataloging in Publication Data

Jackson, John Howard, 1932–
  Legal problems of international economic relations.

  (American casebook series)
  1. Foreign trade regulation—Cases. 2. Tariff—
Law and legislation—Cases. 3. International economic
relations. 4. Foreign trade regulation—United States—
Cases. 5. Tariff—Law and legislation—United States—
Cases. I. Davey, William J., 1949–   . II. Title.
III. Series.

K3943.A58J3 1986   343'.087   86–15656

ISBN 0–314–22309–6

Int'l.Econ.Rel.2d Ed. (J & D) ACB
3rd Reprint—1993

Preface to the Second Edition

This edition, we admit, is overdue. Almost a decade has passed since the first edition, and the changes in international circumstances relevant to the subject of this book have been startling. The basic theme of the first edition—the impact of international economic interdependence and the struggle of legal institutions to cope with that circumstance—has been confirmed many times over. The words of the preface to the first edition (most of which are printed below) are thus in many ways prophetic.

We have re-examined the basic premises of the first edition, and explored ways to make the second edition more useful. This has not been easy. We have benefitted from our own experiences in teaching with the first edition. We have also benefitted from the suggestions and criticisms of the many student and other faculty users of the first edition. Many suggestions called for additions to the book, however, and to keep the book manageable additions always entail subtractions. It will be easily seen that both the subtractions and the additions for this edition have been substantial. We do not claim the perfect balance between the myriad of competing desires of teachers and students of this subject, but we hope and expect that we have considerably improved the book with our efforts.

An important basic goal of both editions, however, needs to be repeated. It is very easy to tally up multiple dozens of subjects which a potential international legal practitioner would find useful when he or she begins to grapple with real world problems. We do not intend to offer a complete coverage of these dozens of subjects, nor even a substantial portion of them. We aim, instead, to offer the student, professor, or current practitioner, the means to achieve a basic understanding of the international economic system as it operates in real life, and as it is constrained or aided by a number of fundamental legal institutions, including national and international constitutional documents and processes. In doing this adequately, we have necessarily had to minimize the coverage of many other practical topics. In a number of cases, however, many of those topics have been covered in other courses in the curriculum.

Our goal for this book, and courses based upon it, is to penetrate deeply into subjects which can have great importance to the government or private practitioner, but which are essentially not covered in other law courses. In addition our goal is to build for the student a knowledge of the "foundations" of the legal system and institutions of international economic relations. This implies knowledge of the constituent international instruments and processes, and the ways those interact with the important national constituent instruments and processes. The words of the Preface to the First Edition explain this in more detail.

In preparing this revision, however, we have had several other subsidiary objectives in mind. First, after reflection, we decided to improve the overall organization of the book, to make the presentation of material to students easier to understand, and also to make it easier for a teacher to select from the book so as to tailor the materials for his own preferred course outline. (The overall structure of the book is explained at the beginning of Chapter 1.)

In dramatically cutting early parts of the book, we have made room in Part III of the book for a number of short survey chapters of topics, some of which were not included in the first edition. We did this as a response to requests so that teachers would have considerable freedom, hopefully after exploring the fundamental and constitutional aspects of the subject contained in the first two parts, to select subjects they wished to emphasize. We anticipate that for some of those teachers, those who wish to explore subjects of Part III in more detail, the notes and bibliographical references will assist in the preparation of additional materials for students. The only satisfactory alternative to this approach was a multi-volume casebook, which is not practical for this course.

Finally, in Part IV, we have included some material designed to stimulate additional thinking about the strengths and weaknesses of the present international economic system, and to pose some questions which face national and international policy makers. Once students have mastered the fundamentals of this subject, it has been our experience that they have found it exciting to participate in discussion of some of the "forefront issues" of current international economic policy.

In general the material in this book is current as of about March 1, 1986. In some cases we have been able to update material to reflect events occurring subsequent to that date.

JOHN H. JACKSON
WILLIAM J. DAVEY

Ann Arbor, Michigan
Champaign, Illinois
June 1986

A Personal Note

The author of the first edition wishes to express his delight and gratitude that he is joined for the second edition by Professor William Davey, an outstanding young scholar and law teacher who has not only impressive academic credentials, but who has had direct and substantial experience in the practice of law, both abroad and in the U.S., dealing with the subject of this book. His efforts to improve this book have been extraordinarily helpful.

JHJ

*

Preface to the First Edition

Preparing a book on the subject of international economic regulation is like trying to describe a landscape while looking out the window of a moving train—events tend to move faster than one can describe them. Certain other law subjects have similar problems, but in the case of international economic law, this problem is compounded by the lack of definition of the borderlines of the subject. In its broadest extent, a study of international economic transactions and governmental actions relating to them, could be a subpart of dozens of existing law subjects in the law school curriculum. It certainly involves subject material considered in international law, conflicts of law, constitutional law, contracts and sales, corporations, tax, anti-trust, civil procedure, and administrative law.

As yet there is no generally agreed subject matter selection for this course in the United States law curricula, not even an agreed "core", as you would find in most courses in the law school curriculum. This is both the challenge and the danger of preparing published materials.

No doubt as time goes on, we shall see the course subject matter selection "shake down," become more cohesive and develop some agreement among law teachers. For the moment, however, this is not the case, and consequently any casebook on this subject must involve a series of decisions about scope, emphasis, and selection of subjects and materials, that can be appropriately challenged.

For these reasons it is perhaps especially important that this author explain the bases for his choices, and the premises on which he has developed this book. There are many of them.

First, and foremost, this book is constructed so as to emphasize the *legal system* and legal process of international economic relations in context.

The objective of this book is to look at the legal principles and processes as they affect decisions regarding international economic relations, whether the decisions be those of private citizens or enterprises, or government officials. Thus there is an integration of national regulation and international law, and to a lesser extent private transaction law (which however is not emphasized in this course because it is often a part or at least analogous to material learned in other courses.) For example, United States constitutional and regulatory rules have an intimate and weighty connection and influence on the international rules of GATT (The General Agreement on Tariffs and Trade.) One must study both to fully understand how they operate, because they interact.

Secondly, the emphasis is on trade in goods and related monetary problems, because these are generally at the center of international economic relations. Many other subjects are important, e.g. various "invisibles" or service transactions such as shipping, insurance, tourism—but although these may be touched upon from time to time, constraints of space and time suggest a priority treatment for the center of gravity of international economic relations. The principles learned there, however, are almost always transferable to other economic relation subjects e.g. the constitutional problems of division of governmental authority within a nation, the practicalities of negotiating new international rules, the "constitutional" status of international norms, the difficulties of international dispute settlement procedures, the particular weight of special interest groups and their influence compared with broader but more diffuse foreign policy objectives or the interests of the consumers, the operation of legislative bodies, the decision and voting processes of international organizations, the economic complexity of some of the rules, and the difficulty of fact finding.

Thirdly, the emphasis of this book is on the legal processes in *context,* but the emphasis is on *law.* The context obviously includes difficult conceptional and empirical questions of economics and political science, of sociology, history and especially overall foreign policy. But the emphasis here is on those subjects which have developed relatively sophisticated *rule* systems. There are many important subjects which have not yet developed such rule systems, and while touched upon they have not been selected for extensive treatment. (A course in economics, or world politics, therefore, might involve quite a different selection.) For example, both expert controls and problems of developing countries merit considerable policy attention. But rule systems or the influence of law on those subjects, is not (yet) weighty. Both subjects are dealt with in this book, but the focus on the primary goal of understanding the operation of *law,* means that it is necessary to eschew some tempting elaborations of policy questions when they, as yet, depend so little on law. This does not foreclose, of course, the opportunity for a particular teacher to construct for his class a rule formulating exercise based on the current and temporary materials bearing on the policy issues. Nor does this reflect any view of the author regarding the relative importance in a broader context of nonlegal materials or information. It reflects his view that it is useful for law students to examine closely to what extent their particular skills and knowledge could contribute to solution of the myriad international economic problems.

A word at this point might be in order as to the differences perceived by the author between a "legal" or lawyer's approach on the one hand, and the approach of an economist or political scientist on the other. Such a word, of course, risks angering one or the other of these groups, but may nevertheless be interesting and provocative to the reader. It seems to this writer that the lawyer is often more concerned with precision, with individual problems, and with the practical limitations on realizing objectives, than his counterparts from other disciplines. The economist skillfully analyzes the overall or macro effects of various policies, and sees them in statistical terms. Often the political scientist does likewise. The lawyer is frequently forced to resolve individual problems, either those of particular citizens or those of a particular circumstance, often involving competing policy goals—both (or all of them) valid, but necessitating compromise. Likewise the lawyer is often a person who is asked to *implement* a policy and faces practical obstacles to such implementation. Could one say that the economist tells us what should be done, and then the lawyer worries about how to do it? In some cases, however, the lawyer is forced to (uncomfortably) play the role of the guardian of long run goals (preserving a constitution, for example) against those who strive for short term expediency.

Obviously these reflections are not entirely accurate, but it seems clear that there is a difference in role as well as approach between those trained as lawyers and those trained in other disciplines—for better or worse.

Fourthly, a basic goal of these materials is to be sensitive to their use in the setting of the American law school curricula, so as to avoid unnecessary duplication of other courses, and to present to the student a coherent subject matter that he is not likely to obtain elsewhere. This is the reason, for example, for deemphasizing private transaction law in this book, while focusing on government regulation. It is also a reason for minimizing duplication of material often included in either public or private (conflicts) international law. To a certain degree this author sees this course as a logical sequel to the course in public international law. However this book is designed to accommodate the many students who take it without first having taken international law.

Fifthly, closely related to the previous "premise", is the notion that this course should be sensitive to the problems faced by practitioners—lawyers or officials, but should also offer the student something which he may never again (in practice) have the opportunity to get—namely, an opportunity to examine at length and in depth the overall operation of the "legal system" governing international economic affairs. The day to day problems faced by practitioners will quickly give the young lawyer experience in "how to do it", and great expertise on rather precise narrow topics. What is hard to obtain after leaving law school is the opportunity to spend a considerable amount of time achieving a comprehensive understanding of the total system and the interrelationships of its parts. This book emphasizes this comprehensive viewpoint.

Sixthly, so as to minimize the otherwise rapid obsolescence of both this book and students' learning, attention has been directed more toward the "constitutional" or fundamental aspects of the subject, eschewing too much concern with very recent "current events." In this respect the timing of this book has some advantages and some disadvantages. United States law has just undergone an enormous overhauling. The Trade Act of 1974 has revised the comparable 1962 statute, and added many subjects. Probably this law will remain in place for more than a decade, and the reader will discover that this law forms a sort of "leitmotiv" for this book, consistently appearing in almost every chapter as it bears on our subject matter. The GATT—which represents at the international level the basic "statute" is in great need of change, but the likelihood of much change in the near future seems remote. Trade negotiations underway in Geneva as this is written could bring fruition for some changes in the near future, but competent observers suspect results will take somewhat longer. On the other hand this book catches the international monetary system in the middle of fundamental revision—and the materials reflect that and focus on the likely results of that revision.

Finally, although designed primarily as an instructional tool for law courses, this book has also been designed so as to be useful for research and reference. Concerning almost every subject there has been included a "research footnote", that is, a relatively long footnote listing some of the more general and useful recent secondary works concerning the subject, which should assist a person—be he student or practitioner—to approach the subject so as to help solve his problem.

A few other observations and explanations about the nature of these materials are in order. It is clear that court cases as such cannot form the "backbone" of instruction of this subject matter. There are too few such cases, and the real context of the problems too often ranges more broadly. Thus many other materials are included. In particular documents are important, and the supplement contains the text of key documents. Most chapters contain many queries or problems, and often these must be discussed in the context of the documents in the supplement. Consequently the class time needed for such discussion may be greater than would appear from the number of pages devoted to a topic. Often class discussion can center around the problems—in the light of the materials furnished, including the documents.

This book is designed primarily for a three semester hour course (45 classroom hours) although it is clear that a course of such length cannot cover all of this book. A four hour (60 classes) course would likely be both necessary (and sufficient) to complete all of this book. A shorter course has the added luxury of some selection.

JOHN H. JACKSON

Ann Arbor, Michigan
June, 1977

Acknowledgments

This second edition of the book has built considerably on the first edition, and thus we continue to be in the debt of all those who contributed so much to the first edition. As the book evolved into its second edition, we were particularly indebted to the comments and reactions received from teachers and students who used the first edition, in particular those who have taken our courses in international trade law at the University of Michigan Law School and the University of Illinois College of Law. In addition, we are much indebted to our friends and colleagues, both within and without the legal profession, both here and abroad, who have patiently engaged in discussions with us and/or reviewed drafts of the manuscript covering some of the difficult issues raised in a book with such a broad scope as this one. In this regard we owe special thanks to Jacques H.J. Bourgeois of the EC, Dean Peter Hay of Illinois, Peter Kenen of Princeton, Harold Koh of Yale and Daniel K. Tarullo of Harvard.

While it is not possible to name all of those who have contributed significantly to our work and thinking in preparing this edition, a few individuals who have worked with us closely are particularly worthy of recognition. These include our research assistants since the appearance of the first edition in 1977: Edwin Vermulst, William Ingram, Judi Wilson Marshall, Karin Siefert, Melanie Julian Muckle, Rory Perry, Raymond Check, Loveen Moody, & David Laverty and Il Young Byun, all of Michigan, and Robert Cross and Mark Brodeur of Illinois. In addition, the devoted work of our secretaries, Barbara A. Shapiro and Donna Ross, has been particularly valuable.

*

Summary of Contents

*

Table of Contents

PART II. REGULATORY PRINCIPLES AND IMPORT RESTRAINTS: THE CORE OF THE SYSTEM

PART IV. MANAGING WORLD ECONOMIC INTERDEPENDENCE

*

Table of Cases

The principal cases are in bold type. Cases cited or discussed in the text are in roman type. References are to pages. Cases cited in principal cases and within other quoted materials are not included.

Table of Statutes and Constitutions Cited

References are to pages and footnotes.
(See also Table of International Agreements, and the Index)

Table of International Agreements or Similar Documents

*

A Note on Style and Abbreviations

We have indicated deletions from quoted materials by asterisks, except that we have not indicated deletions of footnotes, citations or internal cross references. The footnotes in this book have been numbered sequentially in each section, with the exception of footnotes in quoted material, which are numbered as in the original and are indicated by an asterisk.

The following is a list of common abbreviations used in the book:

List of Common Abbreviations

ASP	American Selling Price	Euratom	European Atomic Energy Community
BNA ITR	Bureau of National Affairs, International Trade Reporter—Current Reports	FCN	Friendship Commerce and Navigation
BOP	Balance of Payments	FOB	Free on Board
BTN	Brussels Tariff Nomenclature	FTO	Foreign Trade Organizations (Non-market)
CAP	Common Agricultural Policy of the EC	GATT	General Agreement on Tariffs and Trade
CIEC	Conference on International Economic Cooperation (the North-South Dialogue)	GSP	Generalized System of Preferences
CIEP	Council on International Economic Policy (U.S. Government)	IBRD	International Bank for Reconstruction and Development ("World Bank")
CIF	Cost, Insurance and Freight	IMF	International Monetary Fund
CIT	Court of International Trade	ITA	International Trade Administration, U.S. Department of Commerce
Comecon	Council for Mutual Economic Assistance (Communist countries)	ITC	International Trade Commission (U.S. Government; formerly the "Tariff Commission")
COREPER	Committee of Permanent Representatives		
EC	European Communities	ITO	International Trade Organization
E.C.R.	European Court Reports; Official Reports of the Court of Justice of the EC (in English)	ITRD	Bureau of National Affairs, International Trade Reporter—Decisions (published bi-weekly and later in bound volumes)
ECSC	European Coal and Steel Community		
EEC	European Economic Community	LDC	Less Developed or Developing Countries
EFTA	European Free Trade Association	MFN	Most-Favored-Nation clause or treatment

MTN	Multilateral Trade Negotiations
NME	Nonmarket Economies
NTB	Nontariff Barrier
OECD	Organization of Economic Co-operation and Development
OMA	Orderly Marketing Agreement
OTC	Organization for Trade Cooperation
PPA	Protocol of Provisional Application of the GATT
SDR	Special Drawing Rights (in the IMF)
STC	State Trading Corporations
STR	Special Trade Representative (U.S. Government)
TEA	Trade Expansion Act of 1962 (U.S.)
UNCITRAL	United Nations Commission on International Trade Law

UNIDROIT	International Institute for the Unification of Private Law
UNSITC	United Nations Standard International Trade Classification
USITC	United States International Trade Commission (formerly Tariff Commission—USTC)
USTR	United States Trade Representative (formerly the Special Trade Representative (STR))
VRA	Voluntary Restraint (or Orderly Marketing) Agreement
Williams Commission	Commission on International Trade and Investment Policy (U.S. Government, July 1971)

LEGAL PROBLEMS OF
INTERNATIONAL ECONOMIC RELATIONS
Second Edition

*

Part I

THE LEGAL STRUCTURE OF THE REGULATION OF INTERNATIONAL ECONOMIC RELATIONS

Chapter 1

THE POLICIES UNDERLYING INTERNATIONAL ECONOMIC RELATIONS

SECTION 1.1 INTERNATIONAL ECONOMIC RELATIONS AND THE LAW

(A) THE INTERDEPENDENCE PHENOMENON AND THE BRETTON WOODS SYSTEM

"Interdependence" may be an overworked word, but it accurately describes our world today. The United States depends on exports and imports for an increasing percentage of its national economy, and many other countries have a much higher dependence on trade (see Section 1.2). Under these conditions, economic influences flow with great rapidity from one country to the next. Thus, despite all the talk about sovereignty, independence, and equality of nations, these concepts are fiction if used to describe today's world. What is the sovereignty of a country whose economy is so dependent on trade with other countries that its government cannot unilaterally determine its own domestic interest rate, or set its own tax policy, or establish its own program of incentives for business or talented individuals? As a result there is much frustration among governments and their leaders today because they find it difficult to carry out their program goals on behalf of their constituents, such as providing full employment or increasing economic welfare.

To a great extent contemporary international economic interdependence can be attributed to the success of the institutions put in place just after World War II, what we call in this book the Bretton Woods System, which includes the IMF (International Monetary Fund) and GATT (the General Agreement on Tariffs and Trade). GATT in particular has been a major force over the last four decades in greatly reducing tariff barriers to trade in industrial goods, at least among the democratic market-oriented industrial countries. To be sure, decreases in the costs of transportation and communication may have had the largest role in increasing levels of trade and interdependence, but without the rules of the Bretton Woods System, governments could easily have acted to negate the effect of such cost decreases.

With the decline of tariffs almost to irrelevancy, however, other much more complex barriers or distortions of trade have become relatively more important. Nontariff barriers are myriad, and the ingenuity of man to invent new ones assures us that the problem of trade barriers will never go away. This is why one of the most important problems facing the world today is institutional—the question of whether national and international governmental institutions (such as GATT) have the capacity to meet the challenges of private and governmental behavior which could undermine the inter-linked trade and investment world in which we find ourselves.

As the focus of international trade and economic policy has shifted from tariffs, enterprises troubled by foreign competition have been compelled to look for other ways to obtain protection from such competition. In particular, they have turned to laws designed to provide relief from unfair trade practices. In many cases it is appropriate that they do so. It has been recognized, however, that in some cases attempts are being made to respond to practices that are unfair only in the eyes of the domestic industries that would like freedom from the challenges that competition brings.

There is an increasing number of situations which involve very difficult balancing of contradictory economic, cultural, and political goals. The essential policy behind unfair trade practice rules is the notion of the "level playing field." This is the idea that enterprises should be able to compete in the open markets of the world on the basis of market economic principles which apply equally to all participating enterprises. Unfortunately, we are well aware that many societies do not have the affinity for market economics that we in the United States do. Thus, at the very base of the policies toward "unfair" trade in international relations, we are troubled by deep and fundamental differences of opinion about the appropriate economic role of governments.

In addition to problems concerning trade in goods, there are a number of other important and perplexing issues of international economic relations. Monetary issues take a central place among these. With fundamental shifts in the Bretton Woods System regarding international discipline on monetary matters, the world has experienced a degree of volatility of exchange rate changes that appears to be much greater than was predicted would accompany the change to "floating" exchange rates. When an exchange rate changes by 20 or 30 percent within even one year, many product-specific import barriers which are often of a magnitude of less than 10 percent (in terms of ad valorem tariff equivalent) appear relatively less important. Interdependence is brought home by statistics that indicate that over $150 billion move across national borders EVERY DAY, often commanded merely by several keystrokes on a computer terminal.[1]

Beyond the traditional core subjects of trade in goods and monetary matters, international economic policies and legal problems have become increasingly complex and diverse. Subjects such as taxation, trade in services, application of antitrust rules, all have their impact on economic relations between nations.

1. N.Y. Times, November 25, 1985, at D5.

A central feature of this book is the focus on the way national legal systems interact and intertwine with international legal rules and institutions. Illustrations of this feature can be found scattered through the chapters of this work. One prominent example, to which we return in a later chapter, was briefly summarized by one of the authors in another book as follows: [2]

> An example from an earlier period of history illustrates the focus of this inquiry. Immediately after World War II, several initiatives converged into a proposal to establish an International Trade Organization (ITO). After years of international negotiations, the 1948 draft Havana Charter was completed. This charter would have established an ITO to become the framework for international rules designed to prevent the kind of destructive national government "beggar-thy-neighbor" policies many thought had contributed to the causes of the war. Despite these elaborate preparations, the effort to create an ITO ultimately failed (although an earlier effort to create monetary rules and a monetary fund—the IMF—had succeeded). The ITO effort failed largely because of the domestic constitutional and political structure of the country then economically preeminent—the United States. It failed despite the fact that the major leadership for the effort to create it had come from the United States itself. But this leadership was that of the executive branch or presidency in the United States. Under the U.S. constitutional and legal requirements, for the government to formally accept the ITO charter, the executive branch had to get the approval of the U.S. Congress, and this the Congress refused to give. In 1950 it was clear that it would be futile to continue trying to obtain this approval, and the ITO was stillborn.

> At the same time as the efforts to create an ITO were occurring, another set of international economic rules was being drafted. These were embodied in an agreement entitled The General Agreement on Tariffs and Trade, commonly called the GATT. Unlike the ITO, the GATT did come into force, largely because particular laws at that time allowed the executive branch to commit the United States to the GATT obligations without further approval of Congress. In fact the GATT gradually had to fill the vacuum created by the ITO failure, and today it has come to play the central role in the international economic system as it relates to trade in goods. It plays this role uneasily, however, with a defective constitutional structure not designed to support it.

(B) OVERVIEW AND STRUCTURE OF THE BOOK

For purposes of analysis, the law of the international trade transaction can be divided into three "levels." The first is the private law of the transaction, which includes the contract and sales laws of the two nations involved, conflict of laws ("private international law"), insurance law, corporate law, and maritime law. For reasons indicated in the Preface, this book does not focus on the private law of international transactions. Nevertheless Chapter 2 is designed to give a brief survey of this law, to assist those

2. J. Jackson, J.–V. Louis & M. Matsushita, Implementing the Tokyo Round: National Constitutions and International Economic Rules 1–2 (1984). Reprinted by permission of the authors.

readers who wish to do so to "review" their knowledge of some typical transactions in the context of business that crosses national borders.

The second level of law of the international trade transaction is the national governmental regulation that is imposed on the transaction. Here must be considered the law of customs tariffs, export and import controls, quality and packaging standards, internal taxes (which may discriminate against foreign goods), and special mixing or purchasing requirements (such as "Buy American" laws). Each nation has its own set and those of the United States, for instance, are wide-ranging, diverse, and pervasive—every export transaction and every import transaction requires at least one report to the United States Government. The purposes to be achieved by these laws are varied, often contradictory, and sometimes related to political pressures of special-interest groups at the expense of broader benefit to the nation as a whole. One troubling facet about these laws in the United States is that they are administered by a wide variety of agencies and the laws themselves are sprinkled throughout the United States Code so that it is difficult to find the relevant statutes or to co-ordinate the policies of different agencies.

The third and last level of law that affects the international trade transaction is the international law, or law of international economic institutions. Usually this law applies only to nations and not directly to individuals or business units. Thus the effect of this international law is indirect, but it may be profound. The fact that it is indirect has probably contributed to the lack of knowledge about it among traders or their lawyers. Mr. Smith, exporter, doesn't file reports with an international organization and often has never heard of the international law or organization that affects his trade. If either the nation where he lives and exports or the nation to which he exports has laws or regulations that violate an international legal obligation, Mr. Smith will probably be ignorant of that also. Even if he is not ignorant of these facts, he may feel—sometimes correctly, sometimes incorrectly—that there is little he can do about it.

Part I (Chapters 1 through 5) of this book is designed to follow this "three-level" analysis, and to present an overall comprehensive view of the "constitutional" working of the international legal system as it applies to international economic relations. In the remainder of this first chapter we introduce the subject further, and focus on the basic economic and other policies which motivate national and international governmental institutions in their development and application of the rules. Then Chapter 2 provides us with a brief "reminder" of the structure of the underlying transactions. (In our view this material is not unfamiliar to the student, often building on or directly applying material that he has confronted in other basic law courses.) Chapters 3 and 4 then turn to national government legal systems. The United States is the focus of a rather extended treatment in Chapter 3, partly because the book is designed for courses in that country, but also because for better or worse the U.S. economy is so influential on world economic relations; Japan and the European Community are the focus in Chapter 4. Chapter 5 then establishes the ground work for an understanding of the "international constitution" of our subject.

Part II of this book, in Chapters 6 through 10, then takes up the core subjects involved in the regulation of imports. Each chapter discusses one central "regulatory principle," relating the national law to the international rules and institutions. These five chapters, cover basic import restrictions, most-favored-nation obligations, national treatment rules, safeguards and escape clauses, and finally laws designed to permit responses to "unfair" actions of governments or firms engaged in exporting.

These chapters should be viewed not only as an exposition of important trade policy issues, but as sort of a "case study" of the contemporary real life operation of national and international legal rules relating to economic relations among nations. The rules explored in these chapters are possibly the most complex and refined of any international rules which exist today. How they operate (or fail to operate) in the circumstances of modern economies and sovereign state constitutional and other legal constraints, is instructive beyond the borderlines of the substance involved in these rules. The potential for governments to look upon these rules and their institutional context such as GATT and its dispute settlement mechanisms, as a source of analogy for other areas of endeavor (such as flows of investment capital, or cross-border trade in services) is apparent.[3]

In Part III of this book, we turn to a series of other perplexing and increasingly important subjects of international economic relations. We view these chapters as primarily overview chapters, and would recommend that particular teachers select among them according to their (or their students') interests, perhaps adding to the necessarily short selections which we have been able to include in this book. Subjects such as monetary affairs, export controls, politically motivated economic sanctions, commodity problems, trade in services, investment questions, the multinational corporation, antitrust rules and policies, and taxation are covered in this way. The list could easily be longer, but this book and the course contemplated for it are already too crowded.

In Part IV (Chapters 20 through 22) we turn to consideration of the diversity of economic systems in today's world, and look specifically at several different systems to explore how they fit into the basic Bretton Woods system. The brief answer is: not too well! One of the challenges of the near future, is how the elaborate GATT system, which was designed primarily for market economies of mostly advanced industries, can accommodate the special problems of either nonmarket economies, or developing countries. Even in the industrial economies with relatively similar structures, there is sometimes difficulty applying the GATT rules or other policies.

Last, in Chapter 23, we step back from the mosaic of detail involved in this book, and try to draw some preliminary conclusions about the current national and international rules and institutions which could have such a profound effect on the economic and even geo-political future of the world. Don't expect any final answers! We find we are better at asking questions than providing either predictions or sweeping conclusions. To a certain

---

3. See, e.g., Kindleberger & Goldberg, Towards a GATT for Investment: A Proposal for Supervision of the International Corporation, 2 Law & Poly.Intl.Bus. 295 (1970).

extent all the chapters of this book lead up to this last one, so the reader might find it useful to peruse that chapter in progressing through the book.

The first section of all chapters is designed for student background reading, so that class discussion can begin with the second section. Problems for analysis and discussion have been distributed throughout the book, and in many chapters class discussion may center on these problems.

The Preface outlines a number of themes and purposes of the course for which this book is designed, but to suggest a few of the types of questions one might expect to be related to the materials of this book, consider the following:

(1) Suppose your business client is trying to decide whether to build a plant in Europe so as to manufacture and sell small appliances there, or alternatively to expand its manufacturing capacity in the United States with a view to shipping products to Europe for sale there. How can it find out what are the trade barriers to exporting to Europe? How stable are those barriers (or lack of barriers) likely to be over a 20 year period? Consider also the reverse situation—goods shipped from Europe to the United States.

(2) If a plant to manufacture tires is established in a developing country such as Mexico to benefit from lower cost labor, what are the long term probabilities that the product of that plant will be able to be imported into a) the United States, b) Europe, or c) Japan without incurring an increase in government barriers to such imports? Would these imports benefit from zero or low tariffs accorded to developing country products?

(3) What authority does the U.S. President have to cut off or reduce imports from a country which imposes unfair burdens on exports to it from the U.S.?

(4) Can a private firm get its government (e.g., U.S. or EC) to bring pressure to bear on foreign governments which are restraining imports produced by that firm?

(5) What arguments can government representatives use and what international procedures exist for bringing pressure on a government which breaches the international trade rules? Should these procedures be revised?

(6) If imports suddenly increase and compete so as to cause a domestic firm to consider going out of business, are there any government remedies or aids available to that firm or its workers? How do measures available fit into overall foreign economic policies of the country?

(7) To what degree are international trade policies formulated by public or citizen participation? For example, to what degree do legislatures participate in that policy formulation?

(8) Can a private firm, if it expends time and resources to develop a foreign export market, rely upon the stability of the international rules so that its investment will pay satisfactory returns? Could foreign governments quickly change the rules of international trade to prevent

a firm's export sales from taking advantage of its advertising and good will efforts?

(9) How does trade policy contribute to or relate to overall foreign policy objectives? To the problem of keeping the peace? To human liberties?

(10) Do the international trade rules apply directly in United States domestic court lawsuits between two private firms or individuals?

(11) More broadly: How are the government decisions affecting international trade made?

(12) Is the international economic legal system adequate to the stresses of today or the near future? Should it be reformed? *Can* it be reformed? If so, how?

SECTION 1.2   THE GROWTH AND IMPORTANCE OF INTERNATIONAL TRADE

Trade between different areas of the world has occurred throughout history. Indeed, much of the world was discovered and explored by those seeking new trading opportunities—from the Phoenicians in the Mediterranean and the North Atlantic to Marco Polo to the Portuguese and Spanish explorers of the fifteenth and sixteenth centuries. The risks of trading expeditions in these times were great but they were viewed as worth taking in light of the potential profits.

Initially, nations viewed the value of trade in terms of the gold it earned for the exporting nation and its citizens. To expand those earnings by gaining control of the sources of export commodities, as well as to secure export markets, the European nations established colonies throughout the world. To maximize their earnings from trade, they often severely restricted imports. In the nineteenth century, however, in part due to economists, who (as we see in the next subsection) argued that gains from trade would be maximized if trade occurred without restrictions, nations began to reduce their import restrictions. The trend toward reduction was reversed in the 1870's, but the volume of trade continued to grow until World War I. The period between World War I and World War II was not a good time for trade. Increasing tariffs, particularly those adopted in the early 1930's, led to sharp declines in the volume of world trade, thereby deepening the Great Depression.

Following World War II, many national leaders were convinced that it would be mutually advantageous—economically and otherwise—to promote international trade. This book is essentially a study of the institutions and structure that were put in place immediately after the war. The focus will be on the central agreement of that structure—the General Agreement on Tariffs and Trade, better known as GATT. The principal goal of GATT was to establish agreed-upon limitations on tariffs and to control the use of certain non-tariff barriers to trade. As a result of seven subsequent series of negotiations—called rounds, such as the Kennedy Round in the 1960's and the Tokyo Round in the 1970's—significant reductions in tariffs have occurred. From 1934 to 1952, i.e. from the time of the Smoot-Hawley tariff through the Reciprocal Trade Agreements Program to the initial implementation of GATT, average U.S. tariffs on dutiable imports fell from 53% to 12.8%.[1] Little reduction occurred in the next decade. However, as a result of the Kennedy and Tokyo Rounds, it is estimated that U.S. tariffs will average only 5.7% on dutiable imports.[2] Similar reductions have occurred in the tariff rates of other industrialized countries.

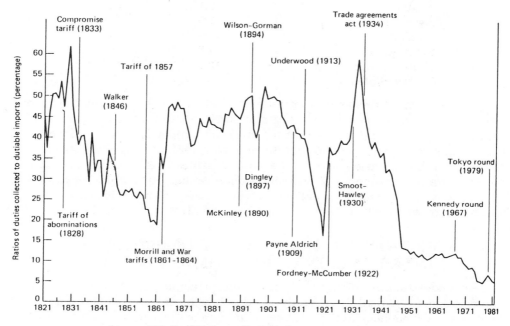

Average U.S. Tariff Rates on Dutiable Imports

Source: Peter B. Kenen, The International Economy © 1985, p. 226. Reprinted by permission of Prentice-Hall, Englewood Cliffs, New Jersey.

Overall, the GATT system has led to significant increases in the volume of world trade. Between 1963 and 1973, world exports grew at a rate of approximately 8½% per year in volume. Even with the economic slowdown of the early 1980's, world exports grew at a rate of about 3% per year between 1973 and 1983. In each case, the growth in export volumes was about 50% greater than the growth in total production during the same period.[3] In the case of manufactures, total world output grew 259% from 1963 to 1983; total world exports grew 429%.[4] As a consequence, international trade has continued to grow more important to national economies.

The degree of importance varies, of course. One way to measure it is to compare the value of a country's exports with its total gross national product. For 1967 and 1983, the following statistics can be found: [5]

1. P. Morici & L. Megna, U.S. Economic Policies Affecting Industrial Trade 8 (1983).

2. S.Rep. No. 96–249, 96th Cong., 1st Sess. 164 (1979).

3. GATT, International Trade 1983/84, at 2 (Table 1) (1984).

4. Id., Appendix, Table A1.

5. The OECD Member Countries, OECD Observer, No. 38, at 19, 24–25 (Feb. 1969); The OECD Member Countries, OECD Observer, No. 133, at 13, 18–19 (Mar. 1985).

Exports as a Percentage of Gross National Product

Country	1967	1983
Canada	17.9	22.8
France	10.4	17.6
Germany	17.9	25.8
Japan	9.1	12.7
Netherlands	31.9	49.6
Sweden	18.9	29.9
Switzerland	21.8	26.4
United Kingdom	13.2	20.2
United States	3.9	6.1

The increasing relative importance of world trade has meant that the economic welfare of one country is often tied closely to that of another. For example, the OECD estimates that a significant proportion of the economic growth that occurred in Japan and Europe from 1982 to 1984 was attributable to their increased exports to the United States.[6] As we will see, this increasing interdependence of national economies has put increasing strains on the GATT system, particularly during times of recession and slow economic growth such as occurred in the early 1980's.

SECTION 1.3 ECONOMIC THEORY AND INTERNATIONAL ECONOMIC POLICY

An understanding of the basic economic principles relating to international trade is critical to a study of the law of international economic relations. Economists are not always in agreement on how these basic principles should be translated into policy, and their views are not always accepted in any event. Nonetheless, their views on the desirability of international trade and the effects of interferences with trade have played an important role in shaping the legal framework in which trade occurs. While much of the economics literature is too theoretical and technical for our purposes,[1] the basic principles can be grasped by non-economists.[2] This section introduces a few of those principles, to which we will refer throughout the book, as well as a sampling of more advanced economic thought in the field of international trade. Here we consider 1) comparative advantage and gains from trade; 2) the effect of restraints on trade; and 3) the validity of arguments in favor of trade restraints.

6. See Growth and Imbalances, OECD Observer, No. 134, at 35, 41 (May 1985).

1. For recent surveys of the economics literature on international trade, see Stern, Tariffs and Other Measures of Trade Control: A Survey of Recent Developments, 11 J. Econ. Literature 857, 882–88 (1973) and Deardorff & Stern, Current Issues in U.S. Trade Policies: An Overview, in R. Stern (ed.), U.S. Trade Policies in a Changing World Economy (forthcoming).

2. For book-length expositions of the economic issues raised by international trade in addition to those excerpted in this chapter by Kindleberger and Kenen, see B. Soderstein, International Economics (2nd ed. 1980); F. Root, International Trade & Investment (5th ed. 1984); P. Ellsworth & J. Leiter, The International Economy (6th ed. 1984); J. Bhagwati & T. Srinivasan, Lectures on International Trade (1983); J. Bhagwati, International Trade: Selected Readings (1981). For more basic discussions of those issues, see P. Samuelson & W. Nordhaus, Economics, chs. 38–39 (12th ed. 1985); R. Lipsey, P. Steiner & D. Purvis, Economics, chs. 41–42 (7th ed. 1984).

(A) COMPARATIVE ADVANTAGE AND GAINS FROM TRADE

CHARLES P. KINDLEBERGER, INTERNATIONAL ECONOMICS

17–21, 27, 33 (5th ed. 1973) [3]

LAW OF COMPARATIVE ADVANTAGE

The classical economists asked what goods would be traded between two countries because they thought the answer for trade between countries was different from that for trade within a country. Within a country, a region produces the goods it can make cheaper than other regions. The value of a commodity within a country, moreover, is determined by its labor content. If the product of a certain industry can be sold for more than the value of the labor it contains, additional labor will transfer into that industry from other occupations to earn the abnormal profits available there. Supply will expand until the price is brought down to the value of the labor it contains. Similarly, if a commodity sells for less than the worth of its labor, labor will move away into other lines until the gap is closed. The tendency of wages toward equality within a country results in prices of goods equal to their labor such as to equalize the return to labor in all occupations and regions. If wages are higher in California than in Massachusetts, labor will migrate to California. This will lower wages in California and raise them in Massachusetts, and the movement will continue until the return to labor is equated in the two regions. After labor has spread itself among several regions to equalize wages, these regions will produce and sell to each other what each region can make the cheapest. Its advantage in such commodities over other regions will be absolute. Therefore the theory of trade applicable to regions of a country is the theory of absolute advantage.

Classical economists thought that the labor theory of value valid in trade within a country cannot be applied between nations, since factors of production are immobile internationally. If wages are higher in the United States than in Britain, they stay higher, for migration cannot take place on a scale sufficient to eliminate discrepancies. Under these circumstances, the classical economists asked, what will the United States sell to Britain and Britain to America?

Let us assume two countries and two commodities. If each country can produce one good cheaper (i.e., with less labor) than it can be produced in the other, as in the case of domestic trade, each will have an advantage in the production of one commodity and a disadvantage in the production of the other. Each country will then be anxious to export the commodity in which it has an advantage and import the commodity in which it has a disadvantage. The position is suggested in the following table, where wheat can be produced more cheaply in the United States and cloth more cheaply in Britain. The United States has an absolute advantage in wheat and an absolute disadvantage in cloth. It will export wheat and import cloth, which, with the numerical values given, may be assumed to exchange one for

---

3. Reprinted by permission from International Economics, Fifth Edition, by Kin-   dleberger (Homewood, IL: Richard D. Irwin, Inc., 1976c).

the other at something like the rate of one yard of cloth for one bushel of wheat:

Production of One Man in One Week

Product	In United States	In United Kingdom
Wheat	6 bushels	2 bushels
Cloth	2 yards	6 yards

But suppose that the labor content of both wheat and cloth is less in the United States than in Britain. Suppose that instead of merely 2 yards of cloth per week a man in the United States can produce 10. The position is then as follows:

Production of One Man in One Week

Product	In United States	In United Kingdom
Wheat	6 bushels	2 bushels
Cloth	10 yards	6 yards

It is evident that labor is more efficient in the United States than in the United Kingdom, and wages in the United States will be higher on that account. By assumption, however, migration will not take place to equalize wage rates.

Trade cannot now follow the decree of absolute advantage and a new principle is needed to take its place. This was developed by David Ricardo more than 150 years ago, in the law of comparative advantage. Ricardo observed that in cases similar to ours, while the United States had an absolute advantage over Britain in both wheat and cloth, it had a greater advantage in wheat than in cloth. He concluded that a country would export the product in which it had the greater advantage, or a comparative advantage, and import the commodity in which its advantage was less, or in which it had a comparative disadvantage. In this example the United States would export wheat and import cloth, even though it could produce cloth more efficiently than Britain.

The reasoning underlying this conclusion may be demonstrated arithmetically. Without international trade, wheat and cloth would exchange for one another in each country at their respective labor contents, which would differ as between the two countries. In the United States, 6 bushels of wheat, or one week's labor, would buy 10 yards of cloth. In Britain, by the same token, 6 bushels of wheat—three weeks' labor in the less productive country—would buy 18 yards of cloth. If the United States through trade can get more than 10 yards of cloth for 6 bushels of wheat (or more than $1\frac{2}{3}$ yards of cloth per bushel of wheat), it will pay it to do so. It cannot hope to get more than 18 yards of cloth for 6 bushels of wheat (3 yards of cloth for a single bushel). This is the price which cloth producers in Britain can get without trade, and there is no reason for them to enter into foreign trade and be worse off.

Similarly, if Britain can get more than 2 bushels of wheat for 6 yards of cloth (more than one third of a bushel of wheat per yard of cloth), it will pay it to export cloth and buy wheat. But it cannot hope to get more than six tenths or three fifths of a bushel per yard—the American wheat farmers' price without trade.

For effective comparison, the prices should be quoted the same way. At any price for cloth cheaper than 10 yards (of cloth) for 6 bushels (of wheat), that is, for any more than 10 yards for 6 bushels, the United States will gain by shifting resources out of cloth into wheat and importing cloth. Similarly, at a price of cloth which would involve Britain giving up less than 18 yards for 6 bushels (equal to 6 yards for 2 bushels), it will pay Britain to move its labor out of wheat into cloth and import wheat in exchange for cloth rather than grow grain itself. Trade raises the price of wheat and lowers the price of cloth in the United States; it raises the price of cloth and lowers the price of wheat in Britain. Even when one country can produce both commodities more efficiently than another country, both can gain from specialization and exchange, provided that the efficiency advantage is greater in some commodity or commodities than in others.

On the basis of this type of demonstration, the classical economists concluded that international trade does not require offsetting absolute advantages but is possible where a comparative advantage exists. It goes without saying but must be said, as it is frequently forgotten, that a comparative advantage is always (and by definition) accompanied by a comparative disadvantage.

PRODUCTION POSSIBILITIES CURVES

The labor theory of value on which this analysis rested was subsequently rejected as invalid. The tendency for the return to labor to be equal throughout a country was seen by observation to be weak and faltering. Labor is not homogeneous. If there is an increase in the demand for barrels, the wages of coopers will rise above those of smiths, with whom they are not interchangeable. It became recognized that there is not one great class of labor with a single wage but a series of noncompeting groups among which the tendency to equalization of wages, at least in the short run, is weak or nonexistent.

A more fundamental objection, however, which would apply even if labor were homogeneous and commanded one price in a perfectly competitive market, is that goods are not produced by labor alone but by various combinations of all the factors of production: land, labor, and capital. To compare the labor content of two commodities—say, gasoline and textiles, or meat and shoes—gives an erroneous view of relative values. Gasoline production requires far more capital per unit of labor than textiles, and meat output more land than shoes. Variable proportions of factors in the production of different commodities make it impossible to use the labor theory of value, however qualified.

An escape from this impasse has been provided by Gottfried Haberler in the theory of opportunity costs. The cost of wheat in the long run is how much cloth a country has to give up to get additional units of wheat. It makes little difference whether the factors which leave the production of cloth are all suited to the output of wheat or not. The question is simply how much of one commodity must be given up to get more of the other.

The notion of opportunity cost is illustrated in international trade theory with production possibilities or transformation curves. Instead of saying that a week's labor will produce either 6 bushels of wheat or 10 yards of cloth, one says that all the factors of production can produce either 6 bushels of wheat or 10 yards of cloth per some appropriate unit of time, or some intermediate combination of them. In figure 2.1, where the vertical axis represents wheat and the horizontal axis cloth, the U.S. curve means that the resources of the United States, in the absence of foreign trade, can be used entirely to produce wheat, in which case 6 bushels (per capita per week) can be produced, exclusively for cloth, in which case output will consist of 10 yards per man-week, or some appropriate intermediate combination, such as 3 bushels of wheat and 5 yards of cloth. The production possibilities curve does not tell what will in fact be produced. More information is needed for this purpose, on the side of demand. It merely sets out what the possibilities are.

FIGURE 2.1. Production Possibilities Curves, Constant Opportunity Costs

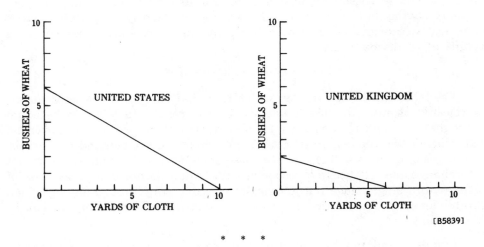

[B5839]

* * *

FACTOR PROPORTIONS

If international trade is based on differences in comparative costs, the curious student will proceed to the next question: What makes for differences in comparative costs? Why do the transformation curves of various countries differ?

The answer given to this question by Swedish economist Bertil Ohlin is two-fold: Different goods, he stated, require different factor inputs; and different countries have different factor endowments. If wheat is technologically best produced with lots of land relative to labor and capital, countries that have an abundance of land will be able to produce wheat cheaply. This is why Australia, Argentina, Canada, Minnesota, and the Ukraine export wheat. On the other hand, if cloth requires much labor relative to capital and land, countries that have an abundance of labor—Hong Kong, Japan,

India—will have a comparative advantage in cloth manufacture and be able to export it.

* * *

* * * Differences in comparative costs come about not only because of differences in factor endowments but also through specialization in different commodities. To a degree the choice of whether the United States or Britain specializes in one kind of an automobile or another, or this tractor or that, may be determined by historical accident. The fact is that, with each country specialized, a basis for trade exists, since each can produce one good cheaper than the other.

MILTIADES CHACHOLIADES, INTERNATIONAL TRADE THEORY AND POLICY

305–06 (1978) [4]

Several distinguished economists have argued recently that perhaps the composition of trade depends on dynamic factors such as technical change. In particular, it has been argued that what gives the United States its ability to compete in world markets is its ability to supply a steady flow of new products.

The technological-gap theory makes use of the sequence of innovation and imitation, particularly as they affect exports. As a new product is developed in a country and becomes profitable in the domestic market, the innovating firm, which enjoys a temporary monopoly, has initially an easy access to foreign markets. Initially, the country's exports grow. Later on, however, the profits of the innovating firm prompt imitation in other countries which may actually prove to have a comparative advantage in the production of the new commodity after the innovation is disseminated. * * * But as the innovating country loses, through imitation, its absolute advantage in one commodity, a new cycle of innovation imitation begins in another. Thus, the innovating country may continue to develop new products and may continue to have a temporary absolute advantage in products which are eventually more efficiently produced by other countries.

* * *

The technological-gap theory fails to explain why the gap is what it is, and why it is not larger or smaller. Raymond Vernon generalized the theory into the product cycle which stresses the standardization of products. In particular, the product-cycle theory suggests three product stages: new product, maturing product, and standardized product. In addition, the input requirements change over the life-cycle of a new product. For instance, at the new-product stage, production requires much highly skilled labor for the development and improvement of the product. As the product matures, marketing and capital costs become dominant. Finally, at the standardized-product stage, the technology stabilizes and the product enjoys general consumer acceptance. This leads to mass production which largely requires

---

4. Reprinted by permission of McGraw–Hill Book Co. See also E. Leamer, Sources of International Comparative Advantage (1984); Balassa, Changing Patterns of Comparative Advantage in Manufacturing Goods, 61 The Rev. of Econ. & Stat. 259 (1979); Majumdar, An Industry Study of Dynamic Comparative Advantage, 32 Kyklos 559 (1979).

raw materials, capital, and unskilled labor. Accordingly, as the product matures and becomes standardized, comparative advantage may shift from a country relatively abundant in skilled labor to a country which is abundant in unskilled labor.

* * *

Why does the United States have a comparative advantage based on technology and innovation? Several factors are usually cited for this phenomenon. First, the United States has a per capita income which is high by international standards—a fact which creates unique consumption patterns and a favorable market for new or improved products. Second, the development of new or improved products requires much skilled labor which is relatively abundant in the United States. Third, because of the high U.S. labor costs and the alleged tendency of innovations to be labor saving, there is a greater incentive to innovate in the United States. * * * Finally, the development and marketing of new or improved products may be associated with economies of scale which tend to be realizable in large, high-income markets such as that of the United States. This last point is, of course, closely related to the first.

Notes and Questions

(1) The readings from Kindleberger and Chacholiades suggest a number of variables that affect a nation's comparative advantages: factor endowment, historical accident, research and development expenditures. The impact of some such variables can be affected by government and private action—including by such non-trade-related activities as promoting education in engineering and sciences. By doing so, a nation over time may be able to create a comparative advantage in particular types of products. Does this ability to create and shift comparative advantages make comparative advantage a meaningless concept? We will later consider whether implementation of such conscious policies is somehow unfair and whether countries that do not do so should be able to restrict trade with those that do in order to reestablish the "natural" balance of comparative advantages.[5]

(2) In the early 1980's, the appreciation in the value of the U.S. dollar relative to the currencies of the principal trading partners of the United States was a major cause of large U.S. balance of trade deficits. Normally, such deficits would lead to a decline in the value of the dollar, but this did not occur, apparently in large part because investors in foreign countries used the dollars earned by trade to invest directly in the United States or in dollar-denominated assets. The ability of such capital flows to affect exchange rates and thereby the balance of trade for reasons not necessarily related to traditional measures of comparative advantage—such as manufacturing efficiency—has caused some economists to question whether comparative advantage is still a meaningful concept. In particular, can the theory of comparative advantage be useful for planning and policy purposes if a manufacturing plant entailing a large investment with a useful life of 10 years can be rendered comparatively disadvantageous as a result of an exchange rate shift caused by capital flows in its first year of operation? If that occurs, should the plant be scrapped, moth-balled or

5. See Chapter 22 infra. The efficacy of such policies is disputed. See Kindleberger, Government Policies and Changing Shares of World Trade, 70 Am.Econ.Rev. 293 (1980).

operated with the hope that exchange rates will shift again? What assistance should a government offer in such an event?

In recognition of problems caused by the overvalued dollar, the United States and four other major trading nations—France, Germany, Japan and the United Kingdom—tried in 1985 to lower the value of the dollar, in an effort to make its value reflect more closely "fundamental economic conditions." [6] Whether such efforts will be successful is not clear as of this writing (December 1985).

(B) INTERFERENCE WITH FREE TRADE

Economists generally believe that free international trade is beneficial to a nation because when each nation specializes in making the products that it can make most efficiently and trades for the other products it needs, overall welfare is increased in each nation. Economist Paul Samuelson once wrote, "[T]here is essentially only one argument for free trade or freer trade, but it is an exceedingly powerful one, namely: Free trade promotes a mutually profitable division of labor, greatly enhances the potential real national product of all nations, and makes possible higher standards of living all over the globe." [7]

It is important to understand, however, that there is a gain only in an overall sense. Within a national economy certain sectors, particularly those that produce goods made more efficiently abroad and that may be expected by economic theorists to shift from their present activities because of import competition, are likely to pressure their governments to interfere with free trade in order to afford them protection from such competition. For example, if domestic consumption of widgets is 1 million units per year at $10 each, and foreign producers could sell widgets in the United States market at $8 each, a $2 per widget tariff will enable domestic producers to keep the U.S. market to themselves. Unless a consumer uses many widgets, his loss is only a small amount ($2 per widget) and he has little interest in organizing a lobbying effort against the tariff. In contrast, producers and labor unions can afford to make large campaign contributions to influence politicians to preserve the $2 tariff and protect their profits and jobs. Indeed, since such lobbying is relatively cheap compared to the gains that may be obtained, industries may lobby for protection even when import competition is not causing problems. In this subsection, we consider the general effect of tariffs and whether they may be justified in certain circumstances.

(1) The Effect of Tariffs

The two most common types of restraints on imports are tariffs (a tax levied on imports at the time of importation, which usually has the effect of increasing the prices at which the imports are sold) and quotas (an upper limit on the quantity or value of imports allowed during a given time period).

6. N.Y. Times, Sept. 23, 1985, at 1. See generally Section 11.1(D) infra; Hearings on the Causes and Effects of the Cumulative Appreciation of the Dollar Against the Currencies of Other Major Industrial Nations Before the Subcomm. on Intl. Finance & Monetary

Policy of the Senate Comm. on Banking, Housing & Urban Affairs, 98th Cong., 2d Sess. (1984).

7. P. Samuelson, Economics 692 (9th ed. 1973).

The effects of tariffs and quotas are demonstrated by diagrams in the Appendix to this Chapter. Here, we will discuss these effects on an intuitive level.

The availability of imported goods limits the price that domestic producers can charge. If they charge more than the price of the imported goods, consumers will purchase more imports. Imposition of a tariff typically results in (i) an increase in government revenue equal to the amount of the tariff collected and (ii) an increase in the consumer price of the import. A higher price for the imported product means domestic producers can increase their prices. Thus, imposition of a tariff on a product typically results in a number of effects: domestic consumption of the product will fall because of the higher price; domestic consumers will pay more for each unit of the product and thus will have less to spend on other products; the domestic producers will increase their revenues per unit of product; the government's revenue will increase. As shown in the Appendix, economists generally believe that the loss to consumers, though spread among many, exceeds the gains of the producers and the government.

Economists analyze quotas by comparing them to tariffs that have similar price effects. The main difference is that the benefits of the price increase go the foreign producer unless the government sells rights to use the quota. Economists generally prefer tariffs to quotas because quotas may have a more adverse effect on competition. Even if the government sells rights to use quotas so that foreign producers do not obtain monopoly profits, the existence of quotas may put domestic industry in a position to reap such profits. Apart from these economic considerations, there are numerous practical considerations that influence the choice between tariffs and quotas. For example, it is argued that quotas tend to conceal from the public the degree of protection being afforded domestic producers. On the other hand, economic planning may be easier if the precise amount of imports can be predicted—quotas may allow this, while tariffs make such prediction more difficult.

(2) Justifications for Tariffs

The arguments raised by the potential beneficiaries of trade restrictions are numerous and varied. Most of the arguments have no foundation in economic analysis, although some are based on a belief that certain unrealistic assumptions underlie the theory of comparative advantage. We will discuss these latter arguments in subsequent subsections.

First, so-called mercantilist arguments are put forward. Those arguments, which were generally accepted prior to Ricardo, assert that the wealth of a nation is increased by promoting exports and restricting imports. The arguments make sense if accumulation of money *per se* is desirable. Most economists believe that money has value only to the extent it can be exchanged for goods. Thus, a country that sends more goods abroad than it imports will eventually reduce the well-being of its inhabitants, at least in terms of the amount and variety of goods available to them.

Second, it is argued that tariff protection will give domestic producers a larger market share, thereby creating more jobs in the domestic economy. But as the analysis in the Appendix of the effect of a tariff shows, a tariff on a particular product is likely to reduce the total quantity of goods that consumers are able to buy with a given amount of income and result in overall economic inefficiency, both of which will result in the nation's economy being worse off, even if one sector benefits. Of course, this argument may have more force in a period of high unemployment. But even in such a case, use of trade restrictions is inefficient and unnecessary in the sense that there are more direct ways to combat unemployment. Moreover, this is a policy that tries to "export" unemployment to the country whose imports are reduced. That country may retaliate by imposing tariffs itself, leading to an ever decreasing volume of world trade that is likely to leave everyone worse off. Such a chain of events helped prolong the Great Depression and is one of the principal reasons that nations have tried to agree on trade rules since World War II.

Third, it is argued that interference is necessary to protect workers in a high-wage nation from "pauper labor" in developing countries. It is suggested that producers in the high-wage nation cannot compete against producers in such countries because of the difference in labor costs. Of course, direct labor costs are only one factor in production costs; it is also necessary to consider other factors, such as intensity of capital use and labor productivity. A highly productive labor force using advanced production machinery and techniques may well produce goods that can be sold at a lower price than those produced by "pauper labor." Moreover, if it cannot, the theory of comparative advantage suggests that it should produce goods where it does have an advantage.

Fourth, it is sometimes argued that tariffs should be imposed to equalize costs in the importing and exporting nations. The result of such an action would be to prevent all trade since the basis of international trade depends on comparative cost differences.

Fifth, it is argued that some peculiar national interests require trade restrictions: the need to protect an industry necessary for national defense or some other national goal; the need to enable a new industry having a potential comparative advantage to develop to the size necessary to achieve that comparative advantage (the "infant industry" argument); the need to diversify the economy of a developing country—either by expanding the range of products exported in order to reduce dependence on the export earnings of a few products or by promoting balanced internal growth. These arguments may have merit, but as discussed below, other economic policies would probably be better suited to achieve those goals.

(3) Optimal Tariffs, Retaliation and Strategy

ALAN V. DEARDORFF AND ROBERT M. STERN, CURRENT ISSUES IN U.S. TRADE POLICIES: AN OVERVIEW [8]

NATIONAL MONOPOLY POWER AND THE OPTIMAL TARIFF

The idealized assumptions of the classic argument for free trade imply the optimality of free trade only for the world as a whole. For individual countries the optimality of free trade requires the additional assumption

---

8. From R. Stern, note 1 supra. This and other excerpts from this publication in this section are reprinted by permission of The MIT Press.

that the country is too small to have any influence, through its policies, over the prices at which it trades. Without that assumption it is well known that free trade is not optimal from a national perspective, and instead that there exists an optimal degree of trade intervention, known as the optimal tariff, that works by turning the country's terms of trade in its favor.

* * *

This argument is sometimes thought to require that the country in question be large, and therefore to apply only to such large industrialized countries as the U.S. However, the argument really applies to some extent to any country that is not insignificantly small. Furthermore, the size that is important is not the size of the country as a whole, but rather its share of world trade in markets in which it exports and imports. Since many countries tend to specialize their exports in a fairly small range of goods— exactly as trade theory predicts they should, incidentally—even quite small countries may have enough market power over the prices of their exports for the optimal tariff argument to apply.

Now the optimal tariff argument has the important feature that it involves a benefit for the intervening country only at the expense of the country's trading partners. Indeed, since free trade is known to be optimal for the world as a whole, it must be true that the rest of the world loses more than the tariff-levying country gains. Furthermore, the rest of the world, were it able to act collectively, would have the same sort of power over the terms of trade as does the original country and it is therefore quite inappropriate to think of a single country as levying an optimal tariff in isolation. The possibility that other countries may do the same, either in retaliation or simply because they too think they recognize an opportunity for gain, must surely be considered.

This feature of the optimal tariff argument—that it involves gain by one country at other countries' expense—is one that [is found] in some of the newer arguments for trade intervention. To address such arguments in a common framework, we will refer to such trade policies as being "exploitative intervention." Such policies typically are available to more than one, if not many, countries, each of which can have adverse effects on the others, and therefore require that strategic issues be considered. Like other forms of exploitative intervention to be considered below, the optimal tariff argument is likely to find countries in the classic position of the Prisoners' Dilemma. That is, each country has available a policy that will benefit itself at the expense of others, but, if all countries simultaneously pursue that policy, all are likely to lose.

* * *

* * * The appropriate policy * * * depends on what policies will be undertaken abroad, on how those policies may depend on the policies that we ourselves pursue or claim that we will pursue, and so forth. Thus exploitative intervention policies, even without the complications of imperfect competition to be discussed, inevitably raise the complicated and perhaps unsolvable strategic issues.

AVINASH DIXIT, HOW SHOULD THE U.S. RESPOND TO OTHER COUNTRIES TRADE POLICIES [9]

Schelling identifies three basic kinds of strategic moves: commitments, threats, and promises. A commitment is an unconditional, irreversible prior policy choice. A free trade clause in the constitution would be an example, so would an undertaking to provide interest-free export credits. Once we have made such a choice, the foreigners' policies must be made in the light of ours, but they do not have to take into account any further repercussions on our actions. By contrast, threats and promises are prior choices of contingent policy rules. The rules themselves are irreversible, but the actual actions they dictate depend on what other countries do in the meantime. A countervailing duty code, or an aggressive reciprocity law, are examples of threats; a formula for reciprocal tariff cutting is an example of a promise. Threats are further divided into deterrent and compellent ones. The [countervailing duty code] is of the former kind; its purpose is not one of collecting revenue, but of preventing foreigners from subsidizing their exports. Aggressive reciprocity is for compellence; we threaten damaging actions unless others open their markets. With both threats and promises, but especially with the latter, there is a further difference between unilateral and mutual use. Sometimes it suffices for just one country to use the policy; at other times, such as Prisoners' Dilemma situations, both or all countries must participate to sustain the desired outcome.

If the action we commit ourselves to, or threaten, or promise, were our optimal response to the other country's action after the fact, there would be no need for us to do anything in advance. At the most, and just to be sure, we might remind the others of the coming response. It is only when such is not the case that we have to adopt the action or the policy rule in advance. Two questions arise. First, why might it be advantageous to take a prior action that is not optimal after the fact? Second, how can it be taken in such a way that the others believe us?

The answer to the first is that if we can take the action demonstrably and credibly, it alters the others' expectations, and therefore their actions. The "fact" in "after the fact" itself changes, and this can be beneficial to us. For example, a deterrent threat, such as retaliation leading to a trade war, may be too costly for us to carry out if the occasion arises. But if others see that we are resolved to do so, then they will not take the first steps that lead to the crisis. The occasion for the trade war will not arise, and the whole situation will have changed to our benefit. As another example, the promise of tariff concessions may be costly once their concession has been received, but it would not have been forthcoming had our promise not been credible. The whole package of concessions may be better for us than the status quo.

The second question is trickier. The others would need assurance that we would not renege on our promises. Nor would they fear our threats if they know that we had the freedom to back down if the matter were put to the test. They would not consider our commitments binding if they believed

9. From R. Stern, note 1 supra.

that we had avenues of retreat from them. The problem of achieving credibility is a subtle one in both theory and practice.

(4) Domestic Distortions and Second–Best Policies

ALAN V. DEARDORFF & ROBERT M. STERN, CURRENT ISSUES IN U.S. TRADE POLICIES: AN OVERVIEW
Page 19 supra.

"SECOND-BEST" ARGUMENTS FOR INTERVENTION

A crucial assumption underlying the classic gains-from-trade proposition is that everything within the domestic economy is working properly. Thus, it is assumed that all domestic markets are perfectly competitive, that prices and wages adjust freely so that markets clear, and that there are no externalities in production or consumption. If any of these conditions fails to hold, then there exists a "domestic distortion" and the first-best optimal results of free trade are no longer assured. Instead, the very distortionary effects that trade interventions are known to have could conceivably be used to offset the domestic distortion and make the economy better off.

* * *

Such use of trade intervention is said to be "second best" * * *. Because a tariff always distorts both producer and consumer behavior, while the externality in question concerns only one of these groups, a better policy is possible that addresses the original distortion more directly. * * *

The general principle is that trade intervention, by introducing two distortions rather than one, may succeed in solving one problem but only at the same time that it causes another. Trade policy is like doing acupuncture with a fork. No matter how carefully you insert one prong, the other is likely to do damage.

Such examples are rife in the theory of protection. The classic example is the infant-industry argument, where a tariff is said to protect a young industry while it learns to be efficient. The assumption here is that some market failure—such as an imperfection in the loan market or the impossibility of keeping new technical knowledge from being copied—makes it impossible for competitive firms to take advantage of what would otherwise be a profitable opportunity. A tariff or other import restriction can therefore be used temporarily to make the operation profitable even in the short run while the learning process is under way. Naturally, though, the success of such a policy depends crucially on a correct diagnosis of which industries really do offer the potential for such improvement over time. Also it may be difficult politically to remove protection once it has been put in place, even though this particular rationale for protection is explicitly temporary.

As in the case of the externality discussed above, the infant industry argument may be valid in the sense that a tariff may indeed be beneficial. But it is also true that some other policy would be superior. Once again a production subsidy, equal in size to the tariff, would yield exactly the same benefits to producers as the tariff, without causing the additional costly distortion of consumer choice. And even better might be a policy that subsidizes or guarantees loans to the industry, if the capital market was the real source of the distortion, or a policy that permits firms to appropriate technology if that was the problem. The general principle is simply that first best policies deal directly with the distortions involved, and distortions rarely involve the double effect on both producer and consumer choice that would be best addressed with trade intervention.

Many other arguments for intervention can similarly be traced to the presumption of a distortion somewhere in the domestic economy. Tariffs to protect "essential" industries, for example, depend on the private sector being unable to perceive or take advantage of the fact that these industries are essential, which often means that they confer social benefits on others in society. Tariffs to discourage consumption of undesirable goods similarly assume an undesirable social effect of such consumption, or else that consumers themselves have a distorted view of their own welfare. And finally, tariffs for employment and balance-of-payments purposes assume rather obviously that certain markets—labor and foreign exchange—are for some reason failing to adjust to equilibrium.

All of these arguments may be valid if the distortions on which they rest are correctly diagnosed, but once again they could be better dealt with by means of some other policies that deal more directly with the distortions in question.

ROBERT E. BALDWIN, THE INEFFICACY OF TRADE POLICY

19–20 (1982) [10]

For an approach that is touted by many pressure groups and government officials as an effective remedy for a host of economic ills, the use of trade policy does not receive high marks for effectiveness. Occasionally, it may produce effects exactly opposite to those desired. In a not insignificant number of instances, it can be expected to have no effect at all in furthering the desired objective and may even promote some other undesirable outcome. More frequently, it probably operates in the direction intended, but policy-makers either underestimate the extent of offsetting pressures or misunderstand the nature of its indirect consequences. Therefore, it does not fully accomplish its intended purpose. Furthermore, an important conclusion of the preceding analysis is that the ineffectiveness of trade policy tends to be greater when quantitative measures rather than tariffs are used to restrict imports.

Perhaps economists have understood this all along. Maybe we have not dwelt upon the inefficacy of trade policy because we know that usually the more effective trade policies are in achieving the purposes for which they are intended, the greater the resulting decline in national economic welfare.

It is also interesting to note that those trade policies that are growing in popularity, namely discriminatory measures such as orderly marketing agreements, voluntary export restraints, and selective embargoes, are the

10. Essays in International Finance, No. 150, Princeton University, Dept. of Economics, Dec. 1982. Copyright © 1982. Reprinted by permission of the International Finance Section of Princeton University.

Int'l.Econ.Rel.2d Ed. (J & D) ACB—3

very ones likely to be least effective. Pressure groups seem to believe that they have a better chance of gaining public support if they focus upon a particular country or set of countries and a product line where a surge of imports or an apparently unfair practice can be observed fairly clearly. Government officials also like this approach, since it avoids political pressures from other countries supplying the same or similar products who cannot be accused of disruptive or unfair behavior. Thus, protection may be easier to achieve when framed in this narrow manner. But it does not usually take very long for recipients of this type of trade-policy assistance to discover that their political achievement confers little economic benefit.

(5) Conservative Social Welfare Function

W. M. CORDEN, TRADE POLICY AND
ECONOMIC WELFARE

107–08 (1974) [11]

Let us now introduce the conservative social welfare function, a concept which seems particularly helpful for understanding actual trade policies of many countries. Put in its simplest form it includes the following income distribution target: any significant absolute reductions in real incomes of any significant section of the community should be avoided. This is not quite the same as setting up the existing income distribution as the best, but comes close to it, and so can indeed be described as 'conservative'. In terms of welfare weights, increases in income are given relatively low weights and decreases very high weights.

The conservative social welfare function helps to explain the income maintenance motivation of so many tariffs in the past and the reluctance to reduce income maintenance tariffs even when it has become clear that the need for them is more than temporary. It can be regarded as expressing a number of ideas.

Firstly, it is 'unfair' to allow anyone's real income to be reduced significantly—and especially if this is the result of deliberate policy decisions—unless there are very good reasons for this and it is more or less unavoidable.

Secondly, insofar as people are risk averters, everyone's real income is increased when it is known that a government will generally intervene to prevent sudden or large and unexpected income losses. The conservative social welfare function is part of a social insurance system.

Thirdly, social peace requires that no significant group's income shall fall if that of others is rising. Social peace might be regarded as a social good in itself or as a basis for political stability and hence perhaps economic development. And even if social peace does not depend on the maintenance of the incomes of the major classes in the community, the survival of a government may.

Finally, if a policy is directed at a certain target, such as protection of an industry or improving the balance of payments, most governments want

11. Reprinted by permission of Oxford University Press.

to minimize the adverse by-product effects on sectional incomes so as not to be involved in political battles incidental to their main purpose.

Notes and Questions

(1) As a matter of policy, should the United States attempt to improve its terms of trade at the expense of its trading partners? If our partners cannot effectively retaliate with trade-related measures, would such a policy entail any other risks for the United States?

(2) Is there anything inherent in the U.S. governmental system that makes it more or less difficult for the United States to use threats and promises to gain advantages in dealing with its trading partners?

(3) Why do you think that first-best policies are often thought to be politically unacceptable? Why can't governments explain why a particular economic policy is superior to others?

(4) Does Professor Corden's analysis attempt to justify or explain trade policies? Do you think that the conservative social welfare function is in fact widely accepted or that potential losers simply lobby legislators more effectively for special treatment than the larger group of potential gainers?

(C) MEASUREMENT OF GAINS FROM TRADE

Economists have some difficulty in measuring gains from removing trade restrictions. As the following excerpts demonstrate, both intuitive and econometric arguments can be made.

GATT STUDIES IN INTERNATIONAL TRADE, TRADE LIBERALIZATION, PROTECTIONISM AND INTERDEPENDENCE

23–29 (1977) [12]

The benefits to be expected from trade liberalization may be classified into consumption gains, production gains, economies of scale gains, gains from a more competitive domestic economy, and a contribution to domestic price stability. The first three constitute the basic motivation for the pursuit of freer trade, while the latter two are "fringe benefits" in the sense that they contribute to the achievement of goals which are being pursued principally through policies other than trade liberalization.

*   *   *

CONSUMPTION GAINS

Everyone is a consumer, and most are also producers. In their role of consumer, people benefit directly from the lower price.   *   *   *

PRODUCTION GAINS

Many people also gain in their role of producers—that is, as suppliers of labour services, capital, and land. Inefficiently produced domestic output is replaced by imports, permitting the reallocation of some domestic land, labour, and capital away from low productivity industries and into more

---

12. R. Blackhurst, N. Marian & J. Tumlir, Trade Liberalization, Protectionism and Inter- dependence (GATT Studies in Intl. Trade, No. 5, Geneva 1977).

productive employment in those industries in which the country has a comparative advantage. * * *

ECONOMIES OF SCALE GAINS

* * * Trade liberalization enlarges the market in which each country's tradeable goods industries compete, bringing with it the opportunity to gain from the cost reductions that under certain circumstances accompany increases in the scale of operations.

* * *

GAINS FROM A MORE COMPETITIVE DOMESTIC ECONOMY

Enlargement of the market via trade liberalization brings important benefits through its impact on the degree of competition between foreign and domestic firms in the domestic market. This is particularly true for those industries in which efficient size firms are so large relative to the domestic market that there are only a few firms in each country.

* * *

* * * By providing increased competition, trade liberalization will force [sheltered] firms to abandon complacent attitudes and adopt efficient production technology. It is also likely to stimulate a search for new technologically superior processes. Both considerations point to a positive correlation between the degree of exposure to world market competition and the rate of technological progress in export and import-competing industries.

* * *

CONTRIBUTION TO DOMESTIC PRICE STABILITY

Although it is now widely accepted that inflation is fundamentally a monetary problem requiring a monetary solution, trade liberalization can be a very useful adjunct to the basic policy package. To begin with, the lower (than otherwise) prices will have a one-time beneficial effect on the wholesale and consumer prices indices. * * *

There is a second effect, related to the benefit from more competition, which is lasting and much more important. Efforts to control inflation, particularly in recent years, have frequently been made more difficult by the price and wage behavior of uncompetitive business and labour groups. * * * In the presence of effective competition from foreign producers, and a credible commitment by the government not to return to the previous (higher) level of protection, there will be a parallel restraint on both prices and wages, the restraint on one being more tolerable because the other is also under restraint. * * *

ALAN V. DEARDORFF & ROBERT M. STERN, AN ECONOMIC ANALYSIS OF THE EFFECTS OF THE TOKYO ROUND OF MULTILATERAL TRADE NEGOTIATIONS ON THE UNITED STATES AND THE OTHER MAJOR INDUSTRIALIZED COUNTRIES

(1979) [13]

[W]e expect the main results of the MTN to be as follows:

(1) Employment will increase by a small amount in all countries except Japan and Switzerland. The increase for the United States is about 15 thousand workers. In percentage terms, these changes are no more than a few tenths of one per cent of the labor force in any country and still less in the U.S.

(2) Exchange rates will change to a small extent. The U.S. dollar will depreciate very slightly (two tenths of one percent), as will such currencies as the French franc and the British pound. The deutsche mark and the yen will appreciate very slightly.

(3) Import and therefore consumer prices will fall to a limited extent in all countries. For the U.S., the decline is less than one-tenth of one per cent.

(4) Economic welfare will be increased in all countries except Switzerland. The welfare gain for the U.S. is estimated at between $1 and $1.5 billion dollars, which is less than one tenth of one per cent of U.S. gross domestic product.

All of these changes, small as they are, assume that the changes in tariffs and [non-tariff barriers] that have been negotiated are to be implemented all at once. In fact, they will be phased in over a number of years, so that the effects that will occur in any one year will be even smaller than noted.

STEPHEN T. EASTON & HERBERT G. GRUBEL, THE COSTS AND BENEFITS OF PROTECTION IN A GROWING WORLD

(1982) [14]

The theoretical contribution of this paper consists of the arguments and empirical evidence suggesting that the costs of protection should be considered to grow at the rate at which international trade has grown in recent decades and can be expected to grow in the future as a result of reduced transportation costs and economies of scale in the production of differentiated goods, while the benefits of protection should be considered to grow at only the rate of real output growth. Under the assumption that real growth of output is less than real growth in international trade, the excess of the present value of costs over benefits generally is an increasing function of time and can become quite large in the longer run. * * *

---

13. Subcomm. on Intl. Trade, Senate Finance Comm., 96 Cong., 1st Sess. III–IV (Comm. Print 96–15, 1979).

14. Reprinted by permission. 36 Kyklos 213, 226–27 (1982).

Our speculative examination of real world phenomena in the light of our theoretical model suggest to us that probably the net present value of the costs of protection are very high, absolutely and in relation to GNP, certainly much higher than is implied by models considering only instantaneous costs. If we are correct in our speculation, then international trade economists can use the idea of a growing economy to make their case for free trade with much more confidence in its empirical validity than has been true in the past.

SECTION 1.4 POLITICAL GOALS AND INTERNATIONAL ECONOMIC POLICY

Economists support free international trade as a means of maximizing global production. Individual nations, however, always have domestic and foreign political goals that are motivated by policy concerns other than maximizing output.

(A) WAR AND PEACE

Probably the most important foreign policy goal related to international economic policy is the prevention of war. Many statesmen and scholars believe that recent history establishes a clear relationship between implementation of certain international economic policies and war. The importance of this relationship was particularly evident in the case of World War II. As economist Richard Cooper has argued:

RICHARD N. COOPER, TRADE POLICY AND FOREIGN POLICY [1]

The most disastrous single mistake any American president has made in international relations was Herbert Hoover's signing of the Hawley-Smoot Tariff Act into law in June 1930. The sharp increase in American tariffs, the apparent indifference of the U.S. authorities to the implications of their actions for foreigners, and the foreign retaliation that quickly followed, as threatened, helped convert what would have been otherwise a normal economic downturn into a major world depression. The sharp decline in foreign trade and economic activity in turn undermined the position of the moderates with respect to the nationalists in Japanese politics and paved the way for the electoral victory of the Nazis in Germany in 1932. Japan promptly invaded China in 1931, and the basis for the Second World War was laid.

Valuable lessons were learned from the Hawley-Smoot tariff experience by the foreign policy community: the threat of tariff retaliation is not always merely a bluff; tariffs do influence trade flows negatively; a decline in trade can depress national economies; economic depression provides fertile ground for politically radical nostrums; and political radicals often

1. From R. Stern (ed.), U.S. Trade Policies in a Changing World Economy (forthcoming). Reprinted by permission of The MIT Press.

See also J. Jackson, World Trade and the Law of GATT, ch. 2 (1969), particularly at 38ff.

seek foreign (military) adventures to distract domestic attention away from their domestic economic failures. The seeds of the Second World War, both in the Far East and in Europe, were sown by Hoover's signing of the Hawley-Smoot tariff.

———

This close relationship between the causes of the war and international economic policies was recognized by U.S. wartime leaders. For example, Harry Hawkins, then Director of the Office of Economic Affairs of the Department of State, said in a 1944 speech,[2]

> We've seen that when a country gets starved out economically, its people are all too ready to follow the first dictator who may rise up and promise them all jobs. Trade conflict breeds nonco-operation, suspicion, bitterness. Nations which are economic enemies are not likely to remain political friends for long.

At the end of the war, the United States government, in suggesting a draft charter for an international trade organization, stated: [3]

> The fundamental choice is whether countries will struggle against each other for wealth and power, or work together for security and mutual advantage. * * * The experience of cooperation in the task of earning a living promotes both the habit and the techniques of common effort and helps make permanent the mutual confidence on which the peace depends.

(B) GENERAL FOREIGN POLICY GOALS

Not all foreign policy goals are aimed at, or even consistent with, promoting peace. Indeed, among the principal general foreign policy goals that affect international economic policies are the desire of one nation to strengthen its allies and to avoid strengthening its potential enemies and to convince (or to attempt to force) foreign countries to change their behavior or policies. For example, the United States at times may have promoted policies not completely in its economic self-interest in order to promote growth and economic strength in Western Europe and Japan. On the other hand, the United States maintains trade restrictions in respect of trade and other economic relations with the Soviet Union, as well as many other countries that are viewed as potential enemies. In the recent past use of trade restrictions designed to force policy changes has become more common. They are viewed as an acceptable alternative to the use of force, and while their effectiveness may often be questioned, they serve as a symbolic objection to the policies of the foreign state, thereby satisfying the domestic political need to do something to register such objections. These kinds of restraints and their effectiveness will be considered in detail in Chapter 13.

(C) DOMESTIC POLITICAL GOALS

Attempts to achieve domestic political goals may also affect international economic policies.[4] In particular, imposition of trade restrictions may

2. U.S. Dept. of State, Commercial Policy Series 74, at 3 (Pub. No. 2104, 1944).

3. United States Proposals, Dept. of State Pub. No. 2411, at 1–2 (1946).

4. See J. Jackson, note 1 supra, at 53–57.

occur to achieve such goals as the promotion of domestic full employment; the reduction of income disparities among groups in the national population; the protection of particular groups from competition—domestic or foreign; the development of specific industries (or, in the case of developing countries, industrialization in general); the reduction of dependency on a few export industries; the prevention of pollution and other detriments to the "quality of life" in a nation; and the promotion of certain religious beliefs. The achievement of these goals need not necessarily lead to restrictions on trade. As was noted in Section 1.3, many of these goals can best be achieved by government subsidies or other government intervention in the domestic market. Trade restrictions are, however, sometimes viewed as a politically expedient method of achieving these goals.

APPENDIX. AN ECONOMIC ANALYSIS OF TARIFFS, QUOTAS AND SUBSIDIES

PETER B. KENEN, THE INTERNATIONAL ECONOMY

17–19, 175–77 (1985)[1]

PRODUCTION, CONSUMPTION, AND TRADE IN A SINGLE COMMODITY

The effects of differences in relative costs cannot be examined by looking at markets one at a time. It is necessary to look at an entire national economy, and then compare it with another. Therefore, international economic analysis cannot make much use of standard partial-equilibrium price theory—of ordinary demand and supply curves. It must use general-equilibrium theory most of the time. Demand and supply curves can be used, however, to show how the opening of trade in a single commodity affects production and consumption in the domestic market, and they can be used to quantify the gains from trade.

EQUILIBRIUM BEFORE TRADE IS OPENED

In Figure 2–1, the domestic demand curve for cameras is D_H, and the domestic supply curve is S_H. When there is no international trade in cameras, equilibrium will be established at E. The domestic price of a camera will be OP, domestic production will be OQ, and production will necessarily equal consumption. The diagram, however, says much more.

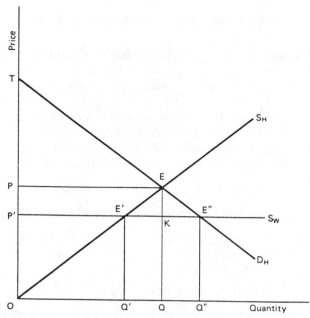

FIGURE 2-1

Effects of the Opening of Trade in the Market for a Single Good

Before trade is opened, the domestic price is OP, and the quantity OQ is produced to satisfy domestic demand. When trade is opened at the world price OP', domestic production falls to OQ', domestic consumption rises to OQ'', and the quantity $Q'Q''$ is imported to close the gap. The production effect is $Q'Q$, and the corresponding welfare gain is $E'KE$. The consumption effect is QQ'', and the corresponding welfare gain is $KE''E$.

When domestic markets are perfectly competitive, the supply curve is the sum of the marginal cost curves of domestic firms. Accordingly, the area under the supply curve measures the total cost of camera production. (Strictly speaking, it measures the total variable cost, but fixed cost plays no role in this analysis.) If OQ cameras are produced, total cost is given by the area of the triangle OQE. But total payments to producers (revenues) are given by the area of the rectangle $OQEP$. Therefore, the area of the triangle OEP serves as a measure of profit or *producer surplus*.

The area under the demand curve is meaningful, too. Under somewhat restrictive assumptions that need not detain us here, it measures the cash equivalent of the utility that consumers derive from their purchases of cameras. If OQ cameras are consumed, that cash equivalent is the area $OQET$. But consumers pay $OQEP$ for their cameras. Therefore, the area of the triangle PET serves as a measure of net benefit or *consumer surplus*.

EQUILIBRIUM AFTER TRADE IS OPENED

Suppose now that trade in cameras is opened and that the world's supply curve is S_W. The world price of cameras, OP', is lower than the old domestic price, OP, and the world price must come to prevail in the domestic market if there are no transport costs or tariffs. Domestic firms will cut back production to OQ'. Domestic consumers will step up their purchases to

OQ''. The gap between domestic demand and supply, $Q'Q''$, will be filled by imports.

What are the effects on economic welfare? Producer surplus will be $[OE'P']$. It will fall by $P'E'EP$. Consumer surplus will be $P'E''T$. It will rise by $P'E''EP$. As the increase in consumer surplus exceeds the decrease in producer surplus by $E'E''E$, consumers can compensate producers and come out ahead. The area $E'E''E$ measures the gain from the opening of trade in cameras. Note that it can be divided into two parts. The decrease in domestic output, $Q'Q$, contributes $E'KE$. This is the *production effect*. The increase in domestic purchases, QQ'', contributes $KE''E$. This is the *consumption effect*.

* * *

EFFECTS OF A TARIFF WITH A CONSTANT WORLD PRICE

At the start of Chapter 2 [*see above*], we used a simple diagram to study the effects of trade in a single market. The same diagram can be used to study the principal effects of a tariff.

EFFECTS IN A SINGLE MARKET

In Figure 8–1, the demand curve for cameras is D_H, and the domestic supply curve is S_H. If there is no trade at all, equilibrium will be established at E. If there is free trade and the foreign supply curve is S_W, equilibrium will be established at F. The domestic price will equal the world price, OP_1. Domestic consumption will be OC_1, domestic production will be OQ_1, and imports will be Q_1C_1 (equal to $F'F$).

Suppose that the importing country imposes a tariff at an ad valorem rate equal to P_1P_2/OP_1. As the foreign supply curve is perfectly elastic, the world price will stay at OP_1. But the domestic price will rise to OP_2. Domestic consumption will fall to OC_2, domestic production will rise to OQ_2, and imports will fall to Q_2C_2 (equal to $G'G$). The *consumption effect* of the tariff is C_1C_2. The *production effect* is Q_1Q_2 and is also called the *protective effect*. The two together measure the *restrictive effect*, the amount by which the tariff reduces import volume. The government collects P_1P_2 of tariff revenue on each imported camera, which means that it collects $G'GTT'$ in total tariff revenue. At this point in our work, we will assume that all such revenue is returned to households; the government reduces other taxes or raises transfer payments, so tariffs do not cut consumers' incomes.

What are the effects on economic welfare? Consumer surplus falls by P_1FTP_2. Producer surplus rises by $P_1F'T'P_2$. The difference is $F'FTT'$. But $G'GTT'$ of this loss is offset by returning tariff revenue to households, so the net loss is reduced to $F'G'T'$ *plus* FGT. The area $F'G'T'$ is the welfare loss associated with the protective effect; the area FGT is the loss associated with the consumption effect. The total welfare loss is related to the restrictive effect of the tariff. * * *

COMPARING TARIFFS AND QUOTAS

Figure 8–1 can be used to compare an import quota with an import tariff. Start again with free trade and suppose that the government imposes a quota that has the same restrictive effect as the tariff analyzed in Figure

8–1. It limits the volume of imports to Q_2C_2. The domestic price must rise to OP_2 to clear the domestic market. Domestic production will rise to OQ_2, imports will be Q_2C_2, and the two together will equal domestic consumption, which falls to OC_2. The consumption and protective effects of the quota are identical to those of the tariff when the two devices have identical restrictive effects.

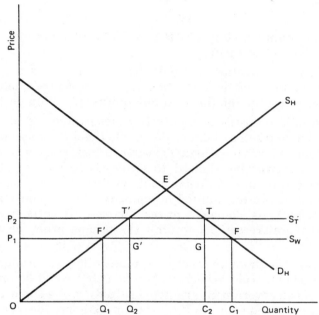

FIGURE 8-1

Effects of a Tariff in a Single Market

In the initial free-trade equilibrium, domestic consumers buy OC_1 at the price OP_1 determined by the foreign supply curve, S_W. Domestic producers supply OQ_1, and imports are Q_1C_1. An import tariff raises the domestic price to OP_2, so domestic consumers buy OC_2, domestic producers supply OQ_2, and imports are reduced to Q_2C_2. The consumption effect of the tariff is C_1C_2. The production (protective) effect is Q_1Q_2. The two together measure the restrictive effect. The government collects P_1P_2 of tariff revenue on each imported unit, or $G'GTT'$ in total tariff revenue.

There is, of course, one difference between the quota and the tariff. The tariff yields $G'GTT'$ in tariff revenue. The quota does not yield any. The revenue equivalent $G'GTT'$ goes as a windfall profit to importers standing at the head of the line when tickets are handed out. Under the assumption adopted previously, however, this difference is relatively unimportant. When the government returns its tariff revenue, consumers as a group get back what they pay out. When a quota is used instead of a tariff, importers collect what consumers pay out, but importers are consumers, too. Therefore, the welfare loss with the quota is $F'G'T'$ *plus* FGT, just as it was with the tariff.

The equivalence between a quota and a tariff can break down in two instances: when markets are not perfectly competitive and when the various demand and supply curves are subject to random shifts. Such random shifts need not affect the *expected* levels of production and consumption. Under a tariff, however, shifts in the foreign supply curve cause fluctuations in domestic output. Under a quota, they do not. (Furthermore, random fluctuations have different consequences for expected welfare under a tariff and under a quota.)

Notes

(1) The losses symbolized by F'G'T' and FGT are sometimes referred to as "deadweight losses" of tariffs.

(2) In the case of quotas, it would be possible for the government establishing the quota to charge a fee for a license to use the quota, in which case it could recover some of the windfall profits of the importers.

(3) If a domestic industry is relatively concentrated, i.e. if only a few firms dominate the market, a quota could enable them to charge oligopolistic prices because no matter how high domestic prices rise, only a specified quantity of imports will be allowed to enter the country. Oligopolistic producers might not be in such a favorable position when a tariff is used. With a tariff imports are not limited in quantity, they are only made more costly by the tariff. As domestic prices increase, imports become more competitive and therefore can act to limit the pricing practices of domestic producers.

(4) If the aim of a quota or tariff is to protect domestic industry, and it usually is, there is one other government action that could accomplish that result as well. If the government granted a subsidy to the domestic industry for each camera produced equal to P_2P_1, the domestic producers could afford to produce a quantity of cameras equal to Q_2 the same as if the P_1P_2/OP_1 tariff had been imposed. This would be true because their revenues would be the same as if the price were P_2 and they would therefore produce the amount associated with that price. Consumers would have the benefits of the free trade price of P_1. The government (and through taxes all citizens), of course, would have to pay for the subsidy, but if the subsidy was funded by a nondistorting tax, the economy could be better off than if a tariff or quota were used.

Chapter 2

INTERNATIONAL COMMERCIAL TRANSACTIONS

SECTION 2.1 INTRODUCTION

This book focuses on international and national regulation of international economic transactions, particularly sales of goods across international borders.[1] While it is beyond the scope of this book to treat in any detail the private law of international transactions, we will highlight in this chapter some of the major legal problems faced by private parties in structuring such sales. A general understanding of the underlying transactions should be useful in putting the regulations studied later into their real-world context. Many of the legal issues faced in structuring international transactions do not differ significantly from those faced in structuring domestic sales, and as such are well known to lawyers and law students. Thus, this chapter will consider only those aspects of international transactions that are likely to be governed by rules of law applicable particularly to international transactions or that raise legal problems that are not commonly found in domestic transactions. Such problems generally arise because of the increased risks involved in international transactions and because of the diversity of legal rules that may be applicable to such transactions.

The additional risks and problems involved in an international transaction stem from a number of factors: (1) a seller may hesitate to ship goods to a distant buyer without assurance of payment; a buyer may hesitate to pay a distant seller before he has inspected the goods or at least knows that the goods have been shipped; (2) at least one of the parties will have to deal in a foreign currency; (3) often the parties will not share a common native language, increasing the risk of a misunderstanding over the basic terms of the transaction; (4) the transaction will typically be subject to more government regulation than a domestic transaction and in addition will be subject to the regulation of more than one government; (5) more than one legal

---

1. There are a wide variety of international economic transactions that do not directly involve trade in goods. For example, such transactions include contracts for engineering, advisory and other services, licenses of patents and technology, insurance and shipping contracts and agreements between corporate affiliates located in different countries. These subjects will be treated in several later chapters, particularly Chapters 15 (services), 16 (investment) and 17 (multinational enterprise).

35

system and one set of business customs will be involved, which may also give rise to misunderstandings and which raises the difficult questions of which law and which customs are to be applied in event of a dispute; and (6) if a dispute arises or a contract is breached, the determination and enforcement of contract obligations will be more difficult since foreign courts and foreign legal rules may be involved.

Some of the foregoing problems are probably insolvable: only a pattern of successful transactions will dispel mistrust; the very nature of an international transaction dictates the use of foreign exchange. On the other hand, some of the problems could be minimized or even eliminated if customs and practices could be standardized and made uniform throughout the world. Indeed, we will find in this chapter as we consider the structure of typical international sales transactions and the problems of dispute settlement that many efforts have been made toward unification of laws and standardization of customs.[2] Extensive references will be made to the products of these efforts since they are a good indication of what the laws and customs are or are evolving towards in most countries. Moreover, it is important for lawyers to be aware of these efforts because they may be referred to in contract negotiations or proposed as alternatives to applying U.S. law.

Efforts to unify the laws and customs applicable to international transactions have taken three forms: conventions signed by nations who thereby agree to apply the conventions' rules in the defined situations; model laws that are proposed by international organizations for adoption into national law; and statements of customs or practice that parties may incorporate into their agreements.[3] A number of organizations play an active role in these efforts.[4] The International Chamber of Commerce (ICC) has published definitions of trade terms and rules regarding letters of credit and also

2. Such efforts should not be unfamiliar to U.S. or European readers. In the United States, the National Conference of Commissioners on Uniform State Laws traces its history back to 1892 and has promulgated numerous uniform laws, most notably the Uniform Commercial Code, which has been adopted in 49 states. Similarly, the American Law Institute (ALI) has published "restatements" of the law in a number of fields. In the particular area of interest of this book, the ALI published the Restatement of the Law, Second, Foreign Relations Law of the United States (1965). It is currently engaged in revising and updating that volume. See ALI, Restatement of the Law, Foreign Relations Law of the United States (Revised) (Tentative Draft No. 6—2 vols., April 12, 1985). In Europe, the European Community has been very active in recent years in promoting the harmonization of laws of its member states. The wide range of activities undertaken to harmonize laws and establish Community-wide rules are described generally in its annual reports. See, e.g., Commission of the European Communities, Eighteenth General Report on the Activities of the European Communities—1984, at 79–90, 152–63 (1985).

3. For a collection of conventions, model laws and customs, see K. Zweigert & J. Kropholler, Sources of International Uniform Law (3 vols. 1971, 1972, 1973). For a comprehensive study of the international efforts to unify private law and a summary of the work of the Hague Conference on Private International Law and UNIDROIT, see R. David (ed.), International Encyclopedia of Comparative Law, Vol. II, The Legal Systems of the World: Their Comparison and Unification, ch. 5, The International Unification of Private Law 133–48 (1971).

4. The current activities of the numerous groups concerned with the unification of laws are described in UNIDROIT, Digest of Legal Activities of International Organizations and Other Institutions (6th ed. 1984). In addition, UNIDROIT published a quarterly "News Bulletin" containing a report on its activities, as well as the activities of other bodies working on related topics, and a bibliography of literature on unification and court decisions interpreting existing conventions. It also publishes a biannual law review entitled "Uniform Law Review". Among UNIDROIT's current activities are drafting an international trade law code, uniform rules on international fi-

provides arbitration services. The Hague Conference on Private International Law has drafted numerous conventions in the area of trade law, covering such subjects as the choice of law in the international sale of goods, the law applicable to agency, the recognition of foreign companies, the recognition and enforcement of judgments in civil and commercial matters and products liability. The International Institute for the Unification of Private Law (UNIDROIT) was founded by the League of Nations in 1924, with the aim of examining "ways of harmonizing and coordinating the private law of states * * * and to prepare * * * for the adoption by Governments of uniform rules of private law." It has recently adopted a convention on agency in the international sale of goods. The United Nations Commission on International Trade Law (UNCITRAL) was formed in 1966 by the United Nations General Assembly for the specific purpose of promoting the unification and harmonization of international trade law. It has sponsored rules on carriage of goods by sea and the Vienna Convention on Contracts for the International Sale of Goods as well as rules for arbitration. The United States participates in the Hague Conference and UNIDROIT, as well as in UNCITRAL as a U.N. member.[5] In recent years, the number of unifying agencies may have become so great as to result, at least occasionally, in disunification.[6]

There are a number of other legal subjects, in addition to commercial law, that a practitioner active in the field of international trade is likely to encounter. We will treat a number of these subjects in more or less detail in later chapters—international taxation (Chapter 19), antitrust (Chapter 18), different types of "foreign investment," from the creation of agencies or distributorships to licensing to direct investment (Chapter 16), expropriation (Chapter 16) and the conduct of business abroad by multinational enterprises (Chapter 17). Other subjects sometimes encountered by practitioners, such as the Act of State doctrine and foreign sovereignty immunity, we will touch only briefly, as they are more appropriately treated in a basic course on public international law.

We turn now to the focus of this chapter—international sales transactions. In this regard, the reader's attention is directed to the problem set out in Section 2.4, which attempts to draw together the principal materials discussed in the chapter.

nancial leases and rules on certain aspects of international factoring. UNCITRAL publishes a "Yearbook" every year or so on its activities. Volume XIII:1982 covering 1982 was published in 1984 as U.N.Doc. A/CN.9/SER.A/1982. Among UNCITRAL's current activities are drafting conventions on bills of exchange and international promissory notes and on international checks, as well as work in the area of dispute settlement. Among the Hague Conference's current projects is a draft revision to its convention on the law applicable to contracts for the international sale of goods.

5. 22 U.S.C.A. § 269g. See Pfund, U.S. Participation in International Unification of Private Law, 19 Intl.Law. 505 (1985); Bolgar, In Memoriam, Hessel E. Yntema: The American Journal of Comparative Law 1952–1966, 15 Am.J.Comp.L. 21, 50–51 (1966–67); Nadelmann, The United States Joins the Hague Conference on Private International Law, 30 Law & Contemp.Prob. 291 (1965).

6. For example, UNCITRAL's work in two areas, the Hamburg Rules (see Section 2.2(C)) and the Vienna Convention on Contracts for the International Sale of Goods (see Section 2.2(B)), is designed to replace prior, and not particularly old, uniform laws.

SECTION 2.2 INTERNATIONAL SALES TRANSACTIONS [1]

(A) OUTLINE OF THE TRANSACTION

CLIVE M. SCHMITTHOFF, EXPORT TRADE: THE LAW AND PRACTICE OF INTERNATIONAL TRADE

6–7 (7th ed. 1980) [2]

Contracts for the international sale of goods exhibit a characteristic which is not present in contracts for the sale of goods in the home market. They are entwined with other contracts, in particular with the contract of carriage by sea, air or road under which the goods are exported, and the contract of insurance by which they are insured. In many export transactions the delivery of the shipping documents to the buyer or his agent plays, as will be seen, an important role in the performance of the contract of sale; the shipping documents consist normally of the bill of lading, the marine insurance policy and the invoice and thus represent elements of the three contracts referred to. The situation is even more involved when payment is made under a bankers' documentary credit because this frequent method of payment in the export trade requires the addition of two further contracts to the export transaction, namely the contracts of the bank with the buyer and seller respectively. In short, the export transaction presents itself to the business man as a natural and indivisible whole and he is apt to pay little attention to its constituent parts, like the motorist who thinks of the components of his car only when he notices a fault in them. We have to analyse the individual contracts which constitute the export transaction because this is the best method of appreciating the functioning of the machinery of exports as a whole. From this point of view, the contract for the sale of goods abroad is the principal and central legal arrangement involved in the export transaction, and all other contracts, such as contracts of carriage, insurance and credit, have a supporting and incidental character.

———

When a seller sells to a buyer located in the same country, the transaction can be very simple, especially if the seller delivers the goods or the buyer picks them up and if the price is paid immediately or billed on open account. In a sale across national boundaries, however, certain factors complicate the transaction, and the transaction itself often becomes very complex and involves a whole cluster of contracts. A diagram of a typical international trade transaction could be as follows:

S = Seller

B = Buyer

1. Additional and more detailed materials on international sales transactions can be found in: A. Lowenfeld, International Private Trade (2d ed. 1981); C. Schmitthoff, Export Trade: The Law and Practice of International Trade (7th ed. 1980); P. Vishny, Guide to International Commerce Law (1984).

2. This and other excerpts from this publication in this section are reprinted by permission of Stevens & Son Ltd., London.

SB = Seller's Bank

BB = Buyer's Bank

C = Carrier

I = Insurance company

Solid lines indicate direct contractual relationships, dotted lines indicate beneficiaries of a contract.

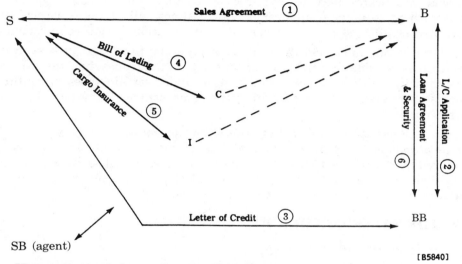

[B5840]

Here we see at least six separate contracts:

(1) The basic sales agreement between Seller in Country A and Buyer in Country B;

(2) Buyer's application to his Bank for issuance of a letter of credit, accepted;

(3) The letter of credit itself, whereby Buyer's Bank commits itself to Seller upon certain conditions; this letter is probably forwarded through Seller's Bank (or a bank near Seller) which will act as agent;

(4) Seller's contract for shipping the goods to Buyer, which is usually in the form of a bill of lading;

(5) Seller's contract for insurance of the cargo;

(6) If Buyer is borrowing from his bank to pay for the goods, he may give a security interest in the goods he is buying to his bank.

Seller will forward a "draft" (bill of exchange) with the bill of lading, and the draft will raise independent, contractual relations when accepted by Buyer or Buyer's Bank. Furthermore, Seller may have his own financing arrangements related to the transaction (e.g., he may have borrowed money on the strength of Buyer's order in order to process and ship the goods). Additionally, Buyer may have contracted for an independent inspection company to certify as to the quality of the goods at the time they are shipped. Finally, several carriers or intermediaries such as freight forwarders may be involved in shipping the goods. Each additional participant raises the possibility of additional contractual relations.

To add to the complexity of the transaction, there may be governmental requirements and regulations that impinge on each of the various contracts mentioned above. For instance, tariff levels obviously affect Buyer's choice of purchase. But in addition, government quotas may prohibit Buyer from importing, or Seller from exporting. Laws may affect the shipping contract and the power of banks to issue letters of credit and to finance international trade. Exchange controls may limit Buyer's ability to pay for the goods. Special certificates may be required by customs authorities in order to enable them to enforce applicable laws. Almost all of these aspects are governed or affected in some measure by international legal commitments.

Finally, one must add the conflict of laws questions that lurk at every bend. It is possible that the various contracts in the transaction will each be governed by a different law. And indeed, under certain types of conflicts analyses, different issues concerning the same contract may be subject to different laws.

In any particular transaction, the following questions may arise: (1) Is there a contract? (2) If so, what are its terms, i.e. what performance is required by the contract? (3) Has there been a breach? If so, by whom? (4) Who had the risk of loss? (5) How could the transaction be structured differently so as to avoid particular problems?

(B) THE SALES CONTRACT

(1) General Considerations

In analyzing an international sales transaction, it is essential to consider whether the parties have concluded an enforceable contract and what are their respective duties and obligations. Although there are variations among legal systems in respect of contract formation, they are generally not of great importance.[3] The precise scope of a party's rights and obligations, and his rights in event of breach by the other party, are more likely to vary under different legal systems. These problems may be minimized if the parties choose a governing law known to and acceptable to both of them since most courts accept the parties' right to choose the law applicable to their agreement.[4] Choosing a law may not be enough, however. If the

---

3. For example, while civil law systems do not require consideration to be found in order to have a valid contract, the presence of consideration is not usually an issue in a commercial transaction. Some of the differences in contract formation law between the UCC and civil law, and the way those differences were resolved in the Vienna Convention on Contracts for the International Sale of Goods are highlighted in Winship, Formation of International Sales Contracts under the 1980 Vienna Convention, 17 Intl.Law. 1 (1983).

4. The parties' right to choose applicable law may be limited if they can show no reasonable basis for picking the chosen law or if application of the chosen law would contravene important public policies of the state whose law would otherwise apply. See generally E. Scoles & P. Hay, Conflict of Laws 632–

52 (1982). A recently enacted New York statute, however, authorizes parties to a contract to choose New York law and to agree to submit disputes to New York courts even in the absence of a reasonable relationship with New York if the related transaction involves $250,000 (for choice of law) or $1,000,000 (for choice of courts). N.Y.—McKinney's Gen.Oblig.Law § 5–1401–02 (Supp.1985). A number of international conventions may determine the choice of law in international transactions in the absence of an agreement thereon by the parties. See, e.g., U.N. Convention on Contracts for the International Sale of Goods Art. 1 (1980) (the "Vienna Convention"); European Communities Convention on the Law Applicable to Contractual Obligations (1980), [1980] Eur.Comm.O.J. No. L266 (not yet in force). The Hague Conference is drafting a conven-

chosen law has to be interpreted in a court that is unfamiliar with it, the effect of choice may be negated by misunderstanding on the part of the foreign judge. Consideration must also be given to specifying the forum (whether a court or arbitral panel) that the parties want to interpret the contract. More and more, courts seem to be more willing to accept the choice of forum made by the parties.[5] Of course, even a "favorable" choice of law and choice of forum provision may be negated if it is not possible to enforce any judgment obtained in the other country without relitigating the issues in dispute.[6]

In choosing applicable law it is important to bear in mind that in some countries special rules apply to international sales transactions. Ten or so countries have subscribed to the Hague Convention Relating to a Uniform Law on the International Sale of Goods.[7] In the future, many more, including at least some who subscribed to the Hague Convention, will probably ratify the UNCITRAL-sponsored replacement—the Vienna Convention on Contracts for the International Sale of Goods.[8]

(2) The CIF Contract

In an effort to unify the common understanding of the typical forms of international sales transactions, the International Chamber of Commerce (ICC) has published detailed definitions of the principal terms used to describe these transactions.[9] Although these definitions lack the force of law, they may be adopted by the parties and are likely in any event to be accepted by courts in diverse countries as representing the common meaning of a particular term. Perhaps the best known, if not the most common, type of sales contract is the CIF contract.

tion to be applicable to choice of law when the Vienna Convention is not.

5. See generally E. Scoles & P. Hay, note 4 supra, at 351–63. See also Convention on the Jurisdiction of Courts and the Recognition and Enforcement of Judgments in Civil and Commercial Matters, [1972] Eur.Comm.O.J. No. L299/32.

6. See Section 2.3 infra.

7. The ratifying countries include Belgium, the Federal Republic of Germany, Israel, Italy, the Netherlands and the United Kingdom.

8. See generally J. Honnold, Uniform Law for International Sales under the 1980 United Nations Convention (1982); N. Galston & H. Smit (eds.), International Sales: The United Nations Convention on Contracts for the International Sale of Goods (1984); Vergne, The "Battle of Forms" Under the 1980 United Nations Convention on Contracts for the In-

ternational Sale of Goods, 33 Am.J.Comp.L. 233 (1985); Winship, Bibliography: International Sale of Goods, 18 The Intl.Lawyer 53 (1984). In general, the Vienna Convention would apply to a contract between two traders each located in a different ratifying nation and when the applicable conflict-of-law rules refer a court to the law of a ratifying nation. Article 6 of the Convention permits the parties to a contract subject to the Convention's rules to agree to vary any particular provision of the Convention. The United States signed the Convention and the Senate is now considering whether to ratify it. See Hearing on Treaty Document 98–9: Proposed United Nations Convention on Contracts for the International Sale of Goods Before the Senate Foreign Relations Comm., 98th Cong., 2d Sess. (1984).

9. For a general survey of standardization efforts in this area, see C. Schmitthoff, note 1 supra, chs. 2 & 3.

INCOTERMS: CIF

COST, INSURANCE AND FREIGHT * * * (NAMED PORT OF DESTINATION)

(5th ed. 1980)[10]

CIF means "Cost, Insurance and Freight." This term is the same as C & F but with the addition that the seller has to procure marine insurance against the risk of loss of or damage to the goods during the carriage. The seller contracts with the insurer and pays the insurance premium. * * *

A. The seller must:

1. Supply the goods in conformity with the contract of sale, together with such evidence of conformity as may be required by the contract.

2. Contract on usual terms at his own expense for the carriage of the goods to the agreed port of destination by the usual route, in a seagoing vessel (not being a sailing vessel) of the type normally used for the transport of goods of the contract description, and pay freight charges and any charges for unloading at the port of discharge which may be levied by regular shipping lines at the time and port of shipment.

3. At his own risk and expense obtain any export license or other governmental authorization necessary for the export of the goods.

4. Load the goods at his own expense on board the vessel at the port of shipment and at the date or within the period fixed or, if neither date nor time has been stipulated, within a reasonable time, and notify the buyer, without delay, that the goods have been loaded on board the vessel.

5. Procure, at his own cost and in a transferable form, a policy of marine insurance against the risks of carriage involved in the contract. The insurance shall be contracted with underwriters or insurance companies of good repute on FPA terms, and shall cover the CIF price plus ten per cent. The insurance shall be provided in the currency of the contract, if procurable.

Unless otherwise agreed, the risks of carriage shall not include special risks that are covered in specific trades or against which the buyer may wish individual protection. Among the special risks that should be considered and agreed upon between seller and buyer are theft, pilferage, leakage, breakage, chipping, sweat, contact with other cargoes and others peculiar to any particular trade. When required by the buyer, the seller shall provide, at the buyer's expense, war risk insurance in the currency of the contract, if procurable.

6. Subject to the provisions of article B.4 below, bear all risks of the goods until such time as they shall have effectively passed the ship's rail at the port of shipment.

---

10. ICC No. 350, Incoterms, Copyright © 1980 by ICC Services S.A.R.L. All rights re- served. Reprinted with the permission of the ICC Publishing Corporation.

7. At his own expense furnish to the buyer without delay a clean negotiable bill of lading for the agreed port of destination, as well as the invoice of the goods shipped and the insurance policy or, should the insurance policy not be available at the time the documents are tendered, a certificate of insurance issued under the authority of the underwriters and conveying to the bearer the same rights as if he were in possession of the policy and reproducing the essential provisions thereof. The bill of lading must cover the contract goods, be dated within the period agreed for shipment, and provide by endorsement or otherwise for delivery to the order of the buyer or buyer's agreed representative. Such bill of lading must be a full set of "on board" or "shipped" bills of lading, or a "received for shipment" bill of lading duly endorsed by the shipping company to the effect that the goods are on board, such endorsement to be dated within the period agreed for shipment. If the bill of lading contains a reference to the charter-party, the seller must also provide a copy of this latter document.

Note: A clean bill of lading is one which bears no superimposed clauses expressly declaring a defective condition of the goods or packaging. The following clauses do not convert a clean into an unclean bill of lading: a) clauses which do not expressly state that the goods or packaging are unsatisfactory, e.g. "second-hand cases", "used drums", etc.; b) clauses which emphasize the carrier's non-liability for risks arising through the nature of the goods or the packaging; c) clauses which disclaim on the part of the carrier knowledge of contents, weight, measurement, quality, or technical specification of the goods.

8. Provide at his own expense the customary packing of the goods, unless it is the custom of the trade to ship the goods unpacked.

9. Pay the costs of any checking operations (such as checking quality, measuring, weighing, counting) which shall be necessary for the purpose of loading the goods.

10. Pay any dues and taxes incurred in respect of the goods up to the time of their loading, including any taxes, fees or charges levied because of exportation, as well as the costs of any formalities which he shall have to fulfill in order to load the goods on board.

11. Provide the buyer, at the latter's request and expense (see B.5), with the certificate of origin and the consular invoice.

12. Render the buyer, at the latter's request, risk and expense, every assistance in obtaining any documents, other than those mentioned in the previous article, issued in the country of shipment and/or of origin and which the buyer may require for the importation of the goods into the country of destination (and, where necessary, for their passage in transit through another country).

B. The buyer must:

1. Accept the documents when tendered by the seller, if they are in conformity with the contract of sale, and pay the price as provided in the contract.

2. Receive the goods at the agreed port of destination and bear, with the exception of the freight and marine insurance, all costs and charges incurred in respect of the goods in the course of their transit by sea until their arrival at the port of destination, as well as unloading costs, including lighterage and wharfage charges, unless such costs and charges shall have been included in the freight or collected by the steamship company at the time freight was paid. * * *

3. Bear all risks of the goods from the time when they shall have effectively passed the ship's rail at the port of shipment.

4. In case he may have reserved to himself a period within which to have the goods shipped and/or the right to choose the port of destination, and he fails to give instructions in time, bear the additional costs thereby incurred and all risks of the goods from the date of the expiration of the period fixed for shipment, provided always that the goods shall have been duly appropriated to the contract, that is to say, clearly set aside or otherwise identified as the contract goods.

5. Pay the costs and charges incurred in obtaining the certificate of origin and consular documents.

6. Pay all costs and charges incurred in obtaining the documents mentioned in article A.12 above.

7. Pay all customs duties as well as any other duties and taxes payable at the time of or by reason of the importation.

8. Procure and provide at his own risk and expense any import license or permit or the like which he may require for the importation of the goods at destination.

Notes

(1) The division of duties between the seller and the buyer under the CIF term is only one possible allocation. Other Incoterms either increase or decrease their respective duties. If a seller sells "ex-works," the seller's only duty is to put the goods at the buyer's disposal at the seller's factory. At the other extreme, if the sale is made "delivered duty paid" virtually all of the responsibility for performing the duties listed in the CIF term will fall on the seller. The most common Incoterm other than CIF is probably "FOB—Free on Board (named port of shipment)." Under an FOB contract, the seller must arrange for the goods to be loaded on board a ship named by the buyer at the place of shipment. The seller has no responsibility for arranging carriage or insurance. Because of their comprehensive consideration of the tasks that must be performed by someone in an international sales transaction, the Incoterm definitions provide a handy planning checklist, even if they are not used in a given transaction.

(2) The CIF contract is designed for shipments by sea where the seller delivers the goods to the ship. The analogous situation where multiple carriers are used (e.g., truck from seller's premises to seller's port, ship to buyer's port, truck to buyer's premises) is defined by the Incoterms as "Freight/Carriage and Insurance paid to (named point of destination)." The FOB equivalent when a ship is not being used is "Free Carrier (named point)."

(3) The Uniform Commercial Code's definition of CIF is less detailed than and varies slightly from the Incoterms definition. For example, under the UCC, the seller is required to obtain war risk insurance and is authorized to charge the buyer therefor. UCC § 2–320. See also UCC §§ 2–319, 2–321, 2–322.

(4) A CIF contract is a shipment contract, not a destination contract. As the Incoterms definition makes clear, the seller's obligation under a CIF contract is to arrange for insurance and freight and to deliver the goods to the carrier. The seller takes the risk that shipping or insurance costs will be higher than anticipated, but the seller is not responsible for seeing that the goods actually reach their intended destination. If they are lost, the risk of loss falls on the buyer. Moreover, a CIF contract is often more accurately called a contract for the delivery of documents rather than one for the delivery of goods. When the seller presents to the buyer or the buyer's agent evidence of insurance and a document of title from the carrier covering the goods, the buyer is normally obligated to pay for the goods even though they have not arrived and he has had no opportunity to inspect them. Under a CIF contract, if non-conforming goods are shipped, the buyer will be out-of-pocket until a settlement is reached. Buyers sometimes try to reduce this risk by requiring, as a condition to payment, a certificate from an independent inspection agency that the goods conform to the contract. In light of the many events—wars, embargoes, etc.—that may prevent delivery of goods after shipment in an international transaction, the risk-of-loss allocation to the buyer may be significant. These risks occur not infrequently. Indeed many of the classic cases in contract law on impossibility or frustration involve international sales contracts.

(5) The duties of a buyer and seller under a CIF contract are fairly well established. The consequences of a breach are less so. If a buyer fails to pay when the documents are properly presented, the seller will retain possession of the documents (and therefore of the goods) and will be entitled to normal contract damages. But what if the seller fails to perform? The buyer will be entitled to damages, but courts have split over the question of the proper date at which damages should be measured—the date the goods were due to arrive or the date the documents should have been presented to the buyer—and the proper market in which to measure damages—should the buyer's damages be based on the market price of similar goods in the seller's market or the buyer's market? The majority view seems to be that damages are measured in the buyer's market at the last date on which properly tendered documents could have been received by the buyer under the contract. See D. Sassoon & H. Merren, C.I.F. and F.O.B. Contracts §§ 305, 306 (3rd ed. 1984). Can that date ever be precisely determined?

(C) THE CONTRACT OF CARRIAGE AND THE BILL OF LADING [11]

CLIVE M. SCHMITTHOFF, EXPORT TRADE: THE LAW AND PRACTICE OF INTERNATIONAL TRADE

Page 38 supra, at 345–47

Nature of the Bill of Lading. The principal purpose of the bill of lading is to enable the owner of the goods, to which it relates, to dispose of them

---

11. See generally 2A Benedict on Admiralty (7th rev. ed. 1985); G. Gilmore & C. Black, The Law of Admiralty, ch. III (2d ed. 1975); T. Schoenbaum & A. Yiannopoulos, Admiralty and Maritime Law, ch. 6 (1984); R. Colinvaux, Carver's Carriage by Sea (13th ed., 2 vols. 1982); E. Ivamy & W. Payne, Carriage of Goods by Sea (10th ed. 1976); A. Mitchelhill,

rapidly although the goods are no longer in the hands of the owner but already in the custody of the shipowner. When goods belonging to a merchant in London are on the high seas in transit from London to Singapore, the bill of lading representing the goods enables their owner to pledge the goods with his bank in London or to sell them to a buyer in New York. The bill of lading is a creation of mercantile custom, a typical institution of international trade. It came into use in the sixteenth century. A book on mercantile law, published in 1686, stated that "bills of lading are commonly to be had in print in all places and several languages." The character of the bill of lading as a document of title was first recognised by the courts in 1794 in Lickbarrow v. Mason.

From the legal point of view, a bill of lading is—

(1) a formal receipt by the shipowner acknowledging that goods of the stated species, quantity and condition are shipped to a stated destination in a certain ship, or at least received in the custody of the shipowner for the purpose of shipment;

(2) a memorandum of the contract of carriage, repeating in detail the terms of the contract which was in fact concluded prior to the signing of the bill; and

(3) a document of title to the goods enabling the consignee to dispose of the goods by indorsement and delivery of the bill of lading.

THE INTERNATIONAL RULES RELATING TO BILLS OF LADING

Although the clauses contained in a duly tendered and signed bill of lading represent, in law, the terms of agreement between the shipper and the shipowner, the shipper has little discretion in the negotiation of these terms. The terms of the contract which he concludes, are fixed in advance, and his position is not unlike that of a railway passenger who, when buying a ticket, concludes an elaborate standard contract with the railway authority for the carriage of his person from one locality to another. The shipper, like the railway passenger, is protected by Act of Parliament against abuse of the greater bargaining power of the other party. As far as the shipper is concerned, this protection is now contained in the *Carriage of Goods by Sea Act 1971.* * * *

The Act of 1971 was preceded by the *Carriage of Goods by Sea Act 1924* which has an interesting history: the clauses in bills of lading exempting the shipowner from liability had become so complex and diffuse that the usefulness of bills of lading as "currency of trade" was seriously threatened. This was particularly unsatisfactory to holders of bills of lading who were not the original parties to the contract of carriage and consequently had no influence on its formation, such as further purchasers of goods, bankers who accepted the bills as security for advances, or insurers who were subrogated to the rights of the shipper. On the initiative of the International Law Association the *Hague Rules* 1921 relating to Bills of Lading were formulated and diplomatic conferences held in Brussels in 1922, 1923 and 1924

Bills of Lading: Law and Practice (1982); P. Gram, Chartering Documents, ch. 6 (1981); Tetley, Waybills: The Modern Contract of Carriage of Goods by Sea (pts. 1 & 2), 14 J. Maritime L. & Commerce 465 (1983), 15 J. Maritime L. & Commerce 41 (1984).

recommended their international adoption. In the United Kingdom, effect was given to the Hague Rules by the Carriage of Goods by Sea Act 1924. The Hague Rules imposed on the carrier certain minimum responsibilities which he could not reduce, e.g. to exercise due diligence to provide a seaworthy ship, to load, handle, stow, carry, keep, care for and discharge the goods and to issue a bill of lading in a particular form, and put upon him the liability for the proper and careful conduct of these operations while giving him certain maximum exemptions which he could not increase.

———

The United States gave effect to the Hague Rules in the Carriage of Goods by Sea Act (known as "COGSA"), 46 U.S.C.A. §§ 1300–1315. As demonstrated in the following case, the Act has a complicated system of allocating and shifting the risk of loss and the burden of proof between the shipper and the carrier.

QUAKER OATS CO. v. M/V TORVANGER

United States Court of Appeals, Fifth Circuit, 1984.
734 F.2d 238, cert. denied, ___ U.S. ___, 105 S.Ct. 959, 83 L.Ed.2d 965 (1985).

TATE, CIRCUIT JUDGE:

[Suit by cargo owner against carrier for damages to cargo of a chemical, tetrahydrofuram, shipped from Japan to the United States. Cargo samples taken following cargo loading indicated that the peroxide content of the cargo was at commercially acceptable levels. Samples taken on one part of the cargo on arrival at destination indicated unacceptably high peroxide levels].

Both parties agree that this dispute is governed by COGSA, which regulates the rights and liabilities arising out of the carrier's issuance of a bill of lading with respect to cargo damage or loss.*1 "To enforce their respective rights under the Act, litigants must engage in the ping-pong game of burden shifting mandated by Sections 3 and 4." The plaintiff establishes a prima facie case by proving that the cargo for which the bill of lading issued was "loaded in an undamaged condition, and discharged in a contaminated condition." The "bill of lading shall be prima facie evidence of the receipt by the carrier of the goods as therein described." 46 U.S.C. § 1303(4).

Once the plaintiff has presented a prima facie case, "the carrier then has the burden of proving that it exercised due diligence to prevent the

---

* 1. The carrier's responsibilities and liabilities under the Act are as follows:

Seaworthiness

(1) The carrier shall be bound, before and at the beginning of the voyage, to exercise due diligence to—

(a) Make the ship seaworthy;

(b) Properly man, equip, and supply the ship;

(c) Make the holds, refrigerating and cooling chambers, and all other parts of the ship in which goods are carried, fit and safe for their reception, carriage, and preservation.

Cargo

(2) The carrier shall properly and carefully load, handle, stow, carry, keep, care for, and discharge the goods carried.

46 U.S.C.A. § 1303(1)–(2).

damage or that the harm was occasioned by one of the excepted causes delineated in 46 U.S.C. § 1304(2)." *2

If the carrier rebuts the plaintiff's prima facie case with proof of an excepted cause listed in § 4(2)(a)–(p) of COGSA, 46 U.S.C. § 1304(2)(a)–(p), the burden returns to the plaintiff to establish that the carrier's negligence contributed to the damage or loss. If the plaintiff is then able to establish that the carrier's negligence was a contributory cause of the damage, the burden shifts to the carrier "to segregate the portion of the damage due to the excepted cause from that portion resulting from [the carrier's] own negligence."

In addition to rebuttal of the prima facie case by proof of one of the specific exception causes of cargo damage, 46 U.S.C. § 1304(2)(a)–(p), the carrier may also rebut the prima facie case by relying on the catch-all exception in § 1304(2)(q) of COGSA, which provides that the carrier may exonerate himself from loss from any cause other than those listed in 4(2)(a)–(p) by proving that the loss or damage occurred "without the actual fault and privity of the carrier. * * *" 46 U.S.C. § 1304(2)(q). The carrier's burden of establishing "his own freedom from contributing fault . . . is no mere burden of going forward with evidence, but a real burden of persuasion, with the attendant risk of nonpersuasion." Consequently, the burden of proof does not return to the plaintiff, but rather judgment must hinge upon the adequacy of the carrier's proof that he was free from any fault whatsoever contributing to the damage of the goods entrusted to his carriage.

* 2. The excepted causes are listed in the Act as follows:

(2) Neither the carrier nor the ship shall be responsible for loss or damage arising or resulting from—

(a) Act, neglect, or default of the master, mariner, pilot, or the servants of the carrier in the navigation or in the management of the ship;

(b) Fire, unless caused by the actual fault or privity of the carrier;

(c) Perils, dangers, and accidents of the sea or other navigable waters;

(d) Act of God;

(e) Act of war;

(f) Act of public enemies;

(g) Arrest or restraint of princes, rulers, or people, or seizure under legal process;

(h) Quarantine restrictions;

(i) Act or omission of the shipper or owner of the goods, his agent or representative;

(j) Strikes or lockouts or stoppage or restraint of labor from whatever cause, whether partial or general: *Provided*, That nothing herein contained shall be construed to relieve a carrier from responsibility for the carrier's own acts;

(k) Riots and civil commotions;

(*l*) Saving or attempting to save life or property at sea;

(m) Wastage in bulk or weight or any other loss or damage arising from inherent defect, quality, or vice of the goods;

(n) Insufficiency of packing;

(*o*) Insufficiency or inadequacy of marks;

(p) Latent defects not discoverable by due diligence; and

(q) Any other cause arising without the actual fault and privity of the carrier and without the fault or neglect of the agents or servants of the carrier, but the burden of proof shall be on the person claiming the benefit of this exception to show that neither the actual fault or privity of the carrier nor the fault or neglect of the agents or servants of the carrier contributed to the loss or damage.

46 U.S.C.A. § 1304(2). In exculpating the carrier, the district court relied on (q), providing in effect that the carrier may escape liability by proving that the damage occurred "without the fault" of the carrier.

[The district court found that plaintiff had established a prima facie case by showing that the tetrahydrofuram was delivered to the carrier in good condition and that a part of it was no longer in good condition on arrival. The court also found that the carrier rebutted that prima facie case by showing that it had used due diligence " 'with respect to the preparation of the loading and storage equipment, the loading of the cargo, and the care of the cargo during the voyage * * *,' thus 'return[ing] to [plaintiff] the burden to show that the peroxide formation was caused at least in part by [the carrier's] negligence.' "]

* * * Consequently, if all the evidence is true, the evidence shows no cause for the peroxide contamination. However, that contamination must have resulted either from some defect in the chemical or its processing for shipment, for which the carrier would not be responsible—which the evidence does not prove; or else that contamination must have resulted during shipment from some failure of the vessel's officers or of the vessel—which again is not proved.

* * * None of the specific excepting causes (including the "inherent defect" exception, 46 U.S.C. § 1304(2)(a)–(p), were proved by the carrier, so the burden did not shift back to the shipper to prove that carrier negligence contributed to the damage. Under COGSA, the carrier's proof of the remaining general catch-all exception to liability relied upon, § 1304(2)(q), is not shown by its simple and to be expected evidence that its crew did all it was supposed to do * * *. The statute provides, more stringently, that the carrier shall prove that its fault did *not* contribute to the accident: "the burden of proof shall be on the person claiming the exception to show that neither the actual fault or privity of the carrier nor the fault or neglect of the agents or servants of the carrier contributed to the loss or damage." 46 U.S.C. § 1304(2)(q).

For purposes of this catch-all no-fault exception to liability, 46 U.S.C. § 1304(2)(q), the presumption of fault—resulting from the arrival of cargo, damage free when shipped under bill of lading, but contaminated on arrival—is thus not rebutted by simple proof of the carrier's own due diligence, evidence peculiarly within its knowledge and control during the period of the shipment of the cargo entrusted to its care. For the § 1304(2)(q) exception to come into play, the carrier must first prove what that "other cause" was. But the district court found that "no one knows what caused the cargo to form peroxide in the way it did" and indeed concluded that the cause of the damage was a "mystery."

To rebut the presumption of fault when relying upon its own reasonable care, the carrier must further prove that the damage was caused by something other than its own negligence. Once the shipper establishes a prima facie case, under "the policy of the law" the carrier must "explain what took place or suffer the consequences." "[T]he law casts upon [the carrier] the burden of the loss which he cannot explain or, explaining, bring within the exceptional case in which he is relieved from liability."

Here, contrary to the policy of the statute, the trial court placed the burden upon the shipper, not the carrier, to explain the unexplained or unexplainable loss. Its judgment must therefore be reversed, and the case remanded for entry of judgment awarding the plaintiff the damages sustained.

Notes

(1) The cases dealing with COGSA's various duties and exceptions are legion. See, e.g., Mobil Sales and Supply Corp. v. M.V. "Banglar Kakoli", 588 F.Supp. 1134 (S.D.N.Y.1984) (Judge Weinfeld carefully considers shippers' allegations that damage to their cargo was caused by improper stowage, geographic deviation and mishandling by the carrier and carrier's claim that the losses were caused by improper packing, perils of the sea, restraints of princes, and/or errors in navigation); The S.S. Asturias, 40 F.Supp. 168 (S.D.N.Y.1941).

(2) The bill of lading should indicate any defects in the cargo delivered to the carrier or any unusual shipping terms (e.g., that the goods are being carried on deck). If it does not, it is considered a "clean" bill of lading. This concept is important because presentation of a clean bill of lading is usually a condition to the buyer's obligation to pay under a CIF contract. The ICC has attempted to standardize practice in this area. See The Problem of Clean Bills of Lading (ICC Pub. No. 283, 1963). Bills of lading have typically been used in maritime shipping, and they have not been readily adaptable to new modes of shipment that utilize multiple carriers. As a consequence, the ICC has adopted a Combined Transport Document to serve the function of a bill of lading in such cases. See Uniform Rules for a Combined Transport Document (ICC Pub. No. 298, 1975).

(3) The Hague Rules were amended in 1968 in order to, inter alia, increase the carrier's maximum liability per package and to define the concept of package, which had become outmoded with extensive use of large "packages" (i.e. containers) to ship numerous smaller packages. For a perceptive and exhaustive discussion of the problems courts have faced in defining "package", see Mitsui & Co. v. American Export Lines, Inc., 636 F.2d 807 (2d Cir.1981) (Friendly, J.). In their amended form the Hague Rules are known as the Hague-Visby Rules. The United States has not adopted the amendments. The United Kingdom did in 1971. Fundamental changes to the Hague-Visby Rules have been made in the UNCITRAL-sponsored U.N. Convention on the Carriage of Goods by Sea 1978, also known as the Hamburg Rules. The Hamburg Rules in general place greater burdens on the carrier than do the Hague-Visby Rules. Among other changes, the long list of exceptions to the carrier's liability is deleted and it is provided that the carrier is liable for any loss incurred while the goods were in its charge unless it proves that it took all measures that could reasonably be required to avoid the loss. It is unclear whether the Hamburg Rules will be widely adopted as shipowners in general oppose them. See S. Mankabady (ed.), The Hamburg Rules on the Carriage of Goods by Sea (1978).

(4) There are also conventions on the carriage of goods by air, road and rail. See the 1929 Warsaw Convention for the Unification of Certain Rules Relating to International Transportation by Air (the United States is a party); [12] the 1956 Convention on the Contract for the International Carriage of Goods by Road (the United States is not a party); the 1961 International Convention Concerning the

---

12. 49 Stat. 3000, TS 876. See Trans World Airlines, Inc. v. Franklin Mint Corp., 466 U.S. 243, 104 S.Ct. 1776, 80 L.Ed.2d 273 (1984) (upholding per package damage limitation).

Transportation of Merchandise by Rail (the United States is not a party). The Warsaw Convention has been amended several times, most recently in 1975.

(D) CARGO INSURANCE [13]

CLIVE M. SCHMITTHOFF, EXPORT TRADE: THE LAW AND PRACTICE OF INTERNATIONAL TRADE

Page 38 supra, at 288

INSURANCE OF EXPORTS

It is customary to insure goods sold for export against the perils of the journey. According to the method of transportation, a marine, aviation or overland insurance is effected.

The term "marine insurance" is somewhat misleading because the contract of marine insurance can, by agreement of the parties or custom of the trade, be extended so as to protect the assured against losses on inland waters or land which are incidental to the sea voyage. In the export trade it is usual to arrange an extended marine insurance in order to cover the transportation of goods from the warehouse of the seller to the port of dispatch, and from the port of arrival to the warehouse of the overseas buyer. Marine insurance is an institution of great antiquity; it was known in Lombardy in the fourteenth century, the first English statute dealing with it was passed in 1601, and Lloyd's Coffee House, the birthplace of Lloyd's London, is first mentioned in the records of 1688. The law relating to marine insurance is codified in the Marine Insurance Act 1906. This enactment provides a standard policy, known as Lloyd's S.G. policy, which the parties may adopt if they so desire whether they insure the risk with underwriters at Lloyd's or elsewhere.

The International Chamber of Commerce has prepared a publication entitled *Tables of Practical Equivalents in Marine Insurance,* in which the similarities and differences existing in marine insurance terms, clauses and covers in 13 important centres of the world are analysed and compared from the marine insurance point of view.

In the law relating to aviation or overland insurance no standard policy has been developed yet and Lloyd's S.G. policy is used with suitable alterations.

Notes

(1) Marine or cargo insurance can be an extraordinarily complicated subject and one that cannot be dealt with in detail here. Much litigation occurs between the insurers of the cargo and those who insure the ship, since placing the risk of loss on one or the other of the cargo owner or the ship determines which insurer will have to pay. The interpretation of the exceptions to the carrier's liability under the Hague Rules is not always easy. Numerous cases

13. See generally C. Schmitthoff, note 1 supra, ch. 23; G. Gilmore & C. Black, note 11 supra, ch. II; T. Schoenbaum & A. Yiannopoulos, note 11 supra, ch. 8; M. Mustill & J. Gilman, Arnould's Law of Marine Insurance and Average (16th ed., 2 vols. 1981); E. Ivamy, Marine Insurance (3rd ed. 1979).

have had to grapple with such concepts as "peril of the sea", etc. See, e.g., Boston Ins. Co. v. Dehydrating Process Co., 204 F.2d 441 (1st Cir.1953).

(2) According to the Incoterms, in a CIF contract, the seller is obligated to obtain insurance on "FPA terms" and is not obligated to obtain coverage of special risks. Under typical FPA terms, the insurance is payable only if there is a total loss of the cargo or an individual package making up part of the cargo. Such a policy is well-suited to shipment of items like bulk steel—if the ship makes it to the destination, the steel will probably arrive undamaged—but may not be adequate if the cargo is machinery or some other item that may be damaged, although not destroyed, en route. The possible need for special insurance should always be considered in international commerce.

(3) War risk insurance is not required to be provided by the seller under the Incoterms definition of CIF contract, although it is so required according to the UCC definition. In either case, war risk insurance is the buyer's expense. War risk insurance insures against somewhat different risks, such as "all consequences of hostilities or warlike operations." As might be expected, interpretive difficulties arise, as illustrated by the case of Standard Oil Co. of New Jersey v. United States, 340 U.S. 54, 71 S.Ct. 135, 95 L.Ed. 68 (1950), in which the United States Supreme Court held that the war-risk clause did not cover loss to the petitioner's ship caused by a collision with a navy minesweeper, because the "evidence failed to show that the warlike phase of the minesweeper's operation had caused the collision." The Court noted the close factual questions involved, stating (at 60):

> This Court, moreover, has long emphasized that in interpreting insurance contracts reference should be made to considerations of business and insurance practices. The particular English cases relied on by petitioner produced such an unfavorable reaction among that country's underwriters that they revised the clause here involved to avoid the injurious effects of those decisions. The terms of American war risk policies have also been altered.

> The proximate cause method of determining on the facts of each case whether a loss was the "consequence" of warlike operations may fall short of achieving perfect results. For those insured and those insuring cannot predict with certainty what a trier of fact might decide is the predominant cause of loss. But neither could they predict with certainty what particular state of facts might cause a court to discover liability "as a matter of law." Long experience with the proximate cause method in American and English courts has at least proven it adaptable and useful in marine and other insurance cases. There is no reason to believe that its application in this case will disappoint the just expectations of insurer or insured.

(E) FINANCING EXPORTS

(1) The Letter of Credit [14]

If a seller of goods trusts the buyer, the seller may ship the goods to the buyer and bill the buyer on open account. Within the United States most

---

14. See generally J. Dolan, The Law of Letters of Credit (1984); H. Harfield, Bank Credits and Acceptances (5th ed. 1974); H. Harfield, Letters of Credit (1979); C. Schmitthoff, note 1 supra, ch. 21; G. Gilmore & C. Black, note 11 supra, at 114–30; R. Purvis & R. Darvas, Commercial Letters of Credit, Shipping Documents and the Termination of Disputes in International Trade (1975).

ordinary sales are made this way. But in the international trade transaction this mode of business is much riskier because of the various factors discussed in Section 2.1. A seller can minimize those risks in a number of ways: (1) require the buyer to pay in advance, although the buyer may refuse to pay before evidence of shipment is presented; (2) send an agent (or hire one already in the buyer's locale) to collect from the buyer at the time the shipment arrives and is turned over to the buyer, although if the buyer doesn't pay, the goods will have to be resold in a foreign country, perhaps at a loss; (3) require the buyer to deposit money with an acceptable bank with instructions to pay the amount to the seller on presentation of acceptable shipping documents, although this may be inconvenient and expensive for the buyer; or (4) require the buyer to arrange for a bank, which the seller is willing to trust, to promise the seller that the bank, on its own account, will pay the seller when the seller presents acceptable shipping documents. The last alternative describes the typical letter of credit transaction. When payment to the seller is made, the bank then collects from the buyer. Thus the bank becomes a sort of escrow agent for the trade transaction. The convenience and relative safety of this mode of dealing has made it the backbone of international commerce.

The steps involved in the typical letter of credit transaction are as follows: Seller (S) and Buyer (B) contract for S to ship widgets, and B to pay for them, and as part of this contract B promises to open an irrevocable letter of credit (L/C) in S's favor. The following occurs:

(1) B goes to his bank in Paris and asks it to open the L/C. If the bank does not trust B it may ask for a deposit, but usually B is a regular customer of the bank. The bank will then open the L/C and airmail or cable an "advice" to S that the credit is open.

(2) S, thus assured, ships the goods and prepares the documents.

(3) S will want to present the documents in his own locale. If B's bank has a branch there, fine. If not, B's bank can send the L/C to a correspondent bank in S's locale to handle the presentment. In this case only B's bank in Paris stands behind the L/C.

(4) If S prefers to trust only his local bank, B may open the L/C at a distance with S's bank. But often, S's bank doesn't know B. So B opens the L/C at his own bank, and then B's bank opens a new L/C with S's bank, in favor of S. This is a "confirmed" letter of credit.

(5) S is called the "beneficiary" in this transaction.

(6) The banks involved charge a modest commission for their various services. The higher the risk that the bank assumes, the higher the commission (e.g., to confirm an L/C is riskier than merely transmitting an advice of credit.)

In an effort to standardize practices in the letter of credit area, the ICC has published and from time to time updates the Uniform Customs and Practice for Documentary Credits ("UCP") (ICC Pub. No. 400, 1983). The vast majority of letters of credit incorporate the UCP.

The principal issues that arise in cases involving letters of credit are (1) when can a bank be enjoined from making payment under a letter of credit and (2) when is a bank excused from performing its payment obligation under a letter of credit?   Consider the following materials:

UNIFORM CUSTOMS AND PRACTICE FOR DOCUMENTARY CREDITS

(1983) [15]

ARTICLE 3

Credits, by their nature, are separate transactions from the sales or other contract(s) on which they may be based and banks are in no way concerned with or bound by such contract(s), even if any reference whatsoever to such contract(s) is included in the credit.

ARTICLE 4

In credit operations all parties concerned deal in documents, and not in goods, services and/or other performances to which the documents may relate.

*   *   *

ARTICLE 7

a.   Credits may be either

i revocable, or

ii irrevocable.

*   *   *

c.   In the absence of such indication [i.e. that it is irrevocable] the credit shall be deemed to be revocable.

ARTICLE 8

A credit may be advised to a beneficiary through another bank (the advising bank) without engagement on the part of the advising bank, but that bank shall take reasonable care to check the apparent authenticity of the credit which it advises.

*   *   *

ARTICLE 10

a.   An irrevocable credit constitutes a definite undertaking of the issuing bank, provided that the stipulated documents are presented and that the terms and conditions of the credit are complied with:

i if the credit provides for sight payment—to pay, or that payment will be made;

ii if the credit provides for deferred payment—to pay, or that payment will be made, on the date(s) determinable in accordance with the stipulations of the credit;

iii if the credit provides for acceptance—to accept drafts drawn by the beneficiary if the credit stipulates that they are to be drawn on the issuing bank, or to be responsible for their acceptance and payment at maturity if the credit stipulates that they are to be drawn on the applicant for the credit or any other drawee stipulated in the credit;

iv if the credit provides for negotiation—to pay without recourse to drawers and/or bona fide holders, draft(s) drawn by the beneficiary, at sight or at a tenor, on the applicant for the credit or on any other drawee stipulated in the credit other than the issuing bank itself, or to provide for negotiation by another bank and to pay, as above, if such negotiation is not effected.

b. When an issuing bank authorizes or requests another bank to confirm its irrevocable credit and the latter has added its confirmation, such confirmation constitutes a definite undertaking of such bank (the confirming bank), in addition to that of the issuing bank, provided that the stipulated documents are presented and that the terms and conditions of the credit are complied with:

[Similar to (i)–(iv) above]

* * *

ARTICLE 15

Banks must examine all documents with reasonable care to ascertain that they appear on their face to be in accordance with the terms and conditions of the credit. Documents which appear on their face to be inconsistent with one another will be considered as not appearing on their face to be in accordance with the terms and conditions of the credit.

ARTICLE 16

a. If a bank so authorized effects payment, or incurs a deferred payment undertaking, or accepts, or negotiates against documents which appear on their face to be in accordance with the terms and conditions of a credit, the party giving such authority shall be bound to reimburse the bank which has effected payment, or incurred a deferred payment undertaking, or has accepted, or negotiated, and to take up the documents.

b. If, upon receipt of the documents, the issuing bank considers that they appear on their face not to be in accordance with the terms and conditions of the credit, it must determine, on the basis of the documents alone, whether to take up such documents, or to refuse them and claim that they appear on their face not to be in accordance with the terms and conditions of the credit.

c. The issuing bank shall have a reasonable time in which to examine the documents and to determine as above whether to take up or to refuse the documents.

d. If the issuing bank decides to refuse the documents, it must give notice to that effect without delay by telecommunication or, if that is not possible, by other expeditious means, to the bank from which it received the documents (the remitting bank), or to the beneficiary, if it received the documents directly from him. Such notice must state the discrepancies in respect of which the issuing bank refuses the documents and must also state whether it is holding the documents at the disposal of, or is returning them to, the presentor (remitting bank or the beneficiary, as the case may be).

The issuing bank shall then be entitled to claim from the remitting bank refund of any reimbursement which may have been made to that bank.

e. If the issuing bank fails to act in accordance with the provisions of paragraphs (c) and (d) of this article and/or fails to hold the documents at the disposal of, or to return them to, the presentor, the issuing bank shall be precluded from claiming that the documents are not in accordance with the terms and conditions of the credit.

f. If the remitting bank draws the attention of the issuing bank to any discrepancies in the documents or advises the issuing bank that it has paid, incurred a deferred payment undertaking, accepted or negotiated under reserve or against an indemnity in respect of such discrepancies, the issuing bank shall not be thereby relieved from any of its obligations under any provision of this article. Such reserve or indemnity concerns only the relations between the remitting bank and the party towards whom the reserve was made, or from whom, or on whose behalf, the indemnity was obtained.

ARTICLE 17

Banks assume no liability or responsibility for the form, sufficiency, accuracy, genuineness, falsification or legal effect of any documents, or for the general and/or particular conditions stipulated in the documents or superimposed thereon; nor do they assume any liability or responsibility for the description, quantity, weight, quality, condition, packing, delivery, value or existence of the goods represented by any documents, or for the good faith or acts and/or omissions, solvency, performance or standing of the consignor, the carriers, or the insurers of the goods, or any other person whomsoever.

ARTICLE 18

Banks assume no liability or responsibility for the consequences arising out of delay and/or loss in transit of any messages, letters or documents, or for delay, mutilation or other errors arising in the transmission of any telecommunication. Banks assume no liability or responsibility for errors in translation or interpretation of technical terms, and reserve the right to transmit credit terms without translating them.

*   *   *

ARTICLE 25

Unless a credit calling for a transport document stipulates as such document a marine bill of lading (ocean bill of lading or a bill of lading covering carriage by sea), or a post receipt or certificate of posting:

a. banks will, unless otherwise stipulated in the credit, accept a tansport document which:

i appears on its face to have been issued by a named carrier, or his agent, and

ii indicates dispatch or taking in charge of the goods, or loading on board, as the case may be, and

iii   consists of the full set of originals issued to the consignor if issued in more than one original, and

iv   meets all other stipulations of the credit.

* * *

ARTICLE 31

a.   Unless otherwise stipulated in the credit, or inconsistent with any of the documents presented under the credit, banks will accept transport documents stating that freight or transportation charges (hereinafter referred to as "freight") have still to be paid.

* * *

c.   The words "freight prepayable" or "freight to be prepaid" or words of similar effect, if appearing on transport documents, will not be accepted as constituting evidence of the payment of freight.

* * *

ARTICLE 32

Unless otherwise stipulated in the credit, banks will accept transport documents which bear a clause on the face thereof such as "shipper's load and count" or "said by shipper to contain" or words of similar effect.

* * *

ARTICLE 35

a.   Insurance documents must be as stipulated in the credit, and must be issued and/or signed by insurance companies or underwriters, or their agents.

b.   Cover notes issued by brokers will not be accepted, unless specifically authorised by the credit.

* * *

ARTICLE 37

a.   Unless otherwise stipulated in the credit, the insurance document must be expressed in the same currency as the credit.

b.   Unless otherwise stipulated in the credit, the minimum amount for which the insurance document must indicate the insurance cover to have been effected is the CIF (cost, insurance and freight . . . "named port of destination") or CIP (freight/carriage and insurance paid to "named point of destination") value of the goods, as the case may be, plus 10%. However, if banks cannot determine the CIF or CIP value, as the case may be, from the documents on their face, they will accept as such minimum amount the amount for which payment, acceptance or negotiation is requested under the credit, or the amount of the commercial invoice, whichever is the greater.

ARTICLE 38

a.   Credits should stipulate the type of insurance required and, if any, the additional risks which are to be covered. Imprecise terms such as "usual risks" or "customary risks" should not be used; if they are used, banks will accept insurance documents as presented, without responsibility for any risks not being covered.

* * *

ARTICLE 41

a. Unless otherwise stipulated in the credit, commercial invoices must be made out in the name of the applicant for the credit.

*   *   *

c. The description of the goods in the commercial invoice must correspond with the description in the credit. In all other documents, the goods may be described in general terms not inconsistent with the description of the goods in the credit.

KMW INTERNATIONAL v. CHASE MANHATTAN BANK, N.A.

United States Court of Appeals, Second Circuit, 1979.
606 F.2d 10.

OAKES, CIRCUIT JUDGE:

[Chase Manhattan Bank ("Chase") appeals the issuance of a preliminary injunction restraining it from honoring an irrevocable letter of credit issued by it for KMW's account in favor of Banque Etebarate ("Etebarate") of Iran. KMW had contracted to sell telephone poles to an Iranian government entity. Under the contract it was required to obtain a performance guarantee of 10% of the contract price, or about $350,000. It fulfilled that obligation by arranging for a letter of credit of $350,000 in favor of Etebarate, which then issued the required performance guarantee. The letter provided Chase would pay upon receipt of "[Etebarate's] authenticated cable certifying [that] the amount drawn is the amount [Etebarate has] been called upon to pay Khuzestan Water and Power Authority, P.O. Box 13, Ahwaz, Iran, under [Etebarate's] guarantee issued at the request of KMW International due to nonperformance by KMW International under the terms of Khuzestan Water and Power Authority purchase order # 4229 dated August 1, 1978."

[The Water and Power Authority was required to pay KMW by means of a separate letter of credit. KMW's obligation to ship the telephone poles was deferred until a date within three to ten months after it received the letter of credit in its favor. No such separate letter of credit was opened, and the court assumed that KMW therefore had no obligation to ship any telephone poles under its contract. After the downfall of the Shah and his government, KMW sought the injunction at issue on the grounds that any demand under the letter of credit or under any performance guarantee issued by Etebarate "of necessity would be false and fraudulent," that the contract had been wholly frustrated because of nonperformance of that contract by the Water and Power Authority, and that unknown persons in Iran might make fraudulent drawings under the performance guarantee or under the letter of credit. At the hearing on the injunction it was disclosed that the United States Embassy in Tehran had informed the State Department that it had received a report from the Tehran representative of the Water and Power Authority that there was "no change" in its status, that it was functioning and that nothing had changed concerning the status of its contractual obligations. KMW claimed it had been unable to communicate with the Authority.]

The legal standard in the Second Circuit for preliminary injunctive relief clearly calls for a showing of (a) possible irreparable harm and (b) either (1) likelihood of success on the merits or (2) sufficiently serious questions going to merits to make them a fair ground for litigation and a balance of hardships tipping decidedly toward the party requesting the preliminary relief. * * *

In the first place, KMW has not shown that it will suffer possible irreparable injury absent the injunction. KMW claims a possible loss of $347,539.55. This circuit does not recognize as irreparable harm a loss that may be adequately redressed by a monetary award. Appellant claims, however, that the financial damage which it may suffer is irreparable, since it will have no real remedy, at least by way of resort to Iranian courts, if Chase were to pay a demand which appears to comply with the terms of credit but is in fact fraudulent. But this damage is purely conjectural. At the time the preliminary injunction was granted, Chase had received no demand for payment whatsoever; that a later demand would necessarily be fraudulent is at best speculative. * * *

Furthermore, when KMW entered into its contract with the Water and Power Authority it assumed the business risks of international transactions. These risks included the possibility that even if a dispute about performance of the underlying contract should arise and international litigation ensue, which we assume can occur in this case, KMW's funds would be paid out under the irrevocable letter of credit and held in foreign hands. A preliminary injunction shifts the burden to Chase to pursue that international litigation. Such a shifting of risk is unwarranted where, as here, one party to an international business transaction has previously subjected itself to the risks and hazards of foreign political turmoil. * * *

As a matter of law, a bank's obligation under a letter of credit is totally independent of the underlying transaction. UCP General Provisions and Definitions Paragraph c and Article 8(a) provide:

> c. Credits, by their nature, are separate transactions from the sales or other contracts on which they may be based and banks are in no way concerned with or bound by such contracts.

> 8(a). In documentary credit operations all parties concerned deal in documents and not in goods.

By virtue of the letter of credit, Chase is subject to the UCP. As a leading commentator has pointed out, "The financial value of the letter of credit promise is predicated upon its degree of legal certainty." B. Kozolchyk, Commercial Letters of Credit in the Americas § 18.04[1], at 394–95 (1966). The issuing bank's obligation under an international irrevocable letter of credit may not be modified without the consent of both the customer and the beneficiary. UCP Article 3(c). There is nothing in the U.C.C. or the UCP which excuses an issuing bank from paying a letter of credit because of supervening illegality, impossibility, war or insurrection. Indeed, Article 8(c) of the UCP provides the opposite, viz., that a bank suspecting noncongruence with terms and conditions of credit "must determine, on the basis of the documents alone, whether to claim that payment, acceptance or negotiation was not effected in accordance with the terms and conditions of the credit."

There is, as we have suggested, limited authority for enjoining payment under a letter of credit when the documentation presented is fraudulent or there is "fraud in the transaction." This authority has recently been construed in the New York courts as to permit injunctive relief only in case of a "clear showing of the active intentional fraud complained of," not merely anticipated fraud as claimed here. There is no question that prior to suit Chase had received no demand for payment whatsoever, so that the injunction cannot as a matter of law be upheld on the grounds stated in N.Y. U.C.C. § 5–114 that "a required document * * * is forged or fraudulent * * *." Nor is there any basis here for finding "fraud in the transaction" unless that phrase is given some meaning we have been unable to divine from the New York cases. * * * Insurrection or supervening impossibility are not equivalents of fraud. The "unsettled situation in Iran" is simply insufficient to release any party from obligations under the letter of credit which are separate from the underlying contract.

Although there has been a change of government in Iran, the United States has so far as appears recognized the present government as the de jure government. The present Iranian government is therefore entitled by operation of law to enforce the rights of the Water and Power Authority, an agency of a province of Iran, under the performance guarantee secured by the letter of credit.

Even if the foregoing demonstrated a fair ground for litigation, the balance of hardships would not tip decidedly in favor of KMW, which as we have said assumed the risk of doing business in Iran in the first instance.

Both in the international business community and in Iran itself, Chase's commercial honor is essentially at stake. Failure to perform on its irrevocable letter of credit would constitute a breach of trust and substantially injure its reputation and perhaps even American credibility in foreign communities. Moreover, it could subject Chase to litigation in connection with not only this matter but also other banking affairs in Iran.

We take judicial notice of the fact that the Iranian banks have been nationalized since the argument on this appeal. However, we do not see that this changes our views on this controversy.

Although we conclude that the preliminary injunction must be vacated, * * * [p]ursuant to our general equitable powers and in the interest of justice, see 28 U.S.C. § 2106, we direct Chase to provide KMW with three days' notice in writing of receipt of a demand for payment before making payment thereon. This three-day notice corresponds to the three-day period which N.Y.U.C.C. § 5–112 allows issuing banks to decide whether to honor or dishonor demands upon letters of credit. In view of the circumstances currently existing in Iran, we consider that anything less than three days would not be in compliance with the spirit if not the letter of Article 8d of the UCP which requires that "[t]he issuing bank shall have a reasonable time to examine the documents and to determine * * * whether to make such a claim [that payment, acceptance or negotiation was not effected in accordance with the terms and conditions of the credit]." Such notice permits KMW either to provide evidence of fraud or to take such other action as KMW deems appropriate. Chase indicated on argument that it would have no objection to such a direction.

Notes and Questions

(1) In Rockwell Intl. Systems, Inc. v. Citibank, N.A., 719 F.2d 583 (2d Cir. 1983), Judge Oakes upheld the issuance of a preliminary injunction against honoring letters of credit issued by Citibank in favor of an Iranian bank to secure Rockwell's performance of its contract with the Iranian War Ministry. Rockwell was found to have demonstrated irreparable harm in the absence of an injunction because it was unclear that any effective forum would be open to Rockwell if the letters were honored. The jurisdiction of the Iran—U.S. Claims Tribunal was held to be "at best * * * unsettled". The contracts required resort to Iranian courts and the post-revolutionary Iranian judicial system was conceded by the parties to be incapable of affording an adequate remedy. The court also found that Rockwell had demonstrated a likelihood of success on the merits of a fraud defense because it had shown that the War Ministry suspended Rockwell's performance pending negotiations. "We think that the essence of the fraud exception is that 'the principle of the independence of [a] bank's obligation under the letter of credit should not be extended to protect' a party that behaves so as to prevent performance of the underlying obligation * * *; the 'fraud' inheres in first causing the default and then attempting to reap the benefit of the guarantee." 719 F.2d at 589. In this case Judge Oakes said nothing about Rockwell's accepting the risks of international litigation. Should courts ever interfere with the parties' agreement to shift the risk and place of litigation? If only U.S. courts do so, what will happen? The so-called Iranian letter of credit cases are discussed in Weisz & Blackman, Standby Letters of Credit After Iran: Remedies of the Account Party, 1982 U.Ill.L.Rev. 355.

(2) The most famous statement of the fraud exception is contained in Sztejn v. J. Henry Schroder Banking Corp., 177 Misc. 719, 31 N.Y.S.2d 631 (1941). The court refused to dismiss a request for preliminary injunction to enjoin payment on a letter of credit by the issuing bank where it was alleged that the seller had shipped cowhair, other worthless material and rubbish instead of bristles, as called for by the contract. The court held: "This is not a controversy between the buyer and seller concerning a mere breach of warranty regarding the quality of the merchandise; on the present motion, it must be assumed that the seller has intentionally failed to ship any goods ordered by the buyer. In such a situation, where the seller's fraud has been called to the bank's attention before the drafts and documents have been presented for payment, the principle of the independence of the bank's obligation under the letter of credit should not be extended to protect the unscrupulous seller. It is true that even though the documents are forged or fraudulent, if the issuing bank has already paid the draft before receiving notice of the seller's fraud, it will be protected if it exercised reasonable diligence before making such payment. However, in the instant action Schroder has received notice of Transea's active fraud before it accepted or paid the draft."

(3) The large international banks issue thousands of letters of credit annually. Typically the decision whether to pay is essentially determined by a clerk who simply checks to see if each document called for by the letter of credit has been submitted. Any deviation from the requirements of the letter need not be

accepted. In Courtaulds North America, Inc. v. North Carolina National Bank, 528 F.2d 802 (4th Cir.1975), the letter of credit required the presentation of invoices stating that they covered "100% acrylic yarn." The invoices presented stated "Imported Acrylic Yarn". In reversing a judgment against the bank that refused to pay, the court stated, "[T]he letter of credit dictated that each invoice express on its face that it covered 100% acrylic yarn. Nothing less is shown to be tolerated in the trade. No substitution and no equivalent, through interpretation or logic, will serve. Harfield, Bank Credits and Acceptances (5th Ed. 1974), at p. 73, commends and quotes aptly from an English case: 'There is no room for documents that are almost the same, or which will do just as well.' " 528 F.2d at 806. Is this fair if conforming goods were actually shipped? Should a good-faith buyer be required to tell its bank to waive this sort of discrepancy? Why might the buyer not want to do so? What if the bank paid without a waiver from the buyer?

(2) Sources of Export Finance

Letters of credit are typically used in international sales transactions. While their use eliminates concerns about credit worthiness, it highlights the need that a buyer or seller has to finance its own commitment. The seller has to acquire and ship the goods before it is paid; the buyer has to pay before it receives them. There are both private and public sources of export finance. Among the private sources are all those available for domestic use, although some types are particularly common in international transactions. One, of course, is the letter of credit. It is worth mentioning that the letter of credit is a very flexible device. A buyer may insist, for example, that on presentation of the required documents payment will be due in 60 days. The seller thus finances the buyer, although if the seller wishes to be paid immediately it can discount the 60 day draft it receives. Somewhat similarly, the seller may use the buyer's obligation under the letter of credit to finance its manufacture or acquisition of the goods to be sold to the buyer. This may involve the use of the buyer's letter of credit if it is transferable or it may involve the use of a new letter based on the buyer's letter, a so-called back-to-back letter of credit. Since the documents presented to obtain payment under a letter of credit typically include the document of title, the letter of credit device can easily serve to give the buyer's bank a security interest in the goods until the buyer pays the bank. Finally, it should be mentioned that exporters sometimes agree to ship on open account to buyers if the seller can obtain credit insurance, which protects the seller against certain risks of nonpayment.

Most governments sponsor export promotion programs of one sort or another, including in most cases agencies that provide export credits. The extent to which these programs can provide favorable credit terms is limited by international agreements concerning minimum permissible interest rates and export subsidies that will be discussed in Chapter 10. While the terms of specific programs change frequently, there are a number of institutions that offer favorable loans to finance exports or that guarantee the obligations of foreign buyers.[16] In the United States, the Export-Import Bank of

16. See OECD, The Export Credit Financing Systems in OECD Member States (1982); EX–IM Bank, Report to Congress on Export

the United States (the EX–IM Bank) provides such programs.[17]   The United States also has programs designed to supply various types of foreign aid, including loans, to developing countries and to assist the export of agricultural commodities.   In addition, a number of international or regional banks, such as the World Bank, the European Investment Bank, the Inter-American Development Bank, the Asian Development Bank and the African Development Fund have programs that assist in financing exports to developing countries.[18]

SECTION 2.3   RESOLVING INTERNATIONAL COMMERCIAL DISPUTES

Among the greater risks involved in an international transaction, compared with one that is purely national, are the problems that arise when a dispute occurs.   The dispute, if serious enough, may require litigation in a foreign country with a different legal system.   If the party is lucky enough to be able to obtain jurisdiction and receive a court judgment in its favor in its "home territory," then it may be faced with enforcing that judgment in a foreign country.   Often arbitration is used as a technique to reduce the risks involved in a dispute, and to provide a (hopefully) less expensive procedure for resolving disputes.   This section will briefly survey these two general subjects of resolving disputes: arbitration, and litigation and judgments.

(A)   ARBITRATION AND ENFORCEMENT OF ARBITRAL AWARDS[1]

Arbitration has generally been favored as a dispute settlement mechanism in international transactions, although it is not without hazards. There are many arbitration procedures in use today.   They range from those sponsored by trade associations for resolving disputes involving particular commodities to those sponsored by national or city arbitration associations to

Credit Competition and The Export-Import Bank of the United States (1982).

17.   The EX–IM Bank's activities are discussed in its Annual Report.   See also H.R. Rep. No. 98–175, 98th Cong., 1st Sess. (1983) on legislation extending the life of the Bank. Other U.S. agencies supplying export credits and similar assistance for exporters include the Federal Credit Insurance Association, the Overseas Private Investment Corporation, the Commodity Credit Corporation, the Private Export Funding Corporation and the Agency for International Development.   See generally U.S. Dept. of Commerce, A Guide to Financing Programs, Business America 3 (April 15, 1985).

18.   The activities of the regional banks and U.S. participation in their activities is discussed in H.R.Rep. No. 98–175, note 17 supra, at 47–63.   See also U.S. Dept. of Commerce, note 17 supra.

1.   The Commercial Arbitration Yearbooks published annually under the auspices of the International Council for Commercial Arbitration provide extensive information on rules and national laws affecting arbitration, important arbitral awards and extensive bibliographic information.   See also International Commercial Arbitration (Oceana looseleaf); G. Delaume, Transnational Contracts, Applicable Law and Settlement of Disputes (A Study in Conflict Avoidance) (Oceana looseleaf); R. David, Arbitration in International Trade (1985); K. Seide, The Paul Felix Warburg Union Catalog of Arbitration (3 vols. 1974); L. Brown, A Selected Bibliography of International Commercial Arbitration (1976, 1978, 1980).   Surveys contrasting the rules and practices of the principal arbitral bodies can be found in McLaughlin, Arbitration and Developing Countries, 13 The Intl. Lawyer 211 (1979); Note, A Survey of Arbitral Forums: Their Significance and Procedure, 5 N.Car.J. of Intl.L. & Comm.Reg. 219 (1980).

those sponsored by international bodies. Among the best known national or city associations are the American Arbitration Association, the London Court of Arbitration and the Stockholm Chamber of Commerce. The International Chamber of Commerce and the International Centre for Settlement of Investment Disputes are the two principal international bodies providing arbitration services.[2] In an effort to provide more uniformity in arbitral practices, UNCITRAL has developed a set of procedural rules and a model national law to be applicable to international arbitration.[3] There is an immense volume of material available on arbitration. Here we will consider only the problems of enforcing arbitral awards and of making arbitration the exclusive method of resolving disputes.

CHARLES L. EVANS & ROBERT W. ELLIS, INTERNATIONAL COMMERCIAL ARBITRATION: A COMPARISON OF LEGAL REGIMES

(1973) [4]

C. THE UNITED NATIONS CONVENTION

Against the background of very limited success with both bilateral and multilateral attempts to establish an international regime for the uniform enforcement of transnational arbitral agreements and awards came the 1958 United Nations Convention on the Recognition and Enforcement of Foreign Arbitral Awards.

The "New York" Convention, as it is commonly referred to, begins in article I by establishing a broad coverage applicable to all awards made in the territory of a State "other than the State where the recognition and enforcement of such awards are sought." The breadth of coverage, however, may be limited by two reservations contained in article I(3). These provide that any country may "on the basis of reciprocity declare that it will apply the Convention to * * * awards made only in the territory of another contracting State," or that it "will apply the Convention only to differences arising out of legal relationships * * * which are considered as commercial under the national law of the state making such declaration."

2. In addition to conciliation and arbitration services, the ICC offers special procedures for providing impartial experts to resolve technical disputes and for adapting contracts in light of changed circumstances. ICC, Guide to Arbitration (Pub. No. 382, 1983). On ICC arbitration generally, see ICC, Rules for the ICC Court of Arbitration (Pub. No. 291, 1980); ICC, Multiparty Arbitration (Pub. No. 404, 1982); ICC, ICC as Appointing Authority under the UNCITRAL Arbitration Rules (Pub. No. 409, 1982); W. Craig, W. Park & J. Paulsson, International Chamber of Commerce Arbitration (1984).

The ICSID is available only to resolve investment disputes between nationals of one state and another state where both states are parties to the Convention pursuant to which the ICSID was established. See G. Delaume, note 1 supra, ch. XV; J. Cherian, Investment Contracts and Arbitration (1975); Soley. ICSID Implementation: An Effective Alternative to International Conflict, 19 Intl.Law. 521 (1985).

3. See U.N.Commn. on Intl.Trade L., Model Law on International Commercial Arbitration (adopted June 21, 1985), 24 Intl.Legal Materials 1302 (1985); Kerr, Arbitration and the Courts: The UNCITRAL Model Law, 34 Intl. & Comp.L.Q. 1 (1985); Herrmann, UNCITRAL's Work Towards a Model Law on International Commercial Arbitration, 4 Pace L.Rev. 537 (1984); Broches, A Model Law on International Commercial Arbitration? A Progress Report, 18 Geo.Wash.J.Intl.L. & Econ. 79 (1984).

4. 8 Texas Intl.L.J. 17, 53–55. Reprinted by permission of the Texas International Law Journal.

Arbitration agreements are given transnational validity by article II. Each state is required to "recognize" written agreements in which the parties agree to submit to arbitration their present or future differences on "a defined legal relationship * * * concerning a subject matter capable of settlement by arbitration."

The term "recognize" is not further clarified, but "it seems clear that it does not require a Contracting State to grant specific performance of the agreement by ordering a recalcitrant party to arbitrate." Furthermore, the courts of the forum state are empowered to decide whether the subject matter of the agreement is "capable of settlement by arbitration." This latitude in determining arbitrability impairs predictability and to that extent may weaken the Convention. Nonetheless, article II(3) addresses itself to the enforcement of an agreement and commands a court of a contracting state, "when seized of an action in a matter" to which the parties have agreed to arbitrate, to refer the parties to arbitration, "unless it finds that the said agreement is null and void, inoperative or incapable of being performed."

Article III is the heart of the Convention, for it requires that each contracting state "recognize arbitral awards as binding and enforce them in accordance with the rules of procedure * * *" of the forum state. In addition, the forum state may not impose "substantially more onerous conditions or higher fees or charges on the recognition or enforcement of arbitral awards to which this Convention applies than are imposed on * * * domestic awards." Hence principles of national treatment and non-discrimination are provided for in the enforcement of foreign awards. Article IV supplements article III in providing that to obtain recognition and enforcement pursuant to article III, the party must, at the time of application, supply the original arbitration agreement and award, or duly certified copies thereof, in the official language of the forum state.

Article V establishes five grounds upon which recognition and enforcement of the award may be refused by the court upon request and proof by the party defendant. Two additional grounds permit the enforcing court on its own motion to refuse recognition and enforcement of a foreign award. The grounds requiring a motion and supporting evidence by the defendant are, briefly, the absence of a valid arbitration agreement, deprival of a fair opportunity to be heard, that the award or an inseverable part of it exceeds the submission to arbitration, improper composition of the arbitral tribunal or improper arbitral procedure, and that the award is not binding or has been set aside or suspended in the country of origin. The two further grounds invokable by the court on its own motion are that "[t]he subject matter of the difference is not capable of settlement by arbitration under the law of that country" and that "[t]he recognition or enforcement of the award would be contrary to the public policy of that country."

The final operative provision of the Convention is article VI. It simply gives the enforcing authority discretionary power to adjourn the decision on the enforcement of the award and require security from the defending party "if an application for the setting aside or suspension of the award has been made to a competent authority *   *   * " in the country in which the award was rendered.

The anticipated advantages of this new international regime over former bilateral and multilateral treaties have been summarized as follows:

> [I]t was already apparent that the document represented an improvement of the Geneva Convention of 1927. It gave a wider definition of the awards to which the convention applied; it rendered and simplified the requirements with which the party seeking recognition or enforcement of an award would have to comply; it placed the burden of proof on the party against whom recognition or enforcement was invoked; it gave the parties greater freedom in the choice of the arbitral authority and of the arbitration procedure; it gave the authority before which the award was sought to be relied upon the right to order the party opposing the enforcement to give suitable security.

While the Convention thus realigns the burden of proof as to grounds for avoiding enforcement and eliminates the troublesome requirement that the award be proved "final" in the state of origin, it does not attain the goal of uniformity. Since supplementing legislation in each state is required and reservations as to reciprocity and exclusion of non-commercial disputes are available, problems of uniform application arise, as under the Geneva treaties. Furthermore, the system is exposed to the vagaries of law among the states as perpetuated by the national treatment and non-discrimination formulas. In the final analysis, whether the Convention will represent a significant step toward the uniform recognition and enforcement of international arbitration agreements and awards depends upon the good faith of the contracting states.

As is evident from this survey, legal machinery suitable for the efficacious use of international commercial arbitration is available at the national level in commercially important states and at the international level through multilateral treaties and conventions. Differences between the various national systems, however, have implications for transnational enforcement of awards which, although not generally impairing enforceability per se necessitate that great care be taken in the drafting and implementation of arbitral agreements. One answer to this disparity, as yet not fully realized, is the uniformity in the recognition and enforcement of foreign awards promised by the United Nations Convention.

ROBERT LAYTON, ARBITRATION IN INTERNATIONAL COMMERCIAL AGREEMENTS: THE NOOSE DRAWS TIGHTER

(1975) [5]

By a 5–4 vote, the United States Supreme Court has given its imprimatur to favoring arbitration in the international context where its decision prevented assertion of claims under the federal securities laws. Alberto Culver, an American company incorporated in Delaware and based in Illinois, had sought to avoid arbitration under an international agreement on the ground that the federal securities laws gave it the right to litigate in the federal courts its claim that it had been defrauded in buying a complex

5. 9 Intl.Law. 741, 741–43. Reprinted by permission of the American Bar Association.

of business rights. In expanding its overseas operations, Alberto Culver had bought from Scherk, a German citizen, certain trademarks and the outstanding securities of two companies organized under the laws of Germany and Liechtenstein. The contract, which was negotiated in the United States, England and Germany, closed in Switzerland and contained a "broad" arbitration clause, as well as express warranties that the trademarks were unencumbered. Upon later discovery that the trademarks were encumbered, Alberto Culver asserted in a complaint in the Federal District Court in Illinois that the purchase had been induced by fraudulent representations in violation of § 10(b) of the Securities Exchange Act of 1934 and Rule 10b–5 thereunder. Scherk moved to stay the action pending arbitration in France. The District Court denied the motion and enjoined Scherk from proceeding to arbitration and was upheld by the Court of Appeals. The Supreme Court reversed and directed that the arbitration provision be enforced.

In Scherk v. Alberto Culver Company, the Court pointedly noted that with respect to any contract touching two or more countries:

> A contractual provision specifying in advance the forum in which disputes shall be litigated and the law to be applied is, therefore, an almost indispensable pre-condition to achievement of the orderliness and predictability essential to any international business transaction. Furthermore, such a provision obviates the danger that a dispute under the agreement might be submitted to a forum hostile to the interests of one of the parties or unfamiliar with the problem area involved.

To Justice Stewart of our Supreme Court the overriding consideration was preventing damage to "the fabric of international commerce and trade" and imperilling the "willingness and ability of businessmen to enter into international commercial agreements." Most significant to the majority was the fact that the subject matter of the contract concerned business enterprises located abroad. In so doing, the Court departed from its prior decision in Wilko v. Swan, where it had refused to compel arbitration in connection with a domestic dispute in which one of the parties sought to enforce alleged rights arising under the federal securities law which were claimed to override the provisions of an arbitration clause in a brokerage agreement. Justice Stewart held that in the context of an international contract the considerations which motivated the Court in *Wilko* become chimerical because the availability of speedy resort to foreign courts could hinder access to the American court chosen by a defrauded purchaser. In sum, the Supreme Court in the *Alberto Culver* case held that the agreement of parties to arbitrate "any dispute arising out of their international commercial transactions" would be respected and enforced by the federal courts.

The significant conclusion to be drawn from *Alberto Culver* is that once corporate counsel have acceded to a broad arbitration and forum selection clause, the prospect of ever avoiding resolution of any dispute before a panel of arbitrators is gone. Claims of fraud in the inducement of the contract itself are exclusively for the arbitrators as are claims of frustration or termination of the contract.[6]

---

6. See Scherk v. Alberto-Culver Co., 417 U.S. 506, 94 S.Ct. 2449, 41 L.Ed.2d 270 (1974); Mitsubishi Motors Corp. v. Soler Chrysler-Plymouth, Inc., 473 U.S. ___, 105 S.Ct. 3346, 87 L.Ed.2d 444 (1985).

Note

After reviewing the court decisions under the New York Convention, Pieter Sanders concluded that courts generally enforce awards. Sanders, A Twenty Years' Review of the Convention on the Recognition and Enforcement of Foreign Arbitral Awards, 13 Intl.Law. 269 (1979).[7]

(B) LITIGATION AND ENFORCEMENT OF JUDGMENTS [8]

Litigation of international commercial disputes is often fraught with difficulties. It may be difficult to obtain jurisdiction over the defendant, to obtain evidence from outside the court's jurisdiction and to enforce any judgment ultimately obtained. Courts in the United States will exercise jurisdiction over a foreign defendant who has not consented to jurisdiction only if adequate notice of the lawsuit has been given and sufficient minimum contacts exist between the defendant and the forum.[9] Obtaining evidence from abroad is often very difficult if the witness is uncooperative, although there is a 1970 Hague Convention on the Taking of Evidence Abroad in Civil or Commercial Matters and a 1965 Hague Convention on the Service Abroad of Judicial and Extrajudicial Documents in Civil or Commercial Matters to which the United States and several large European countries are parties.[10] Finally, once a judgment is obtained, there is the difficulty of enforcing it.

ROBERT B. VON MEHREN, TRANSNATIONAL LITIGATION IN AMERICAN COURTS: AN OVERVIEW OF PROBLEMS AND ISSUES

(1984) [11]

A plaintiff who has secured a judgment from an American court against a foreign defendant has good reason to be pleased but may face further problems in attempting to have the judgment satisfied. If the defendant is unwilling to comply with the judgment and has insufficient assets in the United States against which the judgment can be enforced, it will be necessary for the plaintiff to initiate proceedings abroad for the recognition

---

7. See Commercial Arbitration Yearbooks, note 1 supra and G. Gaja (ed.), International Commercial Arbitration: The New York Convention (Oceana looseleaf).

8. See generally B. Ristau, International Judicial Assistance (Civil and Criminal) (1984); Symposium—Transnational Litigation, 18 The Intl. Lawyer 522 (1984), including Gaw, Bibliography: International Judicial Assistance, at 555–62; Practicing Law Institute, International Litigation (1980).

9. World-Wide Volkswagen Corp. v. Woodson, 444 U.S. 286, 100 S.Ct. 559, 62 L.Ed.2d 490 (1980). There are special rules for service of process on foreign defendants. Fed.R.Civ.P. 4(i).

10. See generally von Mehren, Recognition and Enforcement of Foreign Judgments—Gen-

eral Theory and the Role of Jurisdictional Requirements, 167 Recueil des Cours 1 (1980); G. Delaume, note 1 supra, chs. IX and X; G. Roman, Recognition and Enforcement of Foreign Judgments In Various Foreign Countries (1984); Woodward, Reciprocal Recognition and Enforcement of Civil Judgments in the United States, the United Kingdom and the European Economic Community, 8 N.Car.J. of Intl.L. & Comm.Reg. 299 (1983).

11. From (J. Moss ed.), Private Investors Abroad—Problems and Solutions in International Business in 1984 (1985), at 1, 22–30. Copyright © 1985 by Matthew Bender & Co., Inc., and reprinted with permission from Southwestern Legal Foundation *Private Investors Abroad (1984)*.

and enforcement of the American judgment. Indeed, there may even be obstacles to enforcement of an American judgment within the United States.

United States is Not a Party to Bilateral or Multilateral Conventions

There is no settled, customary rule of international law regarding the transnational recognition and enforcement of judgments. The courts of each nation traditionally have applied that nation's own rules in determining whether to honor a judgment rendered in another nation. There are essential similarities in the standards applied in different nations—for example, as among the United States and other common-law nations; however, real certainty in the area has been achieved only with the conclusion of bilateral or multilateral conventions. Such international agreements currently govern recognition and enforcement between or among many nations of Europe and the British Commonwealth. Unfortunately, the United States is not at present a party to any such agreement.

* * *

Finally, the United States and the United Kingdom negotiated unsuccessfully from 1973 until 1980 for a bilateral convention on foreign judgments. Scholars in this country have long been advocating the conclusion of treaties governing judgment recognition practice, and the U.S.-U.K. Convention would have been the first such treaty. Besides harmonizing the practices of these two nations, which do not greatly diverge in any event, this treaty was expected to be the first in a network of agreements designed to regularize recognition practice in the United States and improve the prospects for recognition and enforcement of United States judgments abroad. The project foundered largely because of the objections of insurance interests and others on the British side concerning the very high damages available in American courts.

General Principles of Comity

In the absence of treaties, the reciprocal recognition practice of the United States and other nations is governed by general principles of international comity, embodied in national or local statutory and case law.

* * *

While the requirement of reciprocity or mutuality as an element of comity in this area has since lost favor in the American law,[*53] it typically remains a centerpiece of the law in civil-law nations.

Thus, the courts of many European and Latin American nations will not as a matter of course give conclusive effect to an American money judgment, even if satisfied that the rendering American court had jurisdiction and that fundamental fairness attended the proceedings. Under their national laws, in the absence of a treaty, these foreign courts must additionally be satisfied that the rendering American court would grant reciprocal recognition to their countries' judgments. Moreover, while the actual practice with respect

---

* 53. The Uniform Foreign Money-Judgments Recognition Act does not make reciprocity a precondition for recognition and enforcement of foreign-country judgments, and the Restatement (Second) of Conflicts of Law, § 98, Comment e (1971), questions whether considerations of reciprocity are material.

to foreign-country judgments in the United States under the common law generally has not placed any greater—and probably has placed fewer— obstacles before European judgments than the European courts have placed before American judgments, because of the absence of statutory law and the dearth of case authority in many American jurisdictions, it has often been difficult for the proponent of the American judgment to establish the elements of reciprocity.

For example, in the Federal Republic of Germany, judgments of countries with which there is no treaty relationship, including the United States, may be recognized and enforced as long as none of the grounds set forth in Section 328 I of the Code of Civil Procedure for refusal of recognition is present. These grounds have to do with the propriety of jurisdiction of the foreign court, the adequacy of service of process, the consistency of the judgment with "good morals or the purpose of a German law," and, finally, the existence of reciprocity.*[54]

The German courts have traditionally interpreted the reciprocity requirement quite strictly. * * *

Recent decisions of the German Supreme Court have been considerably more liberal in interpreting the reciprocity provision. Currently the existence of reciprocity will be assumed by German courts where recognition and enforcement of German judgments abroad encounter difficulties essentially no greater than the obstacles that would conversely be imposed by Germany. Partial reciprocity, i.e., reciprocity for the particular class of judgment at issue, is held to be sufficient. It is also now settled that the foreign rules need not be identical with the German provisions but that the rules as a whole must be essentially equivalent.

In the absence of a uniform American law regarding the treatment of foreign judgments, no determination can be made as to whether reciprocity exists between Germany—or any other nation—and the United States as a whole. In this connection, one commentator has analyzed the Uniform Foreign Money-Judgments Recognition Act (the Uniform Recognition Act) against the German provisions governing recognition and enforcement of foreign judgments. His conclusion is that the laws are almost completely equivalent and thus that, for money judgments, reciprocity exists with those American states that have adopted the Uniform Recognition Act.

It would actually appear that American states that follow the pure common-law requirements for according conclusive effect to foreign judgments—jurisdiction, proper notice, opportunity to be heard, absence of fraud, finality, and consistency of public policy of the forum—should also now be held in Germany to have a relationship of reciprocal recognition and enforcement, since these are similar to the conditions set forth in the German Code of Civil Procedure. There can be no assurance of this, however. The courts of France, while not requiring reciprocity, do require

*[54]. Steiner and Vagts, Transnational Legal Problems (Foundation Press 1976), p. 804. The following discussion is based upon this text and upon Brensch, "The Recognition and Enforcement of Foreign Money Judgments in the Federal Republic of Germany," 11 Int'l Law. 261 (1977).

conditions similar to the common-law requirements noted above to be met before granting conclusive effect to a foreign judgment.

SECTION 2.4 PROBLEM

Sam Golddust of the Golddust Widget Corporation brings you a number of documents related to an international transaction that has gone awry and asks your advice on the company's rights against the other parties to the transaction.

A complete answer to this question would require consideration of statutes not reproduced in this book, such as the Uniform Commercial Code, as well as issues typically covered in courses covering such subjects as contracts, commercial transactions, conflicts, etc. The materials in this chapter, however, do suggest these issues and sources of law to resolve them. In your answer, you should note such issues and the sources you would consult to resolve them.

DOCUMENTS

1. Telex to Comptoir des Widgets, Paris, July 16, 1986.

We are able to offer you 100 crates of 12 gross widgets per catalog specifications for $100,000 CIF Le Havre.

Golddust Widgets, New York.

———

2. Telex to Golddust Widgets, July 17, 1986

We accept your offer of July 16, 1986, provided widgets arrive Le Havre on or before September 1.

Comptoir des Widgets

———

3. Letter to Comptoir des Widgets, July 18, 1986
    Gentlemen:

We herewith confirm our telex exchange by which you contract to buy 100 crates of 12 gross widgets C.I.F. Le Havre for $100,000. The normal shipping time ex New York is less than two weeks and we will ship next week, after notice of letter of credit opening. Please sign the attached copy of this letter and return it for our files.

Sincerely

Sam Golddust, President

Golddust Widget Corp.

———

4. Bill of Lading No. 86–21748
    Tramp Lines
    August 2, 1986

Shipped in apparent good order and condition by Golddust Widget at the port of New York on board the S.S./M.V. Slowpoke the following goods

Int'l.Econ.Rel.2d Ed. (J & D) ACB—4

marked and numbered as hereunder, and to be delivered from the Ship's deck, where the Ship's responsibility shall cease, in the like order and condition at or off the port of Le Havre or so near thereto as the ship may safely get and lie always afloat unto Comptoir des Widgets, Paris, France or his or their assigns, subject to the liberties, exceptions and conditions set forth on either side hereof.

Freight for the said goods and primage (if any) to be paid by the shippers in advance on delivery of the Bill of Lading in cash without discount, unless otherwise agreed upon.

Shipper's Marks & Nos.	Shipper's Description of Goods	
Golddust Widgets 3 ply, Spec. 10932 12 gross (100 crates)	Crates in apparent good order and condition except 5 crates are apparently used packing crates	
Freight		$6,792
Arbitrary beyond		$–0–
Other charges		$3,000
	Total	$9,792
By Sam Golddust, Shipper	Tramp Lines Ltd. Per Peter Slowpoke, 1st mate	

---

5. Invoice No. 7184

    Golddust Widget Corp.

    August 2, 1986

    Sold to: Comptoir des Widgets, Paris

    100 crates of 12 gross each, widgets packed in sawdust (CIF Le Havre)

    Balance due: $100,000

    Terms: Net cash

---

6. Letter of Credit No. T4578

    July 22, 1986

Drafts drawn under this credit must be marked "Drawn under Banque Generale L/C No. 8432, Citybank, New York, T 4578"

To: Golddust Widget Corp.

We have been requested by Banque Generale, Paris by telex to advise you that they have established their irrevocable credit no. 8432 in your favor for account of Comptoir des Widgets, Paris available to the aggregate sum of $100,000 by your drafts drawn at sight on us and accompanied by the following documents:

    —commercial invoice in triplicate

    —full set of clean on board ocean bills of lading, to order and blank endorsed, freight prepaid, notify Comptoir des Widgets, Paris

—marine insurance policy

evidencing shipment 1200 gross triplated widgets, packed shockproof shipment latest August 21, 1986

The above mentioned correspondent engages with you that all drafts drawn under and in connection with the terms of this credit will be duly honored on delivery of documents as specified if presented at this office on or before September 7, 1986.

We confirm the credit and thereby undertake that all drafts drawn and presented as above will be duly honored by us.

This credit is subject to the Uniform Customs & Practice for Documentary Credits (1983 revision), ICC.

Citybank

---

7. Certificate of Insurance

    Waterperil Insurance Co.

    August 1, 1986

    Vessel: S.S.S. Slowpoke

    Loading: New York

    Destination: Le Havre

    Details: 100 crates, Golddust widgets, 3-ply, spec. 10932 12 gross.

    Insured Voyage: New York/Le Havre by ship

    Cert. Ins. No. WI 876

THIS IS TO CERTIFY that insurance is effected in accordance with Open Cover no. T/Z 80/52, dated January 12, 1960 in respect of above shipment.

It is understood and agreed that this certificate represents the value declared on the Original Stamped Policy and conveys all rights under the said Policy as fully as if the property insured were covered by a special policy direct to the Holder of this Certificate.

WATERPERIL INS. CO.

As agents

Loss, if any, payable after collection from Underwriters to this Holder of the appertaining documents and on surrender of the original certificate to WATERPERIL INS. CO., N.Y.

---

8. Telex to Golddust Widgets, N.Y.

    August 10, 1986

    SSS Slowpoke apparently lost at sea, cause unknown. All cargo apparently lost. We decline payment.

    Comptoir des Widgets, Paris.

Chapter 3

THE UNITED STATES CONSTITUTION AND REGULATION OF INTERNATIONAL ECONOMIC AFFAIRS

SECTION 3.1 INTRODUCTION TO CHAPTERS 3 AND 4

In this and the next chapter, we begin our study of national governmental regulation of international trade. Transactions that cross national boundaries are among the most regulated of all transactions. In addition to the regulations that would apply to purely domestic affairs, governments traditionally have exercised an additional measure of control, for a variety of political and economic policy reasons, over transactions with persons in foreign nations. The objectives of these controls could be many: protecting the balance of payments and national reserves, influencing international political alignments, protecting domestic business from competition of foreign goods, preserving natural resources, enhancing national security, etc. There is an enormous number of different kinds of regulations. It is intended in these chapters to examine some of the basic constitutional problems that impinge on the way nations regulate their international trade. In Part II of this book, we will examine in some detail the specifics of various regulations, such as tariffs, antidumping and countervailing duties, and a plethora of non-tariff barriers.

This chapter will focus on the problems faced in regulating international economic transactions under the U.S. Constitution; Chapter 4 will then briefly view comparable problems in other important trading entities, particularly the European Community and Japan. After this introduction, the materials in this chapter are divided into five more sections. Section 3.2 provides an overview of the constitutional division of powers in the United States between the President and Congress. Then, in Section 3.3, we focus on one particular aspect of that division—U.S. constitutional provisions that affect the negotiation and implementation of international agreements. Next, in Section 3.4, we look at the mosaic of legislation in the United States by which Congress has delegated extensive authority to the President in respect of international economic affairs, focusing especially on the series of trade acts which began with the 1934 Reciprocal Trade Agreements Act. We then turn in Section 3.5 to the role of the courts in reviewing Executive Branch action in this area. Finally, in Section 3.6, we consider problems related to the federal structure of the United States.

There are a number of very perplexing and relatively unanswered questions in U.S. constitutional law relating to international affairs generally and international economic affairs in particular. Some introductory comments at the beginning of sections below will pose some of these questions. However, the following excerpt should assist the reader to appreciate the relationship of various questions to each other and help focus attention on how issues concerning international constitutional divisions of regulatory power have important impacts on practical day-to-day affairs.

J. JACKSON, J.–V. LOUIS & M. MATSUSHITA

LAW AND WORLD ECONOMIC INTERDEPENDENCE

(1984) [1]

The world after World War II has effectively shrunk to the point where we watch foreign wars on our living room television sets, where more than $160 billion move across national borders every day, where an economic depression in one country rapidly transmits its effects into other countries, where political violence in a Middle Eastern country causes farmers in Iowa to go bankrupt. The degree to which goods and services can flow across national boundaries in this interdependent world has helped create growing material prosperity in that world, but it has also created extremely difficult problems of public and private management. The international governmental system, which includes the International Monetary Fund (IMF) and the General Agreement on Tariffs and Trade (GATT), was created mainly in the 1940s to assist in this management process, but in recent years there has been legitimate concern about whether it can cope with changed circumstances for the last two decades of this century and thereafter. A number of efforts have been undertaken to change the system, but national and international procedures and rules for such change are incredibly complex, and in some circumstances may be so rigid that change is prevented. The degree to which law, both national and international, either contributes to this rigidity or facilitates the processes of change is an issue of some importance. This book examines one part of that issue, focusing on national constitutional systems that affect the development of international agreements on economic matters. It does this by examining, for three key legal systems, the acceptance and implementation of the complex and extensive series of agreements resulting from the Tokyo Round of negotiations held under the aegis of the GATT.

An example from an earlier period of history illustrates the focus of this inquiry. Immediately after World War II, several initiatives converged into

---

1. From J. Jackson, J.-V. Louis & M. Matsushita, Implementing the Tokyo Round: National Constitutions and International Economic Rules 1–2 (1984). Reprinted by permission of the authors.

a proposal to establish an International Trade Organization (ITO). After years of international negotiations, the 1948 draft Havana Charter was completed. This charter would have established an ITO to become the framework for international rules designed to prevent the kind of destructive national government "beggar-thy-neighbor" policies many thought had contributed to the causes of the war. Despite these elaborate preparations, the effort to create an ITO ultimately failed (although an earlier effort to create monetary rules and a monetary fund—the IMF—had succeeded). The ITO effort failed largely because of the domestic constitutional and political structure of the country then economically preeminent—the United States. It failed despite the fact that the major leadership for the effort to create it had come from the United States itself. But this leadership was that of the executive branch or presidency in the United States. Under the U.S. constitutional and legal requirements, for the government to formally accept the ITO charter, the executive branch had to get the approval of the U.S. Congress, and this the Congress refused to give. In 1950 it was clear that it would be futile to continue trying to obtain this approval, and the ITO was stillborn.

At the same time as the efforts to create an ITO were occurring, another set of international economic rules was being drafted. These were embodied in an agreement entitled The General Agreement on Tariffs and Trade, commonly called the GATT. Unlike the ITO, the GATT did come into force, largely because particular laws at that time allowed the executive branch to commit the United States to the GATT obligations without further approval of Congress. In fact the GATT gradually had to fill the vacuum created by the ITO failure, and today it has come to play the central role in the international economic system as it relates to trade in goods. It plays this role uneasily, however, with a defective constitutional structure not designed to support it.

This sequence of events amply demonstrates the importance of national constitutional and legal constraints on the process of formulating, implementing, or changing international rules. The compartmentalization of legal processes into international on one hand and national on the other can lead to serious misunderstandings of the world today. In fact, that world is a complex intertwining of national and international legal, economic, and other constraints and forces. The current expression *international interdependence,* so apt and yet so trite, often conjures up an image of economic forces and influences, but the legal systems of nations have also become interdependent, not only among themselves but also with the international legal systems that now are influencing daily events.

The constitutional, governmental policy and structural questions considered here need not be viewed as unique to international economic relations. Many of the issues discussed come up in a large variety of subject areas, including many domestic subjects. The constant struggle between the President and Congress in the U.S. Government conditions much of the national political life of the United States. The study of this struggle in this book can, therefore, also be viewed as sort of a "case study" of constitutional law and politics. One of the interesting (and for lawyers perplexing) aspects of this struggle is that relatively little of it gets to the courts, especially the Supreme Court. This is more so for international affairs, but the fact is that the daily strife often ends in accommodations and compromises, or stand-offs, which none of the parties to a particular contest want to test in the courts. Students and lawyers who are used to relying on court opinions for most of their knowledge about the "law", therefore, often feel somewhat at sea when dealing with many of the issues taken up in this chapter as well as other chapters in this book. Fortunately, we have a few court opinions to help us find our way into the foyer of the subject, but often these opinions raise more questions than they resolve. The rest of the way is relatively uncharted, and recourse must be had to a variety of historical and legal documents as well as to general reporting about various incidents that are relevant.

SECTION 3.2 THE UNITED STATES CONSTITUTION AND INTERNATIONAL ECONOMIC RELATIONS

(A) INTRODUCTION

It is impossible to extricate the question of distribution of powers over foreign economic affairs from the general problem of distribution of powers over foreign affairs in United States governmental and constitutional prac-tice. The reader is probably familiar with the broad themes of this story: [1] The great increase in Executive power during the 1930's and during and after World War II; the concern in the 1960's and early 1970's (particularly in relationship to the Vietnam War) that the Executive had become too strong; the revulsion at the disclosures of misuse of Executive power during the "Watergate" episode; and the ensuing struggle of Congress to restore some of its power in the international affairs area. However, in this book, and particularly this chapter, we endeavor to focus on the problem of international economic affairs, as opposed to foreign affairs generally. In many ways, the struggle of Congress to regain some authority over interna-tional economic affairs was best manifested in the passage of the 1974 Trade Act, which will be discussed in Section 3.4.

There are some puzzling and very important questions involved in the issue of distribution of powers. For example, how can international negotia-tions, especially economic or trade negotiations, be carried on by a democra-cy such as the United States? Particularly when the Executive Branch is theoretically separate from the Legislative Branch, some important difficul-ties occur. It is perhaps impossible for Congress, as such, to negotiate

1. See J. Nowak, R. Rotunda & J. Young, Constitutional Law 190–201 (2d ed. 1983); L. Tribe, American Constitutional Law 157–72 (1978); W. Lockhart, Y. Kamisar & J. Choper, Constitutional Law: Cases-Comments-Ques-tions 194–237 (5th ed. 1980); P. Kauper, Con-stitutional Law: Cases and Materials 264–285 (4th ed. 1972); T. Franck (ed.), The Tethered Presidency: Congressional Restraints on Exec-utive Power (1981); T. Franck & E. Weisband, Foreign Policy by Congress (1979); A. Schles-inger, The Imperial Presidency (1973); L. Henkin, Foreign Affairs and the Constitution (1972); F. Wilcox, Congress, the Executive and Foreign Policy (1971); Symposium on Presi-dential Power, 40 Law & Contemp. Prob. Nos. 2 & 3 (1976).

economic subjects; its members are usually too beholden to particular parochial constituents, and consequently have difficulty formulating overall negotiating positions and objectives that are in the broader national interest. In addition, who speaks for Congress? It is doubtful that even the duly constituted leadership of either House of Congress can speak for that House, much less for Congress as a whole, on international trade matters. Consequently, a foreign negotiator will not negotiate seriously with someone whom he feels cannot "deliver" on the commitments made. The Executive Branch is not quite in the same position. Generally, at least within the scope of the authority contained in the Executive Branch, whether by constitutional right or through statutory delegation by previous Act of Congress, the commitments of high officials negotiating on behalf of the United States can be formulated so as to represent the commitments of the President and the Executive Branch. Insofar as further legislation is necessary, however, there is a realm of uncertainty about the commitments, comparable to that described above for the Legislative Branch. Trading partners of the United States remember all too well commitments made during the course of the Kennedy Round of negotiations on tariffs and trade, which never came into effect because Congress never enacted the legislation required to implement them.

Consequently, the dilemma facing thoughtful students of international economic affairs in the United States today is that, on the one hand, there appears to be a need to limit or circumscribe the very extensive authority that has grown up in the Executive Branch over international economic affairs; on the other hand, it is not clear that the United States will be able to bargain effectively in international economic negotiations if such limitations are imposed. The Executive Branch appears to be the only viable agent for such negotiations, and the feebler is its power, the less effective will be its negotiating ability, unless it can somehow persuade its trading partners that Congress is prepared to deliver on those commitments that require congressional action. As discussed in Section 3.4 below, the procedures followed in negotiating and implementing the Tokyo Round Agreements may suggest a way to do this.

The materials of this section are divided into two substantive subsections. In Section 3.2(B), the President's "inherent" powers are examined. In Section 3.4, we return to presidential powers, but there in the context of the President's delegated powers under various statutes. Needless to say, there is not an easily defined distinction between the President's inherent powers and his delegated powers. The approach of the courts, or for that matter of Congress and the Presidency itself, towards delegated powers can be either broad or narrow. The philosophy of the *Curtiss-Wright* case, giving broad leeway to presidential inherent powers, would also lead to a broad approach with respect to statutory delegations. In Section 3.2(C) we give a brief overview of congressional powers, again a subject that recurs in later sections.

All this leads to a number of questions which the reader should keep in mind in reading the materials below. One broad question (probably unanswerable) is whether the President or Congress has generally implemented those policies that are in the best interests of the United States as a whole. For those who, like many economists (see Chapter 1), believe that a "liberal" or "freer" trade policy (allowing more imports) is in the best long-run interest of the United States as a whole, the question can be more specifically phrased: In general is the Presidency or Congress likely to be more protectionist?

More specifically, in considering the materials one can ask: Was the *Curtiss-Wright* case correct (and was Justice Sutherland's dicta correct)? What is the impact of *Youngstown* and *Dames & Moore* on Sutherland's view of presidential foreign affairs powers?

What exactly did the *Guy Capps* case stand for? Does the Court of Appeals opinion have any viability today? What could we expect federal courts to do today in the event of a court challenge to an international agreement entered into by the President concerning economic matters but without congressional participation? How far will the courts likely go to limit the President's foreign affairs activities because of a lack of statutory delegated powers? How viable today would a challenge to presidential actions be under the arguments used in the *Consumers Union* case?

Finally, some other questions: How does the existence of legislation make a difference to presidential power when the legislation does not explicitly authorize what the President wants to do? What is "preemption" by Congress? And, as to all these questions, should the answers differ in the context of foreign affairs as opposed to domestic affairs?

(B) THE PRESIDENT'S INHERENT FOREIGN AFFAIRS POWERS

UNITED STATES v. CURTISS–WRIGHT EXPORT CORP.

Supreme Court of the United States, 1936.
299 U.S. 304, 57 S.Ct. 216, 81 L.Ed. 255.

MR. JUSTICE SUTHERLAND delivered the opinion of the Court.

On January 27, 1936, an indictment was returned in the court below, the first count of which charges that appellees, beginning with the 29th day of May, 1934, conspired to sell in the United States certain arms of war, namely fifteen machine guns, to Bolivia, a country then engaged in armed conflict in the Chaco, in violation of the Joint Resolution of Congress approved May 28, 1934, and the provisions of a proclamation issued on the same day by the President of the United States pursuant to authority conferred by § 1 of the resolution. In pursuance of the conspiracy, the commission of certain overt acts was alleged, details of which need not be stated. The Joint Resolution (c. 365, 48 Stat. 811) follows:

"*Resolved by the Senate and House of Representatives of the United States of America in Congress assembled,* That if the President finds that the prohibition of the sale of arms and munitions of war in the United States to those countries now engaged in armed conflict in the Chaco may contribute to the reëstablishment of peace between those countries, and if after consultation with the governments of other American Republics and with their coöperation, as well as that of such other governments as he may deem necessary, he makes proclamation to that effect, it shall be unlawful to sell, except under such limitations and exceptions as the President prescribes, any arms or munitions of war in any place in the United States to the countries now engaged in that armed conflict, or to any person, company, or association acting in the interest of either country, until otherwise ordered by the President or by Congress.

*   *   *

[The President proclaimed a prohibition on arms sales and the defendant violated the prohibition and was indicted. The lower court quashed the indictment and the United States appealed.]

Whether, if the Joint Resolution had related solely to internal affairs it would be open to the challenge that it constituted an unlawful delegation of legislative power to the Executive, we find it unnecessary to determine. The whole aim of the resolution is to affect a situation entirely external to the United States, and falling within the category of foreign affairs. The determination which we are called to make, therefore, is whether the Joint Resolution, as applied to that situation, is vulnerable to attack under the rule that forbids a delegation of the lawmaking power. * * *

It will contribute to the elucidation of the question if we first consider the differences between the powers of the federal government in respect of foreign or external affairs and those in respect of domestic or internal affairs. That there are differences between them, and that these differences are fundamental, may not be doubted.

The two classes of powers are different, both in respect of their origin and their nature. The broad statement that the federal government can exercise no powers except those specifically enumerated in the Constitution, and such implied powers as are necessary and proper to carry into effect the enumerated powers, is categorically true only in respect of our internal affairs. In that field, the primary purpose of the Constitution was to carve from the general mass of legislative powers *then possessed by the states* such portions as it was thought desirable to vest in the federal government, leaving those not included in the enumeration still in the states. Carter v. Carter Coal Co., 298 U.S. 238, 294, 56 S.Ct. 855, 865, 80 L.Ed. 1160. That this doctrine applies only to powers which the states had, is self evident. And since the states severally never possessed international powers, such powers could not have been carved from the mass of state powers but obviously were transmitted to the United States from some other source. During the colonial period, those powers were possessed exclusively by and were entirely under the control of the Crown. By the Declaration of Independence, "the Representatives of the United States of America" declared the United [not the several] Colonies to be free and independent states, and as such to have "full Power to levy War, conclude Peace, contract Alliances, establish Commerce and to do all other Acts and Things which Independent States may of right do."

As a result of the separation from Great Britain by the colonies acting as a unit, the powers of external sovereignty passed from the Crown not to the colonies severally, but to the colonies in their collective and corporate capacity as the United States of America. Even before the Declaration, the colonies were a unit in foreign affairs, acting through a common agency— namely the Continental Congress, composed of delegates from the thirteen colonies. That agency exercised the powers of war and peace, raised an army, created a navy, and finally adopted the Declaration of Independence. Rulers come and go; governments end and forms of government change; but sovereignty survives. A political society cannot endure without a supreme will somewhere. Sovereignty is never held in suspense. When, therefore, the external sovereignty of Great Britain in respect of the colonies ceased, it immediately passed to the Union.

*   *   *

It results that the investment of the federal government with the powers of external sovereignty did not depend upon the affirmative grants of the Constitution. The powers to declare and wage war, to conclude peace, to make treaties, to maintain diplomatic relations with other sovereignties, if they had never been mentioned in the Constitution, would have vested in the federal government as necessary concomitants of nationality. * * * As a member of the family of nations, the right and power of the United States in that field are equal to the right and power of the other members of the international family. Otherwise, the United States is not completely sovereign.

*   *   *

* * * In this vast external realm, with its important, complicated, delicate and manifold problems, the President alone has the power to speak or listen as a representative of the nation. He *makes* treaties with the advice and consent of the Senate; but he alone negotiates. Into the field of negotiation the Senate cannot intrude; and Congress itself is powerless to invade it. As Marshall said in his great argument of March 7, 1800, in the House of Representatives, "The President is the sole organ of the nation in its external relations, and its sole representative with foreign nations." Annals, 6th Cong., col. 613. The Senate Committee on Foreign Relations at a very early day in our history (February 15, 1816), reported to the Senate, among other things, as follows:

"The President is the constitutional representative of the United States with regard to foreign nations. He manages our concerns with foreign nations and must necessarily be most competent to determine when, how, and upon what subjects negotiation may be urged with the greatest prospect of success. For his conduct he is responsible to the Constitution. The committee consider this responsibility the surest pledge for the faithful discharge of his duty. They think the interference of the Senate in the direction of foreign negotiations calculated to diminish that responsibility and thereby to impair the best security for the national safety. The nature of transactions with foreign nations, moreover, requires caution and unity of design, and their success frequently depends on secrecy and dispatch." U.S. Senate Reports, Committee on Foreign Relations, vol. 8, p. 24.

It is important to bear in mind that we are here dealing not alone with an authority vested in the President by an exertion of legislative power, but with such an authority plus the very delicate, plenary and exclusive power of the President as the sole organ of the federal government in the field of international relations—a power which does not require as a basis for its exercise an act of Congress, but which, of course, like every other governmental power, must be exercised in subordination to the applicable provisions of the Constitution. It is quite apparent that if, in the maintenance of our international relations, embarrassment—perhaps serious embarrassment—is to be avoided and success for our aims achieved, congressional legislation which is to be made effective through negotiation and inquiry within the international field must often accord to the President a degree of discretion and freedom from statutory restriction which would not be admissible were domestic affairs alone involved. Moreover, he, not Congress, has the better opportunity of knowing the conditions which prevail in foreign countries, and especially is this true in time of war. He has his confidential sources of information. He has his agents in the form of diplomatic, consular and other officials. Secrecy in respect of information gathered by them may be highly necessary, and the premature disclosure of it productive of harmful results. Indeed, so clearly is this true that the first President refused to accede to a request to lay before the House of Representatives the instructions, correspondence and documents relating to the negotiation of the Jay Treaty—a refusal the wisdom of which was recognized by the House itself and has never since been doubted. * * *

The marked difference between foreign affairs and domestic affairs in this respect is recognized by both houses of Congress in the very form of their requisitions for information from the executive departments. In the case of every department except the Department of State, the resolution *directs* the official to furnish the information. In the case of the State Department, dealing with foreign affairs, the President is *requested* to furnish the information "if not incompatible with the public interest." A statement that to furnish the information is not compatible with the public interest rarely, if ever, is questioned.

* * *

* * * A legislative practice such as we have here, evidenced not by only occasional instances, but marked by the movement of a steady stream for a century and a half of time, goes a long way in the direction of proving the presence of unassailable ground for the constitutionality of the practice, to be found in the origin and history of the power involved, or in its nature, or in both combined.

* * *

The judgment of the court below must be reversed and the cause remanded for further proceedings in accordance with the foregoing opinion.

Reversed.

MR. JUSTICE MCREYNOLDS does not agree. He is of the opinion that the court below reached the right conclusion and its judgment ought to be affirmed.

MR. JUSTICE STONE took no part in the consideration or decision of this case.

Note

A particularly strong criticism of the Sutherland view of history is found in Berger, The Presidential Monopoly of Foreign Relations, 71 Mich.L.Rev. 1 (1972), who states at 26–28: [2]

2. Reprinted by permission of Raoul Berger. Other strong criticisms of Sutherland's historical theory and his view of presidential power over foreign affairs include Levitan, The Foreign Relations Power: An Analysis of Mr. Justice Sutherland's Theory, 55 Yale L.J. 467 (1946); Fulbright, American Foreign Policy in the Twentieth Century Under an Eight-

It remained for our time to furnish a powerful impetus to presidential expansionism in the shape of some ill-considered dicta in United States v. Curtiss-Wright Export Corporation, per Justice Sutherland, to which the Court lent credit in United States v. Pink. Despite searching criticism, *Curtiss-Wright* has become the foundation of subsequent decisions and has all too frequently been cited for an omnipresent presidential power over foreign relations. The case proceeded from a Joint Resolution which authorized the President, upon making certain findings and engaging in consultations with other American Republics, to declare unlawful the sale of munitions to countries then engaged in armed conflict in the Chaco, namely Bolivia and Paraguay, if it "may contribute to the reestablishment of peace between those countries." The sole issue was whether this was an improper delegation, a question that might adequately have been answered under the Field v. Clark line of cases. But the aims of Justice Sutherland soared beyond this modest goal; he would launch a theory of inherent presidential power over foreign relations. To this end he confined the enumeration of powers doctrine to "domestic or internal affairs"; in foreign affairs, he explained, in terms recalling the descent of the Holy Ghost, "the external sovereignty of Great Britain * * * immediately passed to the Union." In this he was deceived. It hardly needs more than Madison's statement in *The Federalist No. 45,* that "[t]he powers delegated by the proposed Constitution are *few and defined* * * * [they] will be exercised principally on *external* objects, as war, peace, negotiation, and foreign commerce," to prove that the powers over *foreign relations* were enumerated and "defined." Deferring for a moment further comment on Sutherland's aberrant theory, let it be assumed that somehow the *nation* or Union obtained "inherent" powers over foreign relations, and it still needs to be shown how the power came to be vested *in the President.* For, as Justice Frankfurter pointed out, "the fact that power exists in the Government does not vest it in the President." The "inherent power" theory, moreover, would circumvent the manifest intention of the Framers to create a federal government of limited and enumerated powers and defeat their purpose to condition presidential action in the field of foreign relations on congressional participation. Before examining the history Sutherland avouched, another ground of his opinion should be noticed: the "plenary and exclusive power of the President as the sole organ of the federal government in the field of international relations," for which he trotted out Marshall's "sole organ" dictum and the Senate Committee Report of 1816, earlier discussed.

McDougal and Lans, who relied heavily on these dicta, acknowledged that Sutherland's analysis "unquestionably involves certain metaphorical elements and considerable differences of opinion about historical facts," but concluded that he "may have been expressing a thought more profound than any involved in quarrels about the naming of powers." This is to conclude that Sutherland was right for the wrong reasons. Apparently the "profound" thought was the "important fact * * * that the imperatives of survival have required the Federal Government to exercise certain powers." No "imperatives of survival" were at stake in *Curtiss-Wright* or in *Pink* nor has there been any demonstration that the powers of the federal govern-

eenth Century Constitution, 47 Cornell L.Q. 1 (1961); Borchard, Treaties and Executive Agreements—A Reply, 54 Yale L.J. 616, 648 (1945); Lofgren, United States v. Curtiss-Wright Export Corporation: An Historical Reassessment, 83 Yale L.J. 1 (1973); Schlesinger, Congress and the Making of American Foreign Policy, 51 Foreign Affairs 78 (1972).

ment were and are inadequate, still less how supraconstitutional powers came to rest in the President. Instead, the issue is whether the President may act without the participation of the Senate in the exercise of powers conferred on President and Senate *jointly.* ⸤The "quarrel," therefore, is not about the mere "naming of powers," but about presidential claims to exclusive power notwithstanding that the Constitution and Founders unmistakably meant the treaty power to be exercised jointly with the Senate.⸥

YOUNGSTOWN SHEET & TUBE CO. v. SAWYER

Supreme Court of the United States, 1952.
343 U.S. 579, 72 S.Ct. 863, 96 L.Ed. 1153.

MR. JUSTICE BLACK delivered the opinion of the Court.

We are asked to decide whether the President was acting within his constitutional power when he issued an order directing the Secretary of Commerce to take possession of and operate most of the Nation's steel mills.

* * *

In the latter part of 1951, a dispute arose between the steel companies and their employees over terms and conditions that should be included in new collective bargaining agreements. Long-continued conferences failed to resolve the dispute. * * * The indispensability of steel as a component of substantially all weapons and other war materials led the President to believe that the proposed work stoppage would immediately jeopardize our national defense and that governmental seizure of the steel mills was necessary in order to assure the continued availability of steel. Reciting these considerations for his action, the President, a few hours before the strike was to begin, issued Executive Order 10340. * * * The order directed the Secretary of Commerce to take possession of most of the steel mills and keep them running. The Secretary immediately issued his own possessory orders. * * * Congress has taken no action.

Obeying the Secretary's orders under protest, the companies brought proceedings against him in the District Court. * * * Holding against the Government on all points, the District Court on April 30 issued a preliminary injunction restraining the Secretary from "continuing the seizure and possession of the plants * * * and from acting under the purported authority of Executive Order 10340." On the same day the Court of Appeals stayed the District Court's injunction. Deeming it best that the issues raised be promptly decided by this Court, we granted certiorari on May 3 and set the cause for argument on May 12, 343 U.S. 937, 72 S.Ct. 775.

Two crucial issues have developed: *First.* Should final determination of the constitutional validity of the President's order be made in this case which has proceeded no further than the preliminary injunction stage? *Second.* If so, is the seizure order within the constitutional power of the President?

* * *

II

The President's power, if any, to issue the order must stem either from an act of Congress or from the Constitution itself. There is no statute that expressly authorizes the President to take possession of property as he did here. Nor is there any act of Congress to which our attention has been directed from which such a power can fairly be implied. Indeed, we do not understand the Government to rely on statutory authorization for this seizure. There are two statutes which do authorize the President to take both personal and real property under certain conditions. However, the Government admits that these conditions were not met and that the President's order was not rooted in either of the statutes. The Government refers to the seizure provisions of one of these statutes (§ 201(b) of the Defense Production Act) as "much too cumbersome, involved, and time-consuming for the crisis which was at hand."

Moreover, the use of the seizure technique to solve labor disputes in order to prevent work stoppages was not only unauthorized by any congressional enactment; prior to this controversy, Congress had refused to adopt that method of settling labor disputes. When the Taft-Hartley Act was under consideration in 1947, Congress rejected an amendment which would have authorized such governmental seizures in cases of emergency. Apparently it was thought that the technique of seizure, like that of compulsory arbitration, would interfere with the process of collective bargaining. Consequently, the plan Congress adopted in that Act did not provide for seizure under any circumstances. Instead, the plan sought to bring about settlements by use of the customary devices of mediation, conciliation, investigation by boards of inquiry, and public reports. In some instances temporary injunctions were authorized to provide cooling-off periods. All this failing the unions were left free to strike after a secret vote by employees as to whether they wished to accept their employers' final settlement offer.

It is clear that if the President had authority to issue the order he did, it must be found in some provisions of the Constitution. And it is not claimed that express constitutional language grants this power to the President. The contention is that presidential power should be implied from the aggregate of his powers under Article II of the Constitution. Particular reliance is placed on provisions in Article II which say that "The executive Power shall be vested in a President * * *"; that "he shall take Care that the Laws be faithfully executed"; and that he "shall be Commander in Chief of the Army and Navy of the United States."

The order cannot properly be sustained as an exercise of the President's military power as Commander in Chief of the Armed Forces. The Government attempts to do so by citing a number of cases upholding broad powers in military commanders engaged in day-to-day fighting in a theater of war. Such cases need not concern us here. Even though "theater of war" be an expanding concept, we cannot with faithfulness to our constitutional system hold that the Commander in Chief of the Armed Forces has the ultimate power as such to take possession of private property in order to keep labor disputes from stopping production. This is a job for the Nation's lawmakers, not for its military authorities.

Nor can the seizure order be sustained because of the several constitutional provisions that grant executive power to the President. In the framework of our Constitution, the President's power to see that the laws are faithfully executed refutes the idea that he is to be a lawmaker. The Constitution limits his functions in the lawmaking process to the recommending of laws he thinks wise and the vetoing of laws he thinks bad. And the Constitution is neither silent nor equivocal about who shall make laws which the President is to execute. The first section of the first article says that "All legislative Powers herein granted shall be vested in a Congress of the United States. * * *" After granting many powers to the Congress, Article I goes on to provide that Congress may "make all Laws which shall be necessary and proper for carrying into Execution the foregoing Powers and all other Powers vested by this Constitution in the Government of the United States, or in any Department or Officer thereof."

The President's order does not direct that a congressional policy be executed in a manner prescribed by Congress—it directs that a presidential policy be executed in a manner prescribed by the President. The preamble of the order itself, like that of many statutes, sets out reasons why the President believes certain policies should be adopted, proclaims these policies as rules of conduct to be followed, and again, like a statute, authorizes a government official to promulgate additional rules and regulations consistent with the policy proclaimed and needed to carry that policy into execution. The power of Congress to adopt such public policies as those proclaimed by the order is beyond question. It can authorize the taking of private property for public use. It can make laws regulating the relationships between employers and employees, prescribing rules designed to settle labor disputes, and fixing wages and working conditions in certain fields of our economy. The Constitution does not subject this law-making power of Congress to presidential or military supervision or control.

It is said that other Presidents without congressional authority have taken possession of private business enterprises in order to settle labor disputes. But even if this be true, Congress has not thereby lost its exclusive constitutional authority to make laws necessary and proper to carry out the powers vested by the Constitution "in the Government of the United States, or any Department or Officer thereof."

The Founders of this Nation entrusted the law-making power to Congress alone in both good and bad times. It would do no good to recall the historical events, the fears of power and the hopes for freedom that lay behind their choice. Such a review would but confirm our holding that this seizure order cannot stand.

The judgment of the District Court is affirmed.

[Justice Jackson wrote a concurring opinion which contained the following often quoted passage:]

    1. When the President acts pursuant to an express or implied authorization of Congress, his authority is at its maximum. * * *

    2. When the President acts in absence of either a congressional grant or denial of authority, he can only rely upon his own independent powers, but there is a zone of twilight in which he and Congress may have concurrent authority, or in which its distribution is uncertain. Therefore, congressional inertia, indifference or quiescence may sometimes, at least as

a practical matter, enable, if not invite, measures on independent presidential responsibility.   *   *   *

3. When the President takes measures incompatible with the expressed or implied will of Congress, his power is at its lowest ebb, for then he can rely only upon his own constitutional powers minus any constitutional powers of Congress over the matter. Courts can sustain exclusive Presidential control in such a case only by disabling the Congress from acting upon the subject. Presidential claim to a power at once so conclusive and preclusive must be scrutinized with caution, for what is at stake is the equilibrium established by our constitutional system.

[The remainder of Justice Jackson's concurring opinion is omitted, as are concurring opinions of Justices Clark, Frankfurter, Douglas and Burton, and dissenting opinions of Justices Vinson, Reed and Minton.]

Note

There have been very few Supreme Court cases since the end of World War II that have addressed the President's foreign affairs powers, and fewer still that have done so in the context of international economic relations, although the lower federal courts have had to struggle with such problems. Apart from *Youngstown* (which makes very little reference to foreign affairs, although part of the argued justification for the President's action was the needs of the Korean War), these cases required the Court to determine whether the President had acted in accordance with specific statutory delegations of authority and are therefore discussed in Section 3.4(B) below. One case, however, touched on the question of inherent presidential powers in foreign affairs.

DAMES & MOORE v. REGAN, 453 U.S. 654, 101 S.Ct. 2972, 69 L.Ed.2d 918 (1981), involved a challenge to President Carter's orders transferring certain blocked Iranian assets under U.S. jurisdiction, nullifying attachment orders previously obtained thereon and suspending claims against Iran pending in U.S. courts. The orders were issued as part of the agreement by which American hostages held in Iran were released. In his opinion for an essentially unanimous Supreme Court, Justice Rehnquist quoted from both *Curtiss-Wright* and Justice Jackson's concurrence in *Youngstown*. In upholding the transfer and nullification orders, he gave a broad reading to the scope of the authority delegated to the President by Congress in the International Emergency Economic Powers Act ("IEEPA") (see Section 3.4(B) below). Although he concluded that neither IEEPA nor the Hostage Act of 1868 specifically authorized the President to suspend claims, Justice Rehnquist noted that "both statutes [are] highly relevant in the looser sense of indicating congressional acceptance of a broad scope for executive action in circumstances such as those presented in this case." 453 U.S. at 677, 101 S.Ct. at 2985. After reviewing what he considered to be congressional acquiescence in past cases where a president had negotiated the settlement of international claims, Justice Rehnquist concluded: "In light of all of the foregoing—the inferences to be drawn from the character of the legislation Congress has enacted in the area, such as the IEEPA and the Hostage Act, and from the history of acquiescence in executive claims settlement—we conclude that the President was authorized to suspend pending claims." 453 U.S. at 686, 101 S.Ct. at 2990. The significance of this case is colored by the special factual setting in which it arose. The orders were necessary to implement the agreement under which the hostages were to be released. Given a more pedestrian factual situation, the Court might not have been so accommodating to the President.[3] See Section 3.5(C) below.

UNITED STATES v. GUY W. CAPPS, INC.

United States Court of Appeals, Fourth Circuit, 1953.
204 F.2d 655.[4]

PARKER, CHIEF JUDGE:

This is an appeal by the United States from a judgment entered on a verdict directed for the defendant, Guy W. Capps, in an action instituted to recover damages alleged to have been sustained by the United States as the result of alleged breach by defendant of a contract with respect to the importation of seed potatoes from Canada. The District Court denied a motion to dismiss the action. United States v. Guy W. Capps, Inc., 100 F.Supp. 30. Upon the subsequent trial, however, the court directed a verdict and entered judgment for defendant on the ground that there was no sufficient showing of breach of contract or damage to the United States.

The contract sued on has relation to the potato price support program of 1948 and the executive agreement entered into between Canada and the United States. * * * In a manifest attempt to protect the American Potato Market in which this price support program was operating from an influx of Canadian grown potatoes, the Acting Secretary of State of the United States, on November 23, 1948, entered into an executive agreement with the Canadian Ambassador, who was acting for the Canadian Government, to the effect that the Canadian Government would place potatoes in the list of commodities for which export permits were required and that export permits would be granted therefor only to Canadian exporters who could give evidence that they had firm orders from legitimate United States users of Canadian seed potatoes and that "Canadian exporters would also be required to have included in any contract into which they might enter with a United States seed potato importer a clause in which the importer would give an assurance that the potatoes would not be diverted or reconsigned for table stock purposes". In consideration of this agreement on the part of the Canadian Government, the United States Government undertook that it would not impose "any quantitative limitations or fees on Canadian potatoes of the 1948 crop exported to the United States" under the system of regulating the movement of potatoes to the United States outlined in the Canadian proposal and would not consider the Canadian Government's guarantee of a floor price with respect to certain potatoes to be the payment of a bounty or grant and would not levy any countervailing duty on such potatoes under the provisions of section 303 of the Tariff Act of 1930. * * *

Defendant, a corporation engaged in business in Norfolk, Virginia, entered into a contract in December 1948 with H.B. Willis, Inc., a Canadian

---

3. See Symposium: Dames & Moore v. Regan, 29 UCLA L.Rev. 977 (1982).

4. The action taken by the Supreme Court in this case is discussed in the note following the case.

exporter, to purchase 48,544 sacks of Canadian seed potatoes. * * *
Defendant's officers admittedly knew of the agreement with Canada and
stated in a telegram to an official of the United States Department of
Agriculture that the potatoes were being brought in for seed purposes.
Defendant sent a telegram to the exporter in Canada on the same day that
the potatoes were billed stating that they were for planting in Florida and
Georgia. Defendant sold the potatoes while in shipment to the Atlantic
Commission Company, a wholly owned agency of Great Atlantic & Pacific
Tea Company, a retail grocery organization. No attempt was made to
restrict their sale so that they would be used for seed and not for food, and
there is evidence from which the jury could properly have drawn the
conclusion that they were sold on the market as food displacing potatoes
grown in this country and causing damage to the United States by requiring
greater purchases of American grown potatoes in aid of the price support
program than would have been necessary in the absence of their importation.

On these facts we think that judgment was properly entered for the
defendant, but for reasons other than those given by the District Court. We
have little difficulty in seeing in the evidence breach of contract on the part
of defendant and damage resulting to the United States from the breach.
We think, however, that the executive agreement was void because it was
not authorized by Congress and contravened provisions of a statute dealing
with the very matter to which it related and that the contract relied on,
which was based on the executive agreement, was unenforceable in the
courts of the United States for like reason. We think, also, that no action
can be maintained by the government to recover damages on account of
what is essentially a breach of a trade regulation, in the absence of express
authorization by Congress. The power to regulate foreign commerce is
vested in Congress, not in the executive or the courts; and the executive may
not exercise the power by entering into executive agreements and suing in
the courts for damages resulting from breaches of contracts made on the
basis of such agreements.

In the Agricultural Act of 1948, Congress had legislated specifically with
respect to the limitations which might be imposed on imports if it was
thought that they would render ineffective or materially interfere with any
program or operation undertaken pursuant to that act. Section 3 of the act,
which amended prior statutes, provided in the portion here pertinent, 62
Stat. 1248–1250, 7 U.S.C.A. § 624:

[The court here quoted from the Agricultural Act of 1948, a statute that
amended section 22 of the Agricultural Marketing Agreement Act and called
upon the President to impose quantitative restrictions on imports of products
when such imports would otherwise undermine a price maintenance program for U.S. agricultural products.]

* * *

There was no pretense of complying with the requirements of this
statute. The President did not cause an investigation to be made by the
Tariff Commission, the Commission did not conduct an investigation or make
findings or recommendations, and the President made no findings of fact and

issued no proclamation imposing quantitative limitations and determined no representative period for the application of the 50% limitation contained in the proviso. All that occurred in the making of this executive agreement, the effect of which was to exclude entirely a food product of a foreign country from importation into the United States, was an exchange of correspondence between the Acting Secretary of State and the Canadian Ambassador. Since the purpose of the agreement as well as its effect was to bar imports which would interfere with the Agricultural Adjustment program, it was necessary that the provisions of this statute be complied with and an executive agreement excluding such imports which failed to comply with it was void. * * *

It is argued, however, that the validity of the executive agreement was not dependent upon the Act of Congress but was made pursuant to the inherent powers of the President under the Constitution. The answer is that while the President has certain inherent powers under the Constitution such as the power pertaining to his position as Commander in Chief of Army and Navy and the power necessary to see that the laws are faithfully executed, the power to regulate interstate and foreign commerce is not among the powers incident to the Presidential office, but is expressly vested by the Constitution in the Congress. It cannot be upheld as an exercise of the power to see that the laws are faithfully executed, for, as said by Mr. Justice Holmes in his dissenting opinion in Myers v. United States, 272 U.S. 52, 177, 47 S.Ct. 21, 85, 71 L.Ed. 160, "The duty of the President to see that the laws be executed is a duty that does not go beyond the laws or require him to achieve more than Congress sees fit to leave within his power". In the recent case of Youngstown Sheet & Tube Co. v. Sawyer, 343 U.S. 579, 72 S.Ct. 863, 867, 96 L.Ed. 1153, * * * [t]he rule was well stated by Mr. Justice Jackson in his concurring opinion * * * as follows: [quoting the third numbered paragraph of the concurrence, see previous case].

We think that whatever the power of the executive with respect to making executive trade agreements regulating foreign commerce in the absence of action by Congress, it is clear that the executive may not through entering into such an agreement avoid complying with a regulation prescribed by Congress. Imports from a foreign country are foreign commerce subject to regulation, so far as this country is concerned, by Congress alone. The executive may not by-pass congressional limitations regulating such commerce by entering into an agreement with the foreign country that the regulation be exercised by that country through its control over exports. Even though the regulation prescribed by the executive agreement be more desirable than that prescribed by Congressional action, it is the latter which must be accepted as the expression of national policy.

It is argued that irrespective of the validity of the executive agreement, the contract sued on was a valid contract between defendant and the Canadian exporter and that since the contract was made for the benefit of the United States, this country may maintain action upon it.* The answer

---

* There is a holding to that effect in a decision of the United States District Court for the Eastern District of New York in the case of United States v. Carpenter, 113 F.Supp. 327.

is that the contract was but the carrying out of the executive agreement entered into in contravention of the policy declared by Congress; and the courts of the United States will not lend their aid to enforcing it against the public policy of the country so declared. As stated, the regulation of imports from foreign countries is a matter for Congress and, when Congress has acted, the executive may not enforce different regulations by suing on contracts made with reference thereto. As said by the Supreme Court in Oscanyan v. Arms Co., 103 U.S. 261, 277, 26 L.Ed. 539, "Contracts permissible by other countries are not enforceable in our courts, if they contravene our laws, our morality or our policy."

We think the action for damages may not be sustained for the additional reason that Congress has created no such right of action. * * * This is not a case where the government stands in the shoes of a private person and sues on a contract which it has made as such. It is a case where the government sues in its sovereign capacity to recover damages which it claims to have sustained while engaged in the exercise of governmental powers, as the result of the violation of a contract made between other persons. No such cause of action exists under federal law; and we do not think that analogies drawn from private contract law, permitting suit by one for whose benefit a contract is made to sue thereon, can properly be followed here. "The exercise of judicial power to establish a new liability would amount to an unwarranted intrusion by the courts into a field properly within the control of Congress and as to a matter concerning which it had seen fit to take no action". Gartner v. United States, 9 Cir., 166 F.2d 728, 730. * * *

For the reasons stated, we do not think that the United States can maintain the action for damages. The judgment for defendant will accordingly be affirmed.

Affirmed.

Note

The case was affirmed by the U.S. Supreme Court at 348 U.S. 296, 75 S.Ct. 326, 99 L.Ed. 329 (1955), but on completely different grounds. It dismissed the U.S. complaint against the defendant, noting that there was no showing of bad faith, neglect or carelessness on the part of defendant, since A & P also sold potatoes for seed purposes.

In his book, SUPER CHIEF—Earl Warren and His Supreme Court—A Judicial Biography 165–66 (1983), Bernard Schwartz described the Supreme Court's approach in the *Guy Capps* case as follows:[5]

> * * * The court of appeals decided against the government in an opinion by Judge John J. Parker, whose nomination to the Supreme Court by President Hoover had been turned down by the Senate. Parker ruled that the executive agreement contravened the provisions of a federal statute that governed limitations on agricultural imports. In such a case, the executive agreement could not be given effect.

5. Reprinted by permission of New York University Press.

The Supreme Court had never decided the constitutional issue disposed of by Parker. At the November 20, 1954, conference Warren proposed that the issue should not be dealt with. Referring to the decision below against the government, the Chief said, "Let it stand." But he proposed reaching that result without deciding the constitutional question. Instead, he would prefer to have the case go on the grounds given by the district court, that neither a valid contract nor damages had been proved. Warren, too, stated that he would exonerate the defendants from damages, as there was no adequate proof of any contract violation or damages. All the others agreed, and on February 7, 1955, an opinion of the Court following the Chief's approach was delivered by Burton.

At least two of the Brethren indicated their views on the constitutional issue. Warren himself had stated at the conference that "the Government was entitled to make such agreements." He recognized that the relevant statute provided for imposing import limitations through the Tariff Commission, under the President's direction. But, he asserted, it "was not the only procedure allowable for the President. It contemplated other international agreements." Burton's opinion of the Court did not, however, touch even inferentially upon the executive agreement issue. As Frankfurter had stressed at the conference, the opinion was written to "allow no basis to quote us on the issue."

In *Capps,* Frankfurter explained in a later memorandum to the Brethren, "in order to avoid entanglement in the explosive issue * * * the whole Court exercised not a little astuteness to have the case go off on a different ground to such an extent that the fact that the power to make treaties and executive agreements was in issue was not even mentioned but was discreetly covered up by reference to 'other questions' which we said there was no occasion to consider."

CONSUMERS UNION OF U.S., INC. v. KISSINGER

United States Court of Appeals, District of Columbia, 1974.
506 F.2d 136, cert. denied, 421 U.S. 1004, 95 S.Ct. 2406, 44 L.Ed.2d 673 (1975).

McGOWAN, CIRCUIT JUDGE:

These consolidated cross-appeals are directed respectively to two declarations made by the District Court in a suit challenging efforts by the Executive Branch of the United States Government to bring about reductions in steel imports by means of self-imposed limitations on foreign producers. Arrayed against each other are a complaining consumers organization, on the one side, and, on the other, the State Department, and foreign and domestic steel producers, individually and in association. In the form eventually taken by the litigation in the District Court, we consider that the only question before us is whether the actions of the Executive were a regulation of foreign commerce foreclosed to it generally by Article I, Section 8, Clause 3 of the Constitution, and in particular by the Trade Expansion Act of 1962, 19 U.S.C. § 1801 et seq. To the extent that the District Court declared no such conflict to exist, we affirm its decision.

I

Steel imports into the United States increased more than tenfold over the period 1958–68, with the great bulk of imports coming from Japan and the countries of the European Communities. The effect of this development on the domestic steel industry, which is deemed to be of great importance to the nation's security as well as to its peacetime economy, became a matter of widespread concern. In 1968 bills with substantial backing were introduced in Congress to impose mandatory import quotas on steel.

The Executive Branch regarded the problem created by steel imports as temporary in nature and thus amenable to a short-term solution. It concluded, moreover, that unilaterally imposed mandatory quotas would pose a danger of retaliation under the General Agreement on Trade and Tariffs, prove inflexible and difficult to terminate, and have a seriously adverse impact on the foreign relations of the United States. Import limiting agreements negotiated with other governments were likewise rejected on the State Department's advice that negotiated official restrictions, if achievable, would have political consequences for the foreign governments that would also affect our external affairs adversely. Accordingly, the Executive Branch concluded in 1968 that voluntary import restraint undertakings by foreign producers offered the best hope of alleviating the domestic industry's temporary problems at the least cost to United States foreign, economic and trade policies.

After an initial showing of interest by the foreign producer associations, State Department officials entered into discussions that lasted from June to December, 1968, and resulted in letters being sent to the Secretary in which the Japanese and European producer associations stated their intentions to limit steel shipments to the United States to specified maximum tonnages for each of the years 1969, 1970, and 1971.[*4] During 1970, domestic industry and union representatives urged the State Department to seek renewal of the restraints beyond 1971 to provide greater time within which to achieve needed changes, and the House Ways and Means Committee issued a report to like effect. When various executive organs, such as the President's Council of Economic Advisors, had made the same recommendation, the President directed the Secretary to seek extensions of the limitation representations. Such extensions, covering 1972 through 1974, were forthcoming in letters dated early in May, 1972, and announced by the President on May 6.

The two 1972 letters are substantially alike. Each states the signatories' intention to limit exports of steel products to the United States both in aggregate tonnage and, within such limits, in terms of product mix. Each represents that the signatories "hold themselves [itself] ready to consult with representatives of the United States Government on any problem or question

---

* 4. The letters to the Secretary, dated December 23, 1968, were approvingly read by President Johnson after their receipt, and were transmitted by the Secretary on January 14, 1969, to the respective Chairmen of the Senate Finance Committee and the House Ways and Means Committee. The recipients thereupon issued a joint announcement welcoming the voluntary restraints and releasing the texts of the producers' and the Secretary's letters. No mandatory import quota legislation was recommended by the committees thereafter.

that may arise with respect to this voluntary restraint undertaking" and expect the United States Government so to hold itself ready.*6   In addition, each states that its undertaking is based on the assumptions that (1) the effect will not be to place the signatories at a disadvantage relative to each other, (2) the United States will take no unilateral actions to restrict imports by the signatories to the United States, and (3) the representations do not violate United States or international laws.

II

The original complaint in this action contained two separate and distinct claims.   They were respectively denominated "FIRST CLAIM (Antitrust)" and "SECOND CLAIM (Unlawful Action by State Department Officials)". The first claim sought declaratory and injunctive relief with respect to what were said to be continuing violations of Section 1 of the Sherman Act, 15 U.S.C. § 1.   The court was asked to declare the 1972 letters of intent to be in violation of that statute, and to enjoin all of the named defendants from engaging in any act to effectuate the import reductions contemplated by those letters.

The second claim, as its title implies, sought relief only with respect to the State Department defendants, who were said to have violated the law by "facilitating, bringing about and negotiating" the limitations set forth in the 1972 letters of intent without compliance with Section 301 or Section 352 of the Trade Expansion Act of 1962.   The relief sought was a declaration that the 1972 export limitations are illegal, and an injunction addressed to all the defendants, prohibiting acts in furtherance of the arrangement.

After answers had been filed by some of the defendants and a motion to dismiss or alternatively for summary judgment had been made by the State Department defendants, the parties stipulated that the first claim in the complaint be dismissed with prejudice, and an amended complaint was filed. The violation of law alleged in the amended complaint was that the State Department officials had acted to regulate foreign commerce within the meaning of Article 1, Section 8, Clause 3 of the Constitution, and of the laws relating to the regulation of foreign trade set forth in Title 19 of the U.S. Code, including Sections 301 and 352 of the Trade Expansion Act of 1962. The foreign producer defendants were said to be violating the same laws to the extent that they took steps to effectuate the limitations sought by the defendant State Department officials acting in excess of their authority. The relief sought was a declaration that the actions of the State Department officials in seeking the export limitations were *ultra vires,* and an injunction against the defendants from furthering the 1972 letters of intent in any way.

[In its ruling on summary judgment motions of each side, the District Court declared (1) that the steel arrangements were not exempt from the antitrust laws and that the Executive had no power to exempt them and (2) that the Executive could enter the arrangements without complying with

* **6.** It is undisputed that "[i]n negotiating the arrangements and all of their specific terms, the State Department officers explained to the foreign producers that they were being asked to make the requested commitments by the Executive Branch of the United States Government on the ground that they were in the national interest of the United States."   JA 155a.

the 1962 Act so long as they were not otherwise illegal. The District Court then indicated that it thought that there were very serious antitrust issues present. At the outset of its opinion, the Court of Appeals noted that the antitrust issues were no longer in the case and that the District Court's views had no judicial force and effect.]

We turn, then, to the District Court's declaration that, in respect of the actions of the Executive culminating in the undertakings stated in the letters of intent, "the Executive is not preempted * * * and that there is no requirement that all such undertakings be first processed under the Trade Expansion Act of 1962." That statute, as its name suggests, had as its principal purpose the stimulation of the economic growth of the United States and the maintenance and enlargement of foreign markets for its products.

This was to be achieved through trade agreements reached by the President with foreign countries. Title II of the Act provided that, for a period of five years (1962–67), the President was authorized to enter into such agreements whenever he determined that any existing tariff duties or other import restrictions of either the United States or any foreign country were unduly burdening and restricting the foreign trade of the United States. Upon reaching any such trade agreement, the President was delegated the unmistakably legislative power to modify or continue existing tariffs or other import restrictions, to continue existing duty-free or excise treatment, or to impose additional import restrictions, as he determined to be necessary or appropriate to the carrying out of the agreement. 19 U.S.C. § 1821. In connection with the first two of these powers, the Tariff Commission was given an advisory function, which included public hearings; and public hearings were also directed to be held, by an agency designated by the President, in connection with any proposed trade agreement. 19 U.S.C. §§ 1841, 1843.

Title III of the Trade Expansion Act of 1962, recognizing that domestic interests of various kinds may be adversely affected by concessions granted under trade agreements, authorizes the making of compensating adjustments of various kinds. Section 301 (19 U.S.C. § 1901) provides that the Tariff Commission shall undertake investigations of injuries allegedly being done to domestic businesses or workers by such things as increased imports flowing from a trade agreement. After holding public hearings, the Tariff Commission shall make a report to the President. If it affirmatively finds injury to domestic industry, the President may under Section 351 increase or impose tariff duties or other import restrictions, 19 U.S.C. § 1981, or alternatively he may under Section 352 negotiate agreements with foreign governments limiting the export from such countries to the United States of the article causing the injury. 19 U.S.C. § 1981. If this latter option is taken, the Act provides that the President is authorized to issue regulations governing the entry or withdrawal from warehouse of the article covered by the agreement.

The foregoing description of the Trade Expansion Act of 1962 covers, among others, Sections 301 and 352. They are the only provisions expressly identified in the amended complaint as constituting the allegedly preemptive exercise by Congress of its constitutional power to regulate foreign commerce that, so it is said, forecloses the actions of the Executive challenged in this case. The description extends also to Sections 302 and 351, which are referred to in plaintiff-appellant Consumers Union's brief, as is also Section 232, 19 U.S.C. § 1862. This last is the so-called national security clause which provides that the President shall not decrease or eliminate tariffs or other import restrictions if to do so would impair the national security. The Director of the Office of Emergency Planning is directed to investigate any situation where imports threaten to impair the national security; and if he finds such threat, and the President concurs, action shall be taken "to adjust the imports" of the article in question, which means that the article may by regulation be excluded from entry or withdrawal from warehouse.*10

What is clear from the foregoing is a purpose on the part of Congress to delegate legislative power to the President for use by him in certain defined circumstances and in furtherance of certain stated purposes. Without such a delegation, the President could not increase or decrease tariffs, issue commands to the customs service to refuse or delay entry of goods into the country, or impose mandatory import quotas. To make use of such delegated power, the President would of course be required to proceed strictly in accordance with the procedures specified in the statutes conferring the delegation. Where, as here, he does not pretend to the possession of such power, no such conformity is required.

The steel import restraints do not purport to be enforceable, either as contracts or as governmental actions with the force of law; and the Executive has no sanctions to invoke in order to compel observance by the foreign producers of their self-denying representations. They are a statement of intent on the part of the foreign producer associations. The signatories' expectations, not unreasonably in light of the reception given their undertakings by the Executive, are that the Executive will consult with them over mutual concerns about the steel import situation, and that it will not have sudden recourse to the unilateral steps available to it under the Trade Expansion Act to impose legal restrictions on importation. The President is not bound in any way to refrain from taking such steps if he later deems them to be in the national interest, or if consultation proves unavailing to meet unforeseen difficulties; and certainly the Congress is not inhibited from enacting any legislation it desires to regulate by law the importation of steel.

The formality and specificity with which the undertakings are expressed does not alter their essentially precatory nature insofar as the Executive Branch is concerned. In effect the President has said that he will not initiate steps to limit steel imports by law if the volume of such imports remains within tolerable bounds. Communicating, through the Secretary of

* 10. The Katz affidavit asserts that consideration was given to the utilization of both Section 352 and Section 232. The former "could not seriously be considered" because it was in terms made available by Congress only for the purpose of softening injuries to domestic commerce caused in major part by prior concessions in trade agreements; and this was not a major cause in this instance. As to Section 232, national security was only one of the factors contributing to the problem, and the attempt to solve it by a method which armed the President with legislative power to stop foreign imports at the water's edge would have had an unfortunate impact on foreign trade policy and international relationships.

State, what levels he considers tolerable merely enables the foreign producers to conform their actions accordingly, and to avoid the risk of guessing at what is acceptable. Regardless of whether the producers run afoul of the antitrust laws in the manner of their response, nothing in the process leading up to the voluntary undertakings or the process of consultation under them differentiates what the Executive has done here from what all Presidents, and to a lesser extent all high executive officers, do when they admonish an industry with the express or implicit warning that action within either their existing powers or enlarged powers to be sought, will be taken if a desired course is not followed voluntarily.

The question of congressional preemption is simply not pertinent to executive action of this sort. Congress acts by making laws binding, if valid, on their objects and the President, whose duty it is faithfully to execute the laws. From the comprehensive pattern of its legislation regulating trade and governing the circumstances under and procedures by which the President is authorized to act to limit imports, it appears quite likely that Congress has by statute occupied the field of *enforceable* import restrictions, if it did not, indeed, have exclusive possession thereof by the terms of Article I of the Constitution. There is no potential for conflict, however, between exclusive congressional regulation of foreign commerce—regulation enforced ultimately by halting violative importations at the border—and assurances of voluntary restraint given to the Executive. Nor is there any warrant for creating such a conflict by straining to endow the voluntary undertakings with legally binding effect, contrary to the manifest understanding of all concerned and, indeed, to the manner in which departures from them have been treated.[*12]

In holding, as we do, that the District Court did not err in declining to characterize the conduct of the Executive here under attack as in conflict with the Trade Expansion Act of 1962, we are not to be understood as intimating any views as to the relationship of the Sherman Act to the events in issue here. The Sherman Act is not, as noted above, one of the regulatory statutes charged as preempting the field, and the question of its possible substantive applicability vanished from this case with the original complaint.

The declaration in the District Court's order with respect to antitrust exemption is vacated, and the declaratory aspect of that order is confined to the proposition that the State Department defendants were not precluded from following the course they did by anything in the Constitution or Title 19 of the U.S.Code. As so confined, the order appealed from is affirmed.

It is so ordered.

DANAHER, SENIOR CIRCUIT JUDGE (concurring):

* * *

[*12.] In 1969 the Japanese, and in 1972 all foreign producers, exported to the United States more steel or particular types of steel product than their undertakings contemplated. In no case were the "excess" goods denied entry into the United States. Rather, consultations were sought and the next year's voluntary quota reduced by the amount of the excess.

Our dissenting colleague regards the arrangements with the foreign private concerns as "solemn negotiated bilateral understandings". The record shows that the private producers themselves limited their own exports. Our colleague sees the Executive in position to call upon nonjudicial exercises of power if the foreign producers violate the arrangements. He suggests, e.g., that there could be "possibly a call to reduce assistance programs" to the *country* of a foreign producer. He ventures "Suppose the President directed customs officials to deny entry to United States ports of commodities violating the undertaking." None of these things happened.

* * *

* * * Perhaps it is not too much to "suppose" (our colleague's word) that President Johnson said "Why don't you get those people in here and see if you can reason together with them?"—or words to that effect.

* * *

* * * If it be a penchant of our press to coin applicable expressions, "jawboning" could here be taken as apt and that is what happened, nothing else.

LEVENTHAL, CIRCUIT JUDGE (dissenting):

With all respect, I must record my disagreement with the ruling of the majority that the President had the authority to negotiate detailed arrangements with foreign steel producers to limit their shipments of products to the United States.

In my view, this case is controlled by Congress's exercise of its plenary authority over the regulation of foreign commerce through passage, over the past forty years, of legislation establishing a comprehensive scheme occupying the field of import restraints. While there is room for a role based on inherent authority of the executive, in this case the actions taken by the President are inconsistent, by fair implication, with the scheme Congress has provided. My point is not that the President has taken the kind of action that Congress had forbidden to the Executive. On the contrary, the statutes passed by Congress established a broad executive discretion, and with a subject like steel imports and the kind of expansive scope of the "national security" provision (which emerged in the 1950's and now appears in § 232 of the Trade Expansion Act of 1962) that permits a restriction of imports which threaten to impair the national security by weakening the internal economy, there is a likelihood that the President would have been able to make the findings required by that law. But Congress has made the exercise of executive authority over import restraints dependent on public ventilation of the issues and has prescribed a procedure with safeguards and right of comment by affected interests. The President has concededly not followed that procedure, and this course cannot stand consistently with the statutory pattern.

* * *

I am not persuaded by the majority's pronouncement that the statutes are not pertinent to the present case because the arrangements, incorporated in letters from foreign steel producers which describe themselves as "voluntary restraint undertakings," did not contemplate the mandate of judicial enforceability. These undertakings by the President and foreign steel producers were carefully structured in considerable detail, obviously after detailed consultation with American steel interests, without exposure to the kind of input by purchasers that would have been provided if the Congressional procedures had been followed. These undertakings are bilateral, and established obligations. Their bite persists notwithstanding the majority's effort to coat them bland vanilla. The majority tolerates executive detours around the limits staked by Congress in the field it has occupied. Its concept that a different route is available for executive arrangements discerned as not intended for judicial enforcement is, in my view, unsound.

* * *

The contention, accepted by the majority, that the President's action is valid, notwithstanding its lack of statutory authorization, is based on two propositions: (1) the action is within the President's independent "foreign affairs" power; and (2) the import restraint achieved as a result of the President's action is not pre-empted by the Congressional regulatory structure.

[While recognizing the existence of presidential power in foreign affairs independent of Congress, even in commercial affairs, Judge Leventhal concluded on the basis of Justice Jackson's concurring opinion in *Youngstown* that "the executive cannot, through its communications, manage foreign commerce in a manner lying outside a comprehensive, regulatory scheme Congress has enacted pursuant to its Article I, § 8 power."]

The proper inquiry, then, is whether the executive action in obtaining the agreements for steel import restrictions comports with the Congressional program for foreign trade, or whether Congress, by occupation of the field of foreign import restraints, has precluded the President's taking action on an independent basis without complying with the standards and procedures provided by Congress as a condition of executive effectuation of import restraints.

The majority says that the steel import restraints are in harmony with the statutory program because they are not enforceable in courts of law; they are said to be mere precatory expressions which Congress never intended to circumscribe by the procedural requirements applicable to mandatory import controls.

This response presents an issue that focuses on the nature and effect of the undertakings before us. Turning first to effect, Presidents may engage in many activities that have a perceivable economic impact upon the volume of commodities imported. The effects vary in terms of their stability, their specificity, and their duration. At one pole would lie general Presidential exhortations—say, to consumers to "Buy American"—or general alarms, announcing that protective legislation will be sought if imports are not contained. Such appeals are valid even though they may have the effect of inhibiting some market behavior, and no one would view them as prohibited by even the strongest Congressional "free trade" legislation. At the other extreme is a Presidential proclamation that foreign-trade commodities will not be allowed to enter, which plainly cannot be reconciled with the existing statutory structure, or legitimated by reference to some aura of "inherent" Presidential authority. In between is a continuum of restrictions. In my view, the comprehensive statutory program constrains some but not all of the activities in this continuum. Here, the undertakings have an economic effect that parallels that of import quotas proclaimed by the President.

Turning to its nature, the Presidential action here goes far beyond a speech or announcement—even one preceded by "feelers" to foreign governments to ascertain how much they will tolerate. Far from being mere expressions of desire and intent, these are solemn negotiated bilateral understandings.

The arrangements are not unilateral announcements but the culmination of bilateral discussions that were not only participated in, but initiated by State Department officials. Although the final letters that embody the specific limitations are astutely couched in a litany of a "voluntary restraint undertaking" on the part of the foreign steel producers, the circumstances are instinct with bilateral undertaking.

Obviously, foreign firms that have vigorously marketed their products in the United States do not voluntarily withhold production without some reciprocal aspect indicating that forbearance is to their advantage. Here, the undertakings of the foreign producers rest on Government assurances that disadvantages would be equalized among producers; that the United States Government—or at least the not uninfluential Executive Branch— would not take or start other measures to limit steel imports or increase duties; and that the transaction would not violate any law of the United States.

The specificity of the limitations imposed by the undertakings also indicates that they were the result of bilateral bargaining and agreement.

Significantly, by the terms of the arrangements, the parties contemplate continuing consultations. The foreign steel producers "hold themselves ready to consult" on any question that may arise on the interpretation of their "undertaking." Does one accompany a unilateral declaration of intent with an offer to "consult" about what he has declared? When the foreign producers go on to say that their undertakings are based on their expectation that the United States Government will consult with them on questions that arise, and the White House releases these letters, along with a detailed Fact Sheet, as a "welcome development" that is the product of Executive negotiation can it be meaningfully denied that there is a reciprocal undertaking by the United States Government to engage in consultations with the producers?

The inference of bilateral undertaking is strengthened when the arrangement is placed in the context of historical practice. Export forbearance by foreign producers has historically been obtained by diplomatic exchange of notes between the United States and foreign governments. The diplomatic notes themselves have referred to an "agreement" or "gentlemen's agreement" to limit shipments.*[6]

* 6. See the 1935 limitation on imports of Japanese cotton goods and the 1936 limitation on imports of Japanese cotton rugs. * * *

International agreements are not limited to those embodied in formal documents, authenticated with ceremony, but include, as here, the specifying of an arrangement, together with mutual assurances and understandings as to how all parties will behave in response. To cast the steel restraints as unilateral undertakings rather than as agreements is to exalt form over substance.

The majority asserts that, unlike agreements negotiated pursuant to statute, which may be enforced by executive regulations and ultimately by judicial sanctions, the steel arrangements are unenforceable. But it is by no means clear that the Executive is without sanctions if the producers fail to abide by the arrangements. The very specificity of the limitations described by the letters makes violations easy to detect and the arrangements easy to enforce. That the threat of sanctions may carry considerable weight is indicated by the cooperation of the Japanese producers in making compensatory adjustments when they exceeded the quota for 1969 established by the original agreement. The remedy was a reduction of the 1970 quota by the amount of the overshipment. See Fifteenth Annual Report of the President of the United States on the Trade Agreements Program 28 (1970). Similarly, when the Japanese producers exceeded their aggregate quotas for 1972, "consultations" resulted in an agreement by the Japanese producers to charge the 1972 overshipments against 1973 quotas. See Seventeenth Annual Report of the President of the United States on the Trade Agreements Program 44 (1972).

If, as the Government argues, the President has inherent power to negotiate these and similar restraints, I fail to see why the courts would or should refrain from enforcement if sought. Products shipped to the United States in excess of the restraints might be denied entry, or domestic firms might be enjoined from handling them.

The common law of international agreements respects voluntary undertakings even in the absence of the "consideration" that is required under historic Anglo-American common law for domestic agreements to be enforceable in most state courts. If there must be a diplomatic peppercorn, there is consideration in the fact that the undertakings by the producers were plainly not meant to be revocable at will, and were based on a United States Government undertaking for consultation in the event problems arose and for avoidance of unilateral action against imports and tariffs. As I earlier indicated, this undertaking was binding on the Government which released and thus acknowledged this aspect of the letter arrangements. Further, principles of promissory estoppel may bind the foreign parties, even in the absence of a finding of initial consideration, once the Executive has relied on their representation that they intend to abandon any right they may have had to exceed the stated limitations on imports—as it has relied here by failing to take other steps to limit imports.

Even if judicial enforcement was not contemplated by the parties, the arrangements still embody a restraint. Trade agreements between foreign nations, and indeed many international agreements, may be "enforceable" only in the sense that they depend for enforcement on "good faith" performance by the parties. That does not make them any the less solemn agreements, that are both intended to affect the conduct of the parties and likely to have that result.

Moreover, the Executive may call on non-judicial resources if foreign producers violate the arrangements. Actions that would ordinarily be resisted as inconsistent with amicable relations, possibly a call to reduce assistance programs to the country in question, could hardly be assailed in the face of foreign producer bad faith.

A deliberate breach may well have an outcome intermediate between direct judicial enforcement and complete non-involvement on the part of the judiciary. Suppose the President directed customs officials to deny entry to United States ports of commodities violating the undertaking, and suppose such actions were sought to be enjoined. It seems to me entirely likely that the parties might have contemplated both this executive action, and the judicial consequence—on the assumption that the negotiations were valid— that the courts had no basis for holding the executive action invalid.[*7]

What is the significance of the reiteration that these undertakings were "voluntary" on the part of the foreign producers? It is commonplace for a businessman to decide "voluntarily" that he will enter into an agreement, although the agreement, once entered into, has binding effect. The mandate may issue from a court of law or arbitration. But the obligations enforced in a court of commercial good faith and good will are as rigorous and insistent as a blackrobed judgment. Congress has expressly authorized negotiated limitations in the orderly marketing agreement provision, § 352 of the Trade Expansion Act of 1962. And the national security provision authorizes restrictions imposed by Presidential proclamation, which embraces the authority to arrange restraints to which foreign producers consent.

In my view, the steel quotas before us present an import restraint having a composite characteristic, in terms of effect and nature, as to be subject to the procedures and requirements set forth in the Trade Expansion Act of 1962.

This is the critical question in the case—where to draw the line. There is a continuum of restraints, as noted above. In my view, the critical distinction is between executive actions that rest wholly in the domain of appeals and exhortations, and executive actions that culminate in obligations. A good faith agreement with the kind of specificity present here puts an obligation on the foreign producer, in any realistic assessment. Accordingly, I think the executive negotiation and acceptance of these undertakings are activity in a field that has been preempted by Congress, and can only be engaged in by following the procedures set forth in the Congressional enactments.

* * *

I am unimpressed with defendants' citation of statements from the legislative history of various trade provisions as indicating a legislative intent that agreements could be reached without prescribed procedures.

* 7. This assumes the court would pass on the merits. A court might well dismiss an action on another ground, like lack of clean hands.

If the entire legislative history is appraised, weight must be given to the two occasions—in the passage of the 1962 law, and again in 1971—when Congress has declined to give the President authorization to impose import restraints without observing procedural requirements. However, the legislative history, as conventionally ascertained, does not give an independent view of Congressional intent, and this must be discerned from basic analysis of the statutes passed by Congress. The deep-seated and comprehensive Congressional insistence on procedural safeguards can best be appreciated in the light of pertinent history.

The ascertainment of pertinent legislative intent depends not only on express wording of the Trade Expansion Act of 1962, and specific notations in its immediate legislative history, but on its character as a culmination of comprehensive enactments on the subject of executive actions resulting in obligatory foreign trade restraints, including agreements by the executive regarding imports. The Congressional pattern makes clear that such executive action is tolerated only if it is accompanied and safeguarded by procedural protections that ensure a right of comment by those whose interests may be affected. This not only avoids the vice of complete secrecy within the Government, it also avoids the vice of cozy confidentiality, in which the public is informed only when the matter is a fait accompli.

[Judge Leventhal then summarized existing legislation relating to imports, including general trade negotiating authority (which at the time of the events in this case had expired), a number of specific statutes regulating particular commodities, the general escape clause statute, statutes for regulating imports for national security purposes, etc.]

The procedures by which Congress has circumscribed executive power to shape the terms of foreign trade are no mere technicalities. While freeing the making of international trade policy from the encumbrances of the legislative process, Congress has sought to maintain public ventilation of the issues relevant to policy formation. To say, as the majority opinion does, that the steel arrangements worked out by the President fall within an inherent Presidential authority not preempted by Congress is to allow the circumvention of these procedural safeguards whenever that suits the Executive. If detailed letters of intent are no different from general appeals to industry, the President would be within his authority to enter into such letters-of-intent arrangements with all industry on every aspect of domestic, as well as foreign commerce. This is dangerous doctrine.

Whatever may be the President's prerogative when Congress has not spoken, it is untenable, in my view, to assert a continuing inherent Executive authority to negotiate import restraints outside and in disregard of a consistent and comprehensive Congressional pattern for protective procedures.

The Government and the foreign steel producers urge on the court that Presidents have long negotiated restraints similar to the steel quotas without specific statutory authority, and that this tradition validates the President's action here. An appeal to past executive practice is not without relevance, but it is not decisive and often raises as many questions as it purports to answer.

So far as this case is concerned, it suffices to say that while defendants cite examples of import restraints, * * * they fail to present a history of import restraints consistently negotiated by the President without regard for the procedures established by Congress and so represented to the Congress.

* * *

* * * When it enacted the Trade Expansion Act of 1962, Congress had an opportunity to review all of the President's power to regulate imports. In my view, the Act has scope as a Congressional preemption which "occupies the field" of import restrictions. This approach is heightened by the fact the 1962 Act included authority under § 201 that was expressly limited to run to June 30, 1967. Congress deliberately contracted Presidential latitude by permitting the expiration of that authority, as of July 1, 1967, notwithstanding Executive requests for extension.

[Had his views prevailed, Judge Leventhal indicated that he would have declared executive participation in the agreements invalid only prospectively, so that such participation prior to the Court's judgment would have been assumed to have been valid in considering any action for damages or other relief. He also indicated that he would have withheld any order for 90 days to allow the President to implement controls pursuant to statutory authority.]

Notes and Questions

(1) Section 607 of the Trade Act of 1974 (Documentary Supplement) contains a congressional grant of immunity from antitrust laws with respect to the voluntary arrangements on steel examined in this case. An interesting question is whether the procedures followed in this case could be used today in light of the escape clause provisions in the 1974 Act (Sections 201–03).

(2) So-called "voluntary export restraints" (also called auto-limitations and export restraint arrangements), are measures which seem to have spread rapidly in recent years. There is considerable worry that these "grey area" measures are undermining the international regime of liberal trade. The United States government has been at the forefront of a challenge to these measures, yet the United States has itself indulged rather frequently in their use. We will examine the issues raised by this increase in the use of such restraints in detail in Section 9.4 infra. As indicated in the *Consumers Union* case, the legal status in the United States of these measures is complicated by the U.S. antitrust laws, and is anything but clear. An interesting and somewhat controverted question is whether the *Consumers Union* case has in practice had the practical effect of adding to presidential authority or the effect of subtracting from (or at least inhibiting use of) such authority. Some say that although the plaintiffs in this case lost the "battle", they won the "war", because the implicit threat of court challenge, not completely absolved by the case, has caused the Executive Branch to be cautious about using so-called voluntary restraint arrangements as a tool of international economic policy.

(3) If consumers were to be precluded from challenging foreign restraints instigated by the U.S. government, do you think that it would be more or less likely that international economic rules limiting such restraints would be observed by the United States?

(C) CONGRESS AND CONTROL OF INTERNATIONAL ECONOMIC RELATIONS

In Section 3.4 we will examine legislation concerning the international economic relations of the United States (and many delegations of authority to the President) and in that context deal with many problems arising out of the relationship between the Executive and Congress. In this subsection, however, we examine the fundamental constitutional position of Congress in these affairs, and explore a few of the issues regarding that position that can be appropriately juxtaposed with presidential powers, as taken up in the previous subsection.

In the United States' system of government, with its division of powers and its checks and balances, the Legislative Branch would inevitably have a significant role to play in matters so prominent as international economic policy. In the United States Constitution, however, the role of the legislature in these affairs is made even stronger by the explicit constitutional grant of power to Congress "to lay and collect taxes, duties, imposts and excises, * * *", and "to regulate commerce with foreign nations and among the several states. * * *" [6] Congress is very conscious of its special role in international economic policy,[7] and even though the conduct of general foreign policy, particularly political and defense matters, may rest largely in the Executive Branch, when it comes to economic foreign policy, Congress does not hesitate to assert itself. The events of the "Watergate Scandal" leading to President Nixon's resignation in 1974 have affected the relationship between Congress and the Executive Branch greatly, and it would be expected that these events would influence Congress' approach to international policy also.

The basic dilemma, as stated before, is the problem of Congress exercising its power and control over international economic policy while accommodating the necessity of the United States acting and negotiating through spokesmen who have the authority to commit the United States. In no case in recent years has Congress faced this dilemma more starkly than in its 1974 and 1979 legislation relating to the Tokyo Round of Multilateral Trade Negotiations (see Section 3.4(E)–(F) below).

Here we will look briefly at the structure of Congress and at two constitutional issues that Congress must bear in mind in resolving its dilemma—the constitutional limits on delegation of legislative authority and the unconstitutionality of such congressional oversight devices as the legislative veto. First, it should be useful to survey briefly some aspects of the structure and organization of Congress that bear upon its work. As American readers know, Congress is divided into two Houses: the House of Representatives (435 representatives selected from districts of roughly equal population throughout the United States, so that representation is proportionate to population) and the Senate (2 senators from each of the 50 states, regardless of the population of the state). What is not often apparent in elementary studies of Congress is the vast difference between the procedures

---

6. U.S. Const. Art. I, § 8, cls. 1, 3.

7. Senate Comm. on Finance, Trade Reform Act of 1974, S.Rep. No. 1298, 93d Cong., 2d Sess. 14 (1974).

and methods of work of the two Houses, and consequently of the types of influences that are brought to bear. Any description of Congress, of course, runs into the difficulty that the procedures and rules of Congress change from time to time.

In both Houses of Congress, the committee structure is very important.[8] Some of the committees are almost as old as Congress itself, and there has developed a maze of jurisdictional guidelines which allocate various subjects to various committees. Relevant to international economic policy, for example, is not only trade and tariff policy (which is assigned in the Senate to the Senate Finance Committee), but a number of banking and monetary issues (House Banking, Finance and Urban Affairs Committee; Senate Banking, Housing and Urban Affairs Committee), matters concerning aid (House Foreign Affairs Committee, Senate Foreign Relations Committee), the giving of advice and consent on the ratification of treaties (Senate Foreign Relations Committee), export promotion of agricultural surplus and quotas against the import of certain agricultural goods (Senate Agriculture, Nutrition and Forestry Committee, House Agriculture Committee), and certain other matters relating to commerce that are sometimes assigned to the commerce committees of the two Houses. In addition, the Joint Economic Committee often deals with issues of international monetary policy.

Each of these committees tends to have a different membership configuration, and consequently is more or less influenced in different ways by different groups in the United States. For example, in the House of Representatives, the Ways and Means Committee is perhaps the most powerful and most prestigious of all committees. The bulk of this committee's work has to do with taxation. It also has jurisdiction over a wide variety of social legislation, such as unemployment compensation, social security and medical aid. In addition, since tariffs are taxes, it deals with trade policy.

The committee structure, as well as other procedures, differs markedly between the House and the Senate. Because of its size, the House depends more heavily upon committees, and there is a more stringent rule against membership in more than one important committee. Consequently, the typical congressman in the House finds that a great deal of his daily legislative activity revolves around the committee. Committee sessions occupy most of his time. Likewise, the rules structure in the House provides control on amendments that may be offered on the floor when a bill is reported by a committee to the whole House.[9]

In the Senate, however, these matters differ. Senators often belong to several very important committees, and find their day broken up racing from one committee to another. In addition, the Senate floor debates are considerably less controlled; amendments are generally permitted and de-

8. L. Froman, The Congressional Process (1967); J. Lees, The Committee System of the United States Congress (1967); Peabody & Polsby (eds.), New Perspectives on the House of Representatives (2d ed. 1969); R. Bolling, Power in the House (1974); J. Manley, The Politics of Finance: The House Committee on Ways and Means (1970); Curtis, The House Committee on Ways and Means: Congress Seen Through a Key Committee, 1966 Wis.L. Rev. 121.

9. See articles by Rohde, Peabody and Gardner, 411 Annals 39, 133, 169 (1974).

bate is unlimited, unless closure is voted. Consequently, the importance of the committee is somewhat less. Attendance at committee meetings seems to be less also. Senators represent a larger constituency, and for this or other reasons seem to rely more heavily on staff personnel.

(1) The Constitution and Delegation of Authority by Congress

The general issue of the extent to which Congress may delegate its authority is sometimes thought to be largely an issue of the past. In the 1930's, several "New Deal" statutes were declared unconstitutional on these grounds.[10] Since that time, however, no statute has been invalidated for this reason by the Supreme Court, although Justice Brennan, in a concurring opinion dealing with the Subversive Activities Control Act of 1967, noted the danger of congressional delegation of power which allows "overbroad, unauthorized, and arbitrary application of criminal sanctions in an area of protected freedoms. * * *" In that opinion Justice Brennan felt that the statute was constitutionally insufficient because it "contains no meaningful standard" and no procedures to contest administrative designations under it.[11]

In the cases litigating the validity of the 1971 wage-price freeze, the courts sustained a broad congressional delegation of authority to the President to impose such controls. The challenged statute provided simply, "The President is authorized to issue such orders and regulations as he may deem appropriate to stabilize prices, rents, wages, and salaries at levels not less than those prevailing on May 25, 1970." In Amalgamated Meat Cutters & Butcher Workmen of North America, AFL–CIO v. Connally, 337 F.Supp. 737 (D.D.C.1971), Judge Leventhal said (at 745):

> We may usefully begin with the modest observation that the Constitution does not forbid every delegation of "legislative" power. This was recognized explicitly at least as long ago as Norwegian Nitrogen Products Co. v. United States, 288 U.S. 294, 305, 53 S.Ct. 350, 354, 77 L.Ed. 796 (1933), where Justice Cardozo stated that the tariff provision under consideration involved "in substance a delegation, though a permissible one, of the legislative process."
>
> There may thus be added to the outworn doctrines interred in the cause of wisdom the conception developed in Field v. Clark, 143 U.S. 649, 692–693, 12 S.Ct. 495, 505, 36 L.Ed. 294 (1892), which centers the validity of a delegation by Congress to the President on whether he "was the mere agent of the lawmaking department to ascertain and declare the event upon which its expressed will was to take effect." That officials may lawfully be given far greater authority than the power to recognize a triggering condition was recognized within twenty years in the famous *Grimaud* case where a unanimous Court "admitted that it is difficult to define the line which separates legislative power to make laws, from administrative authority to make regulations." There is no analytical difference, no difference in kind, between the legislative function—of prescribing rules for the future—that is

---

10. See J. Nowak, R. Rotunda & J. Young, Constitutional Law 161–63 (2d ed. 1983).

11. United States v. Robel, 389 U.S. 258, 272–73, 88 S.Ct. 419, 428, 19 L.Ed.2d 508 (1967).

exercised by the legislature or by the agency implementing the authority conferred by the legislature. The problem is one of limits.

* * * Congress is free to delegate legislative authority provided it has exercised "the essentials of the legislative function"—of determining the basic legislative policy and formulating a rule of conduct—held satisfied by "the rule, with penal sanctions, that prices shall not be greater than those fixed by maximum price regulations which conform to standards and will tend to further the policy which Congress has established." The key question is not answered by noting that the authority delegated is broad, or broader than Congress might have selected if it had chosen to operate within a narrower range. The issue is whether the legislative description of the task assigned "sufficiently marks the field within which the Administrator is to act so that it may be known whether he has kept within it in compliance with the legislative will."

The *Yakus* ruling of Chief Justice Stone carries forward the doctrine earlier articulated by Chief Justice Taft in *Hampton* that there is no forbidden delegation of legislative power "if Congress shall lay down by legislative act an intelligible principle" to which the official or agency must conform.

Notes and Questions

(1) As Judge Leventhal indicates, the delegation issue has often arisen in the context of tariff and trade legislation, the classic case being Field v. Clark, 143 U.S. 649, 12 S.Ct. 495, 36 L.Ed. 294 (1892). In J.W. Hampton, Jr., & Co. v. United States, 276 U.S. 394, 48 S.Ct. 348, 72 L.Ed. 624 (1928), for instance, the Court upheld a statute saying, (at 409):

* * * The same principle that permits Congress to exercise its rate making power in interstate commerce, by declaring the rule which shall prevail in the legislative fixing of rates, and enables it to remit to a rate-making body created in accordance with its provisions the fixing of such rates, justifies a similar provision for the fixing of customs duties on imported merchandise. If Congress shall lay down by legislative act an intelligible principle to which the person or body authorized to fix such rates is directed to conform, such legislative action is not a forbidden delegation of legislative power. If it is thought wise to vary the customs duties according to changing conditions of production at home and abroad, it may authorize the Chief Executive to carry out this purpose, with the advisory assistance of a Tariff Commission appointed under Congressional authority. This conclusion is amply sustained by a case in which there was no advisory commission furnished the President—a case to which this Court gave the fullest consideration nearly forty years ago.

(2) In STAR–KIST FOODS, INC. v. UNITED STATES, 275 F.2d 472 (C.C. P.A.1959), the Court of Customs and Patent Appeals upheld presidential action in reducing tariffs on imports of tuna fish. Although the statutory duty rate was 25% ad valorem, the President had proclaimed a rate of 12½% in order to carry out a trade agreement with Iceland, entered into pursuant to his statutory trade agreements negotiating authority. A domestic tuna producer challenged the lower rate by challenging the validity of the agreement on two grounds: (1) that the statutory authority for entering into the agreement was an unconstitutional delegation of Congress' powers to legislate, tax and regulate foreign

commerce, and (2) that the agreement had not been submitted to the Senate for advice and consent. The court rejected both arguments. The following are some excerpts from the opinion:

A constitutional delegation of powers requires that Congress enunciate a policy or objective or give reasons for seeking the aid of the President. In addition the act must specify when the powers conferred may be utilized by establishing a standard or "intelligible principle" which is sufficient to make it clear when action is proper. And because Congress cannot abdicate its legislative function and confer carte blanche authority on the President, it must circumscribe that power in some manner. This means that Congress must tell the President what he can do by prescribing a standard which confines his discretion and which will guarantee that any authorized action he takes will tend to promote rather than flout the legislative purpose. It is not necessary that the guides be precise or mathematical formulae to be satisfactory in a constitutional sense.

* * *

Of course the [trade] acts ⌐ ` 1890, 1922, and 1934 are different, but we comprehend only a difference in degree. In each one Congress has allowed the President broad discretion, not only with respect to when he can act, but also in the exercise of the conferred powers. Under the act of 1890, he could suspend articles from the free list "for such time as he shall deem just." And under the Flexible Tariff Act of 1922, the President was authorized to modify duties to equalize the competitive opportunities of American and foreign producers in the markets of the United States. Although he was to be assisted by the Tariff Commission, and was to consider as far as was *"practicable"* certain enumerated factors, as well as any other factors he himself deemed to be relevant, the final decision as respected equalization was his and *his alone*. While it is true that under that act the President was required to seek the advice of the Tariff Commission before he could act, the Court in the Hampton case recognized that an advisory commission is not necessary. Consequently, the absence of such a provision in the Trade Agreements Act is inconsequential. Neither is the absence in the act of 1934 of a suggested list of factors to consider in applying the standard determinative of any of the issues.*5 Under both the 1922 and the 1934 acts, the President was given the power to increase or decrease duties up to 50 per centum of the specified rates. The difference lies only in the procedure set out in the 1922 act to *assist* the Chief Executive in making *his* decision.

* * *

After making the enabling finding, the President is authorized to act in a manner such "that the purpose above declared will be promoted by the means hereinafter specified." Those means are to enter into foreign trade agreements and to proclaim certain modifications in various import restrictions. It becomes immediately apparent, therefore, that the President is limited to action which will advance the policies of the act, and which will tend to secure the benefits considered desirable by the Congress. Not only must they advance the Congressional policy, but with respect to rate modifications, the problem with which appellant is most concerned, they

---

* 5. In Field v. Clark, there were no enumerated factors for consideration in applying the standard, and in J.W. Hampton, Jr., & Co. v. United States, the fact that there was a suggested list of items to consider was not held to be a controlling feature of the case.

must be "required or appropriate" to carrying out the trade-agreement as well.

* * *

We now come to the other contention of appellants, that the trade agreement with Iceland executed by the President pursuant to the Trade Agreements Act is null and void because it is, in fact, a treaty and lacks the concurrence of the Senate, required by Article II, § 2 of the Constitution and, further, that since the agreement is illegal the proclamation which effectuated the agreement is also without legal effect.

This procedure was established by Congress so that its policy and the basic philosophy which motivated the passage of the Trade Agreements Act could be realized. From reading the act, it is apparent that Congress concluded that the promotion of foreign trade required that the tariff barriers in this and other countries be modified on a negotiated basis. Since the President has the responsibility of conducting the foreign affairs of this country generally, it gave to him the added responsibility of negotiating the agreements in pursuance of the spirit of the act. Such a procedure is not without precedent nor judicial approval. The Supreme Court in Altman & Co. v. United States, 224 U.S. 583, 601, 32 S.Ct. 593, 597, 56 L.Ed. 894, recognized that not all commercial compacts are treaties, saying:

> * * * While it may be true that this commercial agreement, made under authority of the Tariff Act of 1897, § 3, was not a treaty possessing the dignity of one requiring ratification by the Senate of the United States, it was an international compact, negotiated between the representatives of two sovereign nations, and made in the name and on behalf of the contracting countries, and dealing with important commercial relations between the two countries, and was proclaimed by the President. If not technically a treaty requiring ratification, nevertheless it was a compact authorized by the Congress of the United States, negotiated and proclaimed under the authority of its President.

(3) In light of cases such as *Hampton* and *Star-Kist,* how would you evaluate the chances for success of an argument that Congress exceeded its powers in delegating authority to the President? Exactly what are the limits on congressional delegation? Some legal scholars believe that there has been a revival of concern about delegation on the Supreme Court in recent years. They cite such cases as the *Chadha* case discussed in the next subsection. One such scholar has concluded: [12]

> The delegation doctrine is alive, but not well articulated or coherently applied by the Supreme Court. The Court continues to invalidate governmental action out of concern that Congress has delegated decisions that should be made in the legislative process, but under rubrics other than delegation, such as due process or vagueness, or even special, narrow versions of the delegation doctrine, such as a stringent approach to cases involving certain rights or favoring statutory constructions that avoid constitutional clashes. Nowhere has the Court attempted to explain how its various approaches to delegation by Congress relate to one another. Thus, the Court's approach to delegation simultaneously fails to serve the doc-

12. Schoenbrod, The Delegation Doctrine:
Could the Court Give It Substance?, 83 Mich.
L.Rev. 1223, 1289 (1985).

trine's purposes and, because it is incoherent, invites judicial usurpation of legislative powers.

(2) Constitutional Limitations on Congressional Supervision of Delegated Powers

The fact that Congress has delegated power to act in an area to the President does not indicate that Congress has no interest in what the President does. Indeed, Congress carefully monitors presidential action through hearings and other means. One method developed by Congress to increase the effectiveness of its oversight procedures was the legislative or congressional veto. Although it first appeared in the 1930's, its use mushroomed in the 1970's—there are five examples in the 1974 Trade Act alone.[13] A typical congressional veto provision requires the President to report to Congress action taken pursuant to a delegated authority and permits Congress or one House thereof to veto or disallow the action within a certain time period. The use of such provisions was challenged in IMMIGRATION & NATURALIZATION SERVICE v. CHADHA, 462 U.S. 919, 103 S.Ct. 2764, 77 L.Ed.2d 317 (1983), where the U.S. Supreme Court, in an opinion by Chief Justice Burger, struck down a provision that authorized either House of Congress, by resolution, to invalidate a decision by the Attorney General, made pursuant to authority delegated by Congress, to allow a particular deportable alien to remain in the United States. In *Chadha,* the Attorney General's decision to allow Chadha to remain in the United States was "vetoed" by the House of Representatives.

In deciding Chadha's challenge to the procedure, the Supreme Court first reviewed the Constitutional structure under which legislation is adopted in the United States. In doing so, it focused on three particular aspects of that structure: First, the need for both Houses of Congress to participate in enacting legislation; second, the role of the President in the legislative process, and, in particular, his right to veto legislative action, in which case a two-thirds vote in each House is required to enact legislation; and third, the bicameral nature of Congress, which consists of two houses, whose members are selected for two different terms of office and apportioned differently among the States. The Court concluded that the act of ordering Chadha's deportation was a legislative act in purpose and effect. Absent the act, Chadha would have had the legal right under existing legislation to remain in the United States. The action by the House of Representatives changed the effect of that legislation and altered Chadha's legal rights. The Court held that this legislative act was invalid because it did not conform to the structure outlined above—it was not taken by both Houses and it was not presented to the President (thereby depriving him of his veto right). In the words of the Court: "Congress must abide by its delegation of authority until that delegation is legislatively altered or revoked." 462 U.S. at 955, 103 S.Ct. at 2786. Justices White and Rehnquist dissented, with Justice White arguing, inter alia, that it should be sufficient for the initial legislation containing the legislative veto provision to comply with the Constitution's requirements for legislative acts. He stated (462 U.S. at 986, 103 S.Ct.

---

13. Sections 203(c), 302(b), 402(d), 407(c)(2), 407(c)(3).

at 2802): "If Congress may delegate legislative power to independent and executive agencies, it is most difficult to understand Article I as forbidding Congress from also reserving a check on legislative power for itself." Justice White also noted that as a practical matter the legislative veto was a useful political invention.

There is some thought that the Court's opinion goes much too far for the needs of the facts of the particular case, and some would argue that there is still a chance of persuading the Court to distinguish two-House vetoes from one-House vetoes, or to distinguish cases involving general issues (such as the adoption of generally applicable rules by an agency) from those involving specific individuals, as was the case in *Chadha*. In addition, there is a substantial question as to the degree to which the veto procedure is severable from the remaining portions of a statutory delegation of power to the President when Congress granted that delegation only on the condition of the veto procedure. Only time and future cases will resolve these and many other questions raised by the decision.[14]

One particularly interesting alternative to the legislative veto is the so-called "fast track" procedure, which was used in 1979 to implement the Tokyo Round agreements into U.S. law and in 1985 to implement the U.S.-Israel Free Trade Agreement. Essentially, as used in these situations, the President is authorized to take a particular action (e.g., negotiate an agreement), but congressional approval is required to implement the results of the negotiation. Since the form of congressional approval is a statute that could be vetoed by the President, the concerns of *Chadha* would seem to be met. The 1979 procedures are described in Section 3.4(E) below.

SECTION 3.3   INTERNATIONAL AGREEMENTS AND U.S. LAW

(A)   INTRODUCTION—THE RELEVANT QUESTIONS

We turn in this section to an exploration of a series of key legal questions relating to international agreements in United States law, namely: (1) What is the legal authority of U.S. officials, such as the President or his officers, to negotiate internationally with a view to entering into an international agreement? (2) What is the legal authority and procedure for U.S. officials to accept an international agreement as a binding obligation of the United States under international law? and (3) What is the legal authority and procedure for implementing an international agreement in the domestic law of the United States? The second of these questions relates to so-called "treaty making" authority, although in the United States there are international agreements that are not called treaties. In the United States, the

---

14. See Franck & Bob, The Return of Humpty-Dumpty: Foreign Relations Law after the Chadha Case, 79 Am.J.Intl.L. 912 (1985); Elliott, INS v. Chadha: The Administrative Constitution, the Constitution, and the Legislative Veto, 1983 Sup.Ct.Rev. 125; Tribe, The Legislative Veto Decision: A Law By Any Other Name?, 21 Harv.J. on Legis. 1 (1984); Breyer, The Legislative Veto After Chadha, 72 Geo.L.J. 785 (1984); Levitas & Brand, Congressional Review of Executive and Agency Actions After Chadha: The "Son of Legislative Veto" Lives On, 72 Geo.L.J. 801 (1984); Spann, Spinning the Legislative Veto, 72 Geo. L.J. 813 (1984); Spann, Deconstructing the Legislative Veto, 68 Minn.L.Rev. 473 (1984).

third question involves consideration of whether the agreement is "self-executing." In some other countries, the question is whether it is "directly applicable." [1]

As to the first of these questions, the generally accepted viewpoint is that the President and his officers can negotiate on any subject at any time. This does not necessarily imply the authority to accept as binding the results of the negotiation. The negotiation will often be "ad referendum", with the understanding that the President will have to obtain authority to accept the agreement which results from the negotiation. The limits of this "pure negotiating" authority have not often been probed by the Courts or by Congress; the *Consumers Union* case, Section 3.2 supra, is perhaps the best available judicial discussion of this topic.

Of course, the authority to "negotiate" may be relatively useless if representatives of other countries feel that the President or his officers will not be able to obtain authority to accept the results of the negotiation. This is a question of "negotiation credibility" to which we have alluded and which we will discuss again. It should be noted that in other countries or legal systems, such as the European Community, there may not reside in executive officials even the authority to negotiate. That is to say, before any discussions with foreign representatives that could be characterized as potentially leading to an international agreement can occur, there must be some sort of authorization procedure.[2]

(B) POWER TO ENTER INTO INTERNATIONAL AGREEMENTS—EXECUTIVE AGREEMENTS AND THE PRESIDENT'S POWER

In U.S. law a distinction is made between treaties and executive agreements. The Constitution requires the Senate to advise and consent by a two-thirds vote to the ratification of a treaty, but it makes no mention of executive agreements. In international law, no such distinction is made—both "treaties" and "executive agreements" are considered to be treaties as that term is used in international law. The use of this different terminology—unfortunately unavoidable now—is a source of some confusion.

In fact one can discern the following different types of international agreements under U.S. law:

(1) Treaties, in the U.S. constitutional sense, requiring advice and consent of two-thirds of the Senate.

(2) Congressional Executive Agreements previously authorized, where Congress has enacted legislation delegating to the President the authority to enter into an international agreement (example: typical trade agreements authority, such as section 101 of the Trade Act of 1974).

(3) Congressional Executive Agreements subsequently authorized, where after an agreement is negotiated, the President seeks authority from Congress to accept the agreement as a binding international obligation of the United States (example: Bretton Woods Agreements Act, 22 U.S.C.A. §§ 286–86x (1982)).

---

1. See Chapter 4.2(C) infra.   2. See Chapter 4.2(C) infra.

(4) Presidential Executive Agreements, sometimes termed "inherent" presidential agreements, where the President accepts an agreement as a binding obligation of the United States without any participation by Congress, on the basis of his "inherent" or constitutional authority (examples: agreements on the disposition of armed forces in foreign countries under the Commander-in-Chief Clause).

(5) Treaty Executive Agreements, where a treaty approved by the Senate leaves certain details of implementation to be worked out by various governments at a later time, and may thus explicitly or implicitly authorize the President to enter into international agreements to accomplish such implementation. (The same could be said of authorizations contained in Congressional Executive Agreements.)

It has been noted often that executive agreements have been growing in use, as compared to treaties. From the Executive Branch's point of view they are speedier and easier, and avoid the minority Senate veto (of one third, plus one) that could block a treaty. But from the point of view of Congress, of course, the executive agreement threatens to diminish the congressional role in foreign affairs, thus risking direct domestic legal effects of self-executing agreements without congressional participation.

Under President Roosevelt, the United States entered into 105 treaties and 123 executive agreements in the eight years from 1933 to 1940. Under President Truman, the United States entered into about the same number of treaties (132), but 10 times as many executive agreements (1,324) in the eight years from 1945 to 1952. The comparative usage rate of treaties and executive agreements in the Truman years has continued up to the present day. Under President Nixon, the United States entered into 63 treaties and 846 executive agreements in the four years from 1969 to 1973. According to the State Department in 1975, 97% of the executive agreements concluded since World War II had been effected through statutory authority of some kind, although that number may not include all informal day-to-day operating agreements and classified agreements.[3]

This great increase in the use of executive agreements has been very worrisome to those who criticize unchecked Executive Branch power, particularly in light of Supreme Court decisions (discussed in subsection C infra) that held executive agreements, as federal law, prevailed over inconsistent state law by reason of the Supremacy Clause. We will first consider two contrasting viewpoints on the executive-agreement question and then consider attempts in Congress to restrict the use of executive agreements. You should note that the first extract was undoubtedly influenced by the failure of the U.S. Senate to advise and consent to U.S. membership in the League of Nations following World War I. Query: To what extent do the authors' arguments relate to particular kinds of executive agreements (e.g., presidential executive agreements) as opposed to executive agreements in general?

3. Hearings on S. 632 and S. 1251 Before the Subcomm. on Separation of Powers of the   Senate Comm. on the Judiciary, 94th Cong., 1st Sess. 467 (1975).

MYRES S. McDOUGAL AND ASHER LANS, TREATIES AND CONGRESSIONAL–EXECUTIVE OR PRESIDENTIAL AGREEMENTS: INTERCHANGEABLE INSTRUMENTS OF NATIONAL POLICY

(1945)[4]

* * * The wise statesmen who drafted the Constitution of the United States not only gave the President a *permissive* power, "with the advice and consent of the Senate," "to make treaties, provided two-thirds of the Senators present concur," but they also gave both to the President and to the whole Congress broad powers of control over the external relations of the Government which are meaningless if they do not include the instrumental powers, first, to authorize the making of intergovernmental agreements and, secondly, to make these agreements the law of the land. Throughout our national history, these broad grants to the President and the Congress have, furthermore, been in fact interpreted, by all branches of the Government, in hundreds of instances, to include such instrumental powers. The result is that our constitutional law today makes available two parallel and completely interchangeable procedures, wholly applicable to the same subject matters and of identical domestic and international legal consequences, for the consummation of intergovernmental agreements. In addition to the treaty-making procedure, which may—as the nation has found from bitter experience—be subjected to minority control, there is what may be called an "agreement-making procedure," which may operate either under the combined powers of the Congress and the President or in some instances under the powers of the President alone. The practices of successive administrations, supported by the Congress and by numerous court decisions, have for all practical purposes made the Congressional-Executive agreement authorized or sanctioned by both houses of Congress interchangeable with the agreements ratified under the treaty clause by two-thirds of the Senate. The same decisive authorities have likewise made agreements negotiated by the President, on his own responsibility and within the scope of his own constitutional powers, appropriate instruments for handling many important aspects of our foreign relations. Initial choice of the procedure to be followed for securing validation of any particular intergovernmental agreement lies with the President since it is constitutional practice unquestioned since Washington's day that the President alone has the power to propose or dispose in the actual conduct of negotiations with other governments. When a specific agreement is submitted to the Congress for approval or implementation, the Congress may of course question the procedure by which the President seeks validation of the agreement, but if the Congress is to act rationally—that is, appropriately to secure the best long-term interests of the whole nation—it should shape its action in terms of the policy issues involved in the specific agreement and not in terms of some misleading and unhistorical notion that the treaty-making procedure is the exclusive mode of making important international agreements under our Constitution.

4. 54 Yale L.J. 181, 534 (1945), at 187–89. Reprinted by permission of the Yale Law Journal Company, Inc. and Fred B. Rothman & Company.

This suggestion that the Constitution of the United States affords interchangeable procedures for effecting international agreements meets, it must be admitted, with a resistance that is difficult to understand in view of the historical record and of this nation's traditional preference for democracy. Some resistance comes from those who genuinely favor democratic, majority control of our foreign affairs but who, confused about a supposed exclusiveness of the treaty-making clause, think that a constitutional amendment is the only way out. The chief resistance comes, however, from those who explicitly favor minority control of foreign affairs because they fear what majority control may be able to achieve in an integrated, responsible foreign policy. Sometimes the dominant theme of resistance is mere defense of Senatorial prerogative, upon an assumption often none too unconscious that the safety of the nation and the sanctity of the Constitution would be imperiled if one-third of the Senate could not dictate the nation's foreign policy. At other times the theme is, more bluntly, that there are special minority interests in the country that must be given a delusive protection however much the interests of the whole nation, including the long-term interests of all its minorities, may suffer.

RAOUL BERGER, THE PRESIDENTIAL MONOPOLY OF FOREIGN RELATIONS

(1972) [5]

II. Executive Agreements

A. *Evolution*

Executive agreements are not mentioned in the Constitution, in the Constitutional Convention, or in the Ratification Conventions; indeed the term is of comparatively recent vintage. Starting from a trickle, executive agreements made by the President alone—which can involve large financial, and possibly military commitments—have, since 1930, mounted to a flood. Many of these agreements the State Department refuses to reveal even to the Senate, the constitutional participant in the making of international agreements. Even apologists for executive agreements agree that secret agreements are undesirable and that they should be subject to debate and the "salutary influence of public opinion."

* * *

Article II, section 2, of the Constitution provides that the President "shall have power, by and with the Advice and Consent of the Senate, to make Treaties. * * * " At the adoption of the Constitution, the word "treaties" had a broad connotation; * * * Hamilton construed "treaty" in the broadest terms:

> [F]rom the *best opportunity of knowing the fact,* I aver, that it was understood by *all* to be the intent of the provision to give that power the most ample latitude—to render it competent to all the stipulations which the exigencies of national affairs might require; competent to the making of

5. 71 Mich.L.Rev. 1, 33–37 (1972). Reprinted by permission of the Michigan Law Review Association.

treaties of alliance, treaties of commerce, treaties of peace and every other species of convention usual among nations * * *. And it was emphatically for this reason that it was so carefully guarded; the cooperation of two-thirds of the Senate, with the President, being required to make any treaty whatever.

Those indefatigable advocates of executive agreements, McDougal and Lans, state that "there are no significant criteria, under the Constitution * * * or in the diplomatic practice of this government, by which the *genus* 'treaty' can be distinguished from the *genus* 'executive agreement' other than the single criterion of the procedure or authority by which the United States' consent to ratification [by the Senate] is obtained." It follows that the express provision for treaty-making by the Senate and President jointly—which embraces "all the stipulations which * * * national affairs might require * * * and every other species of convention"—covers the field, and therefore, as Justice Jackson stated in the *Youngstown* case, the presidential claim to power is "clearly eliminated." On the historical facts, the question, in the words of Professor Philip Kurland, is, "Should the Constitution really be read to mean that by calling an agreement an executive agreement rather than a treaty, the obligation to secure Senate approval is dissolved?"

* * * However impenetrable the intention of the Framers may be in other respects, they made clear beyond doubt that the specific objective of the treaty clause was to preclude the President, acting alone, from entering into international agreements.

Note: The Bricker Amendment and Similar Proposals: Congressional Control of Executive Agreements

During the 1950's a series of proposals for constitutional amendment, many sponsored principally by Senator John Bricker of Ohio, were made to place limits on international agreements and their domestic legal effect. Some of these failed by only one vote to get the necessary two-thirds Senate vote. The main themes of Bricker's proposals were to require congressional approval of all international agreements and to require Congress to adopt legislation before an international agreement could have legal effects in the United States.

Although the Bricker Amendment failed, the concerns behind it have, if anything, become more prominent in the light of worries about presidential power during the Vietnam War and the "Watergate" crisis of the Presidency. In 1972, Congress enacted the "Case-Zablocki Act," which included the following:

The Secretary of State shall transmit to the Congress the text of any international agreement, * * * other than a treaty, to which the United States is a party, as soon as practicable after such agreement has entered into force with respect to the United States but in no event later than sixty days thereafter. However, any such agreement the immediate public disclosure of which would, in the opinion of the President, be prejudicial to the national security of the United States shall not be so transmitted to the Congress but shall be transmitted to the Committee on Foreign Relations of the Senate and the Committee on International Relations of the House of Representatives under an appropriate injunction of secrecy to be removed only upon due notice from the President. 1 U.S.C. § 112b (1982).

The State Department has adopted specific guidelines on the use of treaties and executive agreements. It revised them in 1974, in part to meet congressional concerns.

CIRCULAR NO. 175

U.S. DEPT. OF STATE, FOREIGN AFFAIRS MANUAL
(1985)

§ 720.2 General Objectives

The objectives [of these procedures] are:

a. That the making of treaties and other international agreements for the United States is carried out within constitutional and other appropriate limits;

*   *   *

c. That timely and appropriate consultation is had with congressional leaders and committees on treaties and other international agreements;

*   *   *

§ 721.3 *Considerations for Selecting Among Constitutionally Authorized Procedures*

In determining a question as to the procedure which should be followed for any particular international agreement, due consideration is given to the following factors along with [constitutional requirements]:

a. The extent to which the agreement involves commitments or risks affecting the nation as a whole;

b. Whether the agreement is intended to affect State laws;

c. Whether the agreement can be given effect without the enactment of subsequent legislation by the Congress;

d. Past U.S. practice with respect to similar agreements;

e. The preference of the Congress with respect to a particular type of agreement;

f. The degree of formality desired for an agreement;

g. The proposed duration of the agreement, the need for prompt conclusion of an agreement, and the desirability of concluding a routine or short-term agreement; and

h. The general international practice with respect to similar agreements.

In determining whether any international agreement should be brought into force as a treaty or as an international agreement other than a treaty, the utmost care is to be exercised to avoid any invasion or compromise of the constitutional powers of the Senate, the Congress as a whole, or the President.

§ 721.4 *Questions as to Type of Agreement to Be Used; Consultation With Congress*

*   *   *

c. Consultations on such questions will be held with congressional leaders and committees as may be appropriate.

*   *   *

In recent years there have been numerous proposals that would go further than the Case-Zablocki Act. Three such bills were the subject of 1975 hearings held by the Subcommittee on Separation of Powers of the Judiciary Committee of the United States Senate (94th Congress, 1st Session). These three bills all provided that an executive agreement must lie before Congress for a sixty day period, during which Congress or the Senate could adopt a resolution of disapproval which would prevent the agreement from coming into force.[6]

Notes and Questions

Like two gladiators in a constitutional arena, Congress and the President are currently circling each other and probing to try to define what will be the appropriate relationship between them. Exactly what the division of power will ultimately be, or should be, is difficult to say at the moment. Consider some of the following problems.

(1) GATT (the General Agreement on Tariffs and Trade) is an executive agreement which was accepted for the United States in 1947 under the then existing Trade Agreements Act authority, which read:[7]

Sec. 350. (a) For the purpose of expanding foreign markets for the products of the United States (as a means of assisting in the present emergency in restoring the American standard of living, in overcoming domestic unemployment and the present economic depression, in increasing the purchasing power of the American public, and in establishing and maintaining a better relationship among various branches of American agriculture, industry, mining, and commerce) by regulating the admission of foreign goods into the United States in accordance with the characteristics and needs of various branches of American production so that foreign markets will be made available to those branches of American production which require and are capable of developing such outlets by affording corresponding market opportunities for foreign products in the United States, the President, whenever he finds as a fact that any existing duties or other import restrictions of the United States or any foreign country are unduly burdening and restricting the foreign trade of the United States and that the purpose above declared will be promoted by that means hereinafter specified, is authorized from time to time—

(1) To enter into foreign trade agreements with foreign governments or instrumentalities thereof; and

(2) To proclaim such modifications of existing duties and other import restrictions, or such additional import restrictions, or such continuance, and for such minimum periods, of existing customs or excise treatment of any article covered by foreign trade agreements, as are required or appropriate to carry out any foreign trade agreement that the President has entered into hereunder.

Arguments have been made for decades that the acceptance of GATT went beyond the scope of statutory or other authority of the President. One of the

---

6. See Hearings, note 3 supra.

7. Reciprocal Trade Agreements Act, 59 Stat. 410 (1945); comparable to Trade Expan-sion Act of 1962, § 201, 19 U.S.C.A. § 1821 and Trade Act of 1974, § 101, 19 U.S.C.A. § 2101.

authors has argued in another publication [8] that there existed ample legislative history and precedent to support the view that GATT was authorized by the statute quoted. But consider the following GATT clauses in that regard.[9] Did any exceed the scope of presidential authority?

(a) Clause obligating countries to treat imports as they treat domestically produced goods (national treatment; Article III).

(b) Clause establishing a voting procedure with a waiver authority (Article XXV).

(c) Part IV of GATT, added in 1965 and effective for the United States on June 27, 1966, relating to special treatment favoring developing countries, but generally phrased in terms of "desirable" action rather than obligation (See Articles XXXVI, XXXVII and XXXVIII).[10]

(2) The 1967 "Anti-Dumping Code," was accepted by the President without explicit statutory authority, on the argument that it required changes only in administrative practices of the Executive Branch, which were within the delegated authority of that Branch. Is this an appropriate use of executive agreements? Does it matter whether the agreement requires changes in long established administrative practices, although the changes would not be inconsistent with any statute? [11]

(3) Examine section 102 of the Trade Act of 1974. Does this section add to or detract from the President's authority to complete executive agreements on trade and economic matters if he acts *not* under the authority of that statute?

(4) In October, 1975, the United States entered into an agreement with the Soviet Union concerning shipments of grain from the United States. The terms of this agreement included a commitment by the United States not to impose export controls on grain sales to the U.S.S.R., and agreement that the U.S.S.R. would purchase six million metric tons each year for five years, but that if purchases would exceed eight million metric tons, "official consultation would occur." This agreement was completed as an executive agreement, without congressional action. The validity of this process was challenged by the National Farmers' Organization, which threatened to sue in the courts of law, to establish the lack of validity of the agreement. In your view, did the President or the Executive Branch have authority to enter into the grain agreement? [12]

(5) The Organization for Economic Cooperation and Development (see Section 5.3(B) infra for brief description) is governed by a 1960 convention to which

---

8. Jackson, The General Agreement on Tariffs and Trade in United States Domestic Law, 66 Mich.L.Rev. 249 (1967).

9. See Chapter 5, infra for more details on GATT.

10. Part IV of GATT has never been "proclaimed" by the President. Consequently, it is probably not domestic law since GATT is generally not self-executing; see Jackson, note 8 supra, at 289.

11. Members of Congress have complained about Executive Branch changes in long established administrative practices, particularly when done to fulfill an executive agreement not approved by Congress. Under the Trade

Act of 1974, a special new procedure has been set up for the approval of nontariff barrier agreements, and in commenting on that procedure, the congressional reports make it abundantly clear that when such agreements change an established administrative practice (or regulation), they should be submitted for congressional approval. See, e.g., Senate Comm. on Finance, Trade Reform Act of 1974, S.Rep. No. 93–1298, 93d Cong., 2d Sess. 75 (1974).

12. See BNA International Trade Reporter's U.S. Export Weekly (ITEX), No. 78, Oct. 21, 1975, at A–14; and No. 79, Oct. 28, 1975, at A–2.

the United States is obligated as a treaty. The convention includes the following articles:

Article 2

In the pursuit of these aims, the Members agree that they will, both individually and jointly:

(a) promote the efficient use of their economic resources;

(b) in the scientific and technological field, promote the development of their resources, encourage research and promote vocational training;

(c) pursue policies designed to achieve economic growth and internal and external financial stability and to avoid developments which might endanger their economies or those of other countries;

(d) pursue their efforts to reduce or abolish obstacles to the exchange of goods and services and current payments and maintain and extend the liberalisation of capital movements; and

(e) contribute to the economic development of both Member and non-member countries in the process of economic development by appropriate means and, in particular, by the flow of capital to those countries, having regard to the importance to their economies of receiving technical assistance and of securing expanding export markets.

* * *

Article 5

In order to achieve its aims, the Organisation may:

(a) take decisions which, except as otherwise provided, shall be binding on all the Members;

(b) make recommendations to Members; and

(c) enter into agreement with Members, non-member States and international organisations.

Article 6

1. Unless the Organisation otherwise agrees unanimously for special cases, decisions shall be taken and recommendations shall be made by mutual agreement of all the Members.

2. Each Member shall have one vote. If a Member abstains from voting on a decision or recommendation, such abstention shall not invalidate the decision or recommendation, which shall be applicable to the other Members but not to the abstaining Member.

3. No decision shall be binding on any Member until it has complied with the requirements of its own constitutional procedures. The other Members may agree that such a decision shall apply provisionally to them.

A memorandum by the then Legal Adviser of the United States Department of State, Abram Chayes, is included in the record of the Senate debates, and one paragraph states:

The argument has been intimated that since the Organization under article 5 is authorized to take decisions and since the executive branch will be representing the United States in the Organization, the convention will operate to give the Executive power to agree on decisions in the substantive fields covered by articles 1 and 2. This argument is based on the erroneous assumption that the convention in any way concerns itself with the distribution of powers within the United States or any other member state. Properly viewed, articles 1 and 2 merely set forth a general agreement between the member nations on broad lines of public policy and define the area of concern of the Organization. Under article 5 the Organization may take decisions, but the convention is silent as to the process by which a member nation, within its own internal system, arrives at the point where it may cast an effective vote in favor of a particular decision. Articles 1 and 2 are void of any grant of power to the Executive. Thus, the power of the United States to cast a favorable vote and bind the United States in any particular case must be sought in a source outside the convention.

In addition, a statement for the record includes the following: [13]

Thus, if a decision were proposed to the Council for the establishment of a committee of representatives of member governments to study the promotion of tourism, the executive branch would consider it had power to agree to such a decision. Similarly, if a decision were proposed to the Council for the establishment of a fund for the period of a year, contributed to by all members, to encourage tourism in member countries, the U.S. executive would consider it had power to agree to such a decision, if the U.S. Congress had authorized and appropriated funds for the promotion of tourism to the United States. If no such congressional authorization and appropriation existed, the executive branch through its representative would either veto the decision, or abstain (thus permitting the decision to become binding as to other member countries) or approve, subject to compliance with U.S. constitutional procedures. In this last event, appropriate U.S. congressional action would have to be taken before the decision could be binding on the United States. Similarly, a decision might be proposed to the Council involving an international agreement of a type which would require Senate advice and consent under U.S. treaty procedure. In this case, again the U.S. representative could veto, abstain, or approve subject to compliance with U.S. constitutional procedures. In this last event, Senate advice and consent would need to be given before the decision could be binding on the United States. In conclusion, it is our view that paragraph 3 of article 6 allows for full compliance with U.S. constitutional procedures and the division of functions between the Executive and the Congress.

(C) DOMESTIC LEGAL EFFECT AND IMPLEMENTATION OF INTERNATIONAL AGREEMENTS IN U.S. LAW

The question of whether and to what extent an international agreement has domestic legal effects involves at least three subquestions that courts and officials do not always clearly distinguish. First, does the international agreement, or any part of it, have "direct applicability" or a "self-executing effect" in U.S. law, so that at least some litigants in U.S. courts are entitled to rely on its provisions, and courts must accept those provisions as applicable law?

13. 107 Cong.Rec. 4157 (1961).

Second, there is a separate question of "hierarchy of norms." If the international agreement is inconsistent with a prior or subsequent federal or state statute or constitutional provision, which prevails?

The third question is whether a particular party to litigation can rely on a provision of an international agreement. This question is closely related to the first discussed above, and often courts do not distinguish these two questions, but there can be a distinct difference between them. The third question concerns the "standing" of the party. Even if a provision of an international agreement is self-executing, is the particular party who claims the benefit of that provision a party entitled to make such a claim under the meaning of that provision?

(1) Self-Executing International Agreements

The question of whether a treaty has direct domestic law effect is, under United States law (in contrast to the law of a number of foreign nations), a question of whether the treaty is "self-executing" and purports directly by its own terms to give rights to individual citizens, rather than simply imposing the international legal obligation upon the national government to effectuate those rights. One classic case is Sei Fujii v. State of California, 38 Cal.2d 718, 242 P.2d 617 (1952), which held that certain provisions of the United Nations Charter were not self-executing. The California court said (242 P.2d at 620–22), "it must appear that the framers of the treaty intended to prescribe a rule that, standing alone, would be enforceable in the courts" and concluded that the United Nations Charter "pledges the various countries to cooperate" and "represents a moral commitment," but that the provisions at issue "were not intended to supersede existing domestic legislation, and we cannot hold that they operate to invalidate the alien land law [of California]."

If the provisions of an international agreement are not self-executing, and if implementation of the agreement requires some changes in domestic U.S. law (not always the case), then some additional action by government bodies will be necessary. This raises the question of authority to implement an agreement. A number of different forms of implementation are possible. Congress may enact a statute that will implement the agreement (e.g., many portions of the Trade Agreements Act of 1979, discussed in Section 3.4 below) or the President or other officials may have authority to implement the agreement by issuing or changing regulations (e.g., the implementation of the Tokyo Round Agreement on "Licensing", discussed in Section 6.4 below). Such authority may exist in previous enactments of Congress, or be granted in a new enactment (sometimes the same Act which authorizes entry into the agreement), or stem from the President's "inherent" powers.

Sometimes the question of "self-executing" is made a subject of understanding between the Executive Branch and the Senate during the treaty ratification process. For example, the 1962 International Coffee Agreement was ratified after Senate approval, but the Senate record notes understandings between the Senate and the Executive Branch (which were crucial for obtaining Senate approval) that the treaty would not be self-executing.[14]

14. 109 Cong.Rec. 9126 (1963).

Two years after ratification of the treaty in December, 1963, implementing legislation was finally enacted.[15]

Questions

How does a court determine when an international agreement is self-executing? What sort of language in the agreement itself does it look to? If the language of the agreement is ambiguous, what other sources will a court address? Intent of the draftsmen as expressed in the "preparatory work" for the agreement? Is the issue of any appropriate concern to the foreign parties, or is it solely a U.S. constitutional law question? If the latter, would U.S. courts look primarily or solely to the intentions expressed by the U.S. negotiators? Would that category be deemed to include Congressmen or Senators? Suppose the Senate, in its advice and consent, expressed its view that an international agreement was not self-executing as drafted, should that view prevail? Suppose it is clear from the record that the Senate advice to favor ratification was premised on the belief that the agreement was not self-executing, is that determinative? We will have occasion to consider in Chapter 5 the question of whether GATT is a self-executing agreement. See generally S. Riesenfeld, The Doctrine of Self-Executing Treaties and *U.S. v. Postal:* Win at Any Price?, 74 Am.J.Intl.L. 892 (1980).

(2) Hierarchy of Norms: Which Rules Take Precedence?

If faced with a conflict between state and federal law or between an international agreement and a statute, a court must try to reconcile the opposing provisions. In doing so, a court should normally try to construe a statute so it does not conflict with international law or an international agreement of the United States.[16] If it is unable to do so, then it must decide which is superior. In the United States, federal law prevails over state law (see Section 3.6 below). Federal statutes and international agreements are deemed to be of the same rank, and thus generally it is considered that the later in time will prevail, at least in the case of treaties.[17] The following materials consider (1) whether the Treaty-Making Power expands federal constitutional authority and (2) the position of executive agreements vis-à-vis state law.

THE TREATY POWER AND DOMESTIC LEGAL EFFECT

The reader probably recalls the United States Supreme Court case of Missouri v. Holland, 252 U.S. 416, 40 S.Ct. 382, 64 L.Ed. 641 (1920), which

15. International Coffee Agreement Act of 1965, Pub.L. No. 89–23, 79 Stat. 112 (codified at 19 U.S.C.A. § 1356a et seq.).

16. American Law Institute (ALI), Restatement of the Law (Second), Foreign Relations Law of the United States § 3(3) (1965) (Restatement); ALI, Restatement of the Law, Foreign Relations Law of the United States (Revised), Tentative Draft No. 6, § 134 (Vol. 1, April 12, 1985) (Tentative Revised Restatement).

17. Restatement, note 16 supra, § 141. There is some controversy on the question of

whether a subsequent noncongressionally authorized executive agreement overrides a prior congressional statute. See, e.g., the *Guy Capps* case discussed in Section 3.2 supra; Swearingen v. United States, 565 F.Supp. 1019 (D.Colo.1983); Tentative Revised Restatement, note 16 supra, § 135 and comments; Note, Superseding Statutory Law by Sole Executive Agreement: An Analysis of the American Law Institute's Shift in Position, 23 Va.J.Intl. L. 671 (1983).

held that a valid treaty (with Canada relating to migratory birds) must prevail over state law, even if a United States federal statute on the subject might be considered an unconstitutional interference with state power in the absence of a treaty. Justice Holmes said in this case: [18]

> * * * Acts of Congress are the supreme law of the land only when made in pursuance of the Constitution, while treaties are declared to be so when made under the authority of the United States. It is open to question whether the authority of the United States means more than the formal acts prescribed to make the convention. We do not mean to imply that there are no qualifications to the treaty-making power; but they must be ascertained in a different way. It is obvious that there may be matters of the sharpest exigency for the national well-being that an act of Congress could not deal with but that a treaty followed by such an act could, and it is not lightly to be assumed that, in matters requiring national action, "a power which must belong to and somewhere reside in every civilized government" is not to be found.

Subsequent cases suggest some limitations on the treaty-making power, such as constitutional civil liberties limitations (viz. Reid v. Covert, 354 U.S. 1, 77 S.Ct. 1222, 1 L.Ed.2d 1148 (1957), holding that United States civilian dependents of armed forces members overseas could not constitutionally be tried by a court martial, even though an executive agreement or treaty would so provide; see also Kinsella v. United States, ex rel. Singleton, 361 U.S. 234, 80 S.Ct. 297, 4 L.Ed.2d 268 (1960)).

The case of Power Authority of New York v. Federal Power Commission, 247 F.2d 538 (D.C.Cir.1957), considered a "reservation" attached by the Senate to the 1950 Treaty between the United States and Canada relating to uses of the waters of the Niagara River,[19] which purported to reserve the right to provide for development of the United States share of the waters of the Niagara River only pursuant to an Act of Congress which specifically authorized it. But for this "reservation," the Federal Power Commission would, under prior statute, have had authority to grant petitions for such water development. The Court (two to one) held that since the "reservation," "relates to a matter of *purely domestic* concern," it had no domestic law effect, being put forth by the Senate under the treaty power, without participation of the House of Representatives.

EXECUTIVE AGREEMENTS AND DOMESTIC LEGAL EFFECT

UNITED STATES v. BELMONT

Supreme Court of the United States, 1937.
301 U.S. 324, 57 S.Ct. 758, 81 L.Ed. 1134.

[President Roosevelt, pursuant to the so-called "Litvinov Assignments", agreed to grant diplomatic recognition to the Union of Soviet Socialist Republics in exchange for, inter alia, the assignment to the U.S. government of assets owned by a Russian corporation and located in the United States.

18.   252 U.S. at 433, 40 S.Ct. at 383.

19.   1 UST 694, TIAS No. 2130, 132 UNTS 223.

The corporation had been nationalized by the Soviet government. In a challenge to the title of the United States to the assets, the Court stated:]

We take judicial notice of the fact that coincident with the assignment set forth in the complaint, the President recognized the Soviet Government, and normal diplomatic relations were established between that government and the Government of the United States, followed by an exchange of ambassadors. The effect of this was to validate, so far as this country is concerned, all acts of the Soviet Government here involved from the commencement of its existence. The recognition, establishment of diplomatic relations, the assignment, and agreements with respect thereto, were all parts of one transaction, resulting in an international compact between the two governments. That the negotiations, acceptance of the assignment and agreements and understandings in respect thereof were within the competence of the President may not be doubted. Governmental power over internal affairs is distributed between the national government and the several states. Governmental power over external affairs is not distributed, but is vested exclusively in the national government. And in respect of what was done here, the Executive had authority to speak as the sole organ of that government. The assignment and the agreements in connection therewith did not, as in the case of treaties, as that term is used in the treaty making clause of the Constitution (Art. II, § 2), require the advice and consent of the Senate.

A treaty signifies "a compact made between two or more independent nations with a view to the public welfare." B. Altman & Co. v. United States, 224 U.S. 583, 600, 32 S.Ct. 593, 596, 56 L.Ed. 894. But an international compact, as this was, is not always a treaty which requires the participation of the Senate. There are many such compacts, of which a protocol, a modus vivendi, a postal convention, and agreements like that now under consideration are illustrations. See 5 Moore, Int.Law Digest, 210–221. The distinction was pointed out by this court in the *Altman* case, supra, which arose under § 3 of the Tariff Act of 1897, authorizing the President to conclude commercial agreements with foreign countries in certain specified matters. We held that although this might not be a treaty requiring ratification by the Senate, it was a compact negotiated and proclaimed under the authority of the President, and as such was a "treaty" within the meaning of the Circuit Court of Appeals Act, the construction of which might be reviewed upon direct appeal to this court.

Plainly, the external powers of the United States are to be exercised without regard to state laws or policies. The supremacy of a treaty in this respect has been recognized from the beginning. Mr. Madison, in the Virginia Convention, said that if a treaty does not supersede existing state laws, as far as they contravene its operation, the treaty would be ineffective. "To counteract it by the supremacy of the state laws, would bring on the Union the just charge of national perfidy, and involve us in war." 3 Elliot's Debates 515. And see Ware v. Hylton, 3 Dall. 199, 236–237. And while this rule in respect of treaties is established by the express language of cl. 2, Art. VI, of the Constitution, the same rule would result in the case of all international compacts and agreements from the very fact that complete power over international affairs is in the national government and is not and cannot be subject to any curtailment or interference on the part of the several states. Compare United States v. Curtiss-Wright Export Corp., 299 U.S. 304, 316, et seq., 57 S.Ct. 216, 219, 81 L.Ed. 255. In respect of all international negotiations and compacts, and in respect of our foreign relations generally, state lines disappear. As to such purposes the State of New York does not exist. Within the field of its powers, whatever the United States rightfully undertakes, it necessarily has warrant to consummate. And when judicial authority is invoked in aid of such consummation, state constitutions, state laws, and state policies are irrelevant to the inquiry and decision. It is inconceivable that any of them can be interposed as an obstacle to the effective operation of a federal constitutional power. Cf. Missouri v. Holland, 252 U.S. 416, 40 S.Ct. 382, 64 L.Ed. 641, 11 A.L.R. 984; Asakura v. Seattle, 265 U.S. 332, 341, 44 S.Ct. 515, 516, 68 L.Ed. 1041.

Note

Even though an international agreement is not directly applicable or self-executing in domestic law, it can still be very relevant to that law. As noted earlier, when domestic law and an international agreement or a rule of customary law relate to the same subject, the courts and the Executive Branch "will endeavor to construe them so as to give effect to both, if that can be done without violating either." [20]

In addition, if a statute or regulation was formulated with the intention of implementing an international agreement, the courts have even more reason to conclude that the legislative intention was to conform to and carry out the international agreement.

(3) An Individual's Right to Invoke International Agreements; Standing

Even if an international agreement is self-executing, it remains to determine if a particular individual is entitled to invoke the agreement's provisions.[21] In other words, does that individual have "standing"? For example, an international agreement may be self-executing in that federal government officials have authority to implement its provisions in their daily official tasks (e.g. apply a particular tariff to Company A, or restrain the exports of Company B). On the other hand, a particular challenger (e.g. Company X) may not be sufficiently affected by the provision for the courts to grant it the right to invoke it.

A case that touches on these subjects is DIGGS v. RICHARDSON, 555 F.2d 848 (D.C.Cir.1976). The case concerned a United Nations Security Council resolution calling upon U.N. members to have no dealings with South Africa that impliedly recognized the legality of its continued occupation of Namibia. Plaintiffs alleged that the resolution was self-executing and that U.S. government officials had violated its terms by discussing the harvest of fur seals in Namibia with South African officials. They asked for

---

20. Tentative Revised Restatement, note 16 supra, at 79.

21. See L. Henkin, R. Pugh, O. Schachter & H. Smith, International Law: Cases and Materials 161 (1980).

an injunction against further contacts between those officials. The U.S. government argued that Security Council resolutions are not legally binding on U.N. members, that the resolution at issue was not self-executing, that the plaintiffs lacked standing and that the case concerned a political question not appropriate for judicial resolution.

The Court of Appeals affirmed the dismissal of the case by the lower court (555 F.2d at 851):

> on the ground, related to the issue of standing, but analytically distinct, that even assuming there is an international obligation that is binding on the United States—a point we do not in any way reach on the merits—the U.N. resolution underlying that obligation does not confer rights on the citizens of the United States that are enforceable in court in the absence of implementing legislation.
>
> *   *   *
>
> In determining whether a treaty is self-executing courts look to the intent of the signatory parties as manifested by the language of the instrument, and if the instrument is uncertain, recourse must be had to the circumstances surrounding its execution. *   *   *
>
> Applying this kind of analysis to the particular Security Council Resolution on which plaintiffs rely, we find that the provisions here in issue were not addressed to the judicial branch of our government. They do not by their terms confer rights upon individual citizens; they call upon governments to take certain action. The provisions deal with the conduct of our foreign relations, an area traditionally left to executive discretion. See, e.g., C. & S. Air Lines v. Waterman Corp., 333 U.S. 103, 111, 68 S.Ct. 431, 92 L.Ed. 568 (1948).

See also Tel-Oren v. Libyan Arab Republic, 726 F.2d 774, 808–10 (D.C.Cir. 1984) (Bork, J., concurring), cert. denied, ___ U.S. ___, 105 S.Ct. 1354, 84 L.Ed.2d 377 (1985).

SECTION 3.4   PRESIDENTIAL AUTHORITY AND TRADE LEGISLATION IN THE UNITED STATES

(A)   INTRODUCTION

Although the President of the United States has only limited constitutional powers regarding the conduct of international economic relations, over the years Congress has delegated vast authorities to the President. These delegations, embodied in numerous statutes enacted over decades, often are so general or ambiguous as to give the President considerable freedom to act. In this section we will survey these delegated authorities and examine how they have been interpreted by the courts. We will also note recent congressional attempts to withdraw some of the more sweeping powers.

This section is divided into five substantive subsections. Subsection B will discuss generally the delegated powers of the President and how they have been interpreted by the courts. Subsections C through E will briefly survey the history and substantive provisions of the "core" international trade legislation of the United States. Subsection F will then survey the U.S. government agencies that conduct international economic relations.

(B) THE PRESIDENT AND DELEGATED INTERNATIONAL ECONOMIC POWERS

The President has been delegated a considerable amount of "emergency" power over international economic affairs. Congress has struggled to find the appropriate line between giving the President too much discretion and yet giving him enough authority so he can be effective when necessary. We look first at some of these delegations, and then turn to powers contained in non-emergency trade legislation. Finally in this subsection we examine how the courts have reacted to these delegations.

(1) The President's Emergency Powers

The extent of the President's power, particularly in so-called "emergencies," has been a source of concern to Congress. In a November, 1973 report, a Special Senate Committee on the Termination of the National Emergency published a list and the texts of emergency powers statutes, filling a volume of almost 600 pages! That report said: [1]

> Since March 9, 1933, the United States has been in a state of declared national emergency. In fact, there are now in effect four presidentially proclaimed states of national emergency: In addition to the national emergency declared by President Roosevelt in 1933, there are also the national emergency proclaimed by President Truman on December 16, 1950, during the Korean conflict, and the states of national emergency declared by President Nixon on March 23, 1970, and August 15, 1971.

> These proclamations give force to 470 provisions of Federal law. These hundreds of statutes delegate to the President extraordinary powers, ordinarily exercised by the Congress, which affect the lives of American citizens in a host of all-encompassing manners. This vast range of powers, taken together, confer enough authority to rule the country without reference to normal constitutional processes.

> Under the powers delegated by these statutes, the President may: seize property; organize and control the means of production; seize commodities; assign military forces abroad; institute martial law; seize and control all transportation and communication; regulate the operation of private enterprise; restrict travel; and, in a plethora of particular ways, control the lives of all American citizens.

In 1976, Congress adopted the National Emergencies Act that provided for the termination of most of the President's emergency powers after a period of two years.[2] Exempted from these termination provisions was the Trading With the Enemy Act (TWEA), originally enacted in 1917.[3] This Act has been used in recent years to regulate economic relations between the

---

1. S.Rep. No. 93–549, 93d Cong., 1st Sess., Forward (1973). See also S.Rep. No. 94–922, 94th Cong., 2d Sess. (1976).

2. Pub.L. No. 94–412, 90 Stat. 1255 (codified at 50 U.S.C.A. § 1601 et seq.). The Act contained legislative veto provisions that are probably unconstitutional in light of the *Chadha* decision discussed in Section 3.2(C) supra.

3. 50 U.S.C.A.App. § 1 et seq. Provisions of the act are quoted in the *Yoshida* case, discussed later in this subsection.

United States and a number of countries considered to be unfriendly, such as Cuba, North Korea and Vietnam. It was also used from 1968 to 1974 to regulate foreign direct investment by U.S. citizens. In 1977, Congress adopted the International Emergency Economic Powers Act (IEEPA),[4] which is set out in the Documentary Supplement. IEEPA restricted use of TWEA to time of war, and thus IEEPA is now the principal peacetime source of presidential emergency authority in international economic affairs.

IEEPA authorizes the President, if he declares a national emergency, inter alia, to regulate (a) foreign exchange transactions, (b) transfers or payments involving interests of a foreign country or national, and (c) property in which a foreign country or national has any interest, in order to deal with an unusual or extraordinary external threat to the national security, foreign policy or economy of the United States.[5] IEEPA has served as a basis for controlling Iranian assets in the United States and implementing the Iran-U.S. hostage accord (see the discussion of the *Dames & Moore* case in Section 3.2(B) supra), controlling trade between the United States and Nicaragua[6] and imposing limited economic sanctions on South Africa,[7] as well as continuing export controls in effect on expiration of the Export Administration Act.[8] The President is required to consult with Congress "in every possible instance" before exercising any powers under IEEPA and to report regularly to Congress on actions taken.[9]

The frustration of Congress in trying appropriately to limit the President's discretion and yet give him the scope he needs is poignantly illustrated by the following extracts from a statement of Congressman Don Bonker (Democrat from the State of Washington, member of the House Foreign Affairs Committee and chairman of its sub-committee on International Economic Policy and Trade). This statement was made on July 18, 1985, at a conference concerning the newly adopted renewal of the Export Administration Act (see Chapter 12 infra).[10]

> Before I get into the national security section of the new law, I want to talk about the foreign policy section for just a moment. I have with me a copy of the committee report for the supplemental appropriations bill that we took up recently. The first page of the report says that the American agricultural community is near bankruptcy because of past foreign policy

4. Pub.L. No. 95–223, title II, 91 Stat. 1626 (codified at 50 U.S.C.A. § 1701 et seq.). Congress permitted certain actions taken under TWEA—such as the regulations dealing with Cuba—to be renewed from time to time by the President. 50 U.S.C.A. § 1706(a)(2). The so-called grandfather powers under the TWEA were interpreted by the U.S. Supreme Court in Regan v. Wald, 468 U.S. 222, 104 S.Ct. 3026, 82 L.Ed.2d 171 (1984) (upholding President's right to revise regulations under grandfather powers). On IEEPA generally, see Marks & Grabow, The President's Foreign Economic Powers after Dames & Moore v. Regan: Legislation by Acquiesence, 68 Cornell L.Rev. 68 (1982); Note, The International Emergency Economic Powers Act: A Congressional Attempt to Control Presidential Emergency Power, 96 Harv.L.Rev. 1102 (1982).

5. 50 U.S.C.A. §§ 1701, 1702(a)(1).

6. Executive Order No. 12573 of May 1, 1985, 50 Fed.Reg. 18629. See Chapter 13 infra.

7. Executive Order No. 12532 of Sept. 10, 1985, 50 Fed.Reg. 36861 (1985). See Chapter 13 infra.

8. See Section 12.3 infra.

9. 50 U.S.C.A. § 1703.

10. Remarks before July 18, 1985 conference on the Export Administration Amendments Act of 1985, reported in 4 Intl.Bus.Rev. (Aug.1985), at 3. See Section 13.3 infra.

controls. It went through and listed at least four different executive branch actions that called for either trade embargoes or termination of contracts on agricultural exports. It then listed recent statements by the Administration that it will never again consider embargoes on agricultural products, in full recognition that they do not work and that they harm American farmers. At the same time that this page in the committee report was being printed, the President was imposing a new trade embargo on Nicaragua. Where was the authority? The EAA had expired.

The President found the authority in the International Emergency Economic Powers Act (IEEPA). So when the State Department appeared before the committee I asked, "If the EAA had been alive and well, and if we had no contract sanctity provision, which would you have chosen, IEEPA or the EAA to impose that embargo?" The official response was IEEPA. All of the work that we have put into contract sanctity to protect American businessmen with long-term commitments in the world community goes out the window because the President at any time, through a mere whim, can invoke IEEPA.

(2) The President's Specific Delegated Powers

In addition to the "emergency" authority discussed above, there is a plethora of statutes that authorize regulation by the President of international economic relations. The principal statutes dealing with trade matters include the series of trade agreements acts (discussed in Sections 3.4(C)–3.4(E) below) and the following provisions:

The Escape Clause, which provides that when increasing imports are the substantial cause of serious injury to competing U.S. industry, the President can proclaim certain limitations regarding those imports for a period generally not to exceed five years.[11]

Antidumping Legislation, which allows added duties to be imposed, inter alia, if imports into the United States are priced at a level that is below the price at which those goods are sold in the home market of the producer.[12]

Countervailing Duty Legislation, which allows added duties to be imposed to offset any subsidies which the imported goods enjoy.[13]

Section 301 Complaints Procedure Legislation, which allows for complaints to be made to the U.S. government about foreign government practices violating trade agreements or otherwise adversely affecting U.S. commerce and authorizes the President to take retalitory measures if he finds the complaint to be meritorious and the foreign government unwilling to change its practices.[14]

11. Trade Act of 1974, §§ 201–203; 19 U.S. C.A. §§ 2251–2253. See Chapter 9 infra. A similar statute, applicable to goods from non-market economies, is contained in Section 406 of the Trade Act of 1974. 19 U.S.C.A. § 2436.

12. Trade Agreements Act of 1979, § 101; 19 U.S.C.A. §§ 1673–1673i. See Section 10.2 infra.

13. Trade Agreements Act of 1979, § 101; 19 U.S.C.A. §§ 1671–1671f. See also 19 U.S.C.A. § 1303. Both provisions are discussed in Section 10.3 infra.

14. Trade Act of 1974, §§ 301–306; 19 U.S. C.A. §§ 2411–2416. See Section 10.4 infra.

Unfair Trade Practices Legislation, which authorizes complaints to be made to the International Trade Commission (ITC) that imports are involved in such unfair trade practices as patent or copyright infringement, monopolization, etc. and authorizes the ITC to ban all imports of those goods, subject to a presidential override. (This is often simply called the Section 337 procedure.)[15]

Textile and Agricultural Products Import Legislation, under which the President is authorized to restrain imports of textiles and a number of agricultural products.[16]

The National Security Exception, under which imports harming an American industry may be restricted to the extent that they endanger national security.[17]

Meat Import Legislation, under which imports of meat may be restrained based on projections of domestic supply and demand.[18]

The Generalized System of Preferences, under which the President can authorize duty-free imports of many goods from most developing countries.[19]

The Export Administration Act, under which the President has broad authority to control exports for national security, political and scarcity reasons.[20]

There are many other statutes that also authorize the President to act in respect of international economic relations,[21] including legislation concerning: international monetary and investment matters, certain specific bilateral relations (e.g. U.S.–Canada automotive products, U.S.–Israel Free Trade Area, the so-called "Carribbean Basin Initiative"), the Export-Import Bank, credit for export sales of agricultural commodities, stockpiling strategic materials, provision of aid and assistance to developing countries, appropriations and structure of U.S. government agencies, etc.

(3) *Judicial Control of Delegated Authorities*

The courts have generally treated the President kindly when interpreting his statutory powers. Since 1945, the U.S. Supreme Court has never found the President to have exceeded his powers in the area of international

---

15. Tariff Act of 1930, § 337; 19 U.S.C.A. § 1337. See Section 10.5 infra.

16. Agricultural Adjustment Act of 1933, § 22; 7 U.S.C.A. § 624; Agricultural Act of 1956, § 204; 7 U.S.C.A. § 1854.

17. Trade Expansion Act of 1962, § 232, as amended, Trade Act of 1974, § 127; 19 U.S.C.A. §§ 1862–63.

18. Meat Import Act of 1979, § 1; 19 U.S.C.A. Note to § 1202.

19. Trade Act of 1974, title V; 19 U.S.C.A. §§ 2461–65.

20. 50 U.S.C.A.App. §§ 2401–2420. See Chapters 12 and 13 infra.

21. A convenient compendium of U.S. legislation relating to foreign affairs is "Legislation on Foreign Relations," published annually by the Senate Foreign Relations Committee and the House Foreign Affairs Committee. See, e.g., Legislation on Foreign Relations Through 1984, Sen.Print. No. 99–12, 99th Cong., 1st Sess. (1985). Volume II contains a section entitled "Foreign Economic Policy: Tariff and Trade Laws," in which the principal trade laws are set out. Volume III, which includes Treaties and Other Materials, is published from time to time and also contains a section on "Foreign Economic Policy: Tariff and Trade." Other categories of legislation of importance to international economic relations include "Foreign Assistance," "Agricultural Commodities," and "Financial Institutions." A recent check for all USC sections containing the words "international trade" or "international economic" resulted in 252 sections!

economic relations (but only a few cases of this type have been considered by the Supreme Court). The Executive Branch has not fared as well in the lower federal courts, but, as is discussed in Section 3.5(C) infra, that is usually because the contested action involved application by lower ranking government officials of specific statutory standards established by Congress in a detailed regulatory scheme such as the antidumping legislation, as opposed to the exercise by the President or his officers of a more discretionary power.[22]

Here we will examine how courts have interpreted the President's discretionary authority in general. In Section 3.5(C) infra, we will look more generally at judicial control of executive action and examine the expanded jurisdiction and some recent decisions by the specialized federal courts dealing with international economic relations.

The reader should note that the following five cases are considered in chronological order. Can a pattern be detected in these cases regarding court treatment of Presidential actions pursuant to statutory delegations? Are the courts becoming more or less willing to give expansive definitions of the President's powers? Given that the most recent cases considered are Supreme Court cases, what future trends are likely? The Vietnam War occurred principally from 1965 to 1975, and the Watergate scandal from 1973 to 1974. These events triggered considerable mistrust of the Presidency, which was reflected in congressional attitudes. (For example, the congressional actions on emergency powers, designed to restrain presidential use of them, came during these periods.) Do the cases seem to reflect any of these events?

In UNITED STATES v. SCHMIDT PRITCHARD & CO., 47 C.C.P.A. 152 (1959), cert. denied, 364 U.S. 919, 81 S.Ct. 283, 5 L.Ed.2d 259 (1960), an importer of bicycles challenged a duty increase on bicycles ordered by the President following a determination by the Tariff Commission, in an Escape Clause proceeding, that the U.S. bicycle industry had been seriously injured by imports. The first challenge was procedural. After an initial report by the Tariff Commission, the President asked for a supplemental report. Although the initial report was submitted within the statutorily required time period, the supplemental report was not. In reversing the Customs Court, which had upheld the challenge, the Court of Customs and Patent Appeals held that it was sufficient that the initial report was timely. It noted that Congress was fully aware of the President's practice of asking for supplemental reports and had indicated its approval, even though it had not revised the Escape Clause legislation to take their use into account. "[W]e think Congress must be deemed to have approved and, in effect, ratified this prior administrative interpretation and application." 47 C.C.P.A. at 158. The second challenge stemmed from the President's decision to increase the duties on bicycles by an amount different from that recommended by the Tariff Commission. In upholding the Custom Court's decision that this action was unlawful, the appeals court noted that the relevant statute

22. The major exceptions to this statement are the *Guy Capps* case, discussed in Section 3.2(B) supra, and the *Schmidt, Pritchard* case, discussed in this subsection.

provided "the President may make *such adjustments in rates of duty,* * * * as *are found and reported by the Commission* to be necessary to prevent or remedy serious injury." 47 C.C.P.A. at 159. It then concluded, "The powers of the President with respect to trade agreements are delegated to him by Congress under its Constitutional powers. It requires no elaborate argument to support the proposition that Congress in so delegating its powers may prescribe whatever procedures and limitations it sees fit." 47 C.C.P.A. at 162.

In AIMCEE WHOLESALE CORP. v. UNITED STATES, 468 F.2d 202 (C.C.P.A.1972), the Court of Customs and Patent Appeals affirmed a decision by the Customs Court upholding a duty increase on English bicycles ordered by the President in implementation of an agreement between the United States and various foreign countries pursuant to the "renegotiation" authority under GATT Article XXVIII. The court noted that the renegotiation was held in order to implement the duty increase voided in *Schmidt Pritchard*. The importer argued that the President had no authority to increase duties pursuant to a trade agreement, but only pursuant to the Escape Clause procedures, which required a Tariff Commission investigation. The court rejected this argument. It noted that the statute provided that the President was required to notify the Tariff Commission of his intention to enter into a foreign trade agreement, that the Tariff Commission was required to make a report within six months thereafter and that the President could not act until he had received the Commission's report or six months had elapsed. The court concluded (468 F.2d at 205–06):

> There is nothing in the wording of the statute which would indicate that the commencement or the completion of an escape-clause investigation is necessary before the President can negotiate an agreement under section 350 of the 1930 Act. The legislative history of the 1958 amendments to section 3(b) of the Act indicates that the President may still negotiate duty increases *even though* an escape-clause investigation has been started. Moreover, as pointed out by appellee, although the Trade Agreements Extension Act of 1958 changed the time period in the above-quoted provision from 120 days to six months, it did nothing about the fact that the President could negotiate an agreement after the expiration of that period even if he never received the Commission's report. Thus the statute authorizes negotiations at a time when the Commission may not yet have determined that a duty increase was called for. In sum, appellants' argument that commencement of an escape-clause investigation was a prerequisite to negotiation is without merit.

> Appellants also contend that Proclamation 3394 is invalid because of the failure to declare the finding of fact required by section 350(a):

> > * * * the President, whenever he finds as a fact that any existing duties or other import restrictions * * * are unduly burdening and restricting the foreign trade of the United States and that the purpose above declared will be promoted by the means hereinafter specified, is authorized * * *

The Customs Court pointed out that there is no requirement that the President *recite* that he made the finding. The court [correctly] considered that it may be presumed in this case that the President made the requisite finding of fact and properly exercised his authority under section 350.

Question

The following "bootstrap powers" question can be considered (although it is not squarely addressed in *Aimcee*): Under authority which is limited in time can the President enter into an international executive agreement which contains in itself a clause allowing that agreement to be modified under certain conditions, even though such modifications might occur at a point of time after which the President's authority to enter the original agreement has expired? To what degree can a President with authority to enter an international agreement, provide in such international agreement for further authority to enter into future agreements or amendments?

In UNITED STATES v. YOSHIDA INTERNATIONAL, INC., 526 F.2d 560 (C.C.P.A.1975), reversing, 378 F.Supp. 1155 (C.C.P.A.1974), a Japanese importer of zippers had sued to recover the amount of tariffs collected pursuant to a "tariff surcharge" proclaimed by President Nixon in August 1971 to correct a significant "balance of payments" deficit.[23] The President's proclamation declared a national emergency, and cited authority under the Tariff Act of 1930, the Trade Expansion Act of 1962 and other provisions of law to "modify or terminate, in whole or in part" the prior implementation of trade agreements. The proclamation did not explicitly cite as authority the Trading With the Enemy Act. Each of the two trade acts provided that the "President may at any time terminate, in whole or in part, any proclamation" made under the act.

The Customs Court, ruled that the President had exceeded his authority (378 F.Supp. at 1162–63):

> We conclude that the authority granted by statute to "terminate, in whole or in part, any proclamation" does not include the power to determine and fix unilaterally a rate of duty which has not been previously legally established. On the contrary, the "termination" authority, as statutorily granted, merely provides the President with a mechanical procedure of supplanting or replacing existing rates with rates which have been established by prior proclamations or by statute. * * *
>
> There is a logical reason for placing a limitation on the tariff changes which may be effected by proclamations giving effect or carrying-out

23. See Comment, Attacks on the United States Import Surcharge Under Domestic and International Law: A Pragmatic Analysis, 6 J.Intl.L. & Econ. 269 (1972); Note, The United States Response to Common Market Trade Preferences and the Legality of the Import Surcharge, 39 U.Chi.L.Rev. 177 (Fall, 1971); Jackson, The New Economic Policy and United States International Obligations, 66 Am.J. Intl.L. 110 (1972); Pollard and Boillot, The Import Surcharge of 1971: A Case Study of Executive Power in Foreign Commerce, 7 Vand.J.Transnatl.L. 137 (1973); Note, United States Trade Law at the Crossroads: Presidential Power in the Trade Area After Yoshida International, Inc. v. United States and the Trade Act of 1974, 8 N.Y.U.J.Intl.L. & Pol. 63 (1975); Student Comment, Recent Developments Affecting the Scope of Executive Power to Regulate Foreign Commerce, 16 B.C.Ind. & Com.L.Rev. 778 (1975).

trade agreements but not on those which merely terminate other proclamations, since the latter can do no more than restore rates which have already been legally established, and are thus inherently limited.

General headnote 4(d) of the tariff schedules codifies this principle and provides clear legislative direction with respect to the effect resulting from the termination of a proclamation:

> [W]henever a proclaimed rate is terminated or suspended, the rate shall revert, unless otherwise provided, to the next intervening proclaimed rate previously superseded but not terminated or, if none, to the statutory rate.

The Court of Customs and Patent Appeals reversed and upheld presidential authority, but on different grounds. The appeals court agreed with the Customs Court's interpretation of the trade acts "termination" authority (later amended in the 1974 act, incidentally), but found authority for the President's actions in the Trading With the Enemy Act (TWEA). The Customs Court had rejected the argument that TWEA authority to regulate imports encompassed the authority to impose duties. In reversing, the appeals court stated (526 F.2d at 573):

> Our duty is to effectuate the intent of Congress. In so doing, we look first to the literal meaning of the words employed. Analysis of the statute and its wording provides the threshold determination of what was delegated by the Congress.

> The express delegation in § 5(b) of the TWEA is broad indeed. It provides that the President may, during "any" period of national emergency declared by him, through "any" agency he designates, or "otherwise," and under "any" rules he prescribes, by means of instructions, licenses, "or otherwise," "regulate," "prevent" or "prohibit" the importation of "any" property *[17] in which "any" foreign country or a national thereof has "any" interest, and that the President may, in the manner provided, take "other and further measures," not inconsistent with the statute, for the "enforcement" of the Act.

> The Act authorizes the President to define "any or all" of the terms employed by Congress in § 5(b).

> It appears incontestable that § 5(b) does in fact delegate to the President, for use during war or during national emergency only, the power to "regulate importation." The plain and unambiguous wording of the statute permits no other interpretation. As was said of a war power in Lichter v. United States, 334 U.S. 742, 782, 68 S.Ct. 1294, 1315, 92 L.Ed. 1694 (1948), the primary implication of an emergency power is that it should be effective to deal with a national emergency successfully. The delegation in § 5(b) is broad and extensive; it could not have been otherwise if the President were to have, within constitutional boundaries, the flexibility required to meet problems surrounding a national emergency with the success desired by Congress.

---

* 17. Appellee's argument that the TWEA is limited to importations of property having an "enemy taint" is foreclosed by the statuto-ry reference to "any" property of "any" foreign country or national thereof. * * *

Notes and Questions

(1) No petition for certiorari in the Yoshida case was made. Certiorari was denied in another case involving the same issues. Alcan Sales, Div. of Alcan Aluminum Corp. v. United States, 534 F.2d 920 (C.C.P.A.), cert. denied, 429 U.S., 986, 97 S.Ct. 506, 50 L.Ed.2d 598 (1976).

(2) The subject of balance of payments trade measures is taken up in Section 11.4 infra. The *Yoshida* case should be reviewed when that section is discussed.

(3) A key issue in using the "termination" authority is the "intermediate rates" issue. If the statutory tariff is 25%, and the tariff has been successively lowered as a result of tariff negotiations, to 15% in 1955; to 12% in 1960; and to its current rate of 8% in 1968; can the President then set a rate by a "termination" proclamation of:

(a) 12%?

(b) 15%

(c) 25%

(d) 14% or 20%?

(e) 30% (clearly not!)

The argument against the Customs Court position on "termination" authority is made in Note, Yoshida International, Inc. v. United States: Was the 1971 Import Surcharge Legally Imposed?, 73 Mich.L.Rev. 952 (1975).

(4) Is there a diplomatic reason for failing to mention the TWEA in the proclamation? Cf. the *Consumers Union* case in Section 3.2(B). Are the trading nations affected "enemies"? Does this matter in United States law? In public understanding of the measure abroad? Would the proclamation be effective if promulgated today, in the light of the National Emergencies Act, which requires the President to specify the provision of law he is relying upon?

(5) Under the "termination" authority, could the President have removed the surcharge?

(6) The total sum of surcharge tariffs collected between August and December 1971 is estimated to be about $500 million—a substantial sum. Would the size of the sum make any difference to the court in its determination? Should the fact that the surcharge costs had in many cases been passed on to the ultimate consumer in the price of the goods make any difference in this court proceeding?

(7) Even if the Government lost this case, would it have achieved the objectives of the surcharge measure? Should the likely delay of court challenge to a surcharge affect the policy decision to go ahead with it, even if its legality is doubtful?

(8) Under international law, a tariff surcharge is probably inconsistent with GATT obligations to the extent that it raises some tariffs above the "bound" or agreed rate. Should GATT compatibility (not mentioned by the Court) have been relevant in the *Yoshida* case? (See Chapters 5, 6 and 11).

(9) The court noted that section 122 of the Trade Act of 1974 contains a new measure specifically governing tariff surcharges for balance of payments reasons. Was the court correct in drawing no conclusion from the inclusion of the new measure in the Act?

(10) In the light of section 122 of the Trade Act, how would a new Yoshida case under a new proclamation, identical to that of August 1971, be decided? Is the President's authority now greater or less than it was in 1971? In a floating exchange rate system, is there ever justification for a tariff surcharge for balance-of-payments reasons? Would the U.S. statute or GATT articles XII–XIII ever apply in such a system? Note the GATT reference to "reserves." (We return to this question in Section 11.4 infra.)

In FEDERAL ENERGY ADMINISTRATION v. ALGONQUIN SNG, INC., 426 U.S. 548, 96 S.Ct. 2295, 49 L.Ed.2d 49 (1976), the U.S. Supreme Court considered the National Security Exception, which allows the President to "adjust" imports so that they "will not threaten to impair the national security" if the Secretary of the Treasury determines that imports are threatening to do so. The issue was whether the President's authority to adjust imports of oil products, which historically had been used to impose quotas, also authorized imposition of a fee system, under which the importation of oil products would be subject to payment of a substantial fee per unit of product. In unanimously reversing the Court of Appeals for the D.C. Circuit and upholding the President's action, the Supreme Court brushed aside a suggestion that Congress had impermissibly delegated excessive powers to the President and focused on the proper interpretation of those powers. In doing so, it stated (426 U.S. at 561–62, 96 S.Ct. at 2303):

In authorizing the President to "take such action, and for such time, as he deems necessary to adjust the imports of [an] article and its derivatives," the language of § 232(b) seems clearly to grant him a measure of discretion in determining the method to be used to adjust imports. We find no support in the language of the statute for respondents' contention that the authorization to the President to "adjust" imports should be read to encompass only quantitative methods—i.e., quotas—as opposed to monetary methods—i.e., license fees—of effecting such adjustments.

Indeed, reading respondents' suggested limitation into the word "adjust" would be inconsistent with the range of factors that can trigger the President's authority under § 232(b)'s language. Section 232(b) authorizes the President to act after a finding by the Secretary of the Treasury that a given article is being imported "in such quantities or *under such circumstances* as to threaten to impair the national security." (Emphasis added.) The emphasized language reflects Congress' judgment that "not only the quantity of imports * * * but also the circumstances under which they are coming in: their use, their availability, their character" could endanger the national security and hence should be a potential basis for Presidential action. 104 Cong.Rec. 10542–10543 (1958) (remarks of Rep. Mills). It is most unlikely that Congress would have provided that dangers posed by factors other than the strict quantitative level of imports can justify Presidential action, but that that action must be confined to the imposition of quotas. Unless one assumes, and we do not, that quotas will always be a feasible method of dealing directly with national security threats posed by the "circumstances" under which imports are entering the country, limiting the President to the use of quotas would effectively and artificially prohibit him from directly dealing with some of the very problems against which § 232(b) is directed.

Turning from § 232's language to its legislative history, again there is much to suggest that the President's authority extends to the imposition of monetary exactions—i.e., license fees and duties. * * *

In examining the legislative history, the Court particularly stressed the statement by one of the legislation's sponsors that the legislation authorized the President "to take whatever action he deems necessary to adjust imports * * * [including the use of] tariffs, quotas, import taxes or other methods of import restriction." 426 U.S. at 564, 96 S.Ct. at 2304. The Court of Appeals had based its decision principally on the fact that when the National Security Exception was extended in 1962, a proposal to give the President the power to impose duties was rejected. It concluded that Congress must have believed at the time that the President had no such power. In considering this argument, the Supreme Court wrote (426 U.S. at 569–70, 96 S.Ct. at 2307):

We disagree, however, with the Court of Appeals' assessment of the proposed amendment. The amendment was in reality far more than an articulation of the authority that the Government finds to be contained in § 232(b). Unlike § 232(b), the rejected proposal would not have required a prior investigation and findings by an executive department as a prerequisite to Presidential action. Moreover, the broad "national interest" language of the proposal, together with its lack of any standards for implementing that language, stands in stark contrast with § 232(b)'s narrower criterion of "national security" and § 232(c)'s articulation of standards to guide the invocation of the President's powers under § 232(b). In light of these clear differences between the rejected proposal and § 232(b), we decline to infer from the fact that the Senate amendment was proposed, or from the fact that it was rejected, that Congress felt that the President had no power to impose monetary exactions under § 232(b).

Only a few months after President Nixon invoked the provision to initiate the import license fee system challenged here, Congress once again re-enacted the Presidential authorization encompassed in § 232(b) without material change. Making no mention of the President's action, both the Senate Committee report and the conference report recited the language of the statute itself to reaffirm that under § 232(b) the President "may take such action, and for such time as he deems necessary to adjust imports so as to prevent impairment of the national security." The congressional acquiescence in President Nixon's action manifested by the re-enactment of § 232(b) provides yet further corroboration that § 232(b) was understood and intended to authorize the imposition of monetary exactions as a means of adjusting imports.

Notes and Questions

(1) The Court of Appeals decision in *Algonquin*, 518 F.2d 1051 (D.C.Cir.1975), was a two-to-one decision overruling the trial court which had upheld the government. Judges Tamm and Leventhal were the majority, with Judge Robb dissenting. The majority opinion concentrated on the legislative history of section 232. Judge Robb argued that "the legislative history of section 232 is hopelessly ambiguous and inconclusive" and he followed what in his view was the "plain and broad language of section 232(b)." He also added (at 1063):

The majority is driven to its conclusion by its concern that "[i]f our system is to survive, we must respond to even the most difficult of problems in a manner consistent with the limitations placed upon the Congress, the President, and the Courts by our Constitution and our laws." While I share this concern, I believe the court should not interfere in this dispute between the President and Congress. The power to regulate foreign commerce belongs to Congress, and it may delegate as much or as little as it chooses to the President. If it determines it has gone too far, Congress may withdraw the delegated power from the President. Here the delegated power is broad, and Congress has had repeated opportunities to limit it or withdraw it altogether. It has not done so, and I think this court should not do so.

(2) Judge Leventhal was the dissenter in the *Consumers Union* case discussed in Section 3.2(B) below. In both cases, he took a position narrowly construing presidential powers. Could his view on the appropriate scope of presidential power have affected his reading of the legislative history of section 232?

(3) What is the relevance of the *Curtiss-Wright* case, also discussed in Section 3.2(B), on construction of a statutory delegation of power to the President? If you were a judge today, how would you proceed to view delegations of power relating to international economic affairs to the President? What weight would you give to legislative history?

––––––––––

In ZENITH RADIO CORP. v. UNITED STATES, 437 U.S. 443, 98 S.Ct. 2441, 57 L.Ed.2d 337 (1978), the U.S. Supreme Court had to determine whether the Japanese practice of remitting otherwise applicable commodity taxes on export of a product constituted a "grant" or "bounty" under section 303 of the Tariff Act of 1930. If such remissions were considered to be grants or bounties, the Secretary of the Treasury would have been required to assess countervailing duties to offset them on Japanese products imported into the United States. The Customs Court had ruled that such duties had to be imposed, despite the longstanding position of the Treasury Department, dating back to 1898—one year after the initial passage of the basic countervailing duty statute in 1897, that such remissions were not grants or bounties. In unanimously upholding the Court of Customs and Patent Appeals, which had reversed the Customs Court, the Supreme Court concluded that the legislative history indicated that only remission of taxes in excess of what would otherwise be due constituted a bounty. It continued (437 U.S. at 455–58, 98 S.Ct. at 2448–49):

Regardless of whether this legislative history absolutely compelled the Secretary to interpret "bounty or grant" so as not to encompass any nonexcessive remission of an indirect tax, there can be no doubt that such a construction was reasonable in light of the statutory purpose. This purpose is relatively clear from the face of the statute and is confirmed by the congressional debates: The countervailing duty was intended to offset the unfair competitive advantage that foreign producers would otherwise enjoy from export subsidies paid by their governments. * * *

In deciding in 1898 that a nonexcessive remission of indirect taxes did not result in the type of competitive advantage that Congress intended to counteract, the Department was clearly acting in accordance with the shared assumptions of the day as to the fairness and economic effect of that practice. The theory underlying the Department's position was that a foreign country's remission of indirect taxes did not constitute subsidization of that country's exports. Rather, such remission was viewed as a reasonable measure for avoiding double taxation of exports—once by the foreign country and once upon sale in this country. ＊ ＊ ＊

The Secretary's interpretation of the countervailing-duty statute is as permissible today as it was in 1898. The statute has been re-enacted five times by Congress without any modification of the relevant language, and, whether or not Congress can be said to have "acquiesced" in the administrative practice, it certainly has not acted to change it. At the same time, the Secretary's position has been incorporated into the General Agreement on Tariffs and Trade (GATT), which is followed by every major trading nation in the world; foreign tax systems as well as private expectations thus have been built on the assumption that countervailing duties would not be imposed on nonexcessive remissions of indirect taxes. In light of these substantial reliance interests, the longstanding administrative construction of the statute should "not be disturbed except for cogent reasons."

The Court then distinguished one of its 1903 cases, which it found to be "opaque" and not clearly contrary to the government's position.

Notes and Questions

(1) The *Zenith* litigation was contemporaneous with substantial portions of the Multilateral Trade Negotiations, including discussion of the draft Subsidies Code. Had the Court ruled in Zenith's favor, negotiations over the Subsidies Code could well have collapsed. To emphasize this possibility and the view that such a decision would be a violation of U.S. obligations under Article VI of GATT, both the EC delegation and the Japanese Embassy in Washington conveyed diplomatic notes to the Department of State, which asked the Solicitor General to distribute them to the Court. The notes and accompanying correspondence are reproduced at 17 Intl. Legal Materials 934 (1978). The Clerk of the Supreme Court did distribute the notes, but later advised the Solicitor General that Court rules did not contemplate such a distribution. He pointedly suggested that an *amicus* brief was the proper method for a foreign government to express its views on a pending Supreme Court case.

(2) Could the administering authority of the countervailing duty law (now the Commerce Department) decide in future cases that, as a matter of U.S. law, non-excessive remission of indirect taxes does, in at least some instances, constitute a bounty or grant within the meaning of the law?

(3) Would the analysis in *Zenith* have been different if there had already existed a provision such as § 1001 of the Trade Agreements Act of 1979, which amends § 516A of the Tariff Act of 1930 (19 U.S.C.A. § 1516a) to state that a reviewing court "shall hold unlawful any [final countervailing duty] determination ＊ ＊ ＊ found ＊ ＊ ＊ to be unsupported by substantial evidence on the record, or otherwise not in accordance with law"?

(4) In both *Algonquin* and *Zenith* the Supreme Court viewed the legislative history as a source to find support for Executive Branch interpretations of statutes, but seemed to reject use of such history to negate explicit language or

long established practice. What does this suggest for Congress' ability to control the Executive Branch?

(5) The next Supreme Court case to consider the President's powers in international economic matters was *Dames & Moore,* discussed in Section 3.2(B) supra. A few days before the *Dames & Moore* decision, the Supreme Court decided Haig v. Agee, 453 U.S. 280, 101 S.Ct. 2766, 69 L.Ed.2d 640 (1981) in which it upheld a long-standing administrative practice and interpretation of a statute where there had been apparent congressional acquiescence. More recently, in Regan v. Wald, 468 U.S. 222, 104 S.Ct. 3026, 82 L.Ed.2d 171 (1984), the Supreme Court gave a broad reading to the President's grandfather powers in respect of the TWEA under IEEPA.[24] What conclusions can be drawn from these three cases and the five discussed in this section? The reader should reconsider this question after studying Section 3.5.

(4) Note: Statutes Governing the Administrative Process as It Relates to International Economic Relations

As might be expected, the extensive control over private transactions exercised by United States regulation of international economic affairs involves a number of questions that are also found in other areas of government economic regulation, many of which are more appropriately taken up in a course in administrative law. Nevertheless, there are several issues that promise to be peculiarly significant for the conduct of foreign affairs generally, and the problems of international economic regulation particularly. Essentially the question is whether foreign affairs issues should be exempted from "fair procedure" or similar statutes. Here we consider how three such significant statutes treat matters involving international economic relations.

THE ADMINISTRATIVE PROCEDURE ACT (APA)

"Military and foreign affairs functions" are exempt under section 4 of the APA from its rule-making procedures (5 U.S.C.A. § 553(a)(1)); under section 3 of the APA, from its adjudicatory procedures (5 U.S.C.A. § 554(a) (4)); and under section 2 of the APA from its information-supplying requirements (5 U.S.C.A. § 552(b)(1)).[25] There are many who argue that the exemption is much too broad and tends to deprive citizens of a meaningful opportunity to have their "day in court," with respect to the implementation of policies which affect their business or occupations.[26] A 1970 American Bar Association resolution advocated a narrowing of the exemptions, and the Administrative Conference of the United States (an agency of the United States government designed to improve administrative procedures) recommended at its annual session in 1973 that the APA categorical exemption for "military or foreign affairs" rule-making should be eliminated.[27]

24. See note 4 supra.

25. See Mast Industries, Inc. v. Regan, 596 F.Supp. 1567 (CIT 1984).

26. Bonfield, Military and Foreign Affairs Function Rule-Making Under the A.P.A., 71 Mich.L.Rev. 221 (1972).

27. Administrative Conference of the United States, Report of the Committee on Rulemaking and Public Information, "Recommendation B: Elimination of the 'Military or Foreign Affairs Function' Exemption from A.P.A. Rulemaking Requirements" (1973).

THE FREEDOM OF INFORMATION ACT (FOIA)

The Act (5 U.S.C.A. § 552(b)) exempts matters that are specifically authorized under criteria established by an Executive Order to be kept secret in the interest of national defense or foreign policy and are in fact properly classified pursuant to such Executive Order, as well as trade secrets and commercial or financial information obtained from a person and privileged or confidential. There have been numerous cases concerning FOIA, but only a few have touched on foreign affairs issues.[28]

THE FEDERAL ADVISORY COMMITTEE ACT

The Federal Advisory Committee Act, 5 U.S.C.A. App. §§ 1–15, contains elaborate provisions with respect to public access to meetings, minutes and documents of federal "advisory committees." Since many activities of the United States government concerning international economic problems involve a large number and variety of advisory committees, this Act can pose a number of complex legal problems. The difficulties of this Act were considered sufficiently troublesome that when the Trade Act of 1974 was enacted, with its many elaborate provisions concerning advisory committees (for example, Section 135), some specific exemptions from the Advisory Committee Act were written into the Trade Act (see Section 135(f)), and particular provisions for trade secrets and commercial or financial information were made. The Senate report on the Trade Act noted: "If the advisory committees are to play an effective role in the negotiations they should be privy to our negotiating objectives, strategy, and tactics. These are not subjects which can be discussed in public meetings, which may include representatives from other governments and the press." [29]

(C) THE UNITED STATES TRADE ACTS AND THE RECIPROCAL TRADE AGREEMENTS PROGRAM

Professor F.W. Taussig, in his classic "The Tariff History of the United States" states, "The early economic history of the United States may be divided into two periods. The first, which is in the main a continuation of the colonial period, lasted till about the year 1808; the embargo marks the beginning of the series of events which closed it. The second began in 1808, and lasted through the generation following. It was during the second period that the most decided attempt was made to apply protection to young industries in the United States.[30]

From a time in the 18th century, when the British colonies in North America were essentially required to import virtually all manufactured items, to the 1930's, the history of U.S. tariffs is one of ups and downs, often

---

28. See, e.g., Neal-Cooper Grain Co. v. Kissinger, 385 F.Supp. 769 (D.D.C.1974); Note, National Security Information Disclosure Under the FOIA: The Need for Effective Judicial Enforcement, 25 B.C.L.Rev. 611 (1984); Note, Secrecy in the Conduct of United States Foreign Relations: Recent Policy and Practice, 6 Cornell Intl.L.J. 187 (1973).

29. S.Rep. No. 93–1298, 93d Cong., 2d Sess. (1974).

30. F. Taussig, The Tariff History of the United States 8 (8th ed. 1931). For other works on U.S. tariff history, see U.S. Senate, History of the Committee on Finance, 91st Cong., 2d Sess. 49 (S.Doc. No. 91–57, 1970).

related to domestic problems (such as the Civil War and the need for federal government revenues). Taussig continues the story,[31]

> The successive acts from 1883 to 1922 are all explicable on the ground of some special occasion for a general revision: either an admitted need of overhauling, or a party overturn, or some financial or economic stress. For several years before the act of 1883, it had been agreed on all hands that the rates established during and after the Civil War needed to be readjusted. The three acts of 1890, 1894, 1897 were the results of federal elections and political upsets. President Cleveland, largely influenced by fiscal difficulties, had thrown down the gauntlet on the tariff question in his famous message of 1887; that was the issue in the election of 1888; the Republicans, having elected President Harrison and a Congressional majority, passed the McKinley act of 1890. Their defeat in 1892 led to the Wilson "free trade" act passed by the Democrats in 1894. The return of the Republicans to power in 1896 was naturally followed by the act of 1897 with its accentuated protective duties. Among all in the list the tariff of 1909 was least occasioned by a specific exigency; yet the financial crisis of 1907 and the contested election of 1908 were factors. That of 1913, with its lowered rates, was the result of the Democratic victory in the election of 1912. Finally, the act of 1922 is explicable from the nationalistic feeling fostered by the war and the disastrous economic collapse of 1920–21. Nothing of this sort can be said in explanation of the tariff of 1930.

In describing the passage of the Tariff Act of 1930, the infamous "Smoot-Hawley" Tariff, Taussig goes on to note:[32]

> The difficulty, as already intimated, was mainly in our political system. The accepted procedure, not new in 1930 but then more firmly established than in previous years, deserves description. In each of the two committees which deal with the tariff—that on Ways and Means in the House and that on Finance in the Senate—the traditions and methods are ideal for log-rolling.

Since the Smoot-Hawley Tariff Act of 1930, thoughtful persons in Congress have recognized the difficulty of Congress' developing a tariff in the national interest. As one senator stated in 1934:[33]

> [O]ur experience in writing tariff legislation * * * has been discouraging. Trading between groups and sections is inevitable. Log-rolling is inevitable, and in its most pernicious form. We do not write a national tariff law. We jam together, through various unholy alliances and combinations, a potpourri or hodgepodge of section and local tariff rates, which often add to our troubles and increase world misery.

From this experience, and the leadership of Cordell Hull, Congress enacted the Reciprocal Trade Agreements Act of 1934, by which it delegated to the President the authority to negotiate international trade agreements for the reciprocal reduction of tariffs. For over forty years of operation of that program, Congress has entrusted to the President a major portion of U.S. international economic policy.

31. F. Taussig, note 30 supra, at 489–90.

32. Id., at 491.

33. 78 Cong.Rec. 10379 (1934) (remarks of Senator Cooper).

The language of the 1934 Act not only delegated negotiating authority to the President, but also gave the President authority to "proclaim" the resulting modifications of tariff and import restrictions, i.e. an implementing authority. This language, which has been included in every trade negotiating authority enacted since, was probably chosen for the original act more as a result of tradition and precedent than for any calculated purpose. As one of the authors has noted: [34]

> As early as 1798, an act empowered the President to undertake commercial intercourse with a foreign country (France) and "to make proclamation thereof." This terminology was followed in a series of other international trade statutes during the ensuing century. The 1897 Tariff Act, for example, gave the President power to enter into "commercial agreements" with foreign governments, and separately to suspend duties on products subject to the agreement "by proclamation to that effect." The Supreme Court, in passing on the constitutionality of the delegation of power to the President under the Tariff Act of 1890, held that no "legislative power" was delegated because the President could only issue a proclamation based on particular findings of fact specified in the statute. Later tariff statutes reinforced this practice of establishing a proclamation power as the normal means for the President to implement tariff changes.

The Senate Report on the 1943 Act stated: [35]

> Under the Trade Agreements Act changes in our tariff rates are made, so far as our domestic law is concerned, by the President's proclamation under the authority of the Trade Agreement Act. Changes in the tariff rates are not made by the agreements, per se. * * * It is precisely the same procedural principle as that on which the Interstate Commerce Commission is authorized by Congress to fix fair and reasonable railroad rates.

The authority granted in the 1934 Act extended for a period of three years, and this authority was renewed for various periods in a series of subsequent acts, extending almost to the present.[36] The 1945 renewal of the Act was crucial because it was the foundation of the U.S. acceptance of membership in GATT (discussed in Chapter 5). By the time of the 1945 Act,

34. Jackson, The General Agreement on Tariffs and Trade in United States Domestic Law, 66 Mich.L.Rev. 249, 283 (1967). Reprinted by permission of the Michigan Law Review Association.

35. S.Rep. No. 258, 78th Cong., 1st Sess. 47, 48 (1943).

36. Act of June 12, 1934, c. 474, 48 Stat. 943 (codified at 19 U.S.C.A. § 1351), as amended, Joint Resolution of March 1, 1937, c. 24, 50 Stat. 24 (three-year extension); Joint Resolution of April 12, 1940, c. 96, 54 Stat. 107 (three-year extension); Joint Resolution of June 7, 1943, c. 118, 57 Stat. 125 (two-year extension); Act of July 5, 1945, c. 269, § 1, 59 Stat. 410 (three-year extension); Act of June 26, 1948, c. 678, § 2, 62 Stat. 1053 (one-year extension); Act of September 26, 1949, c. 585, § 3, 63 Stat. 697 (three-year extension); Act of June 15, 1951, c. 141, § 2, 65 Stat. 72 (two-year extension); Act of August 7, 1953, c. 348, title I, § 101, 67 Stat. 472 (one-year extension); Act of July 1, 1954, c. 445, § 1, 68 Stat. 360 (one-year extension); Act of June 21, 1955, c. 169, § 2, 69 Stat. 162 (three-year extension); Act of August 20, 1958, Pub.L. No. 85–686, § 2, 72 Stat. 672 (four-year extension). After a five-year extension enacted in 1962 expired, see note 38 infra, the Trade Act of 1974, § 101; 19 U.S.C.A. § 2111, reestablished similar tariff negotiating authority in respect of tariffs, which expired in January 1980. A different authority included in the 1974 Act regarding non-tariff barriers was enacted for a similar period and since has been extended to 1988. Trade Act of 1974, § 102, as amended, Trade Agreements Act of 1979, § 1101; 19 U.S.C.A. § 2112.

the U.S. had entered into 32 reciprocal trade agreements, all of them bilateral in nature.[37]

The Trade Expansion Act of 1962, which extended the trade agreements authority for five years, was an important milestone in this sequence of acts.[38] This Act established the authority for U.S. participation in the "Kennedy Round" of GATT trade negotiations, the sixth such round, and established the legal framework for a fundamental shift in the procedures of negotiation as well as setting up the position in the U.S. government of the "Special Trade Representative" (discussed in subsection F below). This Act also revised the Escape Clause (as discussed in later chapters), and has sometimes been termed the "high water mark" of post World War II liberal trade policy in U.S. legislation, since the revised Escape Clause made it more difficult for domestic industries to obtain relief from import competition.

(D) THE TRADE ACT OF 1974

(1) Background to the 1974 Act

After the completion of the Kennedy Round of negotiations in 1967, there was considerable criticism in Congress of the results of that negotiation from the point of view of U.S. domestic producers. When the trade agreements authority ran out on June 30, 1967, it was anticipated that it would be promptly renewed. However, protectionist pressure in the United States, reinforced by international economic problems that had arisen partly because of the Vietnam War, and partly because of the inflexibility of the Bretton Woods System (particularly as it involved fixed exchange rates), made the political climate difficult, to say the least, for a trade bill. A trade bill is always a relatively unpopular measure in Congress, since it involves the necessity of congressmen voting for a statute with national policy advantages, which often transgresses on the particular economic interests of some of their constituents. With a presidential and congressional election coming up in 1968, it was natural that legislative efforts for trade agreements authority be postponed until after that election. As a consequence, when the trade agreements authority for the President ran out in June 1967, it was not until the end of 1974 that it was renewed—the first significant gap in that authority since the original 1934 Act was passed.

In 1969, the new Administration had introduced in Congress a trade bill which was partly designed to renew the tariff and trade agreements authority that had expired.[39] For a variety of reasons that will not be detailed here, this bill ultimately failed to pass Congress. What had started to be legislation with a liberal trade orientation, evolved in the House Ways and Means Committee into a piece of legislation that was considered by many economists and businessmen to be overly protectionist and potentially damaging to United States international relations. While the bill passed the House, it

---

37. See Hearings on Extension of the Reciprocal Trade Agreements Act Before the House Comm. on Ways and Means, 79th Cong., 1st Sess. 38, 636, 932 (1948).

38. Act of October 11, 1962, Pub.L. No. 87–794, 76 Stat. 872.

39. The Trade Act of 1969, H.R. 14870. See also Foreign Trade and Tariffs: Written Statements and Other Material Submitted by Administration Witnesses to House Comm. on Ways and Means, 91st Cong., 2d Sess. (Comm. Print, 1970).

floundered in the Senate (with the aid of a filibuster threat) and finally it failed passage in the late days of the 91st Congress,[40] at the end of 1970.

Meanwhile, in May 1970, the President had established a Commission on International Trade and Investment Policy, known as the Williams Commission.[41] The Commission was composed of a number of businessmen, labor leaders and academics, and had a professional staff headed by an economist as executive director, Professor Isaiah Frank. The Commission reported in July, 1971, with a 400-page volume containing the basic report, and two appended volumes containing a series of papers that it had commissioned on a variety of subjects. It was perhaps the most comprehensive official commission for the study of United States international trade policy which had ever been organized. The Williams Commission report avoided doctrinaire extremes of free trade or protectionism, but generally reported a need for further liberalization of United States trade, while protecting United States trading interests from the shocks of surging imports and unfair activities from abroad. Most notable of its recommendations were probably those which advocated the renewal of tariff and trade agreements authority, and those which recommended a revision of the escape clause and adjustment assistance program so as to make these remedies more available.[42]

To a great degree, the Williams Commission report (unlike many other commission reports) furnished the intellectual foundations for the subsequent developments leading finally to the adoption of the Trade Act of 1974. One of the reasons for this was that a number of persons who were involved with the Williams Commission, either as Commission members or as staff members, later entered federal government service in various positions where they had an opportunity to influence the development of the 1974 Trade Act.

Throughout the deliberations on the Trade Act of 1974, Congress was constantly confronted with difficult policy choices. The Trade Act of 1974 was the most significant single piece of United States legislation concerning international economic matters at least since the 1962 Trade Expansion Act, and possibly since the innovation of the 1934 Act. Partly this was because the Trade Act was the longest and most complex trade statute ever passed by Congress to that date. Not only did it renew and revise the traditional trade agreements authority, but in a series of other titles the Trade Act of 1974 dealt more or less comprehensively with United States relations with Communist countries, the establishment of a preferential tariff system for developing countries, revision of the rules bearing on United States law regarding imports which have been affected by unfair foreign actions, and a sweeping revision of the portions of the law dealing with the escape clause and adjustment assistance.

40. Trade Act of 1970, H.R. 18970. See H.R.Rep. No. 1435, 91st Cong., 2d Sess. (1970); S.Rep. No. 1431, 91st Cong., 2d Sess. 233–406 (1970); 116 Cong.Rec. 37564–68, 38427–9, 39931–43, 41806–27, 42151–56, 43646 (1970). See also Metzger, The Mills Bill, 5 J.World Trade L. 235 (1971).

41. Commission on International Trade and Investment Policy, United States International Economic Policy in an Interdependent World, Report (1971).

42. Id.

(2) The Path of a Trade Act Through Congress

Although there have been two major trade enactments since the 1974 Act (with more threatened as this is written), the 1974 Act was the latest "typical" broad trade enactment. The 1979 Act followed special procedures for implementation of international trade agreements, and the 1984 Act was a hurly-burly last minute exercise that resulted from a series of political trends, not typical of the series of trade agreements acts which started in 1934. For this reason a look at the typical path of trade legislation in Congress naturally refers mostly to the history of the 1974 Act, at least for broader legislation which has been proposed after careful planning by the Executive Branch.

A bill relating to United States international trade almost invariably involves tariffs. The United States Constitution requires that "revenue" measures originate in the House of Representatives. Since tariffs were originally a "revenue measure," it has been the consistent tradition of U.S. constitutional history for bills relating to tariffs to originate in the House of Representatives. This is perhaps an anomaly, since today tariffs have less significance for revenue generating than they do as regulations on the flow of trade into the United States.

In the House of Representatives, the Ways and Means Committee has jurisdiction over taxes and revenue-raising measures, and once again the fiction that tariffs are a revenue matter has led over the years to the tradition of tariff and trade bills being referred to the Ways and Means Committee, the most powerful committee in the House. Sometimes, however, it has been proposed that jurisdiction over trade be transferred to other committees such as the Commerce Committee, or the Foreign Affairs Committee. On occasion some other committee (such as one of these two) will consider a bill which touches on trade (such as the "automobile domestic content" bills in 1983 and 1984), and this can result in a bit of jurisdictional tugging and pulling in the procedures of the House, which can influence the substance of the legislation. The Ways and Means (or other) committee will usually hold public hearings, and then begin what is called the "mark-up", during which the committee redrafts the bill in the manner it feels best reflects national and constituent interests. When it has finished this process, the committee will vote on whether to "report out" the bill. If it does so, the bill goes to the whole House for consideration "on the floor."

A commonly expressed overall strategy for a trade bill (and for a number of other kinds of bills also), is to work carefully with the House Ways and Means Committee to achieve a sound bill which then goes to the House floor under a closed rule (no amendments). When the bill passes the House and goes to the Senate, it is usually referred to the Senate Finance Committee. Allegedly "chaos" then ensues and a number of damaging provisions (in the view of those who espouse this strategy) will be added by the Senate Finance Committee or on the floor of the Senate under the relatively undisciplined procedures of the Senate. Subsequently then, the Senate version and the House version are reconciled in "conference" (generally a committee with an equal number of members of both Houses drawn primarily from the two committees that have worked on the bill), and in conference it is hoped that the damaging provisions will be largely eliminated and most of the House version restored.

This strategic vision, however, depends on a number of assumptions, including good committee work by the Ways and Means Committee, a closed rule in the House, and effective bargaining by the House members of the conference committee. For a variety of reasons, this scenario does not always occur (if ever).

Under the established procedures of the House, when a committee reports a bill it then goes to the Rules Committee. The Rules Committee must decide on "the rule" under which the bill is to be debated on the floor of the House. The Ways and Means Committee had traditionally sought and obtained closed rules for the bills which it brought to the floor of the House.

However, reformers in the mid-1970's forced this to change, so that in the case of the 1974 Act, the "rule" permitted several amendments to the bill. One of these would have stricken Title IV which deals with trade with communist countries (and was embroiled in a dispute mentioned below). Another would have stricken Title V which provided for preferential treatment for imports from developing countries (the "GSP" or Generalized System of Preferences). In addition, the so-called "Jackson-Vanik" forces, led by Senator Jackson and Representative Vanik, who had been instrumental in linking the trade and financial policy of the United States towards the U.S.S.R. to the emigration policy of the latter, sought and obtained from the Rules Committee a rule which would permit the extension of the bill's linkage of emigration not only to most-favored-nation (MFN) treatment (as stated in the bill), but to the granting of United States government credits to the countries concerned.[43]

Once a bill passes the House, it is then sent to the Senate. The trade bill passed the House in 1973, and then had the misfortune of reaching the Senate at the beginning of 1974, in the middle of two crises: Watergate, and the oil price shock. In the Senate, such a bill goes to the Senate Finance Committee, which has a jurisdiction very similar to the House Ways and Means Committee. Only after much maneuvering was this committee persuaded in 1974 to take up the trade bill and to hold public hearings. Even then it proceeded at a pace designed to prevent the bill from becoming law, until after President Nixon had resigned, and Gerald Ford had become President and made a concentrated effort to push the trade bill.[44]

---

43. This provision was popularly known as the "Jackson-Vanik" provision. It was placed in the title of the bill which authorized the President to extend MFN treatment to some Communist nations under certain conditions. It added as one of those conditions, that the Communist country must allow free emigration in order to qualify for MFN treatment from the United States.

44. In the Fall of 1974 the Senate Finance Committee began to "mark up" the bill in earnest. It did so recognizing that the 93d Congress would expire at the end of 1974 (a new Congress being elected in November of 1974). When the 93d Congress expired, all bills not then passed would also expire, and a trade bill would have to begin over again in the House—an effort that was not likely to be tried again in the near future. Consequently, the Finance Committee, and subsequently the Senate, was engaged in a race with the deadline. Some respite occurred when it was decided that the Congress would come back in session after the November election. The Finance Committee finally reported its bill on November 26th, and the bill was taken up on the Senate floor December 13th, where it passed after a filibuster attempt was successfully defeated by a cloture vote (requiring a two-thirds margin), and after 26 floor amendments were added to the bill.

When the Senate has passed a bill, the House and Senate versions must be reconciled, and this is normally done by a "conference committee" drawn from the substantive committees of each House. An agreed identical conference version of the bill is then sent to each house, usually for quick passage so that an enrolled bill can be sent to the President for his signature (or veto). The 1974 Trade Act was finished only during a post-election special session, and only after a number of trade-offs with other issues troubling Congress which had little or nothing to do with trade. The President signed the bill into law on January 3, 1975, but it is still called the "Trade Act of 1974." [45]

(3) Negotiating Authority for Nontariff Barriers

It is difficult to negotiate agreements on nontariff barriers (NTBs). The problem facing Congress is how to place limitations on the authority to negotiate such agreements, without at the same time destroying the credibility of United States negotiators. The approach of the 1973 trade bill as introduced (on behalf of the administration) in the House was to provide that NTB agreements be submitted to Congress for "veto" within a specific period of 90 days. Basically the House of Representatives accepted this approach, while embellishing it with some important procedural additions to prevent abuse of the process under House of Representatives rules of procedures. The Senate, however, coming to consideration of the bill at the height of the Watergate presidential crisis, would not accept the veto procedure as written. In particular, it was argued that changes in United States domestic law (which might result from implementation of a NTB agreement) should only occur through the constitutional process of adoption of a statute. (Later the U.S. Supreme Court ruled, in *INS v. Chadha*, see Section 3.2(C)(2) supra, that legislative vetoes were unconstitutional.) But recognizing that it was this usual procedure that had failed in previous attempts to implement international NTB agreements, the Senate was willing to go along with a special set of rules to apply both to the Senate and the House deliberation of statutes

45. The House conferees were somewhat weakened by the absence of Representative Mills, and observers contended that the House conferees were not as able to make their desires prevail over the Senate on the bill as had been the case in the past. However, the great bulk of the Senate amendments were technical and easily accepted by the House, and on a number of key provisions the House was able to prevail.

In virtually the last few hours of the congressional session, the conference report was returned to each House and there adopted, so that the final bill could be enrolled and sent to the President. Neither House, at the time it voted to approve the conference bill, had in front of it the definitive text of the bill to be adopted. The press of time would not permit that.

The bill was sent to the President, and signed by him on January 3d, at which time the President made a statement that indicated some strong reservations about certain portions of the bill.

The apparent chaos and confusion that is endemic to a decision-making process that involves a large number of compromises on a large number of complex provisions, is frustrating indeed. Perhaps the heart of the matter is compromise, since there is great divergency of viewpoints concerning the appropriate policy for the United States to take in international economic affairs. No one obtained his favored bill, and due to the unfortunate coincidence of the crisis in the Presidency, plus the reform developments in the House of Representatives, there was a decided lack of overall leadership in connection with the development of the bill. Generally, it has been thought impossible to obtain a trade bill in the United States without strong presidential leadership—the Trade Act of 1974 must be counted an exception to that rule.

designed to implement the NTB agreements (and for approval of the agreements also). The key ingredients of such a procedure, in the eyes of some observers, were threefold: 1) preventing a committee or committee chairman from "bottling up" legislation so that it could not come to the floor for a vote; 2) providing for consideration in each House of the NTB agreement and implementing legislation without the possibility of amendment, since amendment would require returning to the international bargaining table and redoing the bargain which had already been agreed internationally; and 3) providing for limitation of debate on the floor of both Houses (to prevent a Senate filibuster, for example).

The version adopted by the Senate was accepted by the House, and basically provides that NTB agreements and implementing statutes be rapidly considered by both Houses of Congress (within an overall time limit which is usually 90 days) under special procedures that satisfy the three criteria mentioned above.[46]

Other provisions of the 1974 Trade Act provide for extensive "prenegotiation procedures" by which various sets of public hearings are held so that American citizens can comment on the possible effect of tariff reductions or NTB agreements before American negotiators are authorized to make concrete offers at the international bargaining table. Many of these procedures follow those which have been in effect for previous trade rounds, but in the 1974 Act there is an additional set of procedures relating to the establishment of particular economic sector negotiating advisory committees of private citizens or business representatives, having to do with major fields of manufacturing or agricultural endeavor (e.g., steel, aluminum, electronics, etc.)[47]

(E) THE TRADE AGREEMENTS ACT OF 1979

JOHN H. JACKSON, UNITED STATES LAW AND IMPLEMENTATION OF THE TOKYO ROUND NEGOTIATION

(1984)[48]

For the United States to both accept and implement the major nontariff agreements of the MTN required congressional approval, and under the Trade Act of 1974 this was to be accomplished by normal legislation, which, however, was to be considered by the Congress under the "fast-track" procedure described earlier. The procedures turned out to operate in a very interesting fashion, which is revealing of the United States governmental and constitutional processes.

Under the "fast-track" procedure, the President was required to notify the Congress ninety days before he signed any NTB agreements, and to consult with key congressional committees during that time. Congress had been kept informed generally throughout the course of the Tokyo Round

---

46. Trade Act of 1974, §§ 102, 151.

47. Id., §§ 131–35.

48. From J. Jackson, J.—V. Louis & M. Matsushita, Implementing the Tokyo Round:

National Constitutions and International Economic Rules 162–68 (1984). Reprinted by permission of the author.

negotiations, and key congressional committees had developed professional staff whose full time was devoted to following the course of the negotiations. When the President notified the Congress in early January 1979, about the tentative NTB agreements, his officials sent to the Congress detailed information about the status of the negotiations, including the tentative drafts of the various agreements that were contemplated. Anticipating this, congressional staff, in consultation with key senators and congressmen, had designed a procedure for the consultation that closely paralleled the normal procedure followed in work on bills, except that in this case no bill had yet been introduced in the Congress.

When a committee of Congress begins to formally consider a bill that has been introduced and to prepare that bill for report to the floor of the whole House, its session is often called a *markup*, indicating that the committee is marking up the bill with its proposed changes. The consultations with the executive branch during the ninety days before completion of the international agreements were called *nonmarkup* sessions, and followed very closely this type of procedure. One important difference was that the sessions were not open to the public.

The principal committees devoting time to this subject were the Senate Finance Committee and the House Ways and Means Committee (particularly the latter's Subcommittee on Trade). These committees met extensively with executive branch officials, including the trade negotiators, and on some subjects entered into detailed negotiations about the matters that should be included in a statute implementing the international agreements. Particularly close attention was given to the antidumping and countervailing duty laws. Perhaps most surprising, the members of Congress informed the executive branch that they desired to have their own staff (including the legal staff of the House and the Senate), develop the actual text of the bill the President would introduce.

Further procedures also indicated the parallel with normal legislative processes. On certain issues the Ways and Means Committee and the Finance Committee did not agree, so they held a "nonconference" joint session at which they resolved their differences in order to present a united front to the executive branch. Throughout this process the executive branch officials participated, influenced the deliberations, and were in a position of some bargaining power, since it was understood that it was the President's bill that would be ultimately introduced and that could not be amended afterward.

After the international agreements were initialed in Geneva, the executive branch prepared the bill that the President introduced to the Congress. Understanding the political realities, the President's officials took almost the exact text of the draft bill that had been prepared by the congressional committees and staff. The President then arranged to have the bill introduced in June 1979.

Once the bill had been introduced, the basic substantive work was over, since it could not be amended. Thus, from the point of view of the Congress, the consultation period, including the nonmarkup and the nonconference, that went on before the bill was introduced was crucial in shaping the bill so that it would gain enough support in both houses of Congress to be able to pass. Thus, after the bill was introduced the normal procedures for enacting legislation were a formality. To no one's surprise, the bill passed. What was surprising was the overwhelming vote in favor of the bill: 90 to 4 in the Senate, and 395 to 7 in the House.

One interesting development in these congressional procedures for approval of the MTN agreements was the involvement of foreign nation interests. Early in the ninety-day consultation procedures, * * * officials of the EEC realized * * * that the shape of the statute the Congress was formulating would have a profound effect on the practical implementation of the MTN agreements. Once the statute became U.S. law, it would be hard to persuade the Congress to change it. * * * The fact that the United States procedures were moving faster than those of any other country would also be highly influential. Consequently, the EEC took the logical step: they hired professional (legal and economic) representation in Washington, D.C. to monitor as closely as possible what was going on in the congressional consultation with the executive branch officials. These representatives reported quickly and frequently to the EEC officials, and thus on certain issues EEC negotiators could raise questions with their American counterparts. If the EEC objected to a direction they saw the congressional-executive sessions taking, it could and did make it known that it would deem certain statutory formulations a breach of the international obligations assumed by both the EEC and the United States.

* * *

In all this extensive consultation between the executive branch and the Congress, with the tugging and compromising that inevitably goes on in the legislative process, the testimony of participants was that the congressional committees were responsive to executive branch objectives that nothing be included in the U.S. statute that would require the United States to be in default of any of its international obligations under the MTN results. It appears that congressmen and senators were very careful to prevent any such measures from being included in the proposed statute. To confirm this observation, after the bill was forwarded to the Congress in final form there was an official statement by the EEC Commission to the effect that in the opinion of the EEC officials, on the whole, the bill reflected the spirit and the letter of the MTN agreements.

Several aspects of this procedure for enacting the Trade Agreements Act of 1979 are particularly interesting and potentially significant. First, the Congress was evidently pleased with the procedure. The heavy involvement of the congressional committees in the drafting process gave the Congress confidence and a feeling of security that the executive branch was not trying to foist something upon Congress without giving it an opportunity to influence the results. * * *

The Congress' satisfaction with the procedure is evidenced not only by statements in the committee reports and other legislative history, but more concretely by the fact that it extended by eight years the period prescribed for the procedure under the 1974 act. In addition, in Section 3(c) of the 1979 act the Congress adopted virtually the same procedure for amending U.S.

law implementing the MTN agreements when such amendments are necessary to fulfill a "requirement of, amendment to, or recommendation under
such an agreement. * * * " Thus, if an international disputes panel rules
against the United States on a question of interpretation of an MTN
agreement, and U.S. law prevented the executive branch from implementing
the international interpretation, this procedure could be followed to change
U.S. law.

The "fast-track" procedure thus holds considerable potential for the
future, as a means of accommodating the interests of both the executive
branch in its international dealings and the Congress with its responsiveness
to constituents. One might even hope that the rancor between these two
branches of government over international trade policy during the past
several decades may be considerably softened by the "fast-track" procedure.
This could have important implications for the future of the GATT–MTN
system.

The second interesting aspect of the procedures for enacting the 1979 act
is a somewhat unusual problem concerning the techniques of interpreting it.
Normally U.S. courts are influenced in their interpretation of a statute by
its legislative history. This history consists of, among other things, the
committee hearings and debates, the committee reports, and statements on
the floor of both houses while the bill was being considered. * * * Under
the "fast-track" procedure, however, a bill was introduced by the executive
branch and could not be amended. Thus the executive branch was in theory
the draftsman, and its intent was arguably the intent of the draftsman. The
executive branch sent to Congress, along with the drafted bill, a Statement
of Administrative Action indicating its intentions in administering the new
legislation. Thus this statement is an important part of the legislative
history, and arguably is the definitive source of legislative intent. However,
[the House Report] * * * stakes out a claim to be considered as a prime
source of legislative history, just as it would normally be for other legislation. Moreover it also presents a view of the role of the Statement of
Administrative Action, and notes that those statements "are not part of the
bill and will not become part of U.S. statutes. * * * They will not provide
any new, independent legal authority for executive action."

Finally, the role of the MTN agreements themselves in the legislative
history must be considered. As will be seen below, it is clear that the
agreements do not themselves become U.S. law, but the committee reports
state, "This bill is drafted with the intent to permit U.S. practice to be
consistent with the obligations of the agreements, as the United States
understands those obligations." Thus it seems fair to conclude that the
trade agreements (and presumably *their* preparatory work) can be used as at
least a secondary source of legislative history of the 1979 act when other
sources fail to resolve an issue.

One additional aspect of the Trade Agreements Act of 1979 should be
noted. The act clearly covers a number of matters not explicitly required by
any of the MTN agreements or other negotiation results. * * * Nevertheless, although the "fast-track" procedure purports to be a means of implementing and approving the trade negotiation results, since the form of the

congressional action is that of a typical statute adopted through the normal constitutional procedures (and not through a procedure such as legislative veto or delegated regulations), the statute provides its own authority for even those matters that go beyond the necessities of implementing the MTN results.

With respect to the domestic law implementation of the Tokyo Round agreements, the 1979 act is quite interesting. We have previously discussed the problem of "self-executing" treaties in U.S. law (see Section 3.3 supra).

JOHN H. JACKSON, UNITED STATES LAW AND IMPLEMENTATION OF THE TOKYO ROUND NEGOTIATION
Supra, at 169–70.

The Trade Agreements Act of 1979 has two clauses that address this subject, which, although not models of clarity themselves, are clarified by the relevant committee reports and Statement of Administrative Action. The clauses are Sections 3(a) and 3(f).

Section 3(a) states:

SEC. 3. RELATIONSHIP OF TRADE AGREEMENTS TO UNITED STATES LAW.

(a) United States Statutes to Prevail in Conflict.—No provision of any trade agreement approved by the Congress under section 2(a), nor the application of any such provision to any person or circumstances, which is in conflict with any statute of the United States shall be given effect under the laws of the United States.

Section 3(f) states:

(f) Unspecified Private Remedies Not Created.—Neither the entry into force with respect to the United States of any agreement approved under section 2(a), nor the enactment of this Act, shall be construed as creating any private right of action or remedy for which provision is not explicitly made under this Act or under the laws of the United States.

The Statement of Administrative Action on the MTN agreements is unequivocal: "The Trade Agreements negotiated are not self-executing and accordingly do not have independent effect under U.S. law." The Senate and House reports follow suit, saying that "the trade agreements are not self-executing."

(F) THE STRUCTURE OF U.S. GOVERNMENT FOR CONDUCT OF FOREIGN ECONOMIC RELATIONS—AN OVERVIEW AND PERSPECTIVE

It is impossible here to give the reader any fixed or precise "road-map" of decision-making and exercises of regulatory power in the Executive Branch of the United States, because these functions are constantly shifting and changing.[49]   At the apex, of course, is the White House and the aides and assistants immediately surrounding the President.   Each President tends to operate with these individuals in a different way, and so the lines of authority tend to shift from one President to the next, and indeed even during the term of office of a particular President.   Some Presidents have designated one particular "assistant" through which all international economic matters will funnel to the President.   Other Presidents have even designated a small "agency" in the White House to perform this coordinating function (such as the "CIEP," Council on International Economic Policy, for most of the 1970's.)   Most Presidents have also utilized "Cabinet Committees" of various types, which meet and make recommendations to the President.   President Reagan has had three such cabinet level committees with apparently overlapping jurisdiction on international trade, one of which is set up by statute, the others by presidential order.   The most significant agency for trade matters affiliated with the Office of the President is that of the U.S. Trade Representative (USTR), described below.

When one moves down from the apex of United States government policy formation and coordination, going beyond the borders of the Executive Office of the President, one finds considerably more stability in the allocation of functions relating to various statutory delegations of authority over international economic policy.   These functions are widely dispersed among various governmental agencies or departments.   Many of these agencies or departments have developed particular constituencies, with special interest in the regulatory measures, that lead the departments to guard their jurisdiction jealously.   It is not surprising, therefore, that occasions will arise when the United States government will be taking actions through one department, which are, or at least appear to be, inconsistent with actions taken by another department.   The following is a very brief summary of some of the agencies involved in international economic policy.   Overall, it is quite easy to count over four dozen agencies in the Executive Branch with jurisdiction touching on international economic matters, and over a dozen independent agencies or authorities with such concerns.   Add to these the dozen and a half congressional committees and subcommittees giving attention to these matters, and one can begin to appreciate the difficulty of originating and implementing a consistent overall international economic policy for the United States.

In recent years there have been a number of proposals to centralize and unify executive branch authority over international trade into a single department, sometimes called the "DITI" (Department of International Trade and Industry).   These proposals have been very controversial.   Some of them would merge the USTR with most of the current Commerce Department to create such new department.   Some would even include in

---

49. A description of trade policy functions as of December 1984, as well as a summary of U.S. trade laws, is found in Subcomm. in Trade, House Comm. on Ways & Means, Overview of Current Provisions of U.S. Trade Law 128–39 (98th Cong., 2d Sess. Comm. Print: WMCP: 98–40, 1984). Much of the informa-tion of this sub-section can also be found in the United States Government Manual. Other information has been obtained from interviews or from one of the author's general knowledge obtained from his work in Washington.

this department the current independent commission called the "International Trade Commission" (see below.) [50]

(1) Agencies Affiliated to the Executive Office of the President

The most significant agency on trade matters in the Executive Branch is the office of the United States Trade Representative (USTR). Originally entitled the "STR" (Special Trade Representative) in the 1962 Act which started this agency, its permanence was recognized by a change of name in a 1980 Presidential reorganization order. The 1974 Act had already elevated the head of this agency (always called the Trade Representative, with status of Ambassador Extraordinary and Plenipotentiary) to cabinet level. (The only other non-department head at this level is the U.S. Ambassador to the United Nations.) [51]

This agency is charged with negotiations with foreign nations on trade and a number of other economic matters, and coordinates much of the United States government policy formulation on such matters. Statutes have set up a group of inter-agency committees, and USTR officials are often charged, either by statute or presidential order, to chair such committees. The agency has always been small, however, usually numbering only slightly more than 100 professional level staff persons. It often relies on other agencies or departments for staff work, and receives help from persons detailed from other agencies.

Inter-agency committees on trade include the basic working committee "TSC", Trade Staff Committee, and its sub-committees for specific subjects. Middle level officials of many departments and agencies, often all those discussed below, sit on this committee, which drafts instructions and cables for U.S. representatives abroad, prepares testimony and bills for Congress, etc. When agreement is not possible at this level, matters tend to be considered by an intermediate level supervising committee on which the representatives are usually from the Assistant Secretary level. When disagreement continues, the matter will go to a cabinet level committee, such as the statutory Trade Policy Committee chaired by the USTR. Finally matters will be referred to the President for his decision.

In addition to the agencies or offices mentioned in the preceding paragraphs which deal with coordination and policy formation, a number of other agencies reporting directly to the President have concerns relating to international economic policy. The Office of Management and Budget (OMB) has a major division devoted to international affairs, and a portion of this monitors international economic policy, from a budgetary and a substantive point of view. The Council of Economic Advisors has been giving increasing attention to international economic affairs, since these affairs have important effects on the domestic economy. The Central Intelligence Agency is on call to respond to needs for studies or other information of various policy-making officers.

50. See 2 BNA Intl. Trade Rptr. 88, 421 (1985).

51. See Trade Expansion Act of 1962, Pub. L. No. 87–794, §§ 241–42, 76 Stat. 878 (codified in part at 19 U.S.C.A. § 1872); Trade Act of 1974, Pub.L. No. 93–618, § 141, 88 Stat. 1999 (codified at 19 U.S.C.A. § 2171); Reorganization Plan No. 3 of 1979, 93 Stat. 1381; Executive Order No. 12188 of Jan. 2, 1980, 45 Fed.Reg. 989.

(2) Department of State

The Department of State, as the principal United States department for foreign affairs, obviously is deeply concerned with international economic matters, although its reputation in Congress for handling these matters is not good. The Department has a major bureau entitled The Bureau of Economic and Business Affairs, directed by an assistant secretary of state. In addition, there is an undersecretary for economic affairs at a higher level. The Agency for International Development (AID) and the Overseas Private Investment Corporation (OPIC) are closely affiliated to the Department of State. The State Department tends not to be the recipient of specific delegated authorities under congressional statutes relating to various regulatory actions, but the Department's central role in international diplomacy and in world-wide communications for the United States inevitably gives it an important role in international economic affairs. Often when international agreements are to be negotiated and concluded, this is done through State Department personnel and logistical support.

(3) Department of the Treasury

The Treasury directly controls the implementation of some of the key regulations of international economic affairs. Principal and most extensive of these is the United States Customs Service (formerly Bureau of Customs), which collects tariffs at the border and performs a number of other regulatory functions in connection with imports and exports. It previously administered the countervailing duty and antidumping laws of the United States, but these duties were moved to the Commerce Department in 1980, as described below. An Undersecretary for Monetary Affairs, and his office, have considerable responsibilities in international monetary affairs, representing the United States at monetary conferences and in major international financial and monetary organizations such as the International Monetary Fund and the International Bank for Reconstruction and Development. The Treasury has some of its staff placed directly abroad, as attachés to embassies. In addition, the Treasury controls the "exchange stabilization fund," a large sum of money derived from United States direct account participation in international exchange markets, on behalf of policies relating to the dollar. In recent years, the Treasury has had a major role in East-West trade matters, in energy and commodity policy, bilateral trade commissions, and national security restrictions under section 232 of the 1962 Trade Expansion Act.

(4) Department of Commerce

The Department of Commerce has been delegated direct implementing responsibility for the export control legislation and regulations and since 1980, for countervailing and antidumping duties. In the 1980 reorganization, a major agency called the ITA—International Trade Administration, (not to be confused with the ITC—International Trade Commission), was established in the Department, with subdivisions for export controls, for import administration (antidumping and countervailing duties) and for export promotion activities.

(5) Department of Agriculture

International trade in agricultural goods has for decades been one of the troubled subjects of international economic policy. The Department of Agriculture has been delegated a number of responsibilities relating to international trade in agricultural and commodity goods, both as to importation and exportation. On the export side, the Commodity Credit Corporation provides liberal credit terms for the export of various United States produced agricultural goods. Likewise, the Department and the CCC have major roles under Public Law 480, the Agricultural Trade Development and Assistance Act of 1954 (under which food aid is shipped abroad). On the import side, the Department zealously protects regulations limiting the importation of agricultural goods, under section 22 of the Agricultural Adjustment Act of 1933. The Foreign Agricultural Service (FAS) locates attaché personnel at major United States embassies around the world, works to promote the exportation of agricultural products from the United States, and helps develop United States policy for trade in agricultural goods and commodities.

(6) Department of Labor

In addition to general participation in policy formulation, the Department of Labor has responsibility for the worker adjustment assistance program under the Trade Act of 1974. Consequently, it is this department that determines the availability of special unemployment and relocation compensation for workers who have been affected by imports to the United States (see Chapter 9).

(7) Department of Defense

The Defense Department has a major office for international security affairs, and is involved, perhaps somewhat less directly than the other departments mentioned above, in the formulation of major economic policy, particularly as it relates to national security. One area of intense interest to the Department of Defense has been the export control program, particularly the export of strategic materials or implements of war.

(8) Other Departments

Other departments with roles to play in international economic affairs include the Department of Justice, particularly its Office of Legal Counsel and the Foreign Commerce Section of the Antitrust Division, the Department of Energy, with a major role on oil import matters and energy policies, and the Department of Transportation, with a major role in civil aviation.

(9) Independent Agencies

Perhaps the most important independent agency relating to international economic and trade affairs is the United States International Trade Commission (formerly the United States Tariff Commission), which plays an advisory role on important issues, including the escape clause (see Chapter 9). In addition to this Commission, the Export-Import Bank of the United States provides credits for exports from the United States; various regulatory commissions, including the Federal Energy Regulatory Commission (FERC), the Federal Trade Commission (FTC), and the Foreign Claims Settlement Commission, all have some activity relating to international economic policy.   In addition, the Federal Reserve Board system regulates the international banking activities of American banks abroad, and to a certain extent foreign banks in the United States, as well as handling, through the Federal Reserve Bank of New York, the foreign exchange activities of the United States.   (The Comptroller of the Currency also has some jurisdiction in this area.)

SECTION 3.5   THE COURTS AND FOREIGN RELATIONS

(A)   INTRODUCTION

The cases in the previous sections of this chapter suggest considerable hesitancy on the part of the courts to "second-guess" the President in his conduct of foreign affairs.   As Professor Henkin has written "[F]oreign affairs make a difference.   The courts are less willing to curb the political branches and have even developed doctrines of special deference to them. They have asserted judicial power to develop doctrines to safeguard the national interest in international relations against both judicial interference and invasion by the States." [1]

A prime example of such action by the federal courts is the Act of State doctrine under which courts in the United States generally decline to examine the validity of acts of a governmental nature taken by a foreign sovereign government within its own territory.   This doctrine has been held by the Supreme Court to be a matter of federal law, and therefore must be applied by state courts.[2]   Although the Supreme Court has recognized that there may be exceptions to the doctrine, its hesitancy to intrude into foreign affairs is highlighted by the fact that the principal exception to the Act of State doctrine was created by Congress in reaction to the *Sabbatino* decision.[3]   Similarly in the area of sovereign immunity—the general principle that a sovereign government cannot be sued without its consent, it has been Congress and not the courts that has taken the lead in expanding the jurisdiction of U.S. courts into areas that those courts had been hesitant to enter.[4]   These two topics are treated extensively in most international law casebooks and will not be examined here.[5]

---

1. L. Henkin, Foreign Affairs and the Constitution 206 (1972).

2. Banco Nacional de Cuba v. Sabbatino, 376 U.S. 398, 84 S.Ct. 923, 11 L.Ed.2d 804 (1964).

3. 22 U.S.C.A. § 2370(e)(2).   This exception, created by the so-called Second Hickenlooper Amendment, provides that a U.S. court shall not invoke the Act of State doctrine in cases of expropriation that are illegal under principles of international law unless the President suggests to the court that the doctrine should be applied.

4. See Foreign Sovereign Immunities Act of 1976, Pub.L. No. 94–583, 90 Stat. 2891.

5. See, e.g., W. Bishop, International Law 659–700, 876–99 (3rd ed. 1971); L. Henkin, R. Pugh, O. Schachter & H. Smit, International Law: Cases and Materials 123–35, 490–524 (2d ed. 1980), H. Steiner & D. Vagts, Transnational Legal Problems 637–728 (2d ed. 1976); J. Sweeney, C. Oliver & H. Leech, The International Legal System 288–420 (2d ed. 1981).

In this section, we will look first at a leading Supreme Court case, where the Court goes out of its way to avoid reviewing action taken by a regulatory agency because the President had the final say over the agency's ultimate decision. We will then look at how lower federal courts have reviewed a variety of executive decisions taken under the various statutes regulating international trade. In doing so, we will give particular attention to the recent creation and actions of the specialized federal courts in this area: the Court of International Trade and the U.S. Court of Appeals for the Federal Circuit.

(B) JUDICIAL REVIEW AND FOREIGN AFFAIRS

CHICAGO & SOUTHERN AIR LINES, INC. v. WATERMAN S.S. CORP.

Supreme Court of the United States, 1948.
333 U.S. 103, 68 S.Ct. 431, 92 L.Ed. 568.

MR. JUSTICE JACKSON delivered the opinion of the Court.

[By a five to four decision, the Supreme Court reversed a court of appeals decision and dismissed the petition of an airline company (Waterman) which was protesting the award of an international air route (between the U.S. and a foreign country) to Chicago and Southern.]

Congress has set up a comprehensive scheme for regulation of common carriers by air. Many statutory provisions apply indifferently whether the carrier is a foreign air carrier or a citizen air carrier, and whether the carriage involved is "interstate air commerce," "overseas air commerce" or "foreign air commerce," each being appropriately defined. 49 U.S.C. § 401(20), 49 U.S.C.A. § 401(20). All air carriers by similar procedures must obtain from the Board certificates of convenience and necessity by showing a public interest in establishment of the route and the applicant's ability to serve it. But when a foreign carrier asks for any permit, or a citizen carrier applies for a certificate to engage in any overseas or foreign air transportation, a copy of the application must be transmitted to the President before hearing; and any decision, either to grant or to deny, must be submitted to the President before publication and is unconditionally subject to the President's approval. Also the statute subjects to judicial review "any order, affirmative or negative, issued by the Board under this Act, except any order in respect of any foreign air carrier subject to the approval of the President as provided in section 801 of this Act." It grants no express exemption to an order such as the one before us, which concerns a citizen carrier but which must have Presidential approval because it involves overseas and foreign air transportation. The question is whether an exemption is to be implied.

This Court long has held that statutes which employ broad terms to confer power of judicial review are not always to be read literally. Where Congress has authorized review of "any order" or used other equally inclusive terms, courts have declined the opportunity to magnify their jurisdiction, by self-denying constructions which do not subject to judicial control orders which, from their nature, from the context of the Act, or from the relation of judicial power to the subject-matter, are inappropriate for review.

The Waterman Steamship Corporation urges that review of the problems involved in establishing foreign air routes are of no more international delicacy or strategic importance than those involved in routes for water carriage. * * *

We find no indication that the Congress either entertained or fostered the narrow concept that air-borne commerce is a mere outgrowth or overgrowth of surface-bound transport. * * *

The "public interest" that enters into awards of routes for aerial carriers, who in effect obtain also a sponsorship by our government in foreign ventures, is not confined to adequacy of transportation service, as we have held when that term is applied to railroads. That aerial navigation routes and bases should be prudently correlated with facilities and plans for our own national defenses and raise new problems in conduct of foreign relations, is a fact of common knowledge. Congressional hearings and debates extending over several sessions and departmental studies of many years show that the legislative and administrative processes have proceeded in full recognition of these facts.

*   *   *

But when a foreign carrier seeks to engage in public carriage over the territory or waters of this country, or any carrier seeks the sponsorship of this Government to engage in overseas or foreign air transportation, Congress has completely inverted the usual administrative process. Instead of acting independently of executive control, the agency is then subordinated to it. Instead of its order serving as a final disposition of the application, its force is exhausted when it serves as a recommendation to the President. Instead of being handed down to the parties as the conclusion of the administrative process, it must be submitted to the President, before publication even can take place. Nor is the President's control of the ultimate decision a mere right of veto. It is not alone issuance of such authorizations that are subject to his approval, but denial, transfer, amendment, cancellation or suspension, as well. And likewise subject to his approval are the terms, conditions and limitations of the order. 49 U.S.C. § 601, 49 U.S.C.A. § 601. Thus, Presidential control is not limited to a negative but is a positive and detailed control over the Board's decisions, unparalleled in the history of American administrative bodies.

Congress may of course delegate very large grants of its power over foreign commerce to the President. The President also possesses in his own right certain powers conferred by the Constitution on him as Commander-in-Chief and as the Nation's organ in foreign affairs. For present purposes, the order draws vitality from either or both sources. Legislative and Executive powers are pooled obviously to the end that commercial strategic and diplomatic interests of the country may be coordinated and advanced without collision or deadlock between agencies.

*   *   *

In this case, submission of the Board's decision was made to the President, who disapproved certain portions of it and advised the Board of the changes which he required. The Board complied and submitted a revised order and opinion which the President approved. Only then were they made public, and that which was made public and which is before us is only the final order and opinion containing the President's amendments and bearing his approval. Only at that stage was review sought and only then could it be pursued, for then only was the decision consummated, announced and available to the parties.

While the changes made at direction of the President may be identified, the reasons therefor are not disclosed beyond the statement that "because of certain factors relating to our broad national welfare and other matters for which the Chief Executive has special responsibility, he has reached conclusions which require" changes in the Board's opinion.

The court below considered, and we think quite rightly, that it could not review such provisions of the order as resulted from Presidential direction. The President, both as Commander-in-Chief and as the Nation's organ for foreign affairs, has available intelligence services whose reports neither are nor ought to be published to the world. It would be intolerable that courts, without the relevant information, should review and perhaps nullify actions of the Executive taken on information properly held secret. Nor can courts sit in camera in order to be taken into executive confidences. But even if courts could require full disclosure, the very nature of executive decisions as to foreign policy is political, not judicial. Such decisions are wholly confided by our Constitution to the political departments of the government, Executive and Legislative. They are delicate, complex and involve large elements of prophecy. They are and should be undertaken only by those directly responsible to the people whose welfare they advance or imperil. They are decisions of a kind for which the Judiciary has neither aptitude, facilities nor responsibility and have long been held to belong in the domain of political power not subject to judicial intrusion or inquiry. We therefore agree that whatever of this order emanates from the President is not susceptible of review by the Judicial Department.

* * *

* * * The dilemma faced by those who demand judicial review of the Board's order is that, before Presidential approval, it is not a final determination even of the Board's ultimate action, and after Presidential approval, the whole order, both in what is approved without change, as well as in amendments which he directs, derives its vitality from the exercise of unreviewable Presidential discretion.

* * *

MR. JUSTICE DOUGLAS, with whom MR. JUSTICE BLACK, MR. JUSTICE REED and MR. JUSTICE RUTLEDGE concur, dissenting.

* * *

* * * Congress made reviewable by the courts only orders "issued by the Board under this Act." Those orders can be reviewed without reference to any conduct of the President, for that part of the orders which is the work of the Board is plainly identifiable.[*5] The President is presumably concerned only with the impact of the order of foreign relations or military

---

* 5. The Board had consolidated for hearing 29 applications for certificates to engage in air transportation which were filed by 15 applicants. The President's partial disapproval of the proposed disposition of these applications did not relate to the applications involved in this case. As to them, the action of the Board stands unaltered.

matters. To the extent that he disapproves action taken by the Board, his action controls. But where that is not done, the Board's order has an existence independent of Presidential approval, tracing to Congress' power to regulate commerce. Approval by the President under this statutory scheme has relevance for purposes of review only as indicating *when* the action of the Board is reviewable. When the Board has finished with the order, the administrative function is ended. When the order fixes rights, on clearance by the President, it becomes reviewable. But the action of the President does not broaden the review. Review is restricted to the action of the Board and the Board alone.

* * *

Judicial review would assure the President, the litigants and the public that the Board had acted within the limits of its authority. It would carry out the aim of Congress to guard against administrative action which exceeds the statutory bounds. It would give effect to the interests of both Congress and the President in this field.

Notes and Questions

(1) In HAIG v. AGEE, 453 U.S. 280, 101 S.Ct. 2766, 69 L.Ed.2d 640 (1981), the Supreme Court upheld State Department regulations applied to revoke the passport of an American citizen who was engaged in a campaign to expose the identities of agents of the Central Intelligence Agency. In so doing, it stated (453 U.S. at 290–92, 101 S.Ct. at 2773–74):

> The [1926] Passport Act does not in so many words confer upon the Secretary a power to revoke a passport. Nor, for that matter, does it expressly authorize denials of passport applications. Neither, however, does any statute expressly limit those powers. It is beyond dispute that the Secretary has the power to deny a passport for reasons not specified in the statutes. * * * Particularly in light of the "broad rule-making authority granted in the [1926] Act," *Zemel* [v. Rusk], 381 U.S., at 12, 85 S.Ct., at 1278 [1965], a consistent administrative construction of that statute must be followed by the courts " 'unless there are compelling indications that it is wrong.' " This is especially so in the areas of foreign policy and national security, where congressional silence is not to be equated with congressional disapproval. * * * Applying these considerations to statutory construction, the *Zemel* Court observed:

>> "[B]ecause of the changeable and explosive nature of contemporary international relations, and the fact that the Executive is immediately privy to information which cannot be swiftly presented to, evaluated by, and acted upon by the legislature, *Congress—in giving the Executive authority over matters of foreign affairs—must of necessity paint with a brush broader than that it customarily wields in domestic areas.*" 381 U.S., at 17, 85 S.Ct., at 1281 (emphasis supplied).

Matters intimately related to foreign policy and national security are rarely proper subjects for judicial intervention. In Harisiades v. Shaughnessy, 342 U.S. 580, 72 S.Ct. 512, 96 L.Ed. 586 (1952), the Court observed that matters relating "to the conduct of foreign relations * * * are so exclusively entrusted to the political branches of government as to be largely immune from judicial inquiry or interference." Id., at 589, 72 S.Ct., at 519; accord,

Chicago & Southern Air Lines, Inc. v. Waterman S.S. Corp., 333 U.S. 103, 111, 68 S.Ct. 431, 436, 92 L.Ed. 568 (1948).

The opinion by Chief Justice Burger in this 7–2 decision was issued three days before *Dames & Moore v. Regan*, discussed in Section 3.2(B) supra.

(2) Are the policy reasons for deference to presidential discretion when exercised in the area of foreign affairs persuasive? Do these reasons adequately provide a rationale for distinguishing between foreign and domestic affairs as to the degree of judicial review that is appropriate? Do any of the reasons stated as applying to foreign affairs also apply to domestic affairs? If the world continues on a course of greater and greater economic (and other) interdependence, and more of everyone's affairs become intertwined with international transactions or policies, will a policy of greater deference to executive prerogative in foreign affairs cause serious inroads into the U.S. constitutional system of checks and balances? of protection of individual citizen rights?

(3) The February 1, 1977 issue of Forbes magazine at page 23, described the procedure for presidential determinations under § 801 of the Federal Aviation Act as "a political cesspool," in reporting on an application by Delta Airlines for a transatlantic route from London to Atlanta and Texas which had been recommended by the CAB, but sent back by President Ford for a new analysis. The Forbes article suggested that the President's action may have been politically motivated because the outgoing administration was "piqued at the South, which voted for Carter." The article concludes: "If there is a moral to this, it is that Section 801 causes more trouble than it is worth. The State Department negotiates landing rights with other countries; by itself the CAB should decide which U.S. carriers fly under them. Other regulators—in international banking and telecommunications, for example—deal with foreign policy issues." (The CAB no longer exists; its functions were taken over by the Department of Transportation.)

(C) THE COURT OF INTERNATIONAL TRADE AND LOWER FEDERAL COURT INTERPRETATION OF TRADE STATUTES

(1) The Court of International Trade

Most litigation involving international trade statutes in the United States now occurs in the Court of International Trade (CIT). The CIT was formerly known as the Customs Court. It received its new name in a 1980 statute that also significantly expanded its jurisdiction.[6] The CIT is an Article III court of nine judges, no more than five of whom may belong to any one political party. It is based in New York, but sits throughout the United States. Its decisions are appealable to the U.S. Court of Appeals for the Federal Circuit (formerly the Court of Customs and Patent Appeals), and ultimately to the Supreme Court.

---

6. Customs Courts Act of 1980, Pub.L. No. 96–417, 94 Stat. 1727. The exclusive jurisdiction of the Court of International Trade was made broader in 1980 in part to avoid the problem of conflicting decisions on trade issues arising in the District Courts. Prior to the 1980 Act, there was confusion as to the extent of the Customs Court's exclusive jurisdiction and some parties preferred to litigate in District Courts because the limited powers of the Customs Court often meant they could not obtain what they viewed as appropriate relief (e.g. injunctions). See H.Rep. No. 96–1235, 96th Cong., 2d Sess. 19 (1980). See generally Recent Developments, The Customs Courts Act of 1980, 13 Law & Poly. Intl. Bus. 281 (1981).

The CIT has exclusive jurisdiction under 28 U.S.C.A. § 1581 over appeals or actions involving (a) denials of protests by the U.S. Customs Service, (b) challenges by U.S. competitors of import classification decisions, (c) antidumping and countervailing duty cases, (d) trade adjustment assistance to workers, firms and communities, (e) country of origin determinations, (f) disputes over the confidentiality of information submitted to the International Trade Commission, (g) customshouse brokers' licenses, (h) challenges by importers of classification decisions and (i) the United States as a defendant that arise out of any law providing for revenues from imports; tariffs, duties, fees or other taxes on imports; and embargoes or quantitative restrictions on imports (other than those imposed for public health and safety reasons).[7] It also has jurisdiction under 28 U.S.C.A. § 1582 of civil actions by the United States to recover duties, penalties and customs bonds. Although some actions in the CIT may only be brought by a narrowly defined class, the 1980 Act in general greatly expanded access to the CIT to include most persons with a real interest in challenging or defending a trade-related action.[8]

The scope of review in the CIT depends on the type of action brought. A trial "de novo" is held in actions brought by the United States under § 1582 and in cases where jurisdiction is based on § 1581, category (a), (b), (e), (f) or (g) of the preceding paragraph.[9] In antidumping and countervailing duty cases, certain government actions are reviewed to determine if they were arbitrary, capricious, an abuse of discretion or unlawful; while others are reviewed to determine if they were supported by substantial evidence in the agency record or unlawful.[10] In trade adjustment assistance cases, the determinations of the agency are considered conclusive if supported by substantial evidence in the record, but the CIT has the authority for good cause shown to order the agency to take further evidence.[11] In all other actions, the CIT's review is made pursuant to the Administrative Procedure Act, which generally establishes a substantial-evidence standard for agency action taken on a record and an arbitrary-capricious standard for other agency action.[12]

(2) Standards of Review

This somewhat complex structure of review for international trade actions taken by the Executive Branch largely reflects a desire by Congress to limit Executive discretion under certain trade statutes. Given the opportunity, private litigants quickly began to challenge Executive action more frequently. Indeed, challenges of preliminary decisions in antidumping and countervailing duty cases became so burdensome that Congress limited them in 1984.[13] We will consider recent CIT and Federal Circuit decisions in some detail when we examine the various U.S. trade statutes in Part II. Here we

7. There is an exception to the CIT's jurisdiction for imports of obscene materials.

8. See 28 U.S.C.A. § 2631.

9. 28 U.S.C.A. § 2640(a).

10. 28 U.S.C.A. § 2640(b); 19 U.S.C.A. § 1516a.

11. 28 U.S.C.A. § 2640(c); 19 U.S.C.A. § 2395(b).

12. 28 U.S.C.A. § 2640(d); 5 U.S.C.A. § 706.

13. Trade and Tariff Act of 1984, § 623 (elimination of interlocutory appeals), Pub.L. No. 98–573, 98 Stat. 2948, amending 19 U.S.C.A. § 1516a.

will only try to give a flavor of the strictness of the scrutiny provided by the CIT and the Federal Circuit and of how it seems to vary depending on the nature of the challenged action.

Customs Classification. In Stewart-Warner Corp. v. United States, 748 F.2d 663 (Fed.Cir.1984), the issue was whether speedometers attached to exercise cycles should be classified as "bicycle" speedometers or "other" speedometers. The Court of Appeals explained the standard for review as follows: "The meaning of customs classification terms, such as 'bicycle speedometers,' is an issue of law which we review independently, while the question whether a particular item fits that meaning is a question of fact which we review under the clearly erroneous standard. In a classification challenge * * * the Customs Service's decision is presumed correct, and the burden of proving otherwise rests upon the challenger." 748 F.2d at 664–65. The Court then concluded that the CIT erred in reversing the Custom Service's decision that the speedometers were "other" speedometers. Its decision depended in large part on applying the rule that in a classification based on use (like bicycle speedometers), the controlling use is the chief use of product (which here was on exercise machines).

Escape Clause. Maple Leaf Fish Co. v. United States, 762 F.2d 86 (Fed. Cir.1985), arose under the so-called Escape Clause, which we will consider in detail in Chapter 9. The issue was the standard of review to be applied to a challenge to the President's decision to order import relief measures after the International Trade Commission (ITC) had found that the U.S. prepared and preserved mushroom industry was being injured by imports of those products. Maple Leaf claimed that (1) the ITC investigation did not cover frozen mushrooms and that the President therefore had no authority to impose additional duties on them and (2) if the investigation did cover frozen mushrooms, the ITC had no basis for its finding of injury in respect thereof. The Court ruled (762 F.2d at 89):

> The question then is to what extent the courts can review the challenged actions of the Commission and the President in such a case. The critical element is that the area of the "escape clause" legislation undoubtedly involves the President and his close relationship to foreign affairs, our nation's connections with other countries, and the external ramifications of international trade. More than that, Congress has vested the President with very broad discretion and choice as to what he decides to do affirmatively, or even whether he should do anything. * * *
>
> In international trade controversies of this highly discretionary kind—involving the President and foreign affairs—this court and its predecessors have often reiterated the very limited role of reviewing courts. For a court to interpose, there has to be clear misconstruction of the governing statute, a significant procedural violation, or action outside delegated authority. On the other hand, "[t]he President's findings of fact and the motivations for his action are not subject to review."

Multifiber Arrangement. In upholding action taken by the Executive Branch in respect of limitations on textile imports against challenges alleging statutory, administrative and constitutional defects, the Court of Appeals for the Federal Circuit stated:

We accentuate, again, that legislation conferring upon the President discretion to regulate foreign commerce invokes, and is reinforced and augmented by, the President's constitutional power to oversee the political side of foreign affairs. "In the intercourse of nations, changes in economic relationships have many an important political corollary." In the area of international trade, "intimately involved in foreign affairs," "congressional authorizations of presidential power should be given a broad construction and not 'hemmed in' or 'cabined, cribbed, confined' by anxious judicial blinders."

American Assn. of Exporters & Importers—Textile & Apparel Group v. United States, 751 F.2d 1239, 1248 (Fed.Cir.1985).

Antidumping Duties. In Alberta Gas Chemicals, Inc. v. United States, 515 F.Supp. 780 (CIT 1981), an importer challenged the finding of injury to domestic industry made by the International Trade Commission (ITC), a prerequisite for imposing antidumping duties, as we shall see in Chapter 10. In rejecting that finding, the CIT reviewed the legislative history of the relevant statute and found that the ITC had not properly applied the statute. "In summary, the record before the Commission shows simply a mere *possibility* that injury might occur at some remote future time. Such showing, viewed in the context of the 'real and imminent' standard enunciated by Congress, compels the conclusion that the record lacks substantial evidence of likelihood of injury." 515 F.Supp. at 791.

Countervailing Duties. In Michelin Tire Co. v. United States, 4 Intl. Trade Rptr. Dec. 1450 (December 22, 1983), the CIT described its review of the case as follows:

> In its first decision on the subject, the Court, among other things, found that the grants were no longer linked to the repayment of certain loans and therefore should not have their benefit allocated over the period of the loans. The Court remanded the question of the proper allocation period. In the next opinion, the Court disapproved the method by which the International Trade Administration of the Department of Commerce (ITA) had allocated the face value of the grants over *half* the useful life of the assets which they were used to purchase. The Court criticized the method as an arbitrary allocation of benefit. The Court remanded the matter again and spoke approvingly of a method which would recognize the time value of money over the life of the assets purchased. In the latest administrative determination the ITA has used a method which takes into account the time value of money. It incorporates this method into a calculation known as the present value of an annuity, a technique which has its most familiar use in the calculation of the standard home mortgage repayment schedule.

> The Court, although it approves the recognition of the time value of money, finds the annuity method used by the ITA to be incorrect for use in the valuation of these grants.

Adjustment Assistance. In Katunich v. Donovan, 594 F.Supp. 744 (CIT 1984), an appeal of the Secretary of Labor's decision to refuse to grant benefits under the Trade Act of 1974, the CIT stated (594 F.Supp. at 753):

> In light of the Secretary's admission that "1980 would have been a better year for the present analysis," it was incumbent upon the Secretary to make a greater effort to obtain the required information. The record

does not reveal any efforts made by the Secretary to obtain the necessary information for a meaningful evaluation of plaintiffs' petition.

The court, therefore, finds that the method utilized by the Secretary in interpreting the existence of "increases of imports" evidences inconsistent application of data, and reliance upon incomplete data which renders it defective. Furthermore, the Secretary has not proffered a valid reason for the court to consider a base period other than the one enunciated in prior cases.

In view of the foregoing, it is the determination of this Court that the method utilized in this case which led to the Secretary's determination that "increases of imports" did not contribute importantly to plaintiffs' separation from employment, is not supported by substantial evidence, and is not in accordance with law. 594 F.Supp. at 753.

Summary. If any conclusion can be drawn from the foregoing, it would seem to be that where courts are dealing with detailed statutory provisions, with legislative history that indicates dissatisfaction with past administration of those laws, such as the antidumping and countervailing duty laws, they are willing to exercise serious oversight of Executive Branch actions on the grounds that Congress has specified in some detail what rights it wishes to be protected. On the other hand, where courts are dealing with broad grants of power to the President or ministerial actions involving Customs administration, they are unlikely to second guess the Executive Branch. The reader should consider in reading Part II whether these conclusions are well-grounded. Also, are these cases consistent with the cases we examined in Section 3.4(B) above?

(3) *The Costs of Judicial Review*

The large increase in trade-related cases brought in the federal courts in the last few years has caused some to wonder if the costs of judicial review of complex administrative procedures are too high. One of the authors of this book has contrasted the benefits of the present system—promotion of open, informed, consistent decision-making by trade officials, giving every interested party a "day in court" and thereby promoting acceptance of decisions—with the costs—the risk of creating inflexible rules, unjustified harassment of weaker parties, large fees payable to lawyers and economists. His conclusions are set out in Chapter 23. As we analyze the operation of the many U.S. trade laws, particularly in Chapters 9 and 10, the reader should attempt to form a view of whether the costs would seem to outweigh the apparent benefits.

SECTION 3.6 FEDERAL–STATE RELATIONS AND INTERNATIONAL ECONOMIC REGULATION

(A) INTRODUCTION

The United States has a federal form of government under its Constitution. A constitutional U.S. federal law overrides an inconsistent state law, although the Constitution places some limits on the powers of Congress and the federal government. The evolution of the division of powers between the federal government and the state governments has a long and complex history.   There are two important questions involved here.   First, what constitutional limitations are there on state government exercise of power when such activity affects international commerce (as almost everything does today).   Second, the reverse situation: what limitations are there on the federal government which result from reserved powers to the states under the Constitution?   As to the latter, as a practical matter, there are today few, if any, limits upon the federal government's ability to regulate economic and commercial affairs generally.[1]

JOHN H. JACKSON, UNITED STATES LAW AND IMPLEMENTATION OF THE TOKYO ROUND NEGOTIATION

(1984) [2]

Since the structure of the U.S. government under its Constitution is federal in nature—that is, it consists not only of a central government but also of state governments that have considerable independent authority and sovereignty—it might be thought that the division of powers between the federal and state governments would be an important constraint on the scope of federal government action in the area of foreign affairs.   Indeed, at the outset of the republic, the states were first independent sovereignties after obtaining independence from Great Britain.   It was these states that joined together, first into a confederacy, and later into the United States under the Constitution of 1788.

There has been a long and extraordinarily detailed history of constitutional evolution and accommodation between state powers and the federal powers.   However, as to the division of these powers in foreign affairs, the Supreme Court has had relatively few occasions on which to pronounce. Furthermore, in domestic affairs, the evolution of U.S. constitutional law has been generally in the direction of concentrating power in the federal government.   It is reasonably well established today that the federal government has supremacy, if it chooses to exercise it, over almost all issues that have any commercial overtones.

* * *

In foreign affairs, there is virtually no Supreme Court opinion that rules against the exercise of federal power on the grounds that it conflicts with state power, as long as the exercise of federal power was itself otherwise constitutional.   Thus, although the Supreme Court has held that state powers sometimes prevail over international treaties (such as in the offshore oil cases), the basis for this decision was itself an exercise of federal power, namely an act of Congress.

The courts and federal authorities can rely on a number of clauses in the Constitution in arguing that the exercise of federal power will prevail over state power in the areas of foreign relations.   Such clauses include the commerce clause, the supremacy clause, the treaty clause, and clauses on

1. See Section 3.3(C)(2) supra; J. Nowak, R. Rotunda & J. Young, Constitutional Law 138–81 (2d ed. 1983).

2. From J. Jackson, J.—V. Louis & M. Matsushita, Implementing the Tokyo Round:

National Constitutions and International Economic Rules 142–43 (1984). Reprinted by permission of the author.

presidential power, including his power to receive ambassadors, and his authority as Commander in Chief.

Notes and Questions

(1) In 1976, the Supreme Court (in a 5–4 decision) placed some limits on the power of the federal government to regulate state and local governments in National League of Cities v. Usery, 426 U.S. 833, 96 S.Ct. 2465, 49 L.Ed.2d 245 (1976), where it held that certain provisions of the Fair Labor Standards Act could not be applied to state and local government employees. The Court ruled essentially that the federal government could not impair the attributes of state sovereignty by regulating the wages of state employees and thereby interfering with the integral governmental functions of states. That case was overruled in a 5–4 decision in 1985. Garcia v. San Antonio Metropolitan Transit Authority, ___ U.S. ___, 105 S.Ct. 1005, 83 L.Ed.2d 1016 (1985). It remains to be seen whether the Court, as predicted by one dissenter, will reverse itself again soon.

(2) The questions that remain to some degree unanswered in the area of Federal-State relations concern the power of the states to regulate and tax foreign commerce. The Constitution authorizes the federal government to regulate such commerce, but what state power exists when the federal government has not acted or prohibited state action? The cases in this section have been selected to highlight important issues of Federal-State relations as applied to international trade. We come back to some of these issues later in the book, particularly in Chapters 5 (GATT as a restriction on state and local government action) and 8 (regarding governmental purchases). At this time the reader should consider such questions as

(A) Can states ever regulate goods imported from a foreign country? (or exports to be sent to a foreign country?) If they are not pre-empted, how far can they go? Are the tests of the limits on state power over interstate commerce also to be applied to foreign commerce, or will those tests be different?

(B) To what degree can states tax imports from another country? Tax foreign companies?

(C) Is there any limit on what the federal government of the United States can do by way of preventing state government actions (regulation, taxes, government purchases, etc.) which affect foreign commerce? (imports or exports? services as well as goods?)

These questions cannot all be answered, at least not definitively, but the materials in the next three sub-sections, treating respectively state regulation, state taxation, and state government purchasing and other proprietary actions, can suggest some directions.

(B) STATE REGULATION AND FOREIGN COMMERCE

TUPMAN THURLOW COMPANY v. MOSS

United States District Court, M.D. Tennessee, Nashville Division, 1966.
252 F.Supp. 641.

PER CURIAM.

* * *

Both Acts challenged in this proceeding were enacted by the 84th General Assembly of Tennessee, the Labeling Act having been passed on February 16, 1965, and the Licensing Act on March 16, 1965. The Labeling

Act requires that any person selling or offering for sale in the State of Tennessee any meats or meat foods which are the products of any foreign country to the United States "shall so identify each product and its foreign origin." If any product is offered for sale in bulk or portions whereby labeling is not feasible, it is provided that "a conspicuous sign in lieu of the label shall be displayed near the stock or display of the product." If foreign meats are combined with domestically produced meat into one product, the product shall be so labeled. In the event preservatives of any kind are used in any packaged meat product, the preservative shall be identified, along with the quantity used, and clearly displayed on any such package.

* * *

The Licensing Act requires the registration and the annual licensing of "each person, firm, or corporation in the State of Tennessee engaged in the business of manufacturing, buying, selling, handling, processing, packing or distributing imported meat or imported meat products, either at retail or wholesale." Imported meat and imported meat products are defined as "meats whose source of origin was beyond the continental limits of the United States and are or will be sold to the ultimate consumer as fresh or raw meat." * * *

* * * All registration and license fees are appropriated to the Department of Agriculture, "to be used separately in carrying out the provisions of this Act and none of the funds or fees collected under this Act can be paid to or used for or by any other governmental agency." * * *

Before discussing the substantive issues as to the constitutionality of the Acts when measured in terms of the Commerce Clause, we consider first the contentions of the defendants that the plaintiff is without standing to challenge the validity of the Acts. * * *

Plaintiff is a New York corporation with no office or place of business in Tennessee. For several years it has been engaged in foreign and interstate commerce as a dealer in imported meats. It purchases meat which is grown, slaughtered and packaged in foreign countries, imports such meat into the United States, and resells it within and among the several states of the United States, including Tennessee. Its business is exclusively in interstate or foreign commerce. Its practice is to solicit orders from customers in Tennessee and then to have the meat imported into the United States in sealed cartons, each of approximately sixty pounds in weight, under conditions of refrigeration which cause the meat to remain hard frozen, and to be delivered in that form to its customers in Tennessee. * * *

The allegations of the complaint, amply sustained by the evidence, are to the effect that the passage of the Labeling and Licensing Acts by the General Assembly of Tennessee has caused plaintiff's Tennessee customers to refuse to purchase its imported meat, thus for all practical purposes destroying the Tennessee market for its direct sales.

* * *

* * * Under such circumstances, although the plaintiff is not directly within the terms of the Acts, it nevertheless is so directly and immediately affected by their operation that it has standing to challenge their validity upon the ground that they constitute an undue burden upon interstate commerce.

* * *

Turning to the substantive issues, we find no escape from the conclusion that the Labeling and Licensing Acts, whether considered separately or essentially as one regulatory measure, impose unreasonable and discriminatory restrictions and burdens upon interstate and foreign commerce, and so run afoul of the Commerce Clause. The line of demarcation between a permissible and impermissible state regulation affecting interstate commerce has been charted in manifold decisions of the Supreme Court from the earliest days of our Republic to the present time. While the Commerce Clause as construed by the Supreme Court does not prohibit all state regulatory measures affecting interstate commerce, the Supreme Court has invariably outlawed those state restrictions which unduly and unreasonably burden or restrain interstate commerce when evaluated in terms of legitimate state or local interests, or those state restrictions and regulations which unreasonably discriminate against such commerce. * * *

The burdensome and discriminatory character of the present legislation can scarcely admit of doubt when it is considered in the light of the pertinent facts. In sweeping terms the Labeling Act requires that "each quarter of each carcass, each carton, each retail package, or individually packaged item shall be plainly identified with a brand or label stating that it is a foreign product and naming the country of its origin." * * * The evidence discloses that manufacturers and processors of meatfoods and products, such as weiners, bologna, hamburgers, baby foods, and other products, customarily, use foreign and domestic meats indiscriminately without any effort to keep the one separate from the other. The Labeling Act would require such products to be labeled to show the fact of co-mingling and the country in which the foreign meat had its origin. It would be necessary for Tennessee handlers of plaintiff's meat or meat products to keep track of or trace the origin of such meat, purchased either directly or through wholesalers or manufacturers, in order that the ultimate product sold to consumers in the State of Tennessee could be identified and labeled with the country of origin, or labeled in such way as to indicate that foreign and domestic meats both had been used. That these requirements of labeling are exceedingly burdensome is self-evident. Indeed, it is reasonable to infer that in co-mingling domestic and foreign meats, compliance with the Act would be a practical impossibility. Yet these onerous burdens apply under the Act only to foreign meat and to products in which foreign meat is used as an ingredient. Meats produced anywhere within the United States are exempt, with the result that the discriminatory burden on interstate and foreign commerce is unmistakably clear. * * *

If we understand the defendants' position, it is not seriously contended that the Licensing Act, considered apart from the Labeling Act, can be sustained as a valid measure under the Commerce Clause. The defendants' theory is that "reading both the Labeling and Licensing statutes together necessitates the conclusion that the purpose of the legislation was to impose a license fee in order to defray the costs of supervising enforcement of these statutes."

* * *

It seems clear, however, under the Tennessee rule, since the two Acts were passed at the same session of the General Assembly and deal with the same subject matter, that they should be read together as one regulatory scheme. On this basis, assuming that the major purpose of the Licensing Act is to raise funds to supervise enforcement of the Labeling Act, which we hold to be invalid, it would appear that the two Acts would necessarily be required to share the same fate. Furthermore, as so read and construed, the discriminatory character of the statutory exactions in the Licensing Act would still remain, in that there would be no logical or reasonable basis for imposing the substantial burdens of the Act upon handlers of foreign meats while exempting those who handle domestic meats.

Defendants undertake to support the present legislation solely upon the ground that it constitutes a proper exercise of the state's police power to protect the consumer from fraud and deception.*5 It is insisted that for almost a century states have been enacting legislation pursuant to their police power, with the approval of the Supreme Court, to protect citizens from being deceived or misled in their purchase of commodities, especially foods and food products, at retail.

In seeking to answer the question how consumers in Tennessee are misled by the sale of meat in that state which was originally imported, defendants point to the fact that the plaintiff's imported meat is frozen in the country of origin [, but usually sold as a fresh processed product, thereby deceiving consumers into believing the product was never frozen].

The argument is met with a number of insuperable difficulties. There is no evidence that food products, such as those referred to by the defendants, are supposed by a consumer to be a fresh product, in the sense that the meat content has never been frozen, although we may suppose that this could be true as to hamburger meat. Nor is there any evidence that such products are generally offered for sale or represented to the public as fresh products. But whether these assumptions by the defendants are correct or not, it is difficult to see how the Labeling Act could have been designed to protect the consumer from deception, when the same protection is not afforded him in purchasing the same products which have been manufactured from frozen domestic meat. If the consumer is entitled to be advised, albeit indirectly,

* 5. Since the Labeling Act expressly provides that the Commissioner of Agriculture, in implementing the Act, shall issue no regulation requiring a higher standard of purity and sanitation than is required to govern the federal inspection of foreign meat, no serious contention can be made that the labeling requirement was designed as a valid health measure under the police power of the state. There is no proof that foreign meat, per se, is unwholesome or impure, or that it poses a health problem. Plaintiff's foreign meats are imported and sold in sealed cartons, labeled with country of origin, and inspected by federal inspectors at port of entry, in accordance with federal laws and regulations which impose standards of wholesomeness and purity. Such foreign meats are deemed and treated as domestic meat within the provisions of 34 Stat. 674. The requirement in the Labeling Act for disclosure of any preservatives used in a packaged product could have been designed as a health regulation, but the difficulty is that its burden falls on foreign meat only with no like requirement as to domestic meat. Such a distinction is purely arbitrary, further emphasizing the discrimination against interstate and foreign commerce.

that he is purchasing foreign meats which have been frozen, he is entitled to receive the same information about domestic meats which have been frozen.

* * *

* * * The present labeling requirement, in contrast, would do nothing except inform the public that a meat product had its origin in a foreign country without conveying any information as to its nature, quality or quantity. In addition, as noted, it imposes substantial burdens upon meat and meat products of foreign origin without imposing the same burdens upon meat and meat products of domestic origin.

It is further insisted by the defendants that the present legislation does not offend the Commerce Clause because it operates only on goods which have come to rest in Tennessee so as to become part of the common property of the state. The cases cited by the defendants involving the "come to rest" and original package doctrines, merely recognize, because of the nexus with the state thus established, the power of the state to impose taxes or regulations upon those foreign goods which are designed to compete in the domestic market. Conceding that the imported meats in the present case are designed to compete in the domestic market, and that the state therefore has the power to regulate, it remains evident that the state may do so only if the regulations apply equally to foreign and domestic meats, and thus make possible equal competition in the domestic market.

* * *

In accordance with this opinion a form of judgment will be submitted declaring the Labeling Act and the Licensing Act to be in conflict with the Commerce Clause and therefore void, and permanently enjoining the State Commissioner of Agriculture and the State Chemist and Director of Foods Division, Department of Agriculture, from enforcing the provisions of such Acts.

Notes

(1) See Annotation, Commerce Clause of Federal Constitution as Violated by State or Local Regulation on Prohibition Affecting Business of Selling, Distributing, Packaging, Labelling, or Processing Food Intended for Human Consumption—Supreme Court cases, 25 L.Ed.2d 846 (1971).

(2) In PORTLAND PIPE LINE CORP. v. ENVIRONMENTAL IMPROVEMENT COMMISSION, 307 A.2d 1 (Me.1973), the Supreme Court of Maine in a lengthy and remarkably complete analysis of federal-state power relationships concerning international trade, upheld a complex state regulatory enactment designed to fix responsibility and compensation for oil spills occurring in Maine waters. Under the state scheme, an annual license fee was imposed per barrel of oil transferred over coastal waters of the state, and this fee was used to create a revolving fund to cover clean-up costs of spills, and research and development concerning environmental damage due to the transfer of oil in those waters.

Among the many challenges to the state regulation were a challenge based on the U.S. constitutional clause (Article I, Section 10, Clause 2), that prohibits states (without consent of Congress) from laying imposts or duties on imports or exports, "except what may be absolutely necessary for executing * * * Inspection Laws", and a challenge based on the Commerce Clause.

In rejecting these challenges, the Court stated:

The constitutionality of the one-half cent per barrel license fee imposed upon terminal operators depends upon the answers to three questions:

Is the license fee an impost or a duty?

Is the license fee imposed "on" imports or exports?

Is the oil, at the time the fee is imposed, an import or an export?

Treating the latter question first, we find that under decided law, the oil is an import when the license fee is imposed. Because the petroleum products come to Maine from foreign points of origin, the prohibition of the Import-Export clause is applicable. Woodruff v. Parham, 75 U.S. (8 Wall.) 123, 19 L.Ed. 382 (1869).

Since Brown v. Maryland, 25 U.S. (12 Wheat.) 419, 6 L.Ed. 678 (1827), the Supreme Court has steadfastly maintained a mechanistic approach in deciding when the prohibition of the Import-Export Clause ceases and the power of the state to tax arises. The "original package" and related doctrines are the result of literal interpretations of the prohibition. The absolute prohibition has left little room for judicial construction as to what types of imposts or duties may or may not be permissible as well as little room to determine what is and what is not an impost. See Youngstown Sheet & Tube Co. v. Bowers, 358 U.S. 534, 79 S.Ct. 383, 3 L.Ed.2d 490 (1959), (Frankfurter, J., dissenting).

* * *

The transfer fee is imposed upon oil which, at the outset, is an import under Woodruff v. Parham and which has not ceased to be an import by reason of use or sale. Therefore, the imposition of the transfer fee must be evaluated under the Import-Export Clause.

* * *

The license fee imposed by the Act now before us, is imposed upon the off-loading of oil rather than upon the oil itself. The license fee is completely unrelated to the value of the oil. It may be argued that the fee is imposed directly on the goods rather than on the activity of off-loading because it is based upon volume. But although volume is not an unusual method of taxing goods, it is here an accurate gauge of the activity being taxed.

It is also of importance that the volume of oil offloaded is directly related to the danger that the Act seeks to guard against.

* * *

The state urges that the license fee is not an impost or a duty under the Import-Export Clause. The prohibition of that clause, as of any constitutional provision must be determined by ascertaining the purpose of its provisions. Cook v. Pennsylvania, 97 U.S. (7 Otto) 566, 24 L.Ed. 1015 (1878).

The State's first contention is that only "general revenue measures" are proscribed as imposts or duties. This position is supported by the statement of the purpose of the Import-Export Clause found in Youngstown Sheet & Tube Co. v. Bowers, supra.

* * *

The deciding factor in determining whether a fee is a prohibited impost or duty is not whether the tax is a general revenue measure, but whether the tax is a "burden" upon imports or exports.

* * *

The imposition of these costs is essential to provide services which are in the best interests of plaintiffs. The prompt containment of oil spills will prevent or lessen damages caused by the spill.

* * *

We hold that plaintiffs' challenge to the Act based upon the Import-Export Clause must fail for two reasons. First, the license fee is not imposed *"on Imports or Exports."* Because the transfer fee is imposed on an *activity* related to the importation of oil *rather than on the property imported,* the fee is not sufficiently direct to be "on Imports" under Article I, Section 10, Clause 2.

Second, the license fee is not a duty or impost since the overall effect of the Act is the establishment of a regulatory scheme for controlling oil pollution which is essential to protect the public interest and affords benefits to those subject to the license fee.

Plaintiffs' challenge of the Act under the Commerce Clause is in two parts.

* * *

The test for a taxing measure incorporated as part of a "police power" regulation requires a different formulation of the "burden test" from that employed to evaluate the kind of taxes before the Court in *McGoldrick.*

Included in the "just share" of state tax burdens imposed on interstate commerce is the cost of preventing and remedying harm caused by a danger inherent in the interstate commerce being taxed.

* * *

Similar charges upon interstate and foreign commerce have been approved by the Supreme Court [if a three-part test is met:]

First, the tax must not discriminate against interstate and foreign commerce. The license fee imposed by the Act does not so discriminate. While the majority of oil transferred over Maine waters is in interstate or foreign commerce, the license fee is also imposed upon transfers resulting from intrastate shipment.

Second, the license fee must "reflect a fair if imperfect approximation" of the conduct which gives rise to the danger against which the Act seeks to guard. The license fee is not imposed upon *all* overwater transfers of oil. Marinas fueling vessels of 75 feet or less in overall length, where the purchaser and consumer of the fuel are the same entity, and storage facilities with a capacity of no more than 500 barrels are exempted from paying the license fee.

* * *

Third, those engaged in interstate and foreign commerce have the burden of proving that the license fees collected are "excessive" in relation to costs incurred by the taxing authorities. Since there is no experience under the Act from which the amount of money necessary to accomplish the purposes of the Act can be established and since the plaintiffs have given us no factual basis for their claim the fees are excessive, the plaintiffs have failed to sustain their burden.

We cannot, as a matter of law, find that the $4,000,000 limit of the Fund is irrational in light of the catastrophic damages which may be caused by an oil spill.

* * *

Plaintiffs' second Commerce Clause contention is that the regulatory system imposed by the Act is in conflict with federal law thus destroying the required uniformity of controls upon interstate and foreign commerce.

* * *

Early in our history the Supreme Court distinguished instances where the states were precluded from exercising power by the dormant Commerce Clause and instances where the states were free to regulate unless those regulations came in conflict with federal law. Willson v. Black Bird Creek Marsh Co., 27 U.S. (2 Pet.) 245, 7 L.Ed. 412 (1829). The Court held in *Cooley* that the distinction turned upon whether the subject which the state sought to regulate was a national or a local concern.

* * *

The Maine Act does not discriminate in favor of the intrastate commerce and plaintiffs have advanced nothing to show that compliance with Maine's regulations will place plaintiffs in the dilemma facing the truckers in Bibb v. Navajo Freight Lines, Inc., 359 U.S. 520, 79 S.Ct. 962, 3 L.Ed.2d 1003 (1959).

(3) In RAY v. ATLANTIC RICHFIELD CO., 435 U.S. 151, 98 S.Ct. 988, 55 L.Ed.2d 179 (1978), the Supreme Court ruled on the constitutionality of a Washington state statute that regulated the design, size and movement of oil tankers in Puget Sound. The Court struck down portions of the state law dealing with design and size of tankers, but upheld a state rule requiring tug escorts. The Court noted that in the area of tanker safety standards, "Congress expressed a preference for international action and expressly anticipated that foreign vessels would or could be sufficiently safe for certification by the [federal government] if they satisfied the requirements arrived at by treaty or convention: it is therefore clear that [the federal act] leaves no room for the states to impose different or stricter design requirements than those which Congress has enacted with the hope of having them internationally adopted or has accepted as the result of an international accord. A state law in this area * * * would frustrate the congressional desire of achieving uniform, international standards." 435 U.S. at 167–68, 98 S.Ct. at 999.

(4) In similar cases, both the New York State Court of Appeals and the Federal District Court for the Southern District of New York upheld the New York statute authorizing the prohibition of sale within the state of the skin or hide of endangered species, against challenges based on the "supremacy" and "commerce" clauses of the U.S. Constitution. Both courts ruled that the federal Endangered Species Conservation Act of 1969 did not preempt state law, that the state could ban species not on the federal list, and that the commerce clause was not violated. A.E. Nettleton Co. v. Diamond, 27 N.Y.2d 182, 315 N.Y.S.2d 625, 264 N.E.2d 118 (1970), appeal dismissed sub nom. Reptile Prod. Assn. v. Diamond, 401 U.S. 969, 91 S.Ct. 1201, 28 L.Ed.2d 319; Palladio v. Diamond, 321 F.Supp. 630 (S.D.N.Y.1970), affirmed, 440 F.2d 1319, cert. denied, 404 U.S. 983, 92 S.Ct. 446, 30 L.Ed.2d 367 (1971).

(C) STATE TAXATION OF FOREIGN COMMERCE

JAPAN LINE, LTD. v. COUNTY OF LOS ANGELES

Supreme Court of the United States, 1979.
441 U.S. 434, 99 S.Ct. 1813, 60 L.Ed.2d 336.

MR. JUSTICE BLACKMUN delivered the opinion of the Court.

This case presents the question whether a State, consistently with the Commerce Clause of the Constitution, may impose a nondiscriminatory ad valorem property tax on foreign-owned instrumentalities (cargo containers) of international commerce.

I

The facts were "stipulated on appeal," and were found by the trial court as follows:

Appellants are six Japanese shipping companies; they are incorporated under the laws of Japan, and they have their principal places of business and commercial domiciles in that country. Appellants operate vessels used exclusively in foreign commerce; these vessels are registered in Japan and have their home ports there. The vessels are specifically designed and constructed to accommodate large cargo shipping containers. The containers, like the ships, are owned by appellants, have their home ports in Japan, and are used exclusively for hire in the transportation of cargo in foreign commerce. Each container is in constant transit save for time spent undergoing repair or awaiting loading and unloading of cargo. All appellants' containers are subject to property tax in Japan and, in fact, are taxed there.

Appellees are political subdivisions of the State of California. Appellants' containers, in the course of their international journeys, pass through appellees' jurisdictions intermittently. Although none of appellants' containers stays permanently in California, some are there at any given time; a container's average stay in the State is less than three weeks. The containers engage in no intrastate or interstate transportation of cargo except as continuations of international voyages. Any movements or periods of nonmovement of containers in appellees' jurisdictions are essential to, and inseparable from, the containers' efficient use as instrumentalities of foreign commerce.

Property present in California on March 1 (the "lien date" under California law) of any year is subject to ad valorem property tax. A number of appellants' containers were physically present in appellees' jurisdictions on the lien dates in 1970, 1971, and 1972; this number was fairly representative of the containers' "average presence" during each year. Appellees levied property taxes in excess of $550,000 on the assessed value of the containers present on March 1 of the three years in question. During the same period, similar containers owned or controlled by steamship companies domiciled in the United States, that appeared from time to time in Japan during the course of international commerce, were not subject to property taxation in Japan, and therefore were not, in fact, taxed in that country.

[The California Supreme Court upheld the imposition of the tax.] [*4]

* * *

The Constitution provides that "Congress shall have Power * * * To regulate Commerce with foreign Nations, and among the several States, and with the Indian Tribes." Art. I, § 8, cl. 3. In construing Congress' power to "regulate Commerce * * * among the several States," the Court recently has affirmed that the Constitution confers no immunity from state taxation, and that "interstate commerce must bear its fair share of the state tax burden." Instrumentalities of interstate commerce are no exception to this rule, and the Court regularly has sustained property taxes as applied to various forms of transportation equipment. If the state tax "is applied to an activity with a substantial nexus with the taxing State, is fairly apportioned, does not discriminate against interstate commerce, and is fairly related to the services provided by the State," no impermissible burden on interstate commerce will be found. Complete Auto Transit, Inc. v. Brady, 430 U.S. 274, 279, 97 S.Ct. 1076, 1079, 51 L.Ed.2d 326 (1977).

Appellees contend that cargo shipping containers, like other vehicles of commercial transport, are subject to property taxation, and that the taxes imposed here meet *Complete Auto*'s fourfold requirements. The containers, they argue, have a "substantial nexus" with California because some of them are present in that State at all times; jurisdiction to tax is based on "the habitual employment of the property within the State," and appellants' containers habitually are so employed. The tax, moreover, is "fairly apportioned," since it is levied only on the containers' "average presence" in California. The tax "does not discriminate," thirdly, since it falls evenhandedly on all personal property in the State; indeed, as an ad valorem tax of general application, it is of necessity nondiscriminatory. The tax, finally, is "fairly related to the services provided by" California, services that include not only police and fire protection, but also the benefits of a trained work force and the advantages of a civilized society.

These observations are not without force. We may assume that, if the containers at issue here were instrumentalities of purely interstate commerce, *Complete Auto* would apply and be satisfied, and our Commerce Clause inquiry would be at an end. Appellants' containers, however, are instrumentalities of foreign commerce, both as a matter of fact and as a matter of law. The premise of appellees' argument is that the Commerce Clause analysis is identical, regardless of whether interstate or foreign commerce is involved. This premise, we have concluded, must be rejected. When construing Congress' power to "regulate Commerce with foreign Nations," a more extensive constitutional inquiry is required.

When a State seeks to tax the instrumentalities of foreign commerce, two additional considerations, beyond those articulated in *Complete Auto*, come into play. The first is the enhanced risk of multiple taxation. It is a commonplace of constitutional jurisprudence that multiple taxation may well be offensive to the Commerce Clause. In order to prevent multiple

---

* 4. The California Supreme Court also rejected appellants' argument that California's tax constituted "Imposts or Duties" proscribed by U.S. Const. Art. I, § 10, cl. 2. Appellants reiterate this argument here; in view of our disposition, we do not consider it. * * *

taxation of interstate commerce, this Court has required that taxes be apportioned among taxing jurisdictions, so that no instrumentality of commerce is subjected to more than one tax on its full value. The corollary of the apportionment principle, of course, is that no jurisdiction may tax the instrumentality in full. * * *

Yet neither this Court nor this Nation can ensure full apportionment when one of the taxing entities is a foreign sovereign. * * *

* * * Due to the absence of an authoritative tribunal capable of ensuring that the aggregation of taxes is computed on no more than one full value, a state tax, even though "fairly apportioned" to reflect an instrumentality's presence within the State, may subject foreign commerce " 'to the risk of a double tax burden to which [domestic] commerce is not exposed, and which the commerce clause forbids.' "

Second, a state tax on the instrumentalities of foreign commerce may impair federal uniformity in an area where federal uniformity is essential. Foreign commerce is preeminently a matter of national concern. "In international relations and with respect to foreign intercourse and trade the people of the United States act through a single government with unified and adequate national power." Although the Constitution, Art. I, § 8, cl. 3, grants Congress power to regulate commerce "with foreign Nations" and "among the several States" in parallel phrases, there is evidence that the Founders intended the scope of the foreign commerce power to be the greater. Cases of this Court, stressing the need for uniformity in treating with other nations, echo this distinction. * * *

[I]n discussing the Import-Export Clause, this Court, in Michelin Tire Corp. v. Wages, 423 U.S. 276, 285, 96 S.Ct. 535, 540, 46 L.Ed.2d 495 (1976), spoke of the Framers' overriding concern that "the Federal Government must speak with one voice when regulating commercial relations with foreign governments." The need for federal uniformity is no less paramount in ascertaining the negative implications of Congress' power to "regulate Commerce with foreign Nations" under the Commerce Clause.

A state tax on instrumentalities of foreign commerce may frustrate the achievement of federal uniformity in several ways. If the State imposes an apportioned tax, international disputes over reconciling apportionment formulae may arise. If a novel state tax creates an asymmetry in the international tax structure, foreign nations disadvantaged by the levy may retaliate against American-owned instrumentalities present in their jurisdictions. Such retaliation of necessity would be directed at American transportation equipment in general, not just that of the taxing State, so that the Nation as a whole would suffer. If other States followed the taxing State's example, various instrumentalities of commerce could be subjected to varying degrees of multiple taxation, a result that would plainly prevent this Nation from "speaking with one voice" in regulating foreign commerce.

* * *

Analysis of California's tax under these principles dictates that the tax, as applied to appellants' containers, is impermissible. * * *

First, California's tax results in multiple taxation of the instrumentalities of foreign commerce. By stipulation, appellants' containers are owned, based, and registered in Japan; they are used exclusively in international commerce; and they remain outside Japan only so long as needed to complete their international missions. Under these circumstances, Japan has the right and the power to tax the containers in full. California's tax, however, creates more than the *risk* of multiple taxation; it produces multiple taxation in fact. Appellants' containers not only "are subject to property tax * * * in Japan," but, as the trial court found, "are, in fact, taxed in Japan." Thus, if appellees' levies were sustained, appellants "would be paying a double tax."

Second, California's tax prevents this Nation from "speaking with one voice" in regulating foreign trade. The desirability of uniform treatment of containers used exclusively in foreign commerce is evidenced by the Customs Convention on Containers, which the United States and Japan have signed.

Under this Convention, containers temporarily imported are admitted free of "all duties and taxes whatsoever chargeable by reason of importation." The Convention reflects a national policy to remove impediments to the use of containers as "instruments of international traffic." California's tax, however, will frustrate attainment of federal uniformity. It is stipulated that American-owned containers are not taxed in Japan. California's tax thus creates an asymmetry in international maritime taxation operating to Japan's disadvantage. The risk of retaliation by Japan, under these circumstances, is acute, and such retaliation of necessity would be felt by the Nation as a whole. If other States follow California's example (Oregon already has done so), foreign-owned containers will be subjected to various degrees of multiple taxation, depending on which American ports they enter. This result, obviously, would make "speaking with one voice" impossible. California, by its unilateral act, cannot be permitted to place these impediments before this Nation's conduct of its foreign relations and its foreign trade.

Because California's ad valorem tax, as applied to appellants' containers, results in multiple taxation of the instrumentalities of foreign commerce, and because it prevents the Federal Government from "speaking with one voice" in international trade, the tax is inconsistent with Congress' power to "regulate Commerce with foreign Nations." We hold the tax, as applied, unconstitutional under the Commerce Clause.

Appellees proffer several objections to this holding. They contend, first, that any multiple taxation in this case is attributable, not to California, but to Japan. California, they say, is just trying to take its share; it should not be foreclosed by Japan's election to tax the containers in full. California's tax, however, must be evaluated in the realistic framework of the custom of nations. Japan has the right and the power to tax appellants' containers at their full value; nothing could prevent it from doing so. Appellees' argument may have force in the interstate commerce context. In interstate commerce, if the domiciliary State is "to blame" for exacting an excessive tax, this Court is able to insist upon rationalization of the apportionment. As noted above, however, this Court is powerless to correct malapportionment of taxes imposed from abroad in foreign commerce.

Appellees contend, secondly, that any multiple taxation created by California's tax can be cured by congressional action or by international agreement. We find no merit in this contention. * * * For to say that California has created a problem susceptible only of congressional—indeed, only of international—solution is to concede that the taxation of foreign-owned containers is an area where a uniform federal rule is essential. California may not tell this Nation or Japan how to run their foreign policies.

Third, appellees argue that, even if California's tax results in multiple taxation, that fact, after *Moorman,* is insufficient to condemn a state tax under the Commerce Clause. In *Moorman,* the Court refused to invalidate Iowa's single-factor income tax apportionment formula, even though it posed a credible threat of overlapping taxation because of the use of three-factor formulae by other States. That case, however, is quite different from this one. In *Moorman,* the existence of multiple taxation, on the record then before the Court, was "speculative," on the record of the present case, multiple taxation is a fact. In *Moorman,* the problem arose, not from lack of apportionment, but from mathematical imprecision in apportionment formulae. Yet, this Court consistently had held that the Commerce Clause "does not call for mathematical exactness nor for the rigid application of a particular formula; only if the resulting valuation is palpably excessive will it be set aside." This case, by contrast, involves no mere mathematical imprecision in apportionment; it involves a situation where true apportionment does not exist and cannot be policed by this Court at all. *Moorman,* finally, concerned interstate commerce. This case concerns foreign commerce. Even a slight overlapping of tax—a problem that might be deemed *de minimis* in a domestic context—assumes importance when sensitive matters of foreign relations and national sovereignty are concerned.

Finally, appellees present policy arguments. If California cannot tax appellants' containers, they complain, the State will lose revenue, even though the containers plainly have a nexus with California; the State will go uncompensated for the services it undeniably renders the containers; and, by exempting appellants' containers from tax, the State in effect will be forced to discriminate against domestic, in favor of foreign, commerce. These arguments are not without weight, and, to the extent appellees cannot recoup the value of their services through user fees, they may indeed be disadvantaged by our decision today. These arguments, however, are directed to the wrong forum. "Whatever subjects of this [the commercial] power are in their nature national, or admit only of one uniform system, or plan of regulation, may justly be said to be of such a nature as to require exclusive legislation by Congress." Cooley v. Board of Wardens, 12 How. 299, 319, 53 U.S. 299, 13 L.Ed. 996 (1852). The problems to which appellees refer are problems that admit only of a federal remedy. They do not admit of a unilateral solution by a State.

The judgment of the Supreme Court of California is reversed.

It is so ordered.

Substantially for the reasons set forth by Justice Manuel in his opinion for the unanimous Supreme Court of California, 20 Cal.3d 180, 141 Cal.Rptr.

905, 571 P.2d 254, MR. JUSTICE REHNQUIST is of the opinion that the judgment of that court should be affirmed.

Note

Recently, there have been a number of Supreme Court cases regarding state taxation of foreign commerce. For example, in Xerox Corp. v. Harris County, Texas, 459 U.S. 145, 103 S.Ct. 523, 74 L.Ed.2d 323 (1982), the Court relied on the Supremacy Clause to disallow local property taxation of goods manufactured in Mexico, shipped to the United States and held in a customs bonded warehouse while awaiting shipment to Latin America. Earlier, in Michelin Tire Corp. v. Wages, 423 U.S. 276, 96 S.Ct. 535, 46 L.Ed.2d 495 (1976), the Court had ruled that imports could be taxed once they were no longer in transit (e.g., stored in a warehouse awaiting further distribution within the United States).

Another state taxation case involving international business that is of particular interest is Container Corp. of America v. Franchise Tax Board, 463 U.S. 159, 103 S.Ct. 2933, 77 L.Ed.2d 545 (1983). In this case, which is set out in Section 19.4 infra, the Supreme Court upheld the so-called unitary tax applied by California to the income of corporations doing business in the state. Under California's rules, the tax is based on the proportion of a corporation's total payroll, property and sales that are in California, a formula that many businesses believe unfairly inflates their income subject to California tax.

In Wardair Canada, Inc. v. Florida Dept. of Revenue, No. 84–902, 54 U.S.L.W. 4687 (June 18, 1986), the Court gave a narrow reading to *Japan Line* and permitted Florida to impose a tax on aviation fuel used by an air carrier engaged exclusively in international commerce, over the dissent of Justice Blackmun and the opposition of the Solicitor General. The Court found no explicit federal policy to preempt such state taxation, which was not expressly prohibited by the applicable international agreements.

(D) STATE GOVERNMENT PURCHASES AND OTHER PROPRIE-TARY ACTION

SOUTH–CENTRAL TIMBER DEVELOPMENT INC. v. WUNNICKE

Supreme Court of the United States, 1984.
467 U.S. 82, 104 S.Ct. 2237, 81 L.Ed.2d 71.

JUSTICE WHITE delivered the opinion of the Court with respect to Parts I and II, and delivered an opinion with respect to Parts III and IV, in which JUSTICE BRENNAN, JUSTICE BLACKMUN, and JUSTICE STEVENS joined.

* * *

I

In September 1980, the Alaska Department of Natural Resources published a notice that it would sell approximately 49 million board-feet of timber in the area of Icy Cape, Alaska, on October 23, 1980. The notice of sale, the prospectus, and the proposed contract for the sale all provided, pursuant to 11 Alaska Admin.Code § 76.130, that "primary manufacture within the State of Alaska will be required as a special provision of the contract." Under the primary-manufacture requirement, the successful bidder must partially process the timber prior to shipping it outside of the

State. The requirement is imposed by contract and does not limit the export of unprocessed timber not owned by the State. The stated purpose of the requirement is to "protect existing industries, provide for the establishment of new industries, derive revenue from all timber resources, and manage the State's forests on a sustained yield basis." When it imposes the requirement, the State charges a significantly lower price for the timber than it otherwise would.

*   *   *

Petitioner, South-Central Timber Development, Inc., is an Alaska corporation engaged in the business of purchasing standing timber, logging the timber, and shipping the logs into foreign commerce, almost exclusively to Japan. It does not operate a mill in Alaska and customarily sells unprocessed logs. *   *   *

We must first decide whether the court was correct in concluding that Congress has authorized the challenged requirement. If Congress has not, we must respond to respondent's submission that we should affirm the judgment on two grounds not reached by the Court of Appeals: 1) whether in the absence of congressional approval Alaska's requirement is permissible because Alaska is acting as a market participant, rather than as a market regulator; and 2) if not, whether the local-processing requirement is forbidden by the Commerce Clause.

II

Although the Commerce Clause is by its text an affirmative grant of power to Congress to regulate interstate and foreign commerce, the Clause has long been recognized as a self-executing limitation on the power of the States to enact laws imposing substantial burdens on such commerce. It is equally clear that Congress "may redefine the distribution of power over interstate commerce" by "permit[ting] the states to regulate the commerce in a manner which would otherwise not be permissible." The Court of Appeals held that Congress had done just that by consistently endorsing primary-manufacture requirements on timber taken from *federal* land. Although the court recognized that cases of this Court have spoken in terms of *express* approval by Congress, it stated:

> But such express authorization is not always necessary. There will be instances, like the case before us, where federal policy is so clearly delineated that a state may enact a parallel policy without explicit congressional approval, even if the purpose and effect of the state law is to favor local interests.

We agree that federal policy with respect to federal land is "clearly delineated," but the Court of Appeals was incorrect in concluding either that there is a clearly delineated federal policy approving Alaska's local-processing requirement or that Alaska's policy with respect to its timber lands is authorized by the existence of a "parallel" federal policy with respect to federal lands.

Since 1928, the Secretary of Agriculture has restricted the export of unprocessed timber cut from National Forest lands in Alaska. *   *   * The export limitation with respect to federal land in Alaska * * * applies to exports to other States, as well as to foreign exports.

* * *

It is true that most of our cases have looked for an express statement of congressional policy prior to finding that state regulation is permissible. * * * We noted that on those occasions in which consent has been found, congressional intent and policy to insulate state legislation from Commerce Clause attack has been "expressly stated."

* * *

There is no talismanic significance to the phrase "expressly stated," however; it merely states one way of meeting the requirement that for a state regulation to be removed from the reach of the dormant Commerce Clause, congressional intent must be unmistakably clear. The requirement that Congress affirmatively contemplate otherwise invalid state legislation is mandated by the policies underlying dormant Commerce Clause doctrine. It is not, as Alaska asserts, merely a wooden formalism. The Commerce Clause was designed "to avoid the tendencies toward economic Balkanization that had plagued relations among the colonies and later among the States under the Articles of Confederation." Unrepresented interests will often bear the brunt of regulations imposed by one State having a significant effect on persons or operations in other States. Thus, "when the regulation is of such a character that its burden falls principally upon those without the state, legislative action is not likely to be subjected to those political restraints which are normally exerted on legislation where it affects adversely some interests within the state." On the other hand, when Congress acts, all segments of the country are represented and there is significantly less danger that one State will be in a position to exploit others. Furthermore, if a State is in such a position, the decision to allow it is a collective one. A rule requiring a clear expression of approval by Congress ensures that there is, in fact, such a collective decision and reduces significantly the risk that unrepresented interests will be adversely affected by restraints on commerce.

The fact that the state policy in this case appears to be consistent with federal policy—or even that state policy furthers the goals we might believe that Congress had in mind—is an insufficient indicium of congressional intent. Congress acted only with respect to federal lands; we cannot infer from that fact that it intended to authorize a similar policy with respect to state lands. Accordingly, we reverse the contrary judgment of the Court of Appeals.

III

We now turn to the issues left unresolved by the Court of Appeals. The first of these issues is whether Alaska's restrictions on export of unprocessed timber from state-owned lands are exempt from Commerce Clause scrutiny under the "market-participant doctrine."

Our cases make clear that if a State is acting as a market participant, rather than as a market regulator, the dormant Commerce Clause places no limitation on its activities. The precise contours of the market-participant doctrine have yet to be established, however, the doctrine having been applied in only three cases of this Court to date.

The first of the cases, Hughes v. Alexandria Scrap Corp., involved a Maryland program designed to reduce the number of junked automobiles in the State. A "bounty" was established on Maryland-licensed junk cars, and the State imposed more stringent documentation requirements on out-of-state scrap processors than on in-state ones. The Court rejected a Commerce Clause attack on the program, although it noted that under traditional Commerce Clause analysis the program might well be invalid because it had the effect of reducing the flow of goods in interstate commerce. The Court concluded that Maryland's action was not "the kind of action with which the Commerce Clause is concerned," because "[n]othing in the purposes animating the Commerce Clause prohibits a State, in the absence of congressional action, from participating in the market and exercising the right to favor its own citizens over others."

In Reeves, Inc. v. Stake, the Court upheld a South Dakota policy of restricting the sale of cement from a state-owned plant to state residents, * * *. The Court relied upon "the long recognized right of trader or manufacturer, engaged in an entirely private business freely to exercise his own independent discretion as to parties with whom he will deal." In essence, the Court recognized the principle that the Commerce Clause places no limitations on a State's refusal to deal with particular parties when it is participating in the interstate market in goods.

The most recent of this Court's cases developing the market-participant doctrine is White v. Massachusetts Council of Construction Employers, Inc., in which the Court sustained against a Commerce Clause challenge an executive order of the Mayor of Boston that required all construction projects funded in whole or in part by city funds or city-administered funds to be performed by a work force of at least 50% city residents. The Court rejected the argument that the city was not entitled to the protection of the doctrine because the order had the effect of regulating employment contracts between public contractors and their employees. Recognizing that "there are some limits on a state or local government's ability to impose restrictions that reach beyond the immediate parties with which the government transacts business," the Court found it unnecessary to define those limits because "[e]veryone affected by the order [was], in a substantial if informal sense, 'working for the city.'" The fact that the employees were "working for the city" was "crucial" to the market-participant analysis in *White.*

The State of Alaska contends that its primary-manufacture requirement fits squarely within the market-participant doctrine. * * * However, when Maryland became involved in the scrap market it was as a purchaser of scrap; Alaska, on the other hand, participates in the timber market, but imposes conditions downstream in the timber-processing market. Alaska is not merely subsidizing local timber processing in an amount "roughly equal to the difference between the price the timber would fetch in the absence of such a requirement and the amount the state actually receives." If the State directly subsidized the timber-processing industry by such an amount, the purchaser would retain the option of taking advantage of the subsidy by processing timber in the State or forgoing the benefits of the subsidy and exporting unprocessed timber. Under the Alaska requirement, however, the choice is made for him: if he buys timber from the State he is not free to take the timber out of state prior to processing.

The State also would have us find *Reeves* controlling. * * * Although the Court in *Reeves* did strongly endorse the right of a State to deal with whomever it chooses when it participates in the market, it did not—and did not purport to—sanction the imposition of any terms that the State might desire. For example, the Court expressly noted in *Reeves* that "Commerce Clause scrutiny may well be more rigorous when a restraint on foreign commerce is alleged," that a natural resource "like coal, timber, wild game, or minerals," was not involved, but instead the cement was "the end product of a complex process whereby a costly physical plant and human labor act on raw materials," and that South Dakota did not bar resale of South Dakota cement to out-of-state purchasers. In this case, all three of the elements that were not present in *Reeves*—foreign commerce, a natural resource, and restrictions on resale—are present.

Finally, Alaska argues that since the Court in *White* upheld a requirement that reached beyond "the boundary of formal privity of contract," then, *a fortiori,* the primary-manufacture requirement is permissible, because the State is not regulating contracts for resale of timber or regulating the buying and selling of timber, but is instead "a seller of timber, pure and simple." Yet it is clear that the State is more than merely a seller of timber. In the commercial context, the seller usually has no say over, and no interest in, how the product is to be used after sale; in this case, however, payment for the timber does not end the obligations of the purchaser, for, despite the fact that the purchaser has taken delivery of the timber and has paid for it, he cannot do with it as he pleases.

* * *

The limit of the market-participant doctrine must be that it allows a State to impose burdens on commerce within the market in which it is a participant, but allows it to go no further. The State may not impose conditions, whether by statute, regulation, or contract, that have a substantial regulatory effect outside of that particular market. Unless the "market" is relatively narrowly defined, the doctrine has the potential of swallowing up the rule that States may not impose substantial burdens on interstate commerce even if they act with the permissible state purpose of fostering local industry.

* * *

There are sound reasons for distinguishing between a State's preferring its own residents in the initial disposition of goods when it is a market participant and a State's attachment of restrictions on dispositions subsequent to the goods coming to rest in private hands. First, simply as a matter of intuition a State market participant has a greater interest as a "private trader" in the immediate transaction than it has in what its purchaser does with the goods after the State no longer has an interest in them. The common law recognized such a notion in the doctrine of restraints on alienation. * * *

Second, downstream restrictions have a greater regulatory effect than do limitations on the immediate transaction. Instead of merely choosing its own trading partners, the State is attempting to govern the private, separate economic relationships of its trading partners; that is, it restricts the post-purchase activity of the purchaser, rather than merely the purchasing activity. In contrast to the situation in *White,* this restriction on private economic activity takes place after the completion of the parties' direct commercial obligations, rather than during the course of an ongoing commercial relationship in which the city retained a continuing proprietary interest in the subject of the contract. In sum, the State may not avail itself of the market-participant doctrine to immunize its downstream regulation of the timber-processing market in which it is not a participant.

IV

Finally, the State argues that even if we find that Congress did not authorize the processing restriction, and even if we conclude that its actions do not qualify for the market-participant exception, the restriction does not substantially burden interstate or foreign commerce under ordinary Commerce Clause principles. We need not labor long over that contention.

* * *

We are buttressed in our conclusion that the restriction is invalid by the fact that foreign commerce is burdened by the restriction. It is a well-accepted rule that state restrictions burdening foreign commerce are subjected to a more rigorous and searching scrutiny. It is crucial to the efficient execution of the Nation's foreign policy that "the Federal Government * * * speak with one voice when regulating commercial relations with foreign governments." * * *

[JUSTICE MARSHALL did not participate. JUSTICE POWELL, joined by the CHIEF JUSTICE, concurred in only Parts I and II of the Court's opinion and would have remanded the case for a factual determination of whether Alaska was acting as a market participant and whether its rules substantially burdened interstate commerce.

[JUSTICE REHNQUIST, joined by JUSTICE O'CONNOR, dissented. He found the market participant/market regulator distinction unconvincing and noted that Alaska could clearly accomplish the same result through other means, such as selling only to Alaskan processors, thus suggesting the Court was too attentive to form over substance.]

Note

Justice White, the author of the opinion in *South-Central Timber,* had dissented in the case cited as establishing the state-as-market-participant doctrine, *Alexandria Scrap,* and in the two subsequent cases involving its application—*Reeves* and *Stake.* Since these various cases have been decided by narrow margins, with different Justices comprising the majority in different cases, the precise meaning of the whole doctrine is somewhat in question.

BETHLEHEM STEEL CORP. v. BOARD OF COMMRS.

Court of Appeal, Second District, Division 5, 1969.
276 Cal.App.2d 221, 80 Cal.Rptr. 800.

STEPHENS, ACTING PRESIDING JUSTICE.

These consolidated appeals are from summary judgments rendered in two superior court actions denying Bethlehem Steel Corporation (Bethlehem) injunctive relief and damages against the Department of Water and Power of the City of Los Angeles (the Department).

[The cases were brought by Bethlehem to enjoin the Department from performing or awarding contracts where foreign steel was to be used and for other relief. Bethlehem asserted that such contracts violated the California Buy American Act.]

The California Buy American Act (Govt.Code §§ 4300–4305) requires that contracts for the construction of public works or the purchase of materials for public use be awarded only to persons who will agree to use or supply materials which have been manufactured in the United States, substantially all from materials produced in the United States.[*1]

The crucial and determinative issue presented by these appeals is whether this act, as applied to certain purchases of steel products manufactured abroad, violates the United States Constitution. We have concluded that the California Buy American Act is an unconstitutional encroachment upon the federal government's exclusive power over foreign affairs, and constitutes an undue interference with the United States' conduct of foreign relations.

The United States Constitution itself does not, in so many words, vest in the national government the power to conduct external relations. Instead, it parcels out certain aspects of the foreign-affairs power among the political departments. As one writer has pointed out, "the organic provisions delegating such specific powers fall far short of covering comprehensively the whole field of foreign affairs."

Whether we must conclude from this that the nation does not possess foreign-affairs powers other than those specifically enumerated is answered in an unqualified negative: "As a sovereign power possessed by the nation, the power over foreign affairs is *inherent, exclusive,* and *plenary.* It is inherent, since * * * it does not depend for its existence upon the affirmative grants of the Constitution. It is exclusive in the Federal Government, both because of express prohibitions on the states in this field and because only the Union is vested with the attributes of external sovereignty. For national purposes, embracing our relations with foreign nations, we are but one people, one nation, one power. [Footnotes omitted.]"

* 1. Government Code section 4303 provides:

"The governing body of any political subdivision, municipal corporation, or district, and any public officer or person charged with the letting of contracts for (1) the construction, alteration, or repair of public works or (2) for the purchasing of materials for public use, shall let such contracts only to persons who agree to use or supply only such unmanufactured materials as have been produced in the United States, and only such manufactured materials as have been manufactured in the United States, substantially all from materials produced in the United States."

As stated in United States v. Curtiss-Wright Export Corp., 299 U.S. 304, 315–316, 57 S.Ct. 216, 219, 81 L.Ed. 255: "The broad statement that the federal government can exercise no powers except those specifically enumerated in the Constitution, and such implied powers as are necessary and proper to carry into effect the enumerated powers, is categorically true only in respect of our internal affairs." (See also Burnet v. Brooks, 288 U.S. 378, 396, 53 S.Ct. 457, 77 L.Ed. 844.) The powers of external sovereignty do not depend upon the affirmative grants of the Constitution, but are vested in the federal government as necessary concomitants of nationality.

The exclusivity of the federal government's power in this sphere is predicated upon the "irrefutable postulate that though the states were several, their people in respect of foreign affairs were one." (United States v. Curtiss-Wright Export Corp., supra, 299 U.S. at 317, 57 S.Ct. at 219.) The several states are bereft of power in this field since "in respect of our foreign relations generally, state lines disappear." (United States v. Belmont, supra, 301 U.S. at p. 331, 57 S.Ct. at p. 761; see also *Chinese Exclusion Case,* 130 U.S. 581, 606, 9 S.Ct. 623, 32 L.Ed. 1068.) Hence, the external power of the United States is exercisable "without regard to state laws or policies" and "is not and cannot be subject to any curtailment or interference on the part of the several states." (Ibid.)

The California Buy American Act, in effectively placing an embargo on foreign products, amounts to a usurpation by this state of the power of the federal government to conduct foreign trade policy. That there are countervailing state policies which are served by the retention of such an Act is "wholly irrelevant to judicial inquiry" (United States v. Pink, 315 U.S. 203, 233, 62 S.Ct. 552, 86 L.Ed. 796) since "[i]t is inconceivable that any of them can be interposed as an obstacle to the effective operation of a federal constitutional power." (United States v. Belmont, supra, 301 U.S. 324, 332, 57 S.Ct. 758, 761, 81 L.Ed. 1134.) Only the federal government can fix the rules of fair competition when such competition is on an international basis. Foreign trade is properly a subject of national concern, not state regulation. State regulation can only impede, not foster, national trade policies. The problems of trade expansion or nonexpansion are national in scope, and properly should be national in scope in their resolution. The fact that international trade forms the basis of this country's foreign relations is amply demonstrated by the following. At the present time the United States is a party to commercial treaties with 38 foreign nations. In addition, there are tax treaties presently in effect between the United States and 31 countries. The United States is a party to many other international treaties and agreements regulating, directly and indirectly, its commercial relations with the rest of the world. See, for example, the General Agreement on Tariffs and Trade; The United Nations Charter; The International Monetary Fund Agreement of 1945; The Universal Copyright Convention; The Warsaw Convention; The International Finance Corporation; The International Development Association; The International Bank for Reconstruction and Development; The International Civil Aviation Organization; The Organization for Economic Cooperation and Development; International Trade in Cotton Textiles; Long Term Agreement Regarding Such Trade; The International Coffee Agreement. Certainly, such problems are beyond the purview of the State of California. As stated in United States v. Pink, supra, 315 U.S. 203, 232, 62 S.Ct. 552, 566, 86 L.Ed. 796: "These are delicate matters. If state action could defeat or alter our foreign policy, serious consequences might ensue. The nation as a whole would be held to answer if a State created difficulties with a foreign power."

The argument is nevertheless advanced that until such time as the federal government acts, either by conflicting legislation *8 or international agreement,*9 state legislation is unobjectionable. In Purdy & Fitzpatrick v. State of California, 71 Cal.2d ____, ____ *, 79 Cal.Rptr. 77, 84, 456 P.2d 645, 652 our Supreme Court stated: "We need not await an instance of actual conflict to strike down a state law which purports to regulate a subject matter which the Congress simultaneously aims to control. The opportunity for potential conflict is too great to permit the operation of the state law. [Footnote omitted.]" A state law may not stand "as an obstacle to the accomplishment and execution of the full purposes and objectives of Congress." (Hines v. Davidowitz, supra, 312 U.S. 52, 67, 61 S.Ct. 399, 404, 85 L.Ed. 581.) *11 Suffice it to say that the force of Bethlehem's argument as is premised upon City of Pasadena v. Charleville (1932) 215 Cal. 384, 10 P.2d 745 and Heim v. McCall (1915) 239 U.S. 175, 36 S.Ct. 78, 60 L.Ed. 206 has been rendered extremely doubtful, if not completely emasculated, by Purdy & Fitzpatrick v. State of California, supra.

The California Buy American Act, like the Oregon escheat statute in Zschernig v. Miller, 389 U.S. 429, 434–435, 88 S.Ct. 664, 667, 19 L.Ed.2d 683,

* 8. Our attention has been directed to the federal Buy American Act (47 Stat. 1520, as amended in 63 Stat. 1024). This Act does not appear to be in direct conflict with the California Act so as to preempt the latter. Conversely, the existence of the federal Act cannot serve as a justification for state legislation since, as we have previously stated, it is the sole province of the federal government to act in this sphere. However, in contrast to the California Act, the federal Act appears to serve as an equalizer in considering foreign invitational bids, rather than as an embargo altogether on such bids. (See Executive Order No. 10582, Dec. 17, 1954, 19 F.R. 8723, as amended by Executive Order No. 11051, Sept. 27, 1962, 27 F.R. 9683.)

* 9. It is vigorously asserted by defendants and denied by plaintiff that the Buy American Act is violative of the General Agreement on Tariffs and Trade (GATT, 61 Stat., Pts. 5 and 6, as amended), of which this nation is a signatory. In Baldwin-Lima-Hamilton Corp. v. Superior Court, 208 Cal.App.2d 803, 819–820, 25 Cal.Rptr. 798, as one column of a twin pedestal upon which its decision was based, the court held that the California Buy American Act had been *superseded* by GATT. In Territory v. Ho, 41 Hawaii 565, similar legislation was invalidated on the premise that it was in *conflict* with GATT. Since we have concluded that the federal power, whether or not exercised, is exclusive in this field, we find

it unnecessary to delve into an extensive analysis of the effect of GATT.

* Advance Report Citation: 71 A.C. 587, 598.

* 11. An editorial dated October 15, 1964 in the New York Journal of Commerce commented: "Something of a dilemma confronts the present Administration and will also confront any future administration in consequence of the urge that prompts many State Legislatures to enact measures that restrict the flow of international commerce within their borders * * * The nature of this dilemma was suggested in a Washington dispatch to this newspaper yesterday. In brief, its message was to the effect that Washington's opportunity to win meaningful tariff concessions from foreign countries in the current Kennedy Round may be much curtailed by 'Buy American' or by simply 'Buy Local' laws adopted in many states." After giving a number of examples, the editorial concludes: "In the circumstances, about the best we can hope is that the State Legislatures will try harder in the future to temper the urge to protect their own producers with realization that the cumulative effect of procurement restrictions among many states can produce impossible rigidities in national policy. Even those who do not approve of the national foreign trade policy should realize that if it is to be determined by the future policies of 50 different entities, there won't be any policy at all."

"has more than 'some incidental or indirect effect in foreign countries,' and its great potential for disruption or embarrassment makes us hesitate to place it in the category of a diplomatic bagatelle." [*12]   Such state legislation may bear a particular onus to foreign nations since it may appear to be the product of selfish provincialism, rather than an instrument of justifiable policy.   It is a type of protectionism which invites retaliative restrictions on our own trade.   While the present California statute is not as gross an intrusion in the federal domain as others might be, "it has a direct impact upon foreign relations, and may well adversely affect the power of the central government to deal with those problems." (Zschernig v. Miller, supra, 389 U.S. 429, at page 441, 88 S.Ct. 664, at page 671, 19 L.Ed.2d 683.) [*14]

Our system of government is such that the interest of the cities, counties and states, no less than the interest of the people of the whole nation, "imperatively requires that federal power in the field affecting foreign relations be left entirely free from local interference." (Hines v. Davidowitz, supra, 312 U.S. at page 63, 61 S.Ct. at page 402.)   Effectiveness in handling these delicate problems requires no less. (United States v. Pink, supra, 315 U.S. 203, 229–230, 62 S.Ct. 552, 86 L.Ed. 796.)   To permit state legislation to concurrently operate in this sphere would very certainly "imperil the amicable relations between governments and vex the peace of nations." (Oetjen v. Central Leather Co., 246 U.S. 297, 304, 38 S.Ct. 309, 311, 62 L.Ed. 726; see Ricaud v. American Metal Co., 246 U.S. 304, 308–310, 38 S.Ct. 312, 62 L.Ed. 733.)

The present legislation is an impermissible attempt by the state to structure national foreign policy to conform to its own domestic policies.   It illustrates the dangers which are involved if federal policy is to be qualified by the variant notions of the several states.   We conclude that the California Buy American Act is an unconstitutional intrusion into an exclusive federal domain.

The judgments are affirmed.

Reppy, J., concurs:

Aiso, Justice (concurring).

I concur in Acting Presiding Justice Stephens' opinion holding the California Buy American Act (Govt.Code, §§ 4300–4305) unconstitutional as an undue interference with the federal government's conduct of foreign relations.   I desire to add a few supplementary observations.

---

* **12.** In a concurring opinion, Justice Stewart observed: "Today, we are told, Oregon's statute does not conflict with the national interest.   Tomorrow it may.   But, however that may be, the fact remains that the conduct of our foreign affairs is entrusted under the Constitution to the National Government, not to the probate courts of the several States." (Zschernig v. Miller, supra, at p. 443, 88 S.Ct. at p. 672.)

* **14.** In *Zschernig*, the court pointed out numerous instances where state courts have delved into "foreign policy attitudes" and noted in some detail how the Oregon statute, as applied, was unconstitutional.   Nevertheless, Justice Douglas, in his majority opinion, makes it clear that conceptually such legislation based on its history, as well as its operation, was patently "an intrusion by the State into the field of foreign affairs which the Constitution entrusts to the President and the Congress." (Zschernig v. Miller, supra, at p. 432, 88 S.Ct. at p. 666.)

Juxtaposition of the text of the California Buy American Act alongside those of GATT and the Trade Agreements Act (19 U.S.C.A. § 1351) as amended and extended, not only makes manifest the seriousness of the potential, if not presently actual, interference by California with the federal government's power to conduct its foreign affairs, but lays bare California's unconstitutional intrusion into the congressional power "[t]o regulate Commerce with foreign Nations." (U.S. Const., Art. I, § 8, cl. 3.)

The power to regulate commerce with foreign nations is an express grant by the people to the federal government. (Gibbons v. Ogden (1824) 22 U.S. (9 Wheat.) 1, 187–189, 6 L.Ed. 23, 68.) "It is an essential attribute of the power that it is exclusive and plenary. As an exclusive power, its exercise may not be limited, qualified or impeded to any extent by state action. [Citations.] The power is buttressed by the express provision of the Constitution denying to the States authority to lay imposts or duties on imports or exports without the consent of the Congress. Article 1, § 10, cl. 2. [¶] The Congress may determine what articles may be imported into this country and the terms upon which importation is permitted." (University of Illinois v. United States (1932) 289 U.S. 48, 56–57, 53 S.Ct. 509, 510, 77 L.Ed. 1025, 1028.)

Notes

(1) The *Bethlehem Steel* case was not appealed to the California Supreme Court.

(2) In K.S.B. TECHNICAL SALES CORP. v. NORTH JERSEY DISTRICT WATER SUPPLY COMMISSION, 75 N.J. 272, 381 A.2d 774 (1977), the New Jersey Supreme Court upheld a state "Buy American" statute which applied to purchases of equipment for a government water supply service, noting that although GATT applies with as much vigor as a treaty and is deemed supreme over state law under the U.S. Constitution, the specific exception in GATT Article III, paragraph 8, for government purchases exempted from the GATT national treatment obligation the purchases involved here.

On the question of whether the state statute was an impermissible intrusion by New Jersey into the field of foreign affairs, the court distinguished the *Zschernig* case cited in *Bethlehem* on the grounds that the New Jersey statute was nondiscriminatory (thus state officials would not need to evaluate or differentiate between foreign countries or their policies) and distinguished the *Bethlehem* case itself on the grounds that the New Jersey statute was narrower than the California one in that it provided that domestic materials did not need to be used if their cost was unreasonable or if it would be impractical or inconsistent with the public interest to do so.

Finally, the New Jersey court noted U.S. Supreme Court authority to the effect that a state can discriminate against non-residents when it acts in a proprietary capacity as a buyer or a seller. (See *South-Central Timber* case above.)

(3) In LUCCHINO v. BRAZIL, SOUTH KOREA, SPAIN, MEXICO, AND ARGENTINA, 82 Pa.Cmwlth. 406, 476 A.2d 1369 (1984), the court upheld a state statute that banned the purchase by state government agencies of steel, iron and aluminum products imported from countries which in turn discriminate against such products made in Pennsylvania. The court found that the matter being

commercial, neither sovereign immunity nor the Act of State Doctrine applied, and also found evidence that the defendant countries had discriminated against the relevant Pennsylvania products. The state court relied heavily on determinations of the federal administrative agencies concerning such practices as dumping or subsidization by the countries named as to the products concerned, and concluded (476 A.2d at 1376–77):

> 6. The statutes, regulations, policies, procedures and practices of the respondent foreign countries Brazil, South Korea, Spain, Mexico and Argentina, as set forth in the Findings of Fact, have the practical effect of granting and/or bestowing a preference, discount or other competitive advantage to steel, iron or aluminum products manufactured in said respondent foreign countries, the effect whereof discriminates against the same or substantially similar steel, iron and aluminum products manufactured in this Commonwealth and furthermore places said products manufactured in this Commonwealth at a competitive disadvantage.

> * * *

> 11. The violations of the Pennsylvania Trade Practices Act by each of the respondent foreign countries * * * entitles petitioner to the relief he seeks and thereby makes it unlawful for any public agency to specify, purchase, or permit to be furnished or used, in any public works, steel, iron and aluminum products made in any of the respondent foreign countries which have been determined by this Court to discriminate pursuant to the Act.

The *Lucchino* case was subsequently removed to federal court and later dismissed on procedural grounds. 50 BNA Antitrust & Trade Reg.Rptr. 921 (1986).

(4) The relation of government purchases to imports is taken up in Chapter 8 infra. One of the cases treated there is the California case of *Baldwin-Lima-Hamilton,* a lower court California case of 1962 (preceding *Bethlehem*) which held the California Buy American Act to be contrary to GATT article III, partly on grounds that the supplying of electricity by a city utility involved the production of goods for resale under the exception to the exception of GATT article III, paragraph 8.

(5) From the foregoing cases, how far would you say that the states may go in regulating matters affecting international trade? To what extent can their actions be overruled by federal action—either by Congress in enacting legislation or by the President in entering into a trade agreement on nontariff barriers to trade?

(6) Could the U.S. federal government enter into and implement an international agreement regulating government procurement by state and municipal governments? See Section 8.4 infra.

Chapter 4

NATIONAL GOVERNMENT REGULATION OF INTERNATIONAL ECONOMIC TRANSACTIONS

SECTION 4.1 INTRODUCTION

Although much of this book emphasizes problems of U.S. law and the U.S. Constitution, partly because of its expected audience but also because the United States is so important to world trade, it is also important to explore the legal systems of other countries in the world. Space and time prevent doing this in any great depth, or for more than just a few selected and illustrative cases. Nevertheless the purpose of this chapter is to help the reader to understand how some problems similar to those we explored in Chapter 3, would be handled in certain other countries. Not only is this important for persons engaged in transactions in or with other countries, but it is also important for obtaining an overall sound understanding of the operation of the international economic system. Just as the U.S. Constitution may impose certain constraints on statesmen seeking to "manage" the international economy, so also may the legal and constitutional structures of other countries, especially those (like the European Community and Japan) which have great weight in international trade and economic transactions.

In Chapter 3, we saw that the ability of the United States to engage effectively in trade negotiations was very much affected by the constitutional division of powers between the federal government and the states and between the President and Congress. It may also be affected by the relative openness of the U.S. legislative process and the degree to which individuals have access to the courts to challenge state or federal actions that are allegedly inconsistent with U.S. international obligations. The other members of the GATT trading system also must deal with splits in authority between different constituent elements of their governments and with judicial systems with rules that differ from those applicable in U.S. courts. In this chapter, we examine such problems mainly from the perspective of the European Community (EC) and Japan.

We conclude with a brief look at the legal framework in which trade is conducted in two developing countries, and in a group of state trading countries. As we discuss the GATT rules in later chapters, the reader should consider the extent to which the special needs of these countries require or merit special treatment. The complexities of managing economic interdependence as it affects the West, the East and the developing world will be explored in depth in Part IV.

In studying the materials in this chapter, the reader should focus on the following questions:

(1) How have the different institutional conflicts present in the United States, the EC and Japan affected the formation of international economic law in the past and how might they affect the scope and results of future negotiations on changes in such law?

(2) Does the possibility of an individual challenging government acts as inconsistent with international economic law (or the lack of such a possibility) mean that international agreements will be adhered to more (or less) faithfully?

(3) What implications should the answers to these questions have in constructing institutions and norms of international economic law (a question particularly relevant in reading Chapter 5 where the current system is outlined)? [1]

(4) Which entities of the government structure have the authority to regulate international trade?

(5) What is the relationship between parliamentary institutions, executive organizations, and the judiciary, in this regard?

(6) Do federal states or customs unions have special problems with the authority of the central government over external trade and other matters?

(7) What bodies have the power to enter into an international agreement?

(8) What is the legal effect of such an agreement in the internal law of a country?

(9) In which cases does such an agreement prevail over other internal law, or not?

The materials in the following sections will not answer all these questions with regard to all countries discussed, but these questions have motivated the selection and emphasis of materials in those sections.

The focus of this chapter will be the European Community and Japan, because of their importance in world trade and their importance in the trade of the United States. In 1983, the EC was the largest single trading entity, accounting for 33% of world trade (approximately one-half of which was internal EC trade), while Japan accounted for 8% and the United States for 11%.[2] These statistics may even understate the importance of the EC, as it is allied by preferential trading agreements with the other major countries of Western Europe and with numerous former colonies, concentrated mostly

---

1. These questions are explored in some detail in J. Jackson, J.–V. Louis & M. Matsushita, Implementing the Tokyo Round, chs. 1 & 5 (1984).

2. General Agreement on Tariffs & Trade, International Trade 1983/84, Table A5 (1984) (based on exports).

in Africa, but spread throughout the world. Its policies thus have an enormous impact on world trade. U.S. imports from the EC and Japan represented about 19% and 18%, respectively, of total U.S. imports in 1984.[3]

In terms of economic power, the United States, the European Community and Japan (the three entities are sometimes call the "trilateral group") have the overwhelmingly dominant role to play in the development of Western international economic policy. Probably either the United States or the European Community has an effective veto over most proposals for international economic policy, and together they almost certainly have such a veto. Likewise, together they often have the power of initiative, in the sense that if they are agreed that a certain policy should be followed to promote certain international economic goals, on many issues (but certainly not all issues) this agreed position will prevail. It is thus extremely important to have a basic understanding of their institutions as they are involved with international trade.

We will look first and in greatest depth at the European Community, both here and in other chapters of this book. The European Community is the most successful example of an economic union formed in modern times. The governmental system which was launched by the Treaty of Rome in 1957, and has been evolving towards a more unified system, contains a group of problems, as well as the evolution of solutions to those problems, which may foreshadow some of the problems and solutions which will face the broader international trade community. If GATT continues to evolve and liberal trade policies continue to prevail, some of the problems of coordinating other kinds of economic policy are certain to arise. This has been the experience of the EC which, in organizing a free trade area and customs union, found that it had to address problems concerning the free flow of workers between nations, the free flow of capital between those nations and ultimately the coordination of government fiscal and monetary policies, leading to greater harmonization of antitrust policy and taxation, company law and most government economic policy generally. No one expects a world international economic system to evolve as far as has the European Community, but an examination of how the EC has faced certain coordination problems can shed light on possible solutions of analogous problems in the wider international context. When the EC faces the difficulty of how to handle member state government subsidization of exports, it reaches for solutions some of which may be applicable to the similar problems faced in the context of GATT and multilateral trade negotiations on a wider scale. Likewise, coordinating government purchasing procedures is a problem common both to the EC and to multilateral trade negotiations in GATT. An understanding of the legal system of the European Community, and how it differs from the legal system (if one can call it that) of the broader GATT community, can assist the reader—whether he be a scholar or practitioner— in appreciating the pros and cons of comparative approaches to his problems.

3. U.S. Dept. of Commerce, Business America 5 (Mar. 4, 1985).

SECTION 4.2   THE EUROPEAN COMMUNITY [1]

(A) THE INSTITUTIONS AND ACTIVITIES OF THE EUROPEAN COMMUNITY

The European Community (EC), sometimes referred to as the European Common Market, is in fact three communities: the European Coal and Steel Community (ECSC) established in 1951 by the Treaty of Paris, the European Economic Community (EEC) established in 1957 by the Treaty of Rome and the European Atomic Energy Community (Euratom) also established by a Rome treaty in 1957. The original members of the EC were Belgium, France, Italy, Luxembourg, the Netherlands and West Germany. They were joined in 1973 by Denmark, Ireland and the United Kingdom, in 1981 by Greece and in 1986 by Portugal and Spain. Norway agreed to join in 1973, but did not do so after its proposed accession was voted down in a national referendum. Further enlargement is not likely in the near future, as the principal remaining nonmember states of Western Europe—Austria, Finland, Sweden and Switzerland—will probably remain officially nonaligned by reason of tradition, treaty or location, although they each have extensive preferential trading arrangements with the EC.

There are four Community institutions: The Commission, the Council, the European Parliament and the Court of Justice.[2] Although the same institution has acted in respect of each community since the institutions of the various communities were merged in the 1960's, the institution's power in each instance is derived from the treaty establishing the particular community and thus varies somewhat depending on the community for which it is acting.

The *Commission,* which is based in Brussels, was designed under the EC treaties to be the most "European" of the institutions.[3] It consists of 17 commissioners who are appointed by joint action of the member states for four-year terms as independent persons and not as representatives of particular governments. Each member state has the right in practice to choose one (two in the case of the largest member states) of the commissioners to be appointed. The member states also choose the President and Vice Presi-

1. See generally H. Smit & P. Herzog, The Law of the European Economic Community (6 vols. 1976); E. Stein, P. Hay & M. Waelbroeck, European Community Law and Institutions in Perspective: Text, Cases and Readings (1976), with Supplement (1985) (extensive bibliographic references); J. Mégret, M. Waelbroeck, J.–V. Louis, D. Vignes & J.–L. Dewost (eds.), Le Droit de la Communauté Economique Européenne (12 vols. 1970). For one volume works, see D. Lasok & J. Bridge, An Introduction to the Law and Institutions of the European Communities (3rd ed. 1982); A. Parry & J. Dinnage, Parry & Hardy: EEC Law (1981); P. Mathijsen, A Guide to European Community Law (3rd ed. 1980); D. Wyatt & A. Dashwood, The Substantive Law of the EEC (1980).

2. See generally Commission of the European Communities, The Institutions of the European Community (European File, Pub. No. 17/84, Nov. 1984); J. Lodge (ed.), Institutions and Policies of the European Community (1983); H. Wallace, W. Wallace & C. Webb (eds.), Policy Making in the European Community (2d ed. 1983).

3. See generally Treaty Establishing the European Economic Community (1957) (the "Treaty of Rome"), arts. 155–63; Treaty Establishing a Single Council and a Single Commission of the European Communities, ch. II (1965) (the "Merger Treaty").

dents of the Commission. The President in recent years has represented the EC at the annual international economic summit meetings of Western leaders.

The Commission is the executive arm of the EC. It is charged with ensuring that the treaties are observed and that the decisions of Community institutions are faithfully implemented. It administers the programs and enforces the regulations put in place by the Council, and it plays an important role in proposing new legislation to be enacted by the Council. Each commissioner is responsible for a particular part of the Commission's work. The Commission staff numbers some 10,000 officials.

The *Council*, also based in Brussels, is composed of one representative from each member state.[4] The actual membership of the Council varies depending on the issue before it—national transport ministers discuss transport issues; national agricultural ministers consider agricultural questions. The Council is the legislative body of the EC and adopts regulations and other acts proposed by the Commission. Those acts often delegate considerable implementation authority to the Commission. Each member state has a permanent representative to the EC. These permanent representatives, known as the Committee of Permanent Representatives (COREPER), have an extensive staff. COREPER looks after the interests of the member states between Council meetings and plays an important role in preparing for Council meetings, a role that gives it considerable influence on actions ultimately taken by the Council.

The Council voting structure depends on which particular power under which of the treaties it is exercising. In some cases each member state has one vote and a simple majority prevails; in other cases a "qualified majority" is required involving votes weighted by the relative importance of the member states; and in still other cases, unanimity is required.[5] The Treaty of Rome provided for a "transitional phase" and at the end of the transition a number of "unanimity" voting requirements were to become "qualified majority" voting requirements.[6] In 1965, France opposed the movement to a qualified majority system and after much travail the "Luxembourg Compromise" was agreed upon. In any case which by treaty could be decided by majority, a member state, under the Compromise, can assert that the issue is "very important" and then the Council attempts to arrive at a solution to which all can agree. If agreement fails, the Compromise, with studied ambiguity, noted that France feels discussion must continue; other member states noted that a "divergence" exists on this point. Although from time to time the Council makes decisions by majority vote (e.g., in May 1982 the Council adopted a decision on agricultural prices over the objections of Great Britain), the French view of the Compromise seems to have in fact generally prevailed for 20 years, despite considerable criticism. In December 1985, a meeting of European leaders agreed on a reduction of certain unanimous voting requirements applicable in respect of measures establishing free movement within the internal market.[7]

4. See generally Treaty of Rome, arts. 145–54; Merger Treaty, ch. I.

5. Treaty of Rome, art. 148.

6. See, e.g., Treaty of Rome, art. 43.

7. See Reform of EEC Treaty and Political Cooperation Treaty: Results of Luxembourg

The treaties give executive authority to the Commission and provide for Community legislation to be adopted by the Council, but usually only upon proposal of the Commission. The Council can amend a Commission proposal only by unanimous vote; to adopt most proposals a "qualified majority" is required.[8] In practice, considerable negotiation occurs between the two bodies and the Council, with its power to reject any proposal, is often able to insist on its viewpoint.

The Council and the Commission may act under their various authorities by several means: [9]

Regulation: a binding act that is directly applicable in all Member States.

Directive: an act binding "as to the result to be achieved" but which leaves to national authorities the "choice of form and methods."

Decision: an act binding in its entirety upon those to whom it is addressed.

Recommendations and opinions: acts which have no binding force.

The struggle for power between the Council and Commission basically reflects the desire of the member states to retain their national sovereignty vis-à-vis the EC. The dominating role of the member state governments has been particularly emphasized in recent years by the regular meetings held by the leaders of the member states to discuss and often decide upon the direction of EC policy. Although these meetings are not provided for in the treaties, the decisions by the leaders are later implemented by member state representatives in the Council and its sub-bodies. These "summit meetings" have become fairly regular (three or so times a year) and have been called the "European Council."

The *European Court of Justice* (sitting at Luxembourg) is one of the most interesting, and from a juridical point of view, most impressive institutions of the European Community.[10] Thirteen judges, assisted by six "Advocates General," one of whom recommends a decision to the court in each case, form a judicial institution which has been given an impressive array of powers and has exercised them in a remarkably forthright way. The Court's work has on the whole enhanced both the unity and the central powers of the EC institutions. An American lawyer is struck by some of the parallels between Court of Justice case developments and those of the United States Supreme Court.[11] In effect, the European Community operates within a system of judicial review (court power to annul unconstitutional acts) which is both very similar to that of the United States and very different from the judicial systems in some of the major EC member states. Given the relatively subordinate role of the judiciary in many European government systems, it is striking to find such a strong judicial role played at the European Community level.[12]

Summit, Agence Internationale d'Information pour la Presse, Europe, December 5, 1985 (Nos. 1383/1384). The agreement was implemented in early 1986.

8. See Treaty of Rome, art. 149.

9. Id., art. 189.

10. Id., arts. 164–87.

11. For an informed discussion of such parallels, see T. Sandalow & E. Stein (eds.), Courts and Free Markets (2 vols. 1982).

12. The works cited in note 1 supra contain extensive comments on the European

Under the provisions of the EEC Treaty, the Commission or a member state is authorized to sue another member state in the Court for failing to fulfil a Treaty obligation.[13]   Likewise, the Commission, the Council or a member state can ask the Court to review acts of the Council or Commission for violations of the Treaty or EEC rules, for lack of competence, for infringement of essential procedural requirements or for misuse of powers.[14] They may also sue the Commission or Council for failure to act when required to do so.[15]   In addition, in certain cases, when an individual is directly affected by a Community action, recourse can be had to the Court.[16] Finally, and of particular importance, a party litigant in the court of a member state may be able, in asserting the applicability of Community law, to obtain a Court of Justice ruling on that law by requesting the member state court to refer the Community law issue to the Court of Justice.   If there is no appeal of the member state court's decision, Article 177 requires that court to refer the Community law issue to the Court of Justice.[17]

Often, issues of Community law, whether they be interpretation of the basic treaties themselves or of "secondary legislation" (as regulations and other actions of EC institutions are called), can and will be brought to the Court of Justice.   To a remarkable degree, then, one observes that much Community activity is conducted with reference to the fact of its ultimate "challengeability" in the Court.   In short, lawyers are important, their expertise is growing, and possibly so also is their influence (although Europe, especially the Continent, has traditionally been less influenced by lawyers, private or public, than the United States has been).   In connection with the EC exercise of powers relating to international economic power, then, the EC legal norms can be expected to have considerable importance.

The final EC institution to be discussed here is the *European Parliament* which meets in Strasbourg.[18]   Members of the European Parliament are directly elected by the voters of the various member states.   The number of parliamentary seats allocated to each member state is in rough proportion to that state's number of votes under the weighted voting procedure in the Council.   The Parliament has the right to give nonbinding advice on proposed legislation, to ask questions of the Council and Commission and have

court. In addition, the following works may be consulted: G. Bebr, Development of Judicial Control of the European Communities (1981) (with extensive bibliography); L. Collins, European Community Law in the United Kingdom (3rd ed. 1984); R. Lecourt, L'Europe des Juges (1976); H. Schermers, Judicial Protection in the European Communities (1976); A. Toth, Legal Protection of Individuals in the European Communities (2 vols. 1978).

13. Treaty of Rome, art. 169–71.

14. Id., arts. 173–74.

15. Id., art. 175–76.

16. Id., arts. 173, 175. There is a body of complex decisional law on the question of when a private party is authorized to bring an action in the Court of Justice. Essentially, if the contested action is not in the form of a decision addressed to it, a private party must show that the action (such as a regulation) is of direct and individual concern to it. Compare Koyo Seiko Co. v. Commission [1979] E.C.R. 1337 (exporter to EC permitted to challenge antidumping duty) with Alusuisse Italia S.p.A., [1982] E.C.R. 3463 (importer not permitted to challenge antidumping duty).

17. If the answer to the question is obvious, a reference to the Court of Justice may not be required. CILFIT Srl v. Ministry of Health, [1982] E.C.R. 3415. See Bebr, The Rambling Ghost of "Cohn-Bendit": Acte Clair and the Court of Justice, 20 Comm.Mkt.L.Rev. 439 (1983); Rasmussen, The European Court's *Acte Clair* Strategy in *CILFIT,* 9 Eur.L.Rev. 242 (1984).

18. Treaty of Rome, arts. 137–44 (The European Parliament is referred to in the treaties as the Assembly).

them answered and to pass a motion of censure which would then require the resignation of all of the members of the Commission (something it has never done).   In addition, it has the power to suggest changes to the annual Community budget, and except in respect of expenditures "necessarily resulting from this Treaty or from acts adopted in accordance therewith" (e.g. the common agricultural policy, described in Section 14.2(C) infra), the power to determine the ultimate budget (except that any increase is limited by specified guidelines).[19]   The Parliament is constantly seeking to expand its powers and influence, an effort not generally supported by the member states.

The EC is engaged in a broad range of activities.[20]   It was recognized at the outset that the creation of a true common market would require more than a simple elimination of tariff barriers.   Indeed, in order to fulfill the goal of free movement of goods, services, workers and capital, it was imperative that the EC have the power to deal with many subjects.   Today, it administers a single common agriculture policy applicable throughout the Community, and essentially oversees the operation and subsidization of the EC steel industry. In addition, it actively promotes, and often requires, harmonization of a wide variety of laws and regulations that affect trade, particularly in the area of product standards and border formalities.   The other areas where it has been active in harmonization include company law, intellectual property law, consumer protection law, environmental law and laws relating to health, safety, employment and social security.   It enforces the antitrust (called "competition") rules spelled out in the treaties, including supervision of member state subsidies to private enterprise.   It promotes economic development through its regional assistance programs and its programs to develop new high-technology industries in Europe.   While the member states have retained their sovereignty in matters of general economic policy, the EC promotes the coordination of economic and monetary policy and operates the European Monetary System.   To finance its numerous programs, which in 1984 necessitated a budget of 29.3 billion ECU, the EC relies mainly on customs revenue and its share of member state value added tax revenue.[21]

The wide range of these activities has inevitably raised questions of how closely integrated politically the EC should become.   Although the EC treaties focus on economic matters, it has been understood from the beginning that some of their framers viewed them as having the longer range objective of European political union.   Indeed, it is hard to see how the progress toward economic unity could have avoided major political implications.   For years one of the major issues in the EC has been the question of how much and how fast the EC should evolve toward political union.   For the immediate future, the integration of Greece, Portugal and Spain and the continuing controversy over the operation and financing of the EC's agricul-

19.   Treaty Amending Certain Financial Provisions of the Treaties Establishing the European Communities and of the "Merger Treaty", art. 12 (1975).

20.   Each year these activities are described in the Commission's annual report. See, e.g., Commission of the European Communities,

Eighteenth General Report on the Activities of the European Communities—1984 (1985).

21.   The ECU or European Currency Unit is a monetary unit, the value of which is based on a market basket of member state currencies.   At January 24, 1986, 1 ECU was equivalent to $0.895.

tural program may divert attention from the unification question, but it is a question that will not go away.

The difficulties faced by the EC often lead one to wonder if it will survive—at least in any form beyond a customs union. These doubts may be premature. "To the casual observer of Community politics and the occasional participant in the policy-making process, the EC projects a Jekyll and Hyde image. On the surface much of the political activity—elaborate European Council meetings and persistently unproductive Council of Ministers' sessions—yields no result. The EC does not seem very far removed from other kinds of international organizations; its member governments do not appear to be responding to any 'Community spirit'. Yet there is another side. To the lawyer, trader, consumer, or farmer, the EC is a complex political and economic organization through which demands are channelled, resources claimed and power and influence sought. Community politics take on substance and reality in spite of the political flux and posturing on the surface." [22] The fact that the lofty goals of the EC's framers have not been completely achieved sometimes obscures the great progress toward achieving them that has occurred.

From the perspective of international economic relations, two questions concerning the EC are of particular importance: (1) To what extent is legislation or other action taken by the EC enforced in the individual member states, i.e. the relation of Community law to national law? (2) What powers does the EC have in the realm of international economic affairs and to what extent does it share them with the member states? We will look at each of these issues in turn.

(B) THE FORCE OF COMMUNITY LAW IN THE MEMBER STATES [23]

There may be a no more perplexing or complex set of questions regarding the international trade law of the EC than those questions which concern the relationship between the juridical acts (regulations, directives, basic treaty rules, external agreements) of the EC and the legal rules which exist within the legal systems of each of the member states. The subject has occasioned a vast literature. Here, we explore first the view of the European Court of Justice and then briefly consider how these issues are viewed in several of the principal member states. In reviewing this material the student should consider how the issues discussed in Sections 3.3 (International Agreements and U.S. Law) and 3.6 (Federal-State Relations) would be resolved in the EC.

22. Webb, Theoretical Perspectives and Problems, in H. Wallace, W. Wallace & C. Webb, note 2 supra, at 1.

23. See generally Pescatore, The Doctrine of "Direct Effect": An Infant Disease of Community Law, 8 Eur.L.Rev. 155 (1983) and the works cited in notes 1 and 12 supra.

(1) The View of the European Court

AMMINISTRAZIONE DELLE FINANZE DELLO STATO
v. SIMMENTHAL S.p.A.

Court of Justice of the European Communities, Case 106/77
[1978] E.C.R. 629.

[An Italian beef importer brought an action in Italian court to recover certain veterinary and public health inspection fees it was required to pay when importing beef from France. The importer claimed the fees were obstacles to the free movement of goods and as such were forbidden by Community law. The Italian court posed the following questions to the European Court of Justice pursuant to Article 177:]

(1) Since, in accordance with Article 189 of the EEC Treaty and the established case-law of the Court of Justice of the European Communities, directly applicable Community provisions must, notwithstanding any internal rule or practice whatsoever of the Member States, have full, complete and uniform effect in their legal systems in order to protect subjective legal rights created in favour of individuals, is the scope of the said provisions to be interpreted to the effect that any subsequent national measures which conflict with those provisions must be forthwith disregarded without waiting until those measures have been eliminated by action on the part of the national legislature concerned (repeal) or of other constitutional authorities (declaration that they are unconstitutional) especially, in the case of the latter alternative, where, since the national law continues to be fully effective pending such declaration, it is impossible to apply the Community provisions and, in consequence, to ensure that they are fully, completely and uniformly applied and to protect the legal rights created in favour of individuals?

(2) Arising out of the previous question, in circumstances where Community law recognizes that the protection of subjective legal rights created as a result of "directly aplicable" Community provisions may be suspended until any conflicting national measures are actually repealed by the competent national authorities, is such repeal in all cases to have a wholly retroactive effect so as to avoid any adverse effects on those subjective legal rights?

[The Court of Justice replied as follows:]

The main purpose of the *first question* is to ascertain what consequences flow from the direct applicability of a provision of Community law in the event of incompatibility with a subsequent legislative provision of a Member State.

Direct applicability in such circumstances means that rules of Community law must be fully and uniformly applied in all the Member States from the date of their entry into force and for so long as they continue in force.

These provisions are therefore a direct source of rights and duties for all those affected thereby, whether Member States or individuals, who are parties to legal relationships under Community law.

This consequence also concerns any national court whose task it is as an organ of a Member State to protect, in a case within its jurisdiction, the rights conferred upon individuals by Community law.

Furthermore, in accordance with the principle of the precedence of Community law, the relationship between provisions of the Treaty and directly applicable measures of the institutions on the one hand and the national law of the Member States on the other is such that those provisions and measures not only by their entry into force render automatically inapplicable any conflicting provision of current national law but—in so far as they are an integral part of, and take precedence in, the legal order applicable in the territory of each of the Member States—also preclude the valid adoption of new national legislative measures to the extent to which they would be incompatible with Community provisions.

Indeed any recognition that national legislative measures which encroach upon the field within which the Community exercises its legislative power or which are otherwise incompatible with the provisions of Community law had any legal effect would amount to a corresponding denial of the effectiveness of obligations undertaken unconditionally and irrevocably by Member States pursuant to the Treaty and would thus imperil the very foundations of the Community.

The same conclusion emerges from the structure of Article 177 of the Treaty which provides that any court or tribunal of a Member State is entitled to make a reference to the Court whenever it considers that a preliminary ruling on a question of interpretation or validity relating to Community law is necessary to enable it to give judgment.

The effectiveness of that provision would be impaired if the national court were prevented from forthwith applying Community law in accordance with the decision or the case-law of the Court.

It follows from the foregoing that every national court must, in a case within its jurisdiction, apply Community law in its entirety and protect rights which the latter confers on individuals and must accordingly set aside any provision of national law which may conflict with it, whether prior or subsequent to the Community rule.

Accordingly any provision of a national legal system and any legislative, administrative or judicial practice which might impair the effectiveness of Community law by withholding from the national court having jurisdiction to apply such law the power to do everything necessary at the moment of its application to set aside national legislative provisions which might prevent Community rules from having full force and effect are incompatible with those requirements which are the very essence of Community law.

This would be the case in the event of a conflict between a provision of Community law and a subsequent national law if the solution of the conflict were to be reserved for an authority with a discretion of its own, other than the court called upon to apply Community law, even if such an impediment to the full effectiveness of Community law were only temporary.

The first question should therefore be answered to the effect that a national court which is called upon, within the limits of its jurisdiction, to apply provisions of Community law is under a duty to give full effect to those provisions, if necessary refusing of its own motion to apply any conflicting provision of national legislation, even if adopted subsequently, and it is not necessary for the court to request or await the prior setting aside of such provision by legislative or other constitutional means.

The essential point of the *second question* is whether—assuming it to be accepted that the protection of rights conferred by provisions of Community law can be suspended until any national provisions which might conflict with them have been in fact set aside by the competent national authorities—such setting aside must in every case have unrestricted retroactive effect so as to prevent the rights in question from being in any way adversely affected.

It follows from the answer to the first question that national courts must protect rights conferred by provisions of the Community legal order and that it is not necessary for such courts to request or await the actual setting aside by the national authorities empowered so to act of any national measures which might impede the direct and immediate application of Community rules.

* * *

THE COURT, in answer to the questions referred to it by the Pretore di Susa by order of 28 July 1977, hereby rules:

A national court which is called upon, within the limits of its jurisdiction, to apply provisions of Community law is under a duty to give full effect to those provisions, if necessary refusing of its own motion to apply any conflicting provision of national legislation, even if adopted subsequently, and it is not necessary for the court to request or await the prior setting aside of such provisions by legislative or other constitutional means.

Notes and Questions

(1) The *Simmenthal* case is one of many where the European Court of Justice has expressed its view of the position of Community law *vis à vis* the laws of the various member states. Over time it has grown more forceful in asserting the superiority of Community law, but the bases for decisions such as *Simmenthal* were laid many years ago. Consider in this regard the following case.

In N.V. ALGEMENE TRANSPORT—EN EXPEDITIE ONDERNEMING VAN GEND & LOOS v. NETHERLANDS INLAND REVENUE ADMINISTRATION, Case No. 26/62, [1963] E.C.R. 1, the Court was asked whether Article 12 [24] of the EEC Treaty had direct application within the territory of a Member State, i.e. whether nationals of a State could, on the basis of Article 12, lay claim to individual rights which national courts had to protect. The Court responded as follows:

24. Article 12 provides: "Member States shall refrain from introducing between themselves any new customs duties on imports or exports or any charges having equivalent effect, and from increasing those which they already apply in their trade with each other."

To ascertain whether the provisions of an international treaty extend so far in their effects it is necessary to consider the spirit, the general scheme and the wording of those provisions.

The objective of the EEC Treaty, which is to establish a Common Market, the functioning of which is of direct concern to interested parties in the Community, implies that this Treaty is more than an agreement which merely creates mutual obligations between the contracting states. This view is confirmed by the preamble to the Treaty which refers not only to governments but to peoples. It is also confirmed more specifically by the establishment of institutions endowed with sovereign rights, the exercise of which affects Member States and also their citizens. * * *

In addition the task assigned to the Court of Justice under Article 177, the object of which is to secure uniform interpretation of the Treaty by national courts and tribunals, confirms that the states have acknowledged that Community law has an authority which can be invoked by their nationals before those courts and tribunals.

The conclusion to be drawn from this is that the Community constitutes a new legal order of international law for the benefit of which the states have limited their sovereign rights, albeit within limited fields, and the subjects of which comprise not only Member States but also their nationals. Independently of the legislation of Member States, Community law therefore not only imposes obligations on individuals but is also intended to confer upon them rights which become part of their legal heritage. These rights arise not only where they are expressly granted by the Treaty, but also by reason of obligations which the Treaty imposes in a clearly defined way upon individuals as well as upon the Member States and upon the institutions of the Community.

* * *

The wording of Article 12 contains a clear and unconditional prohibition which is not a positive but a negative obligation. This obligation, moreover, is not qualified by a reservation on the part of states which would make its implementation conditional upon a positive legislative measure enacted under national law. The very nature of this prohibition makes it ideally adapted to produce direct effects in the legal relationship between Member States and their subjects.

* * *

It follows from the foregoing considerations that, according to the spirit, the general scheme and the wording of the Treaty, Article 12 must be interpreted as producing direct effects and creating individual rights which national courts must protect.

(2) The extent to which a directive can override national law was analyzed in Pubblico Ministerio v. Ratti, [1979] E.C.R. 1629. The court held that "after the expiration of the period fixed for the implementation of a directive a Member State may not apply its internal law—even if it is provided with penal sanctions—which has not yet been adapted in compliance with the directive, to a person, who has complied with the requirements of the directive." In an answer to another question the Court ruled that a national law inconsistent with the terms of a directive could be enforced until the time at which the directive was required to be implemented.

(3) Readers familiar with U.S. constitutional history should recognize similarities between the cases quoted above and such U.S. Supreme Court cases as Martin v. Hunter's Lessee, 14 U.S. (1 Wheat) 304, 4 L.Ed. 97 (1816). What differences between the constitutional structures of the United States and the European Community explain differences in the approach and effect of these cases?

(4) Consider to what extent the superiority of Community law over national law might allow member state governments to implement unpopular programs opposed by national legislatures by not vigorously opposing such programs in Community institutions. What could a national legislature do to prevent this? In terms of implementing controversial international trade policies, is it easier, harder, or no different, to do so in the EC?

(2) The Views of the Member States

Generally the courts of the member states of the EC have accepted that Community law must be taken into consideration and prevails over inconsistent national law, but as the following material makes clear that acceptance cannot be said to be complete and universal.

(a) The United Kingdom

Traditionally, in the United Kingdom treaties have been applied as domestic law only if Parliament so applied them and subsequent action by Parliament could override the Treaty. The European Communities Act of 1972 addresses this problem as follows:

EUROPEAN COMMUNITIES ACT, 1972
(1972, c. 68, 20–21 Eliz. II 3.)

2.—(1) All such rights, powers, liabilities, obligations and restrictions from time to time created or arising by or under the Treaties, and all such remedies and procedures from time to time provided for by or under the Treaties, as in accordance with the Treaties are without further enactment to be given legal effect or used in the United Kingdom shall be recognised and available in law, and be enforced, allowed and followed accordingly; and the expression "enforceable Community right" and similar expressions shall be read as referring to one to which this subsection applies.

(2) Subject to Schedule 2 to this Act,[25] at any time after its passing Her Majesty may by Order in Council, and any designated Minister or department may by regulations, make provision—

(a) for the purpose of implementing any Community obligation of the United Kingdom, or enabling any such obligation to be implemented, or of enabling any rights enjoyed or to be enjoyed by the United Kingdom under or by virtue of the Treaties to be exercised; or

(b) for the purpose of dealing with matters arising out of or related to any such obligation or rights or the coming into force, or the operation from time to time, of subsection (1) above;

25. Schedule 2 basically excepts actions that would increase taxes, impose retroactive obligations or create new criminal offenses punishable by imprisonment for more than two years.

and in the exercise of any statutory power or duty, including any power to give directions or to legislate by means of orders, rules, regulations or other subordinate instrument, the person entrusted with the power or duty may have regard to the objects of the Communities and to any such obligation or rights as aforesaid.

* * *

(4) The provision that may be made under subsection (2) above includes, subject to Schedule 2 to this Act, any such provision (of any such extent) as might be made by Act of Parliament, and any enactment passed or to be passed, other than one contained in this Part of this Act, shall be construed and have effect subject to the foregoing provisions of this section; but, except as may be provided by any Act passed after this Act, Schedule 2 shall have effect in connection with the powers conferred by this and the following sections of this Act to make Orders in Council and regulations.

One of England's leading jurists, Lord Denning, expressed the status of Community law in England as follows: "Under § 2(1) and (4) of the European Communities Act 1972 the principles laid down in the Treaty are 'without further enactment' to be given legal effect in the United Kingdom; and have priority over 'any enactment passed or to be passed' by our Parliament. * * * If on close investigation it should appear that our legislation is deficient or is inconsistent with Community law by some oversight of our draftsmen then it is our bounden duty to give priority to Community law. * * * If the time should come when our Parliament deliberately passes an Act with the intention of repudiating the Treaty or any provision in it or intentionally of acting inconsistently with it and says so in express terms then I should have thought that it would be the duty of our courts to follow the statute of our Parliament." Macarthys Ltd. v. Smith, [1979] 3 All Eng.R. 325, 329 (Court of Appeal). See generally L. Collins, European Community Law in the United Kingdom (3rd ed. 1984).

(b) France

French courts also usually recognize the priority of Community law in France. The Cour de Cassation (Supreme Civil and Criminal Court) has explicitly so held. See Clave Bouhaben von Kempis v. Epoux Geldof, [1976] 2 Comm.Mkt.L.R. 152; Administration des Douanes v. Société Cafés Jacques Vabre, 12 Comm.Mkt.L.Rev. 336 (1975); Audeoud, Berlin & Manin, The Application of Community Law in France: Review of French Court Decisions from 1974 to 1981, 19 Comm.Mkt.L.Rev. 289 (1982). There are some exceptions to this general rule to be found in the decisions of the Conseil d'Etat (Supreme Administrative Court). See, e.g., In Re Cohn-Bendit, 16 Comm. Mkt.L.Rev. 702 (1979) (direct effect of a Community directive denied in apparent disregard of the settled case law of the Court of Justice); Syndicat Général des Fabricants de Semoules de France, 9 Comm.Mkt.L.Rev. 395 (1970); Bermann, French Treaties and French Courts: Two Problems in Supremacy, 28 Intl. & Comp.L.Q. 458 (1979).

(c) Federal Republic of Germany

In 1974, the German Constitutional Court suggested that it would not apply Community law if it was at variance with basic rights guaranteed by the German Constitution. Decision of May 29, 1974, [1974] 2 Comm.Mkt. L.R. 540. Subsequent cases seem to limit that decision such that Germany also seems generally to recognize the superiority of Community law. See E. Stein, P. Hay, M. Waelbroeck & J. Weiler, European Community Law and Institutions in Perspective 59–60 (1985 Supp.).

Questions

When the German Constitutional Court suggested Community law could not override basic rights guaranteed by the German Constitution, its principal concern was that EC rules are established by the Commission and the Council without any effective control being exercised by a parliament representing the people. We have commented before on how a member state government could effectively implement laws and programs through Community legislation that it could not convince its own parliament to adopt. What safeguards could be set up within the European Community or member state governments to insure appropriate citizen, political and parliamentary participation in the law-making process? Would the concern of the German court be alleviated if the European Court recognized the existence of fundamental rights? See Hauer v. Land Rheinland-Pfalz, [1979] E.C.R. 3727, 3745 ("[T]he Court is bound to draw inspiration from constitutional traditions common to Member States, so that measures which are incompatible with the fundamental rights recognized by the constitutions of those States are unacceptable in the Community * * *").

(C) THE COMMUNITY'S POWER IN EXTERNAL RELATIONS [26]

(1) The Scope and Exclusivity of Community Powers

INTERNATIONAL AGREEMENT ON RUBBER

Court of Justice of the European Communities, Opinion No. 1/78.
[1979] E.C.R. 2871.

[The Commission asked the Court to give its opinion, as it is authorized to do pursuant to Article 228 of the EEC Treaty, on whether the Community was competent to conclude the International Rubber Agreement. The Council argued that the Community was not because the agreement dealt with matters beyond the competence of the Community—general economic policy, the supply of a "strategic product" essential for defense and was in part a sort of aid to developing countries. The Court rejected these arguments:]

[I]t is clear that a coherent commercial policy would no longer be practicable if the Community were not in a position to exercise its powers

---

26. In addition to the works cited in note 1 supra, see E. Volker & J. Steenbergen, Leading Cases and Materials on the External Relations Law of the E.C. (1985); A. Bleckman, Division of Powers Between the European Communities and Their Member States in the Field of External Relations (1981); Pescatore, External Relations in the Case-law of the Court of Justice of the European Communities, 16 Comm.Mkt.L.Rev. 615 (1979); Leopold, External Relations Power of the EEC in Treaty and in Practice, 26 Intl. & Comp.L.Q. 54 (1977).

also in connection with a category of agreements which are becoming, alongside traditional commercial agreements, one of the major factors in the regulation of international trade.

* * * [I]t would no longer be possible to carry on any worthwhile common commercial policy if the Community were not in a position to avail itself also of more elaborate means devised with a view to furthering the development of international trade. It is therefore not possible to lay down, for Article 113 [27] of the EEC Treaty, an interpretation the effect of which would be to restrict the common commercial policy to the use of instruments intended to have an effect only on the traditional aspects of external trade to the exclusion of more highly developed mechanisms such as appear in the agreement envisaged. A "commercial policy" understood in that sense would be destined to become nugatory in the course of time. Although it may be thought that at the time when the Treaty was drafted liberalization of trade was the dominant idea, the Treaty nevertheless does not form a barrier to the possibility of the Community's developing a commercial policy aiming at a regulation of the world market for certain products rather than at a mere liberalization of trade.

Article 113 empowers the Community to formulate a commercial "policy", based on "uniform principles" thus showing that the question of external trade must be governed from a wide point of view and not only having regard to the administration of precise systems such as customs and quantitative restrictions. The same conclusion may be deduced from the fact that the enumeration in Article 113 of the subjects covered by commercial policy (changes in tariff rates, the conclusion of tariff and trade agreements, the achievement of uniformity in measures of liberalization, export policy and measures to protect trade) is conceived as a non-exhaustive enumeration which must not, as such, close the door to the application in a Community context of any other process intended to regulate external trade. A restrictive interpretation of the concept of common commercial policy would risk causing disturbances in intra-Community trade by reason of disparities which would then exist in certain sectors of economic relations with non-member countries.

[The Court noted, however, that the Agreement anticipated substantial costs to be borne by the parties to it. It therefore ruled:]

2. The question of the exclusive nature of the Community's powers depends in this case on the arrangements for financing the operations of the buffer stock which it is proposed to set up under that agreement. If the burden of financing the stock falls upon the Community budget the Community will have exclusive powers. If on the other hand the charges are to be borne directly by the Member States that will imply the participation of those States in the agreement together with the Community.

3. As long as that question has not been settled by the competent Community authorities the Member States must be allowed to participate in the negotiation of the agreement.

27. Article 113 is set out in part in note 30 infra.

COMMISSION v. COUNCIL

RE THE EUROPEAN ROAD TRANSPORT AGREEMENT (ERTA)

Court of Justice of the European Communities, Case No. 22/70.
[1971] E.C.R. 263.

[The Commission sought the annulment of Council action regarding the negotiation and conclusion by the EC member states of an agreement concerning international road transport. The agreement was abbreviated "ERTA" in English, but the case is often referred to by the French abbreviation "AETR". At issue was the question of who had the power—the member states or the Community—to negotiate and conclude the AETR.]

In the absence of specific provisions of the Treaty relating to the negotiation and conclusion of international agreements in the sphere of transport policy—a category into which, essentially, the AETR falls—one must turn to the general system of Community law in the sphere of relations with third countries.

* * *

To determine in a particular case the Community's authority to enter into international agreements, regard must be had to the whole scheme of the Treaty no less than to its substantive provisions.

Such authority arises not only from an express conferment by the Treaty—as is the case with Articles 113 and 114 for tariff and trade agreements and with Article 238 for association agreements—but may equally flow from other provisions of the Treaty and from measures adopted, within the framework of those provisions, by the Community institutions.

In particular, each time the Community, with a view to implementing a common policy envisaged by the Treaty, adopts provisions laying down common rules, whatever form these may take, the Member States no longer have the right, acting individually or even collectively, to undertake obligations with third countries which affect those rules.

As and when such common rules come into being, the Community alone is in a position to assume and carry out contractual obligations towards third countries affecting the whole sphere of application of the Community legal system.

With regard to the implementation of the provisions of the Treaty the system of internal Community measures may not therefore be separated from that of external relations.

Under Article 3(e), the adoption of a common policy in the sphere of transport is specially mentioned amongst the objectives of the Community.

Under Article 5, the Member States are required on the one hand to take all appropriate measures to ensure fulfilment of the obligations arising out of the Treaty or resulting from action taken by the institutions and, on the other hand, to abstain from any measure which might jeopardize the attainment of the objectives of the Treaty.

If these two provisions are read in conjunction, it follows that to the extent to which Community rules are promulgated for the attainment of the objectives of the Treaty, the Member States cannot, outside the framework of the Community institutions, assume obligations which might affect those rules or alter their scope.

According to Article 74, the objectives of the Treaty in matters of transport are to be pursued within the framework of a common policy.

With this in view, Article 75(1) directs the Council to lay down common rules and, in addition, "any other appropriate provisions".

By the terms of subparagraph (a) of the same provision, those common rules are applicable "to international transport to or from the territory of a Member State or passing across the territory of one or more Member States".

This provision is equally concerned with transport from or to third countries, as regards that part of the journey which takes place on Community territory.

It thus assumes that the powers of the Community extend to relationships arising from international law, and hence involve the need in the sphere in question for agreements with the third countries concerned.

Although it is true that Articles 74 and 75 do not expressly confer on the Community authority to enter into international agreements, nevertheless the bringing into force, on 25 March 1969, of Regulation No. 543/69 of the Council on the harmonization of certain social legislation relating to road transport (Official Journal No. L 77 p. 49) necessarily vested in the Community power to enter into any agreements with third countries relating to the subject-matter governed by that regulation.

This grant of power is moreover expressly recognized by Article 3 of the said regulation which prescribes that: "The Community shall enter into any negotiation with third countries which may prove necessary for the purpose of implementing this regulation".

Since the subject-matter of the AETR falls within the scope of Regulation No. 543/69, the Community has been empowered to negotiate and conclude the agreement in question since the entry into force of the said regulation.

These Community powers exclude the possibility of concurrent powers on the part of Member States, since any steps taken outside the framework of the Community institutions would be incompatible with the unity of the Common Market and the uniform application of Community law.

[The Court ultimately concluded that since the negotiations had started before the Community had powers in this particular area, it was appropriate for both the Community and the member states to be involved in the negotiations. The Court therefore rejected the Commission's request.]

Questions

(1) How does the foreign relations power of the European Community compare with that of the United States federal government? With the Presi-

dent's power under the United States Constitution? With the *Curtiss-Wright* case?

(2) Is there an "implied powers doctrine" in the European Community?

(3) How would the United States Congress challenge the President on the constitutionality of an act of the latter? How would the President challenge the Congress in a similar situation? Is court litigation an appropriate means of resolving such disputes?

(4) The Court of Justice dismissed the Commission's complaint in the *ERTA* case, but would you term the Commission, the Council or the member states the "winners" of this case? What about the *Rubber Agreement* case? Since 1981 commodity agreements like the Rubber Agreement have been negotiated and concluded as "mixed agreements" with the involvement of both the Commission and the member states.[28]

(2) *The Implementation of the Common Commercial Policy* [29]

The Treaty of Rome provides in Article 113 for the implementation by the EEC of a common commercial policy toward third countries.[30] To implement the common commercial policy, the Community has (1) entered into agreements with third countries on various trade-related matters and (2) taken a number of unilateral actions that affect trade. The process followed by the Community in entering into agreements with third countries is epitomized by its negotiation and implementation of the Tokyo Round Agreements.

JEAN–VICTOR LOUIS, THE EUROPEAN ECONOMIC COMMUNITY AND THE IMPLEMENTATION OF THE GATT TOKYO ROUND RESULTS

(1984) [31]

The separation of the functions of the Commission and the Council is an important feature of the institutional structure of the Community. Generally, the Commission appears as the initiator of Community actions. It makes formal proposals to the Council, which has to use the proposals as the basis for its decisions. As far as external relations are concerned, and especially

---

28. [1981] Eur.Comm.Bull. No. 3, point 2.2.17.

29. See generally E. Volker (ed.), Protectionism and the European Community (1983); Steenbergen, The Common Commercial Policy, 17 Comm.Mkt.L.Rev. 229 (1980); Le Tallec, The Common Commercial Policy of the EEC, 20 Intl. & Comp.L.Q. 732 (1971).

30. Article 113 provides in relevant part:

1. After the transitional period has ended, the common commercial policy shall be based on uniform principles, particularly in regard to changes in tariff rates, the conclusion of tariff and trade agreements, the achievement of uniformity in measures of liberalisation, export policy and measures to protect trade such as those to be taken in case of dumping or subsidies.

* * *

3. Where agreements with third countries need to be negotiated, the Commission shall make recommendations to the Council which shall authorize the Commission to open the necessary negotiations. The Commission shall conduct these negotiations in consultation with a special committee appointed by the Council to assist the Commission in this task and within the framework of such directives as the Council may issue to it.

31. From J. Jackson, J.–V. Louis, M. Matsushita, Implementing the Tokyo Round: National Constitutions and International Economic Rules 24–26, 36–38. Reprinted by permission of the author.

when there is a prospect of negotiating an international agreement that will be binding on the Community and its Member States, the Commission acts in its capacity as the Community's negotiator in close connection with the Council.

The Committee of Permanent Representatives (COREPER), an internal organ of the Council, must be mentioned, because it plays an important role in the relations between the Commission and the Council. The members of the COREPER are the Permanent Representatives themselves who are the ambassadors of the Members States [to] the European Communities (called COREPER II) or the[ir] Deputies (COREPER I). Due to their political character, the subjects related to external relations are treated by COREPER II. The COREPER prepares the deliberations of the Council and undertakes a close examination of every measure proposed by the Commission, especially in the field of external relations.

There is indeed a "constant tension between Council and Commission in the conduct of external relations", because the "foreign policy domain is notoriously the most jealously guarded area of national sovereignty. The Council has been reluctant to transfer powers of negotiation to the Commission and when it has done so, under the terms of the Treaty, it has been diligent in keeping the Commission on a tight rein." The MTN (the Multilateral Trade Negotiations) at the Tokyo Round are a good example of those tensions.

THE EEC NEGOTIATING PROCESS IN THE TOKYO ROUND

The ordinary negotiating process of a trade agreement—either bilateral or multilateral—concluded by the EEC generally includes different stages, which can be described as follows:

1. Preliminary talks between the Commission and the state(s) concerned

2. Report by the Commission to the Council, including a recommendation to open formal negotiations with the third state

3. The Commission's authorization by the Council to negotiate along the lines of the directives (mandate) approved by the Council on the recommendation formulated by the Commission and, as usual, carefully examined by the COREPER

4. Negotiation of the agreement by the Commission, with the assistance of a special committee composed of representatives of the Member States in charge of international economic relations (called the Committee of Article 113, or the 113 Committee)

5. Authentication of the formal result of the negotiations by way of an exchange of letters or the initialing (*paraphe*) of the agreement by the Commission

6. Report by the Commission to the Council, which approves the result of the negotiations by a regulation or a decision and decides to proceed to the final conclusion of the agreement

7. Formal conclusion through a complex procedure (approval plus conclusion) or by the signature on behalf of the Community, of the persons designated by the Council

If the agreement is deemed to be mixed, that is, if for reasons of the allocation of competence between the EEC and its Member States it (the Lomé Convention, for example) must be accepted not only by the EEC but also by the Member States, then the Member States must follow certain additional procedures. This procedure, which is dictated partly by the joint requirements of Articles 113 and 228 of the EEC Treaty and partly by the practice followed by the Community, had to be adapted to multilateral negotiations like the MTN.

*   *   *

The Commission's view was that the EEC had the authority to conclude the MTN agreements without the intervention of the Member States, on the basis of either Article 113 of the EEC Treaty or other provisions of the EEC and ECSC treaties, read in light of the jurisprudence of the Court of Justice, starting with the European Road Transport Agreement [ERTA] decision of March 31, 1971. *   *   *

The ad hoc group of the Council, on the other hand, following the opinion of the Council's legal service, took the position that some provisions of the MTN agreements to be concluded—in particular, the standards, government procurement, and civil aircraft codes—transcended the field of commercial policy under Article 113 of the EEC Treaty, and since common rules did not exist on the internal EEC level for all the matters covered by those codes, there was a possibility that Member States should conclude those particular agreements jointly with the Community.

The so-called Rubber Agreement opinion issued by the Court of Justice on October 4, 1979, seems to have brought the conceptions of both legal services closer together.

*   *   *

The French presidency was anxious to find a compromise based on objective—if not legal—criteria. The solution proposed took into account the hard kernel of the positions of France and Great Britain. There was some legal justification for the Member States' conclusion of the ECSC Tariff Protocol, and it was considered that lack of time made it impossible to thoroughly examine the foundation of the two countries' thesis as far as the standards and civil aircraft codes were concerned. It was suggested that the political consensus achieved in the Council should not affect the legal thesis advocated by the Commission and the Member States.

So it was finally decided, after much debate, that the Community alone should sign the bi- and multilateral agreements, but that the Member States (all the Member States and not merely some of them, as had been proposed during the discussions in the Council) could also sign and accept the Tariff Protocol (as far as ECSC products were concerned), the Standards Code, and the Civil Aircraft Agreement.

In spite of the Presidency's wish to avoid the appearance of arbitrariness in the Council's solution, it is difficult to understand this solution as anything but a purely diplomatic compromise. No objective reason seems to exist for adopting different solutions for the Standards Code and for the Government Procurement Code.

Note

The common commercial policy has not yet been fully implemented. Numerous bilateral agreements dealing with commercial matters that antedate the implementation of the common commercial policy remain in effect between Member States and third countries, and the Council regularly authorizes the tacit renewal of these agreements. Some of these agreements, such as those that restrict certain Japanese imports into France and Italy, represent serious gaps in the Community's management of EC trade relations.

Nonetheless, much of the common commercial policy is in place. At its base is the common customs tariff that classifies and establishes tariff rates for all products imported into the EC.[32] Generally speaking there are two tariff rates for each product: the autonomous rate applicable to those countries not accorded most-favored-nation treatment and the conventional rate applicable, inter alia, to goods from GATT members. In addition, the Community has entered into numerous preferential agreements that provide for duty-free entry of goods originating in a country entitled to the preference and otherwise satisfying the terms of the applicable agreement. The Community has such agreements with most European and Mediterranean countries and most developing countries, some of which are described in Sections 7.3(B), 14.3(B) and 20.3 infra.

Pursuant to Article 113, the Community has adopted common rules for imports in general,[33] for imports from state-trading countries [34] and for imports from the People's Republic of China.[35] Under these rules, restrictions may be imposed on imports causing injury to a Community industry. Over time the Commission has attempted to reduce the power of the member states to impose quantitative restrictions unilaterally but while such powers have been limited, they have not yet been totally eliminated.

In addition, the Community has adopted procedures pursuant to which antidumping duties may be imposed upon dumped products and countervailing duties may be imposed upon subsidized products.[36] It has also adopted procedures allowing imposition of duties or quotas or the suspension or withdrawal of trade concessions in response to injurious illicit commercial practices of other nations.[37]

32. Regulation No. 950/68, [1968] Eur. Comm.O.J. No. L172/1. The lengthy annexes to the regulation are updated annually and specify the details of product classification and tariff rates.

33. Regulation No. 288/82, [1982] Eur. Comm.O.J. No. L35/1.

34. Regulation No. 1765/82, [1982] Eur. Comm.O.J. No. L195/1. Many imports from state-trading countries are subject to quantitative restrictions in the different member states. See Regulation No. 3286/80, [1980] Eur.Comm.O.J. No. L353. The EC does not purport to regulate intra-German trade (i.e. trade between East and West Germany). See

Protocol [to the Treaty of Rome] on German internal trade and connected problems.

35. Regulation No. 1766/82, [1982] Eur. Comm.O.J. No. L195/21.

36. Regulation No. 2176/84, [1984] Eur. Comm.O.J. No. L201/1. See generally Davey, An Analysis of European Communities Legislation and Practice Relating to Antidumping and Countervailing Duties, in The 1983 Annual Proceedings of the Fordham Corporate Law Institute 39–128 (1984).

37. Regulation No. 2641/84, [1984] Eur. Comm.O.J. No. L252/1.

In respect of exports, the EC imposes virtually no controls, except from time to time on the export of certain kinds of scrap metal that are in short supply. The EC does regulate in some respects the export credit policies of the member states and negotiates agreements in respect thereof in the OECD.

Questions

(1) In light of the foregoing materials, who has the power in the EC (i.e. the member states, the Commission or the Council) to negotiate an agreement with the United States on agricultural tariffs? On steel quotas? On trade in such services as insurance and banking? On reform of the international monetary system? How would you use the *ERTA* and *Rubber* cases to support your answer?

(2) If the answers to the foregoing questions differ, and all of these subjects are treated in one global negotiation, what problems could arise because of the need to coordinate between the EC and its member states on global compromises (i.e. a trade off involving tariffs on agricultural and international monetary reform)? In light of the Louis article, do you think these problems would be more serious than those normally faced by the EC? Why? (The new round of GATT negotiations may raise some of these issues, especially if services are a subject of negotiation.) If the member states must participate in negotiations on certain subjects, it would be necessary to consider the type of questions we have considered in this section in respect of each member state. We cannot in this overview attempt such a country-by-country analysis of negotiating authority. It is worth noting, however, that the typical form of member state government is parliamentary, which means that there is less of a problem coordinating the legislative and executive branches than in the United States because they are in principle under control of the same leaders. Other problems may exist, however, such as those of the federal-state type in federal countries like Germany.

(3) As a negotiator for the United States, how would you satisfy yourself that an EC negotiating team consisting of Commission officials was authorized to negotiate pursuant to Article 113(3)? To enter into a particular agreement? Is the involvement of the Article 113 Committee sufficient protection? [38]

(4) If the Council (consisting of member state representatives) has to approve any agreement negotiated by the Commission, and if the Article 113 Committee (also consisting of member state representatives) oversees negotiations, why does it matter whether the member states participate directly in negotiations?

(5) How would you compare and contrast the problems raised here with those raised in Sections 3.2 and 3.4 supra?

---

38. In 1985, Commission officials agreed with U.S. officials to reduce export subsidies on pasta products as part of an overall temporary settlement of a U.S.–EC dispute involving a variety of agricultural products. Although ultimately approved by the Council, the Commission was criticized by some for not having obtained a negotiating mandate from the Council. Agence Internationale D'Information Pour La Presse, Europe, July 17, 1985, at 8 (No. 4133 n.s.); id., July 20, 1985, at 7–8a (No. 4136 n.s.).

(3) Internal Legal Effect of International Agreements Under Community Law [39]

INTERNATIONAL FRUIT CO. v. PRODUKTSCHAP

Court of Justice of the European Communities, Case Nos. 21–24/72.
[1972] E.C.R. 1219.

* * *

The second question [referred to this Court] asks whether Regulations Nos. 459/70, 565/70 and 686/70 of the Commission—which laid down, by way of protective measures, restrictions on the importation of apples from third countries—are "invalid as being contrary to Article XI of the General Agreement on Tariffs and Trade (GATT)", hereinafter called "the General Agreement."

* * *

Before the incompatibility of a Community measure with a provision of international law can affect the validity of that measure, the Community must first of all be bound by that provision.

Before invalidity can be relied upon before a national court, that provision of international law must also be capable of conferring rights on citizens of the Community which they can invoke before the courts.

It is therefore necessary to examine whether the General Agreement satisfies these two conditions.

It is clear that at the time when they concluded the Treaty establishing the European Economic Community the Member States were bound by the obligations of the General Agreement.

By concluding a treaty between them they could not withdraw from their obligations to third countries.

On the contrary, their desire to observe the undertakings of the General Agreement follows as much from the very provisions of the EEC Treaty as from the declarations made by Member States on the presentation of the Treaty to the contracting parties of the General Agreement in accordance with the obligation under Article XXIV thereof.

That intention was made clear in particular by Article 110 of the EEC Treaty, which seeks the adherence of the Community to the same aims as those sought by the General Agreement, as well as by the first paragraph of Article 234 which provides that the rights and obligations arising from agreements concluded before the entry into force of the Treaty, and in particular multilateral agreements concluded with the participation of Member States, are not affected by the provisions of the Treaty.

39. See generally Bourgeois, Effects of International Agreements in European Community Law: Are the Dice Cast?, 82 Mich.L.Rev. 1250 (1984); Schermers, The Direct Application of Treaties with Third States: Note Concerning the Polydor and Pabst Cases, 19 Comm.Mkt.L.Rev. 563 (1982); Bebr, Agreements Concluded by the Community and Their Possible Direct Effect: From International Fruit Company to Kupferberg, 20 Comm.Mkt.L.Rev. 35 (1983); Hartley, International Agreements and the Community Legal System: Some Recent Developments, 8 Eur.L. Rev. 383 (1983); Petersmann, Application of GATT by the Court of Justice of the European Communities, 20 Comm.Mkt.L.Rev. 397 (1983).

The Community has assumed the functions inherent in the tariff and trade policy, progressively during the transitional period and in their entirety on the expiry of that period, by virtue of Articles 111 and 113 of the Treaty.

By conferring those powers on the Community, the Member States showed their wish to bind it by the obligations entered into under the General Agreement.

Since the entry into force of the EEC Treaty and more particularly, since the setting up of the common external tariff, the transfer of powers which has occurred in the relations between Member States and the Community has been put into concrete form in different ways within the framework of the General Agreement and has been recognized by the other contracting parties.

In particular, since that time, the Community, acting through its own institutions, has appeared as a partner in the tariff negotiations and as a party to the agreements of all types concluded within the framework of the General Agreement, in accordance with the provisions of Article 114 of the EEC Treaty which provides that the tariff and trade agreements "shall be concluded * * * on behalf of the Community."

It therefore appears that, in so far as under the EEC Treaty the Community has assumed the powers previously exercised by Member States in the area governed by the General Agreement, the provisions of that agreement have the effect of binding the Community.

It is also necessary to examine whether the provisions of the General Agreement confer rights on citizens of the Community on which they can rely before the courts in contesting the validity of a Community measure.

For this purpose, the spirit, the general scheme and the terms of the General Agreement must be considered.

This agreement which, according to its preamble, is based on the principle of negotiations undertaken on the basis of "reciprocal and mutually advantageous arrangements" is characterized by the great flexibility of its provisions, in particular those conferring the possibility of derogation, the measures to be taken when confronted with exceptional difficulties and the settlement of conflicts between the contracting parties.

Consequently, according to the first paragraph of Article XXII "Each contracting party shall accord sympathetic consideration to, and shall afford adequate opportunity for consultation regarding, such representations as may be made by any other contracting party with respect to * * * all matters affecting the operation of this Agreement."

According to the second paragraph of the same article, "the contracting parties"—this name designating "the contracting parties acting jointly" as is stated in the first paragraph of Article XXV—"may consult with one or more contracting parties on any question to which a satisfactory solution cannot be found through the consultations provided under paragraph (1)."

If any contracting party should consider "that any benefit accruing to it directly or indirectly under this Agreement is being nullified or impaired or that the attainment of any objective of the Agreement is being impeded as a result of", *inter alia*, "the failure of another contracting party to carry out its obligations under this Agreement", Article XXIII lays down in detail the measures which the parties concerned, or the contracting parties acting jointly, may or must take in regard to such a situation.

Those measures include, for the settlement of conflicts, written recommendations or proposals which are to be "given sympathetic consideration", investigations possibly followed by recommendations, consultations between or decisions of the *contracting parties*, including that of authorizing certain contracting parties to suspend the application to any others of any obligations or concessions under the General Agreement and, finally, in the event of such suspension, the power of the party concerned to withdraw from that agreement.

Finally, where by reason of an obligation assumed under the General Agreement or of a concession relating to a benefit, some producers suffer or are threatened with serious damage, Article XIX gives a contracting party power unilaterally to suspend the obligation and to withdraw or modify the concession, either after consulting the contracting parties jointly and failing agreement between the contracting parties concerned, or even, if the matter is urgent and on a temporary basis, without prior consultation.

Those factors are sufficient to show that, when examined in such a context, Article XI of the General Agreement is not capable of conferring on citizens of the Community rights which they can invoke before the courts.

Accordingly, the validity of Regulations Nos. 459/70, 565/70 and 686/70 of the Commission cannot be affected by Article XI of the General Agreement.

Notes and Questions

(1) The Court of Justice has adhered consistently to the position that GATT provisions are not directly applicable, see SIOT v. Ministero delle Finanze v. SPI, [1983] E.C.R. 731; Amministrazione delle Finanze dello Stato, [1983] E.C.R. 801. In its view the "great flexibility of [GATT's] provisions, in particular those concerning the possibilities of derogation", Amministrazione delle Finanze dello Stato v. SPI, supra, at 828, means that GATT obligations are not sufficiently unconditional to be directly applicable.

(2) In a number of cases, however, the Court of Justice has, implicitly or explicitly, held international agreements to be directly applicable. These cases involved the EC's Association Agreement with Greece, the Yaounde Convention and the EC-Portugal free trade agreement. Haegeman v. Belgian State, [1974] E.C.R. 449; Bresciani v. Amministrazione Italiana delle Finanze, [1976] E.C.R. 129; Hauptzollamt Mainz v. C.A. Kupferberg & Cie., [1982] E.C.R. 3641. Although the Court's reasoning has not always been completely clear, it appears that the Court will hold a provision of an international agreement concluded by the EC to be directly applicable if the provision sets forth an unconditional obligation that is central to the purpose of the agreement. Compare Hauptzollamt Mainz v. C.A. Kupferberg & Cie., supra, with Polydor Ltd. v. Harlequin Records Shop Ltd., [1982] E.C.R. 329. In the *Kupferberg* case the Court stated (at 3665):

* * * In order to reply to the question on the direct effect of the first paragraph of Article 21 of the Agreement between the Community and Portugal it is necessary to analyse the provision in light of both the object and purpose of the Agreement and its context.

The purpose of the Agreement is to create a system of free trade in which rules restricting commerce are eliminated in respect of virtually all trade in products originating in the territory of the parties, in particular by abolishing customs duties and charges having equivalent effect and eliminating quantitative restrictions and measures having equivalent effect.

Seen in that context the first paragraph of Article 21 of the Agreement seeks to prevent the liberalization of the trade in goods through the abolition of customs duties and charges having equivalent effect and quantitative restrictions and measures having equivalent effect from being rendered nugatory by fiscal practices of the Contracting Parties. That would be so if the product imported of one party were taxed more heavily than the similar domestic products which it encounters on the market of the other party.

It appears from the foregoing that the first paragraph of Article 21 of the Agreement imposes on the Contracting Parties an unconditional rule against discrimination in matters of taxation, which is dependent only on a finding that the products affected by a particular system of taxation are of like nature, and the limits of which are the direct consequence of the purpose of the Agreement. As such this provision may be applied by a court and thus produce direct effects throughout the Community.

(3) How does the decision in *International Fruit* on the direct applicability of GATT compare to the decisions discussed in Section 3.3(C) supra on self-executing international agreements and standing?

(4) Assuming that a treaty concluded by the EC was found to be directly applicable, how would a conflict between the treaty and the Treaty of Rome be resolved? The treaty and prior Community legislation? The treaty and subsequent Community legislation? The treaty and a member state constitution? The treaty and prior member state legislation? The treaty and subsequent member state legislation?

SECTION 4.3 JAPAN

Japan is obviously one of the "key players" on the world economic scene, often mentioned as part of the "trilateral" group (with the United States and the EC) which has very great influence in world trade matters. In recent years there has been an extraordinary amount of attention paid to the trade and economic policies of Japan, often with a tinge (or more) of bitterness and perhaps jealousy. Substantial bilateral trade deficits with Japan have accentuated these attitudes in the U.S. and the EC and elsewhere. Japan is alleged to pursue an "export push" policy, while protecting its own market from imports. Yet there are many who say that these allegations are not proved, and it is at least clear that the issues are very complex. In later parts of this book we touch on some of these matters, but here we focus on the basic constitutional and legal structure of Japan's international economic relations.

In considering these materials, the reader should review the questions posed in Section 4.1 supra.

L.J. ADAMS, THEORY, LAW AND POLICY OF CONTEMPORARY JAPANESE TREATIES 13–17

(1974) [1]

The present Constitution of Japan includes several articles related to treaties. The portions of the relevant articles include, first, Article 7 which reads in part:

> The Emperor, with the advice and approval of the Cabinet, shall perform the following acts in matters of state on behalf of the people:
>
> (1) Promulgation of amendments of the constitution, laws, cabinet orders and treaties; * * *

Article 61 of Chapter IV, concerning the approval of treaties by the Diet, provides that the special procedures regarding passage of the budget also applies to treaties:

> The second paragraph of the preceding article applies also to the Diet approval required for the conclusion of treaties.

The procedures concerning passage of the budget are stipulated in Article 60, paragraph 2. This provision states:

> Upon consideration of the budget, when the House of Councillors makes a decision different from that of the House of Representatives, and when no agreement can be reached even through a joint committee of both Houses, provided for by law, or in the case of failure by the House of Councillors to take final action within thirty days, the period of recess excluded, after the receipt of the budget passed by the House of Representatives, the decision of the House of Representatives shall be the decision of the Diet.

Articles 65 and 73 of Chapter V provide that the executive power be vested in the Cabinet, and in Article 73 certain functions are delineated with respect to the conduct of foreign affairs by the Cabinet. Article 73 reads in part:

> The Cabinet, in addition to other general administrative functions, shall perform the following functions:
>
> (1) Administer the law faithfully, conduct affairs of state;
>
> (2) Manage foreign affairs;
>
> (3) Conclude treaties. However, it shall obtain prior or, depending on circumstances, subsequent approval of the Diet; * * *

Finally, Article 98 of Chapter X states that:

> This Constitution shall be the supreme law of the nation and no law, ordinance, imperial rescript or other act of government, or part thereof, contrary to the provisions thereof, shall have legal force or validity.

1. Reprinted by permission of the author.

2. The treaties concluded by Japan and established laws of nations shall be faithfully observed.

Within the above legal framework, it is appropriate to analyze the legal aspects of the conclusion and validity of treaties under the present Japanese constitution.

MITSUO MATSUSHITA, JAPAN AND THE IMPLEMENTATION OF THE TOKYO ROUND RESULTS

(1984) [2]

CONSTITUTIONAL AND LEGAL FRAMEWORK OF JAPANESE GOVERNMENT ACTIONS IN INTERNATIONAL ECONOMIC RELATIONS

The Constitutional Framework of the Government

The Basic Constitution

Under the Japanese Constitution, there are three basic organs of the state: the National Diet, the Cabinet, and the Judiciary.

Under Article 42 of the Constitution, the National Diet consists of the House of Representatives and the House of Councillors; the former is the lower house and the latter the upper. The National Diet is the highest organ exercising state power (Article 41), and the members of both houses are elected by the people. The National Diet is the legislature, and a legislative proposal becomes law when it has been approved by both houses. * * * Whenever the House of Councillors' decision on a treaty is different from that of the House of Representatives, the decision of the House of Representatives is regarded as the decision of the National Diet if unanimity cannot be obtained in a joint conference of both houses, or the House of Councillors has not acted on the proposal for a treaty within thirty days after it received a decision of the House of Representatives approving it.

Administrative power is vested in the Cabinet, which is composed of the Prime Minister and other ministers. The Prime Minister is appointed from among the members of the National Diet by a resolution of the National Diet (Article 67), all political parties participating. In practice, the controlling party selects its leader, and then this person is elected as Prime Minister when the National Diet meets for this purpose.

The Cabinet is jointly responsible to the National Diet where the exercise of the administrative power is concerned. The Prime Minister appoints the ministers, and the majority of them must be appointed from among the members of the National Diet. The Cabinet must resign when the House of Representatives passes a resolution of nonconfidence or rejects a confidence resolution, unless the House is dissolved within ten days. The Cabinet is charged to execute general administrative duties, including (1) executing laws; (2) establishing and maintaining diplomatic relationships; (3) concluding treaties; (4) preparing the budget and introducing it in the National Diet; (5) issuing Cabinet orders; and (6) granting clemency.

2. From J. Jackson, J.—V. Louis & M. Matsushita, Implementing the Tokyo Round: National Constitutions and International Economic Rules 78–95. Reprinted by permission of the author.

The third branch of the government is the Judiciary, which consists of the Supreme Court and lower courts. Courts have the power of judicial review. Article 98(1) declares that the Constitution is the supreme law of the land, and laws, orders, imperial decrees, and other regulations contrary to its provisions are null and void. Article 98(2) declares that treaties to which Japan is a party and the established international law shall be faithfully observed.

The Japanese governmental system is that of a parliamentary-cabinet system, as opposed to a presidential system. There is a fusion of the legislative and the executive authorities. However, the Judiciary is independent, and it can exercise judicial review of both legislative and administrative actions.

The Policy-Making Process in the Japanese Government

Extraparliamentary processes are vitally important in the policy-making process in Japan. Policies, including economic policies, often take the form of legislation. Even though, as explained above, a law is passed by the National Diet, in reality the process preceding the parliamentary process is vitally important. Often ideas for policies are conceived in various ministries and in the Liberal Democratic Party (LDP), which is the party currently in control. Sometimes the LDP formulates policies. The process involved is very complex, and a brief sketch must suffice.

When an idea for a policy is formulated in a ministry, officials in charge discuss the matter with key LDP persons, and after obtaining their informal approval, draft a legislative proposal that is sent to the Legislation Bureau of the Cabinet. After the Legislation Bureau amends it, the proposal is sent to the LDP again for a more formal examination. Then it is examined in a Cabinet meeting. When the Cabinet has given its approval it is introduced in the National Diet. As long as the LDP holds the majority in both houses, a legislative proposal made by the Cabinet after extraparliamentary consent by the LDP is likely to pass, unless there is an unusual situation—unless, for example, the opposition party offers a very strong obstruction of the debate, or the National Diet runs out of time to examine the proposal because other bills have taken up too much time. Normally, however, the Cabinet bill would pass without amendment.

The extraparliamentary process therefore, is as important, or perhaps more important, than the parliamentary process in formulating economic policies. Most of the bills are formulated through this process by the government and introduced in the Diet.

If the matter is very controversial, the opposing parties may offer a strong resistance in the National Diet. However, the most they can do is to engage in delaying tactics, and if the LDP is determined to pass a proposal it is usually enacted into law despite the opposition.

In the area of foreign and international economic policies, the opposition parties have raised relatively few opposing arguments to proposed bills, possibly because they were too complex and technical and not very interesting to the opposition. Most of the international controversies in the Diet center on political issues like the Security Treaty between the United States and Japan. Thus there was not much opposition to the signing and implementation of the Tokyo Round agreements.

The Cabinet can enter into an international agreement with other nations without the Diet's approval, and such an agreement is binding on the Japanese government as a matter of international law. However, as long as the Diet has not given its approval, the agreement cannot be legally enforced in Japan if there is a conflicting domestic statute or if the agreement contains provisions that restrict the rights of citizens.

Interministerial Rivalries in Formulating and Executing Foreign Economic Policies

Although there is relatively little legislative opposition in the area of foreign or international economic policies, one cannot say that there is no conflict and struggle in making and executing policies having to do with the foreign economic relations of Japan. Quite often there are tensions and conflict concerning foreign economic policies among the various agencies and ministries in charge of formulating and executing them. The major government agencies in charge of economic policies include the Ministry of International Trade and Industry (MITI), the Ministry of Agriculture, Forestry and Fisheries (MAFF), the Ministry of Finance (MOF), the Economic Planning Agency (EPA), the Ministry of Health and Welfare (MHW), and the Ministry of Foreign Affairs (MFA). Except for MFA, which is in charge of foreign diplomacy, and EPA, which oversees a global economic policy, each of the ministries supervises and promotes some industrial sectors, and it is the ministry in charge of a particular industry that is usually responsible for formulating the industrial or agricultural policy concerning it.

Sometimes the policies of various ministries collide. For example, MFA may have a policy of maintaining a friendly relationship with foreign nations and may wish to abolish import quotas for some agricultural products imported from overseas. However, MAFF, as the advocate and promoter of the Japanese agriculture, may have a different policy and wish to restrict imports from abroad. MITI is in charge of supervising and promoting mostly industrial goods, and may have a restrictive policy for industrial products that are not internationally competitive and a liberal trade policy for products that are. Even though the Cabinet is the forum in which such conflicts are to be reconciled, and, therefore, the Cabinet's deciding on a measure concerning foreign economic policy usually means that the conflict has been resolved, sometimes such conflicts persist and are difficult to solve. In these cases the LDP may act as a moderator in the conflicts and may try to reconcile the different attitudes by suggesting a compromise.

In any event, the bureaucracy plays a vital role in Japanese politics and also in economic policy. It is in the key ministries where the best human resources and information about industries are pooled together. It is natural, then, that the real power struggle takes place there, in the very heart of the Japanese power structure. In this sense, something comparable to the conflict and tension between the Congress and the executive branch in the United States might be seen in the relationship among the key ministries.

These ministerial conflicts and rivalries are not openly reported, however, even though they may be common knowledge among those who know something about the Japanese government. No official report or comments are made. Therefore, we must be satisfied with some reports that have trickled out through newspaper accounts. Some examples of such ministerial conflicts on trade may be useful at this point.

During the late 1970s there were increased European imports into Japan of adjusted butter (an ingredient used in confectionery). In 1975 imports of this item were about 3,000 tons; in 1980 they climbed to a high of 17,000 tons. MAFF, fearing that this would have some impact on domestic farmers, planned an import restriction. However, MFA and MITI objected very strongly, fearing that such a measure would touch off a trade conflict between Japan and the European exporting countries. Discussions were held among those ministries, and finally a compromise was reached: MAFF would withdraw its plan to restrict imports of adjusted butter from Europe, and the Japanese government would instead request the European producers or their governments to adopt some voluntary measure to restrain exports from those countries to Japan. In this instance, MAFF basically represented the interests of domestic producers and other ministries emphasized the importance of a good relationship among trading partners.

In the United States-Japan negotiations on textiles and autos, there were conflicts of policies between MITI and MFA. In the 1974 textile negotiations, MITI emphasized the importance of protecting domestic producers of the products and opposed Japanese concessions to the United States. MFA emphasized the importance of friendly relations and took a more flexible attitude toward such concessions.

In the auto negotiations, MITI took the position that it should have charge of the negotiations with the United States, since whatever agreement might be made would have to be implemented domestically through administrative guidance or legal measures—and MITI has some control and influence over the auto industry in Japan and MFA does not. MFA, on the other hand, maintained that it should be commissioned to negotiate with the United States, since such negotiations are part of diplomacy, over which it has exclusive control and authority. The minister of MITI, when asked his view regarding the negotiating authority in the Committee on Commerce and Industry of the House of Representatives in the National Diet, answered, "Properly MITI should be in charge of this negotiation." Actually, MFA conducted the negotiations, but MITI was extensively involved—a sort of compromise between the two positions.

The Relationship Between the Constitution, Treaties, and Domestic Laws

The Constitution and Treaties

Article 73(3) of the Japanese Constitution provides that the Cabinet is empowered to enter into treaties with other nations. However, a proviso states that the Cabinet must obtain prior, or, depending on the circumstances, subsequent approval of the National Diet. This requirement is designed to guarantee that the National Diet will have some control over the treaty-making power of the Cabinet, since treaties sometimes involve provisions that restrict the rights of private individuals.

*   *   *

It is generally held that whether an agreement is a treaty in the sense of Article 73(3) depends on whether it affects the rights of individuals—that is, whether it contains provisions binding or prohibiting the conduct of private individuals. If it does, it is regarded as a treaty and must be approved by the National Diet.

Some examples of international agreements for which no approval of the National Diet is necessary are: (1) an international agreement pertaining to technical details of diplomacy; (2) an international agreement providing for detailed rules for implementing a treaty that has already been approved by the National Diet; and (3) an international executive agreement within the framework of the powers delegated to the Cabinet by legislation.

In practice, the requirement that the National Diet approve a treaty is not strictly observed. Often the government takes the view that agreements are within the framework of authority that has previously been delegated by legislation, and therefore need not be submitted to the Diet. The 1974 United States-Japan Textile Agreement is such an example. There are also a number of commercial agreements between various nations and Japan providing for rights and obligations of the governments involved which seem to affect the rights of individuals and yet were dealt with as executive agreements and not as treaties. *   *   *

A view often expressed by Japanese government officials is that if an international economic agreement is not self-executing but requires domestic legislation in order to implement it, the Cabinet need not submit the agreement to the National Diet for approval. Rather, implementation will take place either through domestic legislation already enacted by the Diet, or, if such legislation is lacking, the government will introduce the necessary legislation for Diet approval. When the United States and Japan made their textile agreement, the opposition parties asked the Japanese government why it had entered into such an agreement, which would have a serious impact on the freedom of trade in Japan, without submitting it to the National Diet. The Director General of the Cabinet Legislation Bureau answered as follows:

> If * * * an international agreement is enforced not as such but through a domestic law, then restrictions of the rights of individuals are governed by that domestic law. In this situation, we believe that such an agreement need not be submitted to the National Diet. When our government and a foreign government have agreed on a matter under the Constitution, it is not necessary to put such agreement under the democratic control of the National Diet as long as such agreement is not enforced directly (that is, such agreement does not impose obligations and restrictions upon the conduct of citizens in Japan) and is not in conflict with a treaty which has been approved by the National Diet. It is to be understood as an executive agreement of which no such approval is necessary.

The General Agreement on Tariffs and Trade (GATT) was submitted to and approved by the National Diet. Accordingly, it is a treaty in the sense of Article 73(3), and it is therefore probably correct to say that the Cabinet already had broad power to enter into executive agreements in order to implement provisions of the GATT. However, some MTN codes have been submitted to the National Diet and have already been approved. Also, as will be explained later, some amendments to the domestic legislation were made in order to incorporate those MTN agreements into Japanese domestic laws on tariffs and trade. The Cabinet could have chosen not to submit those agreements to the National Diet for its approval on the theory that they are implementations of the GATT and the Cabinet has already been given the power to enter into executive agreements for its implementation. Even though the reason the Japanese government submitted them to the National Diet for approval was not made clear, we can guess that it did so because, although the provisions of the GATT were general, much of the language of the codes was more specific. Consequently, the government felt it necessary to submit them to the National Diet to make sure that it had no objection to their contents.

* * *

Constitutionality of the MTN Codes in Japan

As explained in the preceding paragraphs, the GATT and various MTN codes are treaties in the sense of the Japanese Constitution. What is the legal situation when a treaty is in conflict with a provision of the Constitution? For example, if a provision of one of the MTN codes or the domestic laws implementing them conflicts with a constitutional provision, which is given priority? This problem may occur, for example (if it occurs at all) when an enterprise or individual subject to a regulation imposed by the domestic statute incorporating an MTN code objects and brings an action against the agency enforcing such a rule, alleging that the code or the law violates a provision in the Japanese Constitution. Another possible situation is one in which the question of constitutionality is raised in the National Diet. For example, one of the MTN codes or one of the laws implementing a code might adversely affect the interests of small business in Japan, and some members or political parties supported by small business might raise the question of its constitutionality. As a matter of domestic legal priority, it is not settled whether a constitutional provision or a treaty prevails when the two are in conflict. There are two conflicting schools of thought, one maintaining that the Constitution prevails and the other asserting that a treaty prevails. The first bases its rationale on, among other things, the amendment procedure of the Constitution. In order to amend the Constitution a referendum is required, but the conclusion of a treaty needs only the approval of the National Diet. This theory maintains that should a treaty be given priority over the Constitution, it would mean that the Constitution, which must otherwise be amended by means of a national referendum, can be amended in substance by the conclusion of a treaty that conflicts with it. This would be contrary to the basic principle of the sovereignty of the people, which is regarded as one of the fundamental principles of the Constitution.

On the other hand, the theory that maintains that a treaty prevails over the Constitution holds that the Constitution is based on the principle of internationalism, and thus, since it is the expression of the national will of only one nation, it must yield to a treaty, which is the expression of the will of the international community.

Without going into detail, it must be stated that the former theory is more persuasive than the latter, since to hold that a treaty prevails over the Constitution would mean that the most fundamental rights provided for in the Constitution (such as the Bill of Rights) could be overridden if the Cabinet decided to enter into a treaty repudiating them. This seems an absurd proposition.

In the *Sunakawa* case, the Supreme Court in an indirect way took the position that the Constitution prevails over a treaty. The case concerned the effect of the Status of Forces Agreement between the United States and Japan, which was based on the Security Treaty between those two countries. The Supreme Court stated that the Security Treaty had great political importance, and was not subject to judicial review of the courts *unless some of its provisions were clearly and obviously unconstitutional.* In this particular case the Court adopted the doctrine of political question and thereby avoided a judicial review of the constitutionality of the treaty. It is, however, noteworthy that in dicta the Court recognized the possibility of judicial review of a treaty, depending on the nature of the treaty, when some of its provisions seem clearly and obviously unconstitutional.

One constitutional provision relevant to the MTN codes is Article 22, which guarantees the freedom of occupation. This is interpreted to include the freedom of trade or business, which, however, can be restricted if that is necessary for the public welfare. Since the freedom to engage in export, import, or other types of international economic transactions is regarded as part of the freedom of occupation, such activities are covered by Article 22. Under the MTN Government Procurement Code, for example, the Japanese government is in principle obligated to maintain open tendering procedures in government procurement contracting, and, as will be explained later, some changes have been made in the domestic regulations concerning government procurement. Under the new rules, the government agencies and some government corporations must use open tendering or selective tendering rather than individually negotiated contracts in purchasing instruments from suppliers. A supplier who under the individually negotiated contract procedure has supplied some instruments to the government corporation operating telecommunications might be defeated in bidding under the new open tendering system, because his price is higher. This supplier might bring an action against the government alleging that the new domestic bidding system is contrary to the freedom of contract that is a part of the constitutional guarantee of freedom of occupation, since freedom of contract should include a government corporation's freedom to select a supplier as it sees fit. Moreover, he might argue that this contract system deprives the corporation of the right to choose suppliers and deprives him of the right to be chosen as the supplier. Or the government corporation might raise a claim alleging that it enjoys the right to select a supplier, and cannot be deprived of that right by the MTN code. What is the constitutional implication of such allegations?

There is a line of cases that has interpreted Article 22. The issue was whether domestic legislation restricting the rights of individuals was justified under the Constitution because it was designed to achieve some socioeconomic goal. The Supreme Court has held that a judgment on whether a restriction is in fact necessary to achieve such a goal is best made by the legislative branch of the government and should in principle be left to the discretion of the National Diet. Under this reasoning, if a law that restricts the rights of individuals is designed to achieve some social or economic policy (for example, the protection of small enterprises), the Court will refrain from making a judgment on the wisdom of such restriction. It is easy to see that under this rule any legislation that is designed to achieve an economic policy (including international economic policy) and that restricts freedom of trade will be considered justified unless it is flagrantly unreasonable. Domestic regulations on government procurement based on the MTN code are most likely to be regarded as regulations enacted for the purpose of embodying an international economic policy. Thus it is almost certain that any regulation implementing the MTN Government Procurement Code will be held constitutional.

Most of the MTN codes and implementing domestic laws are designed to achieve some economic policy goals. For example, the Antidumping Code and the Countervailing Duty Code and implementing laws in Japan may be regarded as measures aimed at maintaining a fair trade rule in international trade, and should be justified under the Constitution.

Therefore, on the whole, there should be little problem with the constitutionality in Japan of the MTN codes and of domestic laws that implement them.

The Legal Effect of the MTN Codes in Japan, and Conflicting Domestic Laws and Regulations

Under the prevailing Japanese doctrine on the Constitution and international law, there is no question that a treaty that has been duly approved by the National Diet and that contains matters regulating activities of individuals in Japan is self-executing. Accordingly, the MTN codes that have been approved by the National Diet have the effect of domestic laws. Nevertheless, the Japanese government usually enacts domestic laws with the same contents as the treaties to make certain that the treaties have that effect. As will be noted later, the Japanese government has enacted domestic laws that are designed to implement the MTN codes, and therefore generally have the same contents as the Codes.

What about the relationship between the MTN codes or the implementing laws and those laws and regulations that may come in conflict with them? To state the conclusion first, whenever there is a conflict between a treaty and a domestic law or regulation, the treaty overrides the domestic law or regulation regardless of whether the National Diet approves the treaty before or after it approves the conflicting domestic law or regulation. There is no court decision on this precise point yet. However, the commentaries agree that a treaty should be given higher priority than a domestic law or regulation regardless of when it was approved by the Diet. Accordingly, we can conclude that if there is a conflict between a domestic law or regulation and a provision in the MTN codes or implementing laws, the latter will prevail.

The writings maintaining that a treaty overrides a conflicting domestic law are based on Article 98(2) of the Constitution, which declares that a treaty and the established international law shall be faithfully observed. To admit that there can exist a law that conflicts with a treaty would be contrary to this constitutional command. It is also maintained that the effectiveness of Article 98(2) is guaranteed only by maintaining the supremacy of a treaty over a conflicting domestic law, and that the constitutional provision restrains the National Diet from enacting a law that would deny the effect of a treaty the Diet has already approved.

As already indicated, we can predict with reasonable certainty that courts will go along with this theory when a problem comes up. There can be a conflict between a treaty and domestic legislation or between a treaty and an administrative action based on legislation, but whatever the case, it appears certain that the treaty will prevail.

Government inaction can also be a violation of the MTN codes. For example, if the government has not taken a measure required under one of the codes, its inaction can be regarded as a violation. Legal remedies in such cases will be discussed later.

It must be noted that only a treaty that has been approved by the National Diet is covered by Article 98(2) and is given a higher priority than a domestic law. An international agreement that has been entered into between the Japanese government and a foreign government but not approved by the National Diet has no such legal effect. This conclusion can be easily derived from the doctrine that the National Diet's approval of a treaty is required to guarantee that the legislative power of the Diet is not infringed on by Cabinet treaty making.

Of course, in practice, a court will always try to reconcile an international agreement with domestic legislation, and will not lightly find a conflict.

An Overview of the Basic Japanese Public Laws Regulating International Trade

Various Japanese public laws regulate and control international transactions—i.e., exports, imports, investments, and related matters. In addition, many administrative regulations implement those basic laws. One salient feature of the laws and their enforcement is that the enforcement agencies (the various ministries) are given wide powers to enact rules and regulations. Unless one is familiar with those administrative regulations, it is difficult to understand the realities of the enforcement. Moreover, some laws that regulate domestic affairs (for example, various safety standard laws for appliances, foods, cars, and so forth) also have a great impact on international trade. There may also be de facto barriers to trade, such as the distribution system, business customs and practices, the language, and so on. Also it has been claimed that industrial policy exercised by the Japanese government has constituted barriers to entry into the Japanese market vis-à-vis foreign commodities and enterprises. It is impossible to describe all of the relevant laws, regulations, and customs. We must be satisfied with a description of the most basic laws on trade.

*   *   *

Export Control

The major laws controlling exports from Japan are the Control Law and the Transactions Law. The former authorizes MITI to enforce an export approval system for some designated commodities, and the latter permits private exporters to enter into export agreements between themselves with some governmental supervision.

The Control Law

Article 47 of the Control Law provides: "Export of goods from Japan shall be permitted with the minimum restrictions thereon consistent with the purpose of this Law." As this language makes clear, the basic principle is the freedom of export, and restrictions should be kept to the minimum. It is also clear that export controls must be consistent with the purpose of the law. The purpose of the law is enunciated in Article 1: "This Law has as its objective the healthy development of the national economy together with international balance of payments equilibrium and currency stabilization." (This means, in short, economic objectives.) Accordingly, any restriction of exports imposed for any other purpose would be held outside the scope of the law and therefore *ultra vires*.

Under Article 48 of the Control Law, MITI is authorized to enforce an export approval system through a cabinet order. Article 48 provides: "Any person desiring to export goods from Japan may be required to obtain the approval of the Minister of International Trade and Industry for particular types of goods and/or for particular destinations and/or for methods used for transactions or payments, as provided for by Cabinet Order." In 1949 the Cabinet issued the Export Trade Control Order (the Export Order) authorizing MITI to institute an export approval system.

*   *   *

The constitutionality of export controls under the Export Order has been challenged at least twice. In the COCOM case, the plaintiffs had planned to exhibit some products in a trade show in mainland China, but their request for export approval had been denied by MITI for the reason that those products were contraband under the COCOM agreement. The plaintiffs maintained that MITI could only establish export controls if they were necessary to achieve the objective of the law, namely, "the maintenance of the balance of international payments and the sound development of international trade or national economy." The export control in question, it was argued, was exercised for international political or strategic goals and thus fell outside the scope of the law.

The Tokyo District Court noted that since the right of individuals to export was a constitutional right that could only be restricted if that was necessary for the purpose of public welfare, and since the public welfare in this particular case was expressed in the purpose of the Control Law (Article 1), the controls exerted by MITI were for the purpose of international politics or strategy, which was outside the scope of the Control Law. In particular, the court stated that the exercise of controls infringed on the constitutional guarantee of freedom of occupation and was unconstitutional. But the plaintiffs were denied money damages indemnity for the reason that the government officials showed no malicious intent or negligence in making the decision on this contraband.

*   *   *

MITI often uses administrative guidance as a means of control in conjunction with the Export Order. Such guidance (an informal request) may ask exporters to keep up an export price, or hold down the quantity of exports to a certain country. If this guidance is not complied with, then MITI usually invokes an order. A prominent example of this was the 1981 auto export restraint. Because the United States Congress threatened to pass a law setting up quota limitations on the imports of autos from foreign countries, MITI decided that it would be a better policy to implement voluntary export restraints. Accordingly, MITI requested that each auto exporter keep the number of autos exported to the United States within the maximum indicated by MITI. If this maximum number would likely be exceeded, then MITI would invoke the compulsory export approval system under the Export Order. As this example shows, administrative guidance is often a preliminary stage before export controls are invoked.

The Transactions Law

The Transactions Law permits exporters to enter into export agreements, under which they fix export prices, set a quantity to be exported, or determine other terms of business. Basically, the function of the Transactions Law is to authorize private exporters to enter into export agreements and to exempt such agreements from the Anti-Monopoly Law. If an agreement only contains terms of export trade (i.e., export price, quantity, and so on), it must be filed with MITI, and if it contains terms restricting domestic trade (i.e., purchase terms of merchandise to be exported), MITI's approval must be obtained.

Formally, the Transactions Law provides only for private export agreements and does not involve government export control except for an order issued under Article 28. (This will be explained later.) However, the government is actually heavily involved. Usually MITI advises exporters to enter into export agreements whenever it foresees some possible trade conflict with an importing country. In this way, export agreements are used to carry out governmental trade policy. MITI sometimes advises exporters to enter into an export agreement fixing a price or setting a quantity with a threat that if its advice is ignored it will promptly invoke compulsory export control as provided for in the Export Order.

Article 28 of the Transactions Law authorizes MITI to issue an order binding export prices, quantity, or other terms of business when an agreement entered into among exporters is not sufficient to establish orderly export conditions. This provision is invoked when an exporters' agreement is not effective due to activities of outsiders or when the terms of business set up by the agreement (export price or export quantity, and so on) are not satisfactory. Such an order is binding on every exporter, including the participants in the agreement, and is sometimes called outsider regulation.

However, this is a misnomer, since insiders are bound by it as well. The order can be issued only after an export agreement has been entered into and proven to be ineffective. The fact that the governmental order is premised on a private agreement indicates that private agreements are regarded as a part of a broader governmental trade policy.

Import Control

There are several major laws designed to control imports: the Control Law, the Transactions Law, and the Customs Tariff Law. Moreover, the Tariff Law provides for procedures relating to imports and the collection of duties. In addition, there are also a number of laws that prohibit or restrict importation of some products into Japan.

The Control Law

Article 52 of the Control Law provides for an import approval system. It states "In order to ensure healthy development of foreign trade and national economy, any person desiring to effect imports may be required to obtain approval therefor as provided for by Cabinet Order." It should be noted that unlike Article 47 and Article 48(2), which concern export control, this Article contains no language that requires that import controls be kept within the limits dictated by "the maintenance of the balance of international payments and the sound development of international trade or national economy." Although the language in Article 52 authorizing import controls "in order to ensure healthy development of foreign trade and national economy" may suggest that an import control exercised for a purpose other than that of ensuring of healthy development of foreign trade and national economy is *ultra vires,* the outer limit of the government's power to control imports is not as clearly defined as it is for export controls. The legislative purpose of the legal structure pertaining to import controls may be interpreted to mean that the freedom to import is not emphasized as much as the freedom to export.

It should also be noted that there is no explicit requirement of a finding of injury to a domestic industry before an import control under the Import Order can be initiated. However, since Article XIX of the GATT does require such a finding before import controls are invoked, and since Japan is a signatory of the GATT, the Japanese government should find an injury to a domestic industry before it enforces an import restriction on a particular item.

Under Article 52 of the Control Law, MITI is authorized to establish an import quota system (IQ). If an IQ system is established for a specific item, a person desiring to import this item must obtain MITI's approval before applying for an import license for the product. In the 1950s and 1960s this IQ system was widely used to restrict imports of many kinds of items. However, since the late 1960s, the number of items under the IQ system has dropped sharply, due to the trend toward liberalization. Some items are still controlled: (1) meat and dairy products, (2) marine products, (3) miscellaneous beans and oil-stuff seeds, (4) fruits, vegetables, and preparations containing them, (5) cereals, (6) coal, and (7) hides and leather products. Import control under the Control Law is exercised for various purposes, among which the most important is the protection of domestic industries.

In addition to the Control Law, there are a number of laws regulating or prohibiting the importation of certain items, as specified in each statute. In 1982 the number was twenty-seven. The names of some of the more important laws are: the Plant Quarantine Law, the Forest Seedling Law, the Law for the Prevention of Infectious Diseases in Domestic Animals, the Wildlife Preservation and Game Law, the Food Sanitation Law, the Fertilizer Control Law, the Drugs, Cosmetics and Medical Instruments Law, the Narcotics Control Law, the Stimulant Drugs Control Law, the Staple Food Control Law, the Tobacco Monopoly Law, the Alcohol Monopoly Law, the High Pressure Gas Control Law, the Explosives Control Law, and the Consumer Product Safety Law.

Some of these laws contain a provision that restricts or prohibits the importation of the item covered by the law. Others only set up standards of quality to be observed by the sellers of the item in question, whether it is domestically manufactured or imported. Still others require the sellers of such items to obtain a license from public authorities. However, they all affect imports in one way or another.

KENNETH W. ABBOTT AND CONRAD D. TOTMAN, "BLACK SHIPS" AND BALANCE SHEETS: THE JAPANESE MARKET AND U.S.–JAPAN RELATIONS

(1981) [3]

Without doubt, the Japanese economy was tightly closed during the period immediately following World War II and even into the 1960s, with imports and foreign capital largely barred by an extensive system of tariffs, quotas and other direct controls on trade, investment and foreign exchange transactions. Japan's postwar economic situation, particularly its serious lack of foreign exchange, virtually required such a restrictive policy; indeed, the major problem for Japan at the time was how to export enough in the short run to be able to pay for the imported energy, food and other basic items necessary for reconstruction, if not for survival. Most objective observers agree, however, that Japan kept its rigid official barriers to foreign economic activity in place considerably longer than was justified by the postwar balance of payments emergency.

The late 1960s and 1970s saw significant changes in this system of restraints. For one thing, Japan and the United States began to engage in extensive discussions and negotiations over the closed market issue. These negotiations, furthermore, were often unusually one-sided, with America pressing Japan to modify its restrictive practices and Japan gradually giving ground. Largely as a result of this kind of pressure, the Japanese economy has opened dramatically, especially in terms of such direct official restraints as tariffs, quotas and investment controls. Japanese import and foreign

---

3. Nw.J.Intl.L. & Bus. 103, 108–09, 116–17. Reprinted by special permission of the Northwestern Journal of International Law and Business, © by Northwestern University School of Law, Vol. 3, No. 1.

direct investment statistics confirm this opening, and demonstrate that many foreign sellers and investors have been able to take advantage of the new opportunities. As foreign businesses have begun to expand their activities in Japan, however, they have encountered other Japanese rules and practices that impede further penetration. Some of the newly identified impediments seem to be merely more subtle manifestations of the same official policies previously implemented through direct restraints. Others, however, seem not to reflect official policy at all, or to do so only in part, but to derive primarily from the characteristics of Japanese society and culture. Businessmen and government officials in the United States and other countries have increasingly turned their attention to these two less familiar, and very different, types of impediments to foreign economic activity, while continuing to press for removal of the remaining direct official restraints. As a result, the closed market issue has taken on a much more complex character than it had even ten to fifteen years ago.

*   *   *

There have been drastic, even "revolutionary" changes in the trade barriers that in earlier days protected the Japanese economy from foreign penetration. The Wise Men,[4] and most other informed observers, now agree that the tightly closed market of the 1950s and 1960s no longer exists.

The first barriers to be significantly reduced were the traditional, positive restraints on imports—tariffs and quotas. By the start of the Tokyo Round in 1975, Japanese tariffs had on the whole been reduced to a level comparable to that of the U.S., although a few high ad valorem rates effectively excluded some products, such as tobacco. Since 1975, multilateral and bilateral negotiations have led to further reductions. On more than one occasion, Japan has unilaterally lowered its tariffs in response to American pressure. During the MTN, Japan agreed to tariff reductions averaging 46 percent on 2600 categories of products; as mentioned above, the average reduction on products of particular interest to the U.S. was even higher. When the tariff reductions agreed on during the Tokyo Round are fully effective, Japan's average industrial tariff rate will be only 3.2 percent, slightly lower than that of the U.S. Since the end of the Tokyo Round, moreover, the high tobacco tariffs have been moderated, agreed semiconductor tariff reductions have been accelerated, and tariffs on auto parts have been eliminated altogether.

Postwar Japan relied heavily on quotas to restrict imports. By 1978, however, only twenty-seven quotas remained, and almost all of them protected politically influential groups engaged in farming and fishing. As regards manufactured goods, Japan has become the target of many more quantitative restraints than it maintains, at least if one considers "voluntary" Japanese export restraints like those on autos, most of which are simply disguised quotas.

4. The Wise Men were eight private individuals from Japan and the United States who were appointed by President Carter and Japanese Prime Minister Ohira to study and recommend ways of improving long-term bilateral relations between the United States and Japan.

MITSUO MATSUSHITA, LEGAL FRAMEWORK FOR IMPORT TRADE AND INVESTMENT IN JAPAN

3–10 (1985) [5]

Administrative guidance is often used to achieve governmental purposes in export/import regulation and also foreign investment control. Administrative guidance has played a vital role in regulating export in the orderly marketing cases. In import regulation, administrative guidance was also used. One important example is that of naphtha import control. In the petrochemical industry, there was an import control by administrative guidance concerning import of naphtha. In this industry, naphtha is a very important material, but importation of this material was restricted by administrative guidance. Under the Petroleum Business Law, a person who desires to import a petroleum product including naphtha shall file a report with MITI and then import the product. This means that the statute only requires a person who wants to import to file a report and nothing more. However, MITI had the policy of not allowing importation of naphtha by petrochemical companies but allowing importation only by oil refineries. There MITI exercised administrative guidance to the petrochemical industry to the effect that petrochemical companies shall not file a report with MITI. This was not a legal order (MITI had no such authority), but only advice given informally by the government. From a legal standpoint, therefore, it was possible for petrochemical companies to file a report and import naphtha despite the opposition of MITI. However, this would be rare in Japan.

The petrochemical industry in Japan became impatient with this situation, since the industry had to purchase naphtha from the oil refining industry which had the permission from MITI to import it, and this resulted in the price of naphtha being higher than it would have been. The petrochemical industry finally decided to make "a report in force." At this point, a compromise was reached between MITI and the industry, and in 1982, the policy of MITI was changed to allow in substance the importation of naphtha by the petrochemical industry.

Another important case of import control by administrative guidance is that of the Lions Oil Company. In 1984, Lions intended to import gasoline from Singapore and, for this purpose, to file with MITI a report under the Petroleum Business Law to import gasoline from Singapore. MITI, of course, objected to it strongly, but Lions also insisted that it would import gasoline. While negotiations were proceeding between Lions and MITI, gasoline was shipped from Singapore to Japan. According to news reports, MITI, having considered that it would be difficult to persuade Lions to give up [its import plan,] decided to pressure financial institutions to suspend financing to Lions if Lions insisted on importing gasoline. Lions finally gave in and decided to abandon the plan to import gasoline, and gasoline which had been shipped from Singapore to Japan was imported not as gasoline but as "naphtha."

5. Reprinted by permission of Dean Rusk Center, University of Georgia, from a book entitled Dynamics of United States—Japan Trade (1986).

The above two cases are instances in which an import control was exercised by way of an administrative guidance rather than by a legal order. In these two cases, MITI had no formal and legal authority to prohibit import, and, if the companies had forced their ways through by filing reports, there was little MITI could have done to legally prevent it from happening. Therefore, it was necessary for MITI to utilize some other ways (for example, to talk banks into [not] giving financial credit to the violator).

*   *   *

The other issue is the relationship between GATT and a domestic law restricting import. Article 98(2) of the Japanese Constitution provides that a treaty and the established international law should be given a due respect. This constitutional provision has been interpreted to signify the supremacy of a treaty or the international customary law if it is firmly established. Therefore, when a domestic law or an administrative regulation is contrary to a provision of a treaty or a rule in the international law which has been firmly established, then the treaty or the rule will be given the overriding effect over the domestic law or administrative regulation which is contrary to it.

GATT enjoys the status of a treaty in the Japanese legal system since GATT was signed by the Administration and then approved by the National Diet. Therefore, where a conflict arises between a provision in GATT and a domestic law or regulation, the provision in GATT should be interpreted to override the law or regulation.

There are few court decisions addressing these legal issues. However, a decision by the Kyoto District Court which was handed down recently touches upon these issues, and, therefore, an explanation and analysis of this decision is due.

On July 29, 1984, the Kyoto District Court handed down a decision upholding legislation which provided for the exclusive power of a government agency to import raw silk. Involved in the decision are some important legal issues, i.e., the discretionary power of the National Diet in enacting a law which restricts the freedom of enterprises to engage in import trade, the relationship between GATT and such a law and some related matters.

The facts involved in the case are briefly summarized in the part of this paper which deals with the Chinese Silk Case. Other relevant facts are explained below. The National Diet enacted a law which authorized the price stabilization program of raw silk in the domestic market and also [provided] for the exclusive right given to a government agency to import raw silk from abroad. Under the scheme of the legislation, the government establishes the upper and lower limits to the price of raw silk, and when the market price of the product comes below the lower limit (or there is a threat that this may happen), the agency purchases raw silk from the market in order to support the price. When it goes up above the upper limit, then the agency sells the product into the market to make the price come down. Even though this legislation provides measures both for lower prices and higher prices, it is clear that the legislative purpose is to deal with lower prices rather than higher prices.

To operate this price stabilization program effectively, it was thought necessary to introduce a restriction on import of raw silk, since, if raw silk from abroad were allowed to come in freely when the domestic price is too low and the government agency purchases it, it would have a disruptive effect on the stabilization program.

In light of this, the law was amended to provide for import restriction. Under this amendment, a government agency (Sanshi Jigyodan, the Silk Business Agency) is empowered to import raw silk from abroad exclusively, and no other person is allowed to import the product in principle. The agency is not permitted to sell the imported raw silk into the domestic market when the price of it comes below the lower limit or there is a threat thereof. Also, when the agency sells the imported raw silk, the sale price must not be below the standard price to be determined by the government.

In short, this regime is designed to protect the domestic raw silk producers by establishing the price stabilization program and also the import control. Because of this legislation and other economic factors, the price of raw silk in Japan has been much higher than the international market price.

However, the above scheme has caused adverse impacts on producers of fabrics for neckties in Japan. No import restriction was introduced with regard to fabrics for ties, even though a tariff has been imposed. European producers of ties purchase raw silk from Mainland China and Korea (the two major producing countries), produce ties at much lower costs compared with those of Japanese producers due to the difference of purchase prices of silk and export ties to Japan.

The Japanese producers of fabrics complained that they could not compete with European ties imported into Japan and brought a suit against the government, alleging that the legislation in question was contrary to Article 22(1) and Article 29(2) of the Japanese Constitution which guarantees the freedom of trade and private property respectively, Article 17 of GATT which provided that a state trading agency must act on the basis of commercial consideration in foreign trade operations and some related issues.

The decision of the Kyoto District Court held, in essence, as follows. The freedom of trade and the guarantee of private property are not absolute, and they are subject to restrictions for the public welfare. Therefore, when a restriction of such constitutional rights is necessary to achieve some socio-economic policy, such a restriction is not contrary to the Constitution as long as the restriction remains within the area necessary for achieving such a governmental policy.

The question as to what kind of policy should be adopted and enforced in socio-economic matters should best be left to the judgment and discretion of the legislature, since the legislature is the organ most suitable for examining such questions on the basis of empirical data, adjusting various adverse interests involved and drawing upon the best conclusion. Therefore, unless legislation aimed at achieving a socio-economic policy goals clearly steps outside the orbit of reasonableness, a court should not pass judgment on the wisdom of such legislation.

The court also stated that the government has provided for some aids to the Japanese producers of tie fabrics, that a high tariff wall had been erected and that the government would be able to [impose] an import restriction [on] necktie fabrics under Article 19 of GATT if the conditions surrounding the fabrics industry in Japan became seriously deteriorated. After these statements, the court concluded that, considering that the government had attempted to establish compensatory measures to remedy the plight of the fabrics industry, the legislation in question could not be held as unreasonably restraining the freedom of trade of the fabrics producers in Japan, even if it amounted to a restriction of such freedom.

One of the issues raised by the fabrics producers was the illegality of this legislation under Article 17(1)(a) of GATT stipulating that every contracting party agrees that a state trading agency under its control operate its transactions on the basis of commercial considerations only in terms of price, quality and availability. Article 2(4) of GATT also stipulates that, whenever a tariff concession under GATT has been made for a commodity which is an object of state trading, a contracting party shall not engage in a practice in which the commodity in question is sold in the domestic market at a price level which is above the actual import price plus tariff and the profit earned.

The Japanese fabrics producers argued that the government agency in charge of importing raw silk amounted to a state trading agency and, since the agency was not allowed to sell in the domestic market the imported raw silk below the stabilization price, this sales policy envisaged in the legislation was in violation of Article 17 of GATT.

The court rejected this argument raised by the fabrics producers and upheld the validity of the legislation for the following reasons.

" * * * The exclusive importership and the price stabilization system under consideration * * * are designed to protect the business of raw silk producers from the pressure of imports for a while, and this has the same substance as the emergency measure permitted under Article 19 of GATT. Even though it is reasonable to state that, judging from the nature of such an emergency measure, there should be a limit to the duration period of it, such a limit should not be regarded as absolute. Since this duration period should be decided in relation to the duration period of the pressure of imports, Article 12–13–2 of the law providing for enforcing the exclusive importership for a while cannot be regarded as unreasonable."

With regard to the effectiveness of Articles in GATT in relation to domestic laws, the court stated as follows. " * * * A violation of a provision of GATT has its impact on the violating country, for it pressures the country toward rectifying the violation by being confronted with a request from another member country for consultation and retaliatory measures to be taken. However, it cannot be interpreted to have more effect than the above. Therefore, it cannot be held that the legislation in question is contrary to GATT and null and void and that legislating such a law was illegal."

The decision is significant in the sense that it is one of the rare court decisions dealing with import problems. What is striking is the judicial passivism in respect to the discretion of the legislature in dealing with policy matters such as trade policy. The court pointed out that the wisdom of introducing or rejecting an import control should be left to the legislative discretion and that courts can intervene only in some exceptional situations where the legislature has clearly overstepped the reasonable boundary. This judicial attitude coincides with the previous Supreme Court decisions dealing with domestic economic policies which held that the reasonableness of a government restriction imposed on activities of private enterprises should be basically judged by the legislature rather than by courts. This judicial attitude may indicate that courts are probably not an effective countervailing force to import restrictions in Japan.

The validity of the court's holding on the relationship between GATT and a domestic regulation is rather dubious. The court held that the import restriction in question would be held lawful since the same kind of measure would be allowed under Article 19 of GATT. However, Article 19 requires that a country invoking a safeguard measure find "serious injury" caused by an increase in import. In this case, however, not only "serious injury" had not been found but also there had been no procedure in the law to find such an injury. Moreover, this exclusive importership was established in 1976, and there is no sign that this will be relaxed or abolished. Even admitting that the duration of restriction may be determined relative to import pressure against which the restriction provides protection, the unlimited duration period as provided for in this legislation seems too excessive.

Finally the court seems to imply that the fact that a domestic law is contrary to a provision of GATT does not affect the validity of the law in Japan, although it may invite a request for consultation and retaliation by another member country which is affected by such a law. This position seems to ignore Article 98(2) of the Constitution providing that a treaty and the established rules in international law should be accorded a due respect and the established legal interpretation in Japan that a treaty overrides a domestic law contrary to the treaty regardless of the times at which the treaty and the domestic law were enacted.

Note

There is now an extensive literature on Japan and its international economic relations, some of it rather critical. In Part IV of this book we return to some of the more recent and perplexing issues regarding trade with Japan (and other industrial countries), including questions about whether GATT and the traditional Bretton Woods system is adequate to regulate appropriately a number of new governmental and societal practices which affect international trade, such as consumer taste and other preferences for domestic goods, the tolerance of monopoly and cartel behavior, the effect of certain structures of retail trade, administrative guidance techniques for influencing enterprise action without legal sanctions, industrial policy and practices termed "targeting." In addition to references listed there, however, the reader may be interested in some of the following additional references which relate to the subject of this section, i.e. the more constitutional or systemic aspects of Japanese government regulation of international economic relations: E. Vogel, Japan as Number One: Lessons for America (1979); C. Higashi, Japanese Trade Policy Formulation (1983); E. Hahn,

Japanese Business Law and Legal Systems (1984); J.T. Sawada, Subsequent Conduct and Supervening Events (1968).

SECTION 4.4 NONMARKET ECONOMIES

We will consider the problems of nonmarket economies or state trading countries in detail in Chapter 21, where we will take another look at the Soviet Union. It is useful here, however, to consider the general framework in which the so-called Eastern trading area conducts international trade. A considerable volume of trade occurs between nations of the Communist bloc, and the roles of government and government-controlled entities in this trade differ significantly from those found in most members of the international trading system. The reader should keep these materials in mind as we study the GATT system and consider the extent to which special rules are needed to deal with nonmarket economies.

THOMAS W. HOYA, EAST–WEST TRADE: COMECON LAW—AMERICAN–SOVIET TRADE

11–13, 15–16 (1984) [1]

In each Comecon country, the basic means of production are owned by the state, and the economy is centrally planned. Foreign trade is also centrally planned, and is run as a state monopoly. Each country's ministry of foreign trade administers most of the foreign trade monopoly.

A state monopoly of foreign trade does not, however, mean that each Comecon government in its sovereign capacity negotiates, signs, and performs foreign trade contracts. Rather, the work of contracting, exporting, and importing is done primarily by FTOs, which are state foreign trade organizations that are legal entities juridically separate from, albeit administratively totally subordinate to, the state. Such a Soviet or East European foreign trade organization is commonly referred to in English as an "FTO," the abbreviation used in this book.

Each FTO is state owned and is subject to administrative direction from some office of the central government, usually the ministry of foreign trade. In terms of legal characteristics, nevertheless, an FTO resembles a private corporation in a Western market economy. It is an independent juridical person having an individual name and a seal, and it concludes contracts and commercial transactions as a principal. An FTO may sue and be sued in its own name, and it does not plead sovereign immunity.

Each FTO has its own assets, which are separate from the assets of the state and from those of other state owned organizations. Only the assets of the particular FTO are liable for satisfaction of the obligations of that FTO. Neither the state, nor other state owned organizations, nor the employees or agents of the FTO in their individual capacities, are liable for obligations of the FTO. In the same way, the FTO bears no responsibility for any obligations of the state, other state owned organizations, or the FTO's employees or agents in their individual capacities.

---

1. Reprinted with permission from Hoya, American-Soviet Trade pp. 11–16 (Oceana T.W., East-West Trade—Comecon Law— Publications, Inc., 1984).

The typical FTO has a monopoly in its country over the export and import of a designated range of goods. Normally, it functions as a middleman. What it exports, it has not produced itself but has obtained from a domestic operating enterprise; and what it imports, it transfers for use or consumption to a domestic operating enterprise.

In the Soviet Union, about seventy FTOs conduct almost all the nation's exporting and importing. In the other Comecon countries, most foreign trade is conducted by FTOs. Each country typically has several dozen of them. One recent development is that, in the East European countries, certain large domestic operating enterprises are increasingly being authorized to sell directly to foreign customers without having to channel the exports through the middleman FTOs. This new approach is being tried especially in Hungary. These large East European operating enterprises are, like the FTOs, independent juridical entities, with segregated assets. They conclude commercial transactions in their own names, bring lawsuits, and answer suits without interposing sovereign immunity.

KINDS OF COMECON TRADE AGREEMENTS

Foreign trade within Comecon is basically bilateral, and it is arranged primarily through three kinds of bilateral agreements: long-term trade agreements, annual trade protocols, and contracts. A long-term trade agreement is entered into between two governments, and specifies the bilateral trade that is to take place during the next five years. During these five years the two governments spell out their trade in more detail on a yearly basis by executing annual trade protocols. For each individual export and import transaction required to achieve this prescribed trade, a contract is signed by the parties that will actually carry out the transaction—normally the exporting FTO of one country and the importing FTO of the other.

The long-term trade agreement and the annual trade protocols, since they are entered into by sovereign governments, belong to the first type of international trade agreements described at the beginning of this Chapter. The contracts concluded between the FTOs belong to the second type (viz., contracts signed between the parties that actually conduct trade).

In addition to the trade agreements, annual protocols, and contracts, there exist many additional legal agreements within Comecon, both multilateral and bilateral, that form part of the overall legal framework of intra-Comecon trade. But essentially this trade is set legally as each country's government and FTOs negotiate bilateral trade agreements, annual protocols, and contracts with the government and FTOs of each of its Comecon trading partners.

* * *

This long-term agreement sets forth which goods in what amounts are to be supplied by each country to the other, with deliveries broken down by years. * * * These agreements do in fact, claim authorities in Comecon, indicate the main outline of trade for their operative periods. During 1966–1970, about 85–90 percent of trade among the Comecon countries was, according to a Hungarian economist, covered by the bilateral long-term trade agreements that had been signed for these five years.

Since Comecon lacks an effective multilateral payments system, generally a long-term agreement schedules the trade between the two countries so that, unless credit is to be provided to pay for any deficit, their trade will balance bilaterally.

* * *

Beginning in the early 1970s and continuing through the early 1980s, some FTOs' contracts are being negotiated before, rather than after, execution of the inter-governmental long-term agreements and annual protocols. This practice is growing chiefly in those countries where decentralization of the economy is most advanced, which means especially Hungary, and also Poland, Czechoslovakia, and the G.D.R. Under the traditional system used by Comecon's centrally planned economies, the FTOs normally sign their contracts only after execution of the annual protocol, because the protocol determines the deliveries for which the contracts are to be concluded. This traditional system is still used for most foreign trade by all the Comecon countries, including the four mentioned above.

But for a modest, but steadily increasing, portion of trade, particularly involving these four countries, the FTOs sign their contracts prior to execution of the pertinent inter-governmental agreements and protocols. Then the foreign trade ministries, after consultation with their FTOs, seek to negotiate inclusion in these inter-governmental documents of the deliveries for which contracts have been concluded.

Note

A recent example of a U.S. governmental view of nonmarket economies (NME) was given in a countervailing duty case by the International Trade Administration as follows: [2]

Most NME systems are characterized by centrally administered prices. Descriptions of these systems report that prices are reformed, revised or changed with varying frequency. Thousands of prices can be changed at a time by the planners.

Prices in Czechoslovakia are similarly controlled. * * *

* * * Even where so-called "market" prices exist for consumer goods, non-price rationing is evident in the reported 10-year wait for an apartment in Prague.

SECTION 4.5 DEVELOPING COUNTRIES

No developing country can be said to be truly representative of the others. The diversity of developing country governmental systems and the variety of ways those systems deal with international economic relations, is very great indeed. The perception of many industrial country governments seems to be, however, that many developing countries have a large measure of government involvement in their economies, such that these countries also might be called "nonmarket." We cannot in this book delve very deeply

---

2. Carbon Steel Wire Rod from Czechoslovakia, 49 Fed.Reg. 19371, 19372 (1984) (Final Negative Determination).

into the myriad constitutional and governmental arrangements of the more than 100 developing countries, particularly since it is often impossible to find perceptive information about them published in English.[1] The following excerpts we have selected as illustrating several interesting features of the legal and constitutional systems regulating international trade and economic relations of two prominent developing countries. In later chapters in this book we discuss other particular features of the international as well as national legal systems which bear on these relations.

As indicated in other sections of this chapter, a major question in examining the legal and constitutional structure of various nations, is the degree to which such structure "meshes" well with the international rules, such as those of GATT. In later parts of this book, for example, we learn about the difficulty of applying GATT rules to nonmarket economies, or to state trading agencies. Likewise we discuss the criticisms which developing countries have had about the international regulatory system for international trade.

RAJ KRISHNA, INDIA'S FOREIGN TRADE
(1967)[2]

THE CONSTITUTIONAL FRAMEWORK

*The Legislative Power Pertaining to Matters Connected
With Foreign Trade*

The Indian Constitution aims at the centralization of international trade by keeping it out of the ambit of States' regulatory power. Following the Government of India Act, 1935, but at the same time widening the scope of the provision contained therein, the Constitution empowers Parliament to legislate in respect of "import and export across customs frontiers; definition of customs frontiers" and also "trade and commerce with foreign countries". An important distinction between the two constitutional instruments is that whereas the power to define customs frontiers is now conferred on Parliament, under the Act of 1935, only the Union Government was competent to do so. Parliament can also legislate as regards the "establishment of standards of quality for goods to be exported out of India or transported from one State to another." Pursuant to this power Parliament has enacted the Indian Standards Institution (Certification of Marks) Act, 1952 and the Export (Quality Control and Inspection) Act, 1963. It is not uncommon for the Government to enter into export trade in specific commodities or to create a monopoly in favour of a corporation owned or controlled by the State, on the ground that it was necessary for properly maintaining the quality of the commodity sought to be exported.

---

1. Useful sources in English on foreign trade laws include such U.S. Department of Commerce publications as "Country Market Surveys" and "Overseas Business Reports." The Bureau of National Affairs publishes the "Export Shipping Manual" as part of its International Trade Reporter. The Manual has detailed coverage of the import regulations of many countries.

2. 1 J. World Trade L. 329, 332. Reprinted by permission of the Journal of World Trade Law.

The levying of customs duties is likewise within the exclusive legislative competence of Parliament. A tax or a levy becomes a customs duty when it is imposed on the act of importation or exportation. Unlike the United States Constitution there is no provision in the Indian Constitution prohibiting the imposition of duty on exports. Parliament again is competent to legislate in respect of "foreign exchange" and "foreign loans." No legislation with respect to "foreign loans" has been enacted but such loans, no doubt, can be regulated under the foreign exchange regulations.

* * *

It may be pointed out that a State can enter foreign trade without any specific legislation authorizing it to do so. To remove all doubts, Article 298 was inserted in 1956 which expressly provides that the "executive power" of the State includes the right to carry on a trade or business. But a total or complete monopoly in trade can be created in the States' favour only under a statute.

* * *

Over the years the imports of a number of commodities have been canalized through the S.T.C. [State Trading Corporation] and the local enterprises have to meet their requirements directly from the S.T.C. In Glass Chatons v. Union, where the canalization of the imports of glass chatons through the S.T.C. was challenged by the importers, the Supreme Court held that it was a reasonable restriction imposed in the interest of the general public. The Court, however, did drop the hint that

> while the decision that import of a particular commodity will be canalized may be difficult to challenge, the selection of the particular channel or agency decided upon in implementing the decision of canalization may well be challenged on the ground that it infringes Article 14 of the Constitution or some other fundamental rights.

In *Daya's* case the Supreme Court held that canalization of exports of manganese ore was also in the interest of the general public. In this case the petitioner alleged that there was practically no internal demand for manganese ore and that as he was prevented from exporting the commodity, he was compelled to sell it to the S.T.C. at a price which the S.T.C. dictated and which was unfair. This contention was not pressed before the Court. The Court, however, made the significant observation that the S.T.C.

> being owned and controlled by the Central Government is an agency or instrument of Government for effectuating its commercial policy. If in the performance of its duties as such public authority it acts in any improper or unfair manner it would be subject to the control of the Courts.

* * *

The Supreme Court has declared that in normal trades the executive cannot be given regulatory powers, unregulated by any rule or principle. In Bhatnagars and Co., Ltd., v. Union the validity of the Imports and Exports (Control) Act, 1947 was challenged on the ground that it prescribed no guiding principles for the exercise of discretionary powers by the Government as regards the regulation of imports and exports. The Supreme Court in its endeavor to protect the existing controls surprised the legal profession by holding that although no policy was discernible in the Import and Export

(Control) Act, 1947, there was such a policy in the repealed predecessor whose provisions it purported to continue.

SANG HYUN SONG, FOREIGN TRADE REGULATIONS OF KOREA

569–70, 575–78 (1983) [3]

TRADE POLICY

While adhering to a general goal of trade liberalization, the Government of Korea continues to maintain controls over foreign trade and exchange transactions. Recently, however, the Korean Government took a number of positive steps toward freer trade—a new tariff table has been adopted, lowering tariffs from an arithmetical average of 38.8% to 31.3% in line with Korea's commitment to the General Agreement on Tariffs and Trade (GATT); the special customs duty law, a special levy in addition to the regular tariff, has been abolished; and the Foreign Trade Transactions Law has also been amended, opening the door for trade with Communist countries in time of need.

Korea must import many of the raw materials needed for producing goods for local consumption and for export. Furthermore, the implementation of the country's ambitious Economic Development Plans has and will continue to require substantial importation of capital goods.

* * *

The Semi-Annual Trade Plan, which becomes effective on January 1 and July 1 of each year, is announced and implemented by the Ministry of Commerce and Industry (MCI). The plans generally give priority to the importation of capital goods required for development, raw materials not available domestically, and other essential commodities.

* * *

IMPORT TARIFF SYSTEM

Tariff Structure

Korea maintains a three-column import tariff schedule. This schedule is made up of general rates, temporary rates, and GATT rates. There is also a separate set of concession tariff rates relating to trade negotiations among developing countries (TNDC rates). Very few special temporary rates, GATT rates and TDC rates are now in effect. * * *

Import duties are not assessed on capital goods and raw materials imported in connection with foreign investment projects. * * *

Raw materials used in the production of export goods are also exempt from payment of customs duties. In addition, certain machinery, materials and parts used in designated basic industries—such as electric power, iron and steel, the machinery industry, shipbuilding, petroleum refining, agriculture, mining, and petro-chemical industry may enter Korea either free of duty or at reduced rates.

* * *

3. From Sang Hyun Song (ed.), Introduction to the Law and Legal System of Korea (1983). Reprinted by permission of Sang Hyun Song.

NON-TARIFF IMPORT CONTROLS

Import Licensing

An import license, obtainable from the Korea Exchange Bank or from any one of the 15 other Class A foreign exchange banks and valid for 6 months, is required for every transaction and before a letter of credit can be opened in favor of a foreign supplier. Under the negative list system of licensing introduced in July 1967, all commodities may be freely imported (i.e., applications for import licenses are automatically approved) unless they are included on a negative list, which includes commodities that are either prohibited or restricted. * * * The bulk of Korean imports are licensed on an automatic approval basis. Processed foods, apparel, certain paper wares and some luxury goods make up the items in the prohibited import category.

* * *

Exchange Controls

All foreign exchange transactions are subject to exchange controls administered by the Ministry of Finance and the Bank of Korea. The Ministry of Commerce and Industry is authorized, however, to grant or deny import (or export) licenses, depending upon the current trade plan and the general availability of exchange. Any import permit issued by the MCI entitles the holder to buy the required foreign exchange. For automatic approval commodities, as noted earlier, exchange may be purchased directly from a foreign exchange bank. Exchange certificates are required for all foreign exchange expenditures, with some exceptions.

All foreign exchange proceeds, with very few exceptions, must be surrendered to the Korea Exchange Bank, or the foreign exchange banks, against payment in won or be exchanged into equivalent foreign exchange certificates. The exceptions are largely limited to transportation and insurance companies, and foreign non-residents.

* * *

KOREA'S EXPORT CONTROLS

Under the negative list system, the Semi-Annual Trade Plan specifies those items that are banned from export trade and those that are restricted, all other items being automatically approved for export. In order to export restricted items an export permit issued by the Ministry of Commerce and Industry or other government agencies or a recommendation by an appropriate end-user association, must be obtained, while automatic approval items simply require an export approval certificate issued by an authorized foreign exchange bank. Export permits are issued only when an authorized organization has already given its approval. This procedure is intended to improve the quality of products exported from Korea and to eliminate excessive competition among exporters.

Most export commodities, including marine and agricultural products and many manufactured goods, must pass export quality and quantity inspection by the relative inspection institute designated by the Korean Government, prior to receiving customs clearance.

Chapter 5

INTERNATIONAL ECONOMIC REGULATION AND THE BRETTON WOODS SYSTEM

SECTION 5.1 INTRODUCTION TO INTERNATIONAL ECONOMIC LAW AND INSTITUTIONS

(A) OVERVIEW

Having considered the law of the private transaction and the law of national regulation, we now take up the institutional and constitutional aspects of international regulation of economic relations. In this Section and Section 5.2, we examine some of the fundamentals of international law, both customary and treaty based.[1] We will consider how international norms come into being and what is their effect, particularly in the context of economic relations.

In Section 5.3 we turn to an examination of the multilateral treaties and institutions on which so much of international economic regulation is based today. We look generally at some of the constitutional problems of international economic organizations—how disputes are resolved, how voting rights are distributed, and then turn to the Bretton Woods system, which is at the core of today's international economic system. (There are those who think that the Bretton Woods system is now dead, or that it no longer is meaningful for international economic policy. In the sense of the whole body of

---

1. Many of the questions we consider are usually discussed in more detail in courses on international law and organizations. Readers not generally familiar with those materials, may find the following references useful: W. Bishop, International Law: Cases and Materials (3d ed. 1971); Bishop, General Course of Public International Law, 115 Receuil des Cours 147 (1965); I. Brownlie, Principles of Public International Law (3d ed. 1979); L. Henkin, R. Pugh, O. Schachter & H. Smit, International Law: Cases and Materials (1980); N. Leech, C. Oliver & J. Sweeney, Cases and Materials on the International Legal System (2d ed. 1981); M. McDougal & W. Reisman, International Law in Contemporary Perspective (1981); H. Steiner & D. Vagts, Transnational Legal Problems: Materials and Text (3d ed. 1986); B. Weston, R. Falk & A. D'Amato, International Law and World Order (1980); American Law Institute, Restatement of the Law (Second), Foreign Relations Law of the United States (1965) (now being revised); see also Zagayko, Guide to a Basic Library on International Law, 53 Law Library J. 118 (1960).

norms introduced by that system in the 1944–1948 period, they may be right. We use the phrase "Bretton Woods system" more broadly here, however, to designate the institutional and constitutional system, which although much changed, nevertheless traces its lineage directly to the 1944–1948 period and still operates in the context of the institutions created then.)

In the next three sections of this chapter, we take up the institutional and constitutional structure of the General Agreement on Tariffs and Trade, known as GATT. As indicated at the outset of this book, GATT and the international trading rules surrounding it, are the most detailed and extensive of those which exist for international economic regulation today. Thus, apart from their central significance, they also form a model or prototype of a legalistic type system of international regulation which is obviously influencing thinking about how to structure other areas of economic international endeavor, such as rules on trade in services (see Chapter 15 infra). Some may feel that GATT is a defective or flawed model, one that should be avoided, but even if that is the case it will be necessary to understand the model and its strengths and weaknesses in order to profit from its history in designing any other system.

Finally, in the last section of this Chapter we pose a series of problems, designed to show how the materials of Part I of this book (particularly Chapters 3 through 5) fit together in the context of particular policy questions, and designed to prepare the reader for materials which come later in the book.

(B) THE PROBLEM OF EFFECTIVENESS OF INTERNATIONAL LAW

One of the most perplexing aspects of international law, whether economic law or otherwise, is the question of "effectiveness." There is often a tendency, particularly on the part of persons (official or otherwise) who have not had direct experience with international matters, to discount the impact of international rules. This is probably at least partly because that impact sometimes differs substantially from the impact of domestic law rules, and because it is often difficult to understand the more subtle impact of international rules. Many attributes of an effective domestic or national legal system do not exist in the context of international legal norms. Therefore, some conclude, since there often is no "sanction," or no "monopoly of power in the state," the rules are not truly rules (in the sense that John Austin would define them).[2]

We cannot in this book go deeply into this interesting philosophical question, even though it does vitally affect the subject of this book. Nevertheless a few comments or reflections are worthwhile, to remind the reader of the dimensions of this problem. It is true, as we have seen and will see further, that international norms (like domestic norms) are sometimes breached. It may even be true that some international norms are more likely to be breached than domestic legal norms. This does not lead to the conclusion that international norms are always or even frequently breached,

2. See J. Austin, The Province of Jurisprudence Determined (Library of Ideas ed. 1954).

or that they are irrelevant. There are various reasons, including the desire for reciprocally advantageous treatment by other nations, why nation-states will feel that it is important to obey international legal norms.[3]

STATEMENT OF GATT DIRECTOR GENERAL ARTHUR DUNKEL, MARCH 5, 1982 [4]

[I]nternational economic policy commitments, in the form of agreed rules, have far-reaching domestic effects, indeed effects so important that they are indispensable for democratic governance. They are the element which secures the ultimate coordination and mutual compatibility of the purely domestic economic policies. They form the basis from which the government can arbitrate and secure an equitable and efficient balance between the diverse domestic interests: producers vs consumers, export industries vs import-competing industries, between particular narrowly defined industries. Last but not least, only a firm commitment to international rules makes possible the all-important reconciliation, which I have already alluded to, of the necessary balance on the production side and on the financial side of the national economy.

I am still convinced that it is in the national interest of every trading nation to abide by the rules, which were accepted as valid for good times and bad, and to frame their internal policies accordingly. One of the major benefits of international disciplines is that they offer equal opportunities and require comparable sacrifices from all the countries involved in international competition. Those who believe in the open trading system must recognize and accept the need to correct those rigidities in their economic and social systems which obstruct the process of continuing adjustment on which economic growth depends.   *   *   *

In later sections, as well as in later chapters, we will have occasion to discuss further, the problem of "effectiveness" of international norms, and, in particular of GATT rules. The following readings include a useful and brief overview of some of the theories concerning this subject.

OSCAR SCHACHTER, TOWARDS A THEORY OF INTERNATIONAL OBLIGATION

(1971) [5]

As a subject, the "foundation of obligation" is as old as international law itself; it had a prominent place in the seminal treatises of the founding fathers—Suarez, Vittoria, Grotius, Pufendorf et al—and it remained a central issue in the great controversies of the nineteenth century. In our

3. In Chapter 17 we consider the effect of nonbinding codes of conduct aimed at multinational enterprises. There too we find that the nonbinding nature of the codes does not mean that they are without force.

4. Address in Hamburg, West Germany; GATT Press Release No. 1312, March 5, 1982.

5. From S. Schwebel (ed.), The Effectiveness of International Decisions (Papers and proceedings of a conference of the American Society of International Law) 9 (1971). This and other excerpts from this publication in this chapter are reprinted by permission of A.W. Sijthoff International Publishing Co. N.V., Leyden.

century it has had a lesser place; it was largely overtaken by the discussion of "sources" and evidence, centered around Article 38 of the Statute of the International Court. Although subordinated, it was not neglected and each of the leading scholars of the twentieth century found himself impelled to advance a fresh analysis. No single theory has received general agreement and sometimes it seems as though there are as many theories or at least formulations as there are scholars. We can list at least a baker's dozen of "candidates" which have been put forward as the basis (or as one of the bases) of obligation in international law:

    (i) Consent of states

    (ii) Customary practice

    (iii) A sense of "rightness"—the juridical conscience

    (iv) Natural law or natural reason

    (v) Social necessity

    (vi) The will of the international community (the "consensus" of the international community)

    (vii) Direct (or "stigmatic") intuition

    (viii) Common purposes of the participants

    (ix) Effectiveness

    (x) Sanctions

    (xi) "Systemic" goals

    (xii) Shared expectations as to authority

    (xiii) Rules of recognition

On looking at this wide array of ideas concerning the "true" or "correct" basis of obligation in international law it may be wondered, on the one hand, whether the choice of a "basis" has any great practical significance and, on the other, whether the diversity of opinion does not reveal a radical weakness in the conceptual structure of international law.

For some pragmatically-inclined international lawyers, the issue is not likely to be regarded as important. As long as the obligation itself—the legal norm or prescription—can be identified in one of the so-called formal sources—treaty or custom or in general principles of law—it seems to matter little what the underlying basis of the obligation may be. It is, therefore, understandable that most contemporary treatises and textbooks on international law pass quickly and lightly over the problem of the "foundation." Like the chaplain's opening prayer at public meetings, it has little effect on what is said afterwards. The practical international lawyer is supposed to be concerned not with the foundation of obligation but with the so-called "sources," formal and material.

But this is more easily said than done. Somehow conceptions as to the basis of obligation arise time and again, and not only in theoretical discussion about the binding force of international law. They come up in concrete controversies as to whether a rule of law has emerged or has been terminated; whether an event is a violation or a precedent; and whether practice under a treaty is accepted as law. They are involved in dealing with situations in which solemn declarations, couched in legal terminology, are adopted by official bodies which have no formal authority to lay down prescriptive rules. They come up when there is substantial variance between what is preached and what is practiced; or when consensus (or expectations) are limited in geographical terms or in duration. These are not, of course, new problems and over the years they have been the subject of much jurisprudential writing. But in the last few years the general problem has assumed a new dimension. The peculiar features of contemporary international society have generated considerable normative activity without at the same time involving commensurate use of the formal procedures for international "legislation" and adjudication.

It may be useful to recall the main factors which have emerged in international life in the last few years to give enhanced importance to problems of indeterminacy of obligation.

First, there has been the much-discussed "quasi-legislative" activity by the General Assembly and other United Nations bodies purporting to lay down, expressly or by implication, requirements of State conduct or to terminate or modify existing requirements.

Second, there has been a recognition of so-called "rules of the game," based on implicit understandings or unilateral actions and acquiescence. This has been a notable feature of Great Power behavior in regard to their use of armed force.

Third, there have been the social revolutions which have overturned traditional orders and have challenged the assumptions on which prior conceptions of authority were based.

Fourth, the growing interdependence of States—especially in economic and technological activities—has vastly increased patterns of cooperation and reciprocal behavior which have not been institutionalized in the traditional modes of lawmaking.

Fifth, the increased "permeability" of national States has resulted in a diminishing barrier between matters of international concern and those of domestic jurisdiction. Related to this is the fact that the United Nations Charter—particularly its articles relating to respect for human rights and self-determination of peoples—has brought domestic activities before collective organs for appraisal on the basis of international criteria.

Sixth, the expansion of science and technology with international impact both beneficial and harmful has given rise to informal means of setting standards and exercising supervision without entering into tight and tidy legal instruments.

The mere statement of these trends indicates how extensive and far-reaching are normative processes which cannot easily be placed into the categories of treaty and customary law, at least as these terms have been applied traditionally. Lawyers are made uncomfortable by this and they ceaselessly endeavor to pour the new wine into the old bottles and to market it under the time-honored labels. They will treat many of the cases as problems of treaty interpretation; others will be dealt with on the assumptions applicable to traditional customary law. But when we examine the arguments and the grounds for decision, we find more frequently than not that the test of whether a "binding" rule exists or should be applied will involve basic jurisprudential assumptions. Even the International Court of Justice, which is governed expressly by Article 38 of its Statute as to the sources of law, has demonstrated time and again that in their deliberative process the judges have had to look to theory to evaluate practice.

JOHN H. JACKSON, WORLD TRADE AND THE LAW OF GATT
757, 760, 762 (1969) [6]

Departures from legal norms always occur in a legal system, to one degree or another. There is nothing unique about GATT or international legal norms in this respect. Many domestic laws fall into disuse or are abused. There is usually a price to be paid, however, for the widespread existence of practice that is inconsistent with the legal obligations. The price is not always easy to measure, but often the phrase "disrespect for the law" is used as a shorthand expression for it. The existence of practice that is inconsistent with legal rules, particularly when such divergent practice results in profit of one kind or another, usually increases the incentive for other departures from the rule and, therefore, the number of other departures. Consequently, one of the values of a legal rule—the enhancement of stability and predictability—is lost. Of course the practice of departing from legal rules can be limited to specific types of rules, and this can support an argument that the "custom" is itself a norm that now assists attainment of the goals of the legal system. But there are two detriments associated with such "customary" norms. First, the customary norms are usually less well-defined than legislated or agreed norms and therefore promote activity that is less stable and less predictable. Secondly, and perhaps more serious, when the customary activity is directly inconsistent with the legal norm, there are conflicting signals emitted in the prediction process and there is a danger that the custom of departing from the legal rule will encourage (or at least not discourage) departures from other legal rules.

* * *

Thus it can be seen that a variety of techniques have been utilized in GATT to achieve some of the basic objectives of the international community with respect to international trade and commerce. The four mentioned above can be summarized as: (1) legal norms, backed by a complaint or a dispute-settling procedure; (2) elaborate discussion and consultation, with a view to alerting other nations to future national policies; (3) the use of Working Parties, subcommittees, and discussions in plenary sessions to bring moral force upon countries to conform their individual national policies and practices to either the legal norms or the stated objectives of GATT; and (4) the use of negotiation and bargaining as a means to formulate new obligations and to settle differences about old obligations.

One of the features in GATT—and most likely a feature in many international organizations and institutions today—that makes it more com-

6. Reprinted from World Trade and the Law of GATT by John H. Jackson, copyright 1969, by the Bobbs Merrill Company, Inc. Reprinted by permission. All rights reserved.

plex to evaluate the degree of "compliance" with the existing legal norms is the confusion and ambiguity that exists about the nature of some of those norms. Some of these norms can be separated into two groups. One group might be labeled "norms of obligations" while another group may be labeled "norms of aspiration." This dichotomy touches a basic problem of legal philosophy that exists in domestic law also. It requires elaboration.

Norms of obligations can be used to designate those legal norms toward which the attitude is that a person or country should feel obligated to follow. This feeling of obligation may stem from an idea of moral duty or a pragmatic recognition of consequences that might follow if the norm is broken but, in either case, the term designates more than just a "statement of purpose or objective."

A "norm of aspiration," on the other hand, can be used to designate a mode of conduct that everyone thinks is desirable, but toward which there is no feeling of obligation. Nations generally feel obligated to fulfill their treaty agreements. But when an international body votes a "recommendation," even if a nation voted in favor of the recommendation, it may not feel obligated to carry out that recommendation.

* * *

This somewhat elaborate discussion leads to the following point: there is a danger in mixing "norms of obligation" in the same instrument with "norms of aspiration," when the distinction between the two is not clearly signaled to the participants of that instrument. The danger is that some countries will consider a particular phrase to be a "norm of obligation" while others will consider the same phrase to be a "norm of aspiration." This can lead to tensions and disputes in international affairs and it can also be very misleading to particular participants in the institution. When many countries follow certain international obligations, the premium (in terms of economic reward) to a country that decides to depart from that obligation may be even greater than it would have been had there been no obligation at all. Just as in domestic society when the production or sale of an opiate drug is prohibited, the profit to be realized by successful evasion of that prohibition is immensely greater than would be the case if there were no prohibition at all. In certain circumstances, the same may be true in international economic relations. Another side of the same coin is the fact that certain activities that are inconsistent with an international legal norm have a greater chance of succeeding when other nations are inhibited from retaliation by the existence of that or other similar norms.

OSCAR SCHACHTER, TOWARDS A THEORY OF INTERNATIONAL OBLIGATION
Supra, at 30–31

First there is the criticism of those who will consider that "legal obligation" may be dissolved by having it depend on expectations, perceptions and probable compliance. In their view "legality like virtue is not a matter of degree" and while we may have compassion we should have no uncertainty when the fallen damsel has indeed fallen. But actually most of us will view virtue as a matter of degree and we should recognize that legal obligation—whether national or international—also may involve "degrees" and that it will depend on attitudes, expectations and compliance. True, these factors will in turn depend on law. The circularity is there, but it is not vicious; it simply takes account of interactions and influences. To be sure, at a given point one may have to decide in a concrete context whether or not an obligation exists (this can also be stated in operational terms) and that judgment will have to be made on the basis of the relevant variables. The more serious risk is to live in a "make-believe" world where the "law is always the law" and as a consequence in cynical reaction to reject a large body of normative phenomena that are actually operative in international behavior. To impose hard-and-fast categories on a world filled with indeterminancies and circularities can only result in a pseudo-realism which does justice neither to our experience nor to our higher purposes.

A second objection may come from those who believe that diverse political and cultural determinants preclude any truly international obligations in today's world. But this is a question of empirical fact, not of *a priori* judgment, and, as we indicated above, our experience provides enough evidence to indicate that divergent systems and beliefs exhibit concordances on a wide array of international norms. We have ample proof that mankind shares common characteristics and needs and its efforts to satisfy those needs provide a realistic basis for an international normative structure. In our view the specific features of that structure must be identified and validated in terms of shared expectations and attitudes, rather than in trans-empirical terms.

SECTION 5.2 INTERNATIONAL LAW: ROLE OF CUSTOM AND TREATIES—INDIVIDUAL RIGHTS AND STATE RESPONSIBILITY

(A) SOURCES AND CUSTOM

Traditionally, the sources of international law have been enumerated similarly to the list found in Article 38 of the Statute of the International Court of Justice: [1]

Article 38.—1. The Court, whose function is to decide in accordance with international law such disputes as are submitted to it, shall apply:

a. international conventions, whether general or particular, establishing rules expressly recognized by the contesting states;

b. international custom, as evidence of a general practice accepted as law;

c. the general principles of law recognized by civilized nations;

d. subject to the provisions of Article 59, judicial decisions and the teachings of the most highly qualified publicists of the various

---

1. Statute of the International Court of Justice, annexed to the Charter of the United Nations; signed at San Francisco, June 26, 1945; entered into force for the United States on Oct. 24, 1945 (59 Stat. 1031, 1055; TS 993; 3 Bevans 1153).

nations, as subsidiary means for the determination of rules of law.

2. This provision shall not prejudice the power of the Court to decide a case ex aequo et bono, if the parties agree thereto.

Yet it is generally recognized that rules or standards which effectively influence international action do not always fall within the above categories. The problem of recognizing the development of a new rule from the sources listed is often formidable. A few statements quoted below should suffice to remind students of some of these problems.

AMERICAN LAW INSTITUTE, RESTATEMENT OF THE LAW (SECOND), FOREIGN RELATIONS LAW OF THE UNITED STATES

§ 1, comment *e* (1965) [2]

* * * The growth of practice into a rule of international law depends on the degree of its acceptance by the international community. If a state initiates a practice for which there is no precedent in international law, the fact that other states do not object to it is significant evidence that they do not regard it as illegal. If this practice becomes more general without objections from other states, the practice may give rise to a rule of international law. Because failure to object to practice may amount to recognition of it, the objection by a state to a practice of another is an important means of preventing or controlling in some degree the development of rules of international law.

––––––––––

In a book devoted to, "The Concept of Custom in International Law," D'Amato [3] notes the "tremendous amount of disagreement among scholars and publicists over the rules of customary international law," and Professor Wolfgang Friedmann [4] has written that,

> [M]any important areas of international law are still governed by custom, although the momentum of international legal development is now more and more achieved by treaties. But international society is certainly not primitive in the physical sense of the word—as nations were in the days preceding the industrial revolution. The dramatic difference in the speed and intensity of communications, as between our time and even the beginning of the century, is of basic importance for the methods of international lawmaking.

D'Amato notes: [5]

2. American Law Institute, Restatement of the Law (Second), Foreign Relations Law of the United States, § 1, comment *e*, at 3 (1965). This and other excerpts from this publication in this chapter are reprinted by permission of the American Law Institute. Copyright 1965 by The American Law Institute. See also American Law Institute, Restatement of the Law, Foreign Relations Law of the United States (Revised), Tentative Draft No. 6, § 102 (Vol. 1, April 12, 1985).

3. A. D'Amato, The Concept of Custom in International Law 5 (1971).

4. W. Friedmann, General Course in Public International Law, 127, 132 Receuil des Cours 41 (1969).

5. A. D'Amato, note 3 supra, at 104.

What has not been sufficiently recognized in the literature of international law is a secondary, yet significant, effect of treaties. Not only do they carve out law for the immediate parties, but they also have a profound impact upon general customary law for nonparties. For a treaty arguably is a clear record of a binding international commitment that constitutes the "practice of states" and hence is as much a record of customary behavior as any other state act or restraint. International tribunals have clearly recognized this effect of treaties upon customary law, and historically treaties have a decisive impact upon the content of international law.

C.H. ALEXANDROWICZ, THE LAW–MAKING FUNCTION OF THE SPECIALIZED AGENCIES OF THE UNITED NATIONS
156 (1973)

Apart from treaty-making and quasi-legislative action, the Specialised Agencies also contributed to the generation, within their framework, of customary rules and general principles of law. The process of establishing or developing general principles of law within the Specialised Agencies is *sui generis*. It may be recalled that these principles are found in the main legal systems of the world and States recognising them as a source of international law do not recognise them in a constitutive but in a declaratory way. They do not draw their legal existence from such recognition, they exist prior to it as legal norms at a universal level. Whenever a Specialised Agency sees to it that a particular principle, which is essential for the operation of its legal mechanism, is introduced into the municipal laws of member States, it sets into motion a process which tends to endow the principle with uniform and global validity. Thus, according to Dr. C.W. Jenks, freedom of trade union association can now be considered a general principle of law. It owes its existence to persistent ILO action which penetrated into the major legal systems of the world.   *   *   *

IAN BROWNLIE, PRINCIPLES OF PUBLIC INTERNATIONAL LAW
8 (3d ed. 1979)

Opinio juris et necessitatis. The Statute of the International Court refers to "a general practice *accepted as law*". Brierly speaks of recognition by states of a certain practice "as obligatory", and Hudson requires a "conception that the practice is required by, or consistent with, prevailing international law". Some writers do not consider this psychological element to be a requirement for the formation of custom, but it is in fact a necessary ingredient. The sense of legal obligation, as opposed to motives of courtesy, fairness, or morality, is real enough, and the practice of states recognizes a distinction between obligation and usage. The essential problem is surely one of proof, and especially the incidence of the burden of proof. The position is probably as follows. The proponent of a custom has to establish a general practice and, having done this in a field which is governed by legal categories, the tribunal can be expected to presume the existence of an *opinio juris.* In other words, the opponent on the issue has a burden of proving its absence. * * *

(B) INTERNATIONAL CUSTOMARY NORMS OF ECONOMIC RELATIONS

When we search for customary norms of international law that relate to economic transactions, there is precious little to be found apart from the extensive developments on expropriation of property. There are, however, many international law norms which, although not focused on economic affairs, nevertheless have considerable importance to them. The basic norm of "Pacta Sunt Servanda"—the rule that treaties must be followed in good faith—is a foundation for treaty-based law (which is very important to economic regulation). The general subject of treatment of aliens, of which expropriation of property is a part, is also highly relevant to economic interaction among nations. Even international norms on human rights have been increasingly injected into discussions and negotiations on economic affairs. But let's try to ascertain what, if any, customary international norms exist specifically for economic affairs.

GEORG SCHWARZENBERGER, THE PRINCIPLES AND STANDARDS OF INTERNATIONAL ECONOMIC LAW

(1966) [6]

I. THE FORMS OF INTERNATIONAL ECONOMIC LAW

Compared with the other two law-creating processes of international law—international customary law and the general principles of law recognised by civilised nations—the emphasis in International Economic Law is on treaties.

a. Treaties

The economic interest of States made short work of natural-law fallacies. Writers have asserted freedom of commerce or navigation as natural rights and deduced such rights from any first principles they cared to adopt as the starting points of their arguments. Yet, unless they were quick to reduce their claims to imperfect rights, they merely served to lend a spurious respectability to untenable claims. This was what happened when, in 1824, an ill-advised United States Secretary of State relied for evidence of the absolute right of freedom of navigation on the River St. Lawrence, on natural law in general and Grotius, Pufendorf, Wolff and Vattel, in particular. All that his British counterpart had to do was to take him at his word and raise the issue of reciprocal British privileges on navigable rivers in the United States not covered by British treaty rights.

* * *

6. Schwarzenberger, The Principles and Standards of International Economic Law, 117 Receuil des Cours 1, 12, 14 (1966). Reprinted by permission of the Hague Academy of International Law.

b. International Customary Law

In relative significance, international customary law lags behind treaties in International Economic Law. Even so, it fulfills three important functions:

> 1. It provides the background against which consensual international economic law must be construed.

> 2. In its rules on international responsibility and warfare on land and at sea, international customary law provides the bulk of the rules governing the laws of international economic torts and economic warfare.

> 3. By the treaties and parallel national practices to which, in an evolution extending over nearly a millenium, International Economic Law has given rise, it has made two major contributions to international law at large. By way of generalisation of rules originally limited to foreign merchants, it has laid the foundations for the rules of general international customary law on the freedom of the seas in times of peace and war, and for the rule on the minimum standard for the treatment of foreign nationals.

The growth of the rules on the exhaustion of local remedies, denial of justice, the outlawry of piracy *jure gentium,* and the transformation of the right of shipwreck into the law of salvage are further illustrations of the contributions made by International Economic Law to general international customary law.

GEORG SCHWARZENBERGER, EQUALITY AND DISCRIMINATION IN INTERNATIONAL ECONOMIC LAW

(1971) [7]

* * * In the absence of bilateral and multilateral treaty obligations to the contrary, international law does not ordain economic equality between States nor between their subjects. Economic sovereignty reigns supreme. It is for each subject of international law to decide for itself whether and, if so, in which form, it desires to grant equal treatment to other States and their subjects or give privileged treatment to some and discriminate against others.

———

Sometimes it is claimed that the principle of "non-discrimination", often termed the "Most-Favored-Nation" obligation, is a norm of customary international law, a question to which we will return in Chapter 7. In addition, in the international discourse of today there is often argument over whether there exists in international law some general obligation to assist developing countries in their efforts to make economic progress. Some of these ideas have been incorporated into treaty-based law (such as Part IV of GATT, or

7. Schwarzenberger, Equality and Discrimination in International Economic Law, 25 Yearbook of World Affairs 163, 163 (1971).

resolutions of the United Nations Conference on Trade and Development), so it may no longer be necessary to base such arguments solely on customary law. Again these are subjects to which later chapters, particularly Chapter 20, return. Finally, in Chapter 17 we discuss the legal effect of "voluntary" codes of conduct that have been adopted for multinational enterprises. As we will see, some commentators refer to such codes as "soft" law—technically not legally binding, but capable in some cases of creating "moral obligations" that are impossible to ignore.

(C) TREATIES IN INTERNATIONAL LAW

Perhaps the most important source of international obligation and the one which writers tend to think is most often followed, treaties, nevertheless, pose a series of difficult questions. The basic "core" principle is "pacta sunt servanda." But how are treaties formed? Who do they bind? How are they changed? What effect do they have on domestic law of nations which are parties to the treaty? How are treaties terminated? How are they interpreted? Various attempts have been made to codify or systematize rules relating to these questions, the most prominent being the American Law Institute 1965 Restatement (Second) of the Foreign Relations Law of the United States, and the U.N. International Law Commission Convention on the Law of Treaties, put in final form at a conference at Vienna in 1969.[8] The Convention came into force in 1980.

VIENNA CONVENTION ON THE LAW OF TREATIES

ARTICLE 26. PACTA SUNT SERVANDA

Every treaty in force is binding upon the parties to it and must be performed by them in good faith.

ARTICLE 27. INTERNAL LAW AND OBSERVANCE OF TREATIES

A party may not invoke the provisions of its internal law as justification for its failure to perform a treaty. This rule is without prejudice to article 46.

* * *

ARTICLE 31. GENERAL RULE OF INTERPRETATION

1. A treaty shall be interpreted in good faith in accordance with the ordinary meaning to be given to the terms of the treaty in their context and in the light of its object and purpose.

2. The context for the purpose of the interpretation of a treaty shall comprise, in addition to the text, including its preamble and annexes:

---

8. The Vienna Convention on the Law of Treaties, with annex, done at Vienna, 23 May, 1969 (text: UNGA U.N. Doc. A/Conf. 39/27, May 23, 1969; see also U.N. Conf. on the Law of Treaties, UNGA U.N. Docs. A/Conf. 39/1–28); see further, I. Sinclair, The Vienna Convention on the Law of Treaties (2d ed. 1984); T. Elias, The Modern Law of Treaties (1974); S. Rosenenne, The Law of Treaties: A Guide to the Legislative History of the Vienna Convention (1970).

The revised Restatement closely follows the Vienna Convention. See American Law Institute, Restatement of the Law, Foreign Relations Law of the United States (Revised), Tentative Draft No. 6, pt. 3 (Vol. 2, April 12, 1985).

(*a*) any agreement relating to the treaty which was made between all the parties in connexion with the conclusion of the treaty;

(*b*) any instrument which was made by one or more parties in connexion with the conclusion of the treaty and accepted by the other parties as an instrument related to the treaty.

3.   There shall be taken into account, together with the context:

(*a*) any subsequent agreement between the parties regarding the interpretation of the treaty or the application of its provisions;

(*b*) any subsequent practice in the application of the treaty which establishes the agreement of the parties regarding its interpretation;

(*c*) any relevant rules of international law applicable in the relations between the parties.

4.   A special meaning shall be given to a term if it is established that the parties so intended.

ARTICLE 32.   SUPPLEMENTARY MEANS OF INTERPRETATION

Recourse may be had to supplementary means of interpretation, including the preparatory work of the treaty and the circumstances of its conclusion, in order to confirm the meaning resulting from the application of article 31, or to determine the meaning when the interpretation according to article 31:

(*a*) leaves the meaning ambiguous or obscure; or

(*b*) leads to a result which is manifestly absurd or unreasonable.

ARTICLE 33.   INTERPRETATION OF TREATIES AUTHENTICATED IN TWO OR MORE LANGUAGES

1.   When a treaty has been authenticated in two or more languages, the text is equally authoritative in each language, unless the treaty provides or the parties agree that, in case of divergence, a particular text shall prevail.

* * *

ARTICLE 34.   GENERAL RULE REGARDING THIRD STATES

A treaty does not create either obligations or rights for a third State without its consent.

* * *

ARTICLE 46.   PROVISIONS OF INTERNAL LAW REGARDING COMPETENCE TO CONCLUDE TREATIES

1.   A State may not invoke the fact that its consent to be bound by a treaty has been expressed in violation of a provision of its internal law regarding competence to conclude treaties as invalidating its consent unless that violation was manifest and concerned a rule of its internal law of fundamental importance.

2.   A violation is manifest if it would be objectively evident to any State conducting itself in the matter in accordance with normal practice and in good faith.

* * *

ARTICLE 60.   TERMINATION OR SUSPENSION OF THE OPERATION OF A
TREATY AS A CONSEQUENCE OF ITS BREACH

1.   A material breach of a bilateral treaty by one of the parties entitles the other to invoke the breach as a ground for terminating the treaty or suspending its operation in whole or in part.

2.   A material breach of a multilateral treaty by one of the parties entitles:

(a) the other parties by unanimous agreement to suspend the operation of the treaty in whole or in part or to terminate it either:

   (i) in the relations between themselves and the defaulting State, or

   (ii) as between all the parties;

(b) a party specially affected by the breach to invoke it as a ground for suspending the operation of the treaty in whole or in part in the relations between itself and the defaulting State;

(c) any party other than the defaulting State to invoke the breach as a ground for suspending the operation of the treaty in whole or in part with respect to itself if the treaty is of such a character that a material breach of its provisions by one party radically changes the position of every party with respect to the further performance of its obligations under the treaty.

3.   A material breach of a treaty, for the purposes of this article, consists in:

(a) a repudiation of the treaty not sanctioned by the present Convention; or

(b) the violation of a provision essential to the accomplishment of the object or purpose of the treaty.

* * *

ARTICLE 62.   FUNDAMENTAL CHANGE OF CIRCUMSTANCES

1.   A fundamental change of circumstances which has occurred with regard to those existing at the time of the conclusion of a treaty, and which was not foreseen by the parties, may not be invoked as a ground for terminating or withdrawing from the treaty unless:

(a) the existence of those circumstances constituted an essential basis of the consent of the parties to be bound by the treaty; and

(b) the effect of the change is radically to transform the extent of obligations still to be performed under the treaty.

* * *

ARTICLE 64.   EMERGENCE OF A NEW PEREMPTORY NORM OF GENERAL
INTERNATIONAL LAW (JUS COGENS)

If a new peremptory norm of general international law emerges, any existing treaty which is in conflict with that norm becomes void and terminates.

IAN McTAGGART SINCLAIR, THE VIENNA CONVENTION ON THE LAW OF TREATIES
(1984) [9]

* * * The fact that "international Conventions" are listed first among the sources of international law on which the International Court can draw may imply a value judgment as to the place which treaties occupy in the hierarchy of sources, if such a hierarchy exists; on the other hand, it may simply be indicative of the logical concept that, the consent of States (whether express or tacit) being the method whereby rules of international law are effectively created or accorded recognition within the framework of an international society of individual nation States, one should first apply those rules to which assent has been specifically and expressly given before having recourse to rules (such as those deriving from international custom and general principles of law) whose validity depends more on the notion of tacit, rather than express, consent.

(D) BILATERAL ECONOMIC TREATIES

No attempt will be made here to canvass or catalogue the myriad of bilateral economic treaties. Perhaps most important of these, at least among "market economies" (non-Socialist states) are the "FCN" (Friendship-Commerce-Navigation) treaties, the various treaties for the avoidance of multiple taxation, a long line of "commercial treaties" dealing with tariffs and customs matters (often superseded by modern multilateral agreements) or particular commercial treaties dealing with a specific product group (e.g., textiles or meat).[10] More recently a number of bilateral treaties have been completed entitled "economic cooperation agreements," often providing a loose framework for developing trade between market and nonmarket economies.[11] In addition, a number of countries, including the United States, have developed a program for negotiating bilateral investment treaties, focused on the problem of protecting their citizen investors who invest in foreign countries, and also dealing with some of the problems of the capital importing countries, a subject to which we will return in Chapter 16.

The brief materials that follow should help to lend perspective to materials in the rest of this book that focus on modern multilateral agreements as a source of international regulatory obligation.

ERIC V. YOUNGQUIST, UNITED STATES COMMERCIAL TREATIES: THEIR ROLE IN FOREIGN ECONOMIC POLICY
(1967) [12]

FUNCTIONS OF THE FCN TREATY

As its title suggests, the traditional friendship, commerce and navigation treaty is designed to establish an agreed framework within which mutually

---

9. I. Sinclair, note 8 supra, at 2.

10. See, e.g., U.S. Dept. of State, Treaties in Force (A list of Treaties and Other International Agreements of the United States in Force).

11. See, e.g., U.S.-China Accord on Industrial and Technological Cooperation, signed and entered into force, January 12, 1984.

12. Youngquist, United States Commercial Treaties: Their Role in Foreign Economic Pol-

beneficial economic relations between two countries can take place, creating a basic accord governing day-to-day intercourse between them. It is bilateral, rather than multilateral in nature. Such a treaty is "one of the most familiar instruments known to diplomatic tradition" and probably the simplest type of general agreement with meaningful provisions available in United States treaty practice. It sets forth the terms upon which trade and shipping are conducted, and governs the rights of individuals and firms from one state living, doing business, or owning property within the jurisdiction of the other state. In its earlier forms such a treaty might also contain detailed provisions dealing with consular matters and customs treatment of specific items, or clauses setting forth the understanding between the parties on topics of current bilateral concern. In the treaty with France in 1778, for example, particular stress was placed on protection of goods and ships in case of war.

In current United States practice, the FCN treaty is a comprehensive statement of the understanding between the parties intended "to deal with the whole citizen, in his person and his property, who have lawful concerns in another country. * * *" Such a treaty normally covers the following main subjects: (a) rights of entry for business and residence; (b) protection of individuals and companies; (c) rights and privileges of individuals and companies with respect to: (1) practice of professions; (2) acquisition of property; (3) patents; (4) taxes; (5) remittance of earnings and capital; (6) competition of state-owned enterprises; (7) expropriation or nationalization; (8) access to courts; (d) trade (duties and quantitative restrictions); (e) shipping; and (f) referral of disputes under the treaty to the International Court of Justice.

* * *

The commercial treaty occupied a central foreign policy role during the formative years of the Republic. It served both as a symbol of peaceful relations and a protector of vital commercial interests. In a world of exclusively bilateral relations, it was virtually the sole instrument for important peacetime agreements between nations. The history of this country's foreign economic policy is written in the negotiations on commercial treaties.

* * *

After the peace in 1815, the United States sought to extend the network of its commercial treaties.

* * *

The FCN treaty underwent no radical development either in form or purpose during the years between the Civil War and the beginning of the 20th Century. It was not until after World War I that a conscious effort was made to adjust commercial treaties to the sweeping changes that had taken place in the United States economy and to the new and important role of the United States in the world economy.

* * *

icy, Studies in Law and Economic Development, Vol. II, study no. 1, at 72, 73–76, George Washington University International Law Society (May, 1967). Reprinted by Permission of the George Washington University International Law Society. "Studies in Law and Economic Development" continues as the *Journal of International Law and Economics*.

THE MODERN FCN TREATY PROGRAM—1945 TO PRESENT

After World War II—as after the First World War, the United States decided to revise the FCN treaty and employ it in a program aimed at modernizing its commercial treaty relations with other countries.

* * *

These postwar FCN treaties retained many of the traditional provisions of the older treaties. They differed from their predecessors primarily in that they placed greater emphasis on the right of establishment and promotion of private foreign investment, as opposed to trade and shipping, which were the areas of greatest concern in negotiation of earlier FCN treaties. This change in emphasis was a direct reflection of the increased foreign investment role of American business firms after World War II as well as the fact that, after 1934, the trade promotion aspects of commercial treaties had largely been taken over by the reciprocal trade agreements program, and that the General Agreement on Tariffs and Trade (GATT) provided the principal forum for negotiating tariff adjustment and furthering trade promotion objectives after World War II. * * *

Note

As of October 1985, the United States was a party to 48 FCN treaties, of which 25 have come into force since the end of World War II.

(E) THE INDIVIDUAL AND INTERNATIONAL LAW

AMERICAN LAW INSTITUTE, RESTATEMENT OF THE LAW (SECOND), FOREIGN RELATIONS LAW OF THE UNITED STATES

§ 1, comment *f* (1965)

f. Rights of Individuals Under International Law. International law imposes upon states duties with respect to individuals. Thus, it is a violation of international law for a state to treat an alien in a manner which does not satisfy the international standard of justice under the rule stated in § 165. However, in the absence of a specific agreement, an individual does not usually have standing to complain of such a violation before an international tribunal. Generally, it is the state of which he is a national that has the standing to bring the complaint. Moreover, the state of nationality may usually decide whether to exercise the right. For example, under the rule stated in § 73, a diplomatic representative is immune from the exercise of the jurisdiction of the state to which he is accredited. The state that he represents may, however, waive this immunity.

International law does not prohibit states from granting to individuals rights which they may enforce directly. See the Convention of December 20, 1907 for the Establishment of a Central American Court of Justice, which provides that individuals may bring complaints in that court, whether or not the state of their nationality supports their claims. Doc. No. 12, G/9, 14 U.N.Conf. Int'l Org.Docs. 477 (1945), [1907] Foreign Rel.U.S. 697 (1910). And as indicated in § 2 below, a state may provide a remedy under its domestic law to give effect to a rule of international law. Also, as indicated in § 3(b), an individual or corporation may enter into an agreement with a foreign state by the terms of which disputes arising out of the agreement are to be decided according to principles of international law.

W. PAUL GORMLEY, THE PROCEDURAL STATUS OF THE INDIVIDUAL BEFORE INTERNATIONAL AND SUPRANATIONAL TRIBUNALS

(1966) [13]

Today there exist a number of very important instances in which individuals, groups, and nongovernmental entities have: 1) a right of petition, and 2) a right of action. Beginning with Roman Law, its subsequent impact on the civilized world, and culminating with the contemporary regional movement, one essential conclusion arises, namely *the individual has emerged as a subject of international law.* Therefore, it is no longer valid to hold that only fully sovereign States are procedural subjects of international law. Nevertheless, the individual has yet to achieve a *locus standi* equal to that possessed by States. This conclusion applies to all regional and international institutions examined in this study. Though a subject of the law, considerable improvement must still be made in order to give meaning to the worth and dignity of human beings.

(F) INTERNATIONAL STANDARDS OF NATIONAL CONDUCT

WILLIAM W. BISHOP, JR., INTERNATIONAL LAW: CASES AND MATERIALS

(1971) [14]

Introductory Note. This field of law, corresponding roughly to the private law of tort or delict, may be thought of as the responsibility of states for injuries to aliens, or as the protection of nationals abroad, or as the law of international claims. It is, of course, but one aspect of the broader field which might be called state responsibility, including in addition responsibility for breaches of treaties, for unlawful acts of force, and for violations of international law generally.

HENRY J. STEINER & DETLEV F. VAGTS, TRANSNATIONAL LEGAL PROBLEMS: MATERIALS AND TEXT

(1986) [15]

The growth of the law of state responsibility reflected the more intense identification of the individual (or later, the corporation) with his country that accompanied the nationalistic trends of the 18th to early 20th centuries. That growth would not have taken place but for Western colonialism and economic imperialism which reached their zenith during this period. Trans-

---

13. W. Gormley, The Procedural Status of the Individual Before International and Supranational Tribunals 185 (1966). See also American Law Institute, Restatement of the Law of the United States (Revised), Tentative Draft No. 6, Part II—Introductory Note, at 85–86 (Vol. 1, April 12, 1985).

14. W. Bishop, International Law: Cases and Materials 742 (3d ed. 1971). Reprinted by permission of W.W. Bishop, Jr.

15. H. Steiner and D. Vagts, Transnational Legal Problems: Materials and Text 402 (3d ed. 1976).

national business operations centered in Europe, and later in the United States as well, penetrated Asia, Africa and Latin America. Thus security of the person and property of a national inevitably became a concern of his government. That concern manifested itself in the vigorous assertion of diplomatic protection and in the enhanced activity of arbitral tribunals. Often the arbitrations occurred under the pressure of actual or threatened military force by the aggrieved nations particularly in Latin America.

WILLIAM W. BISHOP, JR., INTERNATIONAL LAW: CASES AND MATERIALS

Supra, at 742

What happens procedurally is that a national of state A who feels himself wronged by state B takes the matter up with the foreign office of his own country. If state A, the claimant's government, believes there has been a violation of international law by state B, it may, if it considers it desirable to do so, take the matter up through diplomatic channels with the foreign office of state B. A settlement may be reached at this stage, after presentation of the claim internationally and some negotiation; both foreign offices may agree that the claim is not good under international legal standards, or the respondent state may admit liability and make reparation. If the two states cannot agree, the claim may be submitted to arbitration, or held until enough claims have accumulated between the two states for them to create an arbitral claims commission, or dealt with as part of a lump sum settlement, often followed by adjudication before a national tribunal such as the Foreign Claims Settlement Commission of the United States.

SECTION 5.3 MULTILATERAL ECONOMIC TREATIES AND INSTITUTIONS: THE BRETTON WOODS SYSTEM

(A) INTRODUCTION

As already indicated, probably the most important multilateral international economic institutions today are GATT (General Agreement on Tariffs and Trade) and the IMF (International Monetary Fund). These two institutions, and the broader concept of the "Bretton Woods System," to which they belong, are discussed in greater detail later in this chapter. However, there are many other multilateral international economic institutions, some of them quite important. In addition, there are some general "constitutional" problems, which are common to a number of different international economic institutions, or which relate to broader themes of possible reforms and creation of new institutions. This section will first introduce some of these broader "constitutional" questions and give the reader a brief description of the Organization for Economic Cooperation and Development (OECD) and the United Nations Conference on Trade and Development (UNCTAD), two of the more important multinational economic institutions other than GATT and the IMF.

The constitutional aspects of international institutions can, in themselves, provide a fascinating and lengthy study. There are many perplexing subjects, and some will be considered in connection with particular functional problems.[1]   Three issues in particular merit further introduction here. However, it should be noted that it is not the purpose of this chapter to suggest reforms or proposals for reform of substantive rules of international economic law, subjects better treated in the functional chapters in Part II of this book.   Constitutional or institutional issues to be introduced in this section are: (1) the effectiveness of rules and the problem of sanctions; (2) the problem of voting in the procedures for formulating new rules or amending old rules; and (3) questions about institutional procedures for the resolution of disputes.   Some of these issues will again be considered in later sections of this chapter, which focus more particularly on the institutional aspects of GATT.

(1) Effectiveness of Rules and the Problem of Sanctions

HENRY G. SCHERMERS, INTERNATIONAL INSTITUTIONAL LAW

§§ 1292–1342 (1980) [2]

The constitutions of international organizations do not provide for heavy sanctions, but many of them make provision for some degree of coercion. This coercion can usually be introduced in all cases where there is a major breach of obligations, but sometimes its use is restricted to particular situations, such as the non-payment of contributions.   *   *   *

In some constitutions possible sanctions are not specified.   The general congress of the organization is empowered to take any coercive measures which it deems appropriate.   In other cases the general congress is restricted to specific sanctions.   Usually these sanctions deprive members from rights or privileges which flow from their participation in the organization.

Two general questions should be posed: (1) May international organizations impose sanctions on Members which violated obligations other than those contained in the constitution of the organization?   (2) May sanctions be taken which are not provided for in the constitution of the organization?   A strict interpretation of powers would suggest a negative answer to both questions.   An international organization's task is limited.   It has no power to go beyond the field attributed to it.   Expediency would also plead for a negative answer, at least to the first question.   A delegation of meterologists to a meeting of the World Meterological Organization (WMO), for example, must decide whether WMO Members fulfil their obligations under the WMO

---

1.   For an example of a study dealing with such issues, see the report of a panel of the American Society of International Law which considered reforms relating to the institutions of world trade. American Society of International Law, Re-Making the System of World Trade: A Proposal For Institutional Reform, Report of the Panel on International Trade Policy and Institutions, Studies in Transnational Legal Policy No. 12 (1976). More generally see R. Jordan, International Organizations: A Comparative Approach (1983); H.

Schermers, International Institutional Law (1980); F. Kirgis, International Organizations In Their Legal Setting: Documents, Comments and Questions (1977) with 1981 Supplement.

2.   This and other excerpts from this publication in this chapter are reprinted by permission of Sijthoff & Noordhoff International Publishers B.V., Alphen aan de Rijn, The Netherlands.

constitution. They may not be the most suitable people to judge whether a certain State is an aggressor or has violated basic principles of international law. On the other hand, international organizations are not isolated units: they form part of a general international structure and therefore should abide by the rules of that structure.

[Professor Schermers discusses a series of possible sanctions, including:

(a) Suspension of voting rights, which he says, "is mainly used as sanction for the non-payment of financial contributions."

(b) Suspension of representation.

(c) Suspension of services of the organization: He cites particularly cases where the International Monetary Fund may declare a member ineligible to use its resources, noting the following cases:

(1) If a Member fails to fulfil any of its obligations under the constitution.

(2) When the FUND is of the opinion that a Member is using its resources in a manner contrary to its purposes.

(3) If a Member fails to exercise appropriate control to prevent the use of the FUND's resources to meet a large or sustained outflow of capital.

(d) Suspension of rights and privileges of membership.

(e) Expulsion from specific organs: He notes that "[n]o constitutions provide for expulsion from particular organs as a sanction, but, a Member normally has no constitutional right to participate in an organ, apart from the general congress. * * *" (at § 1303).

(f) Expulsion from the organization.

(g) Sanctions through other organizations:]

8. SANCTIONS THROUGH OTHER ORGANIZATIONS

Expulsion from some organizations automatically leads to ejection from others. States expelled from the UN cease to be Members of UNESCO. States expelled from the International Monetary Fund (FUND) cease to be Members of the International Bank for Reconstruction and Development (BANK); States that are no longer Members of the BANK cease to be Members of the International Finance Corporation (IFC) and the International Development Association (IDA). In the latter cases the provision seems logical. Membership of IFC and IDA is only open to Members of the BANK: membership of BANK is limited to Members of FUND. In the case of UNESCO the loss of membership following expulsion from the UN seems less appropriate. UNESCO has a separate membership, the conditions of which differ from those of UN-membership. Expulsion from the UN might be for reasons which do not justify expulsion from a specialized agency. It is difficult to see why States, expelled from the UN, lose their membership of UNESCO while other States which (perhaps for the same reason) are not admitted to the UN may become Members of UNESCO. More acceptable are the constitutional provisions of the International Maritime Consultative Organization, also accepted by the International Civil Aviation Organization in an amendment to its constitution of 1947. According to these provisions, the General Assembly of the UN has the right to expel Members of the specialized agencies concerned by addressing a specific decision to them. In taking this decision, the General Assembly can take account of the situation in the specialized agency. It can make the decision for Members and non-Members of the UN alike.

The General Assembly of the UN has no right to expel Members of the other specialized agencies. The agencies are obliged to submit UN recommendations to their appropriate organs. Whether they will be pursued depends on the organs themselves. Only decisions of the Security Council for the maintenance or restoration of international peace and security are binding on the specialized agencies. The Security Council could therefore instruct an agency to impose sanctions on a Member. These instructions may only be issued, however, where the agency is constitutionally empowered to apply the sanctions concerned. The Security Council may not require a specialized agency to take measures which it is incompetent to take.

[Prof. Schermers continues with his list:

(h) Military enforcement: He notes principally the practice of the League of Nations and the United Nations.

(i) Other sanctions

(j) Sanctions by other members.]

(2) *Voting in International Institutions*

One of the more perplexing questions of current international economic affairs is the problem of the appropriate structure for voting in international organizations. There are strong proponents for equal voting, "one nation—one vote," and equally strong proponents for other systems. The following excerpts may suggest some of the policies involved in connection with this question, but they do not suggest the intensity with which various views are held.

ROBERT A. KLEIN, SOVEREIGN EQUALITY AMONG STATES: THE HISTORY OF AN IDEA

(1974) [3]

The resolutions of the United Nations are theoretically capable of expressing the general will of its members. The claim to legitimacy, however, is wide open to question. There is a gross disproportion between voting power and real power. The smallest and financially weakest states, representing a minority of the total population in the organization, possess a majority of the votes. Paying a fractional share of the assessments of the organization, they are able to outvote those paying the highest rates. At budget time, when expenditures for the coming year come up for approval, the major powers, paying two-thirds of all UN costs, feel the full impact of

3. Reprinted from Sovereign Equality Among States: The History of an Idea, at 148–49, by Robert A. Klein, by permission of the University of Toronto Press. © University of Toronto Press 1974.

majority rule. They find themselves chosen to foot the bill for projects which they voted against and which the majority, by themselves could never afford.

All this is manifestly unjust: to the states involved and to the real human beings making up the population represented in the organization. Because members are not bound by a single code of behaviour, because they are not devoted to common basic values and aspirations, because they are not committed to accepting the will of the majority, what emerges from the UN and proceeds to speak for the international community is a particularly corrupted voice. In playing out the myth of democracy and sovereign equality, irresponsibility is reflected in a stream of resolutions on a wide variety of matters based on emotion and without regard to the consequences for the organization or for world order.

Attempts to apply the concept of sovereign equality to the raw facts of international existence have left a path marked by ambiguity, contradiction, and frustration. Ponder, for example, the reasoning of the General Assembly with regard to the inhabitants of the colony of Gibralter who, by a massive vote, elected to remain under British rule. In 1713 Spain transferred the rock to Britain under the terms of the Treaty of Utrecht. In recent years Spain has contested before the appropriate organs of the United Nations the ancient cession of its territory. A 1966 resolution of the General Assembly invited the two parties to start negotiations and both accepted.

In 1967 the minister of state for Commonwealth Affairs, Mrs. Judith Hart, explained that Britain could not simply transfer one population to the rule of another country without regard to the opinions and desires of the people concerned. To do so clearly violated the Charter based on the equal rights and self-determination of peoples. It also violated Britain's sacred trust under the same instrument to promote the well-being of the inhabitants (Article 73). In accordance with the spirit of these provisions, the British government decided to let the people of Gibraltar choose: either to retain their association with Britain or to elect to live under Spanish sovereignty. Both the United Nations and the Spanish government received invitations to send observers. Each refused. According to their reasoning the matter did not involve a colonial situation but the territorial integrity of Spain. The fate of Gibraltarians was a matter to be determined solely by bilateral negotiations between the British and Spanish governments.

Britain, nevertheless, held the referendum. Forty-four voters chose to be affiliated with Spain; over 12,000 elected to remain under British rule. In spite of this overwhelming expression the General Assembly sought to nullify the result. Resolution 2429 XXIII declared the continuation of the colonial situation in Gibralter incompatible with the purposes of the Charter and previous Assembly resolutions. Britain was given a deadline: to end its rule by 1 October 1969.

That day has long since come and gone. Neither Spain nor Britain has changed its position. The UN is powerless to enforce its resolution. Spain and Britain have resumed bilateral talks. But the contradictory levels of meaning embodied in the idea of equality and its corollary, the principle of self-determination, stand exposed. * * *

HENRY G. SCHERMERS, INTERNATIONAL INSTITUTIONAL LAW

Supra, at §§ 681–83

B. Weighted Voting

(i) Desirability

Several systems of weighted voting have been considered in order to compensate the inequality of Members.*[135] The main argument in favour of this procedure is one of equity, that it is unfair for the interests of a large population to be set aside in favour of the interests of two or three other populations which, even when combined, are smaller.

Another argument for weighted voting is its limiting effect on "dealing" with votes. In matters where States have votes but no substantial interests, they may vote for a proposal in order to gain support in other matters instead of basing their vote on the issue involved. The effect of such abuses is decreased by giving States relatively fewer votes in matters in which they are disinterested.

The main problem of weighted voting is the ground on which extra weight should be given. Should it be population, national income, power, or some other criterion?

As a rule, the size of the population seems the most suitable factor, but in several fields this does not seem appropriate. States like China and India, which would thus obtain the largest voting strength, have relatively little interest in foreign trade, air navigation, or safety at sea, which are of great importance to smaller States such as the Netherlands and Norway.

Several other criteria have been considered. Voting power proportional to financial contribution unduly favours the richer States (contributions are based on financial capacity, rather than on the interests involved). Furthermore, this weighting may create problems if the decisions are so important that States would be prepared to pay larger contributions in order to obtain extra votes. Jenks wrote in 1945:

> Weighted voting is most readily attainable in an organization the functions of which are sufficiently circumscribed and well-defined to afford some simple basis for the selection of criteria of relative importance capable of securing general acceptance. Where an organization has a wide range of responsibilities, the factors to be taken into account in assessing the relative interest of its Members either in its work as a whole or in particular decisions are likely to be too varied and imponderable and the relative weight to be attached to the different factors is likely to be the subject of acute controversy.

* 135. Catharine Senf Manno, Selective Weighted Voting in the UN General Assembly, 20 Int.Org. (1966), pp. 37–62, and further literature quoted there (p. 37); Carol Barret and Hanna Newcombe, Weighted Voting in International Organizations, Peace Research Reviews, April 1968; Joseph Gold, Weighted Voting Power: Some Limits and Some Problems, 68 AJIL (1974), pp. 687–708.

Only when the interests involved are specific and isolated from other interests is it relatively easy to find a key for a weighted voting system. If an organization covers many different interests, the use of a weighted voting formula might be considered only for some isolated subjects and either a non-weighted or a differently weighted voting system for other subjects. This will inevitably lead to problems relating to the category to which a particular question belongs. Clear preliminary definitions may limit such problems, but cannot exclude them.

(3) Dispute Resolution

A particularly difficult question that international organizations face is resolving disputes between members concerning interpretation of and compliance with the rules of the organization. We examine this question in some detail in Section 5.6 infra in respect of GATT. The following excerpt offers a general overview of the problems involved in dispute resolution and how they are sometimes handled in international organizations.

HENRY G. SCHERMERS, INTERNATIONAL INSTITUTIONAL LAW

Supra, at §§ 1193, 1203–06

Whoever applies a rule in the first instance will also interpret it. He will execute it in the way he thinks it should be understood. This is why the Member States and the organs of the organization, to whom most of the rules apply, have an extensive power to interpret their rights, their obligations and their competence under the law of an international organization. As long as their interpretations remain unchallenged, the Members will continue to interpret their obligations in the way they think they should be interpreted and the organs will continue to exercise the competences to which they think they are entitled. Sometimes the original interpretation by the applicant is challenged. This challenge creates a dispute between two parties.

Questions of interpretation are actually disputes, or prospective disputes, on the interpretation of the rule by the applicant. For that reason, it is difficult to separate questions of interpretation from disputes. Conversely, most disputes can be traced back to questions of interpretation.

* * *

Many international organizations expressly charge their policy-making organs with interpretation and settlement of disputes on questions concerning their legal order. Others do so without the express authorization of their constitutions, which leads to disputes with the Members involved.

There are several reasons why policy-making organs may be more suitable for settling disputes than courts:

(a) Policy-making organs can compromise. They can look for a solution acceptable to all parties concerned. In court, however, the open clash of two governments and the resulting victory of one party over another can be harmful to the governments involved in the dispute.

(b) Policy-making organs can solve problems by further legislation. They need neither limit themselves to the wording of a text nor to the intention of the parties; they do not have to look back; they can look forward and create a new situation, abandoning the old conflict. Policy-making organs can more easily override specific articles and give priority to the purposes of the organization.

(c) Courts are formalistic. They often occupy an immense amount of time, forbid the States concerned to participate fully in their deliberations, use strict rules on the burden of proof and give insufficient consideration to political arguments. Policy-making organs can produce better results by mutual consultation. The parties to the dispute are present and participate fully in formulating a solution.

(d) Many international organizations are unwilling to leave decisions to outside bodies, either because these bodies are not composed of experts in the matter covered by the organization, or because they cannot apply a weighted voting formula.

It was probably mainly for the latter reason that the financial agencies and the commodity councils charged their executive organs with all questions of interpretation. Another reason may have been the difficulty of agreeing on a sufficiently representative external tribunal.

The organizations which use a weighted voting system, in particular the International Monetary Fund (FUND) and the International Bank on Reconstruction and Development, have adopted official interpretations of several provisions of their constitutions. Observers have been satisfied with this procedure, but not particularly for the reason that weighted voting can be used in interpreting texts. In legal discussions, where the individual opinion of the participating experts may be more important than the interests they represent, weighted voting is not very suitable. The FUND, therefore, introduced a Committee on Interpretation which takes its decisions by a non-weighted majority. The general congress of the organization (Board of Governors) can only overrule the Committee on Interpretation by a majority including 85 per cent of the voting power.

*   *   *

Several international organizations leave the interpretation of their legal order, in the first instance, to their general congress (or to their board). There may be a possibility of appeal to an arbitral tribunal, to the International Court of Justice, or to either one. Thus, they benefit from the advantages offered by settlement in the policy-making organ, without excluding a final settlement by a judicial organ.

(B)   A NOTE ON INTERNATIONAL ECONOMIC ORGANIZATIONS: THE OECD, UNCTAD AND OTHERS

There are numerous international economic organizations.[4] This note focuses on two that are of particular importance in international trade

4. See generally Union of International Associations (ed.), Yearbook of International Organizations (published annually) (hereinafter "YIO"); A. Peaske (ed.), International Governmental Organizations: Constitutional Documents (5 vols. 3d ed. 1974–79); M. van Meerhaeghe, International Economic Institutions (2d ed. 1971) (hereinafter "IEI"); D.

relations: the OECD and UNCTAD. In addition, it gives a brief listing of other important international economic organizations and sources of additional information thereon.

(1) OECD

The Organization for Economic Cooperation and Development (OECD)[5] was established in 1961[6] as an expanded successor to the Organization of European Economic Cooperation. The OECD's aims are to promote growth, full employment, trade "on a multilateral, nondiscriminatory basis" and financial stability. Twenty-four countries are members[7] and one other has special status.[8] All members have a seat on the Council, which meets annually at the ministerial level and weekly at the head-of-delegation level. An Executive Committee of 14 members prepares the Council's work. The Council nominates the secretary-general for a five-year term. Committees function under OECD auspices on the topics of economic policy, economic and development review, trade and development assistance. Numerous ad hoc committees have been assembled. A member is bound by a decision or recommendation,[9] except when it has not voted for it,[10] once it "has complied with the requirements of its own constitutional procedures."[11] The possibility that United States membership might enhance the powers over foreign economic policy of the Executive Branch vis-à-vis Congress was the most serious reservation expressed by many senators in approving the treaty.[12] The OECD engages in economic research and has, among other activities, adopted codes or guidelines applicable to capital movements and multinational enterprises.[13]

(2) UNCTAD

The United Nations Conference on Trade and Development (UNCTAD)[14] was first convened in Geneva in 1964, and later that year became a permanent organ of the General Assembly of the United Nations.[15]

Bowett, The Law of International Institutions (4th ed. 1982); C. Alexandrowicz, World Economic Agencies (1962); and R. Cox & H. Jacobson (eds.), The Anatomy of Influence: Decision Making in International Organization (1973).

5. See generally OECD, Annual Reports; Ohlin, The Organization of Economic Cooperation and Development, 22 Intl.Org. 231 (1968); M. van Meerhaeghe, note 4 supra, ch. 9; OECD, OECD at Work (1969); H. Aubrey, Atlantic Economic Cooperation: The Case of the OECD (1967); M. Camps, "First World" Relationships: The Role of the OECD (Council on Foreign Relations, 1975).

6. Convention on the Organization for Economic Co-operation and Development, Dec. 14, 1960, 12 UST 1728, TIAS No. 4891.

7. Australia, Austria, Belgium, Canada, Denmark, Finland, France, the Federal Republic of Germany, Greece, Iceland, Ireland, Italy, Japan, Luxembourg, Netherlands, New Zealand, Norway, Portugal, Spain, Sweden, Switzerland, Turkey, United Kingdom, United States.

8. Yugoslavia.

9. Convention, note 6 supra, Art 5(a).

10. Id., Art. 6.2.

11. Id., Art. 6.3.

12. See Section 3.3(B) supra.

13. See Sections 11.4 and 17.3 infra.

14. See generally Cordovez, The Making of UNCTAD, 1 J. World Trade L. 243 (1967); Gardner, The United Nations Conference on Trade and Development, 22 Intl.Org. 99 (1968); K. Hagras, United Nations Conference on Trade and Development (1965); B. Gosovic, UNCTAD Conflict and Compromise (1972); Walters, UNCTAD: Intervenor Between Poor and Rich States, 7 J. World Trade L. 527 (1973); Ramsey, UNCTAD's Failures, The Rich Get Richer, 38 Intl.Org. 387 (1984).

15. G.A.Res. 1995, 19 U.C. GAOR Supp. 15, at 1, U.N.Doc. 1/5815 (1965).

The aims of the Conference are to promote trade in the interest of development, to formulate principles and policies concerning such trade, to initiate multilateral trade agreements, and to act as a center for harmonizing governmental policies affecting the area. As of February 1983, the Conference had 166 members,[16] each of which had an equally weighted vote. The Conference meets in plenary session every four years,[17] its Trade and Development Board (open to all members) meets annually, and there are seven main Committees of the Board: dealing with Commodities, Manufactures, Preferences, Transfer of Technology, Invisibles and Financing related to Trade, Economic Cooperations among Developing Countries and Shipping, which meet between Conferences. The UNCTAD secretariat in Geneva operates as part of the United Nations secretariat, its budget being approved by the General Assembly and its Secretary-General being chosen by the U.N. Secretary-General with confirmation by the General Assembly. The Conference has reached agreement on a number of international conventions, dealing with such topics as liner conferences, multimodal transport and various commodities. It has also helped to formulate guidelines for international economic activity,[18] and a set of principles for control of restrictive business practices.[19] It is working on codes governing technology transfer and conduct of transnational corporations.

(3) *Other International Economic Institutions*

The *International Bank for Reconstruction and Development*[20] (IBRD or *World Bank*) was conceived at the Bretton Woods Conference in 1944, established in 1945 and became a specialized agency of the U.N. in 1947. Its aims are to promote growth, trade and balance of trade equilibrium of its members, "by facilitating the investment of capital for productive purposes" with its own loans at conventional rates of interest and guarantees for foreign investors, and by providing technical assistance. Its initial efforts were primarily directed to the reconstruction of European members, but it soon turned to infrastructural projects in developing countries, especially electric power and transportation projects. Only those countries which are members of the IMF may join the World Bank. As of 1985, the Bank had 148 members.[21]

16. YIO, note 4 supra.

17. Conferences have been held at Geneva (1964), New Delhi (1968), Santiago (1972), Nairobi (1976), Manila (1979) and Belgrade (1983). Proceedings of the conferences are published by the United Nations.

18. Charter of Economic Rights and Duties of States, G.A.Res. 3281, 29 U.N. GAOR Supp. 31, at 50, U.N.Doc. A/9631 (1975). See Section 20.4 infra.

19. G.A.Res. 35/63 (December 5, 1980). See Section 18.4 infra.

20. Articles of Agreement of the International Bank for Reconstruction and Development, opened for signature Dec. 27, 1945, 60 Stat. 1440, TIAS No. 1502, 2 UNTS 134. See 22 U.S.C.A. § 286. See generally IBRD,

World Bank Annual Reports; E. Black, The Diplomacy of Economic Development (1960); IBRD, The World Bank, IFC and IDA (1962); E. Mason & R. Asher, The World Bank Since Bretton Woods (1973); R. Lavalle, La Banque Mondiale et Ses Filiales (1972); J. Weaver, The International Development Association (1965); J. Baker, International Finance Corporation (1968); J. Cherian, Investment Contracts and Arbitration (1975); Broches, The Convention on the Settlement of Investment Disputes Between States and Nations of Other States, 136 Receuil des Cours 331 (1972); Szasz, The Investment Disputes Convention and Latin America, 11 Va.J.Intl.L. 256 (1971).

21. U.S.Dept. of State, Treaties in Force 237 (1985).

The *International Finance Corporation* [22] (IFC) was set up in 1956 by the World Bank as a separate entity to perform a function which the Bank was precluded from doing by its own Articles: the making of loans to private enterprises without a repayment guarantee of the local government. Its membership stood at 126 nations in 1985.[23]

A second World Bank related organization is the *International Development Association* [24] (IDA), established in 1960. The IDA offers loans on more generous terms than the World Bank: there is no interest, except for a minimal service charge; the repayment schedule is longer and more flexible; repayment may be by "soft" national currency instead of "hard" foreign currency. As of 1985, the organization was composed of 116 countries.[25]

A third offshoot of the World Bank is the *International Center for Settlement of Investment Disputes* [26] (ICSID), created in 1966 to encourage private foreign investment and settlement of disputes between Contracting States and foreign investors. By 1985, 82 countries were parties to the Convention.[27]

A fourth agency related to the World Bank may soon come into existence: *The Multilateral Investment Guarantee Agency*, which is discussed briefly in Section 16.5 infra and which will insure investments in developing countries against noncommercial risks.

The *International Labor Organization* [28] (ILO) was formed in 1919 as a result of the Treaty of Versailles and was affiliated with the League of Nations before it became a Specialized Agency associated with the U.N. in 1946.[29] Its purposes are to promote improvement in working and living standards, full employment, collective bargaining, and related goals.

The convention to establish the *International Maritime Organization* (IMO) was drawn up in 1948, but did not come into force until 1958, because of delays in ratification.[30] Some concerns of the IMO have been governmental regulations and practices affecting shipping of goods in international trade, unfair or unnecessary restrictions by governments, restrictive practices by shipping concerns, safety of human life, collisions, pollution and

22. Articles of Agreement of the International Finance Corporation, opened for signature July 20, 1956, 7 UST 2197, TIAS No. 3620, 264 UNTS 117. See 22 U.S.C.A. § 282.

23. U.S.Dept. of State, Treaties in Force 238 (1985).

24. Articles of Agreement of the International Development Association, opened for signature Sept. 24, 1960, 11 UST 2294, TIAS No. 4607, 439 UNTS 249. See 22 U.S.C.A. § 284.

25. U.S.Dept. of State, Treaties in Force 239 (1985).

26. Convention on the Settlement of Investment Disputes Between States and Nationals of Other States, opened for signature March 18, 1965, 17 UST 1270, TIAS No. 6090, 575 UNTS 159. See Section 2.3 supra.

27. U.S.Dept. of State, Treaties in Force 257 (1985).

28. See generally A. Alcock, History of the International Labor Organization (1971); G. Johnston, The International Labor Organization (1970); D. Morse, The Origin and Evolution of the I.L.O. and Its Role in the World Community (1969); and C. Jenks, Social Justice in the Law of Nations (1970).

29. Instrument for the amendment of the Constitution of the International Labor Organization, opened for signature Oct. 9, 1946, 62 Stat. 3485, TIAS No. 1868, 15 UNTS 35.

30. Convention on the Intergovernmental Maritime Organization, opened for signature March 6, 1948, 9 UST 621, TIAS No. 4044, 289 UNTS 48 (effective March 17, 1958). Prior to a 1975 amendment effective in 1982, IMO was known as the Intergovernmental Maritime Consultative Organization (IMCO). See generally S. Mankabady, The International Maritime Organisation (1984).

rules of civil liability. The IMO is intended to act as a consultative and advisory organ, and numerous conventions have resulted from its attention to the topics listed.

The *International Civil Aviation Organization*[31] (ICAO) was established by the three companion agreements emerging from the International Civil Aviation Conference of 1944: The Convention on International Civil Aviation,[32] the International Air Services Transit Agreement,[33] and the International Air Transport Agreement.[34] The three agreements impose increasingly burdensome obligations for the freedom of access to airspace, and the number of signatories varies accordingly.[35] In December 1983, the ICAO membership stood at 152.[36] The International Air Transport Association[37] was established in 1945 as a nongovernmental organization of companies from ICAO member countries which provide air transport internationally. It acts as a trade association and has engaged in regulating schedules and fares of international flights, coordinating the activities of its members and drafting conventions on standards.

(C) THE BRETTON WOODS SYSTEM AND WORLD ECONOMIC RELATIONS

At the core of contemporary international regulation of economic relations is a group of institutions and multilateral international agreements which can be termed the "Bretton Woods System." There are numerous other institutions and agreements besides those that are generally considered part of the Bretton Woods System, and the next section of this book will take up some of those other institutions. However, as a starting point for the understanding of international regulation of economic relations, the Bretton Woods System, comprising the International Monetary Fund (IMF), the International Bank for Reconstruction and Development (IBRD—the "World Bank"), and the General Agreement on Tariffs and Trade (GATT) stand undisputed. These institutions and agreements were developed during a series of conferences beginning near the end of World War II, extending to the end of the 1940's. In 1944, the Bretton Woods conference itself was held at Bretton Woods, New Hampshire, in the United States. This conference developed the institutions and agreements on the financial side of economic relations, namely the IMF and IBRD. The GATT, however, was developed

31. See generally ICAO, Memorandum on ICAO (12th ed. 1984); S. Rosenfield, The Regulation of International Commercial Aviation: The International Regulatory Structure (1984); P. Haanappel, Pricing and Capacity Determination in International Air Transport: A Legal Analysis (1984); T. Buergenthal, Law-Making in the International Civil Aviation Organization (1969).

32. Convention on International Civil Aviation opened for signature Dec. 7, 1944, 61 Stat. 1180, TIAS No. 1591, 15 UNTS 295 (effective April 4, 1947).

33. 59 Stat. 1693, EAS No. 487, 84 UNTS 389 (effective Jan. 30, 1945).

34. 59 Stat. 1701, EAS No. 488, 171 UNTS 387 (1953) (effective Feb. 8, 1945).

35. T. Buergenthal, note 31 supra, at 6, 154; see also C. Alexandrowicz, note 4 supra, ch. 6. The United States is not a party to the International Air Transport Agreement.

36. ICAO, note 31 supra.

37. See generally 137 Receuil des Cours 411–506 (1972); J. Braucker, IATA and What It Does (1977).

in a series of conferences beginning in the Fall of 1946, and extending to mid-1948.[38]

GERALD M. MEIER, THE BRETTON WOODS AGREEMENT—25 YEARS AFTER

(1971)[39]

I. THE BRETTON WOODS SYSTEM AS A CODE OF INTERNATIONAL ECONOMIC CONDUCT

The term "Bretton Woods system" incorporates the GATT as well as the IMF and World Bank, because the Bretton Woods Conference looked forward to the creation of an ancillary institution that would reduce obstacles to international trade and give effect to the principle of multilateral nondiscriminatory trade. Although the initial plans for the Havana Charter and the creation of an International Trade Organization were not carried out, the GATT emerged as a multilateral agreement embodying commercial policy provisions essentially similar to the Havana Charter chapter on commercial policy. While the IMF was intended to repair the disintegration that had befallen the international monetary system prior to the War, and the World Bank was designed to stimulate and support foreign investment, which had declined to insignificant amounts, the GATT was intended to reverse the protectionist and discriminatory trade practices that had multiplied during the pre-war depression years. The Fund and GATT were to collaborate on exchange policies and trade policies. In combination, the Fund, the Bank, and GATT were designed to help the advanced industrial countries achieve the multiple objectives of full employment, freer and expanding trade, and stable exchange rates. The shaping of the postwar international economy, therefore, can be understood only by considering the operation of the GATT along with the IMF and World Bank and by addressing the question of whether these institutions have been mutually supportive or have operated at cross purposes.

* * *

A. The Uneasy Triangle

The overriding international economic policy question for most nations has been whether they can attain simultaneously the multiple objectives of high levels of employment (as stated in article I of the Fund Agreement), trade liberalization (as proposed by GATT), and balance-of-payments equilibrium with stable exchange rates (as proposed by the IMF). To the extent that these objectives conflict, some policy tradeoffs must occur.

In their efforts to achieve full employment, countries have often resorted to import restrictions. Even though international trade theory would label the advocacy of trade restrictions in order to promote full employment as a "non-argument" or as a "third, fourth, or nth best" policy measure,

---

38. See generally J. Horsefield (ed.), The International Monetary Fund, 1945–1965 (3 vols. 1969); IMF, The International Monetary Fund 1966–1971 (1984); E. Mason & R. Asher, The World Bank Since Bretton Woods (1973); R. Lavalle, R. Banque Mondiale et ses Filiales (1972); R. Gardner, Sterling-Dollar Diplomacy (rev. ed. 1969).

39. 39 Stanford L.Rev. 235, 237, 245–46 (1971). Reprinted by permission of the Board of Trustees of the Leland Stanford Junior University.

governmental policies have often in reality had this neomercantilistic aspect. The pursuit of full employment also can entail balance-of-payments disequilibrium or departure from the condition of a fixed exchange rate. As a country undertakes expansionary domestic measures to achieve full employment, it is probable that its imports will increase and/or its exports fall so much that a deficit arises in the country's international payments balance. Some tradeoff must then occur between full employment and balance-of-payments equilibrium with stable exchange rates, or between full employment and trade liberalization. Finally, if a balance-of-payments deficit arises, the country will likely attempt to remedy the situation either by undertaking measures that restrict employment and contract income, in order to reduce imports and stimulate exports, or by imposing trade restrictions.

When confronted by these policy conflicts, most governments have allowed the objective of full employment to dominate national economic policymaking even at the cost of a retreat from trade liberalization or pressure on their balance of payments. The central challenge to the operation of the Bretton Woods system has therefore been how to allow nations to pursue their domestic economic objectives without having to forgo the gains from trade or suffer balance-of-payments disequilibrium.

RICHARD N. COOPER, THE NEXES AMONG FOREIGN TRADE, INVESTMENT, AND BALANCE–OF– PAYMENTS ADJUSTMENT

(1971)[40]

By longstanding convention, questions of foreign trade, international investment, and balance-of-payments policy have been treated as separate issues, governed by separate rules and subject to separate consultations among countries. This separation is built into the celebrated triad of international codes of behaviour and institutional supervision proposed during the Second World War. The International Monetary Fund was to look after the international monetary system; its rules were embodied in the Articles of Agreement and an institution was established to interpret, adjudicate, and police them and by short-term lending to facilitate adherence to them. An International Trade Organization was to look after the problems of foreign trade; a long code laid down the rules, and an organization was to have been created to serve the same functions in trade that the IMF did in currency arrangements. In the end, the ITO never came into existence, but its function was partially fulfilled by the General Agreement on Tariffs and Trade (GATT), which laid down general rules governing foreign trade policies and provided a forum for negotiating changes in trade policies (notably tariffs) and for reconciling trade disputes between countries. Finally, the International Bank for Reconstruction and Development (IBRD, or World Bank, as it has generally come to be called) was established to facilitate the flow of long-term capital from the capital-rich areas (initially,

40. U.S. Commission on International Trade and Investment Policy (Williams Commission), Papers II, at 515 (1971).

the United States) to regions needing capital for reconstruction from the devastation of war or for economic development. This institution reflected the expectation that normal flows of private capital would have dried up because of large-scale defaults and other difficulties of creditors during the 1930's, so that some official intermediation would be necessary in order to revive long-term foreign investment. The IBRD then laid down its own conventions regarding conditions it would require on its loans. In addition, the still-born international trade charter contained provisions covering such private investment (especially direct investment) as might resume after the war. These provisions never came into force, so the international economic "system" was left incomplete in this regard.

This institutional division of responsibility at the international level reflected a similar division of responsibility within many countries, including the United States. Ministries of Finance looked after international matters (including capital movements insofar as these bore directly on the balance of payments); Ministries of Trade or Foreign Ministries (the State Department in the United States until 1962, the President's Special Trade Representative thereafter) looked after trade and tariff policies, although many functional ministries had a role when trade in particular products were in question (e.g., agriculture, minerals); and Ministries of Industry generally looked after international investment, largely in terms of facilitating outward or inward investment and policing inward investment (the Commerce Department largely had this function in the United States, although its responsibilities were often vague).

To be sure, various links among trade, investment, and balance-of-payments policies were recognized. A country has to be a member of the IMF, and hence in principle must agree to its code of conduct, before it can be a member of the World Bank. Certain derogations from the GATT trading rules can be made in the name of balance-of-payments requirements, but only with the approval of the IMF; and so on. But these links were de-emphasized under the institutional arrangement and they have frequently been ignored even within governments in the discussion of major policy issues. Yet recent history strongly suggests inseparability of these three elements, and the President's Commission on International Trade and Investment Policies is right to bring them together.

(1) The International Monetary Fund [41]

In Chapter 11 we will take a more detailed look at the International Monetary Fund (known as the IMF or simply the Fund) and its legal rules and operations. In this subsection, however, a few of the basic constitutional and structural aspects of the IMF will be taken up, so that these can be compared and contrasted with other institutions (such as GATT), and so that we will have an overall view with which to approach some of the problems

41. For information about the IMF, the reader is directed to the numerous works by Sir Joseph Gold, former General Counsel and now Senior Consultant to the Fund. See, e.g., J. Gold, Legal and Institutional Aspects of the International Monetary System: Selected Essays (2 vols. 1984); J. Gold, Developments in the International Monetary System, the International Monetary Fund, and International Monetary Law Since 1971, 174 Recueil des Cours 107 (1982).

concerning the "constitutional" questions of international economic law, as posed in the last section of this chapter. For example, it is important to know in this connection, what are the necessary steps (both internationally and nationally) which must be taken in order to amend the IMF Articles of Agreement. In addition, it is important to know who has the definitive authority to interpret the IMF articles, how decisions are made, what is the nature of the voting and what procedures exist for dispute resolution and sanctions.

The IMF's structure and rules were extensively revised by the Second Amendment to the Articles of Agreement of the IMF, which came into effect on April 1, 1978. (The revised version of the articles is set out in the Documentary Supplement.) The United States has participated in the IMF (and other Bretton-Woods institutions, such as the World Bank), under the authority of the Bretton-Woods Agreements Acts of 1945, as amended.[42] Several salient provisions of that act are as follows:

BRETTON WOODS AGREEMENTS ACT
As amended, §§ 4(b)(4), 5, 26; 22 U.S.C.A. §§ 286b(b)(4), 286c, 286e–6

Sec. 4(b)(4). Whenever, under the Articles of Agreement of the Fund or the Articles of Agreement of the Bank, the approval, consent or agreement of the United States is required before an act may be done by the respective institutions, the decision as to whether such approval, consent, or agreement, shall be given or refused shall (to the extent such decision is not prohibited by section 5 of this Act) be made by the Council [a group consisting of the Secretaries of State, Treasury and Commerce, the Chairman of the Board of Governors of the Federal Reserve System, the President of the Export-Import Bank and a representative of the President], under the general direction of the President. No governor, executive director, or alternate representing the United States shall vote in favor of any waiver of condition under article V, section 4, or in favor of any declaration of the United States dollar as a scarce currency under article VII, section 3, of the Articles of Agreement of the Fund, without prior approval of the Council.

Sec. 5. Unless Congress by law authorizes such action, neither the President nor any person or agency shall on behalf of the United States (a) request or consent to any change in the quota of the United States under article III, section 2(a), of the Articles of Agreement of the Fund; (b) propose a par value for the United States dollar under paragraph 2, paragraph 4, or paragraph 10 of schedule C of the Articles of Agreement of the Fund; (c) propose any change in the par value of the United States dollar under paragraph 6 of schedule C of the Articles of Agreement of the Fund, or approve any general change in par values under paragraph 11 of schedule C; (d) subscribe to additional shares of stock under article II, section 3, of the Articles of Agreement of the Bank; (e) accept any amendment under article XXVIII of the Articles of Agreement of the Fund or article VIII of the Bank; (f) make any loan to the Fund or the Bank or (g) approve either the disposition of more than 25 million ounces of Fund gold for the benefit of the Trust Fund established by the Fund on May 6, 1976, or the establishment of

42. 22 U.S.C.A. § 286–86x.

any additional trust fund whereby resources of the International Monetary Fund would be used for the special benefit of a single member, or of a particular segment of the membership, of the Fund. Unless Congress by law authorizes such action, no governor or alternate appointed to represent the United States shall vote for an increase of capital stock of the Bank under article II, section 2, of the Articles of Agreement of the Bank, if such increase involves an increased subscription on the part of the United States. Neither the President nor any person or agency shall, on behalf of the United States, consent to any borrowing (other than a borrowing from a foreign government or other official public source) by the Fund of funds denominated in United States dollars, unless the Secretary of the Treasury transmits a notice of such proposed borrowing to both Houses of the Congress at least 60 days prior to the date on which such borrowing is scheduled to occur.

Sec. 26. The United States Governor of the Fund is directed to vote against the establishment of a Council authorized under Article XII, Section 1 of the Fund Articles of Agreement as amended, if under any circumstances the United States' vote in the Council would be less than its vote in the Fund.

———————

Congress has attempted to keep control of U.S. participation in the IMF in other ways as well. For example, the U.S. representative is to work against any extension of assistance to a country whose government harbors terrorists, 22 U.S.C.A. § 286e–11, and to seek to assure that no IMF decision will undermine the U.S. policy regarding comparable treatment of public and private creditors. 22 U.S.C.A. § 286e–8. In 1983, Congress adopted numerous directives to the Executive Branch as to what policies it should espouse and when it should consult with senior Members of Congress in respect of the IMF. See Pub.L. No. 98–181, title 8, 97 Stat. 1267. One addition requires the U.S. representative to work to have the IMF, as a condition of extending financial assistance, obtain the beneficiary's agreement to eliminate unfair trade and investment practices that the U.S. Trade Representative determines to be deleterious to the international trading system. 22 U.S.C.A. § 286gg(b).

(2) Structure of the Fund and Voting

IMF SURVEY, SUPPLEMENT ON THE FUND
(Sept. 1985)

Membership in the Fund is open to every country that controls its foreign relations and is able and prepared to fulfill the obligations of membership. The structure of the Fund is set forth in the Articles of Agreement, which provide in Article XII that "the Fund shall have a Board of Governors, an Executive Board, a Managing Director, and a staff" and which define their powers and duties.

The highest authority of the Fund is the Board of Governors, in which each of the member countries—currently numbering 149—is represented by a Governor and an Alternate Governor. In most cases, the Fund's Governors are ministers of finance or central bank governors in their countries or hold comparable rank. The Board of Governors meets once a year but may vote by mail at other times.

The Articles, as amended effective April 1, 1978, provide that the Board of Governors may decide to establish a new Council at the ministerial level, which would "supervise the management and adaptation of the international monetary system, including the continuing operation of the adjustment process and developments in global liquidity, and in this connection [would] review developments in the transfer of real resources to developing countries." The Council, which is intended to be a decision-making body, would also consider proposals to amend the Articles of Agreement.

Pending establishment of the Council, a 22-member Interim Committee on the International Monetary System, established by a resolution adopted at the 1974 Annual Meetings, advises the Board of Governors in the areas outlined above, which would become the responsibility of the Council. In addition, the Interim Committee advises the Board of Governors "in dealing with sudden disturbances that might threaten the international monetary system."

The Board of Governors has delegated many of its powers to the Executive Board, which is "responsible for conducting the business of the Fund" and is therefore in permanent session at the Fund headquarters in Washington. The Executive Board regularly deals with a wide variety of administrative and policy matters, issues Annual Reports to the Board of Governors, conducts discussions to complete the process of consultations with members, and from time to time produces comprehensive studies on crucial issues.

* * *

Members' quotas in the Fund, which at present amount to approximately SDR 89.3 billion, determine their subscription to the Fund, their drawing rights on the Fund under both regular and special facilities, and their share of any allocation of SDRs; and they are closely related to their voting power.

Every Fund member is required to subscribe to the Fund an amount equal to its quota. An amount not exceeding 25 percent of the quota has to be paid in reserve assets. The remainder is paid in the member's own currency. The voting power of a member is determined by 250 "basic votes" plus 1 vote for each SDR 100,000 of quota.

Reviews of quotas of Fund members are held at intervals of not more than five years to determine whether quotas should be increased to take into account the growth of the world economy and changes in relative economic positions among members as reflected in the quota calculations. The Fund has generally sought to apply objective quantitative criteria, through the use of quota formulas, as a means of indicating the order of magnitude of appropriate quota increases for individual members.

IMF, THE INTERNATIONAL MONETARY FUND: ITS EVOLUTION, ORGANIZATION AND ACTIVITIES
18–19 (4th ed. 1984)

VOTING

The Fund uses a system of weighted voting power. Each member has a basic allotment of 250 votes; in addition, it has one vote for each part of its quota that is equivalent to SDR 100,000. The basic allotment is intended to recognize the sovereign equality of states and strengthen the voting position of the economically smaller members. The variable allotment is designed to recognize differences in subscriptions and to protect the interest and ensure the cooperation of those members that account for the greater part of international trade and financial transactions. As of November 1984, total votes in the Fund were 930,018. Votes allotted to individual members ranged from 179,433 (approximately 19 percent of the total) for the United States to 270 for the Maldives (see Appendix I).

Governors and Executive Directors, or their Alternates in their absence, cast the number of votes allotted to the members that have appointed or elected them. Elected Executive Directors cast all the votes of their countries as a unit (see Appendix II); however, this does not prevent them from indicating during Board meetings the positions of individual members of their groups. With respect to the Council, provision has been made for Councillors appointed by groups of members to cast separately the votes allotted to each member in the group.

Most decisions taken by the Board of Governors or the Executive Board are adopted by a simple majority of the votes cast. However, for more important decisions, a larger majority is required. Broadly, a 70 percent majority of the total voting power is needed to resolve such operational issues as rates of charges on the use of the Fund's resources and the rate of interest on holdings of SDRs. An 85 percent majority (often referred to as a "high" majority) is required to decide matters concerned with, for example, the structure of the Fund, changes in quotas, the allocation of SDRs, and the disposition of the Fund's gold. The United States alone, or the members of the European Community or the group of developing countries when voting together, can veto proposals subject to a high majority. In practice, formal votes are rarely taken by the Executive Board. In most cases, decisions in the Board are arrived at by consensus; however, these decisions usually take cognizance of the distribution of voting power among members.

Voting in the IMF—September 13, 1985 [43]

	Votes	% Fund Total
United States	179,433	19.29
United Kingdom	62,190	6.68
Germany, Federal Republic of	54,287	5.84
France	45,078	4.85
Japan	42,483	4.57
Saudi Arabia	32,274	3.47

43. IMF, Directory, September 13, 1985.

Other countries have formed into fifteen groups, each of which elects an executive director who casts the total of the group's votes. Each group has from four to twenty-three nations, and total votes ranging from 1.95 percent of the IMF total to 4.77 percent. Groups may have members from a particular geographical area (India-Bangladesh-Bhutan-Sri Lanka), or language (seven Latin American countries plus Spain), or be widely dispersed. EC members are spread over six different groups, apart from the three that have their own executive directors.

Questions

What power does the United States have in the process of amending the Articles of the Fund? See Article XXVIII. What about the EC? Under Article XVI, § 4, decisions regarding allocations and cancellations of special drawing rights require approval by 85% of the Fund's voting power. What powers do the United States and the EC have in these decisions?

(3) Interpretation of the Articles of the Fund

JOSEPH GOLD, THE RULE OF LAW IN THE INTERNATIONAL MONETARY FUND
43–46 (1980)

QUESTIONS OF INTERPRETATION

Article XXIX is an obvious provision under which specific complaints or disputes can be considered. The original provision was modified by the First Amendment of the Articles, but no substantial change was made in it by the Second Amendment. The heart of the provision is the following sentence:

> Any question of interpretation of the provisions of this Agreement arising between any member and the Fund or between any members of the Fund shall be submitted to the Executive Board for its decision.

The provision was unusual when adopted because it created jurisdiction for the Fund to settle within the organization itself questions of interpretation of the Articles that arose between any member and the Fund or between members. The provision required members seeking a resolution of these questions to submit them to the Fund and to no other authority, required the Fund to decide the questions when submitted to it, and provided that the decisions of the Fund on the questions were to be final. The sentence quoted above referred to questions and not to complaints or disputes in order to broaden the category of issues to which the provision related, but there was no doubt that a question of interpretation that was the subject of, or arose from, a complaint or dispute fell within the scope of the provision. None of these aspects of the original provision has been modified.

* * *

Once the Executive Board has adopted a decision on a question of interpretation, any member, and not merely the member that raised the question or the members between which the question arose, may require, within three months of the decision, that the question be referred to the Board of Governors. If the question is referred to the Board of Governors, the procedure that must be followed is one that was created by the First Amendment in order to meet the criticism that the Board of Governors might be predisposed to endorse the decision of the Executive Board. It was also argued that the size of the Board of Governors would impede its ability to act as an effective appellate body. The solution was the creation of a Committee on Interpretation of the Board of Governors, which must consider a question of interpretation that has been decided by the Executive Board but is referred to the Board of Governors.

The composition of the Committee, its procedures, and the voting majorities required for its decisions are left open by Article XXIX. The Board of Governors must close this gap, but has not done so yet. One reason for the omission has been the difficulty of establishing a Committee to exercise important functions if its composition does not reflect the composition of the Executive Board. A Committee of 20 or 21 persons has been resisted by some critics as inappropriate for the task of interpretation. Article XXIX does provide, however, that each member of the Committee shall have only one vote. The decisions of the Committee are the only decisions of the Fund that are taken without the application of weighted voting power. This part of the provision also represents a compromise in the negotiation of the First Amendment with members that were critical of weighted voting power in matters of interpretation. They held that the weight of argument and not of voting power should prevail in the resolution of these questions. The compromise responded also to the objection that on some questions of interpretation the Fund might be acting as a judge in its own cause.

A decision of the Committee is a decision of the Board of Governors unless the Board of Governors decides, by a majority of 85 per cent of the total voting power, not to accept the decision of the Committee. If a decision were not accepted, the Board of Governors probably would substitute a decision of its own. While the result of a reference to the Board of Governors is pending, the Executive Board may determine whether, and to what extent, it will act on its own decision.

A dispute in 1947 about the interpretation of a Resolution of the Board of Governors led to the appointment of a Committee on Interpretation of the Executive Board, which has continued in existence to this day. The functions of this Committee are to report to the Executive Board and to make recommendations on questions of interpretation referred to it by the Executive Board. This Committee must be distinguished from the Committee on Interpretation of the Board of Governors. The Committee of the Executive Board is not mentioned in the Articles, and it could be disbanded at any time by the Executive Board. Moreover, its recommendations are in no way binding on the Executive Board, which takes decisions on whether to adopt the recommendations, in contrast to the decisions of the Board of Governors, which are, in effect, whether to overrule the decisions of its Committee.

The Executive Board's Committee has been dormant for many years. This dormancy and the inactivation of the Committee of the Board of Governors have caused no inconvenience because questions of interpretation have been less divisive than they were in the early years of the Fund. In those early years, particularly when the Fund's financial activities were modest, there was usually substantial opposition to any proposed interpretation, whether formal or informal, that could affirm jurisdiction for the Fund.

Experience and the volume of transactions have dispelled any reflex tendency of this kind.

An explanation of the disuse of the formal procedure for interpretation is that in these matters, as well as in others, the Fund has preferred informal procedures. Only ten questions of interpretation have been settled by recourse to the formal procedure. The last of these interpretations was adopted on July 24, 1959. Nine of the interpretations were adopted at the request of individual members or at the instance of the Fund on the assumption that questions had arisen between a member and the Fund, although this assumption was not based on anything like a dispute between a member and the organization. There was tacit agreement, concurred in by the Fund and members, that clarifications by way of interpretation would be helpful for various reasons. The remaining interpretation was the result of a dispute between the Fund and a member.

A multitude of other questions of interpretation have been settled by decisions of the Executive Board without resort to the formal procedure. These decisions are reached by the same legal techniques as are formal decisions on questions of interpretation and are treated with the same respect by members and the Fund. Few of the decisions reached by the informal procedure have been prompted by anything resembling complaints or disputes.

Questions

(1) Why do you think that there is a preference for informal resolution of interpretative questions?

(2) In Chapter 11 we will see that private parties can be affected directly by interpretations of the Articles of the Fund. Would a national court be bound to follow a formal interpretation of a provision of the Articles? An informal interpretation? The U.S. Federal Communications Commission once held that a formal interpretation was binding on it. See J. Gold, The Interpretation by the International Monetary Fund of Its Articles of Agreement, 3 Intl. & Comp.L.Q. 256 (1954).

(4) Sanctions

JOSEPH GOLD, SOME CHARACTERISTICS OF OPERATION—THE AVOIDANCE OF SANCTIONS

(1969) [44]

A student of the development of the Fund must note how little use the Fund has made of sanctions. This characteristic of the way in which the Fund has operated has had a formative influence on Fund law and practice. The Articles authorize the Fund to take certain actions of which some are clearly sanctions and others have been regarded as comparable to sanctions if only because there is a tacit view that they involve an adverse judgment on the member against which the action is taken. One of the most obvious

---

44. From J. Horsefield (ed.), note 38 supra, vol. II, at 578.

sanctions is a declaration of ineligibility to use the Fund's resources either because a member "is using the resources of the Fund in a manner contrary to the purposes of the Fund" or because a member "fails to fulfill any of its obligations" under the Articles. If a member makes an unauthorized change of par value despite the objection of the Fund in circumstances in which the Fund is entitled to object, this is technically not a failure by the member to fulfill any of its obligations, but it becomes automatically unable to make purchases unless the Fund decides to forestall ineligibility.

The most radical of all obvious sanctions is the compulsory withdrawal of a member from the Fund. This can be required if after a reasonable period a member persists in its failure to fulfill any of its obligations under the Articles or if a difference between the Fund and a member persists on its unauthorized change of par value.

* * *

* * * The most dramatic employment of a sanction in the history of the Fund was the declaration of Czechoslovakia's ineligibility in November 1953 and the decision in September 1954 to compel it to withdraw because of its failure to provide information under Article VIII and consult under Article XIV. There have been no other declarations of ineligibility or decisions to compel withdrawal, although ineligibility proceedings were initiated against Cuba in February 1964 for failure to repurchase after it had requested and been refused a postponement beyond five years from its purchase, and in these circumstances Cuba withdrew voluntarily. France became ineligible in January 1948 when it adopted an unauthorized par value, but ineligibility was automatic under Article IV, Section 6 and called for no declaration by the Fund. Under Article XV, Section 2, if a difference between a member and the Fund on an unauthorized change of par value continues, the member may be required to withdraw. The Fund took no further action in the case of France, and eligibility was restored by the Fund in October 1954, even though a new par value was not established until December 1958. Only two members have had to pay rates of charge in excess of 5 per cent per annum, and then for no more than brief periods. The Fund has made no formal representations under Article XIV, Section 4, and has not published any report under Article XII, Section 8.

The sparing use of sanctions can be evaluated only if it is known to what extent sanctions could have been applied, but it is not easy to arrive at a judgment on that question. One reason for the difficulty is that the practices and procedures that have been developed to avoid sanctions, particularly in connection with the use of the Fund's resources, make it unnecessary to determine whether members are making an improper use. There have been numerous failures by members to observe their obligations to seek the prior approval of the Fund for the introduction of multiple currency practices or restrictions on payments and transfers for current international transactions, but in most cases these failures were the subject of consultation with the Fund after the adoption of the measures and the Fund then took decisions to approve them. Many of the failures to observe obligations in the code of conduct were the result of oversight, but there have been a few cases in which the violation has been a conscious choice under what was thought to be the pressure of events. There have been no more than a handful of cases in which members have failed to honor their financial obligations meticulously. Only in rare instances have charges been paid or repurchases made after the due date, and there has never been a protracted or permanent default. Although there is no legal or logical distinction between financial and other obligations, financial institutions and their members have a special sensitivity about the prompt and full performance of financial obligations.

One must conclude that there has been a high degree of law observance by members, but not complete impeccability, and sanctions could have been applied more frequently than they have been. * * *

Note

The IMF has recently experienced some difficulties in respect of members who have fallen behind in meeting their financial obligations to the Fund. As a consequence, the Executive Board has adopted a policy that restricts the right of members in arrears to use certain facilities of the Fund. See IMF, Annual Report—1985, at 73–74.

SECTION 5.4   THE GENERAL AGREEMENT ON TARIFFS AND TRADE [1]

(A) THE TROUBLED HISTORY OF GATT'S ORIGINS [2]

National leaders never intended that GATT become the central international trade organization. The original idea was to create a broader international organization to be named the "International Trade Organization" (ITO), but history was not kind to that idea.

1. In addition to the materials cited or quoted in the text of this section, the reader may find the following references useful in further research on this subject: J. Jackson, World Trade and the Law of GATT (1969); G. Curzon, Multilateral Commercial Diplomacy (1965); D. Carreau, P. Juillard & T. Flory, Droit International Economique (2d ed. 1980); K. Dam, The GATT: Law and International Economic Organization (1970); T. Flory, GATT, Droit International et Commerce Mondial (1968); R. Hudec, The GATT Legal System and World Trade Diplomacy (1975); K. Kock, International Trade Policy in the GATT, 1947–1967 (1969); P. Lortie, Economic Integration and the Law of GATT (1975); O. Long, La Place du Droit et Ses Limites Dans La System Commercial (1984); E. McGovern, International Trade Regulation (1982); G. & V. Curzon, The Management of Trade Relations in the GATT, in A. Shonfield, G. Curzon, V. Curzon, T. Warley & G. Ray, International Economic Relations of the Western World 1959–1971, Vol I: Politics and Trade (1976); P. Verloren van Themaat, The Changing Structure of International Economic Law (1981); Executive Branch GATT Studies, Nos. 1–13, Senate Comm. on Finance, Subcomm. on International Trade, 93d Cong., 1st Sess. (Compilation of 1973 Studies prepared by the Executive Branch: Comm. Print, March 1974); Evans, Legal Code or Voluntary Contract?, 10 J. Common Market Studies 96 (1971); Hudec, GATT or GABB?, 80 Yale L.J. 1299 (1971); Dam, The GATT as an International Organization, 3 J. World Trade L. 374 (1969). GATT publishes an annual report entitled "GATT Activities in 19——." It also publishes a compilation of Basic Instruments and Selected Documents (BISD), which in recent years has been added to annually and which includes the major actions taken by GATT. See also GATT, Status of Legal Instruments (looseleaf).

2. See J. Jackson, note 1 supra, ch. 2; R. Gardner, Sterling-Dollar Diplomacy ch. XVII (rev.ed. 1969); W. Brown, The United States and the Restoration of World Trade (1950); C. Wilcox, A Charter for World Trade (1949); W. Diebold, The End of the I.T.O. (Essays in International Finance No. 16, Princeton University, 1952).

The initiatives towards the development of a GATT and an ITO began during World War II and came principally from the United States. Two strands of American economic policy converged to encourage these initiatives. The first strand was the general "Reciprocal Trade Agreements" program of the United States, originating with the 1934 Act that enabled the President to negotiate mutual reductions of tariffs.[3] Weaknesses of the bilateral approach were becoming apparent, however, and a multilateral approach seemed to offer some solutions for those weaknesses.

A second strand of American policy recognized the role of international economic affairs in causing World War II, and sought to prevent a reoccurrence of such an event. It was recognized by American policy makers that organizations to regulate national practices affecting international monetary flows, as well as trade, would be needed, and in 1944 a monetary conference was held at Bretton Woods.[4]

In 1945 Congress again extended the Reciprocal Trade Agreements Act.[5] Late in that year, the United States Department of State invited a number of other nations to enter into multinational negotiations for the reduction of tariffs. At about the same time the United Nations was beginning its work, and the U.N. Economic and Social Council (ECOSOC) was established. At the first ECOSOC in February 1946, the United States introduced a resolution, which was adopted, calling for the convening of a "United Nations Conference on Trade and Employment" with the purpose of drafting a charter for an international trade organization.[6]

The first preparatory committee for this effort convened in the Fall of 1946 in London, to consider a "suggested charter for an international trade organization" drafted by the United States government.[7] Following this meeting, a drafting subcommittee met at Lake Success, New York, early in 1947,[8] and then the full preparatory conference convened again in Geneva from April to October, 1947.[9] At this conference, the multilateral tariff negotiations were conducted, in addition to the continuing work of a draft charter for an ITO which was to be concluded at the Havana conference during the early part of 1948.

The General Agreement on Tariffs and Trade (GATT) was drafted at the Geneva conference, simultaneously with the tariff negotiations and the work on the ITO charter. The basic idea for GATT was that it would be an agreement to embody the results of the tariff negotiations, but that it would also include some of the general protective clauses which would prevent evasion of the tariff commitments. It was not contemplated that GATT would be an organization; indeed, when early drafts of GATT included

3. See Section 3.4(C) supra.

4. See J. Jackson, note 1 supra, chs. 1, 2, 18; R. Gardner, note 2 supra.

5. An Act to Extend the Authority of the President Under § 350 of the Tariff Act of 1930, 79th Cong. 1st Sess., 59 Stat. 410 (1945).

6. U.S. State Dept. Press Release, Dec. 16, 1945, reproduced in 13 Dept. State Bull. 970 (1945); 1 U.N. ECOSOC Res. 13, U.N. Doc. E/22 (1946); see J. Jackson, note 1 supra, § 2.2.

7. See London Report, First Session of the Preparatory Committee (1946); U.N. Doc. EPCT/CII/1–66 (1946).

8. See New York Report, U.N. Doc. EPCT/34 (1947); U.N. Doc. EPCT/C.6/W.58 (1947).

9. See U.N. Docs. EPCT/A/SR/1–43; EPCT/B/SR/1–33 (1947); U.N. Doc. EPCT/TAC/SR. 1–28 (1947).

terminology that suggested an organization, these were intensely criticized in hearings before the U.S. congressional committees [10] on the grounds that the President had no authority to accept international organization membership for the United States without congressional approval. It was understood that an ITO charter would be submitted to Congress (or to the Senate). The tariff agreements and GATT were being negotiated under the authority of the Reciprocal Trade Agreements Act extension of 1945. However, GATT was intended to be a subsidiary agreement under the ITO charter, and to depend upon the ITO charter and the ITO secretariat for servicing and enforcement. Indeed, most of the general clauses of GATT were drawn from comparable clauses drafted for the ITO, and it was understood that most of these GATT clauses would be changed to conform to the corresponding version of the ITO charter that emerged from the later Havana conference.[11]

The United States tariff agreements authority would have expired in the middle of 1948 and it was obvious that an ITO charter would not be in effect by then. Partly for these reasons the United States and other countries desired to have GATT accepted and implemented as soon as possible. Because some countries would require parliamentary action in order to accept many general clauses of GATT, GATT itself was not applied. Instead, a "Protocol of Provisional Application" (PPA) was signed in late 1946, by the 22 original members of GATT, and this protocol became effective on January 1, 1948.[12] It is only through this protocol that GATT is applied. Originally it was thought that after the ITO charter came into force, the Protocol of Provisional Application would fall by the wayside, and GATT would be applied definitively.

The Havana conference in early 1948 completed the draft charter of the ITO, but since the United States was the strongest economy in the post-war world, and since the initiative for an agreement came from the United States, other countries waited to see if the United States would accept the ITO. The ITO was several times submitted to Congress and extensive hearings were held upon it, but by the late 1940's the aura of international cooperation that prevailed immediately after World War II had faded, and the composition of Congress had shifted to a stance less liberal on trade matters and less internationally oriented. Recognizing the inevitable, in December 1950, the Executive Branch announced that it would not re-submit the ITO charter to Congress for approval, and for all practical purposes the ITO charter was dead.[13]

The death of the ITO meant that GATT was, by default, the central organization for coordinating national policies on international trade. By now somewhat enlarged by its additional members, the GATT countries recognized that the GATT agreement was ill-adapted to perform the role

10. See Hearings on the Trade Agreements Act and the Proposed ITO Before the House Ways and Means Comm., 80th Cong. 1st Sess. (1947); Hearings on Operation of the Trade Agreements Act and Proposed ITO Before the Senate Finance Comm., 80th Cong. 1st Sess. (1947).

11. See J. Jackson, note 1 supra, § 2.4.

12. Protocol of Provisional Application to the General Agreement on Tariffs and Trade, Oct. 30, 1947, 61 Stat. pts. 5, 6, TIAS No. 1700, 55 UNTS 308; see also J. Jackson, note 1 supra, § 3.2.

13. See W. Diebold, note 2 supra; J. Jackson, note 1 supra, § 2.5.

that had been thrust upon it. Consequently it was decided to overhaul GATT and establish a small organization to operate it, to be known as the Organization for Trade Cooperation (OTC). The ninth session of the Contracting Parties of GATT, (October 1954 to May 1955),[14] was the "review session" at which a number of amendments to GATT were prepared, and a draft charter for the OTC completed.

The OTC charter met the same fate as the earlier ITO charter—Congress would not accept it.[15] A number of the amendments to GATT, however, were ultimately brought into force, accepted for the United States under the authority of the current Trade Agreements Act. Subsequently, GATT was amended only once—the 1964 amendments to add Part IV relating to developing countries.[16]

One legacy of this troubled history has been a long festering quarrel in the United States over the "legality" of GATT, a subject that we take up below in subsection (D).

(B) OUTLINE OF THE GATT AGREEMENT

The GATT agreement, including the remarkably detailed commitments on tariffs that comprise the "Tariff Schedules," fills many volumes of treaty text. The "General Articles" of GATT comprise the basic trade policy commitments of the contracting parties. These articles, now numbering thirty-eight and covering eighty or ninety pages of text (see Documentary Supplement) contain a number of detailed rules and obligations designed generally to prevent nations from pursuing "beggar-thy-neighbor" trade policies which would be self-defeating if emulated by other nations. Consideration of various of these GATT obligations will be found throughout this book, particularly in Part II. Here, however, we give a brief overview of the general clauses of GATT.

GATT is not a single agreement, but is a series of over one hundred agreements, protocols, procès-verbaux, etc.[17] Some of these protocols are amendments to the text of the general articles of GATT, while many are corrections or revisions (in the light of renegotiations) of the tariff schedules. Special "side agreements" have been completed in the context of GATT, which fill out details of obligations on certain subjects, but these apply only to the signatories of the side agreements.

The beginning point for understanding the GATT obligations is Article II, relating to the tariff schedules themselves.[18] The detailed commitments by each country to limit tariffs on particular items by the amount negotiated and specified in its tariff schedule, is the central core of the GATT system of international obligations. The obligations relating to the tariff schedules are contained in Article II of GATT, which makes the schedules an integral part of GATT and its treaty commitments. Basically, for each commodity

---

14. See GATT, 3d Supp. BISD (1955); Agreement on the Organization for Trade Cooperation, GATT Doc. Final Act, 9th Session; see also J. Jackson, note 1 supra, § 2.5.

15. See J. Jackson, note 1 supra, at 51.

16. Id., § 3.4. and Appendix C, at 888–897, list of GATT Protocols and Agreements.

17. See J. Jackson, note 1 supra, ch. 3., and Appendix C. at 888–897 for list of GATT Protocols and Agreements, as of 1969. The Tokyo Round Agreements are described in Section 5.5 infra.

18. See Chapter 6 infra; J. Jackson, note 1 supra, ch. 10.

listed on a country's schedule, that country agrees to charge a tariff which will not exceed an amount specified in that schedule; it can, if it wishes, cnarge a lower tariff, however.

To a certain extent, the remaining obligations of GATT are designed to reinforce the basic tariff obligation; i.e., to prevent evasion of the tariff obligation by the use of other nontariff barriers, which would inhibit imports. Perhaps the principal exception to this statement is the important obligation contained in Article I, the "Most Favored Nation" clause (MFN). This clause makes a central feature of the GATT obligation system, the non-discrimination principle which had theretofore been contained in a number of bilateral treaties. Under this clause, each member of GATT is obligated to treat other GATT members at least as well as it treats any other country with regard to imports or exports.

A third important obligation of GATT is contained in Article III—the national treatment obligation. While MFN provides a non-discriminatory principle for the treatment of imports from foreign nations, the national treatment obligation specifies that imports shall be treated no worse than domestically produced goods, under internal taxation or regulatory measures.

A number of other clauses of GATT limit the type of governmental actions that can be taken to affect imports or exports. Some analyses of international trade policy suggest that there are four basic ways of affecting imports: tariffs, quotas, subsidies and state trading mechanisms. Tariffs in GATT are permitted, but are limited by Article II as discussed above. Quotas, however, are prohibited by Article XI, unless one of the detailed exceptions applies.

Subsidies in GATT are regulated by Article XVI, which, however, does not provide much restraint on what a nation can do. Article VI allows a government unilaterally to use countervailing duties to offset foreign subsidies on goods. Article VI and Article XVI are the subject of a Tokyo Round agreement.

State trading refers to a system of regulating imports by requiring that all imports be made by a government agency or corporation, or by a private corporation to which has been given the monopoly of imports on a commodity. Article XVII of GATT contains some rather general and fairly loose obligations pertaining to state trading. One of the difficult current problems of GATT is the question of how to relate free enterprise or market-type economies, to the socialist-type economies (such as those of Eastern Europe), when the latter utilize state trading corporations for virtually all of their international trade.

In addition to the major obligations outlined above, GATT contains a number of obligations relating to the application of tariffs through customs procedure. These obligations limit systems of valuation for customs purposes (Article VII), the types of fees and formalities that can be utilized in connection with importation or exportation (Article VIII), the types of marks of origin that can be required (Article IX), and provide a requirement for publication and fair administration of trade regulations (Article X).

In addition to *obligations,* however, GATT contains a large number of exceptions. Again, many of these will be discussed in later chapters, but the following overview will give an idea of their scope. It has been said that the GATT is "riddled with exceptions", and that "a lawyer could drive a four-horse team through any obligation that anybody had." Nevertheless, exceptions may be necessary to allow an agreement to be viable, giving it sufficient flexibility so that wholesale derogation from its obligations will not occur.

The most important exception to GATT is also its most general, namely the waiver authority of Article XXV. The CONTRACTING PARTIES, acting jointly can, by a specified vote, waive any obligation of GATT.

A second important exception to GATT is the escape clause of Article XIX, providing for the use of temporary restraints on imports in cases where imports are causing serious injury to domestic industry.

Important exceptions to GATT obligations are contained in Articles XII–XIV relating to trade policy in the event of a balance of payments crisis. Basically, these articles allow the use of quotas (despite the prohibition of Article XI) in such cases.

Customs unions and free trade areas are, under Article XXIV, allowed to deviate from the MFN principle so as to give certain preferred status to the trade of members of the customs union or free trade area.

Article XX and Article XXI contain some important general exceptions which allow deviation from GATT obligations for purposes of implementing national health and safety regulations, and national security.

(C) PROVISIONAL APPLICATION AND GRANDFATHER RIGHTS

The GATT Agreement, central as it is to international trade regulation, has never itself been applied. As explained above, GATT is applied by the "Protocol of Provisional Application" (PPA), signed October 30, 1947, which reads as follows: [19]

PROTOCOL OF PROVISIONAL APPLICATION OF THE GENERAL AGREEMENT ON TARIFFS AND TRADE

1. The Governments of the Commonwealth of Australia, the Kingdom of Belgium (in respect of its metropolitan territory), Canada, the French Republic (in respect of its metropolitan territory), the Grand-Duchy of Luxemburg, the Kingdom of the Netherlands (in respect of its metropolitan territory), the United Kingdom of Great Britain and Northern Ireland (in respect of its metropolitan territory), and the United States of America, undertake, provided that this protocol shall have been signed on behalf of all the foregoing Governments not later than 15 November 1947, to apply provisionally on and after 1 January 1948:

   (a) Parts I and III of the General Agreement on Tariffs and Trade, and

   (b) Part II of that Agreement to the fullest extent not inconsistent with existing legislation.

19. Protocol of Provisional Application to the General Agreement on Tariffs and Trade, Oct. 30, 1947, 61 Stat. pts. 5, 6, TIAS No. 1700, 55 UNTS 308; see also J. Jackson, note 1 supra, § 3.2.

2. The foregoing Governments shall make effective such provisional application of the General Agreement, in respect of any of their territories other than their metropolitan territories, on or after 1 January 1948, upon the expiration of thirty days from the day on which notice of such application is received by the Secretary-General of the United Nations.

3. Any other Government signatory to this Protocol shall make effective such provisional application of the General Agreement, on or after 1 January 1948, upon the expiration of thirty days from the day of signature of this Protocol on behalf of such Government.

4. This Protocol shall remain open for signature at the Headquarters of the United Nations, (a) until *15 November 1947,* on behalf of any Government named in paragraph 1 of this Protocol which has not signed it on this day, and (b) until *30 June 1948,* on behalf of any other Government signatory to the Final Act adopted at the conclusion of the Second Session of the Preparatory Committee of the United Nations Conference on Trade and Employment which has not signed it on this day.

5. Any Government applying this Protocol shall be free to withdraw such application, and such withdrawal shall take effect upon the expiration of sixty days from the day on which written notice of such withdrawal is received by the Secretary-General of the United Nations.

———

Each time a country has later become a member of GATT, it has done so under a protocol with essentially the same terms (but different dates) or through a procedure by which it is deemed to come within such a protocol.[20] While GATT Article XXXI allows a country to withdraw from GATT after six months' notice, the PPA shortens that notice period to 60 days.

The most important clause of the PPA, however, is the "existing legislation clause" of paragraph 1(b), the clause giving rise to what are known as "grandfather rights." In commenting on GATT's domestic legal status in the United States, one of the authors has said:

JOHN H. JACKSON, THE GENERAL AGREEMENT ON TARIFFS AND TRADE IN UNITED STATES DOMESTIC LAW

(1967) [21]

More interesting, however, is the case of pre-GATT legislation. Because the Protocol of Provisional Application applies Part II of GATT subject to "existing legislation," the usual rule making executive agreements superior to prior inconsistent legislation is reversed. Although the Administration has undertaken to furnish Congress and, later, GATT headquarters with a listing of such prior inconsistent legislation, there are several interpretative difficulties relating to the terms "existing" and "inconsistent" in the Protocol.

20. See J. Jackson, note 1 supra, §§ 3.2, 4.4.

21. 66 Mich.L.Rev. 249, 294 (1967). This and other excerpts from this publication in this chapter are reprinted by permission of the Michigan Law Review Association.

As to "existing," the question naturally arises: "existing when?" This ambiguity was considered in an early GATT session and was resolved there when the Contracting Parties "accepted" a ruling by their chairman that "existing legislation" refers "to legislation existing on 30 October 1947, the date of the Protocol as written at the end of its last paragraph." The argument that the relevant point of time is the date on which a given nation signed the protocol was not adopted. Another puzzle relating to the meaning of "existing" is the treatment of amendments to Part II. For example, a sequence such as the following could occur: (1) October 30, 1947, the Protocol of Provisional Application is signed agreeing to apply GATT; (2) in 1950, United States legislation consistent with the existing GATT is enacted; (3) in 1955, a protocol amending GATT enters into force, and this protocol is inconsistent with the 1950 statute. What would be the status of the 1950 legislation? Technically, the later in time would prevail, which here is the GATT protocol. Since the GATT amending provision states that amendments are applicable only to those nations which accept them, the President can always refuse to accept an amendment which is inconsistent with domestic law if he desires to avoid the inconsistency.

An interpretative difficulty also turns on the word "inconsistent." The following hypotheticals will assist in forming the issues:

A. Legislation at the time the United States entered GATT *authorized* the President to impose quotas on widgets, and previously the President had imposed such a quota.

B. Similar legislation existed when the United States entered GATT, but the President only later imposed the widget quota.

C. Existing legislation *required* the President to impose the quota whenever he found fact X, and the President had previously found that fact and imposed the quota.

D. Similar legislation existed when GATT was entered, but only later did the President find fact X and impose the quota.

Under interpretations developed in the practice of GATT, cases *A* and *B* would not be "inconsistent" and would be violations by the United States of its *international obligation* if the quotas were permitted to continue. Cases *C* and *D,* however, are "inconsistent" and would not be such violations. The GATT interpretation is that measures are within the "existing legislation" clause, provided that the legislation on which it is based is by its terms or expressed intent of a mandatory character—that is, it imposes on the executive authority requirements which cannot be modified by executive action. This interpretation is supported by statements in the preparatory work of GATT which will be discussed below.

But what is the domestic law effect of cases *A* through *D?* Where the legislation, although inconsistent with Part II of GATT, is not deemed a violation of the international obligation pursuant to the "inconsistent legislation" clause (cases *C* and *D*), it would seem clear that it should be considered superior to GATT as domestic law even though GATT is subsequent. This puts the domestic law interpretation of the "inconsistent legislation" clause in line with the international obligation, and recognizes the superiority of the domestic law.

In case *B,* the quota imposed, being subsequent to GATT, would prevail in domestic law under the "later in time" rule, even though this would be a clear violation of the international obligation. Case *A,* however, is more difficult. If for domestic law purposes an inconsistency is found, then the "later in time" rule would provide that the previously established quota was abrogated automatically when GATT became domestic law. But the scope of the President's proclamation should be determinative of this question as to domestic law, and the impact on the previous inconsistent quota would depend on the tenor and interpretation of the subsequent GATT proclamation.

Some of these principles apply generally to GATT members of course, and mean that most countries can claim some major exemptions from GATT obligations.[22]

Questions

(1) Suppose a GATT member later amends a pre-GATT statute that established a "grandfather right"; is that country obligated to bring its legislation into conformity with GATT obligations? Suppose an Executive Branch proposal for legislation would do this, but the legislature refused to go along; has a GATT international obligation been violated? In the Trade Act of 1974, the United States countervailing duty law was changed without, however, bringing the old law into conformity with GATT.[23] Did the United States thereby violate GATT?

(2) In today's context (almost 40 years of the PPA), can GATT nations legitimately ask for a negotiating quid pro quo if they are willing to "relinquish" a grandfather right? In other words, must other GATT members "pay" with reciprocal benefits for the benefit received when a pre-GATT statute is made to conform to GATT rules? Would intervening exchange rate changes or other trade policy measures be relevant to consideration of this question? Consider the following materials.

22. The United States has claimed that only the following provisions of its law now or did benefit from this GATT exemption: Regarding Article I of GATT, a former preference in the processing tax accorded to Philippine coconut oil; regarding Article III, former processing taxes imposed on certain imported edible oils; certain former sections of the Internal Revenue Code imposed internal taxes on various imported dairy products; a discriminatory tax is imposed on imported perfumes containing distilled spirits (26 U.S.C.A. §§ 5001, 5007); regarding Article VI, the Tariff Act of 1930, § 303 (as amended, 19 U.S. C.A. § 1303) concerning countervailing duties, does not require the presence of injury or threat thereof to domestic industry; certain provisions contravene Article VII of GATT (19 U.S.C.A. § 1336); regarding Article XI, there is a prohibition on the export of tobacco seeds (7 U.S.C.A. §§ 516, 517), and the President is required under the Agricultural Adjustment Act of 1930 (as amended, 7 U.S.C.A. § 624) to impose import quotas on certain imported products which could interfere with domestic agricultural programs; certain copyright laws are also affected (17 U.S.C.A. §§ 601–03); see GATT Doc. L/2375/Add 1, at 17–19.

23. See Section 10.3 infra.

BRAZILIAN INTERNAL TAXES [24]
First Report adopted by the Contracting Parties on 30 June 1949

11.   In all the remaining cases the rates of tax on the domestic product had been increased, and the differential of 100 per cent on the rate imposed on imported products had been retained, with the result that the absolute difference between the two rates had been increased although the proportionate relationship had been retained.   The Brazilian delegate, supported by one other member of the working party, took the view that, since this proportionate relationship had already been established by the law of 1945, any increase in the absolute difference in the rates was permitted during the period of provisional application, so long as this proportion was retained.

12.   The other members of the working party, however, took the view that the Protocol of Provisional Application limited the operation of Article III only in the sense that it permitted the retention of an absolute difference in the level of taxes applied to domestic and imported products, required by existing legislation, and that no subsequent change in legislation should have the effect of increasing the absolute margin of difference.   To take a case in point, the Brazilian law of 1945 required the tax on domestic liqueurs to be 3 cruzeiros and the tax on imported liqueurs 6 cruzeiros.   The law of 1948 had raised the tax on domestic liqueurs to 18 cruzeiros and the tax on imported liqueurs to 36 cruzeiros.   These members of the working party felt that while the Brazilian Government was entitled to raise the tax on the domestic product to 18 cruzeiros, the new tax on imported liqueurs could not in these circumstances exceed 21 cruzeiros if the increase were to be compatible with the requirements of Article III and the Protocol; it was evident to them that the structure of the law of 1945 (which imposed a margin of 100 per cent on imported products) could have been modified when the rates had been altered.

BRAZILIAN INTERNAL TAXES
Second Report adopted by the Contracting Parties on 13 December 1950 [25]

1.   The working party was asked to examine a draft law (No. 483–50) modifying the present legislation on consumption taxes which has been prepared by the Government of Brazil and submitted to its legislature, and to advise on the conformity of the draft with relevant provisions of the General Agreement and the Protocol of Provisional Application.

* * *

3.   The Brazilian delegation informed the working party that the draft law was a first step in what would be a gradual process of removing all the discriminatory taxes.   The draft law was intended to remove the new or increased discrimination between domestic and foreign products which had been introduced since 30 October 1947, and, in addition—although this was not required so long as the Agreement was being applied only on a provision-

---

24. GATT/CP.3/42; GATT, BISD Vol. II, 181 (1952).

25. GATT/CP.5/37; GATT, BISD Vol. II, 186–87 (1952).

al basis—it provided, on some commodities, for the removal of some of the discrimination which had existed prior to that date.

4. With reference to the removal of the margins of discrimination which existed prior to 30 October 1947, the Brazilian delegation stated that its Government reserved the right to incorporate such margins of discrimination into the customs duties. The delegation of Brazil advanced economic and legal arguments to support this view. The representative of Chile suggested that there might be justification in this case on various, and particularly economic, grounds for the conversion of the internal tax discrimination into customs duties. The representatives of France, Greece, the United Kingdom and the United States, on the other hand, pointed out that while a government would have the legal right to convert internal tax margins into customs duties in respect of tariff items not included in its schedule to the General Agreement, it would not have that right in respect of scheduled items except through the procedures of the Agreement for the modification of concessions. The Chairman expressed the view that the working party's terms of reference did not permit it to reach a conclusion on this matter. The majority of the working party agreed with his view, and felt that it would not be necessary to decide this issue in present circumstances. The representative of Brazil stated that in that event his Government would reserve the right to modify the draft law to retain only those provisions which are strictly necessary to eliminate the new or increased discrimination introduced since 30 October 1947.

U.S. MANUFACTURING CLAUSE [26]

[The so-called U.S. Manufacturing Clause dates back to the Chace Act of 1891 in which the U.S. Congress specified that copyright protection in the United States would only be granted if manufacture took place in the United States. The coverage of the Clause was progressively reduced through amendments to the law between 1909 and 1976. The 1976 amendment provided for the Clause to expire on July 1, 1982. In June 1982, Congress extended the life of the Clause for a further four years. The President vetoed the bill but Congress repassed it with the two-thirds majority necessary to override a veto.

[A GATT panel report finding that the U.S. act was inconsistent with U.S. GATT obligations (Articles III and XI were invoked) was adopted by the GATT Council in May 1984.]

35. The Panel then examined whether this inconsistency with Article XI could be justified under the Protocol of Provisional Application, under which the United States applies the General Agreement. It noted that, according to paragraph 1(b) of the Protocol, Part II of the General Agreement is to be applied "to the fullest extent not inconsistent with existing legislation", that is mandatory legislation in force on 30 October 1947. It also noted that the central point of difference between the two parties to the dispute related to whether the Manufacturing Clause, despite the postpone-

---

26. The description of the facts is taken from GATT, GATT Activities in 1983, at 45–46 (1984). The excerpts from the panel report are taken from GATT, 31st Supp. BISD 74 (1985); GATT Doc. No. L/5609.

ment by legislation of July 1982 of the expiry date of 1 July 1982 inserted in the Clause in 1976, could still qualify as "existing legislation" under the Protocol of Provisional Application.

36.   In order to examine the arguments advanced by the two parties on this matter, the Panel, noting that the Manufacturing Clause had been amended on 13 July 1982, first asked itself whether the mere fact that the Clause had been amended after 30 October 1947 meant that it had lost the cover of the "existing legislation" provision of the Protocol of Provisional Application.   The Panel noted that in the case of the Brazilian internal taxes the CONTRACTING PARTIES had accepted that legislation inconsistent with Part II of the GATT could be modified without losing its status of "existing legislation" provided the degree of inconsistency with the General Agreement was not increased.   The Panel further noted that one of the basic purposes of the provisional application of Part II of the GATT had been to ensure that the value of tariff concessions was not undermined by new protective legislation.   To permit changes to "existing legislation" that did not increase the degree of inconsistency of such legislation with the General Agreement would thus be in accordance with this purpose of the Protocol of Provisional Application.   The Panel therefore considered that changes to the Manufacturing Clause that did not alter its degree of inconsistency with the General Agreement, or which constituted a move towards a greater degree of consistency, would not cause it to cease to qualify as "existing legislation" in terms of paragraph 1(b) of the Protocol of Provisional Application.   In this regard, the Panel noted with satisfaction that certain of the amendments made by the United States since 1947 to the Manufacturing Clause had reduced its degree of inconsistency with the General Agreement.

37.   The Panel then asked itself whether or not the legislation of 13 July 1982 postponing the expiry date of the Manufacturing Clause had merely amended the Manufacturing Clause without increasing its degree of inconsistency with the General Agreement.   The Panel considered that the answer to this question depended on whether the introduction by the United States in 1976 of an expiry date of 1 July 1982 for the Manufacturing Clause had constituted a move towards GATT conformity, which had been reversed by the 1982 legislation, or whether the 1976 amendment had represented only an announcement of the possibility of a future move.   The Panel considered that the response to this question depended in turn on whether, in the circumstances of the particular case, the insertion of the expiry date could justifiably have been considered by trading partners as a change in United States policy (with delayed implementation) or merely as the announcement of the possibility of a future change in policy.   After a careful evaluation of the evidence before it, in particular of the evidence in paragraphs 24–29, and having regard to the fact that the expiry date inserted in the Clause in 1976 was the first such provision introduced since the legislation came into force in 1891, the Panel found that the European Communities had been justified in reaching the conclusion that the expiry date inserted in 1976 had constituted a policy change.   The Panel therefore found that the insertion of the expiry date of 1 July 1982 for the Manufacturing Clause by Public Law 94–553 had represented a move towards greater GATT conformity.   In consequence, the Panel further found that the legisla-

tion of 13 July 1982 postponing this expiry date had, in the circumstances of this particular case, constituted a reversal of this move towards greater GATT conformity and, therefore, increased the degree of inconsistency with the General Agreement of the Manufacturing Clause.

38. The Panel then considered whether this increase in the degree of inconsistency with the General Agreement of the Manufacturing Clause could be justified in terms of paragraph 1(b) of the Protocol of Provisional Application because the postponement of the expiry date had not increased the degree of inconsistency to a level in excess of that which had existed on 30 October 1947. The Panel was of the view that the basic issue in this respect was whether the "existing legislation" provision of the Protocol of Provisional Application should be interpreted as opening a "one-way street" permitting only movements from the situation on 30 October 1947 to the situation required by Part II of the GATT or a "two-way street" permitting also movements back towards the 1947 situation.

39. Since the text of the Protocol itself and previous decisions of the CONTRACTING PARTIES concerning the Protocol are not clear on this point, the Panel examined which of these two interpretations would be in accordance with the purposes of the Protocol of Provisional Application and of the General Agreement. It noted that the Protocol had been conceived of as providing a temporary dispensation to enable contracting parties to apply Part II of the General Agreement without changing existing legislation or acting inconsistently with it. Given this purpose of the Protocol, the Panel believed that, once a contracting party had reduced the degree of inconsistency of "existing legislation" with the General Agreement, there could be no justification for a subsequent move to increase the degree of GATT inconsistency of such legislation, albeit to a level not exceeding that which had existed on 30 October 1947. The Panel further noted that one of the basic aims of the General Agreement was security and predictability in trade relations among contracting parties. The Panel believed that it would not be consistent with this aim if contracting parties were free to reverse steps that had brought legislation inconsistent with GATT and justified under the Protocol of Provisional Application into line with the provisions of the General Agreement. The Panel therefore found that the Protocol of Provisional Application did not authorize contracting parties to enact legislation increasing the degree of GATT inconsistency of "existing legislation", even if that degree of inconsistency remained not in excess of that which had obtained on 30 October 1947. The Panel therefore found that the United States legislation of 13 July 1982 postponing the expiry date of the Manufacturing Clause could not be justified under the Protocol of Provisional Application.

Note

It can be argued that the grandfather rights problem of GATT, which has had such importance in the past, is now largely over. The most critical grandfather right was the U.S. right to impose countervailing duties to offset subsidies without establishing injury to U.S. industry. (We come back to that in Section 10.3 supra.) Many other grandfather rights have gradually disappeared over the years through changes of domestic law, etc. In 1955 the GATT tried to inventory these rights and collected country notifications. It might be argued that unnotified rights were then lost, but unfortunately some notifications "reserve" against this possibility.

The EC has a particular situation. Not only did some member states not notify any measures in the 1955 exercise, but external trade of the EC, pursuant to the 1957 Treaty of Rome, is now regulated by EC institutions. In bringing this about, the EC issued regulations and other legal measures, and unless these expressly preserved grandfather rights, it can be argued that they are subsequent legislation and therefore not entitled to grandfather treatment. In short, harmonization may have extinguished all or nearly all GATT grandfather rights at least as to matters within the EC common commercial policy.

When the United States accepted the Tokyo Round agreement on subsidies, it largely (but not completely) gave up its countervailing duty grandfather right, and besides that and the Manufacturing Clause (mentioned above), the U.S. claims very little else (although the 1955 waiver for U.S. legislation on agriculture restrictions discussed in Section 14.2 infra, created a new set of exceptional rights). Whether there are other significant grandfather rights still extant has been very difficult to ascertain. The issue may gradually fade away.

(D) VALIDITY OF GATT IN U.S. LAW AND DOMESTIC LAW APPLICATION

GATT is an executive agreement entered into by the President of the United States. Because Congress never explicitly approved GATT, questions have been raised from time to time as to whether the President had the authority to enter into GATT and as to the status of GATT in domestic U.S. law, i.e. is it a self-executing agreement and does it apply to the states? [27]

As to the question of GATT's self-executing nature, one of the authors has argued that although GATT itself was to be self-executing, application under the Protocol of Provisional Application is not self-executing. Nevertheless, under statutory authority giving the President the power to "proclaim" trade agreements,[28] if the President had the authority to enter into GATT, he had the authority to make GATT part of United States domestic law, which he did for all of GATT except Part IV.

As to the more basic question of whether the President exceeded his powers under his trade agreement authority when he entered into GATT, consider the following:

JOHN H. JACKSON, THE GENERAL AGREEMENT ON TARIFFS AND TRADE IN UNITED STATES DOMESTIC LAW

Supra, at 259–60

From examining the text of the [trade agreements authority], one can see that it places no *explicit* hurdle against multilateral trade agreements.

---

27. In Section 3.3 supra, we dealt generally with the problems in U.S. law of international agreements, both in respect of how they are properly accepted by the United States as binding agreements and their application as domestic law.

28. See discussion in Section 3.4(C) supra.

Furthermore, it was stressed in testimony before the congressional committee that the 1947 GATT negotiations would in reality be "bilateral," as before, with the results of the many bilateral negotiations simply drawn together in one instrument, for the sake of convenience. Even an opposing Congressman commented that merely because the result was one instrument signed by all, did not in itself mean that the President had exceeded his statutory authority. Thus, one can conclude that GATT does not go beyond the statutory authority merely because of its multilateral nature.

A more serious statutory assault on GATT is the argument that specific provisions of GATT exceed the authority delegated to the President by the Trade Agreements Act. Careful analysis is required to evaluate this argument, but to discuss each clause of GATT here would be tedious and lengthy. Appendix A outlines the sources, if the reader wishes to pursue the matter as to any specific article of GATT. Without reference to specific GATT provisions, however, the arguments for the statutory validity of our adherence to GATT can be summarized as follows: (1) the language of the Statute can be read to permit United States entry into GATT, since it authorizes "trade agreements" either without explicit limitation or with limitations that can be interpreted not to preclude an agreement such as GATT; (2) the legislative history shows that provisions such as those in GATT were contemplated by Congress; (3) prior trade agreements known to Congress had provisions like those of GATT, thus further evidencing congressional intent; (4) later actions of Congress can be taken as recognizing or accepting GATT; and (5) several court cases, while not directly litigating the validity of GATT, have resulted in decisions and opinions that necessarily imply its validity.

———

In the early years of GATT, congressional antagonism led Congress on at least one occasion to specify in a statute that "no trade agreement * * * shall be applied in a manner inconsistent with the requirements of this section." [29] In extensions of the trade agreements authority in 1953, 1954, 1955 and 1958, Congress inserted a clause which read, "the enactment of this Act shall not be construed to determine or indicate the approval or disapproval by the Congress of the Executive Agreements known as the General Agreement on Tariffs and Trade." [30] In the Trade Act of 1974, Congress for the first time explicitly provided authority to appropriate funds to meet the U.S. obligation to contribute to the GATT budget. (Prior to that action the President had used other funding sources under his control, such as his contingency funds, but always reported to Congress on his action.) The 1974 statutory clause (Section 121(d)) reads (still somewhat begrudgingly!): "This authorization does not imply approval or disapproval by the Congress of *all* articles of the General Agreement on Tariffs and Trade" (emphasis supplied).

It would seem that an issue like this, after such a long history of recognition by the U.S. government of the validity and binding nature of

29. 65 Stat. 75 (1951).

30. 72 Stat. 673 (1958); 69 Stat. 162 (1955); 68 Stat. 360 (1954); 67 Stat. 472 (1953).

GATT, would be laid to rest. Yet in a 1983 report by the House Commerce Committee concerning a proposal for a "domestic content" requirement on automobiles sold in the United States, the Committee stated: "GATT is an executive agreement, never ratified by the Senate under the Constitution." [31] A footnote to the statement reads as follows:

> The American Law Division of the Congressional Research Service (CRS) in a June 6, 1983 memorandum commented on the legal nature of GATT and said:

> > Some ambiguity surrounds the precise legal nature of the General Agreement on Tariffs and Trade (GATT). GATT came into force for the United States on January 1, 1948, pursuant to a Protocol of Provisional Application to which the United States agreed to (sic) by way of an executive agreement. Some courts apparently refuse to give full legal effect to GATT since Congress never ratified it. See, e.g., Sneaker Circus, Inc. v. Carter, 457 F.Supp. 771, (E.D.N.Y.1978), aff'd 614 F.2d 1290 (2d Cir.1979).

> > The Conference Report (H.Rept. No. 93–1644, December 19, 1974, p. 27) concerning the Trade Act of 1974 notes a provision was added to section 121 of the Act stating that the authorization of appropriations for payment by the United States of its share of expenses to GATT "does not imply approval or disapproval by the Congress of all articles of the GATT."

The footnote is somewhat misleading. The Second Circuit did not find it necessary to address this issue in *Sneaker Circus*. In the lower court, Judge Costantino had stated, "Plaintiff's claim that the President's action violated the General Agreement on Tariff and Trade * * * is likewise without merit, since Congress has never ratified GATT," 457 F.Supp. at 795, citing United States v. Yoshida Intl., Inc., 526 F.2d 560, 575 n. 22 (C.C.P.A.1975). (The *Yoshida* court did *not* hold that GATT was not a binding international agreement.) Judge Costantino's statement seems to be directly inconsistent with the Supreme Court's holding in the *Belmont* case, discussed in Section 3.3 supra. In any event, he went on to note that "even if GATT were applicable," its provisions were complied with. Id.

In any event, having made the above quoted statement, the Committee did not claim that GATT was an invalid agreement, but rather went on to argue that the proposal was consistent with GATT. The fact that the Committee felt it necessary to argue that the proposal was GATT consistent is itself very interesting to the question of appraising the effectiveness of GATT.

The authors are aware of no U.S. state or federal court which has held GATT not to be a binding international agreement for the United States, and many cases have applied the rules of GATT.[32] The situation as to the agreements resulting from the GATT-sponsored Tokyo Round negotiation is entirely different, as was discussed in Section 3.4(E).

31. H.Rep. No. 98–287, 98th Cong., 1st Sess., part I, at 22 (1983).

32. See e.g., Baldwin-Lima-Hamilton Corp. v. Superior Ct., 208 Cal.App.2d 803, 25 Cal. Rptr. 798 (1962) (Section 8.4(A) infra); Bethle- hem Steel Corp. v. Board of Commrs., 276 Cal. App.2d 221, 80 Cal.Rptr. 800 (1969) (Section 3.6(D) supra); Territory v. Ho, 41 Hawaii 565 (1957) (Section 8.3(B) infra).

There is, however, a perplexing question of the relation of GATT obligations to state laws in the United States. This stems from the language of GATT Article XXIV, paragraph 12, which reads:

> 12. Each contracting party shall take such reasonable measures as may be available to it to ensure observance of the provisions of this Agreement by the regional and local governments and authorities within its territory.

The following extract may help to focus the issues presented by this paragraph.

JOHN H. JACKSON, THE GENERAL AGREEMENT ON TARIFFS AND TRADE IN UNITED STATES DOMESTIC LAW

Supra, at 302–04

Simple and straightforward as it appears, this language contains an ambiguity that has an important impact on the domestic law application of GATT. The opposing interpretations can be expressed as follows:

(A) The language does not change the binding application of GATT to political subdivisions, but it recognizes that in a federal system certain matters are legally within the power of subdivisions and beyond the control of the central government. In such a case, the central government is not in breach of its international obligations when a subdivision violates GATT, as long as the central government does everything *within its power* to ensure local observance of GATT.

(B) On the contrary, this language indicates that GATT was not intended to apply as a matter of law against local subdivisions at all, and even when the central government has legal power to require local observance of GATT, it is not obligated under GATT to do so, but merely to take "reasonable measures."

If the second interpretation is correct, then GATT cannot be invoked as a matter of law in any state proceeding involving state law. This precise issue has risen in several cases, including a very recent California case. The unanimous conclusion of the courts thus far has been that GATT does apply to and override state or territorial law. However, the State Department took the contrary position in a letter to the Hawaii Territorial Supreme Court in the earliest of these cases. This letter, signed by the then State Department Legal Advisor, Herman Phleger, referring to Article XXIV:12, stated:

> This provision * * * has always been interpreted as preventing the General Agreement from overriding legislation of political subdivisions of contracting parties inconsistent with the provisions of the Agreement; by placing upon contracting parties the obligation to take reasonable measures to obtain observance of the Agreement by such subdivisions, the parties indicated that as a matter of law the General Agreement did not override such laws. * * * In light of the provisions of paragraph 12 of Article XXIV * * * the reliance by the Supreme Court of the Territory on Article VI, clause 2 of the United States Constitution to invalidate the legislation would appear to have been based on a misconception of the General

Agreement and of its effect on the legislation of the parties to it ✳ ✳ ✳ it is suggested that you might desire to request a rehearing of the case on the basis that the particular constitutional grounds relied on are not appropriate in view of paragraph 12 of Article XXIV.

This letter is consistent with the testimony of a State Department official in hearings before a Senate Committee in 1949, one-and-one-half years after GATT was signed. ✳ ✳ ✳

The actual drafting history of GATT, however, leaves one with a somewhat different impression. The language of article XXIV:12 was drawn directly from an identical provision that was in the draft ITO Charter at the time the GATT draft was formulated.

✳ ✳ ✳

What, then, can be concluded from the preparatory history of article XXIV:12? The fragments of that history which were recorded suggest that this clause was intended to apply only to the situation in which the central government did not have the constitutional power to control the subsidiary governments. Australia and other countries made reference to this situation. The United States delegate did likewise, adding his tentative judgment that the United States did not find itself in this circumstance. Thus, it can be argued that interpretation (A) which was presented at the outset of this section is the correct one, despite the opposing view expressed in the 1949 Senate Finance Committee hearings.

(E) AMENDING GATT

Article XXX of GATT establishes the basic amending procedure, requiring two-thirds acceptance of amendments for most of GATT, but unanimous acceptance for amendment of Part I [33] (which includes the Article I MFN clause and Article II governing the tariff bindings). Amendments, however, apply only to those countries which accept them, giving rise to the possibility of confusing divergence among the obligations of members, as well as some interesting procedural dilemmas (e.g., suppose an amendment changes a two-thirds vote requirement to a majority vote requirement, which would be required if some nations refused to accept the amendment.) [34] In GATT's early years, amendments were fairly frequent (in all there have been 13 amendment agreements that have entered into force). [35] As membership (and diversity of viewpoint) has increased, however, it has been increasingly difficult to amend GATT. Since the 1955 GATT Review Session agreements, only one amendment of GATT has occurred—the amendment adding Part IV (relating to developing countries). Several of the 1955 amendments never came into force and were finally dropped, [36] because several members held out from the unanimity requirement. It is generally considered today almost impossible to amend GATT because of the stringent vote and proce-

33. Unanimity is also required to amend Articles XXIX and XXX of the GATT, which in turn govern amendments. See also J. Jackson, note 1 supra, § 3.6.

34. See J. Jackson, note 1 supra, § 3.6. Suppose, for example, a GATT working party were constituted to review actions taken by a country under an amended article. May the GATT member which had not accepted the amendment participate in the working party?

35. A number of these early amendments were designed to help shape GATT for its more important role due to the demise of the ITO.

36. See J. Jackson, note 1 supra, at 79, 67.

dural requirements, coupled with the wide divergence of interests among the greatly enlarged membership.

Some GATT articles are substantially out of date and new circumstances have arisen which GATT does not cover, yet amendments have not been made. As indicated above, interested nations have instead looked to "side agreements," negotiated and often administered in the context of GATT, but applicable only to those who join the side agreement. As discussed in Section 5.5, this occurred particularly in the Tokyo Round.

The increasing use of side agreements, however, poses some problems and some risks. One risk is the danger that not all appropriate interests will be adequately considered in the formulation of the agreement. Problems posed include the MFN status of actions under the agreement (theoretically each member of an agreement must extend the benefits of that agreement's obligations to all GATT members if the subject matter falls within Article I of GATT) and the relationship of the GATT dispute settlement mechanism to disputes under a side agreement.

(F) CONTRACTING PARTIES ACTING JOINTLY AND ARTICLE XXV OF GATT

The draftsmen of GATT at the Geneva conference in 1947 tried to avoid giving GATT the characteristics of an "organization", particularly after U.S. congressional hearings and criticism of proposals that "looked like" an organization.[37] Nevertheless, a multilateral agreement of the importance and complexity of GATT requires some "tending," so provision was made for the "CONTRACTING PARTIES" to act "jointly" on various matters, so as to achieve some necessary flexibility. Several dozen clauses in GATT grant various voting and decision authorities to the CONTRACTING PARTIES [38] (expressed in capitals when designated in their collective capacity), but Article XXV sets forth a general voting system (one nation—one vote, with decisions by majority of votes cast unless otherwise specified) and states that,

> 1. Representatives of the contracting parties shall meet from time to time for the purpose of giving effect to those provisions of this Agreement which involve joint action and, generally, with a view to facilitating the operation and furthering the objectives of this Agreement.

This language is remarkably broad, and although cautiously utilized (at least in the early years) is the basis for much GATT activity. For the United States, for instance, this language could pose a danger. First, the United States is increasingly outvoted in a GATT with 91 members,[39] over two-thirds of which are developing countries, and over two-thirds of which are formally associated in one status or another with the European Community. Second, a nation's vote is cast by the Executive Branch of its government, and for the United States (possibly other countries as well) an Executive decision to vote for a measure could result in its accepting a binding international obligation, without participation of its Legislative Branch. In practice, however, this is probably not a realistic danger, since the preparatory work, the failure of the ITO and OTC, the criticism of Congress, and the

---

37. See note 10 supra.

38. See J. Jackson, note 1 supra, at 128.

39. GATT, 31st Supp. BISD viii (1985). Hong Kong became the 91st party in 1986.

worry over voting strength, have led the Contracting Parties to be cautious in voting additional obligations. A short withdrawal notice period and the relative ease of breaching obligations have also been sources of caution. Most efforts in GATT get accomplished through a process of negotiation and compromise, with varying degrees of formality and a tacit understanding that agreement is necessary among countries with important economic influence. Yet the waiver power, and the shortcomings of the enforcement and dispute settlement procedures (see below), have been abused.

One important question of the scope of authority under Article XXV is whether the CONTRACTING PARTIES have the power to make definitive interpretations of the General Agreement, which interpretations are binding

GATT MEMBERSHIP AS OF FEBRUARY 1985

Contracting Parties to the General Agreement (90)

Argentina	Ghana	Norway
Australia	Greece	Pakistan
Austria	Guyana	Peru
Bangladesh	Haiti	Philippines
Barbados	Hungary	Poland
Belgium	Iceland	Portugal
Belize	India	Romania
Benin	Indonesia	Rwanda
Brazil	Ireland	Senegal
Burkina Faso	Israel	Sierra Leone
Burma	Italy	Singapore
Burundi	Ivory Coast	South Africa
Cameroon	Jamaica	Spain
Canada	Japan	Sri Lanka
Central African Republic	Kenya	Suriname
Chad	Korea, Rep. of	Sweden
Chile	Kuwait	Switzerland
Colombia	Luxembourg	Tanzania
Congo	Madagascar	Thailand
Cuba	Malawi	Togo
Cyprus	Malaysia	Trinidad and Tobago
Czechoslovakia	Maldives	Turkey
Denmark	Malta	Uganda
Dominican Republic	Mauritania	United Kingdom
Egypt	Mauritius	United States
Finland	Netherlands	Uruguay
France	New Zealand	Yugoslavia
Gabon	Nicaragua	Zaire
Gambia	Niger	Zambia
Germany, Fed. Rep. of	Nigeria	Zimbabwe

Acceded Provisionally (1)   Tunisia

Countries applying the General Agreement on a de facto *basis (31)*

Algeria	Grenada	St. Lucia
Angola	Guinea-Bissau	St. Vincent
Antigua and Barbuda	Kampuchea	Sao Tomé and Principe
Bahamas	Kiribati	Seychelles
Bahrain	Lesotho	Solomon Islands
Botswana	Mali	Swaziland
Brunei Darussalam	Mozambique	Tonga
Cape Verde	Papua New Guinea	Tuvalu
Dominica	Qatar	United Arab Emirates
Equatorial Guinea	St. Christopher and Nevis	Yemen, Democratic
Fiji		

on all members. For example, the CONTRACTING PARTIES, in a decision of 9 August, 1949, ruled: [40]

> The reduction of the rate of duty on a product, provided for in a schedule to the General Agreement, below the rate set forth therein, does not require unanimous consent of the CONTRACTING PARTIES.

From time to time, various working groups or panels of GATT report their interpretations of the General Agreement, and these reports will be "adopted" by the CONTRACTING PARTIES. In addition, once in a while the chairman of the CONTRACTING PARTIES will make an "interpretative ruling", and no objection will be raised in the CONTRACTING PARTIES' meeting.[41]

Queries: (1) Do any of these interpretations have formal binding status on GATT members, and if so, why? Does Article XXV, paragraph 1 provide the legal underpinning for binding interpretations? [42] Contrast the formal authority and procedure for interpretation contained in the Articles of Agreement of the International Monetary Fund.[43] The interpretation of treaties under international law in general is discussed at Section 5.2(C) supra.

(2) Would a country's vote on an interpretative measure affect whether that country would be bound by the interpretation? What about a statement of approval (on the record) by a country's representative in a working group meeting which approves a particular interpretation?

(G) WAIVERS

Article XXV, paragraph 5 provides, in very broad language, power to the CONTRACTING PARTIES to waive any GATT obligation "in exceptional circumstances not otherwise provided for * * *" by a two-thirds majority of votes cast, including at least half of all the Contracting Parties. This authority has been widely used [44] (over 50 times) and raises an important question: How can the waiver power be distinguished from an amendment of GATT? The following document bears on this problem:

ARTICLE XXV:5(a)

Applicability of the Provisions of Article XXV:5(a) to Obligations defined in Part I of the General Agreement [45]

1. In Review Working Party II at the Ninth Session the representative of Cuba asked for a legal opinion as to whether the CONTRACTING PARTIES could grant, by the majority specified in paragraph 5(a) of Article XXV, a waiver of obligations which a contracting party has assumed under Part I of the Agreement. The Executive Secretary gave his opinion that the CONTRACTING PARTIES could grant such a waiver by a two-thirds majority. (See the last section of paragraph 6, Third Supplement, page 208). At

---

40. GATT, BISD Vol. II, 11 (1952); see also J. Jackson, note 1 supra, at 21.

41. See GATT, BISD Vol. II, 12 (1952) (Ruling by the Chairman on 24 August, 1948).

42. See J. Jackson, note 1 supra, at 132 and 23.

43. See Section 5.3(C)(3) supra.

44. See generally J. Jackson, note 1 supra, ch. 22, and particularly at 549, the chart of waivers granted by the CONTRACTING PARTIES under Art. XXV.

45. GATT Doc. L/403, 7th Sept. 1955.

the request of Cuba the Working Party recommended that the Legal and Drafting Committee be asked to consider this question, but it was later agreed that the matter should be included as an item on the Agenda of the Tenth Session.

2.   In order to facilitate the discussion at the Tenth Session there are presented below references to the relevant material and an explanation of the facts which led the Executive Secretary to the conclusion referred to above.   The relevant considerations, discussed below, fall under three headings:

Analysis of the text of paragraph 5(a) of Article XXV and of paragraph 1 of Article XXX;

Legislative history of these provisions; and

History of the application of these provisions by the CONTRACTING PARTIES.

Analysis of Texts

3.   *Article XXV:5(a)*—The relevant portion of this paragraph reads:

In exceptional circumstances not elsewhere provided for in this Agreement, the CONTRACTING PARTIES may waive an obligation imposed upon a contracting party by this agreement; *Provided* that any such decision shall be approved by a two-thirds majority of the votes cast and that such majority shall comprise more than half of the contracting parties.   .   .   .

(a) In the absence of any other qualification the words "may waive an obligation" must refer to any obligation under the Agreement.   If the drafters had intended this power to be limited to Parts II and III of the Agreement it would have been a simple matter to include such a qualification.   This was not done.

(b) The phrase "not elsewhere provided * * *" could not have been intended to exclude those provisions that can only be amended by unanimity.   Any such interpretation of the phrase would necessarily exclude as well those provisions of the Agreement that are subject to amendment by a two-thirds vote, and the waiver provision would for practical purposes be inoperative.

(c) The words "in exceptional circumstances not elsewhere provided for in this Agreement" are clearly designed to limit the use of the waiver provision to individual problems to which the agreement as written does not provide an adequate solution and where an amendment would result in a modification both broader in its application and more permanent than is required.

4.   *Article XXX:1*—Paragraph 1 of Article XXX reads:

Except where provision for modification is made elsewhere in this Agreement, amendments to the provisions of Part I of this Agreement or to the provisions of Article XXIX or of this Article shall become effective upon acceptance by all the contracting parties, and other amendments to this Agreement shall become effective, in respect of those contracting parties which accept them upon acceptance by two-thirds of the contracting parties and thereafter for each other contracting party upon acceptance by it.

The phrase "Except where provision for modification is made elsewhere
* * *" provides a clear exception for action taken under the provisions of
Article XXV:5(a), for—

  (i) if the waiver of an obligation in Part I is *not* considered to represent a
  "modification" it can hardly be a change that would require the application of the amendment procedure; and

  (ii) if such a waiver *is* considered to be a "modification", this phrase
  provides an explicit exception from the unanimity requirement for
  amendment of Part I.

Legislative History

5.   The report of the First Session of the Preparatory Committee for the
ITO shows that the application of the waiver provision to all the provisions
of the Charter, was not accidental but the result of careful deliberation. The
discussion that took place is recorded in the report of the First Session on
page 22, as follows:

> In discussing the powers of the Conference to suspend, in exceptional
> circumstances, obligations undertaken by members, under the general com-
> mercial policy divisions of the Charter, it was suggested that this power may
> be extended to cover all obligations under the Charter. It was stressed that
> the waiving of such obligations was intended to apply only in cases of an
> exceptional nature, involving hardship to a particular member, which were
> not covered by specific escape clauses. It was finally agreed that all the
> obligations undertaken by members, pursuant to the Charter, should come
> within the purview of this general provision.

6.   The relevant part of Article XXV:5(a) was adopted by the Tariff
Agreement Committee at the Second Session of the Preparatory Committee
in Geneva in September 1947 and was taken directly from the corresponding
provision in the draft ITO Charter (paragraph 3 of Article 77 in the final
Charter) without any change in substance. Article XXX, however, represents a very substantial change from the amendment article of the Charter
(Article 100 in the final Charter), which required only a two-thirds vote for
any amendment.

7.   These facts suggest the possibility that the drafters of the General
Agreement, in taking over the waiver provision from the Charter, overlooked
the fact that it had become inconsistent with the new and tighter amendment provision. The legislative history, however, does not support such a
thesis.

  (a) In the Tariff Agreement Committee there was a lengthy discussion
on the unanimity provision in the new amendment article and its relationship to those other provisions under which obligations in Part I might be
modified without a unanimous vote. This discussion is recorded on pp. 4–33
of document E/PC/T/TAC/PV/15.

  (i) Because the schedules were to be made an integral part of Article II
    of the Agreement it was generally agreed that any change in a
    schedule could have the effect of modifying the provisions of Part I.
    Therefore specific attention was paid to the relation between the

provisions of Articles XVIII, XIX, and XXIII on the one hand and the unanimity requirement for amendment of Part I.

(ii) The Committee rejected a proposal that any inconsistency between those provisions be removed by permitting the amendment of any part of the agreement upon two-thirds acceptances, as in the draft Charter.

(iii) Specific suggestions were made that Article XXX should contain an explicit exception to cover the various articles of the Agreement under which provision was made for altering the schedules of the Agreement. Others argued that the list of exceptions might not be sufficiently complete.

(iv) The solution that was adopted by the Committee, and accepted without dissent, was the inclusion of the initial phrase that appears in paragraph 1 of Article XXX "Except where provision for modification is made elsewhere in this Agreement * * *".

(b) There was no reference during the above discussion in the Committee to the waiver provision. But the reasoning that led the Committee to the solution referred to above would be equally applicable to any provision in the Agreement that involved the modification of an obligation in Part I. In any event, the discussion that took place shows that the Committee was well aware of the possible effect of the unanimity provision on other provisions in the Agreement and adopted the exception in Article XXX specifically to prevent any conflict from arising.

History of Application

8. The CONTRACTING PARTIES have previously considered the issue discussed in this memorandum and have decided that the waiver provisions of Article XXV do apply to Part I of the Agreement. The Working Party which considered the waiver relating to the European Coal and Steel Community included the following discussion in its report, which was approved by the CONTRACTING PARTIES on 10 November 1952 (Basic Instruments and Selected Documents, 1st Supplement, page 86):

> The Working Party considered, in particular, whether it would be appropriate to grant a waiver under paragraph 5(a) of Article XXV, in order to permit the six countries to participate in the European Coal and Steel Community without violating their obligations under the General Agreement. The Working Party concluded, after consideration of the contentions of the Czechoslovak representative, that such action would be appropriate. The Working Party is of the view that the text of paragraph 5(a) of Article XXV is general in character; it allows the CONTRACTING PARTIES to waive any obligations imposed upon the contracting parties by the Agreement in exceptional circumstances not provided for in the Agreement, and placed no limitations on the exercise of that right.

9. The CONTRACTING PARTIES, invoking in each instance the provisions of Article XXV:5(a), have granted the following waivers of obligations under Part I of the Agreement: [nine listed]

10. In four of the cases listed in the foregoing paragraph (numbers 3, 6, 8(b) and 9), votes were recorded against the granting of the waiver. In no

case did the CONTRACTING PARTIES record a vote by "all the contracting parties". In cases 2, 3, 6 and 8(b) Cuba, and in cases 3 and 6 Czechoslovakia, questioned the legality of the procedure followed; in the other cases the procedure was not challenged.

Conclusion

11. From the above analysis it appears—

(a) that the CONTRACTING PARTIES intentionally made a distinction in the Agreement between an amendment and a waiver granted in exceptional circumstances;

(b) that they made an effort to avoid the possibility of conflict between Article XXX and other Articles by writing an exception in Article XXX;

(c) that they explicitly decided that the provisions of Article XXV:5(a) may be applied to any obligation under the Agreement; and

(d) that they have, in many cases, granted waivers of obligations of Part I by less than a unanimous vote.

Note

Generally, one views a waiver as a measure to excuse one or more countries from a GATT obligation, and not as a means for imposing new obligations. Yet a waiver may *condition* an excuse from an obligation on certain facts or performances which result in new obligations. In addition, a waiver of major GATT trade policy obligations for one country alters the balance of benefits under the agreement to other countries. For instance, suppose five major countries agreed reciprocally to limit tariffs on aluminum bars to 5%, but later a waiver allows one of those countries to raise tariffs at will to protect its domestic producers. The effect of the obligation of the other four countries is substantially altered. Alternatively, suppose a waiver is granted to two of those countries to allow them to give tariff-free treatment to each other's aluminum exports without granting like treatment on an MFN basis to the others. Again, the "left-outs" will find their competitive position substantially altered.

Many waivers are for a limited duration in time, but some important ones are not so limited, including the 1955 waiver [46] to the United States which released it from GATT obligations for restrictions on imports of agricultural commodities which were mandated by Congress under a 1951 statute, and the 1965 waiver to the United States for participation in the United States-Canadian Automotive Products Agreement.[47]

46. Waiver to the United States regarding the restrictions under the Agricultural Adjustment Act, GATT, 3d Supp. BISD 32 (1955); Import Restrictions Imposed by the United States under section 22 of the United States Agricultural Adjustment Act of 1933 (as amended), Report adopted on March 5, 1955, (GATT Doc. L/339), GATT, 3d Supp. BISD 141 (1955). The 1955 United States Agriculture waiver has had a profound effect on GATT, perhaps bearing a large amount of responsibility for the fact that agricultural trade restrictions are only ineffectively regulated by

GATT. See J. Jackson, note 1 supra, ch. 27, and Chapter 14 infra.

47. United States-Canadian Automotive Products Agreement; signed at Johnson City, Texas, Jan. 16, 1965; entered into force definitively Sept. 16, 1966 (17 UST 1372; TIAS No. 6093); see also Waiver granted to the United States—Imports of Automotive Products; Decision of Dec. 20, 1965, GATT, 14th Supp. BISD 37 (1966); see further the discussion of the United States-Canadian Automotive Products Agreement, Section 7.4(B) infra.

Many waivers include a special consultation procedure or a periodic review procedure, to enable countries which may be harmed in later years to have an opportunity to urge changes in application, and the United States-Canadian Automotive Products Agreement waiver establishes a procedure by which the waiver may be partially revoked if it proves harmful to other countries.[48] In addition, many waivers expressly recognize the retained right of GATT members to invoke Article XXIII.[49]

One very important waiver is that of 1971 allowing developed countries to depart from MFN to the extent necessary to grant tariff preferences to developing countries.[50] One objection to using the "waiver" approach for implementing the preference system was that the "exceptional circumstances" provided for in Article XXV, paragraph 5, could not be applied to a generalized system of preferences.[51] Arguably an amendment would have been legally better, but the difficulties of amending GATT led to a rejection of that "option" and a waiver was utilized. The waiver does have a 10 year time limit and provisions for consultation.[52] One result of the Tokyo Round was an "understanding" adopted by the Contracting Parties of GATT regarding "Differential and More Favourable Treatment" for developing countries (see Chapter 20 infra). It is generally considered that this action operates to authorize perpetually preference systems favoring developing countries.

Questions

(1) Would it be sound policy to require all waivers to be limited to no more than 5 years? Would new procedures for amendment of GATT then be necessary?

(2) Is Article XXIII adequate insurance to a GATT member which is harmed by the operation of a waiver?

(3) Is the voting system for waivers fair, or should it more explicitly recognize economic power or vulnerability?

(4) Should general provision be made for the revocation of any waiver, by a special vote? (Implemented by GATT amendment, or automatic inclusion of standard language in each waiver.)

(5) Should countries which are benefitted by a waiver be allowed to vote for it?

(6) Should all waivers be subject to annual consultation and study-review by the CONTRACTING PARTIES?

(H) ADMINISTRATION OF THE AGREEMENT: COMMITTEES, THE COUNCIL, AND THE SECRETARIAT: A NOTE [53]

In early years of GATT there was a reluctance to establish committees (other than *ad hoc* committees) or other subbodies of the Contracting Parties

---

48. Waiver granted to the United States—Imports of Automotive Products, GATT, 14th Supp. BISD 37, 38–39 §§ 2–5 (1966).

49. See, e.g., Waiver to Uruguay regarding Import Surcharges, GATT, 10th Supp. BISD 51, 53, §§ 5, 6 (1962).

50. For discussion of the GSP system, see Chapter 20 infra.

51. See Gros Espiell, GATT: Accommodating Generalized Preferences, 8. J.World Trade L. 341 (1974), particularly at 349 & n. 33.

52. Generalized System of Preferences, Decision of 25 June, 1971, GATT Doc. L/3545; GATT, 18th Supp. BISD 24 (1972).

53. See generally, J. Jackson, note 1 supra, chs. 6 and 7.

to GATT, which might suggest characteristics of an international organization. Nevertheless, the work of GATT necessitated some organizational structure and when the ITO failed to materialize, committees of a more permanent nature began to develop in GATT. Today there is a fairly extensive committee structure, including committees of signatories set up under the Tokyo Round Agreements.

The committee structure, however, was not enough. There was a need for a more or less permanent body which could meet on short notice at GATT headquarters in Geneva, to further the work of GATT. After failure of the second try to establish an international trade organization (the OTC of the 1955 proposals), a 1960 session of CONTRACTING PARTIES established a Council composed of representatives of all the Contracting Parties "willing to accept the responsibilities of membership", and convenable upon three days' notice. The terms of reference of the Council are as follows: [54]

> (a) To consider matters arising between sessions of the CONTRACTING PARTIES which require urgent attention, and to report thereon to the CONTRACTING PARTIES with recommendations as to any action which might appropriately be taken by them at the next regular session, at a special session which may be called by the Council, or by a postal ballot.

> (b) To supervise the work of committees, working parties, and other subsidiary bodies of the CONTRACTING PARTIES operating intersessionally, providing guidance for them when necessary, examining the reports of such bodies, and making recommendations thereon to the CONTRACTING PARTIES.

> (c) To undertake preparation for sessions of the CONTRACTING PARTIES.

> (d) To deal with such matters with which the CONTRACTING PARTIES may deal at their sessions, and to exercise such additional functions with regard to matters referred to above, as may be expressly delegated to it by the CONTRACTING PARTIES, including action on behalf of the CONTRACTING PARTIES in performing functions under the provisions of the General Agreement, other than action under paragraph 5 of Article XXV, and under decisions and other formal actions taken by the CONTRACTING PARTIES.

Although this appears to be a broad jurisdiction, actions require a vote equal to the number required for an action by the CONTRACTING PARTIES, and provision is made for appeal to the CONTRACTING PARTIES in the following form: [55]

> If a contracting party considers it is adversely affected by the exercise by the Council of any of its above functions which involve recommendations to individual contracting parties or the making of determinations or taking of decisions, it may suspend the operation of such action by the Council through the submission of a written appeal to

54. See GATT Docs. SR. 16/11, 160 (1960); W. 16/15 corrigendum 1, 2 (1960); see also J. Jackson, note 1 supra, at 155.

55. GATT, 9th Supp. BISD 8, 9 (1961).

the CONTRACTING PARTIES. The CONTRACTING PARTIES may, either generally or in particular cases or types of cases, provide that such recommendations, determinations, or decisions of the Council shall become final if no appeal has been lodged within a specified reasonable period. In particular cases individual contracting parties may, either before or after action has been taken by the Council, waive their right of appeal and agree to accept the action as final.

In practice, since many country representatives act only upon instructions from their capitals, the Council allows the work of GATT to proceed, with the critical or "voting issues" to be referred to capitals for instructions. The Council, except in the Summer, meets about once a month. It has greatly lessened the work of the annual sessions of the CONTRACTING PARTIES which are now much shorter than those of the early years of GATT.

In 1975 the CONTRACTING PARTIES decided to institute a "Consultative Group" with a restricted, but roughly representative, membership of eighteen nations. This group was designed as a sort of "steering" group of key and representative GATT members. It meets several times a year, but has not yet developed much potential.[56]

The Secretariat of GATT is in a truly anomalous position.[57] There is no provision in the General Agreement itself for a Secretariat, pursuing the idea that GATT was not an organization. After the 1948 Havana Conference completed the draft charter for ITO, and Interim Commission for the ITO (ICITO) was set up to prepare the groundwork for that organization. This Commission performed the Secretariat services for the General Agreement, ostensibly under a procedural rule that called for reimbursement to ICITO for the services received by GATT. In technical form, this arrangement still exists today.

(I) MEMBERSHIP OF GATT [58]

(1) How to Become a GATT Member

There are basically two ways for a country to become a contracting party to GATT (other than as an original signatory to the Protocol of Provisional Application for GATT). Article XXXIII specifies the "normal" procedure for membership. This article requires a decision of two-thirds majority of the existing contracting parties, and accession to GATT on terms "to be agreed between such government and the CONTRACTING PARTIES." The article, however, only hints at the most important prerequisite to becoming a member through this procedure—the "ticket of admission" required from the acceding country by way of trade and tariff commitments negotiated at the time of entry.

Suppose, for example, an industrialized country wishes to join GATT today. The existing members of GATT, through seven previous tariff and

---

56. See further on the activities of the "Consultative Group," GATT Press Releases 1163 (July 11, 1975), 1170 (Nov. 25, 1975), 1171 (Nov. 26, 1975), 1175 (Feb. 26, 1976) and 1181 (June 24, 1976). The membership of the Group in 1984 was as follows: Argentina, Australia, Brazil, Canada, Columbia, Czechoslovakia, Egypt, the European Community and its member countries, Finland, India, Japan, Ni-geria, Pakistan, Spain, Switzerland, United States, Zaire and a Nordic and an ASEAN country. See GATT, GATT Activities in 1983 (1984).

57. See generally, J. Jackson, note 1 supra, ch. 6 and § 7.3, nn. 1–24.

58. See J. Jackson, note 1 supra. For current membership, see note 39 supra.

trade negotiating rounds, have each committed themselves not only to the general provisions of the Agreement, but in most cases to extensive and detailed tariff commitments contained in a schedule for each country. For a new country to enter GATT without agreeing to comparable tariff commitments, would allow it to obtain a "free ride" in receiving the previously negotiated concessions of the existing members. Consequently, the existing members appropriately desire a negotiation with the applicant country, which must result in the applicant agreeing to a series of tariff concessions which the existing members feel are reciprocally balanced to those commitments which they have already made in GATT. Often this negotiation is held in the context of a general trade or tariff round (e.g., Japan negotiated for entry during the 1955 Geneva Round).

A first step for membership may be no more than to obtain "observer status" for the applicant. Following this, there may be a declaration by the CONTRACTING PARTIES of special commercial relationships, often providing that existing GATT members will extend GATT treatment, including MFN to the new participant, if the new participant reciprocates. Sometimes such a declaration is called a declaration of "provisional accession" and it results in "de facto" application of GATT. Finally, a protocol for accession itself will be negotiated, and after the necessary decision by the CONTRACTING PARTIES, will be open for signature (although as soon as the applicant country signs, the protocol becomes effective under its terms, since the CONTRACTING PARTIES' vote is acceptance for GATT.) The process suggests that the CONTRACTING PARTIES acting jointly, have the status of a legal entity under international law, enabling them to enter into an international agreement directly with the country.

A second way by which countries become members of GATT, is through "sponsorship" under Article XXVI, paragraph 5(c). This paragraph applies primarily to countries which have recently become independent, and which, before independence, were ruled by a country which was a GATT member, and which had applied GATT to the applicant territory. The first country to accede to GATT under these provisions was Indonesia in 1950. Since that time over 30 nations have become members of GATT in this manner. The procedure requires sponsorship of the former parent country, but when that occurs the new country is "deemed to be a contracting party". Suppose, however, that the new country does not wish to become a contracting party? To accommodate a period of uncertainty regarding trade policy for newly independent countries, GATT has developed the practice of giving "de facto" application of GATT to a new country, for a period of time, to allow that country to decide whether it wishes to become a GATT full member.[59]

One of the key legal questions that arises in connection with this procedure is what obligations the new country takes on under GATT, in the light of the fact that there have been a number of amendments to GATT, and that GATT is applied by the Protocol of Provisional Application. A working party in 1956 stated that:[60]

59. See J. Jackson, note 1 supra, § 4.5.

60. GATT, 10th Supp. BISD 73, para. 19 (1962).

there can be no doubt that a government becoming a contracting party under Article XXVI:5(c) does so on the terms and conditions previously accepted by the metropolitan government on behalf of the territory in question.

Under this interpretation, the sponsored new member would apply GATT as its parent sponsor was applying it on the date of sponsorship, including the "grandfather" clauses of the Protocol of Provisional Application or similar accession protocol.

More significant, perhaps, is the fact that a sponsored country need not negotiate a "ticket of admission." If the parent country had negotiated a separate schedule on behalf of the customs territory which has now become a country, the commitments in that tariff schedule would become the schedule of the newly independent country in GATT. The practice, however, was that these separate sub-schedules for colonial territories were very brief, often containing only a few tariff commitments. In some cases, there were no such tariff sub-schedules. The sponsored country that becomes a new member of GATT takes as its tariff schedule that which had been applied to it by the former parent. In a number of cases, this means that such a country has no schedule, i.e., no tariff commitments in GATT (which means that that country can raise its tariffs to any level it desires without being inconsistent with any GATT commitment).[61]

The possibility of membership for the People's Republic of China has raised some interesting legal questions. China was one of the original 1948 Contracting Parties to GATT, but the government representing China at GATT, the "Nationalist Chinese" on Taiwan, withdrew China from GATT in 1950. In recent years, the government of the People's Republic of China (mainland China), has assumed China's seat in certain international organizations, including the United Nations and the International Monetary Fund. China has recently joined the Multifiber Arrangement associated with GATT, and has become an observer at GATT.[62] It is not entirely clear whether China will soon desire membership in GATT, or what legal form such membership would take. Some argue that the withdrawal of China from GATT was attempted by a government which was not in control, and therefore was not effective. However, China's absence from GATT for many decades would be a counter argument.

Hong Kong has participated in GATT, because of the extension of GATT by the parent country (the United Kingdom) to Hong Kong. The United Kingdom and China have entered into an agreement by which Hong Kong will become a part of China in 1997. Hong Kong became a contracting party of GATT in 1986.

(2) Opting Out of GATT Relationships with a New Member

When GATT was negotiated, the original text required a unanimous decision to accept a new member. After the 1948 Havana Conference,

61. Eighteen GATT contracting parties have no current GATT schedule. See GATT, Status of Legal Instruments (looseleaf). Each of these members acceded to the GATT under the Article XXVI:(5)(c) procedure; see further, J. Jackson, note 1 supra, §§ 4.5 and 10.1.

62. Journal of Commerce, January 7, 1984, at 5.

however, this provision was changed to a two-thirds majority. Nevertheless, it was felt that no country should be forced to accept a trade agreement with another country without its own decision to do so. Consequently, Article XXXV was added to the GATT Agreement, giving to each contracting party, and to an applicant for membership, a one time option (at the time the applicant becomes a contracting party) to "opt out" of a GATT relationship with any other contracting party, providing that the two countries concerned have not "entered into tariff negotiations." [63]

Often political considerations enter into the decision to opt out of a trading relationship, as suggested by the option of India and Pakistan against South Africa. The most extensive set of "opt out" applications were those exercised by a number of countries against Japan at the time Japan entered GATT in the middle of the 1950's. Subsequently, a number of those countries withdrew their Article XXXV invocation, often after individual bilateral negotiations with the government of Japan resulting in some special commitments.[64]

A number of the agreements resulting from the Tokyo Round negotiations include an "opt out" clause patterned after the GATT Article XXXV. This figured prominently in a dispute between the United States and India over U.S. application of the Subsidies Code, discussed in Section 7.4(C) infra.

(J) COMPARISON OF THE IMF AND GATT

We have now completed a basic overview of the IMF and GATT. To put their organizational similarities and differences in perspective, the following chart should be useful. You should consider whether one or the other seems to have a superior way of handling a particular problem. Could that problem-handling method be successfully transplanted to the other?

GATT vs. IMF (as of October 1985)

		GATT	IMF
1.	Origin	Various conferences on International Trade Organization (not intended to be organization)	Bretton-Woods Conference (established as international organization)
2.	U.S. Adherence	Executive action—Various statutes conform to GATT	Congressional action—Bretton Woods Agreements Act controls U.S. participation

63. This has been interpreted to mean that the countries have not held a first meeting scheduled by a tariff negotiations committee at which they would normally exchange lists of offers. See GATT, BISD Vol. II, 35 (1952).

64. As stated, the most extensive application of Article XXXV has been against Japan, but many of these invocations have been subsequently withdrawn. As of 1985, only Cyprus and Haiti still applied Article XXXV against Japan. On the application of Article XXXV to Japan, see GATT Doc. L/4234. Pakistan invoked Article XXXV against Bangladesh in November, 1972 (GATT Doc. L/3784), but withdrew its invocation in January, 1975 (GATT Doc. L/4146); see generally J. Jackson, note 1 supra, § 4.6. The United States has invoked Article XXXV in respect of Hungary and Romania (GATT Docs. L/3619 and L/3911).

GATT vs. IMF (as of October 1985)—Continued

		GATT	IMF
3.	Structure	CONTRACTING PARTIES acting jointly	Board of Governors
		Council	Executive Directors
		Consultative Group of 18	
		Director-General	Managing Director
4.	Voting	One country/one vote	Weighted
5.	Amendment	Unanimous for part I; $2/3$ for rest (only apply if vote for or accept)	$3/5$ (up to 85% in some cases)
6.	Interpretation	Joint Action? (Article XXV)	Binding Procedure (Article XXIX)
7.	Disputes	Articles XXII & XXIII	Article XXIX
8.	Sanctions	Retaliatory suspension of obligations toward offending party	Ejection or limitation of rights to use Fund
9.	Finance	Contributions	Self-supporting
10.	Membership	91 (as of Apr. 1986) Articles XXVI & XXXIII	149 (as of Sept. 1985) Terms set by Board

SECTION 5.5   GATT TRADE NEGOTIATING ROUNDS

(A) OVERVIEW

One of the more important roles that GATT has played during the last four decades has been its sponsorship of a series of major multinational trade negotiations. So far there have been seven such trade negotiating "rounds", including the latest which is called the "Tokyo Round", or the "Multilateral Trade Negotiations" (MTN). The rounds are summarized by the following chart: [1]

		Countries Participating	Trade Affected
1.	Geneva, Switzerland 1947	23	$10 Billion
2.	Annecy, France 1948	33	Unavailable
3.	Torquay, England 1950	34	Unavailable
4.	Geneva 1956	22	$2.5 Billion

1. For the first five rounds, see G. Curzon, Multilateral Commercial Diplomacy 81 (1965). For the Kennedy Round, see J. Evans, The Kennedy Round in American Trade Policy 281 (1971). For the Tokyo Round, see GATT, The Tokyo Round of Trade Negotiations: Report by the Director-General of GATT 118 (1979) and GATT, The Tokyo Round of Trade Negotiations: Supplementary Report by the Director-General of GATT 6 (1980) (collectively, the GATT Tokyo Round Reports). See also the following Department of State publications in its Commercial Policy Series (CPS): No. 2983 (CPS No. 109), Analysis of General Agreement on Tariffs and Trade (1947); No. 3651 (CPS No. 120), Analysis of Protocol of Accession and Schedules to the General Agreement on Tariffs and Trade (1949); No. 4209 (CPS No. 135), Analysis of Torquay Protocol of Accession, Schedules and Related Documents (1951); No. 6348 (CPS No. 158), General Agreement on Tariffs and Trade: Analysis of United States Negotiations (1956).

	Countries Participating	Trade Affected
5. "Dillon Round," Geneva 1960–61	45	$4.9 Billion
6. "Kennedy Round," Geneva 1964–67	48	$40 Billion
7. "Tokyo Round," Geneva 1973–1979	99	$155 Billion

The first five of these rounds focused on negotiations for the reduction of tariffs. As it turned out, the sixth round also focused on tariffs, although one of the expressed goals for the round was to turn significantly to non-tariff barriers. The seventh round was predominantly concerned with non-tariff measures, although considerable attention was still given to tariff reductions. The negotiation procedures and problems concerning tariffs will be discussed in the next chapter. This section will present a summary of the important results of the last round.

(B) TOKYO ROUND RESULTS [2]

JOHN H. JACKSON, THE BIRTH OF THE GATT–MTN SYSTEM: A CONSTITUTIONAL APPRAISAL

(1980) [3]

The Multilateral Trade Negotiation (MTN) has now been completed. This is an impressive accomplishment because the MTN was conducted during one of the most difficult periods of peacetime economic stress. Although launched in September 1973, at a General Agreement on Tariffs and Trade (GATT) ministerial-level meeting, the MTN proceeded by fits and starts and suffered long periods of relative inactivity. The negotiations were targeted for substantial completion in the summer of 1978, but the formal initialing of the Agreements actually occurred on April 12, 1979. Neverthe-less, the international negotiations are now formally and substantially over, and the MTN results are entering the implementation phase.

Except for the original drafting of the GATT itself, the MTN results may well be the most far-reaching and substantively important product of the seven major trade negotiating rounds of the GATT. The immediate prede-cessor of the MTN, the Kennedy Round, was very extensive and probably accomplished more in terms of tariff reductions. Unfortunately, the Ken-nedy Round failed to achieve significant progress on the formulation of rules relating to nontariff barriers to trade (NTBs), which have become increasing-

2. For general information on the Tokyo Round, see GATT 26th Supp. BISD (1980); GATT Tokyo Round Reports, note 1 supra; J. Jackson, J.–V. Victor & M. Matsushita, Imple-menting the Tokyo Round: National Constitu-tions and International Economic Rules (1984) (revised version in 81 Mich.L.Rev. 289 (1982)); McRae & Thomas, The GATT and Multilater-al Treaty Making: The Tokyo Round, 77 Am. J.Intl.L. 51 (1983); and the articles in 11 L. & Poly.Intl.Bus. 1257 (1979); 12 L. & Poly.Intl. Bus. 1 (1980); 13 Cornell Intl.L.J. 145 (1980). In addition, the Senate Finance Committee commissioned a series of so-called MTN Stud-ies. Sen. Finance Comm., 96th Cong., 1st Sess. (Comm.Prints 96–11 to 96–15).

3. From 12 Law & Poly.Intl.Bus. 21, 21–24, 36–40, 49–52 (1980). Reprinted by permission of the Journal of Law and Policy in Interna-tional Business.

ly troublesome. The MTN was the first negotiating effort since the origin of the GATT to address significantly the problems of nontariff measures affecting international trade. It produced an extensive series of international Agreements relating to nontariff measures, including Agreements on: (1) subsidies and countervailing duties; (2) antidumping duties; (3) technical barriers to trade; (4) government procurement; (5) procedures for licensing of imports (when licensing is permitted); (6) valuation for customs purposes; (7) a framework of GATT (with subparts relating to developing country privileges and obligations, balance-of-payments measures and dispute settlement procedures); (8) agricultural products; and (9) trade in civil aircraft.

The MTN results are particularly impressive in light of the enormous difficulties through which the international economic system has been passing for the past decade: the economic impact of U.S. military activity in Vietnam; the dramatic increases in oil prices; and slowing economies, high unemployment and rampant inflation. All of this has occurred at a time of increasing economic interdependence (resulting partly at least from three decades of successful trade liberalization under GATT leadership and through the six rounds of GATT trade negotiations). At the same time, major political systems have had to operate on narrow parliamentary majorities—majorities that consequently had to respond to constituent complaints about harm caused by imports. It is little wonder that the MTN was difficult to complete or that it bears the scars and blemishes of the gauntlet it had to run.

Despite these obstacles, the MTN has produced a large variety of complex and technical Agreements. These Agreements should increase considerably the international community's awareness of and surveillance over the activities of national governments that affect international economic relations. In short, the scope of the existing GATT system has been greatly broadened. We have witnessed no less than the birth of a GATT–MTN system for the international surveillance, consultation and regulation of world trade.

It is very difficult at this early stage to appraise the MTN and its future impact. Some studies conducted before the completion of the negotiations used computer modeling techniques to forecast the economic impact of those portions of the MTN that were relatively amenable to quantification (such as tariff reductions, quota liberalization and even government procurement regulations). A majority of the MTN results, however, concern matters not easily quantified. These matters are in the form of obligations that will have varying impacts, depending heavily on the manner in which these obligations are in fact *administered* at the national and international level.

Furthermore, important as the *economic* results of international trade obligations are, the *political* results are equally important. For example, will the system help nations resolve disputes more peacefully in the future? Will the system be perceived as fair, and will it therefore minimize international tensions that inevitably arise when one nation's economic policies cause economic distress in another country? Will the system permit a fair degree of national decisionmaking over internal priorities and goals (*i.e.*, will it permit a fair degree of sovereignty)? Will the system facilitate the degree of international coordination and cooperation essential to general economic progress in the world? Will it enhance the ability of national leaders to cooperate in the resolution of persistent and potentially dangerous world economic problems: extreme poverty, economic welfare disparities and uncertain resource supplies?

* * *

Upon reading the MTN Agreements, one is struck by their remarkable complexity, variety and far-reaching scope. The willingness of nations to yield "sovereignty" (if that is a meaningful concept) on such matters as government procurement is impressive. Yet the overall impact is perplexing. The variety of Agreements and the variety of approaches within the Agreements on both substantive and institutional questions reflect a somewhat fragmented method to the negotiation.

On a number of substantive issues, there seems to be a variety of approaches, probably reflecting the different objectives of national domestic interest groups who influenced different parts of the negotiations. (Of course, because of the complexity of many of these substantive issues, negotiations had to proceed in subgroups.) Thus, some of the Agreements seem tuned toward the direction of trade liberalization to increase the flow of trade, others seem more trade-restricting. Some seem to enhance MFN; other seem to erode it further.

Generally, these substantive problems of international trade can be approached in two divergent ways, each resulting from a particular philosophy. On the one hand, there is the "freer trade" or nongovernmental approach, which attempts to create international rules designed generally to minimize government interference. On the other hand, there is a more "managed" approach, which encourages governments to cooperate and to manage or direct the type and amount of trade flow. The original GATT reflected the views of the first approach; whereas in the MTN Agreements, different Codes seem to take differing approaches. Some of the Agreements seem designed to establish new mechanisms through which governments and international bodies can manage trade. The creation of new "committees" in many of the Codes leans in this direction. Portions of the subsidies Agreement suggest the same. Other Agreements, however, appear to be more in tune with the first approach—that is, with the traditional GATT view—and thus seem designed to limit further governmental interference with international trade.

It is also difficult to discover an overall consistent policy on the institutional and legal questions addressed by this article. The Agreements vary widely on such matters as dispute settlement, degree of precision in rule statements and the extent and nature of international decisionmaking authority.

With respect to the weaknesses of the GATT constitution discussed above, a number of the tougher questions unfortunately were avoided. This is perhaps understandable; to achieve any agreement at all, it might have been necessary to avoid many tough issues that could have sidetracked the negotiations. Yet it must be recognized that many of these tough issues remain and are even more perplexing as a result of the MTN. Some of the comments later in the article illustrate this point.

* * *

Perfection, of course, cannot reasonably be expected in a negotiation among so many nations with so many divergent goals. The real and substantial gains made by the MTN on such matters as government procurement policy, valuation and product standards may more than offset the failure meaningfully to address some problems, particularly when those problems have become almost perennial. A tidy world certainly is not the likely characteristic of any foreseeable trade policy. Yet the MTN bargaining process and the resulting Codes, which stand virtually alone as treaties in themselves, have an overall impact on the GATT legal system. The interrelationships between the various Codes and the GATT will become increasingly complex. Such complexity, in turn, will make it harder for the general public to understand the GATT–MTN system, perhaps resulting in less public support for that system over time. The complexity will hurt those countries that cannot devote additional governmental expertise to GATT representation problems. In addition, such complexity inevitably will give rise to a variety of legal disputes among GATT parties. Finally, it will contribute to the belief that the richer nations can control and can manipulate the GATT system for their own advantage.

It should be noted that many (maybe all) of these MTN-created technical and legal problems with the GATT may be fully justified as fulfilling important policy objectives in the face of the rigidity and unamendability of the GATT and in the face of the GATT's inadequate constitutional structure. In each such case, however, it must be recognized that there is a long-term cost to the usefulness of the GATT and its related agreements. That cost may be worth it. But what is suggested by this discussion and the discussion that follows is that there are still many important, unresolved issues that will require considerable efforts in the years ahead.

* * *

After the MTN, the basic problem of GATT remains: in the face of a larger and more diverse membership, how can GATT decisionmaking be made more efficient and effective? As long as it is subject to the disparity between real economic power and actual voting power of a one-nation, one-vote system, it seems unlikely that powerful nations will trust that system with any meaningful authority.

The MTN largely ignored this institutional question. A "GATT Framework" group was set up to negotiate reforms, but it did not come to any conclusions on these decisionmaking issues. The MTN results, however, do affect the GATT decisionmaking process, possibly in very significant ways. Almost all of the new Codes create their own new international body, called a "Committee on Subsidies and Countervailing Measures" or a "Committee on Government Procurement," and the like. The comparison requirements of these Committees are generally the same: Each signatory or party is entitled to one representative. Voting is not generally mentioned—a striking omission! Thus, it is at least possible, if not probable, that a one-member, one-vote practice could develop and that a majority vote would prevail. Most of these Committees have only consultative powers, but some have important powers in dispute settlement procedures, as discussed above. Even in those cases where the relevant committee has no formal decision-making authority, it is the only official international agency to oversee the operation of a new Code. Therefore, the Committee is likely to have considerable influence, particularly in early years, over the process of interpreting that Code.

Several observations can be made on these GATT–MTN Committees. First, the creation of this new set of international bodies could have some impact. One result will be less centralized decisionmaking and a decrease in the authority of the GATT Contracting Parties. Consequently, although the total GATT–MTN system may have been strengthed by the remarkable increase in scope of the new rules negotiated in the MTN and by the establishment of a new group of Committees and procedures in the GATT system, the GATT Contracting Parties, the Council and other GATT bodies may have been weakened. Only future developments will indicate whether this is good or bad.

Second, even if all of these Committees meet in GATT headquarters and depend on the GATT for secretariat services, each of the new legal entities will exclude some members of the GATT from its deliberations. Such exclusivity may encourage more nations to join each Code; at least, it will exclude from voting those who have no interest in the subject matter. Conversely, in addition to increased administrative burdens on national and international governments, such exclusivity may make it more difficult for some Code nonsignatories to be heard and to remind the Codes' signatories that actions they may take in the Committees may impinge unnecessarily on other nations.

Third, although at this time it is impossible to know the exact composition of these Committees, it is fairly clear that the industrialized nations of the Organization for Economic Cooperation and Development (OECD) are likely to belong to most of them. Presumably, some less developed countries (LDCs) will belong. But it is likely that at the outset the industrialized countries will have a much greater influence in these Committees vis-à-vis the LDCs than is presently the case in the GATT itself. (Some industrialized countries may not find this always an advantage, however, because they will face organized groups—such as the EC—that can vote in a bloc and that, in some cases, can control effectively the Committee's work.) As years go by, more nations may accede to the Codes. In some of the Codes, they may do so by right—i.e., no vote or other procedure of admission is needed. It could happen, therefore, that an entirely new majority will be in control of some of these key Committees in the future. In some Codes, this could have substantial impact on the degree to which nations will be obligated to and do in fact comply with the rules of the particular Codes.

These developments, of course, should not be overemphasized. Little decisionmaking power, apart from the disputes procedures, has been given to these Committees. It seems clear that at best the MTN has not improved the GATT decisionmaking structure, at least from a long-term perspective. The advantages of the MTN may still outweigh these disadvantages. The above analysis demonstrates, however, that little priority was given during the MTN to basic institutional problems and that the work is not completed either for the international community or for the United States and other individual governments.

Finally, because the various Codes differ so much in approach, and because they contain a variety of institutional and separate dispute settlement provisions, the administration of and national representation to these Code institutions will be more costly. A series of "mini-GATTs" could develop: one for government procurement, one for standards, one for subsidies, etc., with government personnel developing specialized competence in their particular mini-GATT. This could lead to bureaucratic infighting among mini-GATT technocrats over jurisdictional areas of each mini-GATT. The infighting could occur at both the secretariat and in national capitals. It also could result in reduced transferability of personnel skills from one mini-GATT to another, such as might be needed to conduct dispute settlement cases, or to meet new problems arising in the coming decades. In short, it can be concluded that the MTN will assist in the further balkanization of international trade policy.

————

The following chart lists the major agreements resulting from the MTN, with information (as of February 24, 1986) about the countries which have accepted the agreements.[4] Since each agreement is a "stand-alone" treaty, in many cases with its own institutional provisions (Committee of Signatories, dispute settlement procedures, etc.), no government is obligated by such agreement unless it has accepted it. It could occur after the passage of time, however, that the practice under an MTN agreement could be taken as "practice" which interprets one or another of the provisions of GATT itself, thus becoming binding on GATT members that have not accepted the agreement. That will be for the future to decide.

MTN Agreement	Countries Accepted	Of Which [5]			
		DC	LDC	NME	non-GATT
Geneva Protocol	29	22	2	5	0
Supplementary Protocol	21	6	15	0	0
Technical Barriers to Trade	33	20	9	4	1
Government Procurement	12	11	1	0	0
Subsidies	25	14	11	0	0
Bovine Meat	22	13	5	4	3
Dairy Products	14	9	2	3	1
Customs Valuation	23	14	5	4	1
Import Licensing Procedures	23	13	6	4	0
Civil Aircraft	18	17	0	1	0
Antidumping	23	12	6	5	0

In addition to the treaty agreements resulting from the MTN, there were several "understandings", developed in a negotiating committee called the "Group Framework Committee". The form which these understandings

4. GATT Doc. L/5808 and additions (1985–86).

5. DC = Developed Country; LDC = Less Developed Country; NME = Non-Market Economy

would take, was decided only at the end of the negotiations. They were adopted by the CONTRACTING PARTIES acting jointly, presumably as decisions under Article XXV of GATT. These were a decision on differential and more favorable treatment for developing countries,[6] a declaration on trade measures taken for balance of payment purposes,[7] a decision on easing developing country use of the safeguard procedures [8] and an understanding on notification, consultation, dispute settlement and surveillance.[9]

In adopting these decisions, the CONTRACTING PARTIES also adopted the following resolution regarding the relationship of the MTN agreements to GATT:

ACTION BY THE CONTRACTING PARTIES ON THE MULTILATERAL TRADE NEGOTIATIONS

Decision of 28 November 1979 [10]

1. The Contracting Parties reaffirm their intention to ensure the unity and consistency of the GATT system, and to this end they shall oversee the operation of the system as a whole and take action as appropriate.

2. The Contracting Parties note that as a result of the Multilateral Trade Negotiations, a number of Agreements covering certain non-tariff measures and trade in Bovine Meat and Dairy Products have been drawn up. They further note that these Agreements will go into effect as between the parties to these Agreements as from 1 January 1980 or 1 January 1981 as may be the case and for other parties as they accede to these Agreements.

3. The Contracting Parties also note that existing rights and benefits under the GATT of contracting parties not being parties to these Agreements, including those derived from Article I, are not affected by these Agreements.

(C) FUTURE NEGOTIATION PROSPECTS

In the 1980's, governments began to give some consideration to the launching of a new—the eighth—trade round of negotiation. One U.S. official expressed the reasons for such move as follows: [11]

> One reason is protectionism itself. If we do not move forward toward freer trade, increased protectionism is the likely result.
>
> A second reason is unfinished business from previous trade rounds. Tariff-cutting has not yet gone far enough to eliminate some significant residual impediments to achieving economic efficiency through trade; agriculture continues to escape full GATT discipline; and the trade rules have to be further adapted to today's trading realities.
>
> A third reason is that trade in areas of new importance, including services and high technology, has an impressive potential to create jobs and wealth if we are wise enough to seek liberalization.

6. GATT 26th Supp. BISD 203 (1980).

7. Id., at 205.

8. Id., at 209.

9. Id., at 210.

10. Id., at 201.

11. Address by Denis Lamb, Deputy Assistant Secretary for Trade and Commercial Affairs, April 25, 1984 (U.S. Dept. of State, Current Policy No. 585).

Finally, negotiations can provide the incentive and the means to integrate the newly industrializing, and increasingly trade-oriented, developing countries into the GATT system.

As of this writing (end of 1985), the Contracting Parties of GATT have formally approved the launching of a new (eighth) round of negotiations in GATT, and have set up preparatory committees to begin planning for it. One of the most controversial issues in this planning is whether the subject of "international trade in services" (such as banking, insurance, engineering, tourism, etc.) will be part of the negotiation. See Chapter 15 infra.

SECTION 5.6 DISPUTE RESOLUTION AND SANCTIONS IN GATT

The question of dispute settlement in international affairs has already been raised earlier in this chapter, and it is part of the broader issue of whether "legalistic" approaches to managing international economic affairs are the best or even an appropriate means to carry out desirable policies. Throughout the rest of this book, we will have a number of occasions to refer to disputes and their resolution under GATT or comparable procedures as part of the "practice" of nations which is relevant to our attempts to ascertain the applicable legal rules for various situations. Even though strict "stare decisis" concepts of precedent do not apply in international law, it is clear that in practice prior "precedents" do have weight in various international discussions and fora. Indeed, sometimes the deliberations of international dispute settlement panels or arbiters give every bit the appearance of common law lawyers arguing precedent.

(A) GATT AND DISPUTES [1]

JOHN H. JACKSON, GATT AS AN INSTRUMENT FOR THE SETTLEMENT OF TRADE DISPUTES

(1967) [2]

There is no single sharply defined dispute-settlement procedure in GATT that can be readily distinguished from the remainder of GATT activity. Or, in the alternative, one can say that there are over 30 such

1. For discussion of the GATT dispute settlement procedures, see J. Jackson, World Trade and the Law of GATT ch. 8 (1969); R. Hudec, The GATT Legal System and World Trade Diplomacy (1975); Hudec, The GATT Legal System and World Trade Diplomacy, 70 Am.J.Intl.L. 393 (1976); Hudec, GATT Dispute Settlement After the Tokyo Round, an Unfinished Business, 13 Cornell Int'l L.J. 145 (1980); Jackson, Jurisprudence of International Trade: The DISC Case in GATT, 72 Am.J.Intl. L. 747 (1978), Jackson, Governmental Disputes in International Trade Relations: A Proposal in the Context of GATT, 13 J. World Trade L. 1 (1979); Jackson, The Puzzle of GATT, 1 J. World Trade L. 131 (1967); de Kieffer, GATT Dispute Settlements: A New Beginning in International and U.S. Trade Law, 2 Nw.J.Intl. L. & Bus. 317 (1980); Lowenfeld, "Doing Unto Others" * * *—The Chicken War Ten Years After, 4 J. Maritime L. & Comm. 599 (1973); 5 J. Maritime L. & Comm. 317 (1974); Walker, Dispute Settlement: The Chicken War, 58 Am.J.Intl.L. 671 (1964); European Community Restrictions on Imports of United States Speciality Agricultural Products: Hearings on HR 238 and HR 320 Before the Subcomm. on Trade of the House Comm. on Ways and Means, 95th Cong., 1st Sess. 21 (1977).

2. Proceedings of the American Society for International Law 144–46 (April, 1967). Reprinted with the permission of the American Society for International Law.

procedures. For instance there are 19 clauses in the GATT Treaty which obligate the parties to GATT to consult in specific instances. By way of illustration, a sentence in the first paragraph of Article VII which concerns limitations on the way nations value goods for customs purposes says that a Contracting Party shall "upon a request by another Contracting Party review the operation of any of their laws or regulations relating to value for customs purposes in the light of these principles." A similar sentence is found in Article VIII, paragraph two, while in Article XIX a sentence in the second paragraph establishes that a Contracting Party which invokes that article "shall afford * * * those Contracting Parties having a substantial interest as exporters of the product concerned an opportunity to consult with it in respect to the proposed action."

Likewise, there are sprinkled throughout GATT at least seven different provisions for compensatory withdrawal or suspension of concessions. These include the renegotiations under Article XXVIII, as well as compensation under Article XIX, Article XVIII, Article XII, Article II, *et cetera.*

In addition, while one is cataloguing different procedures or authority for different procedures of dispute settlement in GATT, it is necessary to include two separate provisions of Article XXV, the one enabling joint action by the Contracting Parties to facilitate the objectives of GATT, and another authorizing waivers from GATT obligations in certain circumstances. Both of these provisions can be vital means to pursue practical dispute resolutions in certain circumstances.

Finally in GATT certain dispute-settlement procedures are sometimes followed which have no specific authority in the treaty itself. For instance, early in the history of GATT, there were occasions of interpretative difficulty which were submitted to the Chairman of the Contracting Parties for a ruling. His ruling was then usually adopted by the Contracting Parties as a whole.

JOHN H. JACKSON, GATT MACHINERY AND THE TOKYO ROUND AGREEMENTS

(1983) [3]

The history of dispute settlement procedures in GATT is the history of improvising on the extremely inadequate language of Article XXIII, which concerns remedies for "nullification and imp[air]ment" of negotiated liberalization commitments. In the early years of GATT there were no established procedures. The contracting parties as a whole could and sometimes would examine complaints by one member against another. During this period a working party or other general committee would occasionally be set up to consider the complaints of one party against another, and report back to the contracting parties. As time went on, due partly to the leadership of Sir Eric Wyndham-White who was then executive secretary of the GATT, the concept of establishing a panel to consider the complaint of one government against another was accepted. (Individuals appointed to be members of a

---

3. © 1983, Institute for International Economics. This and other excerpts from this publication in this chapter are reproduced by permission from W. Cline (ed.), Trade Policy in the 1980s 159, 180–82, 185–87.

panel act in their own capacity, and presumably without instruction from their respective governments.)

A "restatement" of GATT dispute settlement procedures was drafted during the Tokyo Round, and accepted by a decision of the contracting parties. There is a certain amount of ambiguity at almost every step of this procedure. Furthermore, there are ample opportunities for delay. Unfortunately, it is not clear what the legal result of a panel finding is. It appears that there is no legal obligation to carry out a panel finding, at least until the GATT contracting parties approve the panel reports, and even then there has been considerable ambiguity.

There has been only one case in GATT where, under Article XXIII an actual authorization of suspension of concessions was made (a case early in the history of GATT brought by the Netherlands against US dairy import restrictions). In the "chicken war," a "compensatory withdrawal of concession" was exercised by the United States against EC member countries. This case was not an Article XXIII case, however, but was brought under different articles of the GATT which contemplate compensatory action of this type.

The procedures under Article XXIII can be contrasted with certain more "automatic" responses that are authorized by other articles of GATT. For example, under Article VI of GATT a party is authorized to use antidumping duties against goods that are "dumped" and countervailing duties against goods that are subsidized. In these situations the importing country has the right to make the necessary determinations and act unilaterally (provided that it makes its findings and takes these actions in accordance with its international obligations). Likewise, Article XIX of GATT, which is the escape clause, allows an exporting nation unilaterally to take compensatory action against another country that has excluded imports pursuant to a legitimate invocation of the escape clause criteria and procedures. There is no precondition that an international body approve these various unilateral responses. The results, in some ways, suggest that these unilateral responses, which are in effect sanctions, have been more effective in encouraging compliance with the rules of trade than the Article XXIII dispute-settlement procedures.

There is one very important aspect of the provision of Article XXIII that pervades the GATT practice and procedures of dispute settlement. When invoking Article XXIII, a GATT party must argue that benefits it expected under the GATT are being nullified or impaired. Although there is a provision for another type of invocation, in general this requirement of nullification or impairment is central to the right to invoke the GATT procedures. Unfortunately, the phrase "nullification or impairment" is exceedingly ambiguous. An early case in GATT suggested that it related to the concept of "reasonable expectations" of the other party. It is explicitly recognized in the GATT practice that nullification or impairment is *not* coexistent with a *breach* of GATT obligations. A breach of obligation is neither a sufficient nor a necessary prerequisite to the invocation of Article XXIII. A breach of obligation does, however, under the practice of GATT raise a prima facie nullification or impairment.

* * *

DISPUTE SETTLEMENT UNDER THE MTN AGREEMENTS

Many of the MTN agreements contain independent and new dispute-settlement procedures which can operate totally separately from the GATT dispute-settlement procedure. Indeed, of the 11 major MTN agreements, no 2 have identical dispute-settlement procedures in them. Two of the agreements contain no explicit provision with respect to dispute settlement, and presumably rely upon the GATT procedures. Two more agreements refer explicitly to the GATT dispute-settlement provisions as governing disputes on the agreements, (the Licensing Agreement and the framework understandings, the latter of which are really decisions and not agreements). Each of the 7 other agreements contain explicit provisions mentioning dispute settlement, with varying degrees of formality. The Bovine Meat Agreement (Article IV paragraph 6) only provides that "any participant may raise before the council any matter affecting this agreement * * *." In such a case the council will meet within 15 days to consider the matter. But at the other extreme, the Subsidies-Countervailing Duty Agreement (Articles XVII and XVIII) specifies an elaborate set of procedures, including reference to a panel, and report of the panel to the Committee on Subsidies and Countervailing Measures. The Antidumping Agreement (Article XV) also establishes a separate procedure for dispute settlement, including reference to the committee, and then to a panel. The Aircraft Products Agreement provides that the committee shall review a matter brought to it by a signatory. It also provides with respect to any dispute not covered by other instruments negotiated under the auspices of GATT, that the provisions of the GATT Articles XXII and XXIII along with the understanding relating to dispute settlement, shall be applied. The remaining three agreements: Valuation, Technical Barriers, and Government Procurement, each contain a fairly detailed procedure for dispute settlement, following generally a pattern of consultation, then reference to the committee, then reference to a panel, and report by the panel to the committee. However, none of the three procedures is identical to any other, and each agreement contains certain specific differences in the procedure.

Some of the MTN agreements unfortunately use the nullification-impairment language of the GATT Article XXIII itself. In any event, with this plethora of different procedures, there is an increased risk of jurisdictional conflicts, forum shopping, and disputes over procedures. It is too early to tell how serious the problem will be. It is possible that after a brief period of "shakedown" there will be sufficient decisions as to procedure under each code, that procedural matters can be put in the background. It is not clear to what extent a decision as to a procedural matter under one code, will be used as quasi-precedent for the resolution of a similar issue under another code. In a few agreements, it is specified that the code procedure must be utilized by disputing parties who are both signatories to the code, before applying to the general GATT procedure. As mentioned above, it is not clear what will be the situation in those agreements which do not have such language. Neither is it clear the degree to which the "framework understanding" on dispute settlement can be utilized as a guide for procedures under any of the specific codes. Only recently (March 1982) has the first panel procedure under one of the MTN agreements been formally invoked (a dispute involving the subsidization of wheat flour by the European Community, brought by the United States in connection with the subsidies code). Nevertheless, as mentioned earlier in this chapter, a number of disputes or differences have been raised formally in the various supervising committees of the MTN agreements. In a few such cases a formal complaint has been filed, and in one case there has been a ruling that the complaint could not be pursued under the procedure of that code. In most cases discussions within the supervising committees with respect to matter that could give rise to a dispute about interpretation of the MTN agreement involved, have been discussed as general problems, and not in the context of a particular case. To a certain extent, these were interpretive problems left over from the MTN negotiations.

Note

Articles XXII and XXIII are considered the primary dispute-settlement mechanisms in GATT. XXII provides generally for consultation, but XXIII provides a procedure that can be invoked in different types of circumstances and could ultimately result in suspension of certain GATT obligations towards an offending nation. This result, (which has only occurred once in the history of GATT), however, requires a majority vote of the CONTRACTING PARTIES. Such a vote is difficult to obtain, and this difficulty, plus a growing reluctance to "offend" other nations by bringing a concrete complaint against them, resulted in the 1960's in a decline in the use of the Article XXIII procedures.

Problems

(1) Note the provisions that govern a dispute arising under GATT Articles VI, XIX or XXVIII, and note that in each of these cases reaction by the aggrieved nation (with countervailing duties to a subsidy, with compensatory import restraints to an escape clause action, and with compensatory withdrawal of tariff bindings to a prior withdrawal) requires no international permission, i.e. it can be effected unilaterally, if necessary. Compare these provisions with Article XXIII. If your country took an action which could be interpreted as either an escape clause action or a violation of a GATT binding (nullification and impairment), would you prefer a construction of the action as a violation, or as the exercise of a right under Article XIX? Which would most likely result in counter-response from the other side? Is there an anomaly in a situation which "rewards" violations compared to exercise of rights?

(2) Could monopoly or cartel practices give rise to an Article XXIII complaint? One GATT report [4] suggested that such practices should not be the basis of such a complaint, because it was "dangerous" to use Article XXIII in these circumstances. Why? Are there any definable boundaries to the use of this article?

4. GATT, 9th Supp. BISD 172 (1961); see J. Jackson, note 1 supra, at 181.

(B) THE DISPUTE–SETTLEMENT PROCEDURES

UNDERSTANDING REGARDING NOTIFICATION, CONSULTATION, DISPUTE SETTLEMENT AND SURVEILLANCE

Decision Adopted by the Contracting Parties 28 November 1979 [5]

1. The Contracting Parties reaffirm their adherence to the basic GATT mechanism for the management of disputes based on Articles XXII and XXIII. With a view to improving and refining the GATT mechanism, the Contracting Parties agree as follows:

NOTIFICATION

2. Contracting parties reaffirm their commitment to existing obligations under the General Agreement regarding publication and notification.

3. Contracting parties moreover undertake, to the maximum extent possible, to notify the Contracting Parties of their adoption of trade measures affecting the operation of the General Agreement, it being understood that such notification would of itself be without prejudice to views on the consistency of measures with or their relevance to rights and obligations under the General Agreement. Contracting parties should endeavour to notify such measures in advance of implementation. In other cases, where prior notification has not been possible, such measures should be notified promptly *ex post facto*. Contracting parties which have reason to believe that such trade measures have been adopted by another contracting party may seek information on such measures bilaterally, from the contracting party concerned.

CONSULTATIONS

4. Contracting parties reaffirm their resolve to strengthen and improve the effectiveness of consultative procedures employed by contracting parties. In that connexion, they undertake to respond to requests for consultations promptly and to attempt to conclude consultations expeditiously, with a view to reaching mutually satisfactory conclusions. Any requests for consultations should include the reasons therefor.

5. During consultations, contracting parties should give special attention to the particular problems and interests of less-developed contracting parties.

6. Contracting parties should attempt to obtain satisfactory adjustment of the matter in accordance with the provisions of Article XXIII:1 before resorting to Article XXIII:2.

DISPUTE SETTLEMENT

7. The Contracting Parties agree that the customary practice of the GATT in the field of dispute settlement, described in the Annex, should be continued in the future, with the improvements set out below. They recognize that the efficient functioning of the system depends on their will to abide by the present understanding. The Contracting Parties reaffirm that

5. GATT, 26th Supp. BISD 210 (1980).

the customary practice includes the procedures for the settlement of disputes between developed and less-developed countries adopted by the Contracting Parties in 1966 and that these remain available to less-developed contracting parties wishing to use them.

8. If a dispute is not resolved through consultations the contracting parties concerned may request an appropriate body or individual to use their good offices with a view to the conciliation of the outstanding differences between the parties. If the unresolved dispute is one in which a less-developed contracting party has brought a complaint against a developed contracting party, the less-developed contracting party may request the good offices of the Director-General who, in carrying out his tasks, may consult with the Chairman of the Contracting Parties and the Chairman of the Council.

9. It is understood that requests for conciliation and the use of the dispute settlement procedures of Article XXIII:2 should not be intended or considered as contentious acts and that, if disputes arise, all contracting parties will engage in these procedures in good faith in an effort to resolve the disputes. It is also understood that complaints and counter-complaints in regard to distinct matters should not be linked.

10. It is agreed that if a contracting party invoking Article XXIII:2 requests the establishment of a panel to assist the Contracting Parties to deal with the matter, the Contracting Parties would decide on its establishment in accordance with standing practice. It is also agreed that the Contracting Parties would similarly decide to establish a working party if this were requested by a contracting party invoking the Article. It is further agreed that such requests would be granted only after the contracting party concerned had had an opportunity to study the complaint and respond to it before the Contracting Parties.

11. When a panel is set up, the Director-General, after securing the agreement of the contracting parties concerned, should propose the composition of the panel, of three or five members depending on the case, to the Contracting Parties for approval. The members of a panel would preferably be governmental. It is understood that citizens of countries whose governments are parties to the dispute would not be members of the panel concerned with that dispute. The panel should be constituted as promptly as possible and normally not later than thirty days from the decision by the Contracting Parties.

12. The parties to the dispute would respond within a short period of time, i.e., seven working days, to nominations of panel members by the Director-General and would not oppose nominations except for compelling reasons.

13. In order to facilitate the constitution of panels, the Director-General should maintain an informal indicative list of governmental and non-governmental persons qualified in the fields of trade relations, economic development, and other matters covered by the General Agreement, and who could be available for serving on panels. For this purpose, each contracting party would be invited to indicate at the beginning of every year to the

Director-General the name of one or two persons who would be available for such work.

14.   Panel members would serve in their individual capacities and not as government representatives, nor as representatives of any organization. Governments would therefore not give them instructions nor seek to influence them as individuals with regard to matters before a panel. Panel members should be selected with a view to ensuring the independence of the members, a sufficiently diverse background and a wide spectrum of experience.

15.   Any contracting party having a substantial interest in the matter before a panel, and having notified this to the Council, should have an opportunity to be heard by the panel. Each panel should have the right to seek information and technical advice from any individual or body which it deems appropriate. However, before a panel seeks such information or advice from any individual or body within the jurisdiction of a State it shall inform the government of that State. Any contracting party should respond promptly and fully to any request by a panel for such information as the panel considers necessary and appropriate. Confidential information which is provided should not be revealed without formal authorization from the contracting party providing the information.

16.   The function of panels is to assist the Contracting Parties in discharging their responsibilities under Article XXIII:2. Accordingly, a panel should make an objective assessment of the matter before it, including an objective assessment of the facts of the case and the applicability of and conformity with the General Agreement and, if so requested by the Contracting Parties, make such other findings as will assist the Contracting Parties in making the recommendations or in giving the rulings provided for in Article XXIII:2. In this connexion, panels should consult regularly with the parties to the dispute and give them adequate opportunity to develop a mutually satisfactory solution.

17.   Where the parties have failed to develop a mutually satisfactory solution, the panel should submit its findings in a written form. The report of a panel should normally set out the rationale behind any findings and recommendations that it makes. Where a bilateral settlement of the matter has been found, the report of the panel may be confined to a brief description of the case and to reporting that a solution has been reached.

18.   To encourage development of mutually satisfactory solutions between the parties and with a view to obtaining their comments, each panel should first submit the descriptive part of its report to the parties concerned, and should subsequently submit to the parties to the dispute its conclusions, or an outline thereof, a reasonable period of time before they are circulated to the Contracting Parties.

19.   If a mutually satisfactory solution is developed by the parties to a dispute before a panel, any contracting party with an interest in the matter has a right to enquire about and be given appropriate information about that solution in so far as it relates to trade matters.

20. The time required by panels will vary with the particular case. However, panels should aim to deliver their findings without undue delay, taking into account the obligation of the Contracting Parties to ensure prompt settlement. In cases of urgency the panel would be called upon to deliver its findings within a period normally of three months from the time the panel was established.

21. Reports of panels and working parties should be given prompt consideration by the Contracting Parties. The Contracting Parties should take appropriate action on reports of panels and working parties within a reasonable period of time. If the case is one brought by a less-developed contracting party, such action should be taken in a specially convened meeting, if necessary. In such cases, in considering what appropriate action might be taken the Contracting Parties shall take into account not only the trade coverage of measures complained of, but also their impact on the economy of less-developed contracting parties concerned.

22. The Contracting Parties shall keep under surveillance any matter on which they have made recommendations or given rulings. If the Contracting Parties' recommendations are not implemented within a reasonable period of time, the contracting party bringing the case may ask the Contracting Parties to make suitable efforts with a view to finding an appropriate solution.

23. If the matter is one which has been raised by a less-developed contracting party, the Contracting Parties shall consider what further action they might take which would be appropriate to the circumstances.

SURVEILLANCE

24. The Contracting Parties agree to conduct a regular and systematic review of developments in the trading system. Particular attention would be paid to developments which affect rights and obligations under the GATT, to matters affecting the interests of less-developed contracting parties, to trade measures notified in accordance with this understanding and to measures which have been subject to consultation, conciliation or dispute settlement procedures laid down in this understanding.

TECHNICAL ASSISTANCE

25. The technical assistance services of the GATT secretariat shall, at the request of a less-developed contracting party, assist it in connexion with matters dealt with in this understanding.

Annex

AGREED DESCRIPTION OF THE CUSTOMARY PRACTICE OF THE GATT IN
THE FIELD OF DISPUTE SETTLEMENT (ARTICLE XXIII:2)

1. Any dispute which has not been settled bilaterally under the relevant provisions of the General Agreement may be referred to the Contracting Parties [*1] which are obliged, pursuant to Article XXIII:2, to investigate matters submitted to them and make appropriate recommendations or

---

[*1]. The Council is empowered to act for the Contracting Parties, in accordance with normal GATT practice.

give a ruling on the matter as appropriate. Article XXIII:2 does not indicate whether disputes should be handled by a working party or by a panel.*²

2. The Contracting Parties adopted in 1966 a decision establishing the procedure to be followed for Article XXIII consultations between developed and less-developed contracting parties. This procedure provides, *inter alia,* for the Director-General to employ his good offices with a view to facilitating a solution, for setting up a panel with the task of examining the problem in order to recommend appropriate solutions, and for time-limits for the execution of the different parts of this procedure.

3. The function of a panel has normally been to review the facts of a case and the applicability of GATT provisions and to arrive at an objective assessment of these matters. In this connexion, panels have consulted regularly with the parties to the dispute and have given them adequate opportunity to develop a mutually satisfactory solution. Panels have taken appropriate account of the particular interests of developing countries. In cases of failure of the parties to reach a mutually satisfactory settlement, panels have normally given assistance to the Contracting Parties in making recommendations or in giving rulings as envisaged in Article XXIII:2.

4. Before bringing a case, contracting parties have exercised their judgment as to whether action under Article XXIII:2 would be fruitful. Those cases which have come before the Contracting Parties under this provision have, with few exceptions, been brought to a satisfactory conclusion. The aim of the Contracting Parties has always been to secure a positive solution to a dispute. A solution mutually acceptable to the parties to a dispute is clearly to be preferred. In the absence of a mutually agreed solution, the first objective of the Contracting Parties is usually to secure the withdrawal of the measures concerned if these are found to be inconsistent with the General Agreement. The provision of compensation should be resorted to only if the immediate withdrawal of the measure is impracticable and as a temporary measure pending the withdrawal of the measures which are inconsistent with the General Agreement. The last resort which Article XXIII provides to the country invoking this procedure is the possibility of suspending the application of concessions or other obligations on a discriminatory basis vis-à-vis the other contracting party, subject to authorization by the Contracting Parties of such measures. Such action has only rarely been contemplated and cases taken under Article XXIII:2 have led to such action in only one case.

5. In practice, contracting parties have had recourse to Article XXIII only when in their view a benefit accruing to them under the General Agreement was being nullified or impaired. In cases where there is an infringement of the obligations assumed under the General Agreement, the action is considered *prima facie* to constitute a case of nullification or impairment. A *prima facie* case of nullification or impairment would *ipso facto* require consideration of whether the circumstances are serious enough to justify the authorization of suspension of concessions or obligations, if the

---

* **2.** At the Review Session (1955) the proposal to institutionalize the procedures of panels was not adopted by Contracting Parties mainly because they preferred to preserve the existing situation and not to establish judicial procedures which might put excessive strain on the GATT.

contracting party bringing the complaint so requests. This means that there is normally a presumption that a breach of the rules has an adverse impact on other contracting parties, and in such cases, it is up to the contracting parties against whom the complaint has been brought to rebut the charge. Paragraph 1(*b*) permits recourse to Article XXIII if nullification or impairment results from measures taken by other contracting parties whether or not these conflict with the provisions of the General Agreement, and paragraph 1(*c*) if any other situation exists. If a contracting party bringing an Article XXIII case claims that measures which do not conflict with the provisions of the General Agreement have nullified or impaired benefits accruing to it under the General Agreement, it would be called upon to provide a detailed justification.

   6. Concerning the customary elements of the procedures regarding working parties and panels, the following elements have to be noted:

   (i) working parties are instituted by the Council upon the request of one or several contracting parties. The terms of reference of working parties are generally "to examine the matter in the light of the relevant provisions of the General Agreement and to report to the Council". Working parties set up their own working procedures. The practice for working parties has been to hold one or two meetings to examine the matter and a final meeting to discuss conclusions. Working parties are open to participation of any contracting party which has an interest in the matter. Generally working parties consist of a number of delegations varying from about five to twenty according to the importance of the question and the interests involved. The countries who are parties to the dispute are always members of the Working Party and have the same status as other delegations. The report of the Working Party represents the views of all its members and therefore records different views if necessary. Since the tendency is to strive for consensus, there is generally some measure of negotiation and compromise in the formulation of the Working Party's report. The Council adopts the report. The reports of working parties are advisory opinions on the basis of which the Contracting Parties may take a final decision.

   (ii) In the case of dispute, the Contracting Parties have established panels (which have been called by different names) or working parties in order to assist them in examining questions raised under Article XXIII:2. Since 1952, panels have become the usual procedure. However, the Council has taken such decisions only after the party concerned has had an occasion to study the complaint and prepare its response before the Council. The terms of reference are discussed and approved by the Council. Normally, these terms of reference are "to examine the matter and to make such findings as will assist the Contracting Parties in making the recommendations or rulings provided for in paragraph 2 of Article XXIII." When a contracting party having recourse to Article XXIII:2 raised questions relating to the suspension of concessions or other obligations, the terms of reference were to examine the matter in accordance with the provisions of Article XXIII:2. Members of the panel are usually selected from permanent delegations or, less frequently, from the national administrations in the capitals amongst delegates who participate in GATT activities on a regular basis. The practice has been to appoint a member or members from developing countries when a dispute is between a developing and a developed country.

(iii) Members of panels are expected to act impartially without instructions from their governments. In a few cases, in view of the nature and complexity of the matter, the parties concerned have agreed to designate non-government experts. Nominations are proposed to the parties concerned by the GATT secretariat. The composition of panels (three or five members depending on the case) has been agreed upon by the parties concerned and approved by the GATT Council. It is recognized that a broad spectrum of opinion has been beneficial in difficult cases, but that the number of panel members has sometimes delayed the composition of panels, and therefore the process of dispute settlement.

(iv) Panels set up their own working procedures. The practice for the panels has been to hold two or three formal meetings with the parties concerned. The panel invited the parties to present their views either in writing and/or orally in the presence of each other. The panel can question both parties on any matter which it considers relevant to the dispute. Panels have also heard the views of any contracting party having a substantial interest in the matter, which is not directly party to the dispute, but which has expressed in the Council a desire to present its views. Written memoranda submitted to the panel have been considered confidential, but are made available to the parties to the dispute. Panels often consult with and seek information from any relevant source they deem appropriate and they sometimes consult experts to obtain their technical opinion on certain aspects of the matter. Panels may seek advice or assistance from the secretariat in its capacity as guardian of the General Agreement, especially on historical or procedural aspects. The secretariat provides the secretary and technical services for panels.

(v) Where the parties have failed to develop a mutually satisfactory solution, the panel has submitted its findings in a written form. Panel reports have normally set out findings of fact, the applicability of relevant provisions, and the basic rationale behind any findings and recommendations that it has made. Where a bilateral settlement of the matter has been found, the report of the panel has been confined to a brief description of the case and to reporting that a solution has been reached.

(vi) The reports of panels have been drafted in the absence of the parties in the light of the information and the statements made.

(vii) To encourage development of mutually satisfactory solutions between the parties and with a view to obtaining their comments, each panel has normally first submitted the descriptive part of its report to the parties concerned, and also their conclusions, or an outline thereof, a reasonable period of time before they have been circulated to the Contracting Parties.

(viii) In accordance with their terms of reference established by the Contracting Parties panels have expressed their views on whether an infringement of certain rules of the General Agreement arises out of the measure examined. Panels have also, if so requested by the Contracting Parties, formulated draft recommendations addressed to the parties. In yet other cases panels were invited to give a technical opinion on some precise aspect of the matter (e.g. on the modalities of a withdrawal or suspension in regard to the volume of trade involved). The opinions expressed by the panel members on the matters are anonymous and the panel deliberations are secret.

(ix) Although the Contracting Parties have never established precise deadlines for the different phases of the procedure, probably because the matters submitted to panels differ as to their complexity and their urgency, in most cases the proceedings of the panels have been completed within a reasonable period of time, extending from three to nine months.

The 1966 decision by the Contracting Parties referred to in paragraph 2 above lays down in its paragraph 7 that the Panel shall report within a period of sixty days from the date the matter was referred to it.

Note

The GATT agreement itself contains very little procedural framework for dispute settlement. The GATT parties have had to improvise and develop the procedures through practice over the years. In early years, the GATT body to undertake exploration of disputes was called a "working party" (see the Australia-Chile case reproduced below). A working party is understood in the GATT context to mean a body whose members are "nations," so that each nation may send a representative of its own choice. A panel is understood to be composed of individuals acting in their individual capacity, and not as national representatives. The panel members are often chosen from available national representatives to the GATT, but from nations not involved in any way with the dispute. Three person or five person panels have been the rule, and occasionally a non-government person, such as a professor or retired GATT official, has been selected to be a panel member. The difficulty of finding sufficient available and appropriate personnel to staff the many panels necessary for the relatively large number of cases now coming, has been one of the concerns about the viability of the GATT procedures. (As of this writing in January 1986, there were around a dozen GATT dispute settlement procedures in process.)

JOHN H. JACKSON, GATT MACHINERY AND THE TOKYO ROUND AGREEMENTS
Supra, at 182–85

A brief look at some statistics of the actual GATT practice during its 35 year history, may be helpful in getting that practice into perspective. Based on a fairly systematic (but preliminary) inventory of the disputes brought formally in GATT, mostly under Articles XXII and XXIII of GATT we have identified 159 formal dispute cases during the history of GATT. Fifty of these were brought during the 1950s, then there was somewhat of a drop during the 1960s. During the 1970s a renewal of interest in the dispute processes of GATT occurred. This interest seems to have continued, and it appears that there will be quite a large number of formal dispute cases in the GATT during the 1980s, particularly since a number of new dispute-settlement procedures are now available in connection with the various Tokyo Round codes.

Of the 159 cases so far inventoried, 75 percent were brought by developed countries, and 86 percent were against developed countries. It is clear that the dispute-settlement procedures are utilized mainly by the industrial nations. The United States stands out as the primary user of the procedures, being a complainant in 36 percent of the cases and a respondent in 14 percent of the cases. Thus in one-half the dispute-settlement cases in GATT, the United States is either a complainant or the respondent!

Approximately 45 percent—almost one-half of the disputes—involved agricultural products, whereas only 16 percent involved manufactured products. Since approximately 35 percent of the cases do not fall easily within a product category, only a small percentage is left for primary products. Agricultural products are clearly the predominant source of disputes within the GATT.

About one-half of the cases brought are settled or withdrawn before a panel report is issued. In nearly all of the cases in which a panel report was issued, the report was "accepted" or "adopted" by the GATT contracting parties or council and thereby approved by the GATT as a whole.

There were at least eight cases in which there has been a refusal to comply with the results of the dispute-settlement procedure, but as mentioned above, only one case in which an official sanction has been taken under the procedures of Article XXIII of GATT.

(C)　**THE LAW OF ARTICLE XXIII**

A careful look at Article XXIII will reveal a number of troublesome and peculiar characteristics. The article can be invoked under paragraph 1, in three widely divergent circumstances:

(i) Breach of obligation by a contracting party.

(ii) Application of any measure by a contracting party, whether it conflicts with the Agreement or not.

(iii) The existence of any other situation.

These provisions are qualified by a preceding sentence that requires one of the following two to be found:

(i) Benefits accruing under the Agreement are nullified or impaired.

(ii) Attainment of any objective of the Agreement is being impeded.

Even with the qualifying phrase, however, the invoking principles are very broad. Clearly they extend to situations beyond those of a breach of the Agreement, and that is one of the defects of the article in the authors' opinion, since it gives rise to arguments and disputes of a broad policy nature that probably ought not to be handled in the context of a dispute resolution procedure. In fact, (as one of the authors has written elsewhere),[6] the draftsmen of GATT had at least three objectives in mind for Article XXIII, and it is not likely that those objectives are consistent one with another.

The first objective was that Articles XXII and XXIII were to be the framework of a dispute settlement procedure, stressing the general obligation to consult on any matter relating to GATT. The second objective was that Article XXIII would play an important role in obtaining compliance with the GATT obligations. The customary international law analogy of *retorsion* was used. A third goal for these provisions of GATT was to establish a means for ensuring continued "reciprocity and balance of concessions" in the face of possibly changing circumstances. This third goal is more in the nature of an "escape clause" or "changed circumstances" provision.

Much of the practice of GATT under Article XXIII has centered on the clause "nullified or impaired," as it is necessary that there be nullification or impairment for an Article XXIII action complaint to be sustained. Thus, a mere breach of the agreement would not suffice; some "damage" which could be termed "nullification and impairment" would be necessary (somewhat like the analogy of domestic contract law). Needless to say, the question of what is nullification and impairment is important. The following extract from an early GATT working party report on the subject has had a great deal of influence on subsequent GATT practice: [7]

THE AUSTRALIAN SUBSIDY ON AMMONIUM SULPHATE
Report adopted by the CONTRACTING PARTIES on 3 April 1950

I. INTRODUCTION

1. The working party examined with the delegations of Australia and Chile the factual situation resulting from the removal, on 1 July 1949, of nitrate of soda from the pool of nitrogenous fertilizers which is subsidized by the Australian Government. It then considered whether the measure taken by the Australian Government constituted a failure by the Australian Government to carry out its obligations under the Agreement, within the terms of Article XXIII.

Having come to the conclusion that the measure taken by the Australian Government did not conflict with the provisions of the Agreement, the working party then examined whether the Australian measure had nullified or impaired the tariff concession granted by Australia to Chile on nitrate of soda in 1947, and agreed on the text of a recommendation which, in its

---

6. J. Jackson, note 1 supra, at 167–169.

7. The Australian Subsidy on Ammonium Sulphate, Report adopted by the Contracting Parties on 3rd April, 1950 (GATT/CP. 4/39), in GATT, BISD Vol II, 188 (1952); see also Hudec, Retaliation Against Unreasonable Foreign Trade Practices, 59 Minn.L.Rev. 461 (1975).

opinion, would best assist the Australian and Chilean Governments to arrive at a satisfactory adjustment.

The Australian representative stated that his Government was unable to associate itself with the conclusions reached by the working party in paragraph 12 of this report; their views are reproduced in the annex to this report.

II. THE FACTS OF THE CASE

2. Prior to the outbreak of war in 1939, ammonium sulphate was distributed in Australia by a commercial pooling arrangement operated by Nitrogenous Fertilizers Proprietary, Ltd., a private enterprise; that corporation bought ammonium sulphate from the local producers (both by-product and synthetic sulphate) and from foreign sources of supply. The ammonium sulphate from all sources was sold to consumers at a uniform price. The distribution of imported sodium nitrate was effected by independent agencies.

* * *

III. CONSISTENCY OF THE AUSTRALIAN MEASURES WITH THE PROVISIONS OF THE GENERAL AGREEMENT

7. The removal of nitrate of soda from the pooling arrangements did not involve any prohibition or restriction on the import of sodium nitrate and did not institute any tax or internal charge on that product. The working party concluded, therefore, that the provisions of Article XI, paragraph 1, and of Article III, paragraph 2, were not relevant.

8. As regards the applicability of Article I to the Australian measure, the working party noted that the General Agreement made a distinction between "like products" and "directly competitive or substitutable products". This distinction is clearly brought out in Article III, paragraph 2, read in conjunction with the interpretative note to that paragraph. The most-favoured-nation treatment clause in the General Agreement is limited to "like products". Without trying to give a definition of "like products", and leaving aside the question of whether the two fertilizers are directly competitive, the working party reached the conclusion that they were not to be considered as "like products" within the terms of Article I. In the Australian tariff the two products are listed as separate items and enjoy different treatment. Nitrate of soda is classified as item 403(C) and sulphate of ammonia as item 271(B). Whereas nitrate of soda is admitted free both in the preferential and most-favoured-nation tariff, sulphate of ammonia is admitted free only for the preferential area and is subject to a duty of $12\frac{1}{2}$ per cent for the m.f.n. countries; moreover, in the case of nitrate of soda the rate is bound whereas no binding has been agreed upon for sulphate of ammonia. In the tariffs of other countries the two products are listed separately. In certain cases the rate is the same, but in others the treatment is different: for instance, in the case of the United Kingdom, nitrate of soda is admitted free, whereas a duty of £ 4 per ton is levied on ammonium sulphate.

9. In view of the fact that Article III, paragraph 4, applies to "like products", the provisions of that paragraph are not applicable to the present

case, for the reasons set out in paragraph 8 above. As regards the provisions of paragraph 9 of the same article, the working party was informed that a maximum selling price for ammonium sulphate was no longer fixed by governmental action and, in any event, noted that Australia had considered the Chilean complaint and had made an offer within the terms of that paragraph. Since it was not found that any of the substantive provisions of Article III were applicable, the exception contained in paragraph 8(*b*) is not relevant.

10. The working party then examined the question of whether the Australian Government had complied with the terms of Article XVI on subsidies. It noted that, although this Article is drafted in very general terms, the type of subsidy which it was intended to cover was the financial aid given by a government to support its domestic production and to improve its competitive position either on the domestic market or on foreign markets.

Even if it is assumed that the maintenance of the Australian subsidy on ammonium sulphate is covered by the terms of Article XVI it does not seem that the Australian Government's action can be considered as justifying any claim of injury under this article. It is recognized that the CONTRACTING PARTIES have not been notified by the Australian Government of the maintenance of that subsidy but the working party noted that the procedural arrangements for such notifications under Article XVI have been approved by the CONTRACTING PARTIES only at their present session, and that they require notification only after imposition of the measure. Moreover, the Chilean Government has not suffered any injury from this failure to notify the CONTRACTING PARTIES, as it is established that the Chilean Consul-General had an opportunity to discuss this matter with the Australian authorities before the decision to discontinue the subsidy on sodium nitrate had been enforced. The Australian Government has discussed with the Chilean Government the possibility of limiting the effects of the subsidization, and has also discussed the matter with the CONTRACTING PARTIES, in accordance with the provisions of Article XVI.

11. Within the terms of reference of the working party, the examination of the relevant provisions of the General Agreement thus led it to the conclusion that no evidence had been presented to show that the Australian Government had failed to carry out its obligations under the Agreement.

IV. NULLIFICATION OR IMPAIRMENT OF THE CONCESSION GRANTED TO CHILE ON SODIUM NITRATE

12. The working party next considered whether the injury which the Government of Chile said it had suffered represented a nullification of (sic) impairment of a benefit accruing to Chile directly or indirectly under the General Agreement and was therefore subject to the provisions of Article XXIII. It was agreed that such impairment would exist if the action of the Australian Government which resulted in upsetting the competitive relationship between sodium nitrate and ammonium sulphate could not reasonably have been anticipated by the Chilean Government, taking into consideration all pertinent circumstances and the provisions of the General Agreement, at the time it negotiated for the duty-free binding on sodium nitrate. The working party concluded that the Government of Chile had reason to

assume, during these negotiations, that the war-time fertilizer subsidy would not be removed from sodium nitrate before it was removed from ammonium sulphate. In reaching this conclusion, the working party was influenced in particular by the combination of the circumstances that:

(a) The two types of fertilizer were closely related;

(b) Both had been subsidized and distributed through the same agency and sold at the same price;

(c) Neither had been subsidized before the war, and the war-time system of subsidization and distribution had been introduced in respect of both at the same time and under the same war powers of the Australian Government;

(d) This system was still maintained in respect of both fertilizers at the time of the 1947 tariff negotiations.

For these reasons, the working party also concluded that the Australian action should be considered as relating to a benefit accruing to Chile under the Agreement, and that it was therefore subject to the provisions of Article XXIII. In reaching this conclusion, however, the Working Party considered that the removal of a subsidy, in itself, would not normally result in nullification or impairment. In the case under consideration, the inequality created and the treatment that Chile could reasonably have expected at the time of the negotiation, after taking into consideration all pertinent circumstances, including the circumstances mentioned above, and the provisions of the General Agreement, were important elements in the working party's conclusion.

The situation in this case is different from that which would have arisen from the granting of a new subsidy on one of the two competing products. In such a case, given the freedom under the General Agreement of the Australian Government to impose subsidies and to select the products on which a subsidy would be granted, it would be more difficult to say that the Chilean Government had reasonably relied on the continuation of the same treatment for the two products. In the present case, however, the Australian Government, in granting a subsidy on account of the war-time fertilizer shortage and continuing it in the post-war period, had grouped the two fertilizers together and treated them uniformly. In such circumstances it would seem that the Chilean Government could reasonably assume that the subsidy would remain applicable to both fertilizers so long as there remained a local nitrogenous fertilizer shortage. The working party has no intention of implying that the action taken by the Australian Government was unreasonable, but simply that the Chilean Government could not have been expected during the negotiations in 1947 to have foreseen such action or the reasons which led to it.

13. Having thus concluded that there was a *prima facie* case that the value of a concession granted to Chile had been impaired as a result of a measure which did not conflict with the provisions of the General Agreement, the working party came to the conclusion that there was no infringement of the Agreement by Australia. Since Chile had not applied for a release from any of its obligations, under the provisions of the last two

sentences of Article XXIII, paragraph 2, and it was moreover hoped that an adjustment of the matter satisfactory to both parties could be reached (without prejudice to the views of either on the merits of the case), it was not necessary for the working party to consider whether the above-mentioned provisions were applicable to the case.

* * *

15. As the declared intention of the Australian Government in maintaining the subsidy on ammonium sulphate was to give financial aid, not to the producers of a certain type of fertilizer, but to the producers of certain crops, whose selling price was limited by price control and who preferred to use ammonium sulphate for technical reasons, irrespective of price considerations, the working party came to the conclusion that a satisfactory adjustment would be achieved if the Australian Government could consider the possibility of modifying the present arrangements in such a way as to achieve that object while giving to the two types of fertilizers equal opportunity to compete on its market.

* * *

17. The following is the text of the draft recommendation submitted by the working party to the CONTRACTING PARTIES:

RECOMMENDATION REGARDING THE COMPLAINT OF CHILE CONCERNING THE AUSTRALIAN SUBSIDY ON SULPHATE OF AMMONIA

The CONTRACTING PARTIES recommend that the Australian Government consider, with due regard to its policy of stabilizing the cost of production of certain crops, means to remove any competitive inequality between nitrate of soda and sulphate of ammonia for use as fertilizers which may in practice exist as a result of the removal of nitrate of soda from the operations of the subsidized pool of nitrogenous fertilizers and communicate the results of their consideration to the Chilean Government, and that the two parties report to the CONTRACTING PARTIES at the next session.

Annex

STATEMENT BY THE AUSTRALIAN REPRESENTATIVE

THE APPLICABILITY OF ARTICLE XXIII, PARAGRAPH 1(B), TO THE COMPLAINT OF CHILE REGARDING THE AUSTRALIAN SUBSIDY ON AMMONIUM SULPHATE

* * *

3. In view of the above and the fact that the working party has also found that the Australian subsidy on ammonium sulphate is completely in accordance with the provisions of the Agreement—including the provisions specifically relating to subsidies, Australia cannot consider it a sound argument that what a country might now say was its *reasonable expectation* three years ago in respect of a particular tariff concession should be the determining factor in establishing the existence of impairment in terms of Article XXIII. If it were accepted by the CONTRACTING PARTIES, then this interpretation of Article XXIII would require a complete re-examination of the principles on which Australia (and, we had supposed, all other countries) had hitherto granted tariff concessions. The history and practice

of tariff negotiations show clearly that if a country seeking a tariff concession on a product desires to assure itself of a certain treatment for that product in a field apart from rates of duty *and to an extent going further than is provided for in the various articles of the General Agreement,* the objective sought must be a matter for negotiation in addition to the actual negotiation respecting the rates of duty to be applied.

4.   If this were not so, and if an expectation (no matter how reasonable) which has never been expressed, discussed or attached to a tariff agreement as a condition is interpreted in the light of the arguments adduced in the report of the working party, then tariff concessions and the binding of a rate of duty would be extremely hazardous commitments and would only be entered into after an exhaustive survey of the whole field of substitute or competitive products and detailed analyses of probable future needs of a particular economy.

* * *

Note.—Agreement on this matter was reached between the two governments and notified to the CONTRACTING PARTIES on 6 November 1950.

Note

Although a mere violation of GATT is not a sufficient condition for the utilization of Article XXIII, in later years there developed a concept of "prima facie" nullification or impairment, which has been applied to two or three types of circumstances.[8] If prima facie nullification or impairment is found to exist by a GATT panel, the theory is that the panel is obligated to recommend cessation of the measures complained against, unless the offending nation is able to carry the burden of proof against such recommendation, including a burden of proof that no nullification or impairment has occurred. The three situations to which the prima facie doctrine has been applied include: 1) a violation of GATT obligations (in general); 2) the use of quantitative restrictions (whether a violation of GATT or not) on products which are bound in a schedule; and 3) the introduction or increase of a domestic subsidy on a product, after a tariff-limiting commitment in GATT has been agreed to, which subsidy has the effect of increasing the competitiveness of the domestic product so that imports will be decreased.

(D) SANCTIONS AND COMPENSATION

The Article XXIII sanction, often termed "compensation", has only been utilized once. Possibly the requirement of prior approval of the sanction by the CONTRACTING PARTIES in cases where they conclude that "the circumstances are serious enough" limits the effectiveness and credibility of the sanction. Certainly United States leaders view matters this way, and they refused to require that a United States retaliation in GATT against foreign violations of GATT be tied to a CONTRACTING PARTIES' permission under Article XXIII.[9] For example, the House of Representatives Ways

---

8. This is discussed more fully in J. Jackson, note 1 supra, at 182.

9. See the testimony of Ambassador William D. Eberle, Special Representative for Trade Negotiations in Hearings on H.R.

10710, Trade Reform Act of 1973, Before the Senate Comm. on Finance, 93d Cong., 2d. Sess., pt. 1, at 307, 283–290; Hearings on H.R. 6767, Trade Reform Act of 1973, Before the

and Means Committee Report on the proposed 1974 Trade Act section relating to retaliation said: [10]

> Your committee is particularly concerned that the decisionmaking process in the GATT is such as to make it impossible in practice for the United States to obtain a determination with respect to certain practices of our trading partners which appear to be clear violations of the GATT. For example, it is highly unlikely that the United States could obtain a GATT decision that the various preferential arrangements which the European Community has created with both developed and developing countries are inconsistent with article XXIV (customs unions and free-trade areas), and hence illegal. So long as decisions in the GATT are made on the basis of political consensus of the contracting parties, the United States will have no assurance that questions of consistency with the GATT will be resolved impartially. The committee believes that it is essential for the United States to be able to act unilaterally in any situation where it is unable to obtain redress through the GATT against practices which discriminate against or unreasonably impair U.S. export opportunities.

The only time Article XXIII "suspension of concessions" was authorized was in the Netherlands' complaint against United States import restrictions on cheese imports.[11]

Authorization for these measures was renewed several times, but ultimately lapsed without visibly affecting the U.S. practices complained against. It should be noted that Article XXIII "suspensions" are *not* limited by the text of that article to "compensatory" amounts (as compared to "punitive" amounts) and are not limited to actions by a nation which has been harmed. Theoretically a "sanction" could authorize suspensions of major concessions by many, if not all, GATT members and could even be the basis for an effective expulsion.

(E) REFORM OF GATT DISPUTE SETTLEMENT PROCEDURES

Many weaknesses of GATT Article XXIII must be now apparent: (1) it is imprecise, confusing, and possibly so broad as to call into question its fairness and objectivity; (2) the process involves a major infusion of political considerations, reducing trust in the objectivity of the procedures; (3) sanctions are in a sense self-defeating, merely compounding trade restraints which have uneconomic effects; (4) complaints by a small nation against a large one probably have little effect insofar as they depend on sanctions. In addition, in later years there has developed a hesitancy to utilize the procedures, and a difficulty of finding appropriate disinterested persons to form a panel.

In 1965 and 1966 a GATT Committee on Legal and Institutional Framework created an Ad Hoc Group on Legal Amendments to consider proposals to amend Article XXIII. Such proposals included the provision of financial compensation to a less-developed country (LDC) damaged by actions violating GATT, the automatic release of an LDC from GATT obligations toward an

House Comm. on Ways and Means, 93d Cong., 1st Sess., pt. 2, at 361.

10. Trade Reform Act of 1973, Report of Comm. on Ways and Means, H.R.Rep.No. 93–571, H.R. 10710, 93d Cong., 1st Sess. 66–67.

11. Netherlands Measures of Suspension of Obligations to the United States, Determination of 8th Nov., 1952, GATT, BISD 1st Supp. 32 (1953).

offending developed GATT member and a provision for collective GATT action against an offending party.[12]   A procedure for LDC complaints was adopted as a GATT decision in 1966,[13] providing for time limits and heavy reliance on mediation by the Director-General of GATT, but the proposals mentioned above were not adopted.

We have already noted the efforts in the Tokyo Round to reform the GATT dispute settlement system, and the result (an "understanding" which is essentially a restatement of existing practice).   Efforts for reform continue, amid considerable criticism of the procedures.   A 1981 GATT report noted that

> the number of disputes brought before GATT was even higher than the record level reached in 1980—and in some cases it seemed that the issues raised might be too wide in scope and too important in terms of national policy, to be dealt with by the semijudicial panel procedures.[14]

At the 1982 annual meeting of the Contracting Parties of GATT, a meeting held for "ministerial level" officials and therefore called the "1982 Ministerial Meeting" (higher than normal level), a further attempt was made to accomplish some improvement of the dispute settlement procedures.   The Ministerial Declaration resulting from that meeting reaffirmed the Tokyo Round Declaration, and added (inter alia): [15]

DISPUTE SETTLEMENT PROCEDURES

The CONTRACTING PARTIES:

* * *

* * * agree further that:

(i) With reference to paragraph 8 of the Understanding, if a dispute is not resolved through consultations, any party to a dispute may, with the agreement of the other party, seek the good offices of the Director-General or of an individual or group of persons nominated by the Director-General.   This conciliatory process would be carried out expeditiously, and the Director-General would inform the Council of the outcome of the conciliatory process.   Conciliation proceedings, and in particular positions taken by the parties to the dispute during conciliation, shall be confidential, and without prejudice to the rights of either party in any further proceedings under Article XXIII:2.   It would remain open at any time during any conciliatory process for either party to the dispute to refer the matter to the Contracting Parties.

* * *

(iv) The secretariat of GATT has the responsibility of assisting the panel, especially on the legal, historical and procedural aspects of the matters dealt with.

(v) The terms of reference of a panel should be formulated so as to permit a clear finding with respect to any contravention of GATT

12.   GATT, 14th Supp. BISD 139 (1969).

13.   Procedures under Art. XXIII, Decision of 5th April, 1966, GATT, 14th Supp. BISD 18 (1966); see also, R. Hudec, The GATT Legal System and World Trade Diplomacy, chs. 18–22 (1975).

14.   BNA, 128 ITIM 206 (May 19, 1982).

15.   GATT, 29th Supp. BISD 13 (1983).

provisions and/or on the question of nullification and impairment of benefits. In terms of paragraph 16 of the Understanding, and after reviewing the facts of the case, the applicability of GATT provisions and the arguments advanced, the panel should come to such a finding. Where a finding establishing a contravention of GATT provisions or nullification and impairment is made, the panel should make such suggestions as appropriate for dealing with the matter as would assist the Contracting Parties in making recommendations to the contracting parties which they consider to be concerned, or give a ruling on the matter, as appropriate.

* * *

(viii) The recommendation or ruling made by the Contracting Parties shall be aimed at achieving a satisfactory settlement of the matter in accordance with GATT obligations. In furtherance of the provisions of paragraph 22 of the Understanding the Council shall periodically review the action taken pursuant to such recommendations. The contracting party to which such a recommendation has been addressed, shall report within a reasonable specified period on action taken or on its reasons for not implementing the recommendation or ruling by the Contracting Parties. The contracting party bringing the case may also ask the Contracting Parties to make suitable efforts with a view to finding an appropriate solution as provided in paragraph 22 of the Understanding.

(ix) The further action taken by the Contracting Parties in the above circumstances might include a recommendation for compensatory adjustment with respect to other products or authorization for the suspension of such concessions or other obligations as foreseen in Article XXIII:2, as the Contracting Parties may determine to be appropriate in the circumstances.

(x) The Parties to a dispute would fully participate in the consideration of the matter by the Contracting Parties under paragraph (vii) above, including the consideration of any rulings or recommendations the Contracting Parties might make pursuant to Article XXIII:2 of the General Agreement, and their views would be fully recorded. They would likewise participate and have their views recorded in the considerations of the further actions provided for under paragraphs (viii) and (ix) above. The Contracting Parties reaffirmed that consensus will continue to be the traditional method of resolving disputes; however, they agreed that obstruction in the process of dispute settlement shall be avoided. It is understood that decisions in this process cannot add to or diminish the rights and obligations provided in the General Agreement.

The rather oblique language of paragraph (x) of this declaration recognizes the problem that sometimes a consensus has been blocked by the "losing party" in a panel report. It has been suggested privately that this language authorizes a Chairman of the Contracting Parties to "find" a consensus which does not include one or more of the parties to the dispute itself.

Note

A reluctance by large powers to comply with GATT dispute settlement rulings in several prominent cases during 1983 and 1984 has led to worries about the workability of the GATT procedures. These worries were particularly prominent in connection with the *Wheat Flour* case and the *Pasta* case, described below. In addition other worries about the dispute settlement process have been expressed.[16]

A number of cases brought to the GATT dispute settlement procedure recently have suggested a variety of defects in the process. In various later parts of this book we will examine GATT dispute panel findings in connection with various substantive issues of GATT law. Of particular interest, both substantively and procedurally (in some cases illustrating some of the defects discussed above) are the following cases:

(1) DISC: The EC complained in 1973 that the 1971 U.S. legislation allowing certain corporate income tax deferral related to export sales amounted to an export subsidy inconsistent with GATT obligations. The United States responded with similar claims about certain territorial income tax practices of France, Belgium and the Netherlands. The procedure became very prolonged, lasting over a decade. A panel ruled that all four countries acted inconsistently with GATT rules, but a GATT Council resolution altered the impact of that ruling, and ultimately the United States changed its law in an attempt to comply with GATT. This case is discussed in Section 10.3 infra.

(2) CHICKEN WAR: In the 1960's the EC applied an external tariff for poultry which was higher than a member state's GATT bound concession, requiring a negotiation for "compensation." [17] The United States and the EC could not agree on an appropriate amount of "compensating trade concession," so that the GATT Director-General appointed a small expert panel (not under article XXIII, but actually an ad hoc procedure under article XXVIII) which recommended a figure which was accepted by both sides. The U.S. then raised restraints on imports for several products primarily shipped by EC countries, including small trucks (a German product). The action seemed to have no effect on EC poultry protection, and a particular irony developed in the late 1960's and early 1970's when Japanese companies began importing substantial numbers of

---

16. An interesting congressional discussion critical of GATT dispute settlement procedures can be found in European Community Restrictions on Imports of United States Specialty Agricultural Products: Hearings on HR 238 and HR 320 before the Subcomm. on Trade of the House Comm. on Ways and Means, 95th Cong., 1st Sess. 21 (1977). See also U.S. Intl. Trade Commn., Review of the Effectiveness of Trade Dispute Settlement under the GATT and the Tokyo Round Agreements (Pub.No. 1793, 1985); Hudec, GATT Dispute Settlement After the Tokyo Round, An Unfinished Business, 13 Cornell Intl. L.J. 145 (1980); Jackson, Jurisprudence of International Trade: The DISC Case in GATT, 72 Am.J.Intl. L. 747 (1978), and Jackson, Govern-

mental Disputes in International Trade Relations: A Proposal in the Context of GATT, 13 J. World Trade L. 1 (1979). The Tokyo Round nontariff measure "codes" each contain dispute settlement procedures. See, for example, Article 18 of the Subsidies/Countervailing Agreement. This "Balkanization" of the disputes procedure has been commented on by Jackson in "MTN and the Legal Institutions of International Trade," a report prepared at the request of the Subcomm. on International Trade of the Senate Comm. on Finance, 96th Cong., 1st Sess. (Comm. Print No. 96–14, 1979).

17. For additional references on the Chicken War, see Sections 6.3(C) and 10.5(C) infra.

such trucks to the U.S. and found themselves affected by the U.S. small truck tariff which had been raised on an MFN basis. By this time the Volkswagen company (of Germany) had begun production of such products within the United States, and thus found itself the beneficiary of a U.S. policy originally designed to harm it!

(3) INDIA AND COUNTERVAILING DUTIES: In 1980, India, after joining the Tokyo Round agreement on subsidies and countervailing duties, complained to GATT when the United States refused to apply that agreement to India. A GATT panel was constituted, where India argued that the United States opting out of a Subsidies Code relation with it (as permitted in the Code) was a violation of the MFN clause of GATT. The parties settled, however, before the panel took any action. See Section 7.4(C)(2) infra.

(4) Other interesting cases include:

WHEAT FLOUR: The U.S. complained against EC export subsidies on wheat flour, and a panel under the Tokyo Round code made some ambiguous findings in 1983, which were highly criticized (see Section 10.3(B) infra).

PASTA: Another Subsidies Code panel found in 1983 that the EC system of subsidizing EC pasta exporters to compensate for the difference in price of flour inputs as compared to the world market price for those inputs, was inconsistent with Code obligations. The EC refused to accept this finding, and the matter (as of December 1985) is still pending in GATT (see Section 10.3(B) infra).

MANUFACTURING CLAUSE (reducing copyright protection for English language works printed abroad when imported into the United States): The EC charged the U.S. with violating GATT with this clause, and a panel supported the EC view in 1984 (see Section 5.4(C) supra).

CANADIAN FOREIGN INVESTMENT REVIEW ACT: The United States complained that this Canadian act and policy violated GATT Article III (and other provisions) by requiring non-Canadian investors to make commitments to buy Canadian products for the manufacturing facilities being invested in. The GATT panel supported the U.S. view (see Section 8.2(C) infra).

SPANISH SOYBEAN OIL CASE: The United States complained against Spain alleging that the Spanish Government, by subsidizing production and consumption of olive oil, was discriminating against U.S. soybean oil. In June 1981 a GATT panel ruled in favor of Spain. However, at the GATT Council's meeting November 3, 1981, the United States successfully blocked a move to have the Council adopt this report as an official document. Instead the Council merely "noted" the report which means that it will not serve as a precedent.[18]

EC CITRUS PREFERENCES: A GATT panel on a complaint of the United States against the EC for its preference on citrus imports, ruled that the EC practice, although it may not be necessarily illegal under GATT, nevertheless nullified or impaired U.S. benefits.[19] The EC has thus far blocked adoption of the panel report by the GATT Council.

In June 1985, the United States Government took action to raise the tariffs on pasta imports, partly as a sanction to retaliate against practices of the EC in its citrus import policy, which had been determined by a GATT panel (but not yet by the GATT Council) to be "nullifying or impairing" U.S. benefits in GATT.

18. BNA ITEX No. 364, at C–6 (June 30, 1981); id. No. 382, at 154 (Nov. 10, 1981).

19. 2 BNA Intl. Trade Rptr. 192 (1985).

The EC then decided to counter-retaliate. The two governments then suspended their actions and continued to negotiate to resolve the problem, but failed to do so and the retaliatory actions were reinstated.[20]

SECTION 5.7 THE INTERNATIONAL ECONOMIC REGULATORY SYSTEM VIEWED AS A WHOLE: PROBLEMS TO CONSIDER

This completes Part I of this book, designed to present various legal problems relating to the overall "constitutional" structure of the international economic regulatory system affected both by international agreements and by national government decisions.

Before beginning the Part II material on various functional regulatory principles, however, it may be worthwhile to review and reconsider the Part I material as a whole. Most of the questions in the first problem below are designed to be answered from the material in chapters one through five, and particularly chapters three through five. Problems 2 and 3 anticipate questions we will consider in part II.

Problems

(1) Chart all the decision making steps required for the following possible international economic regulatory initiatives, both at the international level and at the national level (use the United States, the EC and at least one EC member state as the participants at the "national" level); consider what added steps are likely if court litigation is proposed to test the validity of the processes chosen:

(a) Proposal to reform the international balance of payments adjustment system to provide for IMF prior approval to the use of a tariff surcharge for balance-of-payments reasons, followed by GATT review of the specific exceptions and methods of implementation of the tariff surcharge.

(b) A code on harmonization of procedures for purchases or procurement of governments at the local, state, and national levels.

(c) An amendment to GATT to provide permanent exceptions to Article I (the MFN clause) for developing countries; alternatively, a new waiver for the same purpose.

(d) A separate international agreement on procedures for resolving international trade disputes affecting the application of GATT and a series of other trade agreements related to GATT.

(e) An agreement among GATT members to mutually reduce all tariffs to zero, with stated exceptions and a formula for other exceptions (e.g. a "zero tariff club" of industrialized nations, either with or without MFN application).

In solving the problems above, be sure to consider:

(a) consistency with and procedures in GATT and the IMF.

(b) U.S. Executive Branch authority

(c) U.S. congressional procedures and committee processes

(d) U.S. State government powers

20. 2 BNA Intl. Trade Rptr. 835, 1389 (1985).

(e) procedures for U.S. court testing of the actions before or after they are taken

(f) EC authority (or lack thereof) in GATT matters and in IMF matters

(g) allocation of decision making and/or consultation authority in the EC Council, Commission, and European Parliament

(h) procedures for challenging the actions in the EC Court of Justice

(i) necessity of member state parliamentary action

(j) potential litigation tests within an EC member state.

(2) In the next chapter we turn to a series of specific regulatory areas for more detailed study in the light of the legal framework that has been developed in chapters one through seven. The following therefore are some problems which can be considered in the following chapters, but which depend also on the materials of the preceding chapters:

(a) Your client is a U.S. manufacturer of large electric turbines which desires to expand its exports to the European market. Many turbines are purchased by government owned utilities or similar agencies, and your client finds that tariffs of 20% plus government purchasing ("buy at home") rules make it virtually impossible to compete in Europe against European made goods of like nature. What can you do on behalf of your client to urge and encourage the U.S. government to take measures that would assist your clients exports to Europe?

(b) Suppose imports of tennis rackets from Italy have deeply penetrated the U.S. market and caused your client, The Tiny Tennis Co., to lose sales and shut down plants. Your client wants you to begin proceedings under U.S. law or with appropriate U.S. agencies to introduce import restrictions on tennis rackets. What are your chances of success? What legal rights, if any, does your client have for help of the type he seeks?

(c) Your client is considering opening a plant in Ireland (an EC member) to produce small kitchen appliances, with a view to exporting most of the plant's output to other countries in Europe and the United States. His long term investment will depend heavily upon the stability of the import regulations in those other countries. He consults you to ask to what degree he can depend on the present level of import restrictions on toasters and other small appliances over a period of ten years.

(3) Finally, consider the following hypothetical situation:

Assume that your client is a foreign manufacturer, such as a computer manufacturer in Japan. Your client has developed a new product, which is selling well in its own market. It has just begun to capture a small part of the United States market, and the manufacturer would like to embark on a program to increase those sales. To do that, however, it may have to utilize some technology from the United States, particularly in the software area, where U.S. companies have an advantage. The Japanese company is reviewing four options:

a. Export sales of the product manufactured in Japanese factories, to be sold in U.S. retail outlets. A Japanese government agency offers interest rates below the current market rates for development of additional plant facilities. In addition, the Japanese government offers special inducements for companies to utilize robots. Finally, there are special "start-up costs" tax deductions from Japanese income taxes that are available. The U.S.

tariff for importing the product is five percent and bound under GATT and will decline in the next few years to three percent. Under current exchange rates, the Japanese company calculates it can sell in the U.S. market at a price about twenty percent below its competitors, but such a price would be below the price it charges for its product in the Japanese market. It could lower its Japanese prices, however.

b. A second option is initiating a joint venture with a small U.S. manufacturer, to manufacture the product in the United States and sell it here.

c. A third option is to buy a small U.S. firm, which will then manufacture the product and sell it in the United States.

d. A fourth option is for the Japanese company to establish its own manufacturing facility in the United States, under supervision of Japanese personnel sent here.

What would be the considerations necessary for evaluating the relative merits of these options? Obviously the first option relates to the material in this book. The other options would draw upon other subjects of law.

*

Part II

REGULATORY PRINCIPLES AND IMPORT RESTRAINTS: THE CORE OF THE SYSTEM

Chapter 6

TARIFFS, QUOTAS AND NONTARIFF BARRIERS

SECTION 6.1 INTRODUCTION

(A) INTRODUCTION TO PART II

In Part I of this book, Chapters 1 through 5, we examined the international economic "system" and institutions in a general way, with a focus on fundamental and institutional legal questions. The objective of Part I, as stated at its outset, was to give the reader an understanding of the "three levels" of the international economic system (private transactions, national regulation and international regulation), how these levels fit together, and what the principal legal notions are that constrain or motivate operations and policy in this system.

Now, in Part II, we turn to a series of "functional" subjects, dealing with specific aspects of economic relations. Naturally the starting point (Chapter 6) is the basic import restraint—primarily the tariff and secondarily the quota. The objective in each of these functional chapters is to examine a particular feature of international trade regulation as it operates in several of the "levels of analysis" presented in Part I. That is, if Part I is viewed as "horizontal" in structure, presenting the total system in layers (private transactions at the bottom, national regulation next, and international regulation on top), then Part II is structured "vertically," that is to say, a functional subject is explored through all three levels of analysis (or at least through the top two—national and international—since the focus of the book as a whole is upon government regulation).

The five chapters of Part II (Chapters 6 through 10) deal with the most fundamental aspects of regulation of international economic relations. These are topics which are central to trade policy. Almost any person who is thrust into some aspect of international trade policy—whether it be in government or in private life—will find that discourse generally assumes a knowledge of these topics. Another characteristic of these topics is that they are "more legal" than subsequent subjects, in the sense that a body of rules and principles—usually identified with a legal system—has grown up over decades, and there is a *comparatively* high degree of consensus and compliance with the rules, as well as certain techniques of enforcement.

Many of the topics considered in Part I will be found to occur in the various subjects considered in Part II. For example, United States constitutional problems relating to the relationship of Congress and the President will be a prominent feature of a number of the subjects considered in this part, e.g., the validity of the 1967 Anti-Dumping Code in United States law, the escape clause process and export restraint agreements. The focus of the functional chapters in this part will be upon the GATT rules and United States law, since these two sets of legal principles contain detailed provisions important to international trade.

Chapters 7 and 8, dealing respectively with the most-favored-nation obligation and the national treatment obligation, consider the two most fundamental and general subjects of international trade regulation. Chapter 9 then deals with the so-called Escape Clause, which provides some flexibility in the system of rules. Often Escape Clause measures are called "safeguards," which translates to mean "safeguards for domestic industry against undue foreign competition." Chapter 10 turns to a series of trade measures that are responses to actions taken by foreign exporters or countries in order to promote exports to the detriment of importing country producers. Many techniques of such promotion could be called "unfair." In addition, this chapter will consider generally some of the potential "retaliation" techniques that are available to countries, focusing again on United States law.

(B) THE ECONOMICS OF IMPORT RESTRAINTS

We began in Chapter 1 with an overview of the economic theories that underlie international economic policies and a consideration of noneconomic factors, such as national goals established for political reasons, that affect those policies. We have seen how the view that free trade is desirable and reduces the likelihood of armed conflict played a central role in the creation of GATT. Throughout the rest of the book, and particularly in Part II, the reader will see how the factors introduced in Chapter 1 have affected the creation of the international rules and national practices under them. In particular, we will see how GATT enshrines the basic principles of free international trade, but at the same time allows exceptions to them, particularly in cases where imports are viewed as unfairly traded or as injurious to local industry, and we will see played out time and again the struggle between advocates of a broader national interest—free trade—and those defending the interests of a particular industry.

We will not review here the material in Section 1.3 and the Appendix to Chapter 1, but the reader who is not generally familiar with the principles discussed there would do well to review them. We will refer to additional economic writings in Part II as they bear on particular subjects, such as dumping and subsidies.

(C) INTRODUCTION TO CHAPTER 6

In Chapter 6 we focus on tariffs and quotas, although we also introduce the problem of nontariff barriers (NTBs). In Section 6.2 we look at tariffs from the national perspective, which essentially involves consideration of the basic issues of customs law. In Section 6.3, we continue to focus on tariffs, but from the international perspective as we consider the basic GATT obligations in respect of tariffs. Finally, in Section 6.4, we examine quotas as they are regulated internationally and as they are applied in the United States.

At the end of each principal section of this chapter, there are a series of problems or questions designed to assist the student in understanding and exploring the material presented in the section. It may be helpful in understanding the materials presented if the reader examines those questions at this point, rather than later.

(D) THE VARIETIES OF IMPORT RESTRAINTS: TARIFFS, QUOTAS, AND NONTARIFF BARRIERS

The basic and most prominent government restraint on imports is the tariff, which is, of course, a tax imposed at the border on imported goods. Generally there are three types of tariffs: ad valorem, specific and mixed. The ad valorem tariff is a tax calculated by a percentage of the value of the goods being imported. Thus, a 10% ad valorem tariff would cause a $10.00 tariff for an item which is valued at $100 upon importation. A specific tariff is a flat charge per unit or quantity of the goods, such as $1.00 per ton or 5 cents per pound. A mixed tariff combines these two concepts, such as 5 cents per pound plus 10% of value. In addition to these types of tariffs, there is the "tariff quota." A tariff quota provides a different tariff rate depending upon the amount already imported into a country. For instance, a tariff quota might provide that all imports during a year which total less than 1 million tons shall have a tariff charge imposed at 10%. Once the 1 million ton mark has been reached, however, all additional imports shall have a tariff imposed at 20%.

Generally speaking, a country that has a tariff system has a set of regulations which are applied by the customs agents (who implement the tariff), and these regulations include the "tariff schedule," which is a detailed list of commodities and products with the particular government tariff indicated beside the product. An example of a portion of the United States tariff schedule (in force during 1985) is given in Section 6.2(G) infra. The United States tariff schedule is generally a "two column" tariff schedule, although it currently has three. The tariff which is applied to imported goods depends upon the source or origin of those goods. Column 1 of the United States tariff is the "MFN" rate, that is, the column applied to imports from countries receiving from the United States non-discriminatory or "most-favored-nation" treatment (see Chapter 7). Column 2 of the United States tariff schedule is the "statutory rate," which generally is the rate imposed by the Smoot-Hawley Tariff Act of 1930,[1] as amended from time to time over the subsequent decades. The column 2 rate is applied to products imported into the United States from those countries which do not receive MFN treatment from the United States (generally Communist countries). Finally, there is a third column—the Special column. The rate in that

---

1. Ch. 497, 56 Stat. 590 (1930), codified in 19 U.S.C.A. §§ 1202–1677g. For the current complete schedules, see U.S. International Trade Commission, Tariff Schedules of the United States Annotated (1985) (16th ed., Supp. 3, 1985).

column applies to imports from countries who are beneficiaries of a special U.S. tariff preference. Such beneficiaries include those who qualify for the Generalized System of Preferences (GSP), discussed in Section 20.3 below, and those GSP beneficiaries who are considered to be among the least developed developing countries (LDDCs). Normally, qualifying imports from GSP beneficiaries are duty free. However, in respect of imports that do not qualify for GSP treatment, LDDCs are entitled to receive the MFN rate that will appear in Column 1 when the Tokyo Round tariff reductions are completely phased-in; the LDDCs essentially receive the benefit of those reductions early.[2] The other beneficiaries of the Special column are certain Caribbean countries and Israel, in respect of which the United States has special preferential trading arrangements (see Section 7.3(C) infra).

Conceivably, a country could have many more columns in its tariff schedule. If it did not grant MFN to other nations, it could have a tariff schedule with as many columns as there are nations with whom it trades. Obviously, this would be a very complex tariff system to apply, and the origin of goods could be very critical in terms of the rate actually applied. Thus, questions of how the customs agents would ascertain true origin (and prevent fraud) would loom large. Countries which have traditionally been part of the British Commonwealth preferential system would conceivably have at present a four column tariff schedule (the preferential tariffs (Commonwealth and general), the MFN rate, and the rate for the countries not extended MFN treatment).[3]

As discussed in Chapter 1, whatever tariff is charged upon a good will normally have to be added to the price of the good when it is sold in the importing country's domestic market. Since the domestically produced goods are not subject to the tariff charge, they can be priced as high or almost as high as the tariffed imported goods and still compete with those goods; consequently, the domestic producer captures a higher total price for his goods.

While tariffs are the most basic and simple import restraint, there is a plethora of other ways by which countries can restrain imports. Most of these other ways are termed "nontariff barriers," and they number literally

---

2. See S.Rep. No. 96–249, 96th Cong., 2nd Sess. 170–71 (1979).

3. For example, the following is a portion of the Canadian Tariff Schedule (Can.Rev.Stat. ch. 17 (1984):

Tariff Item		British Preferential Tariff	Most-Favoured-Nation Tariff	General Tariff	General Preferential Tariff
44003–1	Boats, open, including sail boats, skiffs and canoes; *yachts and pleasure boats, not exceeding 9.2 metres in length overall*	15 p.c.	16.3 p.c.	25 p.c.	10.5 p.c.
	on and after January 1, 1984	15 p.c.	15.9 p.c.	25 p.c.	10.5 p.c.
	on and after January 1, 1985	15 p.c.	15.6 p.c.	25 p.c.	10 p.c.
	on and after January 1, 1986	15 p.c.	15.3 p.c.	25 p.c.	10 p.c.
	on and after January 1, 1987	15 p.c.	15 p.c.	25 p.c.	10 p.c.
44005–1	Yachts and pleasure boats, exceeding *9.2 metres* in length overall	15 p.c.	20 p.c.	25 p.c.	13 p.c.
	on and after January 1, 1984	15 p.c.	18.8 p.c.	25 p.c.	12.5 p.c.
	on and after January 1, 1985	15 p.c.	17.5 p.c.	25 p.c.	11.5 p.c.
	on and after January 1, 1986	15 p.c.	16.3 p.c.	25 p.c.	10.5 p.c.
	on and after January 1, 1987	15 p.c.	15 p.c.	25 p.c.	10 p.c.

in the hundreds if not thousands.[4] One most prominent nontariff barrier (NTB) is the "quota" or "quantitative restriction." The quota is a specified amount or quantity of a particular good which a country will allow to be imported. The quota may be "global," in the sense that it will be expressed as a total amount from all origins or sources which can be imported; or a quota may be broken down into "country" quotas so that a certain quantity will be allowed from, say, Japan, another quantity from Australia, etc. Quotas will be analyzed in more detail in Section 6.4 infra.

International trade policy has generally favored tariffs over virtually all the other types of import restraints. Tariffs, it is argued, are more visible, capture for the government much of the "monopoly profit" which they create, do not need licensing to administer, do not require government funds to support (in contrast to a subsidy), and give a specific amount of protection, so that if a foreign based industry can become efficient enough to reduce its prices by a margin that exceeds the tariff, it will still be able to import into the tariff imposing country. (Thus, the tariff limits the monopoly benefit given to domestic producers.) Tariff reduction is also easier to negotiate. Moreover, quotas are thought to entail the risk of government corruption in the licensing process. They also tend to conceal from the public the degree and cost of the protection being afforded domestic producers. On the other hand, economic planning may be easier if the precise amount of imports can be predicted—quotas may allow this, while tariffs make such prediction more difficult.

Besides quotas, there are numerous other ways to restrain imports. At the time that GATT was drafted (1947–48), four techniques of import restraint were considered to be the primary methods of restraint: [5] the tariff, the quota, subsidies and state trading monopolies. The tariff and quota have already been briefly described. A subsidy can be used as a protective or import restraint device if it is granted for the domestic production of goods, so that such products can be priced lower in the domestic market than the imported goods. While tariffs and quotas will generally cause goods that are imported to be priced higher than they would otherwise be, when a subsidy is used for protection, the result, in contrast, is that domestic goods are priced lower than they would otherwise be. Consequently, the use of a subsidy will generally result in favoring the consumer, since all goods, both domestic and foreign, will be at a lower price. The favored domestic goods might be sufficiently low in price such that the foreign imports could not compete at all, and therefore no imports would occur.

State trading monopolies operate as follows: the government decrees that a particular corporation (usually government-owned) shall be the only entity allowed to import a certain type of commodity (such as tobacco or steel). The state trading corporation will then purchase goods abroad and

4. See generally discussion of nontariff barriers in Section 8.1 infra, and discussion and NTB inventory in House Comm. on Ways and Means, 93d Cong., 1st Sess., Briefing Materials on Foreign Trade and Tariffs 54–150 (Comm. Print 1973).

5. See generally J. Jackson, World Trade and the Law of GATT 305–08, 625–38 (1969).

resell them on the domestic market in competition with domestically produced goods. The degree of protection that this device affords will depend upon the "mark-up" which the state trading corporation imposes on the goods. If it purchases goods for $100 each and resells them on the domestic market for $200 each, it has imposed a 100% mark-up. This can operate similarly to a 100% tariff, by reducing the demand for imported goods in competition with domestic goods. A state trading corporation can also operate its purchases and sales to have the effect of a quota. It may simply refuse to purchase more than a specified amount of foreign goods for domestic resale, thereby limiting the quantity of imports to that amount.

Observers have noted that the GATT approach to these four basic protective devices differs considerably from one to another. Basically, GATT is designed to prefer the tariff. Many of the provisions of GATT are designed to prevent the use of nontariff barriers for protective reasons, but tariffs are permitted by GATT. However, the GATT structure provides for multilateral, international negotiation on the level of each tariff (as described in Section 6.3 below). If a country has not agreed to a limit on the tariff for a particular product, it is permitted by GATT to impose any tariff it wishes, even 100% or 1000%. On the other hand, GATT flatly prohibits the use of quotas (with certain specified exceptions to be discussed later). Thus, the quota is the "disfavored" device. As to the use of subsidies or state trading for restraining imports, GATT attempts (rather wistfully) to regulate these devices, but the rules provided in GATT for this purpose are weak and ambiguous. In later chapters these rules will be discussed. (See Chapter 10 for a discussion of subsidies and Chapter 21 for a discussion of state trading monopolies.) An argument made by developing countries has been that devices such as subsidies or state trading, which are more useful for strong industrialized countries, are only weakly regulated by GATT; whereas quotas, which the developing countries have felt are necessary to their systems of economic planning, are severely restrained by GATT.

Beyond the basic four protective devices discussed above, there is a large number of other measures. The discovery of new protective devices appears to be an endless process. As soon as the international system establishes restraints or regulations on a particular protective device, government officials and human ingenuity seem able to turn up some other measures to accomplish at least part of their protective purposes. Consequently, it can be argued that any international economic regulatory system must be designed so as to cope with the constant change in protectionist techniques.

Recognizing that GATT had been more successful in negotiating restraints on the level of tariffs than it had been in reducing nontariff barriers, in the latter part of the 1960's, GATT undertook an exercise to inventory and catalog nontariff barriers of all participating countries. The objective of the inventory was to gather information about the different kinds and effects of nontariff barriers, so that later international trade negotiations could begin to deal with these barriers in a systematic way. By 1973, the inventory contained well over 800 NTBs, listed by country.

Other efforts have been made subsequently to inventory NTBs, and attempts have been made to evaluate their economic impact, often by trying to compute a "tariff equivalent effect" of NTBs. This has proved to be very difficult to do.[6]

Examples of NTBs found in the United States by the GATT study included (1) arbitrary customs valuation and administrative procedures, (2) technical standards that had a greater effect on imports than on U.S. products, e.g. inspections performed only in the United States and standards that were not well known, (3) packaging and labeling requirements, and (4) requirements that government agencies buy only domestic goods.[7] Specific examples of standards that were considered to be NTBs included: [8]

> Marketing orders under the Agricultural Marketing Agreements Act of 1937, as amended, pursuant to which sixteen fruits, vegetables, and nuts were subject to regulations in respect of quality, grade, size, and maturity standards in order to enter the U.S. market. Twelve of the 16 commodities were then being regulated.

> Standards imposed under the Wholesome Meat Act, designed to protect the health and welfare of consumers by assuring that meats are wholesome, not adulterated, and properly marked, labeled, and packaged.

> Certain provisions of U.S. sanitary and health laws and regulations were viewed by foreign suppliers as NTBs (e.g., prohibition of meat imports from countries with hoof and mouth disease).

> Under then existing law, the IRS classified sparkling cider as sparkling wine, in accordance with written specifications. The law was non discriminatory and applied equally to domestic and foreign cider.

> A 1922 ICC regulation on gas cylinders required such cylinders to be tested in the United States prior to sale. As a result, imports on a commercial basis were virtually precluded.

A number of the problems mentioned above were dealt with in Tokyo Round agreements, including the Customs Valuation Code (discussed in Section 6.2(D)), the Import Licensing Agreement (discussed in Section 6.4), the Agreement on Technical Barriers to Trade, known as the Standards Code (discussed in Section 8.5) and the Agreement on Government Procurement (discussed in Section 8.4). We will deal with the varied forms of NTBs throughout Part II because many NTBs are arguably governed by GATT rules on most-favored-nation treatment, national treatment or subsidies.

---

6. The U.S. Trade Representative submitted the first "National Trade Estimate" report to Congress in October 1985. The report contained an extensive list of trade barriers faced by U.S. exports. 2 BNA Intl. Trade Rptr. 1390 (1985).

UNCTAD has been developing a computerized NTB inventory. Regarding NTB effects, see P. Morici & L. Megna, U.S. Economic Policies Affecting Industrial Trade—A Quantitative Assessment (National Planning Association, 1983); D. Tarr & M. Morkre, Aggregate Costs to the United States of Tariffs and Quotas on Imports: General Tariff Cuts and Removal of Quotas on Automobiles, Steel, Sugar, and Textiles, An Economic Policy Analysis (Bureau of Economics Staff Report to the Federal Trade Commission, 1984); The Consumer Cost of U.S. Trade Restraints, Fed.Res. Bank N.Y.Q.Rev., Summer 1985, at 1–12; A. Deardorff & R. Stern, Methods of Measurement of Nontariff Barriers (prepared for the United Nations Conference on Trade and Development, UNCTAD document UNCTAD/ST/MD/28, 2 January 1985).

7. House Comm. on Ways and Means, note 4 supra, at 144–50.

8. Id., at 147–48.

However, the ingenuity of man is such that new varieties of trade barriers crop up constantly. Although their effect on trade is clear, many of these barriers are not easy to fit within the traditional categories of import restraints. They involve subtle concepts such as the effect of government "targeting" policies, or societal differences such as language or quality preference. A major question facing international trade negotiators, as well as theorists, is which NTBs are really trade barriers that should be controlled and which are actions that affect trade but are really legitimate government policies that are not intended to discriminate against foreign products or are simply societal preferences that give one country certain advantages over another so that trade is possible in the first place.

SECTION 6.2 NATIONAL TARIFFS AND CUSTOMS LAW

(A) INTRODUCTION

The subject of national tariffs and customs law is very detailed and specialized. Consequently, we will examine only a few of the more interesting problems. We will first describe briefly the few GATT rules that are applicable to tariff administration and then focus on U.S. customs law and practice. Reference will be also made to international efforts to adopt uniform rules and procedures.

A number of GATT articles (particularly Articles VII through X) attempt to impose some international standards on the customs procedures followed by member nations. For example, Article X requires that customs laws and regulations be published promptly and that a tribunal be available to administer appeals from decisions by customs officials. Under Article VIII, limits are imposed on fees and formalities that can be required. For example, fees must be "limited in amount to the appropriate cost of services rendered and shall not represent an indirect protection to domestic products." Article VIII, paragraph 3 reads:

> No contracting party shall impose substantial penalties for minor breaches of customs regulations or procedural requirements. In particular, no penalty in respect of any omission or mistake in customs documentation which is easily rectifiable and obviously made without fraudulent intent or gross negligence shall be greater than necessary to serve merely as a warning.

Article IX places limits on the use of origin marking requirements, in particular by requiring MFN treatment, while Article VII deals with valuation of goods, a subject also dealt with in a Tokyo Round agreement and to which we return below.

In order to administer tariffs, which are mostly ad valorem, national officials must make three determinations in connection with the importation of particular goods. First, they must "classify" the goods, identifying them under one of the categories in the tariff schedule. (Are they handkerchiefs or scarves? Shoes or sandals?) Second, the goods must be valued so that the ad valorem tariff rate can be applied. Third, the origin of the goods must be determined so that it is possible to apply the appropriate tariff rate within the specific category. After those steps are completed, the customs officials can "liquidate" the entry, that is, specify the exact amount of dollars and cents that is due as tariff on the shipment.

(B) OVERVIEW OF U.S. CUSTOMS LAW [1]

When foreign goods reach the United States, they must be either entered at the port of arrival or transported in bond to an inland port of entry for similar entry procedures.[2] Entry may be accomplished by the consignee (importer), his authorized regular employee or his agent.[3] After entry has been filed, the port director of customs will designate representative quantities for examination by customs officials, make an estimate of duties for deposit and release the bulk under bond.[4] The examination is necessary to determine the value and classification of the goods for customs duty assessment and to ensure that country of origin or other special marking requirements have been met, that no prohibited articles are present, that the shipment has been correctly invoiced and that no quantitative discrepancies exist. It is also at this time that a number of health and safety regulations are applied. Among these are portions of the Flammable Fabrics Act, the United States Food, Drug, and Cosmetic Act, the Trademark Act, the Copyright Act, the Federal Alcohol Administration Act, Foreign Quarantine Regulations and the Federal Seed Act.[5] These acts may prohibit the importation of goods which do not meet their standards. Likewise some statutes impose quotas on the amount of goods which can be imported and customs officials, usually in conjunction with a licensing system, will administer these quotas.

The final determination of the rate and amount of duty is termed "liquidation." The importer is notified of any variance from the estimate

1. The U.S. tariff schedules are contained in 19 U.S.C.A. § 1202 and are published separately in updated form by the International Trade Commission. See, e.g., United States Intl. Trade Commn., Tariff Schedules of the United States Annotated (1985) (16th ed. 1985). The basic laws affecting customs are codified in 19 U.S.C.A., and the rules and regulations of the Customs Service are collected in 19 C.F.R.

The court with exclusive primary jurisdiction over customs matters is the Court of International Trade (formerly the Customs Court), whose decisions are published in Federal Supplement. Appeals are to the Court of Appeals for the Federal Circuit (formerly the Court of Customs and Patent Appeals), whose decisions are published in Federal Reporter 2d. For a discussion of those courts and a brief selection of their jurisprudence, see Section 3.5(C) supra.

There are a number of useful secondary sources on customs law, including in particular R. Sturm, Customs Law and Administration (3d ed. looseleaf); Bureau of National Affairs, International Trade Reporter (consisting of two basic volumes on trade laws, weekly reports and a selection of recent decisions in

the area that are issued periodically as bound volumes entitled "International Trade Reporter Decisions" or "ITRD"); D. Serko, Import Practice: Customs and International Trade Law (1985). For EC customs law, see D. Lasok & W. Cairns, The Customs Law of the European Economic Community (1983).

2. Merchandise may also be imported by mail. See 19 CFR Pt. 145 (1985).

3. Entry may also be made by the exporter or his agent in the United States. The primary requirements are that the surety for any required bond be incorporated in the United States and that the party or agent be authorized to accept service of process in the state of the port of entry. For regulations pertaining to the entry of merchandise, see 19 CFR Pts. 141–42 (1985).

4. Some classes of goods not intended for sale (e.g., goods imported for repair, professional equipment and samples) may be imported free under bond for their exportation within 1 year. 19 CFR §§ 10.31–.40 (1985).

5. 15 U.S.C.A. § 1198; 21 U.S.C.A. § 381; 15 U.S.C.A. §§ 1124–1125; 17 U.S.C.A. §§ 106–109; 27 U.S.C.A. §§ 203–206; 42 CFR Pt. 71 (1974); 7 U.S.C.A. §§ 1581–1586.

deposited; any increase must be paid, and any excess is automatically refunded. A voluntary reliquidation may be made within ninety days to correct errors made in valuation or classification adverse to either the government or the importer.

If the importer wishes to contest the liquidation, he must file a protest with the appropriate customs office to secure an administrative review. The protest must be filed within ninety days.[6]

If the protest is denied and all assessed duties have been paid, the denial may be appealed to the Court of International Trade, which has exclusive jurisdiction over all such actions. The Court, headquartered in New York, sits at any United States port of entry.[7] In the Court of International Trade, there is a trial de novo of the issues,[8] but the Customs official is presumed to have acted correctly. Neither the Government nor importers are bound by prior decisions.[9]

(C) CLASSIFICATION FOR CUSTOMS PURPOSES

(1) United States Law

The first United States tariff schedule came into being only four months after the Constitution of the United States became effective. The current Tariff Schedules of the United States (TSUS)[10] became effective on August 31, 1963. The TSUS are designed to describe, either generally or specifically, all items that might be imported. Frequently, however, imported merchandise (especially new products) may be described by more than one TSUS description with widely disparate rates of duty. (A new classification system entitled the "Harmonized Commodity Description and Coding System" has been prepared under the auspices of the Customs Cooperation Council, Brussels, Belgium. This is described at the end of subsection (C)(2) below.)

The rules used to determine classification issues in close cases are complex and somewhat obscure. We will not attempt to cover these rules in a comprehensive fashion, but the following extracts should give the reader a flavor of the issues involved in classification. Particular attention should be given to the way the following classification principles are defined and used:

(1) Common meaning or "eo nomine"

(2) Commercial designation

(3) Chief use

(4) Relative specificity (of two classification categories)

(5) "Entireties" rule

(6) Parts of articles/unfinished articles

---

6. 19 U.S.C.A. § 1514(c).

7. See Section 3.5(C) supra for a description of the jurisdiction of the Court of International Trade.

8. 28 U.S.C.A. § 2640(a)(1).

9. United States v. Stone & Downer Co., 274 U.S. 225, 47 S.Ct. 616, 71 L.Ed. 1013 (1927); United States v. Ralph Boone, 188 F.2d 808, 38 C.C.P.A. 89 (1951).

10. 19 U.S.C.A. § 1202; see also U.S. Intl. Trade Comm., Tariff Schedules of the United States Annotated (1985) (TSUSA) (16th ed. 1985).

TARIFF SCHEDULES OF THE UNITED STATES (1985)
General Headnotes and Rules

10. For purposes of these schedules—

*   *   *

(c) an imported article which is described in two or more provisions of the schedules is classifiable in the provision which most specifically describes it; but, in applying this rule of interpretation, the following considerations shall govern:

(i) a superior heading cannot be enlarged by inferior headings intended under it but can be limited thereby;

(ii) comparisons are to be made only between provisions of coordinate or equal status, i.e., between the primary or main superior headings of the schedules or between coordinate inferior headings which are subordinate to the same superior heading;

(d) if two or more tariff descriptions are equally applicable to an article, such article shall be subject to duty under the description for which the original statutory rate is highest, and, should the highest original statutory rate be applicable to two or more of such descriptions, the article shall be subject to duty under that one of such descriptions which first appears in the schedules;

(e) in the absence of special language or context which otherwise requires—

(i) a tariff classification controlled by use (other than actual use) is to be determined in accordance with the use in the United States at, or immediately prior to, the date of importation, of articles of that class or kind to which the imported articles belong, and the controlling use is the chief use, i.e., the use which exceeds all other uses (if any) combined;

(ii) a tariff classification controlled by the actual use to which an imported article is put in the United States is satisfied only if such use is intended at the time of importation, the article is so used, and proof thereof is furnished within 3 years after the date the article is entered;

(f) an article is in chief value of a material if such material exceeds in value each other single component material of the article;

(g) a headnote provision which enumerates articles not included in a schedule, part, or subpart is not necessarily exhaustive, and the absence of a particular article from such headnote provision shall not be given weight in determining the relative specificity of competing provisions which describes such article;

(h) unless the context requires otherwise, a tariff description for an article covers such article, whether assembled or not assembled, and whether finished or not finished;

(i) a provision for "parts" of an article covers a product solely or chiefly used as a part of such article, but does not prevail over a specific provision for such part.

*   *   *

9. Definitions—For the purposes of the schedules, unless the context otherwise requires:

* * *

(f) the terms "of", "wholly of", "almost wholly of", "in part of" and "containing", when used between the description of an article and a material (e.g., "furniture *of* wood", "woven fabrics, *wholly of* cotton", etc.), have the following meanings:

(i) "of" means that the article is wholly or in chief value of the named material;

(ii) "wholly of" means that the article is, except for negligible or insignificant quantities of some other material or materials, composed completely of the named materials;

(iii) "almost wholly of" means that the essential character of the article is imparted by the named material, notwithstanding the fact that significant quantities of some other material or materials may be present; and

(iv) "in part of" or "containing" mean that the article contains a significant quantity of the named material.

With regard to the application of the quantitative concepts specified in subparagraphs (ii) and (iv) above, it is intended that the *de minimis* rule apply.

THEODORE B. AUDETT, CUSTOMS LAW—A BRIEF REVIEW AND DISCUSSION

(1970) [11]

It is a long-standing rule of tariff classification that tariff statutes are drafted in the language of commerce, and that the commercial meaning is presumed to be the same as the common meaning unless a different commercial designation is established. Common meaning is a matter of law to be determined by the court, for which purpose the court may consult dictionaries and other authorities, may receive the testimony of witnesses, which is advisory only, and may rely upon its own knowledge. In order to establish a commercial meaning of a tariff term different from the common meaning, it must be shown that at the time of enactment of the provision in question the precise tariff term had a definite, uniform, and general meaning in the trade and commerce of the United States which was different from its common meaning.

It has also been a well-settled rule that in determining which of two or more different tariff provisions governs the classification of an imported article, a *use* provision prevails over an *eo nomine* provision, in the absence of a clearly expressed congressional intent to the contrary. Such contrary intent has been held to be shown by a competing *eo nomine* provision which precisely and specifically describes the merchandise.

* * *

11. 25 Sw.L.J. 441, 450–53. Reprinted by permission of the Southern Methodist University.

Imported articles not more specifically provided for elsewhere in the T.S. U.S. are frequently classified according to the material of which they are composed. Although such tariff descriptions sometimes provide for articles composed "wholly or in chief value of" a specified material and sometimes for articles "of" a specified material, an article must in both instances be composed wholly or in chief value of the named material if it is to be covered by the provision in question. On the other hand, tariff descriptions covering articles "in part of" or "containing" a named material merely require that the article contain a significant part of the named material.

The courts have held that the proper method for determining component material of chief value is to ascertain the cost of the separate parts or component materials to the manufacturer at the time they are in such condition that nothing remains to be done to them except to combine them to make the completed article. This rule is applicable only if the component materials, at the time they are joined together, are in the same condition as in the completed article, which is usually the case. If they are changed in condition after joining together, the general rule does not apply, and their value must be determined in the form in which they appear in the completed article. For example, in a case involving woven fabrics composed of linen, nylon, and wool fibers, which were spun together into a single yarn before being woven into fabric, it was held that spinning costs must be added to the cost of the fibers in order to determine the component material of chief value.

Various provisions for "parts" of certain named articles have long been the source of much confusion and litigation. Prior to the enactment into law of the T.S.U.S., the prevailing rule for determining whether an article should be classified as a "part" of another named article was whether it had been advanced to a point which dedicated it for use as a part of that article. An imported article which was commercially suitable and commercially used as a part of several different articles was held to be not a part of any of them and had to be classified elsewhere in the tariff provisions. As a consequence very similar articles were sometimes subject to widely varying rates of duty, depending upon whether it was determined that, in their imported condition, they were "dedicated" for use as a part of a specific manufacture.

* * *

Even the foregoing brief review of basic classification principles fully indicates the hazards faced by an importer who attempts to determine the rate of duty applicable to merchandise he contemplates importing by consulting the tariff schedules and finding a description which he believes to be appropriate. In recognition of this problem the Bureau of Customs has provided that an importer may obtain a binding opinion on the classification of a prospective import by submitting a written application to the Commissioner of Customs with a complete description of the article, accompanied by a sample, if practicable.

Notes

(1) FRANCESCO PARISI FWDG. CORP. v. UNITED STATES, 296 F.Supp. 315 (Cust.Ct.1969), affirmed, 424 F.2d 1093 (C.C.P.A.1970). The court overruled the importer's protest that a stereocomparator should be classified either as

laboratory apparatus in chief value of metal or as an article having as an essential feature an electrical device or element, and sustained its classification as a "surveying instrument," saying (296 F.Supp. at 319):

> It was incumbent upon plaintiff to either show that the use of the stero-comparator in photogrammetric surveying was not the dominant use or that one or a number of the other uses predominated. Plaintiff took neither of these alternatives and instead chose only to introduce an enumeration and explanation of nonsurveying uses. This is not directly relevant to the issue of chief use.

(2) SEARS, ROEBUCK & CO. v. UNITED STATES, 504 F.2d 1400 (C.C.P.A. 1974). Plaintiff protested the classification of "musical jewelry boxes" imported from Japan as "other articles not specially provided for of a type used for household, table, or kitchen use; toilet and sanitary wares; all the foregoing and parts thereof, of base metal, not coated or plated with precious metal" (item 654.20), rather than as "jewelry boxes of wood lined with textile fabrics" (item 204.50). The court held that "of" wood meant "wholly or in chief value of" wood (TSUS General Headnote 9(f)(i)), and that, as the metal musical mechanism was the component of chief value, the articles could not be classified as jewelry boxes of wood.

(3) STANDARD BRANDS PAINT CO. v. UNITED STATES, 511 F.2d 564 (C.C.P.A.1975). The Court of Customs and Patent Appeals applied the "doctrine of entireties" to packages each containing one-half of an unassembled picture frame and sustained the importers claim that the articles should be classified as "picture and mirror frames of wood" (item 206.60). The court below had sustained the articles' classification as "Wood moldings, * * * whether or not drilled or treated, other than standard wood moldings, not drilled or treated." (item 202.66). Despite the fact that the articles were not assembled prior to resale, they were treated as picture frames and concededly could not be made into anything else.

(4) NICHIMEN CO. INC. v. UNITED STATES, 565 F.Supp. 148 (CIT), affirmed, 726 F.2d 1580 (Fed.Cir.1984). The doctrine of entireties was found not to apply to imports of "chassis" and tape players where the two items were usually combined with other items in order to make products then sold by the importer. "It is now well settled that separate components covered by the same entry, although designed and intended to be used together, are not properly classifiable as an entirety where the components do not comprise a complete commercial entity, but instead must be assembled with additional components to form a complete article of commerce." 565 F.Supp. at 151. The items were therefore classified in separate headings.

(5) WESTERN STAMPING CORP. v. UNITED STATES, 417 F.2d 316 (C.C.P.A.1969). Louis Marx & Co., Inc. imported toy typewriters, which were classified as typewriters (item 676.65) and, hence, admitted duty free. Appellant, an American manufacturer of a similar product, protested the classification and sought to have the articles classified as toys (item 737.90) with a 35% ad valorem duty. The court held that evidence that the article was not suitable for commercial use as a typewriter and that it was marketed solely through toy stores, was not sufficient to satisfy the plaintiff's burden of proof, where one witness admitted being able to type 52 words per minute on the article and where it was not shown that its chief use was for the amusement of children or adults.

(6) CHILDCRAFT EDUCATION CORP. v. UNITED STATES, 742 F.2d 1413 (Fed.Cir.1984), reversing, 572 F.Supp. 1275 (CIT 1983). The issue was whether "Teaching Typewriters" should be classified as toys (item 737.90) or articles primarily used for educational purposes (items 678.50 or 688.40). The Teaching Typewriter presented a series of problems for children to solve by pressing keys. If the right key were pressed, the device would move on to the next problem. The Federal Circuit reversed the finding of the Court of International Trade that the chief use of the imported article was amusement. In doing so, it noted that the fact that the only witness seemed to indicate that "anything [including the typewriters] will amuse a child" did not establish that the chief use was amusement. 742 F.2d at 1415. It therefore relied on the evidence concerning the educational purpose and benefit.

(7) TEXAS INSTRUMENTS, INC. v. UNITED STATES, 475 F.Supp. 1193 (Cust.Ct.1979), affirmed, 620 F.2d 272 (C.C.P.A.1980). Texas Instruments imported visible light emitting diode (VLED) display devices for use in solid state digital watches. The Customs Service classified the devices as watch dials (item 720.40) rather than electrical indicator panels or electric visual signalling apparatus (item 685.70). The Customs Court reversed that decision and was affirmed on appeal. The Court noted that the headnote to the section containing 720.40 states, "This subpart covers watches and clocks, time switches and other timing apparatus with clock or watch movements and parts of those articles." The Court found that the devices were not clock or watch movements and were not put in watches containing such movements. It therefore concluded that they should be classified in item 685.70.

(8) TOYOTA MOTOR SALES, U.S.A., INC. v. UNITED STATES, 585 F.Supp. 649 (CIT 1984), affirmed, 753 F.2d 1061 (Fed.Cir.1985). Toyota imported truck "chassis" consisting of a frame and cab. Although these "chassis" were operable vehicles, they were sold only after an additional item had been added to the frame—usually a cargo box, which made the vehicle a pick-up truck. The issue was whether the "chassis" were unfinished trucks (item 692.02), dutiable at 25%, or automobile truck chassis (item 692.20), dutiable at 4%. The expert witnesses split over whether the item was commonly called a chassis or an unfinished truck, although they agreed that a pickup truck has three parts: cab, chassis and cargo box. The Court concluded that a cab was not part of a chassis, relying in part, as indicative of congressional intent, on the Brussels Tariff Nomenclature which explicitly provides that a motor vehicle chassis fitted with an engine and cab is to be classified as a truck. Finally, the Court considered whether a cargo box was so "essential" to a truck that a chassis with cab could not be considered an unfinished truck. The Court noted that while such an "essentiality" test was once part of U.S. law, the current rule used to determine whether an item is classifiable as an unfinished article is whether it is "substantially complete." The Court found that the chassis-cab was a substantially completed truck, noting that it had the capacity to carry passengers and cargo.

(2) The Brussels Tariff Nomenclature (BTN) and the Harmonized Commodity Description and Coding System

The problems created by widely disparate national tariff classification systems have long been recognized, and efforts to remedy the situation with a uniform classification system began as early as the mid-1800's.[12]

---

12. For a more thorough discussion of the history of efforts to develop a uniform classifi-   cation system, see H. Friedenberg, The Development of a Uniform International Tariff No-

After World War II a European Customs Union Study Group was established in Brussels to develop a classification system for the proposed customs union. This resulted in the Nomenclature for the Classification of Goods in Customs Tariffs, variously known as the Brussels Tariff Nomenclature (BTN) and the Customs Cooperation Council Nomenclature.[13] The convention on the Nomenclature was opened for signature on December 15, 1950. On the same day, a convention was opened to establish a Customs Cooperation Council (CCC),[14] with one of its major purposes being to assume responsibility for supervising the application and interpretation of the Nomenclature. In 1955, the CCC published a revised Nomenclature and a set of explanatory notes.[15] The Nomenclature Committee of the CCC is responsible for updating both the Nomenclature and the explanatory notes and, in addition, issues classification rules to resolve questions of interpretation and application of the Nomenclature.

The classification principles of the Nomenclature called for the arrangement of items progressively from raw materials to finished products as far as possible, both within a chapter and through the Nomenclature as a whole. Additionally, differences based on use or destinations were avoided.[16] The result was a list of 1,097 items arranged in 21 sections and 99 chapters. Each item was given a four-digit number, the first two digits representing the chapter and the last two the numerical position therein.

Use of the Nomenclature is now world-wide.[17] With the exception of the United States and Canada, all major developed trading nations of GATT have made the Nomenclature the basis of their customs tariffs and several regional organizations [18] have adopted the Nomenclature to varying degrees. By 1967, three-quarters of the free-world's exports and imports were classified according to the Nomenclature for tariff purposes.[19] The Common External Tariff of the EC is classified according to the Nomenclature.

In 1968 the United States Senate approved United States membership in the Customs Cooperation Council, and such participation began in 1970. The 1971 Williams Commission Report recommended that the United States adopt the Nomenclature. In 1971 the Office of the Special Representative for Trade Negotiations undertook a study to determine the magnitude of the changes that would have to be made in United States tariff nomenclature to shift to the Nomenclature and concluded that the major problems were

menclature: From 1853 to 1967 with Emphasis on the Brussels Tariff Nomenclature (U.S. Tariff Commn. Pub. No. 237, 1968).

13. Customs Cooperation Council, Nomenclature for the Classification of Goods in Customs Tariffs (5th ed. 1976) (supplemented regularly).

14. 22 UST 320, TIAS No. 7063, 157 UNTS 129.

15. Customs Cooperation Council, Explanatory Notes to the Brussels Nomenclature (2th ed. 1966) (supplemented regularly).

16. H. Friedenberg, note 12 supra, at 40.

17. Official ratification of the BTN requires membership in the CCC, which had reached 95 by January 1, 1985. U.S. Dept. of State, Treaties in Force 226 (1985). Both CCC and non-CCC countries have adopted the BTN without ratification, however, and a total of 132 countries were reportedly using the BTN in May, 1975. U.S. Intl. Trade Commn., Concepts and Principles Which Should Underlie the Formulation of an International Commodity Code, H.R.Doc.No.94–175, 94th Cong., 1st Sess., App. C, at C–23 (1975).

18. Included are the European Economic Community, the European Coal and Steel Community, the European Free Trade Association, the Latin American Free Trade Association and the Common Organization of African States and Madagascar. H. Friedenberg, note 12 supra, at 52–53.

19. Customs Cooperation Council, The Activities of the Council (July, 1967 to June, 1969) 28 (1970).

few.[20] There was resistance in Congress to shifting to the Nomenclature, partly on the grounds that the Nomenclature is now outmoded, and that before the United States shifts, a better and more modern classification system should be devised.

In response to the need to update the Nomenclature, the Customs Cooperation Council has developed, with U.S. participation, the Harmonized Commodity Description and Coding System. The System was opened for signature in June, 1984, and the U.S. International Trade Commission has completed a draft conversion of the TSUS to the new System. It is anticipated that negotiations on implementation (and where applicable, on tariff rate changes) will take place between the United States and the other major trading nations in 1986 and that implementing legislation will be submitted to Congress in 1987 with an effective date in 1988 as the target for implementation.[21]

A third classification system is utilized by the United Nations' statistical commission for reporting of trade statistics and is entitled "Standard International Trade Classification" (SITC).[22] The new Harmonized System is based in part on the SITC.

(3) GATT and Classification

SPAIN—TARIFF TREATMENT OF UNROASTED COFFEE

Panel Report adopted 11 June 1981, GATT, 28th Supp. BISD 102 (1982)

[Prior to 1979, Spain had classified all unroasted, non-decaffeinated coffee under one tariff heading. In 1979, Spain subdivided its classification for such coffee into five parts, to three of which a 7% duty was applied and to two of which no duty was applied. Brazil, which was the principal supplier of the type of coffee subjected to duty, complained to GATT and a panel was established to consider the dispute.]

4.4 The Panel found that there was no obligation under the GATT to follow any particular system for classifying goods, and that a contracting party had the right to introduce in its customs tariff new positions or subpositions as appropriate.* [1] The Panel considered, however, that, what-

---

20. U.S. Tariff Commn., Investigation No. 332–70, Draft Conversion of the Tariff Schedules of the United States into the Format of the Brussels Tariff Nomenclature (1974).

21. 3 BNA Intl. Trade Reptr. 61 (1986). See GATT Concessions Under the Harmonized Commodity Description and Coding System, Decision of 12 July 1983, GATT, 30th Supp. BISD 17 (1984); Trade Policy Staff Comm., Office of U.S. Trade Representative, Conversion of the Tariff Schedules of the United States into the Nomenclature of the Harmonized System, Revised, Showing Administrative Changes Approved by the Trade Policy Staff Committee (1984); Customs Co-operation Council, Introducing the International Con-

vention on the Harmonized Commodity Description and Coding System (1985); Torrence, The Harmonized Commodity Description and Coding System, Customs Today, Spring 1984, at 30; id., Summer 1984, at 9.

22. Department of Economic and Social Affairs, Statistical Office of the United Nations, Series M, No. 34, Standard International Trade Classification, Revised (1961).

* 1. Provided that a reclassification subsequent to the making of a concession under the GATT would not be a violation of the basic commitment regarding that concession (Article II:5).

ever the classification adopted, Article I:1 required that the same tariff treatment be applied to "like products".

4.5 The Panel, therefore, in accordance with its terms of reference, focused its examination on whether the various types of unroasted coffee listed in the Royal Decree 1764/79 should be regarded as "like products" within the meaning of Article I:1. Having reviewed how the concept of "like products" had been applied by the CONTRACTING PARTIES in previous cases involving, *inter alia,* a recourse to Article I:1, the Panel noted that neither the General Agreement nor the settlement of previous cases gave any definition of such concept.

4.6 The Panel examined all arguments that had been advanced during the proceedings for the justification of a different tariff treatment for various groups and types of unroasted coffee. It noted that these arguments mainly related to organoleptic differences resulting from geographical factors, cultivation methods, the processing of the beans, and the genetic factor. The Panel did not consider that such differences were sufficient reason to allow for a different tariff treatment. It pointed out that it was not unusual in the case of agricultural products that the taste and aroma of the end-product would differ because of one or several of the above-mentioned factors.

4.7 The Panel furthermore found relevant to its examination of the matter that unroasted coffee was mainly, if not exclusively, sold in the form of blends, combining various types of coffee, and that coffee in its end-use, was universally regarded as a well-defined and single product intended for drinking.

4.8 The Panel noted that no other contracting party applied its tariff régime in respect of unroasted, non-decaffeinated coffee in such a way that different types of coffee were subject to different tariff rates.

4.9 In the light of the foregoing, the Panel *concluded* that unroasted, non-decaffeinated coffee beans listed in the Spanish Customs Tariffs under CCCN 09.01 A.1a, as amended by the Royal Decree 1764/79, should be considered as "like products" within the meaning of Article I:1.

4.10 The Panel further noted that Brazil exported to Spain mainly "unwashed Arabica" and also Robusta coffee which were both presently charged with higher duties than that applied to "mild" coffee. Since these were considered to be "like products", the Panel *concluded* that the tariff régime as presently applied by Spain was discriminatory vis-à-vis unroasted coffee originating in Brazil.

4.11 Having recalled that it had found the tariff régime for unroasted coffee introduced by Spain through the Royal Decree 1764/79 not to be in conformity with the provision of Article I:1, the Panel further concluded that this constituted *prima facie* a case of impairment of benefits accruing to Brazil within the meaning of Article XXIII.

Note

GATT Article II, paragraph 5 gives members a right to complain against unexpected changes in tariff classifications that cause harm to a trading partner.

Most GATT members adopted the Nomenclature, and GATT often granted waivers to those members to facilitate such adoption (which could occasion some renegotiation rights under other GATT articles).

(D) VALUATION

(1) The GATT Valuation Code and U.S. Law

Prior to the Tokyo Round (1979), the U.S. system for valuation of goods for customs purposes was so complex and cumbersome that it was deemed to be a "non-tariff barrier" by many trading nations.[23] The U.S. law was a pastiche of provisions, some perpetuated from prior laws by special interest lobbying with Congress. No less than nine different standards were applied, depending on the product or circumstance. These were:

Section 402: Export Value

United States Value

Constructed Value

American Selling Price

Section 402a: Foreign Value

Export Value

United States Value

Cost of Production

American Selling Price

Section 402 was the basic U.S. method of valuation. Section 402a was a continuation, under certain circumstances, of the valuation system that was generally in effect prior to the 1956 revision embodied in Section 402. Generally, the items subject to Section 402a were items on the so-called "Final List", a list of items for which the dutiable value would have been five percent less under Section 402 than under Section 402a. Complaints about the U.S. system by its trading partners and U.S. dissatisfaction with the systems used by others led to negotiations in the Tokyo Round on a Customs Valuation Agreement. The background and the results of the negotiations are described in the Senate Report on the Trade Agreements Act of 1979.

SENATE REPORT 96–249
96th Cong., 1st Sess. 108–10 (1979)

The basis and complexity of customs valuation systems used throughout the world vary considerably. Some systems, such as the Brussels Definition of Value (BDV) used by the European Communities (EC) and most of the countries in the world, employ a "notional" standard for valuation purposes. Under this system, the customs value of an imported product is the price at which that product *would be* sold if the actual transaction in question were a perfectly competitive transaction. Adjustments to the actual value to reach

---

23. The former U.S. valuation system is described and contrasted with those of other   countries in U.S. Tariff Commn., TC Pub. No. 180, Customs Valuation (1966).

the ideal value are made, and such adjustments are often criticized as arbitrary and almost always increase the value and, therefore, the tariff liability. Other customs valuation systems, such as the U.S. system, use a "positive" standard, where customs value is usually the price at which goods are sold in the actual transaction. In certain circumstances, such systems also provide for alternative definitions of value for use in those cases where the price cannot be used. Still other systems assess customs duties primarily on the basis of national or official values which are arbitrary and are used to increase duties collected and/or to protect domestic industries, or primarily on the basis of the domestic selling price of the goods in the country of exportation. Other aspects of customs valuation systems making for complexity and controversy include: The existence in some systems of numerous alternative definitions of value; complex laws and administrative regulations making it difficult to easily predict the amount of duty that will be owed; the absence of requirements and procedures for review of valuation decisions; and the absence of published administrative regulations and decisions.

Against this background, negotiations in the MTN on an international set of rules for customs valuation took place with the active participation of the major industrialized countries and many of the developing countries.

*   *   *

SUMMARY OF THE AGREEMENT

Methods of Customs Valuation.—The Customs Valuation Agreement establishes five alternative methods of customs valuation. Each is summarized briefly below in the order in which it would be applied.

1. *The transaction value of the imported goods,* i.e., the price actually paid or payable for the goods with adjustments for certain specified costs, charges, and expenses which are incurred but not reflected in the price actually paid or payable for the goods (including selling commissions, container costs, packing costs, certain royalties and licenses fees, and assists) (article 1 of the agreement).

2. If the transaction value of the imports cannot be determined or used, then the *transaction value of identical goods* sold for export to the same country, and exported at or about the same time as the imported goods (article 2 of the agreement).

3. If the transaction value of identical goods cannot be determined, then the *transaction value of similar goods* sold for export to the same country and exported at or about the same time as the imported goods (article 3 of the agreement).

4. If customs value cannot be determined by looking to transaction value, then the *deductive* value or *computed* value, as the importer chooses. The *deductive* value for the imported goods is determined by the price at which the imported goods, or identical or similar imported goods, are sold in the greatest aggregate quantity to unrelated persons in the country of importation in the same condition as imported (or after further processing), with deductions for commissions or profit, general

expenses, transport and insurance costs, customs duties and certain other costs, charges and expenses incurred as a result of reselling the goods. (Article 5 of the agreement.)

5. The *computed value* of the imported goods, determined by summing the cost of producing the article in the country of exportation, an amount for general expense and profit, and the cost or value of all other expenses necessary to reflect the valuation option (i.e., f.o.b. or c.i.f.) chosen by the signatory. (Article 6 of the Agreement.)

In those rare instances where a value cannot be determined under any of the valuation methods described above, the agreement provides that "the value shall be determined using reasonable means consistent with the principles and general provisions of this code . . . " The customs values determined under this residual method "should be based to the greatest possible extent on previously determined customs values." Several valuation methods are specifically precluded from being used as a basis for determining customs value, including methods such as the American selling price (ASP) and foreign value methods currently used in the United States.

Circumstances Under Which the Transaction Value Will Not Be Used. The most significant circumstance under the agreement which would result in the transaction value not being used is when the transaction in question is between related parties. If the buyer and seller are related, the transaction value may not be used unless an examination of the circumstances surrounding the sale demonstrates that such relationship did not influence the price, or the importer demonstrates that the transaction value closely approximates one of several other enumerated values, subject to other criteria of the agreement.

———

The so-called Valuation Code was implemented into U.S. law by title II of the Trade Agreements Act of 1979 (See Documentary Supplement).[24] It has also been implemented by most other major trading nations, including Canada, the EC and Japan.[25] Despite the special provisions designed to ease adherence by developing countries, many have not done so. The principal reasons given are problems in respect of training customs personnel, determining proper procedures to apply the agreement, loss of revenue, providing guidance to importers and preparation of the necessary laws and regulations.[26]

The Committee on Customs Valuation established by the Code reported in 1983 that experience in the first year "indicated that, in line with the

24. Pub.L. No. 96–39, 93 Stat. 144 (codified at 19 U.S.C.A. § 1401a). For analyses of the Valuation Code, see Sherman, Reflections on the New Customs Valuation Code, 12 Law & Poly.Intl.Bus. 119 (1980); Note, Technical Analysis of the Customs Valuation Agreement, 12 Law & Poly.Intl.Bus. 159 (1980); De Pagter & Van Raan, The Valuation of Goods for Customs Purposes (1981).

25. See Section 5.5 supra for a summary of the total number and types of countries adhering to the Valuation Code.

26. Report of the Committee on Customs Valuation, GATT, 30th Supp. BISD 56, 61 (1984).

Agreement's objectives, the vast majority of customs entries were being valued on the basis of transaction value." [27] It is generally perceived in the United States that valuation disputes have declined with implementation of the Code.[28] The Committee has studied a couple of areas where interpretative difficulties have arisen under the Code, including the proper valuation of computer software and the treatment of interest charges in cases of deferred payment.[29]

(2) Special Problems of Valuation Under U.S. Law

(a) CIF Valuation

The United States has always utilized an FOB method of valuation for customs purposes, whereas most of its trading partners use CIF.[30] This, of course, means that a 10% tariff applied by the United States produces less revenue and is less of a trade barrier than a 10% tariff applied by a country using CIF valuation—the difference being equal basically to 10% of the shipping and insurance costs, a fact negotiators must keep in mind when discussing reciprocal tariff concessions.

U.S. TARIFF COMMISSION, CUSTOMS VALUATION [31]
(1973)

CONSTITUTIONAL REQUIREMENTS FOR VALUATION STANDARDS

A legislative history of the various U.S. valuation standards shows that standards which include freight and insurance in dutiable c.i.f. value have had doubt cast upon their constitutional validity in congressional debates and reports. The doubt was premised on the belief that there was a *lack of uniformity* or the possibility of *preferential treatment*. It seems appropriate, therefore, to include in the report a brief comment on the judicial precedents on the subject. The doubt has been based on two constitutional provisions in Article I, consisting of section 8, clause 1, and section 9, clause 6, which read, respectively:

> The Congress shall have power to lay and collect taxes, duties, imposts, and
> excises, to pay the debts and provide for the common defense and general

27. Id., at 59. A study by the U.S. Customs Service found that over 94% of entries in the ports examined were made on the basis of transaction value. U.S. General Accounting Office, New U.S. Valuation System for Imported Products is Better and Easier to Administer (Report No. B–201765, 1982).

28. Id.

29. Reports of the Committee on Customs Valuation, GATT, 31st Supp. BISD 273, 274 (1985). As a result of a committee decision on software, the EC has determined not to include the value of the software in determining the value of goods containing software. Regulation 1055/85, [1985] Eur.Comm.O.J. No. L 112/50.

30. An FOB price is the price at the point of shipment for the goods only, while a CIF price is the price for the goods plus an amount covering transportation and insurance to buyer's port. See Section 2.2(B)(2) supra. The relevant U.S. statute is 19 U.S.C.A. § 1401a(b) (4)(A) (dutiable value excludes "any costs, charges, or expenses incurred for transportation, insurance, and related services incident to the international shipment of the merchandise" to the United States).

31. Report to Senate Comm. on Finance, 93d Cong., 1st Sess. 83–86 (Comm.Print 1973).

welfare of the United States; *but all duties, imposts, and excises shall be uniform throughout the United States.*

No preference shall be given by any regulation *of* commerce or *revenue to the ports of one state over those of another * * *.*

The underscored provisions are relevant to the subject of discussion.

There appears to be no interpretative judicial precedent on these provisions based on duties *per se.* However, the requirement of uniformity has been examined with reference to other taxes and the principles of the decisions might apply equally to duties. The United States Supreme Court has held that the uniformity required by the Constitution for excise taxes is geographical uniformity, not uniformity of intrinsic equality and operation. By geographical uniformity is meant the laying of the same amount of tax on the same articles in each state, not uniformity in the sense of the collection of the same amount of tax from each state. Thus, a tax may operate unequally by reason of the unequal distribution or existence of the article among the respective states. It seems, however, that this interpretation does not answer the question of the constitutionality of unequal customs *valuation* for duty purposes in different states (which would be the case under a c.i.f. scheme) as opposed to unequal *distribution* of the article in different states.

An f.o.b. customs valuation scheme may also result in unequal valuation. Identical goods entering the United States from different points of origin may be valued unequally because of their different sources. Any inequity, however, would result from the differences associated with the sources of the goods since the valuation of identical goods from the same source would be uniform throughout the United States regardless of which port the goods entered. On a c.i.f. basis, however, identical goods from the same source could be valued differently, depending upon the location of the U.S. port of entry. F.o.b. valuation, therefore, does not favor one state over another or one port over another, since, whatever the valuation may be, it is assessed uniformly throughout the United States. C.i.f. valuation of identical goods from the same source—because it may differ depending upon the U.S. port of entry—can result in unequal valuation among different states or the ports of the same states.

Although the Supreme Court has never addressed itself directly to this customs valuation issue, some lower courts have applied the *Knowlton* concept of geographical uniformity to encompass the same tax rate levied on a changing tax base. The Supreme Court has also interpreted the uniformity clause to require only that "the law shall be uniform in the sense that by its provisions the rule of liability shall be the same in all parts of the United States." Although this last statement must be considered *obiter dictum,* lower courts have used the principle when interpreting the uniformity clause.

As to the preference clause, the Supreme Court has held that a preference resulting from geography, so long as it is reasonable, is not a preference given to the ports of one state over those of another.

(b) American Selling Price

The Tariff Act of 1922 [32] provided that where the statutory tariff did not equalize the difference between foreign and domestic costs of production, the President (by proclamation) could change the valuation basis of the article to the American selling price (ASP). The ASP was the usual wholesale price, including preparation for shipping, at which an article manufactured in the United States was freely offered for sale. The provision was carried into the Tariff Act of 1930 and prior to the Tokyo Round applied to benzenoid chemicals, certain rubber-soled footwear, certain canned clams, and low-value wool-knit gloves. Although less than one percent of United States imports were subject to ASP,[33] the effect where applied was considerable. According to a Tariff Commission study of ASP imports in 1964, a 20% duty on some chemicals and footwear was the equivalent of up to 58% at normal customs value.[34]

The ASP method of customs valuation is not consistent with Article VII of GATT. Because ASP was law prior to GATT, however, it benefited from the "grandfather" clause of the Protocol of Provisional Application.[35] During the Kennedy Round of trade negotiations, a special agreement was reached (1967) whereby the United States would eliminate ASP in exchange for certain European and Japanese tariff and nontariff barrier (NTB) concessions (mainly tariff reductions on chemicals and a French agreement to change their method of taxing automobiles so that United States auto exports would be more competitive in the French market). This agreement required approval by the United States Congress, which was never given. After several extensions of the deadline for acceptance of the agreement and in the face of congressional inaction, European parties to the agreement indicated in 1972 that they were not prepared to accept a further extension, and the agreement lapsed.

The ASP system was eliminated when the United States implemented the Valuation Code as described above. Its only importance today is that it is remembered by U.S. trading partners as a particularly objectionable NTB, one which the President agreed to eliminate in the Kennedy Round, but which he was unable to do because of congressional inaction.

(E) RULES OF ORIGIN

Once goods have been classified and valued, it is necessary to determine their origin so that the proper tariff rate may be applied. Problems of origin have become more significant in recent years as customs unions and free trade areas have been formed and as special preferences have been extended to developing countries. Those problems have been compounded by recent trends toward multinational manufacturing, where different stages in manu-

32. Act of Sept. 21, 1922, ch. 356, § 315, 42 Stat. 941.

33. Estimate based on 1969 imports. U.S. Tariff Commn., Customs Valuation: Report to the Senate Comm. on Finance, 93d Cong., 1st Sess. 71 (Comm.Print 1973).

34. U.S. Tariff Commission, Trade Barriers, pt. II, vol. 6, at 193 n. 1 (TC Pub.No. 665, 1974).

35. See Section 5.4(C) supra.

facturing are performed in different countries, in part to take advantage of lower costs, but also in some cases with an eye toward establishing favorable origin. Here we will consider briefly the effect of origin rules on trade and then consider how origin rules are typically applied.

(1) The Impact of Origin Rules

Origin rules do more than determine tariff rates. Among other things, they affect investment and trading decisions.

U.S. DEPT. OF COMMERCE, EEC AND EFTA RULES OF ORIGIN GOVERNING PREFERENTIAL TRADE

(1974) [36]

COMMERCIAL IMPACT OF EEC AND EFTA ORIGIN RULES

The rules of origin contained in the EEC preferential trade agreements and the EFTA arrangement may be commercially significant to U.S. firms in the following two ways:

1. Difficulties for U.S. exporters may arise indirectly to the extent that a definition of origin for a product limits member country producers from gaining favorable tariff status on the exportation of finished products containing U.S. components. For example, one EEC/EFTA rule of origin stipulates that finished products in Brussels Tariff Nomenclature (BTN) Chapters 84 to 92 will not be granted origin status if they incorporate more than 5% by value of non-origin parts of the same tariff heading as the finished product. Illustrative of this rule is tariff heading 84.10 which covers liquid pumps and parts. A German manufacturer of finished liquid pumps might continue to buy "parts for liquid pumps" from the United States because of superior U.S. quality or lower cost even though such non-origin parts may constitute more than 5% of the value of his finished pump. However, in such an event his products would be assessed the full external duty rate of [sic] exported to Sweden, Norway, Portugal or most of the EEC's preferential partners. Alternatively, he could use only parts manufactured in the preference area and thereby qualify for the preferential rate. Similar pressures for origin sourcing would exist, of course, for production of finished products within EFTA or any of the EEC's preferential partners if a significant element of output was for export to the preference area (e.g., from Spain or Cyprus to the EEC).

2. Investment patterns may be affected by the various rules. A firm planning to build a plant in the EEC, EFTA, or one of the EEC's preferential partners will have to consider sourcing patterns, if sales within the preference area are important. Finished products not manufactured in accordance with the origin criteria will be assessed the importing member country's full duty even though almost all of the value of the finished product originates in the EEC, EFTA, or the EEC preferential partner.

36. Overseas Business Reports, OBR 74–04 (April, 1974), at 6 and 3.

(2) The Application of Origin Rules

The application of origin rules is a complex subject. GATT has no specific tests for origin of goods, leaving each member to determine its own origin rules, although there have been various reports and recommendations on origin in GATT.[37]

At the outset, it should be clear that a good made in country A and transshipped via country B to country X is unlikely to be considered to have "B origin" in country X. The question is how much must be done in country B to give it B origin. Under basic U.S. law, the question is whether the further work done or material added in country B effected a "substantial transformation."[38] If country B is a beneficiary of a particular preference, the rule is likely to be stricter. For example, under the U.S. origin rules for GSP treatment, which affords duty-free entry to certain products of developing countries, the product (1) must be transported directly to the United States from the country of origin and (2) the sum of (a) the cost or value of the materials produced in the beneficiary country plus (b) the direct costs of processing operations performed in such country must not be less than 35% of the value of the product when imported into the United States.[39] Under certain circumstances groups of countries may count as one under these rules, e.g., the Andean pact nations, the ASEAN nations and various Caribbean nations.[40] In 1984, the United States introduced special origin rules for certain textile and textile products designed to make it more difficult for such products to gain origin on the basis of relatively insubstantial manufacturing operations.[41]

37. See J. Jackson, World Trade and the Law of GATT § 17.8 (1969); see also the GATT reports published as follows: GATT, 1st Supp. BISD 100 (1953); GATT, 2d Supp. BISD 53 (1954); GATT, 5th Supp. BISD 33, 102 (1957).

38. 19 CFR § 134.1 (1985) (defined for origin marking purposes). The EC defines origin generally as "the country in which the last substantial process or operation that is economically justified was performed, having been carried out in an undertaking equipped for the purpose, and resulting in the manufacture of a new product or representing an important stage of manufacture." Regulation 802/68, Art. 5, [1968] Eur.Comm.O.J. No L 148/1. It is a mixture of prior EC member state rules on the subject. See generally Forrester, EEC Customs Law: Rules of Origin and Preferential Duty Treatment, 5 Eur.L. Rev. 167, 257 (1980).

39. TSUSA, Headnote 3(e)(v)(C); 19 CFR §§ 10.171–.178 (1985). The EC preferential rules generally focus on whether the four-digit tariff classification number of the product changes, although there are many special exceptions. See generally Forrester, note 38 supra; UNCTAD, Rules of Origin in the General Scheme of Preferences in Favour of the Developing Countries (U.N. Doc. TD/B/AC.5/3/Rev. 1, 1969).

40. TSUSA, Headnote 3(e)(v)(C). In the case of the beneficiaries of the Caribbean Basin Economic Recovery Act, if part of the value of a product consists of materials produced in the United States, an amount not to exceed 15% of the products value that is attributed to the United States may be counted toward the 35% requirement. 19 CFR §§ 10.191–1.98 (1985).

41. 19 CFR §§ 12.130–.131 (1985) (certain combining, cutting, trimming, joining and finishing operations not sufficient to confer origin). See Mast Industries, Inc. v. Regan, 596 F.Supp. 1567 (CIT 1984); Note, The 1984 "Country of Origin" Regulations for Textile Imports: Illegal Administrative Action Under Domestic and International Law, 14 Ga.J.Intl. & Comp.L. 573 (1984).

THE TORRINGTON CO. v. UNITED STATES

Court of International Trade, 1984.
596 F.Supp. 1083, affirmed, 764 F.2d 1563 (Fed.Cir.1985).

[The question presented was whether sewing needles exported to the United States from Portugal, a beneficiary developing country (BDC) under the U.S. Generalized System of Preferences, were in fact of Portuguese "origin" given that the wire from which the needles were made was not.]

The statute relevant to this controversy is 19 U.S.C. § 2463(b) (1982), which was incorporated into the TSUS as General Headnote 3(c)(ii), and provides that an imported eligible article can only be accorded duty-free treatment if "the sum of (A) the cost or value of the *materials produced* in the beneficiary developing country * * * plus (B) the direct costs of processing operations performed in such beneficiary developing country * * * is not less than 35 percent of the appraised value of such article at the time of its entry into the customs territory of the United States." 19 U.S.C. § 2463(b)(2) (emphasis added). The pertinent regulations promulgated by the Secretary of Treasury to carry out this subsection are set forth in part here.

19 C.F.R. § 10.176(a) provides in pertinent part:

(a) *Merchandise produced in a beneficiary developing country or any two or more countries which are members of the same association of countries.* Merchandise which is (1) the growth, product, manufacture, or assembly of (i) a beneficiary developing country * * * and (2) imported directly from such beneficiary developing country * * * may qualify for duty-free entry under the Generalized System of Preferences ("GSP"). However, duty-free entry under GSP may be accorded only if: (i) The sum of the cost or value of the materials produced in the beneficiary developing country * * * plus (ii) the direct costs of processing operations performed in such beneficiary developing country . . . is not less than 35 percent of the appraised value of the article at the time of its entry into the customs territory of the United States.

19 C.F.R. § 10.177(a) provides in pertinent part:

(a) *"Produced in the beneficiary developing country" defined.* For purposes of §§ 10.171 through 10.178, the words produced in the beneficiary developing "country" refer to the constituent materials of which the eligible article is composed which are either:

(1) Wholly the growth, product, or manufacture of the beneficiary developing country; or

(2) Substantially transformed in the beneficiary developing country into a new and different article of commerce.

It is clear that before a non-BDC material can be regarded as a "material produced" in the BDC, with its cost includable in the evaluation by Customs, the non-BDC material must be substantially transformed into a new and different article of commerce, that is, one having a distinctive name, character or use. The question raised by the defendant is whether a two-stage substantial transformation is required. This Court finds that such a two-stage process is required and finds that a substantial transformation of non-BDC material is necessary in order for the non-BDC wire to be regarded as "material produced" in the BDC and to be included in the 35 percent value-added evaluation. Although not explicit, the dual requirement can be gleaned from the statute. The administrative agencies have consistently supported and utilized the dual requirements, and such a requirement is not contrary to the GSP statute and its goals.

Regulations promulgated by Customs define the term "materials produced" to include materials from third countries that are substantially transformed in the BDC into a new and different article of commerce. 19 C.F.R. § 10.177(a)(2). It is not enough to transform substantially the non-BDC constituent materials into the final article, as the material utilized to produce the final article would remain non-BDC material. There must first be a substantial transformation of the non-BDC material into a new and different article of commerce which becomes "materials produced," and these materials produced in the BDC must then be substantially transformed into a new and different article of commerce. It is noted that 19 C.F.R. § 10.176(a) distinguishes between "merchandise produced in a BDC" and the cost or value of the "materials produced in the BDC" which demonstrates the contemplation of a dual substantial transformation requirement. Furthermore, absent such a dual requirement, the GSP's goal of industrialization, diversification, and economic progression for underdeveloped nations could be frustrated. For example, a BDC could import eligible items, merely decorate or assemble these items and thereby satisfy the 35 percent value-added requirement since these direct costs of processing operations would be includable in the calculation. In this manner, BDC's could become mere conduits for the merchandise of developed countries. This is not the type of economic development envisioned by the GSP program. Indeed, the regulations implementing the GSP ought to be interpreted to further, not hinder, the program's stated goals.

[The court then found that the wire had first been substantially transformed into a swagged needle blank, which it found to be a new and different article of commerce. The court then found a second substantial transformation occurred when the blanks were made into needles. See generally Cutler, The United States Generalized System of Preferences: The Problem of Substantial Transformation, 5 N.Car.J.Intl.L. & Com.Reg. 393 (1980).]

(F) SPECIAL PROBLEMS OF U.S. CUSTOMS LAW

It is beyond the scope of this book to consider customs law in any detail, but it may be useful to highlight a few issues of particular interest. In particular, we will consider special rules to assist exports and enforcement issues.

(1) Export Promotion: Foreign Trade Zones and Drawback

The aim of customs law is to tax goods that enter the United States for consumption. To the extent goods are not going to be used in the United

States, no duty is applied. The simplest example of this principle is embodied in the rules on transit; goods passing through the United States on the way to another destination are not subject to duties.[42] In fact, such goods may even be stored and/or processed in the United States in special bonded customs warehouses.[43]

More complex are rules designed to promote U.S. exports. For example, under the foreign trade zone rules goods may enter a designated foreign trade zone in the United States without payment of duty, be processed and then exported.[44] If the resultant product is "exported" to the United States, duty is assessed on the new product, although arrangements may be made so that duties are assessed on the basis of the amount of the imported goods used in the product sold in the United States.

Similarly, since the aim of the customs law is to tax imported goods consumed in the United States, if imported goods are incorporated in a product that is exported from the United States, there are rules that permit 99% of the duties paid on the incorporated product to be recovered.[45] These so-called drawback rules are also designed to promote the United States as a place for manufacture of export goods. The rules for drawback are procedurally complex and any company hoping to avail itself of the rules should make sure it has complied in all respects in advance of exportation. Special rules on "substitution" are designed to allow drawback on a pro rata basis in the situation where domestic-origin and foreign-origin components are used in producing merchandise. Under these rules, if a foreign-origin component was used in a domestically sold item and a like domestic-origin component was used in an exported item, drawback would still be allowed.

Finally, another rule that is designed to promote U.S. manufacturing provides that the value for duty purposes of imported goods assembled abroad of U.S. components is reduced by the value of the U.S. components.[46] This provision provides some incentive for U.S. manufacturers to keep at least part of their production processes in the United States.

(2) Enforcement of Customs Laws

Section 592 of the Tariff Act of 1930 provides that no person shall enter merchandise into the United States by means of a document or statement that is material and false or by means of an omission that is material.[47] Penalties for this civil violation range from the value of the merchandise in

42. See generally 19 U.S.C.A. §§ 1551–65; 19 CFR §§ 18.1–18.45 (1985). Of course, care is taken to exclude the possibility that the goods will be consumed or used in the United States without payment of duty. For example, goods in transit must generally be entered with the customs authorities, transported by bonded carrier and checked out of the United States. See 19 CFR §§ 18.2–18.22 (1985).

43. See generally 19 CFR §§ 19.1–19.49.

44. See generally 19 U.S.C.A. §§ 81a–81u; 19 CFR §§ 146.0–146.49.

45. See generally 19 U.S.C.A. § 1313; 19 CFR §§ 191.0–191.166 (1985).

46. TSUSA, Item 807; 19 CFR §§ 10.11–10.24 (1985).

47. 19 U.S.C.A. § 1592(a)(1) (1982). Clerical errors or factual mistakes are not considered violations unless they are part of a pattern of negligence. 19 U.S.C.A. § 1592(a)(2).

the case of fraud to the lesser of that amount or twice the duties of which the United States is or may be deprived in the case of negligence.[48]

Prior to 1978, the penalty provisions of the U.S. law, which provided for forfeiture in all cases of violation, were claimed to be in violation of GATT Article VIII, paragraph 3, which prohibits substantial penalties for minor breaches.[49]

(G) PROBLEMS

The following problems are designed to focus the reader's attention on issues that may arise under U.S. customs law. Although they may not be susceptible to a complete answer without use of supplementary materials, the materials in the book and Documentary Supplement suggest the major issues to be considered.

(1) Singapan and Hong Kongea are GATT members; Taipore is not. Under GATT Singapan has bound its tariff on widgets at 10%; its normal tariff is 30%. A widget-maker in Taipore exports widgets to Hong Kongea for repackaging and reshipment to Singapan. Singapan charges a 30% duty on the widgets. The reshipper in Hong Kongea comes to you for advice on what GATT rights Hong Kongea has and on what steps it might take to improve Hong Kongea's case. Advise it on the assumption that Singapan has origin rules similar to those in the United States.

(2) Your client wishes to ascertain the likely duty to be assessed on a product, made by its European parent, that it plans to import into the United States for resale. The normal duty rate for the product is 10% and the stated CIF invoice price is $1000. Shipping costs are $50, insurance $10 and packing $5. In addition, your client pays certain royalties to its parent on each resale. Your client has not been doing well financially and the parent has allowed it to defer intercompany payments indefinitely and such amounts are now between 30 and 90 days past due. Discuss the problems that would arise in determining the applicable duty.

(3) Assume your client, a United States corporation, has imported a carload of educational construction kits from its parent Canadian corporation. These kits are designed for teenage children and consist of instructions and parts by which a small (and not too durable) electronic speedometer can be constructed, suitable for attaching to a bicycle or automobile. The kits are marked to sell at a retail price of U.S. $5, but the importer has been invoiced for them at U.S. $1.50 each, including 20 cents each for shipping from a Toronto plant to Detroit.

Consider the following portion of the United States tariff schedule and the materials of this section, above, and advise your client of his probable United States tariff cost per kit; outline arguments to be used with United States customs officials.

---

48. 19 U.S.C.A. § 1592(c). If the violation did not affect the assessment of duties, the penalty for negligence may be 20% of the value. The penalties for gross negligence are twice those for negligence (i.e. four times the duties/40% of the value).

49. See American Bar Assn., Section of Intl.Law, Report to the House of Delegates 2–3 (1975) to accompany resolution on § 502 adopted at the August 1975 meeting.

UNITED STATES TARIFF SCHEDULES ANNOTATED

(16th ed., Supp. 3, 1985)[50]

SCHEDULE 7. SPECIFIED PRODUCTS; MISCELLANEOUS AND NONENUMERATED PRODUCTS

Part 2. Optical Goods; Scientific and Professional Instruments; Watches, Clocks, and Timing Devices; Photographic Goods; Motion Pictures;
Recordings and Recording Media

Item	Stat. Suf- fix	Articles	Units of Quantity	Rates of Duty		
				1	Special	2
		Revolution counters, production counters, taximeters, odometers, pedometers, counters similar to the foregoing articles, speedometers and tachometers, all the foregoing not provided for in subpart C of this part; parts of the foregoing:				
711.90	00	Taximeters and parts	X_____	16.5% ad val.	15% ad val. (D,I) Free (A,E)	85% ad val.
711.91	00	If Canadian article and original motor-vehicle equipment (see headnote 2, part 6B, schedule 6)	X_____	Free		
711.93	00	Bicycle speedometers and parts thereof	X_____	19.6% ad val.	17% ad val. (D,I) Free (E)	110% ad val.
711.98		Other	_____	1.3% ad val.	Free (A,D,E,I)	35% ad val.
	20	Speedometers and tachometers, and parts	X			
	40	Other	X			
711.99	00	If Canadian article and original motor-vehicle equipment (see headnote 2, part 6B, schedule 6)	X_____	Free		

50. The rate in column 1 is the MFN rate; the rate in column 2 is the full statutory rate. The rate in the Special column depends on the identity of the country involved. "A" refers to beneficiaries of the U.S. GSP scheme. "D" refers to least developed developing countries. "E" refers to the beneficiaries of the U.S. Caribbean Basin Initiative. "I" refers to Israel, which is the beneficiary of the U.S.-Israel Free Trade Agreement. An * indicates a further limitation on availability of special treatment exists.

Item	Stat. Suffix	Articles	Units of Quantity	Rates of Duty		
				1	Special	2
712.00	00	Speedometers and tachometers, and parts thereof; all the foregoing if certified for use in civil aircraft (see headnote 3, part 6C, schedule 6)	No._____	Free		35% ad val.

* * *

Part 5. Arms and Ammunition; Fishing Tackle; Wheel Goods; Sporting Goods, Games and Toys

Item	Stat. Suffix	Articles	Units of Quantity	Rates of Duty		
				1	Special	2
		Parts of bicycles: Frames:				
732.30	00	Valued not over $4.16–$^2/_3$ each	No._____	9.2% ad val.	7.2% ad val. (D,I) Free (E)	30% ad val.
732.32	00	Valued over $4.16–$^2/_3$ but not over $8.33–$^1/_3$ each	No._____	42¢ each	36¢ each (D) Free (E,I)	30% ad val.
732.34	00	Valued over $8.33–^1/_3$ each	No._____	5.6% ad val.	4.9% ad val. (D) Free (E,I)	30% ad val.

* * *

Item	Stat. Suffix	Articles	Units of Quantity	1	Special	2
732.42		Other parts of bicycles	_____	11.7% ad val.	10% ad val. (D,I) Free (E)	30% ad val.

* * *

Subpart E. Models; Dolls, Toys, Tricks, Party Favors
Subpart E headnotes:

* * *

2. For the purposes of the tariff schedules, a "*toy*" is any article chiefly used for the amusement of children or adults.

* * *

Item	Stat. Suf-fix	Articles	Units of Quantity	Rates of Duty		
				1	Special	2
		Model trains, model airplanes, model boats, and other model articles, all the foregoing whether or not toys; and construction kits or sets for making or assembling such model articles:				
737.05	00	Models of inventions and of other improvements in the arts, to be used exclusively as models	X_____	Free		Free
737.07	00	Other models, and construction kits or sets: Rail locomotives and rail vehicles; * * * all the foregoing made to scale of the actual article at the ratio of 1 to 85 or smaller	X_____	5.8% ad val.	5.1% ad val. (D) Free (A*,E,I)	45% ad val.
737.09	00	Construction kits or sets with construction units prefabricated to precise scale of the actual article	X_____	6.7% ad val.	5.7% ad val. (D) Free (A,E,I)	45% ad val.
737.15		Other	_____	10.2% ad val.	7.8% ad val. (D,I) Free (A*,E)	70% ad val.
	20	Articles described in item 737.07, made to a scale of the actual article at a ratio larger than 1 to 85	X			
	60	Other	X			

* * *

Item	Stat. Suf-fix	Articles	Units of Quantity	Rates of Duty		
		Toys, and parts of toys, not specially provided for:				
737.80	00	Toys having a spring mechanism	No._____	12.1% ad val.	8.8% ad val. (D) Free (A*,E,I)	70% ad val.
		Other:				
737.85	00	Kites	X_____	10.2% ad val.	7.8% ad val. (D) Free (E,I)	70% ad val.
737.95		Other	_____	9.6% ad val.	7% ad val. (D) Free (A*,E,I)	70% ad val.

SECTION 6.3 GATT AND INTERNATIONAL TARIFF COMMITMENTS: THE BINDINGS

(A) THE OBLIGATION TO LIMIT TARIFFS

It has several times been stated that the central obligation of the General Agreement on Tariffs and Trade is that in Article II, which requires nations to limit their tariffs on particular goods to a specified maximum.[1] Prior to GATT nations negotiated bilateral trade agreements that typically contained reciprocal obligations by which each party undertook to apply a tariff on a particular good at no more than the maximum specified in the agreement.[2] These commitments could be different for the parties; for instance, the United States might agree to a tariff limit of 10% on automobiles in exchange for the United Kingdom agreeing to a 7% tariff limit on bicycles. Under the most-favored-nation (MFN) obligation (discussed in the next chapter), which was found in many such treaties, when a country granted such a "tariff concession," it was required to give like treatment to all countries to whom it owed the obligation of MFN. Thus, if the United States agreed with the United Kingdom that the United States would limit tariffs on a particular commodity to a 10% maximum, it was obligated to limit tariffs to that maximum for like goods coming from any nation to whom the United States had promised MFN treatment.

In bilateral negotiations, therefore, there developed a growing hesitancy to make extensive tariff limit commitments because of the "free ride problem."[3] That is, since any tariff commitment was generalized by the MFN obligation to apply to all MFN countries, those countries that were not part of the original negotiation for the tariff commitment would benefit without having given up anything in return. Consequently, as time went on, it became apparent that bilateral negotiations of tariff reductions would have limited results. Countries tended to negotiate only with trading partners who were "principal suppliers" of particular commodities. Thus a desire for multilateral tariff negotiations developed in GATT.

The current GATT tariff commitments or "bindings," as they are sometimes called, are the result of seven major "rounds" of negotiation (see Section 5.5 supra) and are contained in a series of schedules which are appended to the GATT agreement and incorporated into it by reference in Article II of GATT.[4] Theoretically, each contracting party, that is to say, each nation which is a member of GATT, has a separate schedule which lists its own commitments. Each nation's schedule is, of course, different. A

1. See Section 5.4(B) supra. See J. Jackson, World Trade and the Law of GATT 201–11 (1969). See also R. Caves & R. Jones, World Trade and Payments 281–86 (1973); G. Curzon, Multilateral Commercial Diplomacy 70–123 (1965); K. Dam, The GATT: Law and International Economic Organization 17, 18, 25–55 (1970).

2. See discussion in Section 3.4(C) supra, concerning United States reciprocal trade agreements program.

3. See G. Curzon, note 1 supra, at 57–69; K. Dam, note 1 supra, at 61–64; J. Evans, The Kennedy Round in American Trade Policy 6–7, 143–44 (1971); J. Jackson, note 1 supra, at 219–21, 245–46.

4. A list of schedules for GATT can be found in J. Jackson, note 1 supra, at 884–888. See also GATT, Status of Legal Instruments.

GATT tariff schedule for a nation differs from its national tariff schedule, in that the GATT tariff schedule specifies the treaty-obligated maximum tariff which can be applied for each product listed on the schedule. The national tariff schedule, on the other hand, is the actual rate applied for each product by the customs service of that country. For products which are not on the GATT tariff schedule of that country, the country may charge any tariff it pleases. For products which are listed on the GATT tariff schedule, the country may charge a tariff below the GATT maximum, if it so desires. If it charges a tariff in excess of the GATT maximum, however, it is violating GATT (unless it can establish a GATT exception to its obligation). Such violation will be a violation of international law, but of course the importers will find that they are forced to obey the national law of the importing country, which is contained in that country's national tariff schedule applied by its customs service.

The following is an example of a portion of the GATT tariff schedule of the United States, which can be contrasted with the portion of the United States national tariff schedule which was excerpted at the end of the preceding section.

GATT 79 TOKYO ROUND SCHEDULE
SCHEDULE XX—UNITED STATES OF AMERICA
Part I (continued)

Tariff item number	Description of products	Rate of duty
682.95	Primary cells and primary batteries, and parts thereof	5.3% ad val.
	Storage batteries and parts thereof:	
683.10	Lead-acid type storage batteries, and parts thereof.........................	5.3% ad val.
683.15	Other	5.1% ad val.
683.20	Hand-directed or -controlled tools with self-contained electric motor, and parts thereof	2.2% ad val.
	Vacuum cleaners, floor polishers, food grinders, and mixers, juice extractors and other electromechanical appliances, all the foregoing with self-contained electric motors, of types used in the household, hotels, restaurants, offices, schools, or hospitals (but not including factory or other industrial appliances or electrothermic appliances), and parts thereof:	
683.30	Vacuum cleaners, floor polishers, and parts thereof.....................	3.4% ad val.
683.32	Other	4.2% ad val.
	Shavers, hair-clippers, and scissors, all the foregoing with self-contained electric motors, and parts thereof:	
683.40	Hair-clippers and parts thereof	4% ad val.

Tariff item number	Description of products	Rate of duty
683.50	Other	4.4% ad val.
	* * *	
	Revolution counters, production counters, taximeters, odometers, pedometers, counters similar to the foregoing articles, speedometers and tachometers, all the foregoing not provided for in unit C of this chapter; parts of the foregoing:	
711.90	Taximeters and parts	15% ad val.
711.93	Bicycle speedometers and parts thereof	17% ad val.
711.96	Other	Free
711.97	Speedometers and tachometers, if certified for use in civil aircraft (see note 3, chapter 6C, section 6)	Free

Often the tariff schedule bindings resulting from a major trade round are "phased in" over a period of years. The "Geneva (1979) Protocol" which embraces the tariff concessions resulting from the Tokyo Round specifies, "The reductions agreed upon by each participant shall, except as may be otherwise specified in a participant's schedule, be implemented in equal annual rate reductions beginning 1 January 1980 and the total reduction become effective not later than 1 January 1987." [5] The Protocol establishes a slightly different time schedule for countries which begin tariff reductions on 1 July 1980, and provides for rounding off to the first decimal. The United States phasing provision is contained in the Presidential Proclamation implementing the Tokyo Round tariff reductions.[6]

There are numerous legal problems in connection with the basic GATT Article II obligation, but only a few can be mentioned here.[7] The GATT obligations relating to the tariff commitment can be divided into two groups. The first group consists of those obligations which relate specifically to a tariff binding and are triggered by the existence of such tariff binding on the GATT schedule. A second group of obligations consists of the more general GATT obligations (a sort of "code of good conduct for trade policy"), which relate not only to the treatment of goods which are listed on a schedule, but to all goods. These latter obligations (such as obligations on the use of quotas or national treatment obligations relating to internal taxation and regulations) have as *one* of their purposes the prevention of evasion of the GATT tariff binding. To a certain extent, any nontariff barrier (NTB) is an evasion of the GATT tariff binding, since the objective of obtaining a binding is to allow the exporting country to sell its goods in the obligated country's

5. Para. 2a; GATT, 26th Supp. BISD 3 (1980). The BISD series reproduces the text of the Protocol and Supplementary Protocol entered into at the conclusion of the Tokyo Round. The Protocols with tariff bindings annexed are published separately by GATT.

6. Presidential Proclamation No. 4707 of December 11, 1979, 44 Fed.Reg. 72398.

7. See J. Jackson, note 1 supra, at 211–17.

market. Any NTB which tends to inhibit those sales detracts from the benefits of the exporting country in obtaining the tariff concession.

The group of obligations in the GATT which relate more directly to the tariff binding and are generally limited to goods which are listed on the GATT tariff schedule, include the following:

(1) The tariff maximum or ceiling, as expressed in the schedule (see Article II, paragraph 1 which obligates treatment "no less favorable" than that specified on the schedule).

(2) Other provisions of Article II designed to protect the value of the concession from encroachment by other governmental measures, such as "other charges," new methods of valuing goods, reclassification of goods (see Article II, paragraphs 3 and 5) and currency revaluations (Article II, paragraph 6).

(3) Limits on the protection against imports of a particular product which can be afforded by the use of an import monopoly (Article II, paragraph 4).

(4) A GATT interpretation that new subsidies granted on products covered in a nation's schedule, after the schedule has been negotiated, shall be considered a "prima facie nullification" for purposes of complaints under Article XXIII.

It should be noted that the GATT obligation refers to goods "which are the products of territories of other contracting parties." Thus if A and B are GATT parties and C is not, A cannot buy products from C, ship them to B, and expect the GATT schedule treatment.[8]

Query: what happens when a new product is developed?

GREEK INCREASE IN BOUND DUTY
Report by the Group of Experts, GATT, Doc. L/580 (9 November 1956).

Pursuant to instructions given by the CONTRACTING PARTIES at their meeting on 5 November 1956, the Group examined technical points raised in regard to the German complaint (L/575) that the Greek Government had increased the duty on item 137, e, 3, Gramophone Records, etc., which had been bound both at Annecy and Torquay.

The Greek representative said that his Government had left unaltered the specific duty as bound in Schedule XXV on item 137, e, 3. What they had done was to impose a duty which, with surtax, amounted to 70 per cent ad valorem on "long-playing" records (33⅓ and 45 revolutions per minute). His Government explained this action on the grounds that such records did not exist at the time the Greek Government granted the above concession, that they contained a volume of recordings up to five times that of the old records, that they were lighter than conventional records, that they were made of different material, and that, therefore, as a new product, they were not covered by the item bound at Annecy and Torquay. The Greek representative further pointed out that countries which impose ad valorem duties

8. Id., at 464–69. See Section 6.2(E) supra.

on gramophone records were, because of the higher value of long-playing records, collecting substantially higher duties in monetary terms.

The Group did not feel that it was relevant to the problem to investigate the incidences of the different rates. They noted, however, that if the Greek Government had bound an ad valorem duty for this item, the problem would not have arisen; but they pointed to the essential difference between specific and ad valorem duties and the different consequences which followed the binding of one or the other type of duty.

The Group agreed that the practice generally followed in classifying new products was to apply the tariff item, if one existed, that specified the products by name, or, if no such item existed, to assimilate the new products to existing items in accordance with the principles established by the national tariff legislation. It was noted that when this item was negotiated the parties concerned did not place any qualification upon the words "gramophone record."

The Group consequently reports to the CONTRACTING PARTIES its finding that "long-playing" records (under 78 revolutions per minute) are covered by the description of item 137, e, 3 bound in Schedule XXV (Annecy and Torquay) and, therefore, the rate of duty to be applied to long-playing records is that bound in the schedules under that item. As the action taken by the Greek Government involves a modification in a bound rate, it is the opinion of the Group that the Greek Government should have resorted to the procedures provided in the Agreement for such modification.

In view of the attitude taken by the governments mainly affected, the Group feels the CONTRACTING PARTIES might give sympathetic consideration to any request addressed to them by the Greek Government for authority to renegotiate the item in question.

JOHN H. JACKSON, WORLD TRADE AND THE LAW OF GATT 213–14

(1969) [9]

Partly for political reasons, the CONTRACTING PARTIES did not accept the report of the Group of Experts, but they referred the question to the Intersessional Committee, which later asked an advisory opinion on the classification problem from the Customs Co-operation Council. This organization assists in formulating and administering the Brussels Tariff Nomenclature ("BTN"). The Council refused to give an opinion since the issue did not involve the BTN, but it noted the BTN principle that "[g]oods not falling within any heading of the Nomenclature shall be classified under the heading appropriate to the goods to which they are most akin." It also noted, however, that this principle does not apply where a tariff classification has a residual heading, *i.e.,* "other articles not elsewhere specified," as was the case with Greece. A clarifying communication noted that the Council was not deciding whether the long-playing records could be held to come within an existing heading, the precise issue of the German complaint

9. See note 1 supra.

against Greece. Later, Germany and Greece compromised on a new bound rate for long-playing records under a new subclassification in the Schedule.

Although, as is true of many GATT cases, the result of this dispute is not as clean-cut a precedent as might be desired, it seems that several principles are accepted by most contracting parties: (1) new products must be deemed within bound Schedule items where the description clearly covers them; (2) reference will be made to the national law of the party whose Schedule is under dispute to determine the principles of classification; but the national law is not determinative.

Of course, even if a technical violation of the tariff concession does not occur, a "nullification" that resulted from subdivisions or classification differences regarding a bound item could be the subject of complaint under Article XXIII. This was the result in another GATT case in which Norway complained of treatment by Germany regarding some closely related but admittedly different sardine species.[10] A 1952 report of a Panel on Complaints that was adopted by the CONTRACTING PARTIES found no violation of GATT obligations, but did find "nullification" of a benefit accruing to Norway when similar but distinguishable sardines imported to Germany from other countries were given treatment more favorable than those sardines that Norway exported to Germany. The panel found that the subclassifications existed at the time Germany and Norway negotiated the concession and that these were in the minds of the negotiators. However, since Germany's later actions could not have been reasonably anticipated by Norway and since they upset relationships of the species concerned that Norway had reason to assume would remain stable, "nullification" was found and Germany was urged to take remedial action.

(B) GATT TARIFF NEGOTIATIONS

The various rounds of GATT negotiations have been previously described in general in Section 5.5 supra; here we focus on tariff negotiations. In all trade negotiation rounds, the first important step has been the establishment of a tariff negotiations committee (TNC), consisting of a representative from each of the countries which are participating in the negotiations. Although the negotiation is conducted under the auspices of GATT, is serviced by the GATT secretariat and proceeds with reference to GATT rules, nevertheless there are countries which participate in the negotiations which are not GATT members. Generally, these countries intend ultimately to become GATT members, but there is no legal necessity that they be GATT members during the negotiations. (If they did not become a GATT member, presumably they would have to agree to certain provisions that would have rules comparable to the GATT so the tariff concessions would be protected by the other measures of the General Agreement.) [11]

10. See Section 7.2(C) infra.

11. The countries participating in the Tokyo Round Multilateral Trade Negotiations that were *not* members of GATT, included: Algeria, Bolivia, Botswana, Bulgaria, Costa Rica, Ecuador, El Salvador, Ethiopia, Guatemala, Honduras, Iran, Iraq, Mali, Mexico, Panama, Papua New Guinea, Paraguay, Somalia, Sudan, Swaziland, Thailand, Tongo, Venezuela, Viet-Nam, Yemen, Zambia. Several countries which have only acceded to GATT provisionally also participated. GATT, The Tokyo

The first five negotiating rounds were conducted under procedures following generally those established by the first round and can be summarized as follows: the first step was for each country to submit a "request list" on which it detailed for every other participant the concessions (specified product by product) which it desired the other country to make. Thus, if the United States felt that it had a potential for shipping aircraft to the United Kingdom, it would put on its request list to the United Kingdom a tariff maximum on aircraft which would likely permit more United States sales of that item to the United Kingdom.

Next, each country would analyze the requests submitted to it and prepare an "offer list," which would indicate what tariff concessions it was willing to make in exchange for obtaining favorable treatment on its "requests." Each of the request and offer lists would be furnished to every country participating in the negotiation, so that each could see not only its own pattern of requests and offers, but also those which might pertain between other countries.

A third step was a series of bilateral conferences between negotiating countries to begin to develop the "bargain" between them. The objective was to obtain concessions roughly equivalent in value to those which a country gave up. In general, offers would be extended for particular products to the country which was the "principal supplier" of that product for the offering country. Thus, if country X imported bicycles from countries A, B and C; A supplying 60%, B supplying 30%, and C supplying 10%; then X would make its tariff offer to country A, which supplied most of the bicycles and would stand to benefit most from a concession. Nevertheless, once A and X had come to a tentative agreement, then X would begin negotiating with B with respect to the same concessions, trying to obtain from B some reciprocal concessions for the advantage B would obtain by the concession X was willing to extend to A.

Gradually, toward the end of the conference, more and more concessions would fall into place and third party benefits would be reciprocated as the circle of bilateral negotiations was extended. Finally, at some point near the deadline, all countries would finalize their offer lists. At this point, each country would have to evaluate the total concessions of all the other participants in the conference, to see whether it felt that as a whole they were equivalent in value to the concessions which it was giving. If it felt this was not the case, it would then notify the other participants that it was withdrawing from some of its offers to remove the imbalance. Needless to say, withdrawals from offers could create a ripple effect of counter withdrawals, which could extend through the entire negotiation and destroy the results obtained so far. This stage of the negotiation has been accompanied with a considerable amount of bluff, tension, "midnight oil burning," and hopefully a certain amount of mediation by an impartial secretariat.[12]

Round of Multilateral Trade Negotiations, Report by the Director-General of GATT 184 (1979). For the membership of GATT, see Section 5.4 supra, footnote 39.

12. See J. Evans, note 3 supra, at 221–25, 235–37.

In the early rounds, the focus was on tariffs, but as tariffs generally became lower, NTBs became more significant in their impact on trade. Consequently, in later rounds, there was an attempt to bring NTBs into the negotiations, although most of these attempts were not very successful.

One of the results of a series of tariff negotiating rounds, is that a particular "GATT schedule" for a country is, to a certain extent, a complex "fiction". The schedule technically consists of all the results of a series of tariff conferences and possibly some bilateral negotiations. The tariff on a particular item may have been the subject of negotiation at several of the tariff conferences. At a first conference, for instance, a tariff maximum of 20% may have been set; at a third conference this may have been reduced to 10%; and at a final conference, the maximum may have been set at 5%. The current operative binding is, of course, the latest (which is generally the lowest). However, if for some reason the protocol of application for the latest conference became invalid or was revoked, the previous protocols are still technically enforceable, so that the GATT binding reverts to the next previous concession.

By the time of the "Dillon Round" (1960–61), the 1957 Treaty of Rome had established the European Economic Community, and the EEC was theoretically negotiating as an entity in GATT. The item-by-item approach to tariff negotiations proved extraordinarily cumbersome. The technical problem of dealing with thousands of specific products was formidable enough, but when in each case the EEC had to establish a common position among its members before it could negotiate on an item in GATT at Geneva, it became almost impossible to make progress in the negotiations. Furthermore, by this time, tariffs on many items were low enough that further reductions "hurt," i.e., had more effect. In addition, the United States legislation authorizing the President to negotiate on tariffs was particularly miserly during the Dillon Round, setting a maximum of a 15% cut for each tariff item.

For these various reasons, it was concluded that it would be necessary for future tariff-trade negotiating rounds to establish new procedures and, in particular, it was decided to utilize a "linear technique" for negotiating the reductions. United States legislative authority for the United States to negotiate was obtained (under the 1962 Trade Expansion Act), with the understanding that a linear approach would be followed.[13] An initial GATT ministerial meeting was held in May of 1963, in an attempt to develop the precise negotiating rules, but it was not until May, 1964, at a second ministerial meeting, that the rules were finalized.[14]

Basically, the rules called for a 50% cut as a "working hypothesis," or what some have termed the "initial offer." Unfortunately, however, the agricultural products were generally excepted from the linear rule. On the basis of the 50% linear cut, countries were then entitled to table "exceptions lists," which were to be held to a "bare minimum" and "subject to confrontation and justification." The negotiation among the countries participating

13. J. Evans, note 3 supra, at 140–45.

14. GATT, 12th Supp. BISD 47, para. A4 (1964); GATT, 13th Supp. BISD 109–10 § A (1965). See K. Dam, note 1 supra, at 69–70; J. Evans, note 3 supra, at 184–202; J. Jackson, note 1 supra, at 223–27.

in the linear procedure then focused principally upon the exceptions lists. Products in the agricultural sector were negotiated on an item by item basis (and it is generally conceded that not much trade was covered in these negotiations). Several developed countries, and all of the developing countries, were exempted from the requirement of the initial 50% linear offer. These developed countries (Canada, Australia, New Zealand, South Africa) argued that this exemption was necessary because they depended heavily upon agriculture and raw material exports, and since these products were generally exempt from the linear offer, these countries could not hope for equivalence under reciprocity if they were required to make a 50% cut offer on industrial product imports. Developing countries argued that under Part IV of GATT (added in 1964) they were not required to offer reciprocity and should not be required to make the linear offer,[15] although they desired the industrialized country 50% offer to include products of special interest to the developing countries.

Although nontariff barriers were supposedly a subject of the Kennedy Round, only a few became the subject of serious negotiation. Just before the United States negotiating authority ran out on June 30, 1967, the Kennedy Round participants completed their agreements, consisting of a series of protocols. In addition to the tariff reductions, which were substantial (arguably the greatest reduction of tariffs ever negotiated), agreements on antidumping duties and on wheat and other grains were completed.

GATT, PRESS RELEASE NO. 992
(1967)

3. The GATT secretariat has made a first study of the tariff concessions made by certain of the main industrialized countries—the European Economic Community, Japan, Sweden, Switzerland, the United Kingdom and the United States. In 1964, the last year for which full details are available, the total imports of these countries were valued at $60 billion, of which $23 billion already entered duty free. These countries have made concessions (either duty reductions or the binding of duties already at zero) on imports valued at $32 billion. Duty reductions affect $26 billion, or 70 per cent of these countries' dutiable imports. The majority of these reductions are of 50 per cent or more; these affect imports valued at $18 billion. Another $5 billion are subject to reductions of between 20 and 50 per cent and a further $4 billion are subject to lesser reductions. Trade in dutiable goods in respect of which no reductions were made amounted to $11 billion. Further details are given in Table 1, which relate the depth of the cut to the height of the duty before the negotiations; this shows, for instance, that 30 per cent of trade in products in respect of which no tariff reductions have been negotiated face duties of 5 per cent ad valorem or less.

* * *

7. The developing countries have, during the course of the negotiations, put forward a list of products in which they have an export interest. On 21 per cent of the dutiable items on the list no tariff reductions have been

15. GATT, Art. XXXVI, para. 8; GATT,
Annex I, Ad Art. XXXVI, para. 8.

made, on 26 per cent reductions of less than 50 per cent have been made, on 49 per cent reductions of 50 per cent have been made and on 5 per cent reductions of more than 50 per cent have been made. These results do not differ greatly from the overall results of the negotiations.

Many of the *manufactured products* on the list are of potential, rather than actual, export interest to the developing countries. In the case of dutiable manufactured products of actual interest to developing countries, 24 per cent by value of imports into the main industrialized participants will not be the subject of tariff reductions, 29 per cent will be the subject of reductions of less than 50 per cent and 47 per cent will be the subject of reductions of 50 per cent or more. Comparable figures for all manufactured products are: no reduction, 16 per cent; less than 50 per cent reductions, 29 per cent; reductions of 50 per cent or more, 55 per cent.

Note

The experience of recent negotiating rounds has highlighted a number of problems in the existing techniques of negotiations. Three problems in particular stand out.[16] First, the MFN obligation, providing for a generalization of each nation's concessions to all other GATT members, tends to restrain willingness to make offers and concessions, particularly if one major participant is dragging its feet. A "foot dragger," whose offered concessions are relatively meager would stand to gain from the "free ride" effect of MFN if the other countries went ahead despite the foot dragging.

A second difficulty is apparent in the "reciprocity" principle. Although usually not explicitly stated, all the negotiations in the context of GATT so far have been carried out with the objective in each participant's mind of gaining in concession terms as much as it gives up. However, it is extremely difficult to measure these "gains" and "gives." One might proceed on the basis of trying to evaluate the increase in trade that would occur because of a particular tariff concession and use that as a measure of that concession's "value." However, this would require data concerning the price elasticity of demand in the importing country, which data is generally not available or at least is unsatisfactory. A rougher measure is often used, namely the amount of the tariff reduction times a recent year's import value figure. Thus, if a tariff is reduced from 20% to 10% and the total imports of the product were valued at $1 million in a recent year, the value of the reduction is 10% of $1 million or $100,000. Obviously, this measure has many fallacies. Furthermore, in a period when exchange rates fluctuate more freely, these measures of concession value may have no validity whatsoever; in fact, it may be to a country's advantage to lower its tariffs unilaterally, if that in turn could cause its imports to increase and therefore its currency to decline in value, thus making its exported goods more attractive to foreign markets.

Despite its conceptual problems and possible fallacies, the notion of reciprocity has had enormous political impact during its forty years of life. The idea of equivalent concessions in tariff reductions appeals to laymen and politicians as "fair" and has helped to achieve the great reductions of tariffs that have occurred during that period of time. Perhaps reciprocity can be termed a "useful myth," but it would be nice if some new principles with comparable

16.   See J. Jackson, note 1 supra, at 240–48.

political appeal could be discovered (and perhaps a concept of "sector harmonization" will serve some of these functions).

A third problem of trade negotiations to be mentioned here is the increasingly perplexing problem of nontariff barriers. If tariffs are difficult to negotiate and if the reciprocity principle is mythical in connection with tariffs, the problems of NTBs are manifold worse. Often there is no generally accepted quantitative measure of the value of acceptance of obligations relating to NTBs. Furthermore, the MFN principle again operates to inhibit the development of a strong obligation as to NTBs, tending to reduce such obligations to the least common denominator equivalent to that to which the foot draggers are willing to agree. Again, new principles may be necessary to achieve satisfactory progress in negotiating nontariff barriers: a new type of conditional MFN has been suggested (see next chapter) and sector harmonization may have more validity in the NTB context (e.g., equalizing government procurement practices as to a particular commodity such as steel).

(C) FLEXIBILITY OF TARIFF BINDINGS: REOPENINGS AND RE- NEGOTIATIONS

Although the tariff binding is an obligation to limit the tariff on a particular product to the maximum listed in the tariff binding, GATT contains a number of provisions that give considerable flexibility to this commitment.[17] These provisions are basically of two types: provisions that enable tariff bindings to be suspended or otherwise temporarily departed from; and provisions that enable a particular tariff binding to be changed permanently. The first type is more appropriately the subject of discussion of exceptions to GATT, such as the escape clause exceptions (Chapter 9), retaliation-sanction type provisions of Article XXIII (Chapters 5 and 10), and provisions for waivers under Article XXV (Chapter 5). The second type of provision, however, deals with the procedures for negotiating and renegotiating the permanent schedule obligations themselves. Although the great bulk of tariff reductions are negotiated during one or another of the so-called rounds, nevertheless, GATT is the locus of more or less continuous tariff negotiations. For example, a particular binding may have been accepted by a nation during the Dillon Round and may later prove (due to the change of circumstances or changing political context in the obligated nation) to be impractical or too onerous for the nation to follow. There is provision in GATT whereby that nation is entitled to reopen the matter and substitute other commitments in place of the one which it now desires to remove. In fact, a full survey of all the various types of changes which can be accomplished, as well as the techniques for obtaining new bindings, would include the following:

A. NEW NEGOTIATIONS

1. Bindings resulting from a negotiating "round" (Article XXVIII bis).

2. Negotiations for the accession of new members (under Article XXX- III) (described briefly in Chapter 5).

3. Various other negotiations not specifically authorized by GATT.

17. Id., at 201–38.

(Nations may, of course, negotiate with any other nation on an ad hoc basis for the reduction of tariff maximums below GATT scheduled rates. These negotiations need not be conducted in the context of GATT, but if any member of the negotiation is a GATT member, it is obligated under the MFN clause of Article I of GATT to generalize the treatment promised. While these ad hoc bindings may or may not be included in the schedules of GATT, they nevertheless will affect the trade of all GATT members.)

B. RENEGOTIATIONS, MODIFICATIONS, RECTIFICATIONS

1. Reopening every three years (Article XXVIII, paragraph 1).

2. Special circumstance renegotiations (Article XXVIII, paragraph 4).

3. Reserved renegotiations (Article XXVIII, paragraph 5).

4. Compensatory renegotiations due to formation of a customs union or free trade area (Article XXIV, paragraph 6).

5. Renegotiations by developing countries (Article XVIII, paragraph 7).

6. Withdrawal of concessions under Article XXVII.

7. Rectifications (corrections of mistakes and other minor changes).

This is not the place to discuss each of these methods of change in detail, but a brief summary of several types of the renegotiation provisions may assist the reader in understanding the GATT system.

Originally, GATT was negotiated with the idea that tariff concessions would extend for only a three year period, after which they would be renewed or modified. Article XXVIII of GATT embodied this principle by authorizing, after a three year period, any nation to withdraw any concession or binding. If a binding were withdrawn, however, then the countries "with whom" the original binding had been negotiated or other countries which were major beneficiaries of the obligated tariff treatment, were entitled either to make reciprocal compensatory withdrawals of their own or to obtain from the withdrawing party substitute concessions of equivalent value. Article XXVIII details some of the procedures by which these renegotiations would occur. Subsequently, GATT was amended so that it specified that this "reopener" would occur every three years from January 1, 1958. In some circumstances, a GATT contracting party may at the time of the reopener reserve its right to reopen beyond the technical time limit period provided in Article XXVIII.[18]

Another important renegotiation provision of GATT is that which pertains to the formation of a customs union or free trade area.[19] Under Article XXIV, groups of nations can, under certain circumstances, join together into a customs union or free trade area and depart from the most-favored-nation obligation to the extent necessary to give duty-free treatment to other members of the customs union or free trade area. In the case of a customs

---

18. At the end of 1972, both the United States and the European Economic Community reserved such rights, partly to establish bargaining positions for the negotiations, begun under Article XXVIII of GATT, for compensation to the United States for concessions withdrawn by the United Kingdom, Ireland, and Denmark, when these three countries joined the EEC. See, e.g., Office of the Special Representative for Trade Negotiations, Press Release No. 173 (Dec. 29, 1972).

19. See generally J. Jackson, note 1 supra, at 575–623.

union (as discussed in Chapter 7), a common external tariff is substituted for the individual national tariffs of the members, and when this is done it is very likely that some of the tariffs on the common external tariff will be higher than some individual bindings in GATT for specific members of the union. When this occurs, under Article XXIV, paragraph 6, GATT provides that "the procedure set forth in Article XXVIII shall apply." Unfortunately, the Article XXVIII description of procedures is quite skeletal and a number of difficult problems arise when these procedures are applied to the customs union case. Two important rounds of negotiation in GATT have occurred in connection with these types of rights, both in the context of the development of the European Economic Community.

The EEC Treaty provided for a staged development of a common external tariff (CXT) and the elimination of separate national tariffs (both of which were accomplished earlier than scheduled). Since the CXT tended to be an average level tariff somewhere between the highest and the lowest of the member tariffs, whenever the lowest tariff on a product was bound in GATT for an EEC member, renegotiation rights arose in non-EEC countries. Most of the renegotiations concerned with the development of the EEC occurred simultaneously and as part of the Kennedy Round of negotiations. One of the features of these renegotiations was the withdrawal by the EEC of most bindings on agricultural goods, particularly grains, since the EEC was developing a common agricultural policy (CAP), with provision for variable levies, which would be inconsistent with their bindings in GATT. Since the United States was by then a major exporter of agricultural goods, particularly grains, to the Common Market, it was seriously concerned with the loss of its trading rights and the imbalance in such rights that would allegedly ensue between the United States and the EEC. Two particular disputes arose out of those renegotiation procedures: one called the "Chicken War," and the other called the "Standstill on Grain Rights."

The Chicken War [20] occurred when, after a dramatic increase in the export of United States produced frozen poultry and poultry parts to Common Market countries, the EEC took action to limit imports of these goods, contravening a GATT binding by its new CAP policy. The matter was treated by the United States as a withdrawal of a concession on the part of several European countries, and the United States asserted its renegotiation rights under Article XXVIII. Since the Common Market was unprepared to grant the United States satisfactory substitute concessions, the United States indicated that it would withdraw concessions equivalent in value to the trade it lost because of the EEC policy. The negotiations broke down, however, on the question of what was the value of the trade loss. Article XXVIII is not very satisfactory in the case of a breakdown of a negotiation, since unilateral responses by each negotiating party could draw counter-responses and escalate the conflict. Recognizing the need for some kind of arbitral procedure to prevent such escalation, the Director-General of GATT, Eric Wyndham-White, was induced to suggest the appointment of a special panel composed of representatives from nondisputants, which would be

---

20. K. Dam, note 1 supra, at 87–88; J. Evans, note 3 supra, at 173–80; Galloway, Star Industries Inc. v. United States: Sequel to the Chicken War, 6 Intl.Lawyer 48, 49–52 (1972); Walker, Dispute Settlement: The Chicken War, 58 Am.J.Intl.L. 671 (1964).

charged with determining the precise issue of the amount of the trading rights which the United States had lost. This panel received briefs and oral arguments from both sides, the United States arguing that its trading rights had a value considerably more than that which the EEC was willing to recognize. The panel came to a determination of that value somewhat in between,[21] and the United States and the EEC agreed to abide by that determination. The United States then proceeded to withdraw its own concessions on brandy, trucks, starch and dextrine.[22] Since withdrawals under Article XXVIII are designed to be on an MFN basis, the United States had to choose products which were mostly supplied by countries in the Common Market, so that its withdrawal would hopefully only affect the export trade of the EEC countries. Nevertheless, one country which was hurt by the "fall-out effect" of these withdrawals was Spain, and subsequently a lawsuit was brought in United States courts arguing that the United States President did not have authority to make the withdrawals in the manner which he did. The withdrawals did not result in a change of practice by the Common Market.[23]

The grains rights problem was so difficult that it has still not been resolved. Again, the problem was that the Common Market CAP called for the withdrawal of EEC member state concessions on the importation of grains, which had mostly been with the United States. Because no satisfactory resolution of the matter could be obtained during the Kennedy Round, the EEC and the United States agreed to extend the grains rights to the United States until such time at some future negotiation when the United States would be able to "cash in" its rights.[24]

Another important round of "customs unions renegotiation" occurred when the EEC was enlarged by the admission to membership of the United Kingdom, Denmark and Ireland. The treaty of enlargement became effective January 1, 1973, with the extension of the CXT to the new members' markets. Once again a series of GATT bindings that had been in effect for those new members was withdrawn. An elaborate negotiation took place, which was called the "Twenty-four-Six" negotiation (GATT Article XXIV:6).

Initially the EEC argued that the tariff reductions that the three acceding countries were implementing far outweighed the tariff increases involved in their joining the Common Market and that no other adjustments

---

21. GATT Doc. L/2088 (1963); reprinted in 3 Intl. Legal Materials 116 (1964).

22. Presidential Proclamation No. 3564, 28 Fed.Reg. 13247 (1963).

23. United States v. Star Industries, Inc., 462 F.2d 557 (C.C.P.A.1972), cert. denied, 409 U.S. 1076, 93 S.Ct. 678, 34 L.Ed.2d 663 (1972), sustained the President's authority. See Section 10.5 infra. As one result of the EEC enlargement "XXIV:6 negotiation," the United States reduced the tariff on certain brandy "in order to encourage the resolution of outstanding trade disputes between the United States and the EEC, including the removal of unreasonable import restrictions on poultry from the United States maintained by the EEC." Presidential Proclamation No. 4304, 39 Fed.Reg. 26277 (1974). However, after negotiations were unsuccessful, the rates were increased again. Presidential Proclamations Nos. 4478 and 4480, 41 Fed.Reg. 52287, 53967 (1976).

24. See Agreements between United States and EEC of March 7, 1962, United States TIAS Nos. 5034 and 5035, relating to grains and to wheat. See also Agreement between the EEC and the United States entered into June 30, 1976, suspending agreements of March 7, 1962 (TIAS Nos. 5034 and 5035), relating to quality wheat and other grains. 20 UST 2864; TIAS No. 6761, 723 UNTS 411.

were necessary. The United States position was that it should be compensated for the loss of the lower tariff rates in the three acceding countries. In particular, the United States was unwilling to accept reduced industrial tariffs as an offset to loss of market access in the agricultural area. In 1974, the dispute was settled after the EEC agreed, inter alia, to increase U.S. market access for tobacco, oranges and grapefruits, kraft paper, photographic film, non-agricultural tractors, excavating machinery, diesel and marine engines and outboard motors, engine additives, measuring instruments, pumps, plywood and other items.[25]

(D) THE TOKYO TRADE ROUND AND TARIFF NEGOTIATIONS

In Section 5.5 we described the Tokyo Round generally. Here, we examine the tariff negotiations. The Tokyo Round was supposed to focus (for the first time) on nontariff barriers, and in fact it did. However, the tariff negotiations, especially in the early years of the negotiation, remained very significant. Some have observed that this may have been due to the "momentum" of bureaucratic habits. Others suggested that during periods when the overall negotiation was largely stalled, the continuation of detailed and often mathematical talks about tariffs provided the continuity or "glue" which held the negotiation together, by providing a joint sense of purpose and movement, and a focus for lower level officials to continue their activities thus maintaining the governmental structure necessary to accomplish the intense work that would come when the overall negotiation began to move again.

One of the serious controversies, never adequately resolved in the Kennedy Round, was that between the United States and the European countries in connection with the "disparities issue."[26] Because the Common Market was moving to a common external tariff, and this "CXT" tended to be an average tariff of most of those of the members, the CXT tended to be a more uniform tariff without the "peaks and valleys" that might have pertained in a traditional national tariff schedule. On the other hand, the United States had many "peaks and valleys," and it was argued by the European counterparts that a reduction of 50% in those tariffs that made up the "peaks" would not have an equivalent trade effect to a reduction in a more average tariff by 50%. For example, a 40% tariff could be cut in half and still provide a 20% protection against imports, thus greatly inhibiting those imports. On the other hand, a 20% tariff could be cut in half, and the 10% margin of protection that remained might not suffice to inhibit greatly increased imports. This issue was also an important one in the Tokyo Round. The following shows how it was resolved then.

The Trade Act of 1974 contained the traditional tariff negotiating authority in section 101. Initial proposals for the Act would have obtained

25. White House Press Secretary, Statement by the President, "Background on the United States-European Community Tariff Compensation Negotiations," May 31, 1974.

26. See A. Albregts & A. van de Gevel, Negotiating Techniques and Issues in the Kennedy Round, in F. Alting von Geusau (ed.), Economic Relations After the Kennedy Round 20, 23–31 John F. Kennedy Institute, Center for Atlantic Studies, Tilburg, the Netherlands, Pub. No. 2, A. W. Sijthoff (Leyden, 1969); T. Curtis & J. Vastine, Jr., The Kennedy Round and the Future of American Trade 82–91 (1971); K. Dam, note 1 supra, at 73–76; J. Evans, note 3 supra, at 186–200.

for the Executive unlimited tariff negotiating authority; that is, the authority to agree with foreign trading partners to the total elimination of all remaining tariffs or some result short of that, but unlimited by statute. Partly because of the "Watergate" climate and a weak (and perhaps disinterested) Executive, the tariff authority that finally emerged in the Trade Act limited the extent of possible tariff cuts. Basically, the authority allowed a 60% cut in any tariff existing on January 1, 1975, with provision for abolition of tariffs which on that date were not more than 5% ad valorem. Arguably this was extensive: One can compare it with the 50% tariff authority of the 1962 Act. On the other hand, industrialized tariff levels were then generally between 8% and 9%, so that a 60% cut meant about a 5 percentage point reduction in tariff levels, while in previous negotiations a 50% cut could give an average reduction of 6 percentage points or more. Furthermore, given the swings in exchange rates in the early 1970's (as much as 20% in the dollar's relation to other currencies), exchange rate swings could have many times the influence of the authorized tariff rate changes under the 1974 Trade Act.

The 1974 Trade Act, like some of its predecessor statutes, had extensive procedures for the development and conduct of negotiations on behalf of the United States. Like previous Acts, there was a requirement of a Tariff Commission (now International Trade Commission) study, including public hearings, of possible offers which the United States might make for concessions in the negotiations.[27] Also, there was provision for an Executive Branch interagency study, including public hearings.[28] Generally it was thought that the Tariff Commission would focus on the impact of United States trade concessions on imports and their effect on the United States economy. On the other hand, it was thought that the focus of the parallel proceeding in the Executive Branch (Office of the Special Trade Representative) would be on the export opportunities of the United States. However, there was no air-tight wall between those parallel procedures. In addition, a new layer of procedures was added by the 1974 Act, namely, the "industry liaison" procedures, whereby industry sectors establish a series of committees to consult with, feed information to and possibly give guidance to the United States negotiators.[29]

GATT, THE TOKYO ROUND OF MULTILATERAL TRADE NEGOTIATIONS, REPORT BY THE DIRECTOR–GENERAL OF GATT

46–48 (1979)

2. NEGOTIATIONS ENGAGED: 1977–1979

The deadlock in the Tokyo Round was broken at the meeting in July 1977 between Mr. Strauss [U.S. Trade Representative] and Mr. Haferkamp [EC External Relations Commissioner] in Brussels. As regards the negotia-

27. Trade Act of 1974, section 131. See, e.g., The Journal of Commerce, Jan. 23, 1975, at 1, col. 6.

28. Trade Act of 1974, sections 132–33. See, e.g., Commerce Today, Feb. 17, 1975, at

22; The Journal of Commerce, April 28, 1975, at 1, col. 6.

29. Trade Act of 1974, section 135.

tions on tariffs, it was agreed that a negotiating plan, including a tariff-cutting formula, should be established by 15 January 1978.

At a further meeting in Brussels between Mr. Strauss and Mr. Haferkamp in September 1977, there was agreement that the "working hypothesis" for the tariff-cutting exercise should be established along the lines of the proposal put forward by Switzerland. In the weeks thereafter most developed countries accepted the Swiss proposal as a working hypothesis and agreed to table their detailed tariff offers by 15 January 1978.

Expressed algebraically, with X representing the initial rate of import duty applied, A a coefficient to be agreed upon, and Z the resulting reduced rate of duty, the formula proposed by Switzerland was:

$$Z = \frac{A\ X}{A\ +\ X}$$

On the basis of a proposed coefficient 16, for instance, an initial 10 per cent tariff would be reduced to $(16 \times 10) \div (16 + 10) = 160 \div 26 =$ about 6.15 per cent. A higher tariff would be reduced by a greater proportion, a lower by a less one. If applied without exceptions, this formula would have the effect of reducing the average tariff level of the main industrialized countries by about 40 per cent. The new tariff levels would, in accordance with normal GATT practice, be "bound" against subsequent increase.

The autumn of 1977 was devoted to the preparation of detailed tariff offers in capitals. In mid-January 1978 the tabling of offers on industrial products and the submission of bilateral requests for tariff concessions began. Copies of these initial requests and offers were made available to all countries participating in the Tokyo Round.

By the middle of 1978 countries were proceeding to reciprocal adjustments in their initial offers, involving both improvements and exceptions. A high level of binding of duties by all participants continued to be an important objective. There still remained certain technical problems to be dealt with, such as how to treat specific duties, how to take account of the fact that some tariffs are levied on a c.i.f. and others on an f.o.b. basis, etc.

During the second half of 1978 and the early months of 1979 there were intensive bilateral and plurilateral negotiations among delegations, both in Geneva and in various capitals. The results achieved in these negotiations are described in Chapter II of Part II.

3. THE PROCESS OF NEGOTIATION

There was no formal tariff-negotiating plan as such in the Tokyo Round. A number of problems and differences of view had emerged relating to the various elements that would have been included in such a plan and countries decided that, rather than delay further, it would be better to push ahead with the actual negotiations.

(a) Tariff-cutting Formula

Although the Swiss formula had been generally accepted by the main industrialized countries as a working hypothesis, there were considerable variations in its application. The European Economic Community and the Nordic countries—followed later by Australia—used the coefficient 16, whereas the coefficient 14 was used by the United States, Japan and Switzerland. Canada employed its own formula. These variations were designed to yield an approximately equal average cut in each country's overall tariff. Certain other countries, New Zealand for example, resorted to the item-by-item technique.

(b) Base Dates and Base Rates

Countries used different base dates and base rates. A problem concerning Japan and Australia in particular was whether the legal or the effective rate should be used, the effective rates charged by these countries in recent years often being below the legal rates on which the reductions offered were calculated. It was not possible to reach agreement with the result that, when countries made their offers, it was on the basis of base dates and rates of their own choosing, it being left to the other countries to make an evaluation of this element of the negotiations along with all others.

(c) Staging of Cuts

Staging would be decided upon by the time the Tariff Protocol was opened for signature. As the negotiations developed, an eight-year period seemed to be generally agreed. While, however, some countries considered that the period should begin on 1 January 1980 and go forward annually without interruption, there was also the view that, after the first five years, the situation should be looked at in the light of the economic situation obtaining at that time before a decision was made on the cuts over the remaining three years. It was agreed that, in the case of certain products, special rules concerning staging would apply.

(d) The Developing Countries

The developing countries had hoped at the outset that there would be agreement with the developed countries on special measures to be taken on their behalf.

In the event, and despite intensive discussions between developed and developing countries as well as among the latter, the approach to special and differential treatment in the tariff negotiations remained unspecified.

An examination of initial offers indicated that less than formula reductions, or no reductions, had been offered for a good number of items of which the developing countries were already major suppliers. Such items were often excluded partially from the application of the tariff-cutting formula and did not at that time benefit from GSP treatment. The total or partial exceptions covered textile items for which developing countries were significant suppliers, as well as other sectors such as footwear, leather goods, cutlery, porcelain, wood or wood products, certain types of non-ferrous metals, etc.

In order to compensate in some degree for these partial or total exclusions deeper than formula cuts were offered on a number of other items where developing countries were still minor suppliers and at that time relying mainly on the GSP to achieve a breakthrough into the market.

The developed countries did confirm individually at a later date that their final offers would contain measures providing for special and differential treatment, although they would expect contributions from developing countries commensurate with their level of economic development. They invited developing countries to put forward their requests individually and requests were forthcoming from a number of countries seeking deeper m.f.n. cuts, accelerated implementation of m.f.n. cuts, exclusion of products from exception lists and the maintenance of GSP margins.

Note

There was one particularly important exception to the general rule on negotiating tariff reductions by formula and that was in the case of civil aircraft. In this particular area, a separate agreement was reached that provided for duty-free treatment for civil aircraft and engines and all their parts, components and sub-assemblies, as well as all ground flight simulators. The Agreement on Trade in Civil Aircraft also provided for the elimination of duties on aircraft repairs and called for purchasers of civil aircraft to have the freedom to select suppliers on the basis of commercial and technological factors.[30] The latter provision was designed to reduce pressure on government-owned airlines to buy domestically produced aircraft.

Some countries hoped that a sectoral approach would be used more extensively, but problems such as how to measure reciprocity in such negotiations were not worked out satisfactorily.[31]

GATT, THE TOKYO ROUND OF MULTILATERAL TRADE NEGOTIATIONS, SUPPLEMENTARY REPORT BY THE DIRECTOR–GENERAL OF GATT
3–7 (1980)

A. TARIFF NEGOTIATIONS: CONCLUSION

The opening in the second half of 1979 of two legal instruments for acceptance by governments marked the formal conclusion of the Tokyo Round tariff negotiations.

The first of these instruments—*The Geneva (1979) Protocol to the General Agreement on Tariffs and Trade*—was opened for acceptance on 11 July 1979.

Attached to the Protocol were Schedules of Concessions setting out in full detail tariff-cutting commitments made in the Tokyo Round by the following: Argentina, Austria, Canada, Czechoslovakia, European Communities, Finland, Hungary, Iceland, Jamaica, Japan, New Zealand, Norway, Romania, South Africa, Spain, Sweden, Switzerland, United States and Yugoslavia.

The second instrument was *The Protocol Supplementary to the Geneva (1979) Protocol to the General Agreement on Tariffs and Trade* which was opened for acceptance on 22 November 1979.

---

30. Agreement on Trade in Civil Aircraft, GATT, 26th Supp. BISD 162 (1980). See Piper, Unique Sectoral Agreement Established Free Trade Framework, 12 Law & Poly.Intl. Bus. 221 (1980); Note, Technical Analysis of the Civil Aircraft Agreement, 12 Law & Poly. Intl.Bus. 243 (1980).

31. See GATT, The Tokyo Round of Multilateral Trade Negotiations, Report by the Director-General of GATT 88–89 (1979).

This Supplementary Protocol embodies the results of negotiations continued into the later months of 1979. As a result of these negotiations, countries already with Schedules of Concessions attached to the Geneva (1979) Protocol made certain further concessions, bringing some improvements in benefits to developing countries, while additional developing countries also entered into tariff-cutting commitments.

Schedules of Concessions for the following are attached to the Supplementary Protocol: Australia, Brazil, Canada, Chile, Dominican Republic, Egypt, European Economic Community, Haiti, India, Indonesia, Israel, Ivory Coast, Korea, Malaysia, Pakistan, Peru, Singapore, Spain, Uruguay, Zaire.

Bulgaria took part in the tariff negotiations and was one of the twelve countries that submitted in April 1979 records of tariff commitments. As Bulgaria is not a contracting party to GATT, its Schedule of tariff concessions could not be incorporated in a GATT Protocol but was instead annexed to a separate legal instrument that was drawn up at the same time as the Geneva (1979) Protocol.

Three countries—Colombia, Mexico and the Philippines—carried out tariff negotiations in connexion with their accession to GATT within the framework of the Tokyo Round. The Schedules of Concessions of these countries are, or will be, annexed to their Protocols of Accession.

* * *

B. Tariff Negotiations: Assessment

* * *

The total value of trade affected by m.f.n. tariff reductions and bindings of prevailing tariff rates amounts to $155 billion, measured on m.f.n. imports in 1976 or 1977 excluding petroleum, crude and refined.

Concessions by the European Communities and eight industrial countries (Austria, Canada, Finland, Japan, Norway, Sweden, Switzerland and the United States) covered imports valued at $141 billion, $14 billion in agriculture and $127 billion in industry. Concessions by other developed countries affected imports valued at $0.4 billion in agriculture and $2.7 billion in industry.

Although the participation of developing countries was not subject to the reciprocity rule they made contributions, in the form of tariff bindings or reductions, on $3.9 billion of their imports in 1976 or 1977.

Considering the nine industrial markets enumerated above, the weighted average tariff on industrial products will decline from 7.0 to 4.7 per cent, representing a 34 per cent reduction of customs collection. Measured on the basis of the simple tariff averages, the reduction amounts to 39 per cent and the level of tariffs on industrial products will decline from 10.4 to 6.4 per cent. As a result of the harmonizing effect of the tariff-cutting formula the difference in the nine tariff levels will be reduced by 25 per cent, measured by standard deviation of national averages.

Imports into the nine markets from developing countries affected by m.f.n. tariff concessions amounted to nearly $40 billion; $12 billion in agriculture and $28 billion in industry. In agriculture, tariff action on products of interest to developing countries has been taken mainly in the form of improvements of the Generalized System of Preferences (GSP) in the framework of tropical products negotiations. Concessions on an m.f.n. basis in agriculture resulted in the decline of the weighted average tariff for developing countries from 8.1 to 7.1 per cent.

The nine m.f.n. tariffs facing developing countries' exports of industrial products will be reduced by 27 per cent based on the weighted average tariff and by 38 per cent based on the simple average tariff.

The effect of m.f.n. concessions on the GSP is difficult to assess in view of the imprecision underlying GSP statistics. Products entitled to GSP represented $4.6 billion or 23 per cent of dutiable imports of agricultural products, and $22.5 billion or 65 per cent of dutiable imports of industrial products. GSP contributions would increase the GSP product coverage by $0.9 billion in agriculture, and in industry they would nearly compensate for elimination of GSP preference resulting from m.f.n. concessions at zero rates. The GSP preferential margin would be slightly increased in agriculture as m.f.n. concessions were more important on non-GSP products. In industry, where the GSP coverage is more extensive especially in processed goods, the GSP preferential margin shows a not unexpected decrease as a result of the application of the tariff-cutting formula on items where GSP admission was free of duty.

ACTION BY THE CONTRACTING PARTIES ON THE MTN TARIFF CONCESSIONS
Decision of 28 November 1979 [32]

1. The Contracting Parties note that as a result of the tariff negotiations in the Multilateral Trade Negotiations, the Geneva (1979) Protocol to the General Agreement on Tariffs and Trade and the Protocol Supplementary to the Geneva (1979) Protocol have been drawn up.

2. The Contracting Parties adopt the following decision: in respect of the concessions specified in the Schedules annexed to the Geneva (1979) Protocol to the General Agreement on Tariffs and Trade and the Protocol Supplementary to the Geneva (1979) Protocol, a contracting party shall, when the question arises, be deemed for the purposes of the General Agreement to be a contracting party with which a concession was initially negotiated if it had during a representative period prior to the time when the question arises a principal supplying interest in the product concerned. This decision does not affect initial negotiating rights which are the result of bilateral negotiations and which have been duly notified.

——————

For an econometric analysis of the results, the reader is referred to the Deardorff-Stern article excerpted in Section 1.3 above.

As the Director-General's report indicates, when the Tokyo Round tariff cuts are fully implemented, average tariff rates will be rather low. These low rates are only averages, however, and certain product groups continue to attract high tariff rates. It is probably not surprising that these higher rates are generally found on products that are of export interest to develop-

32. GATT, 26th Supp. BISD 202 (1980).

ing countries (also referred to as GSP beneficiaries).[33]   The following tables
are adapted from the GATT Director-General's Supplementary Report quoted above.

Comparison of MFN Tariff Reductions
Products from all sources vs. Products of interest to GSP nations
(trade weighted averages)

	Depth of tariff cut (%) on products		Post MTN tariff averages on products	
	from all sources	of GSP interest	from all sources	of GSP interest
US				
All industrial products	31	45	4.4	7.9
Semi-finished/finished manufactures	30	24	4.9	8.7
Japan				
All industrial products	49	44	2.8	3.0
Semi-finished/finished manufactures	46	32	5.4	6.8
EC				
All industrial products	29	25	4.7	4.7
Semi-finished/finished manufactures	29	25	6.0	6.7

As the table indicates, on products of interest to developing countries the
depth of tariff cuts was less and remaining tariffs are higher than on the
average.

Excluding raw materials, the major products of export interest to
developing countries (measured by trade value) are textiles, metals, electrical machinery, footwear and travel goods and wood, which taken together
amount to over two-thirds of the processed goods exported by developing
countries to the developed countries.   The following table shows the MTN
results of those sectors.

MAJOR INDUSTRIAL SECTORS OF EXPORT INTEREST
TO DEVELOPING COUNTRIES

	Current Imports	Weighted average tariffs	
	(Billion)	Pre-MTN	Post-MTN
Textiles			
Yarns and fabrics	$1.9	11.3%	8.8%
Clothing	8.5	20.4	16.8

33. See generally Chapter 20 infra for a
view of the Tokyo Round from the developing
country perspective.

	Current Imports	Weighted average tariffs	
	(Billion)	Pre-MTN	Post-MTN
Metals			
Semi-manufactures	$5.6	2.1%	1.7%
Articles of metals	0.8	8.8	5.8
Electric machinery	4.9	8.2	5.6
Footwear & travel goods	2.2	13.3	13.2
Wood			
Semi-manufactures	1.9	5.7	3.5
Articles of wood	0.3	7.8	5.1

As can be seen from the table, there was little reduction in footwear and clothing rates. Indeed, as we will see in Chapter 9, those particular sectors are typically subject to quantitative limitations, as well as high tariffs. The combination of those quantitative limitations and high tariffs is not well accepted in developing countries, who criticize GATT as an organization for industrial giants only.

LIBRARY OF CONGRESS CONGRESSIONAL RESEARCH SERVICE, COMPARISON OF TARIFF LEVELS AMONG MAJOR INDUSTRIAL COUNTRIES: A REVIEW OF THE PROBLEMS OF COMPARISON AND OF RECENT DATA ON TARIFF AVERAGES

(1973) [34]

V. NOMINAL VERSUS EFFECTIVE TARIFFS

The difficulties in interpreting the restrictive impact of tariff levels do not lie solely in the computation of appropriate averages. A real measure of the effective protection afforded national industries by tariffs should take account of the difference between tariffs on imports used in the manufacture of finished products, and tariffs on finished products. Domestic industries utilize raw materials, and semi-manufactures, in the production of finished manufactures. Some of those raw materials and semi-manufactures are imported. Tariffs on these imports increase the cost of production for domestic industry, and thus influence their competitiveness with foreign industries. Tariffs on imports may operate to offset the nominal protection afforded by tariffs on finished manufactures. Effective protection could be considerably reduced.

In practice, however, tariffs on raw materials are usually much lower than tariffs on finished manufactures. In this case, "effective" protection is greatly enhanced. To understand the difference between "effective" and "nominal" tariff rates one must understand just what is being protected. A tariff on a finished manufacture is protection for the "value added" in the process of transforming imported raw (or semimanufactured) inputs into finished outputs.

An example can clarify the explanation. Assume a simple case in which a domestic industry imports all the materials it uses in the manufacturing

34. House Comm. on Ways and Means, 93d Cong., 1st Sess., Briefing Paper No. 3, Trade Agreement Authority and Tariff Levels, 9, 11–17 (Comm.Print 1973).

process. These imports are duty-free, but there is a 10 percent tariff on the finished product. Assume the competitive world price of the materials required to manufacture one unit of output is $50. Assume the competitive world price of the finished good is $100. Businesses in foreign countries which export the raw materials face a choice: to export the raw materials for $50, or to manufacture the finished product themselves and export it for $100. The raw materials will be duty-free, but the finished good will bear a duty of $10. Assuming that, to compete with the domestic manufacturer, the foreign manufacturer cannot raise the price of his export, his revenue from exporting the finished good will be $90, compared to a revenue of $50 from exporting the raw materials. He has earned $40 from the "value added" by his manufacturing process. But the domestic manufacturer, who bears no tariff on the $100 price of the final good, earns $50 from the value added in the domestic manufacturing process. The "effective rate of protection" enjoyed by the domestic manufacturer is the ratio of $10 to $50, or 20 percent, not the nominal tariff rate of 10 percent. The "effective rate of protection" can be defined as "the maximum proportion by which the value added per unit of output by primary resources employed in the domestic industry can exceed the value added per unit of output by primary resources employed in the foreign competitive industry." [*7]

(E) PROBLEMS

Assume that Atlonia and Bugslavia are members of GATT, while Xonia is not. Atlonia's schedule contains the following binding:

Handkerchiefs, cotton _____ 10%.

This concession was negotiated at the most recent round of negotiations, partly pursuant to a request of a country named "Categorica" which at the time was the second largest exporter of handkerchiefs to Atlonia. The largest exporter to Atlonia at that time was "Dominata." Today, the largest two exporters of handkerchiefs to Atlonia are "Exportonia" (first), and "Factonia" (second.) All these countries are members of GATT.

Bugslavia ships products to Atlonia, and the following cases arise. In each case indicate whether the Atlonia practice is consistent with GATT or not. (Refer to the GATT agreement in the Documentary Supplement.)

(1) A tariff is imposed on the imports of cotton handkerchiefs produced in Bugslavia at the rate of:

   (a) 12%.

   (b) 8%.

   (c) Specific rate of one drachma, and the handkerchiefs are valued at 8 drachmas each.

   (d) Same, except value is 12 drachmas each.

(2) Imports are of handkerchiefs made of 50% cotton and 50% synthetic fiber; tariff imposed is 20%.

* 7. Giorgio Basevi, "The United States Tariff Structure: Estimates of Effective Rates of Protection of United States Industries and Industrial Labor." The Review of Economics and Statistics (May 1966).

(3) Besides the tariff, a customs administration fee of 1 drachma per handkerchief is imposed, and mandatory import entry invoice forms are "sold" for 1 drachma each.

(4) All textile imports are valued by the highest price found for like goods in any market of the world.

(5) Textile imports are valued by applying Atlonia production cost factors, using standard Atlonia collective bargaining labor wage rates.

(6) All imports are valued for customs purposes as if their value included the standard Atlonia 10% domestic sales tax applied to all goods, domestic or foreign.

(7) After the binding was negotiated, Atlonia granted to its domestic textile industry an accelerated income tax depreciation rate for new capital expenses by that industry.

(8) Atlonia maintains a state trading monopoly for textile imports and imported handkerchiefs are sold at a 40% mark-up, after they have cleared customs and paid duty.

(9) Atlonia abolishes its state trading monopoly, but establishes an import quota for handkerchiefs at 1 million units per year. (Past imports have never exceeded 700,000 units per year.)

(10) A Bugslavia firm buys handkerchiefs from Xonia and ships them to Atlonia for resale. A tariff of 20% is imposed.

(11) On transistor radios, Atlonia has made no GATT binding. Atlonia now charges a tariff of 10% on imports of this product, but is developing a domestic industry to produce transistor radios. It wishes to exclude imports of these products and consults you, its lawyer, about ways to accomplish this. Advise on the relative merits of the following proposals:

   (a) Impose a ban on imports of the product.

   (b) Subsidize with direct government grant equal to 50% of the cost of producing each item.

   (c) Raise the tariff from 10% to 100%.

   (d) Raise the tariff to 1000%.

   (e) Raise the tariff to 50% ad valorem, but provide that imported transistor radios shall be valued for customs purposes equal to the average price charged in the domestic market for domestically produced transistor radios.

   (f) Impose a requirement that imported transistor radios be stored in a warehouse for one year after importation, before resale.

(12) Suppose Atlonia had bound its tariff on transistor radios at 50%. Would that cause you to change your advice on the alternatives listed in (11)?

(13) Suppose its GATT binding of 50% were on "portable radios," and Atlonia now decided to change its domestic tariff schedule to appear as follows:

Radios:
Portable   50%
Transistor, whether portable or not   100%
All other   10%

Could Atlonia do this without being in contravention of GATT?

(14) Some other techniques for Atlonia to consider (discussed in later chapters):

(a) Leave the tariff at 10%, but impose an internal excise sales tax of 50% which is waived on domestically produced goods.

(b) Require the exchange rate to be used in purchases of transistor radios to allow one-half the amount of Atlonia currency per unit of foreign currency.

(c) Require importers to deposit with an Atlonia bank an amount equal to the value of transistor radio imports, such amount to be refundable after six months (but with no interest).

(d) Allow imports of transistor radios only from countries which import a like amount of such product from Atlonia.

(e) Allow imports of transistor radios only from countries which themselves have a zero tariff on imports of transistor radios.

(15) If Atlonia decides to withdraw its tariff binding on handkerchiefs, what procedures in GATT does it face? Which GATT members will have "negotiating" rights?

(16) If, at a new negotiation, Atlonia is prepared to reduce its tariff on silk handkerchiefs from 20% to 10%, and has recently been importing one million units of this product from Bugslavia, two million from Categorica, and three million from Dominata, all at a wholesale customs entry valuation of the equivalent of $1.00 per unit (before tariff), what value of concessions is Atlonia entitled to ask from each of these countries? How should one measure the value of a concession?

SECTION 6.4   QUOTAS AND THEIR APPLICATION

The nature of a quota and its economic effects have already been described.[1] The following materials will shed light on quota practices in the United States and other countries, and how these practices relate to international obligations.

HARRY H. BELL, ANALYSIS OF ALTERNATIVE PROTECTIVE MEASURES

(1971) [2]

Quantitative Restrictions.—"Quantitative import restrictions are measures that restrict the volume of imports into a country, not by artificially

---

1. See Appendix to Chapter 1

2. From U. S. Commission on International Trade and Investment Policy (the Williams Commission), Papers I, 421, 431–34.

raising the cost of importing—as is the case when a tariff is imposed—but by placing direct limits on the quantity (or value) of imports that may enter the domestic market, irrespective of prices." In contradistinction to nonprohibitive tariffs and tariff-like measures (such as import surcharges, multiple exchange rates, and advance deposits on imports), QR's completely break any link between domestic and world prices. * * *

QR's on imports can conveniently be divided into four main types: global quotas, bilateral quotas, discretionary licensing, and state import monopolies. Import prohibitions are simply a case of a zero quota. "Voluntary" quotas such as those applied under U.S. agreements with a number of textile-producing countries in the framework of the Long Term Arrangement (LTA) for cotton textiles are backed up by the possibility of such strong sanctions that they are only institutionally different from ordinary quotas. A truly voluntary quota would be indistinguishable from an international cartel arrangement.

Global Quotas. Global quotas may be allocated on a first-come-first-served basis, leading to a rather haphazard distribution, but they are more likely to be issued on the basis of the historical record of importing firms. In either case, "since those who can import under a quota system are under no obligation to pass on the lower world price to their customers," the recipients obtain a monopoly windfall profit which, in some countries, may have to be divided with the licensing officials or with the lobbyists whose efforts ensure maintenance of the system.

* * *

Bilateral Quotas. Although global quotas can also be administered so as to discriminate by country of origin, such discrimination is the very nature of bilateral quotas. Since they are usually the object of negotiation, quid pro quo's may be demanded. If the partner has any real bargaining power, i.e., is an important market, this might set into operation a bargaining process that could conceivably degenerate into a system of bilateral trade or even clearing agreements, such as were common in Europe immediately after World War II and are still being used between some developing countries and countries of Eastern Europe.

* * *

Discretionary Licensing. Some form of licensing is always an element in administration of global and bilateral quotas. Automatic issuance of licenses, if really free to all comers, is not really a QR. Discretionary licensing, however, is a type of ad hoc policy measure, the domestic price implications of which are usually as indeterminate as those of other measures in the QR family, although it may be used as a price-stabilizing instrument to temper the adverse domestic price effects of a previously more restrictive quota system. Needless to say, it opens the door wide to corruption when used as a permanent system; uncertainty as to policy changes makes life difficult for exporters, importers, and import-competing industries.

U.S. TARIFF COMMISSION, TC PUBLICATION NO. 243, QUANTITATIVE IMPORT RESTRICTIONS OF THE UNITED STATES

2–7, 80 (1968)

BACKGROUND AND DEVELOPMENT

Historically, quantitative import restrictions have played only a small role in U.S. trade policy; generally, import duties have constituted the principal U.S. import barrier. Before World War I, import duties were the principal deterrent to U.S. imports. The various restrictions imposed on U.S. imports by the War Trade Board during World War I as an emergency measure were abolished soon after the armistice. In the 1920's, the United States continued to rely predominantly on customs duties—e.g., those of the Tariff Act of 1922—for protection of domestic industry. At the 1927 and 1928 international Conferences on the Abolition of Import and Export Prohibitions and Restrictions, the United States sponsored a tightly drawn convention outlawing any form of quantitative import restrictions. The United States ratified the convention unconditionally, but it was accepted by only a few other countries.

At the World Monetary and Economic Conference held in London in 1933, the U.S. delegation strongly urged, "that embargoes, import quotas, and various other arbitrary restrictions should be removed completely as quick as possible." [*2] Later in that year, at the Seventh International Conference of American States at Montevideo, a U.S. resolution, unanimously adopted by the Conference, called for the removal of quantitative restrictions through trade agreements.

The United States subsequently modified somewhat its policy on quantitative restrictions. This action reflected several factors, including the emergency conditions during the depression, the failure of the quantitative restriction prohibition convention to be widely accepted, and the increased resort to quantitative restrictions by other countries. The National Industrial Recovery Act (NIRA) of 1933 marked the initial departure from the earlier U.S. policy. * * *

In mid-1935 basic sections of the NIRA were declared unconstitutional and the legal authority to regulate imports under the codes of fair competition ceased. In 1934, however, new authorization for quantitative restriction on imports was enacted in the Jones-Costigan Sugar Act.[*4] In 1935 authority to impose quantitative restrictions on imports was contained in section 22 of the Agricultural Adjustment Act [*5] and in the Philippine Cordage Act.[*6] The 1946 trade agreement with the Philippine Republic,[*7] the Philippine Trade Agreement Revision Act of 1955,[*8] the Agricultural Act of 1956,[*9] and

---

[*2]. William B. Kelly, Jr., ed., Studies in the United States Commercial Policy, 63 (1963).

[*4]. Ch. 263, § 4, 48 Stat. 672 (1934), 7 U.S.C.A. § 608a.

[*5]. 7 U.S.C.A. § 624.

[*6]. Ch. 240 § 1, 49 Stat. 340 (1935).

[*7]. Ch. 244, §§ 212–216, 504, 60 Stat. 144 (1946), 22 U.S.C.A. §§ 1262–1266, 1354 (1964).

[*8]. Ch. 438, § 201, 69 Stat. 413 (1955) 22 U.S.C.A. § 1372.

[*9]. Ch. 327, § 202, 70 Stat. 188 (1956), 7 U.S.C.A. § 1852.

the Trade Expansion Act of 1962 [*10] also contained authority for imposing quantitative restrictions in particular circumstances.

In 1947 the United States became a party to the General Agreement on Tariffs and Trade (GATT), which in Article XI prohibited quantitative restrictions except under certain circumstances. This country continues to be a party to the GATT along with 73 other countries.

Note

In 1985, the United States had quotas on the following categories of products [3]: (1) Quotas established pursuant to Escape Clause proceedings (see Chapter 9 infra): motorcycles (a tariff quota, higher tariffs apply when quota exceeded), certain stainless steel and alloy tool steel; (2) quotas established pursuant to the Agricultural Adjustment Act (7 U.S.C.A. § 624 (1982): Milk and cream (fluid, evaporated, condensed or dried), cheese and cheese substitutes, chocolate (except for consumption at retail), other dairy products, peanuts, cotton and processed cotton, sugar and products containing sugar; (3) quotas on numerous textiles and textile products established pursuant to bilateral agreements entered into pursuant to the Multifiber Arrangement discussed in Chapter 9; (4) tariff quotas in the TSUS on fresh, chilled or frozen cod, cusk, haddock, hake, pollock and Atlantic ocean perch; on fresh or fluid whole milk; on canned tuna; on white or Irish potatoes and on whisk and other brooms; (5) quotas on coffee under the International Coffee Agreement Act; and (6) quotas on duty-free imports of watches and watch movements from insular possessions (Virgin Islands, Guam and American Samoa). This list does not include products limited by "voluntary" action by exporting countries, which we will discuss in Chapter 9.

The pattern of quotas applied by the United States is not unusual. Most quotas applied by developed countries at the present time are designed to afford protection from imports to farmers, clothing and textile makers and steel producers. Such protection is also afforded in the EC to automakers and producers of electronic products. Since the rationale for this protection has been that the relevant domestic industry had been injured by imports or was the victim of unfair trade practices, we will examine these sectors in more detail in Chapters 9 and 10. The case of agriculture, perhaps the most intractable one facing the GATT trading system, will be examined in Chapter 14.

EXECUTIVE BRANCH GATT STUDIES, NO. 6, THE QUANTITATIVE RESTRICTIONS IN THE MAJOR TRADING COUNTRIES

90–93 (1973) [4]

II. GATT PROVISIONS

Article XI of the General Agreement on Tariffs and Trade (GATT) provides for the general elimination of QRs. It is applicable to QRs on all of a country's trade with the other Contracting Parties, not merely to tariff

---

* 10. 19 U.S.C.A. § 1981.

3. For current quota information, see BNA, International Trade Reporter, Reference File-Quotas.

4. From Subcomm. on International Trade of the Senate Comm. on Finance, 93d Cong., 2d Sess. 90–93 (compilation of 1973 studies prepared by the Executive Branch: Comm. Print. March, 1974).

concessions bound under GATT. There are, however, a number of exceptions to the general requirement to eliminate QRs. They may be used, on a nondiscriminatory basis, to restrict imports of agricultural and fishery products but only when internal limitations are placed on the production or distribution of like products and when certain other conditions are observed.

QRs are also permitted when necessary to safeguard a country's foreign exchange reserves. Trade restrictions imposed for balance of payments reasons must be designed so that they do not unnecessarily damage the interests of the other GATT members. It is also incumbent on the country applying the restrictions to consult with the other GATT members concerning those restrictions so as to insure their progressive relaxation as conditions improve.

The GATT recognizes special trade problems of developing countries by providing that countries "in the early stages of development" may impose restrictions for balance of payments reasons and take certain other restrictive actions on a temporary basis to meet the special problems of their development programs. Other exceptions relate for example to national security, and public health and safety. A formal waiver of the restriction against QRs may be obtained by application to, and approval of, the other Contracting Parties to the GATT. The first major use of this procedure was the U.S. waiver for import restrictions on agricultural products.

III. HISTORY OF THE QR PROBLEM

In the period immediately after World War II, most countries maintained rigid import controls that had been erected during the war. With few exceptions these were continued in order to protect their limited supplies of foreign exchange. This was a period of exceptional demand for imports, reduced production capacity and disrupted trade channels. It was the period of the dollar gap when foreign holdings of dollars were released sparingly and only for essential purchases. Most of our trading partners in Europe maintained total governmental control over imports until late in the 1950's.

So long as these countries were recognized by the International Monetary Fund (IMF) to be still in balance of payments difficulties, the use of QRs was permitted under the GATT. Nevertheless, the United States maintained constant pressure bilaterally and in the GATT and Organization for European Economic Cooperation (now the OECD), for the liberalization of these restrictions as rapidly as the improvement in a country's reserve position permitted.

General recovery of the world economy during the decade of the 1950's culminated in late 1958 when the major trading nations of Western Europe established external currency convertibility. Early in 1960, seven additional countries, including such major trading nations as the United Kingdom, France, Sweden and Australia, announced they were no longer justifying restrictions on balance of payments grounds. Japan maintained controls under a balance of payments justification until 1963.

With the termination of international balance of payments difficulties the situation changed, since the use of QRs was no longer legal under the GATT. Two considerations, however, created difficulty in removing those restrictions that remained. First, most affected politically sensitive agricultural products (e.g. the United States still maintained quotas on various agricultural products under a special provision of the GATT (Article XI, c(1)) and under a waiver it had obtained to permit import restrictions under section 22 of the Agricultural Adjustment Act which might have been inconsistent with the GATT). Second, in the industrial sector, the prolonged period of import restrictions had fostered the survival and growth of a number of uneconomic industries. Governments were under extreme pressure to continue to protect these industries, at least until they could adjust to the new circumstances.

During the 1960's, much of the U.S. effort in the GATT and in bilateral contacts was devoted to obtaining the liberalization of this "hard core" of restrictions and obtaining nondiscriminatory treatment for items continuing temporarily under control. For example, at the initiative of the United States the Contracting Parties required West Germany to submit a schedule for the removal of its remaining restrictions and to undergo an annual review of progress. Similar multilateral pressure was applied to Italy. In 1962, the United States submitted a formal complaint in the GATT against the remaining French import restrictions. The Contracting Parties found that these were illegal. France, in consultation with the United States, established a timetable for the accelerated liberalization of many of them.

By pressure of this kind, residual import restrictions had been reduced by 1968 in almost all developed countries to a relatively small list of products, mostly agricultural. The most serious nonagricultural QRs remaining are those of Japan, which still maintains QRs for certain industrial products.

In late 1967, the member countries of the GATT agreed upon a future work program to lay the groundwork for further trade liberalization and expansion. To carry out this work, the GATT members created two new committees, one of which, the Committee on Trade in Industrial Products (CTIP), was directed to draw up an inventory of all important nontariff barriers affecting international trade, including QRs. The CTIP has completed the factual examination of some 800 notifications submitted by individual countries concerning nontariff barriers of GATT member countries. Following the initial review, in October 1969 the Committee agreed to move to its next stage of work—to search for possible solutions to the major barriers. For this purpose it established five subgroups on different barriers, one of which is now addressing itself to specific limitations on imports and exports, such as QRs.

Japan—Following the 1963 IMF finding that Japan was no longer entitled to maintain import restrictions for balance of payments reasons, Japan lost its GATT right to impose them. Several items were liberalized through April 1964, but very few were removed from the restriction list during the following four years.

Since 1968, the United States has concentrated on accelerating the reduction and removal of Japan's restrictions on trade. In the ensuing consultations between the two countries, the United States has made clear to Japan that if complete liberalization is not achieved within a reasonable time the United States will have to consider appropriate countermeasures. This recognition has resulted in significant quota and license liberalization. Since April 1969, items in 86 Brussels Tariff Nomenclature categories have been liberalized, leaving 33 items currently under restriction. The 11 industrial items remaining under QRs include digital computers, accessories, and components; integrated circuits (with 100 elements or more); leather and leather footwear; coal; and ethyl alcohol. The 22 agricultural items remaining under quota restrictions include beef, pulses, oranges, citrus juices (except lemon), edible peanuts, and certain tomato products. Quotas on most of these products have been increased in recent years.

Note: Agreement on Import Licensing

One of the Tokyo Round agreements was the Agreement on Import Licensing Procedures.[5] The basic provision of the Agreement called for the rules for import licensing procedures, which are normally used to administer a quota program, to be "neutral in application and administered in a fair and equitable manner." [6] Article 1 of the Agreement requires the relevant rules and changes to them and the products to which they apply to be published promptly. It calls for forms and procedures to be kept "simple," and bans refusals of applications for minor documentation errors. It also provides that importations should not be refused for minor deviations in value, weight or quantity from the licensed amount. Additional provisions in Article 3 require that all persons meeting the importing country's legal requirements be eligible to apply for licenses. In allocating licenses, consideration is to be given to an applicant's past performance and to ensuring a reasonable distribution of licenses to new importers, particularly those importing products from the least developed countries or developing countries. The provisions of the Agreement are essentially designed to prevent licensing procedures from constituting trade barriers in themselves.

The GATT Committee on Import Licensing, which was established by the Agreement, has reported that "the Parties consider that the Agreement is adequate to ensure the discipline necessary to prevent trade distortions rising from the operation of licensing procedures." It has noted that the "effectiveness of the Agreement depends on continuing efforts * * * to maintain and increase transparency." [7]

The United States implemented the Agreement through Executive action, it having been determined that no special legislation was necessary.[8] The U.S. general rules on quota procedures are contained in 19 CFR § 132 (1985). Specific license requirements are typically contained in the orders or agreements pursuant to which quotas are established.

Problems

(1) Do GATT Article XI exceptions allow any quotas on agricultural product imports?

5. GATT, 26th Supp. BISD 154 (1980). The status of acceptance of the Agreement is given in Section 5.5 supra.

6. Article 1(3).

7. GATT, 30th Supp. BISD 64 (1984).

8. See S.Rep. No. 96–249, 96th Cong., 1st Sess. 257–58 (1979).

(2) Is United States practice consistent with GATT? Is the practice of other nations consistent with GATT?

(3) Does the escape clause of GATT Article XIX authorize use of quantitative import restraints contemplated by section 203(a)(3) of the United States Trade Act of 1974?

(4) Must quotas be utilized consistently with the MFN obligation of GATT Article I? (See GATT Article XIII.)

Chapter 7

NONDISCRIMINATION AND THE MOST–FAVORED–NATION CLAUSE

SECTION 7.1 THE MOST–FAVORED–NATION OBLIGATION

(A) INTRODUCTION

"The unconditional most-favored-nation (MFN) provision is the cornerstone of the international trade rules embodied in the General Agreement on Tariffs and Trade (GATT).

"The basic rationale for MFN is that if every country observes the principle, all countries will benefit in the long run through the resulting more efficient use of resources. Furthermore, if the principle is observed, there is less likelihood of trade disputes." [1]

The importance of the most-favored-nation principle was further underscored by GATT economists recently when they noted [2]

1. From the economic viewpoint, it ensures that each country will satisfy its total import needs from the most efficient sources of supply, allowing the operation of comparative advantage.

---

1. Executive Branch GATT Studies, No. 9, The Most-Favored-Nation Provision, at 133, Subcomm. on International Trade, Senate Comm. on Finance, 93d Cong., 2d Sess. (Compilation of 1973 studies prepared by the Executive Branch: Comm.Print 1974).

2. GATT Focus, Sept.-Oct. 1984, at 3. For references on MFN in addition to those excerpted in this chapter, see generally Report of the International Law Commission, Draft Articles on Most-Favoured-Nation Clauses and Commentary, in Yearbook of the International Law Commission 1978, at 8–73 (Vol. 2, pt. 2, 1979) (U.N.Doc. A/CN.4/SER.A/1978/Add. 1 (Part 2)); J. Jackson, World Trade and the Law of GATT ch. 11 (1969); League of Nations Economic Comm., Equality of Treatment in

the Present State of International Commercial Relations—The Most-Favoured-Nation Clause, L.N.Doc.C. 379, M. 250. 1936 II.B.; G. Patterson, Discrimination in International Trade: The Policy Issues, 1945–1965 (1966); Gros Espiell, The Most-Favoured-Nation Clause, 5 J. World Trade L. 29 (1971); Sorensen, Most Favored and Less Favorite Nations, 52 Foreign Affairs 273 (1974). In the context of the Tokyo Round, see Hufbauer, Erb & Starr, The GATT Codes and the Unconditional Most-Favored-Nation Principle, 12 Law & Poly.Intl. Bus. 59 (1980); Rubin, Most-Favored-Nation Treatment and the Multilateral Trade Negotiations: A Quiet Revolution, 6 Intl.Trade L.J. 221 (1981).

2. From the trade policy viewpoint, the MFN commitment protects the value of bilateral concessions and "spreads security around" by making them the basis for a multilateral system.

3. From the international-political viewpoint, the commitment to the MFN clause mobilizes the power of the large countries behind the main interest and aspiration of the small ones which is to be treated equally. It represents the only way to realize the ideal of sovereign equality of nations; in more practical terms, it guarantees the access of newcomers into international markets.

4. From the domestic-political viewpoint, the MFN commitment makes for more straightforward and transparent policies and for greater simplicity of administration of protection.

5. Ultimately, the unconditional MFN commitment is of a constitutional significance. It serves as the safe constraint on the delegated discretionary powers of the executive branch in trade matters.

GATT, ARTICLE I, PARAGRAPH 1

1. With respect to customs duties and charges of any kind imposed on or in connection with importation or exportation or imposed on the international transfer of payments for imports or exports, and with respect to the method of levying such duties and charges, and with respect to all rules and formalities in connection with importation and exportation, and with respect to all matters referred to in paragraphs 2 and 4 of Article III, any advantage, favour, privilege or immunity granted by any contracting party to any product originating in or destined for any other country shall be accorded immediately and unconditionally to the like product originating in or destined for the territories of all other contracting parties.

Note

At this point, the reader should examine the remainder of Article I, as well as the interpretative note to Article I in GATT Annex I, Ad Article I (Documentary Supplement). In addition, Sections 102(f), 126, 401 and 501 of the Trade Act of 1974, Sections 301 and 441 of the Trade Agreements Act of 1979, and Section 701 of the 1930 Act (as added by Section 101 of the Trade Agreements of Act of 1979) should be read.

MFN has sometimes been described as the "central" policy of GATT and the post World War II trading system. Certainly it is one of the central policies, and the fact that it is Article I of GATT reinforces its central position. The reader will also recall that the "existing legislation" exception of the Protocol of Provisional Application of GATT does not apply to Part I of GATT, which includes Article I (as well as the tariff concessions article, Article II, discussed in the previous chapter).

The MFN principle of non-discrimination (one of the two major non-discrimination principles of GATT, the other being the national treatment principle, taken up in the next chapter), has been the center of considerable discussion and controversy in recent years. Some would argue that it is being eroded rapidly by a number of exceptions and by various bilateral arrangements between nations which depart from the spirit if not the letter of the MFN obligations. In

Chapter 9 we will discuss one of the most controversial of the recent MFN issues, that concerning the relation of MFN obligations to "safeguard" or "escape clause" actions. In later chapters concerning nonmarket economies and developing countries, respectively, we explore further the relationship of MFN to those types of economies. For example, the Generalized System of Preferences designed to aid less developed countries is a departure from MFN, and one can argue whether it is a wise departure or not.

In this chapter we explore the history, basic policies and traditional operation of MFN obligations. MFN obligations exist in a number of treaties besides GATT, and the lawyer must be sensitive to that fact. The language of the different clauses can have considerable effect on the application of the principle. We also explore whether there is any MFN obligation in customary international law, apart from treaty obligation. These are matters we take up in Section 7.2. In the remaining sections of this chapter we explore some important exceptions to MFN. We start (in Section 7.3) with an examination of the most important exception—that of GATT Article XXIV, for customs unions and free trade areas. In Section 7.4 we look at other exceptions. A very important MFN problem arose after the Tokyo Round negotiation. Two of the Tokyo Round agreements, and the United States statute implementing three of the Tokyo Round agreements, seem to limit the benefits of those agreements to those countries which assumed the obligations of the particular agreement, a sort of "agreement conditional MFN." [3] In considering the materials below, the reader should note the difference between traditional conditional MFN and agreement conditional MFN.

(B) HISTORY AND POLICIES OF MFN

EXECUTIVE BRANCH GATT STUDIES, NO. 9, THE MOST–FAVORED–NATION PROVISION

133–35 (1973) [4]

HISTORY

The concept embodied in the MFN clause has been traced to the 12th century, although the phrase "most-favored-nation" did not appear until the end of the 17th century. The emergence of the MFN provision is largely attributable to the growth of world commerce in the 15th and 16th centuries. At that time England and Holland were competing with Spain and Portugal, and the French and the Scandinavians were challenging the Hanseatic League and the Italian Republics. Each country, seeking maximum advantage for its trade, found itself compelled to grant concessions in return. The

---

3. Agreement on Interpretation and Implementation of Article VI, XVI and XXIII, art. I, GATT, 26th Supp. BISD 56, 57 (1980); Agreement on Government Procurement, art. II:11, GATT, 26th Supp. BISD 33, 35 (1980). As noted below in Section 7.4(C), the Trade Agreements Act of 1979, by which the United States implemented the Tokyo Round agreements, provides that the U.S. obligations under the above two codes, as well as the Standards Code (Agreement on Technical Barriers to Trade, GATT, 26th Supp. BISD 8 (1980)), are owed only to other adherents to the code at issue. All six of the Tokyo Round NTB agreements, i.e. those on Barriers to Trade (Standards), Government Procurement, Subsidies, Valuation, Import Licensing and Dumping have procedural and governance provisions that allow participation only of parties to the particular agreement.

4. Subcomm. on Intl. Trade, Senate Comm. on Finance, 93d Cong., 2d Sess. (Compilation of 1973 studies prepared by the Executive Branch: Comm. Print 1974).

role of the MFN provision was to link commercial treaties through time and between states. At first, the MFN provision applied to concessions granted only to specified states, but gradually the clause became generalized to apply to concessions granted to all countries.

The trend toward wide use of the MFN clause necessarily coincided with the decline of mercantilism. The mercantilist view that in any commercial exchange one nation wins and the other loses does not mix with the concept of reciprocal arrangements implicit in the MFN principle.

The unconditional form of the MFN clause—guaranteed equal treatment without requiring directly reciprocal compensation—was used exclusively until the late 18th century. In fact, conditional MFN—equal treatment conditional upon adequate compensation—was inaugurated in 1778 by the United States. During the first half of the 19th century, the conditional form was common in treaties in Europe and elsewhere. The wave of liberalism that swept Europe in the second half of the 19th century brought a return to use of the unconditional MFN clause in keeping with the free trade sentiment of the time. While European countries ultimately returned to the unconditional form, the United States was consistent until 1923 in its adherence to the conditional form. It should be noted, however, that in practice only a limited amount of United States trade was affected by reciprocal treaties involving conditional MFN. The United States consistently applied a single-schedule tariff to imports from all countries. Reciprocal treaties granting reductions from the general tariff rates were few in number at any given time.

The United States began granting conditional MFN with its first treaty after independence, the United States-France treaty of 1778. Article II provided that, "The Most Christian King and the United States engage mutually not to grant any particular favor to other nations in respect of commerce and navigation, which shall not immediately become common to the other party, who shall enjoy the same favor, Freely, If The Compensation Was Freely Made, Or On Allowing The Same Compensation, If The Concession Was Conditional" (caps added). Similar provisions in treaties with Prussia (1785) and Sweden (1793) served to establish the "American interpretation" that special favors must be specifically bought.

The position of the United States as a newcomer to world commerce largely accounts for its novel interpretation of the MFN clause. With the colonial ties to the British Empire broken, the United States had difficulty establishing an equal footing for trade with other nations. France and Spain, as well as Britain, attempted to exclude the Americans from trading with their overseas possessions. At the same time, these countries sought to penetrate the American market. Given European reluctance to grant initial reciprocity, the United States policy was to establish high duties and grant access to the American market only in return for access to markets controlled by Europe. Under the circumstances then prevailing the conditional MFN clause enabled the United States to maximize its bargaining leverage by offering no gratuitous access privileges.

The American principle of conditional MFN had a growing effect on commercial policy abroad, reaching its peak roughly between 1830 and 1860.

The year 1810 marked the first conditional MFN clause in a treaty between European states (Great Britain and Portugal). In 1824 the clause was introduced to South America, where it remained dominant for the next 25 years. Of all European states, England was the most consistent in adhering to the unconditional MFN form through the first half of the 19th century, although the conditional clause was not uncommon in its treaties during that period.

Beginning with the Cobden treaty between France and England in 1860, the unconditional form of the MFN clause again prevailed in European commercial treaties. The benefits of the Cobden treaty were conditionally extended to other countries by France and unconditionally extended to others by England. It soon became apparent to England that under this arrangement the balance of advantages was in favor of France. To compensate for this, England launched a successful drive to conclude unconditional MFN treaties with other countries. The unconditional MFN clause was used exclusively in Europe after that time, in spite of a return to protectionism on the Continent after 1875.

While the United States and Europe were consistent in following their respective interpretations of the MFN clause during the latter 19th century, practice in other parts of the trading world varied. In South and Central America, for example, both forms of the clause were used with no clear-cut pattern, although the conditional form was used consistently in treaties between American states. Japan also used both forms.

The divergent interpretations of the MFN principle during the late 19th century were largely a manifestation of the economic relationship between the United States and Europe. World War I altered this relationship dramatically. Following the war, the United States no longer stood to Europe as an underdeveloped nation, dependent upon Europe for industrial goods and capital, content to export to Europe its raw materials. American products were now much in demand in Europe and American capital financed European factories. Therefore, in the 1920's United States policy changed, reflecting its broader and more important export interests. By offering complete and continuous nondiscriminatory treatment the United States sought to obtain the same treatment from other countries, thus reducing discrimination against United States exports. Authority for the United States to offer unconditional MFN was included in the Tariff Act of 1922 and implemented in 1923. The Trade Agreements Act of 1934 included an unconditional MFN provision and made it a requirement of United States domestic law.

JOHN H. JACKSON, EQUALITY AND DISCRIMINATION IN INTERNATIONAL ECONOMIC LAW (XI): THE GENERAL AGREEMENT ON TARIFFS AND TRADE

(1983) [5]

It is appropriate to ask what are the basic policies of an MFN obligation. A thorough answer will not be attempted here, but a few of the objectives of

5. From The Yearbook of World Affairs 1983, at 224, 231–32 (London Institute of World Affairs, 1984). Reprinted by permission of Sweet & Maxwell, Ltd.

the MFN clause can be mentioned. Basically, it appears that there are two groups of arguments that buttress the policy of MFN. First, a group we can loosely call "economic reasons," and secondly, a group of political or "not-so-economic" arguments.

With respect to economic arguments for MFN, one can list several: First, a principle of non-discrimination could have a salutary effect of minimising distortions in the "market" principles that motivate some views of economic institutions. By applying government trade restrictions uniformly, without regard for the origin of goods, the market system of allocation of goods and production will have maximum effect. Widgets will tend not to be shipped half way around the world, when widgets just as good, for a comparable price, can be obtained from a neighbouring country. If tariffs are applied more heavily to the neighbouring goods, however, goods from afar may be purchased, and long shipments stimulated, incurring inefficient costs.

Another economic type argument for MFN links the MFN policy to a more general policy of freeing trade from as much government interference as possible. Since MFN has the effect of generalising specific trade liberalising practices, it is argued that more liberalisation *overall* is obtained when MFN prevails than when it does not.

Finally, under this loose grouping of economic arguments, can be mentioned the value of minimising transaction costs. If MFN were fully applied, customs officials would not need to bother with the "origin of goods" question, and customs procedures would be simplified.

A second group of policies stresses the "political" side of MFN. Without MFN, governments could form trade cliques and groupings more readily. These special groupings can cause rancour, misunderstanding and disputes, as those countries "left out" of favours resent their inferior status. Since special preference "deals" between nations, as well as specifically targeted trade restraining actions, are more easily implemented if MFN does not apply, a world trading system is basically a less stable economic environment. The risk ensues that tensions among nations will be more frequent. Such economic tensions have been instrumental in the past for escalating controversies that lead to military action or other breaches of the peace.

JOHN H. JACKSON, WORLD TRADE AND THE LAW OF GATT

250–51 (1969) [6]

One of Wilson's fourteen points in 1918 urged "the establishment of an equality of trade conditions among all the nations consenting to the Peace," which was explained to mean "whatever tariff any nation might deem necessary for its own economic service, be that tariff high or low, it should apply equally to all foreign nations." The League of Nations Covenant likewise mentioned the goal of "equitable treatment for the commerce of all members" and the 1919 peace treaties contained MFN clauses. The League

6. This and other excerpts from this publication reproduced in this chapter are reprinted from World Trade and the Law of GATT, by John H. Jackson, copyright 1969, by The Bobbs-Merrill Company Inc. Reprinted by permission. All Rights reserved.

occupied itself with various economic and financial matters, but one prominent topic was MFN, on which the League prepared a series of reports and studies.

In 1936, the League published a study that included legal language for a recommended MFN clause, as well as a discussion of various problems, ambiguities, and policy questions of scope. At the same time, as chronicled elsewhere, international trade in the interwar period was breaking down and a variety of trade barriers were spreading from nation to nation. In 1930, the United States enacted the infamous Smoot-Hawley tariff and one reaction that has been attributed to this act was the introduction of a preferential trade system for the British Commonwealth. In 1934, the United States accepted Cordell Hull's reciprocal trade agreement program but, although MFN clauses were universally included in the trade agreements negotiated pursuant to that act, the treaties with Commonwealth nations excepted the Commonwealth preferences from MFN operation.

One of the prime post-World War II objectives of the United States was the dismantling of trade preferences, especially the Commonwealth system. The details of the clash between United States and British policy and public opinion in this respect are set forth in Richard Gardner's book *Sterling-Dollar Diplomacy.* The United States' preoccupation with Commonwealth preferences was so intense that an administrative spokesman told Congress in 1947 that eliminating these preferences was almost a *sine qua non* of success at the Geneva Conference. Failure to achieve this result has been blamed as one of the causes for the failure of the United States to accept the Havana Charter, thus causing the ITO to fail to materialize.

◆

In 1956, a GATT official said in a speech: [7]

* * * While the most-favoured-nation clause in GATT is the direct descendant of the unconditional most-favoured-nation clause as enshrined for decades in bilateral agreements, in its multilateral context it has a significance, and perhaps even has a purpose, which goes beyond that of bilateral agreements. The original purpose behind its inclusion in bilateral agreements was simply to make sure that each signatory obtained the best possible treatment from his partner. If that treatment were better than the treatment accorded to others, so much the better. In its multilateral context, however, the significance of the clause goes deeper and is the most essential element in the basic idea that runs through the first experiment in multilateral cooperation in the field of trade. That idea is that *discrimination in any form is likely to lead to more discrimination,* and that *in the long run all countries will suffer from the inevitable distortion of trade patterns which will arise out of discrimination, even though they may be the temporary beneficiaries.* However, because there are undoubted benefits that can be obtained in the short run from reciprocal discrimination, the only way to

---

7. John W. Evans, Director of Commercial Policy of GATT in 1956, from a speech given at the Bologna Center of the School of Advanced International Studies of Johns Hopkins University, Feb. 20, 1956, quoted in G. Curzon, Multilateral Commercial Diplomacy: The General Agreement on Tariffs and Trade and Its Impact on National Commercial Policies and Techniques 67–68 (1965).

prevent a country or a pair of countries from making the move that will set off this chain reaction is to obtain the simultaneous pledge of the largest possible number of trading countries that they will not discriminate against each other.

An example of a "conditional MFN" clause is as follows: "The two High Contracting Parties hereby agree that any favor, privilege, or immunity whatever, in matters of commerce or navigation, which either contracting party has actually granted, or may hereafter grant, to the citizens or subjects of any other State, shall extend, in identity of cases and circumstances, to the citizens of the other contracting party gratuitously, if the concession in favor of that other State shall have been gratuitous, or in return for an equivalent compensation, if the concession shall have been conditional." [8]

The case of John T. Bill Co. v. United States, excerpted below, includes some historical material on the shift of the United States policy from conditional to unconditional MFN.

JOHN T. BILL CO., INC. v. UNITED STATES
Court of Customs and Patent Appeals, 1939
104 F.2d 67, 26 C.C.P.A. (Customs) 67.

GARRETT, PRESIDING JUDGE.

[Importers of German-origin bicycle parts sought to recover duties paid. The Tariff Act provided for a 30% duty, subject to increase up to 50%, to match any duty higher than 30% charged on U.S.–origin bicycle parts by the country of origin of bicycle parts imported into the United States. The bicycles in question had been subjected to a 50% duty on the basis of a U.S. Treasury Decision in which it was noted that Germany charged a duty of 100 marks per 100 kilos on U.S.–origin bicycle parts of worked iron.

[The importers based their arguments for a refund on a 1925 treaty between the United States and Germany, in which each party bound itself "unconditionally" to impose no higher duties on an article originating in the other than it imposed on like articles from third countries. At the time of the importation in question, the 30% rate was being applied by the United States in respect of some other countries.]

That the treaty with Germany was a departure from former practice is a matter of history. It was consciously intended to be such. On the part of the United States the negotiations were conducted under the direction and supervision of the Secretary of State, Honorable Charles E. Hughes. After the treaty had been completed and submitted to the Senate of the United States for its action elaborate hearings were had before that body's Committee on Foreign Relations, beginning January 25, 1924. As a part of the hearings there appears a communication from Mr. Hughes to the Chairman of the Senate Committee on Foreign Relations, from which we quote the following excerpts:

8. Treaty of Friendship, Commerce and Navigation Between the United States of America and the Republic of Paraguay, signed at Asuncion, Feb. 4, 1859; entered into force March 7, 1860: 12 Stat. 1091; TS 272; 10 Bevans 888; but see Reciprocal Trade Agreement and Supplemental Exchanges of Notes, signed at Asuncion, Sept. 12, 1946; entered into force April 9, 1947: 61 Stat. 2688; TIAS No. 1601; 10 Bevans 933; 125 UNTS 179.

The Secretary of State.

Washington, March 13, 1924.

Hon. Henry Cabot Lodge, Chairman Committee on Foreign Relations,
United States Senate.

My Dear Senator Lodge: I understand that questions have been raised
with respect to certain clauses in the treaty with Germany now pending
before your committee. In view of the importance of these clauses, I desire
to emphasize the considerations which led to their inclusion in the treaty.

It is hardly necessary for me to refer to the general situation with
respect to our commercial treaties. With a number of countries we have no
commercial treaties, and the treaties we have should be supplemented and
brought up to date. Important subjects are not covered and as to other
subjects more precise and definite provisions are required. We are therefore
faced with the necessity of negotiating commercial treaties which should be
responsive to our needs, and to this end there has been a most careful study
of the questions presented. In this examination we have been led to
consider the fundamental policies which our commercial treaties should
embody. The result of this examination appears in the pending treaty with
Germany.

I understand that the difficulties which your committee has met, relate
to two classes or provisions: (1) Those providing for 'national' treatment, and
(2) those providing for 'most-favored-nation' treatment.

* * *

(2) *Most-favored-nation treatment.*—I suppose that no one would object
to the inclusion of the usual most-favored-nation provision in our commercial treaties. I take it for granted that we desire to obtain in our treaties
the same benefits for the United States that the other contracting powers
give to third States. The question which has arisen with respect to the
most-favored-nation clauses in the pending treaty with Germany grows out
of the fact that these clauses provide reciprocally for most-favored-nation
treatment without regard to the question whether a favored third State
shall have been accorded the favor gratuitously or in return for special
compensation. In other words, the pending treaty applies what is termed
the "unconditional" most-favored-nation principle. This is indeed a departure from our former practice, but it is believed to be a wise departure.

The traditional policy of the United States in respect to most-favored-
nation treatment was developed on the theory that privileges and concessions in the field of duties on imports or exports should be granted only in
return for privileges and concessions reciprocally accorded. Thus there was
almost uniformly written into the treaties to which we became a party the
provision that most-favored-nation treatment should be conditional. The
benefit of concessions or reductions of duties made to third States by either
contracting power should accrue to the other contracting power freely, if
freely made to the third State, but only in return for an equivalent if made
to the third State for a reciprocal concession or reduction.

In practice, the application of the principle of granting special concessions in return for special concessions involved the upsetting of the equilibrium of conditions which it was in the interest of this country to maintain. It
was the interest and fundamental aim of this country to secure equality of

treatment, but the conditional most-favored-nation clause was not in fact productive of equality of treatment and could not guarantee it. It merely promised an opportunity to bargain for such treatment. Moreover, the ascertaining of what might constitute equivalent compensation in the application of the conditional most-favored-nation principle was found to be difficult or impracticable. Reciprocal commercial arrangements were but temporary makeshifts; they caused constant negotiation and created uncertainty. Under present conditions, the expanding foreign commerce of the United States needs a guarantee of equality of treatment which can not be furnished by the conditional form of the most-favored-nation clause.

While we were persevering in the following of the policy of conditional most-favored-nation treatment, the leading commercial countries of Europe, and in fact most of the countries of the world, adopted and pursued the policy of unconditional most-favored-nation treatment: Each concession which one country made to another became generalized in favor of all countries to which the country making the concession was obligated by treaty to extend most-favored-nation treatment. As the United States attained to a position of first rank as a world power, we, in defense of our essential interests, became an active champion, in fact the foremost champion of the principle of the "open door" in the field of international commercial relations. To be consistent with our professions, and to conserve our interests it has become important that we make our commercial practice square in fact with the theory upon which our policy has been based. This explains the reason why, having examined with most minute care the history of the application of our conditional most-favored-nation principle, the Administration decided to abandon this practice and in its place to adopt the practice of unconditional most-favored-nation treatment. After the matter had been presented to President Harding he wrote me as follows on February 27, 1923:

> "I am well convinced that the adoption of unconditional favored-nation policy is the simpler way to maintain our tariff policy in accordance with the recently-enacted law and is probably the surer way of effectively extending our trade abroad. If you are strongly of this opinion, you may proceed with your negotiations upon the unconditional policy."

The tariff act of 1922 contains provisions which differentiated it from previous tariff legislation. Articles 315, 316, and 317 show that Congress realized that we had entered upon a new era, calling for new methods and a new attitude. The time has come for demanding that conditions of commercial competition be placed upon a bsais [basis] which will both assure our own interests and contribute to the peace of the world by eliminating unnecessary economic contentions. As we seek pledges from other foreign countries that they will refrain from practicing discrimination, we must be ready to give such pledges, and history has shown that these pledges can be made adequate only in terms of unconditional most-favored-nation treatment. We should seek simplicity and good will as the fundamental conditions of international commerce.

There is one apparent misapprehension which I should like to remove. It may be argued that by the most-favored-nation clauses in the pending treaty with Germany we would automatically extend privileges given to

Germany to other powers without obtaining the advantages which the treaty with Germany gives to us. This is a mistake. We give to Germany explicitly the unconditional most-favored-nation treatment which she gives to us. We do not give unconditional most-favored-nation treatment to other powers unless they are willing to make with us the same treaty, in substance, that Germany has made. Most-favored-nation treatment would be given to other powers only by virtue of our treaties with them, and these treaties, so far as we have them, do not embrace unconditional most-favored-nation treatment. We can not make treaties with all the powers at the same moment, but if the Senate approves the treaty which we have made with Germany we shall endeavor to negotiate similar treaties with other powers and such other powers will not obtain unconditional most-favored-nation treatment unless they conclude with us treaties similar to the one with German[y].

* * *

From the language of the treaty, particularly in the light of the foregoing elaborate construction of it by Mr. Hughes, it seems clear to us that the levy of duties at the rate of 50 per centum ad valorem while similar merchandise was being admitted, or was subject to admission, from other countries at the rate of 30 per centum ad valorem, was in contravention of the treaty's provisions.

* * *

The treaty was reciprocal and it was self-executing, requiring no legislation other than its own enactment, so far as any matter here involved was concerned. There is no claim that the rate of duty which Germany was then assessing upon bicycle parts imported from the United States was any higher than the rate imposed upon those parts when imported from other countries, and the fact that such rate was higher than the basic rate imposed by the United States is not of legal moment.

* * *

* * * The agreement between the United States and Germany was that each should receive the benefit of the lowest rate granted by it to any third country, "simultaneously and *unconditionally, without request and without compensation.*" (Italics ours). It was not required that in order to make applicable the rate of 30 per centum ad valorem on bicycle parts imported from Germany that country should give that rate to importations from the United States. It was only required that Germany admit importations from the United States at the lowest rate granted upon importations from any other country.

[The court also rejected the argument that the Tariff Act provision had superceded the treaty provision. It noted that repeal by implication was disfavored, especially in the case of treaties, and held that the Tariff Act could be interpreted to avoid a conflict.]

(C) THE NONDISCRIMINATION OBLIGATION IN CUSTOMARY INTERNATIONAL LAW

From time to time it is argued that countries are obligated under customary international law to extend nondiscriminatory treatment to other nations. The following materials give some idea how this argument has been viewed in recent times. We start with an excerpt from Professor Georg Schwarzenberger who summarizes the state of customary law in the pre-1914 period: [9]

(1) Unless evidence of any limitation of the exercise of territorial sovereignty can be adduced, it is unlimited.

(2) In a state of peace, as distinct from those of war or intermediacy between peace and war (*status mixtus*), and subject only to minor exceptions, the flag State exercises exclusive jurisdiction on the high seas over ships entitled to sail under its flag.

(3) Subject to restrictions regarding innocent passage, the littoral State exercises full sovereignty over its territorial sea.

(4) Freedom of commerce is a purely optional pattern of international economic law. As distinct from freedom of trade, it is compatible with monopoly of trade, preferential treatment and equality of treatment for foreign commerce.

(5) Equality of treatment in international economic law may be absolute or relative. With the object of securing desired forms of, in particular, equality of commerce and navigation, a number of optional standards have been developed in State practice. The most important of these are the standards of most-favoured-nation, national, identical and equitable treatment.

(6) In exceptional circumstances in which colonial or imperialist Powers are obliged to impose self-denying ordinances on themselves, equality of commerce and navigation for all Contracting Parties is established by multilateral treaties, such as the Congo General Act of February 26, 1885. Occasionally, as in the pre-1914 treaties concluded between Western Powers and China and the General Act of Algeciras of April 7, 1906, similar results are obtained by the employment of the standard of the open door.

(7) Economic equality is purely formal. Even if granted on a reciprocal basis, it neither presupposes nor leads necessarily to substantive equality between contracting parties. In this, the concept corresponds closely to freedom of contract under the municipal law of any *laissez-faire* society.

(8) The merger of sovereign States into federal or unitary States terminates treaties of commerce, previously concluded by constituent members of such associations of States. In this eventuality, the issue is reopened on the plane of the sovereignty under international law of the newly created territorial State.

GEORGE E. WARREN CORP. v. UNITED STATES

United States Court of Customs and Patent Appeals, 1934.
71 F.2d 434.

[Plaintiff protested an "excise tax" applied to coal imported from Russia, since under a statutory exemption coal from Canada and Mexico was not so taxed. The United States had no MFN treaty clause with Russia, but plaintiff argued that MFN clauses in treaties with other countries required

9. Schwarzenberger, Equality and Discrimination in International Economic Law (I), 25 Yearbook of World Affairs 163, 164–65 (1971).   Reprinted by permission of Stevens and Sons Ltd., London.

the statutory exemption to apply to all coal imports.   The court rejected that argument, stating (at 436):]

Except for the existence of treaties unabrogated, or unrepealed in an act of Congress itself, Congress certainly has full authority to levy duties upon importations of merchandise discriminatory as between nations. For reasons of comity between nations, as well as for the purpose of shielding the government's revenues, and broadly protecting its interests, the authority has not often been exercised, but this does not imply the nonexistence of the authority itself.   The possibility of its exercise by any and all sovereign nations probably presents the only reason for having most-favored nation treaties. If discrimination were not possible, there would be no occasion for agreements not to discriminate.

Furthermore, if a nation with which no most-favored nation treaty exists must be permitted to have access to a country's markets upon the same terms as a country with which there does exist such a treaty, because of that treaty, what necessity exists for separate and distinct commercial treaties between nations? Most-favored nation treaties are always reciprocal in character, whether they be executory or self-executing. We have none with Russia. Russia may lay whatsoever condition her government may choose to lay upon importations of coal from the United States. Because we have contracts whereby we agree not to discriminate in duties upon the goods of one country, the consideration being that that country accords us the same treatment, are we in any wise legally bound to extend the terms of that treaty to a country which is in no wise bound to reciprocate? We think the answer obviously must be in the negative.

JOHN N. HAZARD, EDITORIAL COMMENT: COMMERCIAL DISCRIMINATION AND INTERNATIONAL LAW

(1958) [10]

The state traders of Eastern Europe are arguing that the principle of equality of states enshrined in the United Nations Charter must be extended to international commercial intercourse to prevent discrimination. This was the theme of the opening session of a recent conference of scholars gathered in Rome to consider the impact of state trading upon the law governing commercial relations of states.[*1]

The issue had been raised by a paper submitted from the American side [*2] arguing that since state trading made possible the purchase of goods

---

10. 52 Am.J.Intl.L. 495. Reprinted by permission of the American Society of International Law.

[*1]. The conference was held under the auspices of the International Association of Legal Science under contract with U.N.E.S.C.O., Feb. 24–March 1, 1958. Emil Sandström (Sweden) presided, and Harold J. Berman (U.S.A.) was general reporter. Participants were Tullio Ascarelli (Italy), Rudolph Bystricky (Czechoslovakia), Alexander Goldstajn (Yugoslavia), Richard N. Gardner and John N.

Hazard (U.S.A.), Trajan Ionasco (Rumania), Feder Kalinytchev (U.S.S.R.), Clive M. Schmitthoff and Kurt Lipstein (U.K.), Henryk Trammer (Poland), André Tunc (France), Luben Vassiliev (Bulgaria), Paul L. Van Reepingen (Belgium), Mario Matteucci (International Institute for the Unification of Private Law), André Bertrand and Samuel Pisar (U.N. E.S.C.O.).

[*2]. For a summary of the paper, see Martin Domke and John N. Hazard, "State Trad-

by state-trading enterprises without thought for such tariffs as might have been established by the state traders themselves for accounting reasons or to tax the parcel-post trade, the traditional most-favored-nation clause had lost its principal value to private merchants seeking to do business in state-trading markets. The clause cannot operate to encourage expansion of trade by opening markets on a non-discriminatory basis to low-cost producers because factors other than cost and tariffs influence the decisions of state-trading buyers. In short, the most-favored-nation clause has proved itself to be no longer a sufficient desideratum for private-enterprise states in their commercial relations with state-trading states to constitute a *quid pro quo* for important tariff concessions by private-enterprise states.

In opposition to the view that the standard most-favored-nation clause has lost its traditional value, it was argued by the state traders at Rome that the clause is the juridical expression in the field of trade of the principle of sovereign equality expressed in Article 2 of the United Nations Charter. Further, it was claimed that the clause is the logical extension of the Charter's Article 1 calling for the development of friendly relations based on respect for the principles of equal rights. To the state traders the clause has value not because it has been traditionally an instrument through which trade has been expanded, but rather because it lays emphasis upon equal treatment, and from equality friendly relations are expected to flow. It becomes in state traders' eyes a contributing factor to the cause of peace. State traders declare that acceptance of the clause should not be considered a national sacrifice to the state-trading countries, for it contributes to the peaceful conditions essential to flourishing trade.

* * *

The Western scholars rose to question the defense of the clause by the state traders. A British scholar asked whether the view expressed did not suggest that a country refusing to grant most-favored-nation treatment was committing a wrong. Such a position, if it were taken, could be questioned, for it was not yet established that most-favored-nation treatment had become merely a reflection of a new standard in customary international law. In reply to this criticism the spokesman for the state traders agreed that he could not demand the granting of most-favored-nation treatment as an international duty, but when it was granted, it was a correct implementation of a principle now enshrined in the United Nations Charter.

A second British scholar held that there are countries not bound by most-favored-nation clauses, yet this does not signify inequality of the participants, for sovereign status is not necessarily tied up with the presence of a most-favored-nation clause in a commercial treaty. To this scholar the clause did not bring in issue equal treatment of states, but it was mainly a device to protect traders, whether private-enterprise firms or state-trading enterprises, and the essence of most-favored-nation treatment is really in the private sphere and without relation to the public-law problem of equality of states. To this comment the state-trading spokesman replied that discrimination against traders in the absence of the clause may affect negatively the

ing and the Most-Favored-Nation Clause," 52
A.J.I.L. 55 (1958).

relations between states, and in consequence the most-favored-nation clause promotes in an indirect way the relations between states, and it has a public-law feature.

An Italian scholar thought that the most-favored-nation clause has come to have a wider content than the reduction of tariffs or the statement of a principle of equality. It can be made to protect a state against discrimination in shipping or access to courts. It is in these spheres which have become subject to increasing discrimination with the centralization of power over the economy of states that the clause now can be useful. Yet, in some European countries the clause has traditionally been limited to applicability to tariffs. If a new function is to be developed for it, that function should be expressly stated. This would preserve the substance of the clause, although its form would be changed.

Notes

(1) In 1966, a United Nations Special Committee attempted to formulate "fundamental rules underlying the concept of international cooperation", and the draft formulation included the following: [11]

The partial consensus eventually reached, including the variations on which agreement was not attained, read as follows:

1. States have the duty to cooperate with one another, irrespective of their different political, economic and social systems, in the various spheres of international relations in order to maintain international peace and security and to promote international economic stability and programs and the general welfare of nations.

2. To this end,

(a) States shall co-operate with other States in the maintenance of international peace and security;

(b) *Alternative I*

States shall conduct their international relations in the economic, social, technical and trade fields in accordance with the principles of sovereign equality and nonintervention with a view to *realizing* international cooperation free from discrimination based on differences in political, economic or social systems;

Alternative II

States shall conduct their international relations in the economic, social, technical and trade fields in accordance with the principles of sovereign equality and nonintervention with a view to *ensuring the realization of* international co-operation free from discrimination based on differences in political, economic or social systems;

(c) States Members of the United Nations have the duty to take joint and separate action in co-operation with the United Nations in accordance with the relevant provisions of the Charter.

11. See Houben, Principles of International Law Concerning Friendly Relations and Co-operation Among States, 61 Am.J.Intl.L. 703, 722–23 (1967). Reprinted by permission of the American Society of International Law.

3. States should co-operate in the economic, social and cultural fields as well as in the field of science and technology and for the promotion of international cultural and educational progress. States should co-operate in the promotion of economic growth throughout the world, especially that of the developing countries.

(2) In 1978, the United Nations International Law Commission concluded its work on 30 draft articles on most-favored-nation clauses and recommended to the U.N. General Assembly that U.N. member states should conclude a convention based on those articles.[12] The articles specifically provide that the basis of MFN treatment is treaty-based.[13] The report on the draft articles stated: [14]

> The Commission observed, however, that the close relationship between the most-favored-nation clause and the general principle of non-discrimination should not blur the differences between the two notions.

> * * *

> [W]hile States are bound by the duty arising from the principle of non-discrimination, they are nevertheless free to grant special favours to other States on the ground of some special relationship of a geographic, economic, political or other nature. In other words, the principle of non-discrimination may be considered as a general rule that can always be invoked by any State. But a State cannot normally invoke the principle against another State which has extended particularly favourable treatment to a third State if the State concerned itself enjoys the general non-discriminatory treatment accorded to other States on a par with the latter. The claim to be assimilated to a State that is placed in a favoured position can be made only on the basis of an explicit commitment of the State granting the favours in the form of a conventional stipulation, namely, a most-favoured-nation clause.

SECTION 7.2   MFN IN OPERATION

(A)   INTRODUCTION

In this section we explore MFN obligations not only in the context of GATT, but also as found in various other agreements. Issues relating to the U.S. MFN obligation and implementation of the 1979 Tokyo Round agreements are taken up in Section 7.4. The problems in subsection (D) of this section illustrate the complexity and variety of legal questions which can arise in connection with MFN obligations.

(B)   THE MFN OBLIGATIONS IN GATT

JOHN H. JACKSON, WORLD TRADE AND THE LAW OF GATT
270–71 (1969)

Although the basic MFN clause of Article I, paragraph 1, applies only to an enumerated list of GATT obligations, when taken together with the other GATT MFN clauses * * *, it is hard to find a GATT obligation that is not

12. See Report of the International Law Commission, note 2 supra, at 16.

13. Art. 8, id., at 25.

14. Id., at 11–12.

subject to the principle of nondiscrimination. By pressing hard and reading closely, arguments can be made that MFN does not apply to a few limited GATT obligations. But of far greater importance is the existence of certain exceptions explicitly included in GATT, some of which are "general exceptions" and can apply to any GATT obligation, such as the waiver power of Article XXV, paragraph 5, the general and security exceptions of Articles XX and XXI, and even the escape clause in Article XIX. Other explicit exceptions refer particularly to MFN obligations or, on analysis, can be seen to affect primarily MFN-type obligations. These include the Article XIV MFN exception for quantitative restrictions in case of balance-of-payments difficulties; the important exception in Article XXIV for customs unions, free-trade areas, and certain cases of frontier traffic and contiguous territory; Article XXXV's nonapplication provision; and the possibility for MFN obligations to be suspended under Article XXIII.*[4]

The GATT MFN article is a fundamental and central obligation of international trade policy, but it is not without interpretive problems, as the draftsmen realized.[1] Apart from Article I of GATT, the General Agreement also contains a number of other MFN or nondiscrimination clauses.[2] Furthermore, interpretations have extended or clarified the application of the MFN principle vis-à-vis other GATT obligations.[3] There is also a series of GATT exceptions to the MFN principle.[4] Some of the pros and cons of MFN have been expressed in Section 7.1. In addition, it will be recalled that MFN has an impact on international trade and tariff negotiations, sometimes inhibiting progress in those negotiations if a major trading country is a "footdragger."[5]

One impact of MFN on tariff negotiations is to encourage the use of narrower and narrower classifications of goods, as negotiating countries try to limit the benefit of a tariff binding to the nation with whom it is

* 4. Included in Article XXIV exceptions to MFN are not only the general clauses for customs unions, etc., but a particular exception in paragraph 11 for trade between Pakistan and India.

1. See generally J. Jackson, World Trade and the Law of GATT ch. 11 (1969); note particularly § 11.2 discussing the draftsmen's views.

2. These other MFN or nondiscrimination-type clauses are: Art. IV, para. (b)—(cinema films); Art. III, para. 7—(international mixing requirements); Art. V, paras. 2, 5 and 6—(transit of goods); Art. IX, para. 1—(marks of origin); Art. XIII, para. 1—(quantitative restrictions); Art. XVII, para. 1—(state trading); Art. XVIII, para. 20—(measures to assist economic development); Art. XX, para. (j)—(measures for goods in short supply); see J. Jackson, note 1 supra, at 255.

3. Particularly GATT Articles XIX and XXVIII; see Section 9.4 infra, re GATT Article XIX, and the *Star Industries, Inc.* case in Section 10.5 infra.

4. See J. Jackson, note 1 supra, at §§ 11.5, and 11.6.; the GATT exceptions to the MFN principle include: Art. I, paras. (1), (2)—(historical preferences) and Annexes A–F; Art. XIV—(balance of payment difficulties); Art. XIX—(escape clause); Arts. XX and XXI—(general and security exceptions); Art. XXIV—(customs unions and free trade area exceptions); Art. XXV, para. 5—(waivers); note particularly the GSP waiver (Chapter 20 infra) and the United States-Canadian Automotive Products Agreement waiver (Section 7.4 infra); it should also be noted that particular antidumping or countervailing duty measures taken by a member can be excepted from the MFN obligation (see Sections 10.2 and 10.3 infra) and note that certain measures such as government procurement may not be covered by Art. I.

5. See Senate Comm. on Finance, Trade Reform Act of 1974, S.Rep. No. 93–1298, 93d Cong.2d Sess. 94 (1974).

negotiating, preventing "free-ride" benefits to third parties. Thus if A and B both export brandy to the United States, and the United States wishes to reciprocate concessions made by A but not B, then the fact (if true) that most of A's brandy is high priced and most of B's brandy is low priced, will suggest to the United States that its "concession" to A shall be only on high priced brandy and not on all brandy. The classic example of this technique was the product description contained in the Swiss-German Treaty of 1904,[6] reducing German tariffs on the importation of "large dapple mountain cattle or brown cattle reared at a spot at least 300 metres above sea level and having at least one month's grazing each year at a spot at least 800 metres above sea level."

The GATT MFN clause, if examined closely, can be seen to apply only to goods, "to any product," and thus not apply to services or consular rights and business establishment. It applies to treatment of *exports* as well as imports. It provides that any treatment by a GATT country to any other country (including non-GATT members) must be granted to all GATT members.

An important policy question is whether the GATT–type MFN obligations should be extended to subject matters such as trade in services (see Chapter 15 infra), when the time comes to negotiate for additional international discipline for that subject matter.

(C) APPLYING MFN

Consider the problems and exercises at the end of this sub-section in the light of GATT Article I, United States law, and the cases and materials which follow:

TREATMENT BY GERMANY OF IMPORTS OF SARDINES

Report adopted by the Contracting Parties on 31 October 1952[7]

I. INTRODUCTION

1. The Panel on Complaints examined with the delegations of the German Federal Republic and Norway the factual situation resulting from (a) the imposition, as from 1 October 1951, of an import duty of 14 per cent on preparations of clupea pilchardus as compared with a duty of 20 per cent for clupea harengus and 25 per cent for clupea sprattus, (b) the application as from 16 November 1951 of a charge equivalent to the German turnover tax at a rate of 4 per cent on preparations of clupea pilchardus and of 6 per cent on preparations of clupea sprattus and clupea harengus, and (c) the removal of quantitative restrictions on preparations of clupea pilchardus while these restrictions were maintained on the preparations of the other varieties. It then considered whether the aforementioned measures taken by the Government of the Federal Republic of Germany constituted, within the terms of Article XXIII: 1 (a), a failure by that Government to carry out its obligations under the Agreement. Having come to the conclusion that the evidence produced by the parties was not such as to warrant a finding that the measures taken by the Government of the Federal Republic of

---

6. See G. Curzon, Multilateral Commercial Diplomacy: The General Agreement on Tariffs and Trade and Its Impact on National Commercial Policies and Techniques 60 & n. 1 (1965).

7. GATT, 1st Supp. BISD 53–59 (1953).

Germany were in conflict with the provisions of Article I:1 or of Article XIII:1 of the General Agreement, the Panel then examined whether those measures had nullified or impaired the tariff concessions granted by Germany to Norway on sub-items 1604 C 1 (*d*)—sprats (clupea sprattus) and 1604 C 1 (*e*) herring, and agreed on the text of a recommendation which, in its opinion, would best assist the German and Norwegian Governments to arrive at a satisfactory adjustment of the question submitted by Norway to the CONTRACTING PARTIES.

II. Facts of the Case

2. Prior to the tariff negotiations conducted at Torquay between Germany and Norway within the framework of the General Agreement, canned products of clupea sprattus and clupea harengus enjoyed the same customs treatment in Germany as the canned products of clupea pilchardus. This equality of treatment had been guaranteed by notes exchanged between the two Governments in 1925 and 1927.

3. The Torquay negotiations were conducted on the basis of the draft of a new German Customs Tariff, following the nomenclature elaborated in 1949 by the European Customs Union Study Group. The canned products of clupea pilchardus, clupea sprattus and clupea harengus were classified under separate sub-items of item 1604 C 1, but the duties proposed were uniformly at 30 per cent *ad valorem*.

*   *   *

III. Consistency of the German Measures With the Provisions of Article I:1 and Article XIII:1

10. The Panel considered whether, by failing to extend to particular preparations of the clupeoid family, of interest to Norway, the advantages, favours and privileges granted by Germany to other preparations of the same family, which are of interest to Portugal, Germany had acted inconsistently with the provisions of paragraph 1 of Article I and of paragraph 1 of Article XIII of the General Agreement.

11. The Panel noted that the difference of treatment was not based on the origin of the goods but on the assumption that preparations of clupea pilchardus, clupea sprattus and clupea harengus are not "like products" within the terms of Article I and Article XIII.

12. The Panel noted also that the General Agreement made a distinction between "like products" and "directly competitive or substitutable products" and that the most-favoured-nation treatment clause in the General Agreement was limited to "like products". The Panel did not feel that it was called upon to give a definition of "like products" or that it was necessary for the consideration of the Norwegian complaint to decide whether the preparations of clupea pilchardus, clupea sprattus and clupea harengus had to be generally treated as "like products". Although the Norwegian complaint rested to a large extent on the concept of "like products" as set out in the Agreement and the German reply addressed itself also to that concept, the Panel was satisfied that it would be sufficient to consider whether in the conduct of the negotiations at Torquay the two

parties agreed expressly or tacitly to treat these preparations as if they were "like products" for the purposes of the General Agreement.

13.   The evidence produced before the Panel shows that in the course of the Torquay negotiations the German delegation has consistently treated the preparation of the various types of clupeae as if they were separate products; the wording of item 1604 and its sub-items was not objected to by other delegations and separate negotiations were in effect conducted on the various sub-items.   The Norwegian delegation tried without success to obtain that preparations of sprats and herrings should be treated as sardines for marketing purposes and, failing that, was content with assurances that equality of treatment in customs matters would be continued.   It would seem, therefore, that the Norwegian Government, in order to secure the extension of advantages or privileges granted to preparations of clupea pilchardus to preparations of clupea sprattus and clupea harengus, relied on assurances which it considered it has obtained in the course of the negotiation rather than on the automatic operation of the most-favoured-nation clause.

*   *   *

15.   The examination of the evidence submitted led the Panel to the conclusion that no sufficient evidence had been presented to show that the German Government had failed to carry out its obligations under Article I:1 and Article XIII:1.

IV.   NULLIFICATION OR IMPAIRMENT OF THE CONCESSIONS GRANTED TO NORWAY ON PREPARATIONS OF CLUPEA SPRATTUS AND CLUPEA HARENGUS

16.   The Panel next considered whether the injury which the Government of Norway claimed it had suffered represented a nullification or an impairment of a benefit accuring to Norway directly or indirectly under the General Agreement and was therefore subject to the provisions of Article XXIII.   It agreed that such impairment would exist if the action of the German Government, which resulted in upsetting the competitive relationship between preparations of clupea pilchardus and preparations of the other varieties of the clupeoid family could not reasonably have been anticipated by the Norwegian Government at the time it negotiated for tariff reductions on preparations of clupea sprattus and clupea harengus.   The Panel concluded that the Government of Norway had reason to assume, during these negotiations that preparations of the type of clupeae in which they were interested would not be less favourably treated than other preparations of the same family and that this situation would not be modified by unilateral action of the German Government.   In reaching this conclusion, the Panel was influenced in particular by the following circumstances:

   (a)   the products of the various varieties of clupeae are closely related and are considered by many interested parties as directly competitive;

   (b)   that both parties agreed that the question of the equality of treatment was discussed in the course of the Torquay negotiations;   and

(c) although no conclusive evidence was produced as to the scope and tenor of the assurances or statements which may have been given or made in the course of these discussions, it is reasonable to assume that the Norwegian delegation in assessing the value of the concessions offered by Germany regarding preparations of clupeae and in offering counter concessions, had taken into account the advantages resulting from the continuation of the system of equality which had prevailed ever since 1925.

18. In the light of the considerations set out above, the Panel suggests to the CONTRACTING PARTIES that it would be appropriate for the CONTRACTING PARTIES to make a recommendation to Germany and Norway in accordance with the first sentence of paragraph 2 of Article XXIII. This recommendation should aim at restoring, as far as practicable, the competitive relationship which existed at the time when the Norwegian Government negotiated at Torquay and which that Government could reasonably expect to be continued.

BELGIAN FAMILY ALLOWANCES
(ALLOCATIONS FAMILIALES)

Report adopted by the Contracting Parties on 7 November 1952 [8]

I. EXAMINATION OF THE LEGAL ISSUES INVOLVED

1. The Panel on Complaints examined the legal issues involved in the complaint submitted by the Norwegian and Danish delegations regarding the application of the Belgian law on the levy of a charge on foreign goods purchased by public bodies when these goods originated in a country whose system of family allowances did not meet specific requirements.

2. After examining the legal provisions regarding the methods of collection of that charge, the Panel came to the conclusion that the 7.5 per cent levy was collected only on products purchased by public bodies for their own use and not on imports as such, and that the levy was charged, not at the time of importation, but when the purchase price was paid by the public body. In those circumstances, it would appear that the levy was to be treated as an "internal charge" within the meaning of paragraph 2 of Article III of the General Agreement, and not as an import charge within the meaning of paragraph 2 of Article II.

3. According to the provisions of paragraph 1 of Article I of the General Agreement, any advantage, favour, privilege or immunity granted by Belgium to any product originating in the territory of any country with respect to all matters referred to in paragraph 2 of Article III shall be granted immediately and unconditionally to the like product originating in the territories of all contracting parties. Belgium has granted exemption from the levy under consideration to products purchased by public bodies when they originate in Luxemburg and the Netherlands, as well as in France, Italy, Sweden and the United Kingdom. If the General Agreement were definitively in force in accordance with Article XXVI, it is clear that that exemption would have to be granted unconditionally to all other

8. GATT, 1st Supp. BISD 59–62 (1953).

contracting parties (including Denmark and Norway). The consistency or otherwise of the system of family allowances in force in the territory of a given contracting party with the requirements of the Belgian law would be irrelevant in this respect, and the Belgian legislation would have to be amended insofar as it introduced a discrimination between countries having a given system of family allowances and those which had a different system or no system at all, and made the granting of the exemption dependent on certain conditions.

4. The Panel wishes to stress that this undertaking to extend an exemption of an internal charge unconditionally is not qualified by any other provision of the Agreement. The Panel did not feel that the provisions of paragraph 8(*a*) of Article III were applicable in this case as the text of the paragraph referred only to laws, regulations and requirements and not to internal taxes or charges. As regards the exception contained in paragraph 2 of Article XVII, it would appear that it referred only to the principle set forth in paragraph 1 of that Article, *i.e.* the obligation to make purchases in accordance with commercial considerations and did not extend to matters dealt with in Article III.

5. The Panel then considered whether the fact that the General Agreement was applied only provisionally had a bearing on the Belgian obligations under Article I with regard to internal taxes. It recognized that the Interpretative Note to Article I allowed Belgium to observe those obligations "to the fullest extent not inconsistent with existing legislation", so long as Belgium was applying the Agreement pursuant to the Protocol of Provisional Application. The Belgian law on family allowances dated back to 1930, and the provisions now applicable were enacted in a Royal Decree of 19 December 1939, with the exception of the provision fixing the rate of the levy, which was amended on 27 March 1951.

6. The Panel noted, however, that, in another case, the CONTRACTING PARTIES agreed that the Protocol of Provisional Application had to be construed so as to limit the operation of the provisions of paragraph 1(*b*) of the Protocol to those cases where "the legislation on which [the measure] is based is, by its tenor or expressed intent, of a mandatory character—that is, it imposes on the executive authorities requirements which cannot be modified by executive action."

7. The Panel, although recognizing that the relevant provisions of the Belgian royal decree appeared to be of a mandatory character, noted that, as pointed out by the Danish and the Norwegian representatives and admitted by the Belgian representative, it had been possible for the Belgian executive authorities to grant an exemption to a country whose system of family allowances did not meet fully the requirements of the law. Even if it might be difficult for the Belgian authorities to take similar action in similar cases, the Panel did not feel that it had been proved to its satisfaction that the Belgian legislation fulfilled all the conditions laid down by the CONTRACTING PARTIES to justify an exception under the Protocol of Provisional Application.

II. Recommendation

8. The Panel felt that the legal issues involved in the complaint under consideration are such that it would be difficult for the CONTRACTING PARTIES to arrive at a very definite ruling. On the other hand, it was of the opinion that the Belgian legislation on family allowances was not only inconsistent with the provisions of Article I (and possibly with those of Article III, paragraph 2), but was based on a concept which was difficult to reconcile with the spirit of the General Agreement and that the CONTRACTING PARTIES should note with satisfaction the statements made at the Sixth and Seventh Sessions by the Belgian representatives and should recommend to the Belgian Government to expedite the consideration and the adoption of the necessary measures, consistent with the General Agreement, including a possible amendment of the Belgian legislation, to remove the discrimination complained of, and to refer to the CONTRACTING PARTIES not later than the first day of the Eighth Session.

Notes and Questions

(1) Note the effect of the Protocol of Provisional Application (discussed in Section 5.4(C) supra). Even though the existing legislation clause is limited to Part II of GATT, it can be seen that it has some effect on Part I (Article I) after all!

(2) How do these two cases relate to the obligations of Article II (discussed in Section 6.3 supra) and to the procedures of Article XXIII (discussed in Section 5.6 supra)? Can the MFN obligation be eviscerated by using extremely narrow product classifications in tariff schedules (see Section 6.2(C)(3) supra)?

(3) The duties in the *John T. Bill Co.* case, Section 7.1 supra, were referred to by the court as countervailing duties. Is there an exception in GATT to the requirement of MFN in respect of such duties? See GATT Article VI, paragraph 3. Are the countervailing duties in *John T. Bill Co.* the same as those referred to in Article VI? What is the obligation in respect of countervailing duties (in the GATT sense) under an FCN treaty containing a MFN obligation in respect of customs duties?

(4) Why wasn't it enough to satisfy the MFN obligation in *John T. Bill* that the duty surcharge provisions applied generally to all countries?

Notecases

The following three notecases are examples of national courts applying MFN clauses.

(1) MARJORIE M. WHITEMAN, 14 DIGEST OF INTERNATIONAL LAW 755 (1970): In an early French case (1913), the French Court of Cassation had to decide whether certain procedural requirements for bringing suit as provided in a French-Swiss Convention on jurisdiction and execution of judgments applied also to German nationals as a result of a most-favored-nation clause in a Franco-German Commercial Treaty. The Franco-German Treaty guaranteed most-favored-nation treatment in their commercial relations including the "admission and treatment of subjects of the two nations". The decision of the Court was

based in part on the following propositions: that "these provisions pertain exclusively to the commercial relations between France and Germany, considered from the viewpoint of the rights under international law, but they do not concern, either expressly or implicitly, the rights under civil law, particularly, the rules governing jurisdiction and procedure that are applicable to any disputes that develop in commercial relations between the subjects of the two States"; and that "the most-favored-nation clause may be invoked only if the subject of the treaty stipulating it is the same as that of the particularly favorable treaty the benefit of which is claimed." (Translation.)

> *Braunkohlen Briket Verkaufsverein Gesellschaft c. Goffart, ès qualités,* Arrêt de la Cour de Cassation du 22 décembre 1913. The decision may be found in *Case Concerning Rights of Nationals of the United States of America in Morocco* (France v. United States of America), II *Pleadings, Oral Arguments, Documents,* I.C.J. (1952) 84–85.

(2) C. TENNANT, SONS & CO. v. DILL, 158 F.Supp. 63 (S.D.N.Y.1957) concerned the imposition in 1957 by the United States of a quota on importation of Paraguayan tung oil. At the time the quota was imposed, plaintiff had a shipment of tung oil en route to the United States and a second followed shortly thereafter. Plaintiff was unable to import all of its tung oil because the first shipment exceeded the available monthly quota. In an action to force the Collector of Customs to admit the tung oil to the United States, plaintiff relied on GATT Article XIII(3)(b) (the "en route clause") and the most-favored-nation clause of the United States–Paraguay International Trade Agreement. The court analyzed plaintiff's argument as follows:

> Paraguay was not a signatory to GATT (see table following 19 U.S.C.A. § 1351). Nevertheless, the plaintiff contends that by reason of the "most-favored-nation" clause contained in Article I of the Paraguayan Trade Agreement, Paraguay is a beneficiary of the en route clause in GATT and that, therefore, the quota restriction here at issue does not apply to plaintiff's en route tung oil. This contention, in my opinion, lacks merit. Article I, subdivision 1, of the Trade Agreement with Paraguay in effect requires the signatories to grant each other unconditional and unrestricted "most-favored-nation" treatment in all matters concerning:
>
> > 1. Customs duties and subsidiary charges of every kind;
> >
> > 2. The method of levying such duties and charges;
> >
> > 3. The rules, formalities and charges imposed in connection with clearing goods through customs;
> >
> > 4. All laws or regulations affecting the sale, taxation, distribution or use of imported goods within the country.
>
> Subdivision 2 of Article I in substance requires that each of the signatories be accorded treatment equal to that accorded any third country with respect to "duties, taxes or charges" or "any rules or formalities."
>
> The subjects covered by subdivisions 1 and 2 of Article I are described with clarity and particularity. The phrase "import restriction" and the word "quota" nowhere appear. Furthermore, these subdivisions do not, in my opinion, contain language from which their applicability to import restrictions involving the fixing of quotas can be implied.
>
> It is interesting to note that Article I of the Trade Agreement with Paraguay is considerably more explicit and restrictive than are certain other

parts of the Trade Agreement. For example, Article III, subdivision 1 of the Agreement employs the language "no prohibition or restriction of any kind" and in Article XII, subdivision 1 the all-inclusive terms "concession" and "customs treatment" are used.

It seems clear, therefore, that the "most-favored-nation" clause contained in the Trade Agreement with Paraguay is not sufficiently broad to entitle Paraguay, and, hence, the plaintiff, to the benefits of the en route provision of GATT.

(3) In Mentula v. State Land Board, 244 Or. 229, 417 P.2d 581 (1966), the Oregon Supreme Court considered a petition of the Consul General of Finland to have proceeds of the estate of a decedent paid to him, to transmit to the sole heir residing in Finland and presumed living. The United States-Finnish Treaty of Friendship and Commerce authorized a Consul General to collect and receive property from estates if he could show that he would remit to the heir. The Treaty also had an MFN clause as to "all the rights, privileges, exemptions and immunities which are enjoyed by officers of the same grade of the most-favored-nation * * *" and on the basis of this the petitioner claimed the estate proceeds *without* the necessity of proving remittance to the heir. The court said (at 233):

> Despite centuries of use in many forms of treaties there is a dearth of authority on the meaning and purpose of the most-favored-nation clause. It is held that "This clause means that each signatory grants to the other the broadest rights and privileges which it accords to any other nation in the treaties it has made or will make." Kolovrat v. Oregon, 1961, 366 U.S. 187, 193, 81 S.Ct. 922, 6 L.Ed.2d 218; Ljubich v. Western Cooperage Co., 1919, 93 Or. 633, 637, 184 P. 551. This tells us that we may look to treaties executed both before and after the treaty with Finland was proclaimed. It does not aid in deciding whether or not the grant of additional general authority to a Consular officer by the most favored nation clause includes the specific authority asserted here. No one would dispute that the most favored nation clause does enhance the authority of a Consul to perform his more normal commercial functions, but does the general grant of most favored nation treatment expand the Consul General's specific grant of authority to collect and receipt for his absent countryman in addition to the restricted authority stated in Article XXIX of this particular treaty? We think it does.

(D) PROBLEMS

A, B and C are nations which are members of GATT. X, Y and Z are nations which do not belong to GATT, but A and X have a bilateral agreement in which each extends MFN to the other as to tariff duties.

(1) A charges a 10% tariff on bicycles from B. C, X and Y also export bicycles to A; what rate are they entitled to?

(2) X charges a 5% tariff on clock radios from Y. What rate are such products from A, B and Z entitled to when imported into X?

(3) A's GATT binding for toy clocks is 10%. Its custom bureau currently charges 5% tariff on toy clocks from Y. What rate should be applied by A to toy clocks from B, C and X?

(4) A's GATT binding for FM radios is 5%, but A's customs bureau is charging a 10% tariff pursuant to a statute just passed by its Parliament.

What recourse do importers of FM radios from B, X or Y have against A? What procedures can be followed?

(5) A charges a tariff of 5% on motorcycle imports, and in addition imposes a quota on motorcycles from B, while prohibiting motorcycle imports from C, X and Y altogether. What rights have B, C, X and Y?

(6) A charges a 5% tariff on imports of autos which weigh less than 2000 pounds; a 20% tariff on other autos. B and X produce only autos weighing less than 2000 pounds; C and Y produce only autos heavier than that. What are the rights of C and Y?

(7) A charges a 5% tariff on imports of autos which operate on less than 20 miles per gallon; a 20% tariff on the rest. B and X autos use less than 20 miles per gallon; C and Y autos more. What are the rights of C and Y?

(8) A charges a 5% tariff on imports of autos without shatter-proof glass; but 20% for autos equipped with shatter-proof glass. A has a large domestic industry which produces shatter-proof glass, and so does B. B sells such glass to its own auto makers and to those of X, both of whom export autos to A. Do B and X have a valid complaint?

(9) A charges a 5% tariff on automobiles from countries with average auto industry wage rates over $4.00 per hour; 20% for autos from other countries. B and X auto wage rates are under $4.00 per hour, C and Y rates are over that amount. Do B and X have a valid complaint?

(10) A charges a 5% tariff on textile imports from countries with a per capita gross national product less than $1000 per year; a 20% tariff on the rest. C and Z are textile exporting countries with per capita annual GNP less than $1000. Do B, X and Y have any recourse?

(11) B imports hand-crafted baskets from Y in bulk lots of 1000, repackages them individually, and exports them to A. A's GATT binding on baskets is 10% but it charges a 30% tariff on these basket imports. Can B complain?

(12) A normally charges 5%, (its GATT binding), on imports of cooking pans. Under a national countervailing duty law, its officials have determined that B's grants of low interest "development loans" to the cooking pan industry, for encouraging exports, are "subsidies" and consequently A imposes a countervailing duty of another 10% on pots and pans produced in B. C, X and Y have similar programs of government export encouraging loans and their cooking pan industries, as well as their basket weaving industries, benefit. However, A does not impose countervailing duties on either cooking pans or baskets from C, X or Y. Does B have a valid complaint?

(13) B's countervailing duty law exempts all imports from countries which have per capita annual GNP of less than $1000. Does A or Y have a valid complaint?

(14) Suppose B's countervailing duty law exemption were not explicit, but merely a "practice" of its officials?

(15) C, a developing country, exports bauxite (for aluminum production). It imposes: a) a ban on bauxite exports to A; b) a 50% export tax on exports of bauxite to X and Y, but not Z or B. What rights do A, X and Y have?

(16) A's laws require its government agencies to purchase only goods produced in A or in B. Does C, X or Y have a valid complaint?

(17) A's laws require its airlines to insure only with companies of A or B. Does C, X or Y have a valid complaint?

(18) A's laws require its airlines to purchase supplies only from firms of A or B (because B has reciprocated with a similar law). Does C, X or Y have valid complaints?

(19) A allows C to establish sales agencies in A's territory, but refuses this privilege to B and X. Can B and X complain?

(20) A's laws provide for valuing imports for tariff purposes by using a currency exchange rate for goods from B, different and more favorable than that for goods from other countries. Does C, X or Y have a valid complaint?

(21) B's customs laws provide for valuation based on an exchange rate for industrial goods, which is less favorable than another rate for agricultural and commodity imports. Most of A's exports are industrial products; most of C's are raw materials and agricultural goods. Does A have a complaint?

(22) A charges 5% on the import of black tea, and 20% on the import of green tea. B produces black tea, while C and X produce green tea. Do C and X have a complaint? Suppose the distinction were between tea priced at under $1.00 per pound and that priced higher?

(23) Before entering GATT, C's law required a 10% sales tax on candy produced domestically or imported from Z; a 20% sales tax on all other imported candy. After entering GATT, C continued this practice. Does A or B have a valid complaint?

(24) Suppose a government decides that sound policy reasons prevent the application of countervailing duties and subsidy rules to a nonmarket economy (because of the difficulty of establishing meaningful price relationships, and because of the administrative difficulties of finding meaningful statistics on which to base countervailing duties, etc., as discussed in Chapter 10 infra). Can market economy countries then argue that MFN is violated when such duties are applied to their exported products?

SECTION 7.3 CUSTOMS UNIONS AND FREE TRADE AREAS

(A) REGIONALISM AND WORLD TRADE

Traditionally there has been an exception to MFN obligations for border traffic and limited regional arrangements, and so when GATT was drafted it was natural to include such an exception in GATT.[1] It was generally

1. See generally J. Jackson, World Trade and the Law of GATT ch. 24 (1969); Uster, The MFN Customs Union Exception, 15 J. World Trade L. 377 (1981). In addition, the reader may find the following references useful: J. Allen, The European Common Market and the GATT (1960); H. Steinberger, GATT und Regionale Wirtschaftszusammenschlüsse, Beiträge zum Ausländischen Offentlichen Recht and Völkerrecht No. 41, Max Planck Institut fur Ausländisches Öffentliches Recht und Völkerrecht, C. Heymanns Verlag K.G. (Cologne, 1963); P. Lortie, Economic Integration and the Law of GATT (1975); V. Curzon, The Essentials of Economic Integration: Lessons of EFTA Experience (1974); Dam, Re-

thought that a customs union or free trade area, whereby associated countries eliminated barriers on each other's trade, would be a further step towards general trade liberalization and therefore should be permitted, as long as the preferential arrangement did not harm the trade of nonmembers. If liberal trade principles were valid, the welfare benefits resulting from the free trade within an area should enhance productivity and wealth sufficiently to cause even more purchases from nonmembers. Yet economists have written extensively about the "trade diverting" as well as "trade creating" results of a free trade area,[2] and the former result could be damaging to world trade policies, including those of nondiscrimination. If, when A and B form a free trade area, the only result is for A to buy tariff-free from B what it used to buy from C (still tariffed), then perhaps the only result is to harm C (to greatly oversimplify). Furthermore, it was recognized that a free trade area exception could be abused to establish trade preferences, defeating the purpose of MFN. Consequently, the exceptions as written into GATT are elaborately circumscribed. If nations are willing to go "all the way" in eliminating trade barriers between themselves, then they will qualify for the exception. Otherwise, in theory, they will not qualify.

In practice matters have worked out far differently. A large number of regional associations have claimed the GATT exception, although arguably only a very few could really qualify. Yet even in questionable cases the preference system has been tolerated, either by an explicit GATT waiver (compare Article XXIV, paragraph 10 with Article XXV, paragraph 5), or merely by inaction. Legal arguments have often been ignored or resulted in a standoff without resolution.

With respect to the European Community in particular, the United States has been faced with some important policy dilemmas.

KRAUSE, THE EXPANSION OF THE EUROPEAN COMMUNITY

(1971) [3]

The United States has been in favor of European integration throughout the entire postwar period. The Organization for European Economic Cooperation (later to become the OECD) was a direct result of U.S. action and it is likely that the EC itself owes much to U.S. encouragement in its formative years. Originally this support was based in part on economic factors. A

gional Economic Arrangements and the GATT: The Legacy of a Misconception, 30 U.Chi.L.Rev. 615 (1963); Walker, Dispute Settlement: The Chicken War, 58 Am.J.Intl.L. 671 (1964); Loveday, Article XXIV of the GATT Rules, 11 Econ.Internationale 1 (1958).

2. See particularly, J. Viner, The Customs Union Issue, Carnegie Endowment for International Peace, New York (1950); J. Meade, The Theory of Customs Unions (1955); T. Scitovsky, Economic Theory and Western European Integration (1958); Lipsey, The Theory of Customs Unions: A General Survey, (a survey of customs union theory development from 1950–1960) in R. Caves and H. Johnson

(eds.), A.E.A. Readings in International Economics, Vol. XI (1968); B. Balassa, The Theory of Economic Integration (1961); J. Vanek, General Equilibrium of International Discrimination: The Case of Customs Unions, Harvard Economic Studies, Vol. CXXIII (1965); M. Krauss (ed.), The Economics of Integration (1973). J. Pelkmans (ed.), Market Integration in the European Community (1984); A. El-Algraa & A. Jones, Theory of Customs Unions (1981).

3. From U.S. Commission on International Trade and Investment Policy (the Williams Commission), Papers II, at 81, 82.

prosperous Europe would not be dependent on U.S. aid, would be a better customer for U.S. exports, and could assume a larger portion of the costs for common defense. In more recent years, it has been recognized that the EC is not an unmixed blessing from an economic point of view. Obviously European prosperity that results from an economic arrangement that excludes the United States may be at the expense of the United States. Thus, continuing U.S. support for the EC and its expansion to include the United Kingdom has come more and more to rest on political and military considerations.

EXECUTIVE BRANCH GATT STUDIES, NO. 4, EFFECTS OF REGIONAL TRADE GROUPS ON U.S. FOREIGN TRADE: THE EC AND EFTA EXPERIENCES

41–42 (1973) [4]

An analysis of the effects of regional trade groups on U.S. foreign trade hinges on a comparison of actual U.S. trade performance with what it would have been in the absence of these regional groups.* It is clear that the preferential trade barrier dismantlement between members of regional trade groups has the effect of increasing the share of partner countries and decreasing the share of outside countries in total imports of the region. In the cases of the European Communities (EC) and the European Free Trade Association (EFTA), U.S. trade in manufactures has not fared badly, at least in absolute terms. However, the many economic forces at work within both trade groups over the past 15 years make it impossible to speculate on how the current U.S. trade picture in manufactures would have changed had these trading blocs not been formed. By contrast, in the agricultural sector it is clear that the Common Agricultural Policy (CAP) of the EC has adversely affected exports of some U.S. products to the EC and to third markets.

(B) THE GATT EXCEPTION FOR CUSTOMS UNIONS AND FREE TRADE AREAS

Close reading of GATT, Article XXIV will reveal that the major MFN exception for trade groupings applies to three types of associations:

(1) A free trade area (defined in Article XXIV, paragraph 8(b); as an association of nations with duty free treatment for imports from members).

(2) A customs union (defined in Article XXIV, paragraph 8(a) as an association of nations with duty free treatment for imports from members and a common level of external tariffs for imports from nonmembers).

(3) An interim agreement leading to one of the above within a "reasonable period of time."

4. Subcomm. on Intl. Trade, Senate Comm. on Finance, 93d Cong., 2d Sess. (Compilation of 1973 studies prepared by the Executive Branch: Comm.Print 1974). See also G. Meier, Problems of Trade Policy 260–61 (1973).

* The analysis for this paper was made in mid-1972. The Executive informs the staff the conclusions would not materially change if 1970 data was included.

Many difficult interpretative problems exist in this troublesome article,[5] including:

(1) What is "substantially all" in the paragraph 8 definitions?

(2) What is a "reasonable time" for an interim agreement to become a customs union or free trade area?

(3) With respect to a customs union, Article XXIV, paragraph 5(a) requires that the external tariff and trade barriers (affecting imports from nonmember nations) "shall not on the whole be higher or more restrictive than the general incidence of the duties and regulations of commerce applicable in the constituent territories prior to the formation of such union."

(4) When a customs union adopts its common external tariffs, it inevitably raises some member nation tariffs above their GATT binding, triggering renegotiation rights under Article XXIV, paragraph 6. This paragraph applies the procedure of Article XXVIII to the renegotiation, but there are many interpretative difficulties with that article also, particularly as it applies to Article XXIV, paragraph 6 renegotiations.

It has been said that, "[n]ot a single Customs Union or Free Trade Area agreement which has been submitted to the Contracting Parties has conformed fully to the requirements of Article XXIV. Yet the Contracting Parties have felt compelled to grant waivers of one kind or another for every one of the proposed agreements" [6]

JOHN H. JACKSON, WORLD TRADE AND THE LAW OF GATT

588 (1969)

In one technical sense, the [above quoted] statement is perhaps misleading: no "waiver," either under Article XXIV, paragraph 10, or Article XXV, paragraph 5, has been granted for a number of the regional arrangements that were brought to GATT to this time. Furthermore, it is at least arguable that the European Economic Community, excluding the Association for Overseas Territories, did fulfill the GATT prerequisites for the automatic regional exception, at least under some interpretations of Article XXIV. But in a larger sense, the quoted statement accurately pinpoints the basic problem of Article XXIV, namely, criteria that are so ambiguous or so unrelated to the goals and policies of GATT Contracting Parties that the international community was not prepared to make compliance with the technicalities of Article XXIV the *sine qua non* of eligibility for the exception from other GATT obligations. It has been pointed out that today more than two thirds of the membership of GATT are nations that belonged to one or another regional arrangement. Since a waiver in GATT requires only a two-

---

5. See generally J. Jackson, note 1 supra, at ch. 24, especially §§ 24.6, 24.7, 24.8.

6. Dam, note 1 supra, at 660–61; also see J. Jackson, note 1 supra, at § 22.4, for the list of waivers granted by the CONTRACTING PARTIES under Article XXV:5 between 1948–1969.

thirds vote, it is not hard to see the potential impact of "regionalism" on GATT and particularly on the Most-Favored-Nation clause.

———

The GATT Article XXIV exception has been analyzed a number of times in GATT. The following three reports give a flavor of how the article has been interpreted. In each case, the working party failed to reach a definitive conclusion.

EXAMINATION OF STOCKHOLM CONVENTION

Report adopted on June 4, 1960 [7]

[In 1960, seven European countries which were not EC members entered into the "Stockholm Convention," which established the European Free Trade Association (EFTA).]

The Working Party considered first whether the requirement relating to "substantially all the trade" in Article XXIV:8(b) was met in the case of the Stockholm Convention. The view was put forward that, as the provisions of, *inter alia,* Articles 3 and 10 of the Convention relating to the elimination of barriers to trade in the free-trade area did not apply to trade in agricultural products, it could not be maintained that duties and other restrictive regulations of commerce were being eliminated on "substantially all the trade." * * *

The member States [of EFTA] agreed that the quantitative aspect, in other words the percentage of trade freed, was not the only consideration to be taken into account. Insofar as it was relevant to consider the qualitative as well as the quantitative aspect, it would be appropriate to look at the consistency of the Convention with Article XXIV:8(b) from a broader point of view and to take account of the fact that the agricultural agreements did facilitate the expansion of trade in agricultural products even though some of the provisions did not require the elimination of the barriers to trade. Moreover, insofar as both qualitative and quantitative aspects were concerned it was incorrect to say that the agricultural sector was excluded from the free-trade area; in fact barriers would be removed on one third of total trade in agricultural products between member States. The figure of 90 per cent for the percentage of total trade between the member States to be freed from barriers was made up of 85 per cent in respect of trade on which barriers to imports into all member States were to be removed and 5 per cent in respect of which barriers to imports into certain member States were to be completely removed. There was a further area, in which the member States did not claim they were achieving free trade, but which was covered by the margin permitted by the phrase "substantially all the trade."

* * *

In view of the divergent opinions which were expressed on the legal issues involved, the Working Party could not reach agreed conclusions concerning the provisions of GATT under which the CONTRACTING PARTIES should consider the Stockholm Convention. The member States considered that as, in their view, the provisions of the Stockholm Convention

7. GATT, 9th Supp. BISD 70, 83–87 (1961).

met all the requirements of paragraphs 5 to 9 of Article XXIV, they were entitled, under paragraph 5 of Article XXIV, to deviate from the provisions of GATT to the extent necessary to permit the establishment of the free-trade area contemplated in that Convention. On the other hand, and without prejudice to the final conclusions on the substance of the matter which might be reached at the seventeenth session, the following views were expressed on the legal aspects of the problem. It was stated by certain members of the Working Party that they had, so far, the greatest difficulty in accepting the contention of the member States and that, even if Article XXIV were applicable, they could not see how the CONTRACTING PARTIES could consider the Convention under any provisions other than paragraph 10 of that Article, if only because all parties to the Convention were not contracting parties to GATT as defined in Article XXXII. Some members of the Working Party took the view that the provisions of Article XXIV were not applicable in the case of the Convention and that the member States should have recourse to a "waiver" under Article XXV.

III. CONCLUSIONS

* * *

In these circumstances, the Working Party recommends to the CONTRACTING PARTIES that they should postpone any action in regard to the Convention and that the question should be included on the agenda of the seventeenth session of the CONTRACTING PARTIES. This would give contracting parties time to reflect on the various points of view expressed in the course of the Working Party's discussions so that they would be in a better position, at the seventeenth session, to reach a conclusion on the issues involved.

ASSOCIATION OF GREECE WITH THE EUROPEAN ECONOMIC COMMUNITY

Report adopted on 15 November 1962 [8]

7. The parties to the Association Agreement indicated that, in deciding on the transitional period of twenty-two years provided for in Article 15 of the Association Agreement for a number of products, account had been taken of the marked difference in the degree of development of the parties to the Agreement. The period of twenty-two years allowed for the creation of the full customs union seemed justified in the light of similar provisions contained in other regional agreements, certain of which did not seem to entail as complete an integration as did the Athens Agreement. The time period contained in that Agreement was moreover in the nature of a guarantee and strict procedures were laid down for the achievement of the customs union within that maximum time-limit. It was stated that the additional ten years in the case of certain products had been considered essential for the fulfilment of the basic aims of the Association Agreement set out in Article 2. The period of twenty-two years might be shortened and the implementation of the Agreement be accelerated as noted in Articles 16:2 and 29.

8. GATT, 11th Supp. BISD 149–54 (1963).

*   *   *

11. Some members of the Working Party felt that the non-applicability of the Association Agreement to coal and steel products left doubt as to whether "substantially all the trade" would be covered by the Association Agreement. The non-applicability of the Agreement to what was now 10 per cent of Greek imports from the European Economic Community was a matter of substance; it stretched the definition under consideration. The representative of the Community pointed out that in this type of calculation trade in both directions should be taken into account and that Greece exported no iron and steel products to the Community. The trade involved was therefore approximately 5 per cent of total trade between the Community and Greece. Moreover, those products were not covered by the Agreement simply because they fell within the scope of a separate body, the European Coal and Steel Community. The representative of Greece stated that the study of problems concerned with Greece's association with that Community was in an advanced stage and that it was the intention of his Government to enter into negotiations as soon as possible. Contracting Parties would be informed if any agreement were concluded.

*   *   *

15. Members of the Working Party who considered that the General Agreement did not permit the application of discriminatory restrictions for balance-of-payments reasons except as provided for under Article XIV, referred to provisions in the Athens Agreement, which, if applied, would in their view violate obligations of the parties to the General Agreement.

*   *   *

16. The parties to the Association held the view that Article XXIV of the General Agreement imposed an obligation on the member countries of a customs union to eliminate, in so far as possible, quantitative restrictions existing between them without necessarily extending such elimination to countries not members of the union. They, therefore, considered that the stipulations of the Agreement, providing for the complete elimination of quantitative restrictions on trade between the partners in the Association, were fully consistent with the General Agreement. In respect of trade with third countries, the Association Agreement did not stipulate the elimination of restrictions but the parties to the Association stated that it was certainly their intention to continue their liberal commercial policies in that respect.

*   *   *

20. Some members of the Working Party raised doubts about the compatibility with GATT of the provisions in paragraph 4 of Protocol 15. GATT requires in Article XVII that State-trading enterprises should act solely in accordance with commercial considerations. These members felt that commitments to purchase fixed annual quantities of tobacco from Greece, as was the case here, might constitute a violation of obligations under Article XVII in that unforeseeable future commercial considerations were being arbitrarily set aside in favour of a firm commitment to buy certain quantities.

EUROPEAN ECONOMIC COMMUNITY—ASSOCIATION AGREEMENTS WITH AFRICAN AND MALAGASY STATES AND OVERSEAS COUNTRIES AND TERRITORIES

Report of Working Party adopted on 4 April 1966 [9]

1. The Working Party was appointed by the Council at its meeting on 6 July 1964 and was instructed to examine, in the light of the relevant provisions of the General Agreement, the provisions of the Convention of Association between the European Economic Community and the African and Malagasy States associated with the Community (hereinafter usually described as the "Yaoundé Convention").

* * *

4. The Working Party noted that, while the original Convention of Association had foreseen the creation of one free-trade area comprising the EEC and a number of African and Malagasy territories, the Community recalled that the Yaoundé Convention created eighteen free-trade areas, each one consisting of the Community and one African or Malagasy State. The representatives of the parties to the Association explained that the new arrangement was due to the fact that the Associated States, which had in the meantime become independent, had decided that their relations *inter se* should not be covered by the Convention of Association. A member of the Working Party said that the fact that the various free-trade areas were institutionally linked together and that they were controlled from outside in the sense that each of them were subject to the influence of the seventeen others gave rise to certain doubts about their legal identity which was a prerequisite under Article XXIV of the General Agreement.

* * *

7. Some members of the Working Party expressed concern that the provisions of Article 3 of the Convention and of Protocol No. 1 to the effect that the Associated States might retain or introduce customs duties or similar charges which corresponded to their development needs or industrialization requirements or which were intended to contribute to their budget, would result in so many exceptions from the tariff reduction that the requirement of Article XXIV:8(b), that the duties should be eliminated on substantially all the trade between the constituent territories, would not be met. The representatives of the Community and the Associated States replied that no such exceptions had been notified during the two-months period specified in Article 1 of Protocol No. 1. They said that the industrialization of the Associated States, which was only just beginning, would not involve the imposition of protective duties except in so far as the industries which were established would be working for the local market and not for export. Moreover, an increase in the volume of the trade covered by protective duties would only involve an increase in the percentage of reciprocal trade not governed by the free-trade area régime if there were no corresponding increase in the total volume of trade. There was, therefore,

9. GATT, 14th Supp. BISD 100–06 (1966). For the conclusions of the CONTRACTING PARTIES adopted on the same date, see id., at 22.

every reason to believe that the portion of trade in protected products would remain small in relation to the total volume. However, if the proportion of protected trade so increased as to risk a violation of the rule of Article XXIV:8(b), it would be up to the parties to the Association at that point, and not before, to take such action as they might consider necessary. One member of the Working Party expressed the view that the term "substantially all" was not to be interpreted in purely statistical terms and that the application for protective purposes of duties or other restrictions to a portion of the trade between members of a free-trade area could hardly be justified.

* * *

14. In reply to the points referred to in the previous paragraph, the representatives of the Community and the Associated States said that the question of reciprocity was not dealt with in Article XXIV, which only required that restrictions on substantially all the trade between the member countries of a customs union or a free-trade area should be removed. Part IV of the General Agreement, which did not exist when the Convention entered into force, did not aim to modify the provisions of Article XXIV. The only test the CONTRACTING PARTIES could apply to a free-trade area was whether it satisfied the requirements of Article XXIV. With regard to the general principle in paragraph 4 of Article XXIV, they said that the precise wording of paragraph 5, which used the terms "Accordingly, the provisions of this Agreement shall not prevent * * * provided that * * *", made it abundantly clear that if the requirements of paragraphs 5 to 9 of Article XXIV were fulfilled, the Agreement was necessarily compatible with the principle set out in paragraph 4. There was no reason to believe that the authors of Article XXIV had overlooked the possibility of free-trade areas between countries at different stages of development. The CONTRACTING PARTIES had moreover already examined free-trade areas where there had been a great difference between the stages of development of the constituent territories.

Notes

(1) The Yaoundé Convention was replaced in 1975 by the so-called Lomé Convention between the EC and 46 African, Caribbean and Pacific Island (ACP) states.[10] The Lomé Convention has twice been renegotiated. The current version (Lomé III) entered into effect in March 1985.[11] Lomé III does not require that any particular treatment be given EC exports to the ACP countries, as the EC has viewed the convention since 1975 as a sort of preference for developing countries. In addition to granting trade preferences, the agreement provides for development assistance from the EC to the 76 current ACP states.

(2) In general, although numerous customs union and free-trade area agreements have been considered by GATT, few have been approved by any formal action by the Contracting Parties. For example, despite extensive discussions the Contracting Parties have never taken a position on the EC or its three enlargements, a fact highlighted in 1983 when the compatibility with Article

10. [1976] Eur.Comm.O.J. No. L 25; see Freideberg, the Lomé Convention: Co-operation Rather Than Confrontation, 9 J. World Trade L. 691 (1975).

11. The Third ACP–EEC Convention, signed at Lomé on 8 December 1984.

XXIV of Greece's accession to the EC was the subject of an inconclusive working party report.[12] Those agreements approved by GATT in the last decade were the ASEAN agreement (Association of South-East Asian Nations: Indonesia, Malaysia, Philippines, Singapore and Thailand) and the Bangkok Agreement (Bangladesh, India, Korea, Laos, Philippines, Sri Lanka and Thailand).[13] Most of the agreements considered without any conclusion being reached concerned the EC or Finland, which has entered into a series of agreements with East European countries.[14]

(C) NOTE: U.S. FREE TRADE AREAS

Recently, the United States has developed an interest in entering into free trade area agreements with specific countries and adopting special preference regimes for certain less developed countries.[15] In 1985, the United States entered into a free trade agreement with Israel.[16] Under the agreement all duties will be eliminated in four stages by January 1, 1995.[17] Certain sensitive products are to be exempt from duty reductions prior to 1990, but are to be brought under the agreement by 1995. The agreement also covers nontariff barriers. For example, Israel commits to eliminate export subsidy programs on industrial products and processed agricultural products within six years. In a number of other respects, such as import licensing and government procurement, the agreement establishes more stringent rules than did the Tokyo Round agreements.[18]

In 1974, Congress indicated that it was the sense of Congress that the United States should enter into a free trade agreement with Canada and the President was authorized to initiate negotiations with Canada on that subject.[19] In 1985, U.S. President Reagan and Canadian Prime Minister Mulroney agreed to study that subject.[20]

---

12. GATT, 30th Supp. BISD 168–90 (1984).

13. GATT, 26th Supp. BISD 224 (1980); GATT, 25th Supp. BISD 6 (1979).

14. See, e.g., GATT, 22d Supp. BISD 47–54 (1976) (Finland-Hungary).

15. We will discuss preferences for less developed countries in Chapter 20 infra. The prime example of a special U.S. preference program is the Caribbean Basin Initiative, established under the Caribbean Basin Economic Recovery Act. 19 U.S.C.A. §§ 2701–2706; 19 CFR §§ 10.191–10.198 (1985); see GATT, 31st Supp. BISD 20 (1985) (waiver granted to U.S. program); Zagaris, A Caribbean Perspective of the Caribbean Basin Initiative, 18 Intl. Lawyer 563 (1984).

16. Negotiation of the agreement was authorized in 1984. Trade and Tariff Act of 1984, title IV; 19 U.S.C.A. § 2112. Under the trade agreement negotiating authority of the 1974 Trade Act, as modified in the 1984 Act for application to a U.S.-Israel trade agreement, congressional approval of legislation implementing the agreement was required. Such legislation was handled under the "fast-track" procedures described in Section 3.4(D)

(3) supra and was approved in June 1985. Pub.L. No. 99–47, 99 Stat. 82. See House Rep. No. 99–64, 99th Cong., 1st Sess. (1985).

17. Agreement on the Establishment of a Free Trade Area Between the Government of the United States of America and the Government of Israel, signed April 22, 1985.

18. Id., arts. 12, 15. The minimum limit for contracts subject to the government procurement provisions is $50,000, about one-third of that of the Tokyo Round Agreement on Government Procurement.

19. Trade Act of 1974, § 612, 19 U.S.C.A. § 2486(a). In 1979, Congress ordered the President to study the desirability of entering into trade agreements with countries in the northern portion of the Western hemisphere. Trade Agreements Act of 1979, § 1104, 19 U.S.C.A. § 2486(b). See U.S.Intl.Trade Commn., Background Study of the Economies and International Trade Patterns of the Countries of North America, Central America and the Caribbean (Inv. No. 332–119, 1981).

20. See BNA, 2 Intl.Trade Reporter: Current Reports 406 (1985).

(D) PROBLEMS

Consider, in the light of the above materials, whether each of the following associations of GATT countries is a valid exercise of the GATT Article XXIV exception to MFN:

(1) Four countries exempt 50% of each other's imports from tariffs; 75%? 85%?

(2) Four countries remove tariffs on all products from each other, except agricultural products (which comprise 10% of the trade).

(3) Two GATT countries make an agreement for a phased establishment of freer trade. The agreement states its purpose is to achieve a free trade area, but specifies no time period within which to accomplish this. The "plan and schedule" provides for an 80% reduction in tariffs between them in four "bites," every five years for 20 years, but only provides that after that time, "further reductions will be negotiated."

(4) A customs union of six members agrees with a free trade area of seven members to form a larger free trade area comprised of the customs union plus the seven other countries.

(5) Could a customs union (e.g., the EC) become a Contracting Party to GATT? See GATT Articles XXVI and XXXIII, and Chapter 5 supra.

SECTION 7.4 PREFERENCES AND MFN EXCEPTIONS

(A) GATT AND THE MFN EXCEPTIONS

EXECUTIVE BRANCH GATT STUDIES, NO. 9, THE MOST–FAVORED–NATION PROVISION

136–37 (1973) [1]

EXCEPTIONS TO THE GATT PROVISION

The GATT recognizes, however, that MFN remains a goal which cannot in all cases, be achieved. It provides for a number of exceptions. Many are required for practical reasons and, in fact, serve to reinforce the GATT rules. Others were required for political and economic reasons. For example, Article XIV permits discrimination in the application of quotas justified on balance of payments grounds. Article VI allows imposition of countervailing and antidumping duties on subsidized exports or imports sold at less than domestic prices, resulting in injury to domestic industries. Paragraph 2 of Article XXIII allows a country to retaliate against another contracting party which has nullified or impaired benefits under the GATT. Article XXI deviations from MFN are permitted for national security reasons.

The most significant GATT exceptions to MFN are found in two Articles related in one way or another to the issue of preferential trade arrangements. These are Article I:2 dealing with tariff preferences in force when

1. Subcom. on Intl. Trade, Senate Comm. on Finance, 93d Cong., 2d Sess. (Compilation   of 1973 studies prepared by the Executive Branch: Comm. Print 1974).

the GATT was drafted and Article XXIV which provides for the formation of customs unions and free trade areas.

Article I (Paragraph 2)

Article I:2 permits contracting parties which, prior to the GATT, granted or received preferences under a variety of arrangements to continue to do so. It also prohibits any increase in the margins of preference granted or received. United States preferences for the Philippines fall under the provisions of this article, as do Commonwealth preferences. The provision was written into the GATT when it became clear that the persistent efforts of the United States to bring an end to historical preferences would not succeed. The countries concerned argued that their historic obligations made it impossible for them to accede to an agreement which did not allow them to continue to meet these obligations.

Developed countries have often sought preferences from or granted preferences to their dependent territories or areas over which they exercised political control. These preferences usually have taken the form of preferential tariff rates. They have usually been specifically excepted from unconditional MFN clauses.

The GATT provisions represented an effort to shift away from such preferential arrangements. However, there has been, since 1958 particularly, a proliferation of such arrangements. Some of these do not fall under the historic exceptions, but are in part a reflection of the traditional aid and trade relations that existed before 1948; others do not fall in this category. Most of these arrangements have been justified by the parties as constituting customs unions or free trade areas. In general, however, the United States has contended that they do not conform with the relevant GATT provisions. These arrangements have thus given rise to the controversy between the United States and its trading partners over the most significant exception to the MFN principle, Article XXIV, which allows the formation of customs unions and free trade areas. As far as preferential relationships of the United States are concerned, the one with the Philippines is being phased out, the arrangement with Cuba is inoperative, and the United States obtained a GATT waiver for the auto pact with Canada.

U.S. TARIFF COMMISSION, TRADE BARRIERS: AN OVERVIEW

110 (1974) [2]

DISCRIMINATORY TARIFF TREATMENT

Preferential Tariff Agreements

* * * Even a modest duty may foreclose participation in a market if other competing foreign suppliers are permitted free entry.

During the past 15 years there has been a proliferation of preferential trade arrangements throughout the world. Numerous customs unions and free trade areas have been formed in which tariffs are removed or reduced

---

2. Report to the Committee on Finance of the United States Senate and its Subcommittee on International Trade, Part I (T.C.Pub. No. 665, 1974).

on products of members but remain unchanged on imports from nonmembers. The European Community and the European Free Trade Association are by far the most important of these.[*1] The United Kingdom, Denmark and Ireland have recently joined the European Community, and the remaining EFTA countries have negotiated significant preferential trading arrangements with the Community. During the past few years, the Community has established preferential trading arrangements with most of the important Mediterranean countries and several African countries (most of which are former colonies of EC members). Under an agreement with Canada in 1965, the United States accorded Canadian automotive products preferential duty-free treatment. Many developed countries have instituted a generalized preference system for products of developing nations in the past few years.

The GATT Statistical Study of Preferential Trade

Concerned with the discrimination which these arrangements involve, the United States in 1971 proposed that the GATT contracting parties make a statistical study of the changes in the proportions of goods imported at most-favored-nation (MFN) rates and at other rates. The study revealed that although the value of goods imported annually by nations of the world has more than tripled since 1955, (a significant growth in spite of the effect of inflation) the percentage of goods imported at most-favored-nation rates has declined steadily. It also showed that the increase in trade under preferential tariff arrangements was on the whole faster than that of total world trade. The study covered imports of 33 contracting parties to the General Agreement and of Hong Kong for 4 selected years in a 15-year period and accounted for about 85 percent of the total imports of the contracting parties in 1970.

* * *

* * * the portion of imports of the contracting parties dutiable at preferential rates increased about 140 percent during the 15 year period covered by the survey. Most of the increase was attributable to the growth in preferential imports of the European Community, which comprised 15.9 percent of the contracting parties' total imports in 1970 and whose share of preferential imports rose from 16.8 percent of the total of such imports in 1955 to 65.4 percent in 1970. Although preferential imports by EFTA countries showed an absolute increase, their share of total preferential imports declined from 15.7 percent in 1961 to 14.4 percent in 1970. U.S. imports under the U.S.–Canadian Automotive Products Agreement constituted 6.2 percent of the total in 1970, the only year included in the survey in which this agreement was in effect. The percentage of imports under other preferential arrangements declined in relation to both total imports of the contracting parties (from 8.4 to 3.4 percent) and total preferential imports (from 83.2 to 14.0 percent) during the period surveyed.

[*1]. Others include the Latin American Free Trade Association, the Caribbean Free Trade Association, the Central American Common Market, the Central African Customs-Economic Union, the Customs Union of West African States, the East African Common Market, the Arab Common Market, the Tripartite Accord (India, Yugoslavia, Arab Republic of Egypt), and a recently negotiated agreement which became effective on February 11, 1973, and established tariff preferences among eight developing countries located throughout the world. An additional eight countries which participated in the negotiations are to be included but have not yet ratified the protocol.

Influence on Trade of Preferential Arrangements

The GATT study provides some insight into the effect of preferential arrangements on trade. As intra-EC imports grew rapidly, the portion of EC imports supplied by the United States in the years surveyed declined from approximately 11.1 percent in 1955 to about 9.5 percent in 1970. In the same period, however, the share of total U.S. exports going to the Community increased from 16.8 to 19.5 percent, an increase that was made possible by the substantial growth of Community imports in the 15 years covered.

In contrast, the U.S. share of total world exports declined from 16.6 to 15.5 percent. The average annual rate of growth of U.S. exports to the European Community exceeded the average rate of growth of total U.S. exports. Exports to the Community grew at 8.1 percent per annum; exports to the world at 7.1 percent per annum. World exports (computed from U.N. commodity trade statistics) grew at an average rate of 8.2 percent a year in the same period. U.S. imports from the EC during the period also rose sharply from $1.1 billion in 1955 to $6.6 billion in 1970, but in absolute terms were consistently below U.S. exports.

Note

A major preferential tariff system is the "Generalized System of Preferences" (GSP) instituted under a 1971 GATT waiver by various industrial countries for the benefit of developing countries. The GSP will be described in detail in Chapter 20. In addition, we will also take up in later chapters problems concerning certain other specific preferences or MFN exceptions, such as whether MFN treatment is required when using the Escape Clause (Chapter 9 infra). In this section we explore several interesting situations involving U.S. application of MFN.

(B) UNITED STATES–CANADIAN AUTOMOTIVE PRODUCTS AGREEMENT [3]

SENATE REPORT NO. 782

89th Cong., 1st Sess. 1 (1965)

This legislation implements the United States-Canadian Automobile Agreement. It authorizes the President to eliminate U.S. duties on motor vehicles imported from Canada and on original equipment parts and accessories imported from Canada for use in the production of automobiles in this country. It also provides adjustment assistance for any workers or firms dislocated because of new trade patterns growing out of the agreement, with special rules of procedure for determining eligibility, applied over a transitional period to insure that the assistance provided for will be available in the event it should be needed.

*   *   *

In fact, more than 90 percent of all motor vehicles produced in Canada are made by subsidiaries of U.S. companies. Workers in both countries, for

---

3. United States-Canadian Automotive Products Agreement, Jan. 16, 1965; entered into force Sept. 16, 1966; 17 UST 1372; TIAS No. 6093; see further Metzger, The United States-Canadian Automotive Products Agreement of 1965, 1 J.World Trade L. 103 (1967).

the most part, belong to the same international union. Motor vehicles generally are identical, and parts and components produced in the United States and Canada are interchangeable. Moreover, the geographic proximity of manufacturing facilities, near to both sides of the border, contributes further to the integrated nature of this industry.

Despite the natural tendencies toward a single integrated North American automotive industry, however, the industry has been divided by tariff and other barriers. Tariff protection of the much larger and economically stronger U.S. industry has, in recent years, been relatively low. The duty on most vehicles imported into the United States is 6½ percent ad valorem and the duty on most parts is 8½ percent ad valorem. Canada, on the other hand, has maintained duties of 17½ percent ad valorem on vehicles and up to 25 percent on automotive parts. Moreover, Canada has maintained a so-called content requirement which, in effect, required that Canadian firms incorporate up to 60 percent of parts and labor of Canadian origin in their automobiles assembled in Canada.

[The executive vice president of the General Motors Corp. illustrated the costly inefficiency of the preagreement situation by pointing out that, in order to meet the various restrictive requirements of Canadian law, a single GM plant in Canada is assembling this year a total of 595 different passenger car and truck models, many more than twice the number in any U.S. plant. The situations of the other U.S. companies in Canada are similar. The agreement will greatly simplify the operations of the U.S. companies by allowing them to reduce the number of different models produced in Canada and to increase the runs of the models produced there. This will lead to considerable economies.]

While the Canadian restrictions helped to build and maintain a viable automobile industry there, this resulted in higher production costs and higher priced products to the Canadian consumer. Not only was the total North American market smaller but Canada's share of production for this market remained far behind her share of consumption in her own market.

1. *Remission plan.*—In an attempt to remedy this situation and to increase production and employment, the Canadian Government in 1963 announced its so-called remission plan designed to stimulate exports of automotive products by remitting duties on imports to producers who increased exports. Several U.S. parts manufacturers believed this plan unfairly disadvantaged them and they registered strong protests. They regarded the Canadian plan as a subsidy and they sought the imposition of countervailing duties by the United States under section 303 of the Tariff Act of 1930. Whether or not countervailing duties had been imposed against imports from Canada, it is clear that the automotive industry was threatened by a period of uncertainty and possible disruption of its trade and production patterns.

* * *

[2. *The agreement.*—] The agreement permits either Government to take action consistent with its obligations under part II of the General Agreement on Tariffs and Trade (GATT) (art. III). Part II of the GATT includes provisions permitting contracting parties to take antidumping measures and escape clause actions. In this connection it should be made clear that nothing in this agreement nor in this enabling legislation acts to dull the operation of our remedial statutes. If a situation calling for application of the antidumping statute should arise, the remedies under that act may be invoked. Similarly, in the event of collusion contrary to the Federal antitrust laws, the provisions of those laws remain fully available.

3. *Letters of undertaking.*—One of the novel features of the solution embodied in the arrangement is the ancillary undertaking by the Canadian automobile companies. By their undertakings the Canadian subsidiaries of U.S. auto companies have expressed to the Canadian Government their intention of expanding their Canadian operations in such a way that the "Canadian value added" (that is, the amount of value added to a product by reason of Canadian industry or services) would be heightened by the end of model year 1968. The total of the additional Canadian value added in the undertaking stated by all the Canadian companies is to be approximately $241 million plus 60 percent of increased Canadian sales, measured in terms of production costs.

These undertakings (reproduced in app. B) were made by the Canadian subsidiaries in order to reassure the Canadian Government that in agreeing to reciprocal elimination of duties the Canadian part of the automotive industry would not be submerged. The Canadians also wished to be sure that the U.S. parent companies would treat the Canadian plants equally and would not overlook the advantages of production and procurement in Canada. Moreover, Canada wished to be sure that Canadian production and employment would participate in the anticipated rapid growth of the Canadian automobile market.

The undertakings of the Canadian companies are subject to necessary qualifications about market conditions and other factors beyond the control of individual companies.

In the view of the committee, although these letters limit the free trade character of the new arrangements, they do not derogate in any significant degree from the objectives of the agreement. Moreover, the committee has been informed that undertakings for increased production stated in the letters end in 1968, that the administration does not approve their renewal or extension.

However, the committee believes that regardless of the duration of the existing undertakings, no new undertakings should be required of U.S. subsidiaries. Therefore, it has amended the bill to insure that elimination of our tariffs on autos and original equipment parts and accessories will remain in effect after model year 1968 only if new undertakings are not required of our auto companies' subsidiary manufacturers in Canada which involve additional commitments to the Canadian Government for further increasing Canadian value added. If such commitments should be required and if the President made a finding to that effect, he would be required to suspend duty-free entry of autos and original equipment parts and accessories unless (1) Congress in effect approved the additional undertakings by enacting new implementing legislation, or (2) he determines that the additional undertakings caused by governmental action have become inoperative.

* * *

The Agreement and GATT

Under the agreement, and as it will be implemented by the bill, duty free treatment is to be limited to automotive products of Canada. This special treatment is admittedly inconsistent with the obligation of the United States, under article I of the General Agreement on Tariffs and Trade (GATT), to accord unconditional most-favored-nation treatment in respect of customs duties to the products of contracting parties to that agreement. However, the agreement deals with a special and unique relationship between the United States and Canadian automobile industries. As stated previously, motor vehicles, parts, and components are produced in the United States and Canada by companies generally sharing a common ownership, are interchangeable, and the geographic proximity of manufacturing facilities, on both sides of the border, contributes to the integrated nature of the industry.

Because the agreement is not expected to affect the prices for automotive products in the United States, there will be no adverse impact on imports from third countries. GATT recognizes in article XXV that there may be exceptional circumstances which may justify a waiver of an obligation. Your committee, like the Committee on Ways and Means of the House, believes that exceptional circumstances warranting a waiver are present, and is advised that the executive branch is invoking the GATT procedures for the purpose of obtaining a waiver.

Moreover, your committee points out that there are many instances where the most-favored-nation principle of the GATT has been set aside in the interest of trade expansion. The European Economic Community and the European Coal and Steel Community are good examples. So too are the European Free Trade Association and the Latin American Free Trade Association. Each of these arrangements departs from the most-favored-nation principle, yet all of them are successful in advancing the economies of their members.

* * *

Minority Views

* * * The hearings have demonstrated that this legislation is special interest legislation of the most restrictive sort, the opposite of free trade, detrimental to our balance-of-payment situation and harmful to American industry and jobs.

* * *

The agreement clearly contemplates the exportation of American jobs to Canada. The automobile makers are committed to expand Canadian production by 1968 to a level of $241 million plus 60 percent of the growth in the Canadian industry. This expanded capacity and its intended employment opportunities can come only out of the United States. This agreement, to expand in Canada rather than in the United States, must have a serious effect upon U.S. labor.

This agreement is equally bad for U.S. business. First and foremost, this agreement opens the vast Detroit market to Canadian parts manufacturers to compete with American businesses without receiving any concessions in return.

However, this is not all. The Canadian subsidiaries have committed themselves to a vast expansion program. One way to satisfy this commitment is the manufacture of parts for use in Detroit as original equipment. Canadian labor is on the average, 70 cents per hour cheaper than comparable American labor. The automobile makers, therefore, have every reason to want to make parts in Canada for shipment to Detroit, getting the benefit of cheaper labor, no import duties, and, at the same time, satisfying their commitment to the Canadian Government. Thus, American parts manufacturers will suffer and American jobs will be lost.

* * *

This agreement has been sold to Americans as free trade. It is not. It is the antithesis of free trade. It removes tariffs, not generally, not even with one nation, but only for a chosen few automobile manufacturers. The Canadian duty on American automobiles is not removed. A dealer in Montana or Maine cannot sell duty-free across the border in Canada. Only an automobile manufacturer can import into Canada free of the 17½ percent Canadian tariff. Not only that, it must be a qualified manufacturer; i.e., one who has provided satisfactory commitments to the Canadian Government.

U.S. duties are not lowered for the benefit of everyone. Parts may be imported duty free only if they are going to an automobile manufacturer. The dealer or supplier who would attempt to sell Canadian made parts to automobile supply stores or automobile repair businesses, or directly to American consumers, must still pay the tariff. This is not free trade and it does not benefit American consumers. Basically, it benefits only a few automobile manufacturers.

* * *

Further, this agreement admittedly puts us clearly in violation of the GATT agreement. Our whole trade policy since the early 1930's has been to reduce trade barriers. The keystone of this policy is the "most-favored-nation" concept. Concessions given to one trading partner are given to all. At the present time, the United States has unconditional most-favored-nation commitments to the GATT. We face severe trading problems in the coming Kennedy round. To violate our agreement at this time, to present the world with a fait accompli and ask for waivers afterward, shows a lack of faith which cannot help but have world repercussions.

* * *

The undersigned are for equitable trade agreements which lead to mutual benefits and mutual prosperity. In this case we have given up the $241 million guaranteed increased production plus 60 percent of the increase over 1964 production. We have also guaranteed maintenance of the level of Canadian value added in 1964. We have in effect closed the Canadian market to us. We opened the U.S. market and got nothing in return. We have taken our Canadian problem in which we are the injured party and Canada is the violator of international agreements, and negotiated an agreement which extinguishes the Canadian violation and places the United

States in violation. We have negotiated away our problem with Canada and negotiated ourselves into a problem with 75 free world members of GATT. We pay for these privileges with a worsened balance-of-payments situation. The undersigned recommend that the U.S. Senate not be a party to such an agreement.

> Abraham Ribicoff
> Vance Hartke
> Albert Gore

CANADA/UNITED STATES AGREEMENT ON AUTOMOTIVE PRODUCTS

Report of the Working Party adopted on 25 March 1965 [4]

I. INTRODUCTION

1. The terms of reference of the Working Party were "to examine the Canada/United States Agreement concerning automotive products and any aspects of that Agreement relevant to the General Agreement, and report to the CONTRACTING PARTIES."

* * *

13. Members of the Working Party noted that Article V of the Agreement which lays down that "access to the Canadian and United States markets provided for in this Agreement may by agreement be accorded on similar terms to other countries" does not require that similar access "be accorded immediately and unconditionally to like products originating in or destined for the territories of all other contracting parties" in the terms of Article I of the GATT. They however observed that, as the Government of Canada had unilaterally extended duty-free treatment for the products described in Annex A to all contracting parties, Article V would, in practice, have significance only with respect to the extension of access to the United States. The representative of the United States confirmed that, so far as it was concerned, this article was intended to permit negotiations with other countries.

III. QUESTIONS RELATING TO ASPECTS OF THE AGREEMENT RELEVANT TO THE GENERAL AGREEMENT

* * *

17. It was the general consensus of the Working Party that, if the United States implemented the Agreement in the manner proposed, United States action would be clearly inconsistent with Article I and it would be necessary for the United States Government to seek a waiver from its GATT obligations.

18. Several members of the Working Party said that they could not accept that the inconsistency with Article I was only with the letter and not with the spirit of the article.

* * *

22. The question was asked whether, in the opinion of the Canadian delegation, the Canadian part of the Agreement was compatible with Arti-

4. GATT, 13th Supp. BISD 112–25 (1965).

cles III:5, III:7 and XVII:1(a), since a Canadian manufacturer could only, generally speaking, import vehicles duty free under the Agreement to an extent directly related to his domestic production, in addition, because of the structure of the Canadian industry, it was not at all certain that a manufacturer who had the privilege of importing vehicles duty free would in fact import from outside the parent corporation and its subsidiaries.

23.   In reply, the Canadian delegate said that there was no doubt in his mind that the Agreement was wholly consistent with the provisions of these Articles of the General Agreement. He stated, moreover, that, under the Agreement, manufacturers were free to choose their sources of imports in the light of commercial considerations and that it could be assumed that vehicles imported duty free by them would in fact come from a variety of sources. He also referred to his statement in paragraph 10, and, in reply to further questions, said that he was not aware of any agreements between firms which limited this freedom of choice.

* * *

Statement Made by the Representative of Canada

I will begin by saying that, while the Automotive Agreement is couched, as is usual in bilateral treaties of this kind, in terms of undertakings entered into by the two parties *vis-à-vis* each other, the Canadian Government is implementing the Agreement in a non-discriminatory manner. As is stated in L/2339, the Agreement will only come into definitive effect after necessary legislative action is taken, but my Government has, by Order-in-Council PC 1965–99 of 16 January (copies of which are available to you), brought the new free-entry conditions envisaged in the Agreement into force with effect from 18 January in so far as Canada is concerned. You will notice that the first paragraph of the Order-in-Council clearly states that the free rates apply to the goods specified when imported "from any country entitled to the benefit of the British Preferential Tariff or Most-Favoured-Nation Tariff." The coverage of the Order parallels that of Annex "A", which is the Canadian Annex of the Agreement. We thus are extending, to each and every contracting party, the same tariff benefits on the same terms, as we have undertaken to grant the United States under the Agreement. My Government has no doubt that its implementation of the Agreement is consistent with both the spirit and letter of Article I of the GATT.

DECISION ON UNITED STATES IMPORTS OF AUTOMOTIVE PRODUCTS

20 December 1965 [5]

The Contracting Parties

Decide, in accordance with paragraph 5 of Article XXV of the General Agreement and in accordance with the procedures adopted by them on 1 November 1956, as follows

1.   The Government of the United States, notwithstanding the provisions of paragraph 1 of Article I of the General Agreement, is free to

5. GATT, 14th Supp. BISD 37–42 (1966).

eliminate the customs duties at present imposed on automotive products of Canada without being required to extend the same tariff treatment to like products of any other contracting party.

2. The Government of the United States shall enter into consultations with any contracting party that requests consultation on the grounds (i) that it has a substantial interest in the trade in an automotive product in the United States market, and (ii) that the elimination of customs duties by the United States on imports of that automotive product from Canada has created or imminently threatens to create a significant diversion of imports of that automotive product from the requesting contracting party to imports from Canada.

3. If, in consultations in accordance with paragraph 2 above, it is agreed there is no significant diversion or imminent threat of diversion of trade in the sense of that paragraph, the waiver shall continue to apply.

4. In the event the parties to consultation in accordance with paragraph 2 above agree there has been a significant diversion or is an imminent threat of diversion of trade, the waiver shall terminate in accordance with paragraph 5, with respect to the automotive product or products in question. If the parties to consultation fail to reach agreement, either may refer the question whether the requesting party has a substantial interest or whether there has been a significant diversion or is an imminent threat of diversion of trade to the CONTRACTING PARTIES. If the CONTRACTING PARTIES decide that the requesting country has a substantial interest and that there has been a significant diversion or is an imminent threat of diversion of trade, the waiver shall terminate in accordance with paragraph 5, with respect to the automotive product or products in question.

5. Unless the requesting party has previously withdrawn its request, any termination of this waiver pursuant to paragraph 4 shall take effect on the ninetieth day after agreement by the parties to consultation, or after a finding by the CONTRACTING PARTIES, with respect to diversion or imminent threat of diversion of trade.

6. In addition to receiving an annual report as referred to in the procedures adopted by the CONTRACTING PARTIES on 1 November 1956, the CONTRACTING PARTIES will, two years from the date when this waiver comes into force and, if necessary, biennially thereafter, review its operation and consider how far in the circumstances then prevailing the United States would continue to need cover to implement the agreement with Canada, having regard to the provisions of paragraph 1 of Article I of the GATT.

WELSH, UNITED STATES–CANADA AUTOMOTIVE TRADE AGREEMENT

(1971)[6]

One of the basic objectives of the Agreement is to encourage integration and realignment of production between the U.S. and Canada—by producing

6. From U.S. Commission on International Trade and Investment Policy (the Williams Commission), Papers II, at 239.

optimum volumes of components and vehicles in both countries in order that the productivity of the automotive industry in both countries, but particularly in Canada, will be improved.

The integration which has been accomplished at substantial expenditures for capital and relocation has resulted in an important improvement in economies of scale in Canada resulting from better utilization of facilities. One Canadian manufacturer reduced by almost 50% the different series of passenger cars produced between 1966 and 1970. There has also been a similar reduction in the number of different automotive components such as engines, transmissions, starting motors, etc. The reduction in different models of vehicles and components has enabled the Canadian Manufacturers to use their machinery and equipment more effectively through longer, larger quantity production runs. Thus, many of the low volume items have been relocated to plants where the benefits of high volume can be obtained. This has happened on both sides of the border, and is still in progress.

Questions

(1) Is it relevant to the analysis of the United States–Canadian Automotive Agreement under the GATT MFN clause that only U.S. automobile manufacturers, and not others, are permitted to import auto parts into the United States duty free?

(2) Is Canada fulfilling its MFN obligations under GATT?

(3) Suppose the United States issued a regulation limiting the importation of autos which do not meet certain energy conservation criteria in gas usage. Can the United States exempt Canadian imports from such a requirement consistently with its GATT obligations?

(4) Would you recommend that the United States government try the automotive agreement approach in other economic sectors or with other countries? Would you approve such agreements if you were another GATT member?

(C) RECENT UNITED STATES LAW AND MFN

(1) The Trade Act of 1974

United States law specifies MFN treatment for most imports. Section 126(a) of the Trade Act of 1974 requires (unless otherwise provided by law) "any duty or other import restriction or duty-free treatment proclaimed in carrying out any trade agreement under this Title shall apply to products of all foreign countries, whether imported directly or indirectly." There are exceptions in the Act for Communist countries, although there is limited authority to extend MFN even to such countries (title IV),[7] and for the Generalized System of Preferences for developing countries (Title V).[8] As indicated in Section 7.3(C) supra, more recent U.S. legislation has authorized

7. For tariff purposes, the following countries do not receive MFN treatment, i.e., the column 2 rate applies (see Section 6.1 supra): Afghanistan, Albania, Bulgaria, Cuba, Czechoslovakia, Estonia, German Democratic Republic, Indochina (any Communist controlled part of Cambodia, Laos or Vietnam), Korea (any Communist controlled part), Kurile Islands, Latvia, Lithuania, Outer Mongolia, Polish People's Republic, Southern Sakhalin, Tanna Tura and the Soviet Union (and the area in East Prussia under provisional Soviet administration). TSUSA, Headnote 3(d) (1985).

8. See Section 20.3 infra.

special preferences in connection with the Caribbean Basin Initiative and the U.S.-Israel Free Trade Agreement.

Apart from the two broad MFN exceptions in the 1974 Act, Section 126(b) of the Act permits the President to depart from MFN in terminating or denying trade concessions towards a "major industrial country" which fails to make concessions which provide equivalent competitive opportunities for United States goods as exist in the United States markets for goods of that country in connection with trade agreements entered into under the Act.

In addition, the Act's authority with respect to negotiation of NTB agreements explicitly states (Section 102(f)) that benefits of such an agreement may be limited to countries which become parties to the agreement.

The Report of the Senate Finance Committee elaborates the reasoning behind these measures.

SENATE REPORT No. 93–1298
93d Cong., 2d Sess. 94–95 (1974)

RECIPROCAL NONDISCRIMINATION

(Section 126)

The Committee feels that the "unconditional" most-favored-nation principle has led, in the past, to one-sided agreements. Under the "unconditional" most-favored-nation principle, the benefits of trade concessions are automatically bestowed upon all countries not specifically denied most-favored-nation treatment, whether or not they have provided reciprocal concessions during the negotiation. Under this principle there is an inherent incentive for countries to "get a free ride," since they would automatically receive the benefits of any trade agreement. The existence of many significant tariff and nontariff barriers in foreign countries and the very small reductions in tariffs of some industrialized countries in the Kennedy Round may be attributable to the realization by certain countries that they could automatically receive all the benefits of the trade agreement without paying any of the costs.

The Committee believes that the nondiscriminatory treatment principle as it applies to multilateral trade negotiations entered into under the authority of the bill should result in concessions by other major industrial countries which provide competitive opportunities in their markets substantially equivalent to those provided in the U.S. market. Since the outset of the successive rounds of multilateral trade negotiations in the post-war period, the possibility has existed that a major industrial country would limit its participation in such negotiations yet nevertheless, through the nondiscriminatory treatment principle, benefit from concessions negotiated by others. In trade parlance this is known as the "free-rider" problem. It is the intent of the Committee to close this loophole by requiring that the United States have as its objective that each major industrial country make a contribution to the lowering of trade barriers substantially equivalent to that made by the United States, and that no major industrial country receive benefits from the negotiations substantially in excess of the concessions it has granted.

At the request of the Special Representative for Trade Negotiations, the Committee agreed to provide expressly that nontariff barrier agreements may be entered into discriminately—on other than a most-favored-nation basis—to assure that a foreign country which receives benefits under a trade agreement is subject to the obligations imposed by the agreement. The Committee feels that the principle of reciprocal nondiscriminatory treatment has the same purpose as the non-most-favored-nation application of nontariff barrier agreements sought by the Executive.

No industrialized country should be given a free ride in this negotiation. Nor should any industrialized country provide protection to its industries while expecting others to lower barriers for their exports. The concept of equivalent competitive market opportunities should be a key guide to this negotiation. No industrialized country should expect to have the best of both worlds anymore. The United States should not grant concessions to countries which are not willing to offer substantial equivalent competitive opportunities for the products of the United States in their market as we offer their products in our market.

The Committee is quite aware that the European Community has concluded, or is in the process of concluding, special commercial agreements with over 80 countries, many of which were former colonies of the member nations. These agreements are discriminatory in nature and often involve so-called "reverse preferences".

Under the Committee amendment, the U.S. negotiator would not seek special advantages for U.S. products in any developed country but *reciprocal* benefits. The Committee believes this was the original intent of the *Reciprocal* Trade Agreements program initiated in 1934 by Secretary of State Cordell Hull.*1

For these reasons, the Committee adopted a "reciprocal" nondiscrimination principle. Under this principle industrialized countries would not get a free ride in this negotiation. The President would be required to determine at the conclusion of all negotiations entered into under this bill, or at the end of the five-year period beginning on the date of enactment, whichever is earlier, whether any major industrial country has failed to make concessions under trade agreements which provide competitive opportunities for the commerce of the United States in such country substantially equivalent to the competitive opportunities provided by concessions made by the United States. The objective would be overall reciprocity—substantially equivalent market access or competitive opportunities on an overall basis. If the President determined that a major industrial country has not made concessions under trade agreements which provide substantially equivalent competitive opportunities for the commerce of the United States, then with

---

* 1. Current U.S. domestic legislation requires that trade agreements concessions negotiated with one country be automatically extended to all others—whether or not an international commitment such as the GATT would entitle others to such concessions—so long as the recipient does not discriminate against U.S. trade. (See section 251 of TEA.)

respect to such country or by article produced by country, in order to restore equivalence of competitive opportunities he should:

(1) proclaim the termination of concessions or refrain from proclaiming benefits of trade agreement concessions made with respect to rates of duty or other import restrictions made by the United States to such country under any trade agreement, and

(2) recommend to Congress that any legislation necessary to carry out a trade agreement entered into under section 102 shall not apply to such country.

The Committee feels that only when there is fairness and reciprocity in commercial relations among the major industrial countries will the groundwork be laid for the continued movement toward freer trade. The Committee's "reciprocal nondiscrimination" principle should not offend any country which is willing to trade with the United States on the basis of equity and reciprocity. Only if a country insists on gaining advantages for its exporters in the U.S. market without being willing to offer U.S. exporters comparable advantages in its markets would it have grounds for concern over this provision.

For purposes of this provision, major industrial countries would include Canada, the European Economic Community, the individual member countries of the Community, Japan, and any other foreign country designated by the President for purposes of this section.

Notes and Questions

(1) Several other provisions of the 1974 Act permit departures from MFN, most notably the new balance-of-payments (BOP) authority and the revised retaliatory authority. Under the BOP section (Section 122(a)(2)) it would be possible to apply a BOP surcharge only against a country with "large or persistent balance-of-payments surpluses." [9] The revised retaliatory authority (Sections 301 and 302) continued the possibility that existed under Section 252 of the 1962 Trade Expansion Act, to retaliate against a foreign unfair action by measures applied only to the trade of that country. Finally, in the escape clause provisions of the new Act, (Section 203(k)), authority is granted, in the application of "import restraints" under an escape clause determination, to depart from MFN.[10]

9. The Treasury Department, which was the source of the BOP provision of the Trade Act, desired that the language put the United States in a posture consistent with the approach then taken by the Treasury (for the United States) in the negotiations for reform of the IMF and its rules concerning BOP difficulties. This was one of the provisions of the Trade Act that was difficult to draft, since it pertained to then concurrent negotiations for changes in international rules of economic behavior. The United States had taken the position that countries with persistent surpluses had an obligation to take measures to alleviate such surpluses, just as traditionally countries with persistent and large deficits had to take remedial actions. An action which a surplus country could take would be to lower its tariffs across the board, a kind of "reverse surcharge." Consequently, the United States statute was worded to allow this, since the United States had been urging that surplus countries should take that type of action. If a country with a surplus failed to take such action, then it was felt that there should be ways to impose a sanction, possibly in the form of a surcharge.

10. See Chapter 9 infra. It is generally considered that there is an international obligation to apply escape clause actions on an MFN basis. Consequently, unless the rule were changed, United States action on a non-

(2) To what extent does the Trade Act of 1974 *authorize* the United States to violate GATT Article I? To what extent might the Act *require* the United States to violate GATT Article I in some circumstances?

(2) U.S. Implementation of the Tokyo Round Agreements and MFN

As has been discussed previously, the Tokyo Round resulted in a whole series of side agreements on various trade issues.[11] Generally, these agreements have procedural and governance provisions that give a voice only to signatories. In that sense, even if the tangible benefits of the agreements accrue to all GATT members because of GATT's MFN requirements, non-signatory members of GATT are treated differently. Much more significantly, two of the side agreements—the Subsidies Code (discussed in Section 10.3 infra) and the Government Procurement Code (discussed in Section 8.4 infra)—only obligate the parties thereto to apply the provisions of the Code to other parties.[12]

In implementing the Subsidies Code and the Government Procurement Code, as well as the Standards Code,[13] the Trade Agreements Act of 1979 provides that the benefits of each of the three codes are available only to other parties of the code in question.[14] For example, the new U.S. countervailing duty law applies only to "a country under the Agreement," which is defined as follows: [15]

> *   *   * a country—

> (1) between the United States and which the Agreement on Subsidies and Countervailing Measures applies *   *   *

> (2) which has assumed obligations to the United States which are substantially equivalent to obligations under the Agreement *   *   *, or

> (3) with respect to which the President determines that—

>> (A) there was an agreement in effect between the United States and that country which—

>>> (i) was in force on June 19, 1979, and

>>> (ii) requires unconditional most-favored-nation treatment with respect to articles imported into the United States,

>> (B) the General Agreement on Tariffs and Trade does not apply between the United States and that country, and

>> (C) the agreement described in subparagraph (A) does not expressly permit

>>> (i) actions required or permitted by the General Agreement on Tariffs and Trade, or required by the Congress, or

MFN basis under Section 203(k) could be a violation of international obligations.

11. See Section 5.5 infra.

12. Agreement on Interpretation and Implementation of Article VI, XVI and XXIII, art. 1, GATT, 26th Supp. BISD 56, 57 (1980); Agreement on Government Procurement, art. II(1), GATT, 26th Supp. BISD 33, 35 (1980).

13. Agreement on Technical Barriers to Trade, GATT, 26th Supp. BISD 8 (1980).

14. Trade Agreements Act of 1979, §§ 101, 301, 422, 19 U.S.C.A. §§ 1671(a), 2511, 2552.

15. Trade Agreements Act of 1979, § 101 (adding Section 701 to Tariff Act of 1930), 19 U.S.C.A. § 1671(b).

(ii) nondiscriminatory prohibitions or restrictions on importation which are designed to prevent deceptive or unfair practices.

According to the Senate Report, only one country—Taiwan—might qualify under paragraph (b)(2), while seven—Venezuela, Honduras, Nepal, North Yemen, El Salvador, Paraguay and Liberia—potentially could qualify under paragraph (b)(3).[16] The more difficult question is whether the MFN obligations of the United States under GATT require the United States to apply the rules of the Subsidies Code to nonsignatories who are GATT members and to signatories that the United States believes have not fully implemented the Code.[17] When the United States refused to apply the Code to India, a signatory, India claimed that the United States had violated its basic obligations under Article I of GATT and invoked the GATT dispute settlement procedures. India later dropped its complaint when the United States found that it qualified under the above-quoted provision.[18]

Notes and Questions

(1) Should India have won if its dispute with the United States had been considered by a GATT panel?

(2) The U.S. legislation implementing the Government Procurement Code limits the benefits of the Code to (1) other Code parties which provide reciprocal benefits to the United States, (2) non major industrial countries which assume the obligations of the Code and provide such benefits, (3) non major industrial countries which provide such benefits and (4) least developed countries.[19] Does this legislation violate Article I of GATT? Consider GATT Articles III:8 and XVII:1 in framing an answer. Could an MFN clause in a typical FCN agreement be invoked to claim MFN treatment in government procurement matters?

(3) The U.S. legislation implementing the Standards Code establishes a procedure through which another Code party or a nonparty found to extend benefits to the United States that are substantially the same as those under the Code may complain to the U.S. Trade Representative that specified standards setting activity in the United States is in violation of the Code.[20] The Trade Representative will then investigate and attempt to solve the problem. Could a GATT member not a Code party successfully argue that the GATT MFN obligations give it a right to be able to invoke the above procedure?

16. Sen.Rep. No. 96–249, 96th Cong., 1st Sess. 45 (1979). See Haufbauer, Erb & Starr, The GATT Codes and the Unconditional Most-Favored-Nation Principle, 12 Law & Poly. Intl. Bus. 59, 70–85 (1980).

17. As discussed in Section 10.3 infra, if the new U.S. law is applied, countervailing duties to offset subsidies will be imposed only if injury to U.S. industry is found by the International Trade Commission. If the old U.S. law is applied, no injury need be shown, and the duties are applicable if subsidies are found.

18. 46 Fed.Reg. 48391 (1981). An Indian representative at GATT stated to the Committee on Subsidies that Indian legislation did not contain provisions in conflict with the Subsidies Code and that it would comply with the Code if it took countervailing action. GATT, 28th Supp. BISD 28 (1982). See also GATT, 29th Supp. BISD 113 (1983) (report of settlement).

19. Trade Agreements Act of 1979, § 301, 19 U.S.C.A. § 2511(b).

20. Trade Agreements Act of 1979, § 422, 19 U.S.C.A. § 2552.

SECTION 7.5 THE FUTURE OF MFN IN GATT

We have seen that the basic MFN requirement in GATT has been eroded by the customs union—free trade area exception and the recent Tokyo Round codes. How serious is this erosion? Consider the following views and whether you agree.

G. HUFBAUER, S. ERB & H. STARR, THE GATT CODES AND THE UNCONDITIONAL MOST–FAVORED–NATION PRINCIPLE

(1980) [1]

CONCLUSION

The unconditional MFN principle has served as a cornerstone of the GATT system. Without unconditional MFN, bilateral trading arrangements that divert trade from third countries and undermine the efficiency of the world economic system could become widespread. It has proven difficult, if not impossible, however, to reduce existing trade barriers and curb distorting internal policies without some measure of reciprocity. In order to preserve the momentum of liberalization, trading nations ignored the unconditional MFN approach at several key junctures in the construction of the GATT system in the 1950s, 1960s and 1970s. Moreover, the recent Tokyo Round negotiations led to several Codes that include a conditional MFN approach. This article has attempted to advance a limited rationale for this latest departure from the unconditional MFN approach—a rationale that does not jettison basic principles of unconditional MFN.

Our analysis suggests that a limited rationale can be constructed for reconciling the conditional aspects of the Code provisions with the unconditional MFN obligations contained in the GATT and bilateral commercial agreements. We shall conclude with some speculative remarks on the consequences of success or failure of a reconciliation effort. The "success" or "failure" of a U.S. effort to reconcile the conditional MFN approach with its obligations under GATT and bilateral agreements will most likely be tested by an international attack under GATT article XXIII.

Success

One view of "success," a view most forcefully expounded by the Curzons, is that extension of the conditional MFN principle will ultimately lead to disintegration of the GATT system. In this view, fragmentation of the universal world trading system is viewed with much the same regret as the breakup of the Holy Roman Empire. This scenario carries considerable weight, particularly in light of those instances in which nations ignore the unconditional MFN principle to allow the application of selective quotas against the exports of a single supplier.

The conditional MFN approach, however, is considerably less destructive, in terms of diverting trade flow and undercutting prior tariff bargains,

1. 12 Law & Poly. Intl. Bus. 59, 91–93 (1980). Reprinted by permission of the Journal of Law and Policy in International Business.

when applied to measures that discipline "internal" government policies. Thus, if conditional MFN can be reconciled in this limited sphere with the traditional requirements of the unconditional MFN approach, it could legitimate further extension of international discipline over national economic policy. Initially, such disciplines might be negotiated among a small group of countries or even bilaterally. For a time, this could mean very different trade regimes as between different pairs of countries. Eventually, however, this process could lead to a new round of generalized MFN discipline over internal economic policies that threaten to harm the economic interests of other nations.

Failure

A successful attack, based on GATT article XXIII, on the conditional MFN aspect of the Codes would have one of three effects. First, if Code signatories simply ignore the application of article I, a deep and obvious schism would appear in the world trading system. The way would be open for widespread bilateral measures that would serve to divert trade from third countries and erode past tariff bargains.

Alternatively, Code signatories might decide that the health of the world trading system is more important than the reciprocity entailed in the particular Codes, and grant unconditional MFN treatment to other GATT members. This decision might well abort the experiment toward international discipline over internal economic policies.

Finally, the GATT contracting parties might grant a waiver, under article XXV, for the conditional aspect of existing Codes. A waiver would establish the principle that further developments along this line also require approval of the majority of GATT members. A waiver approach might slow the use of the conditional technique as a liberalizing measure but should not permanently thwart the international restraint of national economic policies.

Chapter 8

THE NATIONAL TREATMENT CLAUSE AND NONTARIFF BARRIERS

SECTION 8.1 INTRODUCTION

Many trade treaties prior to GATT included a clause which imposed a "national treatment obligation" upon the parties.[1] Consequently, it was natural that when GATT was drafted it would also contain such a clause. The national treatment obligation, like the MFN obligation, is a rule of "nondiscrimination." In the case of MFN, however, the obligation prohibits discrimination as between goods from different exporting countries. The national treatment clause, on the other hand, attempts to impose the principle of nondiscrimination as between goods which are domestically produced, and goods which are imported. It is, needless to say, a central feature of international trade rules and policy.[2] However, the national treatment clause is based on policies that differ from those of the MFN clause. National treatment obligations generally are designed to reinforce the basic policy of trade liberalization—minimizing government interference and distortion of transactions which cross borders. One objective of these obligations is to prevent government practices which evade the tariff obligations. MFN, on the other hand, has the objective of causing governments to treat other governments equally, even if they treat imported goods differently from domestically produced goods.

GATT Article III is the central national treatment obligation. (See Documentary Supplement). Paragraph 2 is aimed at internal taxation (such

1. See J. Jackson, World Trade and the Law of GATT 277 & nn. 7 & 8 (1969).

2. In addition to the references in the text of this chapter, the reader may find the following references useful in further research on the national treatment obligation: Jackson, note 1 supra, ch. 12; U.S. Tariff Commn., Tariff and Nontariff Trade Barriers, pts. 1–4, Report to the Committee on Finance of the United States Senate and its Subcomm. on International Trade (USTC Pub. No. 665 1974); K. Dam, The GATT: Law and Interna-tional Economic Organization ch. 7 (1970); Wonnacott, Tax Adjustments in Internationally Traded Goods; Dept. of State, How Should We Deal with the Border Adjustment Problem?; and Pelikan, Border Taxes and the GATT in U.S. Commission on International Trade and Investment Policy (the Williams Commission), Papers I, at 739–73 (1971); M. von Steinaecker, Domestic Taxation and Foreign Trade: the United States-European Border Tax Dispute chs. 3–6 (1973).

as sales taxes or value added taxes), while paragraph 4 is a broader measure aimed at all government regulation. Paragraph 1 has some general principles which interact with interpretation of the rest of the Article. This is particularly true for the last phrase of paragraph 1 which states that taxes and regulations "should not be applied * * * so as to afford protection to domestic production." A number of other paragraphs of Article III deal with particular situations, and the important paragraph 8 carves out an exception for government procurement.

The relationship of Article III and Article I of GATT is a bit tricky. This comes up particularly in connection with grandfather rights under the Protocol of Provisional Application (PPA), as we have seen in the preceding chapter. (You will recall that grandfather rights permitting existing legislation to be kept in force apply to Part II of GATT which includes Article III, but not to Part I which includes the MFN Article I. However certain cross references and the interpretations found in Annex I of GATT, change this relationship as to certain types of obligations.) Other articles of GATT also have a relationship to Article III. For example, Article XVII regarding state trading practices has sometimes been alleged to impose a "sort of" national treatment obligation although interpretative material suggests the contrary.

One major policy issue concerning the national treatment clause can be easily expressed: In which circumstances is it appropriate for a nation to provide treatment for domestic goods in its national legislation and programs which is more favorable than that for imported goods? Such treatment will tend to disfavor the importation and purchase of imported goods, and consequently it is a form of "protection," which can be even more severe than tariffs. Consequently, a GATT binding to limit a tariff on a particular commodity would be valueless, if there were not some limitations on the types of internal taxation or regulation which a country could impose to afford protection against such imports. To cite one easy example: Suppose tariffs on widgets were bound at 10%, but a country imposed an internal excise or sales tax on all widgets, in an amount of 5% for domestic goods and 10% for imported goods. The effect would be similar to adding 5% to the tariff. Such a practice is proscribed by Article III of GATT.

Many problems, however, are not so simple. A nation may have a wide variety of domestic programs and legislation designed to promote health, welfare and various economic goals. It may regulate the sale of goods in order to prevent pollution of the atmosphere or of water. It may regulate the production of goods so as to assure their reasonable safety when used by the public. It may design a tax structure to assist depressed areas of the country or to re-distribute wealth from the rich to the poor. Few would advocate an international economic system of rules which would prevent nations from exercising their sovereignty to promote domestic policy goals in these various ways. Consequently, in a number of cases, there arises a tension between the liberal trade goals of international economic policy, and national policy goals embodied in a wide variety of national laws and regulations, as well as laws and regulations of local government units.

Article XX of GATT containing the "general exceptions" to GATT obligations has language that imposes a somewhat looser national treatment obligation in certain exceptional cases allowing for government regulation etc. which is deemed justified on social welfare and similar grounds. Article XXI, the "national security" exception, of course, cuts a swath through the national treatment, as well as all other obligations. (We take this up in Chapters 12 and 13).

These exceptions, however, can be abused and can be a form of hidden protectionism. The more the international legal system imposes rules to limit such hidden protectionism, the less freedom there is for national or local governmental units to pursue even their legitimate domestic policies. To a certain extent, the issue is similar to the subject which in the United States is known as "federalism"—the question as to which level of government should appropriately have the authority to make certain types of decisions. If too much decision-making has been centralized at the federal level, then the local governments cannot use initiative and cannot respond to constituents, even though they may be closer to the particular problems of those constituents. On the other hand, there seems to be a natural tendency for local government units to establish policies which favor their constituents at the expense of constituents located in other government units, to the general detriment of the federal system. These are some of the issues that are dealt with in the materials in this chapter.

As the reader now knows, there is a plethora of so-called "nontariff barriers" (NTBs) which present the dilemma between international liberal trade policies, and local domestic policies, described above. Some of these nontariff barriers have been described in Chapter 6. Other NTBs will be taken up in later chapters of this book. One particular problem often associated with national treatment clauses, as well as with international obligations on subsidies, is termed the "border tax adjustment" question— and this will be taken up in Section 10.3 infra.

National treatment clauses will be found in a number of other treaties, particularly bilateral treaties such as FCN treaties where often the obligation is related to the "right of establishment." [3] The Treaty of Rome, establishing the EEC, contains such a clause also, which can be compared with the GATT clause.[4] There is also an elaborate body of international customary international law relating to "treatment of aliens" which imposes national treatment obligations on the way in which a nation treats aliens within its territory in respect of many matters, such as arrest and criminal prosecution, and treatment of property of aliens.[5]

One of the major questions in connection with the possible development of more international rules for trade in services, which we consider in Chapter 15, is the extent to which a national treatment obligation would be acceptable to nations with regard to such subjects as banking, insurance, etc.

In the next section of this chapter, we take up the national treatment obligation generally, noting particularly the difficult conceptual problem than can arise when a domestic tax or regulatory measure is neutral or

3. See Section 5.2(D) supra.

4. Treaty of Rome, art. 30: "Quantitative restrictions on imports and all measures having equivalent effect shall, without prejudice to the following provisions, be prohibited among Member States."

5. I. Brownlie, Principles of Public International Law ch. XXIII (3d ed. 1979).

nondiscriminatory on its face, but in fact has a differential impact on imports. In Section 8.3, we then look to some of the exceptions and particular problems of national treatment. Two of the major problems, however, we take up in separate sections: Government procurement (Section 8.4) and the problem of "technical barriers" or product standards (Section 8.5). Those last two topics were the subject of Tokyo Round agreements.

SECTION 8.2 THE NATIONAL TREATMENT OBLIGATION IN OPERATION

(A) THE GENERAL RULE

ITALIAN DISCRIMINATION AGAINST IMPORTED AGRICULTURAL MACHINERY

Report by the Panel for Conciliation, 15 July, 1958.[1]

I. INTRODUCTION

1.   The Panel for Conciliation examined with the representatives of the United Kingdom and Italy the complaint of the United Kingdom Government (L/649), that certain provisions of Chapter III of the Italian Law No. 949 of 25 July 1952, which provides special credit facilities to some categories of farmers or farmers' co-operatives for the purchase of agricultural machinery produced in Italy, were inconsistent with the obligations of Italy under Article III of the General Agreement and that the operation of this Law impaired the benefits which should accrue to the United Kingdom under the Agreement.

II. FACTS OF THE CASE

2.   In accordance with the Law of 25 July 1952, the Italian Government established a revolving fund which enabled the Ministry for Agriculture and Forestry to grant special credit terms *inter alia* for the purchase of Italian agricultural machinery. To this fund are allocated by budgetary appropriations 25 thousand million lire a year for five fiscal years starting with the year 1952–53; out of these 25 thousand million lire, the Law provides that 7.5 thousand million would be assigned for the purchase of agricultural machinery, an amount which may be modified by the Italian authorities. The loans are granted at 3 per cent, including fees to the Credit Institute, for a period of five years to finance up to 75 per cent of the cost of the machinery. The interest and repayments of the loans are paid into the revolving fund and may be used for further loans. The revolving fund will remain in existence until 1964. Eligible purchasers may benefit from these favourable terms when they buy Italian agricultural machinery; if, on the other hand, they wish to buy foreign machinery on credit the terms would be less favourable. The United Kingdom delegation indicated that loans on commercial terms were presently available at the rate of about 10 per cent while the Italian delegation stated that farmers could obtain from agricul-

1. GATT, 7th Supp. BISD 60 (1959).

tural credit institutions five-year loans on terms substantially more favourable than 10 per cent.

3. The Italian delegation estimated that during the period 1952–1957 the purchasers of about half of the Italian tractors sold in Italy (i.e. about one-third of all tractors sold in the country) benefitted from the credit facilities provided under the Law No. 949.

4. In 1949, i.e. before the entry into force of the Law No. 949, the import duties on various types of tractors and other agricultural machinery, were bound under the GATT and, in particular, the duties on wheeled tractors with internal combustion engines of cylinder capacity up to 7,000 c.c. (Italian Tariff item ex 1218–a–1), which are of particular interest to the United Kingdom, were bound at a rate of 40 per cent ad valorem; in the course of the 1956 tariff negotiations, further concessions were granted by Italy, including a reduction of the rate on these tractors to 32 per cent ad valorem.

III. ALLEGED INCONSISTENCY OF THE EFFECTS OF THE PROVISIONS OF THE ITALIAN LAW WITH THE PROVISIONS OF PARAGRAPH 4 OF ARTICLE III

5. The United Kingdom delegation noted that Article III:4 of the General Agreement provided that products imported into the territory of any contracting party "shall be accorded treatment no less favourable than that accorded to like products of national origin in respect of all laws, regulations and requirements affecting their internal sale, offering for sale, purchase, transportation * * *" etc. As the credit facilities provided under the Italian Law were not available to the purchasers of imported tractors and other agricultural machinery these products did not enjoy the equality of treatment which should be accorded to them. The fact that these credit facilities were reserved exclusively to the purchasers of Italian tractors and other agricultural machinery represented a discrimination and the operation of the Law involved an inconsistency with the provisions of Article III of the General Agreement which provides that laws, regulations and requirements affecting internal sale should not be applied to imported products so as to afford protection to domestic producers. The United Kingdom would not challenge the consistency with the General Agreement of subsidies which the Italian Government might wish to grant to domestic producers of tractors and other agricultural machinery in accordance with the terms of paragraph 8(b) of Article III. However, in the case of the Italian Law the assistance by the State was not given to producers but to the purchasers of agricultural machinery; a case which is not covered by the provisions of paragraph 8(b). Even in the case of subsidies granted to producers the rights of the United Kingdom under Article XXIII of the General Agreement would be safeguarded as was recognized by the CONTRACTING PARTIES in paragraph 13 of the Report on Other Barriers to Trade which they approved during the course of the Review Session.[*1]

* 1. Third Supplement, Basic Instruments and Selected Documents, page 224.

6. The Italian delegation considered that the General Agreement was a trade agreement and its scope was limited to measures governing trade; thus the text of paragraph 4 of Article III applied only to such laws, regulations and requirements which were concerned with the actual conditions for sale, transportation, etc., of the commodity in question and should not be interpreted in an extensive way. In particular, the Italian delegation stated that the commitment undertaken by the CONTRACTING PARTIES under that paragraph was limited to qualitative and quantitative regulations to which goods were subjected, with respect to their sale or purchase on the domestic market.

7. It was clear in their view that the Law No. 949 which concerned the development of the Italian economy and the improvement in the employment of labour was not related to the questions of sale, purchase or transportation of imported and domestically produced products which were the only matters dealt with in Article III.

8. Moreover the Italian delegation considered that the text of Article III:4 could not be construed in such a way as to prevent the Italian Government from taking the necessary measures to assist the economic development of the country and to improve the conditions of employment in Italy.

9. Finally, the Italian delegation, noting that the United Kingdom delegation recognized that the Italian Government would be entitled to grant subsidies exclusively to domestic producers, stressed it would not be logical to exclude this possibility in the case of credit facilities which had a far less pronounced effect on the terms of competition.

10. In the view of the Italian delegation it would be inappropriate for the CONTRACTING PARTIES to construe the provisions of Article III in a broad way since this would limit the rights of contracting parties in the formulation of their domestic economic policies in a way which was not contemplated when they accepted the terms of the General Agreement.

11. The Panel agreed that the question of the consistency of the effects of the Italian Law with the provisions of the General Agreement raised a problem of interpretation. It had the impression that the contention of the Italian Government might have been influenced in part by the slight difference of wording which existed between the French and the English texts of paragraph 4 of Article III. The French text which had been submitted to the Italian Parliament for approval provided that the imported products "ne seront pas soumis a un traitement moins favorable" whereas the English text read "the imported product shall be accorded treatment no less favourable". It was clear from the English text that any favourable treatment granted to domestic products would have to be granted to like imported products and the fact that the particular law in question did not specifically prescribe conditions of sale or purchase appeared irrelevant in the light of the English text. It was considered, moreover, that the intention of the drafters of the Agreement was clearly to treat the imported products in the same way as the like domestic products once they had been cleared through customs. Otherwise indirect protection could be given.

12.   In addition, the text of paragraph 4 referred both in English and French to laws and regulations and requirements *affecting* internal sale, purchase, etc., and not to laws, regulations and requirements governing the conditions of sale or purchase. The selection of the word "affecting" would imply, in the opinion of the Panel, that the drafters of the Article intended to cover in paragraph 4 not only the laws and regulations which directly governed the conditions of sale or purchase but also any laws or regulations which might adversely modify the conditions of competition between the domestic and imported products on the internal market.

13.   The Italian delegation alleged that the provisions of paragraph 8(b) which exempted the granting of subsidies to producers from the operation of this Article showed that the intention of the drafters of the Agreement was to limit the scope of Article III to laws and regulations directly related to the conditions of sale, purchase, etc. On the other hand, the Panel considered that if the Italian contention were correct and if the scope of Article III was limited in this way (which would, of course, not include any measure of subsidization) it would have been unnecessary to include the provisions contained in paragraph 8(b) since they would be excluded *ipso facto* from the scope of Article III. The fact that the drafters of Article III thought it necessary to include this exemption for production subsidies would indicate that the intent of the drafters was to provide equal conditions of competition once goods had been cleared through customs.

14.   Moreover, the Panel agreed with the contention of the United Kingdom delegation that in any case the provisions of paragraph 8(b) would not be applicable to this particular case since the credit facilities provided under the Law were granted to the purchasers of agricultural machinery and could not be considered as subsidies accorded to the producers of agricultural machinery.

15.   The Panel also noted that if the Italian contention were correct, and if the scope of Article III were limited in the way the Italian delegation suggested to a specific type of laws and regulations, the value of the bindings under Article II of the Agreement and of the general rules of non-discrimination as between imported and domestic products could be easily evaded.

16.   The Panel recognized—and the United Kingdom delegation agreed with this view—that it was not the intention of the General Agreement to limit the right of a contracting party to adopt measures which appeared to it necessary to foster its economic development or to protect a domestic industry, provided that such measures were permitted by the terms of the General Agreement. The GATT offered a number of possibilities to achieve these purposes through tariff measures or otherwise. The Panel did not appreciate why the extension of the credit facilities in question to the purchasers of imported tractors as well as domestically produced tractors would detract from the attainment of the objectives of the Law, which aimed at stimulating the purchase of tractors mainly by small farmers and co-operatives in the interests of economic development. If, on the other hand, the objective of the Law, although not specifically stated in the text thereof, were to protect the Italian agricultural machinery industry, the Panel considered that such protection should be given in ways permissible under

the General Agreement rather than by the extension of credit exclusively for purchases of domestically produced agricultural machinery.

IV. ALLEGED NULLIFICATION OR IMPAIRMENT OF BENEFITS ACCRUING TO THE UNITED KINGDOM UNDER THE GENERAL AGREEMENT

17. The Panel considered whether the operation of the Law No. 949 had caused injury to United Kingdom commercial interests, and whether such an injury represented an impairment of the benefits accruing to the United Kingdom under the General Agreement.

18. The Panel and the two parties agreed that under Article XXIII of the General Agreement a case of impairment or nullification may be brought before the CONTRACTING PARTIES whether the impairment was a result of a measure conflicting with the provisions of the Agreement or of a measure which was not inconsistent with the provisions of the Agreement.

* * *

22. On the basis of the statistics presented by the parties and the explanations given, the Panel came to the conclusion that the falling off in imports of tractors and, in particular, of the tractors from the United Kingdom, could not entirely be attributed to the operation of the credit facilities under the Law. It considered, however, that these credit facilities had probably influenced a number of purchasers in the selection of the tractors which they purchased. The Panel considered, furthermore, that if the considered view of the Italian Government was that these credit facilities had not influenced the terms of competition on the Italian market, there would not seem to be a serious problem in amending the operation of the Law so as to avoid any discrimination as regards these credit facilities between the domestic and imported tractors and agricultural machinery.

23. The Panel noted that in the course of the bilateral negotiations between Italy and the United Kingdom the Italian Government mentioned that any modification of the present system might involve special difficulties. The Italian delegation pointed out in particular that if the Law were operated in such a way as to apply to all tractors, whatever their origin, there would be budgetary implications because of the increased appropriations which would be required. Moreover it would be difficult for the Government to justify the use of the proceeds of taxes levied on Italian nationals in a way which would work to the advantage of foreign producers. Finally the limitation of the credit facilities to tractors of domestic origin was necessary to assure national production of agricultural machinery.

24. The Panel considered that the application of the special credit facilities to both imported and domestic machinery need not involve any increase in budgetary appropriations since there could be a different application of the funds within a total already available. In this connexion it noted that the United Kingdom Government was not asking the Italian Government to increase the budgetary appropriation, but rather to extend the availability of the credit facility to permit a fair choice between purchases of tractors of domestic and foreign origin. Further, the Panel noted that the credit facilities were not granted to the Italian producers of agricultural machinery but to the Italian purchasers. Since these facilities were of

advantage to Italian citizens the Panel questioned whether their extension to purchasers of imported machinery would be considered by public opinion as representing a benefit to foreign interests. Finally, as regards the need to assure national production of agricultural machinery, the Panel noted that the Italian industry already had the benefit of tariff protection (which in the case of the tractors under reference, amounted to 32 per cent ad valorem) and that the tariff was an accepted means of giving protection to domestic industry under the General Agreement.

V. Conclusions

25. In the light of the considerations set out above the Panel suggests to the CONTRACTING PARTIES that it would be appropriate for them to make a recommendation to the Italian Government in accordance with paragraph 2 of Article XXIII. The Panel considers that the recommendation should draw the attention of the Italian Government to the adverse effects on United Kingdom exports of agricultural machinery, particularly tractors, of those provisions of Law 949 limiting the prescribed credit facilities to purchasers of Italian produced machinery and suggest to the Italian Government that it consider the desirability of eliminating within a reasonable time the adverse effects of the Law on the import trade of agricultural machinery by modifying the operation of that Law or by other appropriate means.

EEC—MEASURES ON ANIMAL FEED PROTEINS
Report of the Panel adopted on 14 March 1978 [2]

1.1 In April 1976 the Council was informed by the United States that the United States had entered into consultations with the EEC under Article XXIII:1 as a result of the implementation on 1 April 1976, of a compulsory purchase programme for skimmed milk powder by the EEC. On 15 July 1976 the United States referred this matter to the Contracting Parties in accordance with the provisions of Article XXIII:2, since it had not been possible, in intensive consultations with the Community, to reach a satisfactory solution to the trade issues involved.

1.2 At its meeting of 17 September 1976, the Council agreed to establish a Panel with the following terms of reference:

> To examine the complaint by the United States that the EEC import deposits and purchasing requirements affecting non-fat dry milk and certain animal feed proteins are not consistent with the EEC's obligations under the GATT, including the provisions of Articles I, II and III, and to make such findings as will assist the Contracting Parties in making the recommendations or rulings provided for in paragraph 2 of Article XXIII.

* * *

2.3 The objective of the EEC measures was to allow for increased utilization of denatured skimmed milk powder as a protein source for use in feedingstuffs for animals other than calves, with a view to reducing by 400,000 tons the surplus stocks of skimmed milk powder held by governmental intervention agencies.

* * *

2. GATT, 25th Supp. BISD 49 (1979).

2.5   Under these measures, EEC domestic producers or importers of oilseeds, cakes and meals, dehydrated fodder and compound feeds and importers of corn gluten feeds had an obligation to purchase a certain quantity of skimmed milk powder held by intervention agencies and to have it denatured for use as feed for animals other than calves.

* * *

2.14   With respect to customs duty treatment, all of the United States exports subject to the measures enter the EEC under GATT bound rates, with the exception of compound feeds, groundnuts, and other flour or meals of oilseeds or oleaginous fruit, non-defatted, (excluding mustard and castor bean flour) than that of soybeans.

III.   MAIN ARGUMENTS

3.1   In the course of its examination of the EEC measures, the Panel heard arguments from the representatives of the United States and of the European Communities with respect to the following provisions of the General Agreement: Article III:5; Article III:1; Article III:4; Article III:2; Article II:1(b); Article II:2(a); Article I:1 and Article XXIII.

* * *

3.3   The representative of the United States noted that there was no clear definition in the General Agreement on what is a like product and that the term had been variously interpreted depending on the issue in question. He suggested that, in the case of the EEC measures, like products should be considered to be those products used for the same purpose of adding protein to animal feeds.   He maintained that, because of their interchangeability and substitutability for use in feedingstuffs, vegetable proteins including corn gluten, skimmed milk powder as well as animal, marine and synthetic proteins should be considered as like products.

* * *

3.5   The representative of the United States argued that the purchase of denatured skimmed milk powder required by the EEC measures clearly worked as a mixing regulation prohibited under Article III:5.   The purchase requirement had the effect of: (a) raising the price of substitutable vegetable protein products and feeds in order to make skimmed milk powder price competitive, particularly with soybean cakes and meal; and (b) cutting down imports of the vegetable protein products by an amount almost equivalent to 365,000 tons of denatured skimmed milk powder actually disposed of under the measures.

3.6   He said that Article III:5 prohibits regulations which require, directly or indirectly, that any specified amount or proportion of a domestic product be mixed, processed or used and that this provision was reinforced by the language in Article III:6 which exempted mixing schemes already in effect.   He maintained that the purpose and effect of the Council Regulation (EEC) No. 563/76 was to require that a specified amount of skimmed milk powder from domestic intervention agencies stocks, which held only domestically produced products, be purchased and denatured and thereby used as a source of proteins in feedingstuffs, replacing imported vegetable proteins.   In addition, Article III:5 also prohibits mixing regulations to protect domestic production by its reference to the fact that such regulations cannot be applied in a manner contrary to Article III:1.

*   *   *

3.13 [The EC representative] maintained that Article III:1 contains specific practical obligations not to afford protection to domestic production, not just any domestic production, but rather a production directly competing with the imported products covered by the measures. He said that the underlying reasons for the adoption by the EEC of the measure concerning skimmed milk powder were clearly not inspired by any concern to afford protection to domestic production of this product. The essential purpose of the measure was to restrict and reduce existing surpluses. That was confirmed by the adoption and examination of other measures designed to restore a balance in the milk product markets of the EEC and thus to restrain such production. In his view, the fact of wishing to encourage the use of skimmed milk powder for animal feeding for a fairly limited period, and in respect of a small quantity in relation to the annual volume of imports into the Community of protein substances, could not reasonably have been considered as a violation of Article III:1.

*   *   *

3.16 The representative of the European Communities was of the opinion that the measures had not worked to restrict or adversely affect imports. He said that the import data provided sufficient evidence that EEC imports of protein-based products increased over the limited period of application of the measures.

3.17 The representative of the United States argued that the requirement under the EEC measures to purchase denatured skimmed milk powder from intervention agencies, which was entirely of domestic origin, did afford protection to the domestic dairy industry in violation of Article III:1.

3.18 He maintained that the measures protected domestic dairy producers against the natural consequences of surplus and over-production, resulting in the displacement of an almost equivalent quantity of vegetable proteins.

*   *   *

IV. CONCLUSIONS

4.1 The Panel began by examining whether all products used for the same purpose of adding protein to animal feeds should be considered as "like products" within the meaning of Articles I and III. Having noted that the General Agreement gave no definition of the concept of "like product" the Panel reviewed how it had been applied by the Contracting Parties in previous cases.

4.2 The Panel noted, in this case, such factors as the number of products and tariff items carrying different duty rates and tariff bindings, the varying protein contents and the different vegetable, animal and synthetic origins of the protein products before the Panel—not all of which were subject to the EEC measures. Therefore, the Panel concluded that these various protein products could not be considered as "like products" within the meaning of Articles I and III.

*   *   *

4.6   The Panel noted that the Council Regulation (EEC) No. 563/76 referred, in its stated considerations, to the considerable stocks of skimmed milk powder held by intervention agencies and to the objective of increasing the utilization of skimmed milk powder as a protein in feedingstuffs for animals other than calves.   In other words, the Regulation was intended to dispose on the internal market ("utilization") of a given quantity ("stocks") of skimmed milk powder in a particular form ("denatured" i.e. utilizable only for the intended purposes).   The Panel therefore considered that the EEC Regulation was an "internal quantitative regulation" in the sense of Article III:5.   However, the Panel found that this "internal quantitative regulation" as such was not related to "the mixture, processing or use * * * in specified amounts or proportions within the meaning of Article III:5 because, at the level of its application, the EEC Regulation introduced basically an obligation to purchase a certain quantity of skimmed milk powder and the purchase obligation falls under Article III:1.

4.7   Given the reference in Article III:5, second sentence, to Article III:1, the Panel then examined the consistency of the EEC Regulation as an "internal quantitative regulation" with the provisions of Article III:1, particularly as to whether the Regulation afforded protection to domestic production.   The Panel noted that the EEC Regulation considered, in its own terms, that denatured skimmed milk powder was an important source of protein which could be used in feedingstuffs.   The Panel also noted that surplus stocks could originate either from domestic production or imports, but that the intervention agencies from which the buyers of vegetable proteins had to purchase a certain quantity of denatured skimmed milk powder only held domestically produced products.   The Panel further noted that, although globally about 15 per cent of the EEC apparent consumption of vegetable protein was supplied from domestic sources, not all the individual products subject to the EEC measures were produced domestically in substantial quantities.

4.8   The Panel concluded that the measures provided for by the Regulation with a view to ensuring the sale of a given quantity of skimmed milk powder protected this product in a manner contrary to the principles of Article III:1 and to the provisions of Article III:5, second sentence.

*   *   *

4.10   The Panel also examined whether the EEC measures accorded imported protein products less favourable treatment than that accorded to like products of EEC origin within the meaning of Article III:4.   In this regard the Panel noted the economic considerations, including the level of domestic production and of the applicable security deposit, put forward by the EEC to justify the application of the measures to corn gluten of foreign origin only.   The Panel was not convinced that these considerations justified the non-application of these measures to domestic corn gluten and therefore concluded that the measures accorded imported corn gluten less favourable treatment than that accorded corn gluten of national origin in violation of Article III:4.

*   *   *

4.12 The Panel examined whether the protein certificate requirement and other specific administrative requirements accorded to imported products treatment less favourable than that accorded to "like products" of EEC origin in respect of the purchase, sale and distribution of the products in the EEC within the meaning of Article III:4. The Panel was of the opinion that these requirements should be considered as enforcement mechanisms to ensure that the obligation, of either purchasing a certain quantity of denatured skimmed milk powder or of providing a security, had been complied with. The Panel noted that the protein certificate applied only to imports but that there was an equivalent document required for products of national origin except for a relatively short period at the beginning of the application of the EEC measures. The Panel concluded that the various administrative requirements, including the protein certificate, were not inconsistent with the EEC obligations under Article III:4.

* * *

4.18 Having regard to the legal considerations referred to above and taking account of its own findings in relation to Article III:5 and Article III:1 that the EEC measures were an "internal quantitative regulation", the Panel concluded that the EEC measures should be examined as internal measures under Article III and not as border measures under Article II.

Note

Review the excerpt from the Brazilian Internal Taxes report included in Section 5.4(C) supra, and the Belgian Family Allowances case included in Section 7.2(B) supra. A number of other GATT cases have concerned the national treatment obligation. Summaries of some of these follow: [3]

(1) According to an Italian complaint, all continuous artificial fabrics imported into Greece were subject to a luxury tax ranging from 10% to 22%, while all similar domestic goods, except rayon, were not so taxed. The Italians alleged this to be a violation of GATT Article III, paragraph 2. GATT Doc. L/234, at 1 (1954).

(2) Great Britain complained of a 2% differential (4%–6%) in the rate of the Italian turnover taxes applied to domestic versus imported pharmaceutical products. A violation of GATT Article III was alleged. GATT Doc. L/421 (1955).

(3) The Netherlands complained to the CONTRACTING PARTIES of the "Utility System" used by Great Britain to impose its purchase tax, whereby certain domestically produced consumer goods were exempted from the tax while like imports were not. Great Britain agreed that the tax was improper under GATT. GATT Doc. CP.5/SR.20 (1950). Britain later reported an expert committee had been appointed to study the problem. GATT Doc. CP.6/SR.7 (1951). One year later, upon the recommendation of her study committee, Britain abolished the utility system, thus removing the discriminatory aspects of the purchase tax. GATT Doc. SR.7/5 (1952).

(4) The United States asked for discussion of a Cuban sales tax on lumber which was collected only on imports. The United States claimed a violation of

3. Reprinted from World Trade and the Law of GATT, by John H. Jackson, §§ 12.3, nn. 22–25, § 12.4, n. 11. Copyright 1969 by The Bobbs-Merrill Company, Inc. This and other excerpts from this treatise in this chapter are reprinted by permission. All rights reserved.

GATT Article III. GATT Doc. L/63 (1953). The United States withdrew her charges following Cuba's termination of the exemption for domestic lumber. GATT Doc. L/63/Add. 1 (1953).

(5) A Hawaiian territorial law requiring stores selling, and restaurants serving, foreign eggs to give written notice of this to their customers. Australia alleged that this violated GATT Article III, paragraph 4. GATT Doc. L/411 (1955). The complaint was shelved until after a court challenge to the law was completed. GATT Doc. SR.10/13 (1955). The law was subsequently declared unconstitutional. See Territory of Hawaii v. Ho, 41 Hawaii 565 (1957), set out in Section 8.3(B) infra.

(6) Two other GATT cases discussed later in this chapter also involved the national treatment clause: the Canadian Foreign Investment Review Act (Section 8.2(C)) and the U.S. Spring Assemblies case (Section 8.3(D)). Recall also the case of Tupman Thurlow Co. v. Moss, discussed in Section 3.6 supra.

(B) DISGUISED OR DE FACTO DISCRIMINATION

Sometimes a government regulation can be apparently nondiscriminatory on its face, but in actual application cause differences in the conditions of sale of imported goods as compared with domestic goods. The famous "wine-gallon, proof-gallon" controversy litigated in the cases below illustrates this possibility, and it can come up in a variety of other contexts. For example, domestic manufacturers may propose a tax on sales of "all" of a particular product, coupled with a credit for that tax against another government tax which in fact only domestic producers can take. Problems at the end of this subsection illustrate some other similar situations.

The wine-gallon problem was the subject of negotiation in the Tokyo Round, with a resulting agreement by which the U.S., in exchange for certain other concessions from the EC, revised the U.S. system for taxing beverages. (See Trade Agreements Act of 1979, title VIII). Presumably, therefore, the specific facts of the *Schieffelin* case are no longer of interest. The principles, however, continue to apply. Notice in the case the role of a bilateral treaty MFN clause. Also notice the difference in the wording of the bilateral national treatment clause, and the GATT national treatment clause. The earlier case of *Bercut* is noted after *Schieffelin,* but the amicus attorneys in *Schieffelin* surely had a valid point in their arguments about grandfather rights.

Query: Could the language of GATT Article III, especially paragraphs 1 and 2, be applied in the *Schieffelin* fact situation to arrive at a different result?

SCHIEFFELIN & CO. v. UNITED STATES
United States Court of Customs and Patent Appeals, 1970.
424 F.2d 1396.

BALDWIN, JUDGE.

This appeal is from the judgment of the United States Customs Court, Third Division,[*1] overruling two consolidated protests relating to certain 86

[* 1.] Schieffelin & Co. v. United States, 61 Cust.Ct. 397, C.D. 3640 (1968).

proof bottled spirits, imported from Ireland and Scotland, respectively, between March 1964 and April 1965. As filed, the protests were directed only to the internal revenue tax, which was levied at the rate of $10.50 per wine gallon [*2] under section 5001(a)(1) of the Internal Revenue Code of 1954, and the importers claimed that the tax should have been levied on a proof gallon basis at 86% of $10.50, amounting to $9.03 per wine gallon.   *   *   *

The protests were submitted to the Customs Court upon a stipulation including the following:

1. That the merchandise in issue consists of bottled, below proof distilled spirits which are the manufacture of Scotland or Ireland, as hereinafter related, on which tax was assessed at $10.50 per wine gallon under section 5001, Internal Revenue Code.

2. That the merchandise in issue is like bottled distilled spirits of equivalent proof manufactured in the United States *   *   *

3. That a proof gallon of distilled spirits contains 50 percent of alcohol by volume, and a proof gallon is called 100 proof, that is, the number of proof, represents twice the percentage of alcohol.

4. That below-proof distilled spirits contain less than 50 percent of alcohol by volume and the number of proof represents twice the percentage of alcohol. For example, spirits containing 43 percent of alcohol are called 86 proof.

5. That in the United States, the practice of producers of domestic below-proof bottled distilled spirits is to withdraw spirits from bond at or above proof and have the taxes under sec. 5001, Internal Revenue Code, determined on the proof-gallon basis. Thereafter water is added to reduce the proof to the desired level before bottling. In recent years, all distilled spirits legally bottled in the United States have averaged about 85 proof.

6. That the assessment on below-proof bottled distilled spirits on the basis of wine gallons requires payment of higher taxes than would be payable on the basis of proof gallons.

7. That over 90 percent of domestic distilled spirits legally produced for consumption in the United States are withdrawn from bond in bulk at or above proof and are taxed on proof gallons. Over 90 percent of the distilled spirits legally sold at retail in the United States are bottled below proof.

8. That distilled spirits cannot be legally sold in the United States at retail in bulk; only bottled distilled spirits may legally be sold at retail.

*   *   *

Section 5001(a)(1) of the Internal Revenue Code of 1954, 68A Stat. 595, as amended, 26 U.S.C. 5001(a)(1), reads in pertinent part.

[*2.] A "wine gallon" is a standard United States gallon containing 231 cubic inches. The term is generally applied to spirits that are less than 100 proof, i.e., less than 50 percent alcohol by volume. A gallon of 100 proof spirits is called a "proof gallon" and a gallon containing over 50 percent alcohol is designated "over proof" or "above proof."

(a) Rate of tax—

(1) General.—There is hereby imposed on all distilled spirits in bond or produced in or imported into the United States an internal revenue tax at the rate of $10.50 on each proof gallon or wine gallon when below proof * * *.

Section 7852(d) of the Internal Revenue Code, 68A Stat. 922, 26 U.S.C. § 7852(d) provides:

(d) Treaty obligations.—

No provision of this title shall apply in any case where its application would be contrary to any treaty obligation of the United States in effect on the date of enactment of this title.

Section 5006(a)(1) of the Internal Revenue Code (I.R.C.) of 1954 provides that the tax on spirits be determined when they are "withdrawn from bond." The determination is made on withdrawal from internal revenue bond in the case of domestic spirits and, in the case of imported spirits, on withdrawal from customs bond.

Appellants claim that the imposition of the internal revenue tax on the wine gallon basis under Sec. 5001(a)(1) discriminates against their bottled below proof spirits contrary to treaty obligations of the United States and that, under Sec. 7852(d), the provision for so imposing the tax therefore should not apply.

They regard discrimination against the spirits imported from Ireland, Irish whiskey, to be banned by the Treaty of Friendship, Commerce and Navigation between the United States and Ireland, entered into force on September 14, 1950. The portions of that treaty pertinent here are:

Article XVI (1 UST 788 at page 797):

1. Products of either Party shall be accorded, within the territories of the other Party, national and most-favored-nation treatment in all matters affecting internal taxation and sale, distribution, storage and use.

Article XXI (1 UST 788 at page 801):

1. The term "national treatment" means treatment accorded within the territories of a Party upon terms no less favorable than the treatment accorded therein, in like situations, to nationals, companies, products, vessels or other objects, as the case may be, of such Party.

As to the spirits imported from Scotland, i.e., Scotch whiskey, appellants rely additionally on the treaty between the United States and Great Britain, 8 Stat. 228, entered into force July 3, 1815. Under that treaty, products of Great Britain coming into this country are to be accorded most-favored-nation treatment with respect to "duties" levied against them.

Appellants point to the practice, of domestic producers of below proof spirits, of withdrawing the spirits from bond in proof or over proof condition whereby they are subjected to tax on the proof gallon basis and then diluting them to below proof for bottling. The tax of $10.50 per proof gallon so paid is reflected in the cost of domestic spirits bottled at 86 proof, for example, to the extent of only 86 percent of $10.50, or $9.03 per wine gallon. If the foreign produced spirits are imported in bulk at proof or over proof and subsequently bottled at 86 proof, the tax is levied on the bulk spirits on the proof gallon basis just as with domestic spirits and the reflection of that tax on the ultimate bottled product amounts to $9.03 on the gallon just as that on the domestic bottled product. However, the instant imports, having been bottled in Ireland and Scotland, respectively, at 86 proof, were necessarily withdrawn from customs bond in below proof condition so that the resulting tax amounted to $10.50 per *bottled* gallon, or $1.47 per gallon more than the reflected tax on domestic or imported spirits withdrawn from bond in proof or over proof condition and then bottled in the United States at 86 proof.

Appellants' protests are grounded on the charge that the aforementioned circumstances result in discrimination against their imported below proof bottled spirits relative to below proof bottled domestic spirits. They state that the imported Irish whiskey is entitled to national treatment within the United States under Article XVI of the treaty with Ireland, and that, under Article XXI of that treaty, "national treatment" means treatment upon terms no less favorable than the treatment accorded in like situations to products of the United States. With respect to the Scotch whiskey, appellants take the position that the most-favored-nation provisions of the British treaty of 1815 "operate prospectively to encompass the benefits conferred upon products of Ireland in the National Treatment provisions of the Irish treaty, and they encompass specifically the tax here in dispute."

The Customs Court accepted the premise, conceded here by appellee, that the imports from Great Britain are entitled under the most-favored-nation clause of the British treaty to whatever tax treatment is required with respect to the imports of Irish origin. It thus found, and we think correctly, that the case comes down to whether assessment of taxes on the imported merchandise on the wine gallon basis under the stipulated circumstances is in violation of Articles XVI and XXI of the Irish treaty. It observed that the time at which the tax is determined fixes the basis of the assessment and found that "the issue turns on whether the stipulated circumstances involve 'like situations' at the time of tax determination."

In disposing of that question, the court concluded that the *bottling* of the spirits has no bearing on the "taxing event" to which both the domestic and imported products are subject, observing that Sections 5001(a)(1) and 5006(a)(1) are addressed to the spirits and not to the containers which house them. It stated:

> We cannot conclude that the rate of taxation should be the same for both domestic and foreign spirits merely because both products end up in the hands of the consumer bottled and underproof. The criterion on which the taxing event takes place is, with respect to the domestic spirits, the withdrawal of the spirits from bond. Under the stipulated facts at bar the imported spirits are underproof at the time of tax determination, while the domestic spirits are at or overproof at such time. It is this difference in the nature of the taxed commodity which, in our view, militates against plaintiff's claim of discrimination in violation of treaty obligation.

> * * *

> * * * Underproof imported spirits (bottled) and proof or overproof domestic spirits (bulk) at the time of tax determination do not involve "like

situations," and consequently, the provisions of Articles XVI and XXI of the Irish treaty are not applicable here. * * *

The Customs Court relied on Bercut-Vandervoort & Co. v. United States, 46 CCPA 28, C.A.D. 691 (1958), cert. den., 359 U.S. 953, 79 S.Ct. 739, 3 L.Ed. 2d 760 (1959), finding that case "not distinguished upon the relevant facts or the law from the case before the court" and held it *stare decisis* herein. It stated:

> In Bercut-Vandervoort & Co., Inc. v. United States, supra, the protest considered by the United States Court of Customs and Patent Appeals involved distilled spirits which were imported underproof in bottles and on which the internal revenue taxes were assessed on the wine gallon basis. In substance, the provisions of the General Agreement on Tariff and Trade therein considered permitted, on imported products, "a charge equivalent to an internal tax" on like domestic products and prohibited the imported products of a contracting party from being "subject, directly or indirectly, to internal taxes or other internal charges of any kind in excess of those applied, directly or indirectly, to like domestic products."

Appellants concede that the provisions of the Internal Revenue Code of 1939 before this court in *Bercut* are comparable to those of Section 5001(a)(1) of the Internal Revenue Code of 1954 now before us. Also, they make no contention that the "national treatment" provision of the Irish treaty is in any way more restrictive than the similar requirements, expressed in different terms, of GATT which were found not to be violated in *Bercut*.

It is also acknowledged by appellants that Sec. 5001 appears on its face to be non-discriminatory in that it establishes two classifications—proof (and above proof) spirits and below proof spirits—and applies equally to both without regard to whether they are domestic or imported. Rather, they urge that it is examination of other provisions of the law, not considered in *Bercut* which shows that Sec. 5001 is in fact discriminatory as applied in *Bercut* and here. Those provisions are (a)(1) Sec. 5006, I.R.C., supra, which provides that the tax shall be determined when the spirits are withdrawn from bond; (2) Sec. 5233, I.R.C., which provides that spirits cannot be bottled in bond below 100 proof (except spirits for export which are not subject to tax); and (3) Sec. 206(a) of the Federal Alcohol Administration Act, 27 U.S.C. § 206(a), which allows only bottled spirits to be sold to the ultimate consumer. Appellants urge that these provisions were not considered in *Bercut* and that Sec. 5006 had no counterpart in the 1939 Act that the court had before it in that case, and regard them as establishing that the law does not permit domestic *bottled* spirits to be below proof at the time of tax determination. Since bottled imported spirits are the only bottled spirits to which the wine gallon tax can legally apply, they reason, the assessment of the wine gallon tax of Sec. 5001 on their bottled underproof imports is discriminatory.

Her Majesty's Government in the United Kingdom of Great Britain and Northern Ireland submitted a brief in support of the appeal as *amicus curiae* and was represented by counsel at oral hearing. *Amicus* "accepts the premise of the Customs Court that *Bercut* 'is not distinguished [from the present case] upon the relevant facts or the law,'" but it "questions the correctness of the conclusions drawn therefrom."

More specifically, *amicus* points out that the United States undertook the obligations of GATT subject to the Protocol of Provisional Application. That Protocol accepted Part II of the agreement, which part includes Article III embodying the restriction against imported products being subjected to internal taxes or other internal charges in excess of those applied to like domestic products, "to the fullest extent not inconsistent with existing legislation." *Amicus* then concludes that, since the wine gallon provision was existing legislation, the same result could have been reached in *Bercut* on the basis that the Protocol rendered the national treatment provision of Part II of GATT (Article III) ineffective instead of on the grounds on which it was decided—that the national treatment provision was not violated.

As evidence of error on the grounds on which *Bercut* actually was decided, *amicus* refers to the acknowledgment in paragraph 1 of Article III of GATT that internal taxes should not be applied to imported or domestic products so as to "afford protection to domestic production." It then refers to proceedings and documents concerned with the proposed Customs Simplification Act of 1951 (H.R. 1535). That material indicates that the executive branch of the government proposed the elimination of the wine gallon provisions of the Internal Revenue Code and that certain officials apparently regarded those provisions in derogation of the intent of GATT to avoid internal tax discrimination against imported goods. *Amicus* and appellants also point to testimony of certain representatives of domestic producers of spirits, and appellants also to testimony of the Resident Commissioner of Puerto Rico, opposing the elimination of the wine gallon provision as indicating that such elimination would amount effectively to a reduction in the import duties for foreign shippers of cased whiskey. *Amicus* also asserts that, besides itself, "the Common Market, consisting of France, Germany, Italy, Belgium, Luxembourg and the Netherlands," and Canada have "protested the United States excise tax system for spirits imported in bottles (wine gallon) as being contrary to Article III of GATT." *6

We think the Customs Court was plainly correct in regarding the decision in *Bercut* as compelling the conclusion it reached here. Not only is the language in Sec. 5001 equivalent to that in Sec. 2800 of the 1939 Act considered in the earlier case but the covenants in the Irish treaty are no more restrictive than those of GATT which were considered in *Bercut*.

Appellants' reliance here on Sec. 5006 and Sec. 5233 of the I.R.C. of 1954 and Sec. 206(a) of the Federal Alcohol Administration Act as establishing that the law does not permit domestic bottled spirits to be below proof at the time of tax determination does not demonstrate that the present case is distinguished from *Bercut* in any significant respect. As a matter of fact, it was assumed arguendo at the outset in *Bercut* that it was the "universal practice" of domestic producers to withdraw spirits from bond when over proof, and thus pay tax on the proof gallon basis, before diluting them. Thus *Bercut* was in no way premised on a view that domestic underproof

---

* 6. Amicus also refers in a footnote to its brief to "a critical study of *Bercut* in which the conclusions reached support the analysis here made and the position of this brief" in 61 Columbia Law Review, 549–551.

spirits would or could ever be subject to the internal revenue tax in that condition.*7

Neither do we find any significance in the contention of *amicus* [that] *Bercut* might have been decided with the same result on the basis of the adherence of the United States to GATT having been provisional under the Protocol of Provisional Application. The case was actually decided on the broader rationale that application of the wine gallon provisions of the 1939 Internal Revenue Code did not discriminate against imports of bottled under proof spirits under the national treatment provisions of GATT.

The decision in *Bercut* was reached after thorough consideration of the precedents, including the only case which appellants now advance holding that underproof spirits should be subjected to internal revenue tax on the proof gallon, rather than wine gallon, basis. That case, Parrott & Co. v. United States, 156 F.2d 943 (C.A.9, 1946) involved interpretation of a provision of the Internal Revenue Code of 1918 providing that there be levied, collected and paid "upon articles coming into the United States from the Virgin Islands, a tax equal to the internal revenue tax imposed in the United States upon like articles of domestic manufacture." The court found the quoted provision to require that underproof rum, which was alleged to have been distilled in the Virgin Islands at more than 100 proof, be taxed, *not as an importation,* but "as if produced in the United States." We think the court in *Bercut* was correct in distinguishing that case, where the sole issue was interpretation of language of the tax law and that language was entirely different from the prohibitory language of Article III, section 2, of the trade agreement involved in *Bercut*.

The arguments that the unsuccessful attempt of officials of the executive branch of the government in 1951 to persuade Congress to eliminate the wine gallon provisions of the Internal Revenue Code, with certain of the officials urging the change as a means to insure compliance with GATT, and that persons opposing the proposed change referred to it as amounting to a reduction in the protection afforded the domestic (including Puerto Rican) spirits industry, are not considered sufficiently indicative of discrimination to justify overruling *Bercut*. It is of course apparent how foreign producers would find the elimination of the wine gallon provision desirable and it is also understandable that some United States government officials might consider it in the best interests of international trade cooperation to do away with an aspect of the Internal Revenue Code that may well be an irritant to foreign trade negotiators. It is significant to note that there is no history of the GATT negotiations of record to show that that treaty was regarded as compelling the abrogation of a United States tax provision having a long prior history.*9 What is of record does not clearly establish that *Bercut* was

* 7. The parties are apparently in agreement that it is legally possible that bottled domestic below proof spirits could be subjected to taxation on the wine gallon basis. Domestic spirits intended for export (tax free) can be bottled in bond as low as 80 proof. *If* spirits so processed were subsequently diverted to the domestic market instead of being exported, they would be subject to tax on the wine gallon basis.

* 9. As noted in *Bercut*, the classifications of spirits at proof (or above proof) gallon and wine gallon "were established by the Congress in 1868 for purely domestic purposes and have been retained in substance each time the Congress has considered this subject. 15 Stat. 125 (1868); Rev.Stat. § 3251 (1875); 40 Stat. 1105 (1919) as amended, 26 U.S.C. § 2800(a)(1)."

in error, and therefore the principle of *stare decisis* dictates that we should not reverse ourselves. See R.J. Saunders & Co., Inc. v. United States, 54 CCPA 29, C.A.D. 898 (1966).

Referring specifically to the present case, the classification of spirits for internal revenue purposes in the two categories of proof gallon and wine gallon amounts but to a continuation of a practice long established at the time Congress passed the 1954 Internal Revenue Act specifically continuing it. The Irish treaty was already in force at that time. It is apparent that Congress had knowledge through the hearings on the Customs Simplification Act of 1951, discussed at length by appellants and *amicus,* of the controversy relating to the application of the wine gallon tax to bottled imported underproof spirits. In those circumstances, we cannot conceive that Congress, in including in the 1954 Internal Revenue Code, Sec. 7852(d), denying effect to provisions "contrary to any treaty obligation," intended it to apply to the express provision for the wine gallon rate in Sec. 5001.

* * *

The judgment of the Customs Court is affirmed.

Affirmed.

MARJORIE M. WHITEMAN, DIGEST OF INTERNATIONAL LAW
Vol. 14, p. 815 (1970)

In Bercut-Vandervoort & Co., Inc. v. United States it was held that the assessment of imported under-proof gin on a wine-gallon basis instead of on a proof-gallon basis did not violate article III (2) of the General Agreement on Tariffs and Trade although the competitive domestic product was taxed on a proof-gallon basis prior to reduction of proof for sale. The court, citing two previous cases, Bohemian Distributing Co. et al. v. United States, 15 Cust.Ct. 121 (1945), and Vernon Distributing Co. v. United States, 39 C.C.P.A. 205 (1951), stated, *inter alia:*

> From the statute and the cases cited, the following conclusions are drawn. The statute levies a tax on two distinct commodities: (1) Distilled spirits above proof and (2) distilled spirits below proof. The tax attaches to domestic merchandise when it comes into existence and is payable when the same is withdrawn from bond in its condition at that time. The tax attaches to foreign merchandise when it is imported and is payable when the merchandise is entered or withdrawn for consumption in its condition at that time. If the merchandise, domestic or foreign, is above proof when the tax is payable, it is assessed at $10.50 per proof gallon. If the merchandise, domestic or foreign, is below proof when the tax is payable, it is assessed at $10.50 per wine gallon. Where a trade agreement provides that imported articles shall not be subject to internal taxes higher than those payable on like domestic articles, the like domestic articles, where distilled spirits under proof are imported, are domestic distilled spirits under proof at the time the tax was payable. Since both such articles are taxable at the same rate, that is, on the wine-gallon basis, there is no discrimination against the foreign product, and the statute is not in contravention of the trade agreements.

* * *

Where, as here, the taxing statute distinguishes between a product in one condition and the same product in another and different condition the imported and the domestic products must be compared in their condition at the time the tax is applied. Both imported and domestic distilled spirits are taxable and both are taxable in either of two conditions: (1) When under proof and (2) when over proof. Therefore, distilled spirits, under proof when imported, must be compared with distilled spirits, under proof when withdrawn from bond, since, in both instances, that is the time when the tax is applicable. It is clear that both are taxed on the wine-gallon basis, and there has been no discrimination against the imported merchandise.

Bercut-Vandervoort & Co., Inc. v. United States, 151 F.Supp. 942, 946–947 (U.S.Cust.Ct., 3d Div., 1957); certiorari denied 359 U.S. 953 (1959). In a strong dissent Judge Donlon urged application of article III(1) of the General Agreement on Tariffs and Trade as well as of article III(2) and argued that the purpose of the General Agreement was being frustrated because the products taxed were commercially competitive. 151 F.Supp. 948, 949, 952.

Problems

Consider whether each situation described below is consistent or inconsistent with GATT Article III:

(1) Before becoming a GATT member, Xonia imposed internal sales "luxury" taxes on beer—1 drachma per bottle for domestic beer; 2 drachmas per bottle for imported beer. If the law is changed so that domestic beer is taxed the amount in the first column, can Xonia tax imported beer by the amount in the second column, without violating its GATT obligations?

Domestic Goods Tax	Imported Goods Tax
1.50	2.0
1.50	3.0
2	3
2	4
2	5

(2) Suppose the United States imposed a tax on automobiles which cannot operate more efficiently than 15 miles per gallon of gasoline, but rebates 50% of that tax to any domestic automobile company for use solely in research on auto energy conservation.

(3) A special accelerated depreciation income tax deduction is granted to domestic manufacturing companies, but not to foreign manufacturers, even when they derive locally taxable income from sales of imported goods.

(4) Suppose United States purchasers of automobiles are granted a gasoline tax rebate of $100 for the year in which they purchased a new *domestically produced* automobile.

(5) Suppose a proposed bill in the United States House of Representatives would establish a 10% excise tax on the sale of domestically produced or imported cars, but provides that such excise tax shall be one percentage point less than 10% for each 5% improvement in the officially rated gas mileage of each particular current year's make and model, over the model's rating for 1975. That is, if a Ford Pinto was rated at 20 miles-per-gallon in 1975, and 22 miles-per-gallon in 1976, then the 10% improvement would result in an 8% excise tax

on the 1976 model, rather than a 10% tax. Suppose further, that it can be established that the best selling *imported* cars in 1975 had miles-per-gallon ratings of 30% to 50% over most American domestically made models (and that therefore much improvement would be more difficult for the imported makes). Would such a bill, if enacted, be consistent with United States GATT obligations?

(C) PERFORMANCE REQUIREMENTS AND DOMESTIC CONTENT [4]

In recent years several particularly troublesome requirements of certain governments have raised important GATT and trade policy questions. Some governments have imposed so-called "performance requirements" on companies seeking to invest in their country. Such companies may be required, as a condition of a license to build a plant or import foreign capital, to purchase certain supplies domestically and/or to export a certain percentage of their output. Other governments have considered "domestic content" requirements which require products sold within their borders to contain a certain percentage of "domestic content" (value produced within the country, or materials coming from within the country.) The *Animal Feed* case discussed above (subsection (A)), poses some similar problems.

CANADA—ADMINISTRATION OF THE FOREIGN INVESTMENT REVIEW ACT

Report of the Panel adopted on 7 February 1984 [5]

1.1　In a communication dated 5 January 1982, the United States requested the government of Canada to consult under Article XXII:1 on the administration of the Canadian Foreign Investment Review Act. Among the issues which the United States wished to raise in the consultation was the practice of the government of Canada to enter into agreements with foreign investors according to which these are to give preference to the purchase of Canadian goods over imported goods and to meet certain export performance requirements. The communication was circulated to the contracting parties on 7 January 1982 (L/5280). Since the consultation did not lead to a solution, the United States, in a communication dated 19 March 1982, referred the matter to the Contracting Parties in accordance with Article XXIII:2 (L/5308).

* * *

2.2　*The Foreign Investment Review Act.* In December 1973 the Parliament of Canada enacted the Foreign Investment Review Act. According to

4. See generally Fontheim & Gadbaw, Trade Related Performance Requirement under the GATT–MTN System and U.S. Law, 14 Law & Poly.Intl.Bus. 129 (1982); Labor-Industry Coalition for International Trade (LICIT), Performance Requirements (1981); Note, Mexico's Computer Decree: The Problem of Performance Requirements and a U.S. Response, 14 Law & Poly.Intl.Bus. 1159 (1982); Note, Domestic Content Requirements: A Legal and Economic Analysis of Proposed U.S. Legisla-tion and Foreign Content Laws, 17 Geo.Wash. J.Intl.Law & Econ. 407 (1983).

5. GATT, 30th Supp. BISD 140 (1984). See Nixon & Burns, An Examination of the Legality of the Use of the Foreign Investment Review Act by the Government of Canada to Control Intra- and Extraterritorial Commercial Activity of Aliens, 33 Intl. & Comp.L.Q. 57 (1983).

Section 2(1) of this Act, the Parliament adopted the law "in recognition that the extent to which control of Canadian industry, trade and commerce has become acquired by persons other than Canadians and the effect thereof on the ability of Canadians to maintain effective control over their economic environment is a matter of national concern" and that it was therefore expedient to ensure that acquisitions of control of a Canadian business or establishments of a new business by persons other than Canadians be reviewed and assessed and only be allowed to proceed if the government had determined that they were, or were likely to be, of "significant benefit to Canada."

* * *

2.4 *Written Undertakings Given by Investors.* The Act provides that investors may submit written undertakings on the conduct of the business they are proposing to acquire or establish, conditional on approval by the Canadian government of the proposed acquisition or establishment. The submission of undertakings is not required under the Act but, as the administration of the Act evolved, they are now routinely submitted in support of nearly all larger investment proposals. Many undertakings are the result of negotiations between the investor and the Canadian government. Undertakings given by investors may deal with any aspect of the conduct of a business, including employment, investment, research and development, participation of Canadian shareholders and managers, productivity improvements as well as practices with respect to purchasing, manufacturing and exports. There are no pre-set formulas or prescriptions for the undertakings.

* * *

3.1 The *United States* requested the Panel to find that the written undertakings obtained by the Government of Canada under the Foreign Investment Review Act which oblige foreign investors subject to the Act

    (*a*) to purchase goods of Canadian origin in preference to imported goods or in specified amounts or proportions, or to purchase goods from Canadian sources;

    (*b*) to manufacture in Canada goods which would be imported otherwise

are inconsistent with Articles III:4, III:5, XI and XVII:1(*c*) of the General Agreement, and that the undertakings which oblige foreign investors

    (*c*) to export specified quantities or proportions of their production

are inconsistent with Article XVII:1(*c*) of the General Agreement, and that any such undertakings therefore constitute a *prima facie* case of nullification and impairment under Article XXIII of the General Agreement.

* * *

6. *Conclusions*

6.1 In the light of the considerations set out in paragraphs 5.4 to 5.12, the Panel concluded that the practice of Canada to allow certain investments subject to the Foreign Investment Review Act conditional upon written undertakings by the investors to *purchase* goods of Canadian origin, or goods from Canadian sources, is inconsistent with Article III:4 of the General Agreement according to which contracting parties shall accord to imported products treatment no less favourable than that accorded to like products of national origin in respect of all internal requirements affecting their purchase. The Panel further concluded that in relation to Article III:5, there were insufficient grounds to consider the purchase undertakings which refer to specific amounts or proportions under its provisions (paragraph 5.13). Noting that purchase undertakings do not prevent the importation of goods as such, the Panel reached the conclusion that they are not inconsistent with Article XI:1 (paragraph 5.14). Further, having reached a decision on purchase requirements in relation to Article III:4, the Panel did not consider it necessary to make a specific finding on the interpretation of Article XVII:1(c) in the context of this case, and therefore did not reach a separate conclusion regarding the consistency of purchase requirements with this provision (paragraphs 5.15 and 5.16). On the basis of the evidence before it, the Panel could not conclude that the purchase undertakings that were found to be inconsistent with Article III:4 are necessary within the meaning of Article XX(d) for the effective administration of the Foreign Investment Review Act (paragraphs 5.19 to 5.20).

6.2 For the reasons set out in paragraphs 5.17 and 5.18, the Panel found that Canada does not act inconsistently with Article XVII:1(c) of the General Agreement when allowing certain investments subject to the Foreign Investment Review Act conditional upon undertakings by investors to *export* a specified amount or proportion of their production.

[In 5.18, the Panel found that "there is no provision in the General Agreement which forbids requirements to sell goods in foreign markets in preference to the domestic market."

[The Panel recommended that in the future Canada ensure "that any *future* purchase undertakings will not provide more favourable treatment to Canadian products than in relation to imported products." As to the existing purchase undertakings that the Panel had found in violation of GATT, it recommended that Canada bring such "undertakings as soon as possible into conformity with its obligations under the General Agreement."]

Note

In 1985, the Canadian Foreign Investment Review Act was replaced by the Investment Canada Act. Although the Act requires notification and review of certain investments in Canada, it is thought that it will be administered in a way to promote foreign investment in Canada without imposing the sort of restrictions imposed under the Foreign Investment Review Act.[6]

We discuss investment issues more generally in Chapter 16 infra.

---

6. S.C. 1984–85, c. 20. See Glover, New & Lacourciere, The Investment Canada Act: Foreign Investment in Canada, 41 Bus.Law. 83 (1985); Grover, The Investment Canada Act, 10 Can.Bus.L.J. 475 (1985).

CONGRESSIONAL BUDGET OFFICE, THE FAIR PRACTICES IN
AUTOMOTIVE PRODUCTS ACT (H.R. 5133):
AN ECONOMIC ASSESSMENT

1–4 (1982) [7]

It is against this background of deteriorating conditions in the automobile industry that The Fair Practices in Automotive Products Act (H.R. 5133) has been put forward for consideration by the Congress. The bill's objective is to restore auto industry jobs by restricting the number of imported cars and parts that enter the U.S. market.

DOMESTIC CONTENT REQUIREMENTS

The act would institute minimum "domestic content" requirements for most passenger vehicles and light trucks sold in the United States, beginning with model year 1983. The domestic content requirements—calculated as U.S. value added as a percentage of the wholesale price—would have to be met by each domestic and foreign auto manufacturer producing more than 100,000 units for sale in the U.S. market. These requirements would be graduated according to the volume of vehicles sold by each manufacturer. After the first year of implementation, increasingly stringent requirements would be imposed until 1985, when the provisions of the bill are to be fully phased in (see Table 1).

Table 1. Domestic Auto Content Requirements Under the Fair Practices in Automotive Products Act

No. of Vehicles Sold in the U.S.	Required Minimum Percentage U.S. Content Requirement		
	1983	1984	1985
Fewer than 100,000	0	0	0
100,000 to 149,999	8.3	16.7	25.0
150,000 to 199,999	16.7	33.3	50.0
200,000 to 499,999	25.0	50.0	75.0
500,000 or more	30.0	60.0	90.0

Source: H.R. 5133.

EFFECTS ON FOREIGN PRODUCERS

H.R. 5133 would impose penalties on producers who failed to meet their domestic content requirements. Any manufacturer—foreign or domestic—that violated the requirement in any model year would have to reduce its total U.S. sales of vehicles and parts by 25 percent in the following model year. Thus, a manufacturer selling 400,000 units in the United States in

7. Domestic Content Legislation and the U.S. Automobile Industry, prepared for Subcomm. on Trade, House Comm. on Ways & Means, 97th Cong., 2d Sess. 7–10 (Committee Print No. WMCP: 97–33, 1982).

1985 but failing to meet its domestic content requirement would be forced to reduce its sales to the U.S. market to 300,000 units in 1986.

The greatest direct effect of this legislation would be on the six large-volume Japanese auto producers and one German firm—Toyota, Nissan, Honda, Toyo Kagyo, Subaru, Mitsubishi, and Volkswagen. If these firms desired to maintain a high sales volume in the U.S. market, they could realistically comply with the provisions of the bill only by relocating a significant proportion of production to the United States; otherwise they would each ultimately be forced to limit sales in the United States to 100,000 units a year. Even if these foreign auto producers were to relocate their production facilities to U.S. sites, they would need to meet a 75 percent domestic content requirement overall in order to sell as few as 200,000 units per year. This is a stringent requirement that would demand not only the relocation of assembly, stamping, engine, and transmission facilities to the United States, but also the purchase by these foreign producers of substantial amounts of domestically produced parts and materials as well.

Because these firms would probably thereby suffer the loss of the current cost advantages they enjoy, if the proposed domestic content requirement were implemented, no sizable shift of foreign production facilities to the United States would likely occur. Rather, the practical effect of the bill would be the imposition of a rigid import quota of 100,000 units per year on each foreign auto producer. By 1990, the bill would have the effect of reducing auto imports to the United States to about 1.3 million units, approximately one-third of the 3.75 million units that might otherwise have been imported for that year.

PRIMARY ECONOMIC EFFECTS OF DOMESTIC CONTENT REQUIREMENTS

The domestic content requirement legislation would undoubtedly have a profound effect on employment and output in the U.S. automotive and related industries. Assuming that domestic sales of new cars return to earlier high trend rates, H.R. 5133 would displace about 2.4 million foreign cars by 1990, increasing the demand for domestically produced vehicles by about 1.6 million units more than otherwise. Though sizable, this estimated increase in U.S. auto production is smaller than the reduction in imports, because the attendant rise in new U.S. auto prices would dampen domestic sales. Corresponding to this increase in domestic production, the Congressional Budget Office's results suggest that employment in auto and auto-related industries would rise by about 211,000 jobs more than otherwise by 1990.

Despite these effects on the U.S. auto industry, the CBO's analysis of H.R. 5133 implies that the net effects for the U.S. economy in terms of real economic growth, inflation, and employment would be negative though small. In other words, the benefits that would probably accrue to the U.S. automotive industry could be more than offset by the costs imposed on the rest of the economy.

POSSIBLE RESPONSES OF U.S. TRADING PARTNERS

H.R. 5133 would adversely affect the performance of the U.S. economy for a number of reasons. The implied restrictions on auto imports invite retaliatory trade measures on the part of the United States' trading partners, a response sanctioned by the articles of the General Agreement on Tariffs and Trade (GATT). Such measures would raise domestic auto prices and with them, the overall rate of inflation; and they would depress our long-run economic growth potential by misallocating scarce economic resources.

Notes and Questions

(1) The House of Representatives passed the bill described in 1982, but the Senate failed to act upon it.[8] As of this writing, domestic-content legislation to protect the U.S. automobile industry remains pending in Congress.

(2) Would the proposed legislation be consistent with GATT? Consider Articles I, III, XI, XIII and XVII:1. Would the exemptions in Articles XIX or XX apply?

(3) As noted in Section 7.3 supra, the United States has a sort of a free-trade agreement in automobiles with Canada. If the proposed legislation exempted Canada (or otherwise treated Canada differently), would any additional GATT problems arise?

(4) The United States-Japan FCN Treaty requires the United States to accord Japanese products national and most-favored-nation treatment "in all matters affecting internal taxation, sale, distribution, storage and use."[9] Is the proposed legislation consistent with the Treaty?

SECTION 8.3 EXCEPTION FOR NATIONAL SOCIAL AND ECONOMIC PROGRAMS

(A) INTRODUCTION

Article XX of GATT provides a series of potentially broad exceptions to all GATT obligations, including the national treatment obligations. The opening paragraph of this article, however, could be interpreted to impose a loose form of both the MFN and national treatment obligations:[1]

> Subject to the requirement that such measures are not applied in a manner which would constitute a means of arbitrary or unjustifiable discrimination between countries where the same conditions prevail, or a disguised restriction on international trade, nothing in this Agreement shall be construed to prevent the adoption or enforcement by any contracting party of measures: * * *

The difficulty of resolving the many situations where domestic measures are based on legitimate goals, but also impinge on international economic policies, was recognized in the United States Trade Act of 1974, particularly in the framing of section 102 governing NTB agreements. Some of the many possibilities have been explored in Section 8.2 above, and in cases reproduced elsewhere in these materials.[2] The following materials include a few more

---

8. See generally Note, Domestic Content Requirements, note 4 supra; H.Rep.No. 98–287, 98th Cong., 1st Sess. (1983).

9. Treaty of Friendship, Commerce and Navigation, April 2, 1953, arts. XXII(1), XVI(1), 4 UST 2063, TIAS No. 2863.

1. Another important exception to GATT obligations can be found in Article XXI of GATT, concerning national security. This will be taken up in Chapters 12 and 13 infra.

2. See C.S. Tupman Thurlow Co. v. Moss, 252 F.Supp. 641 (D.C.Tenn.1965), and Portland

examples which illustrate the difficulty of reconciling conflicting policy objectives. Sometimes a legitimate domestic policy objective becomes the guise for an unnecessarily "overreaching" effect on imports.

(B) LABELLING

HAWAII v. HO [3]
Supreme Court of Hawaii, 1957.
41 Hawaii 565.

MARUMOTO, J.

In this case, information was filed against defendant for offering or exposing for sale imported chicken shell eggs of Australian origin without complying with section 1308.02 of the Revised Laws of Hawaii 1945. The section is a new section added to chapter 20 of the Revised Laws, relating to sale of eggs, by section 5 of Act 167 of the Session Laws of 1955. It provides that it is unlawful for any person to sell, offer or expose for sale any imported chicken shell eggs of foreign origin unless a placard bearing the words "WE SELL FOREIGN EGGS" printed in legible boldface letters of a size not less than three inches in height is displayed in a conspicuous place where the customers entering can see it.

* * *

[The lower court ruled that the Act deprived defendant of property in violation of due process requirements, was an unconstitutional delegation of powers and was in contravention of GATT. The Supreme Court discussed only the latter ground.]

The General Agreement on Tariffs and Trade is a multilateral agreement originally entered into on October 30, 1947, by twenty-three nations, including the United States and Australia. (61 Stat. Part 5) It was modified by the Geneva Protocol of September 14, 1948. (62 Stat. 3679) It was executed on behalf of the United States by a plenipotentiary of the President. It is not a treaty made by the President by and with the advice and consent of the Senate under Article II, section 2, of the Constitution of the United States. It is an executive agreement made in the exercise of the authority granted to the President "To enter into foreign trade agreements with foreign governments or instrumentalities thereof," under section 350(a) of the Tariff Act of 1930, as amended. The constitutionality of the grant of such authority has been repeatedly questioned in and out of Congress.

Pipe Line Co. v. Environmental Improvement Commn., 307 A.2d 1 (Me.1973), excerpted in Section 3.6 supra.

3. See J. Jackson, World Trade and the Law of GATT 287–288, 111 & n. 11 (1969). A complaint was brought in GATT concerning the Hawaiian egg labelling provision (GATT Doc. L/411 [Sept.1955]), but the complaint was shelved after the court decision reproduced in the text above. In connection with the court litigation, the Dept. of State (through Mr. Herman Phleger, then legal advisor) wrote to Mr. Sharpless, acting Attorney General of Hawaii, February 26, 1957, opposing the conclusion expressed in the court's opinion that GATT was directly applicable, superseding state law. See the text of this letter on file in the Dept. of the Attorney General of Hawaii, as contained and certified in an affidavit of April 5, 1967, by Burtee Kobayshi, Attorney General of the State of Hawaii, filed by the attorneys for plaintiff in Bethlehem Steel Corp. v. Board of Commrs., 276 C.A.2d 221, 80 Cal.Rptr. 800 (1969); partly quoted in Section 5.4(D) supra; also quoted in L. Ebb, Regulation and Protection of International Business: Cases, Comments and Materials 763 (1964).

Nevertheless, Congress has extended from time to time the period during which the President may exercise such authority. The latest extension is contained in Trade Agreements Extension Act of 1955, which extends the authority until the close of June 30, 1958. In the Act, Congress provided, "That the enactment of the Trade Agreements Extension Act of 1955 shall not be construed to determine or indicate the approval or disapproval by the Congress of the executive agreement known as the General Agreement on Tariffs and Trade."

Article VI, clause 2, of the Constitution of the United States provides that "all Treaties made, or which shall be made, under the Authority of the United States, shall be the supreme Law of the Land." Under this constitutional provision, there is no question that a treaty made by the President, by and with the advice and consent of the Senate is the supreme law of the land, overriding all state laws in conflict therewith. This case poses the question: Is an executive agreement, such as the General Agreement on Tariffs and Trade, a treaty within the meaning of this constitutional provision, so that it has the same efficacy as a treaty made by the President by and with the advice and consent of the Senate? We think that it is, under the decisions of the Supreme Court of the United States in United States v. Belmont, 301 U.S. 324, 57 S.Ct. 758, 81 L.Ed. 1134, and United States v. Pink, 315 U.S. 203, 62 S.Ct. 552, 86 L.Ed. 796. * * * [see Section 3.3(C)(2) supra.]

The Territory is *a fortiori* bound by an international agreement having the dignity of a treaty because section 55 of the Organic Act specifically enjoins that its legislative power be exercised consistently with the Constitution and laws of the United States.

Then, in what respects does section 5 of Act 167 contravene the General Agreement on Tariffs and Trade?

The General Agreement on Tariffs and Trade provides in Article III, paragraphs 1 and 4, as follows:

* * *

[The quoted provisions are found in the Documentary Supplement]

Certain exceptions to the above quoted provisions are set forth in Article XX of the agreement, as follows:

* * *

[The quoted provisions are found in the Documentary Supplement]

Section 5 of Act 167, in requiring a conspicuous display of a placard of origin, singles out chicken shell eggs of foreign origin from domestic eggs. No such requirement is imposed in connection with the sale, or offering or exposing for sale, of chicken shell eggs of local or mainland origin. That its purpose is to protect domestic production is indicated by the following statement in Standing Committee Report No. 482 to the President of the Senate, Twenty-Eighth Legislature: "Your Committee conducted a public hearing at which time it was determined that the majority of poultrymen in the Territory were in favor of this measure." Thus, it contravenes the proscription of Article III, paragraph 1, of the General Agreement on Tariffs and Trade that internal laws affecting the internal sale or offering for sale should not be applied to imported products so as to afford protection to domestic production. Furthermore, in imposing an additional requirement on foreign eggs which is not imposed on domestic eggs, it contravenes Article III, paragraph 4, of the agreement which provides that the products of the territory of any contracting party imported into the territory of any other contracting party shall be accorded treatment no less favorable than that accorded to like products of national origin in respect of all laws affecting their internal sale or offering for sale.

The requirement of section 5 of Act 167 does not come within any of the exceptions in Article XX of the agreement. Such requirement is not necessary for the protection of public morals; nor is it necessary for the protection of human, animal or plant life or health.

If it be deemed that a measure to prevent deceptive practices is necessary, such a measure, more comprehensive and nondiscriminatory, is found in section 1308 of the Revised Laws, which provides: "In the case of eggs imported from the mainland United States or foreign countries, regardless of the person producing the same, each egg so imported shall be marked in clear and plain letters, of not less than twelve point type, the letters 'U.S.', if such egg was produced in the mainland United States, or the name of the country, if such egg was produced in a foreign country, before such eggs may be removed from any dock or landing * * *." The exception under Article XX of a measure relating to the prevention of deceptive practices is subject to the requirement that such a measure is not applied "in a manner which would constitute a means of arbitrary or unjustifiable discrimination between countries where the same conditions prevail, or a disguised restriction on international trade." We think that the additional requirement of a placard of origin only in the case of foreign eggs constitutes a disguised restriction on international trade.

The order sustaining the demurrer, dismissing the indictment and discharging defendant from custody is affirmed.

Concurring Opinion of STAINBACK, J.

* * *

While we as a Nation do not, as the Chinese, label all foreigners as "foreign devils," the term "foreign" indicates some inferiority or undesirable quality in the product. This is not the same as requiring the name of a particular country to be placed upon its product, as such may often be regarded as highly complimentary rather than otherwise. For examples: terms such as "French wines," "English woolens," "New Zealand butter," or "Australian wool," would be beneficial as these products are considered of exceptionally high quality throughout the world, while the term "foreign" standing alone does not so indicate but the contrary is implied when such is required by law. The eggs may be from Timbuktu or anywhere on the globe under such a label.

As stated above, ordinarily for a law to be unconstitutional it must clearly violate a provision of the Constitution and in construing the same all doubt is resolved in favor of the constitutionality of the Act, but we have a different rule in construing treaties and that is the so-called rule of *uberrima fides*. Where a treaty admits of two constructions, the one giving the most favorable rights is to be preferred. (Johnson v. Brown, 205 U.S. 309, 27 S.Ct. 539, 51 L.Ed. 816.)

Following this rule, the designation of "foreign eggs" is not as favorable a treatment "in respect of all laws, regulations and requirements affecting their internal sale, offering for sale, purchase, transportation, distribution or use," as is accorded to the sellers of domestic eggs, and therefore the requirement contravenes the General Agreement on Tariffs and Trade.

Notes and Questions

(1) See also GATT Article IX, and J. Jackson, World Trade and the Law of GATT (1969) at 459 ff. The author states (at 460):

> It should be recalled that Article III requires national treatment to be accorded to imported products "in respect of all laws, regulations and requirements." These laws, regulations, and requirements would include marking requirements, as a Working Party report in 1958 indicated. Indeed, the wording of Article III may even imply that regulations with respect to marks of origin should be the same for domestic products as for imported products. This hardly seems reasonable, however, since the specific treatment of questions regarding marks of origin in Article IX suggests that marks of origin are an exception to the national treatment rule of Article III. This is also confirmed by the 1958 recommendation of the Contracting Parties, which urges that marks of origin requirements should be limited to the obligation "to indicate the origin of the imported product."

Do you agree?

(2) An April, 1967 order of the United States Federal Trade Commission changed its labelling rules concerning fur products, by requiring animals formerly designated as "Mink, Japanese" to be henceforth designated as "Japanese Weasel." See 16 C.F.R. § 301.0 (1985). A Wall Street Journal article of May 8, 1967, entitled "FTC Labels a 'Mink' from Japan a Weasel—and the Fur Flies," notes that all mink whether Asian or American are members of the weasel family, and implies that the desire of the FTC to require Japanese mink to be labeled weasel may stem from a desire to protect U.S. mink ranchers from competition of the Japanese fur. Has GATT been violated by the F.T.C. action?

(C) POLLUTION

Pollution regulation poses some special problems for international trade policy. A nation could ban sale or importation of certain goods (domestically or foreign produced) which pose pollution hazards, and this nondiscriminatory treatment would not conflict with GATT. But suppose a tax system was preferred, or suppose the problem was not that the goods polluted, but that the *process* of making the goods caused pollution. Several of these issues are carefully discussed in a 1972 article by Professor Kirgis, a small portion of which is excerpted here:

FREDERIC L. KIRGIS, JR., EFFECTIVE POLLUTION CONTROL IN INDUSTRIALIZED COUNTRIES: INTERNATIONAL ECONOMIC DISINCENTIVES, POLICY RESPONSES AND THE GATT

(1972).[3]

1. THE CONSUMPTION TAX OR EQUIVALENT REGULATION

If country *A* taxes the consumption (sale, use, or disposal) of a product that itself causes pollution damage, regardless of the product's origin, and the tax is uniformly applied without exemption or rebate, there would be no inconsistency with articles I through III. In particular, articles II and paragraph 2 of article III are tailored to turnover and use taxes applied to final products, and impose no obstacle to them so long as they are uniformly applied. The only significant question concerning bound items would arise if the consumption tax were a disguised import duty. It would not be considered such if it were applied equally to domestic products and to imports.

As we have seen, however, if consumption taxes are to be effective inducements to pollution-damage avoidance, they would have to provide exemptions whenever the excess social cost imposed by the taxed commodity has been eliminated. Measures to that end could be expected to be taken primarily at the production stage. Thus, if a product is produced in two or more exporting countries, imports from one country might be taxed (because the producer has not taken steps to eliminate excess social cost from consumption) while those from another are not. Similarly, the tax might exempt some home-produced goods, but not damage-inflicting "like" imports. The question in these cases is whether most-favored-nation treatment, or the equality-of-internal-charge requirement of article III, paragraph 2, requires exemption for the environmentally offensive imports.

Several exceptions to most-favored-nation treatment are written into the General Agreement, and there have been derogations from it with and without benefit of formal GATT waiver. Nevertheless, much of GATT is built around the most-favored-nation principle, and there is no precedent for deviating from it on pollution-control grounds. It retains enough vitality in relations among industrially developed nations to affect the decisions made by national officials seeking to implement any pollution-control approach.

Taken literally, article I would require consumption tax exemption for all imports of like products when the exemption is granted to imports from any external source. The tax would be a "matter" referred to in paragraph 2 of article III (and thus covered by article I); the obligation is to accord all parties any advantage granted to the like product originating in any other country. Any argument to the effect that pollution-engendering and pollution-free imports are not "like products" for most-favored-nation purposes is unpersuasive unless, perhaps, a number of countries adopt such a distinction for tariff classification purposes.

* * *

3. 70 Mich.L.Rev. 859, 889–96. Reprinted by permission of the Michigan Law Review Association. See also S. Rubin & T. Graham (eds.), Environment and Trade (1982).

The "health protection" exception to most-favored-nation treatment is generally recognized to be necessary, but susceptible to abuse. Article XX reflects the fear of abuse, although its attempt to deal with the situation is hardly a model of clarity. The standards are not readily apparent by which to judge whether a discrimination between countries in which the same conditions prevail is or is not "justifiable," nor is the meaning of "disguised restriction on international trade" perfectly clear. Nevertheless, if the taxing country is able to demonstrate a danger to human, animal, or plant health from pollution arising in the consumption of the taxed products, and if it administers the tax evenhandedly among its own products and all foreign products from whatever source, there would seem to be strong grounds for permissibility under article XX(b).

It might still be asked whether the consumption tax approach, with its exemptions for pollution-damage avoidance, is "necessary" to protect health, since other means of protection might be used. An adequate answer is that if some measures are necessary in order to deal with the matter, there is no inconsistency with the "necessary" requirement of article XX unless it could be shown that the measures adopted are clearly unsuited to the health protection objective. This does no violence either to the over-all goals of GATT or to the most-favored-nation principle. Any other view would unduly limit the discretion of GATT members to protect domestic health by means that seem most appropriate to them, and would render article XX(b) too restrictive to have any influence over the actual conduct of national decision-makers.

The applicability of article XX(g), concerning conservation of natural resources, is less clear. It was intended primarily to authorize export controls on products drawn from natural resources that are in danger of being exhausted from overexploitation. It is nevertheless arguable that the consumption tax, which attempts to conserve natural resources "exhaustible" in the sense that they may not survive the pollution inflicted on them (and which involves a restriction on domestic consumption), would fall within the provision. In the light of the clearer applicability of article XX(b), however, such an attempt to stretch article XX(g) is unnecessary.

As with article I, principles of nondiscrimination support article III, paragraph 2, concerning equality of tax treatment between domestic and imported products. A drafting subcommittee at the Havana Conference noted that article III, paragraph 8(b), dealing with the payment of subsidies to domestic producers, "was redrafted in order to make it clear that nothing in Article [III] could be construed to sanction the exemption of domestic products from internal taxes imposed on like imported products or the remission of such taxes." This suggests that the exemption from consumption tax for avoidance of pollution damage by domestic products could run afoul of article III, paragraph 2 in the absence of an applicable exception elsewhere in the General Agreement. The purpose of article III, paragraph 2, however, is to prevent disguised protection for domestic products. When the domestic tax exemption is not simply in favor of the domestic product at the expense of the like imported product—i.e., is available to products from any source—a finding of incompatibility with article III, paragraph 2 would not be required by the remarks of the drafting subcommittee or by the language of article III, paragraph 2, interpreted in light of its purpose. However, it is not necessary to dwell on this point, since the health exception of article XX(b) is also applicable to article III, paragraph 2. As indicated above, this exception would fit the consumption tax case. It is broad enough to encompass bound as well as unbound items.

* * *

2. THE PRODUCTION TAX OR EQUIVALENT REGULATION

a. *Articles I through III.* As we have seen, it would be appropriate for A to deal with pollution arising in the production process (for example from waste disposal) through a production tax or comparable regulation. This may also be a convenient means of attacking some consumption pollution, if a substantial portion of domestic production is sold in the home market. The question is whether a charge on imports designed to offset the domestic producers' cost disadvantage could be imposed consistently with A's GATT obligations stemming from articles I through III.

For ease of tariff administration, the charge would probably be applied equally to imports from all sources, even though the price of the imports might reflect differing (foreign) pollution-control costs. If A did attempt to serve equity by providing an exemption for imports already burdened by significant pollution-control costs (or by charging only unburdened imports), it would be open to a most-favored-nation challenge from suppliers who have not been subjected to strong pollution control. Article I is squarely applicable, unless it could successfully be argued that "discrimination" by reference to pollution-control costs, rather than by country, removes the case.

———

Query: Can Country A impose a tax equivalent to a production tax on imports from Country B of a product subject to a tariff binding without violating the binding? Consider Article XX. Assuming the health hazards are caused by the production of the product, can A rely on Article XX in violating a tariff binding when the health hazards associated with the product are faced by the citizens of B, the producing country, and not by the citizens of A, where it is consumed?

CHARLES PEARSON, IMPLICATIONS FOR THE TRADE AND INVESTMENT OF DEVELOPING COUNTRIES OF UNITED STATES ENVIRONMENTAL CONTROLS

(1976) [4]

82. The critical issue is whether environmentally related product standards are a legitimate reflection of domestic environmental objectives, or whether they are used as covert measures to restrict trade and protect domestic producers. The best distinguishing test is reference to the two principles of national treatment and non-discriminatory treatment of imports.

4. From a study commissioned by United Nations Conference on Trade and Develop- ment, U.N. Doc. TC/B/C.2/150/Add. 1/Rev. 1, at 28–31.

83. The official United States policy towards environmentally related product standards is adherence to the relevant sections of the OECD guiding principles:

9. Measures taken to protect the environment should be framed as far as possible in such a manner as to avoid the creation of nontariff barriers to trade.

10. Where products are traded internationally and where there could be significant obstacles to trade, Governments should seek common standards for polluting products and agree on the timing and general scope of regulations for particular products.

NATIONAL TREATMENT AND NONDISCRIMINATION

11. In conformity with the provision of the GATT, measures taken within an environmental policy, regarding polluting products, should be applied in accordance with the principle of national treatment (i.e. identical treatment for imported products and similar domestic products) and with the principle of non-discrimination (identical treatment for imported products regardless of their national origin).

PROCEDURES OF CONTROL

12. It is highly desirable to define in common, as rapidly as possible, procedures for checking conformity to product standards established for the purpose of environmental control. Procedures for checking conformity to standards should be mutually agreed so as to be applied by an exporting country to the satisfaction of the importing country.

84. The present preliminary review of environment related product standards does not seem to indicate that such standards in the United States are now being used as covert restrictions on international trade.

85. Even if United States product standards are legitimate, as described above, developing countries will wish to know the additional cost and difficulty to their exporters associated with these standards. The costs and difficulties arise from:

(a) Adaption of the product to meet United States standards (small suppliers may become uncompetitive, as short production runs imply higher costs);

(b) The delay and expense of testing and inspection by United States Customs;

(c) The difficulty and expense of attaining inspection approval during the manufacturing process;

(d) Arbitrary or capricious action by customs officials, and associated uncertainty.

*   *   *

102. Looked at from another perspective, the most serious issue is one of information. The covert use of environmental regulations for trade restriction should be monitored. The according of national treatment to imports should be assured. Timely knowledge of areas for impending regulation and details concerning current standards are required. The

procedures for inspection and certification must be known, and the costs and delays kept to a minimum. These are serious issues that affect market access. But they are identical to the issues posed by other non-tariff barriers.

* * *

105. Finally, developing-country exporters would benefit materially if product standards were harmonized, as far as possible, throughout the industrial countries. Harmonization would permit increased production runs and economies of scale, and reduce delay and uncertainty surrounding inspection and certification. The present study indicates considerable scope for harmonization of standards in areas such as pesticide residues, noise abatement and radiation emission levels.

Notes and Questions

(1) How would you draft an international rule to deal with the following:

Country A has stringent pollution controls on smoke emission and sewage discharge from manufacturing plants, the cost of which adds 5% to the price charged for widgets produced in A. Country X (industrialized) and country Y (developing) do not have such controls. Widgets produced in X and Y are shipped to A. These widgets do not themselves pollute in any way, but are 5% cheaper than widgets produced in A and therefore are capturing an increasing percentage of the total rising consumption market in A.

(2) There are numerous bilateral, regional and worldwide agreements that regulate various aspects of environmental protection. Most of these agreements are aimed at specific problems, such as marine oil pollution, or are regional in nature, such as those that deal with a specific river basin.[5] The OECD has been active in promoting harmonized pollution and similar standards so as to reduce barriers to trade.[6]

(D) OTHER LAWS

UNITED STATES—IMPORTS OF CERTAIN AUTOMOTIVE SPRING ASSEMBLIES

Report of the Panel adopted on 26 May 1983 [7]

[A U.S. patent holder obtained an order from the International Trade Commission (ITC) excluding infringing products from entry into the United States pursuant to Section 337 of the Tariff Act of 1930, discussed in Section 10.4 infra. The order excluded, inter alia, the products of a Canadian company, and Canada complained in GATT in 1981.]

IV. Conclusions

49. In accordance with its terms of reference, the Panel examined the exclusion of imports of certain automotive spring assemblies by the United States under Section 337 of the United States Tariff Act of 1930. The

---

5. See generally Bureau of National Affairs, International Environmental Reporter (looseleaf); L. Caldwell, International Environmental Policy: Emergence and Dimensions (1984).

6. For a recent OECD publication in this area, see OECD, Transfrontier Pollution and the Role of States (1981).

7. GATT, 30th Supp. BISD 107 (1984).

provisions of the GATT considered to be relevant were Articles II:1*(b)*, III:1, 2 and 4, XI:1 and XX*(d)*.

* * * The Panel came to the conclusion that its first step should be to consider whether or not the exception provision of Article XX*(d)* applied in this case. The Panel considered that if Article XX*(d)* applied, then an examination of the question of the consistency of the exclusion order with the other GATT provisions cited above would not be required.

* * *

55. The Panel noted that the exclusion order was directed against imports of certain automotive spring assemblies produced in violation of a valid United States patent from all foreign sources, and not just from Canada. It found, therefore, that the exclusion order was "not applied in a manner which would constitute a means of arbitrary or unjustifiable discrimination against countries where the same conditions prevail."

56. The Panel then considered whether or not the exclusion order was "applied in a manner which would constitute a disguised restriction on international trade." The Panel noted that the Preamble of Article XX made it clear that it was the application of the measure and not the measure itself that needed to be examined. Notice of the exclusion order was published in the Federal Register and the order was enforced by the United States Customs at the border. The Panel also noted that the ITC proceedings in this particular case were directed against the importation of automotive spring assemblies produced in violation of a valid United States patent and that, before an exclusion order could be issued under Section 337, both the validity of a patent and its infringement by a foreign manufacturer had to be clearly established. Furthermore, the exclusion order would not prohibit the importation of automotive spring assemblies produced by any producer outside the United States who had a license from Kuhlman Corporation (Kuhlman) to produce these goods. Consequently, the Panel found that the exclusion order had not been applied in a manner which constituted a disguised restriction on international trade.

* * *

58. The Panel considered whether the ITC action, in making the exclusion order, was "necessary" in the sense of paragraph *(d)* of Article XX to secure compliance with United States patent law. In this connection the Panel examined whether a satisfactory and effective alternative existed under civil court procedures which would have provided the patent holder Kuhlman with a sufficiently effective remedy against the violation of its patent by foreign producers including the Canadian producer Wallbank Manufacturing Co. Ltd (Wallbank).

59. The Panel noted that if Kuhlman had pursued the action it had commenced before the United States district court, it could have joined General Motors, Ford and possibly other known users of the automotive spring assemblies in the action and, once the patent had been found to be valid by the court, prevented these parties, but not unknown users, from utilizing the automotive spring assemblies produced by Wallbank by means of an injunction or a cease and desist order. The Panel decided, however, that such a remedy would not have been sufficient to protect Kuhlman's

patent rights because, in practice, it would have been effective only in relation to the automotive spring assemblies produced by Wallbank and supplied to parties joined in the court action. The same remedy would not have been effective against other possible foreign infringers of the United States patent and potential users of the infringing product in the United States. Furthermore, in view of the relatively simple manufacturing process used to produce automotive spring assemblies, these could without major difficulties be produced by other foreign producers infringing Kuhlman's patent and subsequently imported for use in the United States.

60. Against the background of the above considerations, it was the view of the Panel that United States civil court action would not have provided a satisfactory and effective means of protecting Kuhlman's patent rights against importation of the infringing product. * * *

Notes and Questions

As indicated in the Spring Assemblies case, Section 337 provides a sort of analog to various domestic U.S. laws, such as FTC (Federal Trade Commission) statutes and rules regarding unfair trade, common-law contract principles of unfair trade, patent infringement actions, etc. In many cases the United States can argue that an exclusion order stopping imports at the border is a necessary remedy for situations where it is difficult to bring a foreign party into a court under domestic U.S. laws. On the other hand the GATT Panel did not give the U.S. Section 337 process a completely clean bill of health—it noted in concluding remarks that

66. The Panel did not * * * exclude the strong possibility that there might be cases, for example, involving high-cost products of an advanced technical nature and with a very limited number of potential users in the United States, where a procedure before a United States court might provide the patent holder with an equally satisfactory and effective remedy against infringement of his patent right. In such cases the use of an exclusion order under Section 337 might not be necessary in terms of Article XX(d) * * *

Would Article XX, which explicitly mentions patent matters, offer equally an exception for the use of Section 337 in non-patent unfair trade matters?

U.S. law provides protection for something called a "process patent", so that when a party, which produces goods that are not themselves patented, uses a process for production that is patented, compensation can be obtained by the patent holder. What happens when the patented process is used in a foreign country to produce goods which are then shipped to the U.S. market? Is a Section 337-type remedy sufficient protection for the U.S. patent holder? We discuss Section 337 in general in Section 10.4 infra.

(E) PROBLEMS

(1) Could the United States, consistently with its GATT obligations, establish the following auto safety provisions for both domestically manufactured and imported autos:

(a) five passenger seat belts in each car;

(b) each auto must withstand damage in a collision at 10 m.p.h.;

   (c) same as b), if facts establish that most very small cars cannot comply and that imports comprise 90% of the sales of very small cars;

   (d) a new regulation such as b) effective immediately (without notice);

   (e) all imports must be tested for compliance with the regulation described in b) above, by driving the car into a wall at 10 m.p.h.;

   (f) all autos must have tinted glass protecting against sunglare (which adds $200 to the price of each auto); the major source of tinted auto glass is located in the United States. No foreign country imposes such a requirement, so foreign manufacturers do not include such glass in standard cars, and as an option the cost is $400.

(2) Could the United States impose a tax (sales or excise) on each car to be sold in the United States that did not comply with any of the regulations mentioned in problem 1)? For example,

   (a) a flat $500 tax?;

   (b) a 10% tax, regardless of extent of defect?

SECTION 8.4 GOVERNMENT PURCHASES

Because of explicit exceptions in GATT language (see especially Article III, paragraph 8(a)),[1] government purchases are not limited by the national treatment obligation of GATT, and because of the language of Article I, it is generally considered that the MFN obligation also does not apply to government purchases,[2] although Article XVII contains a modest constraint on purchases of state enterprises. Consequently, prior to the Tokyo Round, governments were generally free in their procurement policies to discriminate in favor of domestic goods, or in favor of the goods of one country over another. For example, the U.S. Buy American Act of 1933, as implemented by Executive Order, essentially required federal agencies to buy domestically produced goods unless the price was unreasonable or such purchase was otherwise not in the public interest. In practice, domestic suppliers were favored if their price was not more than 6 or 12 percent (50 percent in the case of Defense Department procurement) above that offered by foreign suppliers. In addition, there were specific statutes that required certain federal government purchases to be made only from domestic suppliers.[3]

The existence of statutes or policies favoring domestic suppliers was a source of considerable aggravation, particularly to certain industries (e.g., aircraft and electric turbines) whose products are often purchased by governments. Moreover, in recent years it seemed that the government owned or operated sector of the economy in many countries represented an increasing

---

1. Compare Article XVII of GATT; see further, S. Metzger, Lowering Nontariff Barriers: U.S. Law, Practice and Negotiating Objectives ch. 3 (1974); R. Baldwin, Nontariff Distortions of International Trade ch. 3 (1970); Hobin, GATT, the California Buy American Act, and the Continuing Struggle Between Free Trade and Protectionism, 52 Calif.L.Rev. 335 (1964); OECD, Government Purchasing in Europe, North America and Japan: Regulations and Procedures (1966); OECD, Government Purchasing (1976).

2. See J. Jackson, World Trade and the Law of GATT 291 (1969).

3. See S.Rep. No. 96–249, 96th Cong., 1st Sess. 131–32 (1979).

percentage of the whole economy, with the result that an increasing amount of economic activity was escaping the discipline of the international trade rules. This was a significant part of the motivation which led major nations to undertake, in the Tokyo Round, to negotiate a code on government purchases (discussed in subsection (B) below). First, however, we examine the original GATT rules on government purchases.

(A) GATT ARTICLE III AND THE EXCEPTION FOR GOVERN-MENT PURCHASES

As noted above, Article III(8) largely exempts government purchases from GATT constraints. Interpretation of that exemption, however, raises a number of difficult questions concerning its scope. For example, what is "procurement by governmental agencies of products purchased for governmental purposes?" If a city-owned electric utility buys equipment, does the purchase fall within the exemption? The cases of Bethlehem Steel Corp. v. Board of Commissioners and K.S.B. Technical Sales Corp. v. North Jersey Dist. Water Supply Commn., discussed in Section 3.6(D) supra, involved this issue. An earlier case in a lower California court dealt with the issue as follows:

BALDWIN–LIMA–HAMILTON CORP. v. SUPERIOR COURT

District Court of Appeal, 1st District Division 1, California, 1962.
208 Cal.App.2d 803, 25 Cal.Rptr. 798.

[In a complicated procedural setting not relevant here, the court considered whether the City and County of San Francisco, in accepting bids for delivery of turbines, generators, valves and pipes for the Canyon Generating Station, could require all goods to be manufactured in the United States pursuant to the "California Buy American Statute" [4] and thereby exclude the use of Canadian and Japanese goods. The court said:]

However, it is also clear, under the authorities relied upon by the city attorney of San Francisco in his opinion rendered to Benas, adopted by the respondent superior court in its memorandum opinion, recognized by Baldwin and not disputed by Allis in their arguments before us, that the California Buy American statute and the above "place of manufacture" clause in the bid call of November 20, 1961, are unenforceable in the situation now before us since they conflict with certain treaties and agreements and thus with the " 'supreme law of the land.' "

At Geneva on October 30, 1947, the United States and 22 other nations entered into a "General Agreement on Tariffs and Trade" (61 Stat., part 5) which for brevity we will hereafter refer to as GATT. Canada was an original signatory thereto. Japan became a signatory thereto effective September 10, 1955.

Paragraph 2 [now 4] of article III of part II of GATT (61 Stat., part 5, p. A18) provides: "The products of the territory of any contracting party

---

4. The California Buy American Act of 1933 (as amended), Cal.Gov't Code §§ 4300–4305; West's Ann.Gov.Code §§ 4300–4305; see also Usher, California's Buy-American Policy: Conflict with GATT and the Constitution, 17 Stan.L.Rev. 119 (1964).

imported into the territory of any other contracting party shall be accorded treatment no less favourable than that accorded to like products of national origin in respect of all laws, regulations and requirements affecting their internal sale, offering for sale, purchase, transportation, distribution, or use. * * *"

Paragraph 5 [now 8(2)] of article III of part II (61 Stat., part 5, p. A19) provides: "The provisions of this Article shall not apply to the procurement by governmental agencies of products purchased for governmental purposes and not for resale or use in the production of goods for sale, * * *."

Under GATT therefore the products of Canada and Japan imported into the United States must be treated no less favorably than like products of such nation of destination. The exception contained in paragraph 5, which we quote immediately above, is not operative in the instant situation since the turbines and other equipment are for use in the generation of electric power for resale and hence for "use in the production of goods for sale." Electricity is a commodity which, like other goods, can be manufactured, transported and sold.

The United States Constitution provides in article VI thereof that "* * * Treaties made * * * under the Authority of the United States, shall be the supreme Law of the Land; * * *" When a state statute conflicts with any such treaty, the latter will control. Compacts and similar international agreements, such as GATT, which are negotiated and proclaimed by the President are "treaties" within the above supremacy clause of the Constitution.

The written opinion of the city attorney of San Francisco to Benas under date of December 29, 1961, which we find attached as an exhibit to Baldwin's complaint in intervention, follows the above reasoning and authorities to hold that the foreign components proposed to be obtained by Baldwin from Canada and Japan were protected by GATT and that the Japanese components were also accorded "'most-favored-nation treatment'" under the "'Treaty of Friendship, Commerce and Navigation,'" signed at Tokyo April 2, 1953. It was in this opinion that the city attorney advised Benas that the California Buy American statute was superseded by the above treaties and that Benas was required to disregard the factor that Baldwin's low bid (bid No. 3) did not conform to the specifications set forth in the "place of manufacture" provision.

We agree that under the foregoing authorities the "place of manufacture" provision contained in the November 20, 1961, bid call has no operative effect in the instant case to restrict or preclude the furnishing of material or equipment produced in Canada or Japan. The result therefore is a nullification of the provision as effectively as if it had not been included in the bid call in the first place. It is superseded, or in other words replaced by the treaty provisions.

Note

The court in Baldwin-Lima refers to the original GATT agreement. Subsequently Article III of GATT was amended by a 1948 Protocol which came into force in 1948. Under the amendment paragraph 5 of Article III became paragraph 8(a), and the wording was modified somewhat.

Problems

(1) Would purchases by the Tennessee Valley Authority (TVA), a Federal Government owned corporation, be limited by GATT Article III? How about purchases of Amtrak?

(2) Would United States Department of State purchases of typing paper and desks be governed by GATT?

(3) Would United States Department of Agriculture purchases of surplus grains from United States farmers be governed by GATT?

(4) Is electricity "goods" or "services," and what difference does it make?

(5) Does GATT Article III, in your view, apply to State laws such as that in California? (See GATT Article XXIV, paragraph 12, and the cases excerpted in Section 3.6(D) supra and Section 5.4(D) supra.)

(6) Would the national treatment obligation of GATT apply to Government purchases of:

(a) Police cars?

(b) Liquor at wholesale, for resale through a State government monopoly?

(B) THE TOKYO ROUND AGREEMENT ON GOVERNMENT PRO-CUREMENT [5]

REPORT OF THE DIRECTOR–GENERAL OF GATT, THE TOKYO ROUND OF MULTILATERAL TRADE NEGOTIATIONS
76–77 (1979)

The lack of international obligations in the area of government procurement and the widespread discrimination that existing legislation, practices and procedures permitted, progressively brought the subject under multilateral scrutiny.

It was first taken up in the OECD where much detailed work was done over a period of years, culminating in a "Draft Instrument on Government Purchasing Policies, Procedures and Practices." This was made available to GATT to form part of the documentation available to the Sub-Group on government procurement in the context of the Tokyo Round.

* * *

While the subject continued to come up from time to time, government procurement did not become a subject for negotiation in the Tokyo Round until July 1976, when it was agreed to establish a Sub-Group, which held its first meeting in October of that year.

---

5. See generally Pomeranz, Toward a New International Order in Government Procurement, 11 Law & Poly.Intl.Bus. 1263 (1979); Anthony & Hagerty, Cautious Optimism as a Guide to Foreign Government Procurement, 11 Law & Poly.Intl.Bus. 1301 (1979); Note, Technical Analysis of the Government Procurement Agreement, 11 Law & Poly.Intl.Bus. 1345 (1979); Note, United States and Japanese Government Procurement: The Impact on Trade Relations, 62 Wash.U.L.Q. 127 (1984).

The creation of a sub-group to deal with this matter was pressed by the developing countries—in particular some of the more advanced—who believed that government procurement held out possibilities for the expansion of their trade and provided scope for special and differential treatment in their favour in accordance with the provisions of the Tokyo Declaration.

The prospect of negotiations on government procurement provoked differing reactions from developed countries. Some, unconvincingly, expressed concern about overloading the Negotiations while others supported the introduction of this area into the Negotiations. Among other things, concern was expressed about the prospects of achieving a real balance in benefits as between countries with systems based on a federal structure and other systems involving greater central control. On the other hand, some developed countries were of the view from the outset that government procurement practices were one of the most important obstacles to world trade and should be dealt with in the course of the Tokyo Round.

The main issues that arose in the negotiations concerned the size of contract and the government agencies that would be subject to the obligations and the treatment of regional and local authorities and developing countries. The following excerpt from the Senate Report on the Government Procurement Code summarizes the terms of the Code and, in describing the extent to which the U.S. Government is bound, provides an overview of existing U.S. "Buy-American" statutes.

SENATE REPORT No. 96–249
96th Cong., 1st Sess. 128–31, 142–43 (1979)

[A] major objective of the United States during the Tokyo Round of Multilateral Trade Negotiations was to establish an international obligation among signatory countries to employ transparent, nondiscriminatory procurement practices. To accomplish this, the Agreement on Government Procurement requires open procurement procedures, including the publication of relevant laws, regulations, and tendering opportunities. Since the provisions of the agreement reflect many aspects of current U.S. procurement practice, few changes in domestic law will be required. At the same time, these requirements are supposed to begin to open up the procurement systems of other signatory countries, thereby enabling American firms to compete for foreign government contracts on an equal footing. The estimated size of this new potential market is $20 billion.

* * *

SUMMARY OF THE AGREEMENT

The agreement is designed to discourage discrimination against foreign suppliers. The benefits of the agreement will be available only to goods originating in the territory of the signatory countries. The agreement establishes open or "transparent" procurement procedures, which are fully publicized, consistently administered, and which cover all aspects of the procurement process. It adopts common "ground rules" of procurement practice which not only reflect the principles of transparent procedures, but which also provide basic norms of international procurement practices to the benefit of all suppliers interested in bidding on contracts abroad. It establishes a disputes mechanism which calls for bilateral consultations between the procuring government and the government of an aggrieved foreign supplier, and sets up multilateral conciliation procedures should bilateral procedures reach an impasse. Finally, the agreement calls for developing countries to be provided with technical assistance where appropriate to help them meet their obligations under the agreement.

Scope. The original U.S. negotiating objective had been to include within the agreement all entities under the direct and substantial control of the government, and to provide a balance of concessions in terms of quantity (total value) and quality (types of products covered). Most of the signatory governments were not prepared to agree to this breath of coverage. Consequently, the agreement will apply solely to those agencies which each signatory country has listed in annex I of the agreement. For the United States, the agreement will not apply to the Department of Transportation, the Department of Energy, the Tennessee Valley Authority, the Corps of Engineers of the Department of Defense, the Bureau of Reclamation of the Department of the Interior, certain parts of the General Services Administration, the Postal Service, COMSAT, AMTRAK and CONRAIL. The agreement does not apply to procurements of State and local governments or to State and local procurements financed through Federal funds.

The agreement does not apply to contracts of less than 150,000 SDR's (special drawing rights—equal to approximately $190,000) [approximately $160,000 in November 1985], and it does not apply to certain classes of purchases. It does not cover the procurement of services, except for those services which are incidental to the purchase of goods. To the extent that there is ambiguity in the scope and meaning of the term "services incidental to the supply of products", the committee is of the opinion that, where feasible, services which are related to the end use of a product (e.g. insurance, financing, etc.) should be covered by the agreement. It will not cover the procurement of arms, ammunition, war materials, and purchases indispensible for national security or national defense purposes. Nor will it apply to purchases by Ministries of Agriculture for farm support programs or human feeding programs such as the U.S. school lunch program.

U.S. coverage under the agreement will not affect our set-aside programs for small and minority businesses, or contracts for goods made in prisons, by the blind, or by the severely handicapped. The requirements in the Defense Department Appropriations Act that certain products (i.e. textiles, clothing, shoes, food, stainless steel flatware, certain specialty metals, buses, hand tools, ships, and ship components) be purchased only from domestic sources are not affected by the agreement.

Tendering Provisions. The first obligation of signatories to the agreement is to publish their procurement laws and regulations and to make them consistent with the rules of the agreement. Furthermore each government agency covered by the agreement is required to publish a notice of each proposed purchase in an appropriate publication available to the public, and to provide all suppliers with enough information to permit them to submit responsive tenders.

The agreement prohibits discrimination against foreign suppliers in all aspects of the procurement process, from the determination of the characteristics of the product to be purchased to tendering procedures to contract performance.

It prohibits the adoption or use of technical purchase specifications which act to create unnecessary obstacles to international trade. It mandates the use, where appropriate, of technical specifications based on performance rather than design, and of specifications based on recognized national or international standards.

A number of tendering (or selection) procedures are authorized by the agreement, provided that equitable treatment of all suppliers is assured and that as many suppliers as is possible are allowed to compete for contracts. "Open tendering procedures" allows all interested suppliers to compete for award of a particular contract. The agreement also allows purchasing entities to pre-qualify suppliers by setting up bidders lists and then limiting competition for particular contracts to pre-qualified suppliers. The agreement prohibits discrimination in the process of pre-qualifying suppliers, and requires that qualified supplier lists, and the requirements necessary to get on them, be published periodically. The use of "single tendering" procedures (or non-competitive procurement) is authorized only under specified circumstances, such as in times of emergency when needed products could not be obtained on a timely basis through other procedures.

While the agreement would not prohibit the granting of an offset or the requirement that technology be licensed as a condition for award, signatories have agreed to recognize that such practices should be limited and used in a nondiscriminatory manner.

Disputes Provisions. Parties to the agreement are required to notify unsuccessful suppliers promptly upon award of a contract, and to provide them, upon request, with pertinent information concerning the reasons why they were not selected, as well as with the name and relative advantages of the winning supplier.

The agreement does not, however, require the price of the winning bid to be revealed publicly, as is the practice in the United States. Parties to the agreement are required to establish procedures for reviewing complaints arising out of any phase of the procurement process. But the agreement does not specifically mandate procedures whereby an aggrieved American bidder could protest an alleged irregularity to an impartial tribunal which could act promptly to direct the award of a contract to the protesting bidder when the protest is supported by relevant facts. The U.S. system can and does allow for the award of contracts to aggrieved bidders, whether foreign or domestic, and the committee expects the U.S. Government to vigorously urge the other signatories to establish similar procedures.

The agreement does enable the government of an aggrieved supplier to enter into bilateral consultations with the procuring government. If consultations prove fruitless, the agreement provides for a "good offices" effort conciliation by a Committee of Signatories to the Agreement. Any party to a dispute can move to have a factfinding panel established. The committee makes rulings and recommendations based on the report submitted to it by the factfinding panel.

*   *   *

The United States has offered approximately $12.5 billion in coverage out of $90 billion in total federal procurement. In other terms, we have offered approximately 15 percent of our total procurement market. This offer includes coverage of most executive agencies with some important exceptions. The 85 percent which will not be covered includes these exceptions as well as purchases of services, construction contracts, and purchases excluded on national security grounds.

From the outset of negotiations it was expected that the telecommunications, heavy electrical, and transportation (mostly railroad) sectors would be problem areas. The U.S. market in these areas is already essentially open to purchasing based on commercial considerations because most of such entities are in the private sector. On the other hand, there is a high degree of government incursion in these areas on the part of our trading partners. The EC was expected to be particularly difficult in the negotiations since it had been unable to agree to the opening of markets in these areas even among its member states. As anticipated, the EC did not offer these entities although the EC did offer the post offices within the Postal-Telegraph-Telephone systems (PTTs) which was an important foot in the door. Our other trading partners followed suit (with the exception, in part, of Japan). As a result, the United States sought to redress his imbalance by withdrawing coverage of:

Department of Transportation;

Department of Energy;

The Bureau of Reclamation;

The Army Corps of Engineers; and

The Tennessee Valley Authority.

In an additional balancing move, the United States did not offer coverage of such government chartered corporations as COMSAT, AMTRAK, CONRAIL, or the U.S. Postal Service, none of which are bound by the Buy American Act.

In regard to purchases by the Department of Defense, certain sensitive products are excluded from coverage. These exceptions are currently covered by the Berry Amendment and include food, clothing including leather gloves and shoes, textiles, buses, vessels or major components thereof, hulls and superstructures. Specialty metals are also excluded.

Purchases of such products as flatware and tools were excluded through our withdrawal of GSA's Regional Office 9 in San Francisco and the National Tool Center.

Finally, there is an explicit provision in the U.S. offer allowing for continued set-aside programs for small and minority business.

Covered U.S. entities purchased a broad range of products, including purchase of such goods as office machines, office furnishings, paper, vehicles, data processing equipment, laboratory equipment, medical supplies and equipment, aircraft, and measuring equipment.

It should be noted that the United States and all its major trading partners have agreed to eliminate discriminatory government purchasing practices by all government entities in regard to aircraft in the context of the Aircraft Agreement. There is no value threshold in the Aircraft Agreement.

Notes and Questions

(1) The Senate report noted also that the offers of certain other countries under the government procurement code were valued as follows: EC: $10.5 billion; Japan: $6.9 billion (with further negotiations on NTT (Nippon Telephone and Telegraph) expected); and Canada: $1.25 billion. Overall the Senate Committee concluded, "it appears that the United States and its major trading partners will be starting from a base of roughly comparable coverage with several notable exceptions mentioned above." Id. at 147.

(2) The status of ratification of the Agreement is indicated in Section 5.5 supra.

(3) Articles I and II of the Agreement read, in part, as follows: [6]

Article I

1. This Agreement applies to:

(a) any law, regulation, procedure and practice regarding the procurement of products by the entities subject to this Agreement. This includes services incidental to the supply of products if the value of these incidental services does not exceed that of the products themselves, but not service contracts *per se;*

* * *

Article II

1. With respect to all laws, regulations, procedures and practices regarding government procurement covered by this Agreement, the Parties shall provide immediately and unconditionally to the products and suppliers of other Parties offering products originating within the customs territories (including free zones) of the Parties, treatment no less favourable than:

(a) that accorded to domestic products and suppliers; and

(b) that accorded to products and suppliers of any other Party.

2. The provisions of paragraph 1 shall not apply to customs duties and charges of any kind imposed on or in connection with importation, the method of levying such duties and charges, and other import regulations and formalities.

3. The Parties shall not apply rules of origin to products imported for purposes of government procurement covered by this Agreement from other Parties, which are different from the rules of origin applied in the normal

---

6. GATT, 26th Supp. BISD 33, 35 (1980).

course of trade and at the time of importation to imports of the same products from the same Parties.

(4) The provisions of U.S. law implementing the Agreement are contained in Sections 301–308 of the Trade Agreements Acts of 1979 (Documentary Supplement).

(5) The Agreement allows developing countries to negotiate exceptions to its general requirements. Section 301 of the Trade Agreements Act authorizes the President to grant the least developed developing countries the benefits of the Agreement, even if they do not reciprocate. For the problem of the conditional nature of the U.S. law in light of the general MFN obligations of GATT, see Section 7.4 supra.

(6) The Agreement applies only to contracting by entities specified in the annexes and does not apply to state and regional governments, although the Agreement provides: [7]

* * *

2. The Parties shall inform their entities not covered by this Agreement and the regional and local governments and authorities within their territories of the objectives, principles and rules of this Agreement, in particular the rules on national treatment and non-discrimination, and draw their attention to the overall benefits of liberalization of government procurement.

The U.S. law does not contain any language on state procurement. In the case of the Standards Code (Section 8.5 below), Congress did indicate its view that states should not engage in standards-related activity that creates obstacles to foreign commerce. Is its failure to do so in the case of government procurement meaningful? Review the cases discussed in Section 3.6(D) and consider how the new U.S. law affects the analysis of a case like *Bethlehem Steel*.[8] Reportedly, the United States was prepared to accept the Code as applicable to governmental subdivisions, but other nations were actively opposed to such a provision.[9]

(7) The Agreement establishes a Committee of Signatories, which meets at least annually, and has a dispute settlement procedure. Among the problems under consideration by the Committee have been whether the Agreement covers leasing and whether taxes and duties should be included in calculating whether a contract is over the threshold.[10] Do you think the Agreement covers leases? Should the answer depend on the type of lease? Should taxes (such as applicable VAT and sales taxes) and duties count in determining whether a contract is subject to the Agreement? More generally, if a contract is to be awarded by bidding, how can its value be determined in advance?

(8) Article IX:6(b) of the Agreement provides for periodic renegotiations to broaden and improve the Agreement and the Committee is charged to explore the possible extension of the Agreement to cover service contracts. A renegoti-

7. Agreement on Government Procurement, art. I:2, GATT, 26th Supp. BISD 33, 35 (1980).

8. Note, State Buy American Laws—Invalidity of State Attempts to Favor American Purchasers, 74 Minn.L.Rev. 389 (1980); Federal Limitations on State "Buy American" Laws, 21 Colum.J.Trans.L. 177 (1982).

9. J. Jackson, J.-V. Louis & M. Matsushita, National Constitutions and the International Economic System in Implementing the Tokyo Round: National Constitutions and International Economic Rules 198, 200 (1984).

10. See GATT, 31st Supp. BISD 247 (1985); GATT, 30th Supp. BISD 36 (1984); GATT, 29th Supp. BISD 41 (1983).

ation procedure was initiated in late 1983, and as of late 1985, it is still in its formative stages.[11]

SECTION 8.5   PRODUCT STANDARDS AND TECHNICAL BARRIERS TO TRADE

U.S. DEPARTMENT OF COMMERCE, FOREIGN INDUSTRIAL NON–TARIFF BARRIERS

(1971) [1]

PRODUCT, SAFETY AND OTHER STANDARDS

These standards, relating to manufactured products, foods and drugs, have an unavoidable deterrent effect on trade, which is increased when standards and regulations differ among countries. They become NTB's when trade is unnecessarily restricted. Of growing importance is the trend toward product quality assurance schemes among countries that can result in exclusion of products from countries unable to comply with certification requirements.

There are indications that serious consideration is being given in Western Europe to a number of standards harmonization systems for industrial products. In fact, a total of twenty-two items—including motor vehicles, electrical equipment and apparatus, measuring instruments, tractors, pressure vessels, food and drugs—have now been compiled by the European Community for possible action. The result of such a trend could be that exports in an increasing number of industrial products will eventually be seriously hindered or even blocked when a government, or group of governments, requires certain standards or requires certification by an authorizing institution that certain qualitative standards have been met. If similar quality standards of countries that do not join the schemes are not accepted as being equivalent in product definition, then serious obstacles to trade can be created. Even though these quality standards systems may be voluntary (as compared to compulsory safety and health standards), they probably will be generally accepted by the industries and governments of those countries who have joined the harmonization scheme.

An example of the product standards and certification problem is the Tripartite Accord on Harmonization of Standards for Electronic Components scheduled to be implemented by the Governments of the United Kingdom, France and West Germany and to be expanded to include all EC and EFTA countries. When fully implemented, U.S. industry is concerned that, without U.S. membership, American firms would be unable to ship electronic components to participating countries without costly testing and approval by

---

11. A study by the General Accounting Office in 1984 concluded that the Agreement thus far has not had a significant impact on international trade. GAO, The International Agreement on Government Procurement: An Assessment of its Commercial Value and U.S. Government Implementation (GAO Report No. NSIAD–84–117, 1984).

1. U.S. Commission on International Trade and Investment Policy (the William Commission), Papers I, at 677, 678. A description of a number of U.S. standards applicable in 1970 can be found in M. Whiteman, 14 Digest of International Law 803 (1970). See also Sections 6.1(D) and 6.2(A) supra.

their testing laboratories, that U.S. firms would be unable to ship standard production items, and consequently that a serious drop in U.S. exports of electronic components would result.

REPORT BY THE DIRECTOR-GENERAL OF GATT, THE TOKYO ROUND OF MULTILATERAL TRADE NEGOTIATIONS

62–63 (1979)

Technical regulations are essential in modern society. They are adopted to protect human and animal life and health; to ensure that products offered to the consumer meet the necessary levels of quality, purity, technical efficiency and adequacy to perform the function for which they are intended; to protect the environment; and for reasons connected with safety; national security; and the prevention of deceptive practices.

However, international trade can be complicated and inhibited by disparities between regulations, adopted at local, State, national or regional levels; by insufficient information on the often complex and detailed requirements; by the introduction of regulations without allowing time for producers, especially foreign ones, to adjust their production; by frequent changes to regulations which create uncertainty; by the drawing up of regulations in terms of design rather than performance in order to suit the production methods of domestic suppliers, thus causing difficulties to suppliers using different techniques; by exacting testing requirements; by the denial of access to certification systems; and finally by the manipulation of regulations, testing or certification to discriminate against imports. The problem has been to strike a balance between the essential needs referred to in the preceding paragraph and the demand of exporters that their goods should not unreasonably or unfairly be excluded from the market.

In the Tokyo Round the negotiations in the field of technical barriers were essentially concerned with the trade aspects. The GATT approach, and the results achieved in the negotiations, complement and do not conflict with the activities of the many other interested international organizations such as the International Organization for Standardization (ISO), the International Electrotechnical Commission (IEC), and the Codex Alimentarius.

Standards are covered in a general way in Article III of the GATT and in Articles XI and XX, but the Code on Standards goes well beyond these provisions.

*   *   *

Standards were prominent in the preparatory work before the Tokyo Ministerial meeting, and many countries notified their difficulties in this area (150 notifications in the non-tariff measures inventory).

Technical barriers was one of the subjects selected for possible *ad referendum* solutions. By the time of the Tokyo meeting in September 1973, a draft "Code for preventing Technical Barriers to Trade" (the Standards Code) had been prepared and was already in a reasonably advanced form.

In examining the following excerpts from the so-called Standards Code, the reader should consider:

(1) To what extent does the Code regulate the substance of standards, as opposed to the procedures for adopting them? If there are substantive requirements, do they in any way exceed or differ from those already established in GATT Article III? Consider whether the United States would be limited under the Code in any substantial way in establishing a health-related standard.

(2) Why do you think that the Code establishes a preference for performance characteristics rather than design or descriptive characteristics?

(3) To what extent does the Code restrict the adoption of national standards if international standards exist in the same field?

(4) To what extent do you think that the Code will promote broader adoption of standards? If the Code does result in more, albeit internationally coordinated, standards, do you think that there may be any adverse effect on international trade flows?

(5) To what extent does the Code effectively restrict the ability of authorities to insist on proof that products comply with national standards?

AGREEMENT ON TECHNICAL BARRIERS TO TRADE [2]

Article 1

* * *

1.3 All products, including industrial and agricultural products, shall be subject to the provisions of this Agreement.

* * *

Article 2

With respect to their central government bodies:

2.1 Parties shall ensure that technical regulations and standards are not prepared, adopted or applied with a view to creating obstacles to international trade. Furthermore, products imported from the territory of any Party shall be accorded treatment no less favourable than that accorded to like products of national origin and to like products originating in any other country in relation to such technical regulations or standards. * * *

2.2 Where technical regulations or standards are required and relevant international standards exist or their completion is imminent, Parties shall use them, or the relevant parts of them, as a basis for the technical regulations or standards [except if they are inappropriate for specified reasons].

2. GATT, 26th Supp. BISD 8 (1980). See generally Nusbaumer, The GATT Standards Code in Operation, 18 J. World Trade L. 542 (1984); Middleton, The GATT Standards Code, 14 J. World Trade L. 201 (1980); Note, Technical Analysis of the Technical Barriers to Trade Agreement, 12 Law & Poly.Intl.Bus. 179 (1980); Note, Prospects for Implementation of the GATT Standards Agreement in the United States, 20 Va.J.Intl.L. 699 (1980); Bourgeois, The Tokyo Round Agreement on Technical Barriers and on Government Procurement in International and EEC Law, 19 Comm.Mkt.L.Rev. 5 (1982).

2.3 With a view to harmonizing technical regulations or standards on as wide a basis as possible, Parties shall play a full part within the limits of their resources in the preparation by appropriate international standard-izing bodies of international standards for products for which they either have adopted, or expect to adopt, technical regulations or standards.

2.4 Wherever appropriate, Parties shall specify technical regulations and standards in terms of performance rather than design or descriptive characteristics.

2.5 Whenever a relevant international standard does not exist or the technical content of a proposed technical regulation or standard is not substantially the same as the technical content of relevant international standards, and if the technical regulation or standard may have a significant effect on trade of other Parties, Parties shall: [publish a notice of their intention to adopt a particular regulation or standard, inform the GATT secretariat of the products affected, provide copies of the proposals to interested parties and consider comments on the proposals, publish the regulations or standards promptly and provide a phase-in period.]

*   *   *

Article 3

3.1 Parties shall take such reasonable measures as may be available to them to ensure that local government bodies within their territories comply with the provisions of Article 2 [with certain exceptions].

Article 4

4.1 Parties shall take such reasonable measures as may be available to them to ensure that non-governmental bodies within their territories comply with the provisions of Article 2, [with certain exceptions].

Article 5

Determination of Conformity With Technical Regulations or Standards by Central Government Bodies

5.1 Parties shall ensure that, in cases where a positive assurance is required that products conform with technical regulations or standards, central government bodies apply the following provisions to products originating in the territories of other Parties:

5.1.1 imported products shall be accepted for testing under conditions no less favourable than those accorded to like domestic or import-ed products in a comparable situation;

5.1.2 the test methods and administrative procedures for imported products shall be no more complex and no less expeditious than the corresponding methods and procedures, in a comparable situa-tion for like products of national origin or originating in any other country;

*   *   *

5.2 However, in order to facilitate the determination of conformity with technical regulations and standards where such positive assurance is required, Parties shall ensure, whenever possible, that their central government bodies:

> accept test results, certificates or marks of conformity issued by relevant bodies in the territories of other Parties; or rely upon self-certification by producers in the territories of other Parties;

even when the test methods differ from their own, provided they are satisfied that the methods employed in the territory of the exporting Party provide a sufficient means of determining conformity with the relevant technical regulations or standards.

———————

The Agreement imposes similar requirements in respect of certification systems. In addition, the Agreement has provisions on publicizing standards and requires parties to maintain enquiry points where information about standards can be obtained. Like other Tokyo Round agreements, the Standards Code has a Committee of Signatories and dispute settlement provisions.

The United States implemented the Standards Code in Sections 401–453 of the Trade Agreements Act of 1979. Several provisions are noteworthy. First, Section 401 explicitly provides that standards-related activity shall not be considered an unnecessary obstacle to foreign commerce if a demonstrable purpose is to achieve a legitimate domestic objective. Second, in Section 403, Congress indicates its view that no state or private person should engage in any standards-related activity that creates unnecessary obstacles to foreign commerce and directs the President to take reasonable measures to promote observance of the Standards Code procedures by states and private persons.

In Sections 421–424 a procedure is established by which another party to the Standards Code (or a non-party that extends equivalent rights and privileges to the United States) may complain to the U.S. Trade Representative that a standards-related activity in the United States violates the Code, in which case the Trade Representative is to review the matter, consult with appropriate agencies and try to resolve the matter on a mutually satisfactory basis. This procedure gives foreign governments a specified procedure through which to complain about U.S. standards.

Notes and Questions

(1) The status of adherence to the Standards Code is set out in Section 5.5 supra.

(2) As noted above, access to the complaint procedure under U.S. law is basically limited to parties to the Standards Code. Does this violate U.S. MFN obligations? (See discussion in Section 7.4 supra.)

(3) Do you think that the lack of a specific federal statute regulating state and private standards-related activity creates a major loophole for U.S. firms? Are the cases discussed in Section 3.6 supra relevant here?

(4) As a foreign government, what rights would you have if you were not satisfied with the results obtained following your complaint under Sections 422 and 423 of the Trade Agreements Act of 1979? Consider Section 421 of that Act.

Chapter 9

ESCAPE CLAUSES, SAFEGUARDS AND ADJUSTMENT POLICIES

SECTION 9.1 INTRODUCTION: THE POLICIES AND HISTORY OF SAFEGUARD MEASURES

(A) THE SAFEGUARDS ISSUE—INTRODUCTION [1]

Probably the most important and controversial issue now facing the world trading community is the question of under what circumstances should a nation be permitted to impose "safeguards", i.e. measures to control imports that are injuring its domestic industry. Article XIX of GATT—often referred to as GATT's escape clause—specifies standards to be met before such measures are imposed, but in recent years new techniques of protecting domestic industry from imports have been developed that are not explicitly dealt with by GATT. Such techniques include so-called "voluntary" export restraints and orderly marketing agreements, which in theory involve no import restraints at all because they are implemented by exporters. The issues surrounding the proper use of safeguards are sufficiently controversial that in the Tokyo Round, no agreement could be reached on a safeguards code, and continuing negotiations have not been fruitful.

---

1. In addition to the materials cited elsewhere in this chapter, see Wolff, The Need for New GATT Rules to Govern Safeguard Actions, in W. Cline (ed.), Trade Policy in the 1980s, at 363 (1983); Merciai, Safeguard Measures in GATT, 15 J. World Trade L. 41 (1981) (with bibliography); Adams & Dirlam, Import Competition and the Trade Act of 1974: A Case Study of Section 201 and Its Interpretation By the International Trade Commission, 52 Ind.L.J. 535 (1977) (extensive analysis of pre-1977 cases); Ris, "Escape Clause" Relief Under the Trade Act of 1974: New Standards, Same Results, 16 Colum.J.Transnatl.L. 297 (1977); Sauermilch, Market Safeguards Against Import Competition: Article XIX of the General Agreement on Tariffs and Trade, 14 Case W.Res.J.Intl.L. 83 (1982); Hindley, Voluntary Export Restraints and the GATT's Main Escape Clause, 3 World Economy 313 (1980); Meier, Externality Law and Market Safeguards: Applications in the GATT Multilateral Trade Negotiations, 18 Harv.Intl.L.J. 491 (1977); Metzger, Injury and Market Disruption from Imports, in U.S. Commission on International Trade and Investment Policy (the Williams Commission), Papers, vol. I, at 167 (1971); Stewart, Import Competition and Government Relief, in id., at 193.

The causes of the underlying desires for safeguards were adverted to in Chapter 1's discussion of the desirability of free trade. Recall that while the overall economic effect of trade liberalization may be beneficial, there are often short-term harmful effects on individuals or groups within a society. Increased imports may promote efficiency and give the consumer more choice at less expense, but the domestic producers of import-competing products may find that they can no longer compete successfully. Businesses may be forced to change their product lines or to go out of business entirely. In such event, workers may become unemployed, business owners may incur losses and communities that were heavily dependent on such businesses may find their tax bases eroded and their economies harmed by the lack of purchasing power from the profits earned and wages paid by those business-es. From a broad perspective, these ill effects may be small compared to the overall gains of the economy. Nevertheless, the harmed businesses and workers can argue that they have been made to bear an undue proportion of the costs for society's general gains and that society through government action should help them "adjust" to their new situation. They analogize to the practice of governments to compensate property owners when property is taken for governmental purposes.

In recent years, problems of adjustment have been magnified by the proliferation of new production facilities in developing countries. Exports from such facilities have created considerable tensions within industrialized countries, where older and less productive facilities combined with higher living standards and costs for labor have made domestically produced goods unable to compete with such exports. At times, the need of the traditionally industrialized societies to ease the harmful effects of such exports and the need of the newly industrializing countries to expand their exports in order to be able to pay their considerable debts and to meet the rising expectations of their populations, seem irreconcilable.

Traditionally, international trade rules and policies have distinguished between the ways in which an importing nation is permitted to respond to fair trade practices, on the one hand, and "unfair" trade practices, on the other hand. Certain safeguard measures are permitted in response to fair trade, i.e., imports that are not "dumped," subsidized, or otherwise consid-ered to be in violation of international rules of conduct, while more extensive counter-measures are permitted to respond to unfair trade practices, such as dumped or subsidized exports. We will follow this theoretical distinction and discuss safeguard measures in response to fair trade in this chapter and then discuss counter-measures permitted in response to unfair trade in Chapter 10. However, in practice it often becomes very difficult to differen-tiate between the two. In escape clause cases, arguments of "unfairness" are made even though not technically relevant, since the existence of unfairly traded imports seems to give an added reason to impose safeguards. Conversely, the rules regarding unfair practices may be invoked even though the "unfair" aspect may only be a technical rules violation (or perhaps even nonexistent, such as in cases brought to harass importers). The basic motivation may be identical to that found in escape clause cases—a desire for time to adjust to international competition.

(B) THE POLICIES OF SAFEGUARDS—COMPENSATING INDIVIDUAL INJURY INCURRED FOR THE BROADER WELFARE OF SOCIETY

We have noted that the basic argument for safeguards is that while free trade is good overall, it is not good for everyone. Therefore, it is argued that safeguards are justified to compensate those individuals and businesses harmed by a government's free trade policy. This argument is not free from substantial criticism. Free trade advocates are apt to point out that businesses are always faced with changing conditions. Changes of consumer taste, changes of production technology, new inventions, declines in government purchasing programs or abandonments of particular weapon systems, all can contribute to loss of business. Arguably, it is management's task to cope with such constant changes, and increased imports are simply another form of such change. A counter-argument is made, however, that problems resulting from changes in government policy are deserving of special treatment. If government has been imposing tariffs or other restraints on imports, and suddenly agrees to eliminate or reduce such import restraints, domestic competing producers can argue that the government decision is the cause of their problems, and therefore the government should do something to alleviate those problems. Of course, the same argument would have equal validity for changes in government procurement policies for weapons systems, although it is less often heard in such cases.

In any event, even if these arguments seem fallacious under close scrutiny from an objective policy viewpoint, they nevertheless have considerable political appeal. Congressmen and senators can cite individual stories of harm to their constituents, which make appealing cases for some government help. Whatever the objective policy validity of such help, the practice has been that governments in fact do respond and do give relief to the persons harmed. Perhaps what makes these situations different from the harm caused by many other types of changing circumstances, is that when imports cause the difficulty, there is the natural inclination of those who have votes in the governmental process to try to impose the burden of adjustment upon those who do not have votes, i.e. upon foreigners. In this connection the reader should review Professor Corden's concept of a "conservative social welfare function," discussed in Section 1.3(B)(5) supra. Professor Corden notes that society seems to place a premium on avoiding significant harm to any group even if it means other groups must forego gains.

There are various ways by which governments can respond to help alleviate the injuries caused by import competition. First, and most obviously, they can reduce imports by imposing new import restraints or moderate increases in imports by phasing in slowly the reduction of such import restraints.[2] For cases where import restraints have already been liberalized, governments may impose some new form (temporary or otherwise) of import restraint, either directly through tariffs or quotas, pursuant to statutory

---

2. The Kennedy Round tariff concessions were phased in over a five-year period, Trade Expansion Act of 1962, Pub.L. No. 87–794, § 253, 76 Stat. 880; see also Presidential Proc- lamation No. 3822, 32 Fed.Reg. 19002 (1967), while the Tokyo Round agreements provided for an eight-year phase-in. GATT, 26th Supp. BISD 3 (1980).

escape clauses (see Sections 9.2 and 9.3 infra), or indirectly through a variety of other possible techniques, such as voluntary restraint agreements or a number of more subtle devices (see Section 9.4 infra). An alternative way to assist individuals or groups which have been harmed by imports, however, is to do so directly by making payments to them from some governmental source. Generally this technique is termed "adjustment assistance" (see Section 9.5 infra).

(C) HISTORY OF ESCAPE CLAUSES [3]

Escape clauses, a general term referring to provisions allowing agreed-upon trade liberalization measures to be modified, have found their way into international and U.S. law in a variety of ways. The U.S. provision first appeared in a Reciprocal Trade Agreement with Mexico in 1943. Since then, it has appeared in other bilateral treaties and in GATT. In 1947, the President issued an Executive Order requiring that an escape clause be included in every trade agreement entered into under the authority of the Reciprocal Trade Agreements Program. This order was amended slightly by subsequent Executive Orders until 1951, when a general statutory escape clause was included in the Trade Agreements Extension Act of 1951.[4] Over the years, Congress has regularly revised the escape clause provisions,[5] and these provisions are often considered a sort of bellwether of congressional

3. See generally J. Jackson, World Trade and the Law of GATT 553–55 & nn. 1–14 (1969).

4. Trade Agreements Extension Act of 1951, ch. 141, 65 Stat. 74.

5. The following are the statutory provisions as from time to time enacted: (emphasis added):

Trade Agreements Extension Act of 1951, Ch. 141, 65 Stat. 74 (1951).

Sec. 6. (a) No reduction in any rate of duty, or binding of an existing customs or excise treatment or other concession hereafter proclaimed under section 350 of the Tariff Act of 1930, as amended shall be permitted to continue in effect when the product on which the concession has been granted is, *as a result, in whole or in part,* of the duty or other customs treatment *reflecting such concession,* being imported into the United States in such *increased quantities, either actual or relative,* as to cause or threaten serious injury to the domestic industry producing like or directly competitive products.

* * *

7. (b) In arriving at a determination in the foregoing procedure the Tariff Commission, without excluding other factors, shall take into consideration a downward trend of production, employment, prices, profits or wages in the domestic industry concerned, or a decline in sales, an increase in imports, either actual or relative to domestic production, a higher or growing inventory, or a decline in

the proportion of the domestic market supplied by domestic producers.

Trade Agreements Extension Act of 1955, Ch. 169, 69 Stat. 1966 (1955).

Sec. 6. (a) Subsection (b) of section 7 of the Trade Agreements Extension Act of 1951, as amended (19 U.S.C. § 1364(b)), is amended by adding at the end thereof the following: "Increased imports either actual or relative, shall be considered as the cause or threat of serious injury to the domestic industry producing like or directly competitive products when the Commission finds that such increased imports have contributed substantially towards causing or threatening serious injury to such industry."

(b) Section 7 of the Trade Agreements Extension Act of 1951, as amended (19 U.S.C. § 1364), is amended by adding at the end thereof the following new subsection:

"(c) As used in this Act, the terms 'domestic industry producing like or directly competitive products' and 'domestic industry producing like or directly competitive articles' mean that portion or subdivision of the producing organizations manufacturing, assembling, processing, extracting, growing, or otherwise producing like or directly competitive products or articles in commercial quantities. In applying the preceding sentence, the Commission shall (so far as practicable) distinguish or separate the operations of the producing organizations involving the like or directly competitive products or articles referred to in such

sentiment toward imports, since escape clause criteria that permit industries to obtain import relief easily tend to nullify the results of trade negotiations.

The following materials outline the history and use of the escape clause. Before reading them, it would be useful to review GATT Article XIX and Sections 201–203 of the Trade Act of 1974,[6] as set out in the Documentary Supplement.

EXECUTIVE BRANCH GATT STUDIES, NO. 8, GATT PROVISIONS ON RELIEF FROM INJURIOUS IMPORTS

124–29 (1973) [7]

USE OF ARTICLE XIX BY THE UNITED STATES AND OTHER COUNTRIES

GATT member countries on the whole have invoked the Article XIX escape clause provision infrequently (see attachment). Since the inception of GATT, 13 member countries, either individually or as members of a regional group, have used the Article a total of 61 times. The United States has invoked it 16 times, and Australia, 16. France, Germany and Italy each invoked the Article twice; and EC has used it twice. Canada used it 8 times, 5 of them for farm products imported mainly from the United States.[*3]

OTHER FORMS OF IMPORT RELIEF UNDER THE GATT

In some circumstances, member countries have preferred to act under GATT provisions other than Article XIX. For instance, member countries may withdraw a tariff concession permanently by entering into renegotiations under regular Article XXVIII procedures. A case in point is the use of this Article by the United States with respect to low-priced stainless steel table flatware.

sentence from the operations of such organizations involving other products or articles."

Trade Expansion Act of 1962, 19 U.S.C. § 1901.

Section 301. * * *

(b)(1) Upon the request of the President, upon resolution of either the Committee on Finance of the Senate or the Committee on Ways and Means of the House of Representatives, upon its own motion, or upon the filing of a petition under subsection (a)(1), the Tariff Commission shall promptly make an investigation to determine whether, as a result in major part of concessions granted under trade agreements, an article is being imported into the United States in such increased quantities as to cause, or threaten to cause, serious injury to the domestic industry producing an article which is like or directly competitive with the imported article.

(2) In making its determination under paragraph (1), the Tariff Commission shall take into account all economic factors which it considers relevant, including idling of productive facilities, inability to operate at a level of reasonable profit, and unemployment or underemployment.

(3) For purposes of paragraph (1), increased imports shall be considered to cause, or threaten to cause, serious injury to the domestic industry concerned when the Tariff Commission finds that such increased imports have been *the major factor in* causing, or threatening to cause, such injury.

Trade Act of 1974, Sections 201, 202 and 203, as amended in 1979 and 1984. (See Documentary Supplement).

6. The U.S. Escape Clause is currently codified at 19 U.S.C.A. §§ 2251–53.

7. Subcomm. on Intl. Trade, Senate Comm. on Finance, 93d Cong., 2d Sess. (Compilation of 1973 studies by the Executive Branch: Comm.Print 1974).

* 3. Precautions must be taken in interpreting this record of usage of Article XIX in view of the many alternative forms of relief available both within and outside the provisions of the General Agreement (see attachment).

Member countries may also take any action, under Article XXI of the GATT, which they consider "necessary for the protection of * * * essential security interests." The Mandatory Oil Import Program of the United States, authorized domestically by Section 232 of the Trade Expansion Act, could be justified under this provision of GATT. Although not widely used, other countries have justified certain import restrictions on national security grounds.

Article XXXV permits a country to withhold the application of its schedule of tariff concessions, or of its obligations under the entire agreement, from another country with which it has not entered into tariff negotiations. A number of member countries have invoked this Article on joining the GATT because of their fear that acceptance of GATT obligations would lead to serious market disruption at home from competitive imports. Developed and developing countries alike have singled out Japan as the primary target of these actions since that country joined the GATT in 1955. For the most part, major trading countries have disinvoked Article XXXV against Japan, but only after obtaining trading commitments from that country in bilateral negotiations. For example, Japan has agreed to restrain exports of selected products to those countries and, in some cases, to consult whenever Japanese exports threaten market disruption in the importing country.

ALTERNATIVE MEASURES TO PROVIDE RELIEF FROM INJURIOUS IMPORTS

Tariffs can be increased unilaterally on items which are not bound under the GATT, that is, products on which tariff concessions have not been granted. Many countries have taken steps to avoid import injury by raising duties on unbound items.

Developing countries are largely insulated from competitive imports which might be injurious to domestic industry through import restrictions. Some of these may be justified on balance-of-payments or economic development grounds. Apart from residual import restrictions, some developed countries maintain discriminatory import restrictions on selected imports. Import restrictions of this type—primarily directed against imports from Japan—are widespread in Western Europe.

EXPORT RESTRAINTS

The use of export restraints has also reduced the need for countries to resort to Article XIX. Export restraints affect shipments of selected goods which are ordinarily free of import restriction but pose a threat to production in the importing country. While such actions might be considered inconsistent with the requirements of GATT Article XI, complaints under that article against such procedures are unlikely to arise, since the controls are imposed at the request of the importing country that would be principally affected by the export restraints.

The most comprehensive example of an export control arrangement is the Long-Term Arrangement Regarding International Trade in Cotton Textiles (LTA) negotiated under the auspices of the GATT. This arrangement affects much of the free world trade in cotton textiles by providing the mechanisms that enable exporting and importing countries to control the growth of trade in cotton textiles through a network of bilateral agreements and by unilateral action. The LTA also assures that exports from participating countries will not be restrained more severely than exports from nonparticipating countries causing market disruption. More recently, export controls aimed at avoiding market disruption have been extended to woolen and man-made fibers in some cases.

SENATE REPORT NO. 93–1298
93d Cong., 2d Sess. 119 (1974)

For many years, the Congress has required that an "escape clause" be included in each trade agreement. The rationale for the "escape clause" has been, and remains, that as barriers to international trade are lowered, some industries and workers inevitably face serious injury, dislocation and perhaps economic extinction. The "escape clause" is aimed at providing temporary relief for an industry suffering from serious injury, or the threat thereof, so that the industry will have sufficient time to adjust to the freer international competition.

By reason of the Congressional requirement, the trade agreements to which the United States is a party contain an escape clause or equivalent provision. Typical and of most general effect is Article XIX.1.(a) of the General Agreement on Tariffs and Trade.

From 1951 through 1962 the escape clause worked reasonably well. The criteria were fair and equitable, and relief was occasionally granted. However, in 1962 the Administration proposed and the Congress adopted rigid and stringent tests of injury and causal relationships between tariff concessions, increased imports and serious injury.

As a result, the provisions of the Trade Expansion Act of 1962 for invoking the escape clause (like the adjustment assistance provisions also adopted in that Act, which contained similar injury tests) have proven to be an inadequate mechanism for providing relief to domestic industries injured by import competition. One result of this inadequacy has been a number of special "voluntary" agreements for industries deemed by the Congress or the Executive to be suffering from excessive imports. The Committee believes it is better to provide a fair and reasonable test for any industry which is being injured by imports—a determination made by an independent factfinding body, such as the International Trade Commission—than to rely on ad hoc agreements for a few select industries.

U.S. COMMISSION ON INTERNATIONAL TRADE AND INVESTMENT POLICY (THE WILLIAMS COMMISSION), REPORT
49–50, 62 (1971)

ELIGIBILITY FOR RELIEF

Under the [Trade Expansion Act of 1962], a prerequisite for either adjustment assistance or escape-clause action is a finding of serious injury or threat of serious injury to the applicant workers, firms, or industry. Increased imports must have been "the major factor" causing that injury, and must in turn have resulted "in major part" from trade agreement concessions.

In practice, these two criteria have proved extremely difficult to meet. The Tariff Commission has interpreted the former to require a showing that increased imports were a more important cause of injury than all other causes combined, and it has given a similarly rigorous interpretation to the latter. The criteria, as written, clearly require that values be assigned to each of the various causes of increased imports and injury.

In practice, the Tariff Commission has rarely found that both these links in the causal chain were sufficiently established. Between passage of the TEA in October 1962, and November 1969, the Tariff Commission made no affirmative findings of serious injury.

In November 1969, the Commission approved three worker petitions. Between that date and June 1971, five industry petitions for escape clause relief, and 79 worker and 14 firm petitions for adjustment assistance were filed with the Tariff Commission. During this period, the Commission completed action on the following cases: four industry petitions—finding no injury in two and dividing evenly on two; 79 worker petitions—finding injury in 10, no injury in 41, and dividing evenly in 28; and 14 firm petitions—finding injury in one, no injury in five, dividing evenly in seven, and discontinuing one.

If import restrictions through the escape clause and the programs for adjustment assistance are to serve their purpose of relieving hardships and facilitating economic adjustment, the eligibility criteria must be made more realistic. However, because of the essential differences between the two forms of relief, it would not be sound policy to alter them to the same extent or in the same way.

The first requirement for adjustment assistance as well as escape-clause action should continue to be the existence of imports that are large enough and increasing at such a rate as to be capable of contributing to the serious injury or threat of serious injury claimed by the petitioners. And in both cases it should be required that a causal relationship be shown between increased imports and the claimed injury. But no useful purpose is served by attempting to retain the link between a previous tariff concession and increased imports.

* * *

CONDITIONS FOR ESCAPE-CLAUSE ACTION

Import restrictions under the escape clause should provide time for adjustment to new conditions of competition, not support a noncompetitive industry indefinitely. Such restrictions should be temporary and rigorously justified by modernization and diversification plans of firms in the industry to be protected. These plans should indicate how a brief period of protection will enable the firms to compete again following removal of import restrictions.

Since an industry-wide plan of adjustment may be either infeasible or inconsistent with antitrust law, individual firms in the industry should be required to submit their plans to the Tariff Commission—without prejudice to the industry's case for an affirmative finding by the Tariff Commission—and, in addition, should be encouraged to solicit the technical advice of the Department of Commerce in formulating such plans. Following an affirmative finding by the Tariff Commission, the plans would be forwarded to the Department of Commerce for use in advising the President on actions to be taken with respect to options permitted under escape-clause procedure.

The purpose of relief provided by import restrictions under the escape clause should be to permit a seriously injured domestic industry to again become competitive without continuing restrictions. Such relief should be extended on a declining basis and for a limited period of time (not more than 5 years) to be specified in the President's proclamation. In petitioning for import restrictions, the firms involved should be required to submit to the Tariff Commission detailed reports of their plans for use of the time requested.

ADMINISTRATION ANALYSIS OF THE PROPOSED TRADE REFORM ACT OF 1973 [8]

Chapter 1.—Import Relief

This chapter constitutes a major revision of the "escape clause" provisions of the Trade Expansion Act. There are four fundamental changes:

(1) Liberalization of existing criteria for determining injury to domestic industry due to imports, including the deletion of the causal link to trade agreement concessions, the substitution of "primary" for "major" cause with respect to the relationship between increased imports and injury, and inclusion of a market disruption determination.

(2) Inclusion of additional factors to be taken into account by the Tariff Commission in determining injury due to imports and by the President in his determining whether and in what form to provide import relief. These factors include efforts by the industry to adjust to import competition and the impact of relief on consumers, exporters, and other domestic industries.

(3) Expanded forms and amounts of import relief which the President may provide, including orderly marketing agreements, other import restrictions, removal of statutory limitations on tariff increases and authority to withdraw application of 806.30 and 807.00 provisions.

(4) Stricter time limits on the duration of import relief and the mandatory phasing out of such relief.

These changes are consistent with the fundamental purpose of import relief under this title, namely to permit a seriously injured domestic industry to become competitive again under relief measures and, at the same time, to create incentives for the industry to adjust to competitive conditions in the absence of long-term import restrictions.

---

8. House Comm. on Ways and Means, 93d Cong., 1st Sess., Press Release and Other Material Relating to the Administration Proposal Entitled the "Trade Reform Act of 1973," Including the Message of the President, Text, Summary and Section-By-Section Analysis of the Proposed Bill (H.R.6767), at 70–72 (Comm. Print 1973).

As can be seen by an examination of Section 201, most of the proposed bill was adopted into law. The major exceptions were the substitution of a "substantial cause" standard for the proposed "primary cause" standard (with "substantial cause" being defined as "a cause which is important and not less than any other cause") and the deletion of the possibility of a market disruption determination, except for Communist country products. The basic provisions of the 1974 version of the escape clause have remained unchanged, although a number of minor or clarifying amendments have been made.[9]

Since the passage of the Trade Act of 1974 up to the time of this writing (February 1986), a total of 55 Section 201 petitions have been brought and acted upon in the United States; 4 are now pending. Of those, the ITC made affirmative rulings in 29, and tie vote affirmative rulings in 3, rejecting 23. Of the 32 cases which were forwarded to the President, the President refused any action in 20 cases; imposed directly some import restraint (such as tariffs or quotas) in 8 cases, and opted to negotiate orderly marketing agreements or otherwise helped arrange export restraints in 4 cases. Thus overall, of the petitions brought, 22% resulted in some import restraint by direct or indirect action.

(D) GENERAL PROCEDURES FOR OBTAINING IMPORT RELIEF: INTRODUCTION TO THE INTERNATIONAL TRADE COMMISSION

The procedures in GATT for invoking Article XIX are spelled out in Article XIX. Under those procedures, if imports are causing injury in the manner specified in Article XIX (the substantive requirements of Article XIX are discussed in the next section), a Contracting Party is authorized to suspend its compliance with its GATT obligations. Before doing so, however, the country is required to inform GATT and, absent critical circumstances, allow the CONTRACTING PARTIES and the affected Contracting Parties to consult with it. If agreement on the action is not reached, the country proposing to take the action is free to do so, and affected Contracting Parties are entitled to suspend substantially equivalent concessions, subject to disapproval by the CONTRACTING PARTIES. One major issue in discussions concerning reform of safeguard procedures is whether GATT ought to be more involved in authorizing or supervising actions taken on escape clause grounds. See Section 9.6 below.

In the United States, as we have noted earlier, the procedures for obtaining escape clause relief have varied significantly over time, often reflecting general congressional attitudes towards the desirability of free trade. Currently under U.S. law, an escape clause proceeding begins with a petition to the International Trade Commission (ITC) by representatives of the allegedly injured domestic industry (such as a trade association, individual firm, union or group of workers), or with a request to the ITC by the President, the U.S. Trade Representative, the Senate Finance Committee, or

---

9. Trade Agreements Act of 1979, Pub.L. No. 96–39, §§ 106(b)(3), 1106(d)(1)–(7), 93 Stat. 193, 312; Trade and Tariff Act of 1984, Pub.L. No. 98–573, §§ 248(a), 249, 98 Stat. 2998.

the House Ways and Means Committee, or upon initiation by the ITC itself.[10] A petition for relief must give information justifying relief, including extensive data on imports, domestic production and injury, as well as an explanation of how the industry is making an effort to compete with the imports. The ITC then determines whether the prerequisites of U.S. law are fulfilled. Its investigation and report must be completed within six months. If it makes an affirmative determination, it then recommends a remedy and passes the matter to the President. The President must act within 60 days of receiving the report. In an escape clause proceeding, in stark contrast to unfair trade proceedings under the antidumping and countervailing duty laws, the President has complete discretion to reject the ITC viewpoint, or alter the recommended remedy, and not infrequently the President has exercised this discretion to reject recommended relief. We discuss congressional attempts to control presidential discretion in Section 9.3 infra. Petitioning industries have often sought to limit a President's discretion by filing their petition nine months or so prior to an election so that the presidential decision will be due shortly before the election.[11]

The International Trade Commission, formerly known as the Tariff Commission, consists of six Commissioners, not more than three of whom belong to the same political party.[12] They are appointed for nine-year terms, with staggered expiration dates. Among other tasks, the ITC is charged with making "serious injury" determinations and recommending appropriate remedies in escape clauses cases, with making "market disruption" findings and recommending appropriate remedies in cases involving Communist country products,[13] with making "material injury" determinations in antidumping and countervailing duty cases [14] and with investigating allegations of unfair methods of competition and unfair acts in the importation of articles into the United States,[15] as well as with fulfilling various other general reporting and study responsibilities in respect of U.S. international trade.[16] One important fact to note is that the ITC is usually involved in

10. The U.S. escape clause procedures are set out in Sections 201–203 of the Trade Act of 1974, which is in the Documentary Supplement. See 19 U.S.C.A. §§ 2251–53. The ITC's general rules are contained in 19 CFR Pts. 200–01 (1985). The procedures specifically applicable to escape clause proceedings and Communist country market-disruption cases are set out in 19 CFR Pt. 206 (1985). The involvement of Congress in initiating actions may be significant. Compare Nonrubber Footwear, Inv. No. TA–201–50, Pub. No. 1545, 6 ITRD 1992 (ITC 1984) (unanimous negative determination; investigation initiated on petition filed by industry) with Nonrubber Footwear, Inv. No. TA–201–55, Pub. No. 1717, —— ITRD —— (ITC 1985) (unanimous affirmative determination).

11. For example, petitions for escape clause relief were filed by producers of stainless steel flatware, nonrubber footwear, steel products, unwrought copper and canned tuna so that the ITC report on injury and any presidential decision on import relief would have to be made at the outset of the 1984 presidential campaign. The ITC ultimately found injury only in the steel and copper cases and the President declined to accord the recommended relief in either instance, although other relief was provided to the steel industry. See Sections 9.4 and 9.6(B) infra.

12. See generally Tariff Act of 1930, title III, 19 U.S.C.A. §§ 1330–41. See generally Practicing Before the International Trade Commission (Practicing Law Institute 1985).

13. 19 U.S.C.A. § 2436; 19 CFR Pt. 206 (1985). See Section 9.2(C) and Chapter 21 infra.

14. 19 U.S.C.A. §§ 1303, 1671, 1673; 19 CFR Pt. 207 (1985). See Sections 10.2 and 10.3 infra.

15. 19 U.S.C.A. § 1337; 19 CFR Pts. 210–12 (1985). See Section 10.4 infra.

16. See 7 U.S.C.A. § 624; 19 U.S.C.A. §§ 1336, 2151, 2643.

only one part of an import-relief proceeding. Typically, another agency will decide whether to grant relief and the scope of the relief to be granted.[17]

The ITC has a large staff of professionals that studies issues that come before it. Interested parties typically submit written materials and present testimony at hearings. In essence, the ITC functions like an administrative agency. Decisions of the ITC are generally reviewable in the Court of International Trade or (in some cases) the Court of Appeals for the Federal Circuit.[18] We will see in Chapter 10 that the courts do not hesitate to second guess the ITC in antidumping and countervailing duty cases. In escape clause cases, however, in large part because of the involvement of the President, court review is typically very limited—essentially to questions of procedural regularity. See Maple Leaf Fish Co. v. United States, 762 F.2d 86 (Fed.Cir.1985). In reading determinations of the ITC, the law student will be struck by the frequent occurrence of separate opinions, and the lack of reliance on prior decisions as having precedential value. This may stem in part from the fact that the commissioners often do not have legal backgrounds.

(E) OVERVIEW OF CHAPTER 9

An escape clause case generally requires under both U.S. and international law (GATT) the following prerequisites:

(1) Increased imports;

(2) Under GATT (but not U.S. law), this increase must be caused by certain factors;

(3) Serious injury to competing domestic industry;

(4) This injury must be a causal result of increased imports.

In addition to the two prerequisites and the two causation requirements listed, issues arising under escape clauses include the type of remedy permitted, whether the remedy must be applied on a most-favored-nation basis, and the question of "compensation" under GATT procedures. Within each of these topics there are important legal questions, such as: What are "like products" for the purpose of comparing imported goods with competing domestic goods, what is an "industry" for the purpose of evaluating injury, and under U.S. law, how important a cause of injury must imports be in order for the ITC to find "affirmatively" in an escape clause case. These matters we take up in Sections 9.2 and 9.3, and then in Section 9.4 we examine various techniques which governments have been using to avoid the discipline of the escape clause procedures, focusing particularly on the troublesome practice of "voluntary restraint agreements." In Section 9.5 we examine "adjustment assistance" programs.

Finally, in Section 9.6 we examine briefly several economic sectors which have been much troubled by economic trends and pressures for "structural adjustment," in significant part triggered by the rise of new

---

17. An exception occurs in Section 337 proceedings, where affirmative action by another agency is not required, although the President can "veto" the ITC decision. See Section 10.4 infra.

18. See generally Section 3.5(C) supra on review by the Court of International Trade.

industries in developing countries, particularly that of textiles, where special national and international institutions have been designed to regulate trade, institutions which do not conform to the policies or the legal norms of GATT and which therefore challenge those policies and norms. We then look at various ideas and processes for national and international reform of escape clause procedures, including a review of the Tokyo Round attempt to negotiate a "Safeguards Code."

SECTION 9.2 THE PREREQUISITES AND CAUSAL REQUIREMENTS OF AN ESCAPE CLAUSE REMEDY

(A) INTRODUCTION AND PROBLEM FOR CONSIDERATION

In this section and in Section 9.3, we will examine the legal issues raised in applying both Article XIX of GATT and the U.S. escape clause, contained in Sections 201–203 of the Trade Act of 1974. The reader should consider, particularly with respect to the causation requirements, how and to what extent U.S. law fails to fulfill GATT obligations or imposes more stringent prerequisites for escape clause relief than GATT requires. We will consider the legal issues raised by escape clause proceedings in the following order. First, in this section, we examine: (1) The requirement of increased imports (and the cause thereof) and (2) the requirement of serious injury to domestic industry (and the cause thereof). Then, in Section 9.3, we consider: (1) Remedies for the importing country; (2) the possibility of selective (non-MFN) remedies; and (3) compensation for exporting countries.

In order to focus attention on some of the issues we will treat, the following problem may usefully be kept in mind. Assume two countries, I, an importing nation, and E, an exporting nation. Both are members of GATT. E ships electronic games for children to I. Statistics for those imports and for consumption of the product in I (where all goods not imported from E are produced within I) are as follow:

Year	Imports	Total Consumption	Imports as % of Consumption
1980	2 million	10 million	20%
1981	3 million	12 million	25%
1982	4 million	12 million	33%
1983	5 million	12 million	42%
1984	5 million	10 million	50%
1985	5 million	8 million	63%
1986	4 million	6 million	66%
1987	3 million	4 million	75%

We will see in this chapter that one prerequisite for the invocation of the escape clause is "increasing imports." Suppose one filed a petition for import relief in 1983, is the prerequisite fulfilled? What if the petition date were 1987? Obviously one question is which time period one should use to evaluate the data. Another question is whether an increasing percentage of domestic consumption attributable to imports fulfills the prerequisite even if imports have not increased in absolute terms.

A second prerequisite for application of the escape clause is "serious injury" to the domestic industry (or threat thereof) caused by imports. If the industry consists of 10 companies, three of which are growing and profitable although overall the industry is contracting, can serious injury be found? Many variations on these facts can occur. If the imports are only of certain components for incorporation into a final product, will that matter? If some members of the domestic industry import these components, will that make a difference? Should electronic toys be treated as a group, or should they be subdivided into groups such as "music toys," "reading toys," and "baseball game toys?" Suppose of the 10 companies, four are located in California and only the California firms are "injured," can a petition to restrain imports succeed? When does mere "injury" become "serious injury?" Is there a key indicator of serious injury that is determinative?

It is also necessary to consider the cause of the injury suffered by the industry. Suppose the decline in sales is due in large part to a recession. Can it be said then that imports are a substantial cause of injury? What if a significant part of the increased market share of imports is due to a perceived quality differential in favor of imports? What if the imports are mainly cheap electronic games that most domestic producers do not make? Suppose that the decline in the overall size of the market is largely due to the fact that children have become jaded by electronic games and fads have shifted their attention to other recreations. Are imports the cause of the problem?

Needless to say, we can't explore all of these issues in detail, but the materials of this section are designed to give the reader an overview of the issues that typically arise in escape clause cases.

(B) INCREASED IMPORTS AND THE CAUSE THEREOF

The first prerequisite for escape clause relief is the existence of increased imports. In this subsection we consider a number of issues related to this requirement: First, what constitutes an increase in imports? In particular, is a relative increase sufficient? Second, what is the domestic industry that is entitled to complain of increased imports? Must domestic industry produce exactly the same product that is being imported in increased quantities? If not, how similar must the domestic and imported products be? Third, to what extent does it matter what "caused" the increased imports? We examine each of these issues below, in each case considering both the requirements of U.S. law and GATT.

(1) Increased Imports

An increase in imports can occur in one of two ways: (1) The absolute volume of imports may increase or (2) the import share of the domestic market may increase, even though the total volume of imports declines. By its terms GATT Article XIX requires that imports be in "increased quantities," but other GATT materials suggest that the increase may be relative.

GATT, Analytical Index: Regarding Article XIX, at 102 (1966) [1]

1. The Analytical Index (2d revision, Feb. 1966) was published by GATT and contains notes on drafting, interpretation and application of the articles of the General Agreement.

(a) *"relatively."* (paragraph 1) This word was inserted between "such" and "increased" at Havana "so as to make it clear that Article 40 could apply in cases where imports had increased relatively to domestic production, even though there might not have been an absolute increase in imports as compared with a previous base period." Havana Reports, Section 11, p. 83.

The GATT Article was not amended to conform to the Charter Article; it was understood, however "that the phrase 'being imported * * * in such increased quantities' in paragraph 1(a) of Article XIX was intended to cover cases where imports may have increased relatively, as made clear in paragraph 1(a) of Article 40 of the Havana Charter." GATT/CP.2/22/Rev.1, Section 30, p. 7 Vol. II/39.

Section 201(b)(2)(C) of the Trade Act of 1974 explicitly provides that the ITC may consider a relative increase in imports in determining whether imports are a substantial cause of injury. The Senate version of the Act would not have permitted such consideration: "The Committee feels that unless imports are increasing absolutely, they cannot be a cause of serious injury." [2] Do you agree?

Another potentially difficult problem is the time period over which the existence of an increase is measured. What if imports have increased in absolute terms over a one- or two-year period, but are below their absolute and relative peaks, which occurred several years earlier?

STAINLESS STEEL AND ALLOY TOOL STEEL

U.S. Intl. Trade Commn. (1976) [3]

VIEWS OF COMMISSIONERS MOORE AND BEDELL

* * *

Increased Imports. The requirement that there be an increase in imports either actual or relative to domestic production, is satisfied when the increase is in absolute terms or when the level of imports is increasing relative to domestic production.

We consider this requirement satisfied because imports increased between 1964 and 1975. We have used this time frame to avoid a determination based solely on a time period in which abnormal economic conditions existed. For example, the time period 1968–74 was not only one of unusual market conditions, but one in which unique governmental actions distorted stainless steel and alloy tool steel import levels. During this period the domestic industry was adversely affected by the Voluntary Restraint Agreement (VRA) and its subsequent changes, a world-wide nickel strike, two recessions, and domestic price controls.

Since 1964, total imports of stainless steel and alloy tool steel have tripled, imports of stainless sheets and strip have more than doubled, and

---

2. Senate Report No. 93–1298, 93d Cong., 2d Sess. 121 (1974).

3. Inv. No. TA–201–5, Pub. No. 756, 1 ITRD 5404 (1976) (The Commission found in the affirmative).

other stainless steel and alloy tool steel articles have increased threefold to tenfold.

The act also states that the Commission should examine whether imports increased relative to domestic production. Imports increased from 116,000 tons in 1973 to 151,000 tons in 1974. During January-September 1975, imports increased to 120,000 tons, compared with 95,000 tons entered during the corresponding period in 1974. The ratio of imports to U.S. production has more than doubled, rising from 9.9 percent in 1973 to 23.1 percent during the most recent period, January-September 1975. Facts developed during the Commission's investigation indicate that imports will continue their upward trend.

*   *   *

VIEWS OF VICE CHAIRMAN MINCHEW

*   *   *

Increased Imports

An increase in imports occurs when the increase is "either actual or relative to domestic production" (section 201(b)(2)(C)). Therefore, the Commission can find "increased imports" when the increase is in "actual" or absolute terms or when the level is declining in actual terms, but is increasing relative to domestic production. It is my view that, in the absence of extraordinary circumstances, the Commission should look at the increase in imports resulting from only the most recent trade concessions, so that the injury considered would be a new and continuing injury from increased imports as opposed to an "old" injury. The Senate Finance Committee Report at page 120 states:

> The increase in imports referred to would generally be such increases as have occurred since the effectiveness of the most recent trade-agreement concessions proclaimed by the President, i.e., as of now, the effectiveness of the Kennedy Round concessions beginning in 1968.

In certain circumstances in the past I have been willing to look at a shorter time frame to determine the trend of increasing imports, as I feel is my prerogative under the statute, but to look back beyond the last trade-agreement concessions would require extraordinary circumstances. In the present case, despite some out-of-the-ordinary occurrences since 1968, I do not feel that these occurrences warrant my looking beyond the 1968 trade-agreement concessions for purposes of determining increased import trends.

*   *   *

VIEWS OF COMMISSIONER ABLONDI

*   *   *

Increased Imports

Inseparably connected to the issue of "increased" imports is the selection of a time period over which imports are to be measured. In my judgment the relevant measuring period in the instant case is confined to the period since 1968.

Section 201(b)(1) of the act requires the Commission to determine "whether an article *is being imported* into the United States in such increased quantities as to be a substantial cause of serious injury, or the threat thereof, to the domestic industry * * * " (Emphasis added).   By using the present tense, Congress clearly intended that the Commission consider only imports which have occurred during a period relative to the alleged injury.   The act requires that imports be related to the injury claimed, and that the injury be current, or "new" injury.   The relevant period of importation, then, must necessarily be close to the time of the injury (that is, to the present time) rather than during earlier periods of importation having little or no impact on present industry conditions.

* * *

It has been argued that the period since 1968 is unrepresentative and that the Commission should therefore consider imports which occurred prior to that time.   I disagree.   The factors cited by advocates of a longer measuring period are insufficient to warrant a departure from the measuring period outlined by Congress.

Many of the factors which are asserted to be the cause of unusual market conditions during the period 1968–74 have been encountered in each investigation conducted by this Commission under section 201.   The effects of recessions, dollar devaluations, and price controls were national in scope and not confined to the speciality steel industry.   Furthermore, market factors which related specifically to speciality steel during the period 1968–74 did not so distort market conditions as to necessitate the adoption of an alternate measuring period.   The nickel strike of 1969 was clearly a temporary condition which served merely to delay imports until the following year.   The two affirmative determinations of this Commission under the Antidumping Act each affected only one product from one exporting country.   Finally, although the Voluntary Restraint Agreement (VRA) did affect import levels, its impact was limited by several factors, including the voluntary nature of the agreement—which in many instances caused imports to vary both above and below quota levels—and the fact that a substantial number of specialty steel exporters were not parties to the agreement.   Clearly, the aforementioned factors are neither unique to the subject industry nor so pervasive as to substantially distort market conditions.   Accordingly, there is no basis on which to adopt a measuring period extending before 1968.

In selecting the appropriate measuring period, it has been the established practice of this Commission under section 301 of the Trade Expansion Act as well as under section 201 of the 1974 Trade Act to analyze imports over a period of time of sufficient length to establish trends and thereby put aberrant or temporary conditions into proper perspective.   Generally, the period of time selected by the Commission has been 5 years or so.   On the basis of such a period, it can be seen that since 1970 total imports of stainless steel and alloy tool steel have declined absolutely and relative to domestic production.   In 1974 total imports were over 7,000 tons less than in 1970.   During 1970–74, annual U.S. production of stainless and alloy tool steel increased steadily from 700,000 tons to more than 1,325,000 tons.   In the same period, the ratio of imports to domestic production was nearly halved, dropping from 24.4 percent to 12.3 percent.

During the recessionary period of 1974 and the first part of 1975, imports did increase relative to domestic production. However, a substantial part of the increase can be attributed to importers' lead times, which at the end of the third quarter of 1974 were roughly twice as long as domestic lead times. Such a differential meant that deliveries on orders placed with foreign producers during the boom period of 1974 continued through the fourth quarter of 1974 and the first and second quarters of 1975—a period during which domestic production fell almost 50 percent below 1974 levels. Clearly, these increases were inconsistent with the general downward trend evidenced during the period 1970–74 and, as such, are not sufficient to satisfy the requirement of "increased" imports.

(2) Domestic Industry and Like or Directly Competitive Products

GATT Article XIX requires that the increased imports injure producers of "like or directly competitive products." The same requirement appears in Section 201(b)(1) of the 1974 Trade Act. The concept of like products is found in other GATT provisions (e.g., Arts. III, VI), but the addition of the words "directly competitive" suggests that a more expansive definition is intended in Article XIX. Indeed, it could be argued that if an industry is seriously injured by imports, that is evidence that it produces "directly competitive products." [4]

CERTAIN CANNED TUNA FISH

U.S. Intl. Trade Commn. (1984) [5]

VIEWS OF COMMISSIONERS ECKES, LODWICK, ROHR AND LIEBELER

Section 201 defines the domestic industry in terms of producers of "an article like or directly competitive with the imported article." "Like" articles are defined in the legislative history as "those which are substantially identical in inherent or intrinsic characteristics (i.e., materials from which made, appearance, quality, texture, etc.)." "Directly competitive" articles are those "which, although not substantially identical in their inherent or intrinsic characteristics, are substantially equivalent for commercial purposes, that is, are adapted to the same uses and are essentially interchangeable therefor." The term "directly competitive" is also defined in section 601(5) of the Trade Act, which provides that articles may be directly competitive with each other at an earlier or later stage of processing.

* * *

In the present case, we must address two issues. First, we must determine what domestic article or articles are like or directly competitive with the imported articles. * * *

The imported articles that are the subject of this investigation include canned tuna packed in oil and canned tuna not packed in oil (i.e., packed in water). We conclude that the domestic article which is like or directly competitive with the imported articles is canned tuna, whether packed in oil,

4. See J. Jackson, World Trade and the Law of GATT 561 n. 16 (1969).

5. Inv. No. TA 201–53, Pub. No. 1558, 6 ITRD 2464 (1984). The ITC did not find injury in this case.

water, or any other medium. No one argued that tuna packed in oil and tuna packed in water were produced by different industries, although they are covered by different tariff items and are dutiable at substantially different rates. We conclude that they are the product of one industry. All major processors produce and market both tuna in oil and tuna in water. Both products are made from the same types of fish. The only difference between the two is the packing solution. While tuna packed in water has grown in popularity in recent years because it is lower in calories than tuna packed in oil, both products are marketed in the same way, are price related, appear together on store shelves, and are used for the same purposes by consumers.

————

The need to define domestic industry and the concept of like (but not directly competitive) products also exist in the unfair trade context, and in the 1984 Trade and Tariffs Act, Congress was persuaded by certain grape growing interests to include on a temporary basis the following provision in the antidumping and countervailing duty laws.[6]

[I]n the case of wine and grape products subject to investigation under this title, the term ["industry"] also means the domestic producers of the principal raw agricultural product (determined on either a volume or value basis) which is included in the like domestic product, if these producers allege material injury, or threat of material injury, as a result of imports of such wine and grape products.

The EC has argued in GATT that this is contrary to GATT obligations and a panel has been appointed to consider the issue.[7] Should the EC prevail?

(3) Cause of Increased Imports

REPORT ON THE WITHDRAWAL BY THE UNITED STATES OF A TARIFF CONCESSION UNDER ARTICLE XIX OF THE GENERAL AGREEMENT ON TARIFFS AND TRADE

(1951)[8]

"HATTERS' FUR CASE"

II. The Requirements of Article XIX

3. In attempting to appraise whether the requirements of Article XIX had been fulfilled the Working Party examined separately each of the conditions which qualify the exercise of the right to suspend an obligation or to withdraw or modify a concession under that Article.

4. Three sets of conditions have to be fulfilled:

(a) There should be an abnormal development in the imports of the product in question in the sense that:

6. Trade and Tariff Act of 1984, § 612(a)(1), Pub.L. No. 98–573, 98 Stat. 3033, 19 U.S.C.A. § 1677(4)(A).

7. 1 BNA Intl. Trade Rptr. 598, 723 (1984); 2 BNA Intl. Trade Rptr. 267 (1985).

8. Sales No.: GATT/1951–3, at 8–14 (Nov. 1951.)

    (i) the product in question must be imported in increased quantities;

    (ii) the increased imports must be the result of unforeseen developments and of the effect of the tariff concession; and

    (iii) the imports must enter in such increased quantities and under such conditions as to cause or threaten serious injury to domestic producers of like or directly competitive products.

(b) The suspension of an obligation or the withdrawal or modification of a concession must be limited to the extent and the time necessary to prevent or remedy the injury caused or threatened.

(c) The contracting party taking action under Article XIX must give notice in writing to the Contracting Parties before taking action. It must also give an opportunity to contracting parties substantially interested and to the Contracting Parties to consult with it. As a rule consultation should take place before the action is taken, but in critical circumstances consultation may take place immediately after the measure is taken provisionally.

III. Existence of the Conditions Required for Action Under Article XIX

* * *

7. *Existence of unforeseen developments: relation of these and of the tariff concession to imports.* The concession granted at Geneva was substantial. Taking a simple average for the 4 value-brackets from $9 to $24 per dozen the duties as from January 1, 1948, were 32.3 per cent. less than the rates of the 1930 Tariff Act.

8. The United States representative stated that about the time the duties were reduced there was a style change greatly favouring hats with nap or pile finishes, a development which was not and could not have been foreseen at the time the concession was granted. As a result of that style change hat bodies with special finishes were imported in increased quantities and represented more than 95 per cent. of the imports of women's fur felt hats and hat bodies in 1949 and in the first six months of 1950. The increased popularity of special finishes, which, as compared with the plain felt hats require much larger amounts of hand labour, which is more expensive in the United States than in the exporting countries, created a special problem for the United States producers who were not in a position to adapt themselves to the change in demand in view of a severe competition from imports. He stated that the United States negotiators at Geneva, while realizing the shifting fashions in the hat trade and expecting some increase in imports, had not been aware of the extent that this particular change in taste had then reached in Europe and had not foreseen the degree of the future shift to special finishes or the effect which it, together with the concession, would have on imports. He considered this statement was sufficient to show unforeseen developments.

9. The Czechoslovak representative stated that the term "unforeseen development" should be interpreted to mean developments occurring after the negotiation of the relevant tariff concession which it would not be

reasonable to expect that the negotiators of the country making the concession could and should have foreseen at the time when the concession was
negotiated. The other members of the Working Party (other than the
United States representative) agreed with this view.

10. On the basis of the interpretation accepted by the majority, the
Czechoslovak representative maintained that:

(a) it is universally known that fashions are subject to constant
changes—"change is the law of fashion";

* * *

Production of Women's Fur Felt Hat Bodies

	1948	1949	1950 (Jan.-June)
Quantities in dozens.................	629,235	565,768	203,235
Percentage of decrease as compared with 1948 figures	————	10%	18%

Consequently, at the time of the investigation, when imports were increasing
rapidly, as indicated above, there had been a substantial decrease in production.

15. A substantial percentage (estimated at over 20 per cent. in 1949
and at over 30 per cent. in the first six months of 1950) of the apparent
demand for hat bodies shifted to special finishes. 80 per cent. of imports in
1949 were of these special finishes. As the total consumption did not
increase substantially it would appear likely that in 1949 and the first six
months of 1950 the imported hat bodies with special finishes replaced to
some extent plain felt hat bodies which would have normally been supplied
by domestic producers.

16. No data were available to assess the financial losses which firms
producing felt hat bodies may have suffered from the increase in imports.
In the industry as a whole the production of women's hat bodies represents
about 25–30 per cent. of the total production of hat bodies and hats, and it
has not been possible to separate the financial results of the production of
women's hat bodies from that of men's hat bodies and hats.

17. Inquiries by the United States Tariff Commission, however, showed
that ten out of fourteen manufacturers questioned by it stated that they
could not make hat bodies in special finishes at prices competitive with
imports.

18. As regards the effects of increased imports on employment, the
figures show a decrease in the number of productive workers on felt hat
bodies (men's and women's) during the period 1947 to 1949. This reduction
was substantial between 1948 and 1949 as indicated below:

Productive Workers Engaged in Making Fur Felt Hat Bodies

	1947	1948	1949
Average number of workers	4,383	4,349	3,717
Percentage decline as compared with 1947 figures	——	1%	15%

* * *

VI.   Conclusions

47.   The following paragraphs contain the conclusions arrived at by the members of the Working Party other than the Czechoslovak and the United States representatives.

48.   These members were satisfied that the United States authorities had investigated the matter thoroughly on the basis of the data available to them at the time of their enquiry and had reached in good faith the conclusion that the proposed action fell within the terms of Article XIX as in their view it should be interpreted.   Moreover, those differences of view on interpretation which emerged in the Working Party are not such as to affect the view of these members on the particular case under review.   If they, in their appraisal of the facts, naturally gave what they consider to be appropriate weight to international factors and the effect of the action under Article XIX on the interests of exporting countries while the United States authorities would normally tend to give more weight to domestic factors, it must be recognised that any view on such a matter must be to a certain extent a matter of economic judgment and that it is natural that governments should on occasion be greatly influenced by social factors, such as local employment problems.   It would not be proper to regard the consequent withdrawal of a tariff concession as *ipso facto* contrary to Article XIX unless the weight attached by the government concerned to such factors was clearly unreasonably great.

49.   For the reasons outlined above, these members came to the conclusion that there was no conclusive evidence that the action taken by the United States under Article XIX constituted a breach of that Government's obligations under the General Agreement.

50.   They wish however to point out that in their opinion, action under Article XIX is essentially of an emergency character and should be of limited duration.

Notes and Questions

(1) In U.S. law prior to 1974, the prerequisites for an escape clause action were similar to those of GATT Article XIX, which requires that increased imports must have resulted from (1) unforeseen developments and (2) GATT obligations.   As urged by the Williams Commission (see Section 9.1(C) supra), the 1974 Trade Act eliminated these requirements.   In commenting upon this change, the Senate Report noted: [9]

The requirement of the Trade Expansion Act that increased imports result *in major part* from trade concessions has been very difficult to satisfy in the past and has become a major barrier to import relief.   The criteria for import relief under the bill would relax the present import relief criteria by: (1) removing the "causal link" requirement that imports result in major part from trade agreement concessions and (2) requiring that increased imports need only be "a substantial cause," rather than "the major cause," of actual or threatened injury.   The increase in imports referred to would generally be such increases as have occurred since the effectiveness of the most recent

9. S.Rep. No. 93–1298, 93d Cong., 2d Sess. 120–21 (1974).

trade agreement concessions proclaimed by the President, i.e., as of now, the effectiveness of the Kennedy Round concessions beginning in 1968.

Modification of the requirement that increased imports be the major cause of actual or threatened injury is necessary because "the major cause" has been interpreted as being a cause greater than all other causes combined (although there is some indication that in recent years the Commission has moved away from this standard). This has proved in many cases to be an unreasonably difficult standard to meet. Substantial cause is defined in the bill to mean a cause which is important and not less than any other cause. This requires that a dual test be met—increased imports must constitute an important cause and be no less important than any other single cause.

The Committee recognizes that "weighing" causes in a dynamic economy is not always possible. It is not intended that a mathematical test be applied by the Commission. The Commissioners will have to assure themselves that imports represent a substantial cause or threat of injury, and not just one of a multitude of equal causes or threats of injury. It is not intended that the escape clause criteria go from one extreme of excessive rigidity to complete laxity. An industry must be seriously injured or threatened by an absolute increase in imports, and the imports must be deemed to be a substantial cause of the injury before an affirmative determination should be made.

(2) In light of the *Hatters' Fur* case, do you think that the omission of the first causation requirement in U.S. law is significant?

(3) What is the test for the "unforeseen developments" criterion of Article XIX in the light of the *Hatters' Fur* case? Would you agree with the following statement?—"If the nature of the development can be foreseen and yet the degree of its impact on imports is that which fulfills the 'unforeseen development' prerequisite, can this not be the case in every substantial increase in imports? If so, there may be built into GATT obligations through the escape clause a limit on the allowable increase of imports of any product." [10]

(4) Are there any circumstances of increased imports into a GATT member country, which are not at least partly the "effect of the obligations" of GATT, as required in Article XIX? Note particularly GATT Articles III and XI. In the absence of Article XI, could not injury always be prevented by imposition of quotas?

(5) Does the omission of the GATT requirements in U.S. law, whether or not significant, violate U.S. international obligations? If so, who can complain and to what are they entitled?

(C) SERIOUS INJURY TO DOMESTIC INDUSTRY AND THE CAUSE THEREOF

The second basic prerequisite for escape clause relief is that the increased imports cause (or threaten) serious injury to domestic industry. Among the questions that must be answered in considering this prerequisite are (1) How is domestic industry defined? Is injury to a part of an industry sufficient? (2) How significant must the injury be? (3) How important a

10. J. Jackson, World Trade and the Law of GATT 561 (1969).

cause of injury must imports be? and (4) What actions must an industry take to help itself? In this subsection, we also look at the special rules applicable in cases of injurious imports from certain nonmarket countries.

(1) Defining the Injured Industry

As we saw in the preceding subsection, the definition of domestic industry is in part related to the question of who produces a like or directly competitive product. However, additional issues arise in considering the definition of industry for analyzing claims of injury. Obviously, an industry can be defined broadly or narrowly, and the definition may be critical to the question of whether injury can be shown. In reviewing the following case, the reader may wish to consider which of the following constitutes an industry for Section 201 purposes: Automobile production generally? Compact car production? Luxury car production? Steering wheel production? Station-wagon production? What about geographical segments of an industry, such as "West Coast steel?"

CARBON AND CERTAIN ALLOY STEEL PRODUCTS
U.S. Intl. Trade Commn. (1984) [11]

[The ITC found several industries injured or threatened with injury and recommended a five-year program of quotas and tariffs. The President rejected their recommendations, but subsequently negotiated a series of voluntary restraint agreements, described in Sections 9.4 and 9.6(B) infra.]

VIEWS OF COMMISSIONERS STERN, ECKES, LODWICK AND ROHR

In this investigation the "imported article" consists of numerous products ranging from semifinished carbon steel products such as ingots, blooms, and billets to more advanced or finished products such as steel wire rope and nails. The breadth of this investigation, covering such a diversity of products, requires the Commission to define like or directly competitive in a manner that reflects the realities of the market and at the same time accomplishes the fundamental purpose of section 201, protection of the productive resources of domestic producers. Thus, the Commission considers both the productive facilities and processes and the markets for these products in determining those articles that may be considered like or directly competitive within the meaning of section 201.

Petitioners, Bethlehem Steel Corp. (Bethlehem) and the United Steelworkers Union (Union), argue that there is a single domestic industry comprised of domestic producers of all basic steel mill products and certain "first tier" finished products. Petitioners contend that all steel products are a class or kind of merchandise and that the advanced products must be included in the domestic industry to prevent circumvention of any relief accorded producers of basic steel products. If the Commission were to find more than one industry, petitioners assert that circumvention would then occur through importation of more advanced products.

11. Inv. No. TA–201–51, Pub. No. 1533, 6
ITRD 2236 (1984).

In arguing that there is one domestic industry within the meaning of section 201, petitioners emphasize the factors common to the articles under investigation. These common characteristics are: (1) a common technological and metallurgical base, (2) production in shared facilities in whole or in part, (3) common melt facilities, (4) relative ease of varying product mix among articles, (5) unitary economies of production, and (6) the high degree of vertical integration among some producers. Further, petitioners argue that two-thirds of the cost of production of finished products is in the production of raw steel. Moreover, they argued that the existence of a continuum of products with no clear dividing lines among product groups makes a single industry approach realistic. Under this approach there would be a single domestic industry consisting of all domestic facilities producing any article like or directly competitive with the imported articles. Thus, the domestic industry would consist of basic steel producers as well as U.S. producers of finished products such as pipe and tube and wire products which are manufactured from basic steel products such as plate and rod, respectively.

Importers and several domestic manufacturers of products that use steel argue that the Commission should find several domestic industries. These parties argue that the criteria set forth in the legislative history and Commission precedent, i.e. (1) inherent and intrinsic characteristics of the articles, (2) basic physical properties, and appearance, and (3) current production and marketing practices, require a finding of multiple industries. Parties opposing a finding of a single domestic industry also argue that there can be no domestic industry or injury finding for a product which is not produced in the United States. Finding a single domestic industry would include many such products in the Commission's determination. Finally, section 201 is derived from the General Agreement on Tariffs and Trade (GATT). Moreover, the provisions of Article XIX, the escape clause, refer to serious injury resulting from trade concessions granted on specific articles. Moreover, the escape clause provides relief to producers of "an article" rather than a "class of articles."

Diversity of products and types of firms producing steel and steel products in the United States characterize this investigation. The imported products that are the subject of this investigation are found in 263 items of the Tariff Schedules of the United States (TSUS). Furthermore, the types of productive facilities range from large integrated producers, which produce raw steel in basic-oxygen or open-hearth furnaces, to nonintegrated producers, which produce steel primarily from scrap in electric furnaces, to non-steel producers, which purchase steel and shape or treat it to produce more advanced products. Integrated steel producers manufacture most of the products which are the subject of this investigation; in addition, nonintegrated producers are also important producers of some products covered by the investigation, such as rod and bar.

Integrated steel producers operate blast furnaces, steelmaking furnaces, electric furnaces, rolling and finishing facilities, as well as own or operate mines which provide iron ore, coal and limestone for the production of iron. These firms, which are concentrated in the Great Lakes region of the United

States, accounted for over 75 percent of raw steel production in 1982 and 1983. In addition to raw steel production, a number of integrated producers operate facilities devoted to shaping and finishing steel products.

* * *

Nonintegrated steel producers typically operate an electric furnace with a relatively limited raw steel capacity and use locally available scrap as raw material. Recently, the comparatively low price of scrap has given nonintegrated producers a cost advantage of as much as $100 per ton over integrated producers. These firms are generally small, regional producers located near a primary market for their product, which results in lower freight costs for these producers. Nonintegrated producers, or minimills, normally specialize their production in a narrow range of products such as bars, wire rods, and light structural shapes.

Nonsteel producers include firms that purchase semifinished steel products or finished steel products such as plates, sheets, or strip and use them as raw material for processing into more advanced products such as pipes and tubes or wire and wire products. Nonsteel producers, or processors, are concentrated in the western part of the United States and these western processors tend to focus on production of wire, pipes and tubes, and railway-type products.

* * *

Based on the record in this investigation, we find that there are nine classes of products that are like or directly competitive with the imported articles.

In prior investigations we have analyzed the effect of imports on a class of products.*[27] We have used this approach, however, in analyzing discrete categories of closely-related products. Although a "class of products" approach is appropriate for the individual nine product groups that we have identified, we believe that including all of the imported articles encompassing both semifinished and finished products in a single class of products exceeds this precedent. Although all of the articles at issue in this investigation share common characteristics in that steel forms the raw material for further processing, there are meaningful differences in the productive facilities and processes for many of these products and wide variance in the U.S. market for each group of products. Moreover, some indicia of serious injury, such as decreased ability to raise capital for investment in steelmaking, have been assessed on a specific firm basis in accord with capital market practices rather than on a product group basis. Thus, we have based our decision regarding the domestic industries on a balancing of all of these criteria.

Notes

(1) The Commission ultimately found that there were nine industries: ingots and similar semifinished products, plate, sheet and strip, wire rod, wire and wire products, railway-type products, bars, structural shapes, and pipes and tubes.

* **27.** Stainless Steel, Inv. No. TA–201–48, USITC Pub. No. 1377 (1983); Nonrubber Footwear, Inv. No. TA–201–50, USITC Pub. No. 1545 (1984); Motorcycles, Inv. No. TA–201–47, USITC Pub. No. 1342 (1983).

(2) Can a geographic sector of an industry invoke escape clause proceedings? Consider the following:

FRESH CUT ROSES

U.S. Intl. Trade Commn. (1980) [12]

In considering whether increased imports of fresh cut roses are a substantial cause of serious injury, or the threat thereof, to the domestic industry, it is first necessary to define the relevant domestic industry that may be suffering the requisite injury. The Trade Act does not define the term "domestic industry," but rather provides guidelines and permits the Commission to use its judgment in light of these guidelines and the relevant economic factors in a given case. Section 201(b)(1) provides that the domestic industry must produce "an article like or directly competitive with the imported article." Section 201(b)(3)(C) also provides that the Commission may treat a regional segment of the national industry as the domestic industry if (a) domestic producers are producing the like or directly competitive article in a major geographic area of the United States; (b) their production facilities constitute a substantial proportion of the domestic industry and primarily serve the market in that area; and (c) imports are concentrated in that area. Although the petitioner did not base its claim for relief on the existence of a regional market within the meaning of section 201, we have considered whether the criteria are met in this case and have concluded that the domestic industry producing an article "like or directly competitive with" fresh cut roses covered by TSUS item 192.18 cannot appropriately be subdivided into a distinct geographic region. Specifically, although the growers in the eastern two-thirds of the United States may technically meet the above statutory conditions, approximately one-half of consumption in that region is supplied by domestic growers outside the geographic area. The impact of imports, therefore, is not isolated on growers in just the eastern region, since imports also compete with roses grown in the western one-third of the United States. We find, therefore, that the appropriate domestic industry consists of all the facilities in the United States devoted to the production of fresh cut roses.

(2) Serious Injury

There are a number of "injury" tests in international and national rules regarding trade, and a comparison of those tests is interesting. The escape clauses (GATT, U.S. and others) speak of "serious injury," but antidumping and countervailing duty laws use the phrase "material injury." Some rules speak only of "injury." The Trade Act of 1974, in Section 406, uses the term "market disruption" as the test of when imports from certain nonmarket countries can be restricted. The statutory test in U.S. law for evaluating petitions for adjustment assistance does not speak of injury, but requires unemployment of a "significant number or proportion of the workers" in the firm or division concerned. Section 337 of the U.S. law—dealing with unfair

12. Inv. No. TA–201–42, Publ. No. 1059, 1
ITRD 5552 (1980).

import competition in general—speaks of acts, the "effect or tendency of which is to destroy or substantially injure an industry." Other tests can be found also.

What is the difference between these various tests? It has never been entirely clear. The "injury" tests of the escape clause and the unfair trade laws are applied to an "industry" (itself a troublesome concept, as noted above), while the injury requirement for worker adjustment assistance focuses upon a particular firm or unit. Apart from that difference, it is generally thought that the "serious injury" requirement of the escape clause is the most stringent (hard to fulfill) test. Since the escape clause is not necessarily a response to unfair activity, it is usually considered important to balance the purposes of that clause with the policies of liberal trade, by requiring a fairly stringent test of injury.

The "material injury" test is thus deemed to be less stringent than "serious injury." Perhaps the policy basis for this difference is that when responding to unfair action, it should not be necessary to establish such a high degree of injury. Where the other tests fall on this spectrum is not always easy to ascertain. Indeed, given the ambiguity of the tests, even with the legislative history behind them, the ITC has a fair degree of discretion in how it applies these tests.

In the case of the U.S. escape clause, the statute requires the ITC to consider, with respect to serious injury, the following: [13]

> the significant idling of productive facilities in the industry, the inability of a significant number of firms to operate at a reasonable level of profit, and significant unemployment or underemployment within the industry.

In evaluating the threat of serious injury, the ITC is to consider: [14]

> a decline in sales, a higher or growing inventory * * * and a downward trend in production, profits, wages or employment (or increasing underemployment).

The law provides that the presence or absence of any factor is not necessarily to be determinative.[15] But consider: if domestic production has not declined can there ever be "serious injury?" Suppose employment declines, but production remains constant? Suppose profits decline, but production remains constant? Suppose an "industry" makes several products and can easily shift from producing one to another, is it injured if it is forced to shift products?

The following two cases highlight some of the difficulties in finding concrete standards for analyzing the seriousness of injury. Do you agree with the results?

---

13. Trade Act of 1974 § 201(b)(2)(A).

14. Trade Act of 1974 § 201(b)(2)(B), 19 U.S.C.A. § 2251(b)(2)(B).

15. Trade Act of 1974, § 201(b)(2)(D), added by Trade and Tariff Act of 1984, Pub.L. No. 98–573, § 249(1)(B)–(D), 98 Stat. 2998, 19 U.S. C.A. § 2251(b)(2)(D).

NONRUBBER FOOTWEAR

U.S. Intl. Trade Commn. (1984) [16]

[In a 5–0 decision, the Commission determined that the domestic nonrubber footwear industry had not been seriously injured and was not threatened with serious injury.]

VIEWS OF COMMISSIONERS STERN, LIEBELER AND ROHR

No Serious Injury

In this investigation, the Commission has made a negative finding because it has concluded that the domestic nonrubber footwear industry is not currently experiencing "serious injury." Section 201 does not specifically define the term "serious injury." The legislative history makes clear, however, that mere injury is not sufficient to meet the statutory standard:

> It is not intended that the escape clause criteria go from one extreme of excessive rigidity to complete laxity. An industry must be seriously injured or threatened with serious injury before an affirmative determination should be made.

We believe that Congress intended that we not make an affirmative finding unless the injury suffered by an industry is indeed severe.

In order to guide the Commission, the statute does list specific economic factors the Commission should consider in reaching its determination as to whether an industry is seriously injured, as follows:

> the significant idling of productive facilities in the industry, the inability of a significant number of firms to operate at a reasonable level of profit, and significant unemployment or underemployment within the industry.

The statute also provides that the Commission may take into consideration any other economic factors it considers relevant. In this investigation, we have found the indicators of the performance of the domestic industry to be mixed; some are characteristic of an industry suffering injury while others are characteristic of a healthy industry. We are mindful of the admonition from Congress in the Trade Act of 1974:

> The Committee did not intend that an industry would automatically satisfy the criteria for import relief by showing that all, or some of the enumerated factors, were present at the time of its petition to the [ITC]. That is a judgment to be made by the [ITC] on the basis of all factors it considers relevant.

We have analyzed and weighed all of the factors we have considered relevant to this industry, including those enumerated. Our analysis of all the indicators of this industry's performance leads us to conclude that it is not currently experiencing serious injury.

Production

The first factor that we have considered is the "significant idling of productive facilities." The data presented to the Commission indicate that

16. Inv. No. TA–201–50, Pub. No. 1545, 6 ITRD 1992 (1984).

total domestic production of nonrubber footwear declined during 1979–83. The major portion of this decline occurred between 1981–82. Between 1982 and 1983, in contrast, the decline in domestic production was small, indicating that production has stabilized.

The Commission received conflicting data on the closings of plants and firms in the industry during the period of investigation. Department of Commerce data indicate that there have been both plant and firm closings during the period of investigation. These data reflect also that the number of such closings was at or below the average annual number of closings in this industry for the last 20 years. Further, the petitioners' data indicate that the closings that occurred during the period of import relief during 1977–81 had a substantially greater effect on capacity than have closings since that time. The Commission also cannot ignore that this industry has historically been characterized by low barriers to entry and exit.

Capacity data provided to the Commission in previous section 201 investigations provide some insight into historical trends in this industry. Industry capacity fell by 150 million pairs during 1967–74, also fell by roughly 200 million pairs between 1974 and 1981. In this investigation, according to information supplied by 152 firms accounting for 87 percent of domestic production in 1983, capacity between 1979 and 1983 increased from 380 million pairs to 414 million pairs.

Overall capacity utilization rates declined slightly between 1979 and 1983. In 1979, capacity utilization stood at approximately 76 percent. This increased to 80 percent during the last two years of import relief and then dropped to 72 percent in 1983. It is significant that the larger firms in the industry by 1983 had largely regained their 1979 capacity utilization rates, despite an 8 percent capacity gain over the period. Smaller firms also appear to have largely stabilized their utilization rates, albeit at levels below their 1979 rates.

In analyzing the performance of the productive facilities in the industry, we conclude that, at this time, although there has been some idling of productive facilities, the evidence does not establish the serious injury required in the statute, especially when viewed in the context of the industry's total performance. The data reveal an industry that is smaller and more concentrated than in prior years. But a smaller and more concentrated industry is not necessarily a seriously injured industry.

Profitability

The second indicator we have analyzed is the profitability of the industry. In its analysis, the Commission considered only the profit data of operations producing domestic footwear.

Overall, profits on domestic nonrubber footwear operations increased during the 1979–83 period. The ratio of net operating profit to net sales increased from 6.8 percent in 1979 to 10.0 percent in 1981, then fell to 8.2 percent in 1982 before rising again in 1983 to 8.8 percent. Compared with other domestic industries and total U.S. production of durable goods, these ratios are impressive. In 1982, total U.S. manufacturing showed a ratio of operating income to net sales of 6.3 percent. For the first three quarters of 1983, that ratio was 6.6 percent.

We have also looked at the performance of the industry using the traditional indicators used by financial analysts. These indicators suggest that a reasonably healthy industry currently exists. As a ratio to total assets, profits reached a five-year high in 1983. Profits as a percentage of net worth, a measure of the returns in this industry, were also sharply above 1979 levels, and in three years, 1980, 1981, and 1983, were over 30 percent.

The liquidity measures of the performance of this industry were also good and displayed upward trends throughout most of the period. The "quick ratio" increased steadily from 1.29 in 1974 to 1.69 in 1983. The current ratio also improved from 2.76 in 1979 to 3.31 in 1983. Further, the measures of debt and fixed assets to net worth and the measure of receivables turnover suggest the financial burdens of debt, fixed assets, and inventories did not increase during the period of investigation.

We have also considered the profitability of the domestic footwear industry based upon the profitability of groups of firms segregated by the size of their production. Based upon this analysis, we conclude that the information supplied to us by the industry does not establish that a significant number of firms are unable to operate at a reasonable level of profit.

Firms producing less than 200,000 pairs annually, and which accounted for 2 percent of production in 1982, showed a ratio of net operating profit to net sales of 5.9 percent in 1979, 10.7 percent in 1981, 7.4 percent in 1982, and 5.3 percent in 1983. Of this group, firms accounting for 56 percent of net sales reported a return of 5 percent and firms accounting for 12 percent reported losses.

Firms producing 200,000 to 500,000 pairs annually, accounting for 6 percent of production, experienced low or negative profitability ratios during the period. Of this group, firms accounting for 40 percent of net sales reported a return of over 5 percent and firms accounting for 37 percent of net sales reported losses. Despite this poor performance, the financial indicators for this segment of the industry have remained relatively constant or have improved. Liquidity measures remained constant, inventory turnover improved, the ratio of net sales to fixed assets improved, and the ratios of profit to total assets and to net worth also increased slightly.

Firms producing 500,000 to 1 million pairs annually, accounting for 7 percent of production, fared better, showing profitability ratios of 4.3 percent in 1979, 6.9 percent in 1981, and 4.6 percent in 1983. Of the group, firms representing 64 percent of net sales reported profits of above 5 percent and firms accounting for only 19 percent of net sales reported losses. The financial indicators of this group of producers also show improving performance over the period of investigation.

The larger companies producing 1 to 2 million pairs annually, accounting for 17 percent of production in 1982 performed considerably better than the smaller firms. The ratios of operating profit to net sales for these firms were 6.3 percent in 1979, 12.6 percent in 1980, and 9.4 percent in 1983. The profitability ratios for firms producing 2 to 4 million pairs annually, which accounted for 15 percent of production in 1982, were 7.0 percent in 1979, 8.5 percent in 1981, and 7.2 percent in 1983. The largest firms, those producing over 4 million pairs annually and accounting for 53 percent of production, showed ratios of net operating profit to net sales of 7.9 percent in 1979, 11.2 percent in 1981, 11.9 percent in 1982, and 11.2 percent in 1983. The financial indicators of the performance of these groups of producers also remained stable or showed improvement.

Thus, the profit data of these three latter categories of firms, representing about 85 percent of domestic production, establish that this industry is not suffering serious injury financially and is, in fact, healthy. Our analysis of all of the segments of the industry indicates to us that only a small number of firms are experiencing injury. We cannot base a finding of serious injury on the ill-health of a very small portion of domestic production.

Employment

A third factor which we have considered is whether there is significant unemployment or underemployment in the industry. It is clear that there are fewer shoeworkers employed in the industry now than in 1981, at the end of the last period of import relief for this industry. In assessing these levels of employment, we recognize that viewed solely in an historical context there is a significant employment problem in the footwear industry. We cannot, however, view employment solely in its historical context. We must also consider employment in the context of the current industry.

Bureau of Labor Statistics estimates show that after a sharp increase in the number of unemployed workers between 1981 and 1982, there was a significant drop in the number of unemployed workers in the industry between 1982 and 1983. At the same time, the Commission's survey indicates that for those firms currently producing footwear, total employment increased slightly between 1982 and 1983 and increased by 7 percent over the period of investigation.

Further, in interpreting employment data, we must also consider the level of compensation paid to workers in the industry. The average hourly compensation paid to production and related workers increased by 31 percent from $4.79 to $6.27 over the 1979–83 period. The Commission does not infer from these wage increases that workers in this industry are overpaid. Wages in this industry have historically been below those in other industries which this Commission has recently examined. Nevertheless, wage trends in this industry do not support a finding of serious injury.

Thus, the employment picture in this industry is mixed. Were we to look solely at the historic employment patterns, we might indeed find that there was significant unemployment and underutilization of capacity in this industry. Our investigation, however, must include other indicia of injury and we do not find, on the basis of the totality of the information before the Commission, including production, profitability, and employment, that the domestic industry is currently experiencing serious injury.

Threat of Serious Injury

With respect to threat of serious injury, the statute directs us to take into account:

> a decline in sales, a higher and growing inventory, and a downward trend in production, profits, wages, or employment (or increasing underemployment) in the domestic industry concerned.

The legislative history states that a threat exists "when serious injury, although not yet existing, is clearly imminent if import trends continued unabated." The Commission traditionally has interpreted the standard to require that threat be real rather than speculative, and that serious injury be highly probable in the foreseeable future. We have considered each of the economic factors enumerated in the statute and have concluded that the data fail to indicate a threat of serious injury at this time. In doing so, we have focused in particular upon the data for 1982 and 1983.

In terms of revenues, net sales of domestically produced footwear have remained essentially stable during the past three years. Although production has declined over the period of investigation, it now appears to have stabilized. According to official statistics, there was only a very slight decline in production between 1982–83. Profits in the industry, although varying by the size of the firm, have been stable or increasing for most firms in the industry during the past two years. As noted above, the unemployment rate in the industry declined during 1983 and the absolute number of employees increased slightly. Further, hourly wages throughout the industry have increased over the period of investigation. Further, the ratio of inventories to shipments, which indicates the potential threat of inventory overhang, remained relatively constant.

NONRUBBER FOOTWEAR

U.S. Intl. Trade Commn. (1985) [17]

[In an investigation initiated by the Senate Finance Committee, the Commissioners found that the domestic nonrubber footwear industry either had been seriously injured by import competition or that it was threatened by such injury. The Commission recommended that quotas be imposed for five years, but President Reagan ultimately decided not to provide any relief to the industry because of the increased costs that would be imposed on U.S. consumers, the possibility of retaliation by shoe-exporting countries and the adverse effect that relief would have on the export earnings of certain major shoe producing countries, which in turn would reduce U.S. exports to those countries.]

VIEWS OF CHAIRWOMAN STERN

1984 and 1985

One year ago [in an investigation initiated by the footwear industry], I joined my colleagues in concluding that the U.S. footwear industry had been successful and would continue to be successful in meeting competition from

---

17. Inv. No. TA–201–55, Pub. No. 1717, ___ ITRD ___ (1985).

abroad. Notwithstanding, I now find the increased imports threaten this industry with serious injury. Why is a different conclusion now warranted? What has changed since 1984 that now justifies a five year period of import relief? How could the Commission which found neither serious injury nor causation one year later find both? Is the present finding the correction of some unacknowledged error? Were increasing imports threatening this industry with serious injury in 1984? Readers will find that I have not recanted. Rather, my present findings stem from changes in the factual situation.

In 1984, imports were penetrating the U.S. market rapidly. Imports had increased an average of 25 percent a year since 1981. In the first quarter of 1984 this pace continued. But the data then indicated that the composition of these imports was such that direct competition with domestic production was limited. The vast majority of the increase in imports between 1979 and 1983 was imports of low-cost footwear, and attributable to a new, strong demand for athletic shoes. Many domestic producers were not seriously affected by this increase in imports—in fact almost half of the imports were imported by the domestic producers themselves. Moreover, the industry's economic indicators, while neither uniformly positive or negative, did not reflect a seriously injured industry.

* * *

In 1985, the Commission has a more complete, and more recent, picture. Now there are distinct, declining trends in production, capacity, shipments, and employment, which could not be foreseen in the last investigation.

* * *

Production. Data from the Department of Commerce in our previous investigation indicated that domestic nonrubber footwear production had declined from 372 million pairs in 1981 to 342 million pairs in 1982. However, in 1983, domestic production appeared to stabilize at 341 million pairs.

Updated information now shows that the overall pattern is one of constant decline in production since 1981. Production fell from 372 million pairs in 1981 to 359 million pairs in 1982. In 1983, production fell to 344 million pairs. The decline continued into 1984, when production reached only 298 million pairs.

Rather than an industry that appeared to be experiencing stability, the picture is now one of a 17 percent decline since 1982, with most of that reduction occurring in 1984. Moreover, production was 20 percent less during the last half of 1984 than in the first part of the year. * * *

Similarly, in the last investigation, capacity appeared to be stabilizing. Although there had been a decline between 1981 and 1982 coincident with the lifting of the [Orderly Marketing Arrangements] with Taiwan and the Republic of Korea, in 1983 capacity stood approximately at its 1982 level.

Now that 1984 figures have been added to previous data, it is clear that capacity has not stabilized. Rather, capacity has fallen 9 percent since 1982. Despite this decline in capacity, domestic producers have been unable to increase their capacity utilization rates. Utilization of domestic capacity has remained at 70 percent since 1983.

This decline in domestic capacity has clearly been the result of a striking increase in the number of firms that have recently closed. While only 3 plants closed in 1980, 11 in 1981 and 1982, and 14 in 1983; in 1984, an alarming 84 plants closed. * * *

Financial Health of the Industry. In 1984, the Commission saw an industry that experienced several years of high and stable profits, as well as an overall healthy balance sheet. Operating income rose from 9.1 percent of net sales in 1980 to 10.1 percent of net sales in 1981. Once import relief was removed in 1982, the industry's profit level fell slightly to 8.0 percent of net sales. However, in 1983, operating profits rose to 8.7 percent of net sales. These profit levels compared favorably with other U.S. manufacturing industries. Financial ratios were also quite healthy.

In 1984, operating income on domestic footwear operations fell to 5.8 percent of net sales. In contrast, average operating profits for all manufacturing increased to 6.8 percent. Moreover, while data in the previous investigation showed the producers of the majority of domestic production were experiencing strong profits, our most recent data show otherwise. * * *

The overall decline in the industry's profitability is apparently attributable to a particularly severe drop in operating profits during the last half of 1984. While the profits were a reasonable 6.4 percent during the first half of 1984, near the level of those for all manufacturing, during the latter half of the year, they fell to 5.3 percent. * * *

Employment. Whereas the employment picture was mixed in last year's investigation, this year's questionnaire data shows that overall employment in this industry has in fact fallen 8 percent since 1983. The number of workers in this industry has fallen gradually since 1981. The drop to only 87,000 workers in 1984, however, is much sharper than in earlier periods.

The new information presented in this investigation thus shows that by the end of 1984 and continuing into 1985, this industry is clearly becoming less able to meet the increasing intensity of global competition than the industry the Commission examined in its last investigation.

Note

The ITC has rejected the claim that harm to some but not most of the firms in an industry is sufficient. See Stainless Steel Table Flatware, Inv. No. TA–201–49, Pub. No. 1536, 6 ITRD 1032 (ITC 1984); Fishing Rods and Parts Thereof, No. TA–201–45, Pub. No. 1194, 3 ITRD 1819 (ITC 1981).

(3) Substantial Cause

In addition to finding "serious injury," the ITC must also find that the serious injury has been caused by the increased imports. As we have discussed in Section 9.1, the U.S. statutory provisions on this second causation issue have changed over time. In the 1951 law, the imports in question had to "cause" or threaten serious injury. In the 1955 amendment, it was provided that it was enough that such imports "contributed substantially" to causing or threatening serious injury, while the 1962 Trade Expansion Act provided that imports had to be "the major factor" in causing, or threatening to cause, serious injury. At present, Section 201 requires that the increased imports be a "substantial cause" of serious injury, with substantial cause defined as an "important" cause that is "not less than" any other cause. Is this "substantial cause" test more or less stringent than that required by GATT Article XIX? What about an "in major part" or "primary cause" test? Review the excerpt from the Senate Report set out in the Notes to subsection (B)(3) supra.

Application of the causation requirement has been difficult, as some of the materials below reveal. Note the importance of the extent to which a "cause" other than imports is disaggregated and treated as several causes, or aggregated and treated as one cause. The latter approach would obviously result in finding a cause much more likely to exceed imports in importance as a cause.

CERTAIN MOTOR VEHICLES
U.S. Intl. Trade Commn. (1980) [18]

On the basis of the information developed in the course of the investigation, the Commission has determined (Commissioners Moore and Bedell dissenting in part) that automobile trucks, on-the-highway passenger automobiles, and bodies (including cabs) and chassis for automobile trucks, * * * are not being imported into the United States in such increased quantities as to be a substantial cause of serious injury, or the threat thereof, to the domestic industries producing articles like or directly competitive with the imported articles.

* * *

VIEWS OF CHAIRMAN ALBERGER
* * *

I have found the decline in demand for new automobiles and light trucks owing to the general recessionary conditions in the United States economy to be a far greater cause of the domestic industries' plight than the increase in imports. While I also believe that the rapid change in product mix necessitated by the shift of consumer preference away from large, less fuel-efficient vehicles is an important cause of the present injury, I do not view this factor to be a more important cause than increased imports.

The Decline in Overall Demand

One noticeable factor in this case is the apparent lack of correlation between the growth in import volume and the state of health of domestic producers. Our investigation reveals that the period 1976–78 was characterized by strong domestic sales and record profits. Yet it was during this period that the largest increase in total imports occurred. Imports actually declined in 1979, when the recession began in earnest. Even Japanese imports grew most dramatically in the prior period, and remained about steady in 1979. While Japanese imports have increased by a more alarming rate in the first 6 months of 1980 (by about 200,000 units over the compara-

18. Inv. No. TA–201–44, Pub. No. 1110, 2
ITRD 5241 (1980).

ble period of 1979), imports from other sources have declined. This juxtaposition of events becomes even more curious when we consider the testimony of petitioners that the injury began in early 1979 and has deepened over the past 18 months. Given the relatively slight import growth in that period, and considering how healthy the monthly sales figures were before 1979, one obviously begins to look for other explanations of the current injury.

One figure that stands out in stark contrast to the rather marginal import increases for 1979–80 is the very large decline in overall consumption of both passenger autos and light trucks. Consumption of passenger autos fell by almost 1 million units in 1979, a decline of 7.8 percent. Moreover, consumption in January-June 1980 was 1.1 million units or 18.5 percent below the figure for January-June 1979. *   *   * While imports did improve their market share substantially during this period by maintaining constant or slightly increasing volume in the face of falling demand, the downturn in demand itself is obviously a variable factor which must be independently assessed for its impact on U.S. producers.

At the most fundamental level, then, it is useful to allocate the decline in domestic producers' shipments in 1979 and 1980 into two basic components: that portion accounted for by the reduced overall consumption of autos and light trucks because of general economic conditions, and that portion attributable to the increasing market share of import vehicles. The relative magnitude of these two causes can be assessed by comparing the actual decline in domestic shipments to the decline that might have occurred if imports had not increased their market share in 1979–80, i.e., if imports and domestic vehicles had shared equally in the overall decline in sales. The difference between these two figures represents the maximum potential loss in sales due to increased imports. This amount can then be compared to the volume of loss attributable *solely* to reduced demand. The following tables, based upon data available in the Commission's report, reveal the results of this exercise for 1979 and for January-June 1980:

Table 1.—**Passenger automobiles: U.S. apparent consumption, U.S. producers' domestic shipments, imports for consumption, imports' share of consumption, 1978 and 1979, and relative increases or declines in imports and producers' shipments in 1979, if the share of imports is held constant at the 1978 level (in thousands of units, except percentages)**

Item	1978	1979
Actual 1978 and 1979 data:		
Apparent consumption	11,185.0	10,315.3
U.S. producers' domestic shipments	8,256.9	7,518.2
Imports for consumption	2,928.1	2,797.1
Ratio of imports to consumption	26.2%	27.1%
Estimated data for 1979, holding import share of consumption constant at 1978 level and using actual 1979 consumption data:		
Imports, if held at 1978 share of consumption	[1]	2,702.6
U.S. producers' domestic shipments, if held at 1978 share of consumption	[1]	7,612.7
Net change from 1978 to 1979:		
Total actual decline in U.S. producers' shipments	[1]	738.7
Net decline due to increasing import share	[1]	94.5
Net decline due to declining demand	[1]	644.2
Share of declining shipments due to declining demand	[1]	87.2%

1. Not applicable.

Source: Compiled from data presented in table 19 of the staff report.

Table 2.—Passenger automobiles: U.S. apparent consumption, U.S. producers' domestic shipments, imports for consumption, imports' share of consumption, January-June 1979 and January-June 1980, and relative increases or declines in imports and producers' shipments in January-June 1980, if the share of imports is held constant at the January-June 1979 level (in thousands of units, except percentages)

Item	Jan.-June 1979	Jan.-June 1980
Actual January-June 1979 and January-June 1980 data:		
Apparent consumption	5,807.7	4,731.7
U.S. producers' domestic shipments	4,369.8	3,099.9
Imports for consumption	1,437.9	1,631.8
Ratio of imports to consumption	24.7%	34.5%
Estimated data for January-June 1980, holding import share of consumption constant at January-June 1979 level and using actual January-June 1980 consumption data:		
Imports, if held at January-June 1979 share of consumption	1	1,168.7
U.S. producers' domestic shipments, if held at January-June 1979 share of consumption	1	3,563.0
Net change from January-June 1979 to January-June 1980:		
Total actual decline in U.S. producers' shipments	1	1,269.9
Net decline due to increasing import share of consumption	1	463.1
Net decline due to declining demand	1	806.8
Share of declining shipments due to declining demand	1	63.5%

1. Not applicable.

Source: Compiled from data presented in table 19 of the staff report.

*   *   *

I believe that these tables demonstrate graphically why imports are not a "substantial cause" of either industry's present malaise. They suggest that declining demand accounted for over 80 percent of the net decline in U.S. producers' domestic shipments of both automobiles and trucks from 1978 to 1979, as compared with less than 20 percent of the decline in U.S. producers' domestic shipments being attributable to imports' increasing share of U.S. consumption. Between January-June 1979 and January-June 1980, about two-thirds of the decline in U.S. producers' domestic shipments was attributable to declining demand and only a third was due to the increased share of the U.S. market accounted for by imports. Thus, even if the import share had been held constant during these critical 18 months, and even if all of those sales which went into the increased import share had instead gone to U.S. producers, domestic firms' sales still would have fallen by over 80 percent of their actual decline in 1979 and by over 60 percent of their actual decline in January–June 1980. While the legislative history cautions against the application of a pure mathematical test, it is necessary to assess the relative impact of these factors, and I think these percentages reveal why one is so overwhelmingly greater than the other.

Petitioners would perhaps dispute the conclusions I draw from the above tables because the tables fail to allow for the theory that an import increase in the earlier period of 1976–78 could be accountable for injury which did not become manifest until 1979. However, even if average imports, consumption and domestic shipments for 1976–78 are compared to the 1979 figures, the decline in demand is still greater than the import factor. Moreover, the above tables really account for the overall import increase since 1975, because they postulate the overall effect of the increased *market share* of imports caused by a drop in domestic sales after three years of steady import growth. Thus, the above analysis gives an accurate picture of the demand *and* import factors since 1975.

It has been argued in this case that the downturn in demand is itself a result of several factors, and that each should be assessed individually to determine whether any single factor is greater than increasing imports. To consider demand in the aggregate, the argument goes, is to cumulate artificially what are clearly separate causal elements in a manner inconsistent with the purposes or legislative history of Section 201. Among the separate and identifiable causes mentioned in this case are inflation, unemployment, rising interest rates, and higher energy costs. Undoubtedly, all of these factors played a part in bringing about the present recession in new vehicle sales. Supporters of the petition contend that none of these factors *alone* played as great a role in bringing about the injury as increasing imports. In fact, the UAW brief contends that increasing imports brought on much of the recession, and so the recession should be viewed as an effect rather than a cause.

All of these contentions seek to isolate and weigh separately the various components of a general economic downturn. In reality, most of the factors mentioned above have worked in unison to bring about what is commonly termed a "recession." Inflation in new vehicle prices coupled with higher credit rates have acted together to drive up the total costs of new motor vehicles. Interest rates have played a particularly important part in the volume of auto sales, because these are long-term consumer durable purchases where credit financing is the norm. Not only have transaction prices for new vehicles and monthly payments for loans increased, but credit has become "tighter," and the refusal rate on auto credit applications has grown. Unemployment and general inflation have acted to reduce the real disposable income of the average consumer, and a normal reaction has been to delay many long-term capital outlays.

All of these phenomena are part and parcel of a generalized recession, which is normally defined as a period of reduced economic activity, and which can be brought on by a multitude of factors. Recessions are often characterized by rising prices, high interest rates and unemployment. But to say they are comprised of a multitude of causes is not to say that reduced demand in a recession cannot be cited as a single cause for purposes of section 201.   In fact, I have cited this very factor in several past cases, particularly where we were considering highly cyclical industries which fluctuate with the general economy.   The reason for such a policy is readily apparent; if decline in demand for the product is a consequence of a general economic downturn, then the inevitable recovery from the recession will restore health to the industry.   This is precisely what happened to the automobile industry after the downturn in 1974–75.   Cyclical downturns in the economy are to be expected, and must not force a reliance on unnecessary import remedies.   The problem which auto producers confront is one which confronts many sectors of the economy (the building industry, for example), and it cannot be solved by import relief.

Of course, it is possible for imports to be a "substantial cause" of serious injury or threat thereof during a recession, but only where the absolute or relative increase is of sufficient magnitude to outweigh or equal the effects of the recession itself.   As the previously cited tables demonstrate, that is not the case in the present investigation.

In addition to concluding that increased imports are not a substantial cause of the serious injury which presently exists, I also believe they could not be a substantial cause of any threat thereof.   U.S. small car production is steadily increasing.   The three major manufacturers have begun introducing their new generation of front wheel drive, fuel efficient vehicles.   We received extensive testimony that such products were fully competitive and would revolutionize the automobile industry.   As such products come on stream the import share of the small car market should decline, particularly if demand picks up.   Of course, if we remain in a deep recession with high interest rates it is probable that the present critical state of the industry will continue for some time.   However, the adjustment already made by domestic firms to changing consumer demand should act to reduce the import share.   Thus, imports should not become a greater causal factor in the next year or two.

* * *

VIEWS OF VICE CHAIRMAN CALHOUN

* * *

I have found two factors which seem to be more important causes of the industry's problems than are increased imports.

First, *the demand for the type of automobile desired by a significant portion of the buying public is shifting from a product line roughly described as larger, less fuel-efficient automobiles to smaller, more fuel-efficient automobiles.* * * *

Second, *there has been an overall decline in demand for automobiles that is largely associated with the general decline in the economy.* * * *

A.   Shift in Demand

With regard to the shift in consumer preference from one type of automobile to another, petitioners argued that if such a shift exists it is nothing more than a shift from the purchase of domestic cars to the purchase of imported cars with a resulting increase in imported automobiles. The reason for the increase in imports, they argued, is unimportant to our determination under section 201. Moreover, their view continued, section 201 is specifically designed to provide a remedy in precisely those circumstances in which domestic sales are displaced by sales of imports. While I do not refute this view of the policy underlying section 201 I must take exception, both in concept and in fact, with the view that in this case the shift in consumer preference merely explains why imports might have increased and is not cognizable as an independent source of injury to the domestic industry.

In concept, the Commission has specifically relied upon a shift in consumer preference from one type of product to another as a phenomenon distinct from a shift to imports *qua* imports. The most attenuated support for this proposition is *Unalloyed, Unwrought Zinc,* Investigation No. TA–201–31, USITC Pub. No. 894 (1978). In that investigation the Commission found that imports were not a substantial cause of serious injury because a decline in demand was a more important cause of the injury to the industry. An important element in the decline in demand for the domestic article was, despite increasing imports, the replacement of the domestic article by a substitute article. Another investigation in which the Commission recognized and relied upon the concept of demand shift as distinct from a shift to imports in assessing causality was *Low-Carbon Ferrochromium,* Investigation No. TA–201–20, USITC Pub. No. 825 (1977). In that case, the Commission found that a technological innovation had caused a fundamental change in the production process employed by the industry and, hence, a drastic shift from the use of low-carbon ferrochromium to the use of high-carbon ferrochromium. As a result the majority concluded that, despite increasing imports, the injury the low-carbon ferrochromium industry might have been suffering was due more to the decline in demand for its product.

For me the decisive precedent for the integrity of demand shift as a concept distinct from a shift to imports in a circumstance of increasing and competitive imports is *Wrapper Tobacco,* Investigation No. TA–201–3, USITC Pub. No. 746 (1975). *Wrapper Tobacco* has a particular precedential appeal because the behavior of imports in the marketplace was especially strong. First, imports had more than tripled their market penetration over a four-year period while domestic production and total consumption were in decline. Second, the prices of the bulk of the imported articles tended to be below the price of the domestic articles, but certain high-grade imports were priced considerably higher than the domestic product. Third, while some of the imports were considered to be of higher quality than the domestic article, most of the imports were used to produce product lines that competed with those using the domestic product.

In the face of this extremely competitive position of imports, the Commission in *Wrapper Tobacco* made a unanimous negative determination. Four Commissioners relied upon the change in consumer tastes from larger cigars to smaller cigars and other tobacco products as the primary reason for the decline in demand they viewed as a cause of injury more important than increasing imports. Thus, the majority of the Commission had no difficulty in concept or in fact in differentiating between a shift from the domestic article and a shift to imports.

* * *

Moreover, where in both concept and in fact a shift in demand is distinguishable from a shift to imports, not to make it a factor in the consideration of causality transforms section 201 from an import relief provision to an industrial relief provision. Under such a view, whenever an industry is in decline because of internal structural changes or exogenous occurrences in the society independent of imports, an industry need only show that imports are increasing concomitant with its difficulty and it could receive relief. While one could make very good arguments supporting the need for an industrial policy which would provide assistance to worthy industries suffering generalized difficulty unassociated with imports, section 201 cannot be so construed. It is plainly and simply an import relief provision and, therefore, our fundamental task on the face of it and from the legislative history is to determine that *imports* are an important cause of the injury and to determine that no other cause is more important than imports. Thus, any other factors that may have contributed to injury must be measured against the contribution made by imports.

Having established the validity of the concept of a product line shift as a factor to be assessed in this case, establishing the fact of the shift and assessing what weight it ought to be given is not difficult. Several preliminary factors make this exercise particularly valuable in finding the substantial cause in this case.

First, there is a significant difference between the level of profit earned by the industry on sales of larger automobiles compared with profits on smaller ones. Indeed, a fundamental strategy for the industry, for years, has been that the great majority of profits on sales of automobiles would be earned on larger automobiles. Smaller cars would be marketed to fill out the product line and, ultimately, to win over larger car purchasers. Thus, the product mix of larger and smaller automobiles has been a particularly important factor in the industry's profitability.

Second, as a practical matter a change in the product mix requires not only a considerable lead time, but also an exceptionally high capital investment.

Together, these two special features of the industry render it especially vulnerable to a relatively quick and sustained shift in consumer preference. Further, they explain why such a shift is an important factor in assessing the substantial cause.

That such a shift has taken place in consumer taste is readily demonstrable. Between 1975 and 1979, large domestic car sales grew at an annual rate of 2.4 percent while sales of imports grew at an annual rate of 6.4 percent. Eclipsing both of these were sales of small domestic cars which grew 9.6 percent during this period. Comparing the first half of 1980 to the first half of 1979, in 1980 sales of large domestic cars declined 48.5 percent, and sales of imports and domestic small cars each grew 1.8 percent. The failure of small domestic cars to keep pace with their earlier rate of sales growth and with the growth rate of imports for the first half of 1980 might be viewed as proof that consumption has, in fact, shifted to imports *qua* imports. But precisely the opposite is the case.

The significant growth in demand for domestic small cars caught up with production during the first half of 1980, exceeding the ability of the domestic producers to supply the market. During the first six months of 1980, several producers were at or above their full capacity for small cars. Others were either experiencing serious recall problems on their major small car models or were suffering from major adverse publicity on their products' quality and safety. Both of these factors had a considerable impact on sales.

The change in consumer purchasing patterns from buying large cars to buying smaller cars is even more striking when measuring car sales as a percent of apparent consumption. In 1975 small domestic car sales were 26.6 percent of total apparent consumption, large domestic cars were 47.6 percent, and imports were 26 percent. In the same year, small domestic cars were 36.1 percent of domestic producers' sales while larger cars accounted for the balance. By 1979, small domestic cars had grown to 31.5 percent of apparent consumption, large domestic cars fell to 41.4 percent and imports were 27 percent. Small domestic cars were 44.1 percent of domestic producer sales. For the first half of 1980, despite the problems of domestic supply shortfalls and quality problems with small domestic cars, this category grew to 36.3 percent of apparent consumption, large domestic cars abruptly fell to 29.2 percent and imports, taking up the slack caused by domestic supply problems, grew to 34 percent of apparent consumption. Small domestic cars, for this period, represented 55.4 percent of domestic producer sales.

These figures convince me that a fundamental demand side structural change is occurring in the automobile industry. They further convince me that this change is not one characterized simply as a shift to imports, even though for the first half of 1980 imports have benefited from the change more than have domestic small cars. This aberration for early 1980 is a result of domestic supply and quality problems. By all measures, consumption has been shifting to smaller cars and domestic smaller cars have benefited from the shift more than have imports.

*   *   *

VIEWS OF COMMISSIONER STERN

*   *   *

Although there is serious injury present in the passenger car industry, I have determined that increased imports do not constitute a substantial cause of the existing serious injury.

*   *   *

Alternate Causes. There is scant legislative direction on which alternative causes should be weighed against increased imports.

The Senate Finance Committee Report does direct the Commission to examine the injury attributable to increased imports or of other causes, "such as change in technology or in consumer tastes, domestic competition from substitute products, plant obsolescence, or poor management." By not shackling the Commission to an approach so finely detailed as to be unworkable in all potential cases, the statute gives the Commission maximum flexibility and discretion. Within these broad boundaries lies the responsibility for the Commission's determination to be "clear, well documented, and *   *   * decisive."

*   *   *

Section 201 and the Case-by-Case Approach. All relevant economic factors must be considered, but the question remains—how? Commission precedent suggests that the answer is to be found in the economic rather than the legal sphere.

The fact that when viewed narrowly, precedents may be cited for viewing particular factors either as causes separate from or as explanations of increasing imports should not be disturbing.*[46] The import relief statute is the broadest jurisdiction assigned to the Commission. The impact of all imports on entire domestic industries is examined. Unlike countervailing duty and dumping cases, there is no well-defined measurable unfair price margin to examine. Section 201 is necessarily broad. It is doubtful that it is theoretically possible for Congress to have made the criteria more specific on the issues of causation that we might have applied in this case and still have an import relief framework applicable to the full range of industries present in the world's largest economy.*[47] Each industry has its own structure and logic. Each case requires the qualitative judgment and intelligence of the Commissioners who must reach a determination. Were these statements not true, the Commissioner's deliberations might better be replaced by computer simulations. Though I am not without self-interest in this matter, I feel there is no mechanical alternative that could give better results than case-by-case analysis.

Causes of Injury

I have attempted to concentrate on those phenomena that are relatively independent. To the extent that an increase in imports seemed to be merely incidental to a far more fundamental phenomenon, I have decided to analyze that fundamental phenomenon as a separate cause. Under the rubric "imports as an independent cause," I shall treat those sales which imports have captured in head-on competition with domestic autos due to attributes such as price, design, and quality that attract customers.

A full understanding of the industry's problems necessitates an examination of a complex web of events. The injury sustained by the automobile industry can best be explained by analyzing four fundamental phenomena:

(1) A general decline in demand due to rapidly increasing costs of car ownership and operation (added to normal—if not precisely predictable—recessionary effects on consumer income and confidence);

(2) A seemingly permanent shift in consumer tastes to relatively smaller, more fuel-efficient autos;

---

* **46.** The legal doctrine of precedents, *stare decisis,* does not strictly apply to administrative agencies. An agency is free to change its policy, or even its interpretation of a statute, so long as it explains the reasons. A section 201 decision may be set aside by the courts only if it is shown to be "arbitrary, capricious, an abuse of discretion, or otherwise not in accordance with law." *See* Administrative Procedure Act, 5 U.S.C. 706(2)(A).

* **47.** Over the last three decades, Congress has passed three different import relief statutes. Although the thresholds of injury and standards for causation (major, principal, substantial) have been debated and changed, Congress has neither sought to delimit narrowly the factors which the Commission should consider nor direct precisely how the causes should be broken down.

(3) A substantially negative accounting impact on profits resulting from huge investments to transform the industry; and

(4) Success of imports in head-to-head competition.

The decline in demand and shift in demand are more important causes of injury to the auto industry than increasing imports, *per se.* I have not been able to evaluate fully the relative significance of the massive capital costs of transforming the industry; however, I believe that their impact on domestic industry performance is at least of the same magnitude as that of imports. It is doubtful that in the absence of the first three causes the remaining injury attributable to imports would be serious.

*   *   *

VIEWS OF COMMISSIONERS MOORE AND BEDELL

*   *   *

As discussed above, imports have increased significantly, in both actual and relative terms. More important, however, imports have captured an ever larger share of the domestic passenger automobile market during the last 3 years. The ratio of automobile imports to domestic automobile consumption increased from 25 percent in 1976 and 1977 to 26 percent in 1978 and 27 percent in 1979, and from 25 percent in the first 6 months of 1979 to 34 percent in the first 6 months of 1980.

Section 201(b)(2) does not limit us to consideration of only certain economic factors in determining whether increased imports are a substantial cause of serious injury. We are to take into account "all" relevant economic factors. We believe that there are a number of other individual causes of injury, such as increased costs of passenger automobiles, the shift in consumer preferences from large to small cars, high interest rates, a shortage of consumer credit, increased gasoline prices, shortages of gasoline (in 1979), the failure of domestic corporate management to anticipate current conditions, and costly Government regulations. We find that none of these other causes, even if considered an important cause of injury, are a more important cause of serious injury to the domestic industry than increased imports.

It is clear that our determination differs from the majority in the interpretation given to the provisions in section 201 of the Trade Act relating to the weighing and comparison of the relevant economic factors contributing to the serious injury experienced by the domestic industry. We believe that the law clearly and unequivocally provides that the Commission shall, to the extent practicable, isolate each of the economic factors relevant to the matter of serious injury for the purpose of comparing each of them with the factor of increased imports. If we were to do otherwise—that is, to aggregate the negative economic factors in comparing them with increased imports—there would be few, if any, Commission decisions favorable to a domestic industry in section 201 cases in times of recession or economic downturn.

In this regard, we refer specifically to the prepared statements read by two of our colleagues at the open Commission meeting of November 10, 1980, at the time of the vote on this matter. Commissioner Stern, in voting in the negative, stated "I find the downturn in economic demand due to general economic conditions, recession, credit crunch, rising costs of car ownership and a major unprecedented shift in demand from large to small cars, brought the domestic industry to its present weakened state." Supporting this point of view was Commissioner Calhoun, who, in voting in the negative, said "My analysis reveals that the general decline in purchases of automobiles and light trucks owing to the downturn of the economy has contributed more so than imports to the serious injury suffered by the automobile industry."

We reject the notion that the statute permits the Commission to aggregate a number of economic factors which in combination are to be weighed against increased imports to find the substantial cause of serious injury. Further, we believe that economic downturns represent the concurrence of a number of adverse factors. We do not believe that Congress envisioned that the Commission would consider an economic downturn per se to be a single economic factor in determining injury in section 201 investigations. Instead, we believe that Congress intended the Commission to examine imports and their impact on the domestic industry over the course of the business cycle— during both good and bad years—in order to ascertain whether import penetration is increasing and, if so, whether the increasing penetration is seriously injuring the domestic industry. This is the approach we have followed in past section 201 cases.

In the present case, as the facts show, imports have been increasing their market share, most significantly during the first 6 months of 1980. We believe that the domestic industry today would be in much better condition—losses would not be so massive and plant closings and layoffs not so severe—had imports not increased their share of the market to the extent that they have. Furthermore, the surge in imports and the share of the market held by imports make it likely that the industry will remain in its present state of serious injury for years to come and increase the likelihood that one or more of the major domestic producers and several of the domestic suppliers will not survive. More than 1 million jobs in passenger-automobile-manufacturing plants, in supplier plants, and at car dealerships, are at stake. Further, the health of the domestic passenger automobile industry affects almost every other basic domestic industry, including the industries producing steel, glass, rubber, machine tools, zinc, and a number of other products.

HEAVYWEIGHT MOTORCYCLES

U.S. Intl. Trade Commn. (1983)[19]

[On September 1, 1982, Harley-Davidson Motor Co. Inc. and Harley-Davidson York, Inc. petitioned the ITC for relief under Section 201 from imports of heavyweight motorcycles, and engines and power train subassemblies for heavyweight motorcycles. The February 1, 1983 final determination was affirmative (2–1) for motorcycle imports, but negative (3–0) for engines and power train subassemblies. Chairman Eckes and Commissioner Haggart found imports to be a substantial cause of threat of serious injury;

19. Inv. No. TA–201–47, Pub. No. 1342, 4
ITRD 2469 (1983).

and Commissioner Stern found that imports were not a substantial cause or threat of serious injury to the domestic industry.]

VIEWS OF CHAIRMAN ECKES

* * *

Finally, imports of finished heavyweight motorcycles pose a "substantial cause" of threat of serious injury. Under section 201(b)(4), a "substantial cause" is "a cause which is important and not less than any other cause." In my view, there is no cause more important than imports threatening injury to the domestic motorcycle industry.

In reaching this conclusion I have considered the significance of the present recession in my analysis. Without a doubt the unusual length and severity of the present recession has created unique problems for the domestic motorcycle industry. Without a doubt the rise in joblessness, particularly among blue-collar workers, who constitute the prime market for heavyweight motorcycles, has had a severe impact on the domestic industry. Nonetheless, if the Commission were to analyze the causation question in this way, it would be impossible in many cases for a cyclical industry experiencing serious injury to obtain relief under section 201 during a recession. In my opinion Congress could not have intended for the Commission to interpret the law this way.

There are other reasons for doubting the domestic recession is a substantial cause of injury or threat to the U.S. industry. During the current recession, imports from Japan have increased their market share from domestic producers, gaining nearly six percentage points. Imports have taken market share from the domestic facilities of Honda and Kawasaki as well as Harley-Davidson.

Moreover, while the current recession has undoubtedly depressed demand for heavyweight motorcycles, economic conditions are beginning to improve in this country. Automobile sales are moving up, and so are housing starts and other important leading indicators. As demand responds to this improvement, the domestic industry will be pre-empted from participating in any growth because of the presence of a one-year supply of motorcycles poised and ready to capture market share. Consequently, not the recession, but the inventory of motorcycles coupled with anticipated future imports constitute the greatest threat of injury in the months ahead.

* * *

VIEWS OF COMMISSIONER HAGGART

* * *

In reaching this conclusion, I have considered other causes of the threat of serious injury, such as high interest rates and the decline in demand for heavyweight motorcycles caused by unemployment. However, I have concluded that the increase in imports of heavyweight motorcycles is a far more important cause of a threat of serious injury.

* * *

VIEWS OF COMMISSIONER STERN

*   *   *

In an affirmative section 201 case, the third condition which must be found is that increasing imports are the substantial cause of serious injury. If any cause other than imports is more important, or if several causes are of equal importance, none of which are important standing alone, a negative determination must be made.

There are two causes more important than imports for the industry's difficulties—problems which only became manifest in 1981. The decline in demand for motorcycles in the United States during 1980 and 1982 and the rapid entry of HAM [Honda] into the U.S. market in 1980 as a domestic competitor each outweigh imports as an important cause of injury. Additional problems buffeting the industry include a decline in export sales in 1981, high interest rates for consumer purchases of motorcycles and Harley's heavy debt burden with the accompanying large interest expenses.

(4) Market Disruption and Nonmarket Economies

With respect to certain Communist countries covered by Title IV of the Trade Act of 1974, a special "escape clause" type proceeding is established by Section 406 of the Act. Since 1975, there have been 10 Section 406 petitions, 2 with ITC affirmative determinations, in both of which actual import restraints were imposed pursuant to other authorities (as of February 1986). A third action received a tie vote affirmative ruling, but the President refused relief. We deal generally with issues concerning nonmarket economies in Chapter 21 infra. The following case gives a flavor of the issues in a Section 406 proceeding.

FERROSILICON FROM THE U.S.S.R.

U.S. Intl. Trade Commn. (1984)[20]

In this investigation, the Commission is required to determine whether imports of ferrosilicon from the Soviet Union cause market disruption. The term "market disruption" is defined in section 406(e)(2) of the Trade Act of 1974 as follows:

> Market disruption exists within a domestic industry whenever imports of an article, like or directly competitive with an article produced by such domestic industry, are increasing rapidly, either absolutely or relatively, so as to be a significant cause of material injury, or threat thereof, to such domestic industry.

Section 406 thus requires that the following three criteria be satisfied in order for market disruption to exist:

   (1) imports of the product of a Communist country are increasing rapidly, either absolutely or relatively,

   (2) a domestic industry producing an article like or directly competitive with the imported article is materially injured or threatened with material injury, and

---

20. Inv. No. TA–406–10, Pub. No. 1484, 6 ITRD 1319 (1984).

(3) such rapidly increasing imports are a significant cause of the material injury or threat thereof.

In the present case, we have determined that imports of ferrosilicon from the Soviet Union are increasing rapidly and that domestic ferrosilicon producers are suffering material injury, but we have found that such imports are not a significant cause of material injury or threat thereof. Because we are unable to find the requisite causal connection between the rapidly increasing imports from the Soviet Union and material injury or threat thereof, we have made a negative determination.

DOMESTIC INDUSTRY

The concept of domestic industry under section 406 is identical to that under section 201 of the Trade Act of 1974. Section 406(a)(2) specifically adopts the definitions of industry set forth under section 201(b)(3). Thus, section 406 defines the domestic industry in terms of domestic facilities producing articles "like" or "directly competitive" with the imported articles subject to investigation.

* * *

IMPORTS ARE INCREASING RAPIDLY

The first of the three statutory criteria requires a finding that the imports are "increasing rapidly, either absolutely or relatively." The Senate Finance Committee Report states that this increase "must have occurred during a recent period of time, as determined by the Commission taking into account any historical trade level which may have existed."

In section 406 cases, the Commission generally examines import trends over the most recent 3 years. In the present case, there were no imports of Soviet ferrosilicon until June 1983. Imports totaled 16,647 short tons during the period June-November 1983. The ratio of Soviet ferrosilicon imports to total U.S. ferrosilicon production accordingly increased from zero for the years 1980–1982 to 3.8 percent for the period January-September 1983, the latest period for which comparable domestic production and import data were available.

In light of the above, we have concluded that imports of Soviet ferrosilicon are "increasing rapidly" for purposes of section 406.

THE INDUSTRY IS MATERIALLY INJURED

The second criterion requires a finding of material injury or threat thereof. The Senate Finance Committee Report states that material injury represents "a lesser degree of injury" than the serious injury standard used in section 201. In determining whether there is material injury in a section 406 case, the Commission has generally examined data concerning domestic production, shipments, inventories, idling of production facilities, industry profitability, and changes in employment.

Although there has been some recent improvement in the condition of the domestic ferrosilicon industry, we have concluded that the domestic industry is materially injured. Domestic production declined from 713,000 short tons in 1980 to 414,000 short tons in 1982, and declined further to 311,000 short tons in January-September 1983 as compared with 344,000 short tons in January-September 1982. Domestic shipments declined from 607,000 short tons in 1980 to 365,000 short tons in 1982, but shipments rose slightly in January-September 1983 to 306,000 short tons as compared with 298,000 short tons in January-September 1982. U.S. producers' end-of-period inventories increased from 145,000 short tons in 1980 to 156,000 short tons in 1982, but inventories declined to 130,000 short tons by September 30, 1983, as compared with 164,000 short tons as of September 30, 1982. The decline in inventories reflected an increase in shipments coupled with a continuation of the decline in production. Capacity utilization declined from 72.1 percent in 1980 to 46.3 percent in 1982. Capacity utilization was only 46.9 percent in January-September 1983, despite a decline in industry capacity. U.S. ferrosilicon producers reported a net operating loss of $29.1 million in 1982 and a net operating loss of $28.7 million in the first 9 months of 1983. Employment in the industry declined from an average of 6494 persons in 1980 to an average of 3940 in 1982, or by 39 percent. Average employment declined an additional 18.5 percent during January-September 1983 to 3439 persons as compared with 4221 persons during January-September 1982.

SOVIET IMPORTS ARE NOT A SIGNIFICANT CAUSE OF MATERIAL INJURY

The third criterion requires a finding that the rapidly increasing imports are a significant cause of the material injury or threat thereof. The term "significant cause" is not defined in the statute, and the legislative history provides us with only general guidance. As stated in the Senate Finance Committee Report:

> The term "significant cause" is intended to be an easier standard to satisfy than that of "substantial cause" [as used in section 201]. On the other hand, "significant cause" is meant to require *a more direct causal relationship* between increased imports and injury than the standard used in [adjustment assistance cases], i.e., "contribute importantly." [Emphasis supplied.]

Thus, Congress intended that there be a direct causal link between the subject imports and material injury. The subject imports need not be a "substantial cause," but must do more than "contribute importantly" to material injury. Since the term "substantial cause" means "a cause which is important and not less than any other cause," a significant cause must be at least an important cause but need not be equal to or greater than any other cause. In order to determine whether the imports under investigation are a sufficiently important cause of material injury, we must look to the facts of each case.

Although the domestic industry is experiencing problems, we do not find a sufficient causal relationship between the industry's difficulties and imports of Soviet ferrosilicon. The severe problems being experienced by the domestic industry antedate the importation of Soviet ferrosilicon, which began only in June 1983. Two factors affecting the health of the domestic ferrosilicon industry which are more important than imports from the Soviet Union are (1) the substantial decline in demand for ferrosilicon as a result of the severe decline in domestic production of steel, and (2) the substantial increase in the volume of imports of ferrosilicon from countries other than the Soviet Union. Therefore, imports of Soviet ferrosilicon have been, at most, an identifiable and contributing cause of injury to the domestic industry, but they are not a significant cause of the industry's difficulties.

Soviet imports, while increasing rapidly since June 1983, remain small relative to total imports of ferrosilicon. Imports from the Soviet Union totaled 11,683 short tons during January-September 1983 as a result of shipments in June and September and were equal to 2.8 percent of U.S. consumption during this period. By comparison, imports from all sources, including the Soviet Union, totaled 110,018 short tons and were equal to 25.8 percent of U.S. consumption during January-September 1983.

The only case where the President implemented import relief under Section 406 involved ammonia from the Soviet Union. In that case the ITC (in a 3–2 decision) found market disruption in 1979 and recommended that import relief be provided for three years,[21] but the President rejected the recommendation in December 1979.[22] Shortly thereafter, however, in January 1980 the President did afford import relief in the form of a quota under Section 406(c), which provides for emergency relief.[23] Following presidential action pursuant to Section 406(c), the ITC must commence a market disruption investigation and if it finds in the negative, the presidential action ceases to apply. In the ammonia case, the ITC found no market disruption the second time around (in a 3–2 decision where the swing vote was a new Commissioner) and the quotas ceased to apply only three months after they were imposed.[24]

(5) Prospects for Successful Adjustment

The underlying philosophy of escape clause relief is that it should be temporary and that it should be designed to allow domestic industry to take the steps that may be required to make it competitive in the future. This philosophy is embodied in Section 203(h) of the 1974 Trade Act, which provides that import relief in an escape clause case should normally not extend beyond five years and should be phased out after three years. The philosophy is also reflected in the 1984 Trade and Tariff Act, which provides that continued assistance to the steel industry is contingent upon the industry making efforts to adjust. See Section 9.6(B) infra.

In recent cases, the ITC has considered, at the request of the Executive Branch, the efforts made by domestic industry to adjust and the prospects for future adjustment. This request reflects the fact that the President is required by Section 202 to consider the probable effectiveness of import relief as a means to promote adjustment and the industry's efforts to adjust when he considers the appropriateness of imposing import relief.

Proposals for reform of international rules on escape clauses often focus on the issue of whether import relief should be granted if other forms of

21. Anhydrous Ammonia from the U.S. S.R., Inv. No. TA–406–5, Pub. No. 1006, 1 ITRD 5270.

22. 44 Fed. Reg. 71809 (1979).

23. Presidential Proclamation No. 4714, 45 Fed.Reg. 3875 (1980).

24. Anhydrous Ammonia from the U.S. S.R., Inv. No. TA–406–6, Pub. No. 1051, 1 ITRD 5355; 45 Fed.Reg. 28847 (1980).

adjustment assistance (such as those discussed in Section 9.5 infra) are available.

Should import relief be granted if there is a serious question whether an industry will ever be economically viable without protection from imports?

UNWROUGHT COPPER

U.S. Intl. Trade Commn. (1984)[25]

VIEWS OF COMMISSIONERS ECKES, LODWICK AND ROHR

* * *

World Price and Factors of Comparative Advantage

The respondents have alleged that the injury to the domestic industry is primarily due to the inability of the domestic industry to compete at the world price because of a lack of comparative advantage.

During the period of investigation world copper prices fell from 85 cents per pound to 63 cents per pound while average U.S. production costs have decreased from 88 cents to 82 cents. In our view market pressures resulting from this relatively low world price have had a significant negative impact on the domestic copper industry's ability to compete with foreign copper producers. The world price, however, cannot be viewed as an isolated cause of injury existing independent of the overall world supply and demand picture as well as factors of comparative advantage. Indeed,

> (s)uch a line of reasoning would result in the entire U.S. market being taken over by imports. * * * It must be clearly understood that imports are the vehicle by which the effects of low world prices are transmitted to the U.S. industry. Increased imports in particular are the cause of those negative effects previously detailed.

Factors of comparative advantage relate to the differing costs and conditions of production experienced by producers in supplying countries. In the copper industry these differing costs across supplying countries include variance in ore grades, transportation costs, wage rates, environmental costs, and the cost of investment capital. It is the interaction of these conditions of production that makes the world price look low from our perspective and perhaps profitable from Chile's. It is also this same interaction, as reflected in low prices, that makes imports attractive and affects their flow into the United States.

Of all the conditions of production affecting the domestic copper industry, declining ore grades have been characterized as an irreparable cause of injury. While we recognize that ore grades are a natural bounty subject to depletion we disagree that the rising costs associated with depletion are irreparable. The domestic industry has already demonstrated that through improved technology domestic producers have improved their production efficiencies and reduced the cost per pound of production.

Moreover, ore grades must be evaluated in their proper context and not just compared across the board. Indeed, if we take into account the

25. Inv. No. TA–201–52, Pub. No. 1549, 6
ITRD 1708 (1984).

coproduction of other metals which are found with copper deposits, even high-cost producers may be viewed as competitive. In addition, the economies associated with a developed country's infrastructure may make copper production in the United States more viable than in certain developing countries with far higher ore grades but significantly greater costs to develop and maintain the necessary infrastructure. Clearly, competitive conditions such as ore grades, wage rates, transportation and environmental costs, and the cost of investment are not immutable.

We reject the notion that the Commission must determine whether the domestic industry has a comparative advantage in a product before making an affirmative recommendation. Such a requirement would thwart the purpose of section 201. It would also ignore the reality that costs and conditions of production change and that section 201 is intended to enable an industry to use a period of shelter in order to adjust to shifts in these costs and conditions.

The relative costs and conditions of production do influence the ability of foreign producers to continue to compete at very low world prices. However, these relative advantages can be offset or limited by technological advances and improved efficiencies or can be subject to changing conditions.

————

President Reagan refused to grant import relief to the copper industry. He based his decision on the negative effect such relief would have on U.S. copper users and on the export earnings of foreign copper-producing countries, which would reduce the ability of such countries to repay their international borrowings and their ability to import U.S. goods.[26]

SECTION 9.3　REMEDIES AND PROCEDURES FOR ESCAPE CLAUSE CASES

The procedures for implementing import relief measures in escape clause cases under GATT and U.S. law have been broadly outlined in Section 9.1(D) supra. In this section we consider particular problems associated with implementing such measures: To what extent can the U.S. President decline to impose relief measures recommended by the ITC? Can such measures be directed only at the countries that are the principal cause of the injury? What compensation is, or should be, available to those countries whose exports are restricted? How is the amount of such compensation set?

(A)　REMEDIES IN ESCAPE CLAUSE CASES

GATT Article XIX imposes no specific limitations on the remedies that may be adopted in escape clause cases, except that obligations under GATT are to be suspended only "to the extent and for such time as to prevent or remedy such injury." Under Section 203 of the 1974 Trade Act, the President has broad authority to take remedial action. He can increase duties, impose quotas or enter into orderly marketing arrangements. Indeed the existence of the President's power to take effective remedial action

---

26.　49 Fed.Reg. 35609 (1984).

where appropriate has not been an issue. Rather, the questions have concerned his willingness to use his powers.

One of the significant legislative issues in the drafting of the 1974 Act was how much discretion to give to the President to depart from findings or recommendations of the ITC. Some urged that the ITC determination and remedy be final; while others urged that for foreign policy reasons as well as broader economic policy reasons, the President should have the final say in all of these cases. Some of these issues are treated in the following extract from the Senate version of the proposed Trade Act of 1974.

SENATE REPORT NO. 93–1298
93d Cong., 2d Sess. 124–26 (1974)

PRESIDENTIAL ACTIONS AFTER RECEIVING COMMISSION DETERMINATION

(Section 202)

This section would require the President to implement import relief or, if the Commission finds that adjustment assistance offers a viable alternative to import relief, to direct that expeditious consideration be given petitions for adjustment assistance. That relief ought not to be denied for reasons that have nothing whatever to do with the merits of the case as determined under U.S. law. In particular, the Committee feels that no U.S. industry which has suffered serious injury should be cut off from relief for foreign policy reasons. In addition, section 202 would provide time limits for Presidential action, and would enumerate factors which the President must take into account in making his determination as to the form and amount of import relief to be provided in the event adjustment assistance is not to be provided in place of import relief.

With respect to import relief the President is, however, given the flexibility to select (within the alternatives afforded under section 203(a)) the type and level of import relief to be provided. If, however, the import relief selected by the President differs from that recommended by the Commission, the Congress may, by concurrent resolution adopted by a majority of the members of each House present and voting, disapprove such relief and direct the President to proclaim, within 30 days after the day on which such resolution was adopted, the relief recommended by the Commission. If, in the event of a tie vote among Commissioners (an eventuality the Committee hopes will not occur), the President may decide whether or not to provide relief, and if he decides to provide relief, what form it should take.

* * *

With regard to the effect of relief on consumers, the Committee feels that the goals of the Employment Act of 1946 should be paramount. Unemployed persons are not happy consumers. The Executive should not confuse the effect on consumers with the effect on importers or foreign producers; they are not the same. If the choice is between (1) allowing an industry to collapse and thereby creating greater unemployment, larger Federal or state unemployment compensation payments, reduced tax revenues, and all the other costs to the economy associated with high unemployment, *or* (2) temporarily protecting that industry from excessive imports at some marginal costs to the consumer, then the Committee feels that the President should adopt the latter course and protect the industry and the jobs associated with that industry.

* * *

IMPORT RELIEF

(Section 203)

The Committee bill would require the President to provide import relief whenever the Commission determined that there is serious injury or, the threat thereof, to an industry in the United States unless the Commission recommends that the adjustment assistance offers a satisfactory alternative. The Committee bill deleted from the House bill the order of preference which would have been imposed upon the President in providing import relief. That order of preference would have been:

(1) increases in, or imposition of duties;

(2) tariff-rate quotas;

(3) quantitative restrictions (quotas);

(4) orderly marketing agreements.

The Committee felt that the order of preference did not make sense, because in any particular case of serious injury, the appropriate remedy might differ.

The Committee has, however, added to those measures which may be taken for relief purposes the extension of adjustment assistance to eligible workers, firms and communities. This would afford the President the flexibility to avoid the imposition of import relief restrictions, in any case where the Commission finds that adjustment assistance would be a more effective remedy than import relief. Under those circumstances, the President would direct that expeditious treatment be given petitions for such assistance.

In lieu of the order of preference in the House bill, section 203(a) of the Committee bill would require the President (in cases where adjustment assistance would not offer a suitable alternative) to provide such import relief under section 203(a) as is necessary, [taking] into account the factors set forth in section 202(c), to prevent or remedy serious injury, or the threat thereof, to the industry in question, and to facilitate the orderly adjustment to new competitive conditions by the industry in question. It is the Committee's intent that the President provide, to the maximum degree consistent with the objectives of this section and the factors he must consider under section 202(c), the relief recommended by the majority of the Commission. That relief may take the form of:

(1) an increase in, or imposition of, duty on the article causing or threatening to cause serious injury to such industry;

(2) a tariff-rate quota on such article;

(3) a modification of, or imposition of, quantitative restrictions on the import into the United States of such article;

(4) orderly marketing agreements with foreign countries limiting the export from foreign countries and the import into the United States of such article;

(5) any combination of such actions.

Accordingly, while the President has flexibility in determining the remedy he must impose, the Committee feels that the remedy should be commensurate with the injury found by the Commission. If the remedial action taken by the President differs from the action recommended to him by the Commission under section 201(b), he shall state the reason for imposing a different remedy. If, under section 203(c)(1), the President reports that he is taking action which differs from the recommendation of the Commission, the Congress could adopt a concurrent resolution, by majority vote of both Houses of Congress within 90 days after the President so reports, disapproving the action taken by the President. * * *

———

In the Act as passed, there was a large but not complete measure of discretion for the President,[1] which can be contrasted with the U.S. laws regarding dumping and subsidies, where there is almost no discretion in the executive. The 1974 Act tried to achieve a balance between those who wanted more and those who wanted no presidential discretion, and sections 202 and 203 reflect this. Note the artful wording of Section 202—the President "shall provide import relief" (some wanted the word "may"). But then later clauses give the President the right to decline to order such relief "in the national economic interest." In Section 203 a legislative veto was crafted to check the President. Since the U.S. Supreme Court's decision in *Chadha,* discussed in Section 3.2(C) supra, the validity of the two House congressional veto provision of Section 203 has been in doubt. In the 1984 Trade and Tariff Act, Congress amended Section 203 to eliminate this veto, and provided that Congress may override the President and cause the recommendation of the ITC to come into effect by adopting a joint resolution to that effect. This effectively eliminates the problems raised by *Chadha* since the President may veto any such resolution. While Congress could override the President's veto by a two-thirds vote of each House, such an event seems unlikely since Congress never felt strongly enough in an escape clause case in the past to even cast a majority vote for a congressional veto.

Before *Chadha,* the possibility of a congressional veto in Section 203 played an interesting role in escape clause cases. The 1974 Act moderately increased the possibility of a congressional veto as compared to prior law (which also had a congressional veto) by allowing a vote of a majority of those "present" to veto the President's action, as compared to a majority of all the members. In several cases congressional vetoes were threatened and in at least one case it was considered a "close call" that a veto was avoided. At the time it was felt that the mere threat of congressional action to overturn a presidential escape clause action was an influence on the President's decision, however.

---

1. The courts have not attempted to control this discretion. See, e.g., Maple Leaf Fish Co. v. United States, 762 F.2d 86 (Fed.Cir. 1985).

In an attempt to avoid inaction by the President after a favorable ITC determination, various petitioning parties have tried to find ways to put pressure on the President to follow the ITC recommendations and actually impose import restraints. One opportunity for such pressure is perceived to be the timing of a case in connection with national elections, particularly the presidential elections. Thus in late 1983 and early 1984, five petitions were filed, timed so that the statutory deadlines would require a presidential decision on the cases a month or two before the November election. Of those five cases, the ITC made affirmative determinations in two, but the President declined to impose import restraints under Section 203 in either case. However, in one of the two cases where injury was found—the steel case, the President promised to negotiate export restraints with steel exporting countries. See Section 9.6(B) below.

(B) MFN AND SELECTIVITY IN ESCAPE CLAUSE REMEDIES

Is it permissible under GATT for a nation to apply an escape clause remedy on a basis other than MFN? Notice that the U.S. law allows for this possibility in certain cases (see Section 203(k) and 126(a) of the 1974 Act).

MARCO C.E.J. BRONCKERS, THE NON–DISCRIMINATORY APPLICATION OF ARTICLE XIX GATT: FACT OR FICTION
(1981) [2]

Paragraph 1 allows a contracting party under certain circumstances to suspend GATT obligations in respect of a *product,* as opposed to a *country.* Thus, one might argue that while product "selection" is permitted under Article XIX, country "selection" is not. In this author's view, however, such a textual argument, only supported by *a contrario* reasoning, fails in the face of a systematic interpretation of the Agreement as a whole. Moreover, the (in this regard) identical wording of a comparable provision in the Havana Charter was not satisfactory to its drafters who did intend to require the non-discriminatory imposition of safeguard measures. For this purpose they added a separate authoritative "Interpretive Note" to record their intention.

The same Interpretive Note has led several authors to believe, not for textual but for historical reasons, that Article XIX would be subject to the MFN principle incorporated in Article I GATT. They recognize that "(t)he m.f.n. requirement (* * * is) not explicit in the text of Article XIX", but submit that "the view that this was the view of the drafters has never been challenged". Apart from the Charter's Interpretive Note, these authors cite a report of a GATT Ad Hoc Committee on Agenda and Intersessional Business from 1953. In the next section we will have a closer look at these historical references.

2. Legal Issues of European Integration 1981/2, at 39–41. Reprinted by permission of Kluwer Law and Taxation Publishers. Also published in M. Bronckers, Selected Safeguard Measures in Multilateral Trade Relations: Issues of Protectionism in GATT, European Community and United States Law 12 (1985).

B. GATT LEGAL HISTORY

Because the origin of the GATT is intertwined with the drafting of the abortive International Trade Organization (ITO), the preparatory work for the Charter of the ITO seems an obvious source for the interpretation of certain GATT provisions. Indeed, the main legal argument proposed in support of the nondiscriminatory application of Article XIX rests on an authoritative interpretation of a Charter provision.

1. Interpretive Note ad Article 40 Havana Charter

The United States insisted on the inclusion of a general escape clause in the Havana Charter, which was to be modelled after similar clauses negotiated by the U.S. in bilateral commercial treaties. Although the U.S. draft did not touch on the question of MFN/selectivity, a later internal United States memorandum has argued that this draft could not but have intended the non-discriminatory application of the escape clause:

> These relevant provisions (of Article XIX) follow closely in substance those in the first detailed escape clause, contained in Article XI of the 1942 trade agreement with Mexico * * *. At the time the United States was putting escape clauses comparable to Article XIX into bilateral trade agreements and was proposing the multilateral negotiation of comparable language it had no authority to take action under such a clause in other than a non-discriminatory manner and therefore must have contemplated its non-discriminatory use.

The logic of this argument is difficult to follow. Does one have to assume that whenever the U.S. invoked the escape clause in a particular bilateral agreement the imports of like products from all other U.S. trading partners would be subject to the same safeguard action? Or would the invocation of one particular escape clause activate all other escape clauses (with respect to like products) in the other bilateral trade agreements negotiated by the U.S.?

Be that as it may, the other draftsmen did not simply adopt the United States proposal and introduced several changes. Yet for our purposes it is important that at the last Havana Conference agreement was reached on an Interpretive Note which embodied the non-discrimination principle. The fact that the drafters of the Charter thought it necessary to make explicit the non-discriminatory application of the escape clause, suggests that the language of the provision itself is inconclusive. This Interpretive Note, incorporated in the Havana Charter to refine the escape clause of article 40 (which is similar to Article XIX GATT), reads:

> It is understood that any suspension, withdrawal or modification under paragraphs 1(a), 1(b) and 3(b) (of article 40–MCB) must not discriminate against imports from any Member country, and that such action should avoid, to the fullest extent possible, injury to other supplying Member countries.

The Note was added to the Charter *after* the GATT had already been signed. It may be doubted whether this interpretation can be applied retroactively to GATT Article XIX.

Fundamentally, the question arises of how relevant, if at all, Charter provisions are to a current interpretation of the GATT. Older literature called attention to Article XXIX of GATT, which provides in paragraph 1:

> The Contracting Parties undertake to observe to the fullest extent of their executive authority the general principles of Chapters I to VI inclusive and of Chapter IX of the Havana Charter pending their [acceptance of it in accordance with their] constitutional procedures.

Formerly it was argued that wherever GATT Articles were identical to Charter provisions, the Interpretive Notes annexed to the Charter would also be binding on their interpretation.

MARK KOULEN, THE NON–DISCRIMINATORY APPLICATION OF GATT ARTICLE XIX(1): A REPLY

(1983) [3]

One can argue that "the obligation" which contracting parties are allowed to suspend refers not only to the obligation to refrain from the imposition of quantitative restrictions but also to the obligation of non-discriminatory application of protective measures. Thus Article XIX(1) would allow the contracting parties to take discriminatory action specifically against the sources of the imports causing or threatening serious injury.

Another interpretation is possible if one stresses the difference between Article XIX(1) and Article XIX(3). In the latter paragraph provision is made for retaliatory measures by countries which are affected by measures under Article XIX(1). This right of retaliation is expressed as follows:

> * * * the affected contracting parties shall then be free * * * to suspend * * * the application to the trade of the contracting party taking such action * * * of such substantially equivalent concessions or other obligations under this Agreement the suspension of which the CONTRACTING PARTIES do not disapprove.

From the use of the expression "the application to the trade of the contracting party taking such action" one can infer that retaliatory measures must be applied in a discriminatory manner, against the contracting party that has taken recourse to Article XIX(1) only. Because of the absence of a comparable requirement in Article XIX(1) it seems reasonable to argue that action under Article XIX(1), in contrast with action under Article XIX(3), is subject to the requirement of non-discrimination.

* * *

At the end of 1947 the Plenary United Nations Conference on Trade and Employment met in Havana to discuss the Geneva Draft of the Charter. During the Conference relatively unimportant changes were made in the text of Article 40 of the Draft Charter. More important is the fact that the delegates took the opportunity to discuss the discriminatory versus non-discriminatory application of measures under this Article. At the instigation of the British delegation it was explicitly agreed that action under sub-

3. Legal Issues of European Integration 1983/2, at 89–95, 110–11. Reprinted by permission of Kluwer Law and Taxation Publishers.

paragraphs 1(a), 1(b) and 3(b)—contrary to action under sub-paragraph 3(a)—would be subject to the non-discrimination requirement. The delegates recognized that the text of the Article was ambiguous in this respect. It was decided to add an Interpretative Note, reading as follows:

> It is understood that any suspension, withdrawal or modification under paragraphs 1(a), 1(b) and 3(b) must not discriminate against imports from any Member.

However in a later stage of the Conference the delegation of Czechoslovakia raised serious objections to the proposed Note. The spokesman of the Czech delegation observed that:

> * * * Article 40 concerned emergency action on imports of particular products and was therefore an exception from the general principle of non-discrimination. The application of Article 40 would in many cases be discriminatory and the footnote might create a chain of withdrawals of concessions. Moreover, if the footnote was retained Article 40 provided no defense measures in the case of social dumping; the non-discriminatory application of quantitative restrictions in that instance would cause hardship to other Members.

The British delegate replied that:

> * * * the intention of the Article was set forth in the Footnote. Paragraph 3(a) offered counter-action against emergency actions: the phrase "to the trade of the Member" showed a discriminatory characteristic not evident in the other paragraphs.

and:

> The general intent of Article 40 was to provide time to rectify possible miscalculations of a concession. Since concessions were negotiated on a non-discriminatory and most-favoured-nation basis their withdrawal should also be on that basis.

Most of the delegates agreed with the statements of the British delegate. It was nevertheless decided to discuss the objections of the Czech delegation in an ad hoc Working Party. This Working Party agreed to amend the Interpretative Note as follows:

> It is understood that any suspension, withdrawal or modification under paragraphs 1(a), 1(b) and 3(b) must not discriminate against imports from any Member and that such action should avoid, to the fullest extent possible, injury to other supplying Member countries.

In this form the Interpretative Note ad Article 40 was included in the Havana Charter.

One wonders what the members of the Working Party exactly intended when they added the last part of the Note. Unfortunately there are no detailed records available of the deliberations of the Working Party. A possible explanation, in the light of the statements of the Czech delegate, is that this sentence was meant to apply in particular to the imposition of quantitative restrictions under Article 40. Thus this sentence would refer to the "representative base period" method of allocating quotas to countries, as recommended in Article 22 of the Charter.

How relevant is the Interpretative Note ad Article 40 of the Havana Charter to a modern interpretation of GATT Article XIX(1), given the fact that the CONTRACTING PARTIES have never explicitly declared this Note to be applicable to Article XIX(1)?

* * *

Thus it was not only the reference to the Havana Charter in Article XXIX(1) GATT, but also the fact that they had all signed the Havana Charter that made the CONTRACTING PARTIES consider themselves bound by interpretative notes to Charter Articles which corresponded to GATT Articles. This consensus regarding the use of the Charter as a source of interpretation of Articles of the General Agreement can be defined, in terms of Article 31 of the Vienna Convention on the Law of Treaties, as a form of " * * * subsequent agreement between the parties regarding the interpretation of the treaty * * *." Therefore the Havana Charter is still of importance to a modern interpretation of the General Agreement; the original intention of the CONTRACTING PARTIES with respect to Articles of the General Agreement can be interpreted in the light of the corresponding provisions of the Havana Charter. The fact that the Havana Charter has never been ratified has not diminished this importance of the Charter in the interpretation of the General Agreement. This has been affirmed in the GATT Analytical Index (Notes on the drafting, interpretation and application of the Articles of the General Agreement) where it is noted that:

> In view of their authoritative status, extracts from the Reports of the Havana Conference have been used extensively for interpretative material where the text of the General Agreement is substantially the same as that of the Charter provisions.

One must conclude that the Interpretative Note ad Article 40 of the Havana Charter was intended immediately to become operative in the application of Article XIX(1) GATT. Although the CONTRACTING PARTIES did not explicitly refer to this Note, the way they, in 1948, established an interpretative link between the Charter and the General Agreement implied that they could not apply Article XIX(1) GATT in any way other than as was laid down in the Note ad Article 40 of the Charter.

Is there evidence that at some moment after 1948 the CONTRACTING PARTIES have, explicitly or implicitly, agreed to modify their original, non-discriminatory interpretation of Article XIX(1)?

* * *

The preceding analysis may be summarized as follows.

1. The Interpretative Note ad Article 40 of the Havana Charter points to the original consensus of the CONTRACTING PARTIES to the General Agreement to apply GATT Article XIX(1) in accordance with the non-discrimination requirements of Article I and Article XIII.

2. Concern with the problem of market disruption has not led the CONTRACTING PARTIES to amend their original interpretation of Article XIX(1) explicitly.

3. Attempts by developing countries to interpret Article XIX(1) in the light of the principle of differential and more favourable treatment of developing countries have been unsuccessful.

4. The available information on the practice of application of Article XIX(1) does not point to the formation of a customary rule permitting discriminatory measures under this Article.

5. During the Tokyo Round of Multilateral Trade Negotiations some contracting parties began to contest that Article XIX(1) is subject to the non-discrimination requirements and applied the Article in a discriminatory manner. As has been made clear by the adoption by the CONTRACTING PARTIES of the Report of the Panel on Norway's restrictions on imports from Hong Kong, this unilateral interpretation has been rejected.

6. The relation between Article XIX(1) and Article XXIV remains unsettled.

MARCO C.E.J. BRONCKERS, RECONSIDERING THE NON-DISCRIMINATION PRINCIPLE AS APPLIED TO GATT SAFEGUARD MEASURES: A REJOINDER

(1983) [4]

II. NON-DISCRIMINATION AND THE INTERPRETATIVE NOTE AD ARTICLE 40 HAVANA CHARTER

Koulen agrees that the text of Article XIX GATT does not clearly set forth a non-discriminatory requirement with regard to the introduction of national safeguard measures. Instead, he derives this requirement from the Interpretative Note ad Article 40 of the Havana Charter (hereinafter: the Note), which allegedly embodies the obligation that safeguard measures may not discriminate against particular sources of supply.

A. *Status of the Note*

Earlier I submitted that, once it became clear that the ITO Charter would never be ratified, the effect of the Note could only be very limited. Koulen on the other hand believes the Note is still controlling. Interestingly enough, he does not seem to regard the Note as part of the GATT's *travaux preparatoires,* although he—rightly—stresses the inter-relationship between the GATT's and the Charter's drafting history. Rather, he relies on an early decision of the contracting parties, adopting the report of a working party to the effect that, whenever the wording of a Charter provision is identical to the text of a GATT Article, the interpretative note to the Charter provision governs the interpretation of the GATT Article. One may quibble about the import of this decision, but one has to grant Koulen that the decision reflects a consensus among the contracting parties during the formative years of GATT. Furthermore, Koulen's position is bolstered by recent GATT panel decisions which have cited Charter interpretations to support their findings.

B. *Meaning of the Note*

Yet even if one is prepared to accept that the Note still controls the application of Article XIX, ambiguities remain. One recalls the language of the Note:

---

4. Legal Issues of European Integration 1983/2, at 114–18. Reprinted by permission of Kluwer Law and Taxation Publishers. Al- so published in M. Bronckers, note 2 supra, at 54.

It is understood that any suspension, withdrawal or modification under paragraphs 1(a), 1(b), and 3(b) must not discriminate against imports from any member, and that such action should avoid, to the fullest extent possible, injury to other supplying member countries.

On the one hand the Note prescribes that safeguards imposed by an importing country must not discriminate against *any* exporter (ITO Member, *c.q.* GATT party) but at the same time the Note instructs that safeguards should not—to the fullest extent possible—adversely affect *other* exporters (those ITO Members, *c.q.* GATT parties not primarily responsible for the disruption in the market of the importing country?). These two requirements seem to be at odds with each other.

Koulen indicates that the second clause of the Note was added at the recommendation of a working party, which was established to contend with the objections of the Czech delegation to the unqualified condition of non-discrimination expressed in an earlier draft of the Note (which only contained the first clause of the final draft). Thus the obvious explanation for the apparent contradiction in the Note is that the final text was the result of compromise. As such, the Note provides uncertain guidance in resolving the issue of non-discriminatory safeguard measures.

To avoid this conclusion, Koulen suggests that the second clause of the Note refers to the so-called "representative base period" method of allocating quota shares to exporting countries. According to this method an importing country, in distributing a quota, allots shares to the different supplying countries in proportion to their import share during a previous representative period. Article 22 of the Charter and its equivalent in the GATT (Article XIII) deem the allocation of quota shares on the basis of an exporter's performance during a previous representative period to be non-discriminatory. Yet in practice this method enables an importing country to disproportionately reduce the import shares of its most competitive (i.e., disruptive) suppliers. Koulen's reading of the second clause therefore is quite ingenious, but fails to explain whether and how this clause affects tariff-type restrictions. The language of the Note's second clause does not limit its instruction to quantitative restrictions, nor is there conclusive evidence for this proposition in its drafting history. Moreover, Koulen does not offer any clues on how to reconcile the principle of non-discrimination (expressed in the Note's first clause) with the objective of the Note's second clause (exempting certain suppliers as much as possible from the restrictions (i.e., injury) effected by a quota or a tariff increase).

It would seem that the Note's language reflects the very dilemma which runs through much of the current debate on selective safeguards. Politically it is not palatable to restrict the imports of countries which arguably do not cause concern, whereas economists would stress that it does not make sense to single out the most threatening (i.e., most efficient, competitive) suppliers. Not surprisingly, proponents of selective safeguard action under Article XIX have on various occasions called attention to the apparent contradiction in the Note.

Given our differing appreciation of the GATT's drafting history, and particularly of the Note, Koulen then proceeds to examine whether at a later point in time the Contracting Parties have modified their original agreement on the non-discriminatory interpretation of Article XIX (either explicitly, or through custom). In light of the ambiguities I perceived in GATT's drafting history, I, on the other hand, inquired whether the practice under Article XIX bore out a consensus among the contracting parties on its non-discriminatory application. My conclusion was that many safeguard measures notified under Article XIX did in fact discriminate against particular suppliers (or had at least selective potential), even though they were global (or non-discriminatory) in appearance. Koulen strongly disagrees with this assertion. Indeed, it is on this point that he and I hold fundamentally different views.

III. NON-DISCRIMINATION AND QUANTITATIVE RESTRICTIONS

Before examining this difference of opinion, one should be clear about the concept of non-discrimination in the context of GATT, specifically with regard to quantitative import restrictions and measures having equivalent effect. In taking escape clause action to protect a domestic industry, GATT contracting parties over the years have more and more resorted to quota-type measures. Through a quota an importing country can better forecast the quantity of imports than would be possible with a tariff, and that is one reason often cited for the trend towards quota-type measures. Yet the distribution of a quota among different exporting countries almost inevitably leads to discrimination, particularly in those cases where only a few of the exporting countries create difficulties for the domestic industry because of their rapid and unpredictable (i.e., dynamic) expansion. It is of course especially in these cases that an importing country is tempted to select its targets in framing safeguard measures.

When an importing country imposes a quota it can basically administer the quota in two different ways. By only fixing the maximum amount (in quantity or value) of products that may be imported, without specifying their country of origin, the importing government lets market forces decide how this "global" quota will be filled. Or the importing government may itself get involved in the distribution of the quota, by allocating quota shares to the different supplying countries. Either way, some exporters are likely to feel aggrieved and will contend that the importing country discriminates against them.

REPORT BY THE DIRECTOR–GENERAL OF GATT, THE TOKYO ROUND OF MULTILATERAL TRADE NEGOTIATIONS
94 (1979)

There were wide divergences of view, even among the developed countries that had tabled the draft integrated text in June 1978. On one side were those who favoured an approach that permitted unilateral, selective action with *ex post facto* review by a Committee on Safeguard Measures immediately thereafter. On the other side were those who were insistent that any selective action be preceded by an agreement on the part of the exporting country, or approval by the Committee. Some others, including the most frequent users of Article XIX in the past, strongly favoured the continued m.f.n. application of the Article.

Developing countries maintained in principle that safeguard measures should be applied on a global basis without discrimination as between sources of supply and in conformity with Articles I and XIII of the GATT. They were also opposed to the provision in the draft integrated text put forward by the seven delegations of developed countries, according to which developed countries would cease to afford special and differential treatment when individual developing countries, or the relevant sectors within those countries, had achieved substantially higher levels of economic development, or the developing country had become internationally competitive in the product concerned.

SUPPLEMENTARY REPORT BY THE DIRECTOR-GENERAL OF GATT, THE TOKYO ROUND OF MULTILATERAL TRADE NEGOTIATIONS
14–15 (1980)

Early in 1979, participants had accepted selectivity as a working hypothesis. However, considering that they had made a major concession in the interest of reaching a mutually acceptable compromise, many countries, developed and developing, insisted on the need for the application of strict rules, criteria and surveillance arrangements relating to the use of selective measures.

For these countries it was essential that a prerequisite for safeguard action must be agreement to such action by the affected exporting country or countries concerned or, in the absence of such agreement, a prior determination by the Committee on Safeguard Measures that would be established under any Code on safeguards to the effect that the conditions and criteria for selective action are fulfilled; that actual, and not only potential material injury to domestic production in the importing country has to be proven; that account has to be taken of damage that might be caused to export industries in developing countries; and that safeguard measures should not be used as a substitute for structural adjustment to changes in conditions of fair competition and shifts in comparative advantage.

For certain industrialized countries some of these conditions were unacceptable. In particular, they were opposed to the need for a prior determination by the Committee on Safeguard Measures. They favoured an approach that would permit unilateral, selective action with *ex post facto* review by the Committee, especially in critical circumstances where delay would cause damage difficult to repair. This, in effect, proved to be a major sticking point.

Despite the intensive negotiations of July 1979 it proved impossible to close the gap on the fundamental issue of selectivity.

JOHN H. JACKSON, THE ROLE OF GATT IN MONITORING AND PROMOTING ADJUSTMENT: THE SAFEGUARDS SYSTEM

(1986) [5]

Where does this all leave us? As is true of so many legal issues in the GATT (or other international obligations), it is hard to say with complete assurance and precision what the interpretation of an international obligation should be. In a pragmatic sense, one would (as United States lawyers often do with respect to the U.S. Constitution and the Supreme Court) try to predict what would be the outcome of the controversy in the meaningful procedures of GATT, such as a panel determination if a dispute were taken under Article XXIII of GATT. More ambiguously, one would try to predict what practice would be considered and tolerated in GATT as consistent with the GATT obligations, over a longer period of time. It is very hard to make such predictions, given the fairly strong opposing stands of important trading partners. It does seem to this writer likely that if the matter were to go to a panel in GATT, that a panel would likely rule on the basis of the Havana Charter and the early GATT report, that MFN is required by Article XIX remedies. The mere fact that there have been departures from a rule over a period of time, and even the fact that those departures have been "tolerated" (but not tolerated as fulfilling or changing the legal obligation) is not evidence of practice or an interpretation of an international agreement. Virtually all agreements are violated at some point or another, and some are violated more than others. A pattern of violations should never be the basis on which to argue that the underlying obligation itself has been changed. Something more would be needed, such as expressions consistent with the customary international law concepts of "opinio juris."

In addition, since there is at least some ambiguity as to the question, it seems important to examine the underlying policies of the GATT agreement as a whole, and particularly of Article XIX in the context of that GATT agreement. Those policies seem to reinforce the concept of MFN. As stated above, it seems dubious that one could argue that the MFN obligation is one of those which is "causally linked" to the increase of imports. In addition, the economic concepts of comparative advantage and the goal of liberal trade policies to allow more efficient producers to develop and enter the market, would reinforce an approach that would negate discriminatory application of Article XIX remedies.

It can be argued pragmatically, however, that so many substantial deviations from the non-discrimination approach in safeguards occur that world welfare would be better served by some, even grudging, recognition of those deviations if they could then be channeled and disciplined so that the worst abuses were inhibited. This is a "second best" (or third best) argument for the real world. The dilemma is that to "recognize" the deviations might be to entrench or encourage more of them. It has been therefore

5. © 1986, Institute for International Economics. Reproduced by permission from G. Hufbauer & H. Rosen (eds.), Domestic Adjustment and International Trade (forthcoming).

argued (somewhat cynically, perhaps) by one diplomat that the "law" should not be changed, while recognizing that

> Professional trade policy administrators know that measures can usually be devised which deal with the category of imports which give rise to the perceived problem.

Note

In a dispute between Norway and Hong Kong over Norway's discriminatory application of quotas to Hong Kong textile products, a GATT panel stated in 1980: [6]

IV. Conclusions

14. The Panel based its consideration of the case on Articles XIX and XIII of the GATT:

(a) The Panel noted that while both parties had advanced extensive data and arguments concerning the history of the case, i.e. especially the situation during 1978 prior to the invocation of Article XIX by Norway, Hong Kong had limited its formal request to a finding on Norway's Article XIX action. The Panel at the same time noted and consequently based its decision on the statements by Hong Kong that the latter was prepared to assume that Norway had the necessary justification for taking this action and that a finding concerning the exclusion from the quotas of the EEC and EFTA countries was not necessary.

(b) The Panel was of the view that the type of action chosen by Norway, i.e. the quantitative restrictions limiting the importation of the nine textile categories in question, as the form of emergency action under Article XIX was subject to the provisions of Article XIII which provides for non-discriminatory administration of quantitative restrictions. In this connexion, the Panel noted the introductory part of paragraph 2 which stipulates that in applying an import restriction on a product, a contracting party "shall aim at a distribution of trade in such product approaching as closely as possible the shares which the various contracting parties might be expected to obtain in the absence of such restrictions ∗ ∗ ∗". To this end, paragraph 2(a) of Article XIII further prescribes that wherever practicable, quotas representing the total amount of permitted imports (whether allocated among supplying countries or not) shall be fixed.

15. In the case before the Panel, Norway had in early 1978 concluded long-term bilateral arrangements with six textile-supplying countries. The Panel noted that Norway had concluded these agreements with the intention of acceding to the MFA [Multifiber Arrangement, see Section 9.6 infra] and notifying the agreements to the TSB pursuant to the appropriate Article of the MFA. The Panel noted also, however, that in the event Norway had not acceded to the MFA and that for these arrangements no derogation or

6. Norway—Restrictions on Imports of Certain Textile Products, GATT, 27th Supp. BISD 119, 125–26 (1981).

provision of Parts I–III of GATT had ever been invoked by Norway. While noting that provision for some developing exporting countries of assured increase in access to Norway's textile and clothing markets might be consistent for those countries with the spirit and objectives of Part IV of the GATT, this cannot be cited as justification for actions which would be inconsistent with a country's obligations under Part II of the GATT. The Panel held that Norway's reservation of market shares for these six countries therefore represented a partial allocation of quotas under an existing regime of import restrictions of the products in question and that Norway must therefore be considered to have acted under Article XIII:2(d). The Panel noted that had the reservation of market shares for the six countries been entered into pursuant to Article XIII:2(d), Norway could have been presumed to have acted under the first sentence of that provision.

16. Since Hong Kong has a substantial interest in supplying eight of the nine product categories in question to the Norwegian market, it had the right to expect the allocation of a share of the quotas in accordance with Article XIII:2(d). The Panel was of the view that to the extent that Norway had acted with effect to allocate import quotas for these products to six countries but had failed to allocate a share to Hong Kong, its Article XIX action was not consistent with Article XIII.

17. In accordance with established GATT practice, the Panel held that where a measure had been taken which was judged to be inconsistent with the provisions of the General Agreement, this measure would *prima facie* constitute a case of nullification or impairment of benefits which other contracting parties were entitled to expect under the General Agreement.

18. On the basis of the conclusions reached above, the Panel finds that Norway should immediately either terminate its action taken under Article XIX or make it consistent with the provisions of Article XIII.

19. The Panel expresses the hope that in the light of this report the parties will be able to arrive at a mutually acceptable agreement.

(C) COMPENSATION TO EXPORTING COUNTRIES

JOHN H. JACKSON, WORLD TRADE AND THE LAW OF GATT
565–66 (1969)

The escape clause action, taken by the party claiming injury from imports, authorizes a retaliatory response from other contracting parties under Article XIX, paragraph 3. The language contemplates that the consultation that is afforded under Article XIX, paragraph 2, by the acting party will generally lead to an agreement. This has uniformly been taken to mean that parties entitled to consult because they have a "substantial interest as exporters of the product concerned" can obtain the agreement of the invoking party to compensatory withdrawal of concessions, or that the consulting parties can accept compensatory concessions by the invoker. Thus, if *A* feels injured by *B*'s widget exports, *A* may withdraw his obligation, *e.g.*, by raising widget tariffs. *B* will then consult and *A* may offer *B* a different concession (*e.g.*, on "gadgets"), which *B* may accept as adequately compensating *B* for the withdrawal by *A*. Or, *B* may withdraw a concession affecting *A*'s exports to *B*, and both may agree that a balance has been struck. In this case the *A* and *B* tariff "Schedules" may effectively be changed, although since the withdrawals and compensations are supposedly temporary, generally they have been excluded from protocols that rectify or modify the Schedules. In practice, however, some of the compensatory concessions tend to become permanent. A delicate question arises when *A* suspends one concession, gives *B* a compensatory concession, and then later reinstates the original concession. Now *A* should either have the right to withdraw the compensating concession or receive from *B* new reciprocal concessions to "pay for" the compensatory concession. Some of these cases get resolved in the course of later major tariff negotiating rounds, as was the case for the United States in the Kennedy Round.

If no agreement is reached, however, the invoking country has the right to proceed with its withdrawal privileges under Article XIX and the exporting country is then given a right to respond in kind. This counterresponse is the prerogative of "affected contracting parties" and is qualified as follows:

(1) Thirty days' written notice of the action must be given (with one exception) and the action must occur no later than 90 days after the initial action by the invoker (but this time limit is uniformly extended by action of the Contracting Parties under the waiver power when such extension is requested);

(2) The counterresponse allowed is to suspend the application of substantially equivalent concessions or other GATT obligations to the trade of the invoker (note that this implies discriminatory treatment against the invoker, contrary to the invoker's right of suspension or withdrawal); and

(3) The Contracting Parties do not disapprove.

In practice, agreements have usually (but not always) been concluded. The Contracting Parties have never "disapproved" of a response to withdrawals, partly because consultation and negotiation among the parties affected as well as other contracting parties sometimes lead to a CONTRACTING PARTIES' decision that approves in advance the response that will be taken.

Notes and Questions

(1) When the United States invokes the escape clause, the President can negotiate to give alternative concessions only during periods when he has been delegated authority enabling him to do so (unless he submits such an agreement to Congress, which is unlikely). During periods when "general tariff negotiating authority" existed, as in 1962–67, and 1974–79, the President could also negotiate escape clause settlements under that authority. However, during periods such as 1967–73, when such authority did not exist, the U.S. Executive Branch felt itself constrained in escape clause cases because it did not have authority to grant alternative concessions. This problem was corrected in the 1974 Act by Section 123. Nevertheless, the general policy problem remains—with tariffs as low as they currently are, it is often very difficult to identify products whose tariffs could be lowered as alternative concessions for compensation in an escape

clause case. This is particularly true in large cases, such as those concerning autos or steel. If there are products in the U.S. tariff schedules which have substantial tariffs (and thus might be attractive for potential cuts for compensation), it is precisely because those products have a substantial and often politically powerful domestic constituency for preserving those tariffs.

(2) It has been suggested (see Section 9.6(C) infra), that the right to compensation should be eliminated. Do you agree?

(D) SAFEGUARDS IN THE EC AND JAPAN

The U.S. safeguards procedures are characterized (like many U.S. governmental institutions) by fairly elaborate public procedures and tendency towards "legalization." Other governments utilize many other techniques, ranging from very informal and highly discretionary actions by government officials to prevent or inhibit troublesome imports, to a variety of processes with varying degrees of formality.

For example, in the EC there are a number of mechanisms for imposing safeguard measures, all of which are potentially speedier and less formal than their U.S. analogues.[7] The EEC's common rules for imports provide as follows:

REGULATION 288/82
[1982] Eur.Comm.O.J. No. L 35/1

Article 3

The Commission shall be informed by the Member States should trends in imports appear to call for surveillance or protective measures. This information shall contain the available evidence on the basis of the criteria laid down in Article 9. The Commission shall pass on this information to all the Member States forthwith.

Article 4

Consultations may be held, either at the request of a Member State or on the initiative of the Commission. They shall take place within eight working days following receipt by the Commission of the information provided for in Article 3 and, in any event, before the introduction of any measure of surveillance or protective measure by the Community.

Article 5

1. Consultation shall take place within an advisory committee (hereinafter called "the Committee") which shall consist of representatives of each Member State with a representative of the Commission as chairman.

*   *   *

7. See Bronckers, A Legal Analysis of Protectionist Measures Affecting Japanese Imports into the European Community, in M. Bronckers, note 23 supra, at 111; E. Volker (ed.), Protectionism and the European Community (1983); J. Steenbergen, G. De Clerg & R. Foque, Change and Adjustment (1983); M. Lejeune, Un Droit des Temps de Crise: Les Clauses de Sauvegarde de la CEE (1976).

Article 16

1.   Where the interests of the Community so require, the Council may, acting by a qualified majority on a proposal from the Commission, adopt appropriate measures:

(a)   to prevent a product being imported into the Community in such greatly increased quantities and/or on such terms or conditions as to cause, or threaten to cause, substantial injury to Community producers of like or directly competing products;

(b)   to allow the rights and obligations of the Community or of all its Member States to be exercised and fulfilled at international level, in particular those relating to trade in primary products.

———

The Japanese rules on import controls were described in Section 4.3 supra by Professor Matsushita and should be reviewed at this time.

SECTION 9.4 VOLUNTARY RESTRAINT AGREEMENTS AND SPECIAL SAFEGUARDS TECHNIQUES

(A) HISTORY AND POLICY

In this section we examine voluntary restraint agreements—their history and economic implications and their regulation under GATT and U.S. law.   Economically, of course, such agreements have the same effect as quotas, which were analyzed generally in Chapter 1 supra.   Here and in Section 9.6 we will look more closely at the economic effects of such agreements, including attempts to quantify their costs.   In particular, we look in this section at one of the better known examples of such restraints, the Japanese restraints on exports of automobiles to the United States. Later in this chapter (Section 9.6(B)), we will look at other economic sectors that have traditionally received some protection from import competition by international agreement, such as the textile and steel sectors.

The taxonomy of various "extra escape clause" techniques for restraining imports which are damaging competing domestic industries is not very precise.   There are a myriad of possibilities, including the use of various "nontariff barriers" which could be deemed to violate GATT rules explicit or implicit.   Recently one of the most commonly used safeguard techniques has been the implementation of export restraints on the part of the exporting country or industry.   Export restraints can be brought about by voluntary restraint agreements (VRAs), which is a generic phrase that covers a number of different species, including orderly marketing agreements (OMAs) and voluntary export restraints (VERs).   Whatever they are called, they are rarely if ever truly "voluntary."

STANLEY D. METZGER, INJURY AND MARKET
DISRUPTION FROM IMPORTS
(1971) [1]

The "voluntary" restraint upon exports is in reality a misnomer—it is an action of restraint by an exporting country taken because of its concern that unilateral quotas would otherwise be imposed against it by an importing country, which might well produce more adverse trade effects than those "voluntarily" agreed to by the exporting country through the more flexible medium of negotiations. For once unilateral quotas are imposed, they bear within themselves the seeds of their own continuity—the same domestic industry groups which were strong enough to secure quotas initially will likely retain sufficient political power to assure their continuation into a relatively long future. In this connection, it is noteworthy that the unilateral American oil import restrictions of 1957 and 1959 have continued to be imposed without interruption down to the present time without apparent signs of early termination, despite costs of the American people estimated at more than $4 billion annually. Cotton and wheat quotas initiated under Section 22 of the AAA have had an even longer life, going back well over 20 years.

On the other hand, exporting countries maintain more control over "voluntary" restraints, whose duration and severity are subject to periodic review through the negotiations process. Thus "voluntary" restraints are considered to be the lesser evil by an exporting country.

The U.S.-Canada Potato Agreement of 1948 exemplifies how a "voluntary" restraint originates. When the U.S. Department of Agriculture considered the institution of a Section 22 action in 1948 concerning potatoes, Canada indicated that it was prepared to control exportation in order to avoid the Section 22 quota (Canada was well aware of the longevity of Section 22 quotas once they had been introduced, having been a large wheat exporter antedating the Section 22 wheat quotas). The Department of Agriculture, for its part, was prepared to see the Canadian export control limited to a single crop year because the potato control could be implemented immediately rather than in the four months' time it would then have taken for the institution of Section 22 quotas and because the Canadian government had indicated to the State Department that adverse political repercussions could be expected to attend U.S. application of unilateral quota controls. The Potato Agreement was the result.

1. U.S. Commission on International Trade and Investment Policy (the Williams Commission), Papers I, at 167, 168–73. For further discussion of past use of VRAs, see generally Smith, Voluntary Export Quotas and U.S. Trade Policy—A New Nontariff Barrier, 5 Law & Poly. Intl. Bus. 10 (1973); U.S. Tariff Commn., Trade Barriers 241–68 (TC Pub. No. 665, 1974) (discussion of restraints on textiles, steel, other Japanese exports, meat, strawberries, tomatoes, mushrooms, coffee, cocoa, footwear, etc.); Fulda, Textiles and Voluntary Restraints on Steel: Protecting United States Industries from Foreign Competition, 13 Va.J. Intl. L. 516 (1973); Bates, The Voluntary Quota System for Regulating Steel Imports, 14 Va.J.Intl.L. 101 (1973); Oman, The Clandestine Negotiation of Voluntary Restraints on Shoes from Italy: An Augury of Future Negotiations Under the Trade Reform Act of 1973?, 7 Cornell Intl.L.J. 6 (1973); Smith, Voluntary Export Quotas and U.S. Trade Policy—A New Nontariff Barrier?, 5 Law & Poly.Intl.Bus. 10 (1973).

The considerations motivating the "voluntary" control over exports which have been negotiated since World War II were foreshadowed by those which underlay the Potato Agreement of 1948. On the U.S. side, strong domestic interests desired to protect themselves against competitive imports. They either believed that they could not qualify for escape clause relief (i.e., Cotton Textiles, Man-made Textile Fibers, Shoes), or, if they might qualify for National Security Amendment relief (i.e., Steel), they were aware of the foreign relations problems involved in imposing unilateral quotas which are often considered to be "unfriendly" acts by America's trading partners. Cognizant Congressional Committees, made aware of these problems by their own experience no less than by that communicated by the Chief Executive, have not desired to force the Administration's hand by passing mandatory legislative quotas; indeed, they have had grave doubts that in the last analysis they could muster the strength to repass such a bill over a determined Chief Executive. Yet, they, like the Administration, have been loathe to treat all domestic industries—those with and those without major political strength—alike. Those without sufficient domestic political strength have simply had to live with the foreign competition which cannot be stemmed under generally applicable domestic legal criteria. Those with such strength have secured the extraordinary remedy of the United States raising to the highest international negotiating levels the matter of securing curtailment of imports from friendly foreign countries, developing and developed alike, in the interest of those who can not show, or at any rate have not attempted to show, serious injury in consequence of increased importation.

THE AGREEMENTS OF THE 1930'S

During the 1930's the United States negotiated a number of "voluntary" restriction arrangements with Japan, covering cotton cloth, cotton floor covering, cotton hose, cotton velveteens, and corduroys. Prior to 1933, imports of cotton textiles had originated mainly from Europe; European imports were of high quality and not directly competitive with domestic production. However, starting in 1933, imports of medium quality cotton textiles competing directly with domestic production began to increase rapidly. Even though total imports of cotton manufactures remained below 5% of domestic sales and 3% of domestic production throughout the 1930's, while such imports from Japan fluctuated around 1% of domestic sales, it was successfully argued by the domestic industry that Japanese imports were (1) rising rapidly, (2) competing directly with domestic production, and (3) because concentrated in a few product lines, constituted a threat to the American industry.

Four "voluntary" agreements were negotiated between Japan and the United States in the 1930's. In two of these cases, the U.S. State Department conducted the negotiations; in the other two cases, the negotiations were conducted by private industry groups in both countries.

1. An agreement on cotton cloth, for two years duration, was concluded in January 1937 and further renewed for two years on December 18, 1938. The agreements limited Japanese exports to 155 million square yards in 1937 and to 100 million square yards for each year thereafter. The signato-

ries were the American Cotton Textile Mission and the representatives of the Japanese cotton textile industry.

2.   An agreement on cotton floor coverings, which entered into force on June 1, 1934, for a one-year period, was twice extended thereafter for the same period. In the 1930's total imports of cotton floor coverings had always exceeded American production, and most imports (99 percent in some years) had originated from Japan.

3.   Thirdly, there was an agreement on cotton hosiery. Before 1933 Germany had been the main exporter of that product to the United States. By 1936, however, Japan's share of total U.S. imports had climbed to 93 percent in volume and 75 percent in value. In 1936, the Japanese Exporters Association began collecting a 5 yen per dozen export tax, approximately the equivalent of a 5 percent ad valorem export duty on average price. On April 16, 1936, a three-year agreement limiting exports was concluded between the National Association of Hosiery Manufacturers and the Japanese Knitted Goods Exporters Association.

4.   Finally, there was an agreement on cotton velveteens and corduroys. In the case of velveteens, an amount equal to between 30 percent and 50 percent of domestic production was imported, more than 90 percent of which came from Japan. In the case of corduroys the percentages were 3 percent and 90 percent respectively. An agreement was reached on February 15, 1937, between the American Association of Velveteens and Corduroys and the Japan Cotton Yarn Piece Goods Exporters Association, limiting imports. The agreement came into force on March 1, 1937, for a period of two years.

As Henry states, the "entire story shows clearly that the U.S.-Japan voluntary export restraint agreements of the 1930's resulted mainly from American pressures and threats of unilateral, permanent, and possibly more restrictive action." "Nothing indicates," he asserts, "that this pattern has been changed since." The Japanese for their part, accepted the agreements as the most practicable means of preserving a portion of their textile exports to the United States, and in the interest of political harmony in this sphere of their relationships with the United States.

*   *   *

The crucial difference between an appropriately structured and administered escape clause, and "voluntary agreements" unconnected with an escape clause case, lies precisely in this necessity for making a reasoned, public case of serious injury caused by imports in the one, and the lack of any such necessity in the other. Assertions can often take the place of reasoned proof when a public, contested case is not involved; it is rare that such a displacement will occur when confrontation and a record are present.

Note

Recall Judge Leventhal's dissent in the *Consumers Union* case, discussed in Section 3.2(B) supra. He too was especially concerned about the lack of public consideration of the relevant issues that occurs when voluntary export restraints are arranged through government or industry action.

———————

Intimately related to the question of whether escape-clause type relief should ever be afforded without public consideration of its desirability, is the question of the relative benefits and costs of such relief. As noted in Section 9.6(C) infra, ventilation of the true costs and benefits of such relief might well result in it being used less frequently. The following cost-benefit study of restraints in the steel industry indicates how such an analysis is conducted.

DAVID G. TARR & MORRIS E. MORKRE, AGGREGATE COSTS TO THE UNITED STATES OF TARIFFS AND QUOTAS ON IMPORTS: GENERAL TARIFF CUTS AND REMOVAL OF QUOTAS ON AUTOMOBILES, STEEL, SUGAR AND TEXTILES

129–31, 141–43 (1984) [2]

[The history of steel import restraints is described by these authors in Section 9.6(B) infra. Here they analyze the effect of the most recent restraint system, which is designed to keep the market share of imports at 18.5%]

The annual costs of such a quota to United States consumers is estimated to be $1,131 million. The annual inefficiency costs to the economy, under the usual method of quota allocation where the foreign countries receive the quota rights, is estimated to be $803 million. Part of what U.S. consumers lose is transferred to domestic and foreign producers. United States producers gain $441 million per year and foreigners extract $573 million per year in quota rents. * * *

[If a quota is imposed, a number of jobs in steelmaking would be created. An estimate of the number of jobs created can be based on the estimates in section II that the 18.5 percent quota will result in an increase in domestically produced steel shipments of 2.636 million short tons. Based on data from the American Iron and Steel Institute, an additional 3.775 employees would be required to produce an additional one thousand short tons of steel mill products. Assuming this ratio would be maintained implies that 2.636 million additional tons of steel produced will result in 9,951 additional jobs.

[In steel Jacobson estimates that displaced workers lose 46.6 percent of their earnings in the first two years after displacement and 12.6 percent in the subsequent four years. The average total compensation of a steel employee in 1983 was $38,574. Suppose, as a result of imposing a quota, a steelworker is never displaced. Then, taking a discount rate of 7 percent yields a present value of $499 million in cumulative saved earnings losses (benefits) from the quota. After termination of the quota, however, the marginal output of the domestic industry which, was induced by and produced jobs only because of the quota, would be eliminated. Thus those workers who are employed because of the quota would be expected to be displaced after the quota is terminated. This means the benefits of the

2. This study is a Bureau of Economics Staff Report to the Federal Trade Commission (FTC). It is stated to represent the views of the FTC's Bureaus of Economics, Consumer Protection, and Competition, but it was not acted upon by the FTC. The FTC did, however, vote to release it.

quota are the deferral of the displacement costs for five years. That is, as a result of a quota the costs of adjustment will not be incurred in the first six years starting immediately, but rather in the six years following the five years of protection.

[By taking the appropriate present values one can calculate that the present value of the cumulative earnings losses of 9,951 steelworkers who would be displaced after five years of protection is $356 million in 1983 dollars. If they were displaced immediately, i.e., no protection were granted, the losses would be $499 million. The difference of $143 million is the benefit of the protection, i.e., it is the value of deferring the earnings losses for five years.]

In order to obtain some perspective on the quantitative importance of the benefits of the quota in relation to the costs, cost-benefit ratios are provided as well as estimates for the costs of the quota per job created. For each job saved by the 18.5 percent quota, the annual costs to consumers is $113,622; the annual inefficiency costs to the economy for each job created by the quota is $80,682. * * * The benefits of the quota are measured by the present value of the saved earnings losses of workers who would otherwise have been displaced. For the purposes of this comparison the present value of the costs to consumers and losses to the economy are taken over five years. It is found that the quota imposes $5 billion and $3.5 billion in costs to consumers and inefficiency costs to the economy over five years, respectively while $143 million in earnings losses are saved. Thus for every dollar of earnings losses saved by otherwise displaced workers, consumers lose $34.60 and the United States economy has excess or inefficiency losses of $24.57.

(B) GATT AND VOLUNTARY RESTRAINT AGREEMENTS

Most voluntary restraint arrangements are probably inconsistent with GATT obligations. However, GATT does not purport to regulate the actions of private companies. Thus, there is a loophole, which allows those governments that are not inhibited by antitrust or other laws to encourage private firm restraints on exports. But with respect to government actions which restrain exports, GATT Article XI is clearly engaged. The sweeping language of that article would seem to embrace virtually any export control maintained by government authority.

The problem in GATT is a more pragmatic one—who will complain? The country establishing export restraints is usually doing so at the behest or signal of an importing nation. The country restraining exports would hardly complain against itself in GATT. The country most affected, namely the importing country that sent the signal, would hardly complain either, since the action is precisely what it had hoped for. Other countries in GATT would find it difficult or awkward to complain, because they normally would not be able to establish that they had been harmed. Thus, there has been a paucity of cases in GATT with respect to export restraints. One possible complainant country in the GATT context might be a country which we would call "C," which felt that as a result of an export restraint arrangement between "A" and "B," exports of "A" were diverted from the "B" market, thus putting greater competitive pressure on the market in "C." This was basically the complaint of the United States steel industry in 1976.[3]

(C) UNITED STATES LAW, VOLUNTARY RESTRAINT AGREEMENTS AND ANTITRUST LAWS

United States law regarding voluntary restraint agreements involves at least two important dimensions: (1) the question of the authority of the Executive Branch to be involved, even informally, in signalling foreign governments to restrain exports to the United States; and (2) the U.S. antitrust laws (which, as we will see in Chapter 18 infra, reach activity abroad that has an "effect" in the United States). The following materials illustrate some of the confusion that surrounds these issues.

(1) Presidential Authority and Voluntary Restraint Agreements

The President's authority to enter into the steel VRAs in the late 1960's was upheld in 1974 in *Consumers Union v. Kissinger*, discussed in Section 3.2(B) supra. The implications of that case were considered by Congress in enacting the Trade Act of 1974 in two significant respects.

First, it was felt that since key members of Congress had been consulted before the steel restraint agreements were encouraged, and since the agreements had been so prominently endorsed by the United States government, the government (including Congress) had an obligation to the private companies to prevent them from being subjected to liability under United States antitrust laws. The obligation was discharged by Section 607 of the Trade Act of 1974, which absolved such liability as to existing or prior voluntary restraint agreements. Conspicuously absent from the absolution, however, was comparable liability that might arise under any future restraint agreements.

A second question considered by Congress was whether the President should have authority to negotiate restraint agreements. Under Section 203 of the Trade Act, "orderly marketing agreements with foreign countries" were authorized as one possible "import restraint" measure that could be taken following an ITC injury determination in an escape clause proceeding. In its report on the proposed trade bill, the Senate Finance Committee suggested that one result of the inadequacy of previous escape clauses was the development of voluntary restraint agreements. The Committee stated: "The Committee believes it is better to provide a fair and reasonable test for any industry which is being injured by imports—a determination made by an independent factfinding body, such as the International Trade Commission—than to rely on ad hoc agreements for a few select industries." [4]

Another provision of the bill, however, seems implicitly to authorize the Executive to negotiate a restraint agreement for footwear (Section 121(a) (12)). The paragraph was added on the floor of the Senate at the behest of Senator Kennedy of Massachusetts—a footwear-producing state—with a statement that the textile type of agreement was desired for footwear. As

---

3. The Section 301 action brought by the U.S. steel industry in this connection is discussed in Section 10.5 infra.

4. Senate Report No. 93–1298, 93d Cong., 2d Sess. 119 (1974).

modified by the House-Senate Conference, the amendment makes reference to Section 107 of the Act which relates to reforms in GATT safeguard mechanisms. It is thus apparently unclear whether a footwear agreement is authorized without first receiving an affirmative ITC finding under Section 201. In fact, footwear orderly marketing agreements were entered into in 1977, but only after escape clause proceedings resulted in an affirmative injury finding by the ITC.

Not counting the 1984 steel case discussed below, the President entered into OMAs following affirmative injury findings by the ITC in escape clause proceedings in respect of specialty steel, nonrubber footwear and color television receivers and assemblies.[5] The President entered into an arrangement in respect of certain steel products from the EC in 1982 without an ITC investigation. His action was at least in part ratified by Congress that year when it authorized the Secretary of the Treasury, if requested in 1982 by the United States and a foreign governmental entity, to require a valid export license issued by such entity to accompany certain steel mill products on importation into the United States as a means of enforcing the arrangement.[6] As noted earlier, the 1984 Trade and Tariff Act specifically authorized the President to enforce steel VRAs for five years.[7] That congressional action followed an affirmative ITC injury determination.[8] However, in cases where the ITC or Congress has taken no action, the authority of the President to promote VRAs is less clear, although the President has claimed such authority, as indicated in the Shenefield letter excerpted below.

Note

In respect of certain products, Congress has granted explicit authority to the President to enter into VRAs without following the escape clause procedures. For example, Section 204 of the Agriculture Act of 1956, as amended, provides: [9]

The President may, whenever he determines such action appropriate, negotiate with representatives of foreign governments in an effort to obtain agreements limiting the export from such countries and the importation into the United States of any agricultural commodity or product manufactured therefrom or textiles or textile products, and the President is authorized to issue regulations governing the entry or withdrawal from warehouse of any such commodity, product, textiles, or textile products to carry out any such agreement. In addition, if a multilateral agreement has been or shall be concluded under the authority of this section among countries accounting for a significant part of world trade in the articles with respect to which the agreement was concluded, the President may also issue, in order to carry out such an agreement, regulations governing the entry or withdrawal from warehouse of the same articles which are the products of countries not parties to the agreement. Nothing herein shall affect the authority provid-

---

5. See Presidential Proclamation No. 4445, 41 Fed.Reg. 24101 (1976) (specialty steel); Presidential Proclamation No. 4510, 42 Fed. Reg. 32430 (1977) (footwear); Presidential Proclamation No. 4511, 42 Fed.Reg. 32747 (1977) (TVs).

6. Pub.L. No. 97–296, § 153, 96 Stat. 1202; 19 U.S.C.A. § 1626.

7. Trade and Tariff Act of 1984, tit. VIII, Pub.L. No. 98–573, 98 Stat. 3043 (also known as the "Steel Import Stabilization Act")

8. Carbon and Certain Alloy Steel Products, Inv. No. TA–201–51, Pub. No. 1553, 6 ITRD 2236 (ITC 1984).

9. 7 U.S.C.A. § 1854.

ed under section 22 of the Agricultural Adjustment Act (of 1933) as amended.

Under this statutory authority, the United States has participated in extensive international regulation of textiles, which is described in Section 9.6(B) infra. As a related matter, recall that the President has powers to impose quotas on certain categories of imports. See Sections 3.4(B) and 6.4 supra.

Questions

(1) Could a steel VRA be put in place today without an ITC affirmative finding under Section 201? How does the 1982 and 1984 legislation concerning steel VRAs affect the President's claim of inherent authority to negotiate VRAs?

(2) Under the reasoning of the *Consumers Union* case, extracted in Section 3.2(B) supra, can the United States Executive Branch enter into any voluntary restraint agreements without previously having an ITC determination? What is the effect of the above-quoted statement in the Senate report?

(3) Can voluntary restraints be arranged between foreign producer firms, if "encouraged" by United States government officials?

(4) Suppose tennis shoes are being imported into the United States in sufficient quantities to annoy United States manufacturers of that product. Such annoyance is known by United States government officials, and these officials indicate to the government of the foreign country which exports most of this product to the United States, that the quantity of their exports is posing a "political problem" inside the United States. As a matter of history, comparable types of problems have sometimes resulted in legislation restricting imports. The foreign government understands the "signal" and decides to impose export restraints. It informs United States government officials of its actions, noting that they will continue for two years, unless the United States government should sooner impose formal import restraints. Has any United States law been violated? If a United States official informs United States private firms which produce that product about the facts of the foreign government statement, has any United States law been violated?

(2) U.S. Antitrust Laws

In a previous section, it was noted that a 1980 petition for escape clause action on automobile imports resulted in a negative ITC determination. At a congressional hearing in 1980, the U.S. Trade Representative was asked whether the President's officials could negotiate a voluntary restraint agreement on automobiles, and his response suggested that the law was not sufficiently clear to allow government negotiation of such an agreement without raising serious antitrust problems.[10] An exchange of letters then ensued, including the following:

LETTER, DATED DECEMBER 29, 1980, FROM ASSOCIATE ATTORNEY GENERAL SHENEFIELD TO SENATOR LEVIN [11]

Dear Senator Levin:

The Attorney General has asked me to respond to your letter of December 8, which posed several questions regarding the antitrust con-

---

10. See BNA ITIM No. 53, at AA-2 (Nov. 19, 1980).

11. The letter is reproduced in BNA ITIM No. 59, at N-1 (Jan. 7, 1981).

straints affecting the ability of the President and his representatives to negotiate with foreign governments "in an effort to bring about import restraints."

You first ask whether the Department of Justice would agree that the President clearly has the constitutional authority to enter into negotiations with a foreign government seeking import restraints. (All of your questions assume that "President" means not only the President but the executive branch officials charged with negotiating responsibility.) The Department agrees that the President possesses such inherent constitutional authority.

Second, you ask if we agree that an agreement between the two governments reached as a result of such negotiations would not be an antitrust violation by the American government negotiators if the foreign government required through its legal process compliance by its national firms. We would agree.

Third, you ask about a situation in which the President asks the foreign government to mandate controls, but the foreign government merely suggests restraint by its national firms. Again we would agree that in all probability the American government negotiators would ultimately be held to have no liability.

Fourth, you ask if we agree that in all of the foregoing hypothetical situations the law is so clear that a suit against the President or his negotiators would be dismissed without discovery. While it is likely that the President and his representatives would prevail ultimately, perhaps on a motion for summary judgment, there is a significant possibility that an artfully drafted complaint could withstand a motion to dismiss prior to at least some limited discovery.

Finally, you ask whether the President and his representatives would likely prevail in an antitrust suit if they urged the foreign government to obtain restraints, without distinguishing between mandatory and voluntary restraints. While we believe that the United States government negotiators would likely prevail in such a suit, the ambiguity inherent in the type of agreement you posit increases the degree of antitrust risk as well as the likelihood that there would be costly and time-consuming discovery before the issue was resolved.

I should add that this response attempts to answer the specific questions you have posed, which relate solely to the potential antitrust liability of the President and United States government negotiators under the circumstances you set forth. I have not addressed the potential antitrust exposure under current United States law for other involved parties, such as the foreign manufacturers.

I hope that these comments have been helpful, and appreciate your concern for the antitrust issues involved in negotiations with foreign governments on import questions.

Sincerely yours,

John H. Shenefield
Associate Attorney General

Notes and Questions

(1) As the Shenefield letter suggests, the concern about U.S. antitrust laws is not limited to U.S. government negotiators. The materials on the automobile VRA in the next subsection include an exchange of letters between the Japanese government and the U.S. Attorney General dealing with antitrust issues.

(2) As a U.S. government negotiator of VRAs how much would you worry about antitrust liability? Would it matter if you were being contacted by or were even consulting with U.S. industry officials as to the terms and acceptability of the VRA?

(3) As a foreign manufacturer, would you participate in such negotiations? To what extent would you insist that your government conduct the negotiations?

(4) As a U.S. manufacturer that is an intended beneficiary of a VRA, what antitrust problems, if any, do you have to consider?

(D) JAPANESE RESTRAINTS ON AUTO EXPORTS TO THE UNITED STATES

As we saw in Section 9.2 supra, in the motor vehicles case, the U.S. auto industry faced difficult economic times in the late 1970's. The attempt by the industry to obtain protection from import competition did not end with the negative ITC determination in 1980.[12] Legislation was introduced in Congress to authorize a VRA in the auto sector and to impose quotas on automobile imports.[13] No legislative action was taken ultimately because in an exchange of views between the U.S. and Japanese governments (U.S. officials adamantly denied that there was a "negotiation"), Japan became "informed" of "our problems" as can be seen in the following letter exchange between Attorney General Smith and Japanese Ambassador Okawara.[14] The exchange highlights the antitrust issues that may arise under U.S. law in connection with VRAs.

LETTER, DATED MAY 7, 1981, FROM JAPANESE AMBASSADOR OKAWARA TO U.S. ATTORNEY GENERAL SMITH

Dear Mr. Attorney General:

I have the honor to inform you that the Government of Japan, through explanations by the United States Government fully understands the difficult situation of the U.S. auto industry.

Based upon the above understanding, the Government of Japan will unilaterally restrain the volume of cars to be exported from Japan to the U.S., according to the scheme explained hereinafter, in order to cooperate with efforts to be taken for the recovery of the automobile industry in the U.S.

---

12. Certain Motor Vehicles, Inv. No. TA–201–44, Pub. No. 1110, 2 ITRD 5241 (ITC 1980). See Section 9.2(C)(3) supra.

13. See, e.g., H.R. 7957, 96th Cong., 2nd Sess. (1980).

14. The letters are reproduced in BNA ITIM No. 77, at M–1 (May 13, 1981).

The Government of Japan considers the orderly export of Japanese products to be one of its basic trade policies so as not to create disruption in the national economies of other countries. On May 1, 1981, the Cabinet members concerned met, considered the attached scheme, and approved it.

It is the Ministry of International Trade and Industry (MITI) that has authority and responsibility for administering concretely Japan's basic trade policies.

The above-mentioned measures concerning Japanese car exports to the U.S. will be put into practice through written directives setting the maximum number of exportable units of passenger cars to the U.S. for each Japanese automobile company, to be given by MITI in accordance with its authority for bringing into action trade policies set forth in Article Three (3) of the establishment law of MITI, as well as Article Forty-eight (48) of The Foreign Exchange and Foreign Trade Control Law (Law No. 228 of 1949).

Adherence to these directives will be secured by reports on car exports to the U.S. which are to be collected separately from each company under the competent authority and responsibility of MITI.

Further, if any firm should fail to make a report or should make a false report in violation of the provisions of Article Sixty-seven (67) of the Foreign Exchange and Foreign Trade Control Law, that firm will be proceeded against for punishment under Articles Seventy-two (72) and Seventy-three (73) of the Law.

If on the basis of the above reports it becomes clear that any company threatens to exceed the limits set forth by MITI, the Government of Japan will promptly make car exports to the U.S. subject to export licensing, by amending the Export Trade Control Order (Cabinet Order No. 378 of 1949) in accordance with Article Forty-eight (48) of the Foreign Exchange and Foreign Trade Control Law. MITI would then enforce the export maximums it has established for each company by refusing to license exports in excess of those maximums. The Government of Japan has the authority under Japanese law to impose this requirement. It would be a violation of Japanese law to export cars without an export license in that situation, and any company engaging in such violation would be proceeded against for imposition of fines, penalties or other sanctions as provided by Article Seventy (70) of the Foreign Exchange and Foreign Trade Control Law.

As the above-mentioned directives setting limits for exportable cars and collecting reports from each company come as a result of the administrative authority inherent in the Government of Japan in accordance with the laws of Japan, each company must obey the orders of the Government of Japan.

The Government of Japan considers that implementation of such an export restraint by the Government of Japan, including the division of the maximum number of exportable units among the companies by MITI, and compliance with the restraints by Japanese automobile companies, would not give rise to violations of American antitrust laws. However, the Government of Japan requests that the Department of Justice, as the authority chiefly responsible for administering the U.S. laws, support the views of the Government of Japan.

*   *   *

Sincerely yours,

Yoshio Okawara
Ambassador of Japan

LETTER, DATED MAY 7, 1981, FROM ATTORNEY GENERAL SMITH TO JAPANESE AMBASSADOR OKAWARA

Dear Mr. Ambassador:

This letter is in response to the request of the Government of Japan, set forth in its letter of May 7, and the two enclosures thereto, for the views of the Department of Justice on antitrust questions regarding measures now being considered by the Government of Japan to unilaterally restrain the export of passenger cars to the U.S. so as to cooperate with the U.S. Government's domestic automobile industry recovery program.

The Government of Japan has advised us that the Ministry of International Trade and Industry (MITI), which it represents has legal authority and responsibility in the Government of Japan for carrying out basic trade policy, including authority to take the measures described in your letter and its two enclosures, and has authority to maintain orderly exports, will establish at its discretion the maximum number of passenger cars which may be exported to the U.S. by individual Japanese companies. MITI will issue a written directive to each company stating the maximum number of cars that company may export to the U.S. in a specified period.

Further, MITI will direct individual companies to submit accurate monthly reports on passenger car exports to the U.S. so as to assure the implementation of the export limitation directive. It is understood, and the directive will state that, in any case in which it becomes clear that any company threatens to exceed the limits set forth by MITI, the Government of Japan will promptly make the export of cars to the U.S. subject to export licensing, in accordance with Article Forty-eight (48) of the Foreign Exchange and Foreign Trade Control Law, (Law No. 228 of 1949), and Article One (1) of the Export Trade Control Order (Cabinet Order No. 378 of 1949 as amended), by amending the Export Trade Control Order. MITI will then enforce the export maximums it established for each company by refusing to license exports in excess of those maximums. The Government of Japan has advised us that MITI has the authority to impose this requirement, that it would be a violation of Japanese law to export cars without an export license in that situation, and that such violation would be punished pursuant to Japanese law by fines, penalties or other sanctions.

In these circumstances, we believe that the Japanese automobile companies' compliance with export limitations directed by MITI would properly be viewed as having been compelled by the Japanese government, acting within its sovereign powers. The Department of Justice is of the view that implementation of such an export restraint by the Government of Japan, including the division among the companies by MITI of the maximum exportable number of units, and compliance with the program by Japanese automobile companies, would not give rise to violations of United States antitrust laws. We believe that American courts interpreting the antitrust laws in such a situation would likely so hold.

* * *

Sincerely,

William French Smith
Attorney General

_____

When the restraints described in the letters expired on March 31, 1985, the United States did not request their renewal.[15] An FTC staff study concluded in 1984 that the restraints were costing consumers at least $1.1 billion (all in 1983 dollars) annually in higher prices and the economy as a whole some $994 million annually in efficiency and other losses. The study estimated that the Japanese auto producers obtained benefits in an amount of $824 million, while U.S. producers' gains were estimated at $115 million.[16] The increased profits to Japanese automakers raises the question of whether the United States would have been better off to have imposed a tariff with the equivalent effect of the VRA. In that case, the increase in Japanese car prices would have gone to the U.S. government, not the Japanese companies. However, the competition in the Japanese auto industry in Japan was such that during much of the restraint period some companies might have incurred losses without the lucrative U.S. market, and the restraints may have been acceptable to Japan only because they allowed Japanese companies to earn these extra profits. Thus, although the restraints may have saved the U.S. industry, they considerably strengthened the already strong Japanese auto industry. The future ramifications of this remain to be seen.

The decision not to request renewal of restraints seemed due at least in part to a belief that the costs to the consumer and the economy could not be justified in light of the record profits being earned by the U.S. auto industry. The renewed health of the U.S. industry may indicate that the auto VRA was a rare case where a safeguard measure accomplished its goal of allowing an industry to adjust to import competition. Such a conclusion is, of course, premature at the moment. At least part of the auto industry continues to push for protectionist legislation. See Section 8.2(C) supra, concerning proposed domestic content legislation for the auto industry. In 1985, Japan continued to restrain its auto exports to Canada and the EC.

15. The Japanese government nonetheless announced that it would not allow auto exports to the United States for the ensuing year to exceed 2.3 million units (an increase of 24% over the levels of the prior year). 2 BNA Intl. Trade Rptr. 276 (1985).

16. D. Tarr & M. Morkre, note 2 supra, at 54.

SECTION 9.5 ADJUSTMENT ASSISTANCE [1]

U.S. COMMISSION ON INTERNATIONAL TRADE AND INVESTMENT POLICY (THE WILLIAMS COMMISSION), REPORT

47–49 (1971)

ALTERNATIVE APPROACHES TO IMPORT COMPETITION

The government can ease adaptation to competition from imports in two ways. First, programs of adjustment assistance can enhance the mobility and upgrade the quality of both our manpower and our capital. Second, methods of temporary protection—"orderly marketing agreements" or import restrictions (tariffs or quotas) under the escape clause—can provide time for industries to achieve a viable competitive position in the same or different lines of activity.

*   *   *

Choosing Among Options

The obligation of the government to aid the adjustment of groups facing competition from imports has already been recognized in U.S. legislation. Three different approaches have been available in recent years.

Before passage of the Trade Expansion Act of 1962 (TEA), the "escape clause" was the primary means available to cushion the impact of imports. The escape clause authorized the President to provide increased protection against imports where an industry needed time to adapt its products or its methods to new conditions. The TEA, while retaining the escape clause, opened up the possibility of providing direct assistance to firms or groups of workers in order to help them make necessary adjustments. It also gave the President authority to negotiate "orderly marketing agreements," under which exporting countries would voluntarily limit their exports to the United States of those products causing adjustment problems.

Adjustment assistance and the two available forms of import restriction differ importantly in their impact on the economy. While adjustment

1. See generally Richardson, Worker Adjustment to U.S. International Trade: Programs and Prospects, in W. Cline (ed.), Trade Policy in the 1980s, at 393 (1983) (with bibliography); Bratt, Issues in Worker Certification and Questions of Future Direction in the Trade Adjustment Assistance Program, 14 Law & Poly.Intl.Bus. 819, 823 (1982); Sorrentino, Trade Readjustment Assistance for Unemployed Workers, 14 U.Toledo L.Rev. 285 (1983). Reischer, Trade Adjustment in Theory and Practice, Subcomm. on Foreign Economic Policy of the Joint Economic Comm., 87th Cong., 1st Sess. (Joint Comm. Print 1961); Fulda, Adjustment to Hardship Caused by Imports: The New Decisions of the Tariff Commission and the Need for Legislative Clarification, 70 Mich.L.Rev. 791 (1972); Clubb & Reischer, The Trade Adjustment Bills: Their Purpose and Efficacy, 61 Colum.L.Rev. 490 (1961); Bratt, Assisting the Economic Recovery of Import-Injured Firms, 6 Law & Poly. Intl.Bus. 1 (1974); Golden, The Politics of Free Trade: The Role of Trade Adjustment Assistance, 14 Va.J.Intl.L. 151 (1973); Manley, Adjustment Assistance: Experience Under the Automotive Products Trade Act of 1965, 10 Harv.Intl.L.J. 294 (1969); Young, America's Labor Pains and Foreign Trade: The Stillbirth of Adjustment Assistance, 13 Va.J.Intl. L. 254 (1972); Weinberg, Adjustment Assistance: A New Proposal for Eligibility, 55 Cornell L.Rev. 1049 (1970); Hoy, Adjustment Assistance Under the Trade Expansion Act: A Critique of Recent Tariff Commission Decisions, 6 Texas Intl.L.F. 67 (1970); GATT, 19th Supp. BISD 28–29 (1973).

assistance is focused on the particular firms or workers injured by increased imports, the impact of tariff relief or "voluntary" export restraints cannot be confined to those firms actually suffering injury. All producers of the protected product, whether or not they have been injured, benefit from lessened competition.

As opposed to adjustment assistance, both escape-clause relief and orderly marketing agreements would also impose in differing degrees the various costs that are associated with increased protection against imports. In a later section of this chapter ("The Costs of Protection") we explain in detail how these costs are incurred.

Adjustment assistance, unlike import restriction, would impose direct monetary costs on the taxpayer. But by creating more flexible industries and more highly skilled workers—thus benefitting the entire economy—successful programs of adjustment assistance should offset part or all of their tax cost.

Use of adjustment assistance also avoids the adverse effects on costs of U.S.-produced goods in both domestic and foreign markets, the restriction on access for those goods to markets abroad, and the strains on U.S. foreign relations that may arise when the escape clause is used or when pressure is applied in an effort to obtain "voluntary" export restraints. Hence the Commission feels that in general the government should encourage adjustment rather than impose restrictions—except in those circumstances, outlined below, where protection may be more appropriate.

Under some circumstances, adjustment assistance will be difficult to apply. An industry may require only a brief period of protection, say five years, but no other aid from government programs to improve its competitive position. Or the industry may be so large that a program of adjustment assistance might need an extraordinarily high budgetary appropriation. As a general principle, therefore, in instances where an entire industry—not simply certain of its firms—is seriously injured, temporary import restrictions, coupled with maximum possible adjustment assistance, would be appropriate.

STANLEY D. METZGER, ADJUSTMENT ASSISTANCE

(1971)[2]

The weaknesses of the escape clause were perceived early in the 1950's. The Randall Commission on Foreign Economic Policy noted in its 1954 report the proposal of David McDonald, then President of the United Steelworkers of America, for adjustment assistance for workers in the form of extended unemployment compensation and retraining and relocation benefits, and bills were introduced that year in both House and Senate (then Senator John Kennedy introduced the first Senate bill) incorporating these conceptions. Indeed, for the next eight years, adjustment assistance bills for workers were regularly dropped in the Congressional hopper but no hearings

2. U.S. Commission on International Trade and Investment Policy (the Williams Commission), Papers, vol. I, at 319, 323–25.

were held on them, nor a serious consideration given them in the 1955 or 1958 trade agreement extension act deliberations in the Congress. The Administration did not adopt the idea until 1962.

There were a number of interacting reasons for the adoption of the adjustment assistance conception in 1962. The Administration was determined to secure major new tariff reduction authority from the Congress in order to make a substantial tariff bargain with the European Economic Community, lowering the Common External Tariff of the EEC so as to preserve the large American export market in Europe. It sought 50% reduction authority—far more than had been sought in the period between 1945 and 1962.

At the same time, the Administration had been made aware of the uneasiness of the Europeans about the instability of tariff concessions once negotiated arising from the operations of the escape clause, and of their consequent reluctance to engage in substantial new negotiations without greater assurances that there would be tighter controls over these trade restrictive measures (quotas and tariffs)—which were the only remedies then available were the escape clause invoked. As earlier noted, while the President had turned down Tariff Commission findings and recommendations in 26 out of 41 cases, he had nonetheless over the years found favorably in the 15 cases. Moreover, the fact that the Commission had interpreted the 1951 Act so that an increase in imports any time after a Tariff concession was conclusively presumed to result "in whole or in part" from the concession, signified to the Europeans that the connection between the operation of the escape clause and its original object—to authorize an "escape" from an injury-causing trade agreement commitment—had become formal rather than real.

In consequence, it was apparent that the Administration had to seek a tightening of the escape clause in the 1962 legislation which would cut back its potential use and create more safeguards so that, if used, it would be truly temporary in duration.

It was also quite clear to the Administration that neither of these objectives—substantial new tariff-reduction authority and tightening of the escape clause—could be obtained without some relief measures being made available which overcame the weaknesses of the escape clause remedies which have been described.

Adjustment assistance to firms and workers was the apparent answer, and the Administration put it forward. By utilizing a variety of domestic economic means to ease the lot of firms and workers who might be impacted by imports, adjustment assistance avoided the foreign relations pitfalls of the escape clause's tariff and quota relief measures. By dealing directly with the adjustment problems of firms and workers regardless whether the industry of which they were a part was suffering serious injury attributable to concession-fed imports, adjustment assistance avoided the no-man's land in which individual firms and workers sometimes found themselves. Adjustment assistance to small firms and groups of workers in consequence promised to offer to them relief which appeared to be substantive, a net gain over what had been available to them theoretically under the escape clause.

That their support for the 1962 legislation, or at least a diminution of their opposition to it, was secured through adoption of the adjustment assistance concept, cannot be considered to be an insignificant factor in the Administration's 1962 action.

SENATE REPORT NO. 93–1298

93d Cong., 2d Sess. 131 (1974)

The worker adjustment assistance provisions enacted in 1962, however, have clearly not been very effective. For the first seven years of the program, no worker was found eligible for its benefits. Since November, 1969, when the first worker certification was issued, only an estimated 47,000 workers in 29 States have been certified as eligible. Total outlays for worker adjustment assistance total less than $69 million over the entire period (an average outlay of about $1,500 per worker). Moreover, the relatively meager information that is available with respect to the operations of the program indicate that, even where workers have been found eligible, the program has often functioned in such a manner that its objectives were frustrated. The petitioning process has proven to be cumbersome and time-consuming. Many recipients did not receive payments under the program until long after they became unemployed because of increased imports.   *   *   *

Note: The Trade Act of 1974 and Recent Amendments

In light of the dissatisfaction with adjustment assistance as it was applied under the Trade Expansion Act of 1962, a number of significant changes were made by the Trade Act of 1974.[3] Although there were important amendments to the 1974 Act in 1981, the 1974 Act established the basic standards for provision of adjustment assistance in the United States. In this Note, we describe the basic changes in adjustment assistance introduced by the 1974 Act, as modified in 1981.

First, to meet criticisms concerning administration of the program prior to 1974, the role of the International Trade Commission was eliminated and the entire administration of the worker adjustment assistance program was placed in one agency, the Department of Labor.[4] It was hoped that the processing of applications would proceed much more quickly so that eligible workers would receive their benefits in a timely fashion. Likewise, an ITC determination is not a step in the process for adjustment assistance for firms [5] or communities,[6] the administration of these programs having been placed primarily in the Department of Commerce.

Second, with respect to the funding of worker adjustment assistance, the 1974 Act made significant changes to the provisions of the 1962 Act. Under the 1962 Act, if workers became eligible for adjustment assistance, federal funds paid the entire amount. Thus, state unemployment compensation funds were

---

3. Trade Act of 1974, §§ 221–83 (codified at 19 U.S.C.A. §§ 2271–394.

4. Trade Act of 1974, §§ 221–50; 19 U.S. C.A. §§ 2271–322. The U.S. Trade Representative has a coordinating function. 19 U.S. C.A. § 2392.

5. Trade Act of 1974, §§ 251–64, 19 U.S. C.A. §§ 2341–54.

6. Trade Act of 1974, §§ 271–74, 19 U.S. C.A. §§ 2371–74.

relieved of having to assist such workers, who otherwise probably would have applied for and received state unemployment compensation. At the time complete federal funding had been introduced, it had been thought politically necessary to provide this "federal funds bait," to overcome the concerns of state officials that the higher federal benefits might cause pressure for increased general unemployment benefits. Under the 1974 Act, federal funds are utilized only to the extent that adjustment assistance payments (administered through the state unemployment offices) exceed the normal state benefits. Thus, at least to the extent that unemployment compensation would be granted to a worker under a state plan, that state's funds pay for that portion.[7]

Third, there were significant changes in the level of benefits available under the program. Under the 1962 Act, the maximum was 65% of the average weekly manufacturing wage; under the Trade Act of 1974, the benefit level was set at 70% of the worker's average weekly wage, and the maximum was raised to 100% of the average weekly manufacturing wage. This meant that workers with higher incomes could receive substantially more than was allowed as a maximum under the 1962 Act. The generosity of the 1974 Act was criticized by the Reagan Administration, which in general has opposed the concept of special adjustment assistance programs, believing that the regular provisions for unemployed workers should be sufficient. Thus, in 1981 the benefits provisions were changed so that the maximum payable benefit is now equal to the applicable unemployment insurance benefit.[8] The principal difference now between regular state unemployment insurance and adjustment assistance is that adjustment assistance may be payable for a longer period of time, up to 78 weeks under certain circumstances.

Fourth, provisions were added in the 1974 Act for adjustment assistance benefits to communities, as well as workers and firms.[9]

Finally, and probably most importantly, the 1974 Act provided for a dramatic shift in the eligibility criteria for benefits. Since economists and other policymakers (including the Williams Commission Report) had indicated a preference for adjustment assistance over import restraints as a means of cushioning adjustment to increased imports, it was provided in the 1974 Act that the criteria for obtaining adjustment assistance would be less stringent than those for obtaining escape clause relief. The table below sets out the differences between the eligibility requirements for escape clause relief and for adjustment assistance:

7. Trade Act of 1974, § 232(d), 19 U.S.C.A. § 2292(d).

8. Trade Act of 1974, § 232(a), 19 U.S.C.A. § 2292(a).

9. Trade Act of 1974, §§ 271–74, 19 U.S.C.A. §§ 2371–74.

Section 201 and Section 222, Trade Act of 1974: Escape Clause and Worker Adjustment Assistance Eligibility Criteria

	Section 201 Escape Clause	Section 222 Worker Adjustment Assistance
Increased imports	actual or relative	actual or relative
Linked to trade concessions	no longer	no longer
Injury	"serious injury" including: —significant idling of facilities; —significant unemployment	significant number or proportion of workers totally or partially separated, *plus* sales or production or both decreased absolutely
Threat?	yes	yes
What is injured?	"industry" (possible geographic area)	workers in firm or appropriate subdivision
Cause of injury	increased imports are a substantial cause (i.e. an important cause not less important than any other cause)	increased imports "contributed importantly" (i.e. are an important cause, but not necessarily more important than other causes)

Escape clause proceedings have reference to the impact of imports on an entire industry, while the adjustment assistance program has primary reference to the impact of imports on the workers of a firm or an appropriate subdivision thereof. It will be noticed, however, that for a workers' petition to succeed, it must be shown that there has been an absolute decrease in sales or production of the firm or appropriate subdivision. This phrase was very carefully framed, so as to provide, as nearly as possible, an objective criterion to prevent adjustment assistance under this program from being used for workers whose separation from employment was not due to imports. The 1981 Act would have provided for a "substantial cause" test to be applied in adjustment assistance cases, but that provision was repealed before it came into effect.[10]

As to the actual operation of the adjustment assistance program, the number of beneficiaries reached some 530,000 workers in 1980 when $1.6 billion in benefits were paid. However, the number of beneficiaries has since fallen off significantly, and the program was estimated in 1985 to cost only some $151 million in the then current fiscal year.[11] It also appears that very few workers have in fact received training, job search or relocation services or payments under the program.[12] In 1985, the Reagan administration again proposed to

10. Pub.L. No. 97–35, § 2501, 95 Stat. 881 (1981), modified, Pub.L. No. 98–120, § 3(a), 97 Stat. 809 (1983).

11. 2 BNA Intl. Trade Rptr 1397 (1985).

12. Bratt, Issues in Worker Certification and Questions of Future Direction in the Trade Adjustment Assistance Program, 14 Law & Poly. Intl. Bus. 819, 823 (1982). For other studies on the operation of trade adjustment assistance programs in the United States, see Employment and Training Report of the President (annual); Sorrentino, Trade Readjustment Assistance for Unemployed Workers, 14 U.Toledo L.Rev. 285 (1983). For a description of adjustment policies in Japan, see Comment, Letting Obsolete Firms Die:

abolish the adjustment assistance program, and handle adjustment problems under other existing federal unemployment relief programs. In early 1986, however, the program was authorized for an additional six years.[13]

As noted in Section 3.5(C) supra, the Court of International Trade reviews legal challenges to administrative decisions made in connection with the program. A fair number of such challenges have been brought.

Questions

(1) The precise role that adjustment assistance should play is a subject of some controversy. Is there any justification for providing more benefits to workers displaced by changes in trade patterns as opposed to changes in technology? Or are such additional benefits simply the price to be paid by the economy for a liberal free trade policy?

(2) What role should the availability of adjustment assistance play in the decision to afford an industry import relief? If sufficient adjustment assistance is available, should import restraints ever be imposed? If so, when?

(3) Should reforms of the international rules on safeguards (discussed in the next section) require use of adjustment assistance along with or in preference to import restraints?

(4) How does the economic analysis presented in Chapter 1 supra affect the answers to the foregoing questions?

SECTION 9.6 SAFEGUARDS AND STRUCTURAL ADJUSTMENT: THE PUZZLE AND PROSPECTS FOR REFORM

(A) INTRODUCTION

From time to time there have been attempts to reform or restructure the international rules on safeguards. Discussions of how to change the safeguard rules inevitably turn to the broader question of how the world trading system and individual nations should handle the problem of "structural adjustment." Many developing countries have invested heavily in industries which pose strong competitive challenges to the competing industries of the industrial countries. Not only do the industries of the developing countries have the advantages of newer plants and equipment, but often they also have the advantage of markedly lower labor costs. In addition, they sometimes have advantages in respect of availability of cheap natural resources and newer technology (often purchased from industrial countries). When the cheaper developing country products are exported to industrial countries, the result has been important political and economic adjustment problems in the older industrialized countries. Solutions to these problems arguably require some sort of structural adjustment, i.e. realignment of production to make it more nearly consistent with the comparative advantages that exist in today's world. In short, the industrial countries have been asked to shrink or eliminate those of their industries that cannot today

Trade Adjustment Assistance in the United States and Japan, 22 Harv.Intl. L.J. 595 (1981).

13. 3 BNA Intl.Trade Rptr. 524 (1986).

compete successfully with developing countries. It is simply not feasible for such actions to be taken without allowing for some adjustment period, which raises the question of what sort of safeguards should be allowed in these situations.

In this section, we will consider a number of proposals for reform of the present rules governing safeguards. Typically, those proposals attempt to deal with some of the major criticisms of the current system that we have considered in the prior sections of this chapter: whether there is a need for international supervision of national safeguards, whether selective (non-MFN) application of safeguards should be permitted, whether and under what circumstances compensation should be provided to exporters affected by safeguards, and how adjustment assistance should be considered in evaluating the need for and extent of safeguards.

Before reviewing proposals for reform, however, it is useful to examine briefly a number of industries where safeguards and structural adjustment problems seem to be most severe.

(B) SELECTED IMPORT-SENSITIVE SECTORS

A definitive list of all of the economic sectors in industrialized countries that have sought import restraints or adjustment assistance of one kind or another is not easily constructed. Some major examples are well known. International trade in steel and textiles, industries which we consider in more detail in this subsection, is extensively regulated by international agreement. International trade in agricultural products, at least among the developed countries, has for many years been subject to numerous import restraints. Indeed, these restraints, which we will examine in some detail in Chapter 14 infra, are so extensive that it is sometimes forgotten that GATT applies to trade in agricultural products. More recently, as we saw in Section 9.4(D) supra, trade in automobiles has been subject to considerable regulation, mainly in the form of restraints imposed by Japan on its exports. Perhaps one indication of U.S. industries in fear of imports can be seen in the list of products not eligible under the 1974 Trade Act for preferential tariff treatment on importation into the United States from developing countries. That list included: textiles and clothing, watches, import-sensitive electronic articles, import sensitive steel articles, certain footwear articles and certain import sensitive glass products.[1]

(1) Steel

The history of steel and steel imports into the United States is a decades long history of the application and removal of a variety of import restraints. We have seen parts of this history in the *Consumers Union* case discussed in Section 3.2(B) supra and in the earlier sections of this chapter, and we will see more of it in Chapter 10 when we consider the so-called trigger price mechanism and various antidumping and countervailing duty cases. Consider the following materials:

1. Trade Act of 1974, § 503(c)(1), 19 U.S. C.A. § 2463.

DAVID G. TARR & MORRIS E. MORKRE, AGGREGATE COSTS TO THE UNITED STATES OF TARIFFS AND QUOTAS ON IMPORTS: GENERAL TARIFF CUTS AND REMOVAL OF QUOTAS ON AUTOMOBILES, STEEL, SUGAR, AND TEXTILES

126–29 (1984) [2]

During the past fifteen years the United States steel industry has enjoyed a significant amount of special protection from imports. During 1969–1974 Japan and the European Economic Community negotiated "voluntary restraint agreements" (VRA's) that limited their exports to the U.S. In 1978 the Administration initiated the "trigger price mechanism" (TPM) as part of its program for the steel industry. The TPM was, in principle, to have established a minimum price for imports below which imports could not enter without being subjected to an expedited antidumping investigation. In 1982 a major effort was undertaken by the majority of the integrated U.S. steel producers to obtain tariff protection under the antidumping and countervailing duty laws. Despite the fact that the Department of Commerce (DOC) made either a negative determination of subsidies or a "de minimus" or insignificant determination of subsidies for a significant portion of the European Economic Community (possibly eliminating the ability of countervailing duties to restrain imports due to additional supply from unrestrained suppliers), the European Economic Community agreed to quotas on steel exports of specific products under the U.S.—E.C. Arrangement.

In early 1984, the United Steelworkers of America and Bethlehem Steel Corporation petitioned the United States International Trade Commission (USITC or ITC) for relief from imports under section 201 of the Trade Act of 1974. In that "Petition" they asked for quotas on imports of carbon and alloy steel products such that imports would be at most 15 percent of domestic apparent consumption. Also in 1984, there was legislation before Congress (the Fair Trade in Steel Act of 1984) that would utilize quotas to limit imports of steel to 15 percent of domestic apparent consumption for five years.

On June 12, 1984, the ITC (by a 3–2 decision) voted that "industries" representing 74 percent of domestic shipments were injured. On July 11, 1984, the ITC recommended to the President that quotas be imposed on almost all of these products (over 97 percent by tonnage).

The President, in response to the affirmative decision by the ITC on the petition rejected quotas through the 201 process; but he directed United States Trade Representative, William Brock, to negotiate with foreign governments. The object of the negotiations would be to get these governments to voluntarily restrain their exports.

After the President's program was announced, Congress passed, in the Trade and Tariff Act of 1984, a nonbinding "sense of the Congress" that

2. This study is a Bureau of Economics Staff Report to the Federal Trade Commission (FTC). It is stated to represent the views of the FTC's Bureaus of Economics, Consumer Protection and Competition, but it was not acted upon by the FTC. The FTC did, however, vote to release it.

imports should be reduced to between 17 and 20.2 percent of U.S. domestic apparent consumption and authorized the President to negotiate agreements to achieve that goal. The bill also provides that continuation of the import relief in any year is contingent on the major steel companies committing "substantially all of their net cash flow from steel operations to reinvestment and modernization of their steel industry." These provisions appear to be the Congressional substitute for the Fair Trade in Steel Act of 1984, but the Trade and Tariff Act of 1984 indicates that if the President's program fails to achieve its goals, Congress will consider appropriate action.

Prior to the announcement of the new restrictions, there were already in place some formal and possibly informal quantitative restraints on steel imports. In October 1982, the United States and the European Community (EC) agreed to limit EC exports of certain carbon steel products to the United States to specified percentages of United States consumption, and the United States companies withdrew the antidumping and countervailing duty petitions they had filed against the companies in the EC. South Africa and Mexico have also agreed to limit their exports of steel into the U.S. In addition, the United Steelworkers-Bethlehem Petition alleges that the "level of exports presently flowing from Japan to the United States [are] based on informal undertakings by the Japanese to the U.S. government." Bethlehem provided details of these undertakings when it stated: In 1983, "The United States Trade Representative negotiated a voluntary restraint promise on steel exports with Japan. As a result, the American steelmakers withdrew their 301 case against Japan." Japan is now said to provide a quarterly "weather forecast" to the U.S. government in which it provides its estimate of the next quarter's steel shipments to the U.S. Thus, the European Community, Mexico, South Africa and possibly Japan were already limiting their exports to the United States.

In announcing the new program, USTR Brock indicated that negotiations to limit imports would be conducted with Brazil, Spain, South Korea, and Japan. It was also reported that an agreement with the European Community on pipe and tube exports would be sought and that Australia and Finland have offered to negotiate voluntary restraint agreements if unfair trade practices cases against them are dropped. In December, the Administration announced that agreements had been reached with Japan, South Korea, Spain, Brazil, South Africa, Mexico, and Australia. The above mentioned agreement with the European Community will remain in effect and Canada is expected to not increase its current market penetration. The goal of the program, however, is to limit imports to 18.5 percent of domestic apparent consumption, where semi-finished steel is excluded from the calculations.

We saw an estimate of the significant costs of steel import restraints in Section 9.4 supra, where we also excerpted a portion of the Tarr and Morkre study.

As a general proposition, the steel industry does not always seem deserving of sympathy. In recent years some companies seem to have spent more on diversification than on steel plant modernization—the case of U.S.

Steel Corporation's acquisition of Marathon Oil comes to mind. Moreover, in the 1970's when the industry's troubles were becoming more and more serious, its labor agreements led to a widening of the already significant gap between the average wage in steel and the average wage in all manufacturing (from 133% in 1970 to 175% in 1981).[3] These factors have caused some to wonder if the industry's management and especially its highly paid workers are not the real cause of its problems and make it undeserving of government assistance at direct or indirect public expense. Nonetheless, the industry certainly can not be accused of making excessive profits in recent years and has thus far existed without direct government subsidies. Moreover, while very high wages continue to be paid to those steelworkers who are employed, tens of thousands have been laid off with little prospect of ever being called back. As a result, there is another side to the steel story.

STATEMENT OF DONALD H. TRAUTHEIM CHAIRMAN, BETHLEHEM STEEL COMPANY AND AMERICAN IRON & STEEL INSTITUTE

(1984) [4]

The major causes of America's steel trade problem are the existence of substantial excess capacity abroad, the increase of foreign government control, subsidization and targeting of steel, and generally ineffective U.S. Trade Law enforcement. All of these had a direct effect on the flow of imports into the U.S. market.

PROFIT RECORD OF STEEL PRODUCERS

After the boom years of 1973–74, the world steel industry underwent a severe downturn. * * * European producers amassed losses approximating 15 billion dollars from 1975 to 1980. While Japanese and North American producers earned profits in that period, margins have generally been thin. When steel segment operations alone are considered, West German, Japanese, and U.S. producers incurred operating losses in several of these years.

* * *

Massive and persistent losses show that the present problems of the world steel industry are structural rather than cyclical. These problems have arisen largely from foreign government actions, yet they have resulted in increased foreign government involvement. Rather than accept the losses in employment and foreign earnings which would result from the bankruptcy or reorganization of steel firms, many governments—especially in Europe and in developing countries—have increased their subsidies for steel industries. This has intensified the underlying problems resulting in the politicization of international steel trade and the near breakdown of the market mechanism. There are many causes of this, but the principal cause is the development of excess capacity worldwide, which began in the late 1960s.

3. Hearings on the U.S. Steel Industry Before the Subcomm. on Intl. Trade of the Senate Comm. on Finance, 98th Cong., 2d Sess. 108 (1984).

4. Id., at 11–24, 91–93.

* * * While European capacity and production maintained a fairly close relationship during the 1960s, they began to diverge sharply after 1975. Since that time, even peak years (such as 1979) have coincided with dangerously low operating rates.

* * *

The construction of excess capacity was not limited to Europe. Table 12 [omitted] shows that during the 1970s the major European countries and Japan had growth in capacity exceeding the growth in consumption, but that the United States did not. In almost all other countries, substantial investments were made to increase capacity which domestic markets could not absorb. As a result, many industries, were, in effect, forced to rely on export markets to boost or maintain operating rates.

It now appears that overaggressive expansion on the part of the Japanese steel industry was a serious strategic mistake. The prosperity and efficiency of the Japanese industry has been based on rapid expansion ahead of the market, providing significant economies of scale. Economies of scale quickly turn into diseconomies, however, when operating rates fall. As world steel demand has remained weaker than the forecasts projected in the early 1970s, excess capacity in the Japanese steel industry has continued to be a persistent problem. That industry is now facing cash-flow constraints, relatively high financial costs, and significant physical inefficiencies due to the logistical problems of running large facilities at much lower rates than those for which they were designed.

Overexpansion has led to even more difficult problems in Europe. It is doubtful that firms run by private managers would have pursued the kind of capacity expansion described in Table 12. In Europe, the availability of government funding (either directly or through loan guarantees) and political pressure for expansion were the key elements leading to the boom in steel capacity between 1965 and 1975. Yet, the politicization of investment decisions during that period has been a major cause of Europe's present crisis of excess steel capacity.

In the advanced developing countries, overexpansion of the steel sector has led to a vicious cycle of growing foreign debt, industry losses, government subsidies and unfair trade. Despite falling demand worldwide, the developing world has added some 50 million tons of new capacity since 1975. Since steel industries in the developing world (especially integrated plants) are for the most part government-owned and protected, this has accentuated the world overcapacity problem. It has done so by intensifying competitive pressures in export markets in general, and in particular in the U.S. market. Thus, U.S. steel imports from countries outside the EC, Canada and Japan, which had averaged 3.5 percent of apparent supply in the period 1979–81, rose to 5.3 percent in 1982 and to 7.6 percent in 1983 (including 8.5 percent in the second half of 1983 and nearly 10 percent so far in 1984).

AGREEMENTS TO ALLOCATE MARKETS

The drive to export has been linked to a related but contradictory response to the crisis of excess capacity: the effort to restrict imports. The most public examples of strict import restrictions are in Europe. Since the onset of the European steel crisis in 1975, the EEC has sought to coordinate an extensive program of market controls, regulating prices and allocating markets. Viscount Davignon of Belgium, who controls the administration of this EEC program, justified it in the following terms:

> The steel industry is a key factor in our independence; Europe cannot therefore allow responsibility for its steel supplies to pass outside the Community for the sake of the international division of labor.*

By the spring of 1978, agreements had been concluded with all major exporters to the European market, stringently limiting imports into the EEC. These limitations have been regularly renewed and are still in effect. Tied to the drive to boost exports, this led to an increase in Europe's positive steel trade balance by the end of the 1970s, a point which also applies to Japan. In effect, these agreements left much of the world steel market subject to a cartel-like arrangement.

The extensive network of European quotas is described in Table 14 [omitted]. It is ironic that European steel exporters have criticized as "protectionist" the legal action against subsidized and dumped imports taken by the U.S. steel industry, while at the same time maintaining strict control over imports into their own market. The Japanese, who have a competitive cost advantage against European producers, shipped only about 300,000 net tons into the EEC during 1983. Japanese shipments to the U.S. market in 1983 were 14 times greater.

In Japan, there have been similar (if less public) restrictions on steel imports, especially from low cost producers in Korea and Taiwan. Recently a published article appeared in the Japan Metal Bulletin, stating that the Japanese Steel Importers Association (formed in November 1983) had in January "voluntarily agreed" to cut back the amount of steel imports to a level not exceeding 3 percent of the total market.

In developing countries, import restrictions have been even more severe. Argentina, for example, requires import licenses for all flat rolled steel products, and such licenses are almost impossible to get. Many other developing countries rely either on high tariffs or licenses to limit steel imports. In Brazil, the most extreme example of protectionism is the so-called "Law of Similars." It means that anything that is made in Brazil cannot be imported without permission, regardless of the sufficiency of domestic production.

SUBSIDIZATION AND NATIONALIZATION

As world steel industry problems intensified, private firms gave way to government control. In late 1978, major steel producers were effectively nationalized in France and Belgium. According to private European steel producers, fully 70% of all the steel companies in Europe are dependent on the state; about half of the EEC's total production is now under direct government control.

The employment effects of steel mill rationalization in certain regions of Belgium and France caused national political concerns. Governments inter-

---

* A.F. Lowenfeld. Public Controls on International Trade (New York, 1979) p. 285.

vened to protect domestic steel producers, representing a camouflaged form of unemployment insurance. Rather than face political unrest, European governments have subsidized continued production in inefficient steel plants. Such practices, however have entailed enormous costs.

Total European subsidies, actual and projected, have been estimated at an incredible 80 billion marks for the period 1975–1985—over $30 billion even at present exchange rates. Government funds have been devoted not just to covering operating losses; they have also been applied to modernization and investment—all under the guise of "restructuring."

* * *

With the exception of Britain, however, many European countries are now subsidizing the replacement of inefficient facilities with new ones—with insufficient reduction in capacity.

* * *

While government involvement in Japan is more subtle, MITI and other agencies are deeply involved in a restructuring program. In general, the Japanese steel industry is reducing large increments of capacity and shifting to a maintenance mode, where investment is designed to raise the efficiency of existing facilities rather than to expand capacity. While Japanese subsidies do not seem to be widespread at this time, the government has controlled raw materials prices (including oil) and management of the adjustment process. As a result, buying and selling cartels have developed in both Europe and Japan; these cartels have even reached some agreements on dividing up other markets.

In countries such as Brazil, Korea and Taiwan—countries which already have significant excess capacity—there are continuing efforts to [expand] capacity based on policies of import substitution and export promotion. Government ownership, control and subsidization of steel is a basic fact of economic life in these countries. In Brazil, Mexico and South Korea government ownership ranges between 68 and 75 percent, and these percentages are all expected to increase in coming years as new government projects come on line. Meanwhile, increasing government subsidies in such countries continue to distort trade and injure U.S. producers. Equally alarming is the fact that our major foreign competitors in Europe and Japan are continuing to provide subsidized financing for their exports of steelmaking equipment to the developing world, yet these same countries severely limit their imports of steel from the plants they help fund.

THE STRUGGLE OVER WHERE RETRENCHMENT WILL OCCUR

Until excess capacity abroad is reduced, our steel trade crisis will persist. Government involvement has generally kept the market from determining where capacity reductions should occur. It is the least efficient facilities which should be retired—yet many of these plants are receiving subsidies in Europe and elsewhere. Should these plants survive and more efficient private plants be closed, the net loss to the world economy in terms of efficiency will be substantial. More significant is the fact that jobs and income will be lost in regions which have resisted playing the subsidies game. This is the key factor in the present steel trade problem.

In some ways the U.S. steel industry was better able to cope with foreign excess capacity than its international counterparts—at least until the catastrophic downturn of 1982–83. This provides some evidence of the advantages of a private, market-based industry. The U.S. industry has not expanded its capacity, *even though it cannot supply all of its home market in a year of strong demand.* Yet in many ways the U.S. steel industry has suffered most from the over-expansion of world steel capacity. Our trade laws have not prevented the U.S. market from being seriously injured by surging imports of unfairly traded steel. The U.S. steel market is the most open major steel market in the world, and U.S. sales are the chief "spoils" in the intense struggle for exports among countries with substantial excess capacity. Most significantly, U.S. producers are dependent on private capital markets for funds. Inefficient operations are sustained abroad via government supports, but no such props exist for U.S. firms, regardless of relative efficiency.

As we have noted, the market mechanism in steel has been more or less dismantled outside the United States. As a result, the price information which the market provides is misleading in regard to where capital should be invested, or where retrenchment should occur. Furthermore, the distorting effects of government intervention have been intensified by recent trends in exchange rates.

The messages given by market prices for steel from many foreign sources do not reflect underlying competitiveness of these sources. The surge of imported steel since 1980 stems largely from intervention by foreign governments and from the disastrous effects of an overvalued dollar. If we look behind these factors, it is demonstrable [that] the underlying competitive standing of the American steel industry is still relatively strong. There is clearly no basis for arguing that immutable factors support further massive contraction in the U.S. industry, or that government policies designed to assist the industry cannot reverse its current decline.

* * *

Thus despite our best efforts, the steel industry's modernization will continue to fall below the level required until an effective trade policy for steel is put in place. That is worth doing, Mr. Chairman, because the American steel industry is cost competitive in its home market. Currently, the costs of production of the U.S. industry average $480 per net ton of steel shipped. In contrast, average landed costs in the U.S. market of Japanese producers (the most efficient major foreign producers, upon whose costs of production the TPM was based) are approximately $520 per net ton (source, WSD). Notwithstanding this, (and using Japan as an example) selling prices in our market are well below costs of production. This is displayed in the chart below and is *also true for most of the foreign sources of imports entering our market.*

* * *

In spite of aging equipment and a lower percentage of continuous casting than in Japan and Europe, American steel producers are more efficient in the use of many inputs than are many of their foreign competitors. Although unit labor costs are unsatisfactory, when compared to those of Japanese and Korean producers, for example, and they must be improved, U.S. carbon steel labor productivity is higher than in these two countries. The strong raw-materials position of U.S. producers, together with the basic strengths of the American economy (e.g., highly developed capital markets, access to advanced technology, and large home market), still provide American steelmakers with significant long-run advantages. Moreover, the U.S. potential for significant further cost reduction is higher than for the other major industries compared.

The present steel crisis is too large to fit into the category of cyclical fluctuation. The severity of this situation is causing sharp changes in the industry. Changes in government policy are urgently needed. An inadequate response will transform the present crisis into a much deeper, more permanent contraction than the level implied by the industry's actual competitive condition—at great cost to the industry, its workers, and to the national economy.

The longer-term competitive prospects of the American steel industry depend upon our Government's response to the flood of subsidized and dumped imports entering the U.S. market. Government action must occur to reestablish the conditions under which private domestic producers can compete with semi-public or fully nationalized foreign competitors. The steel import problem is an example of the overriding problem facing U.S. trade policy; whether the United States can preserve the private character of one of its major industries in a world system in which intervention by foreign governments has become the norm.

(2) Textiles

GATT SECRETARIAT STUDY, TEXTILES AND CLOTHING IN THE WORLD ECONOMY
6–8, 74–76, 82–83 (1984)

The most common feature of trade policies in the textiles (and later clothing) area over the past century is the above-average level of government intervention. With the exception of the United Kingdom and Japan, tariff protection of the textile industry has been commonplace from the nineteenth century to the present. Stimulated by the Great Depression and competition from Japan, the interwar period witnessed a dramatic increase in protection of the mature textile industries against competition from Japan, other newcomers and one another. The first known voluntary export restraint (VER) in textiles, involving Japan's textile exports to the United States, was adopted in 1936.

Most of the developed countries, particularly in Western Europe, began the postwar period with very restrictive trade régimes. As the 1950s progressed, many of these policies were liberalized under the auspices of the GATT and the Organization for European Economic Cooperation (OEEC). Trade policies affecting textiles, and in particular discriminatory policies against Japan, some developing countries, and some East European countries not only remained mainly untouched by this liberalization, but tended to increase in restrictiveness.

During the early postwar years, a number of developing countries either continued to apply import-substitution policies for textiles, or introduced such programmes for the first time. In most instances Article XVIII of the General Agreement was invoked to justify these policies. These protective measures were often part of a restrictive system that covered a wide range of products, in contrast to the developed country measures on textiles, which were maintained or increased at the same time that restrictions on most other non-agricultural products were being reduced.

Japan's accession to the GATT in 1955, the move to external convertibility of West European currencies in 1958 (which removed the balance-of-payments justification for existing quantitative restraints) and the emergence of important developing country exporters combined to create pressure for alternative approaches to controlling "low wage imports" into the industrial countries. It was in this context that the concept of "market disruption" was introduced into GATT discussions (more on this below).

Although cotton textiles and clothing were not the only products caught up in this process, they were clearly the main concern, as is evidenced by the fact that they have been the only products to be formally exempted from the regular GATT rules and given a régime of their own. Initially this took the form of the Short-Term Arrangement Regarding International Trade in Textiles (the STA), which was in force from October 1961 until September 1962. In October 1962 the Long-Term Arrangement Regarding International Trade in Cotton Textiles (the LTA) came into force, lasting (with extensions) until 1973.

These agreements were significant events in GATT's history. An important part of world trade was formally exempted from GATT rules, in particular the non-discrimination rule and the general prohibition of quantitative restrictions. The new rules operated principally to affect exports from Japan and the developing countries.

It is unlikely that there will ever be agreement on the merits and demerits of the STA/LTA. As a major derogation from the General Agreement, and the stepping stone to the Multifibre Arrangement (MFA), they are hardly consistent with the general liberalization of trade in the 1950s and 1960s.

* * *

By the middle of the 1960s, synthetic fibres and yarns were eroding the dominant position of cotton in textiles and clothing, and certain developing countries and countries in Eastern Europe were competing effectively in the market for wool fabrics and clothing. Since the LTA was limited to cotton products, bilateral [quantitative restraints] outside both the GATT and the LTA began to spring up, especially in the trade policies of the United States and Canada.

Pressure to "legitimize" the restrictions on non-cotton textiles and clothing led to the first MFA, which entered into force in January 1974. In exchange for their agreement to negotiate a new arrangement, Japan and the developing countries were able to have an important influence on the terms and conditions. The result was that "The minimum growth rates for quotas, the flexibility provisions and the rules, procedures and implementing arrangements set up by the MFA were all more favourable to developing countries than the corresponding aspects of the LTA." Another important feature of the MFA was the creation of the Textiles Surveillance Body (TSB), with an independent chairman and balanced membership; it supervises the implementation of the MFA and reports to the Textile Committee. Granting these changes and innovations, it remains true that by extending the special rules to non-cotton textiles and clothing, the MFA represented a sizeable increase in the amount of trade formally exempted from regular GATT rules.

In contrast to the divided opinion over the extent to which the LTA and MFA I did or did not contribute to an expansion of world trade in textiles and clothing, there is little doubt that MFA II, which entered into force in January 1978, resulted in a significant tightening of the developed countries' restrictions on imports from developing countries. The negotiations in 1977 had taken place against a background of sluggish output growth, declining employment and increasing imports of textiles and clothing in the United States and, to a much sharper degree, Western Europe. The developed countries successfully pushed for a modification of the rules to make it much easier for them to avoid the requirement that the quotas be increased 6 per cent per year more or less independently of either the market share already achieved or the growth of domestic demand in the importing country. The key to this change, which amounted to a significant step toward establishing upper limits on the share of domestic consumption supplied by the developing countries, was a provision for "jointly agreed reasonable departures" from the MFA's rules (which themselves are a jointly agreed departure from the rules of the General Agreement).

The Protocol for MFA III, which entered into force in January 1982 for a period of four years and seven months, does not contain the "reasonable departures" clause. Two other important changes from the MFA II protocol are the addition of what has become known as the "anti-surge" provision governing the use of unutilized quotas carried over from the previous year, and the establishment of a permanent Sub-Committee of the Textiles Committee to monitor adjustment policies and measures on a regular basis. Regardless of these changes, the actual implementation of MFA III has involved a further tightening in the application of restrictions.

* * *

THE FRAMEWORK OF THE MFA

* * *

There are two sets of balanced rights and obligations in the MFA. First, while participants are permitted to employ its safeguard mechanisms in certain defined circumstances, they are at the same time required to pursue appropriate policies to encourage structural adjustment. Second, the right of the importing country to impose restrictions is balanced by the obligation to respect the provisions of Annex B dealing with base levels, annual growth rates and flexibility of the quotas. These features represented considerable improvements over the LTA in the view of most participants.

* * *

The treatment of restrictions is set out in Articles 2, 3 and 4, which form the core of the MFA. Article 2 deals with the phasing out of pre-MFA restrictions. Article 3 covers situations of *actual* market disruption, and can—in the event that a mutually agreed solution is not possible—involve the unilateral imposition of import restrictions. It is in connection with Article 3 actions that the TSB plays a key role because it is required to make recommendations on actions taken unilaterally. Article 4 deals with situations involving a *real risk* of market disruption. From the viewpoint of the MFA, only bilateral agreements are possible under Article 4 (that is, the invocation of "real risk" of disruption to justify a *unilateral* restraint would fall outside the scope of the MFA). TSB reviews of Article 4 agreements may result in recommendations to the parties concerned.

* * *

In situations of market disruption, the importing country is required to consult with the exporting country. The consultations may result in agreed measures, conforming to the prescriptions in Annex B of the MFA with respect to base levels (the size of the quota in the reference year), growth rates (the annual increase in the size of the quota), and flexibility (the right of the exporting country to "trade off" part of a quota on one product against the quota on another product, or to use part of one year's quota for a particular product in either the preceding or subsequent year). In case no agreement is reached, the importing country is permitted to impose unilateral restrictions.

* * *

Diagnosing a situation of market disruption has always been difficult. The negotiators made considerable efforts to evolve objective criteria, but had to be satisfied with refining the LTA definition. The situation of market disruption was directly related to the existence, or threat, of serious damage to the domestic industry which could be assessed by examination of various factors such as sales, market share, profits, employment, and production. The damage must be clearly connected with a sharp and substantial increase in imports from a particular source, and/or at prices lower than those prevailing in the market for similar products from domestic as well as other import sources. It is also stipulated that the economic interests of the exporting countries should be taken into account when determining whether a situation of market disruption exists. It may be noted at this point that experience in applying the concept of market disruption has not only failed to reduce the degree of subjectivity surrounding it, but has uncovered new problems related to the workability of all the requirements which a country wishing to claim market disruption is supposed to satisfy.

Annex B of the MFA stipulates that new quotas should be large enough to accommodate the actual trade level reached during the twelve-month period terminating two or three months prior to the month when the consultations were sought. When a restraint is renewed, the new quota should not be lower than the previous one. In the case of continuing quotas, the annual growth should not be less than 6 per cent.

Annex B also provides that a particular quota can be exceeded by 7 per cent provided there is a corresponding reduction in another quota (this is called the "swing provision"). Up to 10 per cent of the unused portion of the previous year's quota can be "carried over", or an advance utilization ("carry forward") of up to 5 per cent from the following year's quota is provided for; combined use of carryover and carry forward is set at 10 per cent of the quota. These flexibilities were introduced to partially offset the rigidities of the quota system, thereby increasing the extent to which exporters could respond to changing market conditions.

In "exceptional" circumstances, when a recurrence or worsening of disruption is anticipated, growth can be reduced below 6 per cent and swing reduced from 7 to 5 per cent.

* * *

THE SECOND PROTOCOL

The participants agreed late in December 1981 to renew the MFA for a further term of four years and seven months. This was based on certain understandings regarding its operation in the third phase. Efforts were directed primarily toward reconciling the main concerns of the importing countries with the developing countries' desire to restore discipline to the Arrangement. The solution was found by reiterating full support for the discipline of Annex A and procedures of Articles 3 and 4, and by recognising that the MFA provisions pertaining to base levels, growth rates and flexibility are in the nature of rights belonging to the exporting countries, which can be waived only under specific circumstances. The provision for "reasonable departures" [of MFA II] was not included in the protocol for MFA III.

The EC's concern with the market access enjoyed by the "dominant suppliers" was accommodated by an expression of goodwill on the part of the latter in seeking mutually satisfactory solutions. Another proposal of the EC concerning quota levels was that while the past levels should continue to be the basis for future access, the current level of imports in previously under-utilized quotas for highly sensitive products should be regulated in such a manner as to prevent sharp and substantial increases in imports. This innovation, which came to be known as the "anti-surge procedure", was incorporated in the Protocol, with the proviso that if it was invoked, any resulting solution would include "equitable and quantifiable compensation" to the exporting country.

The clear obligation in the MFA that the use of quantitative restrictions must be accompanied by suitable economic and social policies to facilitate timely adjustment in the domestic industry, was reinforced under MFA III. To this end participants have established a permanent Sub-Committee of the Textiles Committee to monitor adjustment policies and measures on a regular basis.

Notes and Questions

(1) MFA III expires in mid 1986, and negotiations on its extension commenced in 1985. See Das, The GATT—Multi-Fibre Arrangement, 17 J. World Trade L. 95 (1985). See generally V. Aggarwal, Liberal Protectionism: The International Politics of Organized Textile Trade (1985).

(2) The United States has numerous bilateral agreements with textile-exporting countries that limit the volume of exports. As noted in Section 6.2(E) supra, special origin rules have been adopted to ensure the quota systems are not evaded. The United States also imposes significant tariffs on textile imports. In 1980, they were estimated on average to be 27%.[5]

(3) The Tarr and Morkre study, cited earlier in connection with the automobile and steel industries, concludes that in respect of restrictions on imports from Hong Kong, alone, the additional costs incurred as a result of the quotas by U.S. consumers ranged between $318 and $420 million, and that Hong Kong earned monopoly profits of some $218 million.[6]

(4) As the materials demonstrate, the automobile, steel and textile sectors have quite different characteristics. One can therefore ask whether certain characteristics determine or should determine how the sector is treated in the future in respect of safeguards. For example, textiles and clothing are often produced in small plants; most steel and autos are made in large plants. The steel and auto industries are dominated by large companies, but in steel their operations are usually national in scope, whereas the major auto companies have plants and joint venture arrangements throughout the world. At the moment, the automobile industry seems in the best shape. Does that suggest more multinational steel companies would make that industry better off or is there a national security aspect to steel that argues against such a result and will always provide an impetus for excess capacity in most countries? What can be said on this score in respect of textiles and clothing?

(C) REFORMING THE SAFEGUARD RULES: STRUCTURAL ADJUSTMENT AND INDUSTRIAL POLICY

The rules of GATT Article XIX do not seem to be adequate to resolve the structural adjustment problems of such industries as steel and textiles. Indeed, the increase in the use of ad hoc remedies, such as VRAs, outside the GATT framework makes it clear that some sort of reform of that framework is necessary. As a consequence, these issues—safeguards and structural adjustment—have been the subject of extensive study in GATT and other international organizations such as the OECD and UNCTAD. At least partly because of the political structure of the industrialized societies, the problems have so far proved very difficult to resolve. The excerpts from the GATT Director General's report on the Tokyo Round, included in Section 9.3 above, illustrate the relationship of the "selectivity—MFN" issue to these problems. The negotiations on safeguard reforms continue in a committee in GATT, but at this writing (December 1985) the committee has not made much progress.

Prior to the Tokyo Round, a high-level committee of the OECD addressed some of the safeguard issues as follows:

5. Tarr & Morkre, note 2 supra, at 122.   **6.** Id., at 122.

OECD, POLICY PERSPECTIVES FOR INTERNATIONAL TRADE AND ECONOMIC RELATIONS (THE "REY REPORT")
81–84 (1972)

254. In any case there must be a common system of rules and procedures. More precise principles and procedures of a multilateral character should be worked out for the application of safeguard measures. One method would be to revise Article XIX in this sense. However, if such a revision is not possible, a realistic approach might be to have an agreement between the countries prepared to undertake more precise reciprocal commitments in this matter, for example in the form of a protocol to Article XIX of the GATT. This would be somewhat similar to the Declaration giving effect to the provisions of paragraph 4 of Article XVI, or to the Anti-Dumping Code.

* * *

256. The Group discussed at some length the possibility of revising the basic criteria according to which action can be taken in accordance with GATT Article XIX. In particular it considered the desirability of including the concept of market disruption. It concluded, however, that on balance it would not be desirable to develop new basic criteria, particularly since the threat of serious injury which Article XIX requires in itself covers situations involving market disruption.

257. The procedures set out in Article XIX are not very strict. The Group considered the possibility of strengthening them by proposing that explicit prior approval should have to be given in all cases by the Contracting Parties to the GATT. However, such a proposal, at the present stage of international economic relations, would not be realistic and the conclusions which the Group reached for the protocol which might be established are as follows:

(a) The emergency safeguard procedure, introduced into GATT for use only in exceptional cases, has become more and more the rule. In the Group's judgment there should be very few cases in which developments are so rapid that prior consultation could be regarded as unreasonable.

(b) The multilateral consultative procedure should be strengthened by establishing on a permanent basis "a panel of mediators" in the GATT consisting of highly qualified persons with wide experience in international trade problems. Governments would bind themselves to use mediation procedures when one of the parties concerned asks for it, or when in the opinion of the Director General of GATT the use of mediators would facilitate agreement. Views expressed by the panel would be advisory. Different mediators from the panel might be used in different individual cases. Furthermore, if the parties concerned agree, an arbitrator or arbitrators chosen from the panel could be authorised to reach conclusions which would be binding.

* * *

260.   The Group came to the conclusion that the best way to make the safeguard clause more effective is to specify the obligations of the applicant country more precisely, as follows:

(*a*) In the first place, the temporary nature of the protection measures should be emphasised by setting a relatively short time limit on their application.

(*b*) Second, the applicant country should undertake in any case not to reduce its imports below their level at the time the restrictive measures are applied and to allow imports to increase at a reasonable rate.

(*c*) Finally—and this is a fundamental point—application of the safeguard measures should be accompanied by action to bring about domestic adjustment so that the use of the safeguard mechanism will in fact be temporary.

261.   Accordingly, action aimed at domestic adjustment—which should above all include rationalisation or conversion measures—in sectors protected or aided by safeguard measures should be initiated in the importing country. The domestic adjustment programme and its progress would be the subject of consultations with the countries whose trade was restricted and of international review under multilateral procedures.

262.   The Group considers that the right to compensation or retaliation as provided for in the General Agreement should be reviewed in the light of the multilateral procedures suggested. This review should deal in particular with the exercise of this right during the period when these procedures are being invoked and subsequently depending on their outcome.

———————

The Declaration issued at the conclusion of the November 1982 GATT Ministerial Meeting noted the need for a comprehensive understanding on safeguards, which would include "inter alia" the following elements: [7]

SAFEGUARDS

The Contracting Parties decide:

* * *

2.   That to this end, effect should be given to a comprehensive understanding to be based on the principles of the General Agreement which would contain, *inter alia,* the following elements:

(i) Transparency;

(ii) Coverage;

(iii) Objective criteria for action including the concept of serious injury or threat thereof;

(iv) Temporary nature, degressivity and structural adjustment;

(v) Compensation and retaliation; and

7. GATT, 29th Supp. BISD 12–13 (1983).

> (vi) Notification, consultation, multilateral surveillance and dispute settlement with particular reference to the rôle and functions of the Safeguards Committee.

————

The Declaration called for an understanding on these issues to be drawn up and adopted by the time of the 1983 GATT session, but at that session the chairman of the committee charged with this responsibility had to report that the committee had not been able to complete a report. The chairman noted: [8]

> The discussion that has taken place confirmed that so-called "grey-area" actions comprise not only bilateral arrangements of a VER or OMA type between governments providing for quantitative limitations, surveillance systems, price undertakings or export forecasts, but also industry-to-industry arrangements, where the specific role of governments was not always clear, and actions of a unilateral character.

In addition to the various issues raised in the foregoing materials, any safeguards code would have to consider the troublesome ambiguities of GATT Article XIX (such as definition of such terms as "cause," "industry," "like product," and the time frames for measuring increased imports or serious injury, etc.). Another issue that must be faced is whether, as a condition to the invocation of safeguards, a country should be required to prove to an international authority that it has a program for and is administering "adjustment assistance" or is undertaking other activities to encourage structural adjustment.

One approach for reform sometimes suggested is one under which nations would give up their compensation claims in return for enforcement of more disciplined rules on the extent and duration of safeguards. For example, Tumlir argues that if safeguard measures emphasized transparent adjustment assistance, political support for them, except on a truly short-term basis, would not be great as they would be viewed as handouts to a small group in the private sector, whereas negotiated export restraints, even though likely to cost more overall, are largely invisible and unknown to the public, and therefore accepted. He also notes that while an industry will always prefer permanent protection, if it believes that the protection is short term, it will likely strive to adjust quickly.[9]

Recently, another approach to the adjustment problem can be found in the writings of those who advocate that governments should adopt an "industrial policy" to implement actions necessary to ease various problems faced by older industrialized countries, including problems of structural adjustment.[10] In this regard, an interesting provision was inserted in the 1984 Trade and Tariff Act. While authorizing presidential action to enforce an export restraint agreement covering steel exports to the United States for

8. GATT, 30th Supp. BISD 216, 217 (1984).

9. Tumlir, A Revised Safeguard Clause for GATT, 7 J. World Trade L. 404 (1973).

10. See, e.g., R. Reich, An Industrial Policy for America (1983).

a maximum of five years, Congress required, as an annual condition for continuation of such authorization, that the President determine that: [11]

(A) the major companies of the steel industry, taken as a whole, have, during the 12-month period ending at the close of an anniversary referred to in subsection (a)(2)—

(i) committed substantially all of their net cash flow from steel product operations for purposes of reinvestment in, and modernization of, that industry through investment in modern plant and equipment, research and development, and other appropriate projects, such as working capital for steel operations and programs for the retraining of workers; and

(ii) taken sufficient action to maintain their international competitiveness, including action to produce price-competitive and quality-competitive products, to control costs of production, including employment costs, and to improve productivity; and

(B) each of the major companies committed for the applicable 12-month period not less than 1 percent of net cash flow to the retraining of workers; except that this requirement may be waived by the President with respect to a major company in noncompliance, if he finds unusual economic circumstances exist with respect to that company.

It remains to be seen how this will work, or whether it presages further development in the United States of a government industrial policy.

In light of the foregoing, what reforms to the GATT safeguard rules would you suggest?

---

11. Trade and Tariff Act of 1984, § 806, Pub.L. No. 98–573, 98 Stat. 3046. The first report by the President was made on September 30, 1985. 50 Fed.Reg. 40321 (1985).

Chapter 10

RESPONSES TO UNFAIR ACTS IN INTERNATIONAL TRADE

SECTION 10.1 INTRODUCTION

The four preceding chapters have dealt primarily with the substantive obligations of international trade rules, and the exceptions to those rules designed for the orderly adjustment to increased imports. In this chapter, the focus shifts. There are a number of practices of governments or private firms which are designed to influence international trade flows, other than through the use of restraints on imports. In particular, both governments and private firms may wish to promote exports by the use of discriminatory pricing or by subsidies. For decades, certain of these practices have been considered "unfair." First in bilateral, and then in multilateral trade treaties, such as GATT, nations have agreed that unilateral responses to some of these practices should be permitted under international trade rules. The purpose of this chapter is to examine several different types of governmental responses that are designed to counteract foreign trade policy actions which affect trade differently from the free market mechanism. The distinction between escape clause actions and the types of actions considered in this chapter is that escape clause actions are taken for purposes of adjustment to imports, which come about through the natural application of liberal trade policies; whereas the responses considered in this chapter are designed to counteract foreign measures which are considered in some sense "unfair" or "market distorting."

The distinction made in international trade law between "fair" and "unfair" trade, such as is reflected in the differences between titles II and III of the Trade Act of 1974, is not airtight. In practice, there tends to be a blurring of the differences between fair and unfair trade. Arguments about "unfairness" are sometimes made in escape clause proceedings, where fairness is not technically relevant, and the difficulty of defining "unfair" leads to suspicions that some proceedings alleging unfairness are really disguised attempts to obtain escape clause type relief.[1]

1. See, e.g., Stainless Steel and Alloy Tool Steel, Inv. No. TA–201–48, Pub. No. 1377, 5 ITRD 1411 (ITC 1983), which started as a complaint under Section 301 for unfair trade practices. See 47 Fed.Reg. 51717 (1982).

One of the rationales behind the unfair trade rules we will examine is similar to that behind the antitrust and unfair competition laws that exist to a greater or lesser degree in every country. Just as it is believed that certain domestic activities, such as monopolization, price fixing or market sharing are undesirable, it is thought that certain international trade practices are undesirable and should be regulated. The basic idea behind such rules is sometimes expressed as a desire to create a level playing field where the producers of the world all have an equal chance to compete.

We will see that while there is a considerable degree of agreement in the international trading system on the general sort of practices that are unfair, there is some controversy over how to define those practices precisely. Moreover, in the case of one practice—subsidization by governments—there is considerable disagreement over what responses should be permitted. Indeed, it is in the general area of export promotion by governments that the international consensus breaks down. It is agreed that cash bounties paid to exporters to encourage greater exports are unacceptable. But it is not really agreed how to evaluate, and to what extent retaliatory responses should be allowed to offset, government policies that directly or indirectly assist exporters. Such policies may range from operating subsidies, to provision of cheap raw materials, to government policies promoting education and research and development, to government encouragement of the commercialization of certain products, to a full-scale governmental industrial policy.

Moreover, even to the extent that the accepted international rules embodied in GATT reflect the views of the international trading community as to what is unfair, economists have challenged the underlying premises of certain of those rules and have argued that they do not make sense economically (just as they have raised similar questions about national antitrust laws).

The problems we will consider in this chapter can be seen in the following four problems:

(1) Tractor producers in Bavonia export to Avaly and sell their tractors in the Avaly market for less than they sell the same product in the home market of Bavonia. Competing Avaly tractor manufacturers complain that this import competition is unfair and that the tractors are being "dumped" in Avaly.

(2) Caldonia manufacturers produce watches, and the Caldonia government grants to each producer a "subsidy" of the equivalent of $20 for each watch which is exported. Because of the subsidy, Caldonia watchmakers are able to sell their products in the Avaly market for up to $20 less than Avaly-made watches. The Avaly watchmakers cry "foul."

(3) Duglavsky producers of electronic calculators produce and use a special integrated circuit which is patented in Avaly, but refuse to obtain a patent license or to pay royalties to the Avaly patent holder. Nevertheless, they attempt to export some of these calculators to Avaly where they compete with Avaly-made calculators, whose producers pay royalties to the patent holder. The patent holder, as well as the Avaly producers, seeks to prevent those imports.

(4) Xonia normally imports shoes from Avaly, but decides to ban Avaly shoes so as to protect its home shoe industry. Avaly's shoe exporters are disturbed and seek to have Avaly ban imports of silk cloth from Xonia (which are normally substantial).

These cases involve a variety of problems. For example, it has already been noted that some actions affect a country's *exports* in a way which makes other nations feel aggrieved, while other actions affect a country's *imports* in a way which aggrieves others. In some cases the action is by private firms or manufacturers, (e.g., dumping), in others it is by governments (e.g., subsidies). In some cases an action may breach an international obligation, but in other cases there may be no such breach (or there may be no existing international norm on the subject), yet a trading partner will still feel aggrieved and seek a response.

(A) OVERVIEW

In this chapter, we will consider each of these problems. First, in Section 10.2, we will consider the economics, international rules and U.S. laws applicable to the "dumping" of foreign goods. In Section 10.3, we will examine the same questions in respect of subsidies. Section 10.4 will focus on several other U.S. statutes that deal with unfair trade competition, including the extensively used procedures of Section 337 of the Tariff Act of 1930, the rarely invoked provisions of the Antidumping Act of 1916 and a trade-related section of the Internal Revenue Code. Finally, in Section 10.5 we will consider Section 301 of the Trade Act of 1974, a statute giving the U.S. President broad authority to take retaliatory measures against what he determines to be unfair trade practices. References to practices in other countries will be made as appropriate in each section.

Before turning to these detailed discussions, however, there are two general issues affecting all of them that should be considered at the outset. One is sometimes referred to as the problem of interface: How should the world trading system handle problems arising from the fact that different nations have different philosophies of organizing and directing economic activities? The second is the question of how rules on international trade practices should be applied—in a legalistic manner with frequent recourse to courts to establish precise rules of conduct or more flexibly with a view toward government or industry negotiated settlements of disputes?

(B) THE INTERFACE THEORY OF ECONOMIC RELATIONS

Many of the "unfair" trading practices that we will examine have been considered unfair because they interfere with or distort free market economy principles. GATT, of course, was largely based upon such principles. It is not surprising, therefore, that it is often difficult to apply GATT's trading rules to nonmarket economies. In addition, even between the relatively similar western industrial market economies, there are wide differences regarding the degree of government involvement in the economy, by regulation or ownership of various industrial or other economic segments. As world economic interdependence has increased, it has become more difficult to manage relationships between various economies. This problem can be analogized to the difficulties involved in trying to get two computers of different makes to work together. To do so, one needs an "interface" mechanism to mediate between the two computers. Likewise in international economic relations, and particularly trade, some interface mechanism may be necessary to allow different economic systems to trade together harmoniously.

These problems can be easily seen in the two major sections of this chapter. We will see that part of the definition of dumping is selling for export at below-cost prices. But for nonmarket economies, are there meaningful costs and prices? In the case of subsidies, it may be easy to identify cash payments to an exporter, but there are a myriad of government policies that affect the competitiveness of a business. If the goal is really to achieve a "level playing field," does that imply that the world's governments must adopt uniform policies? If not, how will it be humanly possible to analyze (or in these days, to program a computer to analyze) the effect of different policies? Besides, isn't trade to some degree based on differences between countries?

In some cases, the problem involves questions of preventing or inhibiting what are deemed unfair practices, such as dumping, or export subsidies. As the subject of unfair practices develops, however, it becomes clear that it reaches deeply into matters of domestic concern to governments, and the question of unfairness becomes more controversial. In many cases of subsidies, for example, the government providing such subsidies feels that they are an essential and praiseworthy tool of government, sometimes useful to correct disparities of income, or to help disadvantaged groups or regions. With respect to dumping, for example, it is argued that such a practice, a form of "price discrimination," actually has beneficial effects on world and national prosperity, encouraging competition. The rules for responding to some unfair trade practices allow use of import restrictions, such as added duties (and also quantitative measures applied pursuant to settlements of dumping or countervailing cases), which can be anticompetitive and can reduce world welfare. In some cases, exporting nations feel bitterness towards these import restrictions on their trade, and argue that the rules on unfair trade are being manipulated by special interests for effectively protectionist reasons.

An example of the interface problem and the difficulties of defining unfairness can be seen in the following problem, which focuses on so-called variable cost analysis. It may arise in the context of two economies that differ only slightly in respect of their acceptance of basic free market economic principles. As the problem demonstrates, even given such similarities, there may be differences in the way the respective economies operate over the course of the business cycle that may create situations that are considered unfair by some, even though these differences may not have resulted from any conscious unfair policies or practices.

Take an industrial sector (such as steel) in two economies (such as the United States and Japan) with the following characteristics:

Society A Worker tenure (no layoffs of workers)

        Capitalization with a high debt-equity ratio (e.g., 90% debt)

Society B   No worker tenure (wages for workers are therefore variable costs)

Capitalization with low debt-equity ratio (e.g., less than 50%) (dividends can be skipped)

In times of slack demand, economists note that it is rational for a firm to continue to produce as long as it can sell its product at or above its short-term variable costs. This is true because it must in any event pay its fixed costs. Of course, this is true only for limited periods; presumably over the regular course of the business cycle, the firm must not incur losses in the long term.

An analysis of the short-term variable costs of firms in Societies A and B can be done as follows:

Costs of a firm (per unit of production)	Society A	Society B
Plant Upkeep	20 fixed	20 fixed
Debt Service	90 fixed	50 fixed
Dividends (cost of capital)	10 variable	50 variable
Worker costs	240 fixed	240 variable
Cost of Materials	240 variable	240 variable
Total Costs (per unit of production)	600	600
Fixed	350	70
Variable	250	530

As noted above, it will be rational for producers in Society A to continue production so long as they can obtain a price of 250, while producers in Society B need to receive a price of 530. Thus, in a period of falling prices and demand, the producers in Society A can be expected to garner, through exports to Society B, an increasing share of the Society B market. Suppose this happens, and the firms in Society B close. Are Society A's exports to Society B unfair?

There are no easy answers to the questions raised above. Indeed, they are in fact probably more complicated than the foregoing would indicate because whatever general rules exist, it is argued that special considerations should apply to developing countries. We will discuss these issues in more detail in Part IV, where we look at the special problems posed by trade rules and policies that must take account of developing countries (Chapter 20), nonmarket economies (Chapter 21) and divergent economic and social policies in the major market economies (Chapter 22). The reader should bear these issues in mind, however, because they will arise throughout the rest of this chapter.

(C) THE PROBLEM OF LEGALIZATION

As we proceed through this chapter, the reader will note that application of the major statutes on unfair trade practices, such as dumping and subsidization, is characterized, at least in the United States, by complex rules and proceedings and by extensive involvement of lawyers and courts. While our examination of other legal systems will not be extensive, it is fair to say that proceedings in those systems are much more informal, and therefore less costly. It can be argued that the added expense of the U.S.

approach is worth its cost, a matter we will discuss in more detail in Chapter 23 infra.   More frequent judicial review leads to more detailed rules and allows parties to tailor their conduct to avoid violations.   Of course, at the same time it may lead to the creation of unintended loopholes that allow certain conduct because it is considered to be technically outside the rules, even though an unbiased observer would probably conclude that the rules were meant to apply to such conduct, and vice versa.

The lack of precisely defined rules leaves considerable discretion in the hands of those officials who apply the rules.   They may as a result be in a position to use the rules only when appropriate to effectuate the real purpose of the rules.   Their exercise of discretion will be difficult to review, however, and this, of course, presents serious problems of potential abuse, problems which may be magnified since those seeking protection from the officials are constituents of sorts of the officials, while those who will be adversely affected are foreigners.

The reader should consider, as we proceed through Chapter 10, whether the U.S. system has struck the proper balance between flexibility and reasonable cost, on the one hand, and predictability and "over legalization," on the other hand.

SECTION 10.2   DUMPING AND ANTIDUMPING DUTIES [1]

In this section we examine issues concerning the imposition of duties to offset the effects of dumping, which is broadly defined as exporting at prices below those charged on the domestic market or at prices insufficient to cover the cost of the goods sold.   We begin by a consideration of the economic effects of dumping since there is more than a little controversy over whether the internationally sanctioned antidumping rules make sense economically. Then, we look at the international rules on dumping, which are contained in GATT Article VI and in two agreements on the interpretation of Article VI. In subsection (C), we undertake a fairly detailed analysis of U.S. antidumping procedures and law and then briefly consider the EC rules in subsection (D).

1.   There are a number of theoretical and practical books, as well as numerous journal articles, on dumping.   The following articles and books emphasize questions concerning the policies underlying antidumping laws.   See, e.g., J. Viner, Dumping: A Problem in International Trade (1923); Ehrenhaft, Protection Against International Price Discrimination: United States Countervailing and Antidumping Duties, 58 Colum.L.Rev. 43 (1958); DeJong, The Significance of Dumping in International Trade, 2 J. World Trade L. 162 (1968); Barcelo, Antidumping Laws as Barriers to Trade—The United States and the International Antidumping Code, 57 Cornell L.Rev. 491 (1972); W. Wares, The Theory of Dumping and American Commercial Policy (1977); Antidumping Law: Policy and Implementation, 1 Mich.Yb.Intl. Legal Studies (1979); Ehrenhaft, What the Antidumping and Countervailing Duty Provisions (Can) (Will) (Should) Mean for U.S. Trade Policy, 11 Law & Poly.Intl.Bus. 1361 (1979); R. Dale, Anti-dumping Law in a Liberal Trade Order (1980); G. Bryan, Taxing Unfair International Trade Practices: A Study of U.S. Antidumping and Countervailing Duty Laws (1980); Caine, A Case for Repealing the Antidumping Provisions of the Tariff Act of 1930, 13 Law & Poly.Intl.Bus. 681 (1981).

(A) THE ECONOMICS OF DUMPING

BART S. FISHER, THE ANTIDUMPING LAW OF THE UNITED STATES: A LEGAL AND ECONOMIC ANALYSIS

(1973) [2]

I. THE ECONOMICS OF DUMPING

A. *The Definition of Dumping*

Dumping is traditionally defined as selling at a lower price in one national market than in another.   *   *   *

B. *The Economic Motivation for Dumping*

The rationale for dumping products in a foreign market is analogous to that for price discrimination within a domestic market: the discriminating firm can maximize its profits by charging different customers different prices for essentially identical products. For example, if some customers are willing to pay no more than $7, when others will pay $15, for an item, it would be advantageous for the seller to be able to charge the higher price to those customers prepared to pay more. Only when sectorization of markets obtains, however, can goods be sold to the low-price customers without sacrificing the benefits to be obtained from the high-price customers.

The opportunities for profits from dumping will depend upon the interaction of three variables: the demand for the firm's product in its own country and abroad, the barriers to reentry into the exporting market, and the nature of the firm's cost structure. These variables are considered below.

1. *Demand in the Exporting and Importing Countries*

The firm will be more likely to profit from dumping if the home demand for the dumped goods is inelastic. If demand does not slacken in the home market when the dumping firm raises its prices initially (or raises its prices later, if the dumped good is one that can be produced only at increasing costs), then the overall net revenue of the dumping firm will be increased. Profitability of the dumping firm will also be increased if there is high price elasticity abroad for the dumped goods. If foreigners respond sharply to lower prices, more goods will be sold and the firm's revenues will be increased.

2. *Reentry Into the Exporting Country*

Internal price discrimination, i.e., within the same country, is difficult to sustain over a long period of time because there are no barriers to reimportation. In international transactions, the seller will find it far easier to engage in price discrimination between the home market and foreign markets, as he can avail himself of barriers to reimportation in the form of tariffs, quotas, and nontariff barriers to trade. A condition precedent for a successful

2. 5 Law & Poly. Intl. Bus. 85, at 85–93.
Reprinted by permission of Law & Policy in International Business.

dumping scheme is, therefore, the effective insulation of the home market from the world market for the dumped goods. Otherwise, the dumped goods would reenter the domestic market, equalize the home and export prices, and "ruin" the home market for the discriminating firm.

3.   The Cost Structure of the Firm

The final variable in the dynamics of international dumping is the cost function under which the firm must operate. In general, a firm will not dump unless the marginal revenue that it derives from abroad is substantially greater than its marginal costs of production for the dumped goods. Generally, this can be achieved at a lower foreign price only where the cost curve is descending at the margin, i.e., where there is a declining-cost industry involving economies of scale.

The concept of marginal costs helps to explain the three customary subdivisions of dumping—sporadic, intermittent, and continuous (or persistent). Sporadic dumping is of relatively minor concern to the country dumped on, since, typically, it is an unloading of overstock by a foreign producer who prefers to dump his goods in a foreign market rather than endanger his domestic price structure. The firm will ordinarily regard its costs as fixed, its marginal cost as zero, and accept virtually *any* price that can be obtained for the goods abroad.

Generally, intermittent dumping is an element of a larger scheme to secure a foothold in a foreign market. Consequently, the motives here are much more pernicious than those associated with sporadic dumping. The foreign producer seeks to forestall the development of competition, or eliminate it entirely, in the market he selects for the dumping. A frequent technique of such predatory, intermittent dumping is to sell abroad for brief periods at prices below marginal (but not necessarily average) cost. After the foreign competitor is eliminated, the predatory dumper may then raise his prices above marginal costs.

Continuous dumping may be predicated upon an assumption by the foreign producer that its costs over the long term will be cheaper if it manufactures a large number of items in order to realize maximum economies of scale. Since the overproduction might be a burden upon domestic prices, the foreign producer may wish to dump abroad permanently in order to maintain its domestic price structure. A sustained profit from the firm's overall sales will thus be ensured for as long as the average prices charged customers exceed the average cost of production. If the firm desires to pass along the benefits of the dumping to its home customers, lower prices may be made available for the home market. There is no guarantee, however, that the discriminating firm will shift the benefits resulting from dumping to its local customers. Indeed, the interests of the firm and the consumers of the dumping country may be antithetical, i.e., the firm may choose to retain all its profits.

C.   The Effects of Dumping on National Economies

1.   The Exporting Country

As noted above, the *firm* in the exporting country can profit from dumping under certain demand, reentry, and cost conditions. Whether or not a net benefit will accrue to the exporting *country* is, however, another matter. First, other firms in the dumping country may not benefit from the dumping situation, as foreign fabricators having received dumped goods can undersell the home price for finished goods and, thus, underbid home producers in third-country export markets. The effect of the dumping on consumer prices in the dumping country is more complex. If the dumped goods are being produced at declining marginal costs, then consumer prices may fall in the dumping country if the firm chooses to "pass along" the benefits of the dumping to the local consumers. If the goods are produced at rising marginal costs, then the equilibrium home price after dumping will tend to rise, as the dumping firm must "cover" its relatively unprofitable dumping. In the rising cost situation, then, the dumping firm may obtain higher profits; the user industries in the home market, which must compete with foreign goods containing the dumped items, are harmed; and the consumers, facing rising prices, will suffer.

There is, in any case, a misallocation of resources in the exporting country when intermittent or continuous dumping takes place. Such dumping cannot be successful without the artificial conditions of barriers to reentry into the domestic market and some monopolistic control of the home market. These facts, as De Jong notes,

> [c]ondemn the existing economic situation in the exporting country as an inefficient one, because of the misallocation of its productive resources. This country could raise its economic welfare by reducing the output of the dumped article, stop dumping abroad, and expand production of something else.

2. The Importing Country

In the importing country, the most obvious problem caused by dumping is the harm inflicted upon competing producers of the dumped goods. The degree of harm will depend largely upon the quantity of dumped goods and the margin of dumping involved, i.e., the amount by which the dumped goods were underselling the home-market goods. Under the traditional Commission analysis, if a foreigner increased his U.S. market share by 5 percent through his less-than-fair-value (LTFV) exports, the domestic competitors normally would suffer a corresponding loss.

There are also at least three types of "implied injuries" to domestic producers that result from dumping. The first is the amount of growth that would have taken place in the competing industry in the absence of dumping. For example, assume that country X, prior to the sale of LTFV imports, holds 15 percent of the U.S. market in widgets. After the sale of a given amount of LTFV imports, country X still holds 15 percent of the U.S. market in widgets. Has "injury" to competing industries in the United States occurred? The answer is yes: in the absence of LTFV imports, U.S. widget manufacturers would have gained a portion of country X's market share (if the foreign margin of underselling is not substantially greater than the margin of dumping). With LTFV imports, U.S. manufacturers have lost that market opportunity. Thus, while no actual "present" injury has occurred, there is implied injury to U.S. competitors to the extent of lost market opportunities.

The second type of implied injury is the harm suffered by domestic industries with products that are not directly competitive with the dumped imports. Harm to such industries arises because U.S. consumers are tempted to purchase the dumped goods rather than the nondirectly competitive domestic goods. For example, assume that the exporting country dumps television sets but not radios. The LTFV television sets will deflect consumer preferences away from radios in many instances (the degree depending upon the relevant cross elasticities of demand), and thus harm the radio industry in the United States as well as the television industry.

The third type of implied injury is that occurring to user industries in the importing country. Unaware of the source of their low-priced imports, these industries might undertake expansion programs in reliance upon a continued source of supply. If the dumping country terminates the flow of dumped goods, however, the additional facilities would be economically dysfunctional and would represent a misallocation of resources caused by faulty signals from the price system.

The key benefit for the importing country is the lower prices that the dumped goods bring to its consumers. When dumping is sporadic, the benefit of lower prices would appear to outweigh the marginal harm suffered by local producers. When dumping is intermittent or predatory, however, the substantial injury suffered by local industries would appear to outweigh any benefits resulting from lower consumer prices. The most controversial area is that of continuous (or persistent) dumping, which may or may not be economically desirable. If there is a smoothly functioning system of adjustment from import-impacted industries, then the importing country can realize a net benefit from the increased efficiency and lower prices provided by the continuous dumping. If, however, the continuous dumping creates large pools of unemployed manpower, then it can effect a hardship upon the receiving country in excess of the benefits consumers will realize.

* * *

3. Competing Third Countries

Competing producers in third countries will be injured by dumping in the same manner as suppliers in the importing country. As the demand for their goods declines, so will their profits. In contrast to importing countries, however, competing third countries receive none of the potential benefits of dumping, such as lower consumer prices and increased efficiency in the operations of domestic manufacturers. Indeed it would appear that it is the competing third countries that bear the brunt of the disadvantages caused by dumping.

Notes and Questions

(1) The definition of dumping now generally accepted includes exports at prices that do not cover the costs of production. Whatever the desirability of combating international price discrimination, there is probably more controversy over whether trying to prevent below-cost sales makes economic sense.

JOHN J. BARCELO III, THE ANTIDUMPING LAW: REPEAL IT OR REVISE IT

(1979) [3]

THE INNOCENCE OF DUMPING BELOW AVERAGE COST

It is a common misconception that a low dumping price is necessarily unfair if it is below average total cost (unit cost). * * *

Economists and businessmen would agree that a firm (at least a domestic firm), having sunk its investment but facing inadequate demand, should continue to operate in the short run as long as price exceeds average variable rather than average total cost. It would thus make at least some contribution to its fixed costs which, in the short run, would be incurred with or without production. * * * But the argument in the dumping context often has a long-run frame of reference: that a dumper should not be allowed, as a long-run practice, to price below unit cost, because if he does so he is not covering his full costs on the low-priced sales; the earnings from the high-priced sales are being used to subsidize the dumping operations.

Arguments of this kind are fallacious. If the dumper is maximizing his profits by selling his total output in two markets so that marginal cost equals marginal revenue in both markets, he is making the maximum possible contribution to fixed as well as variable costs. A higher price in the export market or a lower one in the home market would reduce his profits and hence reduce his contribution to fixed and variable costs.

Whether a given profit-maximizing firm can sustain its production and pricing patterns in the long run depends on whether its fixed and variable costs are actually being covered by the maximized net revenue being generated. This will occur if average revenue equals or exceeds average cost. If a producer charges different prices in two different markets, average revenue is not equal to price, but falls instead between the two prices. Thus the lower dumping price can fail to meet average cost, while at the same time average revenue may equal or exceed it. If a dumper's average revenue just exactly equals average cost, any price above the profit-maximizing dumping price in the export market would itself be money-losing and nonsustainable, because average revenue would have to fall and thus would fail to cover average cost.

(2) Although laws against price discrimination are often attacked on economic grounds, it is sometimes suggested, as it is in the extract from Fisher, that such laws are justified insofar as they control so-called predatory price discrimination and may be justified insofar as they control long-term or persistent dumping. Not everyone agrees.

JOHN J. BARCELO III, THE ANTIDUMPING LAW: REPEAL IT OR REVISE IT

Supra, at 65–76

ANTIPREDATION—THE PROPER TOUCHSTONE OF ANTIDUMPING LAW

In theory, predatory dumping involves a foreign monopolist who sells his product in the import market at a low money-losing price for a tempora-

---

3. 1 Mich.Yb.Intl. Legal Studies 53, 61–64. This and other excerpts from this publication in this chapter are reprinted by permission of the Michigan Yearbook of International Legal Studies.

ry period, while continuing to earn monopoly profits at home, until he has driven out all competitors in the target market. Thereafter, he raises his price in the newly conquered market to monopoly levels. After recouping the prior losses, he begins to enjoy a continuing stream of monopoly profits. Two elements are central to the concept: money-losing sales and predatory objectives. * * *

A persuasive line of economic analysis suggests that predatory pricing will be rare because it is costly and the benefits are both doubtful and in any event obtainable through less costly means. A monopolist contemplating a predatory attack would have great difficulty predicting both how much he must suffer in losses before all competitors are driven out and how high he could raise the price thereafter without attracting new entry. If entry barriers were low, the price could not be raised much. Even if they were high, but the changeover cost for the displaced productive facilities were low, a slight rise in price would beckon the existing plant back into the market under new management. Predatory pricing designed to induce merger on the predator's terms or collusive price setting might seem more probable because it is less costly. Ancillary predation of this kind would also discourage entry by other firms who might otherwise be attracted by the promise of a lucrative merger without a fight. As Areeda and Turner point out, however, since price-fixing and monopolistic mergers are already illegal, and the tactics just described would be highly visible, predatory pricing even in this context still seems unlikely. Indeed, the empirical evidence available appears to bear out these theoretical predictions that genuine predatory pricing will be uncommon.

The threat of predation seems even less serious in the context of dumping. To be successful, the dumper must drive out not only local producers in the target market but also competing third country exporters. Even if the market for the product in question is regional rather than worldwide, the predator must achieve a monopoly in all the countries in the region. If producers in a single country survive, they are free to export to the target market and undercut the predator's price as soon as he seeks to raise it. A strategy aimed at such a regional monopoly, or even a regional price cartel, would again be highly visible and, if the United States were the target market, would surely invite prosecution under the Sherman Act or the Antidumping Act of 1916.

* * *

FIRST-BEST SOLUTION—THE SHERMAN ACT

For several reasons, in my opinion, protection should not take the form of a special antidumping law. First, the very implausibility of predatory dumping as a genuine threat cuts against the need for special legislation. Second, the presence of price discrimination has little, if anything, to do with the threat of predation. * * *

Third, the existence of a special anti-price discrimination law carries with it the cost of discouraging all price competition, even the healthy variety. * * * Fourth, American producers are already adequately protected from any import competition, including dumping, under the escape clause if there is serious injury to an American industry or under the adjustment assistance provisions if there is serious injury instead to individual firms.

Fifth, and most important, the existing domestic antitrust laws are entirely adequate to protect against the threat of predation from foreign dumpers.

* * *

LONG-RUN DUMPING—INDISTINGUISHABLE FROM OTHER IMPORTS

Economists generally agree that long-run dumping cannot be distinguished from any other long-term flow of imports in its effects on the welfare of an importing nation. The low price improves welfare by expanding the real goods available for consumption in the importing country. Since the supply will continue indefinitely, there is no fear that adjustment costs will be wasteful.

Recently, however, B. Fisher has argued that this is too sanguine a view of long-term dumping. He urges two significant arguments against all forms of dumping other than the inconsequential, sporadic type. First, all dumping leads to resource misallocation on a global scale, and second, failure to impose antidumping duties misses an opportunity to put pressure on countries following excessively protectionist trade policies.

Fisher's first argument raises the problem of second-best. For dumping to occur, there must be monopoly power in the dumper's home market. The existence of that power leads to resource misallocation, because the monopolist restricts his output and charges a price well above marginal cost, the social optimum. A first-best world would be one without such monopoly power.

* * *

* * * The confusion introduced by Fisher's resource misallocation argument lies in his failure to realize, or explain clearly, that it is the existence of monopoly power in the dumper's home market that produces the basic resource misallocation, not dumping. Given this distortion as a starting point, no general conclusions can be drawn *a priori* as to whether dumping will heighten or lessen the distortion. If the objective is to improve efficiency in the world economy, then action must be taken to increase competition in the dumper's home market through, for example, vigorous enforcement of antitrust laws or elimination of restrictions on import competition.

This last point raises Fisher's second argument for opposing long-term dumping—that failure to do so misses an opportunity to put pressure on the dumper's home government to remove excessive restrictions to foreign competition in its own market. If such restrictions exist, they will indeed increase the market power of foreign dumpers, allow such firms to charge higher prices at home, and hence increase the likelihood of dumping. Would an antidumping policy, however, be an effective and appropriate antidote to such a condition?

Surely we are entitled to be skeptical that a government, which by hypothesis has insufficient incentive to reduce import restrictions to benefit its domestic consumers, will do so because its trading partners are imposing antidumping duties on the exports of some of its monopolistic firms. If that government feared that antidumping actions would harm its balance of payments, it would hardly react by unilaterally lowering its own import restrictions and thus worsening its balance of payments. Certainly if the dumping firms themselves complain, they will seek of their government retaliatory increases in trade barriers, not reduced tariffs.

(3) What about the situation where a producer who would normally not supply a market does so at dumping prices during recessionary periods in his home market? Is a *temporary* low price that will injure producers in the importing country bad? The issue seems to turn on whether the costs associated with impermanence (e.g., the need for adjustment and then readjustment of the domestic industry) outweigh the benefits to consumers of cheaper prices and a more competitive marketplace.[4]

(4) In antitrust law, a contrast is sometimes drawn between injury to competition and injury to specific competitors, it being argued that competition is supposed to result in injured competitors so that laws should not be concerned with that result, but rather should focus on preserving and promoting competition. Would you characterize the antidumping rules as you generally understand them at this point as protective of competitors or competition? What about the escape clause discussed in Chapter 9? What should the respective focus of these rules be? Consider the following report:

REPORT OF THE AD HOC COMMITTEE ON ANTITRUST AND ANTIDUMPING OF THE AMERICAN BAR ASSOCIATION SECTION ON ANTITRUST LAW

(1974)[5]

CONCLUSION

Both U.S. antidumping and antitrust law and policy have historic roots, and both were intended to protect and engender the fundamental U.S. economic policy of free and fair competition.

On the one hand, antitrust policy, favoring vigorous competition from all sources, including imports, has played an important role in maximizing consumer choice at competitive prices, and in stimulating industrial efficiency domestically.

On the other hand, antidumping policy seeks to accommodate the legitimate need for legislation which protects American competition from unfair price discrimination by foreign concerns. In this connection, the circumstances giving rise to dumping (e.g., trade barriers or monopolistic practices acceptable in the foreign country) might well be considered in determining whether to condemn such price discrimination.

In the Subcommittee's view, the apparent adverse antitrust ramifications of antidumping law enforcement do not result from economic underpinnings to antidumping policy. Instead, the significant differences we have identified between the two may more properly be ascribed to the fact that those agencies responsible for enforcing the 1921 [Antidumping] Act have not attempted to reconcile that law with United States antitrust law and policy.

---

4. Compare Barcelo, note 3 supra, at 71–75 with W. Wares, note 1 supra, at 84.

5. 43 Antitrust L.J. 653, 691–93 (1974). Reprinted by permission of the American Bar Association.

The Subcommittee believes that antidumping law and enforcement should recognize more affirmatively the countervailing needs and benefits of antitrust law and policy. Although it is not the Subcommittee's purpose to propose specific statutory changes to the 1921 Act, serious consideration might well be given to the evolution and adoption of the following substantive and procedural ideas to achieve this accommodation:

1. Since the 1921 Act is a price-discrimination statute, it would be proper for the Treasury Department to develop more realistic and meaningful criteria to ensure that price discrimination really exists, and for the Tariff Commission to articulate and adhere to proper standards by which to judge whether or not a sufficient lessening of competition has been occasioned by LTFV imports to warrant imposition of dumping duties.

With respect to the price comparison between purchase price or exporter's sale price and fair value (or foreign market value), it is essential that at least the cost-justification criteria operative under the Robinson-Patman Act be available to justify apparent international price differentials. That is, all expenses and costs which are reasonably related to the merchandise under consideration should be taken into account in determining relevant home market and export prices under the Act.

In addition, in seeking to conform our international with our domestic price discrimination statute, the Treasury Department should also consider the circumstances which may have caused the price discrimination (and the legitimate interest of the consumer). For example, it would seem inappropriate to assess dumping duties on "one-shot" dumps due, for example, to an exporter's overstock or the obsolescence of his goods which cannot be sold in the foreign market as readily as in the United States.

With respect to the injury requirement under the 1921 Act, the Tariff Commission should establish, or be required to ensure, that the sanctions of the 1921 Act do not protect individual competitors, but are triggered only if LTFV pricing may substantially restrain or injure *competition*. Not only may the Commission's present predilection—of predicating injury determinations merely on more than trivial disturbances to even a small portion of the industry involved—contribute to the maintenance of inefficient producers, but it also reduces consumer choices on the basis of price, quality and value. In this connection, the concept of injurious dumping should not arbitrarily subsume all instances of discriminatory pricing designed to enable the foreign exporter to meet prevailing U.S. prices.

2. As a statute whose remedies adversely affect importers, exporters and the consumer, procedural safeguards are essential to ensure that interested parties are given a fair opportunity to be heard, challenge and question evidence and witnesses, and be able to obtain a meaningful judicial review of adverse determinations.

In this connection, proceedings should be expedited so that the uncertainty resulting from the (usually prolonged) antidumping proceeding itself does not restrain fair import competition. Secondly, the adjudicatory provisions of Administrative Procedure Act should apply with respect to the administration of the 1921 Act, thus ensuring that the evidence upon which determinations are based has been subjected to time-proven adversarial scrutiny, and that such evidence constitutes the sole basis for determinations under the Act.   Thirdly, in order to ease compliance with the Act, and to enable meaningful judicial review, the Treasury Department and Tariff Commission should be required to articulate the legal and (if not confidential) evidentiary bases for their respective determinations in published, written opinions.

Finally, in order to counter the potentially unwarranted "chilling effect" of a withholding of appraisement, a withholding might be authorized only when there is a reasonable probability that the evidence will establish sales at LTFV and material injury to competition as a result thereof.

Perhaps at the bottom of existing confusion and inconsistencies regarding the 1921 Act and U.S. antitrust policy is the former's post World War I conception as a hybrid tariff and trade law.   In view of the growing commitment on the part of the United States and most other industrial countries to the principles of freer trade, as evidenced by GATT, it may well be appropriate for Congress to reconsider U.S. antidumping law and policy to ensure greater harmonization thereof with the concomitant competitive principles that antitrust seeks to protect.

Application of Antidumping Laws: A Statistical Note

Before turning to an examination of U.S. law, it is instructive to consider how frequently antidumping proceedings are invoked, what results are typical and which countries seem to be most active in imposing antidumping duties. The following table is based on information published by the GATT Committee on Antidumping for the period July 1980—June 1984.

Antidumping Actions

July 1980—June 1984 [6]

Country	Actions Initiated	Provisional Measures	Definitive Duties	Price Undertakings
U.S.	131	81	93	3
EC	120	43	28	63
Japan	0	0	0	0
Canada	153	131	73	0
Australia	141	55	71	17
Austria	1	1	0	0
Finland	3	2	0	2
Sweden	2	0	0	0

From July 1982 to June 1984, the principal targets of U.S. actions were Japan (11), Brazil (8), South Korea (8), China (7), West Germany (6) and Italy (6). The principal EC targets were Czechoslovakia (12), Spain (9) and Japan (8). Canada's principal targets were the United States (8) and South Korea (6).   In the case of Australia, the principal targets were: Japan (18), the United States (18), West Germany (14), Great Britain (9), New Zealand (9), China (8) and

6. GATT, 30th Supp. BISD 70–71 (1984); GATT, 31st Supp. BISD 289–90 (1985).

Belgium (7).[7] In the prior two-year period, U.S. investigations were concentrated on imports from the EC and *vice versa*.[8]

Examination of U.S. statistics indicates that as of February 1986, there have been 389 antidumping actions filed since 1974, including 301 filed since the 1979 statute came into effect. Of these 172 and 160 respectively were steel cases. Since 1979, no dumping was found in 15 cases, and there were 90 determinations of no material injury. Forty-one petitions were pending and 95 had been terminated or withdrawn without a final determination. Thus, since 1979, 60 petitions have been successful, a success rate of 23%.

(B) THE EVOLUTION OF THE INTERNATIONAL OBLIGATIONS

(1) Introduction

During the latter part of the nineteenth century, several European countries, primarily Great Britain and the Netherlands, complained about the dumping of sugar, and in 1902 an agreement was signed to counteract it. Ten European nations adhered to this pact during its eighteen-year life, but there was little success in concluding agreements to cover other products.

Beginning with Canada in 1903, nations started unilaterally to legislate against dumping in order to protect domestic industries from its possible adverse effects. By the time the League of Nations in the 1920's, and the World Economic Conference in 1933, had considered the problem, the national laws were of as much concern as the dumping practices themselves. Nations feared that their trading partners would use the laws as protectionist devices, rather than as simple regulatory measures to deal with patently unfair practices. When the preliminary ITO–GATT work began, the United States offered a proposal for standards modelled upon its own 1921 Antidumping Act. The need for such standards seems to have been generally recognized, and the result was Article VI of GATT, which deals with both antidumping and countervailing duties.[9]

(2) GATT Article VI

The reader should review the provisions of GATT Article VI, which deals with both antidumping and countervailing duties. The key fact about Article VI and GATT regulation of dumping is that GATT does not forbid dumping; GATT only authorizes, as an exception to other GATT obligations, certain unilateral national responses to be taken to offset the effects of dumping if the dumping causes material injury to a domestic industry.

Article VI has been interpreted by two "side" agreements: the 1967 Antidumping Code [10] and the Tokyo Round Agreement on Implementation of Article VI.[11] Like Article VI, they do not prohibit dumping, but seek only to regulate the manner in which antidumping duties are imposed. The lack of a prohibition is not surprising. After all, companies, not governments, dump. Governments could have agreed to make dumping unlawful under

7. GATT, 31st Supp. BISD 289–90 (1985).

8. GATT, 30th Supp. BISD 70 (1984).

9. See generally J. Jackson, World Trade and the Law of GATT 403–424 (1969), for a discussion of the development and meaning of

both Artic'e VI and the 1967 Antidumping Code.

10. Agreement on Interpretation of Article VI, GATT, 15th Supp. BISD 24 (1968).

11. GATT, 26th Supp. BISD 171 (1980).

national law or to make a dumper liable for any damages caused, but they did not do so. As a consequence, it is generally believed that a dumping company is not liable for dumping (beyond the potential assessment of antidumping duties) under national law, although it is conceivable that there could be liability imposed under general statutes regulating trade practices.[12] One can ask whether the fact that dumping is not considered to be illegal (and therefore not punishable by law), increases the likelihood of its occurrence.

There has been only one occasion on which a dispute panel of the GATT contracting parties has considered Article VI, and that was in 1955.

SWEDISH ANTI–DUMPING DUTIES
Report adopted on 26 February, 1955 [13]

INTRODUCTION

1. The Panel on Complaints examined with the representatives of Italy and Sweden the complaint of the Italian Government that the Swedish anti-dumping regulations were not consistent with the obligations of Sweden under the General Agreement and that the administration of these regulations impaired the benefits which should accrue to Italy under that Agreement. * * *

FACTS OF THE CASE

2. On 29 May 1954, the Swedish Government introduced anti-dumping duties on the importation of nylon stockings. In accordance with this Decree, an anti-dumping duty was levied whenever the invoice price was lower than the relevant minimum price fixed by the Swedish Government, the importer being entitled to obtain a refund of that duty if the case of dumping was not established. The Italian complaint was related to that Decree. However, a new decree was issued on 15 October 1954, i.e. before the Italian complaint was considered by the CONTRACTING PARTIES. The main difference between the new decree and the preceding one was that the basic prices were no longer a determining factor for the assessment of the anti-dumping duty but were retained as an administrative device enabling the Swedish Customs Authorities to exempt from anti-dumping enquiries any consignment the price of which was higher than the basic price; the actual determination of dumping policies and the levying of the anti-dumping duty were related to the concept of normal value which was defined in terms similar to those of Article VI of the General Agreement. The anti-dumping duty is assessed in relation to the basic price only when that price is lower than the normal value of the imported product.

* * *

6. The Panel considered these various contentions in detail and came to the conclusions which are summarized in the following paragraphs.

7. Regarding the alleged discrimination against low-cost producers, the Italian argument was as follows: it is agreed that the cost of production of

12. In the United States the Antidumping Act of 1916 makes certain intentional dumping unlawful. See Section 10.4(C) infra.

13. GATT, 3d Supp. BISD 81 (1955).

nylon stockings is different in the various supplying countries. In the absence of anti-dumping duties, the low-cost producer has a substantial price advantage as compared with the high-cost producer. If the high-cost producer subsidizes its exports to the extent necessary to bring down its export price to the level of the Swedish price, he would not be affected by the Swedish anti-dumping regulations. On the other hand, the low-cost producer, if his normal price was equal to or lower than the Swedish basic price, would have lost his price advantage if he were to sell without dumping. If, in order to meet the changed conditions of the competition, he were to resort to dumping practices, he would have to pay in full the anti-dumping duty, even if the amount of dumping in his case were much lower than in the case of the high-cost producer. The Italian Government considered that this would amount to a discrimination against the low-cost producer.

8.   The Panel considered that this argument was not entirely convincing. If the low-cost producer is actually resorting to dumping practices, he forgoes the protection embodied in the most-favoured-nation clause. On the other hand, Article VI does not oblige an importing country to levy an anti-dumping duty whenever there is a case of dumping, or to treat in the same manner all suppliers who resort to such practices. The wording of paragraph 6 supports that view. The importing country is only entitled to levy an anti-dumping duty when there is material injury to a domestic industry or at least a threat of such an injury. If, therefore, the importing country considers that the imports above a certain price are not prejudicial to its domestic industry, the text of paragraph 6 does not oblige it to levy an anti-dumping duty on imports coming from high-cost suppliers, but, on the contrary, prevents it from doing so. On the other hand, if the price at which the imports of the low-cost producers are sold is prejudicial to the domestic industry, the levying of an anti-dumping duty is perfectly permissible, provided, of course, that the case of dumping is clearly established.

9.   The Panel recognized however that the basic price system would have a serious discriminatory effect if consignments of the goods exported by the low-cost producers had been delayed and subjected to uncertainties by the application of that system and the case for dumping were not established in the course of the enquiry. The fact that the low-cost producer would thus have been at a disadvantage whereas the high-cost producer would have been able to enter his goods freely even at dumping prices would clearly discriminate against the low-cost producer.

10.   As regards the second argument relating to the fact that the basic price system is unrelated to the actual prices on the domestic markets of the various exporting countries, the Panel was of the opinion that this feature of the scheme would not necessarily be inconsistent with the provisions of Article VI so long as the basic price is equal to or lower than the actual price on the market of the lowest cost producer. If that condition is fulfilled, no anti-dumping duty will be levied contrary to the provision of Article VI. The Swedish representative stressed that the basic prices were fixed in accordance with that principle. (See also paragraph 22 below.)

* * *

13.   The further contention that the basic prices would in effect prevent any import of the product except at a price which would be fixed arbitrarily by the Swedish authorities and might, therefore, nullify any price advantage which low-cost exporters should enjoy did not appear to the Panel to be conclusive if it is assumed that the system would apply to cases of dumping. Of course, if the system were to be applied when the case of dumping is not established, that particular technique might be more prejudicial to the interests of low-cost producers than other anti-dumping techniques.

14.   In this connection, the Swedish representative pointed out that the ordinary customs duties for nylon stockings were comparatively low, and that the Swedish Government did not make use of its right to raise the rate to the level of 25 per cent at which it had been bound. The Italian representative pointed out that, if the Swedish industry were suffering from competition from low-cost producers, such as Italian producers, the Swedish Government would be entitled, under the General Agreement, to raise its customs duties. The Italian Government would raise no objection to such a measure, as it would not deprive Italy of its competitive advantage over other suppliers.

15.   The Panel then considered the argument developed by the Italian representative to the effect that the Swedish Decree reversed the onus of the proof since the customs authorities can act without being required to prove the existence of dumping practices or even to establish a *prima facie* case of dumping. The Panel considered that it was not competent to deal with the legal rules which may exist in Sweden regarding procedures before customs authorities or the courts. On the other hand, it was clear from the wording of Article VI that no anti-dumping duties should be levied unless certain facts had been established. As this represented an obligation on the part of the contracting party imposing such duties, it would be reasonable to expect that that contracting party should establish the existence of these facts when its action is challenged.

* * *

17.   The general conclusion of the Panel regarding the consistency of the Swedish Decree with the obligations of the Swedish Government under the General Agreement was:

(a)   that the basic price system was not inconsistent with the most-favoured-nation clause or with the provisions of Article VI,

(b)   but that, in practice, the administration of that system might easily run into conflict with those obligations.

Unless the customs authorities were prepared to decide on the alleged cases of dumping in a matter of days after arrival of the consignment, and unless the basic prices were constantly kept under review to make sure that they did not exceed the actual prices prevailing for all the varieties of stockings on the domestic markets of the most efficient producer, there was a certain danger of discrimination against low-cost producers in individual cases. Constant supervision of the operation of the scheme would also be necessary in order to avoid that it might be turned into a general protection against low-cost producers, even in the absence of dumping practices.

ALLEGED NULLIFICATION OR IMPAIRMENT OF BENEFITS ACCRUING TO
ITALY UNDER THE GENERAL AGREEMENT

18. The Panel next considered whether the administration of the Decree had actually caused a serious injury to Italian commercial interests, and whether such an injury represented an impairment of the benefits accruing to Italy under the General Agreement.

*   *   *

22. Apart from the damage caused by those delays, the Italian delegation contended that the main injury suffered by exporters was due to the fact that the Swedish Government was levying an anti-dumping duty on Italian stockings although it had not established that the export prices of the Italian exporters were less than the normal value of those products as required in Article VI of the GATT. The Panel agreed that if the Swedish Decree was being applied in such a manner as to impose an anti-dumping levy in the absence of dumping practices, the Italian Government would be deprived of the protection it would reasonably expect from the terms of Article VI of the Agreement and that it could claim an impairment of benefits.

23. The Swedish representative stated that it appeared doubtful to his delegation that the CONTRACTING PARTIES could consider that question and that it was the right of the national authorities to decide whether dumping had really taken place. The Panel agreed that no provision of the General Agreement could limit in any way the rights of national authorities in that respect. But, for the reasons set forth in paragraph 15 above, it would be reasonable to expect from the contracting party which resorts to the provisions of Article VI, if such action is challenged, to show to the satisfaction of the CONTRACTING PARTIES that it had exercised its rights consistently with those provisions. The Panel felt therefore that, in order to decide whether Italy had suffered an impairment of benefits, it would be appropriate and necessary to examine whether a case had been made out that Italian stocking exporters had resorted to dumping practices.

*   *   *

28. The Panel was of the opinion that if the Swedish authorities considered that it was not possible to find "a comparable price in the ordinary course of trade for the like product when destined for consumption in the exporting country", no provision in the General Agreement would prevent them from using one of the other two criteria laid down in Article VI.

29. The Swedish representative indicated that his Government could not rely on the second criterion which involved a comparison with the export prices to third countries as the Swedish delegation sent to Milan to enquire into this matter had not been in a position to obtain relevant data from the Italian manufacturers. The Italian representative explained that this lack of success was not surprising, since the Swedish delegation included two Swedish manufacturers and the Italian manufacturers were naturally reluctant to disclose confidential information to competitors.

30. The Panel concluded that, in effect, the Swedish authorities were relying on the third criterion which related to the cost of production. The Panel felt that the use by the Swedish authorities of a weighted average as

between the Italian prices could only give a rough estimate of the normal price and that if this approach were retained, it would be reasonable to expect that, if the average included not only the "unmarked" and "marked" first choice stockings of a given type, but also the second and third choices of the same type, the results would be more accurate.

31. In order, however, to see what results the method of calculation adopted by the Swedish authorities would give in a specific instance, the Panel asked the Swedish representative if he could give the actual details of the calculation for one type of stockings. The Panel then compared the data used by the Swedish representative with the official price lists which were used for that calculation and came to the conclusion that, probably through some misunderstandings on a few points, the two sets of figures were difficult to reconcile and that these misunderstandings might explain to a certain extent the divergence of views between the two governments regarding the alleged existence of dumping practices.

32. The Panel felt, therefore, that before it could come to any definite conclusion regarding the difference, if any, between the Italian export prices and the comparable prices on the Italian market, it would be appropriate for the two delegations to try and clarify the facts on which the determination of dumping was based. In its opinion, the best way to arrive at some understanding on this point would be for the Swedish Government to send to Italy a responsible official who, by his functions, would be under an oath of secrecy, and to whom the Italian Government could guarantee free access to the books of the exporters. If such a procedure were acceptable to both parties, and if the Swedish authorities had arrived at definite conclusions regarding the extent to which allowance should be made for the refund of taxes or duties, when the enquiry suggested would be completed, the Panel believes that it would be comparatively easy for the two parties to agree on what is the correct normal price for stockings in Italy, and to determine whether there are any dumping practices as defined in Article VI of the General Agreement. If, however, disagreement should subsist, the Italian Government would be free to refer the matter again to the CONTRACTING PARTIES.

33. In the light of the considerations set out above, the Panel suggests to the CONTRACTING PARTIES that it would be appropriate for them to make a recommendation to Italy and Sweden in accordance with the second sentence of paragraph 2 of Article XXIII. That recommendation should aim at expediting the anti-dumping procedure in Sweden in order to minimize the adverse effects on Italian export trade and at improving the administration of the basic price system, in order to eliminate some of the objections raised by the Italian Government.

Notes and Questions

(1) Do you agree with the statement in Paragraph 8 that Article VI does not require an importing country to treat all suppliers who dump in the same manner? If entities from two different countries were dumping under identical circumstances, is discrimination permitted? Or must it be justified, e.g., on the

ground that no injury was caused by one of the dumpers? What other GATT articles are relevant to the question of discrimination?

(2) In 1960, a GATT committee report stated: [14] "In equity, and having regard to the most-favored-nation principle, the Group considered that where there was dumping to the same degree from more than one source and where that dumping caused or threatened material injury to the same extent, the importing country ought normally to be expected to levy antidumping duties equally on all the dumped imports."

(3) Under GATT, what rights would an Italian exporter have to contest a determination by Sweden that it was dumping? At what point in an antidumping proceeding would such rights, if any, be applicable?

(4) In 1981, the GATT Committee on Antidumping Practices noted that it had discussed special monitoring schemes related to antidumping systems. It adopted an understanding on the subject as follows: [15]

> * * * The Committee recognizes that such schemes are not envisioned by Article VI of the GATT or the Agreement and it is of the view that they give cause for concern in that they could be used in a manner contrary to the spirit of the Agreement. The Committee agreed that such schemes shall not be used as a substitute for initiating and carrying out anti-dumping investigations in full conformity with all provisions of the Agreement. The Committee further agreed that, as monitoring schemes may have the effect of burdening and distorting trade, it is advisable that the effects of such monitoring schemes on international trade continue to be examined with, *inter alia,* a view to assessing the need for strengthening international discipline in this area.

(3) The 1967 Antidumping Code

The rather general terms of GATT Article VI prompted some nations to seek agreement on more specific standards. These efforts, begun in earnest in 1966, culminated in Geneva on June 30, 1967, with the signing of an Agreement on Interpretation of Article VI (the 1967 Antidumping Code) by the United States and 17 other nations.[16] Unfortunately, the U.S. President had received no authorization from Congress to negotiate and enter into such an agreement.[17] As a consequence, even though it is arguable that the Code was consistent with the wording of the then effective U.S. statute,[18] the 1921 Antidumping Act, certain congressional leaders were incensed at the President's action. The ensuing dispute is now of only historical importance since the United States has implemented the Tokyo Round substitute for the Code, but the dispute highlighted the problems of uncertainty that surround the negotiation of agreements by the United States if those agreements may need congressional approval, as well as the rancor that occasionally develops between the President and Congress over trade matters. In addition, the whole affair had an adverse impact on the U.S. image as a responsible

14. GATT, 9th Supp. BISD 196, 198 (1961).

15. GATT, 28th Supp. BISD 52 (1982).

16. GATT, 15th Supp. BISD 74 (1968).

17. The Senate Finance Committee Report on the Trade Expansion Act of 1962, which provided authorization for Kennedy Round negotiations, explicitly stated that the then current antidumping statute was "not intended to be affected." S.Rep. No. 2059, 87th Cong., 2d Sess. 19 (1962).

18. See generally Barcelo, note 1 supra.

participant in trade negotiations, an impact that did not quickly dissipate. The substance of the differences between the old U.S. law and the Code and the ultimate fate of the Code in the United States are explained by Senator Long as follows:

RUSSELL B. LONG, UNITED STATES LAW AND THE INTERNATIONAL ANTI–DUMPING CODE

(1969) [19]

A comparison of the provisions of the Code and pertinent United States statutes shows how the Code limits the discretion of the Tariff Commission in making an injury determination under the Act, and why the Senate Committee on Finance concluded that "there are many areas of significant conflict between the International Antidumping Code and our domestic unfair trade laws."

INJURY TEST

Section 201(a) of the Antidumping Act states that the Commission "shall determine whether an industry in the United States is being or is likely to be, injured, or is prevented from being established by reason of the importation of such merchandise in the United States." There are no explicit criteria which define what constitutes an injury. As already mentioned, the injury test was incorporated into the statute mainly for administrative reasons.

The history of its origin indicates that Congress did not intend that an industry had to be "flat on its back" before dumping duties could be assessed. * * *

Under the determinations made by the Tariff Commission, injury has been construed to mean any harm which is more than *de minimis,* i.e., frivolous, inconsequential or immaterial.

* * *

In contrast to the Act, the Code contains specific criteria for determining what constitutes an injury sufficient to justify assessment of dumping duties, and also requires a rigid causal relationship between dumping and injury. Article 3 of the Code states:

A determination of injury *shall be made only* when the authorities concerned are satisfied that the dumped imports are *demonstrably the principal cause of material injury* or of threat of material injury to a domestic industry or the principal cause of material retardation of the establishment of such an industry. In reaching their decision the authorities *shall* weigh, on one hand, the effect of the dumping and, on the other hand, all other factors taken together which may be adversely affecting the industry.
* * *

* * *

19. 3 Intl.Lawyer 464, 472–89. Reprinted by permission of the American Bar Association.

DEFINITION OF AN INDUSTRY

One of the controversial subjects which has been considered by the Tariff Commission, even prior to the existence of the International Antidumping Code, is the scope to be given to the term in the Act of "an industry in the United States." The Tariff Commission has held, in some instances, that the producers in or serving a portion of the United States rather than all of the producers in the entire country, constituted "an industry" within the meaning of our statute. The competitive market areas were of varying sizes, and have consisted in some cases of one or two states, and in others, parts of one or more states.

* * *

The like-product concept of an industry required by the Code narrows the Commission's discretion as to what industry can be harmed by dumped imports. It permits imports to be compared to only one industry—that which produces the like product. Moreover, as stated, the Code's competitive-market-area criteria for determining the industry are so restrictive that, in the judgment of the Tariff Commission, *four out of five* affirmative determinations might not have been made had the Code been in effect when the determinations were made.

Under the Code's regional-industry concept, "all, or almost all of the producers" within a market area must be injured before there could be an affirmative determination of injury. * * *

In some cases, the Commission has found that sales at less than fair value in a competitive market area were injuring a national industry even though a sizable portion of the total number of producers may not individually have experienced material injury, nor were likely to experience such injury within the foreseeable future.

THE CONFERENCE AGREEMENT

In resolving the dilemma, on the one hand, of not wanting to abrogate an international agreement into which the United States had entered with seventeen foreign nations, but, on the other hand, of not wishing that such agreement change domestic law as it has been applied over a period of more than 46 years of case history, the conferees on the Renegotiation Amendments Act of 1968 reached agreement which provides *inter alia:*

> Nothing contained in the International Antidumping Code, signed at Geneva on June 30, 1967, shall be construed to restrict the discretion of the United States Tariff Commission in performing its duties and functions under the Antidumping Act, 1921.

* * *

* * * Thus, any provision of the Code which limits the discretion of the Tariff Commission in its injury-investigation function is not to be taken into account by that Commission. Such provisions are not to be weighed or used as guides by the administrators in the performance of their responsibilities under the Act. On the contrary, they are to be ignored. Two important features of the Code which did restrict the discretion of the Tariff Commission dealt with (1) the determination of what constitutes an industry for the purpose of an antidumping investigation, and (2) the degree of injury required to invoke the remedy provided by the statute. Both of these features are made inapplicable by the conference report.

The conference agreement on the dumping issue also provided that:

in performing their duties and functions under such act (the Antidumping Act of 1921) the Secretary of the Treasury and the Tariff Commission shall—first, resolve any conflict between the International Antidumping Code and the Antidumping Act, 1921, in favor of the Act as applied by the agency administering the Act; and second, take into account the provisions of the International Antidumping Code only insofar as they are consistent with the Antidumping Act of 1921 as applied by the agency administering the Act.

The intent of this part of the conference agreement was explained to the Senate on October 7, 1968, in the following terms:

The Act as applied by the agency administering it refers to the body of law, rules, and practices built up by the agency in its administration of the Act over the years.

In other words, the committee was saying that it is not enough to look to the cold language of the Act in determining whether any conflict exists with the International Antidumping Code; prior determinations, prior practices and prior procedures must also be considered. The effect of this is that Congress has forbidden the Executive Branch and the Tariff Commission to interpret the Antidumping Act more narrowly in the future than in the past by virtue of the negotiation of the International Antidumping Code.

* * *

SUMMARY

The International Antidumping Code was negotiated without advance authority by Congress, in the face of a strict admonition by the Senate not to change the Antidumping Act in any way. Apart from the question as to whether the President has authority to enter into international agreements with foreign nations in an area which the Constitution reserves exclusively to the Congress, it is settled law that when an agreement has the effect of changing existing domestic law, either directly, or by indirection through giving the law a meaning and a result which Congress never intended, the agreement cannot be given effect until it has been submitted to Congress for implementing legislation.

* * *

The Constitution states that (1) the Constitution, (2) laws made in pursuance thereof, and (3) treaties made under the authority of the United States, shall be the supreme law of the land. Article 1, Section 8 of the Constitution specifically delegates to the Congress the power "to regulate commerce with foreign nations," and clearly an international agreement, which is not a law made pursuant to the Constitution, nor a treaty, but which sets standards which are to be applied by a Commission set up by the Congress in the sphere of "regulating commerce," does not stand on an equal footing with statutory law.

(4) The Tokyo Round Agreement on Antidumping Duties

There were extensive negotiations during the Tokyo Round concerning a code on subsidies, which we will discuss in the next section. When those negotiations were completed, it was agreed that provisions in the 1967 Antidumping Code should be conformed to their analogues in the Subsidies Code.[20] The result was a new Agreement on Implementation of Article VI (set out in the Documentary Supplement), which replaces the 1967 Antidumping Code for those nations that adhere to the new Agreement.[21] Since the United States implemented the Agreement in 1979, we will not separately discuss its provisions here, but will refer to it as appropriate when discussing the current U.S. law. The principal change from the 1967 Code was the elimination of the requirement that dumping be the "principal cause" of injury. As in the case of the other Tokyo Round agreements, a committee of signatories was established, called the Committee on Antidumping Practices. So far, it has issued an understanding on monitoring systems in 1981 and recommendations on the transparency of antidumping proceedings in 1983.[22]

(C) UNITED STATES ANTIDUMPING LAW [23]

(1) Overview

As the foregoing materials have indicated, U.S. antidumping law prior to the Tokyo Round was characterized by a number of facts: It was not entirely consistent with GATT Article VI, or the 1967 Antidumping Code, especially as to the injury test (because U.S. law omitted the word "material"). As to GATT, the U.S. could argue grandfather rights. Even as to the 1967 Code, the U.S. could argue that although its statute did not include the word "material", all U.S. antidumping cases could be shown in fact to satisfy that criterion. The administration of the law by the Treasury Department and the International Trade Commission left a great deal of discretion in the hands of the administrators. There was a growing feeling in Congress that

20. GATT, The Tokyo Round of Multilateral Trade Negotiations, Report by the Director-General of GATT 181 (1979).

21. GATT, 26th Supp. BISD 171 (1980).

22. GATT, 28th Supp. BISD 52 (1982); GATT, 30th Supp. BISD 24 (1984).

23. The articles that have been written on particular aspects of U.S. antidumping law are in general too numerous to cite, although we will cite a few on specific topics. For basic information on U.S. antidumping law, the following looseleaf works that are regularly updated may be consulted: BNA International Trade Reporter (the basic structure of the rules is outlined in the Reference File, significant developments are noted in the weekly Current Reports, and most ITA, ITC and CIT decisions are digested and collected in the Recent Decisions); 1 H. Kaye, P. Plaia & M. Hertzberg, International Trade Practice chs. 21–30; J. Pattison, Antidumping and Countervailing Duty Laws. In addition, see J. Jack-son, R. Cunningham & C. Fontheim (eds.), International Trade Policy: The Lawyer's Perspective (1985); The Commerce Department Speaks Out on Import Administration and Export Administration (Practicing Law Institute, 2 vols. 1984); The Trade Agreements Act of 1979—Four Years Later (Practicing Law Institute 1983); Hearings on Options to Improve the Trade Remedy Laws Before the Subcomm. on Trade of the House Comm. on Ways and Means, 98th Cong., 1st Sess. (2 vols. 1984).

As to basic source material, actions taken by the International Trade Administration (ITA) are published in the Federal Register. Notices of determinations by the International Trade Commission (ITC) are also published in the Federal Register. Such notices identify and explain how to obtain the ITC publication containing the determination. The ITC publications are separate documents and are not published in bound form by the ITC.

the Executive Branch did not take the enforcement of the antidumping laws seriously enough.

Implementation of the Tokyo Round agreements was the occasion for a substantial restructuring of U.S. antidumping law. It can be argued that the changes in substance were not all that great—after all, the Tokyo Round agreement was a somewhat watered-down version of the 1967 Code that the Treasury Department had contended was consistent with U.S. law. The changes in procedure, however, were fundamental in nature. In this overview section, we will focus on the procedural aspects of U.S. law. We will then examine the two principal substantive issues in antidumping law—the existence of dumping and material injury—in later subsections.

As a consequence of the changes in procedure in 1979, antidumping proceedings in the United States have become very formalized and are played out according to a complex set of rules, largely designed to minimize administrative discretion.[24]

To commence an antidumping action, an aggrieved party, typically a manufacturer or association of manufacturers of a like product, files a petition with the International Trade Administration (ITA) of the U.S. Department of Commerce and the International Trade Commission (ITC) alleging that exports from specified countries are being sold at dumping prices in the United States. For purposes of calculating time limits under the Act, we will refer to the filing date as Day 1. The petition must allege the basic elements of an antidumping action—dumping, or in the words of the U.S. statute, sales of foreign merchandise at "less than fair value" (LTFV sales), and material injury to U.S. industry. The petition must contain information reasonably available to the petitioner that supports its allegations. The ITA has until Day 20 to decide if the petition is sufficient to open an investigation. If the ITA decides to open an investigation, it starts an investigation of the dumping allegation. It normally sends questionnaires to those persons alleged to be dumping, which questionnaires inquire into export volumes and prices, and other information germane to the LTFV sales issue. The questionnaires are normally due back in a month or so. The ITA also gathers other relevant information, such as customs data, that may be available to it.

Simultaneously with the activities of the ITA, the International Trade Commission (ITC) considers the question of material injury. The statute requires the ITC to make a preliminary injury determination by Day 45. If the ITC determination is affirmative, both the LTFV sales and injury investigations continue.

In the course of the LTFV sales investigation, the ITA attempts to verify the information it receives, by, inter alia, inspecting records at the compa-

24. The 1979 antidumping statute, which was contained in title I of the Trade Agreements Act of 1979 (see Documentary Supplement), was added to the Tariff Act of 1930 as Sections 731–40 (procedures), Section 751 (reviews) and Sections 771–78 (definitions and procedures). It is codified at 19 U.S.C.A. §§ 1673–73i; 1675, 1677–77h.

The rules of the ITA are found at 19 CFR Pt. 353 (1985). Those of the ITC are at 19 CFR Pt. 207 (1985). The basic statute governing appeals is Section 516A of the Tariff Act, 19 U.S.C.A. § 1516a.

nies accused of dumping. In a normal case, the ITA is required by statute to make a preliminary determination of the dumping margin by Day 160 (Day 110 if the petitioner waives verification and agrees to have the ITA proceed on the basis of the then available information). In an extraordinarily complicated case (as determined by the ITA), the ITA preliminary determination is not due until Day 210. The ITA final dumping determination is due 75 days later (Day 185, 235 or 285, as the case may be), unless it grants a postponement of 60 days at the request of the person against whom the preliminary determination was made.

In the meantime, the ITC injury determination must be made within 45 days after the ITA final dumping determination if the ITA preliminarily found LTFV sales (Day 290, 340 or 390, assuming a 60-day postponement was granted) and within 75 days if the ITA found LTFV sales only in its final determination. The idea behind this incredibly complex scheme is to make sure that the Executive Branch processes petitions promptly, something Congress felt that it did not always do under the former law. Under these rules the typical case should be processed within one year; and even an extraordinarily complicated one should be finished within 14 months.

If a preliminary determination is made that LTFV sales are occurring, the Customs Service will suspend liquidation of the entry of those goods and require provision of security in an amount equal to the estimated dumping margin, unless the margin is de minimis, in which case there is a negative determination. Following final determinations of LTFV sales and injury, a dumping order is issued that requires the Customs Service to collect definitive antidumping duties. The process by which this is done is somewhat complex. Basically, once a year duties are to be assessed retrospectively in respect of the dumping margin found for each importation. Thus, the duty payable varies from company to company and transaction to transaction. Prior to such assessment, estimated duties are paid at the time of importation in an amount equal to the average dumping margin established in the initial investigation or most recent assessment, as the case may be. However, if no request for such an annual assessment is made, the estimated duties become the definitive duties.

An important provision of the law allows the importer, in certain circumstances, to supply detailed information covering the imports made between the first affirmative LTFV sales determination and the ITC injury determination and have definitive duties based on such information assessed 90 days later. Thereafter, the estimated duties are based on the dumping margins established for such imports. This means that if a company does not dump after an investigation is initiated and this procedure is allowed, no definitive or estimated duties will be collected (at least until a future review finds dumping), even if the investigation finds evidence of past LTFV sales.

A part of the congressional effort to broaden the use of the antidumping statute included provision for extensive judicial review of ITA and ITC decisions. Final, as well as many preliminary, decisions were made reviewable in the Court of International Trade (CIT). See Section 3.5(C) supra, for a general discussion of review in the CIT, including review in antidumping cases. The speed of the proceedings necessary to meet the time limits imposed by Congress meant, however, that court review of preliminary determinations was often completed after the final determination was due. The waste inherent in such a system was apparent, and since passage of the 1984 Trade and Tariff Act, generally only final determinations can be appealed.[25] The tendency has been for parties to make extensive use of the judicial review possibilities, and as we will see below, the CIT has not hesitated to substitute its views for those of the ITA and ITC. Under the statute, determinations made on the basis of a record are reviewed to determine if they are supported by substantial evidence and not otherwise unlawful, while other determinations are reviewed to determine if they are arbitrary, capricious, an abuse of discretion or otherwise unlawful.[26]

Notes

(1) *Treatment of Confidential Information.* A particularly difficult problem arises in making judicial review effective in antidumping cases. Much of the information collected by the ITA and the ITC is regarded by the parties supplying it as including sensitive commercial secrets of the highest order: customer names and prices charged; profit, loss and cost information on specific products. There is an obvious need to afford confidential treatment to this information, but without such information it may be impossible to know if the ITA and ITC are properly applying the relevant rules. The solution is contained in Section 777, which authorizes, where necessary and under protective orders, the disclosure of confidential information.[27] Generally, information is disclosed only to the nonaffiliated attorneys of the parties (who may be allowed to disclose it to experts, such as accountants). Inside counsel have not been allowed to participate under this procedure.[28] Although many corporations are very uncomfortable with this process, there have apparently been no major cases of improper disclosure.

(2) *Price Undertakings in U.S. Law.* Article 7(1) of the new GATT Antidumping Code provides that "[p]roceedings may be suspended or terminated without the imposition of provisional measures or anti-dumping duties upon receipt of satisfactory voluntary undertakings from any exporter to revise its prices or to cease exports to the area in question so that the authorities are satisfied that the injurious effect of the dumping is eliminated." The statistics in Section 10.2(A) indicate that undertakings are a common resolution of dumping cases in all countries except the United States and Canada.

The reason that undertakings are not used frequently in the United States is that Section 734 narrowly restricts their use.[29] They are generally permitted only if the exporter ceases exporting to the United States or raises its prices to eliminate the dumping margin. In addition, undertakings may be accepted in extraordinary circumstances (i.e. complex cases where accepting an undertaking

25. Trade and Tariff Act of 1984, § 623, Pub.L. No. 98–573, 98th Cong., 2d Sess., 98 Stat. 3040.

26. 19 U.S.C.A. § 1516a.

27. 19 U.S.C.A. § 1677f.

28. 19 CFR §§ 207.7, 353.30 (1985). See generally Annotation, Access to Confidential or Privileged Material in International Trade Cases Under 19 U.S.C.A. § 1516a(b)(2)(B), 73 ALR Fed. 247 (1985); Sacilor, Acieries et Laminoirs de Lorraine v. United States, 542 F.Supp. 1020 (CIT 1982); Garfinkel, Disclosure of Corporate Documents Under the Trade Agreements Act of 1979: A Corporate Nightmare?, 13 Law & Poly.Intl.Bus. 465 (1981).

29. 19 U.S.C.A. § 1673c.

would be more beneficial to domestic industry than continuing the investigation) if the undertakings cover substantially all of the imports, completely eliminate the injurious effect and eliminate most of the dumping margin. The congressional attitude on undertakings ("suspensions" in U.S. law) was expressed as follows by the Senate Report: [30]

> The suspension provision is intended to permit rapid and pragmatic resolutions of antidumping duty cases. However, suspension is an unusual action which should not become the normal means for disposing of cases. The committee intends that investigations be suspended only when that action serves the interest of the public and the domestic industry affected. For this reason, the authority to suspend investigations is narrowly circumscribed. In particular, agreements which provide for any action less than complete elimination of the margin of dumping or cessation of exports can be accepted only in extraordinary circumstances. That is to say, rarely. Furthermore, the requirement that the petitioner be consulted will not be met by pro forma communications. Complete disclosure and discussion is required.

> The committee intends that no agreement be accepted unless it can be effectively monitored by the United States. This will require establishment of procedures under which entries of merchandise covered by an agreement can be reviewed by the authority and by interested parties. Adequate staff and resources must be allocated for monitoring to insure that relief under the agreement occurs.

> For purposes of section 734(b) and (c), the committee intends the term "substantially all of the imports" to mean no less than 85 percent by volume of the imports of the merchandise subject to the investigation during a recent representative period. This requirement must be met throughout the duration of the agreement. In every case, agreements with exporters must be between the U.S. Government and those exporters. Section 734 is not intended to permit agreements among exporters or between exporters and U.S. persons.

> The standard for the injurious effect determination by the ITC under section 734(h)(2) is lower than the material injury standard defined in section 771(7). Complete elimination of the injurious effect requires that there be no discernible injurious effect by reason of any amount by which the foreign market value exceeds the United States price under the agreement.

Does the U.S. statute implement the GATT Code? Is the congressional direction as to operation of the statute consistent with the apparent intent of the GATT Code?

(2) Determinations of Sales at Less Than Fair Value [31]

The U.S. dumping statute provides that if imports occur at "less than fair value" and are causing material injury, then a dumping duty will be assessed equal to the amount by which the "foreign market value" exceeds

30. S.Rep. No. 96–249, 96th Cong., 1st Sess. 71 (1979).

31. The relevant statutory sections are 772 (definition of U.S. price) and 773 (definition of foreign market value). 19 U.S.C.A. §§ 1677a–77b. The ITA rules are at 19 CFR §§ 353.1–.23 (1985).

the "U.S. price." The U.S. statute does not actually define "less than fair value," although it is generally assumed that if foreign market value (as defined in the statute) exceeds the U.S. price (also defined) then imports are occurring at "less than fair value." Given this statutory imprecision, there would seem to be some slight scope for creative interpretation of "less than fair value" where appropriate for policy reasons, although the U.S. Administration has found it politically difficult to take advantage of this leeway.[32]

The process of finding the U.S. price and the foreign market value is very complex. Typically, invoice prices are the starting point of the process. Various adjustments are then made to those prices. These adjustments are necessary because export sales may be made on quite different terms than sales on the home market, thereby making it inappropriate just to compare invoice prices. To take a simple example, exports may be sold for cash and with a limited warranty, while domestic sales may be made on 30 days credit terms and with warranty. The adjustment process tries to compensate for such differences. It essentially attempts to arrive at comparable "ex factory" prices for the exports and for the like products sold in the home market.

Much work is involved in this effort to establish comparable values. Often, accountants and economic consultants work with the lawyers in these cases, and since comparisons with foreign markets are involved, not only are language skills essential, but analysts must have knowledge of different accounting standards! The adjustment process can be very confusing, but the key is to focus on whether a proposed adjustment expands the difference (called the "dumping margin") between the U.S. price and the foreign market value or decreases it. Generally speaking, the petitioners will want to minimize the U.S. price and maximize the foreign market value, while the exporters will want to do the opposite.

One particular problem is worth noting at the outset. Normally, the first step in establishing the foreign market value is to make a survey of prices on the home market and calculate an average price. But sometimes there are reasons why this cannot be done. For example, the like product may not be sold at home. In such a case, the statute provides alternatives: use of sales to another (third) country, or "construction" of a home market value based on the costs of inputs. In the latter case, the U.S. statute requires a minimum of 10% to be added for "administrative costs," and 8% for "profits." Particularly as to the latter figure, questions have been raised whether the U.S. requirement is consistent with U.S. international obligations under GATT and the Antidumping Code, because often in times of recession, or for certain types of products, profits are not nearly so high as 8%.

The following cases consider some of these various issues. The reader should pay particular attention to such questions as: When and how are the alternative methods of foreign market value used? How are costs constructed? What adjustments are normally allowed? What happens when the relevant transactions are between related parties? What is the same class

32. See Note, Applying Antidumping Law to Perishable Agricultural Goods, 80 Mich.L. Rev. 524 (1982).

or kind of merchandise? What is such or similar merchandise? What is a nonmarket economy? How is a surrogate market country chosen?

We cannot in this book do more than introduce these intricate and complex matters. The materials below do that, and the problems at the end of this section will assist the reader to test his comprehension. It must be remembered, however, we are photographing a moving target—the subject is constantly changing.

(a) Calculation and Comparison of U.S. Price and Foreign Market Value

TUBULAR STEEL FRAMED CHAIRS FROM TAIWAN

Intl. Trade Admin. (1985) [33]

On August 10, 1984, we received a petition in proper form from counsel for Frazier Engineering, Inc., Greenfield, Indiana, on behalf of the U.S. industry producing stacking chairs. * * *

After reviewing the petition, we determined it contained sufficient grounds upon which to initiate an antidumping investigation. We notified the ITC of our action and initiated such an investigation on September 6, 1984. The ITC subsequently found, on September 24, 1984, that there is a reasonable indication that imports of stacking chairs from Taiwan are materially injuring a United States industry. * * * On October 16, 1984, we received a letter from counsel filed on behalf of the producers of stacking chairs, requesting additional time in which to respond to the questionnaires. We subsequently extended the due date for responses to November 9, 1984. On November 9, 1984, we received responses from the producers. Verification of all information submitted to the Department was conducted in Taiwan during the period January 11, 1985, through January 24, 1985. On March 14, 1985, we published our preliminary determination of sales at not less than fair value. The notice stated that, if requested, we would hold a public hearing to afford interested parties an opportunity to comment on the preliminary determination. Neither counsel for petitioners nor respondents requested a hearing. We received one written comment from respondents and it was subsequently withdrawn.

SCOPE OF THE INVESTIGATION

The products covered by this investigation are tubular steel framed stacking chairs, including stacking chairs with plastic slats or expanded metal mesh, as well as of wire grid, as currently classifiable in the *Tariff Schedules of the United States, Annotated* (TSUSA) under item number 727.7065. We investigated sales of these stacking chairs which were made by three Taiwanese producers and sold to the United States during the period of investigation, August 1, 1983, through July 31, 1984. The firms investigated were Taiwan Lounge Chair Industry Co., Ltd., Taiwan Hsin Yeh Enterprise Co., Ltd., and Lu Kuang Enterprise, Co., Ltd. Sales by the above firms accounted for approximately 63 percent of all stacking chairs sold to the United States during the period of investigation.

33. Final Determination, 50 Fed.Reg. 21917.

FAIR VALUE COMPARISON

To determine whether sales of the subject merchandise in the United States were made at less than fair value, we compared the United States price with the foreign market value. In the case of Taiwan Lounge Chair Industry Co. and Lu Kuang Enterprise Co., we compared United States price based on purchase price with foreign market value based on the constructed value of the imported merchandise. For Taiwan Hsin Yeh Enterprise Co., we compared United States price based on purchase price with foreign market value based on the price to third countries.

UNITED STATES PRICE

For Taiwan Lounge Chair, Taiwan Hsin Yeh and Lu Kuang, we used the purchase price of the subject merchandise to represent the United States price, as provided in section 772(b) of the act, because the merchandise is sold to unrelated purchasers prior to its importation into the United States. We calculated the purchase price on the f.o.b. or c. & f. price to unrelated purchasers in the United States or to unrelated trading companies where the manufacturers knew that the merchandise was destined for the U.S. market when it was sold. We made deductions, where appropriate, for inland freight, ocean freight, brokerage charges, bank charges, export promotion fees and stamp tax. We made additions, where appropriate for import duties which were rebated, or not collected, by reason of the exportation of the merchandise to the United States, pursuant to sections 772(d)(1)(B) of the Act.

FOREIGN MARKET VALUE

In all cases, there were either no sales, or insufficient sales, in the home market to use as a basis for foreign market value. For Taiwan Hsin Yeh, we selected sales for export to a country other than the United States (third countries) as a basis for foreign market value pursuant to section 773(a)(1)(B) of the Act. We used third country sales to Australia because Australia was Taiwan Hsin Yeh's largest market for such or similar merchandise for comparison with U.S. sales. We calculated third country price on the basis of the f.o.b. or c. & f. price to unrelated trading companies for sale to Australia. We made deductions, where appropriate, for inland freight, brokerage charges, export bank charges and stamp tax. Where appropriate, we also made additions for import duties, which were rebated or not collected by reason of the exportation of the merchandise, equal to those amounts added to the United States price. An adjustment was also made, where appropriate, for the differences between commissions on sales to the United States and Australia in accordance with § 353.15(c) of the Commerce Regulations. We adjusted for differences in packing; and we also adjusted for physical differences in the merchandise in accordance with § 353.16 of the Commerce Regulations.

In accordance with section 773 of the Act, we calculated constructed value by adding the costs of materials, fabrication, general expenses, profit and packing. For materials and fabrication, we used the appropriate producer's actual cost figures. In the case of Lu Kuang, the amount added for general expenses was the statutory minimum of 10 percent of the sum of material and fabrication costs as prescribed in section 773(e)(1)(B) of the Act. In the case of Taiwan Lounge Chair since the actual general expenses amounted to more than 10 percent of the total cost for materials and fabrication, we used actual general expenses. The amount added for profit was the statutory minimum of 8 percent of the sum of materials, fabrication costs, and general expenses because these companies had no home market sales of merchandise of the same class or kind, and we were unable to determine how much of the companies' overall profit was related to sales to countries other than the U.S.

In calculating foreign market value, we made currency conversions from Taiwan New Dollars to United States dollars in accordance with § 353.56(a) (1) of our regulations, using certified daily exchange rates as furnished by the Federal Reserve Bank of New York.

CELLULAR MOBILE TELEPHONES AND SUBASSEMBLIES FROM JAPAN

Intl. Trade Admin. (1985) [34]

On November 5, 1984, we received a petition from Motorola, Inc. (Motorola) on behalf of the United States cellular mobile telephone and subassembly industry.

* * *

SCOPE OF INVESTIGATION

The products covered by this investigation are cellular mobile telephones (CMTs), CMT transceivers, CMT control units, and certain subassemblies thereof, which meet the tests set forth below. CMTs are radio-telephone equipment designed to operate in a cellular radio-telephone system, i.e., a system that permits mobile telephones to communicate with traditional land-line telephones via a base station, and that permits multiple simultaneous use of particular radio frequencies through the division of the system into independent cells, each of which has its own transceiving base station.

* * *

SCOPE OF INVESTIGATION ISSUES

We have defined the products covered by this investigation as CMTs, CMT transceivers, CMT control units and major subassemblies dedicated exclusively for use in CMTs. The determination to include subassemblies within the scope of the investigation was based on the need to prevent circumvention of any antidumping order on CMTs through the importation of major CMT subassemblies, and the Department's broader conclusion that the investigation properly should include subassemblies. In this regard, Motorola's petition requested that we include "kits of components and subassemblies" in the investigation.

Two of the companies investigated export CMT subassemblies to the United States to related companies which subsequently perform some form

34. Final Determination, 50 Fed.Reg. 45447.

of further manufacture or assembly before selling the completed CMTs to unrelated parties. If the investigation were limited to completed CMTs alone, none of these importations would be subject to an antidumping order, even if all of the subassemblies were of Japanese origin and were being sold at less than fair value, and the complete CMT was "substantially" of Japanese origin.

A number of the respondents have argued that the Department has no authority to include discrete subassemblies (that is, subassemblies that are imported separately rather than in kits) within the scope of this investigation. The crux of their argument is (1) that discrete CMT subassemblies are not the same "class or kind" of merchandise as complete CMTs or CMT kits, (2) that Motorola's petition only included complete CMTs and CMT kits, defined as sets of CMT subassemblies, and (3) that antidumping investigations may only encompass products that are the same "class or kind of merchandise" as those covered in the petition. We address each of respondents' arguments in turn.

I. The Department takes the position that CMT subassemblies that are "dedicated exclusively for use" in CMTs are the same "class or kind" of merchandise as complete CMTs. This determination is based on a consideration of the following factors: (1) General physical characteristics, (2) the expectations of the ultimate purchasers, (3) the channels of trade in which the product is sold, (4) the manner in which the product is advertised and displayed, and (5) the ultimate use of the merchandise in question. These factors have been recognized and utilized by the Court of International Trade as appropriate criteria in determining whether a new product was within the "class or kind" of merchandise described in a prior antidumping finding, and they are likewise instructive where, as here, the question is the initial formulation of the scope of the order. Since the scope of this investigation only includes those subassemblies that are "dedicated exclusively for use" in complete CMTs, both the ultimate use and the ultimate purchaser of the CMT subassemblies are the same as for the complete CMTs, since by definition, the CMT subassemblies could not be used in any other device. Thus, the second and the fifth criteria outlined above are met.

Similarly, based on the evidence in the record, the Department determines that CMT subassemblies, as defined in this investigation, and complete CMTs move in the same channel of trade. Indeed, this is the very reason the Department feels it necessary to include CMT subassemblies within the scope of this investigation since otherwise any resulting order could easily be circumvented. * * *

Similarly, since there is no separate channel of trade for CMT subassemblies, the only respect in which they are advertised and displayed is in the form of complete CMT units. Thus, the fourth criterion is met.

Finally, with respect to the first criterion, the Department does not think that the fact that CMT subassemblies have, in some respect, different physical characteristics from complete CMTs should be controlling in this instance. The only difference between the two is that complete CMTs are, essentially, assembled CMT subassemblies. * * *

II. The Department's view is that respondents are taking an unduly narrow reading of the petition and that the Department's definition of scope is simply a clarification of what was set forth in the petition. Petitioner's definition of kits referred to collections of "key" components, which we have taken to mean "major" subassemblies. The primary purpose of including subassemblies in this investigation is to prevent evasion of the antidumping law. It would be illogical to make a distinction between those subassemblies that are shipped discretely in separate containers and those that are shipped together in one box. Limitations as to packaging would simply be an invitation to evade the antidumping law through changes in packaging.

III. Whether or not Motorola's petitions explicitly covers discrete subassemblies is not dispositive, since the Department has an inherent power to establish the parameters of the investigation so as to carry out its mandate to administer the law effectively and in accordance with its intent.

* * *

FAIR VALUE COMPARISON

To determine whether sales of the subject merchandise in the United States were made at less than fair value, we compared the United States price with the foreign market value.

As required by section 776(b) of the Act, in making our fair value comparisons we used the best information available in calculating both United States price and foreign market value for Matsushita and NEC and foreign market value for MELCO. We used information in the petition as the best information available for Matsushita because it did not submit a response to our antidumping duty questionnaire.

We also used the best information available for NEC because it did not provide a full and complete response to our antidumping duty questionnaire. While NEC did respond to selected sections of the questionnaire, it did not provide the home market sales data requested by the Department. NEC refused to provide the requested data on the grounds that these data were not relevant because its CMTs sold in the home market were not "such or similar" merchandise to the CMTs it sold in the United States, as defined in section 771(16) of the Act. Thus, NEC argued, the Department must calculate foreign market value based on third country sales as provided for in section 773(a)(1)(B) of the Act.

During the course of this investigation, the Department repeatedly advised NEC that if NEC failed to provide home market sales data and the Department determined that NEC's home market sales were of "such or similar merchandise" the Department would have to use best information available. Based on information presented by NEC and an analysis of the data submitted by a technical consultant retained by the Department, we have determined that the CMT sold by NEC in the home market is such or similar merchandise within the meaning of section 771(16) of the Act. As a result, the Department calculated both United States price and foreign market value for NEC using information in the petition as the best information available.

* * *

UNITED STATES PRICE

As provided in section 772 of the Act, we used both the purchase price and exporter's sales price of the subject merchandise to represent the United States price for sales by the Japanese producers.

Purchase price was used for Toshiba, Hitachi and MELCO since the merchandise was sold to unrelated purchasers prior to its importation into the United States or sold to a purchaser outside the United States when it was known at the time of sale that the merchandise was destined for the United States. We calculated the purchase price based on either the f.o.b. or c.i.f., duty paid, packed price to unrelated purchasers for sale in the United States. We made deductions, where appropriate, for foreign inland freight and handling charges, air or ocean freight, marine insurance, U.S. customs duties, and U.S. inland freight and brokerage.

For OKI, we used exporter's sales price (ESP) to represent the United States price because the merchandise was sold to unrelated purchasers after importation into the United States. For these sales, we made deductions, where appropriate, for foreign inland freight and handling charges, air or ocean freight, U.S. customs duties, U.S. inland freight and brokerage, indirect selling expenses incurred in the United States and other direct selling expenses incurred in the United States such as credit, advertising reserve, warranties and post-sale warehousing. In calculating the ESP for OKI, we also deducted the value added to the imported units through further manufacture prior to sale in the United States.

FOREIGN MARKET VALUE

In accordance with section 773(e) of the Act, we calculated foreign market value based on constructed value for OKI, Hitachi and Toshiba as there were not sufficient home market or third country sales of such or similar merchandise for the purpose of comparison. In determining constructed value, we calculated the cost of materials, fabrication, general expenses, profit, and the cost of packing. The specific methodology used to calculate constructed value for each company is listed below:

1. *OKI Constructed Value.* For OKI, the cost of manufacturing was based on weighted-average costs for the months of April through November, 1984. These costs were based on standard costs adjusted to actual costs by the variances reflected in OKI's accounting system. The Department did not use special adjustments to the cost of manufacturing claimed by OKI because the adjustments were either theoretically inappropriate or not quantified and adequately verified. * * * Product-specified R&D expenses, which are necessary expenses incurred in manufacturing, were included as part of the "fabrication" expenses and were amortized over the market-life of the product. For the cellular R&D expenses, the Department used six years based on the foreseeable usefulness of the cellular technology and the estimated life of two generations of the product.

For the general expenses, the Department used the general administrative expenses and the general R&D as provided by OKI and verified by the Department. The interest expense was based on the approximated percentage of interest expense to "cost of goods" of the consolidated corporation.

The interest expense and interest income reflected on the financial statements were adjusted to include only those items which directly or indirectly benefited the production of CMTs. Direct and indirect selling expenses and profit [were] based on verified expense and profit data reported by OKI for the same class or kind of merchandise. As the profit reported by OKI exceeded 8 percent of material, fabrication and general expenses, the Department used the actual profit experience of OKI.

2. *Hitachi Constructed Value.* For Hitachi, the cost of manufacturing was based on the weighted-average costs for the months of April through November, 1984. These costs were based on the actual costs for production completed during this period. The Department adjusted the transfer value of certain parts used in the manufacture of CMTs when it appeared such values did not fairly reflect the usual value for such "sales." The Department did not consider Hitachi's product-specific R&D to be adequately verified. Therefore, we used the corporate average R&D and deducted an amount claimed by Hitachi to be general R&D.

For the general expenses, the Department used a proportional amount of general and administrative expenses of Hitachi Denshi, the subsidiary which manufactures the CMT, and Hitachi, Ltd., the parent corporation. Hitachi, Ltd. performs R&D and other general and administrative functions for Hitachi Denshi.

The Department included interest expense based on the percentage of interest expense to the cost of goods of the consolidated corporation. The direct and indirect selling expenses and profit were based on verified expense and profit data reported by Hitachi for the same class or kind of merchandise. As the profit reported by Hitachi exceeded 8 percent of materials, fabrication and general expense, the Department used the actual profit experience of Hitachi.

3. *Toshiba Constructed Value.* For Toshiba the cost of manufacturing was based on the weighted-average of the actual costs of the production during the months of April through November, 1984. The Department adjusted the transfer value of certain parts when it appeared such values did not fairly reflect the usual value for such "sales".

The Department used the anticipated market-life for the product under investigation to amortize the start-up expense and product specific R&D, which was determined to be three years.

For general expenses, the general and administrative expenses, including general R&D expenses, which were provided by the company and verified by the Department were used. The Department did not accept Toshiba's claim for "negative financing" and used the percentage of interest expense to cost of goods of the consolidated corporation. The direct and indirect selling expenses and profit were based on verified expense and profit data reported by Toshiba for the same class or kind of merchandise. Since the profit reported by Toshiba did not exceed 8 percent of materials, fabrication and general expenses, the Department used the statutory minimum of 8 percent.

Adjustments. We made adjustments under § 353.15 of the Commerce Regulations for differences in circumstances of sale between the two markets. For Hitachi these adjustments were for differences in credit and warranty expenses. For OKI these adjustments were for differences in credit, warranty and advertising expenses. In the case of Toshiba adjustments were made for differences in credit expenses, advertising and warranty expenses.

Since OKI's United States price was based on exporter's sales price, adjustments were made to foreign market value for OKI under § 353.15(c) to account for indirect selling expenses incurred in the home market sales of the "same class or kind of merchandise," up to the amount of indirect selling expenses incurred by OKI on its United States sales. OKI, however, was unable to demonstrate that the home market expenses which it claimed to be direct selling expenses were in actuality direct selling expenses or that they were directly related to home market sales of the same general class or kind of merchandise. Therefore, we have treated those expenses, as well as those identified as indirect selling expenses, as indirect.

*   *   *

Suspension of Liquidation. In accordance with section 733(d)(2) of the Act, we are directing the United States Customs Service to continue to suspend liquidation of the products covered by this investigation from Japan, with the exception of Toshiba, which are entered or withdrawn from warehouse, for consumption, on or after June 11, 1985. The Customs Service shall require a cash deposit or bond in an amount equal to the weighted-average amount by which the foreign market value of the merchandise subject to this investigation exceeds the United States price as shown in the table below. *   *   * This suspension of liquidation will remain in effect until further notice. The margins are as follows:

Manufacturers/sellers/exporters	Weighted-average margin percentage
OKI	9.72
Hitachi	2.99
Toshiba	[1] 0.00
MELCO	87.83
NEC	95.57
Matsushita	106.60
All other manufacturers/producers/exporters	57.81

[1] Excluded.

Notes and Questions

(1) The method of calculating a dumping margin is somewhat unusual and raises serious fairness questions in the minds of some. Take the following example: In the home market, seven sales are shown to occur, one each at a

price of 20, 21, 22, 23, 24, 25, 26. Seven imports into the United States are also made, one at each of those prices. Obviously the average in both cases is 23. But this does not mean that dumping has not occurred. The foreign market value is an average, i.e. 23. But *each* shipment to the U.S. may be compared (after a dumping order issues) to that average, so three of the imports (those made at 20, 21 and 22) are below the average and will be assessed a duty equal to the difference (3, 2 and 1, respectively). Furthermore, as we will see in the next subsection, if it can be shown that the cost of production in the home market is 22, the sales at 20 and 21 will be omitted in calculating the home market average. Thus the home market average will become 24, and even more shipments to the United States will be assessed duties.

(2) How is the problem of sales to related parties handled in calculation of the U.S. price? In calculation of the foreign market value? See Sections 772(c)–(e); Sections 773(e)(2)–(3); 19 CFR § 353.22 (1985). The exporter's sales price is typically used when the foreign manufacturer sells the goods to a related company, such as a distribution subsidiary, that imports the products into the United States and then resells them.

(3) There are subtle distinctions drawn between the goods considered in establishing the U.S. price, the foreign market value and injury. The basic function of the ITA is to determine whether "a class or kind of foreign merchandise" is being sold in the United States at less than its fair value. To do so, it calculates the foreign market value of "such or similar merchandise," a phrase defined in Section 771(16). The ITC determines whether there has been injury to U.S. "industry," a term defined in Section 771(4) to mean the U.S. producers of a "like product," which is itself defined in Section 771(10). The *CMT* case suggests some of the definitional issues that may arise under these concepts. By narrowly defining the class of goods investigated, the likelihood of dumping and injury findings may be increased, but the opportunities for circumvention of a dumping order may be greater.[35]

(4) In respect of adjustments, the basic rules are laid out in Sections 772(d)–(e) and 773(a). The ITA has adopted the following regulations to implement them: [36]

§ 353.14 Differences in quantities

(a) *In general.* In comparing the United States price with such applicable criteria as sales or offers, on which a determination of foreign market value is to be based, comparisons normally will be made on sales of comparable quantities of the merchandise under consideration. Further, reasonable allowances will be made for differences in quantities, to the extent that it is established to the satisfaction of the Secretary that the amount of any price differential is wholly or partly due to such differences in the quantities sold. In determining allowances for differences in quantity, consideration will be given, among other things, to the practice of the industry in the country of exportation with respect to affording in the home market (or third country markets, where sales to third countries are the

---

35. See generally Langer, The Concepts of Like Product and Domestic Industry Under the United States Trade Agreements Act of 1979, 17 Geo.Wash.J.Intl.L. & Econ. 495 (1983).

36. 19 CFR §§ 353.14, 353.15, 353.16 (1985).

basis for comparison) discounts for quantity sales which are available to those who purchase in the ordinary course of trade.

(b) *Criteria for allowances.*   Allowances for price discounts based on quantitative differences in sales ordinarily will not be made unless:

(1) *Six month rule.*   The exporter during the period covered by the antidumping investigation as established under § 353.38 (or during such other period as investigation shows is more representative) had been granting quantity discounts of at least the same magnitude with respect to 20 percent or more of such or similar merchandise sold in the home market (or in third country markets when sales to third countries are the basis for comparison) in the ordinary course of trade; or

(2) *Cost justification.*   The exporter can demonstrate that the discounts are warranted on the basis of savings which are specifically attributable to the production of the different quantities involved.

*   *   *

§ 353.15   Differences in circumstances of sale

(a) *In general.*   In comparing the United States price with the sales, or other criteria applicable, on which a determination of foreign market value is to be based, reasonable allowances will be made for bona fide differences in the circumstances of the sales compared to the extent that it is established to the satisfaction of the Secretary that the amount of any price differential is wholly or partly due to such differences.   Differences in circumstances of sale for which such allowances will be made are limited, in general, to those circumstances which bear a direct relationship to the sales which are under consideration.

(b) *Examples.*   Examples of differences in circumstances of sale for which reasonable allowances generally will be made are those involving differences in credit terms, guarantees, warranties, technical assistance, servicing, and assumption by a seller of a purchaser's advertising or other selling costs.   Reasonable allowances also generally will be made for differences in commissions.   Allowances generally will not be made for differences in advertising and other selling costs of a seller, unless such costs are attributable to a later sale of the merchandise by a purchaser.

*   *   *

§ 353.16   Differences in physical characteristics

In comparing the United States price with the selling price in the home market, or for exportation to countries other than the United States in the case of similar merchandise, due allowance shall be made for differences in the physical characteristics of the merchandise in the markets being compared.   In this regard, the Secretary will be guided primarily by the differences in cost of production, to the extent that it is established to his satisfaction that the amount of any price differential is wholly or partly due to such differences, but, when appropriate, the effect of such differences upon the market value of the merchandise may also be considered.

*   *   *

In a recent case, the ITA commented upon various respondents' requests for adjustments as follows: [37]

Comment 3: Respondent contends that their claim for an allowance for warranty expenses should be allowed because it relates to the kind of merchandise under investigation.

DOC Position: The Department disagrees. The requirement for allowance of such sales expenses is that they be directly related to sales under investigation, not simply to the kind of merchandise under investigation. Recognizing that claims under warranty are often, by their nature, delayed, and thus not captured during the period of investigation, the Department has in the past allowed an average warranty cost based on historical experience. However, in the instant case respondent did not compute, or present evidence to compute, such an average. Therefore, these warranty costs were not allowed.

* * *

Comment 2: Respondent claims that Japanese yen amounts realized by virtue of currency rate fluctuations should be disregarded in deference to the Japanese yen invoiced amount.

DOC Position: The Department disagrees. The transactions in question were denominated in Japanese yen. These contracts mentioned no equivalent dollar amount, nor any agreed upon exchange rate on which a dollar equivalent might be based. The dollar amount remitted by the customer was apparently at the customer's discretion and unquestioned by the manufacturers. As the transaction was yen denominated, the Department considers yen receipts to represent the price of the merchandise.

Comment 3: Respondent claims an allowance for a salesman's visits to customers should be allowed as a circumstance of sale adjustment.

DOC Position: The Department disagrees. Such a circumstance of sale adjustment must be directly related to the sales under investigation to be allowed. The visits in question could not be demonstrated to be related to those sales during the period of investigation, and these expenses were not allowed.

Asahi Comments

Comment 1: Respondent claims advertising costs should be allowed.

DOC Position: The Department agrees in part. Such advertising costs were found to be directly related to the product under investigation and directed to its ultimate consumers. These expenses were allowed with the exception of sample sheets provided free of charge to Asahi's own customers. The Department considers such free trial samples a normal cost of doing business and not a cost directly related to the sales under investigation.

(5) Suppose a French exporter establishes list prices annually and adheres strictly to them. When the prices are set on January 1, the ex-factory price to French customers is 50FF/kg. For U.S. customers, it is a CIF price of $6/kg, where $1/kg represents the cost of shipping and insurance. On January 1, the FF:US$ exchange rate is 10:1. Is the U.S. price a dumping price? On February

37. Fabric Expanded Neoprene Laminate from Japan: Final Determination, 50 Fed.Reg. 23488, 7 ITRD 2045 (ITA 1985).

1, the rate is 9:1. Is the U.S. price a dumping price? For six months, the rate remains at 9:1. Is there dumping? On September 1, the rate falls to 10:1, but shipping costs have increased $0.25/kg. Is the U.S. price a dumping price? Should it be? Consider the following ITA regulation: [38]

> (b) *Special rules for fair value investigations.* For purposes of fair value investigations, manufacturers, exporters, and importers concerned will be expected to act within a reasonable period of time to take into account price differences resulting from sustained changes in prevailing exchange rates. Where prices under consideration are affected by temporary exchange rate fluctuations, no differences between the prices being compared resulting solely from such exchange rate fluctuations will be taken into account in fair value investigations.

See Melamine Chemicals, Inc. v. United States, 732 F.2d 924 (Fed.Cir.1984) (upholding ITA regulation).

(6) Suppose you are a foreign exporter bent on dumping. You decide the best approach is to dump a massive amount of goods into the United States within a short time period and then stop for several months. If an investigation is opened, there will be no imports on which duties can be applied. If one is not opened for a year, you plan to do the same thing again. Are you safe from duties? Consider Section 733(e).[39]

(7) In light of the results of the *CMT* case, would you as an attorney advise your client to cooperate with an investigation? What are the risks of noncooperation?

(b) Sales at a Loss

In Article 2(4), the GATT Antidumping Code provides that when there are no domestic sales "in the ordinary course of trade" or "because of a particular market situation, such sales do not permit a proper comparison," constructed values may be used. U.S. law (Section 773(b)) provides that "sales made at less than cost of production * * * over an extended period of time and in substantial quantities, and * * * not at prices which would permit recovery of all costs within a reasonable period of time in the normal course of trade" may be disregarded in determining foreign market value. What is a reasonable period of time? A persuasive argument could be made that it should be the length of the business cycle (if that could be determined with sufficient certainty) since, as noted in the introduction to this section, economists would expect a profit-maximizing firm to produce at a loss, at least in the short run, if it was recovering its marginal, as opposed to average, costs. In any event the statute does not say and U.S. authorities tend to use a one-year period, which means they frequently disregard sales in reliance on this provision.

Could end-of-season sales be disregarded under this provision? What about sales of electronic products that had incurred such massive development costs that those costs will be recovered only after a year or two of substantial sales volume? How would you treat sales of perishable products? Consider the following case:

38. 19 CFR § 353.56 (1985).   **39.** 19 U.S.C.A. § 1673b(e).

SOUTHWEST FLORIDA WINTER VEGETABLE GROWERS ASSN. v. UNITED STATES

Court of International Trade, 1984, 584 F.Supp. 10.

CARMAN, JUDGE:

This matter is before me on plaintiffs' motion for review of administrative determinations upon an agency record filed pursuant to Rule 56.1 of the Rules of this court, challenging the Final Determination of Sales at Not Less Than Fair Value by the Department of Commerce (Commerce) in the antidumping investigation concerning certain fresh winter vegetables from Mexico, 45 Fed.Reg. 20,512 (March 28, 1980).

* * *

Plaintiffs argue the determination by Commerce that the subject merchandise was not being, and was not likely to be, sold in the United States at less than fair value is unsupported by substantial evidence in the record and is not in accordance with the law. Plaintiffs' contentions in essence are: (1) Commerce erred in using the third country sales methodology rather than the constructed value methodology in determining foreign market value because a substantial number of third country sales at below cost existed making the valuation inaccurate; [and] (2) Commerce improperly refused to disregard a substantial amount of below cost sales in contravention of 19 U.S.C. § 1677b(b).

* * *

I. METHODOLOGY EMPLOYED

To determine whether sales at less than fair value occurred, Commerce had to calculate the "fair value" of the subject merchandise pursuant to the procedures specified for determining foreign market value. See 19 U.S.C. § 1677b (1982). Three methods are available for this calculation: (1) the sales price of the merchandise in the country of export (home market sales), id. § 1677b(a)(1)(A); (2) the sales price of the merchandise in a country other than the United States (third country sales), id. § 1677b(a)(1)(B); or, (3) the "constructed value" of the merchandise (sum of costs for material, fabrication, general expenses and profit), id. § 1677b(a)(2).

Before 1979, the third country sales methodology instead of constructed value methodology was required by statute where the home market sales methodology was not available. Although the mandatory preference for third country sales is no longer required, the legislative history and relevant regulations indicate, nevertheless, a preference for third country sales where there is adequate confirmation subject to timely verification. The criteria employed in selecting the third country sales methodology are in order of significance: similarity of product, volume of sales, and similarity of market from an organizational and development point of view. 19 C.F.R. § 353.5(c).

* * *

In this case, the home market sales methodology was not employed because an insufficient domestic Mexican market existed for fresh winter vegetables. Commerce utilized the third country (Canada) sales method of comparison instead of the constructed value method noting the general preference for third country sales and its greater accuracy in the case at hand. Furthermore, as noted by Commerce, use of constructed value would be wholly unsuitable to the economic realities presented in this case. A principal characteristic of the fresh winter vegetable market is wide price fluctuations, both within a day and over the season. As the Commerce determination reflects, it is a necessary practice for many individual sales to be below the average cost of production. Profitability depends on sales over the course of a season. The use of a price arrived at by constructed value would necessarily give the appearance of dumping even though sellers would be acting in a normal, indeed in a necessary, manner in light of industry demands. Thus, the constructed value methodology is inappropriate because it would require finding that an economically necessary business practice is unfair. As the Senate Report noted: "[T]hird country prices will normally be preferred over constructed value if presented in a timely manner and if adequate to establish foreign market value."

Plaintiffs argue that third country price data in this case is inadequate for the fair value comparison because of the presence of price volatility and the existence of a significant number of sales below the cost of production. This court cannot agree.

First, the proportion of Canadian sales to United States sales (i.e., Canadian sales are approximately 20 percent of United States sales) affords an adequate basis for comparison in using third country sales and is within established administrative guidelines. Second, plaintiffs conceded in their administrative petition that the two markets are almost identical. And third, the record reflects substantial evidence to support the conclusion of price equality.

Furthermore, plaintiffs' contention that constructed value should have been utilized because (1) some growers had too few or no Canadian sales; (2) on some days, growers had sales to the United States, but none to Canada; and, (3) some growers had insufficient above-cost sales to Canada, is without merit. There is no support for the proposition that Commerce was required to utilize constructed value for those transactions that could not be matched with United States transactions for the same grower's product, size and day.

Based on the general preference for the use of third country sales over constructed value, and the existence of adequate data for third country sales, this court cannot find Commerce erred in its use of this methodology.

II. TREATMENT OF BELOW COST SALES

In the case at hand, Commerce concluded that "it would be appropriate to disregard below-cost Canadian sales only if such sales constituted 50 percent or more of a grower's total sales to Canada of the type of produce under consideration." Plaintiffs argue this 50 percent benchmark resulted in the erroneous consideration of a significant number of below cost sales in the determination by Commerce of foreign market value. Neither the statute nor its legislative history, however, supports this contention by plaintiffs.

* * * Commerce is required to disregard below cost sales only when they have been made in substantial quantities over an extended period of time, and are not at prices that permit recovery of all costs within a reasonable period of time in the normal course of trade. As legislative history reflects, "[s]tandards would not require the disregarding of below-cost sales in every instance, for under normal business in both foreign countries and the United States, it is frequently necessary to sell obsolete or end-of-model year merchandise at less than cost. * * * [I]nfrequent sales at less than cost, or sales prices which will permit recovery of all costs based upon anticipated sales volume over a reasonable period of time would not be disregarded."

Commerce found that the fresh winter vegetable markets, in contrast to markets for industrial products or agricultural products with a relatively longer shelf life, normally experience below cost sales, and such sales are common and expected.

Commerce determined that Mexican producers do not have the ability to control their short term output and cannot store their products. They look to make profits over the season as a whole, and do not expect to recover full costs on individual sales. The record reflects that it is not uncommon for some sales by foreign and domestic producers of fresh winter vegetables to be as much as 50 percent below the cost of production.

In short, the statute permits the consideration of below cost sales made in the normal course of trade at prices that permit full cost recovery within a reasonable period of time, and there is substantial evidence in the administrative record to support Commerce's determination that below cost sales in this case up to 50 percent were made in the normal course of trade and at prices that permit full cost recovery within a reasonable period of time. Commerce, therefore, properly regarded the below cost sales in its determination of foreign market value.

Note

(1) The principal case is the subject of a good economic analysis in Note, Applying Antidumping Law to Perishable Agricultural Goods, 80 Mich.L.Rev. 524 (1982).

(2) If manufacturer A makes widgets from scratch and sells them at a loss in the United States, it is dumping. What if manufacturers B and C make widget components and sell them at a loss to D, who assembles them into widgets and sells them in the United States at a small profit? Is D dumping? Is there any real difference in the two cases? The second situation is called downstream dumping, and it is generally agreed it is not covered by existing law, although there have been proposals to change the law to cover it explicitly, one of which was adopted in the House (but not in the final) version of the 1984 Trade and Tariff Act.[40]

40. See House Conference Rep. No. 98–1156, 98th Cong., 2d Sess. 171–72 (1984).

(c) Nonmarket Economies [41]

UNREFINED MONTAN WAX FROM EAST GERMANY

Intl.Trade Admin. (1981) [42]

We have decided that the economy of the GDR [East Germany] is state controlled to the extent that we are unable to determine the foreign market value of unrefined montan wax by normal standards. As a result, we are required by section 773(c) of the Act to use the prices, or the constructed value, of such or similar merchandise in a non-state-controlled country or countries. Our regulations establish a clear preference for a foreign market value based upon sales prices and stipulate that, to the extent possible, sales prices or constructed value should be determined on the basis of prices or costs in a non-state-controlled-economy country at a stage of economic development comparable to the state-controlled-economy country.

An important difficulty in this case is the limited worldwide production of unrefined montan wax. The wax is produced in the FRG [West Germany], but is used for further processing. We were not able to obtain a price or constructed value for wax produced in the FRG.

We then attempted to find other products produced in non-state-controlled economy countries in order to determine if a "such or similar" product existed which could be used to establish the fair value of montan wax from the GDR. We received information on a variety of products both natural and synthetic but we determined that none could be considered such or similar within the meaning of the antidumping law. The natural vegetable waxes were ruled out as commercial substitutes because of the instability of the market for them. The various synthetic products either had not been sold during the period under investigation, had not been used by carbon paper or ink manufacturers, were derived from montan wax imported from the GDR, or had very limited use in the carbon paper industry.

Since there is no commercial production of unrefined montan wax in a non-state-controlled-economy country (other than the United States) and no such or similar merchandise, we constructed a value based on specific components or factors of production in the GDR, valued on the basis of prices in a non-state-controlled-economy country "reasonably comparable" in economic development to the GDR. Counsel for the importer maintains that for purposes of valuing GDR production factors we should use United Kingdom ("U.K."), Canadian, or a combination of U.K. and Canadian prices.

However, we have concluded that to construct a value for montan wax based on a non-state-controlled-economy valuation of the GDR factors of production, we should select values in the Federal Republic of Germany—not the U.K. and/or Canada. Essentially, we found that, of the industrialized countries, the FRG is more comparable to the GDR for purposes of this case than is the U.K. or Canada.

---

41. See generally U.S. General Accounting Office, U.S. Laws and Regulations Applicable to Imports from Nonmarket Economies Could Be Improved (No. ID–81–35, 1981); Horlick & Shuman, Nonmarket Economy Trade and U.S. Antidumping/Countervailing Duty Laws, 18 Intl.Lawyer 807 (1984).

42. Final Determination, 46 Fed.Reg. 38555, 3 ITRD 1056.

Counsel for the importer contends that if the FRG is chosen as a surrogate then the surrogate values should be adjusted to reflect differences between the GDR and the FRG in per capita GNP and wages in the manufacturing sector. We feel, however, that once a reasonably comparable surrogate is chosen, then no adjustments are to be made under section 353.8(c) of the Commerce Regulations.

Both the exporter and counsel for the importer contend that montan wax is a by-product of the production of energy in the form of mined lignite, fuel briquettes, and electricity. As such they would value only those factors that relate to the extraction of the wax directly. They do not believe that any of the pre-extraction costs, such as crushing and drying the lignite, should be allocated to the wax. They cite as arguments the fact that the wax is extracted at a facility which is under the direction of the Coal and Energy Ministry; therefore, the main purpose of the facility is to produce energy. They also argue that the wax represents less than one percent of the total volume, by weight of total production of the Roblingen facility.

We do not feel that these arguments are convincing. Even though the complex, under the direction of the Coal and Energy Ministry, produces energy and related items, a significant investment has been made in a sizable plant to extract and market montan wax. The extraction of montan wax is not essential to the production of energy from lignite. Montan wax has a very high value in relation to the products and the sales are an important part of the economic activity of the facility, a much greater share than the weight of the wax alone would indicate. In addition, great care is taken to segregate the waxy lignite from regular lignite during all phases of mining and processing. For these reasons, we feel that part of the common processing costs in the facility should be allocated to montan wax. Therefore, we have allocated a portion of the costs of transporting lignite from the mine to the plant, as well as a portion of the crushing and drying costs. Because of the differences in value of the resulting products that share these processes, lignite briquettes, montan wax, and electricity, and because the resulting products are not measured in the same units (tons and kilowatt hours) we have allocated the processing costs on the basis of the ratio of the weighted value of the various products. This was done on the basis of the product split of only the high wax lignite that flows through the wax extraction process.

Notes and Questions

(1) Would you cooperate with a U.S. antidumping investigation by supplying price and cost information if you were a producer in a proposed surrogate country? What advantages might result for you? What disadvantages? For example, would you risk an antidumping proceeding if data you provided showed LTFV sales? For whatever reasons, it is not always possible to obtain cooperation. In 1983, the ITA reported the following problem: [43]

43. Shop Towels of Cotton from China: Final Determination, 48 Fed.Reg. 37055, 5 ITRD 1751 (ITA 1983).

The respondent argues that "foreign market value should be based on Pakistani sales to the United States."

DOC Position

Information gathered by the American Consulate in Karachi, Pakistan, from the Towel Manufacturers Association of Pakistan indicates that there may be significant sales of shop towels for consumption in the home market of Pakistan. The Act and Regulations establish an order of preference according to which we must examine a surrogate country producer's home market sales before examining their sales to other countries, including the United States. However, the Government of Pakistan did not grant the Department permission to contact Pakistani shop towel producers. It is the Department's policy not to make such contacts without government permission. The refusal of the Government of Pakistan to grant us permission to contact Pakistani shop towel producers precludes us from examining home market sales in Pakistan. Because of the statutory and regulatory preference for home market as opposed to export sales, in the absence of information concerning home market sales of shop towels in Pakistan, it is inappropriate to use Pakistani sales of shop towels to the United States as the basis for foreign market value in this investigation.

(2) The U.S. regulations specify that the surrogate country is to be at about the same level of development. Nonetheless, is there any real reason to believe that prices and costs in the surrogate country accurately reflect what prices and costs would have been in a nonmarket economy if it were a market economy?

(3) Given the importance of the choice of the surrogate country—it essentially determines whether dumping will be found—should there be more precise standards?

(4) Should a similar "surrogate" approach be used for countervailing duty cases involving products imported to the U.S. from a nonmarket economy? Is it likely to be workable?

(5) What alternative approaches could you design for the policy dilemma of trade between market and nonmarket economies? On the one hand, it is desirable to benefit from the comparative advantage principles of trade through trade with yet another competitor (and desirable for many political reasons to include nonmarket economies in the trading world). On the other hand, the traditional rules of GATT and its related agreements don't work well (to say the least). Would it simply be better to assess imports from a nonmarket economy equal to the difference in price of those goods and some "benchmark", such as the minimum price of similar goods from market economies, or the average domestic price in the United States? The benchmark level would obviously be critical. Could one be set that would balance the policy objectives mentioned above? [44]

(6) How should the recent economic reforms in some Communist countries be handled? In the case of Hungary, the ITA concluded in 1981: [45]

In the petition, Rockwell International alleged that Hungary's economy was state controlled to the extent that sales of merchandise from that

44. See, e.g., S. 1351, 98th Cong., 1st Sess. (1983) (proposed by Senator Heinz).

45. Truck Trailer Axle and Brake Assemblies from Hungary: Final Determination, 46 Fed.Reg. 46152, 3 ITRD 1676 (1981).

country did not permit a determination of foreign market value as prescribed by the Act. The Commerce Department, after a thorough review of the Hungarian economy by the Import Administration staff, and careful consideration of the briefs and materials submitted by the parties, concludes that Hungary is state controlled for purposes of this investigation. Some of the factors involved in determining the state-control issue are as follows:

1. The Hungarian government controls the wage increase levels through a marginal tax rate (50 to 100%) applied to increases greater than the acceptable level. Although new reforms have been introduced in 1980, it would be premature to assess their impact on the period of investigation or the products under investigation.

2. An enterprise's primary source of capital financing is internally generated funds. These funds are controlled by the state (via taxes) for purpose of controlling investment. For additional capital, the sources are the state-owned bank, state grants and state loans, all of which are given under state-controlled terms. Thus external financing (necessary for large investments) is controlled by the state.

3. State agencies control international transactions with "hard currency" countries through a system of import licenses and currency exchange. The Hungarian currency, the forint, is not convertible and is traded officially under a dual exchange rate.

4. Through branch ministries the Hungarian Ministry of Finance has the power to appoint high-level enterprise management, determine management bonuses, develop sectoral plans and control capital investment.

5. It was argued that the 1978 reforms in effect created free-market type economic conditions within the Hungarian economy. To date, virtually all sources agree that there is considerable uncertainty as to the extent that the 1978 reforms are being instituted and enforced.

The structure of the Hungarian economy is undergoing major internal reforms. These reforms, if adopted as expected, may change the Hungarian economy sufficiently to establish "free market" characterization in future cases.

We cannot state categorically that certain factors we have relied on in this case will have the same relevance in any other investigation. Therefore, our determination of state control in no way means that in any future investigation we will necessarily treat Hungary as a state-controlled economy.

(3) Injury Determinations

To impose antidumping duties, it is necessary that the International Trade Commission (ITC) find that imports of merchandise sold at less than fair value have materially injured, or threatened to materially injure, U.S. industry producing the like product or are materially retarding the establishment of such a U.S. industry. As has been noted, prior to 1979 the U.S. statute only required a finding of "injury", without the word "material". One interesting question is whether the statutory change has resulted in any real difference in results. Unfortunately, we can't really answer that question definitively. The United States has argued that even when the word "material" was not in its statute, in cases where duties were assessed, it could always be shown that "material injury" existed. In this subsection, we will consider first the congressional view of the changes made in 1979 and then examine the three key issues that the ITC faces in each investigation: Definition of the domestic industry, evaluation of injury and causation.

SENATE REPORT NO. 96–249
96th Cong., 1st Sess. 87, 74–75 (1979)

* * * Section 771(7) defines the term "material injury," as used in Title VII of the Tariff Act of 1930, as harm which is not inconsequential, immaterial, or unimportant. The term is used in the bill in the context of the ITC determination, in both countervailing duty and antidumping duty investigations, as to whether an industry in the United States is materially injured or threatened with material injury, or the establishment of an industry in the United States is materially retarded, by reason of the less-than-fair-value or subsidized imports. This material injury criterion, which must be satisfied for countervailing or antidumping duties to be applied under Title VII and, with respect to certain duty-free imports, under section 303 of the Tariff Act, is consistent with the analogous criterion of the Agreement Relating to Subsidies and Countervailing Measures and the Agreement Relating to Antidumping Measures, approved in section 2(a) of the bill.

Under the Antidumping Act, 1921, and with respect to duty-free imports under section 303 of the Tariff Act of 1930 (to the extent that the international obligations of the United States require a determination of injury), the ITC now determines whether an industry in the United States is being or is likely to be injured, or is prevented from being established, by reason of the less-than-fair-value or subsidized imports. The ITC determinations with respect to the injury criterion under existing law which have been made in antidumping investigations from January 3, 1975 to July 2, 1979, have been, on the whole, consistent with the material injury criterion of this bill and the Agreements. The material injury criterion of this bill should be interpreted in this manner. This statement does not indicate approval of each affirmative or negative decision of the Commission with respect to the injury criterion, because judgments as to whether the facts in a particular case actually support a finding of injury are for the Commission to determine, subject to judicial review for substantial evidence on the record.

* * *

Section 735(b) contains the same causation term as is in current law, i.e., an industry must be materially injured "by reason of" less-than-fair-value imports. The current practice by the ITC with respect to causation will continue under section 735.

In determining whether injury is "by reason of" less-than-fair-value imports, the ITC now looks at the effects of such imports on the domestic industry. The ITC investigates the conditions of trade and competition and the general condition and structure of the relevant industry. It also considers, among other factors, the quantity, nature, and rate of importation of the imports subject to the investigation, and how the effects of the margin of dumping relate to the injury, if any, to the domestic industry. Current ITC practice with respect to which imports will be considered in determining the impact on the U.S. industry is continued under the bill.

Current law does not, nor will section 735, contemplate that the effects from less-than-fair-value imports be weighed against the effects associated with other factors (e.g., the volume and prices of imports sold at fair value, contraction in demand or changes in patterns of consumption, trade, restrictive practices of and competition between the foreign and domestic producers, developments in technology, and the export performance and productivity of the domestic industry) which may be contributing to overall injury to an industry. Nor is the issue whether less-than-fair-value imports are the principal, a substantial, or a significant cause of material injury. Any such requirement has the undesirable result of making relief more difficult to obtain for industries facing difficulties from a variety of sources; industries that are often the most vulnerable to less-than-fair-value imports.

Of course, in examining the overall injury to a domestic industry, the ITC will consider information which indicates that harm is caused by factors other than the less-than-fair-value imports. However, the petitioner will not be required to bear the burden of proving the negative. That is, that material injury is not caused by such other factors. Nor will the Commission be required to make any precise, mathematical calculations as to the harm associated with such factors and the harm attributable to less-than-fair-value imports.

While injury caused by unfair competition, such as less-than-fair-value imports, does not require as strong a causation link to imports as would be required in determining the existence of injury under fair trade import relief laws, the Commission must satisfy itself that, in light of all the information presented, there is a sufficient causal link between the less-than-fair-value imports and the requisite injury. The determination of the ITC with respect to causation is, under current law, and will be, under section 735, complex and difficult, and is a matter for the judgment of the ITC.

(a) Defining Domestic Industry

Just as in escape clause cases (see previous chapter), and in countervailing duty cases (Section 10.3 infra), to assess the question of whether injury has occurred to a domestic industry, it is necessary to define "industry." Again, this is influenced by the "like product" concept defining imports, and also is subject to some interpretive leeway. The following excerpts illustrate the ITC approach:

HIGH CAPACITY PAGERS FROM JAPAN

U.S. Intl. Trade Commn. (1983)[46]

VIEWS OF CHAIRMAN ECKES AND COMMISSIONER HAGGART

* * *

Imported and domestically produced pagers are manufactured in a variety of models. The threshold issue in this investigation is whether all

46. Inv. No. 731–TA–102 (Final) (Pub. No. 1410), 5 ITRD 1721. See Langer, note 35 supra.

high capacity pagers should be considered "like products." A significant difference between pager models is the availability of a liquid crystal display which provides a combination of tone alert and a numerical readout on the display. Based upon a careful analysis of the characteristics and uses of tone-only and display pagers, we conclude that there are distinct differences in both the characteristics and uses of these respective pagers. The differences between these two types of pagers diminish the degree of substitutionality and competition between tone-only and display pagers in the subscriber market. Therefore, we conclude that tone-only and display pagers are not like products.

* * *

In addition to these differing characteristics and uses, the pricing structure of both the RCC [Radio Common Carrier] and subscriber markets indicates that tone-only and display pagers compete only to a limited extent. There are substantial price differences between these two products. RCCs generally pay a higher unit price for display pagers as compared with tone-only pagers. In addition, the subscriber pays a much higher price for the display pager and the paging service on a display pager. Because RCCs and subscribers perceive a substantial difference between the two products, they are willing to pay a premium for display pagers. Thus, the pricing structure in this market indicates that both RCCs and their subscribers recognize that tone-only and display pagers are distinct products with different characteristics which are used to satisfy different needs.

In addition to the foregoing, the domestic industry has been able to provide the Commission with separate data on tone-only and display pagers in terms of production and profitability. This data is maintained as a matter of course by the domestic producer. The fact that separate data on the producer's profits and production are available allows the Commission to make separate assessments of the effect of imports on the production of distinct products. For the foregoing reasons, we conclude that tone-only and display pagers are distinct like products within the meaning of the statute.

Having resolved the "like product" issue, we next address the scope of the domestic industry. In the context of this investigation, the Commission must determine whether Motorola's production of Metrx and Metro-Pageboy model tone-only pagers should be considered part of the domestic industry in light of the fact that these two models are assembled in Malaysia or Korea and incorporate components sourced in the United States and abroad.

The Commission has not previously addressed the issue of what activities or specific attributes qualify a company as a domestic producer of a like product for the purposes of a final antidumping investigation. All production related activity need not occur in the United States for a firm to qualify as a domestic producer of a like product. Exclusion of firms from the domestic industry that import components or undertake some production related activities abroad would preclude relief to firms having sufficient production related activities in the United States. Our factual determination as to whether Motorola's activities with respect to its Metrx and Metro-Pageboy models are sufficient to include these particular models as part of domestic production is based on an analysis of the overall nature of Motorola's production related activities in the United States with respect to these two pager models.

Although Motorola's most obvious production related activity, the assembly and soldering of the circuit boards, occurs in Malaysia or Korea, significant production related activity occurs in the United States both before and after foreign assembly. These activities involve considerable technical experience and capital investment. The value added to Motorola's Metrx and Metro-Pageboy pagers in the United States constitutes a significant percentage of their component value and direct labor costs. Motorola has two facilities in Florida where the company employs a substantial number of workers in research and development and production activities specifically related to the Metrx and Metro-Pageboy pagers. We have concluded that the level of Motorola's production related activity which takes place in the United States with respect to the Metrx and Metro-Pageboy models is sufficient to include these two models as part of domestic production.

In summary, we conclude that tone-only and display pagers are two distinct like products. For the purposes of this investigation, we also conclude that the domestic tone-only pager industry consists of Motorola's domestic tone-only production, including production of its Metrx and Metro-Pageboy model pagers. Furthermore, we conclude that the domestic display pager industry consists of Motorola's display pager production.

* * *

VIEWS OF COMMISSIONER STERN

* * *

Like product—Generally, "like product" analysis is founded on the following points. First, "like product" covers more than virtually identical articles and may include substantially similar articles. Next, "likeness" is determined on the basis of both characteristics and uses. The definitions of "like product" and "industry" are factual determinations which involve subjective considerations based on the weight of the evidence.

The balance of factors, such as price, similarity of manufacturing processes, interchangeability in use, and customer perceptions as to competition among products is determined on a case-by-case basis. In examining prior Commission decisions regarding "like product", it emerges that certain factors receive more emphasis in specific types of investigations. In investigations involving chemicals, for example, the Commissioner has emphasized similarities in chemical formula and fungibility in uses.

In investigations involving "agricultural" products, the Commission has defined "like product" broadly. Thus, in *Fresh Cut Roses From The Netherlands,* 701–TA–21 (Preliminary), USITC Pub. No. 1041 [1 ITRD 5165] (1980), the Commission defined the domestic industry as producers of roses, and did not separately analyze the effect of imports on hybrid tea roses or sweetheart roses, despite a substantial difference in price and other characteristics. Similarly, in *Frozen Potato Products From Canada,* Inv. No. 701–TA–3 (Preliminary), USITC Pub. No. 1035 [1 ITRD 5161] (1980), the Commission defined the "like product" to include french fries, hash-brown potatoes, potato puffs, baked potatoes, and whole, blanched potatoes.

With respect to products manufactured to particular specifications, the Commission generally defines the domestic industry as those producers capable of satisfying the specifications of the particular type of contract. Thus, the Commission has not atomized the "like product" or "domestic industry." In this type of investigation a "like product" analysis focusing on the distinctions present in each contract or specification would result in a distorted view of the industry. An industry would consist only of the bidders on a specific contract because only those bidders could be construed as satisfying the detailed specifications. Thus, the Commission must often focus on the essential characteristics and uses of the article rather than drawing overly fine line distinctions that would render the term "industry" almost unrecognizable.

In contrast to the Commission's analysis in investigations involving agricultural products and production to specifications, the Commission has found several significant distinctions among "industrial" types of products, such as carbon steel products and pipes and tubes. In these investigations, the Commission has found that competition between separate products, and the existence of separate identifiable facilities, manpower, sales force, and/or research and development associated with the manufacture of each product warranted a finding of separate "like products." Also differences in size, shape or composition, together with varying uses and general lack of competition between products indicate the appropriateness of separate "like product" analysis. This type of analysis has resulted in finding several "like products" in an investigation, and has been applied primarily to industrial goods where differences in size or composition are significant marketplace distinctions perceived by an experienced buyer. These differences do not reflect single transaction requirements and therefore do not contradict Commission precedent in investigations of production to specifications.

There is another line of investigations which includes articles such as portable electric typewriters, televisions, and microwave ovens. Manufacturers market these products in a range of models which appeal to different customers. In some instances, the amount of competition among models is unpredictable or immeasurable. In fact, all of the models could be competing for a particular sale. In these investigations the Commission has emphasized similarity of basic uses, prices, sales force and channels of distribution. The Commission has not required fungibility or complete interchangeability as a condition for varying models to be considered "like products." Thus, in *Television Receiving Sets From Japan*, Inv. No. 751–TA–2, USITC Pub. No. 1153 [2 ITRD 5529] (1981), the Commission adopted the definition of domestic industry found in the original antidumping investigation. Throughout the Commission report distinctions between monochrome and color television receivers and distinctions in the size of the receivers were discussed. The Commission, however, did not make like product distinctions among types of television receivers on these grounds and therefore found one "domestic industry." Consideration of this pattern of prior analysis in this investigation supports my finding that there is a *single* domestic industry producing high capacity pagers.

Paging devices are essentially consumer goods which are sold in a wide range of models. Each model differs slightly from other models and is marketed to appeal to a particular segment of the pager market. This situation, for example, is similar to that in the television industry discussed above where various models differ in terms of color capabilities, size and other aspects. These differences are not sufficient to warrant separate like product analysis in an antidumping investigation.

In terms of characteristics and uses, tone-only and tone and display (display) pagers are essentially the same. Both types of pagers are produced from the same components; the same employees manufacture them in the same plants on the same machinery; and the pagers are sold or rented in the same channels of distribution. There is complete operational interchangeability and some overlap in the paging system subscribers. There is a very high degree of substitutability or interchangeability between these products in terms of their essential use.

Display pagers represent an evolving technology. Although they have an additional feature which differs from tone-only pagers, both types of pagers perform the same essential alerting function. The Commission has required more distinct differences in terms of characteristics and uses than exist here to warrant separate like product treatment of this type of good.

* * *

Domestic Production

* * *

The five suggested criteria included: (1) substantial change, (2) domestic content or value added, (3) major component, (4) commitment to the United States, and (5) degree of control.

* * *

On balance, I find that Motorola's activities in the United States relating to the Metrx and Metro-Pageboy pagers satisfy the domestic production requirement. Although the most obvious production related activity, the assembly and soldering of the circuit boards, occurs abroad, significant production activity occurs in the United States both before and after this foreign processing.

On the other hand, important distinctions exist between Motorola's domestic operations and NEC and Matsushita's operations in the United States. Although all three firms substantially change the pager boards imported into the United States and NEC America has some decision making authority, other factors show significant differences between these firms' operations. NEC and Matsushita use all imported parts in their pager manufacture. Any research and development beyond NEC's patent license from Motorola is done in Japan. NEC and Matsushita currently employ only a limited number of people in the United States directly involved in production related activity on their high capacity pagers. Moreover, final control as to product development and actual production decisions remains in Japan.

Note

Section 771(4)(C) provides that if certain conditions are met, the ITC can base its findings on harm to a regional industry. The key factors are that the regional producers must sell all or almost all of their production in the region, the regional market must not be supplied to any substantial degree by U.S. producers from outside the region and all or almost all of the regional producers must be materially injured. Those requirements are discussed in a series of cases in which the Court of International Trade found the ITC had erred in applying the terms of Section 771(4)(C). Atlantic Sugar, Ltd. v. United States, 519 F.Supp. 916 (CIT 1981); 2 CIT 295 (1981); 553 F.Supp. 1055 (CIT 1982); 573 F.Supp. 1142 (CIT 1983).

(b) Material Injury or Threat Thereof [47]

Generally "material injury" is not so difficult to find as "serious injury" in escape clause cases, and the ITC decisions reflect this. Indeed, one of the factors that the ITC is to consider in evaluating injury is whether the effect of imports has been to depress prices significantly, which is, of course, the essence of competition and therefore not difficult to find. The definition of "material injury" is set out in Section 771(7) and should be reviewed at this time. Judicial review of injury determinations in dumping (and countervailing) cases is much more intensive than in escape clause cases.

HIGH CAPACITY PAGERS FROM JAPAN

U.S. Intl. Trade Commn., supra

VIEWS OF CHAIRMAN ECKES AND COMMISSIONER HAGGART

*   *   *

Domestic production, shipments, and capacity increased rapidly from 1979 through 1982. In the first half of 1983, however, domestic shipments declined substantially from the levels reached in the corresponding period of 1982. Although shipments increased in 1982, profits declined dramatically. This resulted in Motorola experiencing a loss on its sales of tone-only pagers in 1982 and the first half of 1983. This loss resulted from a sharp decrease in the average selling price of tone-only pagers which began in late 1981.

The decline in prices and profitability are the primary indicators of injury to this industry. Examination of the price competition in the tone-only market demonstrates a causal nexus between LTFV imports from Japan and the injury to this industry.

Imports of high capacity tone-only pagers increased steadily from 1980 through 1982. Prices on sales to RCCs in the U.S. market remained virtually unchanged throughout 1980 and the first three quarters of 1981. The imported pagers consistently undersold the domestic tone-only pagers during this period. Significantly, in the fourth quarter of 1981 Matsushita entered the U.S. tone-only pager market and booked orders at prices substantially below Motorola's prices. In response to Matsushita's activities, Motorola reduced its prices on tone-only pagers to retain a large customer in October 1981. Consequently, weighted average selling prices of domestically produced tone-only pagers plummeted during the fourth quarter of 1981.

---

47. Madden, The Threat of Material Injury Standard in Countervailing Duty Enforcement, 16 Law & Poly. Intl. Bus. 373 (1984); Note, ITC Injury Determinations in Countervailing Duty Investigations, 15 Law & Poly. Intl. Bus. 987 (1983).

Matsushita continued to solicit orders at low prices, and in early 1982 Motorola lowered its tone-only prices on both its Metrx and BPR tone-only pager models. Despite Motorola's adjustment of prices, there were significant margins of underselling by the imported product during the last half of 1982. In November 1982, Motorola decreased the price of its BPR 2000 tone-only pager and slightly increased the price of its Metrx pager. As a result of LTFV imports from Japan, the average unit sales price for Metrx pager was approximately $106.00 in 1982 compared with $149.00 in 1981. Industry sources stated that Matsushita's low prices led to Motorola's price decreases in 1981 and 1982. Furthermore, Matsushita's low prices were a factor in three lost sales, which involved a substantial quantity of pagers, occurring during the fourth quarter of 1981 and in 1982.

The drastic decline in average selling prices for tone-only pagers resulted in Motorola incurring significant losses in 1982, despite declines in manufacturing costs and general selling and administrative expenses. The available data supports the conclusion that sales of LTFV imports from Japan prompted Motorola to reduce its prices and thereafter prevented sales at sufficiently high prices to maintain profitability.

Based on the foregoing, we conclude that LTFV imports of tone-only pagers from Japan caused material injury to the domestic tone-only pager industry.

The High Capacity Display Pager Industry

Compared with the tone-only industry conditions in the domestic display pager industry and the role of imports from Japan differ markedly. First, NEC was the initial entrant into the U.S. display pager market in 1981. Motorola did not begin shipping display pagers until July 1982. Initially, NEC captured most of the U.S. display pager market because no significant domestic or foreign competition existed. However, since Motorola introduced its BPR 2000 display pager in the second half of 1982, that company has become the dominant force in the rapidly expanding U.S. display pager market and has captured a substantial portion of that market. Correspondingly, the market penetration of imports has declined drastically.

Significantly, the display pager industry exhibits a different pricing and profitability picture than the tone-only pager industry. Although Motorola asserts that imports of both tone-only and display pagers suppressed prices in the display pager market, the display pager imports undersold the domestic product only in one quarter. This limited underselling has not affected Motorola's ability to be a viable factor in the expanding display pager market. For example, Motorola's weighted-average prices for display pagers have increased significantly in the first quarter of 1983. Furthermore, their profits have improved substantially during the same period. Motorola's capacity utilization for its first year of production of the BPR 2000 display pager was higher than on its other models. During the first quarter of 1983, Motorola's capacity utilization on its display model has remained very high despite increases in production capacity.

In light of these considerations, we conclude that the high capacity tone and display pager industry is not being materially injured by reason of imports of the subject articles from Japan. Based on the following analysis, we also determine that there is no threat of material injury.

Both NEC and Matsushita have taken initial steps to commence production of high capacity pagers in the United States. Currently, NEC is finishing a new facility in Hawthorne, California. Beginning in August 1983, NEC plans to manufacture its display pagers and new tone-only pager in this plant. MEP, the Puerto Rican subsidiary of Matsushita, began assembling pagers in Puerto Rico in January 1983. Eventually, MEP will be assembling and producing tone-only and display pagers in Puerto Rico.

Based on the declining share of the display pager market held by imports from Japan, and Motorola's substantially increasing market share, its increasing average per unit selling prices, production levels and profits, its current high level of capacity utilization, and the importers' intent to produce display pagers in the United States, we determine that the display pager industry in the United States is not threatened with material injury by reason of imports of display pagers from Japan, which are sold at less than fair value.

VIEWS OF COMMISSIONER STERN

* * *

Material Injury to the Domestic High Capacity Pager Industry

Although domestic production, shipments, capacity, and employment increased substantially during the period under investigation, these figures mask the weakened condition of the U.S. high capacity pager industry. Imported Japanese pagers held a significant portion of the U.S. market in 1979. Imports from Japan increased steadily from 1979 through 1981 and in 1982 these imports increased drastically. This substantial increase reflects NEC's introduction of its display pager model into the U.S. market. The domestic industry sold more pagers but at severely depressed prices. Consequently, the financial experience of the industry reveals profitability problems. Motorola's profits continue to show the effects of this price suppression.

The high capacity pager market is highly concentrated with relatively few large buyers accounting for the majority of sales. This concentration in the purchasers side of the market is fairly recent and coincides in time with the entrance of other high capacity pager manufacturers into the U.S. market, such as Multitone Electronics Co., Ltd. of the United Kingdom. Thus, price competition sharpened in the high capacity pager market, and loss of a single large customer can result in the loss of a substantial portion of a firm's sales.

NEC entered the U.S. high capacity pager market in 1976 and Matsushita entered this market in 1981. Prices on sales to Radio Common Carriers (RCCs), which represented the vast majority of total domestic sales remained stable from 1979 through the first three quarters of 1981. At these prices the NEC product did in fact undersell the domestic high capacity pagers. However, in later 1981 Matsushita began taking large orders at prices drastically below Motorola's prices. It was booking orders on both tone-only and tone and display pagers at prices substantially below

Motorola's prices. In response to these actions Motorola dramatically cut its prices to a major customer in order to retain that customer. Then, in early 1982, faced with Matsushita's continuing low price offers, Motorola lowered its prices across the board. During 1982 significant margins of underselling existed, even after Motorola's first price reductions. Customers perceive that Motorola cut its prices because of Matsushita's low prices.

The financial data for the domestic high capacity pager industry shows a reversal in the profitability of this industry in 1982. The industry went from making a profit in 1981 to a significant loss in 1982, and the industry operated at a loss in the first half of 1983, despite declines in costs. The weighted-average unit sales price for tone-only pagers remains at approximately $106.00 as compared with a average-weighted price of approximately $149.00 in 1981. Although a portion of the industry has shown improved profitability in the first half of 1983, this improvement has been insufficient to overcome the effects of less than fair value sales on the industry as a whole.

Based on these considerations, I conclude that the domestic high capacity pager industry is materially injured by reason of imports of high capacity pagers from Japan, which are sold at less than fair value.

ALBERTA GAS CHEMICALS, INC. v. UNITED STATES

Court of International Trade, 1981.
515 F.Supp. 780.

NEWMAN, JUDGE.

[A finding of dumping had been entered in respect of Canadian methanol in 1979. After upholding the determination of LTFV sales, the Court considered the injury question.]

The majority of the Commission found that significant dumping margins (as determined by Treasury) on the LTFV imports from Canada had suppressed U.S. producer prices and that there was a sharply deteriorating trend in the profitability of the domestic industry since 1976. Moreover, the majority found that the declining trend in profitability was the result of rapidly increasing production costs (primarily those for natural gas) without corresponding increases in selling prices, and that the domestic industry was increasingly vulnerable to injury from the LTFV imports. The majority concluded that "continued sales at less than fair value of *expanding supplies* from Canada will suppress or depress U.S. producers' prices and will be almost certain to cause injury to the U.S. industry". (Emphasis added.)

The majority's finding concerning *expanding* supplies was based upon the possibility that AGCL might, at some future time, construct new production facilities. Thus, the Commission's majority stated:

> In July 1976, AGCL obtained approval from the Energy Resources Conservation Board of Alberta to use natural gas as a raw material in the production of methyl alcohol which would be produced in two additional facilities to be constructed at the Medicine Hat, Alberta site. * * * Although AGCL has not made a final determination on whether to proceed with this construction, the outcome of this investigation conceivably may be

a factor in the final decision. If AGCL is permitted to continue to sell at LTFV in this market and the additional capacity under consideration is brought into being, about 700 million pounds of methyl alcohol will be available for export to the United States. The additional supply is the equivalent of more than 10 percent of current U.S. consumption. The U.S. market is a logical market for any increased Canadian production.

Although the dissenting Commissioners recognized that the domestic industry was experiencing "some economic difficulty" (particularly in terms of profitability), they did not relate the domestic industry's (then) current economic problems to the LTFV imports from Canada. With regard to their determination that the domestic methyl alcohol producing industry was not likely to be injured by the LTFV imports, the dissenting Commissioners were "unable to ascertain any factors which would lead [them] to find that the likelihood of such injury is 'real and imminent'." On this score, the dissenters sharply disagreed with the majority's apprehensions concerning expanding supplies of methyl alcohol from Canada, pointing out:

> It is clear that in this case additional exports to the United States by AGCL are unlikely in the imminent future. First, AGCL is producing at virtually 100 percent of capacity and nearly all production is committed under contractual agreements to existing customers. Second, information supplied to the Commission indicates that AGCL's markets outside the United States are expanding and that selling prices in those markets are higher than corresponding U.S. prices. Finally, combined inventories of methyl alcohol held by AGCL and AGCI on March 31, 1979, are relatively small and would not significantly increase U.S. import penetration even if the entire inventory was suddenly diverted to this country.

> AGCL has an expansion plan under consideration that could add two additional plants to existing facilities. However, even if AGCL decides to expand its production facilities, information presented to the Commission clearly indicates that the impact of any such expansion would not be felt in the U.S. market for at least three years. If construction on the new facilities began immediately, AGCL reports that production would not commence until 1982. Furthermore, AGCL's expansion plans are uncertain at present. Financing for the expansion has yet to be obtained. In addition, AGCL has indicated that it would have to evaluate future Canadian energy policies, the results of multilateral trade negotiations and potential new markets for methyl alcohol. We feel that, in view of all these factors, the length of time before any additional methyl alcohol could be exported to the United States is clearly not within the standard of "real and imminent."

The Congressional standard for determining likelihood of injury was articulated by the Senate Committee on Finance, which explained that future injury must be:

> based upon evidence showing that the *likelihood is real and imminent* and not on mere supposition, speculation, or conjecture. [Emphasis added.]

In 1979, Congress again made its intent clear concerning determination of future injury. Congress, in repealing the Antidumping Act of 1921, replaced the language in the statute concerning the likelihood of injury with language directing the Commission to determine whether there exists a "threat of material injury." 19 U.S.C. § 1673 (1980). In that connection, Congress stressed a practical test: there must be "information showing that the threat is real and injury is imminent, not a mere supposition or conjecture."

We have seen that central to the majority's determination of likelihood of injury is AGCL's expansion plans. Nevertheless, the majority conceded that AGCL had not made a final decision on whether to proceed with the construction of the new plants, and speculated that "the outcome of this investigation *conceivably* may be a factor in the final decision" (Emphasis added). The Commission majority further *speculated* that "[i]f AGCL has increased capacity and additional product availability and is able to continue to sell at LTFV to the U.S. market, the likelihood of increased penetration and injury to the domestic industry is apparent."

Patently, the majority's analysis is flawed with supposition and conjecture. As stressed in the dissenting statement, AGCL's expansion plans were uncertain and depended upon several contingencies, and indeed, financing had not even been arranged. More to the point is the undisputed fact that even if AGCL had immediately decided to expand its production facilities, production in such facilities could not commence until 1982 at the earliest, assuming there were no unforeseen delays.

The dissenting Commissioners noted, among other significant factors making additional exports to the United States by AGCL unlikely in the imminent future, is that AGCL (the sole Canadian exporter) was operating at nearly 100 percent of its capacity, and virtually all of the methyl alcohol production was committed to its customers under existing contractual agreements. Consequently, AGCL had no immediate (or "present") ability to increase its production of methyl alcohol or to divert its available capacity to the United States. Hence, it is clear that any injury which might result at some undetermined future time could occur only if new facilities were completed; and under all the facts and circumstances the likelihood of future injury perceived by the Commission majority did not constitute "real and imminent" injury as intended by Congress.

Furthermore, the Commission majority found that "if" AGCL's planned facilities were constructed, that all of the new capacity, estimated to be about 700 million pounds of methyl alcohol, will be "available" for export to the United States. The majority then stated that such estimated additional future supply was the equivalent of more than 10 percent of *current* U.S. consumption, and that "[t]he U.S. market is a logical market for any increased Canadian production." Thus, the Commission majority not only assumed the future increased capacity available for export to the United States, but also implicitly postulated, contrary to the evidence in the record, that there would be no future expansion in the United States consumption of methyl alcohol. The dissenting statement points out that "[o]ver the next several years the market for methyl alcohol is forecasted to expand as methyl alcohol is used in a widening range of applications. Of particular significance are the potential uses of methyl alcohol as fuel for the generation of electricity in power plants and as a gasoline extender and base for synthetic gasoline."

In summary, the record before the Commission shows simply a mere *possibility* that injury might occur at some remote future time. Such showing, viewed in the context of the "real and imminent" standard enunciated by Congress, compels the conclusion that the record lacks substantial evidence of likelihood of injury to the United States methyl alcohol producing industry.

(c) Causation: Cumulation and Margins Analysis

As noted in the Senate Report, the ITC is required by statute to determine if injury has occurred "by reason of imports." There are two particularly difficult conceptual issues faced by the ITC in analyzing causation of injury in antidumping and countervailing duty cases. First is the question of cumulation. In analyzing the injurious effects of imports, is it appropriate to consider the cumulative effect of all imports from those countries whose exports are alleged to have been dumped, or is it appropriate to consider the effect of imports only on a country-by-country basis? Would the fact that only some of the countries involved were parties to the Antidumping Code affect the answer?

Second is the question of so-called "margins analysis." Should the ITC consider the size of the dumping margin in analyzing injury? Or should it only consider whether dumped imports are causing injury?

The following cases consider these issues. They involved countervailing duties, but essentially similar issues arise in antidumping cases.

REPUBLIC STEEL CORP. v. UNITED STATES
Court of International Trade, 1983.
591 F.Supp. 640.[48]

WATSON, JUDGE:

[The ITC made a preliminary finding of no injury. Although the court focuses on the preliminary stage of investigation, it discusses the question of cumulation in both the preliminary and final stages.

[The ITC had refused to consider the cumulative effect of certain imports from various countries because the imports "could not have conceivably contributed to material injury."]

Cumulation is essential to the investigation of injury, and by extension, essential to the enforcement of the countervailing duty law, in two important situations. The first occurs when a number of subsidized sources, no one of which could injure the domestic industry by itself, combine to do injury to the industry. The second occurs when a subsidized source, again not sufficient individually to cause injury to the industry, adds to the injury caused by larger sources. If the countervailing duty law is not administered to take combined or exacerbating effects into account, then it is not being administered reasonably and its fundamental purpose is not being effectuated.

The ITC has not proposed to apply its "contribution" standard for cumulation to cases in which importations are originating from more than

48. See also Gifford-Hill Cement Co. v. United States, 615 F.Supp. 577, 589–90 (CIT 1985).

one producer in a *single* country. These producers are treated as a unit. It is inconsistent for the ITC to treat importations coming from more than one country in a different manner. For the purposes of determining the *possibility* of material injury, distinctions based on the particular sources of importations are immaterial.

For the making of a determination as to whether there is a reasonable indication of injury from a number of different sources, * * * [c]umulation has to be done without any evidence of the specific causal effect of a segment of importations from a particular country. In the beginning of the ITC's role in these proceedings, it is only the entire mass which must display some possibility of injury, not the individual components of the mass. It must be understood that when the Court speaks of a multiplicity of sources having a combined effect, the "contribution" of a particular source of importations is what is required to make it a cause of material injury *in the final sense.* The maximum ultimate effect of a segment of subsidized importations from one of many countries is its contribution to an injury (if the combined results affect the "industry"). For this reason, it follows that if the ITC asks that a particular segment from one country be shown to contribute to injury *as a condition* to being considered or cumulated with others, i.e., as a condition for being investigated, it is asking for a *final* showing of injury, not an *indication* of injury.

Moreover, cumulation, aside from operating in the absence of direct proof of causation, cannot depend on the *volume* or *trend of volume* of a particular segment of importations. The concept of cumulation is specifically needed for instances when the individual segment may only have sufficient size to adversely affect a single member of the industry. The trend of volume has no bearing on the possibility of such an effect. This effect alone may not be sufficient to support a finding of injury to an industry, but it *will* be sufficient to support a final finding of injury which includes that segment if, taken together with other effects, "industry-wide" injury is caused or exacerbated. It follows that if the ITC uses volume or trend as a condition for investigation, it is ignoring the possibility that, even the smallest volumes or declining trends can have a *contributing* effect in the final analysis, after the matter has been properly investigated. For this reason, when cumulation is appropriate there can be no application of the rule of *de minimus,* and no negative inferences from volume or trend.

The Court holds that the proper test for cumulation is whether subsidized or allegedly subsidized imported products are competing with the product of a domestic industry during a period when the effect of these importations is being felt by the domestic industry.

This standard is the only reasonable means of insuring that there is an investigation of the possibility that segments of subsidized importations may be contributing to, or exacerbating, an injury to a domestic industry.

Up to this point, the Court has stressed the necessity of cumulation and has identified the criterion of competitiveness as the standard for cumulation. The next question is whether cumulation can lead to a final injury determination for importations from a given country, without the necessity of a finding that importations from that country were a specific cause of injury.

On this issue the Court holds that cumulation, as important as it is to the *investigation* of injury, cannot, in the end, completely eliminate the need for a causal connection between importations from a country and injury to a domestic industry. The controlling legal consideration is that an injury determination was added to our countervailing duty law to implement the Subsidies Code, an international agreement. The injury determination is something which individual countries, the United States among them, have agreed to make a condition of the assessment of countervailing duties on each other. Common principles of fairness dictate that the final injury determination must be based on some factual connection between the imports from a specific country and an aspect of the injury to the domestic industry.

Note

Section 612 of the 1984 Trade and Tariff Act added a new subsection (iv) to Section 771(7)(C) on the subject of cumulation. Does the new provision change the result of the *Republic Steel* case?

CERTAIN CARBON STEEL PRODUCTS FROM SPAIN

U.S. Intl. Trade Commn. (1983) [49]

ADDITIONAL VIEWS OF COMMISSIONER HAGGART

According to the Senate Report accompanying the Act, Section 705 of the Tariff Act, as amended by section 101 of the Trade Agreements Act of 1979, codifies U.S. obligations under the Subsidies Code into U.S. law. Section 705(b) provides that injury is to be "by reason of imports of the merchandise with respect to which the administering authority has made an affirmative determination under subsection (a) of this section [705(a)].". Article 6, paragraph 4, of the Code states that a countervailing duty will not be imposed on the product of any country which is a party to the GATT unless it is demonstrated that "the subsidized imports, through the effects of the subsidy, [are] causing injury * * *."

Congress could have used the specific language of the Code in the statute; however, it chose not to do so. Instead, Congress elected to require the Commission to make a final determination of whether an industry is materially injured "by reason of imports of the merchandise". Thus, within the context of the issue of causality, the plain meaning of the statute requires us to trace any injury to imports of the subsidized merchandise from a particular country. The statute does not require the Commission to relate the amount of the subsidy to the injury being experienced by a domestic industry.

* * *

The methodology contemplated in Article 6 for tracing the effects of the subsidy to any material injury experienced by the domestic producers in the

---

49. Inv. No. 701–TA–155 (Final) (Pub. No. 1331), 4 ITRD 2030.

importing country is to determine the effects of the volume of subsidized imports on the prices in the product markets of the importing country and their impact on the domestic producers. These are the same effects that sections 771(7)(B) and (C) direct the Commission to consider. Thus, section 771 implements Article 6, paragraphs 2, 3, and 4, of the Code. Therefore, the argument that the statute fails to implement the provision of Article 6, Paragraph 4, of the Code is not persuasive. For these reasons, the literal language of the Code cannot be relied upon to defeat the argument that the Commission must follow the plain meaning of Title VII in making its injury determinations.

Although the statute directs us to determine whether injury is "by reason of imports of the merchandise", we are not precluded from considering the amount of the subsidy or the likely effect of the subsidy as one of the non-specified factors in the Commission's analysis under section 771(7)(B). However, the presence or absence of a causal nexus between the amount of the net subsidy and material injury should not be dispositive with respect to the issue of the cause of any material injury since "the presence or absence of any factor which the Commission is required to evaluate under subparagraph (C) or (D) shall not necessarily give decisive guidance with respect to the determination by the Commission of material injury." If the presence or absence of a specified factor is not decisive, then *a fortiori*, the presence or absence of a nonspecified factor should not be dispositive.

Other considerations support the conclusion that the amount of the net subsidy should not be relied upon in determining material injury by reason of subsidized imports. There is no compelling reason to presume that there is a causal relationship between the amount of the net subsidy calculated by the Department of Commerce and any price differentials in the U.S. market between domestic products and imported subsidized products. Commerce's net subsidy calculation reflects a determination of the value of a foreign subsidy. Essentially, foreign accounting principles are used in determining whether a program is a subsidy and assessing the benefits accruing to the foreign manufacturer because of the subsidy. Caution is warranted in relying upon this net subsidy calculation in light of the fact that accounting calculations may not accurately reflect economic phenomena outside the system within which they are used.

Although there may be some logic in assuming that a less than fair value dumping margin will manifest itself through price differential in the market, this may not be the case with a subsidy. Subsidies may be utilized by foreign producers for a number of purposes such as to improve cash flow, to achieve economies of scale through encouraging production, to encourage employment, or to contribute to product development. Imports still may be a cause of material injury even if there is no evidence of underselling in the market. Thus, a negative determination based on the fact that the net subsidy calculated by the Department of Commerce does not account for a certain portion of the underselling would not comport with the plain meaning of the statute and Congressional intent.

Moreover, the period of investigation covered by the Department of Commerce does not always correspond with the period of investigation covered by the Commission. In these investigations, the period of investigation for the Commission ended in September of 1982. By comparison, the period used by Commerce for measuring subsidization for the Spanish producers was the 1981 calendar year. Thus, certain analytical obstacles exist in drawing conclusions from the relationship between the net subsidies and margins of underselling, when the latter are based on a time period that is not analogous to the period for which the net subsidies were calculated.

In light of these problems, a compelling argument can be made that the amount of the net subsidy calculation may have no methodological connection with any attempt to assess the effects in the U.S. market likely to be caused by certain foreign subsidy practices. Consequently, in these investigations, I have relied on the existence of a causal nexus between the subsidized imports and injury, rather than attempting to relate the amount of the net subsidy to the injury.

* * *

VIEWS OF COMMISSIONER STERN

* * *

In recent cases, I am increasingly struck by the danger of this statute becoming a means of obtaining protection, albeit limited, from fair rather than unfair competition. The Congress has established standards for relief from fair competition which are considerably more stringent than those that apply to unfair competition. Theories on causality which suggest that the level of subsidization is irrelevant to the Commission analysis of the impact of "subsidized imports" on the domestic industry can lead to a breakdown of the carefully constructed framework that Congress has established for providing protection consistent with the public interest and U.S. international obligations.

An affirmative finding in any unfair trade case is premised on a finding of potentially unfair trade, i.e., the existence of subsidization or less than fair value imports. This very basic element was missing in a number of recent cases before the Commission (and yet there were some affirmative votes). Even when the subsidy level is not zero, as in the cases before us here, its significance must still be examined to determine whether it—the potentially unfair trade practice—has resulted or is likely to result in volume or price effects. Only if this has occurred as a result of the subsidy does the potential for material injury or threat of material injury caused by the subsidized imports exist within the meaning of the statute. This is clear from the legislative history. In pointing out that the significance of various factors will differ from industry to industry, the Senate noted:

> Similarly, for one type of product, *price may be a factor in making a decision as to which product to purchase* and a small price differential resulting from the *amount of the subsidy* or the margin of dumping *can be decisive;* for others the size of the differential may be of lesser significance. (Emphasis added.)

The Congress was concerned about price differences resulting from a subsidy which could affect the condition of a domestic industry, and so am I.

As a legal matter, the impact of the subsidy needs to be assessed on the basis of the best information available in a particular case. That this task will at times prove difficult provides neither an excuse nor legal justification for us to avoid making an effort toward such assessment.

Though my position on this matter is taken strictly as a result of the direction of the statute and the legislative history, I point out that it is also based on sound economic and public policy. In brief, if subsidies have no material influence on import prices or volume (as when the subsidy is very small or when it is insignificant in relation to the margin by which the foreign product undersells the U.S. product), corresponding countervailing duties do not correct a problem. Instead, they impose a cost on the U.S. economy and become a nuisance to trade. They result in American penalties for foreign government intervention in their economies even in those instances where the intervention does not materially affect the competing U.S. industry. From a public policy point of view, affirmative Commission findings in cases where the potentially unfair practice itself has not been a cause of injury to the domestic industry fosters a myopic public perception of the factors necessary to strengthen U.S. competitiveness.

An early version of the 1984 Trade and Tariff Act would have authorized the ITC to consider the size of a dumping margin or net subsidy in its determination of injury. It was later deleted. See Maine Potato Council v. United States, 613 F.Supp. 1237, 1242–43 (CIT 1985), quoting 96 Cong.Rec. H7908–09 (daily ed. July 26, 1984).

(4) The Trigger Price Mechanism for Steel Products

The history of the steel industry's efforts to protect itself from foreign competition was described in Section 9.6(B)(1) supra. Those efforts have at times involved massive filings of antidumping petitions directed at steel imports. In fact, since 1974, almost 50% of all antidumping actions have involved steel products. These individual actions have generally not been successful in halting imports, but they have forced the U.S. government to initiate policies that give some protection to the steel industry. One of those policies was the institution of a so-called trigger-price mechanism (TPM) for steel imports. The TPM was introduced in 1978 on the recommendation of a task force headed by Under Secretary of the Treasury Solomon. The TPM essentially provided that the Secretary of the Treasury would institute antidumping investigations, without a complaint by industry, in event of imports of steel below a "trigger price." The trigger price was based on the full costs of production, including appropriate capital charges, of steel mill products by the most efficient foreign steel producer (at that time the Japanese steel industry). By definition then, sales below the trigger price should be sales made at a loss and therefore subject to imposition of antidumping duties. The Treasury Department expected that if an antidumping investigation was opened, it could be concluded much faster than under the normal procedures, i.e. 2 to 3 months, as opposed to 13 months.

The Government had understood that antidumping complaints against the steel products covered by the TPM would be withdrawn following establishment of the TPM, and indeed they were. The TPM itself survived a legal challenge and, by the summer of 1978, a truce of sorts prevailed between government and industry.

The goodwill was not to last long. Domestic steel companies soon began to believe that the TPM was not deterring substantial dumping, particularly by European producers who were able to sell at the trigger prices without risking dumping suits despite their generally higher costs (higher, that is, than the Japanese costs on which the TPM was based). In 1978 and 1979, most Japanese steel products were imported into the United States at relatively constant quantities. Imports from a number of European and developing countries, on the other hand, increased substantially. The U.S. industry also had complaints about the Treasury Department's administration of the TPM. In brief, these complaints held that massive evasion of the system was occurring.

The Administration made clear that it would not maintain the TPM if antidumping cases covering a major portion of U.S. steel imports were filed. In March 1980 cases against most steel imports from seven European countries were filed by United States Steel Corporation. The Department of Commerce immediately suspended the trigger price mechanism. It noted that the TPM was established to monitor the pricing of basic steel mill product imports for purposes of determining when the government should initiate antidumping investigations on an expedited basis and that it was designed as a substitute for individual antidumping petitions by the domestic steel industry. With the filing of the antidumping petitions, it concluded that the basis upon which the TPM was maintained no longer existed.

To say that the world steel trade was in an uproar following these developments is an understatement. European officials intimated that dumping findings could result in a trade war. Customers in the United States were uncertain how long they could continue to buy foreign steel before appraisement was withheld and liability for dumping duties arose.

Meanwhile the work of the Government-labor-business Tripartite Committee established after the Solomon report continued. Once again, the trade issue was becoming more closely woven into general issues of the industry's health and prospects, and in September, President Carter announced measures to increase investment by the industry in the modernization of its plant and equipment, initiatives to foster adoption of advanced technology, programs to help workers and communities adversely affected by imports, and reinstatement of an improved trigger price mechanism.

As expected, U.S. Steel quickly withdrew its dumping petitions, "without prejudice." Meanwhile, U.S. Trade Representative Askew had delivered a letter to Viscount Etienne Davignon, EC Commissioner for Industrial Affairs, formally notifying him of the U.S. Government's reinstatement of the TPM and its expectation that U.S. Steel would withdraw the complaints. Davignon returned a letter to Askew in which he stated EC agreement "on the principle of a TPM consistent with the rules of the GATT and the OECD Steel Consensus." Finally, in two paragraphs of great importance to the United States, he concluded:

We share the view that the limited period of stability provided by the TPM should be used by our industries to pursue and accelerate their restructuring in order to achieve fully competitive enterprises ＊ ＊ ＊

Because of the temporary nature of the system it is evident that after its termination normal rules of international trade are to be applied. Consequently, measures, including those in the field of antidumping and countervailing duties, taken in accordance with the rules of the GATT could not be contested by any party concerned.

Was the TPM authorized by U.S. antidumping law? By the GATT Code? In 1981, the GATT Committee on Antidumping Practices agreed that Article 8:4 of the Code "contained ambiguities, and that in light of different possible interpretations, concluded that Article 8:4 is not essential to the effective operation of the Agreement and shall not provide the basis for any antidumping investigation or for imposition and collection of anti-dumping duties." [50]

(D) EC ANTIDUMPING LAW [51]

The Regulation pursuant to which the EC imposes antidumping duties parallels the GATT Antidumping Code fairly closely. The principal differences in substance between EC law and U.S. law are: (1) Before imposing antidumping duties, the EC considers the interests of the Community, as well as the existence of dumping and material injury. Thus, there is an element of discretion. (2) The amount of the duty imposed may be less than the dumping margin if that is sufficient to offset the injury found, as the GATT Code urges. (3) The antidumping duties imposed by the EC operate prospectively, i.e. the rate is fixed based on the investigation and applies until it is changed as a result of a review, which is normally not held more often than annually. Thus, if a dumping margin of 10% is found and the antidumping duty is set at 10%, all imports for a year will bear the 10% rate, whether they are dumped or not. Because the information used to calculate the margin is usually taken from the six-to-twelve-month period before the investigation is opened and the duty is imposed typically nine months later, the duty often bears little relationship to current dumping margins. While a refund procedure exists through which duties in excess of the actual dumping margins may be claimed, refunds have not often been granted. (4) In constructing the costs of goods, the EC uses what it views as reasonable profit margins and actual overheads, unlike the ITA, which is required by statute to add to its calculations 10% for overheads and 8% for profits. (5) The EC prefers to use constructed values in cases where the domestic market price is unreliable, while the United States prefers export prices to third countries. (6) Generally speaking, and unlike the situation in the United States, findings of no injury are rare.

50. GATT, 28th Supp. BISD 52 (1982).

51. See generally Davey, An Analysis of European Communities Legislation and Practice Relating to Antidumping and Countervailing Duties, in B. Hawk (ed.), 1983 Fordham Corporate Law Institute: Antitrust and Trade Policies of the European Economic Community 41–128 (1983); Vermulst, Dumping in the United States and the European Community: A Comparative Analysis, Legal Issues of European Integration, 1984/2, at 104; J. Cunnane & C. Stanbrook, Dumping and Subsidies: The law and procedures governing the imposition of anti-dumping duties and countervailing duties in the European Community (1983).

Procedurally, there are more significant differences. (1) There are no strict time limits for different phases of the investigation, except that duties may be collected on the basis of a preliminary determination for at most six months. (2) Only one, usually a two-man, team of investigators handles both the dumping and injury investigations. (3) There are no formal hearings and no rules against ex parte contacts. The record essentially consists of written submissions. There is no procedure for attorney inspection of confidential information and while summaries of confidential information are required in theory, they are frequently not prepared. (4) Settlements are common and usually encouraged. The alleged dumpers typically agree to respect certain price levels and report price data regularly to the EC. (5) Appeals to the Court of Justice are possible, at least for disappointed complainants and affected exporters, but there have not been many decisions and it is generally thought that the Court will not interfere in the detailed application of the antidumping rules, so long as procedural safeguards are observed and the Regulation's explicit provisions are observed.

In operation, the EC system is marked by negotiation of settlement agreements, called price undertakings, and discretion. While this sort of system often seems desirable compared to the U.S. tendency to over-lawyer proceedings, it can be quite frustrating at times for participants who are faced with interpreting and abiding by rather amorphous rules.

(E) EVALUATING ANTIDUMPING LAWS

We examined some of the problems economists have found with the antidumping laws at the outset of this section. Here we consider comments by a former administrator of these laws, one who was involved in the 1979 revisions. Do you agree or disagree with his position?

PETER D. EHRENHAFT, WHAT THE ANTIDUMPING AND COUNTERVAILING DUTY PROVISIONS OF THE TRADE AGREEMENTS ACT (CAN) (WILL) (SHOULD) MEAN FOR U.S. TRADE POLICY

(1979) [52]

The principal "reform" wrought by the Trade Agreements Act was its significant reduction in the time periods within which antidumping and countervailing duty proceedings are to be completed. * * * These changes respond to what irritated individual companies—both domestic and foreign—have perceived as a disinterested administration of the laws by Treasury. If there was lackluster "enforcement," it is in part a direct outgrowth of the micro-economic perspective with which the laws must be administered, given their minute focus on the competitive impact of imports by more than 600 individual companies subject to more than 80 dumping findings, and un-counted hundreds more subject to some 150 countervailing duty (CVD) orders. The effort to keep this enormous data base current appears to have

52. 11 Law & Poly.Intl.Bus. 1361. Reprinted by permission of Law and Policy in International Business. See also Testimony of Peter D. Ehrenhaft, Hearings on Options to Improve the Trade Remedy Laws Before the Subcomm. on Trade of the House Comm. on Ways and Means, 98th Cong., 1st Sess., pt. 2, 1048 (1983).

little relationship to the real trade problems of the nation and diverts resources from more significant tasks. * * *

The conclusion is inescapable that most of the cases processed are properly regarded as pimples on the trade landscape. * * *

That invocation of the law has tended to be the preserve of a limited segment of the economy is highlighted by a study prepared by the Office of Economic Analysis of the Customs Service of all antidumping and countervailing duty cases initiated between 1975 and mid-1979. The study confirms that just five industry groups (ferrous metals and products, textiles, industrial chemicals, rubber and plastic materials and automotive equipment) accounted for 86 of the 133 antidumping cases initiated during that period and over 90 percent of the known value of affected imports. Similarly, four groups (food, textiles, leather, and ferrous metals and products) provoked 79 of the period's 108 countervailing duty investigations and accounted for over 76 percent of the value of imports affected. Despite these high concentrations, the trade affected was minor in aggregate terms. This is particularly apparent when it is noted that in the cases with the largest trade volumes, no relief under the laws was ordered: the antidumping proceedings with respect to automobiles were discontinued; the series of steel cases filed in 1977 was withdrawn after the adoption of the "trigger price mechanism"; and most of the textile industry countervailing duty determinations were negative, while the government fashioned a variety of marketing arrangements with foreign textile suppliers.

Two facts stand out from over two years of on-the-job experience administering these statutes. First, most of the largest U.S. companies with significant international operations do not invoke the law, either because they do not feel that the pressure of import competition can be addressed meaningfully through these proceedings, or because they fear retaliation against their export sales. The steel and chemical companies are the sole exceptions, although steel exports are a minor factor; and, in the case of chemicals, most of the proceedings brought appear to involve relatively minor items, such as by-products of other production processes, and not the staples of the trade. Second, when the occasional "large" cases are brought, the micro-economic approach can overwhelm the system. No better illustration exists than the infamous Japanese TV dumping case, in which Treasury fell more than seven years behind in the assessment of duties due to the enormous volume of the affected trade, the number and complexity of the adjustments claimed by the several producers of a variety of different receivers sold in the two markets, and, of course, the possible efforts of some exporters and importers to evade the duties through undisclosed rebates and false invoices. A significant impetus for the creation of the "trigger price mechanism" for imported steel mill products was the pendency of 19 antidumping cases—based not only on price-discrimination charges but on claims of sales below cost as well—involving virtually all of the major steel products imported from the European Community and Japan.

* * *

The Trade Agreements Act has undoubtedly made some desirable improvements in the antidumping and countervailing duty laws. The adjudicatory cast given to proceedings and the extensive administrative detail that has been included both in the statute and, to an even greater extent, in the regulations adopted—and still to be supplemented—tend to assure transparency and certainty.

On the other hand, these same characteristics tend to reduce, if not wholly prevent, the opportunity the law should give decisionmakers to consider other facts that are of possible concern and of no less importance to the priorities of the United States. They overlook political relations with affected foreign governments. Both with regard to the timing and the substance of decisions, the fact that a foreign government is facing an election campaign, the outcome of which may be influenced by U.S. decisions on trade; or that leases for U.S. military bases on its soil are under negotiation; or that a significant purchase of U.S. exports is under consideration by its postal service are all wholly disregarded for the benefit of the particular U.S. producers who happened to have invoked the law. No scope is provided for considering the consistency of the foreign government's behavior with programs of the U.S. government or U.S. producers. The facts that the United States, too, provides preferential export credits through the Export-Import Bank and has regional aid and research and development grants available to eligible companies that may export their output are irrelevant.

More fundamentally, although a series of laws has been enacted to aid the lesser-developed countries, in particular by extending the Generalized System of Preferences to their exports, development goals are extraneous to antidumping and countervailing duty decisions. At a time when the control of inflation is repeatedly cited as the number one priority aim of government programs, the inflationary impact of antidumping and countervailing duty determinations is considered legally irrelevant. At a time when the U.S. economy is threatened by low productivity and lethargic adjustment, these statutes stand in the way of expeditious encouragement to the adjustment process. They may stifle, rather than spur, innovation and efforts to meet competition in the market.

On the procedural side, the acceleration of decisionmaking mandated by the law will prevent a thorough examination of sensitive issues, many of which take more time than is allowed even with significant additions of personnel and an Administration determined to meet all time limits. Judicial review by the Customs Court will be in a forum that traditionally has had a rather narrow perspective of the issues, and may treat countervailing duty cases in particular with a technocratic approach that is insufficiently alert to the impact its decisions may have on the international relations of the United States. To extend to the courts this ability to "interfere" with foreign relations is a peculiar American penchant. And however much Congress wishes to regard a countervailing duty case as a mere adjudicatory dispute, foreign governments may not be willing so to characterize it.

The adoption of more adjudicatory procedures and the availability of expanded judicial review create an impression of certainty in U.S. processes and that willful behavior by foreigners can be checked by the "simple" adoption of rules. To that extent, the new law tends to detract from more meaningful approaches that should be adopted to maintain the vitality of the U.S. economy. Effort might better go to developing positive domestic aids to help keep U.S. industries modern and efficient, and to retrain and relocate U.S. workers to areas in which they can demonstrate their comparative advantage.

(F) PROBLEMS

(1) Firm E in Country X has sold 500,000 pairs of sunglasses to M, a United States importer, at a price of $5.00 per unit. Included in this price are the following: $.40 per unit for extra packaging and handling costs in preparing the sunglasses for a transoceanic voyage; a $15,000 shipment charge for the entire lot (delivery will be in five installments); $.50 per unit to cover the export tax imposed by X. E and M have no particular commercial ties.

Firm E also sells this line of sunglasses in X, at a price of $4.75 a pair. Using only the information here provided, will the Commerce Department find the sunglasses to be sold at less than fair value if a complaint is brought by a United States manufacturer of sunglasses? If so, how much additional duty will be imposed?

(2) Assuming the information in Problem (1), will any of the following factors change your answer?

(a) E has no advertising costs in the United States, but it spends approximately $.12 per unit sold for advertising in X.

(b) Although E offers discount quantity sales to buyers in X, no buyer has ordered more than 500 pairs at one time. All sunglasses sold are produced in the same plant in X, and are stored in the same warehouse before shipment.

(c) M paid in advance for the entire lot, whereas buyers in X always choose to be billed after shipment. The cost of insuring against default and of handling the extra paperwork averages out to $.05 per pair in X.

(d) E offers to refund the purchase price to any consumer in X who is unhappy, for any reason, with the sunglasses. In the past few years, the cost of such refunds (often unreasonably requested) has averaged $.03 on each pair actually sold.

(3) Assume that the Commerce Department finds less than fair value sales in the situation posed in Problem (1). Now consider each of the following situations concerning the United States sunglasses industry. Is the International Trade Commission likely to find injury in any or all of these situations? What arguments can be made on each side of the questions?

(a) M is a Boston importer which has offered the sunglasses for sale only in New England. In the time since the imported sunglasses first came onto the market, sales of domestically manufactured sunglasses in New England have dropped off rather dramatically. In fact, one manufacturer has closed its Rhode Island production facility, laying off some 150 people. However, sales and profits of this and other manufacturers are up over 10% nation-wide since the imports reached the market.

(b) Sales of domestically manufactured sunglasses have increased slightly in New England, but declining sales in the South have resulted in 30% lower profits for domestic manufacturers, all of which are national firms.

(c) Sales of the imported sunglasses in New England have been tremendous, and it appears that M's stock will be depleted before the next installment arrives. Since the sunglasses came onto the market, the percentage of X-made sunglasses among all sunglasses sold has risen from 5% to 40% in the New England market. Domestic manufacturers have experienced no drop in sales, although their plants are not all operating at full capacity.

(d) Same as (c), except that all domestic plants are operating at full capacity.

(e) After several installments of the sunglasses have been received and offered for sale on the New England market, H, a small New Hampshire manufacturer, which sells only in northern New England, has experienced an 80% drop in sales. H's sunglasses have always been more expensive than comparable glasses from other firms, domestic and foreign, but since the introduction of the X-made imports, H's normal markets have dried up. H is in severe financial trouble. All national manufacturers have maintained their previous levels of sales and profits, both in New England and nation-wide.

SECTION 10.3 SUBSIDIES AND COUNTERVAILING DUTIES

(A) INTRODUCTION

THE TOKYO ROUND OF MULTILATERAL TRADE NEGOTIATIONS, REPORT BY THE DIRECTOR–GENERAL OF GATT

53–54 (1979)

Subsidies have become one of the most frequently used and controversial instruments of commercial policy. Together with countervailing duties, they were certain to be a critical and contentious issue in the Tokyo Round.

In the industrial sector the use of subsidies has greatly increased, particularly under the impact in recent years of recessionary world economic conditions, slackening demand and high unemployment. Under the influence of political and social necessity, governments have embarked on massive financial commitments in order, among other things, to prop up ailing industries, to support depressed areas, to stimulate consumer demand or to promote exports. Subsidies have become an important instrument of protection. In some sectors—shipbuilding is a good example—world trade is being conducted less in response to normal market forces than on the basis of competitive subsidization.

A principal difficulty is to draw a distinction between subsidies granted by governments in pursuit of valid economic and social policies and those which, directly or indirectly, intentionally or unintentionally, have the effect of distorting world trade and depriving other countries of legitimate trade opportunities.

Another problem is to define "subsidy." Support given to an industry may go well beyond the simple grant of an export or a domestic subsidy. It could be argued that free State education, providing as it does the skills for industry is a form of government subsidy. This, of course, would be carrying things to extremes, although research grants for universities, e.g. on electronics, is another matter. The fact remains that, because of the range and extent of measures that might be considered subsidies, it has proved impossible to agree on a precise definition or on the criteria to be applied.

———

Since 1979 subsidies have remained one of the most troublesome problems of international trade policy. The problems of definition have not been solved. The governments of the major western trading nations themselves have widely divergent views on the role of government involvement with industry. Even more variety is found when the policies of developing countries are considered. And the problem of definition and agreement on what activities should be permissible becomes incredibly complex when an attempt is made to fit government-controlled economies under the rules.

In this section, we will consider in subsection (B) the rules on use of subsidies found in GATT and the GATT Subsidies Code. A series of problems at the end of subsection (B) is designed to suggest the difficulties inherent in defining subsidies in a meaningful way. We will then turn in subsection (C) to U.S. law on subsidies and countervailing duties. In both of these subsections, the focus will be on the difficult definitional questions raised by this subject: What is a subsidy? What subsidies are appropriately countervailed against? How is the amount of the subsidy calculated? After a brief look at the law of the EC in subsection (D), we will conclude this section with an examination of the so-called border tax adjustment problem.

Before turning to the international rules on subsidies, it is useful to analyze their economic effects, to ask ourselves why we should care about the subsidization practices of other governments and to examine how frequently the rules against subsidies are invoked and by whom.

In international trade policy terms, there are basically two types of subsidies: the "production" subsidy; and the "export" subsidy. The production subsidy is a subsidy granted to an industry merely for the production of a product, regardless of whether the product is exported. The production subsidy, as indicated in Chapter 1, can have many of the effects of a tariff. For example, if U.S. domestic industry produces widgets at a cost of $1.00 each, while foreign industry can produce widgets to sell for a price of $.90 each, the foreign goods should compete successfully against the American-made product. If the United States, on the other hand, grants a subsidy to the widget industry of 20 cents for each widget produced, the United States industry should be able to sell the widget 20 cents cheaper than otherwise. Thus, it can mark its price to a level below that of the imports, and effectively "drive out" the import competition. In this sense, the subsidy can have effects similar to a tariff, although the result would be to lower prices generally of the products concerned (rather than raise them by a tax or tariff), and presumably would thereby favor consumers.

An export subsidy, on the other hand, is one which is paid to an industry for each of its products which is exported. Thus, if the American industry produced widgets at a dollar each, and received a 20 cent subsidy for each widget exported, it could sell its widgets abroad for about 80 cents each. The widgets which are sold in the domestic market, however, would cost a dollar each, and presumably would be priced at about that level. Consequently, one theoretical result of an export subsidy is "bi-level pricing," whereby the goods which are exported are sold abroad at a price below that of the goods retained for the domestic market. In actuality, of course, these effects may not be so simple, because the firm receiving the subsidy may spread the results of that subsidy into the price of both the exported and the domestic goods. Nevertheless, since the subsidy will only be received for goods which are exported, there is an added incentive for the firm to export.

As will be explained below, GATT rules allow an importing nation, which finds that goods shipped to it are subsidized, to respond by imposing "countervailing duties." These are tariffs set equal to the amount of the foreign subsidy, in order to offset the export promotion feature of that subsidy.

In contrast to the problems of dumping and antidumping duties, countervailing duties and subsidies (whether "production" or "export") generally involve foreign *governmental* action. A private firm may "dump" its goods into foreign markets, by setting a price for the goods exported lower than those retained for domestic consumption. Generally, however, it is considered that a "subsidy" originates from the government, either in the form of a specific cash grant, or in the form of some other governmental measure which operates to grant a particular favor to the producer. The major distinction in international trade policy terms, between the problems of antidumping duties and the problems of countervailing duties, is that since the latter quite often involve responses to foreign *governmental* action, they are therefore diplomatically more "sensitive." Each countervailing duty case is a subject of diplomatic consultation and such efforts are sometimes intense. Indeed, over the period of the last few decades, the United States has found that a number of its important trade quarrels with trading partners have involved questions of subsidies or countervailing duties.

GARY C. HUFBAUER & JOANNA SHELTON ERB, SUBSIDIES IN INTERNATIONAL TRADE

5–6 (1984) [1]

THE RATIONALE FOR DISCIPLINING SUBSIDIES

Sovereign governments are free to adopt whatever macroeconomic, industrial, or social policies, including the use of subsidies, that they deem

1. © 1984, Institute for International Economics. Reproduced by permission. See also   D. Wallace, F. Loftus & V. Krikorian, Inter-

necessary to achieve their overall goals. Politicians, producers, and taxpayers may debate the relative merits of supporting one industry versus another, and whether the cost of government financial support is worth the drain on public resources. But in a representative government, the costs and benefits of public policies presumably are settled more or less to the satisfaction of the key interested parties.

An economist might, therefore, ask why the international community should concern itself with the subsidy practices of its member nations. After all, if one nation wishes to subsidize production or exports in the name of infant-industry arguments, second-best policies, or simply to assuage particular industries, isn't the resulting economic distortion principally the misfortune of the subsidizing nation? This question becomes especially pointed when an importing country can enjoy the advantage of cheaper goods made possible by another country's subsidy practices. To be sure, the producers in one country might, with the assistance of public subsidies, drive out foreign producers, capture their markets, and later make good any losses through monopolistic pricing. But shouldn't the international community require evidence of monopolistic intent or result before authorizing countermeasures? Put simply, apart from clear instances of grasping monopoly, why should the international community be the keeper of national export morals?

The answer is also simple: unbridled and competing national subsidies can undermine world prosperity. Whatever the analytic merits of a purist free trade, turn-the-other-cheek approach, the Great Depression taught the world that protective policies can quickly and destructively spread from nation to nation. Because the concentrated interests of producers command greater political support than the diffuse interests of consumers, national governments find it much easier to emulate the vices of protection than the virtues of free trade. This lesson has prompted the international community to fashion guidelines that distinguish between acceptable and unacceptable national subsidy measures and to codify those guidelines both in bilateral treaties and in multilateral agreements. In fact, a major purpose of the General Agreement on Tariffs and Trade (GATT) is to discipline protective import policies. Robert E. Baldwin has ably summarized negotiating history since the 1930s:

> The 1930s experience with export subsidies as well as with competitive devaluation, which has the effect of a general export subsidy and import surcharge, apparently convinced the GATT founders that export subsidies exacerbate international political tensions and should be eliminated. Though consumers in the importing country gain from export subsidization by other nations, domestic-producer groups in the importing countries are forced to curtail output and incur a producer-surplus loss * * *. The view that domestic producers are somehow more entitled to domestic compared to foreign markets is still widely held by the general public. Thus, in the case of export subsidies, it was not necessary for the founders of GATT to implement their international political objective with regard to this distor-

face Three: Legal Treatment of Domestic Subsidies (1984).

tion only gradually (as with tariffs) and export subsidies were banned outright.

Note: Statistics on the Use of Countervailing Measures

The data collected by the GATT Committee on Subsidies and Countervailing Measures reveals that countervailing duties are applied much less frequently than antidumping duties. Moreover, unlike antidumping actions, which are common in the United States, the European Community, Canada and Australia, countervailing duty cases have so far primarily been a U.S. phenomenon.

Antisubsidy Actions

July 1980—June 1984 [2]

Country	Actions Initiated	Provisional Measures	Definitive Duties
U.S.	139	56	30
EC	5	1	3
Japan	1	0	0
Canada	8	7	0
Australia	9	8	0
Chile	114	9	0

Examination of U.S. statistics indicates that as of February 1986 there have been 313 countervailing duty cases since 1974, including 266 processed under the 1979 statutory scheme. Of these 159 and 146 respectively were steel cases. In 12 cases no subsidization was found and in 128 cases no injury was found. Ten cases were pending and 82 were terminated or withdrawn without a final determination. Thus, since 1979, 34 actions have been successful, a success rate of only 13%.

(B) THE EVOLUTION OF THE INTERNATIONAL OBLIGATIONS

GATT regulation of subsidies is a complicated subject and the applicable rules have evolved over time. The original obligations in GATT were amended in 1955 and were expanded upon in the Tokyo Round Subsidies Code in 1979. In this subsection we will look at this evolution of the GATT obligations and then consider several cases where those obligations were at issue.

GATT Article XVI contains the general obligations on subsidies. It consisted originally of one paragraph (XVI:1), with a loose obligation to report all subsidies which operate to increase exports or decrease imports. The article was amended extensively during the GATT 1954–55 review session. An attempt was made at that session to develop meaningful restrictions on the use of subsidies that distort international trade patterns, but this attempt largely failed. Four paragraphs were added to Article XVI, containing two key obligations: one obligation (paragraph 3) prohibits using an export subsidy on primary products which results in obtaining more than "an equitable share of world export trade in that product * * *;" a second obligation (paragraph 4) prohibits a subsidy on the export of non-

2. GATT, 30th Supp. BISD 44–45 (1984);
GATT, 31st Supp. BISD 264–65 (1985).

primary products which results in an export price lower than the comparable price for like goods which are not exported (the so-called "bi-level pricing" condition).[3] These Article XVI amendments, however, were accepted only by certain industrialized nations of GATT. Developing countries objected to the differential treatment of primary and other goods. Consequently, most GATT members are not obligated to refrain from the use of export subsidies.[4]

It will be recalled that introduction of a new subsidy ("production subsidy") on a product which is bound in a country's GATT schedule has been termed a "prima facie nullification and impairment" for purposes of Article XXIII complaints.[5]

Apart from obligations concerning the use of subsidies, GATT authorizes unilateral government responses in the form of countervailing duties. Article VI of GATT governs such measures, prohibiting the use of both antidumping and countervailing duties for the same situation, and imposing a "material injury" requirement as a prerequisite to the use of countervailing duties. If these conditions are met, a government is authorized to apply a countervailing duty on imported goods (in excess of regular bound duty rates), in an amount "equal to the estimated bounty or subsidy" granted directly or indirectly on the "manufacture, production or export."

Thus, on the eve of the Tokyo Round, GATT regulated subsidies on four levels: (1) the loose reporting requirement of Article XVI, paragraph 1; (2) the restraints on export subsidies in Article XVI, paragraphs 3 and 4; (3) the restraints on new production subsidies under Article XXIII; and (4) the authorization of countervailing duties for subsidies under Article VI. In 1960, the GATT Contracting Parties adopted a report of a working party which included an "illustrative list" of practices that would be considered as "export subsidies" for purposes of GATT Article XVI, paragraph 4.[6] This list has been very important for the interpretation of GATT subsidy obligations, and was updated and changed a bit in the Tokyo Round. It is now the Annex to the Subsidies Code. The list is referred to in some of the materials set out below. The reader should note that some parts of the list referred to in the DISC case were changed in 1979. (The Subsidies Code and its Annex are included in the Documentary Supplement.)

3. Paragraph 4 also forbade the extension until December 31, 1957, of any existing subsidization by means of any new or expanded existing subsidies beyond those existing on January 1, 1955. This so-called "standstill" obligation was intended to suffice until the target date of January 1, 1958, when all export subsidies on non-primary goods would be prohibited. Agreement was not reached by that point, however. Consequently, the "standstill" obligation was extended five times, up to the end of 1967. By that time seventeen nations had signed the declaration giving effect to the provisions of Article XVI, paragraph 4, a document which had been issued on November 19, 1960, but which en-

tered into force only as nations signed. For a complete discussion of this subject, see J. Jackson, World Trade and the Law of GATT 372–74 (1969).

4. The countries that accepted the declaration were: Austria, Belgium, Canada, Denmark, France, Federal Republic of Germany, Italy, Japan, Luxemburg, Kingdom of the Netherlands, New Zealand, Norway, Southern Rhodesia, Sweden, Switzerland, the United Kingdom, and the United States.

5. See discussion of the Australia/Chile fertilizer case in Section 5.6(C) supra.

6. GATT, 9th Supp. BISD 185 (1961); see also J. Jackson, note 3 supra, at 385.

THE TOKYO ROUND OF MULTILATERAL TRADE NEGOTIATIONS, REPORT BY THE DIRECTOR–GENERAL OF GATT

54–60 (1979)

3. ISSUES IN THE NEGOTIATIONS

In the beginning of the negotiations, there was a sharp division of opinion as to the relative weight to be given to subsidies and countervailing duties. Some participants took the view that subsidization was the prime distorting factor and that countervailing duties were only necessary to the extent that countries continued to subsidize their exports. Other participants considered that the main aim of the negotiations should be to establish uniform rules for the imposition of countervailing duties.

In 1975 a proposal was tabled that there should be an international code to deal with export subsidies, third country subsidization, import-replacing measures, and offsetting measures. The code should categorize all types of subsidy practices and set out the conditions on which offsetting measures could be taken against such practices. Subsidies should be divided into the following three categories:

— prohibited (practices designed to increase the competitiveness of national producers, thereby distorting international trade);

— conditional (practices directed toward domestic economic, political or social objectives, but which may distort international trade);

— permitted (practices with little or no impact on international trade against which offsetting measures could not be taken).

Although this proposal was not maintained as a basis for the negotiations, elements of it were eventually carried over into the final Agreement.

(a) Subsidies: Approaches to the Negotiations

There was a general impression that in the industrial field the Declaration of 1960 prohibiting export subsidies on industrial products, to which almost all industrialized countries had subscribed, had worked reasonably well. There was, however, discussion of the need to expand and bring up to date the 1960 list of prohibited export subsidies.

A principal concern, on the part of some governments, related to the use of domestic subsidies. Many countries grant various forms of subsidies to assist domestic industries, such as steel and shipbuilding, that are in difficulties. For certain participants it was of major importance to retain a large degree of freedom to grant subsidies for regional purposes, particularly in depressed areas with high levels of unemployment.

While it was generally agreed that domestic subsidies should not be used to cause injury to other countries, their elimination or substantial reduction would, because of the fundamental economic, political as well as social factors in play, obviously present serious difficulties. On the other hand, these measures could have important effects on trade and it was reasonable to expect at least some mitigation of these effects.

In the view of some participants the Agreement should contain a statement that domestic subsidies should not be used to cause injury to others and an indicative list of domestic subsidies should be attached to the Agreement. An indicative list was unacceptable to other participants because the attachment to an Agreement of such a list would tend to give the measures listed a prohibited character, particularly as the list of prohibited export subsidies would also be attached.

By late 1978 a compromise formula was reached which would include a few examples of internal subsidy practices in the provision recognizing the possible adverse effects on trade of such practices.

(b) Countervailing Duties: Approaches to the Negotiations

The attention of several participants was principally focussed on countervailing duties and on a possible code to govern the application of these duties. They had in mind in particular the legislative situation in the United States.

The United States Tariff Act of 1930 did not require "material injury" as a condition for the imposition of countervailing duties and thus did not conform with the requirements of GATT Article VI:6(a). The imposition of countervailing duties against subsidized exports, without regard to any injury criterion, was a mandatory requirement under existing legislation.

Many participants took the firm position that the criterion of material injury in Article VI must be reaffirmed, defined more closely, and respected by all countries. The existence of a significant material injury must be proven and the causal link between injury and the particular subsidy established. The imposition of countervailing duties would [have] to be preceded by consultations with the country granting the subsidy.

For a number of developed countries acceptance by all of the "material injury" criterion was the crux of the negotiations.

Difficult and extensive negotiations—sometimes at a high political level—took place in this context. It was, however, ultimately agreed that the "material injury" criterion would be accepted by all governments adhering to the Agreement.

It was also agreed that signatories of the Agreement would have the possibility of taking counter-measures, not only on the basis of the "material injury" criterion of GATT Article VI, but also through Article XXIII action which should be handled, within strict time-limits, by the Committee of Signatories which, it was envisaged, would be set up under a code. Some participants were very hesitant about this suggestion, as it would seem to offer the easier option of "serious prejudice" under Article XVI instead of the "material injury" criterion of Article VI.

An issue in this context which caused much discussion was whether governments should be entitled to take provisional unilateral action under Article XXIII. Many countries could not accept that such unilateral action be taken in the absence of prior examination by an international body. They recognized, however, the need for quick action and were prepared to see strict time-limits fixed for action by the Committee of Signatories.

(c) Applicability of New Rules

A central issue, as in other parts of the Tokyo Round, was whether any new rules on subsidies and countervailing duties—possibly in the form of a code—should be applied to agricultural and industrial products alike.

From the beginning the main agricultural exporting countries had strongly held that the same rules should apply to both sectors. Other participants took the contrary view. It was agreed that minerals, hitherto classed as primary products to which Article XVI:3 of the GATT applied, should in the future be classed as manufactured products to which Article XVI:4 of the GATT would apply.

The final outcome was that the definition of the ways in which export subsidies on primary products might give the exporting country more than an equitable share of world export trade was made more precise.

Notes and Questions

(1) The status of adherence to the Subsidies Code is set out in Section 5.5(B) supra. The Code established a committee of signatories, known as the Committee on Subsidies and Countervailing Measures. The committee supervises the consultation, conciliation and dispute settlement procedures established by Articles 12, 13, 17 and 18 of the Code. It has also accepted New Zealand and Spain as signatories with reservations and has a working group studying the question of how to value subsidies.

(2) The reader should now review the Agreement on Interpretation and Application of Articles VI, XVI, and XXIII (the Subsidies Code), particularly Articles 8–11 and the Annex in the Documentary Supplement. As we proceed through this subsection and the next on U.S. law, it is critical to distinguish between GATT obligations on the use of subsidies, the violation of which may give rise to claims for compensation by the aggrieved party, and the GATT rules on when imports of products produced or exported with the assistance of subsidies may be subjected to countervailing duties. It is important to remember that even if a subsidy is not prohibited by GATT, GATT may permit it to be offset by countervailing duties, and, in the view of some, vice versa.

(3) What obligations are imposed in respect of nonexport subsidies? What sanctions may be imposed if nonexport subsidies are given in violation of the Code? What would the complaining party have to demonstrate? More specifically, as discussed in the materials in Section 9.6(B)(1) supra, the EC has used subsidies to assist in the restructuring of its steel industry. What arguments could the United States make under Article 8 of the Code to support a claim that it is entitled to compensation from the EC? Do you think the United States might have a chance of obtaining a favorable decision?

(4) What is the distinguishing characteristic(s) between export and nonexport subsidies? How would you establish that a subsidy not on the illustrative list is an export subsidy? In particular, does item (l) mean that the bilevel pricing concept of Article XVI is determinative for subsidies not on the list?

(5) What kind of export subsidies are permitted on nonprimary products? What is a nonprimary product? What rights does an aggrieved country have if a

prohibited export subsidy on nonprimary products is given? What actions can it take unilaterally? To what body might it take its complaints?

(6) What restrictions apply to the use of export subsidies in respect of primary products? What is a "more than equitable share of world export trade?"

The reader should consider how the foregoing questions are dealt with in the following GATT cases. We first look at two cases in GATT (one prior to the Tokyo Round, one subsequent) involving French and EC wheat and wheat flour. Consider how you would rate the success of the Subsidies Code in defining more precisely the rules applicable to primary products. We will then look at cases involving the questions of what is a primary product and what is an export subsidy.

FRENCH ASSISTANCE TO EXPORTS OF WHEAT AND WHEAT FLOUR

Report adopted on 21 November, 1958 [7]

I. INTRODUCTION

1. The Panel for Conciliation examined a complaint by the Government of Australia that as a result of subsidies being granted by the French Government on exports of wheat and wheat flour, inconsistently with the provisions of Article XVI:3, French exports have displaced Australian trade in these products particularly in its traditional wheat flour markets in Ceylon, Indonesia and Malaya, and have thus impaired the benefits which accrue to Australia under the General Agreement.

[The Panel described the French price stabilization system for wheat, which included a system of refunds to bring the French market price in line with the world market price on the export of French wheat. It then determined that the export refunds were financed in large part by government funds and therefore did not qualify as a price stabilization system of the sort permitted by the interpretive notes to Article XVI. The French system has been replaced by the EC system, which is described in the following case.]

The Development of French Exports of Wheat and Wheat Flour

6. In both the inter-war period and the early post-war years, the volume of French exports of wheat and wheat flour respectively has been characterized by wide fluctuations. Since world exports of wheat and of wheat flour have fluctuated less, France's share in the world total has been quite unstable. However, it rose to much higher levels in 1954 and especially in 1955, as regards both [wheat and] wheat flour—particularly the latter. Disregarding effects of the crop failure of 1956, French exports of wheat now account for 7½ per cent of the world total and her exports of wheat flour represent 9 to 10 per cent of world exports.

* * *

7. GATT, 7th Supp. BISD 46 (1959). On export subsidies in GATT generally, see Phegan, GATT Article XVI.3: Export Subsidies and "Equitable Shares," 17 J. World Trade L. 251 (1982): Seyoum, Export Subsidies Under the MTN—An Analysis with Particular Emphasis on Developing Countries, 18 J. World Trade L. 512 (1984).

7. Judging from export unit values, the prices charged for French exports of wheat flour (to destinations outside the franc zone) have in recent years been on the whole lower than those of other exporters. * * * This is further confirmed by the import unit values recorded in Ceylon, Malaya (including Singapore) and Indonesia * * * and by recent quotations for French wheat flour in these markets that were supplied by the Australian delegation and were not disputed by the French delegation.

* * *

Consideration as to Whether the Operation of the French System Resulted in France Obtaining More Than an Equitable Share of the World Export Trade in Wheat and Wheat Flour

15. The Panel considered whether, in the terms of paragraph 3 of Article XVI, France had granted subsidies on the export of wheat and wheat flour in such a manner as to have resulted in France having obtained more than an equitable share of world export trade in these products. The Panel noted that there was no explicit definition in Article XVI of what constituted an "equitable" share in world markets. It was recalled, however, that at both Havana and the Review Session when the provisions of this paragraph were discussed it was implicitly agreed that the concept of "equitable" share was meant to refer to share in "world" export trade of a particular product and not to trade in that product in individual markets.

It was understood, moreover, that in making such a determination the CONTRACTING PARTIES should not lose sight of the desirability of facilitating the satisfaction of world requirements of the commodity concerned in the most effective and economic manner, and that due account should be taken of any special factors affecting world trade in the products under reference with particular regard to the exporting country's share of world trade in those products during a previous representative period.

16. In the first instance, the French representative drew attention to France's established position in world trade as an exporter of wheat and wheat flour. Although curtailed in immediate post-war years as a result of damage incurred during the war, France was again assuming its traditional rôle. This *de facto* status of France as an exporter of wheat and wheat flour has been recognized by the International Wheat Agreement under which export quotas have been accorded to France. Moreover, France's share in the exports of wheat and wheat flour among the five major exporting countries (United States, Canada, Argentina, Australia and France) was considerably less in proportion to her production as compared with the others.

17. The Panel noted that French exports of wheat and wheat flour began to rise in 1954 in absolute quantity to levels very substantially exceeding the quantities exported in any year since 1934 and have since remained considerably higher than in pre-war or early post-war years. This increase in the absolute quantities of wheat and of wheat flour exported by France also represents an increase in France's share of world exports, especially as regards wheat flour.

18. The Panel further considered whether this increase in France's share of world exports, particularly of wheat flour, could be attributed to the

operation of the French subsidy system. The facts above mentioned in paragraph 7 (and also in Appendix Table A) show that French exporters have been able to quote prices for wheat flour lower than those quoted by other exporters, whether at f.o.b. or c.i.f. values. Moreover, judging from export unit values, the price charged by French exporters for wheat flour has in recent years barely exceeded that charged for wheat. While this seems to be the practice followed also in some other European countries, e.g. in Germany, flour is exported even more cheaply than wheat, the export price for flour charged by Australia, Canada and the United States does exceed the export price of wheat by 30 to 50 per cent (see Table 2).

19. In these circumstances, it is reasonable to conclude that, while there is no statistical definition of an "equitable" share in world exports, subsidy arrangements have contributed to a large extent to the increase in France's exports of wheat and of wheat flour, and that the present French share of world export trade, particularly in wheat flour, is more than equitable.

IV. ALLEGED NULLIFICATION OR IMPAIRMENT OF BENEFITS ACCRUING TO AUSTRALIA UNDER THE GENERAL AGREEMENT

20. On the basis of statistical data before it the Panel considered whether and to what extent the operation of subsidies granted by France on the export of wheat and wheat flour had caused injury to Australia's normal commercial interests, and whether such an injury represented an impairment of benefits accruing to Australia under the General Agreement.

21. The Australian representative contended that the effect of the French subsidies had been such as to impair benefits Australia expected under the General Agreement, viz., the assurance that its export trade would not face subsidies going beyond the limits permissible under Article XVI.

* * *

23. On the basis of the statistics submitted and of the explanations provided by the Australian and French representatives, the Panel arrived at the following conclusions:

(a) French exports of wheat flour to the three Southeast Asian countries rose substantially in recent years and accounted for a growing share in France's total wheat flour exports which rose from 13 per cent in 1953–54 to 34 per cent in 1957–58. Australia's exports to these markets fell substantially during this period and their share in Australia's total export of wheat flour declined from 64 per cent in 1953–54 to 50 per cent in 1957–58.

(b) In the three Southeast Asian markets combined, French supplies represented a greatly increased proportion of total imports of wheat flour, accounting for 0.7 per cent in 1954 and 46 per cent in the first half of 1958. The share of Australian supplies, on the other hand, fell from 83 per cent in 1954 to 37 per cent in the first half of 1958.

(c) While other suppliers of wheat flour have recently begun to play a larger part in the Southeast Asian markets, and although it is difficult to estimate to what extent such incursions as these are displacing traditional exporters, it is nevertheless clear that French supplies have in fact to a large extent displaced Australian supplies in the three markets.

(d) As regards the contention of the French representative that the reduction in Australia's exports to these markets was due to limited supplies, it is clear that Australia could not have maintained her combined exports of wheat *and* wheat flour at normal levels in 1957–58. However, Australia could have effected her traditional exports of wheat *flour* in spite of the crop failures, owing to measures taken by the Australian Wheat Board to set aside a quantity of wheat considered necessary to keep up normal exports of flour; this was substantiated by the declaration of the Australian representative that there were no contractual commitments for the export of wheat in the form of grain. Actually, the growth of French subsidized exports to Ceylon and other Southeast Asian countries and the consequent displacement of normal Australian flour exports resulted in the wheat thus available for transformation into flour being exported *as wheat* to other markets.

(e) Since it is obviously more profitable to export wheat flour rather than wheat, Australia has suffered a direct damage which could be evaluated by applying the price difference between wheat flour and wheat to the quantity of Australian exports that were displaced by French exports. It would, however, be difficult to assess this displacement quantitatively with any precision. In addition to this direct damage, there were other incidental adverse effects upon Australia which cannot be measured. Thus, Australia has suffered indirectly by the reduction in the domestic supply of the by-products of flour milling and by the reduction in transport facilities for other Australian export goods to the Southeast Asian markets.

* * *

27. In the light of the considerations set forth in Sections III and IV of this report, the Panel submits the following draft recommendation for the consideration of the CONTRACTING PARTIES.

* * *

The CONTRACTING PARTIES

Recommend that the French Government consider appropriate measures to avoid, in the future, that the system of payments by the Office National Interprofessionnel des Céréales (ONIC) to exporters of wheat and wheat flour operates in such a manner as to create adverse effects on normal Australian exports of flour to Southeast Asian markets, and, more generally, on markets of wheat and wheat flour. These measures might consist of a revision of the methods applied by ONIC for the financing of French exports of wheat and more particularly of wheat flour, or of an agreement by the Government of France to enter into consultations with the Government of Australia before new contracts are entered into by French exporters of flour to the Southeast Asian markets, with a view to minimizing the impact of such contracts on normal Australian trade channels.

EUROPEAN ECONOMIC COMMUNITY—SUBSIDIES ON EXPORTS OF WHEAT FLOUR [8]

[The United States claimed that the EC export refund system applied to wheat flour violated the Subsidies Code because it resulted (1) in the EC obtaining a more than equitable share of the world export market for wheat flour and (2) in prices materially below those of other suppliers to that

---

8. GATT Doc. SCM/42, see GATT, 31st Supp. BISD 259, at para. 17 (1985). The report was reproduced in 18 BNA ITEX 899–916 (1983). It has not been adopted by the GATT Subsidies Committee.

market. The United States claimed nullification and impairment under Article XXIII and serious prejudice to its interests under Article 8 of the Code.]

III. FACTUAL ASPECTS

(a) EEC Export Refunds on Wheat Flour

* * *

3.4 The common organization of the market in cereals provides a single system of internal prices valid for the whole Community, and a common trading system with third countries which is designed to prevent price fluctuation on the world market from affecting cereal prices ruling within the Community.

3.5 In the case of wheat flour, the Community internal price regime consists of a series of price mechanisms designed to maintain an indicative or "target" price for common wheat within the EEC, as well as to ensure the protection of the Community milling industry (Regulation No. 2734/75). As part of the system established to achieve these ends, a threshold price for wheat flour is calculated each year, with periodic adjustments as necessary. The price level thus established serves as the internal EEC price standard for purposes of the Community trading regime.

* * *

3.7 In the case of import of wheat flour into the Community from third countries, a levy is charged which is equal to the threshold price less the import c.i.f. price, normally calculated for Rotterdam on the basis of the most favourable purchasing opportunity on the world market, with appropriate account being taken of differences in quality.

3.8 General rules for granting export refunds on cereals (including wheat flour) and for fixing the amount for such refunds are contained in Regulation (EEC) No. 2746/75. Under this regulation, an export refund may be granted where necessary to cover the difference between the established price for wheat flour within the Community and those prevailing on third markets.

* * *

3.10 In practice, the mechanism described in the regulation for fixing the refund works as follows:

(a) The first two criteria are aimed at determining the cost price f.o.b. European port for wheat flour in bags. An announcement is made weekly for each member State of the market price for domestic milling wheat delivered to mills. This wheat price is then converted by the Commission into a flour price by means of fixed coefficients relating to the quantity of wheat needed to make 1 ton of best quality EEC type flour, the millers' profit margins, the value of the milling offals, and costs incurred for bagging the flour and putting it in on a f.o.b. position. This calculation results, for the whole Community, in a range of f.o.b. wheat flour prices, which are different according to the export points. From this range of prices the Commission selects a price as representative of Community prices (f.o.b.) for wheat flour for purposes of calculating the level of export refund for the Community as a whole. As a general rule, the French prices are selected because France is the EEC member state with the largest surplus of common wheat; it exports most common wheat and flour to third countries, and Rouen is the leading European port for the export of cereal and flour.

(b) The third criteria is aimed at determining other countries' export prices for wheat flour, according to the available information. This determination is made essentially on the basis of world prices for wheat (notably common wheat of a quality comparable to that of European wheat), as the cost of wheat is regarded by the Community producers as the major factor for establishing the price of flour. Certain additional elements are also taken into account, including wheat flour export prices of other suppliers to the extent these are available.

3.11 The Commission fixes the level of export refund based on its assessment of the foregoing information and calculations in light of the relevant EEC Regulations. A regular price study is made weekly, but the rate of refund generally remains unchanged for longer periods. Modifications are made in the refund level when the difference between EEC wheat flour prices and other wheat flour prices changes to a significant degree.

3.12 The level of export refund on a particular shipment of wheat flour is normally that applicable on the day of exportation.

*   *   *

3.14 The funding of the export refund on wheat flour is made by a public contribution out of the budget of the Communities (EAFFG) from the same budget allocation used for the export refund on wheat in the natural state.

*   *   *

3.24 As regards wheat flour prices in the international trade, a world price for flour does not exist, at least in the sense it does for other internationally traded commodities, such as wheat, coffee, sugar, cocoa, etc., nor is there a future market for wheat flour. Published quotations do not represent specific, individual market transactions, but reflect rather an average of such transactions. Wheat flour export prices are fixed freely by the exporters on the basis of their own appreciation of the market, consideration being given, *inter alia*, to their own domestic prices for wheat flour, the quantity of flour involved in the shipment, transportation and other handling costs, and also the price level of wheat in the importing country. As a result, broad price differences often occur in a given market for a given type and quality of wheat flour. These differences in prices are normally sharpened by differences in the quality of wheat flour. Little is known, however, on actual prices paid for individual deliveries. Most transactions are concluded by means of tenders to which little publicity is given. Usually, only the price of the winning tender is known, as private firms generally consider pricing to be a confidential matter.

*   *   *

The panel reached the following conclusions:

1. EEC export refunds for wheat flour must be considered as a form of subsidy which was subject to the provisions of Article XVI of the General Agreement as interpreted and applied by the Code.

2. It was evident to the Panel that the EC share of world exports of wheat flour has increased considerably over the period under consideration when application of EC export subsidies was the general practice, while the share of the U.S. and other suppliers has decreased.

3. The Panel found, however, that it was unable to conclude as to whether the increased share has resulted in the EC "having more than an equitable share" in terms of Article X, in light of the highly artificial levels and conditions of trade in wheat flour, the complexity of developments in the markets, including the interplay of a number of special factors, the relative importance of which it is impossible to assess, and, most importantly, the difficulties inherent in the concept of "more than equitable share."

4. The Panel concluded that, despite the considerable increase in EC exports, market displacement in the sense of Article X:2(A) was not evident in the 17 markets examined by the Panel.

5. With regard to price undercutting in the sense of Article X:3, the Panel found that, on the basis of available information there was not sufficient ground to reach a definite conclusion as to whether the EC had granted export subsidies on export of wheat flour in a manner which resulted in prices materially below those of other suppliers to the same markets.

6. The Panel was not convinced, however, that the application of EC export subsidies had not caused undue disturbance to the normal commercial interests of the United States in the sense of Article XVI:2, to the extent that it may well have resulted in reduced sales opportunities for the United States.

7. The Panel considered it desirable that the EC, bearing in mind the provisions of Article XVI:2, make greater efforts to limit the use of subsidies on the exports of wheat flour. The Panel considered that there were a number of practical aspects of the application of the export refund which might be examined to this end.

8. Finally, from a broader economic and trade policy perspective, the Panel considered the situation as regards export subsidies and other aspects of trade in wheat flour to be highly unsatisfactory and was concerned over what this implied for the effectiveness of the legal provisions in this area. The artificial level and conditions of much of the trade in this product typified the current problems and prospective risks. In this connection it found it anomalous, for instance, that the EC which without the application of export subsidies would generally not be in a position to export substantial quantities of wheat flour, had over time increased its share of the world market to become by far the largest exporters.

9. The Panel considered that certain problems might be reduced by improved transparency and possibly other forms of multilateral cooperation in either the IWC or the GATT. It was of the view, however, that solutions to the problem of export subsidies in this area could only be found in making the pertinent provisions of the Code more operational, stringent and effective in application. Areas which deserve attention in this regard are, inter alia:

(i) a clearer and common understanding of the concept of "more than equitable share," and rendering the concept more operational.

(ii) consideration of whether international understandings relating to sales on other than commercial terms adequately complement and support intended disciplines on export subsidies.

EUROPEAN ECONOMIC COMMUNITY—SUBSIDIES ON EXPORTS OF PASTA [9]

[The United States claimed that EC export refunds on pasta were strictly prohibited by Article 9 of the Subsidies Code. The EC export refund on pasta is essentially equivalent to the refund that would be applicable to the wheat content of the pasta if the wheat had been exported separately. The system of refunds on wheat is described in the preceding case. In this case, the refunds were paid to the pasta makers, not the wheat growers, although both benefited since in the absence of the subsidy, EC pasta could not easily compete on world markets, which would mean lower sales of pasta for the pasta makers and lower purchases of wheat by the pasta makers from EC farmers. The issue in this case is whether such an export subsidy is on a primary product (and thus subject to the "equitable share" rule) or on a nonprimary product (and thus prohibited).]

FACTS RELATED TO THE LEGAL ASPECTS OF THE MATTER

2.11   The negotiating history of Article 9 of the Code starts from the Havana Charter. The corresponding Article (Article 26) prohibited export subsidies on any product except on primary commodities (which were subject to special provisions of Articles 27 and 28).

2.12   Article XVI:4 of the General Agreement corresponds to Article 26:1 of the Havana Charter. It also uses the same definition of the term "primary product" as that provided for in Article 56:1 of the Havana Charter.

2.13   At the 12th Session of the CONTRACTING PARTIES in 1957 the United States sought clarification of the scope of Article XVI and proposed that Article XVI:4 should not prevent a contracting party, in this particular case the United States, from subsidizing exports of processed products (cotton textiles) if such subsidy was essentially the payment that would have been made on the raw material (cotton) used in the production of this processed product if the raw material had been exported in its natural form.

2.14   The US interpretation was not accepted by other contracting parties. No contracting party spoke in favour of it, while several contracting parties clearly rejected it. Some contracting parties proposed that the United States attach a reservation to its signature of the declaration extending the standstill provisions of Article XVI:4. *   *   *

2.15   The United States signed the Declaration extending the standstill provisions of Article XVI:4 on 21 November 1958 "with the understanding that this Declaration shall not prevent the United States as part of its

---

9. GATT Doc. SCM/43, see GATT, 31st Supp. BISD 259, at para. 17 (1985). The report was reproduced in 8 BNA ITIM 468-77 (1983). It has not been yet adopted by the GATT Council. See Section 5.6 supra.

subsidization of exports of a primary product, from making a payment on an exported processed product (not itself a primary product), which has been produced from such primary product, if such payment is essentially limited to the amount of the subsidy which would have been payable on the quantity of such primary product, if exported in primary form, contained in the production of the processed product."

[The Panel noted that the United States reaffirmed its position in 1960 and notified the refunds on cotton products as refunds on primary products in 1963. The Panel also noted that the EC had notified its refunds on processed agricultural products as export refunds and Switzerland had once notified a similar practice. It then reviewed the terms of Article 9.]

2.33   There is no record of any discussion or understanding as to the interpretation of Article 9 nor has any such interpretation been notified to the GATT for the record or attached to any acceptance of the Code. The only reservations made to the Code in general and to Article 9 in particular were those by New Zealand and Spain but they concern only the right to maintain, over a limited period, certain export subsidy practices which are considered as clearly prohibited by the Code.

* * *

IV. Findings and Conclusions

* * *

4.2   The first question the Panel considered was whether or not pasta was a primary product within the meaning of footnote 29 to Article 9 of the Code. It noted that neither party had finally contended that pasta was a primary product. The Panel was of the opinion that pasta was not a primary product but was a processed agricultural product.

4.3   The Panel noted that under the relevant EEC Regulations the EEC system for granting refunds to exporters of pasta products was financed from public funds and that it operated to increase exports of such products from the EEC. The Panel concluded that this system of granting refunds must be considered a form of subsidy in the sense of Article XVI of the General Agreement. Moreover, the EEC had recognized this and had, pursuant to Article XVI:1, notified its system of refunds to exporters of pasta products since 1970.

4.4   The Panel further considered whether the subsidies in question were granted on exports of a primary product (durum wheat), which was incorporated in the processed product (pasta products), and therefore would fall under the provisions of Article 10 of the Code. The Panel noted the view of the EEC that the refund was a cereals refund granted and calculated exclusively in respect of the raw material component (durum wheat) with the intention of placing EEC exports of pasta products who were using domestic durum wheat in the same competitive position as manufacturers using durum wheat, including subsidized EEC durum wheat used in third countries, bought at world market prices. However the Panel considered that the definition of "certain primary products" in Article 9 of the Code, footnote 29, included only a product of farm, forest or fishery "in its natural form or which has undergone such processing as is customarily required to prepare it for marketing in substantial volume in international trade." The

Panel was of the opinion that durum wheat incorporated in pasta products could not be considered as a separate "primary product" and that the EEC export refunds paid to exporters of pasta products could not be considered to be paid on the export of durum wheat. In the Panel's view, the ordinary meaning to be given to the terms of Article XVI of the General Agreement, as interpreted and applied in Articles 9 and 10 of the Code, in their context and in the light of their object and purpose excluded the possibility of considering the export of a processed product in terms of the export of its constituent components, be they primary or processed products. The Panel therefore concluded that the EEC export refunds were granted on the export of pasta products and operated to increase exports of pasta products by refunding a part of the cost of these processed products.

4.5   The Panel then examined whether the language of Article 9 of the Code or its negotiating history gave any indication that would permit the granting of subsidies on exports of processed products, to the amount which would have been granted on one or various primary components, had these components been exported in their natural form. Apart from the discussions in the Committee arising from the present dispute, the Panel noted that there was no record of any discussion or understanding as to the interpretation of Article 9 nor had any such interpretation been notified to GATT for the record or attached to any acceptance of the Code. It also noted that the first draft of the Code circulated in MTN/NTM/W/168 considered a possibility that the prohibition of Article 9 would apply to non-agricultural products (instead of to products other than certain primary products) while agricultural products would be subject to what became Article 10 of the Code. In all subsequent drafts this possibility had been dropped and replaced by differing obligations with respect to "products other than certain primary products" and "primary products." The drafters used the term "certain primary products" instead of "primary products" because minerals had been excluded from the scope of Article 10 and subjected to the disciplines of Article 9. Consequently Article 9 covered all products other than products of farm, forest or fishery in their natural form or which have undergone such processing as was customarily required to prepare them for marketing in substantial volume in international trade. The Panel concluded that the drafters of the Code had clearly recognized that the terms "primary product" and "agricultural product" were not synonyms and that an agricultural product, if it was not a primary product as defined above, should be subjected to different obligations (Article 9) than a primary product (Article 10).

4.6   The Panel noted the differing views of the parties to the dispute concerning the status of the text attached by the United States to the Declaration Giving Effect to the Provisions of Article XVI:4 of the General Agreement. The Panel recognized the well-established principle that the determination of whether a unilateral statement, however phrased or named, was an interpretative declaration or a reservation was dependent not on the particular label attached to the statement by the country concerned but on whether the statement intended to exclude or modify the legal effects of certain provisions of the agreement in their application to that country. The Panel was of the view that the US understanding was intended to limit the legal obligations of the United States under Article XVI:4 and had to be recognized as a reservation rather than an interpretation. This conclusion was confirmed by the history of this understanding, and in particular by the fact that it was referred to as a reservation by the Chairman of the CONTRACTING PARTIES at the 13th Session in 1958 as well as by four contracting parties and that these statements were not challenged by any other contracting party.

4.7   The Panel then considered whether the US reservation to Article XVI:4 had any relevance to the US rights and obligations under the Code. The Panel noted that the United States had not made a formal reservation on its acceptance of the Code. The Panel was of the opinion that the US reservation previously made to Article XVI:4 was not relevant to the US position under the Code since it could not be automatically carried over to the Code. In order for a reservation to be valid under the Code, the United States would have had to make the reservation in compliance with the provisions of Article 19:3 of the Code, which had not been the case. The Panel also noted that the United States had recognized in its submission to the Panel that "the United States gave up the legal right to engage in this practice when the United States signed the Subsidy Code without a reservation." Since the Panel found that there was no US reservation with respect to the US rights and obligations under the Code, it concluded that the United States was not estopped from challenging the EEC practice in question.

4.8   The Panel noted, however, that during the discussion in the Committee some Signatories were of the opinion that such practices as the one under consideration had not been perceived by them as being inconsistent with Article XVI of the General Agreement and these Signatories were therefore of the opinion that these practices could not be inconsistent with Article 9 of the Code. It was possible that some Signatories, when signing the Code, might have believed that they could continue their existing practices of subsidizing exports of some processed agricultural products to the extent that this subsidization was confined to the primary product components. The Panel, however, noted that these beliefs, if they existed, were never transformed into formal, legally effective statements and could not therefore have the effect of changing the meaning of the Code or obligations of Signatories under the Code.

4.9   The Panel examined whether or not there was evidence available which would establish a generally accepted practice which might have permitted the subsidization of exports of processed agricultural products to the extent that this subsidization was confined to the primary product components. The Panel noted that the EEC had, since 1970, notified under Article XVI:1 its subsidies on exports of pasta products and certain other processed agricultural products. At least one other Signatory had regularly notified a similar practice. There were also elements in notifications of some other Signatories which might indicate the existence of similar practices; however, these latter notifications were made, in the view of the Panel, in too general terms to permit any analysis of their scope and nature. The Panel found that the notifications under Article XVI:1 and other evidence available to it did not establish that there was such a generally accepted practice. The Panel viewed the wording of Article 9 as clear and unambiguous and therefore considered that even if the actual practices of some Signatories had become generally accepted, these practices would still have been inconsistent with the provisions of Article 9.

4.10   The Panel considered that the notifications under Article XVI:1 of certain export subsidies on processed agricultural products did neither require nor preclude contracting parties from challenging the legality of such practices. As contracting parties were under no legal obligation to challenge the legality of export subsidies of other contracting parties, the mere abstaining from such a legal challenge could not be relied upon as acquiescence to or construed as approval of the legality of such export subsidies. In this context the Panel noted that another Panel had concluded that the fact that certain practices had been in force for some time without being the subject of complaints was not, in itself, conclusive evidence that there was a consensus that they were compatible with the General Agreement (BISD 23S, page 114, paragraph 79).

4.11   The Panel considered the practical effect of the EEC interpretation of Article 9 of the code. The Panel was of the view that if this interpretation had become a general rule, it would have radically altered the meaning of this Article thereby substantially reducing its scope and impact. Such an interpretation, if generally followed, would have permitted the subsidization of exports of almost all processed products within the purview of Article 9 which contained primary product components which were the product of farm, forest or fishery.

4.12   The Panel considered that paragraph (d) of the Illustrative List of Export Subsidies was not relevant to the case under consideration because the EEC system under examination involved the payment of refunds to exporters of pasta products whereas paragraph (d) related to the delivery by governments or their agencies of inputs for use in the production of exported goods.

4.13   The Panel did not find it necessary to reach a conclusion on the question of "absence of any allegation by the United States in respect of injury", which was raised by the EEC, because footnote 26 to Article 8:4 states: "Signatories recognize that nullification or impairment of benefits may also arise through the failure of a Signatory to carry out its obligations under the General Agreement or this Agreement. Where such failure concerning export subsidies is determined by the Committee to exist, adverse effects may, without prejudice to paragraph 9 of Article 18 below, be presumed to exist. The other Signatory will be accorded a reasonable opportunity to rebut this presumption."

4.14   After having taken all the above considerations into account the Panel concluded that the EEC subsidies on exports of pasta products were granted in a manner inconsistent with Article 9 of the Code.

Note

One member of the Pasta panel dissented. He did not view the meaning of Article 9 as so clear and unambiguous and thought that the general practice of subsidizing processed agricultural exports and the lack of negotiating history or reservations in respect of Article 9 demonstrated that there was a general view that such subsidization was permitted under GATT. The dissent clearly has a point. Can you imagine the EC accepting the Subsidies Code if it had anticipated this decision? The pasta subsidy question has become involved with U.S. charges that the EC unfairly discriminates against U.S. citrus exports by granting preferential treatment to citrus exports from various Mediterranean countries.[10]

DISC—UNITED STATES TAX LEGISLATION
Report of the Panel presented to the Council of Representatives on 12 November 1976 [11]

[The EC complained that a U.S. statute authorizing so-called domestic international sales corporations (DISCs) operated as an export subsidy. DISCs were typically wholly owned subsidiaries of U.S. companies that exported goods. A DISC was permitted to engage essentially only in the export business. Under U.S. Internal Revenue Service tax rules on income allocation between a DISC and its parent and on distributions, 25% of the combined DISC-parent export earnings were allocated to the DISC and the income tax due thereon was deferred until (a) the parent received such earnings from the DISC, (b) the parent ceased to own the DISC, (c) the DISC was liquidated or (d) the DISC ceased to qualify as a DISC. DISCs were used extensively. In 1976, there were over 8000 DISCs and DISC exports in 1974 totalled $43.5 billion, or 61% of total U.S. exports. The percentage was expected to reach 75% in 1976. It was estimated that U.S. exports were several billion dollars higher as a result of DISCs.]

67.   *   *   *   The Panel concluded that [the DISC legislation] conferred a tax benefit and that this benefit was essentially related to exports. The Panel considered that if the corporation income tax was reduced with respect to export related activities and was unchanged with respect to domestic activities for the internal market this would tend to lead to an expansion of export activity. Therefore the DISC would result in more resources being attracted to export activities than would have occurred in the absence of such benefits for exports.

68. The Panel noted that the United States Treasury had acknowledged that exports had increased as a result of the DISC legislation and the Panel considered that the fact that so many DISCs had been created was evidence that DISC status conferred a substantial benefit.

69. The Panel noted that the DISC legislation was intended, in its own terms, to increase United States exports and concluded that, as its benefits arose as a function of profits from exports, it should be regarded as an export subsidy.

10. See Section 10.5(C), note 6 infra. See generally Boger, The United States—European Community Agricultural Export Subsidies Dispute, 16 Law & Poly.Intl.Bus. 173 (1984).

11. GATT Doc. No. L/4422; GATT, 23d Supp. BISD 98 (1977). See Jackson, The Jurisprudence of International Trade: The DISC Case in GATT, 72 Am.J.Intl.L. 747 (1978).

70.   The Panel examined whether a deferral of tax was "a remission" in terms of item (c) or "an exemption" in terms of item (d) of the illustrative list of 1960 (BISD, 9 Suppl. p. 186).

71.   The Panel was not convinced that a deferral, *simply* because it is given for an indeterminate period, was equal to a remission or an exemption. In addition it noted that the DISC legislation provided for the termination of the deferral under specified circumstances.   The Panel further noted, however, that the deferral did not attract the interest component of the tax normally levied for late or deferred payment and therefore concluded that, to this extent, the DISC legislation constituted a partial exemption which was covered by one or both of paragraphs (c) and (d) of the illustrative list.

72.   The Panel noted that the contracting parties that had accepted the 1960 Declaration had agreed that the practices in the illustrative list were generally to be considered as subsidies in the sense of Article XVI:4.   The Panel further noted that these contracting parties considered that, in general, the practices contained in the illustrative list could be presumed to result in bi-level pricing, and considered that this presumption could therefore be applied to the DISC legislation.   The Panel concluded, however, from the words "generally to be considered" that these contracting parties did not consider that the presumption was absolute.

73.   The Panel considered that, from an economic point of view there was a presumption that an export subsidy would lead to any or a combination of the following consequences in the export sector: (a) lowering of prices, (b) increase of sales effort and (c) increase of profits per unit.   Because the subsidy was both significant and broadly based it was to be expected that all of these effects would occur and that, if one occurred, the other two would not necessarily be excluded.   A concentration of the subsidy benefits on prices could lead to substantial reductions in prices.   The Panel did not accept that a reduction in prices in export markets needed automatically to be accompanied by similar reductions in domestic markets.   These conclusions were supported by statements by American personalities and companies and the Panel felt that it should pay some regard to this evidence.

74.   The Panel therefore concluded that the DISC legislation in some cases had effects which were not in accordance with the United States' obligations under Article XVI:4.

* * *

79.   The Panel noted the United States argument that it had introduced the DISC legislation to correct an existing distortion created by tax practices of certain other contracting parties.   However, the Panel did not accept that one distortion could be justified by the existence of another one and considered that, if the United States had considered that other contracting parties were violating the General Agreement, it could have had recourse to the remedies which the General Agreement offered.   On the other hand, the fact that tax practices of certain other countries had been in force for some time without being the subject of complaints was not, in itself, conclusive evidence that there was a consensus that they were compatible with the General Agreement.

80. In the light of the above and bearing in mind the precedent set by the Uruguayan case (BISD, 11 Suppl. p. 100), the Panel found that there was a *prima facie* case of nullification or impairment of benefits which other contracting parties were entitled to expect under the General Agreement.

Notes

(1) The same GATT panel found that the U.S. complaints about the export promoting effects of the Belgian, French and Dutch tax systems were well grounded.[12] Essentially the United States claimed that the territorial basis of those systems—income earned by French companies outside France, for example, was not taxed in France—combined with relaxed standards as to when income was considered to be earned outside the country, effectively operated as an export subsidy. The panel concluded in respect of France that France [13]

> allowed some part of export activities, belonging to an economic process originating in the country, to be outside the scope of French taxes. In this way France had foregone revenues from this source and created a possibility of a pecuniary benefit to exports in those cases where * * * tax provisions were significantly more liberal in foreign countries.

> The Panel found that however much the practices may have been an incidental consequence of French taxation principles rather than a specific policy intention, they nonetheless constituted a subsidy on exports because the above-mentioned benefits to exports did not apply to domestic activities for the internal market.

In responding to the U.S. countercomplaints, the Europeans did not argue that they had grandfather rights. Could they have done so?

(2) In the fall of 1981 a compromise agreement regarding the DISC controversy was reached between the United States and the European Community under which the GATT Council adopted the panel reports "on the understanding that with respect to these cases, and in general, economic processes (including transactions involving exported goods) located outside the territorial limits of the exporting country, need not be subject to taxation by the exporting country and should not be regarded as export activities in terms of Article XVI:4 of the General Agreement. It is further understood that Article XVI:4 requires that arm's-length pricing be observed, i.e., prices for goods in transactions between exporting enterprises and foreign buyers under their or the same control should for tax purposes be the prices which would be charged between independent enterprises acting at arm's length. Furthermore, Article XVI:4 does not prohibit the adoption of measures to avoid double taxation of foreign source income." [14]

(3) The DISC legislation was replaced in 1984 with legislation authorizing so-called Foreign Sales Corporations (FSCs).[15] The new statute essentially provides that if its conditions are met certain income earned by a foreign corporate subsidiary of a U.S. corporation will not be subject to U.S. tax. The statute's presumptions as to income allocation have been questioned in GATT, where the EC has recently reiterated its claim of $10 billion in compensation for damages allegedly caused to it by the DISC legislation.[16]

12. GATT, 23d Supp. BISD 114 (France), 127 (Belgium), 137 (the Netherlands) (1977).

13. 23d Supp. BISD, at 125.

14. GATT, 28th Supp. BISD 114 (1982).

15. 26 U.S.C.A. §§ 921–27.

16. 2 BNA Intl.Trade Rptr. 443 (1985).

Problems

Under GATT, as interpreted by the Subsidies Code, and particularly by the Annex and Article 11(3) of the Code, which of the following are export subsidies and which are nonexport subsidies? Does the nature of the governmental unit (federal, regional, local) affect your answer?

(1) "Tariff drawbacks," by which a firm which exports goods receives a refund of the tariffs which were imposed upon imported raw materials, or component parts, utilized in the production of the goods for export.

(2) A pro rata corporate income tax rebate for goods exported, calculated by applying the ratio of the value of goods exported over the total value of goods produced, multiplied by the corporate income tax.

(3) Export credit financing by a government agency. (a) Assume that the interest rate on the loan is at currently available market interest rates in the country of export. (b) Assume that the interest rate is lower than available market rates, but is at least as high as the government borrowing rate. (c) Assume that the interest rate is lower than available market rates and the government borrowing rate.

(4) Government grants to firms which employ previously unemployed or handicapped workers.

(5) Waivers of city real estate or corporate income tax by a municipality, for a specified period of time.

(6) Provision of a favorable lease rate on a factory built with proceeds of tax-free municipal bonds. Assume the factory exports 70% of its products.

(7) Government grants for on-the-job training for local high school students to work in a local factory that exports most of its products.

(8) Government grants to companies which train workers in certain electronic or "hi-tech" jobs.

(9) Government grants to universities to assist in developing training programs for scientists and technical workers in particular industries. Assume the industries export 50% of their products.

(10) Government research and development contracts with industries, to develop certain technologies (e.g., defense, aircraft or computer technology).

(11) Extensive fire and police protection (which reduces the insurance costs to business).

(12) Government grants to firms for use in encouraging the retirement or relocation of unneeded workers.

(13) Government grants to laid-off workers, which grants relieve firms of legal or moral obligations to make severance payments.

(14) Government grants to firms to enable the closing of unprofitable facilities.

(15) Government renewal of port facilities (a) to keep exporters from leaving economically depressed area or (b) for no specific purpose, although beneficial to exporters.

(16) Government revision of its laws for the protection of intellectual property in a way that benefits exporters of "high-tech" products.

(17) Government failure to enforce strictly its existing antipollution/antitrust laws against export industries. Government has only very lax antipollution/antitrust laws.

(18) Government has extensive social programs that have led to a lower manufacturing wage level in its economy, which exports a significant proportion of manufactured goods produced.

(19) One particularly difficult problem that has arisen in recent years is called "industrial targeting." How, if at all, should GATT treat government policies that have the effect of promoting particular sectors of the economy? Such policies could include encouraging research and development in those sectors (and discouraging the licensing of the technology developed), lax enforcement of antitrust laws, discouragement of foreign investment and promotion of domestic investment in a given sector and discouragement of competing imports. We will consider this difficult problem in Chapter 22 infra.

(C) UNITED STATES COUNTERVAILING DUTY LAW

(1) Historical Overview

U.S. DEPARTMENT OF THE TREASURY, COUNTERVAILING DUTIES

(1971) [17]

I. SUBSTANCE OF PRESENT LEGISLATION

The Countervailing Duty Law (19 U.S.C. § 1303) (Appendix A) was enacted in substantially its present form in 1897. It requires the Secretary of the Treasury to assess a special duty on imported dutiable merchandise, benefitting from the payment or bestowal of a "bounty or grant." The special duty is always equivalent to the "bounty or grant," the purpose of the law being to nullify such benefits. It is for that reason that the special duty is referred to as a "countervailing duty".

In this latter respect, the Countervailing Duty Law does not conform with Article VI 6(a) of the General Agreement on Tariff and Trade (GATT).

* * *

However, the United States is exempted from this injury requirement of the GATT under the Protocol of Provisional Application, which contains a "grandfather clause" providing that this and certain other GATT provisions are not applicable to governments with inconsistent legislation which antecedes the GATT.

The Countervailing Duty Law is mandatory in that the Secretary of the Treasury must assess such a duty if he determines that a "bounty or grant" exists. Although the Treasury Department may launch a countervailing duty investigation on its own initiative, normally such investigations are initiated following a "complaint" from a party claiming to be adversely affected by the payment or bestowal of a "bounty or grant" on foreign imports.

17. U.S. Commission on International Trade and Investment Policy (the Williams Commission), Papers, Vol. I, at 409, 416.

The term "bounty or grant", as used in the legislation, is frequently referred to as a subsidy. The terms are not synonymous, however, for not all undertakings, which may be characterized by some as subsidies, would be construed as a "bounty or grant" under the statute.

II.   TREASURY ADMINISTRATIVE INTERPRETATIONS OF "BOUNTY OR GRANT"

Direct Subsidy

Where a foreign government pays a direct subsidy on its exports to the United States, this clearly constitutes a "bounty or grant." Thus, for example, if country A pays $1 a dozen subsidy on all widget exports, and widgets are dutiable under the provisions of the Tariff Schedules, the Treasury would, in accordance with past administrative and judicial precedents, impose a countervailing duty of $1 a dozen on widgets, in addition to all other duties normally payable. As in the case of the Antidumping Act, it is the importer who is liable for payment of the countervailing duty.

Rebates of Taxes

Under past administrative precedents of the Treasury Department, non-excessive rebates of ordinary indirect taxes and drawbacks of duty do not constitute a "bounty or grant." On the other hand, rebates of direct taxes do constitute a "bounty or grant." Typical of direct taxes under these precedents are income and social security taxes. Typical of indirect taxes are excise and sales taxes. The Treasury's interpretation of the applicability of the Countervailing Duty Law to rebates of direct and indirect taxes is consistent with Article VI 4 of the GATT.

The exemption of rebates of indirect taxes from the term "bounty or grant" does not apply to over-rebates. If for example an exporter in country A has paid $1 in excise taxes on a product he exports to the United States, and he receives a rebate of $1.20 on exportation, under past administrative precedents of the Treasury Department, the imported merchandise would be subject to a countervailing duty of $.20.

More recently, in the Italian Transmission Tower case, the Treasury Department determined a "bounty or grant" to exist on rebates by the Italian Government of excise (indirect) taxes on the exportation of such towers to the United States. The rationale for this decision, which is currently being litigated in the Customs Court (American Express Co. v. United States, Protest 68/59881 Cust.Ct.) was that the excise tax, which was rebated, was not paid directly on the product being exported or components thereof. In short, the Treasury refused to include within its doctrine of acceptable rebates of indirect taxes, excise or other indirect taxes paid for overhead expenses.

III.   JUDICIAL INTERPRETATIONS OF "BOUNTY OR GRANT"

Considerable confusion has arisen in the countervailing duty field over the interpretation of two early Supreme Court opinions, the dicta of which refer to the term "bounty or grant" as applying to all tax rebates, including rebates of indirect taxes. These opinions were rendered in the Downs and Nicholas cases (Downs v. United States, 113 F. 144 (1902) aff'd 187 U.S. 496

(1903); Nicholas & Co. v. United States, 7 Ct.Cust.Appls. 97 (1916), aff'd 249 U.S. 34 (1919)). However, the holdings of the Supreme Court in these two decisions, as distinguished from the dicta, were that over-rebates constitute a "bounty or grant" to the extent of the over-rebate. The Treasury Department has for more than a half century, in its administrative decisions, consistently construed the *Downs* and *Nicholas* opinions in accordance with the holdings rather than the dicta. The Congress has been aware of the Treasury's construction of the *Downs* and *Nicholas* opinions and has not seen fit to require the Treasury to alter its administrative interpretations by revising the statute.

* * *

Countervailing duty investigations contrast sharply with antidumping investigations in a number of respects. In the former, the Customs representatives and the Treasury Department deal with representatives of foreign governments. In antidumping investigations, on the other hand, the Customs representatives and the Treasury normally deal with representatives of foreign companies. This follows from the fact that the Antidumping Act is normally directed at the price discrimination actions of companies, while the Countervailing Duty Law generally relates to the actions of governments. Largely for this reason, countervailing duty investigations are infinitely more delicate to pursue than antidumping investigations. If the Treasury has reason to believe that a "bounty or grant" is probably being paid or bestowed by a foreign government, it normally brings this information informally to the attention of the foreign government representatives concerned and offers them a brief period in which they are provided an opportunity to refute the Treasury's tentative conclusion, or alternatively to take action to eliminate the "bounty or grant."

In cases where a foreign government may refuse to cooperate in furnishing the Treasury Department with the information necessary to reach a conclusion regarding the existence of a "bounty or grant" and its amount, the Secretary of the Treasury is authorized to determine that a "bounty or grant" exists, if he has reason to believe this is the case, and to estimate the amount of the "bounty or grant."

From 1959 to 1967, the Countervailing Duty area tended to be quiescent. An average of less than three "complaints" annually were filed during this period, and none resulted in a determination of the existence of a "bounty or grant". This picture changed in 1967, when the Treasury Department determined that a "bounty or grant" was being paid or bestowed by the Italian Government on exports to the United States of transmission towers. Since 1966 seven countervailing duty orders have been issued, and at the present there are many "complaints" under inquiry or awaiting investigation.

V. POLICY ISSUES INVOLVED IN IMPLEMENTATION OF COUNTERVAILING DUTY LAW

Lack of Discretion

The present legislation is mandatory in that it allows no discretion to the Secretary of the Treasury not to act in cases where he determines a "bounty or grant" is being paid or bestowed on dutiable imports. This lack of policy discretion under the law can be the source of policy problems. Listed below are some examples:

Developing Countries. On occasion, developing countries may claim justification for subsidizing exports as a temporary measure for launching new industries in internationally competitive markets. If discretion were authorized in the Countervailing Duty Law to cover such situations, it would have to be exercised with considerable caution to avoid the danger that it could eliminate motivation to compete effectively in the world markets by producing more efficiently.

Countervailing Duties on Top of Voluntary or Mandatory Quota Restrictions. The Commission is of course well aware of the many United States quota restrictions presently in effect in agricultural and other areas. In many fields, particularly agriculture, foreign governments pay substantial subsidies. The impact of these subsidies on agricultural imports into the United States is frequently softened by U.S. quota restrictions under legislation such as Section 22 of the Agricultural Adjustment Act. Some of the imports subject to Section 22 quota restrictions have also been the subject of countervailing duty "complaints". If the Treasury Department were to countervail the subsidized imports in such a situation, this could conceivably be regarded as an overreaction.

Situations Where United States May Be Subsidizing Exports. Some foreign governments contend that the United States is itself subsidizing exports in various ways. Should the Countervailing Duty Law contain a discretionary provision authorizing the Secretary of the Treasury not to countervail against practices which the United States Government may itself be following?

Notes

(1) Although it is difficult to compare some records, during the period from the first countervailing duty law in 1897 to mid-1973, it appears that there were approximately 84 countervailing duties applied under U.S. law. There were periods of relative infrequency of application of the law, and other periods of greater activity. From 1897 to 1934, for example, there were approximately 35 such duties imposed. Then from 1935 to 1940 there were 24, while from 1941 to 1945 there were none. The 20 year period from 1946 to 1966 saw only 13 imposed (3 in 1951, 2 in 1953, no more than 1 in any other year). Since 1967, however, activity has increased. From 1967 to 1973 there were 12 countervailing duties imposed.[18]

(2) In 1973, the Treasury Department issued a countervailing duty order of considerable importance. The order imposed countervailing duties on tires imported from Canada and made by Michelin Tire Manufacturing Co. of Canada, Ltd.[19] The order was significant because the subsidies countervailed against were domestic subsidies of the sort often granted by governmental units in the

18. These statistics were compiled from the reports issued in Treasury Decisions. The figures from 1897 through 1934 are difficult to compile with precision, inasmuch as the method of reporting the imposition of counter-vailing duties was not very systematic during those years.

19. 38 Fed.Reg. 1018 (1973); 7 Customs Bull. 24 (1973).

United States. Specifically, the following were held to be subsidies: Grants to Michelin by the Canadian and Nova Scotian governments, a special accelerated depreciation provision of the Canadian income tax law made available to Michelin, low-interest loans provided to Michelin by Nova Scotia, and property tax concessions provided by municipalities. These grants and concessions had been made available as part of programs to bolster the relatively (compared to other Canadian provinces) weak economy of Nova Scotia. The imposition of a countervailing duty in these circumstances was apparently the first time that the U.S. statute had been applied to such subsidies, and was rather controversial.[20] Although the grants and concessions were indeed designed to help Nova Scotia's economy, one inevitable result of building plants of the size constructed by Michelin was that a significant proportion (75%) of the tires produced needed to be exported. Since the U.S. market was the only logical export destination, is it arguable that the subsidies were in large part export subsidies because they were intended to be used to construct a plant to export products?

(3) The Trade Act of 1974 made a number of changes in the statute as described in the Williams Commission papers. The principal changes were to require the Treasury Department to make a preliminary decision within six months of the filing date of a petition and a final decision within 12 months. The Act also required the publication of determinations by the Treasury Department and gave disappointed petitioners the right to appeal negative determinations. By so limiting the discretion of the Treasury Department as to the procedural aspects of countervailing investigations, Congress made it likely that there would be a significant increase in the number of petitions filed. At the same time, Congress realized the need for a new international agreement on subsidies and the need for the President to have some flexibility in negotiating such an agreement. The result was that the Secretary of the Treasury was given the right in Section 331(a) of the Act to waive imposition of countervailing duties if certain conditions were met. As a result, the 1974 Act did not lead to increased imposition of countervailing duties.

(4) The U.S. countervailing duty statute originally applied only in respect of dutiable imports. The 1974 Act in Section 331(a) extended coverage of the statute to duty-free articles. It required that a petitioning industry show "injury" as a prerequisite for imposition of countervailing duties. The injury test was added in an attempt to meet the "material injury" requirement of GATT Article VI.

(2) Current U.S. Countervailing Duty Law

The Trade Agreements Act of 1979 implemented the Subsidies Code into U.S. law.[21] The procedural aspects of a countervailing duty case are like

20. See generally Guido & Morrone, The Michelin Decision: A Possible New Direction for U.S. Countervailing Duty Law, 6 Law & Poly.Intl.Bus. 237 (1974).

21. The basic provisions applicable to countervailing duties were added by title I of the 1979 Act to the Tariff Act of 1930 as Sections 701–07 (basic rules), Section 751 (reviews) and Sections 771, 774–78 (definitions and procedures). They are codified at 19 U.S. C.A. §§ 1671–71f, 1675, 1677, 1677c–77h. The former countervailing duty statute, Section 303 of the Tariff Act, 19 U.S.C.A. § 1303, remains applicable in certain cases, generally those involving nonparties to the Subsidies Code.

The rules of the ITA are set out at 19 CFR Pt. 355 (1985). The rules of the ITC are at 19 CFR Pt. 207 (1985). Appeals are governed by Section 516A of the Tariff Act, 19 U.S.C.A. § 1516a.

See Section 10.2, note 23 supra, for general references on U.S. countervailing duty law.

those described in Section 10.2(C) for antidumping cases, except, of course, that the government of the exporter's country is likely to play a more important role since its laws and programs will be the target of the investigation. Similar procedural rules for preliminary and final determinations apply, and similar rights of appeal are provided for. The International Trade Administration (ITA) investigates the existence of a subsidy, including whether the exporter in question benefits from the subsidy, and calculates the value of the subsidy. In respect of products of parties to the Subsidies Code and duty-free products, the International Trade Commission (ITC) considers whether there is material injury to U.S. industry, using essentially the same standards and considering the issues we discussed in Section 10.2 supra, where two countervailing duty cases were extracted.

The time limits in countervailing duty investigations are somewhat shorter than in antidumping cases. After a petition is filed on Day 1, the ITC must make its preliminary injury determination by Day 45 and the ITA must make its preliminary subsidy determination on Day 85 (a few weeks earlier if verification is waived or Day 150 in extraordinarily complicated cases) and its final determination 75 days later (Day 160 or 225, as the case may be). The ITC injury determination is due by Day 270 (Day 300 if the ITA preliminary determination was negative). Special rules apply if so-called upstream subsidies need to be investigated.

In light of the procedural similarities between antidumping proceedings and countervailing duty proceedings, we will limit ourselves in this subsection to a discussion of the important issues unique to the antisubsidy rules. We will focus on four in particular: What is a countervailable subsidy? How is a subsidy valued? When does the law require an injury determination? How should nonmarket economies be treated under the antisubsidy rules?

(a) Countervailable Subsidies

The definition of countervailable subsidies remains the most difficult issue in U.S. countervailing duty law. The following cases offer differing views on where the line should be drawn.

CERTAIN STEEL PRODUCTS FROM BELGIUM

Intl. Trade Admin. (1982) [22]

APPENDIX 4

Comment 1

Some of the petitioners contend that many of the conclusions in our preliminary determinations were erroneous insofar as they found that particular programs of general applicability and availability within a country do not give rise to domestic subsidies. They assert that subsidies must be found

---

22. Final Determination, 47 Fed.Reg. 39304, 4 ITRD 1507. See generally Barshevsky, Mattice & Martin, Government Equity Participation in State-Owned Enterprises: An Analysis of the Carbon Steel Countervailing Duty Cases, 14 Law & Poly.Intl.Bus. 1101 (1982).

to exist from any governmental programs providing benefits, regardless of whether those programs are generally available.

DOC Position

Section 771(5) of the Act, in describing governmental benefits which should be viewed as domestic subsidies under the law, clearly limits such subsidies to those provided "to a specific enterprise or industry, or group of enterprises or industries." We have followed this statutory standard consistently finding countervailable only the benefits from those programs which are applicable and available only to one company or industry, a limited group of companies or industries located within a limited region or regions within a country. This standard for domestic subsidies is clearly distinguishable from that for export subsidies, which are countervailable regardless of their availability within the country of exportation. We view the word "specific" in the statutory definition as necessarily modifying both "enterprise or industry" and "group of enterprises or industries". If Congress had intended programs of general applicability to be countervailable, this language would be superfluous and different language easily could and would have been used. All governments operate programs of benefit to all industries, such as internal transportation facilities or generally applicable tax rules. We do not believe that the Congress intended us to countervail such programs. Further, our conclusion is supported by the clear Congressional intent that "subsidy" be given the same meaning as "bounty or grant" under section 303 of the Act. Never in the history of the administration of this law or section 303 of the Act has a generally available program providing benefits to all production of a product, regardless whether it is exported, been considered to give rise to a subsidy or a bounty or grant. In enacting the Trade Agreements Act of 1979, Congress specifically endorsed that interpretation of section 303. Finally, the fact that the list of subsidies in section 771(5) is not an exclusive one in no way compels the conclusion that domestic benefits of general availability must or can be considered subsidies. Indeed, in view of the statute and its legislative and administrative history, we doubt that we are free to treat such generally available benefits of domestic programs as subsidies; certainly we are not compelled to do so.

OIL COUNTRY TUBULAR GOODS FROM AUSTRIA

Intl.Trade Admin. (1985)[23]

[The ITA determined that the exporter, Voest-Alpine AG, benefitted from subsidies in the form of equity infusions from the Austrian government (0.08%), grants by the Austrian government (1.60%) and subsidized export financing (0.08%), all of which are typical forms of subsidization. The ITA also examined a number of other government programs:]

D. VARIOUS CASH GRANT PROGRAMS

Petitioners alleged that the Federal government provides cash grants, equal to 100,000 Schillings per job created, to companies relocating to, or expanding plants in the special development and coal-mining areas.

23. Preliminary Determination, 50 Fed. Reg. 23334.

The government response stated that a 100,000 Schilling Action program was established by joint resolution between Austria's federal and state governments. Funds from this program are granted (by both the federal and the applicable state government) as a premium in an amount no greater than 100,000 Schillings for each newly created job. To receive these cash grants, a company must meet the following requirements: (1) The recipient must have invested at least 400,000 Schillings in a newly estimated plant or 200,000 Schillings in the expansion of an old plant; (2) the character of the investment must be innovative; and (3) the recipient must make an employment guarantee of at least three years.

Under this program, Voest-Alpine AG was awarded a cash grant for the construction of its new seamless tube mill in Kindberg, Styria. Accordingly, 50 percent of any grant awarded is to be paid by the state (Styria) government and 50 percent by the federal government. The grant was approved in 1981 with payment to be made in two equal installments. The first installment was paid in May, 1983; the second installment is still outstanding. We have no information on the record that the rate of federal support does not vary from state to state and/or that the support is available in all parts of Austria. Because this program may be limited to companies located in specific regions, we preliminary determine this grant to be countervailable.

The methodology used to calculate the benefit was similar to the methodology used in the section entitled "Grants to the Austrian Steel Industry." The undisbursed portion of the grant was not included in this benefit calculation.

We allocated the aggregate benefit over the value of total sales of the oil country tubular goods under investigation. Based on this methodology we find the subsidy conferred by this grant to be 0.06 percent *ad valorem*.

II. Programs Determined Not to Confer a Subsidy

We preliminarily determine that subsidies are not being provided to manufacturers, producers, or exporters in Austria of oil country tubular goods under the following programs:

A. Osterreichische Investitionskredit TOP–1 and TOP–2 Loans

Petitioners alleged that Voest-Alpine AG has received preferential export financing from the government of Austria through TOP–1 and TOP–2 loans. The government of Austria's response stated that the programs are intended to further investments which are important for structural change by providing federal interest rate support for credits given by Austrian banks. These credits are refinanced on the Austrian capital market by the Investitionskredit AG.

According to the government's response, the TOP–1 and TOP–2 programs are not limited to export promotion nor are they limited to a specific industry or group of industries. Therefore, we preliminarily determine that the program does not constitute a subsidy.

B. Labor Subsidies

Petitioners alleged that Voest-Alpine AG has received benefits from labor programs sponsored by the Austrian government.

1. *Government-Funded Labor Training.* The government response stated that under the Labor Market Promotion Act, Law No. 31/1969, companies in Austria may receive funds from the Austrian government for the establishment of in-house training programs to improve worker skills or to teach workers new vocations. In addition, under this law companies in Austria with low levels of capacity utilization may receive funds to be paid to the workers involved in training combined with reduced hours of work. Employees whose working hours are reduced receive support payments compensating them for the loss in earnings sustained. Workers receiving benefits under this program spend the difference between their reduced working hours and their normal working hours in training programs. The government's response stated that funding for these labor training programs is available to all sectors of Austrian industry and not just to the iron and steel industry or to export-related industries. Because this program is not limited to a specific enterprise or industry, or group of enterprises or industries, we preliminarily determine that the program does not constitute a subsidy.

2. *Special Assistant Act.* The Special Assistant Act of 1973, Law No. 642/1973, provides enhanced unemployment benefits for former employees of sectors of the economy hit by the downturn which have been let go and are at least 55 years old for men or 50 years old for women. The Federal Minister of Social Affairs is empowered to determine by decree which sectors of the economy warrant application of the provisions of the law. In a decree issued on March 21, 1983, the iron and steel industry was included within the provisions of this law. The government of Austria's response stated that payments under this law are made directly to the workers who have been laid off by an employer. The employer itself is not entitled to any support or subsidies under this law and is not relieved from payment of any expenses otherwise the obligation of such employer. Because this program provides assistance to workers and does not relieve Voest-Alpine AG of any expenses or obligations, we preliminarily determine that the company does not receive a subsidy under this program.

C. Interest Subsidy Program

Petitioners alleged that Voest-Alpine AG has received interest subsidies from the Austrian government. The government of Austria's response stated that the European Recovery Program Fund of Austria administered a program from 1978–1981 aimed at encouraging industrial projects in Austria. Under this program, qualifying investments were eligible for interest support, reducing the amount of interest payable on commercial loans obtained to finance such investments. Furthermore, the response stated that all companies in Austria were eligible for this program and it was not confined to export-related projects. Because this program is not related to a specific enterprise or industry, or group of enterprises or industries, we preliminarily determine that this program does not constitute a subsidy.

D. Loan Guaranty Program

Petitioners alleged that Voest-Alpine AG has received substantial loan guarantees from the Austrian government. The Austrian government's response stated that loans issued by insurance companies in Austria must meet certain strict requirements for investment security according to section 77 of the Insurance Supervisory Law of October 18, 1976. Because of these requirements, commercial loans by insurance companies must be guaranteed by the government or secured by a pledge of a real estate. The government guarantees insurance company loans to Voest-Alpine AG to enable the insurance companies to find larger-scale legally eligible investments for placement of their investment portfolios, rather than to enable Voest-Alpine AG to raise funds, which it is able to do through other sources. Accordingly, we preliminarily determine that this program does not provide subsidies to Voest-Alpine AG.

E. Local Subsidies To Reduce Moving and Worker Housing Costs— "Pendlerbeihilfe" Program

Petitioners alleged that enterprises willing to move from overcrowded industrial areas to development areas may receive subsidies to reduce moving and worker housing costs. The government of Austria's response stated that their "Pendlerbeihilfe" program was established to cover a portion of the costs incurred by workers, who must commute to a distant new job, due to lay-offs by their prior employer. Workers are only eligible to participate in this program when housing is unavailable in the vicinity of their new job. This program is administered by the state office of the Federal Ministry of Social Affairs and directly benefits the individual worker; benefits do not accrue to the company. Because this program provides assistance to individual workers and not companies, we preliminarily determine that Voest-Alpine AG does not receive a subsidy under this program.

CABOT CORPORATION v. UNITED STATES

Court of International Trade, 1985.
620 F.Supp. 722.

CARMAN, JUDGE:

[The ITA had ruled that the provision of carbon black by a Mexican state-owned oil company at a below world-market price was not a countervailable subsidy.]

A. APPLICABLE LAW: THE INTERPLAY BETWEEN SECTION 1303 AND SECTION 1671

As the "direct descendant" of earlier countervailing duty laws, Bethlehem Steel Corp. v. United States, 7 C.I.T. ___, 590 F.Supp. 1237, 1239 (1984), section 1303 applies to countervailing duty investigations "[e]xcept in the case of an article or merchandise which is the product of a country under the Agreement." 19 U.S.C. § 1303(a)(1). For articles from countries under the Agreement, however, section 1677(5) applies. Mexico was not a country under the Agreement during the period of this investigation, therefore section 1303 is the applicable statute. The ITA stated in its determination, nevertheless, that "[w]hile [the] investigation is governed procedurally by section 303 of the Act, the analysis of programs is based on Title VII of the Act * * *," and therefore applied § 1677(5)(B). This position is not supported by a careful examination of the statutes and the decisions of this court.

Section 1677(5) states first that "subsidy" has the same meaning as "bounty or grant." Thus there is "complete harmony and continuity between the two provisions." Congress enumerated certain countervailable practices. This did not imply a repeal of section 1303 and its interpretation. Thus, the same analysis applies regardless of which statute controls, and the law defining the term bounty or grant informs the interpretation of the term subsidy. Section 1677(5) does not subsume "bounty or grant."

In sum, section 1303 supplies the substantive law in this case. The administrative, legislative, and judicial pronouncements pertaining to section 1303 are accordingly apt. The Court may nevertheless refer to 19 U.S.C. § 1677(5) in interpreting section 1303.

B. THE LEGAL STANDARD: COUNTERVAILABILITY OF GENERALLY AVAILABLE BENEFITS

The chief issue presented to the Court is whether benefits that are available on a nonpreferential basis—that is, benefits obtainable by any enterprise or industry—can be bounties or grants within the meaning of section 1303 and therefore countervailable. Since any industrial user in Mexico could purchase carbon black feedstock and natural gas at the same price (disregarding the regional discount), the ITA viewed PEMEX's provision of these inputs at well below world market prices as not constituting a countervailable practice. The ITA view was based on the "generally available benefits rule," which has evolved within the administrative agency and was adopted by the court in Carlisle Tire & Rubber Co. v. United States, 5 C.I.T. 229, 564 F.Supp. 834 (1983). Two other decisions of this court, however, have rejected the rule as contrary to the countervailing duty statutes, most specifically section 1303, and as therefore unlawful. Agrexco, Agricultural Export Co. v. United States, 9 CIT __, 604 F.Supp. 1238 (1985); Bethlehem Steel Corp. v. United States, 7 CIT __, 590 F.Supp. 1237 (1984). This Court thus faces considerable controversy regarding the rule that generally available benefits provided within the relevant jurisdiction are not countervailable.

The generally available benefits rule as articulated by the defendant is essentially that benefits available to all companies and industries within an economy are not countervailable subsidies. Defendant's conclusions are primarily drawn from 19 U.S.C. § 1677(5)(B), which refers to countervailable domestic subsidies as being those provided to "a *specific* enterprise or industry, or group of enterprises or industries * * *." (emphasis added). Thus, argues defendant, benefits "generally available" to all enterprises or industries are not subsidies under section 1677(5)(B), and therefore do not fall within the meaning of "bounty or grant" as used in section 1303. Defendant bolsters its interpretation by citing Carlisle Tire & Rubber Co. v. United States.

In *Carlisle,* the court upheld the ITA's interpretation of section 1303 as being reasonable. The court relied in part on older case law which described a bounty or grant as a "special advantage," citing Nicholas & Co. v. United

States, 249 U.S. 34, 39 S.Ct. 218, 63 L.Ed. 461 (1919), or "an additional benefit" conferred upon a "class of persons," citing Downs v. United States, 187 U.S. 496, 501, 23 S.Ct. 222, 223, 47 L.Ed. 275 (1903). Apparently the ITA and the court in *Carlisle* view the noncountervailability of generally available benefits as the opposite side of the coin from the countervailability of benefits conferred upon a specific class. There is a distinction, however, which has not been clearly deciphered by the ITA or in prior judicial opinions, but which disrupts the apparent symmetry of the two sides of the coin.

The distinction that has evaded the ITA is that not all so-called generally available benefits are alike—some are benefits accruing generally to all citizens, while others are benefits that when actually conferred accrue to specific individuals or classes. Thus, while it is true that a generalized benefit provided by government, such as national defense, education or infrastructure, is not a countervailable bounty or grant, a generally available benefit—one that may be obtained by any and all enterprises or industries—may nevertheless accrue to specific recipients. General benefits are not conferred upon any specific individuals or classes, while generally *available* benefits, when actually bestowed, may constitute specific grants conferred upon specific identifiable entities, which would be subject to countervailing duties.

The court in *Carlisle* recognized the absurdity of a rule that would require the imposition of countervailing duties where producers or importers have benefited from general subsidies, as "almost every product which enters international commerce" would be subject to countervailing duties,*8 (citing Barcelo, Subsidies and Countervailing Duties—Analysis and a Proposal, 9 L. & Pol'y in Int'l Bus. 779, 836 (1977)). Alternatively, the court in *Bethlehem* recognized the absurdity of a law that would transform an obvious subsidy into a non-countervailable benefit merely by extending the availability of the subsidy to the entire economy. 7 C.I.T. at ___, 590 F.Supp. at 1242. Thus, although a bounty or grant is preferential in nature, bestowed upon an individual class, the generally available benefits rule as

---

*** 8.** A chief concern of the court in *Carlisle* was avoiding the absurd result of countervailing "such things as public highways and bridges, as well as a tax credit for expenditures on capital investment even if available to all industries and sectors." The court's concern seemed directed toward "general subsidies that most governments confer such as national defense, government-subsidized education and infrastructure, and sufficient public health and agricultural extension programs." G. Bryan, Taxing Unfair International Trade Practices 297 (1980). Such subsidies are distinguished from selective subsidies, examples of which are outlined in 19 U.S.C. § 1677(5). Id.

"General subsidies" may also be looked at in economic terms as provisions of *public goods*. Governments provide many such goods and services because of the inability of the price system to effectively provide these goods, which tend to be indivisible and collectively consumable by all citizens whether they pay for them or not. E. Mansfield, Economics Principles, Problems, Decisions 68, 74–78 (4th ed. 1983). This public good analysis is in alignment with the analysis under § 1303. A public good provided by government benefits society in a collective manner. It is not conferred upon any specific enterprise or industry.

With respect to the tax laws such as credits, accelerated methods of depreciation, and special depreciation recapture rules, issues may be more complicated. Each program must therefore be examined on a case by case basis to determine if the benefit accrues to specific beneficiaries or generally to society.

developed and applied by the ITA is not an acceptable legal standard for determining the countervailability of benefits under section 1303.

The appropriate standard focuses on the *de facto* case by case effect of benefits provided to recipients rather than on the nominal availability of benefits. The case must therefore be remanded for further investigation and redetermination. The definition of "bounty or grant" under section 1303 as intended by Congress remains as it is embodied in the case law and later affirmed by Congress in section 1677(5). This definition requires focusing only on whether a benefit or "competitive advantage" has been actually conferred on a "specific enterprise or industry, or group of enterprises or industries." In the case before the Court, the *availability* of carbon black feedstock and natural gas at controlled prices does not determine whether the benefits actually received by these two carbon black producers are countervailable subsidies. The programs appear to effect specific quantifiable provisions of carbon black feedstock and natural gas to specific identifiable enterprises. That additional enterprises or industries can participate in the programs, whether theoretically or actually, does not destroy the programs as subsidies. The programs are apparently available to all Mexican enterprises, but in their actual implementation may result in special bestowals upon specific enterprises.

Once it has been determined that there has been a bestowal upon a specific class, the second aspect of the definition of bounty or grant requires looking at the bestowal and determining if it amounts to an additional benefit or competitive advantage. If so, the benefit might fit within one of the illustrative examples of 19 U.S.C. § 1677(5)(B). The ITA, however, prematurely concluded that "the provision of carbon black feedstock and natural gas clearly involves the provision of goods within the meaning of subsection (ii)," 48 Fed.Reg. at 29568, that is, the subsidy example of providing goods or services at preferential rates. The ITA asserted, "[t]he standard contained in subsection (ii) is 'preferential,' which normally means only more favorable to some within the relevant jurisdiction than to others within the jurisdiction." Thus, concluded the ITA, "even if carbon black feedstock and natural gas were not generally available, we would not find this rate to be a subsidy, because this rate is not preferential * * *." Id.

The ITA has engaged in a tautology, merely extending its generally available benefits rule into the illustrative example of subsection (ii). Although preferential pricing clearly is a countervailable subsidy, subsection (ii), as only one such example of a subsidy, does not include all pricing programs constituting subsidies. The ITA's attention must therefore be directed to the broader question of whether the Mexican pricing programs for carbon black feedstock and natural gas are additional benefits or competitive advantages within the scope of section 1303.*9

---

*9. Plaintiff argues that a price below the world market price is a per se countervailable benefit. The matter is more complex. The availability of inputs at low prices to foreign producers may be the result of various non-countervailable factors such as comparative advantage. See T. Pugel, The Fundamentals of International Trade and Investment, in Handbook of International Business 1–2, 4 (I. Walter ed. 1982). The facts of this case indicate that the Mexican carbon black producers have located themselves (although perhaps pursuant to the NIDP) to take advantage of available carbon black feedstock with specific qualities. This arrangement might allow PEMEX to sell a byproduct which would oth-

Notes and Questions

(1) The problems set out at the end of Section 10.3(B) supra should be reviewed again. Which of the listed practices would be countervailable under U.S. law?

(2) Just as there is controversy over downstream dumping (see Section 10.2(C)(2) supra), there are questions of how to treat so-called upstream subsidies, i.e. subsidies to producers of inputs into a product exported to the United States. In section 613 of the 1984 Trade and Tariff Act, the U.S. practice was codified in Section 771A. Upstream subsidies are treated as subsidies to the producer of the exported good if they bestow a competitive benefit and have a significant effect on the cost of producing the good. A competitive benefit is deemed to be bestowed if the price paid by such producer is less than it would otherwise pay in an arm's length transaction.[24]

(3) Article 9 of the Subsidies Code generally prohibits export subsidies on non-primary products. However, in Article 14(3), a different obligation is stated for developing countries:

> Developing country signatories agree that export subsidies on their industrial products shall not be used in a manner which causes serious prejudice to the trade or production of another signatory.

Whether there is serious prejudice is not relevant to the basic U.S. countervailing duty investigation. However, if the petitioner alleges "critical circumstances," and asks for retroactive application of duties, Section 703(e)(1) requires the ITA to determine whether the Subsidies Code has been violated, as well as whether there have been massive imports in a relatively short time.[25] The ITA typically gives considerable weight to the ITC injury determination in considering the serious prejudice issue.[26]

(4) One of the most difficult subsidy issues has involved natural resource prices that are affected by government policies, an issue involved in the *Cabot Corporation* case. Another example of such a case involved Canadian stumpage programs (i.e. the prices charged by Canadian governments for timber-cutting rights).[27] The petitioners alleged that the benefit was industry-specific and consisted of an assumption of costs by those governments inconsistent with

erwise go unsold. Thus, prices below the world market price or the export price may simply be the result of a symbiotic industrial relationship. Further, PEMEX's refusal to sell carbon black feedstock abroad to plaintiff might be on account of limited Mexican domestic supply.

On the other hand, "generally available" benefits are not necessarily the result of the exercise of comparative advantage. It cannot be concluded merely on the basis of nominal availability and absent further investigation that the prices for carbon black feedstock and natural gas as set by PEMEX are the result of factors such as excess supply and low production cost. See contra Note, Upstream Subsidies and U.S. Countervailing Duty Law: The Mexican Ammonia Decision and the Trade Remedies Reform Act of 1984, Law and Pol'y in Int'l Bus. 263, 291 & n. 126 (1985).

24. 19 U.S.C.A. § 1677-1.

25. 19 U.S.C.A. § 1671b(e)(1).

26. See, e.g., Certain Agricultural Tillage Tools from Brazil: Final Determination, 50 Fed.Reg. 34525, 7 ITRD 1877 (ITA 1985).

27. Certain Softwood Products From Canada: Final Determination, 48 Fed.Reg. 24159, 5 ITRD 1471 (ITA 1983). See generally Bello & Holmer, Subsidies and Natural Resources: Congress Rejects a Lateral Attack on the Specificity Test, 18 Geo.Wash.J.Intl.L. & Econ. 297 (1984); Note, Upstream Subsidies and U.S. Countervailing Duty Law: The Mexican Ammonia Decision and the Trade Remedies Reform Act of 1984, 16 Law & Poly.Intl.Bus. 263 (1984).

commercial considerations. The ITA rejected both arguments. Consider whether its arguments would be accepted by the *Cabot Corporation* court:[28]

> First, stumpage programs do not confer an export subsidy, because they do not operate and are not intended to stimulate export rather than domestic sales, and because they are not offered contingent upon export performance. The mere fact that significant quantities of products made from stumpage are exported to the U.S. does not mean that stumpage programs confer an export subsidy.

> Further, stumpage programs do not confer a countervailable domestic subsidy for the following reasons. First, we determine that stumpage programs are not provided only to a "specific enterprise or industry, or group of enterprises or industries." Rather, they are available within Canada on similar terms regardless of the industry or enterprise of the recipient. The only limitations as to the types of industries that use stumpage reflect the inherent characteristics of this natural resource and the current level of technology. As technological advances have increased the potential users of standing timber, stumpage has been made available to the new users. Any current limitations on use are not due to activities of the Canadian governments.

> * * * Stumpage permits are also held by individual consumers and by industries producing turpentine, charcoal, wood alcohol, and even food additives (i.e., vanillin and lignin).

> * * *

> "[A]ssumption," as used in subsection (iv), means something other than the universe of governmental activities which could have the effect of reducing or absorbing a cost of production. Rather, it refers to a specific type of activity. In the financial and legal terms relevant to subsection 771(5)(B)'s list of domestic subsidies, an "assumption" is the relief from a pre-existing or contractual obligation.

> Under this interpretation, stumpage programs do not constitute the assumption of a cost of production, because the Canadian governments do not relieve the producers of any pre-existing statutory or contractual obligations. To the contrary, the governments impose a cost for the stumpage, which they have owned themselves for well over a century. These imposed costs include not only cash payments for stumpage, but also one or more other costs, such as ground rents, forest management plans, silviculture and road building, as detailed for each province in Appendix B.

> Even if "assumption" were construed more broadly, we determine, based upon available information in the record of these investigations, that Canadian stumpage programs have not effectively reduced, and thereby "assumed," a cost of production. Petitioner claims that because there is an allegedly unified North American market for softwood lumber, shakes and shingles and fence, the Department should compare Canadian stumpage prices to prices for stumpage in the United States. We disagree. First, it has been the Department's policy not to use cross-border comparisons in establishing commercial benchmarks.

> Second, while there may be a unified North American market for each of the products under investigation, there is not a unified market and a

28. 5 ITRD at 1485–87.

unified price for stumpage, because each individual stand of timber is unique due to a variety of factors, such as species combination, density, quality, size, age, accessibility, and terrain and climate. Stumpage prices vary substantially both regionally and locally within Canada and the United States, even within a mill's timber supply area. For example, a publication called *Timber-Mart South* publishes stumpage prices for the southeastern United States. This publication covers thirteen states, each divided into three regions, and lists separate prices for each species within each region of each state.

We believe that a comparison of Canadian stumpage prices with U.S. prices would be arbitrary and capricious in view of: (1) The wide differences between species composition; size, quality, and density of timber; terrain and accessibility of the standing timber throughout the United States and Canada; (2) the additional payments which are required in many provinces in Canada, but not generally in the United States; (3) the fact that in recent years, prices in national forests in the United States have been bid anywhere between two to five years in advance of cut, without taking into account the fluctuations in demand for lumber; and (4) the fact that in recent years the U.S. Forest Service has restricted the supply of timber in certain national forests due to budgetary and environmental constraints.

Alternatively, even if one believes that there is a rational basis for comparing U.S. and Canadian stumpage prices, the record of these investigations includes studies showing that once appropriate adjustments are made to take into account the differences in quality, accessibility, as well as additional cash payments and in-kind services, Canadian prices for standing timber do not vary significantly from U.S. prices. Indeed, in some cases the Canadian price may be higher. Therefore, even if one were to use U.S. prices as a benchmark, there is evidence in the record which establishes that the Canadian governments do not assume costs of production through their stumpage programs.

The House version of what became the 1984 Trade and Tariff Act would have added a new category of countervailable subsidies, called "natural resource subsidies." Essentially, in cases where domestic users of the resource obtained it from a government-controlled entity at an internal price less than the export price (or in the absence of significant exports, at less than the fair market value), where the resource was not available at such internal price to U.S. producers for export to the United States and where the cost of the resource was a significant production cost, a natural resource subsidy would be found in an amount equal to the difference between the internal price and export price. The proposal was deleted from the final version of the Act.[29]

(b) Valuation of Subsidies

When a government grants a defined rebate in cash on each unit exported, the valuation of the subsidy presents no problem. But when the

29. See House Rep. No. 98–725, 98th Cong., 2d Sess. 29–32 (1984); House Conf.Rep. No. 98–1156, 98th Cong., 2d Sess. 170 (1984).

subsidy is alleged to consist of loans at below-market interest rates or equity purchases on noncommercial terms, the valuation of the subsidy is more difficult. Is the relevant issue one of cost to the government or benefit to the recipient? When a large subsidy is received, how is it allocated over time? Many of these questions are too technical for detailed consideration here, but the following extracts will suggest how the ITA handles some of these issues. The extracts summarize the rules for analyzing subsidies in countervailing duty investigations brought by the U.S. steel industry. As we have noted before, many such cases were brought.

COLD–ROLLED CARBON STEEL PRODUCTS FROM ARGENTINA

Intl.Trade Admin. (1984)[30]

SUBSIDIES APPENDIX

* * *

This appendix is a detailed explanation of the current countervailing duty methodology we use to examine grants, loans, loan guarantees, and equity.

* * *

The Senate Report does not suggest what the "value of the subsidy" is or should be. * * * Furthermore, the Signatories to the "Interpretation and Application of Articles VI, XVI, and XXIII" ("the Subsidies Code"), which is implemented (sic) by the TAA, have not yet reached agreement upon rules governing the calculation of subsidies, as envisioned under Article 4, paragraph 2, footnote 2 ("An understanding among signatories should be developed setting out the criteria for the calculation of the amount of the subsidy.")

Given this background, we maintain that we have "wide latitude" in which to determine the value of a subsidy.

* * *

I.   ALLOCATING BENEFITS OVER TIME

Funds provided under government direction or directly by the government provide a subsidy to the extent that the recipient pays less for the funds than it would on the market. In the case of a loan, this is the difference between the cash flows—the company's receipts and payments—on the loan under examination and the cash flows for a comparable commercial loan taken out by the same company. For equity, it is the difference between what the government paid for a share of the company and what the market would have paid for the share. For grants, the saving to the recipient is the face value of the grant; that is, the difference between what the company paid for the funds (nothing), and what it would have to pay on the market to receive the funds (the face value of the grant). The difference in cash flows can arise in a single moment, as with grants (complete receipt of the funds at once), or over several years, as with long-term loans (through periodic repayment).

30. Final Determination, 49 Fed.Reg. 18006, 5 ITRD 2217.

The point(s) at which the difference in cash flows occurs does (do) not always coincide temporarily with the economic effect of the benefit, and therefore does (do) not necessarily provide an appropriate schedule for assessing countervailing duties. The economic effect of the benefit is diffused around the time that the cash flow differential occurs. For example, it would be inappropriate to allocate a $1 billion grant received on March 17, 1981, entirely to March 17, 1981. The grant continues to benefit the company after that date, and thus we would not counteract the economic effect of the grant by assessing countervailing duties to products exported on only that single day. Therefore, to counteract the economic effects of such actions, we must determine an appropriate period over which to allocate benefits, and decide how much of the benefit to allocate to each subperiod (usually a year). In addition, we must choose a discount rate to reflect the time value of money; that is, the fact that a given nominal amount of money has a changing real value over time.

The calculation of some types of subsidies, therefore, is a three step process. First, we must calculate the difference in cash flows between the countervailable program and the appropriate market alternative. Second, we must choose a discount rate for allocating money over time. And third, we must determine a reasonable shape and length for the stream of benefits.

The first step is described under the separate sections below on grants, loans, and equity. In this section, we first consider the discount rate and then discuss the construction of the benefit stream.

A. The Discount Rate

Prior to the cases on certain steel products initiated on February 1, 1982, we allocated the face value of benefits with effects extending beyond the period of receipt in equal increments, over the appropriate time period. In each year we countervailed only that year's allocated portion of the total subsidy. For example, a grant of $100 million spread over 10 years would have been countervailed at a rate of $10 million per year for 10 years, beginning in the year of receipt.

This allocation technique was criticized for not capturing the entire subsidy in that it ignores the fact that money has a changing value as it moves through time. It has been argued that $100 million today is much more valuable to a recipient than $10 million per year for the next 10 years, since the present value (the value in the initial year of receipt) of the series of payments is considerably less than the amount if initially given as a lump sum. We agree with this position, and, in 1982 we changed our methodology of subsidy calculation accordingly (see Appendix 2). As long as the present value (in the year of subsidy receipt) of the amounts allocated over time does not exceed the face value of the subsidy, we are consistent with both our domestic law and international obligations in that the amount countervailed will not exceed the total net subsidy.

The present value of any series of payments is calculated using a discount rate. The discount rate is a measure of the company's time preference for money. If a company is indifferent between receiving $1.00 today and $1.10 next year, its discount rate for the intervening year is 12 percent. We choose a discount rate such that the present value of the cash stream remains constant. For example, if a company receives a countervailable grant of $1000 in 1977, we wish to countervail no more or less than 1000 1977 dollars, regardless of the period over which we allocate the benefit.

A company's time preference for money is determined by its expected rate of return on investment and operations at the time the subsidy is received. This expected rate of return is often called the "opportunity cost of capital." Since this is not easily quantifiable or verifiable, we must choose a surrogate that accurately reflects the company's expected rate of return. We consider the company's actual cost of raising money, or the "weighted cost of capital," as the best surrogate for measuring the expected rate of return, since a rational company will raise money (through debt and/ or equity markets) to the point at which the cost of raising any additional money is greater than its expected rate of return from those funds.

When considering the cost of capital, we seek to determine the marginal cost facing the company at the appropriate time. For our purposes, therefore, the weighted cost of capital is the marginal cost of each type of financing used by the company (usually debt and equity), each weighted by its relative proportion.

We weight-average the marginal costs of debt and equity by each company's total existing proportions of debt and equity. Marginal proportions of debt and equity, although more desirable in theory, are not readily identifiable. Because borrowing and issuing equity do not occur with regular frequency, any choice of a recent period to serve as a marginal measure of relative debt and equity usage would be arbitrary. Moreover, by using total existing proportions, we avoid making a highly speculative guess as to how operations and investment would have been financed absent the subsidy. Because we cannot know how a company would have raised money absent the subsidy program, we assume that the company will use debt and equity in the same proportions at the margin as it has done historically.

For the marginal cost of debt, we prefer to use the commercial rate on bonds issued by the company, or an interest rate on long-term commercial loans received by the company in the period for which we are calculating the discount rate.

In Appendix II, we included a tax adjustment to the marginal cost of debt variable, to account for the fact that taxes normally are not paid on interest, thus lowering the cost of debt to the firm by the amount of taxes not paid. We have decided to abandon the tax adjustment because it is inconsistent with our policy of disregarding the secondary effects, including tax effects, of subsidies.

A company's marginal cost of equity is a function of three variables: a) the risk-free rate on alternative investment, b) the commercial investor's anticipations of the future rate of return on the equity market as a whole, and c) the riskiness of investment in that company relative to the market. Because the latter two factors are not easily identifiable, we cannot calculate a company's actual marginal cost of equity. As a surrogate, we have used the company's marginal cost of debt (which reflects the risk-free rate and the company's riskiness), plus the difference between the national average rate of return on equity and the national average cost of debt (which reflects the anticipated future rates of return on the equity market). We cannot observe the anticipated rate of return on the equity market, and so we have used the actual rate of return on equity for calculating the second variable.

Because equity normally is riskier than long-term debt, investors demand a higher return on equity than on lending. That is, the cost of equity (the *expected* rate of return of equity) is greater than the cost of long-term debt (its interest rate). Our use of an historical measure or as a surrogate for expected returns on equity, however, can lead to the illogical result that the measurement for the cost of equity will be less than that for the cost of debt.

When investors' prior anticipations of rates of return on equity are not realized fully in the present period, the actual rate of return on equity may be less than the cost of debt. The cost of debt may also be greater than the cost of equity when less risky firms finance relatively more with equity, while more risky firms finance relatively more by borrowing. To adjust for such an anomaly, we have set a floor on the surrogate used to measure the national cost of equity. This floor is the national cost of debt. For our purposes, the weighted cost of capital in no instance will be lower than the cost of long-term debt.

We also must consider the appropriate point in time at which to determine the weighted cost of capital for discount rate purposes. Where a grant or a loan is received in a year after the year in which agreement is reached on the principal terms of the grant or loan, we will determine the weighted cost of capital using the year in which agreement was reached rather than the year of receipt or year in which an agreement was concluded formally.

We note that we may not be able to apply in all cases a discount rate based on weighted cost of capitals as described above. This is because we may not be able to obtain information such as the national average long-term debt cost or rate of return on equity. In such cases we then fall back to the next best surrogate available based on the particular facts of the case. For example, for national average rate of return on equity, we may average returns on equity for some number of particular companies. If we believe that the information necessary to construct a reasonable weighted cost of capital figure is unavailable, we generally use instead the company's cost of long-term debt. Possible subsequent choices, in order of general preference, are national average long-term debt costs and the prime interest rate.

Since issuing Appendix II, our experience with applying the weighted cost of capital has been marked by difficulties in finding the required information within the limited time frame for countervailing duty investigations allowed by the Act. Indeed, we have discovered that, in developing countries, necessary information, such as meaningful national average rates of return on equity and long-term interest rates for loans in the home country, may not be available at all. Although we will continue our attempts to use the weighted cost of capital in future cases, we may be forced to change this practice if difficulties in finding the information systematically prohibit us from using it as a discount rate.

B. Construction of the Benefit Stream

To allocate subsidies over time, we need to construct a stream of benefits. In Appendix II, we continue to use an annuity-style schedule, which allocated equal nominal payment to each subperiod. We noted several reasons why we used the annuity-style method instead of the alternative preferred by one judge of the Court of International Trade, the declining balance method. (see Michelin Tire and Rubber Co. v. United States [6 CIT ___, Slip Op. 83–136), December 22, 1983) [5 ITRD 1545] ("Michelin"). First, we argued that the method that gave equal nominal payments was more administratively feasible than the declining balance method. Second, we stated that the declining balance method could result in countervailing duties whose present value exceeded the nominal amount of the subsidies in the year of receipt. Third, we argued that the declining balance method would require us to assign a time value to the portion of a large grant in the year of receipt, which was inconsistent with our decision to allocate very small grants with no time value adjustment to one year only. We have since adjusted the basic declining balance formula so that the amount of the subsidy in the first year will not exceed its nominal value. Our declining balance formula also treats small grants and the first year portion of large grants equally. Given that the declining balance method is only slightly more difficult to apply than the annuity-style method, we do not consider administrative feasibility to be a sufficient reason in this case for our continued reliance on the latter. Although both types of methods are reasonable, we have decided to use the declining balance method. We use this method of allocation, coupled with the discount rate, to allocate certain benefits conferred by grants, loans, guarantees, and equity purchases.

II. GRANTS

In addition to constructing the shape of the allocation stream, we must decide the period over which to allocate benefits. Since the difference in cash flows for grants occurs at only a single moment (when the grant is received) cash flow does not provide guidance in how to allocate the benefit.

It does not help to hypothesize how the company would have raised the funds absent the grant. Firms raise money primarily through sales, secondarily through debt, equity, and non-operating income. Grant money does not resemble any one of these more than any other; all require an obligation in return for the money, which the grant lacks. Moreover, for all of the alternative ways of raising money except debt, it does not make sense to ask the duration of the obligation; the duration of a sale is in some ways near zero, and the duration of equity is in some ways infinite.

We have previously used the average useful life of renewable physical assets in the industry involved as the allocation period. We considered the benefit of a grant to last in some way as long as the average turnover of assets in the industry. However, we recognize first that physical assets are often a fairly small part of the costs of doing business, and second that even in highly capital intensive industries the benefit of funds received—whether from sales, debt, equity, or grants—has no particular relationship to the life of the machinery.

We have concluded that there are no economic or financial rules that mandate the choice of an allocation period. The administering authority therefore must set a standard and hold to it as consistently as possible to allow its actions to be predictable. We have received no objections to the period proposed in Appendix II, and continue to prefer the average useful life of renewable physical assets as the period over which to allocate grants. By using the life of the company's renewable physical assets as our period of allocation, we are simply stating that the effects of a grant, in whatever form, can be spread reasonably over the time in which the company rolls over its renewable physical assets.

In Appendix 2 we allocated solely to the year of receipt all grants of less than one percent of a company's gross revenues. As a result, under Appendix 2 we would find no subsidies (and make a negative determination) for a firm that received only a grant of one percent of the company's gross revenues, because that grant would be allocated over time. However, we would find subsidies for a firm receiving solely a grant of .75 percent of the firm's gross revenues, since that amount would be allocated solely to the year of receipt and would not be *de minimis*. To prevent this anomaly, we will total all grants. If the sum is less than .5 percent of all sales concerned for domestic subsidies or of all export sales concerned for export subsidies, we will allocate such grants only to the year of receipt.

We will allocate all other grants over the average useful life of a company's renewable physical assets (equipment), as determined by U.S. Internal Revenue Service (IRS) in the 1977 Class Life Asset Depreciation Range System (Rev.Proc. 77–10, 1977—1 C.B. 548 (RR–38)). The use of other alternatives, such as accounting useful life as reflected in company records, or tax tables of the country in which the company is based, may yield extremely inconsistent results between companies or between countries. We continue to rely on IRS tax tables as our source because they provide the most practical and fair means of determining average useful life.

III. Loans and Loan Guarantees

A. Long-Term Loans and Guarantees for Companies Considered Creditworthy

In these investigations, various loan activities give rise to subsidies. The most common practices are the extension of a loan on preferential terms or on terms inconsistent with commercial considerations where the government is either the actual lender or directs a private lender to make funds available, or where the government guarantees the repayment of the loan made by a private lender. The subsidy is computed by comparing what a company would pay a normal commercial lender in principal, interest, and other charges in any given year with what the company actually pays on the preferential loan in that year. We determine what a company would pay a normal commercial lender by constructing a comparable commercial loan at the appropriate market interest rate ("the benchmark") reflecting commercial terms.

In Appendix 2, we generally used the national average commercial interest rate as the benchmark. We compared the loan at issue with what the average commercial borrower would have to pay for a loan of similar principal and duration. Upon reconsideration, we have decided that the benchmark for long-term loans will be company-specific, unless the company lacks adequate comparable commercial experience. If the latter, then we will use a national average loan interest rate or the debt experience of a comparable company as the best information available for creditworthy firms. Use of a company-specific benchmark for long-term borrowing enables us to capture the fact that certain companies are more (or less) risky than average, and that commercial lenders will take these risk characteristics into account in setting the conditions of the loan.

For loans denominated in a currency other than the currency of the country concerned in an investigation, the benchmark is selected from interest rates applicable to loans denominated in the same currency as the loans under consideration (where possible, interest rates on loans in that currency in the country where the loan was obtained; otherwise, loans in that currency in other countries, as best evidence). The subsidy for each year is calculated in the foreign currency and converted at an exchange rate applicable for each year.

After finding an appropriate benchmark loan, the next step in determining if, and if so, to what extent, a loan was given on terms inconsistent with commercial considerations is to calculate the payment differential between the benchmark loan and the loan at issue in each year. We then calculate the present value of this stream of benefits in the year the loan was made, using the weighted cost of capital (as described above) as the discount rate. In other words, we determine the subsidy value of a preferential loan as if the benefits had been bestowed as a lump-sum grant in the year the loan was given. This amount is allocated over the life of the loan, using our methodology for allocating benefits over time described above, to yield the annual subsidy amounts.

If a borrowing company receives a payment holiday that is inconsistent with commercial considerations, the subsidy value of the payment holiday is captured in the comparison of the annual payments on the loan at issue with the annual payments on a normal commercial loan with a normal repayment schedule. A payment holiday early in the life of a loan can result in such large loan payments near the end of its term that, during the fiscal years, the loan recipient's annual payments on the subsidized loan may be greater than they would have been on an unsubsidized loan. By reallocating the benefit over the entire life of the loan through the present value methodology described above, we avoid imposing countervailing duties in excess of the net subsidy.

Because loans, unlike grants, have a readily identifiable effect on the company over time, we allocate the benefits over the life of the loan, even for loans expressly given to purchase costly capital equipment. We do not believe a contrary result for loans "tied" to capital equipment is required by the Act.

Loan guarantees are countervailable only if they are provided to a specific industry or group of industries and only if they are on terms inconsistent with commercial considerations. For a creditworthy company, a loan guarantee by the government constitutes a subsidy to the extent the guarantee assures more favorable loan terms than for an unguaranteed loan. To determine if the guarantee is inconsistent with commercial considerations, we first compare the cost of the government loan guarantee with the cost of commercial guarantees. If no difference between government and commercial loan guarantee costs is evident, we then look to see if the government loan guarantee has affected the other terms of the loan.

A special case arises when the government acts as both guarantor and principal owner or majority shareholder of a company. Under these circumstances, a government guarantee is not countervailable if it is normal commercial practice in that country for owners or shareholders to provide guarantees on comparable terms to their companies (see "Final Affirmative Countervailing Duty Determination on Carbon Steel Wire Rod from Trinidad and Tobago" (49 F.R. 480 (January 4, 1984)).

B.   Long-Term Loans and Loan Guarantees for Companies Considered Uncreditworthy

In our view, a company is uncreditworthy if, absent future government support, it would not have been able to obtain commercial loans comparable to those which it did obtain. We consider a company creditworthy if it appears that it will have sufficient revenues or resources to meet its costs and fixed financial obligations, again absent future government intervention. To determine the creditworthiness of a company we analyze its present and past health, as reflected in various financial indicators calculated from its financial statements and accounts. We give great weight to the company's recent past and present ability to meet its costs and fixed financial obligations with its cash flow. Where available, we also consider evidence of the company's future financial position, such as market studies, country and industry economic forecasts, and project and loan appraisals. Because the determination is often highly complex, we consider each case carefully in light of the evidence on the record.

In Appendix 2, we calculated the benefit of a long-term loan to a company considered uncreditworthy by treating it as a countervailable equity infusion and applying our equity methodology. At the time, we stated our preference for using a loan-type calculation to measure the benefit, with a suitable risk premium added to the benchmark. However, we could not find any reasonable and practical basis for selecting a risk premium. Thus, in 1982, we settled for the equity approach, even though we were aware of the flaws in our equity methodology, as discussed in Appendix II.

We now believe that we have a practical and reasonable way to calculate a risk premium. For our purposes, a risk premium is the amount above the highest commonly-available commercial interest rate a creditworthy borrower would have to pay in order to receive a loan. The magnitude of the risk premium is determined solely by the lender's assessment of the riskiness of the company. Thus, to construct a risk premium, we need an observable measurement of risk, as determined by lenders. U.S. bond ratings provide us with such a measurement, since the difference between interest rates associated with different bond ratings are determined solely by risk.

Having settled upon U.S. bond ratings, we must now determine the appropriate spread to adopt as our risk premium. In Appendix II, we proposed using the interest rate spread between the lowest commonly observed bond rating for creditworthy companies and the second lowest, on the basis that the last increment of risk within the range of bond ratings for creditworthy companies best represented the difference in risk between a marginally creditworthy company and an uncreditworthy company. We now consider this spread to be inappropriate, since the difference in risk between the least creditworthy company and the next-to-least creditworthy company has very little relation to the difference in risk between the least creditworthy company and an uncreditworthy company. The spread proposed in Appendix II does not reflect the fact a company's level of risk increases dramatically once it becomes uncreditworthy. A more appropriate measure of the risk between a marginally creditworthy company and an uncreditworthy company is the difference in interest rates associated with the difference between the least creditworthy and most creditworthy bond ratings. Although it is impossible to quantify the risk of an uncreditworthy company precisely, we believe that this spread comes closer to measuring the dramatic increase in risk in lending to an uncreditworthy company than the spread proposed in Appendix II.

For purposes of these final determinations, we have used the difference between *Moody's* Aaa and Baa corporate bond rates. We then calculated the precentage this difference represents of the prime interest rate in the United States. This percentage is applied to the prime interest rate in the country concerned. The resulting risk premium is then added to the highest long-term commercial interest rate commonly available to companies in that country.

We believe this method is practical. Moreover, it seems reasonable, since the spread in riskiness among companies in the United States, which has a highly sophisticated bond market, reasonably reflects market forces determining a measurement of risk. By applying our risk premium, we expect to achieve a meaningful measure of the value to uncreditworthy companies of government support in obtaining loans. As under Appendix 2, we will not impose greater countervailing duties for a subsidized loan (to a creditworthy or an uncreditworthy company) than for an outright grant in the amount of the loan principal, because a loan cannot be worth more to a company than an outright grant of the same amount.

C. Short-Term Loans

Short-term loans (one year or less), like long-term loans, are countervailable to the extent that they are preferential or given on terms inconsistent with commercial considerations. To determine the commercial soundness of short-term loans, we compare the terms on the loan at issue with a benchmark; that is, a comparable commercial loan. Since short-term loans are received and repaid within a year, we allocate any benefits to one year only. Therefore, we do not need to employ present value analysis for short-term loans.

For our benchmark, we use the most appropriate national average commercial method of short-term financing, rather than company-specific experience. We believe the distinction between our treatment of short-term and long-term loans is valid. Lending short-term generally is not as risky as long-term, because of the shorter duration of the repayment obligation and the greater frequency of accompanying security (for example, accounts receivable). Because there is little need for the lender to vary its terms to account for varying risk characteristics among companies, we would not expect company-specific short-term loan terms to vary from national average terms. Additionally, because of the enormous number of short-term loans involved in many cases, the use of company-specific benchmarks would significantly impair our ability to administer the countervailing duty law within the short time limits established by the Act.

We do not treat uncreditworthy companies differently from creditworthy companies when calculating benefits from short-term loans, because of the low level of risk associated with short-term debt, and the frequent existence of security.

D. Forgiveness of Debt

Where the government has permanently assumed or forgiven an outstanding debt obligation, we treat this as a grant to the company equal to the outstanding principal at the time of assumption or forgiveness. Where outstanding debt has been converted into equity (that is, the government receives shares in the company in return for eliminating debt obligations of the company), a subsidy may result. The existence and extent of such subsidies are determined by treating the conversion as an equity infusion in the amount of the remaining principal of the debt. We then calculate the value of the subsidy by using our equity methodology explained below.

IV. EQUITY

It is well settled that government equity ownership *per se* does not confer a subsidy. Government ownership confers a subsidy only when it is on terms inconsistent with commercial considerations.

If the government buys previously issued shares on a market or directly from shareholders rather than from the company, there is no subsidy to the company. This is true no matter what price the government pays, since any overpayment benefits only the prior shareholders and not the company.

If the government buys shares directly from the company (either a new issue or corporate treasury stock) and similar shares are traded in a market, a subsidy arises if the government pays more than the prevailing market price. We strongly prefer to measure the subsidy by reference to market price. This price, we believe, rightly incorporates private investors' perceptions of the company's future earning potential and worth.

It is more difficult to judge the possible subsidy effects of government equity purchases where there is no market price for the shares (as where, for example, the government is already sole owner of the company). In such cases, we must determine the commercial soundness of government equity purchases by assessing the prospects of the company at the time those purchases were made.

To be "equityworthy," a company must show ability to generate a reasonable rate of return within a reasonable period of time. In making our equityworthiness determinations, we assess the company's current and past financial health, as reflected in various financial indicators taken from its financial statements, and, where appropriate, internal accounts. We give great weight to the company's recent rate of return on equity as an indication of financial health and prospects. Like our creditworthiness tests, our equityworthiness analysis also takes into account the company's prospects, as reflected in market studies, country and industry forecasts, and project and loan appraisals, when these types of analyses are available.

For government equity purchases which we deem inconsistent with commercial considerations, we measure the benefit by multiplying the difference between the company's rate of return on equity and the national average rate (the "rate of return shortfall") for the review period by the total amount of the equity purchases made in years in which the company was unequityworthy. Under no circumstances do we countervail in any year an amount greater than that which is calculated treating the government's equity infusion as an outright grant.

CERTAIN STEEL PRODUCTS FROM BELGIUM

Intl. Trade Admin. (1982)[31]

APPENDIX 2. —— METHODOLOGY

* * *

Research and Development Grants and Loans

Grants and preferential loans awarded by a government to finance research that has broad application and yields results which are made publicly available do not confer subsidies. Programs of organizations or institutions established to finance research on problems affecting only a particular industry or group of industries (*e.g.*, metallurgical testing to find ways to make cold-rolled sheet easier to galvanize) and which yield results that are available only to producers in that country (or in a limited number of countries) confer a subsidy on the products which benefit from the results of the research and development (R&D). On the other hand, programs which provide funds for R&D in a wide range of industries are not countervailable even when a portion of the funds is provided to the steel sector.

Once we determine that a particular program is countervailable, we calculate the value of the subsidy by reference to the form in which the R&D was funded. An R&D grant is treated as a "united" grant; a loan for R&D is treated as any other preferential loan.

Labor Subsidies

To be countervailable, a benefit program for workers must give preferential benefits to workers in a particular industry or in a particular targeted region. Whether the program preferentially benefits some workers as

31. Final Determination, 47 Fed.Reg. 39304; 4 ITRD 1507.

opposed to others is determined by looking at both program eligibility and participation. Even where provided to workers in specific industries, social welfare programs are countervailable only to the extent that they relieve the firm of costs it would ordinarily incur—for example, a government's assumption of a firm's normal obligation partially to fund worker pensions.

Labor-related subsidies are generally conferred in the form of grants and are treated as united grants for purposes of subsidy calculation. Where they are small and expensed by the company in the year received, we likewise allocated them only to the year of receipt. However, where they were more than one percent of gross revenues we allocated them over a longer period of time generally reflecting the program duration.

Notes and Questions

(1) By comparing the actual cost of a subsidized loan to the cost that would have been incurred in the marketplace, the amount of the subsidy is the benefit received by the recipient, as opposed to the cost to the government, which may be making the loan at above the rate it has to pay in the market. Notice that in item (k) of the illustrative list of export subsidies in the Annex to the Subsidies Code, export credits are included only if they are provided at rates below the cost to the government. The ITA has specifically refused to apply item (k)'s valuation rule to export credits in derogation of international rules, even if the derogation was authorized by those rules.[32] Is the ITA position reasonable? Should the GATT rules on prohibited subsidies be used in determining when subsidies may be countervailed?

EC officials have argued that since GATT is an agreement of governments and is concerned with what governments do, the value of a subsidy should be based on the cost to the government.

(2) In the *Michelin* case and others, subsidies are given in part to entice companies to locate in regions that are for some reason unattractive: less skilled labor, less developed infrastructure, relatively far from major markets. Companies that locate in these regions may incur higher costs than they otherwise would. In valuing the subsidies, should those costs be treated as an offset? If so, how would you value them? In Section 771(6), the ITA is authorized to deduct application and similar fees and export taxes designed to offset the subsidy.[33] The Senate Report indicates that "costs as a result of locating in an underdeveloped area are not now permitted as offsets."[34] Is this logical or fair if the goal is to create a so-called level playing field?

(c) Injury Determinations: Countries Under the Agreement

Generally, the ITC analyzes the "material injury" requirement in countervailing duty cases in the same manner as it does in antidumping cases. In fact, the reader will recall that some of the cases on injury that we considered in Section 10.2 involved countervailing duties.

32. Rail Passenger Cars from Canada: Final Determination, 48 Fed.Reg. 6569, 5 ITRD 1167 (1983).

33. 19 U.S.C.A. § 1677(6).

34. S.Rep. No. 96–249, 96th Cong., 1st Sess. 86 (1979).

One aspect of injury analysis, however, is unique to countervailing duty cases. As we discussed in Section 7.4(C)(2) supra, the 1979 Act added the requirement that material injury be found by the ITC only in respect of countries "under the Agreement," which was defined in Section 701 of the Act to include other parties to the Subsidies Code, countries which assumed substantially equivalent obligations toward the United States or, in certain cases, countries to which the U.S. was otherwise obligated to give most-favored-nation treatment in this regard.[35] For products originating in countries not under the Agreement, no injury determination is made (unless the product is duty-free, in which case the prior law requirement of a simple injury determination still applies).

U.S. practice in deciding which countries are "countries under the Agreement" and therefore entitled to have an injury test applied is complicated. In practice, the United States has not even treated all parties to the Subsidies Code as countries under the Agreement. This situation has arisen because some developed countries (such as New Zealand) have accepted the Code with reservations and because Article 14 of the Code relaxes the Code's obligations for developing countries. As a consequence, the United States has decided that to become a country under the Agreement for the purposes of U.S. law, a country must have made a commitment to the United States (in a bilateral agreement) that it will fulfil certain Code obligations. To implement this so-called "commitments policy," the United States, pursuant to Article 19:9 of the Code, "opts out" of a Code relationship with any country that is not fully bound under the Code. Thereafter, if a sufficient commitment is made to the United States, the United States applies the Code provisionally in respect of that country and accords it treatment as a country under the Agreement. The commitment required to be made by such a country does not have to include a pledge to abide by all requirements of the Code, but the United States does require a certain "rigor" of commitment, particularly as to export subsidies. This procedure then allows the United States to change a country's "under the Agreement" status if the country's commitment is not honored. Since the United States is only applying the Code provisionally, its action in theory does not violate the Code. Needless to say, this practice has been very controversial in GATT circles where many critics argue that the United States has been acting illegally, and doing so in order to recoup what it lost during negotiations of the Subsidies Code.

Note

The material in Section 7.4(C)(2) supra should be reviewed, particularly with reference to the dispute between the United States and India in respect of the application of most-favored-nation treatment to the Subsidies Code. Is Section 701 consistent with the MFN obligations of the United States under GATT?

35. 19 U.S.C.A. § 1671.

(d) Nonmarket Economies

CARBON STEEL WIRE ROD FROM CZECHOSLOVAKIA

Intl. Trade Admin. (1984) [36]

In our preliminary determination, we stated that nonmarket economy (NME) countries were not exempt from the provisions of section 303 of the Act. This preliminary determination was based on a narrow reading of section 303, which provides that a countervailing duty shall be assessed:

> [w]henever *any* country, dependency, colony, province, or other political subdivision of government, person, partnership, association, cartel, or corporation, shall pay or bestow, directly or indirectly, any *bounty or grant* upon the manufacture or production or export of any article or merchandise manufactured or produced in such country, dependency, colony, province, or other political subdivision of government ＊　＊　＊ (added).

In our preliminary determination, we focused on the phrase "any country," thereby correctly addressing part of the jurisdictional question, i.e., whether any political entity is exempted *per se* from the countervailing duty law. However, upon reconsideration, our preliminary determination did not address adequately the additional jurisdictional question; i.e., whether government activities in an NME confer a "bounty or grant" within the meaning of section 303. Upon reconsideration, we have concluded that bounties or grants, within the meaning of section 303, cannot be found in NME's.

In a market economy, scarce resources are channeled to their most profitable and efficient uses by the market forces of supply and demand. We believe a subsidy (or bounty or grant) is definitionally any action that distorts or subverts the market process and results in a misallocation of resources, encouraging inefficient production and lessening world wealth.

In NME's, resources are not allocated by a market. With varying degrees of control, allocation is achieved by central planning. Without a market, it is obviously meaningless to look for a misallocation of resources caused by subsidies. There is no market process to distort or subvert. Resources may appear to be misallocated in an NME when compared to the standard of a market economy, but the resource misallocation results from central planning, not subsidies.

It is this fundamental distinction—that in an NME system the government does not interfere in the market process, but supplants its—that has led us to conclude that subsidies have no meaning outside the context of a market economy.

In the absence of governmental interventions, market economies are characterized by flexible prices determined through the interaction of supply and demand. In response to these prices, resources flow to their most profitable and efficient uses. To identify subsidies in this pure market economy, we would look to the treatment a firm or sector would receive absent government action. In the absence of the bounty or grant, the firm

36. Final Determination, 49 Fed.Reg. 19370, 6 ITRD 1176.

would experience market-determined costs for its inputs and receive a market-determined price for its output. The subsidy received by the firm would be the difference between the special treatment and the market treatment. Thus, the market provides the necessary reference point for identifying and calculating the amount of the bounty or grant.

However, few modern economies are purely market driven. Governments frequently intervene in the market place to promote social (as opposed to economic) goals, such as full employment or income redistribution. In addition to taxes and subsidies as policy tools, these governments employ various regulations in factor and financial markets. The state sometimes owns selected firms or industries.

Despite the varying degrees of regulation, state ownership and state intervention, we can still identify a bounty or grant. This is primarily because private ownership of resources has remained the rule, rather than the exception, and these governments have not tried to supplant the market as the allocator of resources. A countervailable action in a market economy is a distortion. It encourages a producer to sell abroad rather than in his home market or, in the case of a domestic subsidy, gives preferential treatment to an industry or sector of the economy. In either situation, the subsidy is identifiable as different treatment: Different from the market or different from other firms or sectors. Subsidies in market economy systems are exceptional events. They can be discerned from the background provided by the market system.

No such background exists in an NME. By market standards, the nonmarket environment is riddled with distortions. Prices are set by planners. "Losses" suffered by production and foreign trade enterprises are routinely covered by government transfers. Investment decisions are controlled by the state. Money and credit are allocated by the central planners. The wage bill is set by the government. Access to foreign currency is restricted. Private ownership is limited to consumer goods.

* * *

Assume that the government in a market economy made a payment to a producer on each of his sales. Theoretically, the market economy producer would respond by increasing his output. In an NME, the payment upon sale could be effected merely by increasing the administered price. Would the new, higher price result in increased output by the NME enterprise?

If the NME government controls the inputs the producer needs and does not make these inputs available, then output could not be increased, despite the higher price. Moreover, if the enterprise had to expand its plant to produce more output, and had to rely on the government for investment funds or central management enterprises for the machinery and equipment, then output would not be increased unless the funds or equipment were provided. Thus, the simple price increase, with no further action by the government, would not lead to increased output. The government action would have no economic result. Even if the government gave the producer the investment funds necessary for plant expansion, without the needed inputs, output could not increase. Neither of the actions, the price increase or the government "provision" of capital, would have the effect of a bounty or grant.

In such a situation, we could not disaggregate government actions in such a way as to identify the exceptional action that is a subsidy. Because the notion of a subsidy is, by definition, a market phenomenon, it does not apply in a nonmarket setting. To impose that concept where it has no meaning would force us to identify every government action as a subsidy (or a tax). We are not prepared to do this—we will not impose the market-based concept of a subsidy on a system where it has no meaning and cannot be identified or fairly quantified.

We do not believe that the hypothetical proposed above differs substantially from the situation facing enterprises in NME's. Based on our analysis, we have found that NME systems share certain features that make it impossible to find that a bounty or grant exists. These nonmarket features are, moreover, apparent in Czechoslovakia.

Most NME systems are characterized by centrally administered prices. Descriptions of these systems report that prices are reformed, revised or changed with varying frequency. Thousands of prices can be changed at a time by the planners.

Prices in Czechoslovakia are similarly controlled. For example, the prices of raw materials are to be reformed as part of the seventh Five-Year Plan (1981–85). The prices of technologically advanced products are reportedly set as part of the annual plans. A producer price reform is anticipated in 1984 to increase overall price levels in Czechoslovakia by 6.5 percent–7 percent.

Moreover, centrally administered prices do not play the same role as prices in a market economy system. NME prices do not reflect scarcity. Nor do they equate supply and demand. They are typically calculated by a formula that does not include demand; *i.e.*, the prices that consumers are willing to pay for the good.

Our analysis has shown this to be true in Czechoslovakia. Even where so-called "market" prices exist for consumer goods, non-price rationing is evident in the reported 10-year wait for an apartment in Prague. Producer prices reflect costs and profits with the method of calculation varying from reform to reform.

Where the enterprises' revenues are controlled because output prices are administered, and their costs are controlled through administered input prices, then it seems evident that profits, as they are normally defined (total revenue less total costs), are effectively controlled as well. This is recognized in Attachment C to petitioners' February 10, 1984, submission in the Polish investigation, in which it is stated:

> Profits and losses exist, first of all, as the result of the adoption of particular prices. Overall price revisions are introduced from time to time * * *. These revisions usually change profitability and unprofitability in various sectors of the economy.

Despite limited attempts to bring internal prices more into line with world prices, the reform in Czechoslovakia is not moving away from price planning and central control.

These administered profits play a different role from profits in a market economy. Profit guides capitalists to invest resources where they earn the highest possible return. Profit maximization leads the capitalist to produce goods that are in demand at the least cost. Profits drive market economic systems.

Profit for the NME enterprise manager is only one of many possible success indicators. It is one of the tools typically employed by NME governments to motivate enterprise managers to fulfill targets established in the central plan. Other success indicators, for gauging the enterprise's performance include value-added and/or gross output.

Commentators on NME systems have observed that reliance on a single indicator will not produce the results desired by the central planners. Attempts to maximize value-added, for example, lead to using too much labor input. If profit maximization is pursued, the distortion of the underlying prices will lead to a distorted picture of profits. Because of the distortions arising from the use of success indicators, they are usually supplemented with additional incentives: Bonuses for minimizing costs or using domestically produced inputs or exporting. The result of more and more incentives or bonuses being applied to guide enterprise managers is that decisionmaking is again centralized in the government planning agencies. Instead of being incentives or subsidies in a market sense, they are means of controlling the enterprise.

This is apparently the situation in Czechoslovakia. Detailed, specific targets were set in the seventh Five-Year Plan. For example, steel production is to increase 5 percent, and even the production method is specified. There are strict quotas for production and consumption. Indicators have been introduced which reflect the central planners' goals in such areas as labor productivity, use of fixed assets, reduced consumption of energy, and materials and profitability in terms of value-added. Bonuses exist for over-fulfilling plan targets, particularly export targets.

We see no reason why these success indicators and bonuses would work any differently in Czechoslovakia than in other NME's. We believe that the "incentives" alleged by petitioners function like the other incentives, as more elements of central control. Even those incentives tied to export, some of which might be considered export subsidies in a market economy, do not, in our opinion, operate as export subsidies in an NME.

As described above, enterprises in these countries operate under different conditions than do firms in market economy systems. In Czechoslovakia, for example, foreign trade is operated as a state monopoly. The type and volume of goods to be exported are defined in the material plan.

That the Czech government has introduced "economic mechanisms"—for rewarding overfulfillment of targets, for rationalizing the use of imports, for promoting exports—does not mean that Czech enterprises can respond to those incentives like a competitive firm in a market economy. These mechanisms are imposed upon a system that is not economically rational. Nor are the reforms designed to lead to a rational, market system. Central planning remains the basis for defining the goals and operating conditions for the enterprises.

In this situation, "incentives" have a different meaning than in a market economy system. They are not distortions of market generated signals to competitive firms. They are imposed on a system to generate results: results that the nonmarket economy inherently cannot produce.

Thus, we have found generally for NME's and specifically for Czechoslovakia that prices are administered and that these prices do not have the same meaning as prices in a market economy. Not only are the NME enterprise's output prices controlled, but its costs, which are the prices paid for inputs, also are centrally determined. With administered costs and prices, profits effectively are administered as well. Finally, economic activity is centrally directed through the use of administered prices, plans and targets.

These are the essential characteristics of nonmarket economic systems. It is these features that make NME's irrational by market standards. This is the background that does not allow us to identify specific NME government actions as bounties or grants.

[The ITA concluded also that Congress had never considered the question of applying countervailing duties to nonmarket economies and that a number of commentators had indicated that it would be difficult, if not impossible, to value the subsidies allegedly involved.]

CONTINENTAL STEEL CORP. v. UNITED STATES

Court of International Trade, 1985.
614 F.Supp. 548.

WATSON, JUDGE:

The Court is of the opinion that the Commerce Department has made a basic error in its interpretation and administration of this law. The fundamental error of the Commerce Department is its premise that a subsidy can only exist in a market economy. Stated differently, it is completely at variance with the law to find that the acts at which the countervailing duty law was aimed, do not include the acts of a government of a country with a nonmarket economy.

* * *

The simple fact is that the countervailing duty law makes no distinctions based on the form of any country's economy. Its language and purpose allow no such distinctions to be made.

* * *

In the opinion of the Court the language of this law is perfectly indifferent to forms of economy. The language plainly shows the strongest possible desire to prevent evasion either by means of technicalities of status, or by technicalities of form, or by technicalities of relationship.

We have a law which uses ten exhaustive alternatives to describe the possible conveyor of the subsidy. As an alternative to "pay," which conceivably might be avoided by some other form of conveyance, it uses the general term "bestow." It specifically seeks out benefits given "directly or indirectly." The law takes pains to cover manufacture, production or export lest artificial distinctions be developed between levels of commercial activity. It goes on to specify that it controls in all conceivable methods of importation, whether the article in question is imported into the United States directly or otherwise and whether or not the article is changed in condition by remanufacture or otherwise.

In the midst of this formidable demonstration of careful draftsmanship the law describes the fundamental thing which is paid or bestowed as "any bounty or grant."

The Supreme Court has stated that "a word of broader significance than 'grant' could not have been used." Nicholas & Co. v. United States, 249 U.S. 34, 39 (1918).

* * *

The Commerce Department defines a subsidy as a distortion of the operation of a *market* economy. This is a novel definition. It depends on the premise that only in a market economy can a "distortion" exist because only in such an economy can the alleged subsidy be measured against what the normal or benchmark level of that particular element would be. This in turn presumes that there is no normality or "measurability" in a nonmarket economy, i.e., that central control makes any given economic decision unpredictable or atypical or irrational, so that one act cannot be characterized as more beneficial than another. Into this picture of economic irrationality the Commerce Department adds the additional fillip that even if "incentives" to production do exist in a nonmarket economy they are not beneficial to our sense of the word. They are assertedly some sort of ineffectual attempt to exercise control. They do not actually result in subsidization because the firms, lacking a profit motive and subject to centralized export controls, cannot respond to the incentives.

The determinations state that "even those incentives tied to export, some of which might be considered export subsidies in a market economy, do not, in our opinion, operate as export subsidies in an NME."

This line of analytical legerdemain is developed as follows:

> That the Czech government has introduced "economic mechanisms,"—for rewarding overfulfillment of targets, for rationalizing the use of imports, for promoting exports—does not mean that Czech enterprises can respond to those incentives like a competitive firm in a market economy. These mechanisms are imposed upon a system that is not economically rational. Nor are the reforms designed to lead to a rational, market system. Central planning remains the basis for defining the goals and operating conditions for the enterprises.

> In this situation, "incentives" have a different meaning than in a market economy system. They are not distortions of market generated signals to competitive firms. They are imposed on a system to generate results: results that the nonmarket economy inherently cannot produce.

The quoted passages are amalgams of economic jargon, semantic arbitrariness and unlawful irrationality. Decisions which depend on a premise that economic conduct is irrational or inherently ineffectual cannot be allowed. Economic behavior may be one of the few areas in which rationality and effectiveness can still be presumed in world affairs. Laws cannot be enforced if conduct to which they are directed is not taken at face value. The enforcement of laws requires the investigation of reality, not the formulation of theoretical obstacles.

* * *

The Commerce Department's definition of subsidy includes language stating that a subsidy "results in a misallocation of resources, encouraging inefficient production and lessening world wealth."

There is not the slightest indication in the law or the legislative history to show that the allocation of resources, the efficiency of production or the diminution of world wealth is a concern of the countervailing duty law.

* * *

The term "subsidy" as it applies in the export activity of a nonmarket economy does not present any real difficulties of "meaning." The subsidies alleged to exist here are not acts which are peculiar to nonmarket economies. If there are any difficulties here, they are not difficulties of *meaning,* but problems of *measurement,* which are precisely within the expertise of the agency.

Even if we anticipate problems of meaning in the event that more problematic domestic conduct of these countries becomes subject to scrutiny, it cannot be accepted that this arises from a congenital subsidizing character of all government acts in a nonmarket economy. In other words, it cannot be assumed that central economic control is synonymous with subsidization. This goes back to the fundamental misconception that it takes distortion of a "market" to make a subsidy.

The concept of subsidization is really much broader than that. If it has to be stated in terms of distortion then it is a distortion of a pattern of regularity or even a pattern of reasonably expected fairness. But these subtleties can be left for the future. For the moment, it is sufficient to say that the Commerce Department has the authority and ability to detect patterns of regularity and investigate beneficial deviations from those patterns—and it must do so regardless of the form of the economy.

* * *

Not all the dons of economic academia can persuade this Court that the government of a country with a nonmarket economy cannot show what amounts to favoritism towards the manufacture, production, or export of particular merchandise. The idea violates common sense and conflicts with a rational construction of the law.

It is important to remember that the antidumping law presented an apparent difficulty in dealing with nonmarket economies because its plain language lacked a fundamental reference point needed to measure whether or not sales were being made at less than fair market value. The nonmarket economy did not have the fair home market value against which to measure the price to the United States. This did not deter the enforcing agency from developing that "fair" home market value by reference to surrogate countries with market economies, an administrative practice that was later expressly confirmed by incorporation into the Trade Act of 1974. See S.Rep. 93–1298, 93rd Cong. 2d Sess. 174 (1974).

Questions

(1) Who is right? As this is written, the issue is before the Federal Circuit.

(2) If the countervailing duty provisions do not apply to NME exports and if the antidumping rules can be criticized for their irrelevance to reality (how can one find a true surrogate country), when should the international trading system allow restraints to be placed on NME imports? Is the only reasonable solution the use of Section 406, the "escape clause" for Communist country products? If so, why not abolish antidumping and countervailing duty laws altogether and rely solely on escape clause proceedings in all cases? But what about the "unfairness" element of dumping and subsidies?

(D) COUNTERVAILING DUTIES IN THE EC

The EC has seldom invoked its countervailing duty regulation. Since it is often the target of U.S. investigations, it generally urges interpretations of the rules that make a finding that a subsidy exists less likely and that value it at the lowest possible amount. Nonetheless, the EC has on at least one occasion found that what appeared to be a generally available measure was countervailable.[37]

(E) BORDER TAX ADJUSTMENTS

At the time of this writing quiescent, but at times quite controversial, is the question of whether the remission or noncollection on exportation of consumption or value added taxes is a fair trade practice or should be countervailable. The United States has never applied antidumping or countervailing duties to offset such remissions or exemptions and the GATT Codes explicitly provide that they are not to be treated as export subsidies or added to dumping margins. Nonetheless, in the view of some, the inability of U.S. manufacturers to obtain rebates of the direct taxes allocable to exports and the unimportance of consumption taxes in the United States (at least at the federal level) means that EC and Japanese exports, which are effectively exempt from the significant consumption or value added taxes applied by those countries, will be cheaper than U.S. goods on world markets and therefore have a competitive advantage. Since this advantage is viewed as derived from the fact that these goods do not bear their fair share of national taxes, as U.S. goods allegedly do, U.S. manufacturers and Congress have from time to time pressed the U.S. government to change the long established rules.

37. See Davey, An Analysis of European Communities Legislation and Practice Relating to Antidumping and Countervailing Duties, [1983] Fordham Corp.L.Inst. 39, 113–16 (1984); Cunnane & Stanbrook, Dumping and Subsidies: The law and procedures governing the imposition of anti-dumping and countervailing duties in the European Community 50–60 (1983).

EXECUTIVE BRANCH GATT STUDIES, NO. 1, TAX ADJUSTMENTS IN INTERNATIONAL TRADE: GATT PROVISIONS AND EEC PRACTICES
7–17 (1973)[38]

II. GATT PROVISIONS

Application of Domestic Taxes to Imports

The GATT prohibits levying on imported products any "internal taxes or other internal charges of any kind in excess of those applied, directly or indirectly, to like domestic products" (Article III:2) and enjoins the use of such internal taxes in such a manner as to afford protection to domestic products. The GATT allows countries to impose on imported products (at the time of importation or subsequently) all consumption taxes up to the amount which would have been imposed on those products had they been produced and sold domestically; the GATT prohibits imposing internal taxes on imported products in excess of internal taxes on like domestic products.

* * *

Countries apply the GATT provisions in accordance with their own domestic consumption tax system. In countries where multistage consumption taxes are levied on all transactions, whether wholesale or retail, such as under the tax-on-value added which is imposed at the same rate on imported and domestic goods (discussed in later paragraphs), the tax is levied on imports at the border and on subsequent transactions. In countries without multistage taxes, domestic consumption taxes are usually levied on imports at the import stage, if that corresponds to the stage at which the tax is imposed domestically, or at stages subsequent to the import stage. * * *

The purpose of taxing imports—whether at the time of importation or subsequently—is to ensure that foreign products do not receive more favorable tax treatment than similar domestic products. * * *

Tax adjustments on imports are permitted under GATT only for taxes on products; that is, consumption taxes. The GATT prohibits levying any tax on imported products to compensate for direct taxes, including income taxes, levied on domestic producers. The provision is apparently based on the assumption that income taxes are "paid" by the legal tax payer, whereas consumption taxes are "paid" by the consumer.

Tax Treatment of Exports—"Indirect" Taxes

The GATT permits countries to exempt exported products from domestic consumption taxes and to rebate to exporters such taxes as may have been collected on the exported product. This principle was originally suggested by the United States in September 1946 in its Suggested Charter for an International Trade Organization (ITO) of the United Nations.

* * * Since the original GATT allowed export subsidization, there was at that time no reason for the GATT to specifically note that the

---

38. Subcomm. on Intl. Trade, Senate Comm. on Finance, 93d Cong., 2d Sess. (Compilation of 1973 studies by the Executive Branch: Comm. Print 1974).

exemption or rebate on exports of consumption taxes could not be considered to be a subsidy.

Nevertheless there was a recognition of this principle in the antidumping and countervailing duty article of the GATT (Article VI:4). This article, unchanged since 1947, provides that any consumption tax exemption or rebate on exports shall not be the basis for imposing antidumping or countervailing duties. Our own Antidumping Act, 1921, contains a similar legislated provision. * * *

The GATT provisions permitting rebates of domestic consumption taxes were made more explicit in 1957, following a major Review Session of the GATT Contracting Parties, in Ad Article XVI. The principle was repeated in connection with new provisions which came into effect in 1962 among the major trading countries prohibiting the granting of subsidies on nonprimary products, including a prohibition of the exemption or rebate on exports of domestic charges or taxes *other than* domestic consumption taxes (see below).

It is a universally accepted concept—incorporated in our own domestic law—that since exports are not consumed in the country of production, they should not be subject to consumption taxes in the country of production.

It should be noted that, in accordance with the GATT provisions concerning consumption tax treatment of exports, the United States exempts from or rebates on exported products all state and local sales taxes (46 states and the District of Columbia), as well as Federal and state excise taxes on those exported products. Throughout most of the post-World War II period, our Federal excise taxes were imposed on a wide range of products,[*5] often at relatively high rates. Only a few products are subject to Federal excise tax today.

Even in interstate trade within the United States it is customary to exempt from state consumption taxes or rebate such taxes to manufacturers of "exports" to other states.

Tax Treatment of Exports—"Direct" Taxes

As noted earlier, the major trading countries agreed in the GATT not to grant export subsidies on nonprimary products and defined subsidies to include rebates to exporters of direct (income) taxes and social security taxes.

This provision came into effect in 1962 after the major trading countries entered into a "Declaration Giving Effect to the Provisions of Article XVI:4." This Declaration was developed in a Working Party on Subsidies whose report noted that the governments prepared to accept the Declaration "agree that, for the purpose of that declaration, these practices generally are to be considered as subsidies." Among those listed were:

"(c) The remission, calculated in relation to exports, of direct taxes or social welfare charges on industrial or commercial enterprises;

* 5. For example, alcoholic beverages, tobacco products, motor vehicles and parts, tires and tubes, business machines, household appliances, firearms, fur articles, motor fuels, coal and coke, copper, lumber, vegetable oils and seeds, jewelry, luggage, musical instruments, radios, sporting goods, cosmetics, phonographs and phonograph records, television sets, sugar, and refrigerating equipment.

"(d) The exemption, in respect of exported goods, of charges or taxes, other than charges in connection with importation or indirect taxes levied at one or several stages on the same goods if sold for internal consumption; or the payment, in respect of exported goods, of amounts exceeding those effectively levied at one or several stages on these goods in the form of indirect taxes or of charges in connection with importation or in both forms."

Some countries accepting the Declaration had rebated on exports part or all of their employers' social security taxes (France) and part or all of their corporate income taxes (Japan). The Declaration clarified which taxes would be eligible for adjustment on export.

III. EEC PRACTICES

The European Economic Community (EEC) Council of Ministers decided in 1964 to harmonize by 1970 its member states' consumption tax systems along the lines of the French tax-on-value added (TVA, or "taxe sur la valeur ajoutée [or, in English, the value added tax, or VAT].

The TVA is a consumption or sales tax collected each time a good (whether a raw material, semiprocessed or finished product) is sold, but the tax base at each stage is only the value added by the seller. While the TVA tax base can be computed in different ways, countries currently applying the TVA have chosen the simplest alternative. Under the TVA a businessman has a gross tax liability each month of the total amount of his sales times the tax rate, say 10 percent. His invoices to his customers show this 10 percent as part of the purchase price. From this gross liability he deducts TVA he paid on his purchases. His suppliers will have itemized the TVA payments on their invoices to him. His net TVA liability is the difference between the two figures. * * *

* * * This process is repeated throughout the distribution chain until the product is sold at retail to the final consumer. Since the individual consumer cannot deduct the TVA, the process ends there.

The net tax base (and also the revenue) resulting from all these transactions is the equivalent of that under a retail sales tax at the same ad valorem tax rate. It differs from a retail sales tax principally in that the government gets part of the revenue ultimately paid by the consumer at the earlier stages of production and distribution and therefore it reduces the possibility of tax evasion at the retail stage. * * *

Imports enter the TVA cycle at the border. The tax rate is the same as the rate on the similar domestic product, and is payable at importation, unlike retail sales taxes where most imports are not taxed until sold to an individual consumer. The importer treats the TVA paid on imports as any other purchase he makes for his firm.

* * *

Exports under a TVA system are exempt from tax, as are exports under retail sales tax systems. Therefore, there is no TVA tax refund on exports. As for the tax the exporter paid to his domestic suppliers for the materials used to produce the exported product, he treats them in the same manner as all of the TVA he pays to his suppliers; that is, as a credit for his end-of-the-month accounting to the tax authorities; he omits from the total sales on which tax is due the value of his exports since he has not collected the TVA from his foreign customer. There is thus no inherent incentive in the TVA system for him to export his product rather than sell it in the domestic market. (The possibility of some backward tax shifting—and thus some possible incentive—is discussed below.) * * *

IV. DIRECT AND INDIRECT TAXES: TAX SHIFTING ASSUMPTIONS AND CORPORATE PROFITS TAXES

There is no record of any discussion by the drafters of the GATT of the economic assumptions underlying the differing treatment accorded to direct and indirect taxes on exports and imports. However, the GATT provisions were written as if increases in indirect taxes were fully reflected in the price of goods (i.e., fully shifted forward) while increases in direct taxes were fully absorbed by producers (or shifted back to factors of production), having no effect on price. If these assumptions are correct, the GATT provisions would equalize the amount of indirect taxes levied on competing domestic and imported goods; would avoid granting an incentive to exports by the rebate of (or credit for) taxes not reflected in prices, and would avoid distortions arising from differing direct tax systems. Under such circumstances, the GATT provisions would be trade neutral.

Few people—even European tax authorities—would argue such absolutes. It is generally recognized that the degree of tax shifting for both consumption and profits or other direct taxes depends primarily on the demand for the product, actions of the monetary authorities, the stage of the business cycle and the degree of competition among producers of the goods. Some economists also hold the view that increases in selective consumption taxes are much more easily shifted forward than increases in general consumption taxes. To the extent consumption taxes are not fully shifted forward, and direct taxes are partially shifted forward, countries may derive some trade benefit from the GATT provisions on border taxes, but it is not known how large or how lasting such benefits may be. Relative prices among countries, on which trade advantages largely depend, are subject to a mix of forces and undergo constant change. These advantages, if any, can be erased by a currency appreciation as well as differential rates of inflation, productivity changes, and even shifts in tastes. After a time the first effects of the change may be offset to an indeterminate degree by these other factors. In short, it is impossible to measure the extent of the shifting and its effect on trade in a way which can be used for comparative country analysis. Moreover, there seems no practical way to settle the tax shifting question and quantify effects which the GATT provisions may have on a country's trading position.

* * *

Corporate Income Taxes in Europe and the United States

It is sometimes said that the United States has high corporate income taxes and European countries have high consumption taxes, and that because the GATT rules permit the rebate of consumption taxes but not of corporate income taxes, the United States is disadvantaged by the GATT rules.

In fact, both have high income taxes, especially in the business sector, and in addition the European countries have higher consumption taxes and higher employers' social security taxes than the United States does.

* * *

From the above data, it is impossible to estimate what the effects on a country's trading position would be if GATT provisions were altered to permit the rebate of direct taxes. The ultimate result on a country's trading position would depend on such factors as the size of the rebate, the state of demand for the product, the stage of the business cycle at home and abroad, and the degree of competition among domestic and foreign producers of the good. In addition, competition in trade occurs not at the level of national economies but at the level of individual business firms and specific products. Therefore, the data also do not indicate whether a change in the GATT rules to permit rebate of profit tax to a specific American firm in its exports of a specific product would help or hurt that firm in competition with foreign firms receiving similar rebates. Rebates for direct taxes would necessarily be imprecise, thus affording opportunities for undetected or for competitive overcompensation.

Note

In 1978, the U.S. Supreme Court upheld the Treasury Department's practice of not considering border tax adjustments to be grants or bounties subject to countervailing duties under the U.S. countervailing duty statute. The case in which this issue arose, Zenith Radio Corp. v. United States, is excerpted in Section 3.4(B)(3) supra.

SECTION 10.4   ADDITIONAL REMEDIES FOR UNFAIR TRADE PRACTICES

(A)   INTRODUCTION

Unfair import practices are restricted by a variety of U.S. statutes. One such statute—Section 337 of the Tariff Act of 1930, which deals with unfair methods of competition and unfair acts in connection with importation—has been used fairly extensively by U.S. industry to protect patent rights. Some other laws—the Antidumping Act of 1916, Section 48(a)(7)(D) of the Internal Revenue Code and Section 307 of the 1930 Tariff Act, all described below—have seldom been invoked. Because of its relative importance, this section will focus on Section 337 cases and issues and look only briefly at the other statutes.

(B)   SECTION 337 AND UNFAIR IMPORT PRACTICES

Section 337, which was initially added to U.S. law by the 1930 Tariff Act and then revised by Section 341 of the 1974 Trade Act (Documentary Supplement), provides a means by which U.S. industry can obtain relief from so-called unfair import competition.[1] Before examining the substantive issues arising in respect of the statute's application, we will consider its procedural setting, since that in large part explains its attractiveness to some potential complainants and its nonuse by others.

A Section 337 proceeding is commenced by the filing of a complaint by an aggrieved party.[2] Within 30 days the ITC decides whether to initiate an investigation, and if it does so, the respondent must file a written answer 20 days later. The case is assigned to an ITC administrative law judge (ALJ), who supervises discovery, rules on any motions and eventually issues a decision in the case. There are broad provisions for discovery, including the use of oral depositions, written interrogatories and inspection of documents. Following discovery, a hearing is held before the ALJ, who must normally report an initial determination to the ITC within nine months of the date on which the notice of investigation was published (14 months in a "more complicated" case). The initial determination becomes the Commission's determination unless the Commission orders a review of it or of particular issues. The Commission is required to dispose of a case within 12 months (18 months, if it determines that the case is a "more complicated" one). The President then has 60 days to exercise his right to override the Commission decision.[3]

The Commission is authorized to grant essentially two sorts of relief. First, it may issue an order excluding from entry into the United States any article found to be imported in violation of Section 337.[4] It may issue such an exclusion order on a preliminary basis during the course of the investigation, although importation will be permitted on payment of a bond.[5] Second, the Commission may order the person violating Section 337 to cease and desist such violations.[6] Violations may be punished by a fine equal to the greater of $10,000 a day or the domestic value of the goods entered or sold on such day in violation of the order. Appeals of Commission decisions may be made to the U.S. Court of Appeals for the Federal Circuit.[7]

Two aspects of the foregoing procedural description are especially significant. First, compared to a proceeding in federal court, an ITC proceeding under Section 337 is concluded much more quickly, because of the strict time limits imposed by statute and applicable rules. This means that a complainant under Section 337 must be prepared to establish its claim quickly since the time limits place real constraints on a complainant's ability to conduct leisurely discovery. As a result, the costs of such actions are likely to be high, particularly if extensive discovery must be completed in a short period of time. The result is that Section 337 is generally not considered to be an

---

1. 19 U.S.C.A. § 1337. For general analyses of Section 337, see 1 H. Kaye, P. Plaia & M. Hertzberg, International Trade Practice §§ 4.01–12.21 (looseleaf); U.S. Intl. Trade Commn., Office of the Administrative Law Judges, Compendium of Section 337 Decisions (1981); Walders, Other Import Relief Laws in H. Appelbaum & A. Victor (eds.), The Trade Agreements Act of 1979—Four Years Later 255 (1983); Recent Developments, Section 337: An Activist ITC, 14 Law & Poly.Intl.Bus. 905 (1982).

2. The general procedures applicable to Section 337 cases are set out in 19 CFR Pt. 210 (1985).

3. 19 U.S.C.A. § 1337(g)(2).

4. 19 U.S.C.A. § 1337(d)(2).

5. 19 U.S.C.A. § 1337(e)(2).

6. 19 U.S.C.A. § 1337(f)(2).

7. 19 U.S.C.A. § 1337(c)(2).

attractive remedy in complicated unfair trade practices cases, such as those involving antitrust issues. Rather, it is most attractive for cases involving simpler issues, such as whether there is patent or trademark infringement.

On the other hand, an exclusion order is in essence a judgment enforced by hundreds of customs agents. This may be much more valuable than a judgment that the import infringes a patent in a situation where the complainant is unable to enforce the judgment effectively because of lack of information about sellers and users of the product. Thus, if the Section 337 procedure is not deemed impractical because of time constraints, the remedies available make it very attractive.

With these procedural considerations behind us, we turn now to the substantive requirements of Section 337. Before reviewing the following material, the student should read Section 337(a), focusing on the elements that a complainant must establish to prevail in a Section 337 case.

IN RE CERTAIN CUBE PUZZLES
U.S. Intl. Trade Commn. (1982) [8]

VIEWS OF CHAIRMAN ECKES AND COMMISSIONER HAGGART

I. Procedural Background

On November 17, 1981, complainant Ideal Toy Corp. (Ideal) filed a complaint with the Commission alleging violations of section 337. * * * An investigation was instituted to determine whether there is a violation of section 337 in the unauthorized importation of certain cube puzzles into the United States, or in their sale, by reason of (1) infringement of complainant Ideal's common-law trademark, (2) false designation of origin by copying complainant's trade dress (hereinafter false representation), and (3) passing off of respondents' cube puzzles as those of complainant, the effect or tendency of which is to destroy or substantially injure an industry, efficiently and economically operated, in the United States. Ideal sought a permanent exclusion order and orders to cease and desist.

* * *

II. Unfair Acts

A. Common-law Trademark

A trademark is defined in the Lanham Act as any word, name, symbol, or device, or any combination thereof, adopted and used by a manufacturer or a merchant to identify his goods and to distinguish them from those manufactured or sold by others. This is also the traditional definition of a common-law trademark. A trademark indicates origin or ownership, guarantees quality or constancy, and entitles the owner to advertise goods bearing the mark.

Ideal claims a common-law trademark in the appearance of its cube. Ideal's cube puzzle (called "Rubik's Cube" by Ideal) is a six-sided cube made of black plastic. On each side there are nine smaller cubes, called "cubies."

8. Inv. No. 337–TA–112, Pub. No. 1334, 4 ITRD 2102 (1982).

In the regular or less expensive version of the cube, the outer face of all the cubies on each side of the cube are covered with an adhesive square of the same color when the puzzle is in the starting position. The colors used are red, blue, yellow, green, orange and white. These colors appear against a black grid pattern formed by the black plastic background.

In the deluxe model of the Ideal cube, the same general colors are used but the hues are different from those in the regular model. The colored squares in the deluxe cube are made of plastic and are inserted and glued into the black cubies. In addition, the black background grid is thicker than on the regular cube, the colored sides are slightly raised, and the cube is slightly larger than the regular cube. The expensive version is sold only in a limited distribution network consisting of gift and stationery stores and similar outlets.

The regular cube was sold and the deluxe cube is presently sold in packages which have a cylindrical black plastic base and a cylindrical clear plastic cover through which the cube may be seen. The base and the cover are sealed together by a strip of black and gold tape on which the name "Rubik's Cube" appears. Ideal's regular cubes are presently sold in a square black and green box covered on two sides by clear plastic through which the cube can be seen.

A few respondents sell cube puzzles in packages which are identical to Ideal's packages. Respondents also market their cubes in other packages, including packages which have clear dome-shaped tops and black plastic bottoms. Ideal challenges only the packages that are virtually identical to Ideal's packages.

The alleged trademark in the design of the cube puzzle consists of the solid colors red, blue, yellow, green, orange and white, with the same color on the outer faces of all cubies on each side of the cube, with a square of color appearing against the black plastic on each cubie. According to Ideal, this creates a distinctive grid background. This is the way the puzzle looks in the starting position and the way the cube looks when the puzzle is solved. The player rotates sections of the puzzle and "scrambles" the colors. The colors must be unscrambled to solve the puzzle. It is sold in the starting position so that the purchaser will know that the puzzle can be solved.

The respondents market a number of different cube puzzles, some of which are identical to Ideal's cube. Ideal alleges first that the puzzles identical to its Rubik's Cube infringe Ideal's common law trademark.

Although some of the respondent's cubes may have the same black-background, some respondents vary one or two colors on the sides of the cube by substituting other colors for the colors on Ideal's cube, e.g., purple for blue. Additionally, other cube puzzles have the same colored squares but different background colors, e.g., white, blue, and grey. Ideal also alleges that cube puzzles which vary one or two colors on the side of the cube or which have different background colors infringe Ideal's trademark because they form a grid pattern which is confusingly similar to the black grid background of Ideal's cubes. There are a number of other cube puzzles sold by respondents that have flowers, fruits, colored circles, etc., on them, but these puzzles are not challenged by Ideal.

In order to prove that it has a common-law trademark, Ideal must show (a) that it has a right to use the mark, (b) that the mark is inherently distinctive or has acquired a secondary meaning, (c) that the mark has not acquired a generic meaning, and (d) that the mark is not primarily functional. To prove infringement of that trademark, Ideal must prove there is a likelihood of confusion among consumers who see competing products with a similar appearance. For protection under section 337, a common-law trademark must meet these same criteria.

1. *Ideal's right to use the mark*

[Ideal had purchased the right to use the mark from a Hungarian company.]

2. *Inherent distinctiveness*

*   *   *

Further, the design of Rubik's Cube is not inherently distinctive because it is not unique in the field of cube puzzles. Other puzzles use colors to distinguish the sides of the cube puzzle, although the patches may be circular rather than square and the background may be clear rather than black. Since the design of Rubik's Cube is not unique, it cannot be considered inherently distinctive.

3. *Secondary Meaning*

To establish secondary meaning, a manufacturer must show that, in the minds of the public, the *primary* significance of a product feature or term is to identify the source of the product rather than the product itself. Secondary meaning may be proven by evidence of an association between the mark and the seller in the minds of a substantial number of the buyer group.

*   *   *

Surveys are one means of demonstrating secondary meaning.

*   *   *

*   *   * In August of 1981, Dr. Helfgott in survey A(1) and (2) found that 33 percent of the interviewees identified black-based cubes as Rubik's Cubes. In Study B, out of six cubes, approximately 40 percent of the interviewees identified Ideal's cube puzzle as Rubik's Cube. In a subsequent survey in May of 1982, 72 percent of the interviewees identified Ideal's cube puzzle as Rubik's Cube. These surveys demonstrate that, at least in the New York City area, a significant percentage of consumers identified Ideal's black-based cube as Rubik's Cube or as coming from a single source.

*   *   *

*   *   * We, however, agree with the ALJ that the Russick survey, especially the comments by the interviewees, indicates secondary meaning for Rubik's Cube in the Minneapolis-St. Paul area, and that there is a presumption of secondary meaning throughout the United States.

In addition to both the Helfgott surveys and the Russick survey, there is evidence of meticulous copying, over 2 million dollars in advertising, and 15 million units of sales to date. Although this is "circumstantial" evidence of secondary meaning, when such evidence is combined with the direct evidence of consumer surveys and the fact that the mark is intrinsically a strong mark, we believe that Ideal has established secondary meaning in its Rubik's Cube puzzle.

4. *Genericness*

A generic name of a product, i.e., the name of a product or service itself, e.g. "Aspirin," can never function as a trademark to indicate origin. To be considered generic, the mark must serve to identify the product itself rather than indicating that it comes from one source.

* * *

We determine that the conclusion of both the Helfgott surveys and the comments made during the Russick survey indicate Rubik's Cube is identified with one source, i.e., the black-based puzzle, and therefore, has not become generic.

5. *Functionality*

* * *

The object of the puzzle is to rearrange the puzzle so as to return it to its starting position. Thus, the cube faces must be distinguishable, but not necessarily by the use of square solid-color panels. The fact that the use of color and square patches may make the cubies slightly more distinguishable and, therefore, the puzzle slightly easier to solve than a puzzle using colored patches are functional. The cube has 43,252,003,274,489,856,000 (43 quintillion) possible combinations. It is unlikely, if not impossible, that it could be solved by trial-and-error. The solution must to a degree be planned prior to being completed. Compared with the degree of difficulty of the puzzle itself, the increase in difficulty because of the use of dice versus colors or colored circles rather than colored squares is minimal. Further, the use of colored squares to distinguish the sides of the cube does not enhance or facilitate the actual solution of the puzzle. Therefore, there is no evidence that square color patches on a black background is one of the superior designs available.

6. *Likelihood of Confusion*

In determining the likelihood of confusion, the major consideration is whether a substantial number of reasonable buyers are likely to be confused by similar marks.

* * *

* * * Mr. Weintraub, Ideal's Senior Vice President of Manufacturing, testified that about 50 percent of the approximately 15,000 cube puzzles returned to Ideal as defective Rubik's Cubes puzzles were, in fact, *not* authentic Rubik's Cube puzzles but rather imitations thereof. Finally, the Helfgott surveys demonstrate that numerous black-based cubes made by respondents were identified as Rubik's Cube.

* * *

False Representation

Having established a case of trademark infringement for its cube puzzle, Ideal has also proved a violation of section 43(a) of the Lanham Act for false representation of the source of manufacture.

* * *

C. Passing Off

The ALJ determined that all respondents who sold cube puzzles identical to Ideal's cube puzzles have engaged in passing off. We disagree. However, we determine that certain respondents have engaged in passing off because of additional evidence which indicates their intent to enable distributors to pass off respondents' puzzles as those of Ideal.

An essential element of passing off is that one is engaged in an intentional act that leads the customer to believe he is buying the goods of another.

* * *

F. Domestic Industry

In order for the Commission to find a violation of section 337, complainant must comprise an "industry * * * in the United States." * * *

In the present case, Ideal employs up to 200 people in Newark, New Jersey in an operation which includes quality control, repair, and packaging of cube puzzles that Ideal imports from various overseas sources. When the cube puzzles arrive at the Newark facility, each lot of cubes is subjected to an inspection process in which a certain percentage of cubes within the lot are randomly selected for testing. As a result of this initial quality control inspection, Ideal has rejected 1,000,000 cubes out of the 16,000,000 cubes sold by Ideal.

Subsequent to leaving the initial quality control line, those lots with less than 1 percent defective cube puzzles are visually inspected before packaging. Those lots with 1–3 percent defective cube puzzles are subjected to extensive quality control inspection before packaging.

Ideal's quality control continues well after its Rubik's Cube puzzles leave the quality control line. In addition, Ideal conducts age, drop and shake, and life testing. Thus, because of this extensive quality control operation, virtually every cube is inspected in the United States.

Ideal also conducts some repair activities in the United States. In order to repair the cube puzzles found to be defective through Ideal's extensive quality control procedure, ten full-time employees are employed and they have repaired over 500,000 cube puzzles.

In addition to quality control, Ideal also packages its Rubik's Cube in its Newark, New Jersey facility. All of Ideal's packaging material for its deluxe cube, including the molding of the clear plastic cylinders for the deluxe cubes, and instruction sheets for its regular cube are produced in Newark, New Jersey.

Furthermore, Ideal has expended approximately $200,000 on the production of molds in the United States, and has manufactured molds for use by its manufacturing facilities overseas. Ideal has also spent an additional $50,000 in the United States to improve the design and materials of its cube puzzles and to lower it costs.

We find that Ideal's domestic activities are of the appropriate nature and are significant enough to conclude that their domestic business activities constitute an "industry . . . in the United States."

The significance of Ideal's operations is evidenced by the value added in the United States by Ideal's quality control, packaging and repair operations. Ideal has testified that the imported cost of the cube is approximately $1.00 and that an additional $.92 of value is added to the cube puzzle by the quality control, packaging, and repair activities performed in the United States. We believe that this is significant because approximately 50 percent of the value of the cube puzzle is added by production activities in the United States.

G. Efficient and Economic Operation

We determine that the domestic industry is efficiently and economically operated. The facts that Ideal's cube puzzles have been on allocation and that the repair and packaging could be done more cheaply abroad does not compel a contrary conclusion. Allocation is a standard practice in the toy business. Further, if Ideal expanded its production to fill current demand, and then demand fell, Ideal could be left with warehouses full of cube puzzles. The failure to increase production in this situation does not establish that a domestic industry is not efficiently and economically operated.

H. Injury

Ideal established that over two million infringing cubes were imported since February, 1981. Ideal lost accounts, including Sears Roebuck, Macy's, J.C. Penney, Mervyn's, and K-Mart. Sears alone purchased 350,000–400,000 imported cubes and K-Mart also purchased several hundred thousand cubes. About twenty additional accounts also cancelled some of their orders for Ideal's cube puzzles.

*   *   *

Even though Ideal was on allocation, there was testimony that customers would wait to buy a cube with Ideal's trademark. It is apparent from the vast number of imports and the lost accounts that Ideal was substantially injured by the infringing imports. Further, the record does demonstrate that the imported cube puzzles were sold at a lower price than Ideal's cube puzzles and that Ideal's price reduction was caused in part by the low priced imports.

Ideal is the owner of an exclusive trademark right in the design of the Rubik's Cube. Therefore, each sale of an infringing item is usually a sale that should have gone to Ideal, and once such a sale is made, it is irretrievably lost to complainant. In addition, although not directly applicable to section 337, the federal courts in cases involving injunction proceedings have determined that, in a trademark infringement case, a substantial likelihood of confusion, in and of itself, constitutes irreparable injury to a plaintiff. Thus, it does not matter that Ideal did not suffer a loss or had increasing profits, so long as it lost profits to the imported cubes. Ideal's witnesses estimated that its profit was approximately $1.00 a cube. Thus, on the Sears account alone, Ideal lost approximately $350,000 to $400,000. We think this fact evidences substantial injury to Ideal by the imported infringing cubes.

*   *   *

V. Public Interest

None of the parties has alleged that there are any public interest factors which would preclude a remedy in this case under section 337(d). Neither is there any other information available showing that imposition of a remedy would adversely affect the public health and welfare, competitive conditions in the U.S. economy, the production of like or directly competitive articles in the United States, or U.S. consumers. Therefore, we determine that issuance of an exclusion order is not precluded by consideration of the public interest.

[An exclusion order was held to be appropriate.]

VIEWS OF COMMISSIONER STERN

* * *

I disagree with the majority's conclusion that a domestic industry exists in this case. In *Certain Miniature Battery-Operated, All-Terrain Wheeled Vehicles,* Inv. No. 337–TA–122 (1982) (Toy Trucks), the Commission determined that complainants which imported toy trucks from Hong Kong were not a domestic industry under section 337 based on "the nature and significance of complainants' business activities in the United States" which relate to the toy trucks. In that case, complainants prepared engineering drawings, performed some quality control, packaged some of the toy trucks, and were involved in warehousing, advertising, and sales distribution of toy trucks in the United States. In this case, we have the same general set of facts: Ideal imports the cube puzzles and only performs quality control, repairs, and packaging in the United States. The nature of Ideal's business activities is identical to the business activities performed by the complainants in *Toy Trucks.*

I wish to note further that this case is not like *Certain Airtight Cast-Iron Stoves,* Inv. No. 337–TA–69, USITC Pub. 1126 (1981). In *Cast-Iron Stoves,* the domestic industry consisted of numerous establishments that installed and repaired the stoves. It was in essence a type of industry which transformed the subject product.

Moreover, in *Stoves* and another case, *Certain Airless Paint Spray Pumps and Components Thereof,* Inv. No. 337–TA–90, USITC Pub. 1199 (1982), both installation and repair services were physically related to the product itself. These activities are not those expected of any commercial purchaser. When these types of activities are combined with significant value added in the United States, the article could be considered as transformed into a U.S. product. Thus, the product at least in part is a U.S. product. If this standard is not maintained, however, and protection is extended to purely imported products, the requirement for a U.S. industry in section 337 becomes meaningless. Section 337 becomes a forum in which importers battle importers. I do not believe that this was the intent of Congress.

In this case, the molding of the component parts of the cube puzzles and the assembly work are done entirely abroad—in Taiwan, Hong Kong or Korea. When the cube puzzles enter the United States, they have stickers on them stating "Made in Hong Kong," or "Made in Taiwan" or "Made in

Korea." All of the significant operations in the production process are done abroad and not by Ideal in the United States.

* * *

When quality control, repair and packaging are examined, the value added to Ideal's cube puzzle in the United States is minimal and when packaging is omitted, the value added is *de minimis.*

I can find no rational way to distinguish this investigation from the *Toy Trucks* investigation. Although more quality control and packaging are done in the United States, the same type of domestic activities are performed in this case as were performed in the *Toy Trucks* case. I, therefore, conclude that Ideal should not be considered a domestic industry under section 337.

II. Injury

Had I found complainant's business activities which relate to the subject cubes to constitute a domestic industry, I would have determined that the unfair acts do not have the effect or tendency of substantially injuring the domestic industry. I agree with the ALJ's well reasoned conclusion that there has not been a showing of an effect of substantial injury. Both Ideal's sales and profits have increased markedly since the importation of similar cube puzzles at lower prices.

There is no indication of price suppression or depression. Ideal's purchasers have been on allocation during most of its production of Rubik's Cube, and the imported cube puzzles sell for a lower price than Ideal's cube puzzles. Ideal, therefore, cannot argue that every sale of an imported puzzle was a sale lost to Ideal, because some purchasers might not have waited or have bought a cube puzzle at a higher price. This conclusion is supported by the fact that Ideal could not establish how many cube puzzles were imported using Ideal's color pattern.

* * *

Therefore, I agree with the ALJ that:

The continuous rise in Ideal's sales and profits and its inability to meet current demand for cube puzzles prevent Ideal from showing substantial injury to the domestic industry at this time caused by imports of cubes similar to Ideal's Rubik's Cube.

Notes and Questions

(1) Among the practices that the ITC has indicated could be unfair under Section 337 are patent infringement, trademark infringement, copyright infringement, price fixing, group boycotts, deceptive pricing, combination and conspiracy to restrain and monopolize trade, misrepresentation of the country of origin of the goods, an attempt to monopolize, a refusal to deal, predatory pricing, violation of certain antitrust laws (Sherman Act, §§ 1, 2; Federal Trade Commission Act, § 5) and trade secret misappropriation.[9] Most Section 337 cases seem to involve patents, and not infrequently, the cases are settled before a final ITC determination. Over a dozen settlements were reached in the *Rubik's*

---

9. See U.S. Intl. Trade Commn., Office of the Administrative Law Judges, Compendium of Section 337 Decisions § 101, at 2 (1981).

Cube case. Since 1974, 239 Section 337 actions had been commenced as of February 1986.

(2) In cases where a U.S. registered trademark is involved, it is possible simply to register that trademark with the Customs Service and entry will be denied to articles bearing that trademark. 19 CFR Pt. 133 (1985).

(3) The concept of unfair competition is broad enough to cover actions that violate other U.S. laws, including trade laws. For example, on occasion there have been complaints about an importer's use of predatory pricing, which by its very nature suggests the possibility of dumping. The 1974 Trade Act provided that if the ITC had reason to believe that an investigation might come under the antidumping or countervailing laws, it should notify the authorities administering those laws.[10] In 1979, Section 337(b)(3) was clarified to indicate that the ITC investigation should proceed unless the matter before it is based solely on alleged dumping or subsidization.

(4) The question of what constitutes a U.S. industry is unsettled. As the dissent by Commissioner Stern in the *Rubik's Cube* case indicates, where imported products are involved, the ITC has had difficulty in determining how much activity in the U.S. is necessary to meet Section 337's criteria.[11] If the goal of Section 337 is to protect U.S. industry, doesn't Commissioner Stern have the better argument?

(5) Although the ITC has sometimes been very strict about finding injury under some trade laws, it seems rather willing to find it in Section 337 cases, even though the statutory language—"destroy or substantially injure"—seems to set a rather high standard. The approach followed in the *Rubik's Cube* case is typical. The focus is on the individual company and the standard does not seem to be high—all the Commissioners seemed to agree that truly lost sales would constitute injury.[12]

(6) *The Rubik's Cube* case involves in part what are called counterfeit goods. As successful advertising campaigns have made certain items sell for amounts far in excess of their production costs, the incentive to counterfeit has increased considerably. The issue of whether there should be an international agreement on the subject is presently being considered by a GATT committee. New legislation to combat traffic in counterfeit goods more effectively was proposed in 1985 in both the United States and the EC.[13]

(7) A more difficult issue than that presented by counterfeit goods arises when authentic goods are imported outside the normal channels of the manufacturer's distribution network. The question of how to treat these so-called "grey goods" or "parallel imports" recently led to one of the rare instances where a U.S. President voided an ITC decision under Section 337. The case involved a complaint by the maker of Duracell batteries and was directed at Duracell batteries made by its Belgian subsidiary. The Belgian-made batteries were being bought in Europe and then sold in the United States at prices below those

10. Trade Act of 1974, § 341(b)(3), Pub.L. No. 93–618, 88 Stat. 2053.

11. See generally Note, Litigating Unfair Trade Practices Under Section 337(a) of the Tariff Act of 1930: Defining Domestic Industry, 16 Law & Poly.Intl.Bus. 597 (1984).

12. See generally Brunsvold, Schill & Schwendemann, Injury Standards in Section 337 Investigations, 4 Nw.J.Intl.L. & Bus. 75 (1982).

13. See, e.g., H.R. 3776, 99th Cong., 1st Sess. (1985); Proposal for Council Regulation laying down measures to discourage the release for free circulation of counterfeit goods, [1985] Eur.Comm.O.J. No. C20/7.

charged by Duracell in the United States. The President explained his decision as follows: [14]

Disapproval of the Determination of the United States International Trade Commission in Investigation No. 337–TA–165, Certain Alkaline Batteries

The United States International Trade Commission, following a finding of a violation of Section 337 of the Tariff Act of 1930, as amended, has ordered excluded from entry into the United States imports of certain alkaline batteries that were found to infringe a U.S. registered trademark and to misappropriate the trade dress of the batteries on which the trademark is used.

The President is authorized by Section 337(g)(2) to disapprove a Commission determination for policy reasons. I have notified the Commission today of my decision to disapprove its determination in this case.

The Commission's interpretation of section 42 of the Lanham Act (15 U.S.C. 1224), one of several grounds for the Commission's determination, is at odds with the longstanding regulatory interpretation by the Department of the Treasury, which is responsible for administering the provisions of that section. The Administration has advanced the Treasury Department's interpretation in a number of pending court cases. Recent decisions of the U.S. District Court for the District of Columbia and the Court of International Trade explicitly uphold the Treasury Department's interpretation. Allowing the Commission's determination in this case to stand could be viewed as an alteration of that interpretation. I, therefore, have decided to disapprove the Commission's determination.

The Departments of Treasury and Commerce, on behalf of the Cabinet Council on Commerce and Trade, have solicited data from the public concerning the issue of parallel market importation and are reviewing responses with a view toward formulating a cohesive policy in this area. Failure to disapprove the Commission's determination could be viewed as a change in the current policy prior to the completion of this process.

What should be U.S. policy toward parallel imports? Once a manufacturer (or a unit owned by it) has sold a product, how much control should it have over the product's use or further disposition?

(8) The compatability of Section 337 with GATT, and, in particular, whether Section 337 falls within the exceptions set out in GATT Article XX was treated in the Spring Assemblies case, discussed in Section 8.3(D) supra.

(C) ANTIDUMPING ACT OF 1916

The Antidumping Act of 1916 makes it unlawful to sell articles into the United States, "commonly and systematically," at a price "substantially" less than their actual market value or wholesale price "with the intent of destroying or injuring" a U.S. industry.[15] The act authorizes treble damage actions by injured persons.[16]

---

14. 50 Fed.Reg. 1655 (1985).

15. 15 U.S.C.A. § 72.

16. 15 U.S.C.A. § 72.

Despite the lure of treble damages, the difficulty of proving intent has resulted in no reported cases in which recovery was obtained. This could change, however. See In re Japanese Electronic Products Antitrust Litigation, 723 F.2d 238, 319 (3d Cir.1983) (reversing summary judgment for defendants in actions first filed in 1970), reversed and remanded, Matsushita Electric Industrial Co., Ltd. v. Zenith Radio Corp., ___ U.S. ___, 106 S.Ct. 1348, 89 L.Ed.2d 538 (1986).[17]

(D) THE REVENUE ACT OF 1971

Section 103 of the Revenue Act of 1971, 26 U.S.C.A. § 48(a)(7)(D), provides that if the President determines that a country

> (1) maintains nontariff trade restrictions, including variable import fees, which substantially burden United States commerce in a manner inconsistent with the provisions of trade agreements, or

> (2) engages in discriminatory or other acts (including tolerance of international cartels) or policies unjustifiably restricting United States commerce

he may determine that property manufactured in that country does not qualify for the investment tax credit.

In 1982, Houdaille Industries, Inc. filed a well-publicized petition asking the President to suspend application of the investment tax credit to certain Japanese-origin numerically controlled machine tools. The petition, which is excerpted in Section 22.3 infra, alleged that the Japanese machine-tool industry operated as a cartel under the guidance and direction of the Japanese Ministry of International Trade and Industry (MITI) and that MITI had encouraged the industry to concentrate on high technology machine tools and exports. It was also alleged that the Japanese government had failed to enforce Japan's antitrust laws and allowed the cartel members to share information about new products and to fix prices.[18] The petition was denied after a year-long investigation. No further petitions have been filed under this section and the issues involved may become moot since some 1986 tax reform proposals would abolish the investment tax credit.

A number of issues were left unsettled by the Houdaille petition. For example, subsection (1) clearly concerns barriers to U.S. exports. Should subsection (2) be so limited as well? If the relief requested by Houdaille were granted, would the United States violate its obligations under GATT Article III? Is that article relevant at all to income tax credits or deductions? What is an "international" cartel? How does the alleged involvement of a government affect the petitioner's ability to demonstrate the statutory criteria? Finally, and more practically, would it have made more sense for Houdaille to seek the relief requested in a Section 301 action, discussed in the next section? [19] We discuss in more detail the issues raised by Houdaille and how they should be treated in the international trading

---

17. See generally Almstedt, International Price Discrimination and the 1916 Antidumping Act—Are Amendments in Order? 13 Law & Poly.Intl.Bus. 747 (1981).

18. A copy of the petition can be found in W. Hancock (ed.), Guide to Antidumping & Countervailing Duties and Other Unfair Import Laws 645 (looseleaf).

19. See generally Macrory & Juster, Section 103 of the Revenue Act of 1971 and the Houdaille Case: A New Trade Remedy?, 9 N.Car.J.Intl.L. & Com.Reg. 413 (1984).

system in Chapter 22 infra, where we consider the interrelationship of advanced market economies with each other in light of different legal and cultural heritages.

(E) GOODS MADE BY FORCED LABOR

Section 307 of the Tariff Act of 1930, 19 U.S.C.A. § 1307 (1982), bars the entry into the United States of goods "mined, produced, or manufactured wholly or in part in any foreign country by convict labor or/and forced labor or/and indentured labor under penal sanctions." "Forced labor" is defined as "all work or service which is extracted from any person under the menace of any penalty for its nonperformance and for which the worker does not offer himself voluntarily." See generally 19 CFR §§ 12.42–.45 (1985). Certain Mexican products are currently subject to exclusion under this provision. 19 CFR § 12.42(h) (1985).

In an action arising out of a refusal by a longshoreman's union to unload vessels bringing Russian goods into U.S. ports, in which it was contended that all Russian goods were products of forced labor and therefore not eligible for importation into the United States, a federal district court ruled that

> Congress could not have meant a ban under 19 U.S.C. § 1307 of the type proposed by the defendants to be self-executing. Although the statute does not explicitly so state, Congress must have intended to rest the decision of whether a whole nation's goods should be banned in the hands of the executive branch, rather than those of private citizens, or the judiciary at behest of a private citizen's suit. The disruptive implications for American trade and foreign policy are—as defendants have proven—otherwise too great. * * * In sum, foreign goods which are purportedly the product of forced labor are not barred from entry into the United States under 19 U.S.C. § 1307 until the executive branch declares, pursuant to the regulations set out in 19 C.F.R. §§ 12.42–12.44 (1984), that in fact the goods are the product of forced labor.

Associated Imports, Inc. v. International Longshoremen's Assn., AFL–CIO, 609 F.Supp. 595, 597–98 (S.D.N.Y.1985).

In January 1985, the U.S. Treasury Department determined that there was no reasonable basis to establish a nexus between Soviet forced labor practices and specific imports from the Soviet Union. See McKinney v. United States Dept. of the Treasury, 614 F.Supp. 1226, 1231 n. 11 (CIT 1985) (action challenging Commissioner of Custom's failure to exclude Soviet goods allegedly made with forced labor dismissed as moot in light of the above-noted Treasury determination).

SECTION 10.5 RETALIATION IN TRADE POLICY: SECTION 301 ACTIONS

(A) INTRODUCTION

The possibility that countries aggrieved by specific trade policies may take compensatory or retaliatory action to offset their effect (such as in escape clauses cases) is one of the elements of the international trading system which adds to the "rigor" of the obligations and possibly therefore to the stability of the system. Of course, many countries (especially developing countries) do not have enough economic weight in world trade to take action that would be effective, but many others do.

The structure of the governments of most major U.S. trading partners is such that decisions on retaliatory measures can be taken quickly when the situation arises. Often the government can act without legislative action, and if legislative action is necessary, the government normally commands the votes necessary to obtain it upon short notice, even if the contemplated governmental action might prove to be in violation of international procedures or even international obligations. In the United States, however, the power of the Executive Branch is more limited. Retaliatory actions often must be based upon specific statutory authorization. As we saw in Chapter 3, some of these statutory provisions are broad enough to give the President great discretion in certain situations, but others are fairly precise and narrow.

Beyond the question of whether a government has the power to take retaliatory action is the question of when and how it uses that power. In Chapter 5, we noted that individuals generally have no right of direct access to international procedures, such as those in GATT, to complain about foreign government actions. Consequently, when an individual feels aggrieved by such actions, he must convince his own government to take up his cause on an international plane. The process by which individual problems are brought to the attention of governments may be relatively informal. Citizens may simply go to their foreign ministry or state department, and ask it for assistance. The response to such requests obviously will vary. The government may often not act, especially if it feels the request concerns insignificant matters, or if it feels that it would be inappropriate to raise the matter with the foreign government involved because of broader foreign policy concerns.

In 1962, partly because of the dissatisfaction of Congress with the way in which the Executive Branch had responded to citizen complaints against foreign government action affecting international trade, Congress granted certain explicit powers to the President, authorizing retaliation with trade measures against certain foreign government actions.[1] Although this was by no means the first statute of this type,[2] it was a fairly unique statute. This statute was replaced and considerably expanded by title III of the Trade Act of 1974, and particularly Section 301 thereof, which granted similar powers to the President. The Act also provided explicit procedures under which U.S. citizens could petition the U.S. government for action against harmful foreign government activities. This part of the 1974 Act, from which the "Section 301 Procedure" derives its name, was amended in both 1979 and 1984 (see Documentary Supplement).[3]

1. Trade Expansion Act of 1962, § 252, Pub.L. No. 87–794, 75 Stat. 879.

2. See, e.g., An Act to authorize the President of the United States to lay, regulate and revoke embargoes, 1 Stat. 372 (1794).

3. See Trade Act of 1974, §§ 301–06 (codified at 19 U.S.C.A. §§ 2411–16), as amended, Pub.L. No. 96–39, tit. IX, 93 Stat. 295 (1979); Pub.L. No. 98–573, §§ 304, 306, 98 Stat. 3002 (1984).

(B) PROCEDURES UNDER SECTION 301

The procedures applicable to a Section 301 action are fairly straight forward. When a citizen complaint is filed, the U.S. Trade Representative must decide within 45 days whether to initiate an investigation. His decision must be published. If an investigation is initiated, public hearings must be held if requested.[4] Also, the Trade Representative is required to institute consultations with the relevant foreign parties in the "relevant forum" and to initiate any applicable dispute settlement procedures if no settlement is reached.[5] Section 301 applies to disputes involving services, as well as goods. In the case of goods, the statute essentially requires the United States to initiate consultations and, if necessary, dispute settlement procedures in GATT since that is likely to be the relevant forum. The 1984 amendments provide that such consultations need not be requested until 90 days after the decision is made to proceed with the investigation. Formerly, the requirement of an immediate request for consultations had caused difficulties because the Trade Representative had no time to prepare for such consultations.[6] After a certain period of time, normally 12 months if an international proceeding is not still pending, the Trade Representative must make his recommendations to the President about retaliatory action, and the President then decides whether to proceed with them.[7]

A number of legal issues are raised by Section 301, although Section 301 proceedings tend to be somewhat less "legalistic" than antidumping or countervailing duty proceedings, or even escape clause proceedings. Section 301 is considered primarily a "negotiating tool." Nevertheless, legal issues related to it include: whether a petitioner must allege and show some sort of "injury" as a prerequisite to a decision by the government to launch an investigation; what is the meaning of "unjustifiable," "unreasonable," and the other criteria for complaints; is there any possibility of judicial review over any parts of the Section 301 proceedings? (To this date, there have not been any court cases concerning the Section 301 proceeding.) These and other issues are treated in the following materials.

BART S. FISHER & RALPH G. STEINHARDT, III, SECTION 301 OF THE TRADE ACT OF 1974: PROTECTION FOR U.S. EXPORTERS OF GOODS, SERVICES AND CAPITAL

(1982) [8]

Despite the potentially wide ambit of section 301, its primary use will probably be to enforce trade agreements, multilateral and bilateral, to which the United States is a party. Although GATT is the trade agreement most familiar to U.S. legal practitioners, potential section 301 petitioners may invoke a broad range of agreements in framing a "cause of action," including

4. Trade Act of 1974, § 302, 19 U.S.C.A. § 2412.

5. Trade Act of 1974, § 303, 19 U.S.C.A. § 2413.

6. See Senate Rep. No. 98–308, 98th Cong., 2d Sess 47–48 (1984).

7. Trade Act of 1974, § 304, 19 U.S.C.A. § 2414.

8. 14 Law & Poly.Intl.Bus. 569, 575–78, 595–602. Reprinted by permission of Law and Policy in International Business.

the comprehensive codes supplementing GATT adopted during the Tokyo Round of the Multilateral Trade Negotiations (MTN). * * *

In addition to GATT and the MTN codes, there are numerous international accords to which the United States is a party which might be relied upon by a petitioner under section 301. For example, the OECD Code on Invisible Transactions, the OECD Guidelines on Investment Practices, and the FAO Principles on Food Surplus Disposal could all be considered "hortatory" accords that could, nevertheless, provide the basis for judging the unreasonableness of an action by a U.S. trading partner. Conceivably, the United States need not even be a signatory of the trade agreement invoked, as long as it can be said that the United States has some rights, however vague, under that agreement. Moreover, under section 301, an aggrieved party is not in any sense limited to the rights expressed in international agreements. By its terms, section 301 directs the President to take "all appropriate and feasible action" to counter foreign trade practices that impose an unreasonable or unjustifiable burden on U.S. commerce. Thus, in addition to its legal significance in providing parties a right of access to positive international law, section 301 may prove to be of considerable value in establishing a "common law" of fairness in international markets.

In practice, a petition filed under section 301 by a private party carries an effective threat of potential retaliation, combined with the threat of adverse publicity and a general souring of trade relations. These potential ramifications alone may bring the offending government to the bargaining table. Indeed, astutely using the *threat* of filing a section 301 complaint as leverage to achieve a desired end may lead to better results than actually filing a complaint and pursuing the case through administrative channels. Conversely, a sound legal case coupled with inept commercial diplomacy by either the petitioners or the U.S. government may lead to wasted effort and negligible results. More than any other U.S. trade law, section 301 works through feints and threats, rather than through formal legal processes.

The existence of an expanded role for private industry under the 1979 amendments to section 301 should not mask the central fact that the decision to enforce trade rights of petitioners rests exclusively with the President and is not judicially reviewable in the event no action is taken. Congress intended to give the President wide discretion in formulating his response to a foreign unfair trade practice. Accordingly, the standards which guide the President's decision may have much more to do with the timing of the petition, domestic publicity, relations with Congress, and foreign policy than with the merits of the petition.

* * *

SUBSTANTIVE VIOLATION

Petitioners must allege a substantive violation within one of the four categories outlined in section 301. These include practices which are: (1) contrary to international agreements; (2) unjustifiable; (3) unreasonable; and (4) discriminatory.

1. Practices Contrary to International Agreements

In the easiest case, the challenged governmental conduct is directly prohibited by an international trade agreement. * * *

To the extent that the "agreement" relied upon is informal or hortatory, the likelihood of finding a substantive violation within this category is diminished. By contrast, a showing that the provisions of a binding international agreement have been violated may trigger the dispute resolution process under the agreement itself. In Petition of Great Western Malting Co., for example, the United States requested formal consultations with the European Economic Community (EEC) under GATT Article XXII(1) to discuss EEC subsidies on malt exports to third countries. That request was withdrawn in order that the United States might pursue elimination of the practice in the course of negotiating the MTN Subsidies Code. In the middle to late 1970s, the EEC reduced the amount of the subsidy.

2. Unjustifiable Practices

A foreign governmental act may be "unjustifiable" and yet not be plainly violative of international agreements. According to the Senate Finance Committee Report accompanying the Trade Agreements Act of 1979, the word "unjustifiable" refers to restrictions which are "inconsistent" with international trade agreements. It is unclear whether this category, so defined, includes practices other than those that are contrary to international agreements, although it arguably is broader, embracing conduct which violates the spirit, if not the letter, of binding international agreements. It is also arguable that international instruments, declarations, or state practices which are not themselves "agreements" may nevertheless be invoked under section 301 to challenge unfair but technically legal conduct. Inclusion of "unjustified" in the statute indicates that Congress intended to give private parties broad authority to file section 301 petitions, irrespective of the legal technicalities and status of the agreement upon which the petitioner relies.

3. Unreasonable Practices

The most significant expansion upon the GATT rules and other positive legal obligations is the category of restrictions deemed "unreasonable." The Senate Finance Committee defined the word "unreasonable" as referring to "restrictions which are not necessarily inconsistent with trade agreements, but which nullify or impair benefits accruing to the United States under trade agreements *or which otherwise restrict or burden U.S. commerce.*" The italicized clause suggests that the President may retaliate against a foreign trade practice that in some sense injures U.S. commerce, even though it is legal under international law.*[138]

---

* **138.** Examples of such legal but injurious practices might include the nationalization of domestic manufacturing or financial institutions, the arms length purchase of goods and services from a third party on advantageous but commercially feasible terms, and the simple exploitation of comparative advantage. Because the international law on foreign investment lags far behind that on trade in goods, it is somewhat easier to imagine "legal" but injurious practices in the investment sector.

Whether such a finding is likely depends on the meaning of the reasonableness criterion. Two interpretations are suggested by the cases. The first is a formalist approach, interpreting "unreasonable," as defined in Webster's New Collegiate Dictionary (1979), to mean "not governed by or acting according to reason, not conformable to reason, and exceeding the bounds of reason or irrational." Such a standard is likely to be highly deferential to foreign governments, who might easily justify a particular trade practice as a shrewd political or economic measure, despite its adverse political or economic impact upon the United States or another trade partner. Despite the unfairness of the hypothetical measure, it would be difficult under the circumstances to characterize it as unreasonable within the formalist definition. The second interpretation of "unreasonable" would recognize its normative content, proscribing conduct which is inequitable or in bad faith, irrespective of whether justifications may rationally be posited. This interpretation is significantly less deferential than the formalist approach and allows the President to balance both the justifications for and the international repercussions of a foreign trade practice in determining whether the practice is "reasonable," and, therefore, whether to negotiate, retaliate, or acquiesce. The alternative interpretations are not mutually exclusive; indeed, in the *Border Broadcasters* case, petitioners challenged certain provisions of the Canadian Income Tax Act on the grounds that they were both logically and normatively unreasonable.

The consequent breadth of the reasonableness standards, coupled with the expanded jurisdictional scope of section 301 to include all services as well as products, makes section 301 a potentially powerful weapon for a U.S. industry aggrieved by foreign trade practices. As the *Border Broadcasters* case illustrates, its use is limited more by the President's willingness to pursue the matter than by any requirement that the right asserted be based in international law. In short, the reasonableness category poses virtually no prima facie obstacle to private parties who may, as a result, advance their claims through the President to the limits of diplomacy.

4. *Discriminatory Practices*

A foreign governmental act that is "discriminatory" may also justify presidential action under section 301. The general contours of discrimination may seem clearer perhaps than those of the "unjustifiable" or "unreasonable" doctrines. Nevertheless, the legislative history of section 301 and its progenitors does not address the distinctions, familiar in international trade law, among most favored nation (MFN) treatment, nondiscrimination, and national treatment, each of which might be connoted by the broad "discriminatory" label. Discriminatory conduct clearly includes harassment of a single importer by the national government authorities.

Because of the Act's failure to clarify the distinctions, it is clear that restrictions which uniquely discriminate against U.S. exports are actionable under section 301. Restrictions which discriminate equally against world trade are somewhat more problematic.

Injury

Assuming that jurisdiction and a substantive violation exist, petitioners alleging unjustifiable, unreasonable, or discriminatory foreign conduct under section 301 must also demonstrate that the governmental action of which they complain has caused sufficient injury to "burden or restrict United States commerce." As indicated in the accompanying Table of Cases, actionable injury may take several forms: levies on imports and export subsidies are two common forms of injury. Petitioners have also challenged discriminatory tax treatment, trade agreements among foreign states which indirectly adversely affect U.S. production and prices, assay requirements imposed by a foreign customs service which, though nondiscriminatory in terms, discriminated in effect against U.S. exports, and unfair licensing or surety deposit systems.

In contrast to the required showing of injury in antidumping and countervailing duty proceedings, the showing of injury in section 301 cases is not subject to a statutory test of materiality, although the actual extent to which U.S. commerce is "burden[ed]" or restrict[ed] will obviously influence the likelihood and gravity of any presidential action taken in response to the petition.

The injury criterion of section 301 is also reflected in the requirement that the petitioner be an "interested party" defined in the regulations as:

> a party who has a significant interest; for example, a producer of a like or directly competitive product or a commercial importer or exporter of a product which is affected either by the failure to grant rights to [the] United States under a trade agreement, or by the act, policy, or practice complained of, or any person representing a significant economic interest affected either by the failure to grant a right of the United States under a trade agreement or by the act, policy, or practice complained of in the petition.

No section 301 petition has been rejected on the ground that the petitioner's interest therein was inadequate. Petitioners should not, however, infer that the injury showing in section 301 proceedings is strictly pro forma; U.S. trade law does not redress trifles, and de minimis allegations will not prevail. Nor have categories of per se violations been articulated in the context of section 301. Petitioners alleging such injury, without a reasonable showing of lost sales or profits, diminished capacity utilization, unemployment, or the like, will have failed to satisfy the practical, but not the legal, requirements of section 301.

Notes and Questions

(1) The 1984 amendments defined the words "unjustifiable," "unreasonable" and "discriminatory," and also expanded the definition of U.S. commerce to read as follows: [9]

The term "commerce" includes, but is not limited to—

(A) services (including transfers of information) associated with international trade, whether or not such services are related to specific goods, and

(B) foreign direct investment by United States persons with implications for trade in goods and services.

9. Trade and Tariff Act, Pub.L. No. 98–573, § 304(f)(1), 98 Stat. 3005, amending 19 U.S.C.A. § 2411(e)(1).

It is anticipated that the U.S. government will use this expanded definition in its program to promote international negotiations on trade in services and on international investment and otherwise to remove barriers to U.S. service exports and investment. See Sections 15.2 and 16.2 infra. Actions taken as part of that program in 1985 included Section 301 investigations, initiated by the U.S. government, of Brazilian informatics policy (partial exclusion of U.S. computer makers from the Brazilian market) and Korean restrictions on provision of insurance services.[10]

(2) Since the 1974 Act, there have been (until February 1986) 52 Section 301 petitions, of which 21 were then still pending. Of the 52 that have been filed, 27 have involved the export of goods from the United States. Another 15 have involved questions relating to import of goods into the United States. In addition to those cases relating to goods, however, there have been 10 cases concerning shipping, insurance, border broadcasting and other services. When a petition is brought relating to imports or exports of goods, the United States often files a complaint with GATT or the relevant MTN Code committee. Of the cases brought concerning goods under Section 301, 9 have resulted in a GATT or GATT Code proceeding.[11]

(3) Initiation of a proceeding under Section 301 is discretionary. The Trade Representative has on some occasions found that there is no basis for initiating international consultations or that other trade law remedies should be pursued. In this connection, examine the statute governing the Section 301 procedure, and in light of the following materials, determine whether there is a sort of "injury test" prerequisite to such a proceeding. Also, how should Section 301 be considered to relate to countervailing and antidumping procedures? Should a domestic industry be able to invoke Section 301 if it cannot establish sufficient injury under countervailing or antidumping procedures? (Note that the *Pasta* case in GATT, discussed in Section 10.3(B) supra, resulted from a 301 petition to the U.S. government by competing U.S. manufacturers.)

OFFICE OF THE SPECIAL REPRESENTATIVE FOR TRADE NEGOTIATIONS

[Docket No. 301–10]
43 Fed.Reg. 3962 (1978)

Pursuant to regulations of the Office of the Special Representative for Trade Negotiations the section 301 committee has provided for public hearings and has conducted a review with respect to a petition by the American Iron & Steel Institute. That petition alleged that a bilateral agreement between the European Community and Japan diverted significant quantities of Japanese steel to the United States adversely affecting U.S. commerce. (See *Federal Register* of October 15, 1976, p. 45628.)

The Special Representative for Trade Negotiations has reported to the President the results of that review. Pursuant to Presidential decision of January 18, 1977, further action on the petition is hereby discontinued.

---

10. 50 Fed.Reg. 37608, 37609 (1985).

11. For a general summary of all Section 301 proceedings brought through September 1985, see 2 BNA Intl. Trade Rptr. 1414–22 (1985). GATT proceedings brought as a result of a Section 301 action include complaints about: EC preferences for Mediterranean fruit, EC mixing rules for animal feed, EC minimum import prices for canned fruit, EC subsidies on pasta, sugar, wheat, flour, poultry and canned fruit, and Japanese restrictions on silk imports and leather imports.

The following major factors were significant in the determination to discontinue the section 301 complaint:

(1) During the period covered by the understanding, exports to the EC by the six largest Japanese steel companies, operating as a government approved cartel, were limited to 1.22 million metric tons per year. However, actual exports by these companies were substantially less in both 1976 and 1977, suggesting that depressed market conditions in the EC were a more effective restraint than the understanding.

(2) The pattern of Japanese exports to the United States of steel products covered by the cartel have been generally consistent with domestic market conditions here. The major growth in export volume in 1976 was in product categories where U.S. demand grew substantially (e.g., sheets).

(3) The surge in Japanese steel exports in 1976 and 1977 was widespread and the increases in shipments to the U.S. market were not more pronounced than increases to many other markets. The U.S. share of one-fifth of total Japanese steel exports has remained relatively stable. The surge appears to be principally the result of the depressed domestic demand in Japan and low rates of steel capacity utilization which created pressure on Japanese firms to increase exports.

On the basis of these considerations, there is not sufficient justification to claim that the EC/Japanese understanding created any unfair burden on the United States.

The discontinuation is effective January 30, 1978.

> ROBERT S. STRAUSS
> Special Representative for Trade
> Negotiations

DETERMINATION UNDER SECTION 301 OF THE TRADE ACT OF 1974

47 Fed.Reg. 51717 (1982)
Memorandum for the United States Trade Representative

Pursuant to Section 301(a)(2) of the Trade Act of 1974 (19 U.S.C. 2411(a)(2)), I have determined that the action described below is an appropriate and feasible response to subsidy practices of the European Community (EC), Belgium, France, Italy, the United Kingdom, Austria and Sweden, which are inconsistent with Articles 8 and 11 of the Agreement on the Interpretation and Application of Articles VI, XVI and XXIII of the General Agreement on Tariffs and Trade (Subsidies Code). With a view toward eliminating the harmful effects of such practices, I am directing the United States Trade Representative (USTR) to: (1) request the United States International Trade Commission to conduct an expedited investigation under Section 201 of the Trade Act of 1974 (19 U.S.C. 2251) with regard to the five specialty steel products subject to the 301 investigation; (2) initiate multilateral and/or bilateral discussions aimed at the elimination of all trade distortive practices in the specialty steel sector; and (3) monitor imports of specialty steel products subject to the 201 proceeding. If during the pendency of the International Trade Commission section 201 investigation imports cause damage which is difficult to repair, consideration would be given to what action, if any, might appropriately be taken on an emergency, interim basis under Section 301 of the Trade Act of 1974, consistent with U.S. international obligations.

* * *

Ronald Reagan

THE WHITE HOUSE,
Washington, November 16, 1982.

(C) THE SCOPE OF RELIEF UNDER SECTION 301

A review of Section 301 reveals that the President has broad powers to take retaliatory action, although as indicated below the most appropriate form of relief may require congressional action. The breadth of the President's power is such that a number of questions are raised. For example, must the President's response be on an MFN basis? Must the President act in accordance with U.S. international obligations? More particularly, could the President act without invoking an applicable international dispute-settlement procedure? Is the President limited by the decision resulting from such a procedure? Some of these issues are discussed in the following materials.

SENATE REPORT NO. 93–1298, 93d CONG., 2d Sess.
166 (1974)

Under section 301(b) of the House bill the President would have been required to consider the relationship of any action taken under section 301 to the international obligations of the United States. The Committee on Finance agreed to delete this reference to U.S. international obligations since it felt that retaliation should be against the countries which discriminate against U.S. commerce and not against other countries which do not so discriminate. In addition, the Committee felt that there would be situations, such as in the case of unreasonable foreign import restrictions where the President ought to be able to act or threaten to act under section 301, whether or not such action would be entirely consistent with the General Agreement on Tariffs and Trade. Many GATT articles, such as Article I (MFN principle), Article III (taxes affecting imports), Article XII (balance of payments safeguards), or Article XXIV (regional trade associations) are either inappropriate in today's economic world or are being observed more often in the breach, to the detriment of the United States. Furthermore, the decision-making process under the General Agreement often frustrates the ability of the United States (as well as other contracting parties) to obtain the decisions needed to enable the United States to protect its rights and benefits under the GATT. For this reason, both the House bill and the Committee bill direct the President to seek changes in these GATT articles.

The Committee is not urging that the United States undertake wanton or reckless retaliatory action under section 301 in total disdain of applicable international agreements. However, the Committee felt it was necessary to make it clear that the President could act to protect U.S. economic interests whether or not such action was consistent with the articles of an outmoded international agreement initiated by the Executive 25 years ago and never approved by the Congress.

Under the House bill, the President would have been authorized to act on either a nondiscriminatory (MFN) or selective basis in cases where a country imposed an unjustifiable import restriction, act, policy, or practice. However, in those cases where the particular restriction, act, policy or practice was unreasonable, but not unjustifiable, the President would have been required to act only against the offending country.

The Committee amended the House bill to eliminate this distinction between unjustifiable and unreasonable actions as far as retaliation is concerned. The Committee believed that the President should act only against the country (or countries) which maintains the restriction, act, policy, or practice adversely affecting U.S. commerce, whether it be unjustifiable or unreasonable. The Committee felt that it would be unfair to subject innocent foreign countries to retaliatory actions under section 301, since it is only the offending country(ies) which are to be the "target" of retaliatory measures, or the threat thereof. Thus, while the Committee bill would provide the President with discretion to act on a most-favored-nation (i.e., across-the-board) basis under section 301, if he deems it appropriate, the determination to act on a broad basis would be subject to a two-House Congressional override procedure.

UNITED STATES v. STAR INDUSTRIES, INC.

United States Court of Customs and Patent Appeals, 1972.
462 F.2d 557, cert. denied, 409 U.S. 1076, 93 S.Ct. 678, 34 L.Ed.2d 663.

Before RICH, ALMOND, BALDWIN, and LANE, JUDGES and RE, JUDGE, United States Customs Court, sitting by designation.

BALDWIN, JUDGE.

This appeal is from the decision and judgment of the United States Customs Court, Third Division,*[1] sustaining a protest by Star Industries against the amount of duty assessed on brandy imported from Spain. The brandy had been classified under item 945.16, TSUS. The Customs Court ruled that it should have been classified under item 168.20, TSUS. * * *

At issue in this case is the validity of Presidential Proclamation No. 3564, which brought item 945.16 into existence.

* * *

The events surrounding Proclamation No. 3564 are referred to in international trade circles as "the chicken war." Briefly, it appears that during the late fifties and early sixties United States poultry producers had found a rapidly burgeoning market for frozen poultry in Germany. In 1962, however, the German import fees on poultry were replaced by import fees promulgated by the European Economic Community (EEC). The EEC import fees

*1. 65 Cust.Ct. 662, 320 F.Supp. 1018, C.D. 4155 (1970).

were about three times as high as the German fees they replaced, which adversely affected further importation of U.S. poultry into Germany. The action taken by the President in issuing Proclamation No. 3564 was in the nature of the compensatory withdrawal of previously proclaimed tariff concessions. The higher rates were calculated to increase the duty on EEC goods in an amount which would approximately balance the higher EEC import fees.

Although Spain is not a member of the EEC, the brandy at bar was charged the item 945.16 rate because that rate was instituted on a most-favored-nation basis. The products included under Proclamation No. 3564 were apparently chosen to be those imported almost exclusively from the member nations of the EEC.*6

The statutes specifically relied on for authority in Proclamation No. 3564 read as follows:

Trade Expansion Act of 1962, Section 252(c) (19 U.S.C. § 1882(c)):

(c) Whenever a foreign country or instrumentality, the products of which receive benefits of trade agreement concessions made by the United States, maintains unreasonable import restrictions which either directly or indirectly substantially burden United States commerce, the President may, to the extent that such action is consistent with the purposes of section 102, and having due regard for the international obligations of the United States—

(1) suspend, withdraw, or prevent the application of benefits of trade agreement concessions to products of such country or instrumentality, or

(2) refrain from proclaiming benefits of trade agreement concessions to carry out a trade agreement with such country or instrumentality.

Tariff Act of 1930, Section 350(a)(6) (19 U.S.C. § 1351(a)(6)):

(6) The President may at any time terminate, in whole or in part, any proclamation made pursuant to this section.

* * *

The Customs Court held that the President was not authorized to suspend trade agreement concessions on a most-favored-nation basis under 19 U.S.C. § 1882(c). In its view, only selective action against the instrumentality which maintains unreasonable import restrictions is authorized by that section. The court did not consider that the proclamation could be upheld on the basis of "due regard for the international obligations of the United States," for in its opinion most-favored-nation treatment was not required by Article XXVIII(3) of the GATT. The court rejected appellant's argument that the proclamation was authorized under the termination power of section 1351(a)(6), holding that:

* **6.** See 28 Fed.Reg. 8066 (1963). In addition to brandy, the rates of duty on potato starch, dextrine and modified starches, and trucks valued at $1000 or more were increased by Proclamation No. 3564. According to Walker, Dispute Settlement: The Chicken War, 58 Am.J.Int'l L. 671 (1964) the overall effect of the proclamation on countries which are not members of the EEC has been minor. 58 Am.J.Int'l L. at 681.

> [A]ny limitations written into section 1882(c) affecting the scope of Presidential action taken under that statute would be determinative of the scope of the termination power of section 1351(a)(6) exercised in conjunction with the section 1882(c) action or in aid thereof.

Having thus determined that the President had exceeded his authority in issuing Proclamation No. 3564, the court held the proclamation invalid and void.

* * *

With regard to the reliance stated in Proclamation No. 3564 on Article XXVIII(3) of the GATT, the Customs Court stated:

> As we read paragraph 3 of Article XXVIII of GATT it does not *require* suspension of trade agreement concessions on a most favored nation basis. In fact, favored nation treatment is not even mentioned or implied in paragraph 3. Under paragraph 3 a country having a principal supplying interest or a substantial interest is permitted to withdraw *substantially equivalent concessions initially negotiated with the applicant contracting party.* We construe this language merely to authorize reciprocal action on the part of contracting parties to GATT with respect to modification of tariff concessions, following a break down in negotiations and unilateral withdrawal of concessions by a contracting party.

The last two sentences of the above quote, though correct, are not pertinent to the question of whether unilateral withdrawal of concessions under Article XXVIII(3) must be made on a most-favored-nation basis. We are therefore left with the court's observation that that Article does not specifically mention most-favored-nation treatment, and its conclusions that such treatment is not implied or otherwise required by that Article.

Appellant contends that Article XXVIII(3) must be read within the context of the entire agreement and points to Article I of the GATT, which provides in pertinent part:

[Paragraph 1 Quoted]

Appellant also argues that:

> The very nature of Article XXVIII requires that actions taken under it be on a most favored nation basis. Such concessions cannot be withdrawn only as to a particular party. If withdrawn, the result is that they are also withdrawn as to all parties, i.e., those who obtained the concessions on a most favored nation basis. [Footnote omitted.] Any arrangement whereby the particular concessions are continued as to all such other parties, but not the parties with which they were originally negotiated, is clearly not contemplated by Article XXVIII. In this case, Spanish brandy benefited from the original concession made to France, a member of the EEC, and there is little reason to continue the concession once it has been terminated as to the original contracting party.

Turning to the language of Article XXVIII(3), adverse effects on a plurality of countries from a unilateral withdrawal of concessions were clearly contemplated in this provision. A compensating mechanism is therein provided for three classes of countries which would be adversely effected by a unilateral withdrawal of a concession on a particular commodity, i.e., the country with which the concession was originally negotiated, a country having a principal supplying interest in the commodity, and a country having a substantial interest in the commodity. Article XXVIII(3) is therefore at least not inconsistent with the most-favored-nation principle.

Reading Article XXVIII(3) in context with the rest of the GATT, it is clear that conformity with the most-favored-nation principle is required under that Article. One of the primary purposes of the GATT, recited in its preamble was "the elimination of discriminatory treatment in international commerce." To this end, the most-favored-nation principle was embodied in Article I, quoted supra, and in numerous other GATT Articles. The principle has been described as the heart of the GATT.[10] The GATT does contain some exceptions to the principle, but they are few in number and, when they do appear in the instrument, they are clearly spelled out.[11] There is nothing in Article XXVIII(3) which would indicate that that Article was intended to be an exception to the principle.

Moreover, the "negotiative" history of the Article clearly establishes that the negotiators intended to have the most-favored-nation principle govern actions under it.[12] One of the major changes made in the early drafting of the Article was the substitution of the phrase "withdraw the concession" for the phrase "suspend the application to the trade of the contracting party taking such action of substantially equivalent concessions," the intent being to change the effect of the Article from a discriminatory action to a nondiscriminatory one. Thus should there be any doubt that nondiscriminatory (most-favored-nation) action was required by Article XXVIII(3), the negotiative history of the Article would settle that doubt. Nielson v. Johnson, 279 U.S. 47, 52, 49 S.Ct. 223, 73 L.Ed. 607 (1929) and cases cited; W. Bishop, International Law, 171–72 (2d ed. 1962).

The question remains whether 19 U.S.C. § 1882(c) allows the President to take other than selective or discriminatory action, even when he determines that nondiscriminatory action is required by our international obligations. The Customs Court referred to 19 U.S.C. § 1881, which provides:

> § 1881. Most-favored-nation principle
>
> Except as otherwise provided in this subchapter, in section 1351 of this title, or in section 401(a) of the Tariff Classification Act of 1962, any duty or other import restriction or duty-free treatment proclaimed in carrying out any trade agreement under this subchapter or section 1351 of this title shall apply to products of all foreign countries, whether imported directly or indirectly.

The court considered that section 1881, when read together with the language in section 1882(c) specifying action to be taken with respect to "products of such country or instrumentality" or "a trade agreement with

---

* 10. W. Bishop, International Law, 158 (2d ed. 1962). See generally Jackson, [World Trade and the Law of GATT,] at 249–73; GATT Secretariat, The Most-favoured-nation Clause in GATT, 4 J. World Trade L. 791 (1970).

* 11. See GATT Secretariat, supra, 4 J. World Trade L. at 795–801; Jackson, supra, at 270–272.

* 12. See 18th Meeting of the Tariff Agreement Committee, U.N.Doc. EPTC/TAC/PV. 18 (1947). This is one of a series of documents which have been called the "Primary Source for Drafting of GATT." Jackson, supra, at 904.

such country or instrumentality," created an exception to the most-favored-nation principle in 1882(c) proceedings. Thus the court did not specifically rule on the provisions of section 1882(c) which limit the action the President may take "to the extent that such action is consistent with the purposes of section 1801 of this title, and having due regard for the international obligations of the United States * * *."

The purposes referred to are listed in 19 U.S.C. § 1801 as follows:

> (1) to stimulate the economic growth of the United States and maintain and enlarge foreign markets for the products of United States agriculture, industry, mining, and commerce;

> (2) to strengthen economic relations with foreign countries through the development of open and *nondiscriminatory* trading in the free world; and

> (3) to prevent Communist economic penetration. [Emphasis added.]

Thus the use of section 1882(c) on a nondiscriminatory or most-favored-nation basis would not be inconsistent with the purposes referred to in that section.

With regard to the apparent conflict between our international obligations under the GATT and the statements in section 1882(c) that action is to be taken against the country or instrumentality which maintains the unreasonable import restrictions, we find the following excerpt from the legislative history of the section most enlightening:

> Subsections (a) and (b) of section 252 of the bill together authorize action against burdensome foreign import restrictions. They do not, however, authorize action against foreign import restrictions which, though they may be legally justifiable, impose a substantial burden upon U.S. commerce. The amendment provides that whenever a country which has received benefits under a trade agreement with the United States maintains unreasonable import restrictions which burden U.S. commerce either directly or indirectly, the President may withdraw existing trade agreement benefits or refrain from proclaiming any negotiated trade agreement concessions on such products. Under this subsection the President may act only to the extent consistent with the purposes of the act and in exercising this authority he must take into consideration the international obligations of the United States. Thus, the amendment would not authorize any indiscriminate breach of international obligations of the United States such as *our most favored nation treaties* with regard to the products of other countries.*14 [Emphasis added.]

The amendment referred to is the Senate amendment to H.R. 11970 which added subsection (c) to section 252 of the Trade Expansion Act of 1962 (19 U.S.C. § 1882).

Appellee relies on other legislative history which indicates an intent to provide the President with strong measures to combat foreign trade discrimination. We are of the opinion that the interpretation of section 1882(c) embodied in Proclamation No. 3564 fully complies with that intent. Under that interpretation, section 1882(c) provides for the denial of most-favored-

* 14. S.Rep. No. 2059, 87th Cong.2d Sess. 2–3 (1962), U.S.Code Cong. & Admin.News, p. 3112.

nation treatment where the President decides upon that course "having due regard for the international obligations of the United States." The proclamation indicates in the present case that the President did not choose that course because it would have been inconsistent with our international obligations. However, the measures taken under the proclamation were sharply focused on the instrumentality which was maintaining the unreasonable import restrictions—the EEC. Thus the legislative intent to take strong measures against those who maintain unreasonable import restrictions was upheld, and at the same time we did not breach our international obligations.

For the above reasons, we find that the President did not exceed the authority granted him under section 252(c) of the Trade Expansion Act of 1962 (19 U.S.C. § 1882(c)) in issuing Proclamation No. 3564. That proclamation is therefore valid and the judgment of the Customs Court is reversed.

ROBERT E. HUDEC, RETALIATION AGAINST "UNREASONABLE" FOREIGN TRADE PRACTICES: THE NEW SECTION 301 AND GATT NULLIFICATION AND IMPAIRMENT

(1975) [12]

If there were a Part V of this Article, it would argue—in a balanced way—that the content, tone, and expressed intent of section 301 make it a highly dangerous piece of international brinksmanship. Part V has been forgone in order to focus more sharply on the present problem—what to do with section 301 now that we have it. Although there will be considerable pressure not to use the new retaliation authority during the current round of GATT trade negotiations, the new authority will not be easy to contain. The Executive Branch may feel compelled to resort to section 301 in order to maintain its "credibility" with foreign governments, or with the Congress. Private parties also have the right to initiate proceedings under a separate complaints procedure established by section 301. In view of the particularly disruptive effects which section 301 retaliation could have at the present time, it is important that all participants, private as well as public, have some basic understanding of the relationship between section 301 and the international legal framework in which it will operate.

* * *

C. *GATT* CONSEQUENCES: THE LEGAL FRAMEWORK

The breadth of Presidential authority under section 301 makes it clear that the GATT experience with nullification and impairment cannot be of controlling force under United States law. It does not follow, however, that GATT legal considerations will have no importance in shaping issues and decisions under section 301. The statement of Executive Branch intentions with regard to section 301 remains the most reliable indication of how section 301 discretion will in fact be used. With a major trade negotiation

12. 59 Minn.L.Rev. 461, 463–64, 522. Reprinted by permission of the author.

already in motion, the United States will have every reason to limit aggressive behavior in the near future, and to confine what aggression is necessary to regular GATT channels if at all possible. Even in the long run, the strength or weakness of GATT legal support should remain a critical factor in decisions under section 301. One assumes that any actual or threatened retaliation by the President will claim consistency with GATT if it can. Those who object to proposed action, on the other hand, will invariably call attention to whatever GATT-violation costs the action entails, and negative decisions will almost certainly invoke such GATT costs as a "factor" of decision.

[The author then describes three different ways a section 301 action involving "unreasonable" trade practices could be framed for purposes of GATT: 1) as an Article XXVIII withdrawal, which he terms the "cleanest from the GATT point of view;" 2) as response to a "nullification or impairment" within the meaning of Article XXIII; and 3) "action based solely and squarely on the declared 'unreasonableness' of an otherwise legal trade barrier,"—the riskiest ground.]

* * *

E. A PREVIEW OF SECTION 301: THE CATTLE WAR

The Cattle War began in late 1973 when depressed cattle prices in the United States caused a surge of exports to Canada. The Canadian government responded first with a tariff surcharge which did little to slow the United States exports. The surcharge was removed in early 1974, but shortly thereafter a court decision allowed United States cattle producers to resume using a growth hormone prohibited by Canadian health regulations, and Canada thereupon embargoed all imports from the United States until the United States government could establish an acceptable procedure for certifying absence of the prohibited substance in animals exported to Canada. The embargo lasted from April to August; the delay was viewed by many as a disguised trade restriction. That view was reinforced when Canada imposed import quotas on beef and cattle as soon as the health embargo ended. After further negotiations proved unsuccessful, the United States called public hearings under its trade retaliation statute, citing the entire history of the Canadian import policy and charging in addition that the new Canadian quotas were "highly restrictive." On November 16, the United States imposed quotas of its own on Canadian exports of cattle, beef, veal, swine and pork. The loss to Canada was estimated at 109 million dollars.*[201]

Canada took the position that its action was an escape clause measure authorized by GATT Article XIX. Under Article XIX:3, the United States automatically acquired the right to "suspend * * * substantially equivalent concessions or other obligations," whether or not Canada's action

* **201.** Proclamation No. 4335, 39 Fed.Reg. 40741 (1974). The trade loss is computed in United States Department of Agriculture Press Release No. 3322–74 (Nov. 18, 1974). It may be noted that the existence of two-way trade in the North American cattle market allowed the United States to strike directly against the producers protected by the Canadian quotas, thus giving some reality to the "sanction" in this instance. This is not possible in the typical retaliation case, for the producers being protected by new trade restrictions are usually too weak competitively to be exporting anywhere.

actually conformed to Article XIX requirements. The United States did not even mention Article XIX, however, in its domestic law justification. The United States quotas were imposed under section 252(a) of the Trade Expansion Act of 1962, a subsection which required a finding that the Canadian restrictions were in violation of international commitments. The proclamation imposing the quotas stated that Canada's restrictions violated GATT Article XI, the general prohibition against quotas. Although nothing was said about Canada's Article XIX escape clause justification, the finding of an Article XI violation was necessarily a finding that the Article XIX defense was invalid.

When the United States reported its action to GATT a few days later, no mention was made of the claimed Article XI violation. Instead, the United States merely called attention to Canada's Article XIX escape clause justification, and described its own quotas as a suspension of equivalent concessions—the formula used to describe Article XIX:3 compensation rights. Since the Article XIX:3 rationale did not require a finding of violation, there was no occasion for GATT inquiry into that issue. The result was thus another example of action presented as punitive retaliation under United States domestic law, while justified as nonpunitive compensation under GATT law.

Although the Cattle War retaliation was technically an action under section 252, it can also be regarded as a preview of United States practice and procedure under section 301. The preview is disquieting.

First, the action afforded an opportunity to see how the President would make unilateral determinations that another government's actions are in violation of international obligations. From the rather scant data available, it does not appear that Canada's Article XIX claim could have been rejected out of hand. According to calculations on which the United States based its own measure of retaliation, the surge of United States cattle exports which began in late 1973 would have resulted in a *four-fold* increase over the previous peak year. On the critical issue of "serious injury" to a domestic industry, Canada had reported that it was implementing a program of "deficiency payments" to prevent a drastic cutback in Canadian cattle production, and that quotas were needed to make the program feasible. While these were only pleadings, they did seem to make a prima facie case that needed answering.

The Executive Branch did not answer. It simply ruled that the quotas violated Article XI. There was no formal explanation of why Canada's defense had been rejected, nor even any mention that such a defense existed. Although it is true that the right of retaliation against Canada did not depend on a finding of violation (because of the compensation rights of Article XIX:3), it is nevertheless troubling that the difficult issues involved in establishing this claimed violation could so easily be brushed aside.

Second, the Cattle War decision offered an opportunity to see what if any relevance would be accorded to parallel practices of the United States when considering whether foreign actions are "unreasonable" or "unjustifiable." At least superficially, there was a strong resemblance between the 1974 Canadian quotas and a 1964 statute passed by the United States

Congress. The 1964 statute ordered quotas on imports of meat whenever such imports exceeded 110 percent of the average market share held by imports from 1959 to 1963. The Canadian quotas limited United States imports to their 1969–1973 average. Without a detailed statistical analysis, it is not possible to know whether the two actions were in fact similar.[*209] As far as one can tell, however, no such comparison was attempted. The United States computed its retaliation rights solely on the basis of the larger trade flows which began in late 1973.

The fact that governments sometimes employ double standards in international trade relations is nothing new, nor is the problem peculiar to the United States. Unfortunately, punitive statutes such as section 301 act as a magnet for the worst of these tendencies. A concerted effort will be needed to hold such tendencies in check.

There is no reason to assume that the Cattle War provides the only possible model of decision under section 301, or that all government officials want it to be. Section 301 offers substantial opportunity for participation by interested private parties. Hard questions of the kind involved in the Cattle War can be asked and argued. Participants can also argue for procedures and forms of decision-making that encourage responsive answers. Interested congressmen can play a similar role, if they can be persuaded to do so. Section 301 will probably never work well, but it will work better or worse depending on the quality of participation offered.

Notes and Questions

(1) The Hudec and the Fisher-Steinhardt articles, written at different times, offer differing evaluations of the desirability of the Section 301 procedures. What is your view?

(2) Should the Congress, in granting authority to the President, give him the scope to violate United States international obligations? If so, in what circumstances?

(3) If you were the President's adviser, in what type of cases, if any, would you advise him to disregard the procedures of GATT Article XXIII in exercising his section 301 (Trade Act) authority?

(4) In what other clauses of the Trade Act has the Congress authorized a possible breach of international obligations?

(5) In a statement made July 12, 1976, the United States Trade Representative, Ambassador Fred Dent, warned the EC against applying trade barriers to United States exports of soybeans and soybean oil, stating that "if the EC adopts this tax, or any other measure designed to restrict access of U.S. soybeans and products to its market, the U.S. will move immediately and firmly to defend its trade interests." What makes this threat credible, if it is? Section 301? Would it be a credible threat if the EC knew that the President must obtain congressional authority for any action he contemplates by way of retaliation? Recall the discussion of the theory of retaliation in Section 1.3(B)(3) supra.

* 209. The comparison would have to be made in terms of the impact of imports on local producers. While gross measures such as percentage market shares, rates of import growth, and the like, might be attempted, it would be difficult to get very far without some way of comparing the economic health of the respective industries, particularly in terms of cost-price relationships.

(6) Most Section 301 proceedings result in a negotiated settlement (or at least an attempt to negotiate a settlement) of the underlying dispute. Prior to June 1985, only one retaliatory action had been in fact implemented by the United States.

DETERMINATION UNDER SECTION 301 OF THE TRADE ACT OF 1974

MEMORANDUM FOR THE UNITED STATES TRADE REPRESENTATIVE

45 Fed.Reg. 51173

Under the provisions of section 301(a)(2) of the Trade Act of 1974 (the Trade Act) (19 U.S.C. 2411(a)(2)), I have determined that the action described below is an appropriate and feasible response to the practice of Canada in denying an income tax deduction to Canadian advertisers who contract with U.S. television and radio broadcasting stations located near the U.S.-Canadian border (border broadcasters) for advertising aimed primarily at the Canadian market.

STATEMENT OF REASONS

The Office of the United States Trade Representative initiated an investigation of September 6, 1978 (43 FR 39617) on the basis of a petition filed on behalf of 15 U.S. television licensees. As is reflected in the legislative history to the Trade Act and clarified in the amendment to section 301 in the Trade Agreements Act of 1979 (Pub.L. 96–39, Title IX; 93 Stat. 295), authority to act under section 301 extends to cases involving service industries.

Public hearings were conducted at the request of the petitioner on November 29, 1978, and consultations with the Government of Canada took place on August 15, 1979, in Ottawa. Public hearings relating to the remedies suggested by the petitioner were held on July 9, 1980, to provide an opportunity for parties who might be affected by such actions to comment.

After considering the recommendation of the United States Trade Representative and the evidence developed in the investigation and the hearings, I have determined that the Canadian tax practice with respect to advertising placed with U.S. border broadcasters is unreasonable and burdens and restricts U.S. commerce, within the meaning of section 301.

The longstanding business relationships between U.S. border broadcasters and their Canadian advertisers were disrupted by the enactment in Canada of Bill C–58 in 1976. The bill, which became section 19.1 of the Canadian Tax Law, was intended to strengthen the Canadian broadcast industry as an aspect of Canadian culture. However, while some Canadian broadcasters have benefitted from the law, it denies the U.S. border broadcasters access to a substantial portion of the advertising market in Canada, amounting to approximately $20 to $25 million annually, to which they previously had had access. The law, in effect, places the cost of attaining its objectives on U.S. companies and thus unreasonably and unnecessarily burdens and restricts U.S. commerce.

Consultations were held between U.S. and Canadian broadcasters and between the U.S. and Canadian government, in order to seek a solution which would address the Canadian cultural development objective without having an adverse impact upon the U.S. broadcasting stations. These consultations were not successful in finding a basis for the negotiation of a mutually acceptable solution.

I have determined that the most appropriate response to the Canadian practice is to propose legislation to the Congress which, when enacted, would mirror in U.S. law the Canadian practice. This legislation would amend the U.S. Internal Revenue Code to deny income tax deductions for the costs of advertising primarily aimed at U.S. audiences and placed on broadcast stations located in a foreign country if a similar deduction under the income tax law of that country is denied for advertising principally aimed at its audience and placed on U.S. broadcast stations.

This measured response is most appropriate because it is directed at those interests in Canada which now benefit from the denial, resulting from enactment of C–58, of Canadian advertising revenues to U.S. border broadcasters.

The proposed U.S. law itself will apply to Canada only as long as, and to the degree that, the Canadian law applies. No disruption of other, unrelated markets will be created which might have adverse effects in other areas of the U.S. economy.

This determination is to be published in the Federal Register.

THE WHITE HOUSE,

Washington, July 31, 1980.

Jimmy Carter

Congress did not implement the proposed legislation until 1984.[13]

(7) President Reagan announced substantially higher tariffs on EC-origin pasta in June 1985, in retaliation for EC preferential treatment of citrus fruit originating in certain Mediterranean countries.[14] The increase was suspended in July pending negotiations with the EC and then reinstated when the negotiations were unsuccessful. The EC countered in each instance with higher duties on certain U.S. agricultural products.[15]

(D) RETALIATION UNDER EC LAW

In 1984, the EC adopted procedures allowing it to respond to injurious "illicit commercial practices," which are defined to be "any international trade practices attributable to third countries which are incompatible with international law or with generally accepted rules." [16] The procedures allow for complaints by Community industries and Member States and are similar to those followed in antidumping and subsidy cases.

The Regulation is not as broad as Section 301. For example, the measures authorized are to be "compatible with existing international obligations and procedures," [17] and if an international dispute procedure has

---

13. Trade and Tariff Act of 1984, Pub.L. No. 98–573, § 232, 98 Stat. 2991.

14. 50 Fed.Reg. 25685 (1985). The U.S. had previously complained about EC subsidization of pasta exports and a GATT panel had determined that the subsidies violated GATT rules, which explains the choice of EC pasta as a target for retaliation.

15. See BNA Intl. Trade Rptr. 835, 898, 1389 (1985). At about the same time as the suspension, the EC subsidy on pasta was cut by over 50%. N.Y. Times, July 20, 1985.

16. Regulation No. 2651/84, arts. 1–2, [1984] Eur.Comm.O.J. No. L 252/1.

17. Id., art. 10(3).

been followed, the measures "shall only be decided on after that procedure has been terminated, and taking account of the results of the procedure." [18]

Under the regulation, the EC may act to suspend or withdraw concessions, raise duties or introduce other charges on imports, and introduce quotas or other "measures modifying import or export conditions or otherwise affecting trade with the third country concerned." [19]

Compared with Section 301 does the greater concern in the EC regulation with compliance with international law and procedures make the EC seem a more responsible member of the international trading community than the United States?   Should this sort of appearance matter?

18. Id., art. 10(2).   **19.** Id., art. 10(3).

*

Part III

SPECIAL PROBLEMS OF REGULATING INTERNATIONAL ECONOMIC RELATIONS

Chapter 11

MONETARY AFFAIRS AND TRADE POLICY: OPERATION OF THE INTERNATIONAL MONETARY FUND

SECTION 11.1 INTRODUCTION [1]

(A) MONEY AND TRADE

In economic terms, money and goods are two sides of the same transaction. It is not surprising, therefore, that governmental monetary policy and trade policy are intimately connected. In Chapter 5 we saw evidence of that connection in the fact that the International Monetary Fund ("IMF" or "the Fund") and GATT are each part of the "Bretton Woods System." In Chapter 5, we also examined the basic constitutional and institutional structure of the IMF. In this chapter, we take up a variety of topics which relate to international monetary policy and the regulation of international monetary affairs. First, in this section we look briefly at how foreign exchange transactions operate and how a country's balance of payments is defined. We then look at the problems of floating exchange rates and how such rates affect trade. In Section 11.2, we deal with the operations of the IMF, and, in particular, its lending activities, while in Section 11.3 we look at the obligations that the IMF and others impose on national regulation of foreign exchange transactions. Finally, we conclude this chapter with an examination of the special GATT rules applicable to countries with balance of payments problems.

---

1. A number of works on the IMF and the international monetary system are quoted or cited in the notes in this chapter. In addition, on the IMF generally, see J. Horsefield (ed.), The International Monetary Fund, 1945–1965 (3 vols. 1969); IMF, The International Monetary Fund, 1966–1971 (1984); R. Edwards, International Monetary Collaboration (1985). On the operation of the IMF, see the following IMF publications: Annual Report of the Executive Board; International Monetary Fund Pamphlet Series and the biweekly IMF Survey. On the international monetary system generally, see T. Agmon, R. Hawkins & R. Levich (eds.), The Future of the International Monetary System (1984); F. Mann, The Legal Aspect of Money (4th ed. 1982); R. Triffin, The World Money Maze: National Currencies in International Payments (1966); G. Meier, Problems of a World Monetary Order (2d ed. 1982); M. Shuster, The Public International Law of Money (1973).

The principal focus of this chapter will be balance of payments problems. In recent years, the huge U.S. balance of payments deficit (see chart in subsection (C) infra) has caused considerable concern, particularly in Congress where it has been an important factor in the upsurge of interest in protectionist legislation, some of which was discussed in Chapters 9 and 10 supra. The U.S. deficit is often attributed to the rapid increase in the value of the U.S. dollar that occurred in the early 1980s. Although the exact relationship between exchange rates and trade flows is not agreed upon, it seems clear that in a world of floating exchange rates, where exchange rate shifts of 20 percent over a short period of time are not uncommon, such shifts can overwhelm the effect of traditional trade policy measures such as tariffs, which now typically average less than five percent. Moreover, such exchange rate shifts may often be fueled largely by nontrade related factors, such as capital flows and speculation, meaning that the effect of such shifts on trade flows may not be related to the classical factors of comparative advantage that economists typically assume determine trade flows (see Section 1.3 supra).

(B) THE OPERATION AND UTILITY OF FOREIGN EXCHANGE TRANSACTIONS

(1) Impact of a Trade Transaction on the Balance of Payments and Exchange Rates

Assume that Golddust Widget Mfg. Co. ("Golddust") is a Michigan-based company that exports widgets. Golddust sells widgets to a firm in France by the name of Comptoir des Produits ("Comptoir"). The following are possible ways these sales could be consummated:

(1) Golddust delivers widgets in exchange for some goods Comptoir produces. This barter arrangement would not itself require any international payments (although balance of payments accounting would register this transaction).

(2) Golddust prefers money, so Comptoir pays in French francs. But French francs are only good to Golddust if it wants something from France and Golddust doesn't. So Golddust trades its francs to someone who wants French francs.

(3) Golddust wants United States dollars, so Comptoir purchases some dollars from someone in exchange for francs, and pays Golddust in dollars.

Since using money works better than barter, (2) and (3) above are the preferred modes of transacting business, and in either case, a professional money changer performs an important specialized service function. To be efficient, the money changer (e.g., a bank) must usually maintain a certain balance of different kinds of currencies, so that when clients come for its service, it can serve them.

Now suppose Golddust is shipping to a Buyer in Xonia, where the currency unit is a "dillar," (Symbol = Đ). Suppose U.S. Bank is Golddust's bank, and X Bank is Buyer's bank in Xonia. Suppose U.S. Bank wishes to hold about $100 United States dollars' worth of the foreign currency, and the current rate is 10 dillars for 1 dollar. Golddust ships $10 worth of goods. The following are the effects of this transaction.

Possessed By:

	Golddust	U.S. Bank		X Bank		Buyer
(a) Before shipment	goods	$100	Đ1000	$100	Đ1000	Đ100
(b) Goods shipped, U.S. Bank pays	$10	90	Đ1000	$100	Đ1000	Đ100
(c) X Bank pays U.S. Bank	$10	$100	Đ1000	$ 90	Đ1000	Đ100
(d) Buyer pays his bank	$10	$100	Đ1000	$ 90	Đ1100	goods
(e) X Bank re-establishes dollar balance by buying dollars from U.S. Bank	$10	$90	Đ1100	$100	Đ1000	goods

Now at this point, U.S. Bank is holding more dillars than it desires. If a United States buyer imports from Xonia, it can buy dillars from U.S. Bank. But if fewer buyers in the United States import from Xonia than vice-versa, then U.S. Bank will want to unload its extra dillars (which are essentially good only for goods from Xonia). Thus the imbalance of trade puts a selling pressure on dillars, i.e., U.S. Bank may be willing to lower its price for dillars and give 11 to the dollar.

The result to Xonia and its citizens of these supply and demand pressures operating on the dillar will be:

(1) without Central Bank intervention, the dillar-dollar exchange rate will change as fewer people will want to take dillars, so it will be more expensive for Xonian citizens to import goods that must be paid for in dollars, or

(2) with Central Bank intervention, the dillar-dollar exchange rate may not change and thus there may be no immediate impact on Xonian citizens and their ability to import, but over time the Central Bank will lose reserves, which will have a deflationary impact on the Xonian economy.

Consider again the trade transaction in which Golddust sells widgets to Comptoir. Between the time of contracting and the time when Golddust is able to present the proper shipping documents and draft for payment, several weeks may elapse. If the draft is a time draft, e.g., "90 days sight," even more time may elapse before Comptoir will be required to pay. Suppose further that at the time of contracting, five French francs could be purchased for each U.S. dollar. Now consider Comptoir's position if at the time it must pay in dollars

(a) one U.S. dollar can be purchased for four French francs, or

(b) one U.S. dollar can be purchased for six French francs.

In either case, the effective cost of the goods to Comptoir is going to be about 20 percent different from its expectations at the time of contracting—in (a), in its favor; in (b), to its detriment.

If Comptoir, at the time of contracting, expects that (a) will occur, what should it do? If it expects (b), what should it do? Suppose it doesn't know what to expect, but prefers not to take the risk of (b); what should it do? Can it insure this risk?

(2) Foreign Exchange Transactions

K. ALEC CHRYSTAL, A GUIDE TO FOREIGN EXCHANGE MARKETS

(1984) [2]

The economies of the free world are becoming increasingly interdependent. U.S. exports now amount to almost 10 percent of Gross National Product. For both Britain and Canada, the figure currently exceeds 25 percent. Imports are about the same size. Trade of this magnitude would not be possible without the ability to buy and sell currencies. Currencies must be bought and sold because the acceptable means of payment in other countries is not the U.S. dollar. As a result, importers, exporters, travel agents, tourists and many others with overseas business must change dollars into foreign currency and/or the reverse.

The trading of currencies takes place in foreign exchange markets whose major function is to facilitate international trade and investment.

*   *   *

There is an almost bewildering variety of foreign exchange markets. Spot markets and forward markets abound in a number of currencies. In addition, there are diverse prices quoted for these currencies. This section attempts to bring order to this seeming disarray.

Spot, Forward, Bid, Ask

Virtually every major newspaper, such as the *Wall Street Journal* or the *London Financial Times,* prints a daily list of exchange rates. These are expressed either as the number of units of a particular currency that exchange for one U.S. dollar or as the number of U.S. dollars that exchange for one unit of a particular currency. *   *   *

For major currencies, up to four different prices typically will be quoted. One is the "spot" price. The others may be "30 days forward," "90 days forward," and "180 days forward." *   *   *

The spot price is what you must pay to buy currencies for immediate delivery (two working days in the interbank market; over the counter, if you buy bank notes or travelers checks). The forward prices for each currency are what you will have to pay if you sign a contract today to buy that currency on a specific future date (30 days from now, etc.). In this market, you pay for the currency when the contract matures.

Why would anyone buy and sell foreign currency forward? There are some major advantages from having such opportunities available. For example, an exporter who has receipts of foreign currency due at some future date can sell those funds forward now, thereby avoiding all risks

---

2. 66 The Federal Reserve Bank of St. Louis Review, No. 3, at 5 (Mar. 1984).

associated with subsequent adverse exchange rate changes. Similarly, an importer who will have to pay for a shipment of goods in foreign currency in, say, three months can buy the foreign exchange forward and, again, avoid having to bear the exchange rate risk.

The exchange rates quoted in the financial press (for example, those in table 1) are not the ones individuals would get at a local bank. Unless otherwise specified, the published prices refer to those quoted by banks to other banks for currency deals in excess of $1 million. Even these prices will vary somewhat depending upon whether the bank buys or sells. The difference between the buying and selling price is sometimes known as the "bid-ask spread." The spread partly reflects the banks' costs and profit margins in transactions; however, major banks make their profits more from capital gains than from the spread.

The market for bank notes and travelers checks is quite separate from the interbank foreign exchange market. For smaller currency exchanges, such as an individual going on vacation abroad might make, the spread is greater than in the interbank market. This presumably reflects the larger average costs—including the exchange rate risks that banks face by holding bank notes in denominations too small to be sold in the interbank market— associated with these smaller exchanges. As a result, individuals generally pay a higher price for foreign exchange than those quoted in the newspapers.

* * *

How Does "The" Foreign Exchange Market Operate?

It is generally not possible to go to a specific building and "see" the market where prices of foreign exchange are determined. With few exceptions, the vast bulk of foreign exchange business is done over the telephone between specialist divisions of major banks. Foreign exchange dealers in each bank usually operate from one room; each dealer has several telephones and is surrounded by video screens and news tapes. Typically, each dealer specializes in one or a small number of markets (such as sterling/ dollar or deutschemark/dollar). Trades are conducted with other dealers who represent banks around the world. These dealers typically deal regularly with one another and are thus able to make firm commitments by word of mouth.

Only the head or regional offices of the larger banks actively deal in foreign exchange. The largest of these banks are known as "market makers" since they stand ready to buy or sell any of the major currencies on a more or less continuous basis. Unusually large transactions, however, will only be accommodated by market makers on more favorable terms. In such cases, foreign exchange brokers may be used as middlemen to find a taker or takers for the deal. Brokers (of which there are four major firms and a handful of smaller ones) do not trade on their own account, but specialize in setting up large foreign exchange transactions in return for a commission (typically 0.03 cents or less on the sterling spread). In April 1983, 56 percent of spot transactions by value involving banks in the United States were channeled through brokers. If all interbank transactions are included, the figure rises to 59 percent.

Most small banks and local offices of major banks do not deal directly in the interbank foreign exchange market. Rather they typically will have a credit line with a large bank or their head office. Transactions will thus involve an extra step. The customer deals with a local bank, which in turn deals with a major bank or head office. The interbank foreign exchange market exists between the major banks either directly or indirectly via a broker.

* * *

FOREIGN EXCHANGE MARKET ACTIVITIES

Much foreign exchange market trading does not appear to be related to the simple basic purpose of allowing businesses to buy or sell foreign currency in order, say, to sell or purchase goods overseas. It is certainly easy to see the usefulness of the large range of foreign exchange transactions available through the interbank and organized markets (spot, forward, futures, options) to facilitate trade between nations. It is also clear that there is a useful role for foreign exchange brokers in helping to "make" the interbank market. There are several other activities, however, in foreign exchange markets that are less well understood and whose relevance is less obvious to people interested in understanding what these markets accomplish.

Two major classes of activity will be discussed. First, the existence of a large number of foreign exchange markets in many locations creates opportunities to profit from "arbitrage." Second, there is implicitly a market in (foreign exchange) risk bearing. Those who wish to avoid foreign exchange risk (at a price) may do so. Those who accept the risk in expectation of profits are known as "speculators."

Triangular Arbitrage

Triangular arbitrage is the process that ensures that all exchange rates are mutually consistent. If, for example, one U.S. dollar exchanges for one Canadian dollar, and one Canadian dollar exchanges for one British pound, then the U.S. dollar-pound exchange rate should be one pound for one dollar. If it differs, then there is an opportunity for profit making. To see why this is so, suppose that you could purchase two U.S. dollars with one British pound. By first buying C$1 with U.S. $1, then purchasing £1 with C$1, and finally buying U.S. $2 with £1, you could double your money immediately. Clearly this opportunity will not last for long since it involves making large profits with certainty. The process of triangular arbitrage is exactly that of finding and exploiting profitable opportunities in such exchange rate inconsistencies. As a result of triangular arbitrage, such inconsistencies will be eliminated rapidly. Cross rates, however, will only be roughly consistent given the bid-ask spread associated with transaction costs.

In the past, the possibility of making profits from triangular arbitrage was greater as a result of the practice of expressing exchange rates in American terms in the United States and in European terms elsewhere. The adoption of standard practice has reduced the likelihood of inconsistencies. Also, in recent years, such opportunities for profit making have been greatly reduced by high-speed, computerized information systems and the increased sophistication of the banks operating in the market.

* * *

Interest Arbitrage

Interest arbitrage is slightly different in nature from triangular or space arbitrage; however, the basic motive of finding and exploiting profitable opportunities still applies. There is no reason why interest rates denominated in different currencies should be equal. Interest rates are the cost of borrowing or the return to lending for a specific period of time. The relative price (exchange rate) of money may change over time so that the comparison of, say, a U.S. and a British interest rate requires some allowance for expected exchange rate changes. Thus, it will be not at all unusual to find interest rates denominated in dollars and interest rates denominated in, say, pounds being somewhat different. However, real returns on assets of similar quality should be the same if the exchange rate risk is covered or hedged in the forward market. Were this not true, it would be possible to borrow in one currency and lend in another at a profit with no exchange risk.

Suppose we lend one dollar for a year in the United States at an interest rate of r_{us}. The amount accumulated at the end of the year per dollar lent will be $1 + r_{us}$ (capital plus interest). If, instead of making dollar loans, we converted them into pounds and lent them in the United Kingdom at the rate r_{uk}, the amount of pounds we would have for each original dollar at the end of the year would be $S(1 + r_{uk})$, where S is the spot exchange rate (in pounds per dollar) at the beginning of the period. At the outset, it is not known if $1 + r_{us}$ dollars is going to be worth more than $S(1 + r_{uk})$ pounds in a year's time because the spot exchange rate in a year's time is unknown. This uncertainty can be avoided by selling the pounds forward into dollars. Then the relative value of the two loans would no longer depend on what subsequently happens to the spot exchange rate. By doing this, we end up with $S/F(1 + r_{uk})$ dollars per original dollar invested. This is known as the "covered," or hedged, return on pounds.

Since the covered return in our example is denominated in dollars, it can reasonably be compared with the U.S. interest rate. If these returns are very different, investors will move funds where the return is highest on a covered basis. This process is interest arbitrage. It is assumed that the assets involved are equally safe and, because the returns are covered, all exchange risk is avoided. Of course, if funds do move in large volume between assets or between financial centers, then interest rates and the exchange rates (spot and forward) will change in predictable ways. Funds will continue to flow between countries until there is no extra profit to be made from interest arbitrage. This will occur when the returns on both dollar- and sterling-denominated assets are equal, that is, when

$$(1) \quad (1 + r_{us}) = \frac{S}{F} (1 + r_{uk}).$$

This result is known as covered interest parity. It holds more or less exactly, subject only to a margin due to transaction costs, so long as the appropriate dollar and sterling interest rates are compared.

Speculation

Arbitrage in the foreign exchange markets involves little or no risk since transactions can be completed rapidly. An alternative source of profit is available from outguessing other market participants as to what future exchange rates will be. This is called speculation.

* * *

Speculation is important for the efficient working of foreign exchange markets. It is a form of arbitrage that occurs across time rather than across space or between markets at the same time. Just as arbitrage increases the efficiency of markets by keeping prices consistent, so speculation increases the efficiency of forward, futures and options markets by keeping those markets liquid. Those who wish to avoid foreign exchange risk may thereby do so in a well-developed market. Without speculators, risk avoidance in foreign exchange markets would be more difficult and, in many cases, impossible.

Note

The volume of foreign exchange transactions has increased rapidly in recent years. The Federal Reserve Bank of New York estimates that daily turnover increased from $5 billion a day in 1977 to $33.5 billion a day in 1983.[3]

(C) BALANCE OF PAYMENTS MEASUREMENT AND ACCOUNTING

CHARLES PIGOTT, WHICH TRADE BALANCE?

(1984)[4]

In February, newspapers across the nation reported that the U.S. "trade" deficit for 1983 was $60.6 billion. A month later they reported a 1983 "trade" deficit of $40.8 billion. But the national income account data given in the recent *Survey of Current Business* lists still another version of the "trade" deficit—$7.1 billion. Will the real trade deficit please stand up?

Neither media inaccuracy nor government revisions can be blamed for these discrepancies. Rather, what is commonly referred to as "the trade balance" is actually measured and reported in several different ways. Anyone wanting to know this balance has the following choices: the merchandise trade balance, itself measured in several ways; "GNP net exports", which gives the balance of trade in merchandise *and* services; or the current account balance. While these balances generally move closely together over time, their levels are typically very different. For example, it was the merchandise balance that was $60.6 billion in deficit last year, while the current account and GNP net export deficits were $40.8 and $7.1 billion,

---

3. Andrews, Recent Developments in the U.S. Foreign Exchange Market, Federal Reserve Bank of New York Quarterly Review 38 (Summer 1984).

4. Research Department, Federal Reserve Bank of San Francisco, FRB SF Weekly Letter (April 20, 1984).

respectively. For those who still want to know what the deficit really was, this *Letter* provides a short "guide to the perplexed", explaining the various balances, their relation to one another, and their economic significance.

CURRENT ACCOUNT

The most comprehensive summary of U.S. trade with the rest of the world is given by the current account balance. Indeed, the current account contains the other balances mentioned above and all the transactions in them.

The current account includes all transactions that are "current" in an accounting sense, that is, all payments and receipts for goods and services exchanged with foreigners, as well as transfers. Excluded from the current account are U.S. purchases from or sales to foreigners of financial or real assets. These items, which represent U.S. entities' lending to or borrowing from foreigners, comprise the capital account of the U.S. balance of payments.

If, in any year, total U.S. payments to foreigners on a current basis exceed our receipts from them (that is, we run a current account deficit), our country must borrow from abroad to make up the difference. Conversely, we must lend to foreigners any difference between our sales to them on a current basis and our payments. The current account surplus or deficit therefore also measures the *net* amount the U.S. as a whole is lending to or borrowing from abroad during a given year. Last year, we ran a current account deficit of $40.8 billion; this means that we borrowed a net amount of $40.8 billion from abroad.

The current account itself, though, contains three distinct types of transactions: *merchandise trade, productive services* provided by land, labor, and capital; and *transfers,* which include foreign aid and private remittances as well as payments to foreigners of interest on their holdings of U.S. government debt. These, in turn, are "arranged" into the three basic balances—merchandise trade, GNP net exports of goods and services, and, finally, the current account balance itself.

MERCHANDISE TRADE BALANCE

The merchandise trade account contains all exports and imports of *tangible commodities,* e.g., agricultural products, industrial materials such as steel, consumer manufactures, and capital goods. Actual merchandise trade figures are reported several different ways depending on the extent to which various services involved in transporting them are included.

Imports and exports on a "free-along-side" (f.a.s.) basis are valued as delivered to their point of embarkation for or departure from the U.S. The f.a.s. figures are thus the purest measures of the values of the commodities themselves. Other export/import figures refer to their value "free-on-board" (f.o.b.), that is, inclusive of loading and related costs. Still other figures include the "cost of insurance and freight" (c.i.f.) in addition to the loading costs and the actual (f.a.s.) commodity value.

The first merchandise trade balance figures reported each month by the Commerce Department, and the ones most frequently quoted in the media, are the "census" figures based on the export and import invoices recorded at various U.S. customs stations. These figures value imports at their *point of entry* into the U.S., that is on a c.i.f. basis, while they value exports on an f.a.s. basis. (Commerce reports the balance on an f.a.s. basis for both exports and imports several days following the release of the census data.) The census balance thus includes the transport and other service costs of bringing imports to the U.S. but excludes the service costs involved in getting our exports abroad. Not surprisingly then, last year's census-based deficit of $69 billion was substantially larger than the f.a.s. merchandise deficit of $60.6 billion.

SERVICES

Services provided by factors of production—land, labor and capital—are the second major category of transactions in the current account. Included in such "factor" services are personal travel and tourism, royalties and other fees from professional services, as well as all services associated with transporting and insuring U.S. merchandise trade.

However, the largest and most rapidly growing component of factor services represents payments for services provided by physical capital. These include recorded earnings from U.S. investments abroad as well as payments to foreigners on their investments in the U.S., *except* for the interest they earn on their holdings of U.S. government (federal, state and local) debt. Interest payments to foreigners on government debt are not included in these services (although they are included in the current account) because, according to U.S. national income accounting conventions, they represent a transfer rather than a payment for a current factor service.

Overall, the service balance typically records a large surplus, nearly $54 billion in 1983. This mainly reflects the fact that the U.S. earns considerably more on its investments abroad than it pays to foreigners on their investments here. Indeed, our reported investment receipts totaled $85 billion last year (nearly two-thirds of all service exports), exceeding payments to foreigners on their investments in the U.S. by nearly $47 billion.

The sum of the (f.a.s.) merchandise trade and service balances yields what is known as "GNP net exports." This is the net export figure given in the U.S. national income statistics and it is one of the four major components of U.S. GNP.

TRANSFERS AND THE REMAINDER

The remainder of the current account consists of unilateral transfers such as private contributions, pension payments, official foreign aid, as well as interest payments to foreigners on their holdings of U.S. government debt. The U.S. always runs a large deficit overall in these items, amounting to nearly $33 billion in 1983, $18 billion of which represented U.S. government interest paid to foreigners.

MEANING

On this basis, last year's $41 billion current account deficit was the sum of our $61 billion merchandise trade *deficit,* the $54 billion *surplus* on factor services (together making up the $7 billion deficit on GNP net exports), and our $33 billion *deficit* in transfers and U.S. government interest payments to foreigners (Chart 1).

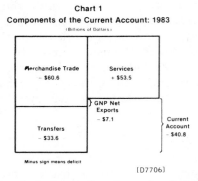

Chart 1
Components of the Current Account: 1983
(Billions of Dollars)

Our merchandise trade balance has been in deficit in all but two of the last fourteen years, while the current account and GNP net exports have more often been in surplus. This pattern is due to the large U.S. surplus in factor services—a surplus that has grown very quickly in recent years mainly because of the rapid increase in receipts from our investments abroad. The services surplus means that the U.S. can have a substantial trade deficit even in years when our total current international payments and receipts (the current account) are in balance. Interestingly, the situation is the opposite for several of our trading partners. Japan, for example, typically runs a substantial deficit in services. Its merchandise trade therefore may be in surplus, as is usually the case, even when its current account is in deficit.

Although the merchandise trade balance gets the most media attention, the GNP net export and current account balances are more economically significant. In particular, GNP net exports provide the best summary measure of the foreign sector's impact on U.S. output and employment, while the current account balance measures the impact of the foreign sector on U.S. financial markets, including the value of the dollar on the foreign exchange markets.

GNP net exports comprise one of the four major components of U.S. GNP (along with private consumption and investment, and government expenditures), measuring the difference between foreign purchases of U.S. goods and services and U.S. purchases of foreign goods and services. As such, variations in GNP net exports have a direct and potentially substantial impact on the growth of our national output. As the foreign sector has grown in importance to the U.S. economy over the last decade, forecasts of U.S. growth have become increasingly sensitive to assessments of GNP net exports.

Finally, the current account's significance lies mainly in the fact that it measures the net flow of U.S. lending to or borrowing from abroad, and hence, the change over time in net U.S. indebtedness to foreigners. (The U.S. is still a net claimant on abroad, but this could change if our present deficits persist.) This flow, in turn, has potentially very important implications for financial conditions in the U.S. and for the value of the dollar on the foreign exchanges. In particular, the nearly $41 billion in funds the U.S.

"imported" from abroad last year helped to meet the credit needs of our private sector and the growing demand for credit by the federal government. Upward pressures on U.S. interest rates would probably have been greater had these foreign funds not been available.

Likewise, concern is growing that the U.S. is borrowing from abroad at an unsustainably high rate through the current account. This has led several observers to predict a sharp decline in the dollar on the foreign exchanges in 1984 (to bring the current account to a more sustainable level). Thus, for financial markets these days, the "trade" balance to watch is mainly our current account.

Note

A country's balance of trade often shifts significantly over time, as is highlighted in the following table: [5]

	1965	1970	1975	1980	1985
	(billions of U.S. dollars)				
United States	4.3	0.5	2.2	−36.2	−143.8
Canada	−0.3	2.4	−2.1	4.9	10.8
Japan	0.3	0.4	−2.1	−10.9	39.6
France	−0.2	−1.0	−0.9	−18.9	−6.6
West Germany	0.3	4.3	15.3	4.9	23.8
Italy	−0.2	−1.8	−3.7	−22.0	−15.8
United Kingdom	−2.3	−2.5	−9.9	−5.4	−8.5
Developing (OPEC)	3.9	6.9	61.4	163.8	24.6
Developing (non-OPEC)	−5.5	−9.2	−41.2	−94.8	−6.4

(D) EXCHANGE RATES AND TRADE

(1) The Transition From Fixed to Floating Exchange Rates

SIR JOSEPH GOLD, DEVELOPMENTS IN THE INTERNATIONAL MONETARY SYSTEM, THE INTERNATIONAL MONETARY FUND, AND INTERNATIONAL MONETARY LAW SINCE 1971

(1982) [6]

13. Exchange rates are at the heart of the international monetary system, the activities of the Fund, and international monetary law. The original Articles represented a major departure from the principle of the past that each country was sovereign in the determination and management of the exchange rate for its currency.

14. The par value system of the original Articles was based on seven principles:

(i) Exchange rates were matters of international concern.

(ii) Exchange stability was desirable, but not exchange rigidity.

5. U.S. Economic Report of the President Feb. 1985 (Table B–105); id. Feb. 1986 (Table B–107).

6. 174 Recueil des Cours 107, 329–33, 229–331.

(iii) Competitive exchange alterations were outlawed.

(iv) Exchange rates were to be fixed and not allowed to float.

(v) Exchange systems had to be unitary; multiple currency practices were prohibited.

(vi) Discriminatory currency arrangements were prohibited.

(vii) Authority over exchange rates was apportioned between the Fund and members, but a member had ultimate authority over the exchange rate for its currency.

15. Each member was responsible for maintaining the effectiveness of the par value of its own currency. A member was required to adopt appropriate measures to ensure that exchange rates in exchange transactions in its territories involving its currency and another member's currency did not develop outside prescribed margins around the parity between the two currencies. The parity was the ratio between the par values established in terms of gold as the common denominator of the par value system. The obligation was an application of the underlying principle that each member is responsible to the Fund for its own currency.

16. The voluntary undertaking of the United States to observe the practice of buying and selling gold freely for its own currency in transactions with the monetary authorities of other members, as that practice was described in the Articles, became the primary norm of the par value system. The US dollar became the main reserve and intervention currency. As a result, the United States was passive in exchange markets.

17. The withdrawal by the United States on 15 August 1971 of its undertaking with respect to transactions in gold led to the floating of all currencies. The view presented by the United States in the discussions on reform of the international monetary system was that its central role in the par value system had been disadvantageous to it. The passivity of the United States had been forced on it by the system as it had developed and had deprived it of means of adjustment that had been available to other members.

18. Other members, however, thought that the par value system had operated unsymmetrically by conferring benefits on the United States not available to them. In the Committee of Twenty [the Committee on Reform of the International Monetary Fund], all agreed that a suitable par value system should be restored, but members pursued different objectives in the search for symmetry in the operation of a par value system. The United States wanted the assurance of symmetry between members in surplus and members in deficit in their balances of payments; other members wanted the assurance of symmetry between the issuers of reserve currencies, principally the United States, and the rest of the membership.

19. The objective of symmetry is inspired by the belief that an international monetary system will not be satisfactory unless it provides equitable treatment for discrete classes of countries. International monetary law, administered through international organizations, particularly an organization like the Fund that is open to universal membership, must be relied on as a principal means to ensure equitable treatment. The issue must be faced

of the extent to which the law of organizations should take the form of fixed rules and how much should be left to the discretion of administering authorities.

20. The Committee of Twenty's *Outline of Reform* set forth the general direction in which the Committee thought that the international monetary system could evolve in the future. A more flexible par value system could be introduced, with floating authorized in particular situations. New ideas, involving for example objective indicators and multicurrency intervention, were adumbrated. The *Outline of Reform* was affected throughout by considerations of symmetry and of the choice between fixed rules and discretionary authority.

21. The Second Amendment abandons the idea of an interim period as contemplated by the *Outline of Reform*. Exchange rate provisions are adopted that will apply at all times; other provisions deal with present conditions and permit evolution in exchange arrangements as conditions change; and further provisions regulate a par value system if conditions permit its introduction, but no express or implied assurance is given that it will be called into being at any time.

22. The principles of the provisions now in operation as compared with the principles in paragraph 14 above are as follows:

(i) Exchange rates continue to be matters of international concern, even though par values are abrogated and members are free, with one exception, to choose their exchange arrangements. The exception is that members may not maintain the external value of their currencies in terms of gold. Members are free also to determine the external value of their currencies. In the exercise of their freedom, members are subject to certain general obligations that apply now and at all times.

(ii) Stability is a principle of the Second Amendment but not in the sense of the steadfastness of exchange rates, which became rigidity in the operation of the par value system. Stability in underlying economic conditions is to be pursued. If achieved, it will produce a stable system of exchange rates among members. If underlying economic conditions are not orderly, exchange rates should not be prevented from responding to such conditions.

(iii) The avoidance of competitive exchange depreciation is still a purpose of the Fund, but the obligation of members has been rewritten. They must avoid manipulating exchange rates or the international monetary system in order to prevent effective balance of payments adjustment or to gain an unfair competitive advantage over other members.

(iv) The Second Amendment avoids any suggestion of the superiority of fixed over floating exchange rates. Criticisms of the way in which floating exchange rates are working have produced a number of proposals for improvements, and some possibilities under the communiqué of the Versailles summit meeting, but not support for return to a par value system.

(v) The desirability of unitary exchange rates continues to be a principle of the Articles, but abrogation of the par value system has affected determination of the practices that are considered multiple currency practices.

(vi) Discriminatory currency arrangements, including broken cross rates, are still prohibited by the Second Amendment. The determination of what constitutes discriminatory currency arrangements has been affected by abrogation of the par value system.

(vii) The balance between the authority of the Fund and of members over the exchange rates for their currencies has shifted radically in favour of members. It is more appropriate to speak of their primary authority instead of the ultimate authority that they had under the par value system.

In Chapter III it was shown that the provisions of the par value system sought a balance between the powers over exchange rates conferred on the Fund and those retained by members. A member had ultimate authority over the exchange rate for its currency, however, because the member could change the par value of its currency notwithstanding the objection of the Fund without violating treaty obligations. Radical changes have followed from the abrogation of the par value system.

The balance between the authority of the Fund and of members under the provisions now in force has shifted in favour of members. Formerly, the Articles prescribed only one form of exchange arrangement, and the Fund's concurrence in the external value of a currency was necessary. Under the present Articles, a member has freedom to choose its exchange arrangement and to determine the external value of its currency. It is more appropriate now to speak of the primary and not the ultimate authority of a member over the exchange rate for its currency.

This change is responsible for the more explicit expression of the vigilance that the Fund must exercise in protecting the international interest. The Fund is directed to exercise this vigilance as overseer of the international monetary system and of the compliance of members with their obligations. The Fund's function of firm surveillance over the exchange rate policies of members has a similar purpose.

Versailles Communiqué

There has been much discontent with the operation of present exchange arrangements because of the behaviour of exchange rates. Differences of opinion have become more pronounced on the extent to which, and the manner in which, members should manage exchange rates in the collective interest. Different opinions are held on the weight to be given to effect on the exchange rate in choosing domestic policies, and on the circumstances in which members should intervene in the exchange markets. The United States has attached less importance to exchange rate considerations than other members, and its view of what are disorderly conditions in exchange markets that justify intervention has been much narrower than the views of others.

These different attitudes have become disturbing politically as well as economically. They have led to a pronouncement on monetary matters in the communiqué issued after the seven-nation summit held in Versailles on 4–6 June 1982. The Heads of States and Government have expressed their concern with the gravity of the world economic situation and have agreed on a number of objectives and lines of action to improve the situation. More stable exchange rates are among the results to be achieved as a result of these lines of action. The communiqué states that:

It is essential to intensify our economic and monetary co-operation. In this regard, we will work toward a constructive and orderly evolution of the international monetary system by a closer co-operation among the authorities representing the currencies of North America, of Japan, and of the European Community in pursuing medium-term economic and monetary objectives. In this respect, we have committed ourselves to the undertakings contained in the attached statement.

The attached statement on "International Monetary Undertakings" reads as follows:

1. We accept a joint responsibility to work for greater stability of the world monetary system. We recognize that this rests primarily on convergence of policies designed to achieve lower inflation, higher employment, and renewed economic growth; and thus to maintain the internal and external values of our currencies. We are determined to discharge this obligation in close collaboration with all interested countries and monetary institutions.

2. We attach major importance to the role of the IMF as a monetary authority and we will give it our full support in its efforts to foster stability.

3. We are ready to strengthen our co-operation with the IMF in its work of surveillance; and to develop this on a multilateral basis taking into account particularly the currencies constituting the [Special Drawing Rights.]

4. We rule out the use of our exchange rates to gain unfair competitive advantages.

5. We are ready, if necessary, to use intervention in exchange markets to counter disorderly conditions, as provided for under Article IV of the IMF Articles of Agreement.

6. Those of us who are members of the [European Monetary System] consider that these undertakings are complementary to the obligations of stability which they have already undertaken in that framework.

7. We are all convinced that greater monetary stability will assist freer flows of goods, services, and capital. We are determined to see that greater monetary stability and freer flows of trade and capital reinforce one another in the interest of economic growth and employment.

Much of this statement paraphrases the present law of exchange arrangements, but the intention of those responsible for the statement may be to ensure a more effective operation of the law. Future developments will show whether important changes in substance or procedure will flow from the statement.

Note

Under the current provisions of the IMF Agreement, a country has considerable flexibility in deciding how to manage its exchange rates—from allowing the rate to float freely to tying it to some other rate or to a formula. See Section 11.3(A)(2) infra. Eight of the members of the EC have joined together in the European Monetary System, where exchange rates are allowed to fluctuate within a narrow band. From time to time, the currency relations are adjusted. Proposals for reform of the international monetary system often are based on some sort of managed float where exchange rates are not pegged to a specific value but are kept within a range around such a value. See, e.g., J. Williamson, The Exchange Rate System (1983).

(2) *Flexible Exchange Rates and Trade*

C. FRED BERGSTEN & JOHN WILLIAMSON, EXCHANGE RATES AND TRADE POLICY

(1983) [7]

Trade policy has traditionally been associated with tariffs, quotas, export subsidies, and other nontariff distortions. Relatively little attention has been paid to the impact of exchange rates on trade policy, despite widespread analyses by international monetary economists of their impact on trade flows. This paper argues that the continued failure to link the trade and monetary aspects of international economic exchange is a major mistake, in terms both of diagnosing the policy problems which now confront the trading system and of dealing with those problems in the foreseeable future.

Misaligned Currencies and Trade Protection

The bifurcation between money and trade, at both the analytical and policy levels, is understandable yet strange. It is understandable for three reasons. First, different officials and, usually, different ministries are responsible for monetary and trade matters in most countries. * * *

Second, there is a legitimate difference between the focus of trade policy on the *level* of trade flows and the focus of exchange rates (and international monetary policy, more broadly) on trade *balances*. As long as trade negotiations are reciprocal in practice as well as in principle, trade policy has a neutral impact on the trade balance. Similarly, the balance of payments adjustment process addresses the problem of the trade balance rather than the trade level. * * *

But the main reason why the money-trade relationship has been so ignored is probably the widespread assumption that the international monetary system will not permit the existence of substantial exchange rate misalignments for prolonged periods. * * *

This bifurcation is strange, however, because exchange rates demonstrably do deviate substantially from their equilibrium paths for substantial

---

7. © 1983, Institute for International Economics. Reproduced by permission from W. Cline (ed.), Trade Policy in the 1980s, at 99–103, 107–09.

periods of time, and because the basic case for liberal trade rests upon the assumption inter alia of balance of payments equilibrium, hence equilibrium exchange rates. If the exchange rate conveys price signals to producers and consumers which are incorrect reflections of the underlying economic relationships, significant distortions can result for production, hence trade.

Persistent overvaluation of a country's exchange rate will, of course, adversely affect the country's price competitiveness in international trade (in both goods and services). Exports will be discouraged and imports will be encouraged. The tradable goods sector of the economy, as a whole, will be disadvantaged with resulting distortions in the distribution of domestic output. The current account will shift adversely, financed via private capital inflows or a decline in the country's external reserves. The amounts of money involved can be quite sizable; for the United States, the typical analysis suggests that the merchandise trade balance declines by about $3 billion for every percentage point decline in US international price competitiveness.

From the standpoint of trade policy, the chief implication is the (additional?) pressure that is generated for protectionist measures. Export- and import-competing firms and workers will tend to seek help from their governments to offset these distortions, which undermine their ability to compete, with some degree of legitimacy since the distortions are accepted—in some cases, even fostered—by those governments. Coalitions in support of trade restrictions will be much easier to form, and much broader in their political clout, because no longer will only the most vulnerable firms and workers be seeking help—and no longer will the countervailing pressures from successful exporters be as effective. As we shall see below, overvaluation of the dollar has proved to be an accurate "leading indicator" of trade policy in the United States—perhaps the most accurate of all such indicators—in the postwar period.

The protectionist impact of an overvalued currency, moreover, may persist beyond the duration of the overvaluation itself. Once adopted, protection is frequently maintained long after its initial cause (or justification) has passed. A return to currency equilibrium, or even "reverse overshooting" to undervalued levels, may not produce elimination of restrictions implemented to offset a previous overvaluation. Exchange rate oscillations may thus produce a ratchet effect on protection, raising it during (the inevitably reversible) periods of overvaluation but failing to undo it when equilibrium is restored.

* * *

THE IMPACT OF MISALIGNMENTS ON TRADE FLOWS

* * *

During the 1960s a number of studies attempted to estimate separately "exchange-rate elasticities" and "tariff elasticities," the former representing the impact on trade flows of exchange rate changes and the latter the impact of tariff changes. The stylized fact emerged that tariff elasticities were substantially larger, by a factor of two or three, than exchange rate elasticities. The usual explanation of this empirical regularity was the greater confidence presumably felt by traders that tariff changes would result in "permanent" changes in competitiveness.

In comparing the relative importance of tariff and exchange rate changes, however, it must be recognized that there has been a much greater degree of fluctuation in exchange rates than in tariffs during the postwar period. The celebrated trade liberalization of the Kennedy Round, for example, which is widely referred to as a 35 percent reduction, cut tariffs by an average of only 4–5 percentage points for the United States and European Economic Community (EEC) and about 7 percentage points for Japan and the United Kingdom. By contrast, real effective exchange rates frequently change by such amounts within very short periods of time—and remain further away from their underlying equilibrium paths (by as much as 10–20 percent) for extended episodes, as noted below. Hence the economic impact of exchange rate changes may at times substantially exceed the impact of tariff changes, even if tariff elasticities are in fact a good bit higher than exchange rate elasticities.

As to the future, tariffs remaining after the Multilateral Trade Negotiations (MTN) cuts will average about 4–6 percent in each of the major industrialized trading areas. Their complete elimination would then be overshadowed by the fluctuations which frequently occur, and the misalignments which periodically persist, in exchange rates. This is not to say that further trade liberalization would not be significant, of course, but that shifts in trade balances are likely to be more influenced by changes in exchange rates than in tariffs (although changes in other forms of protection may well be more important in certain sectors).

The evidence therefore indicates that changes in real effective exchange rates have significant effects on international trade flows—and, through trade, on key domestic economic variables such as output, employment and prices. Deardorff and Stern have made the following estimates of the effects of each percentage point of exchange rate change for the major trading areas (between the second quarters of 1980 and 1981):

Table 3.1 Effects of Exchange Rate Change, Major Trading Areas

	Price level (percentage)	Unemployment	Trade balance (dollars)
United States	0.3	70,000	3 billion
European Community	0.4	100,000	3 billion
Japan	0.5	40,000	1 billion

These estimates suggest that a 20 percent overvaluation could raise unemployment by 1.4 million in the United States or 2 million in Europe, while a similar undervaluation could add 6 percent to the price level in the United States, 8 percent in Europe and 10 percent in Japan.

Notes and Questions

(1) Assuming exchange rate "misalignments" will affect trade flows and increase protectionist pressures, the two key questions become: What causes misalignments and how significant are they? In order to measure misalignments, it is necessary to agree on the proper alignment, a difficult task. Economist John Williamson, one of the co-authors of the foregoing article, calculated his version of proper exchange rates for the English pound, French franc, West German mark, Japanese yen and U.S. dollar and concluded that in the period from 1976 to 1983, only the franc and the mark stayed within a band 10% above and below their proper rates. The pound was outside this 20% band about half of the time (mostly above, but also below for a short period). The yen was once above (1978) and twice below (1980 and 1982) and the dollar was above the band starting in 1981. Williamson ascribes most misalignment to market inefficiencies and macroeconomic policies, such as those pursued by the United States in the early 1980s, when he claims the use of monetary restraint to cool inflation, without complementary fiscal and incomes policies, led to abnormally high interest rates and an overvalued dollar. See J. Williamson, The Exchange Rate System (1983).

(2) The principal article notes some of the effects of misalignment, particularly those on prices and employment. If a firm's prices and costs vis à vis its foreign competitors are significantly affected by a misalignment, the firm may make incorrect decisions on whether to expand or contract output, etc. If the currency of the firm's country is overvalued, the firm may contract its operations too quickly and later have to re-expand them when the exchange rates are properly aligned. This will lead to considerable and unnecessary adjustment costs.

(3) Does the fact that exchange rate changes may play a more important role than tariffs in affecting trade suggest that tariff reduction is no longer a worthwhile goal for GATT?

(4) Would you expect the exchange rate uncertainty that necessarily exists when exchange rates are allowed to float would adversely affect trade because it increases the risks of international transactions (or increases the costs of avoiding the risks)? Economists disagree on the correct answer.[8]

SECTION 11.2 OPERATIONS OF THE INTERNATIONAL MONETARY FUND: INTERNATIONAL LIQUIDITY

The concept of "international liquidity" is important for the regulation of the international monetary system. To illustrate the problem of liquidity, suppose you own thousands of acres of land, but have no money in the bank. When the bills for your purchases of seed and fertilizer are received, you will find it difficult to pay those bills, even though you may be very rich. You are said to be "illiquid." One of the ways you could make yourself more

---

8. Compare R. Blackhurst & J. Tumlir, Trade Relations under Flexible Exchange Rates 12–34 (GATT Studies in Intl.Trade, No. 8, 1980) with Akhtar & Hilton, Effects of Exchange Rate Uncertainty on German and U.S. Trade, Federal Reserve Bank of New York Quarterly Review 7 (Spring 1984). See generally D. Bigman, Exchange Rate and Trade Instability: Causes, Consequences and Remedies (1983).

"liquid" would be to mortgage some of the land, borrowing cash which you would then keep in the bank so as to pay bills as they become due, replenishing this fund with receipts.

Governments and their economies also have bills which become due. In a simple case, if imports exceed exports, the foreign creditors will want to be paid in their currency or an accepted internationally used currency. (If the creditor accepts payment in the local currency, it will want to exchange it for other currencies.) The stocks of foreign currency held by nation are its "reserves."

If the nation wishes to maintain the value of its currency, then it needs to take various actions, one of which is to support its currency on the world exchange markets. To do this, a government uses its own reserves and goes to those markets and buys its currency (thus increasing the demand for its currency and putting an upward pressure on the price of that currency). It could also try, of course, to reduce the use of its currency for payments to foreigners, either by reducing imports or otherwise controlling payments to foreigners (for example, by imposing direct controls on capital transactions). Since it may not wish to interfere with various private transactions or may find that to do so can cause a number of other problems, the existence of reserves and liquidity becomes important to a nation in pursuing its international monetary policy. If it runs out of its own reserves, it may want to borrow reserves from other nations or international organizations, and use these for a period of time until market forces hopefully reverse themselves, and it is able to pay its international obligations.

One of the principal functions of the IMF is to provide liquidity to countries with liquidity or balance of payments problems. The purposes of the IMF are set out in its Articles of Agreement in Article I and Article IV (1) (see Documentary Supplement). The resources of the IMF are basically derived from the subscriptions (quotas) that the members are required to pay, and to a lesser degree from its borrowings. The IMF uses its resources under a variety of programs, which are described below. One of the more controversial issues surrounding the IMF is the extent to which it should attach conditions to its assistance. Because a commitment by the IMF to provide assistance is often insisted upon by international banks before they are willing to lend money to a country or restructure past loans, a country with liquidity problems may have no choice but to negotiate with the IMF.

IMF SURVEY: SUPPLEMENT ON THE FUND
5–9 (September 1985)

Members' quotas in the Fund, which at present amount to approximately SDR 89.3 billion, determine their subscription to the Fund, their drawing rights on the Fund under both regular and special facilities, and their share of any allocation of SDRs [Special Drawing Rights]; and they are closely related to their voting power.

Every Fund member is required to subscribe to the Fund an amount equal to its quota. An amount not exceeding 25 per cent of the quota has to be paid in reserve assets. The remainder is paid in the member's own currency. The voting power of a member is determined by 250 "basic votes" plus one vote for each SDR 100,000 of quota.

INCREASES IN QUOTAS. Reviews of quotas of Fund members are held at intervals of not more than five years to determine whether quotas should be increased to take into account the growth of the world economy and changes in relative economic positions among members.

* * *

QUOTAS OF NEW MEMBERS. For each country applying for membership, appropriate data on the economy are gathered and a calculated quota range is determined using the set of formulas that were agreed to in the latest general quota review. The calculated quota and the relevant data are then compared with those of existing members of comparable economic size and characteristics, and an appropriate quota is recommended. The recommended quota and the proportion in reserve assets in which the subscription is to be paid are considered by a committee of the Executive Board. After agreement with the country, the recommendations are then considered by the full Executive Board and a membership resolution is forwarded to the Fund's Board of Governors. After approval, the country signs the Articles of Agreement and becomes a member.

Members of the Fund may draw on its financial resources under "tranche" policies or the extended Fund facility to meet their balance of payments needs. In addition, there are two permanent facilities for specific purposes—the facility for compensatory financing of export fluctuations (established in 1963, liberalized in 1975 and 1979, and expanded in coverage in 1981 to compensate for fluctuations in cereal import costs) and the buffer stock financing facility (established in 1969).

Furthermore, members may make use of temporary facilities established by the Fund with borrowed resources. For 1974 and 1975, for example, following the sharp rise in oil prices, the Fund provided assistance under a temporary oil facility designed to help members meet the increased cost of imports of petroleum and petroleum products. In 1978, a supplementary financing facility was established with borrowed resources amounting to SDR 7,784 million from 13 member countries or their institutions, and the Swiss National Bank. In March 1981, a policy of enlarged access to the Fund's resources was adopted, allowing the Fund to continue to provide assistance on a scale similar to that under the supplementary financing facility. As of August 31, 1985, borrowing agreements amounting to SDR 15.3 billion had been concluded for this purpose.

This article describes the policies and principles governing members' access to the Fund's general resources under the tranche policies and the permanent facilities. For any purchase, a member is required to represent to the Fund that the desired purchase is needed because of its balance of payments or reserve position or developments in its reserves.

USE OF RESOURCES. When a member purchases from the Fund, it uses its own currency to purchase the currencies of other member countries or SDRs held by the General Resources Account of the Fund. Thus, a purchase results in an increase in the Fund's holdings of the purchasing member's currency and a corresponding decrease in the Fund's holdings of other currencies or SDRs that are sold. Within a prescribed time, a member must reverse the transaction, except for a reserve tranche purchase, by buying back its own currency with SDRs or currencies specified by the Fund. Usually repurchases are required to be made within three to five years after the date of purchase; but under the extended Fund facility, the period for repurchases is within four and a half to ten years, under the oil facility within three and a quarter to seven years, and under the supplementary financing facility and the enlarged access policy, within three and a half to seven years. In addition, a member is expected normally to repurchase as its balance of payments and reserve position improves and the Fund may convert this into an obligation.

RESERVE TRANCHE. If the Fund's holdings of a member's currency not derived from purchases under the facilities described above are less than its quota, the difference is called the reserve tranche. A member using Fund resources in the credit tranches has the option either to use or to retain a reserve tranche position. Purchases in the reserve tranche are subject to balance of payments need but not to challenge, nor are they subject to economic policy conditions, or to repurchase requirements.

CREDIT TRANCHES. Further purchases are made in four credit tranches, each equivalent to 25 per cent of the member's quota. In the past, the total of purchases under credit tranche policies was normally limited to 100 per cent of the member's quota, an amount that would raise the Fund's holdings of the member's currency to 200 per cent of its quota. However, in response to the need for the Fund to finance structural and deep-rooted payments imbalances that confront some members, the Fund is placing greater emphasis on programs involving adjustment periods of longer duration, and provision has been made for waiver of the 200 percent limit.

* * *

All requests for the use of the Fund's resources other than those of the reserve tranche are examined by the Fund's Executive Board to determine whether the proposed use would be consistent with the provisions of the Articles and with Fund policies. For all of these conditional uses, the request must be in support of economic measures designed to overcome a member's balance of payments difficulties. Prior to submission to the Fund of a request to purchase, either immediately or through a stand-by or extended arrangement, a member discusses with Fund staff its adjustment program, including fiscal, monetary, exchange rate, and trade and payments policies for the program period, which is usually the next 12 months but which may be extended up to three years in situations that call for adjustment efforts to be spread over a longer period. A member requesting a direct purchase receives the full amount immediately after approval of the request; under a stand-by or extended arrangement, a member may make the agreed purchases in installments during the period of the stand-by or extended arrangement.

Use of Fund resources in the first credit tranche, which may be appropriate when the payments deficit is relatively small, requires that the member demonstrate reasonable efforts to overcome its difficulties. Use of the first credit tranche may be requested either in the form of a direct purchase or under a stand-by arrangement.

Use of Fund resources in the upper credit tranches requires a member to adopt policies that give substantial assurance that the member's payments difficulties will be resolved within a reasonable period. Such use is almost always made under stand-by or extended arrangements.

The amount available under a stand-by arrangement in the upper credit tranches is phased to be available in portions at specified intervals during the stand-by period, and the member's right to draw is always subject to the observance of certain performance criteria described in the program or to a further review of the situation. The performance criteria typically cover credit policy, government or public sector borrowing requirements, and policy on trade and payments restrictions; they also frequently cover contracting or net use of short-, medium-, and long-term foreign debt, and changes in external reserves. Performance criteria allow both the member and the Fund to assess progress in the implementation of policies during the stand-by or extended arrangement. Any failure to observe the criteria prevents purchases until the Fund and the member determine whether further measures are necessary to achieve the objectives of the program. In this case, the member consults with the Fund in order to reach an understanding on any needed changes.

COMPENSATORY FINANCING. The compensatory financing facility was designed to extend the Fund's financial support to member countries—particular primary commodity exporting countries—encountering payments difficulties caused by temporary shortfalls in export proceeds. Members having a balance of payments need may draw on the Fund under this facility to compensate for such shortfalls, if the Fund is satisfied that the shortfall is temporary and is largely attributable to circumstances beyond the control of the member, and that the member will cooperate with the Fund in an effort to solve its balance of payments difficulties. * * *

The Fund decided in May 1981 to extend financial assistance to members that encounter a balance of payments difficulty caused by an excess in the cost of their cereal imports and presumed to be reversible within a few years. * * *

Purchases under the compensatory financing facility, whether for export shortfalls or for excesses in cereal import costs, as well as those under the buffer stock financing facility (see below), are additional to those which members may make under tranche policies. This means that a member may use the Fund's resources in an amount that could increase the Fund's holdings of its currency beyond 200 per cent of quota, with a waiver of that limit, and that the member's access under other policies is not limited because of these purchases. The provisions for repurchases applying to drawings under the compensatory financing and buffer stock facilities are generally the same as those for drawings under credit tranche policies.

BUFFER STOCK FINANCING. The purpose of the buffer stock financing facility is to assist in the financing of members' contributions to international buffer stocks of primary products when members having balance of payments difficulties participate in such arrangements under commodity agreements that meet appropriate criteria and conform with the principles laid down by the United Nations.

* * *

EXTENDED FUND FACILITY. Under the extended Fund facility, the Fund may provide assistance to members to meet their balance of payments deficits for longer periods and in amounts larger in relation to quotas than under the credit tranche policies. For example, a member might apply for assistance under the facility if it has serious payments imbalances relating to structural maladjustments in production, trade, and prices and if it intends to implement a comprehensive set of corrective policies for two or three years. Or, use of the facility might be indicated by an inherently weak balance of payment position that prevents the pursuit of an active development policy.

In requesting an extended arrangement, a member is expected to present a program setting for the objectives and policies for the whole period of the extended arrangement, as well as a detailed statement of the policies and measures that is will follow in each 12-month period to meet the objectives of the program. Purchases are phased and made subject to performance clauses relating to implementation of key policy measures. Drawings under extended arrangements may take place over periods of up to three years. Purchases outstanding under the extended facility may not exceed 140 per cent of the member's quota (or raise Fund holdings of a member's currency above 265 per cent of the member's quota, excluding holdings relating to compensatory financing and buffer stock financing). Purchases under the extended facility are additional to those a member may make under the first credit tranche. Repurchases under the extended facility must be made in 12 equal installments within four and a half to ten years after each purchase.

ENLARGED ACCESS POLICY. The enlarged access policy replaced the supplementary financing facility following the full commitment of the resources available under the latter. The purpose of this policy is to enable the Fund to provide supplementary financing, in conjunction with the use of the Fund's ordinary resources, to all members of the Fund facing serious payments imbalances that are large in relation to their quotas. The enlarged access policy is used, as was its predecessor, only when the member needs financing from the Fund that exceeds the amount available to it in the four credit tranches or under the extended Fund facility and when its problems require a relatively long period of adjustment. Such drawings are subject to the relevant policies of the Fund, including those on conditionality, phasing, and performance criteria. The period of such stand-by arrangements will normally exceed one year and may extend up to three years in appropriate cases.

The amount of assistance under this policy is determined according to guidelines adopted by the Fund from time to time. Present guidelines specify limits of 95–115 per cent of quota annually or 280–345 per cent over a three-year period; at the same time, a limit of 408–450 per cent of quota, net of scheduled repurchases, applies on the cumulative use of Fund resources. These limits, which may be exceeded in exceptional circumstances, exclude drawings under the compensatory and buffer stock financing facilities.

* * *

CHARGES FOR USE OF RESOURCES. The Fund applies charges for the use of its resources, except for reserve tranche purchases. A service charge of 0.5 per cent is payable on purchases other than reserve tranche purchases. The annual charge for an unpurchased amount under a stand-by or extended arrangement is .25 percent; in the case of extended arrangements, this charge is payable only on the amount that could be purchased during that year. In addition, the Fund levies charges on balances of members' currencies resulting from conditional purchases. The rate of charge on purchases in the four credit tranches and under the extended Fund facility, the compensatory financing facility, and the buffer stock financing facility is determined at the beginning of each financial year on the basis of the estimated income and expense of the Fund during the year and a target amount of net income. The rate of charge effective May 1, 1985, is 7.0 percent a year.

Note

At April 30, 1985, total Fund credit outstanding was SDR 35 billion, an increase from SDR 31.7 billion the previous year. Use of the Fund declined in 1984/85, however. Members drew SDR 6 billion compared to over SDR 10 billion in the two previous years.[1]

ACCESS TO RESOURCES FROM FUND AND USE OF STAND–BY ARRANGEMENTS

Decision of IMF Executive Board, March 2, 1979 [2]

1. Members should be encouraged to adopt corrective measures, which could be supported by use of the Fund's general resources in accordance with the Fund's policies, at an early stage of their balance of payments difficulties or as a precaution against the emergence of such difficulties. The Article IV consultations are among the occasions on which the Fund would be able to discuss with members adjustment programs, including corrective measures, that would enable the Fund to approve a stand-by arrangement.

2. The normal period for a stand-by arrangement will be one year. If, however, a longer period is requested by a member and considered necessary by the Fund to enable the member to implement its adjustment program successfully, the stand-by arrangement may extend beyond the period of one year. This period in appropriate cases may extend up to but not beyond three years.

3. Stand-by arrangements are not international agreements and therefore language having a contractual connotation will be avoided in stand-by arrangements and letters of intent.

1. IMF Survey: Supplement on the Fund, September 1985, at 1.

2. The text of the Decision is set out and each paragraph is commented upon in J. Gold,

Conditionality (1979). See also Pirzio-Biroli, Making Sense of the IMF Conditionality Debate, 17 J. World Trade L. 115 (1983).

4. In helping members to devise adjustment programs, the Fund will pay due regard to the domestic social and political objectives, the economic priorities, and the circumstances of members, including the causes of their balance of payments problems.

5. Appropriate consultation clauses will be incorporated in all stand-by arrangements. Such clauses will include provision for consultation from time to time during the whole period in which the member has outstanding purchases in the upper credit tranches. This provision will apply whether the outstanding purchases were made under a stand-by arrangement or in other transactions in the upper credit tranches.

6. Phasing and performance clauses will be omitted in stand-by arrangements that do not go beyond the first credit tranche. They will be included in all other stand-by arrangements but these clauses will be applicable only to purchases beyond the first credit tranche.

7. The Managing Director will recommend that the Executive Board approve a member's request for the use of the Fund's general resources in the credit tranches when it is his judgment that the program is consistent with the Fund's provisions and policies and that it will be carried out. A member may be expected to adopt some corrective measures before a stand-by arrangement is approved by the Fund, but only if necessary to enable the member to adopt and carry out a program consistent with the Fund's provisions and policies. In these cases the Managing Director will keep Executive Directors informed in an appropriate manner of the progress of discussions with the member.

8. The Managing Director will ensure adequate coordination in the application of policies relating to the use of the Fund's general resources with a view to maintaining the nondiscriminatory treatment of members.

9. The number and content of performance criteria may vary because of the diversity of problems and institutional arrangements of members. Performance criteria will be limited to those that are necessary to evaluate implementation of the program with a view to ensuring the achievement of its objectives. Performance criteria will normally be confined to (i) macroeconomic variables, and (ii) those necessary to implement specific provisions of the Articles or policies adopted under them. Performance criteria may relate to other variables only in exceptional cases when they are essential for the effectiveness of the member's program because of their macroeconomic impact.

10. In programs extending beyond one year, or in circumstances where a member is unable to establish in advance one or more performance criteria for all or part of the program period, provision will be made for a review in order to reach the necessary understandings with the member for the remaining period. In addition, in those exceptional cases in which an essential feature of a program cannot be formulated as a performance criterion at the beginning of a program year because of substantial uncertainties concerning major economic trends, provision will be made for a review by the Fund to evaluate the current macroeconomic policies of the member, and to reach new understandings if necessary. In these exception-

al cases the Managing Director will inform Executive Directors in an appropriate manner of the subject matter of a review.

11.   The staff will prepare an analysis and assessment of the performance under programs supported by use of the Fund's general resources in the credit tranches in connection with Article IV consultations and as appropriate in connection with further requests for use of the Fund's resources.

12.   The staff will from time to time prepare, for review by the Executive Board, studies of programs supported by stand-by arrangements in order to evaluate and compare the appropriateness of the programs, the effectiveness of the policy instruments, the observance of the programs, and the results achieved. Such reviews will enable the Executive Board to determine when it may be appropriate to have the next comprehensive review of conditionality.

SIR JOSEPH GOLD, FINANCIAL ASSISTANCE BY THE INTERNATIONAL MONETARY FUND: LAW AND PRACTICE

13–23 (2d ed. 1980)

* * * The Fund formulates the stand-by arrangement by reference to certain aspects of the letter of intent. The main purpose of this reference is to select those aspects of the program that are to be performance criteria and to ensure that the member will have access to the Fund's resources under the arrangement only if the performance criteria are being observed.

* * *

Performance criteria are as few as are necessary to provide both the Fund and a member reasonable evidence that the program is on course, but the observance of performance criteria is not irrefutable proof that the aims of the program are being achieved or that policies stated in the letter of intent but not incorporated in performance criteria are being followed. If a performance criterion is not being observed, the member will know without having to be told, and the Fund will know because of the periodic reporting of essential data by the member. In these circumstances, the right to make further purchases under the stand-by arrangement will be interrupted. Sometimes the right will revive if the member resumes observance of the performance criterion, but sometimes the right will revive only after a consultation is held between the Fund and the member in which understandings are reached on the advisability of maintaining the original performance criteria or of adapting them or other aspects of the program.

There is no single code of performance criteria for all cases. One performance criterion that is always used is a ceiling on the expansion of credit by the central bank or the banking system, supported in most cases by a ceiling on the expansion of bank credit to the government or the public sector. Balance of payments problems often arise from national overspending, so that it becomes necessary to ensure that aggregate demand for goods and services is brought into line with output. Ceilings on the expansion of domestic credit help to regulate aggregate demand and to enhance the effectiveness of financial policies, including the channeling of sufficient credit to meet the needs of the private sector. If the policies on credit could have detrimental effects on employment and growth, policies must be devised to encourage savings and investment as well as a proper direction of investment.

Almost all stand-by arrangements include performance criteria that deal with the avoidance of all restrictions on payments and transfers for current international transactions as well as restrictions on imports for balance of payments reasons. If existing restrictions have resulted in substantial arrears in payments for current international transactions, a schedule for the aggregate reduction of them may be established as a performance criterion. If external debt service is a present or prospective burden on the balance of payments of undue proportions, limits on the amount and maturity of new short- and medium-term debt may be made a performance criterion. If the exchange rate for the member's currency is not consistent with underlying economic conditions, a performance criterion may take the form of minimum levels of net foreign exchange reserves, the effect of which is to restrain the use of reserves in intervention in the exchange market to support the exchange rate.

The performance criteria that have been cited are not exhaustive. There are others that may be suitable to a member's circumstances. Flexibility is maintained not only to do what is most suitable in the circumstances of each member but also to gain experience in order to broaden the instruments of policy that can be recommended to members.

* * *

The stand-by arrangement and its offshoot, the extended arrangement, are unique legal instruments. * * * They are analogous to the movement away from the classical concept of a relationship between parties governed by a contract that is considered the complete and immutable law of the parties to a concept of a continuing and adaptable relationship, of which "hardship clauses," particularly in long-term contracts, are a symptom. The member's letter of intent and the Fund's decision (the stand-by arrangement) are parallel declarations, and although, unlike parallel lines, they meet this side of infinity, they do not constitute a contract between the member and the Fund. If the member departs from its policies and intentions as stated in its letter of intent, the Fund does not regard the departure as a violation of obligation even if, when a performance criterion is not being observed, the member cannot make further purchases until observance of the performance criterion has been resumed or the outcome of a consultation is known.

* * *

CONDITIONALITY

The fundamental and distinctive characteristic of the Fund's financial assistance is the Fund's doctrine of conditionality. Four strands are woven into it. First, to qualify for the use of the Fund's resources in order to deal with a balance of payments problem, a member must be prepared to pursue policies that are designed to overcome its problem. The policies are often referred to as policies of adjustment of the balance of payments or as a stabilization program. The objective of the program is a balance of payments position that can be sustained over a medium term such as five to eight years ahead. A member's willingness to undertake a program is not a concession to the Fund. Adjustment is inevitable for any member that does not have the means to neglect adjustment. The conditionality of the Fund helps a member to achieve adjustment with the financial, technical, and moral support of the Fund. Second, the policies must be consistent with the purposes of the Fund. For example, the policies should enable the member to avoid the introduction of restrictions on trade and payments for balance of payments purposes and if possible eliminate existing restrictions, because restrictions are likely to intensify and not correct the distortions that give rise to the need for adjustment, and are likely to be harmful to other members. Third, the policies must be designed to overcome the member's problem within a moderate ("temporary") period. Fourth, the policies must be likely to result in augmenting the member's monetary reserves so that it will be able to repurchase its currency from the Fund in accordance with the principle that use of the Fund's resources must be temporary in order that they can revolve for the benefit of all members.

*   *   *

The purpose of conditionality is not to change the basic character or the organization of a member's economy. For example, the degree to which the economy is under government ownership or control is accepted as part of the framework within which a program of adjustment must be made to fit. Similarly, the social objectives or priorities of a member are accepted as beyond negotiation, subject to the proviso that the policies to promote them will permit the member to achieve a sustainable balance of payments position. In short, the Fund does not seek to modify the political or social policies of a member. The character of the Fund is determined by its technical tasks, the principle of universal membership, and the uniform treatment of all members.

*   *   *

It is sometimes said that conditionality is progressively more severe as the amounts made available ascend through the upper credit tranches. This proposition is doubtful because conditionality always has the same objective, the conquest of a member's balance of payments difficulty. It could even be argued that in many instances conditionality is less severe when more resources are made available. It may be easier for a government to give effect to a program over a longer period. Stand-by or extended arrangements for the longer periods that have become a feature of the Fund's practice in recent years tend to be associated with substantial amounts in terms of quota. The apparent truism that more time means more ease is not always true, however, because a program for a longer period may require a perseverance that is politically difficult to maintain.

The word "harsh" is sometimes attached to particular operations involving conditionality. The inevitable determinant of the severity of a program, however it may be measured, is the intensity of a member's problem. Conditionality should be regarded as harsh only if it were to go beyond what was necessary to overcome a problem within the period that was reasonable in the circumstances, but this view does not mean that what is necessary in accordance with this criterion is always beyond controversy.

JOHN WILLIAMSON, THE LENDING POLICIES OF THE INTERNATIONAL MONETARY FUND

(1983) [3]

Little evidence has been found to support the main charges lodged against the Fund. The record of the programs studied by the conference [4] is not one of unqualified success, but the main shortcoming was the failure to secure a lasting switch of resources into the balance of payments, not excessive monetarism, overkill, inappropriate shock treatment, or ideological bias against socialism, as asserted by the left. Neither were the right-wing criticisms of the Fund found convincing. Indeed, the major point on which this study has faulted the Fund is its retreat from anticyclical policy—the tightening of its conditionality in the face of severe world recession.

Notes

(1) The likely continuation for the next few years of the so-called debt crisis facing a number of third-world countries, in particular Mexico, Brazil and Argentina, means the issue of conditionality will continue to draw considerable attention.

(2) Special drawing rights or SDRs were created as a result of the First Amendment to the IMF Articles of Agreement in 1969. They were described by the IMF in 1985 as follows: [5]

The SDR is an international reserve asset created by the Fund and allocated to its members as a supplement to existing reserve assets. The Fund has allocated a total of SDR 21.4 billion in six allocations, and holdings of SDRs by member countries amount to some 5 per cent of total non-gold reserves at the end of May 1985. All member countries of the Fund are participants in the SDR Department and are eligible to receive allocations. They may use SDRs in transactions and operations among themselves; with prescribed holders, of which there are now 14; and with the Fund itself. The SDR is the Fund's unit of account and certain commercial transactions and private financial obligations are denominated in SDRs. The valuation of the SDR is determined on the basis of a basket of five currencies—the U.S. dollar, the deutsche mark, the French franc, the Japanese yen, and the pound sterling. The SDR interest rate is based on yields of short-term obligations in the money markets of the same five countries whose currencies are used in valuation.

* * *

USE OF SDRs. Members with a balance of payments need may use SDRs to acquire foreign exchange in a transaction with designation—that is, ‥here another member, designated by the Fund, provides currency in exchange for SDRs. The Fund designates members to provide currency in exchange for SDRs on the basis of the strength of their balance of payments and reserve positions. However, a member's obligation to provide currency

3. ©1983, Institute for International Economics. Reproduced by permission from J. Williamson (ed.), IMF Conditionality 655.

4. The conference referred to, on the subject of IMF conditionality, was held at Airlie House, Virginia, March 24–26, 1982, under the sponsorship of the Institute for International Economics.

5. IMF Survey: Supplement on the Fund, September 1985, at 12.

does not extend beyond the point at which its holdings are three times its total allocations.

(3) The following is an IMF model form of stand-by arrangement.[6]

Form of Stand-By Arrangement Under Enlarged Access Policy

Attached hereto is a letter [, with annexed memorandum,] dated _____ from (Minister of Finance and/or Governor of Central Bank) requesting a stand-by arrangement and setting forth:

(a) the objectives and policies that the authorities of (member) intend to pursue for the period of this stand-by arrangement;

(b) the policies and measures that the authorities of (member) intend to pursue for the [first year] of this stand-by arrangement; and

(c) understandings of (member) with the Fund regarding [a] review[s] that will be made of progress in realizing the objectives of the program and of the policies and measures that the authorities of (member) will pursue for the remaining period of this stand-by arrangement.

To support these objectives and policies the International Monetary Fund grants this stand-by arrangement in accordance with the following provisions:

1. [For a period of __ years from _____] [For the period from _____ to _____] (member) will have the right to make purchases from the Fund in an amount equivalent to SDR _____, subject to paragraphs 2, 3, 4, and 5 below, without further review by the Fund.

2. (a) Until (end of first year) purchases under this stand-by arrangement shall not, without the consent of the Fund, exceed the equivalent of SDR _____, provided that purchases shall not exceed the equivalent of SDR _____ until _____, the equivalent of SDR _____ until _____, and the equivalent of SDR _____ until _____.

(b) The right of (member) to make purchases during the remaining period of this stand-by arrangement shall be subject to such phasing as shall be determined.

(c) None of the limits in (a) or (b) above shall apply to a purchase under this stand-by arrangement that would not increase the Fund's holdings of (member's) currency in the credit tranches beyond 25 per cent of quota or increase the Fund's holdings of that currency resulting from purchases of supplementary financing or borrowed resources beyond 12.5 per cent of quota.

3. Purchases under this stand-by arrangement shall be made from * * *, provided that any modification by the Fund of the proportions of ordinary and borrowed resources shall apply to amounts that may be purchased after the date of modification.

4. (Member) will not make purchases under this stand-by arrangement that would increase the Fund's holdings of (member's) currency in the credit tranches beyond 25 per cent of quota or increase the Fund's holdings of that currency resulting from purchases of supplementary financing or borrowed resources beyond 12.5 per cent of quota:

6. From J. Gold, Order in International Finance, the Promotion of IMF Stand-By Arrangements, and the Drafting of Private Loan Agreements 43–45 (IMF Pamphlet Series No. 39, 1982).

(a) during any period in the first year in which [the data at the end of the preceding period indicate that]

  (i) [the limit on domestic credit described in paragraph __ of the attached letter], or

  (ii) [the limit on credit to the public sector described in paragraph __ of the attached letter], or

  (iii) * * * [These provisions would incorporate other quantitative performance criteria of the program]

  are not observed, or

(b) if (member) fails to observe the limits on authorizations of new public and publicly guaranteed foreign indebtedness described in paragraph __ of the attached letter; or

(c) during the second or third year of this stand-by arrangement until suitable performance criteria have been established in consultation with the Fund as contemplated by paragraph __ of the attached letter, or after such performance criteria have been established, while they are not being observed;

(d) during the entire period of this stand-by arrangement, if (member)

  (i) imposes [or intensifies] restrictions on payments and transfers for current international transactions, or

  (ii) introduces [or modifies] multiple currency practices, or

  (iii) concludes bilateral payments agreements which are inconsistent with Article VIII, or

  (iv) imposes [or intensifies] import restrictions for balance of payments reasons.

When (member) is prevented from purchasing under this stand-by arrangement because of this paragraph 4, purchases will be resumed only after consultation has taken place between the Fund and (member) and understandings have been reached regarding the circumstances in which such purchases can be resumed.

5. (Member's) right to engage in the transactions covered by this stand-by arrangement can be suspended only with respect to requests received by the Fund after (a) a formal ineligibility, or (b) a decision of the Executive Board to suspend transactions, either generally or in order to consider a proposal, made by an Executive Director or the Managing Director, formally to suppress or to limit the eligibility of (member). When notice of a decision of formal ineligibility or of a decision to consider a proposal is given pursuant to this paragraph 5, purchases under this arrangement will be resumed only after consultation has taken place between the Fund and (member) and understandings have been reached regarding the circumstances in which such purchases can be resumed.

6. Purchases under this stand-by arrangement shall be made in the currencies of other members selected in accordance with the policies and procedures of the Fund, and may be made in SDRs if, on the request of (member), the Fund agrees to provide them at the time of the purchase.

7. The value date of a purchase under this stand-by arrangement involving borrowed resources will be normally either the fifteenth day or the last day of the month, or the next business day if the selected day is not a business day.

(Member) will consult the Fund on the timing of purchases involving borrowed resources.

8. (Member) shall pay a charge for this stand-by arrangement in accordance with the decisions of the Fund.

9. (a) (Member) shall repurchase the outstanding amount of its currency that results from a purchase under this stand-by arrangement in accordance with the provisions of the Articles of Agreement and decisions of the Fund, including those relating to repurchase as (member's) balance of payments and reserve position improves.

(b) Any reductions in (member's) currency held by the Fund shall reduce the amounts subject to repurchase under (a) above in accordance with the principles applied by the Fund for this purpose at the time of the reduction.

(c) The value date of a repurchase in respect of a purchase .:nanced with borrowed resources under this stand-by arrangement will be normally either the sixth day or the twenty-second day of the month, or the next business day if the selected day is not a business day, provided that repurchase will be completed not later than seven years from the date of purchase.

10. During the period of the stand-by arrangement (member) shall remain in close consultation with the Fund. These consultations may include correspondence and visits of officials of the Fund to (member) or of representatives of (member) to the Fund. (Member) shall provide the Fund, through reports at intervals or dates requested by the Fund, with such information as the Fund requests in connection with the progress of (member) in achieving the objectives and policies set forth in the attached letter [and annexed memorandum].

11. In accordance with paragraph __ of the attached letter (member) will consult the Fund on the adoption of any measures that may be appropriate at the initiative of the government or whenever the Managing Director requests consultation

Version A

[because any of the criteria in paragraph 4 above have not been observed or because he considers that consultation on the program is desirable. In addition, after the period of the arrangement and while (member) has outstanding purchases in the upper credit tranches, the government will consult with the Fund from time to time, at the initiative of the government or at the request of the Managing Director, concerning (member's) balance of payments policies.]

Version B

[because he considers that consultation on the program is desirable].

(4) The IMF normally does not publish arrangements actually entered into. They are occasionally published in the country with whom the IMF negotiated. A list of published IMF agreements is contained in R. Edwards, International Monetary Collaboration 251 n. 142 (1985). Edwards publishes the 1981 Arrangement with India. Id. at 251–63. India's Arrangement followed the outline of the IMF form. In its Statement of Economic Policies submitted to the Fund, India outlined its economic plans for the near future. Although many of the plans were outlined only in general terms and were stated to represent present intentions, there were specific commitments in respect of monetary policy

(actions to contain the liquidity of commercial banks and to reduce their loanable funds), ceilings on net credit to government and total domestic credit (the government was to aim at limiting the growth of total liquidity to about 15.7 percent in 1981/82 and domestic credit expansion to 19.4 percent and was to take corrective measures promptly if such ceilings appeared likely to be exceeded) and ceilings on external borrowing and external debt (the government was to limit, with specified exceptions, the contracting or guaranteeing of one to twelve year loans to SDR 1.4 billion, and to limit new one to five year commitments to SDR 400 million).

Problems

Consider the following problems in the light of the materials above, and the IMF Articles of Agreement in the Documentary Supplement.

(1) You have been retained by the Ministry of Development and Finance and the Ministry of Foreign Affairs of a small African nation named Vanzia, a member of the IMF, with a quota of 36 million United States dollars. IMF now holds 30 million dollars' worth of Vanzia currency. Vanzia has been running a deficit on its balance of payments for the last four quarters, amounting to an annual deficit of 50 million United States dollars, because of a drastic decline in the world market price of cocoa, one of Vanzia's principal exports. Vanzia's reserves are now dangerously low and it must take drastic action if its imports of vitally needed machinery are to continue. The Ministry of Development and Finance has put forth a series of proposals, and asks you to evaluate these proposals in the light of the international legal obligations of Vanzia and its trading partners.

(a) Vanzia desires to draw 40 million United States dollars from the IMF. Can it do so? How much can it draw? How does it obtain this right? Suppose some of the dollars were intended to be used by the Ministry for the purchase of machinery for a candy factory? (IMF Article V.)

(b) Vanzia desires to borrow 50 million dollars to obtain foreign exchange to import the necessary foreign machinery for a new candy factory. A bank in the United States was willing to loan the money, but declined on the grounds that the United States Government forbade it. If this were true, has the United States violated any international obligation towards Vanzia? (IMF Article VI.)

(c) Vanzia's currency, the "bobble," now has a value of 20 to the dollar. Can Vanzia act to reduce its value? (IMF Article IV.)

(2) One of the essential machines needed in Vanzia for its development plan is widgets. The Trans-Vanzia Preparation Company has approached the Golddust Mfg. Co. to place a large order of widgets, and plans to buy more. This approach, and United States tax considerations, have led Golddust to consider setting up a branch or corporate subsidiary in Vanzia, and possibly even attempting to manufacture widgets there. Golddust asks your opinion as to the probability of being able to repatriate such profits as it might earn in Vanzia during the next few years.

(3) Suppose Vanzia entered into a stand-by agreement with the Fund. How would that agreement be enforced?

SECTION 11.3 INTERNATIONAL AND NATIONAL REGULATION OF FOREIGN EXCHANGE RESTRICTIONS

(A) OBLIGATIONS UNDER THE IMF AGREEMENT [1]

(1) Restrictions on Foreign Exchange Transactions

Article VIII of the Articles of Agreement of the International Monetary Fund contains a series of obligations regarding what a national government may do in restricting foreign exchange transactions. Basically, it contains obligations requiring member countries to avoid the use of discriminatory currency practices and to avoid restrictions on "current payments." On the other hand, restrictions on capital payments are not prohibited. Examination of the text of the Articles, in the light of the following hypothetical cases, should help demonstrate how they apply:

(1) Vanzia would like to require all payments to persons outside the country to be subject to prior permission of the Ministry of Development and Finance, under a licensing law. Can it do so? (IMF Article VIII.)

(2) Vanzia contemplates entering into a bilateral trade and payments arrangement with Xonia, envisaging the setting up of an account in Vanzia through which payments for specified trade items between the two countries must be made, and prohibiting the payment for specified goods except through that account. What international obligations of Vanzia would be involved? (IMF Article VIII.)

(3) Vanzia has considered selling foreign currency (or foreign exchange) at a favored rate equivalent to $1 United States dollar for only 10 bobbles, to those importers importing goods designated as "vital to the 7-year development plan." Can it do so? (IMF Article VIII.)

(4) In addition, Vanzia is considering several restrictions on imports, including: i) raising tariffs; ii) placing import quotas on non-essential goods; iii) placing an internal sales tax on certain goods if they have been imported. Do any of these measures involve the IMF? (See Section 11.4 infra.)

(2) Maintenance of a Stable System of Exchange Rates

IMF members are obligated by Article IV of the IMF Agreement to collaborate with the Fund and with other members in order to assure orderly exchange arrangements and to promote a stable system of exchange rates. To oversee compliance with those obligations, the IMF exercises surveillance over the exchange rate policies of members and adopts specific principles for their guidance. In a decision on "Surveillance over Exchange Rate Policies," the Executive Board enunciated three general principles: [2]

1. In addition to references cited elsewhere in this chapter, see H. Aufricht, The Fund Agreement: Living Law and Emerging Practice, Princeton Studies in International Finance No. 23 (1969); G. Verbit, International Monetary Reform and the Developing Countries: The Rule of Law Problem (1975); Meier, The Bretton Woods Agreement—Twenty-five Years After, 23 Stan.L.Rev. 235 (1971); Diebold, The Economic System at Stake, 51 Foreign Affairs 167 (1972).

2. IMF Survey: Supplement on the Fund, September 1985, at 10.

A. A member shall avoid manipulating exchange rates or the international monetary system in order to prevent effective balance of payments adjustment or to gain an unfair competitive advantage over other members.

B. A member should intervene in the exchange market if necessary to counter disorderly conditions which may be characterized inter alia by disruptive short-term movements in the exchange value of its currency.

C. Members should take into account in their intervention policies the interests of other members, including those of the countries in whose currencies they intervene.

In September 1985, the United States, France, Germany, Great Britain and Japan agreed to take certain actions designed to reduce the value of the U.S. dollar, which was viewed as being overvalued. Within one month, the effect of their actions had been to reduce the value of the dollar by 10.8 percent vis a vis the Japanese yen and seven percent vis a vis the German mark (see 2 BNA Intl.Trade Rptr. 1182, 1378 (1985)).

(B) THE OECD LIBERALISATION CODES AND THE TREATY OF ROME

As noted in the preceding subsection, the IMF Agreement only limits national restrictions on payments and transfers for current international transactions. Given the diversity of the IMF membership, the IMF Agreement could not reasonably be expected to do more. The advanced industrialized countries, however, have tried to agree among themselves on more stringent limitations on national foreign exchange restrictions.

These efforts have been sponsored by the Organization for Economic Cooperation and Development (OECD), one of the goals of which is to "reduce or abolish obstacles to the exchange of goods and services and current payments and maintain and extend the liberalisation of capital movements." To this end, the OECD has adopted a Code of Liberalisation of Capital Movements and a Code of Liberalisation of Current Invisible Operations.[3] Adherents basically commit themselves to authorize certain specified transactions and to work to liberalize any remaining restrictions. There are broad exceptions to the Codes, allowing derogations if the economic and financial situation of the country justifies them. In addition, many countries adhere to the Codes with reservations. Nonetheless, the fact that the adherents are committed to liberalization and that national restrictions receive international scrutiny on a regular basis has probably played an important role in the gradual liberalization of exchange controls that has occurred in recent years.

The Treaty of Rome, which established the EEC in 1957, contains significant provisions on the use of controls on foreign exchange. Essentially the Treaty calls for the elimination of restrictions on capital movements and related current payments between member states (Article 67). The member states also commit themselves to try to avoid imposing any new restrictions (Article 71). The liberalization of current payments is provided

3. The current versions of each Code are published and updated regularly by the OECD.

for in Article 106. The Treaty also has provisions on coordination of economic policies so as to avoid balance of payments disequilibria (Articles 104 and 105). As noted earlier, the EC has established the European Monetary System, which provides for a managed float of eight member state currencies (not currently included are the currencies of Greece, Portugal, Spain and the United Kingdom). It has also created a monetary unit, the European Currency Unit, or ECU, the value of which is determined by the values of member state currencies.[4]

(C) NATIONAL EXCHANGE CONTROLS

Some governments have controls on payments to be received from abroad by a resident or citizen, or be made abroad by residents or citizens. Those controls are usually quite elaborate since to avoid evasion they must cover all conceivable economic transactions between those subject to the controls and the rest of the world—from simple cash transfers to property exchanges to complex swap or barter arrangements. The IMF publishes an annual report on exchange restrictions, which gives a brief summary of the various exchange controls law then in effect.

In recent years, most major countries have not imposed significant controls on transactions in foreign exchange. The principal exception was the United Kingdom, where controls were not abolished until 1979.

In the 1960's and early 1970's, the United States took a number of actions designed to control capital flows. For example, as a response to its balance of payments difficulties during the 1960's, the United States introduced or enlarged programs to expand exports and reduced its outlays abroad.[5] In addition, it introduced measures to restrain outflows of U.S. private capital. In particular, it introduced in the middle of 1966 an Interest Equalization Tax (IET) on the value of foreign securities bought by U.S. residents, to try to discourage such purchases. In addition, in 1965 a series of voluntary guidelines to commercial banks and business corporations was issued by the Federal Reserve System and the Department of Commerce, encouraging them to restrain loans and investments abroad. In 1968, the voluntary measures were replaced by mandatory investment controls.

After the floating of the dollar, and the other 1971 measures which resulted in a flexible exchange rate system, the measures introduced in the 1960's were considered no longer necessary, and during 1974 the three measures mentioned above: 1) the Interest Equalization Tax; 2) the Department of Commerce Foreign Direct Investment controls, administered by the Office of Foreign Direct Investments; and 3) the Federal Reserve Board "Voluntary Foreign Credit Restraint Program (VFCRP)," were all discontinued.[6] Consequently in 1976, the IMF was able to report for the United States that,

---

4. See generally R. Edwards, International Monetary Collaboration 315–46 (1985). The Annual Reports of the Commission on the Activities of the European Communities report developments each year in the EC's efforts to limit exchange restrictions and develop the European Monetary System.

5. See F. Root, International Trade and Investment 173–79 (5th ed. 1984).

6. See 26th Annual Report on Exchange Restrictions, International Monetary Fund, 1975, at 501–02.

Incoming or outgoing capital payments by residents or nonresidents are not subject to exchange control. In addition, inward and outward direct or portfolio investment are generally free of any other form of approval requirements, although in certain instances compliance with specified banking regulations may be required; with a few exceptions for national security reasons or to protect vital national interests, the United States does not impose special restrictions on inward investment.[7]

(D) PRIVATE RELIANCE ON THE IMF AGREEMENT

Article VIII, section 2, of the IMF Agreement reads as follows:

"Section 2. *Avoidance of restrictions on current payments*

(a) Subject to the provisions of Article VII, Section 3(b), and Article XIV, Section 2, no member shall, without the approval of the Fund, impose restrictions on the making of payments and transfers for current international transactions.

(b) Exchange contracts which involve the currency of any member and which are contrary to the exchange control regulations of that member maintained or imposed consistently with this Agreement shall be unenforceable in the territories of any member. In addition, members may, by mutual accord, cooperate in measures for the purpose of making the exchange control regulations of either member more effective, provided that such measures and regulations are consistent with this Agreement."

This provision has been relied upon occasionally in private litigation, as the cases below illustrate.

BANCO DO BRASIL v. A.C. ISRAEL COMMODITY CO., INC.

Court of Appeals of New York, 1963.
190 N.E.2d 235, cert. denied, 376 U.S. 906, 84 S.Ct. 657, 11 L.Ed.2d 605.

BURKE, JUDGE.

The action upon which the attachment here challenged is based is brought by appellant as an instrumentality of the Government of Brazil to recover damages for a conspiracy to defraud the Government of Brazil of American dollars by illegally circumventing the foreign exchange regulations of Brazil.

Defendant-respondent, Israel Commodity, a Delaware corporation having its principal place of business in New York, is an importer of Brazilian coffee. The gist of plaintiff's complaint is that Israel conspired with a Brazilian exporter of coffee to pay the exporter American dollars which the exporter could sell in the Brazilian free market for 220 Brazilian cruzeiros each instead of complying with Brazil's foreign exchange regulations which in effect required a forced sale of the dollars paid to the exporter to the Government of Brazil for only 90 cruzeiros. Through this conspiracy, the Brazilian exporter profited by the difference between the amount (in

7. 27th Annual Report on Exchange Restrictions, International Monetary Fund, 1976, at 478.

cruzeiros) it would have received for the dollars from the Government of Brazil and the amount it received in the open market in violation of Brazilian law, Israel profited by being able to pay less dollars for the coffee (because the dollars were worth so much more to the seller), and the plaintiff suffered a loss measured by the difference in amount it would have to pay for the same number of dollars in the open market and what it could have paid for them through the "forced sale" had its foreign exchange regulations been obeyed. The evasion was allegedly accomplished through the exporter's forgery of the documents evidencing receipt of the dollars by plaintiff Banco Do Brasil, S.A., and without which the coffee could not have left Brazil.

Plaintiff argues that respondent's participation in the violation of Brazilian exchange control laws affords a ground of recovery because of article VIII (§ 2, subd. [b]) of the Bretton Woods Agreement, a multilateral treaty to which both this country and Brazil are signatories. The section provides: "Exchange contracts which involve the currency of any member and which are contrary to the exchange control regulations of that member maintained or imposed consistently with this Agreement shall be unenforceable in the territories of any member." (60 U.S.Stat. 1411.) It is far from clear whether this sale of coffee is covered by subdivision (b) of section 2. The section deals with "exchange contracts" which "involve" the "currency" of any member of the International Monetary Fund, "and ∗ ∗ ∗ are contrary to the exchange control regulations of that member maintained or imposed consistently with" the agreement. Subdivision (b) of section 2 has been construed as reaching only "transactions which have as their immediate object 'exchange,' that is, international media of payment" (Nussbaum, Exchange Control and the International Monetary Fund, 59 Yale L.J. 421, 426), or a contract where the consideration is payable in the currency of the country whose exchange controls are violated (Mann, The Exchange Control Act, 1947, 10 Mod.L.Rev. 411, 418). More recently, however, it has been suggested that it applies to "contracts which in any way affect a country's exchange resources" (Mann, The Private International Law of Exchange Control Under the International Monetary Fund Agreement, 2 International and Comp.L.Q. 97, 102; Gold and Lachman, The Articles of Agreement of the International Monetary Fund and the Exchange Control Regulations of Member States, Journal du Droit International, Paris (July-Sept., 1962). A similar view has been advanced to explain the further textual difficulty existing with respect to whether a sale of coffee in New York for American dollars "involves the currency" of Brazil, the member whose exchange controls were allegedly violated. Again it is suggested that adverse effect on the exchange resources of a member *ipso facto* "involves" the "currency" of that member (Gold and Lachman, op. cit.). We are inclined to view an interpretation of subdivision (b) of section 2 that sweeps in all contracts affecting any members' exchange resources as doing considerable violence to the text of the section. It says "involve the currency" of the country whose exchange controls are violated; not "involve the exchange resources". While noting these doubts, we nevertheless prefer to rest this decision on other and clearer grounds.

The sanction provided in subdivision (b) of section 2 is that contracts covered thereby are to be "unenforceable" in the territory of any member. The clear import of this provision is to insure the avoidance of the affront inherent in any attempt by the courts of one member to render a judgment that would put the losing party in the position of either complying with the judgment and violating the exchange controls of another member or complying with such controls and refusing obedience to the judgment. A further reasonable inference to be drawn from the provision is that the courts of no member should award any recovery for breach of an agreement in violation of the exchange controls of another member. Indeed, the International Monetary Fund itself, in an official interpretation of subdivision (b) of section 2 issued by the Fund's Executive Directors, construes the section as meaning that "the obligations of such contracts will not be implemented by the judicial or administrative authorities of member countries, for example, by decreeing performance of the contracts or by awarding damages for their non-performance". (International Monetary Fund Ann.Rep. 82–83 [1949], 14 Fed.Reg. 5208, 5209 [1949].) An obligation to withhold judicial assistance to secure the benefits of such contracts does not imply an obligation to impose tort penalties on those who have fully executed them.

From the viewpoint of the individuals involved, it must be remembered that the Bretton Woods Agreement relates to international law. It imposes obligations among and between States, not individuals. The fact that by virtue of the agreement New York must not "enforce" a contract between individuals which is contrary to the exchange controls of any member, imposes no obligation (under the law of the transaction—New York law *) on such individuals not to enter into such contracts. While it does mean that they so agree at their peril inasmuch as they may not look to our courts for enforcement, this again is far from implying that one who so agrees commits a tort in New York for which he must respond in damages. It is significant that a proposal to make such an agreement an "offense" was defeated at Bretton Woods. (1 Proceedings and Documents of the United Nations Monetary and Financial Conference 334, 341, 502, 543, 546—referred to in Nussbaum, Exchange Control and the International Monetary Fund, 59 Yale L.J. 421, 426, 429, supra.)

Lastly, and inseparable from the foregoing, there is a remedial consideration which bars recovery in this case. Plaintiff is an instrumentality of the Government of Brazil and is seeking, by use of an action for conspiracy to defraud, to enforce what is clearly a revenue law. Whatever may be the effect of the Bretton Woods Agreement in an action on "A contract made in a foreign country between citizens thereof and intended by them to be there performed" (see Perutz v. Bohemian Discount Bank in Liquidation, 304 N.Y. 533, 537, 110 N.E.2d 6, 7), it is well established since the day of Lord Mansfield (Holman v. Johnson, 1 Cowp. 341, 98 E.R. 1120 [1775]) that one State does not enforce the revenue laws of another. (Government of India v. Taylor, 1 All.E.R. 292 [1955]; City of Philadelphia v. Cohen, 11 N.Y.2d 401, 230 N.Y.S.2d 188, 184 N.E.2d 167; 1 Oppenheim, International Law, § 144b

---

* All of respondent's acts allegedly in furtherance of the conspiracy took place in New York where it regularly did business.

[Lauterpacht ed., 1947].) Nothing in the Bretton Woods Agreement is to the contrary. In fact its use of the unenforcibility device for effectuation of its purposes impliedly concedes the unavailability of the more direct method of enforcement at the suit of the aggrieved government. By the second sentence of subdivision (b) of section 2, further measures to make exchange controls more effective may be agreed upon by the member States. This is a matter for the Federal Government which not only has not entered into such further accords but has not even enacted the enabling provision into law (U.S.Code, tit. 22, § 286h).

Therefore, the order should be affirmed and the certified questions answered no and yes respectively.

CHIEF JUDGE DESMOND (dissenting).

The order should be reversed and the warrant of attachment reinstated since the complaint alleges a cause of action within the jurisdiction of the New York State courts.

If there had never been a Bretton Woods Agreement and if this were a suit to enforce in this State the revenue laws of Brazil it would have to be dismissed under the ancient rule most recently restated in City of Philadelphia v. Cohen, 11 N.Y.2d 401, 230 N.Y.S.2d 188, 184 N.E.2d 167. But Cohen and its predecessor cases express a public policy which lacks applicability here because of the adherence of the United States to the Bretton Woods Agreement. As we noted in Perutz v. Bohemian Discount Bank in Liquidation, 304 N.Y. 533, 537, 110 N.E.2d 6, 7, the membership of our Federal Government in the International Monetary Fund and other Bretton Woods enterprises makes it impossible to say that the currency control laws of other member States are offensive to our public policy. Furthermore, the argument from City of Philadelphia v. Cohen (supra) and similar decisions assumes erroneously that this is a suit to collect internal taxes assessed by the Brazilian Government. In truth, it is not even an effort to enforce Brazil's currency regulations. This complaint and other papers charge a tortious fraud and conspiracy to deprive plaintiff, an instrumentality of the Brazilian Government, of the dollar proceeds of coffee exports to which proceeds the bank and its government were entitled. This fraud, it is alleged, was accomplished by inserting in coffee shipping permits references to nonexistent exchange contracts and to nonexistent assignments to plaintiff of the foreign exchange proceeds of the coffee exports and by forging the signatures of banking officials and Brazilian officials, all with the purpose of making it appear that there had been compliance with the Brazilian statutes or regulations. The alleged scheme and effect of the conspiracy as charged was to obtain for defendant-respondent coffee in New York at a reduced price, to enable the Brazilian defendants to get more "cruzeiros" per dollar in violation of law and to deprive Brazil of the cruzeiros which it would have received from these coffee sales had the fraud not been committed. According to the complaint and affidavits defendant Israel not only knew of and intended to benefit by the perpetration of this fraud but participated in it in New York by making its purchase agreements here and by here receiving the shipping documents and making payments. The Israel corporation is alleged to have been one of the consignees of some 36,000 bags of coffee exported from Brazil to New York in 1961 without compliance with the Brazilian law and thus to have fraudulently and conspiratorially caused to Brazil damage of nearly $2,000,000. Refusal to entertain this suit does violence to our national policy of co-operation with other Bretton Woods signatories and is not required by anything in our own State policy.

VAN VOORHIS, FOSTER and SCILEPPI, JJ., concur with BURKE, J.

DESMOND, C.J., dissents in an opinion in which DYE and FULD, JJ., concur.

BANCO FRANCES e BRASILEIRO S.A. v. DOE

Court of Appeals of New York, 1975.
36 N.Y.2d 592, 370 N.Y.S.2d 534, 331 N.E.2d 502, cert. denied, 423 U.S. 867, 96 S.Ct. 129, 46 L.Ed.2d 96.

JASEN, JUDGE.

The principal question before us is whether a private foreign bank may avail itself of the New York courts in an action for damages for tortious fraud and deceit and for rescission of currency exchange contracts arising from alleged violations of foreign currency exchange regulations.

Plaintiff, a private Brazilian bank, brings this action for fraud and deceit, and conspiracy to defraud and deceive, against 20 "John Doe" defendants whose identities are unknown to it. The gravamen of plaintiff's complaint is that these defendants over a period of approximately six weeks participated, in violation of Brazilian currency regulations, in the submission of false applications to Banco-Brasileiro of Brazil, which the plaintiff relied upon, resulting in the improper exchange by the bank of Brazilian cruzeiros into travelers checks in United States dollars totaling $1,024,000. A large amount of the fraudulently obtained travelers checks were deposited by defendant "John Doe No. 1" in an account having a code name of "Alberta" at Bankers Trust Company, New York. Other of such travelers checks were deposited by defendant "John Doe No. 2" in an account having the code name of "Samso" at Manfra Tordella & Brookes, Inc., New York. An order of attachment was granted at Special Term against the property of defendants John Doe No. 1 and John Doe No. 2 held by Bankers Trust and Manfra Tordella & Brookes, Inc. Service of summons by publication was authorized by Special Term.

Subsequent to the granting of the order of attachment and the service of the summons by publication, motions were made by the plaintiff for disclosure from Bankers Trust Co. and Manfra Tordella & Brookes of the true names and addresses of John Doe Nos. 1 and 2 and to direct the attorney for defendant John Doe No. 1 to disclose the true name(s) and address(es) of defendant(s) and the basis of the attorney's authority to act, or, in the alternative, to vacate his appearance in the action. The defendant John Doe No. 1, by way of order to show cause, moved to vacate the order of attachment, to dismiss plaintiff's complaint and to intervene in the motion of plaintiff for disclosure from Bankers Trust Co. so as to defend against the disclosure.

Special Term, *inter alia,* denied the motion to vacate the order of attachment and to dismiss the complaint except as to the third cause of action for damages which was dismissed for failure to plead actual damages. Motions for ancillary relief—for discovery and inspection and for disclosure from the attorney for defendant "John Doe No. 1" of the name and address of his client—were granted.

On cross appeals, the Appellate Division, by a unanimous court (44 A.D. 2d 353, 355 N.Y.S.2d 145), relying on Banco do Brasil v. Israel Commodity Co., 12 N.Y.2d 371, 239 N.Y.S.2d 872, 190 N.E.2d 235, cert. den. 376 U.S. 906, 84 S.Ct. 657, 11 L.Ed.2d 605, modified by granting defendants' motion to dismiss the complaint and denying all applications for ancillary relief on the ground that the New York courts were not open to an action arising from a tortious violation of foreign currency regulations.

Plaintiff bank appeals as of right to this court. (CPLR 5601, subd. [a].) We are unable to assent to the decision of the Appellate Division and, accordingly, modify the order appealed from by reinstating the order of attachment and the first two causes of action, with leave to plaintiff, if so advised, to apply to Special Term for permission to serve a supplemental pleading alleging special damages in its third cause of action for damages, and by granting the ancillary relief requested to the extent hereafter specified.

It is an old chestnut in conflict of laws that one State does not enforce the revenue laws of another. * * * But the modern analog of the revenue law rule is justifiable neither precedentially nor analytically.

* * *

In the international sphere, cases involving foreign currency exchange regulations represent perhaps the most important aspect of the revenue law rule. This assumes, of course, that a currency exchange regulation, normally not designed for revenue purposes as such, but rather, to prevent the loss of foreign currency which in turn increases the country's foreign exchange reserves, is properly characterizable as a revenue law. * * *

But even assuming the continuing validity of the revenue law rule and the correctness of the characterization of a currency exchange regulation thereunder, United States membership in the International Monetary Fund (IMF) makes inappropriate the refusal to entertain the instant claim. The view that nothing in article VIII (§ 2, subd. [b]) of the Bretton Woods Agreement Act (60 U.S.Stat. 1401, 1411) requires an American court to provide a forum for a private tort remedy, while correct in a literal sense (see Banco do Brasil v. Israel Commodity Co., supra, p. 376, 239 N.Y.S.2d p. 874, 190 N.E.2d p. 236), does not represent the only perspective. Nothing in the agreement prevents an IMF member from aiding, directly or indirectly, a fellow member in making its exchange regulations effective. And United States membership in the IMF makes it impossible to conclude that the currency control laws of other member States are offensive to this State's public policy so as to preclude suit in tort by a private party. Indeed, conduct reasonably necessary to protect the foreign exchange resources of a country does not offend against international law. (Restatement, Second, Foreign Relations Law of the United States, § 198, comment b.) Moreover, where a true governmental interest of a friendly nation is involved—and foreign currency reserves are of vital importance to a country plagued by balance of payments difficulties—the national policy of co-operation with Bretton Woods signatories is furthered by providing a State forum for suit.

The *Banco do Brasil* case relied upon by the Appellate Division is quite distinguishable.

* * *

There the Government of Brazil, through Banco do Brasil, a government bank, sought redress for violations of its currency exchange regulations incident to a fraudulent coffee export transaction. Here, the plaintiff is a private bank seeking rescission of the fraudulent currency exchange transactions and damages. And no case has come to our attention where a private tort remedy arising from foreign currency regulations has been denied by the forum as an application of the revenue law rule and we decline so to extend the *Banco do Brasil* rationale. Thus, in the instant case we find no basis for reliance upon the revenue law rule to deny a forum for suit. Moreover, where the parties are private, the "jealous sovereign" rationale is inapposite (cf. Loucks v. Standard Oil Co., 224 N.Y. 99, 102–103, 120 N.E. 198, 199 [Cardozo, J.]) even as it might seem inapposite in the *Banco do Brasil* situation where the sovereign itself, or its instrumentality, asks redress and damages in a foreign forum for violation of the sovereign's currency laws. (But cf. Moore v. Mitchell, 2 Cir., 30 F.2d 600, 603 [L. Hand, J., concurring].)

Accordingly, the order of the Appellate Division should be modified in accordance with the views here expressed and the action remitted to the Supreme Court, New York County.

W ACHTLER, J UDGE (dissenting).

We are asked to determine when claims between private parties which spring from jural relationships created by the laws of a foreign country, here Brazil, may be enforced in our courts. The issue turns on the essential nature of the rights and obligations sought to be enforced as the forum court characterizes them. As stated by the United States Supreme Court: "The test is not by what name the statute is called by the legislature or the courts of the State in which it was passed, but whether it appears, to the tribunal which is called upon to enforce it, to be, in its essential character and effect, a punishment of an offense against the public, or a grant of a civil right to a private person."

* * *

It has long been recognized that the courts of one jurisdiction will not enforce the tax laws, penal laws, or statutory penalties and forfeitures of another jurisdiction. * * *

In previous cases our court held that governmental foreign exchange regulation may present an aspect of the exercise of sovereign power by a foreign State to implement its national fiscal policy. Thus, in Banco do Brasil v. Israel Commodity Co. (supra), we decided that our courts were not open to enforce a Brazilian foreign currency exchange regulation. Although the regulation in that case was characterized as a revenue measure, the essence of the matter was that we declined to enforce what we considered to be an exercise of Brazil's sovereign power. Whether a regulation denominated "currency exchange regulation" has or does not have a revenue-producing effect, it must be presumed to have been adopted to accomplish fiscal regulation and ultimate economic objectives significantly similar to, if not identical with, the objectives which underlie what would be characterized as revenue measures—namely, governmental management of its economy by a foreign country. Accordingly, the result is not determined by the threshold appearance of the particular law sought to be enforced or whether such law be denominated by the foreign government as a penal law or a revenue law or otherwise. The bottom line is that the courts of one country will not enforce the laws adopted by another country in the exercise of its sovereign capacity for the purpose of fiscal regulation and management.

*   *   *

Nothing in the Bretton Woods Agreements Act or in any other agreement between the United States and Brazil of which we are aware, however, mandates a complete abrogation of the normal conflicts rule or requires our courts *affirmatively* to enforce foreign currency regulation, as we are invited to do in the present case. This distinction was expressly recognized and held to be dispositive in Banco do Brasil (supra), in which we said (12 N.Y.2d p. 376, 239 N.Y.S.2d p. 874, 190 N.E.2d p. 237): "An obligation to withhold judicial assistance to secure the benefits of such contracts [i.e., those violative of the foreign currency control regulation] does not imply an obligation to impose tort penalties on those who have fully executed them." (See Dicey & Morris, Conflict of Laws [8th ed.], op. cit., p. 161, n. 19; pp. 898–900.)

The appellant seeks to distinguish our decision in *Banco do Brasil* on the ground that the plaintiff in that case was recognized as an instrumentality of the Brazilian Government. I find this unpersuasive.

*   *   *

The majority, however, argues that the time may have come for a change in what historically has been the applicable rule. I recognize that strong arguments can be mounted for a change in view of the increased frequency and importance of international commerce and the significantly different perspective in today's world in which one nation views another nation and its interests. In my opinion, however, the responsibility for any change lies with our Federal Government rather than with the highest court of any single State. Change, if at all, in my view, would better come at the hands of the State Department and the Congress, through the negotiation of international agreement or otherwise in the discharge of the constitutional responsibility of the Federal Government "to regulate commerce with foreign nations" (cf. Bretton Woods Agreements Act). A fitting sense of judicial restraint would dictate that the courts of no single State should enunciate a change, however large that State's relative proportion of foreign commerce may be, particularly since the authoritative effect thereof would necessarily be confined to the borders of that State.

Accordingly, I believe the order of the Appellate Division should be affirmed.

BREITEL, C.J., and GABRIELLI, JONES, FUCHSBERG and COOKE, JJ., concur with JASEN, J.; WACHTLER, J., dissents and votes to affirm in a separate opinion.

J. ZEEVI & SONS v. GRINDLAYS BANK (UGANDA)

Court of Appeals of New York, 1975.
37 N.Y.2d 220, 371 N.Y.S.2d 892, at 900, cert. denied, 423 U.S. 866, 96 S.Ct. 126, 46 L.Ed.2d 95.

[In a New York case, an Israeli partnership sued the New York agent of a Ugandan bank, which had issued an irrevocable letter of credit for the benefit of the partnership. The Uganda government had directed the bank to refuse all payments to Israel or Israeli beneficiaries, but the New York Court of Appeals ruled that the directive did not apply in New York. The court added:]

Defendant urges that enforcement of the letter of credit contract would violate the foreign exchange laws of Uganda in disregard of a treaty. Uganda and the United States are signatories to the Bretton Woods Agreement (60 U.S.Stat. 1401 et seq.) which, in relevant part under article VIII (§ 2, subd. [b]), provides: "Exchange contracts which involve the currency of any member and which are contrary to the exchange control regulations of that member maintained or imposed consistently with this Agreement shall be unenforceable in the territories of any member." Contrary to defendants' position, the agreement, even when read in its broadest sense, fails to bring the letter of credit within its scope, since said letter of credit is not an exchange contract. In Banco Do Brasil, S.A. v. Israel Commodity Co., 12 N.Y.2d 371, 375–376, 239 N.Y.S.2d 872, 874, 190 N.E.2d 235, 236, this court frowned on an interpretation of said provision of the Bretton Woods Agreement which "sweeps in all contracts affecting any members' exchange resources as doing considerable violence to the text of the section."

Note

The position of the New York courts is probably more restrictive than most. For extensive reviews of the cases involving Article VIII, see J. Gold, The Fund Agreement in the Courts (1962, vol. II—1982). In addition, Sir Joseph Gold, who was General Counsel of the IMF for many years, has published updates of the above volumes under the same title as part of the IMF Staff Papers series.

Problems

The African country Vanzia has a law on its books entitled "Foreign Exc!..nge and Trade Control Law," one part of which reads:

Vanzia Exchange Control Act of 1963

Article 26: Any exchange of the bobble for any other currency at a rate less than the value set by the Vanzian Central Bank shall be illegal, and participants in such exchange shall be liable to fine and imprisonment.

* * *

Article 32: An "exchange" within the meaning of this statute shall include any exchange between any two persons, no matter where they are.

On the date in question, the Vanzian Central Bank has set the exchange rate of the bobble at 10 bobbles to the United States dollar. The IMF has "approved" this law under Article VIII, section 2 as part of a stand-by arrangement between Vanzian and the IMF for Vanzian drawings.

Golddust Widget Mfg. Co. succeeded in penetrating the Vanzia market, but in order to make some of its initial sales, it had to take some payments in bobbles. As a consequence, Golddust now has a deposit in the Bank of America, San Francisco, of 20,000 bobbles, another deposit in a private bank in Vanzia ("V Bank") of 50,000 bobbles, and a deposit in a Swiss Bank of 100,000 bobbles. In seeking to convert these deposits into dollars, it has entered into the following contracts:

(a) with Joe Moneybags, United States citizen of San Jose, California to sell 10,000 bobbles on deposit in California for 900 United States dollars;

(b) with Ugu Zimbo, citizen and resident of Vanzia, now in Los Angeles doing business, to sell 10,000 bobbles on deposit in California for 850 United States dollars;

(c) with Hans Schneider of Cologne, Germany, to sell 50,000 bobbles on deposit in Switzerland for 15,000 Deutsch Marks;

(d) with Joe Moneybags, United States citizen of San Jose, to sell 20,000 bobbles on deposit in Switzerland for 6,000 Swiss Francs;

(e) with Agga Xuntz, citizen and resident of Vanzia, to sell 20,000 bobbles on deposit in Vanzia in exchange for 700 United States dollars.

In addition, Golddust has shipped widgets to Vanzia buyers under the following circumstances:

(f) 1000 tin widgets to Bagga Uga for 1000 United States dollars, plus freight and insurance on open line of credit. Bagga Uga has a bank deposit in California sufficient to cover this purchase. Extrinsic evidence would show that these widgets would sell on the United States market for 50 cents each.

Golddust asks your advice on the probability of success of court proceedings anywhere in the world to realize upon these various contracts. Outline your response.

SECTION 11.4　TRADE MEASURES FOR BALANCE OF PAYMENTS REASONS

(A)　INTRODUCTION

In Chapter 9 we looked at trade restrictions imposed to help a particular sector of the economy adjust. In this section we look at a more general problem—trade restrictions imposed to help solve a nation's balance of payments problems.

History has shown that when a nation runs a balance of payments deficit, it is greatly tempted not only to utilize financial measures to correct the imbalance, but also to impose various restraints on international trade, often restricting imports, so as to improve its balance of trade, thereby helping its balance of payments. In general, many economists feel that trade measures should not be utilized for balance of payments reasons.

Nevertheless, nations do indulge in these measures, and the international trade regulation system recognizes that possibility. One major problem of international regulation of this activity is that the activity involves the jurisdiction of two major international organizations, GATT and the IMF. The IMF has the general jurisdiction as well as considerable competence over the broader balance of payments problems. GATT, on the other hand, deals with trade restrictions. GATT has some lengthy articles dealing with the use of trade restrictions for balance of payments reasons, yet information regarding the basic underlying conditions that would lead to such restrictions is often available only in the IMF. During the decades of the existence of these two organizations, there has been an uneasy relationship between them with respect to these problems.[1]

(B) GATT AND TRADE RESTRICTIONS FOR BALANCE OF PAYMENTS REASONS

Some of the most elaborate and complex provisions of the General Agreement on Tariffs and Trade are concerned with the use of trade restrictions for balance of payments reasons. (See Articles XII through XV.) These provisions were the result of extensive debates during the preparatory work.[2] In addition, GATT contains certain obligations relating to exchange rate and currency controls which can operate to restrict imports.

(1) Balance of Payments Restrictions

It will be recalled that Article XI of GATT prohibits the use of quotas generally. The principal exceptions to this prohibition are Article XII and XVIII (applying to developing countries), which both contain provisions that authorize the use of quantitative restrictions or quotas against imports in case of balance of payments difficulties. (There is no explicit authorization in GATT for the use of higher tariffs or tariff surcharges for balance of payments reasons.) It will also be recalled that the most-favored-nation obligation is one of the most important keystones of GATT, contained in Article I of GATT. When quotas or quantitative restrictions are utilized, however, the Article I non-discrimination language may not adequately support the MFN principle, and consequently Article XIII of GATT sets forth a "non-discrimination principle" tailored to use of quotas. For example, Article XIII speaks of the need to administer quotas so as not to damage or reduce imports from countries in a way that would change the historical shares of the importing market. However, even this principle can be departed from in certain, more difficult balance of payments situations, and Article XIV sets forth this exception. Finally, Article XV of GATT tries to establish a satisfactory relationship between GATT and the IMF, requiring the existence of certain facts to be determined by the IMF. Article XVIII,

1. See J. Jackson, World Trade and the Law of GATT ch. 18 (1969). Concerning some of the institutional aspects of the IMF, see American Society of International Law, Report of Panel on International Monetary Policy: Long-Term International Monetary Reform: A Proposal for an Improved International Adjustment Process, (1972); see also UNCTAD, Money, Finance and Development: Papers on International Monetary Reform, U.N.Doc. TD/B/479 (1974).

2. J. Jackson, note 1 supra, at chs. 18 and 26.

section B, deals with the special balance of payments problems of developing countries.

The provisions of Article XVIII differ somewhat, but not drastically, from those of Article XII.[3]

Query: In the context of the current system of "floating exchange rates," can there ever be a case where a member of GATT, whose currency is floating, would be entitled to the Article XII exception? Does a floating exchange rate system change the practical application of Articles XII through XV of GATT?

(2) Tariff Surcharges

The reader will recall that for most industrialized countries which are members of GATT, most of the tariffs (particularly those on non-agricultural goods) are "bound" in the schedules, as a result of negotiated "concessions." [4] There is no general exception in GATT to these "bindings" for balance of payments reasons. Thus, GATT contains the anomaly of allowing quantitative restrictions to be used for balance of payments reasons, but not allowing tariff increases to be so used. On policy grounds, a case can be made that "tariff surcharges" are preferable to quantitative restrictions.[5] A paper by the GATT secretariat written in 1965 outlines some of these reasons: [6]

2. (i) Surcharges were preferred to quantitative restrictions because they were administratively less cumbersome and were less likely to freeze the pattern of trade.

(ii) The substantial revenues obtained from use of surcharges were essential to the success of the country's stabilization programme.

(iii) The surcharges were placed both on bound and unbound items to avoid unfair discrimination between exporters.

3. (i) The conversion of surcharges to internal measures could aggravate industrial conditions, especially in situations where there are accumulation of stocks. The use of such internal measures in place of surcharges could also cause serious internal political difficulties.

(ii) Internal measures alone were not sufficient to restore equilibrium and balance-of-payments and additional measures to restrict imports were necessary.

(iii) In urgent situations, surcharges could be quickly imposed. Otherwise, there could be disastrous delays in bringing a new law before parliament.

Contracting parties have in various instances noted the following considerations in authorizing the use of surcharges:

(i) In one or two instances, the use of surcharges represented a significant simplification over the system of restrictions previously enforced.

---

3. See a chart of these differences in J. Jackson, note 1 supra, at 689.

4. See generally Section 6.3 supra.

5. A tariff surcharge is generally defined as a uniform, ad valorem tariff applied to all goods that are imported (possibly with some exceptions), *in addition to* the tariff normally charged.

6. GATT Doc.Com. TD/F/W.3, at 1–2.

(ii) The effect of the surcharges would be less restrictive than quantitative restrictions permitted under Articles XII or XVIII.

(iii) In addition to its direct effect on the level of reserves, the use of surcharges was in certain instances, necessary to insure success of the government stabilization program.

For a variety of reasons, some of them outlined above, members of GATT (including the United States) have from time to time utilized tariff surcharges for balance of payments reasons.[7] Enough of these instances have occurred that it has even been argued that GATT has been "amended de facto"—a dangerous argument, in the authors' viewpoint.

Query: Should the GATT be amended to allow tariff surcharges for balance of payments reasons? If so, what should be the structure of that amendment? Would it suffice merely to authorize a tariff surcharge in each circumstance where, under Article XII, a quantitative restriction would be authorized?

(3) Tokyo Round Declaration

As a part of the Tokyo Round, the Contracting Parties noted (1) their belief that trade restrictions are an inefficient means of solving balance of payment (BOP) problems and (2) the fact that measures other than quantitative restrictions had been used for BOP purposes. They then agreed as follows: [8]

DECLARATION ON TRADE MEASURES TAKEN FOR BALANCE–OF–PAYMENTS PURPOSES

1. The procedures for examination stipulated in Articles XII and XVIII shall apply to all restrictive import measures taken for balance-of-payments purposes. The application of restrictive import measures taken for balance-of-payments purposes shall be subject to the following conditions in addition to those provided for in Articles XII, XIII, XV and XVIII without prejudice to other provisions of the General Agreement:

   (a) In applying restrictive import measures contracting parties shall abide by the disciplines provided for in the GATT and give preference to the measure which has the least disruptive effect on trade;

   (b) The simultaneous application of more than one type of trade measure for this purpose should be avoided;

   (c) Whenever practicable, contracting parties shall publicly announce a time schedule for the removal of the measures.

The provisions of this paragraph are not intended to modify the substantive provisions of the General Agreement.

2. If, notwithstanding the principles of this Declaration, a developed contracting party is compelled to apply restrictive import measures for balance-of-payments purposes, it shall, in determining the incidence of its

---

7. A list of tariff surcharges coming within the cognizance of GATT can be found at GATT Doc.Com. TD/F/W.3, (1965). Needless to say, there have been a number of subsequent examples that are not included in this list.

8. GATT, 26th Supp. BISD 205, 206–07 (1980).

measures, take into account the export interests of the less-developed contracting parties and may exempt from its measures products of export interest to those contracting parties.

3. Contracting parties shall promptly notify to the GATT the introduction or intensification of all restrictive import measures taken for balance-of-payments purposes. Contracting parties which have reason to believe that a restrictive import measure applied by another contracting party was taken for balance-of-payments purposes may notify the measure to the GATT or may request the GATT secretariat to seek information on the measure and make it available to all contracting parties if appropriate.

4. All restrictive import measures taken for balance-of-payments purposes shall be subject to consultation in the GATT Committee on Balance-of-Payments Restrictions * * *.

(C) UNITED STATES LAW AND BALANCE OF PAYMENTS TRADE MEASURES

Before the Trade Act of 1974, U.S. law concerning the authority of the President to impose a tariff surcharge for balance of payments reasons was not entirely clear. Nevertheless, in August of 1971, President Nixon did impose such a surcharge, which lasted until December of that year and which was upheld in the *Yoshida* case discussed in Section 3.4(B) supra.

Section 122 of the Trade Act of 1974 explicitly authorized tariff surcharges in certain cases (see Documentary Supplement). The following excerpt from the report of the Senate Finance Committee explains its operation.

SENATE REPORT NO. 93–1298

93d Cong., 2d Sess. 87–89 (1974)

* * * Under the Committee bill, the President would be required to impose import restrictions whenever the U.S. faces large and serious balance of payments deficits. However, the President would be permitted to refrain from imposing import restrictions if he determines that they would be contrary to U.S. national interest. If he did not restrict imports, the President would have to inform the Congress and consult with the members of the Senate Finance and House Ways and Means Committees who are to serve as Congressional Advisors under section 161 of the bill, as to the reasons for his determination.

Under the Committee bill, import restrictions proclaimed by the President would not be in effect for a period longer than 180 days (unless a longer period is authorized by Act of Congress). The Committee also felt that the authority to impose surcharges could, in many instances, be applied selectively that is with respect to the articles of commerce from such countries which have substantial surpluses and which do not take adequate steps to reduce or eliminate their surpluses. The Committee does not feel that across-the-board application of balance of payments measures would be the fairest or most effective way to restore equilibrium to the world economy, particularly in circumstances in which one or several countries are responsible for the disequilibrium by maintaining large and persistent balance of payments surpluses.[9] The intent of this provision is to create incentives for surplus countries which have disproportionate gains in reserves to take voluntarily effective adjustment action to eliminate their surpluses. There remains under the Articles of Agreement of the International Monetary Fund a much greater pressure on deficit countries to adjust than on surplus countries.

* * *

Upon the entering into force of new rules regulating the application of surcharges as a part of reform of international balance-of-payment adjustment procedures, the President would be required to impose any surcharge authorized under this section in conformity with such new international rules.

The use of surcharges for balance-of-payments purposes has gained *de facto* acceptance in the General Agreement on Tariffs and Trade over the years. Major industrialized countries which have resorted to surcharges include France in 1955, Canada in 1962, the United Kingdom in 1968, and Denmark and the United States in 1971. Nonetheless, explicit GATT rules on the use of surcharges have never been adopted. Accordingly, the Committee has provided in subsection 122(d)(4) that it is the sense of the Congress that the President seek modifications in international agreements aimed at allowing the use of surcharges in place of quantitative restrictions and providing rules to govern the use of such surcharges as a balance-of-payments adjustment measure within the context of arrangements for an equitable sharing of balance-of-payments adjustment responsibility among deficit and surplus countries.

Subsection 122(e) would provide that actions taken under this balance-of-payments provision must be applied uniformly to a broad range of imported products. However, the President may exempt certain articles or groups of articles because of the needs of the U.S. economy relating to such factors as the unavailability of domestic supply at reasonable prices, the necessary importation of raw materials, and avoiding serious dislocations in the supply of imported goods.

Questions

(1) What type of "new rules" are contemplated in section 122(d)(3)? Must they be a GATT amendment?

(2) Would you recommend a new rule with respect to tariff surcharges, which required that they always be applied on a MFN nondiscriminatory basis? Would you accept a rule that allowed certain differential treatment for countries in strong balance of payments positions?

(3) In 1985, various proposals were made to the U.S. Congress urging it to enact a tariff surcharge. Some advocates saw a surcharge of 20–25 percent as killing two birds with one stone: providing revenue to help reduce the large U.S. federal budget deficit and inhibiting imports to help reduce the large U.S. trade

---

9. Many of the draftsmen had in mind Japan, and to a lesser extent Germany, as countries which had strong reserve positions and which were at certain times unwilling to revalue their currencies.

deficit. Do you think such a proposal is consistent with U.S. GATT obligations? Could the President proclaim such an action without additional congressional authorization under the 1974 Act? Would such action be wise in your view?

The effect of such a surcharge was the subject of some dispute. Many economists argued that it would not accomplish its goals, but would rather strengthen the value of the dollar and thereby cause a drop in exports, with the result of no improvement in the balance of payments problem. In addition, it was argued that a surcharge would particularly harm developing countries with large debt loads because it would cut their export earnings and lead to increased inflation and economic inefficiency in the United States as imports decreased.[10]

(D) THE EC AND BALANCE OF PAYMENTS TRADE MEASURES

The Treaty of Rome allows certain "protective measures" (see Articles 108 and 109). The following is an example of action by the EEC in this regard:

COMMISSION DECISION 76/446/EEC OF 5 MAY 1976

AUTHORIZING THE ITALIAN REPUBLIC TO TAKE CERTAIN PROTECTIVE MEASURES UNDER ARTICLE 108(3) OF THE TREATY.

[1976] Eur.Comm.O.J. No. L120/30.

Whereas the balance of payments situation of the Italian Republic * * * is now—after a relative improvement which had enabled the protective measures to be confined to investments made abroad—suddenly deteriorating once again, the present movement being severely aggravated by speculation;

Whereas this new deterioration is entailing a rapid and excessive depreciation of the lira which represents a serious threat to the working of the common market and which therefore calls for emergency action;

* * *

ARTICLE 1

The Italian Republic is authorized to require the lodging for a period of three months of a non-interest-bearing cash deposit with the Bank of Italy whenever foreign exchange is purchased and whenever lira are deposited on foreign accounts; the deposit shall not exceed 50% of the amount involved in the transaction.

ARTICLE 2

The Italian Republic shall ensure that the Bank of Italy releases the deposit, without delay or formality, three months from the date of its lodging.

* * *

---

10. See, e.g., 2 BNA Intl.Trade Rptr. 1147–49 (1985).

ARTICLE 5

The Commission shall reserve the right to amend or repeal this Decision before the date fixed in Article 6 if it finds that the circumstances motivating its adoption have changed or that its effects are more restrictive than is required for the attainment of its purpose or are having particularly serious consequences for trade, particularly in agricultural products coming under a common organization of the market.

BULLETIN OF THE EUROPEAN COMMUNITIES
No. 5–1976 (June) at 41:

MONETARY SITUATION IN ITALY

2203. After a marked improvement following the adoption by the Italian Government on 18 March of a series of measures designed to help improve the economic situation in Italy, the lira drifted down again, irregularly, in April and the beginning of May: between 17 March and 5 May it depreciated by more than 3% against the dollar and by about 25% since 20 January, the day on which the official quotation of foreign currencies in Italy was suspended.

More effective measures were required immediately to cope quickly with this new build-up of speculative pressure against the lira, which was aggravating Italy's already precarious payments situation.

REQUEST BY THE ITALIAN GOVERNMENT

2204. On 5 May, the Italian Government notified the Commission of the monetary measures which it was planning, namely the introduction of a temporary requirement that for all foreign exchange purchases a non-interest-bearing cash deposit in lire equivalent to half the value of the purchase be lodged and remain frozen for a limited period. What the Italian Government was in fact proposing was the reintroduction and extension to all transactions involving the purchase of foreign exchange of the temporary deposit requirement which it had been authorized to apply, in particular to imports of certain goods, by the Commission Decision of 8 May 1974 taken pursuant to Article 108(3) of the Treaty; as Italy had phased out the deposit requirement altogether by the spring of 1975, the Commission repealed those articles of the Decision relating to this mechanism on 26 May 1975 and left in force only the temporary authorization to require of Italian residents a 50% non-interest-bearing deposit for certain investment transactions in other Member States.

Questions

(1) Is the Italian scheme consistent with GATT obligations? See especially GATT Article XII.

(2) Is the Italian scheme consistent with the OECD Trade pledge? See below.

(3) Italy imposed a new deposit requirement in 1981. See generally Recent Development, 1981 Italian Deposit Requirement: Proper Remedy Under the Treaty of Rome, GATT, or IMF Agreement?, 14 Law & Poly.Intl.Bus. 927 (1982).

(E) THE OECD "GENTLEMEN'S AGREEMENT" TRADE PLEDGE

In the face of the "oil crisis" of 1973, the greatly increased price of oil threatened to cause balance of payments difficulties for a number of Western countries. A fear developed that such countries might begin to apply restrictive import measures as one way to deal with their balance of payments difficulties, and if this occurred, it might result in a series of retaliatory restrictions which could greatly damage world trade, exacerbating and exaggerating the effects of the "oil crisis." In the OECD, therefore, a number of countries decided to develop an agreement, by which they would each mutually pledge not to utilize restrictions on imports as a way of dealing with the balance of payments difficulties caused by the oil crisis. The agreement has been termed a "gentlemen's agreement," without binding force in international law, because many of the countries did not have authority for their Executives to enter into such agreements, and it was considered politically difficult to obtain that authority from Parliaments or Congress.

The 1974 Trade Declaration was modified in 1980 when the OECD adopted a permanent Declaration on Trade Policy. The OECD members pledged, inter alia, to maintain and improve the present open multilateral trading system; to implement the decisions reached at the Tokyo Round; to strengthen their trading relations with developing countries, keeping in mind their special needs and the crucial importance for those countries of export earnings; and to avoid trade practices of a restrictive nature that might have an adverse impact on inflation, productivity and growth potential or inhibit the dynamic development of world trade and its financing.[11]

Query: Why do governments use a voluntary pledge in this context, rather than firm treaty commitments?

(F) GATT OBLIGATIONS RELATING TO CURRENCY PAR VALUES AND EXCHANGE CONTROLS

Recognizing that regardless of the balance of payments condition of a nation, currency par values and exchange controls can be manipulated to defeat the effect of other trade obligations of GATT, the draftsmen of GATT included several obligations relating to these practices. For example, it was well known that a requirement of a license, in order to make a payment in foreign exchange, could effectively prevent the importation of goods or control them through the control exercised in the granting of licenses. In some cases, the obligations of the International Monetary Fund suffice to prevent the abusive practices which would affect trade, and Article XV of GATT recognizes this. However, some of the parties to GATT are not members of the IMF, and consequently it was necessary to include in GATT some substitute for the IMF obligations in these cases. Article XV, para-

---

11. The text of the pledge is reproduced in OECD, Activities of the OECD in 1980, at 93–94.

graph 4, contains such substitutes, and paragraph 6 of that Article provides that a non-Fund member should establish a "special exchange agreement" with the Contracting Parties of GATT, presumably to provide some of the IMF-type obligations.[12] Scattered throughout GATT are various other commitments relating to similar problems.[13] For example, MFN under Article 1 imposes the obligation of nondiscrimination with respect to international transfer of payments; and Article II, paragraphs 3 and 6, limit the possibility of using devaluation or other currency exchange techniques to "impair the value of any of the concessions" under GATT.[14]

12. See generally J. Jackson, note 1 supra, at ch. 18.

13. See J. Jackson, note 1 supra, at 492; commitments relating to exchange controls and currency practices occur in Articles I, para. 1; II, pars. 3 and 6; VI, pars. 2 and 3; VII, para. 4(a) and (c); VIII, paras. 1 and 4, and, of course, the elaborate BOP exceptions in Articles XI through XIV and Article XVIII, Section B.

14. The new floating exchange rate system has posed some new problems for the GATT binding legal rules. If a currency increases in value in relation to other currencies, can that be the basis for an adjustment in the tariff under bindings, pursuant to Article II of GATT? See Roessler, Selective Balance-of-Payment Adjustment Measures Affecting Trade: The Roles of the GATT and the IMF, 9 J.World Trade L. 622 (1975).

Chapter 12

EXPORT CONTROLS UNDER GATT AND NATIONAL LAW

SECTION 12.1 INTRODUCTION

Most of international trade policy and rules developed in the past several decades have been concerned with the problems of market access, with attention being focused on reducing import restraints. In the early 1970's, however, a new form of restraint became the source of considerable concern. This new form involved the utilization of export controls to affect the prices of certain products, particularly certain raw materials and commodities. Normally, in the absence of government interference, if there were an increase in demand compared to supply, the price of a commodity would rise both in the domestic market and on international markets, and if there were an excess supply, prices would fall. In the 1970's, either to avoid a price rise in the domestic market, or to cause a price rise in international markets even in the absence of a true shortage of supply, it was not uncommon for one or more nations, acting individually or jointly, to restrain exports.

This chapter will focus on the general problems of export controls (but will not deal with the subject of export promotion). After a brief historical overview of the use and effects of export controls, we will examine the rules established by GATT in respect of their use and consider a dispute between Brazil and the United States over the use of such controls. We will then look at the U.S. constitutional restraints on the use of export controls and consider the general framework under which the United States regulates exports.

Our examination of export controls in this chapter will be general in scope. Certain specific examples of the use of export controls are treated in other chapters. For example, in terms of the volume of trade affected, probably the most extensive use made of export controls is in the implementation of voluntary export restraints, a subject that we have treated in detail in Section 9.4 supra. The reader will recall that the use of export restraints for such reasons may violate GATT rules, although given the fact that such restraints are imposed at the behest of the importing country, there is often not likely to be any GATT member to complain about the practice. Extensive use of export controls is also made for national security and political reasons, and we will examine such controls in Chapter 13 where we will look in general at trade restrictions imposed for such reasons. Similarly, we will examine the problem of export controls on commodities in the chapter on agricultural goods and commodities (Chapter 14). We begin, however, with an historical overview and a consideration of why export controls are imposed.

C. FRED BERGSTEN, COMPLETING THE GATT: TOWARD NEW INTERNATIONAL RULES TO GOVERN EXPORT CONTROLS

2–10 (1978) [1]

It is often forgotten, however, that access to foreign supplies has sometimes overshadowed, or at least equalled, access to foreign markets among the external economic concerns of nations. Thus, export controls have been of great concern in at least three periods since World War I: the early years after 1918, the late 1930s and the early postwar period running through the Korean War. They usually represented national efforts to export inflation and the effects of shortages, especially of raw materials, just as import controls represented national efforts to export unemployment and the effects of excess production.

Export controls, perhaps even more than import controls, have important security as well as economic implications. We shall shortly see that the major purposes of export controls include holding on to key products (such as food and fuels) to protect a country's own security, denial of the benefits of trade to political adversaries, and the extension of such benefits to allies. Indeed, controls applied for precisely such purposes during the periodic scrambles for resources among countries have frequently been cited among the causes of both world wars. The British export tax on coal, levied in 1901, hit Germany hard and added importantly to the rising tension between them. The U.S. export controls against Japan, along with the long list of export controls erected by most European countries, both reflected and accelerated the disruption of overall relations leading to World War II. Throughout the postwar period, the United States and (to a lesser extent) its allies have used export controls to try to limit the military and economic capabilities of the USSR and other communist countries. And the limitation of oil exports by the Arab producers in late 1973, in an effort to change the Middle East policies of the United States and virtually every other country in the world, has dramatized the issue of "access to supplies" more than any other single event.

* * *

THE PURPOSES OF EXPORT CONTROLS

In fact, the use of export controls is becoming very widespread. Many countries have employed one or another form of such controls in the recent past. For example, the United States has sharply limited, for varying

1. Reprinted by permission of the British-North America Committee, as stated in the booklet quoted.

periods of time, its sales of soybeans, a number of other farm products, metal scrap, and timber. Both Japan and the United States have de facto limited or even embargoed exports of fertilizers and other chemical products, particularly petroleum-based intermediate goods. Brazil has checked its exports of coffee, leather and beef. Export taxes have appeared on Latin American bananas. The most dramatic move was the oil embargo by the Organization of Arab Petroleum Exporting Countries (OAPEC, the Arab group within OPEC), which was intended to block all shipments to the United States, the Netherlands and a few other countries. Canada has adopted legislation enabling it to apply export controls much more readily in the future, and the U.S. Congress is seriously considering similar changes in U.S. legislation. There are dozens of other examples.

These measures have been undertaken for a variety of reasons. * * *

To *avoid "unacceptable" domestic price rises.* The U.S. restrictions on agricultural exports in 1973 were adopted for this purpose. From its inception in 1949, the U.S. Export Control Act (since 1969, the Export Administration Act) has permitted export controls "to protect the economy from the excessive drain of scarce materials and to reduce the inflationary impact of abnormal foreign demand"; this consideration motivated most of the U.S. export controls of the early postwar period, but became insignificant by the late 1950s. If one important exporting country applies controls for this purpose, other exporting countries may emulate the step to prevent the sharp increase in their sales which could otherwise result; the United States has justified its controls on steel scrap exports on precisely these grounds, and numerous countries placed controls on their exports of feedgrains after the United States did so in June 1973.

To *reinforce domestic price controls,* which often exempt export prices and hence encourage foreign sales. In 1973–74, the United States came very close to applying export quotas for this purpose in a number of industries (e.g., petro-chemicals, some of which sold for three times as much abroad) but chose each time to decontrol prices instead. Sometimes the price controls to be reinforced apply to an entire sector; the European Community has recently been applying export taxes to a wide range of farm products to keep their prices from rising to the much higher levels prevailing in world trade. In the original negotiations to form the GATT, New Zealand successfully insisted on an exemption for export controls to buttress domestic price controls because it used them so widely for this purpose. As inflation remains a major problem for most countries, there will probably be increased resort to price controls; hence, there will be continued pressure to use export controls in support thereof.

To *improve the terms of trade of the producing country,* or at least keep them from declining, by forcing up world prices for its commodity exports. This can be done unilaterally by a single country strong enough in a given market to do so, or by a group of producers acting together, or under a commodity agreement including both producers and consumers (as in several existing agreements), for a product in which the price elasticities of world demand and supply are low enough that total revenues can be increased through export controls. Recent efforts include the limits on coffee exports by a number of producing countries, mainly in Latin America, and the taxes placed on banana exports by several Latin American countries. Similar steps are likely in a wide range of additional commodities.

To *capture for exporting countries the scarcity rents generated by other countries' import controls,* which would otherwise accrue to importers in the countries which apply the import controls. This manifestation of the effort to boost a country's terms of trade through export controls appeared widely in the 1930s because of the growing use of import controls during that period.

To *conserve limited resources,* especially for countries reliant on a single commodity. This may improve their terms of trade over time, and usually is based on a judgment that earnings from future production of the commodity will exceed earnings from investments made with the proceeds of current sales. This objective is usually pursued through production cutbacks rather than export controls, however, as has been the case for several years with Kuwaiti and Libyan oil; to do it solely via export controls would require massive stockpiling and hence a heavy additional financial burden.

To *develop domestic processing industries* rather than exporting raw materials. Export restrictions support this process by assuring the access of domestic producers to inputs, which may at times be scarce at any price, and by reducing the costs of those inputs to domestic producers while raising them for foreign producers. The controls may also enable domestic producers to achieve scales of production needed to render them efficient in world markets. For example, Brazil has restricted leather exports to permit growth of its own shoe industry and green coffee exports to boost its production of soluble coffee. A much broader use of this approach can be foreseen in the future as, for example, the oil exporting countries insist both on refining their crude and using the resulting feedstocks to build local petrochemical industries, and the baúxite exporters insist on local alumina production. These uses of export controls can sometimes be justified by analogy to the traditional "infant industry" case for import controls. They improve the overall terms of trade of the producing country, by increasing domestic value-added and hence capturing some of the profits previously made by "downstream" countries. In addition, they bring other benefits such as increased employment.

To *avoid physical shortages* which might cause unemployment and unacceptable levels of economic activity. Japan stopped selling petroleum-based synthetics to other East Asian processors while it feared interruption of its own petroleum supply. A future and longer-term variant of this theme may be export controls to avoid "frittering away" the output undertaken expressly to minimize the international vulnerability of particular countries, such as the rapid expansion of the U.S. coal industry foreseen under "Project Independence."

For *revenue reasons.* Export duties (like import duties) were a major source of government revenue for ancient Greece and Rome, and for Britain and other major European powers until the middle of the nineteenth century. This motive is far less prevalent today, though it remains important for some developing countries.

To *limit the military and economic capability of other countries.* The best examples are the widespread controls applied by the noncommunist industrialized countries (especially the United States) against the communist countries through most of the postwar period. Exports to belligerents are of course often rigidly controlled during wars.

For *foreign policy reasons,* in an effort to induce the denied consumer to change his policy. The oil embargoes against the United States, the Netherlands and a few other countries in 1973–74 were of this type. This and the previous objective are closely related; the main differences are whether the efforts are long-term or short-term, and whether they seek to change the basic orientation of the targeted country or one specific aspect of its foreign policy. Both objectives can be promoted by using export controls both negatively and positively, by denying sales to adversaries and favoring certain countries in the allocation of short supplies; the United States used both techniques during World War II and the postwar reconstruction period, as did the Arab oil suppliers with their three categories of customers during the winter of 1973–74.

Note

The importance of export controls should not be underemphasized, despite the fact that for many decades attention has been focused on market access rather than supply access. Export controls, for example, figured prominently in the relationships between nations prior to World War II and arguably are one of the causes, or at least a trigger, of the outbreak of that war.[2]

SECTION 12.2 INTERNATIONAL REGULATION OF EXPORT CONTROLS

(A) GATT OBLIGATIONS [1]

Exports are mentioned in GATT in at least 13 clauses and are related to obligations in several others.[2] The most significant obligations in GATT relating to treatment of exports are the most-favored-nation treatment obligation of Article I, and the ban on prohibitions and quantitative restrictions of Article XI, which applies to exports as well as imports. Problems stemming from export promotion activities, such as subsidies or dumping, have been treated in Chapter 10. Of course, GATT clauses that apply generally to customs procedures, in many cases apply to those procedures affecting exports as well as imports.[3] The basic problem with GATT obliga-

---

2. J. Herzog, Closing the Open Door: American-Japanese Diplomatic Negotiations 1936–1941, at 92–101, 163–86, Naval Inst. Press (1973); H. Feis, The Road to Pearl Harbor: The Coming of the War Between the United States and Japan 107–09, 205–08, 267–70 (1950).

1. See generally Rom, Export Controls in GATT, 18 J.World Trade L. 125 (1984).

2. GATT Art. I (MFN), para. 1; Art. VI (antidumping), paras. 1, 5, 6(b), 7(a); Art. VIII

(fees and formalities), paras. 1, 4; Art. IX (marks of origin), para. 2; Art. X (publication), para. 1; Art. XI (quantitative restrictions), paras. 1, 2; Art. XIII (nondiscriminatory administration of quantitative restrictions), paras. 1, 5; Art. XVI (subsidies), Section B; Art. XX (general exceptions), paras. (i), (j); see J. Jackson, World Trade and the Law of GATT 497–506 (1969).

3. See, e.g., GATT Arts. VIII and IX:(9).

tions relating to exports, however, stems from two facts: 1) There is no GATT obligation against the use of export taxes or fees; and 2) as to the GATT obligations restraining use of export restrictions, the GATT exceptions are so broad and vague as to almost render those obligations meaningless.

Article XI prohibits export restrictions, but provides an exception for restrictions "temporarily applied to prevent or relieve critical shortages of foodstuffs or other products essential to the exporting contracting party." [4] Article XX provides two broad and vague exceptions for restrictions on exports "necessary to ensure essential quantities of such materials to a domestic processing industry during periods when the domestic price of such materials is held below the world price as part of a government stabilization plan," [5] and restrictions "essential to the acquisition or distribution of products in general or local short supply," provided that an equitable share principle is followed.[6] With these exceptions, a GATT member can almost apply export restrictions at will. In the few cases where it feels restrained by GATT from using quantitative restrictions, it can, of course, utilize export taxes or fees.

There have been few complaints in GATT about export procedures; the following describes those which have occurred:

FRIEDER ROESSLER, GATT AND ACCESS TO SUPPLIES
(1975) [7]

There appear to have been only three complaints against export controls in the history of GATT. In 1948, Pakistan complained that India did not refund excise duties on a number of commodities when they were exported to Pakistan while such refunds were granted for exports to all other destinations. In 1952, a similar complaint was discussed in GATT. This time the parties to the dispute were reversed. India complained that Pakistan discriminated in its taxation of jute exports against India. India explained that jute was exported from Pakistan in the form of wire-bound bales and loose bales and that Pakistan's export duties on loose bales were higher than those on wire-bound bales. Since India took most of its supplies in the form of loose bales it felt that it was the object of discrimination. Both these complaints were withdrawn following bilateral compromises. In 1949, Czechoslovakia brought a complaint against the United States arguing that its practice of export control licences discriminated against Czechoslovakia. The Contracting Parties, however, formally decided that the United States had not "failed to carry out its obligations under the Agreement through its administration of the issue of export licences."

————

The concern of many countries about export restrictions, particularly on oil, resulted in negotiations on the subject of access to supplies of raw materials and finished goods in the Tokyo Round. Prior to the negotiations proposals had been made that would have greatly restricted the ability of

4. GATT Art. XI, para. 2(a).
5. GATT Art. XX, para. (i).
6. GATT Art. XX, para. (j).
7. 9 J.World Trade L. 25, 30.

nations to use export controls, for example, by requiring an escape clause sort of justification for their use (except for national security reasons).[8] Other proposals focused on an item-by-item approach as done in tariff negotiations [9] or on developing separate agreements for particular commodities. The negotiations in the Tokyo Round were difficult because they raised questions concerning national sovereignty over natural resources. The only result was an understanding that the GATT export provisions should be reassessed in the near future.[10] In the meantime, the United Nations Conference on Trade and Development (UNCTAD) has sponsored a number of agreements on specific commodities, which will be discussed in Chapter 14.

(B) A CASE STUDY ON EXPORT TAXES: THE BRAZILIAN COFFEE INCIDENT

The absence of GATT constraints on export taxes and other such controls has meant that most disagreements in this area tend to be resolved either bilaterally between the parties to a dispute or within the terms of various international commodity agreements. The following account of a dispute over Brazilian export taxes on coffee beans gives some idea of the nature of such negotiations.

U.S. COMPTROLLER GENERAL, THE INTERNATIONAL COFFEE AGREEMENT

(1973) [11]

THE SOLUBLE COFFEE CONTROVERSY

Introduction

In the late 1960s U.S. imports of Brazilian soluble (instant) coffee expanded dramatically.

The U.S. coffee industry and labor groups complained that these imports threatened the existence of the domestic soluble industry. In response, the United States attempted to work out an agreement with Brazil which would offset the Brazilian soluble processors' tax advantage. After prolonged negotiations, the governments concluded such an agreement in April 1971.

This review assesses the impact of imports of Brazilian soluble coffee on U.S. production of soluble coffee before the 1971 agreement and evaluates the 1971 agreement.

United States and Brazilian Positions

In 1966 industry and labor groups began protesting the advent of sizable imports of soluble coffee from Brazil. U.S. Government officials became concerned about losing industry support for continued U.S. participation in

---

8. See, e.g., C. Fred Bergsten, Completing the GATT: Toward New International Rules to Govern Export Controls (British-North America Committee, 1974).

9. There is a difference of opinion as to whether the current GATT structure would permit this. Compare J. Jackson, note 2 supra, at 499 & n. 12 with Roessler, note 7 supra.

10. See GATT, The Tokyo Round of Multilateral Trade Negotiations: Report by the Director-General of GATT 152 (1979).

11. Report to the Senate Comm. on Finance, 93d Cong., 1st Sess. (Comm.Print 1973).

the 1962 International Coffee Agreement (ICA). Discussions between the United States and Brazilian Governments began shortly thereafter.

Throughout the ensuing controversy the U.S. Government emphasized, in its official position, the "principle of equal access"; i.e., under a commodity agreement (in this case the ICA) limiting the availability of supply, all parties to that agreement should have equitable and nondiscriminatory access to that supply. The United States argued that Brazilian processors enjoyed two advantages which were manifestly unfair and violated the spirit of the ICA, even though not specifically prohibited by it. Brazilian processors were not taxed on exports of soluble coffee, but a tax was levied on the exports of beans used to make soluble (and roasted) coffee. Brazilian processors also could buy lower cost, lower grade coffee beans which Brazilian authorities had declared to be "non-exportable," but U.S. processors were restricted to higher cost beans even though the lower grades were suitable for making soluble coffee.

In effect, the United States contended that Brazil was using the ICA to put U.S. soluble coffee manufacturers at a competitive disadvantage. Brazil's failure to impose an export tax on soluble coffee exports comparable to that imposed on green coffee (coffee beans before roasting) purchased by U.S. producers gave Brazilian producers an unfair advantage over U.S. producers. If alternative sources of green coffee were freely available to the U.S. producer, the effect of such discrimination would be lessened. However, the ICA restricted the amount of coffee in international trade and limited U.S. soluble producers in seeking alternative low cost supplies of non-Brazilian green coffee.

The United States also feared that the solubles dispute would undermine the price stabilization objectives of the ICA because other coffee-producing countries would attempt to retaliate against this form of price cutting by Brazil.

The Brazilians countered that the U.S. position " * * * dooms Brazil and the other developing countries to remain forever as producers and exporters of raw materials" and claimed that:

—The United States was contradicting its international aid and trade policy which ostensibly sought to provide incentive to less developed countries to industrialize agricultural production and to export agricultural goods.

—The U.S. foreign aid program had financially assisted three of their four new soluble plants.

—United States and European processors had been invited repeatedly to invest in Brazilian soluble production facilities and, thereby, to share in the incentives given to the Brazilian soluble manufacturers.

—Brazil reportedly sold soluble coffee only to established U.S. coffee firms and did not compete with them.

Negotiations for an Agreement

With continued U.S. participation in the ICA at stake, Brazil accepted a new provision in the agreement's renegotiated form in 1968. Included as article 44, this provision prohibited member governments from discriminating in favor of processed coffee exports over green-coffee exports and called for arbitration procedures in case of disputes.

On December 2, 1968, after waiting in vain for Brazil to conform with the new provision, the United States invoked the arbitration procedures of article 44. In early 1969 the neutral country chairman and the U.S. member of the 3-member arbitration panel decided that a situation of the type covered by article 44 existed and that the United States was entitled to take action if Brazil failed to do so. The Brazilian panel member disagreed, stating that no injury to the U.S. industry had been demonstrated and that, therefore, the extent of discrimination, if any, could not be agreed upon.

During the proceedings the U.S. panel member estimated the extent of discrimination at 46 cents per pound of soluble coffee. (This was the export tax of about 17 cents per pound of green coffee times 2.7, the pounds of green coffee estimated to produce 1 pound of soluble coffee.) Even this figure did not account for the Brazilian processor's advantage in having access to the so-called "non-exportable" grades of green coffee. That no injury to the U.S. industry had been demonstrated and that no agreement existed on the extent of discrimination did not alter the fact, in the eyes of the U.S. panel member, that such discrimination existed and called for a remedy under article 44.

Shortly following the arbitration, the United States and Brazil agreed that Brazil would impose a tax on soluble coffee exports to the United States of 13 cents per pound effective May 1, 1969, and to a joint review of the problem in early 1970. The United States viewed the 13 cents per pound tax as a first step in resolving the problem and informed Brazil that the United States reserved the right to take action to insure the imposition of a total tax of 30 cents per pound on Brazilian soluble coffee exports to the United States if no agreement was reached by March 1, 1970. Brazil did not commit itself to the higher tax figure.

The joint review came to an impasse. Brazil stated it would not raise the 13-cent tax, while the United States maintained that further steps were required. U.S. authorities decided to let the deadline pass and to continue negotiations on a new basis since the alternatives were U.S. withdrawal from the ICA or the imposition of an import tax which would only further exacerbate relations. Moreover, important segments of the U.S. industry were changing their positions and protesting the imposition of further obstacles to importing Brazilian soluble coffee.

However, when the Congress authorized U.S. participation in the ICA until July 1971, it was made clear that further U.S. participation was contingent on resolving the solubles dispute by April of 1971. An agreement, reached on April 2, 1971, provided for: (1) a special annual allocation of 560,000 bags of Brazilian green coffee (the approximate green-coffee equivalent of Brazilian exports of soluble coffee to the United States) to U.S. soluble coffee manufacturers on the basis of their respective shares in U.S. soluble coffee production, (2) reimbursement of the tax on the special allocation to U.S. manufacturers in the form of credits against future purchases of coffee, (3) renegotiation, proposed by either country, of the level of the special allocation if Brazilian soluble coffee exports changed by more than 15 percent, (4) removal of the 13 cents per pound tax by Brazil on exports of soluble coffee to the United States, and (5) implementation of the agreement only as long as the ICA remained in force and was implemented by the two countries.

The United States believes that Brazil's soluble export tax advantage has been offset by provision (1) of the April 1971 agreement.

Notes and Questions

(1) Continued participation by the United States in the International Coffee Agreement was authorized (for three years) by Pub.L. No. 98–120, 97 Stat. 809 (1983) (codified at 19 U.S.C.A. § 1356).

(2) Under existing GATT rules, particularly Articles XI and XX, is there any situation in which a GATT member could not legitimately use quota restraints (or an embargo) on exports? Was the United States action in 1973, which embargoed all exports of soybeans for several months, consistent with its GATT obligations? Take an advocate's position on each side of these issues, and then consider whether there is a clearly defensible answer to the questions.

(3) If a GATT member agreed that it would not impose more than a 5% export tax on leather exports, and this commitment was listed in its GATT schedule, what would be the precise nature of that commitment? Consider:

(a) Article II: Is the commitment a "GATT" commitment?

(b) Could a complaint for breach of the commitment be brought under Article XXIII?

(c) If the commitment were withdrawn, would Article XXVIII procedures apply?

(4) Would Article I, MFN obligations apply to the commitment described in question 3? Would it matter whether the commitment was made part of the *schedule* or not?

(5) Is there a way by which the United States could impose a tax, fee, or other charge on exports to restrain them, without using a license-quota system? Would such method be consistent with the United States Constitution (see next subsection)? With GATT?

(6) If your answers to question 3 lead you to believe GATT needs amending to accommodate product-by-product negotiations on export tax "bindings" (commitments as to maximums), how would you amend GATT?

(7) What would you foresee as the negotiating difficulties of formulating a code on export controls? Would you, as representative of a raw material exporting nation (e.g., Canada), be willing to agree to a general code, or would you prefer specific rules for each commodity?

(8) Suppose a GATT member imposes an export tax on a particular commodity, which has the effect of discouraging exports of the commodity and preserving low cost supplies of the commodity for domestic producers of another product. If those producers export that product to another GATT member, are competitors in the importing country entitled to have countervailing duties imposed on the imports on the grounds that the export tax operates as a subsidy? Would your answer depend on whether the country imposing the export tax was the only (or

principal or a major) source of the commodity? Whether the commodity was an essential component of the product?

SECTION 12.3 UNITED STATES EXPORT CONTROL LAW

(A) THE UNITED STATES CONSTITUTION AND EXPORT CONTROLS

Query: Can the United States government impose export fees on goods exported? Can it use quota controls on exports?

MOON v. FREEMAN
United States Court of Appeals, Ninth Circuit, 1967.
379 F.2d 382.

DUNIWAY, CIRCUIT JUDGE.

Appellant seeks review of a decision of the District Court denying return of $168.52 that he was required to pay to the Secretary of Agriculture's agent, Commodity Credit Corporation (CCC), for the purchase of export marketing certificates.

* * *

The constitutional significance of the purchase of export certificates required of appellant cannot be fully understood without some knowledge of the history, purposes and operation of the wheat marketing allocation program for the 1964–65 marketing year. The wheat marketing allocation program for 1964–65 is embodied in the Agricultural Act of 1964, and in the regulations promulgated by the Secretary of Agriculture pursuant to the Act. The overall program was a continuation of the federal government's efforts to regulate farm production and marketing in order to guarantee an annual income for farmers on a parity with that of other segments of the economy.

* * *

Under the terms of the Act wheat farmers who chose to submit to the Secretary's acreage controls became eligible for domestic and export wheat marketing certificates. The quantity of each variety of certificate in circulation and the number that each cooperating farmer was to receive was determined by a rather complicated formula, the substance of which is: The Secretary first estimated how much wheat in the relevant crop year would be sold for processing into food products for domestic consumption and how much would be exported in the form of wheat or wheat products. Then he determined the percentage of the total amount of this wheat that would have to receive certificate support in order to meet the price and income objectives of the Act.

* * * In the year here involved the Secretary estimated that 90 per cent of the wheat which would be marketed should be certificate-supported and that half would go to domestic consumption and half to export. Cooperating farmers therefore were issued domestic certificates on 45 per cent of their approved yield and export certificates on 45 per cent. The certificates were issued at one per bushel of projected yield, and a face value was set on each variety of certificate. The Secretary decided, in line with the broad guidelines of the Act, that domestic certificates should have a value of 70¢ and export certificates 25¢. The farmers received their subsidy by selling these certificates to the Secretary's agent, CCC, or to those required to purchase the certificates under the Act. Those required to purchase certificates could buy directly from a cooperating producer or from CCC.

The purchase requirements of the Act were contained in section 202(16), which provided that: "During any marketing year for which a wheat marketing allocation program is in effect, * * * (ii) all persons exporting wheat shall, prior to such export, acquire export marketing certificates equivalent to the number of bushels so exported. In order to expand international trade in wheat and wheat flour and promote equitable and stable prices therefor the Commodity Credit Corporation shall, upon the exportation from the United States of any wheat or wheat flour, make a refund to the exporter or allow him a credit against the amount payable by him for marketing certificates, in such amount as the Secretary determines will make the United States wheat and wheat flour generally competitive in the world market, avoid disruption of the world market prices, and fulfill the international obligations of the United States. * * *"

* * *

The export certificate portion of the marketing program provided for an adjustment of the certificate price after export so that exports would be encouraged, but the basic purchase requirement remained so that exporters could not undercut wheat prices established by treaty. Refunds on export certificates varied from day to day, depending on the international price of wheat. The record indicates that on numerous occasions the Commodity Credit Corporation actually paid back more than the 25¢ face value of the export marketing certificate, thus providing exporters with a subsidy, although this was not the case on the day appellant sold in export.

Appellant Moon is a wheat farmer in the State of Washington. He elected not to cooperate with the Secretary's production controls for 1964–65. As a non-cooperating producer appellant was not entitled to receive either domestic or export marketing certificates. On January 15, 1965, appellant contracted to sell wheat in export, and on or about January 26, 1965, he exported wheat to Rotterdam. The export certificate liability on this shipment was computed to be $411.93. World wheat prices for the relevant day resulted in a refund of $243.41, and appellant was required to pay a net of $168.52, the sum he seeks to get back in this action.

The trial court held that the export certificate requirement was a legitimate exercise of the federal government's power under Art. I, § 8, cl. 3: "The Congress shall have power * * * to regulate commerce with foreign nations, and among the several States * * *." In asserting that the trial court erred, appellant puts primary reliance upon his theory that Art. I, § 9, cl. 5, is a limitation of the commerce power, as well as of the general power of the federal government to raise revenue. Art. I, § 9, cl. 5, states: "No tax or duty shall be laid on articles exported from any State." Appellant argues that the word "duty" broadens the scope of the clause to proscribe monetary impositions used for regulatory purposes whenever such impositions result in an economic burden on exports.

As authority for this proposition appellant cites the history of the constitutional convention. The most persuasive authority from this source in support of appellant's argument that the export clause was intended as a limitation of the commerce power is that when the clause came from the Committee of Detail for general debate, Mr. Clymer of Pennsylvania moved that the words "for the purpose of revenue" be added after the word "duty." The attempted amendment was defeated. Farrand, The Records of the Federal Convention, Vol. II, p. 363. All of the other convention references cited are either completely ambiguous or consistent with the view that the members of the convention had in mind a limitation only of the power to raise revenue.*[17] And it is clear from a reading of the debate preceding Mr. Clymer's proposal that the members were considering the power of taxation, although they recognized that the power to tax could be used to regulate as well as to raise revenue. See id. at 361–363. No special significance such as appellant suggests was given to the word "duty" in the general debate. The members seemed to consider the word to mean no more than a particular form of taxation.

All of the language appellant cites from Supreme Court cases in support of his theory was used in reference to statutes admittedly passed for the purpose of raising revenue, the only question in the cases being whether the tax or duty was "on exports." Thus, Mr. Clymer's attempted amendment and whatever implications can be drawn from its failure stand alone to support appellant. We do not think that the failure of the amendment is persuasive enough to create a limitation on the commerce power—a grant of power in plenary terms. We are confirmed in this opinion by the approach to the interpretation of the commerce and taxing powers and their limitations adopted by Chief Justice Marshall in Gibbons v. Ogden, by the words of the Constitution which expressly limit both powers, and by Supreme Court cases which reject appellant's theory.

* * *

Regarding the federal power over commerce, Marshall said: "It is the power to regulate; that is, to prescribe the rule by which commerce is to be governed. This power, like all others vested in Congress, is complete in itself, may be exercised to its utmost extent, and acknowledges no limitations, other than are prescribed in the Constitution. These are expressed in plain terms * * *." 22 U.S. (9 Wheat.) at 196, 6 L.Ed. at 70. As to the taxing power he said: "The grant of the power to lay and collect taxes is, like the power to regulate commerce, made in general terms, and has never been understood to interfere with the exercise of the same power by the states * * *. But the two grants [of commercial regulation and taxation]

---

* 17. Mr. Gouverneur Morris of Pennsylvania suggested at one point that the clause would restrict the federal government's power to lay an embargo on exports. Farrand, supra, at 360. But Mr. Ellsworth of Connecticut, a member of the Committee of Detail, did not "conceive an embargo * * * interdicted by this section." Id. at 361. The Supreme Court has since agreed with Mr. Ellsworth, thus implicitly holding that the export clause is no limitation on the use of the most extreme form of export regulation, which would, of course, impose a terminal economic burden on exports. See Mulford v. Smith, 1938, 307 U.S. 38, 48, 59 S.Ct. 648, 83 L.Ed. 1092, 1099.

are not, it is conceived, similar in their terms or their nature. * * * In a separate clause of the enumeration [of federal powers], the power to regulate commerce is given, as being entirely distinct from the right to levy taxes and imposts, and as being a new power, not before conferred. The Constitution, then, considers these powers as substantive, and distinct from each other * * *." Id. at 198–202, 6 L.Ed. at 70, 71.

Rejecting the argument that the limitations imposed by the Constitution on state power to tax commerce showed a power to regulate commerce retained by the states, Marshall said by way of example: " 'A *duty* of tonnage' is as much a *tax*, as a *duty* on imports and exports; and the reason which inducted the prohibition of those *taxes* extends to this also. This *tax* may be imposed by a state, with the consent of Congress, and it may be admitted, that Congress cannot give a right to a state, in virtue of its own power. But a *duty* of tonnage, *being part of the power of imposing taxes*, its prohibition may certainly be made to depend on Congress, without affording any implication respecting a power to regulate commerce. *It is true, that duties may often be, and in fact often are, imposed on tonnage, with a view to the regulation of commerce, but they may be also imposed, with a view to revenue;* and it was therefore, a prudent precaution, to prohibit the states from exercising this power. The idea that the same measure might, according to circumstances, be arranged with different classes of power, was no novelty to the framers of our Constitution. Those illustrious statesmen and patriots had been, many of them, deeply engaged in the discussions which preceded the war of our revolution, and all of them were well read in those discussions. *The right to regulate commerce, even by the imposition of duties, was not controverted; but the right to impose a duty for the purpose of revenue, produced a war* * * *."

Id. at 202, 6 L.Ed. at 71 [emphasis added].

Marshall was not specifically discussing the export clause limitation on the federal government, but we think, and later Supreme Court cases indicate, that the same approach must be taken here. We should not easily suppose that separately stated general powers are limited by words commonly understood to relate only to one of the powers. When the drafters of the Constitution wanted to make it clear that both the commerce power and the taxing power were being limited, they made specific reference. The very next clause to the one now under consideration states "No preference shall be given *by any regulation of commerce or revenue* to the ports of one state over those of another * * *." [Emphasis added.]

Finally, the Supreme Court has heard and rejected the argument made here by appellant that the constitutional convention's failure to add the words "for the purpose of revenue" means that the export clause was intended as a limitation on the commerce power. Pace v. Burgess, 1875, 92 U.S. 372, 23 L.Ed. 657, involved the constitutionality of a charge made for the placing of a special stamp on tobacco to be exported. Under the original Act of 1868 a tax of 32¢ per pound was imposed on all manufactured tobacco except smoking tobacco, which was taxed at 16¢ per pound. The tax was to be paid before the tobacco left the factory. All tobacco intended for export was to have a special stamp bought and affixed before the tobacco left the factory. That stamp cost 25¢ per package, with no restriction on the size of the package. The 1872 Act reduced the charge for the export stamp to 10¢ per package. This stamp charge was said to be a duty on exports, and it was argued that it was immaterial whether the charge was for regulation of commerce, since the constitutional convention rejected "an amendment proposing to insert, after 'duty' * * * the words 'for the purpose of revenue' * * *." 92 U.S. 372 (argument for plaintiff in error). The Court's opinion did not stop to mention the argument. The Court concluded that the monetary charge was not a tax or duty in the sense of Art. I, § 9 cl. 5, but a regulatory measure designed to "facilitate the disposal of tobacco intended for exportation" and a "means devised to prevent fraud and secure the faithful carrying out of the declared intent with regard to the tobacco so marked." 92 U.S. at 374–375, 23 L.Ed. at 659. To the same effect is Turpin v. Burgess, 1886, 117 U.S. 504, 6 S.Ct. 835, 29 L.Ed. 988.

To summarize: Appellant has suggested that the export clause is an across-the-board limitation on the commerce power as well as the taxing power, and that whenever any economic burden is placed upon exports, the export clause is violated. We reject that broad contention. However, the question remains as to the test for determining when a monetary imposition nominally imposed under the commerce power should be considered an exercise of the power to raise revenue and therefore barred by the export clause i.e., when is it a tax and not a regulation.

On this question the District Court adopted the test applied by the Sixth Circuit in Rodgers v. United States, 1943, 138 F.2d 992. That court, in considering whether the penalties imposed for noncompliance with the cotton marketing quotas of the original Agricultural Adjustment Act of 1938 amounted to an unproportioned direct tax, said: "The test to be applied is to view the objects and purposes of the statute as a whole and if from such examination it is concluded that revenue is the primary purpose and regulation merely incidental, the imposition is a tax and is controlled by the taxing provisions of the Constitution. Conversely, if regulation is the primary purpose of the statute, the mere fact that incidentally revenue is also obtained does not make the imposition a tax, but a sanction imposed for the purpose of making effective the congressional enactment." 138 F.2d at 994. We consider this an accurate and precise statement of the rule. It is in line with Chief Justice Marshall's approach in Gibbons v. Ogden, supra; it is exactly the test used by the Supreme Court in Pace v. Burgess, supra, when considering the export clause; and it is also the test used by the Supreme Court and other circuits when searching for the dividing line between monetary impositions that are supported by the taxing power and those that are supported by the commerce power. We agree with the District Court that the Rodgers test applies here.

Our final problem is to determine whether under this test the monetary imposition upon wheat to be exported which is in question here was a tax or duty in the constitutional sense. We start with several Supreme Court admonitions. First, "the presumption is in favor of every legislative act, and * * * the whole burden of proof lies on him who denies its constitutionality." Second, "if the Congress may * * * exercise the [commerce] power, and asserts * * * that it is exercising it, the judicial department may not attempt in its own conception of policy to distribute the duties thus fixed by allocating some of them to the exercise of the admitted power to regulate commerce and others to an independent exercise of the taxing power." And third, a cautionary note from the case of Pace v. Burgess, supra: "The point to guard against is, the imposition of a duty under the pretext of fixing a fee * * *. One cause of difficulty in the case arises from the use of stamps [read 'certificates'], * * * stamps being seldom used, except for the purpose of levying a duty or tax. But we must regard things rather than names. A stamp may be used * * * for quite a different purpose from that of imposing a tax or duty * * *. The sense and reason of the thing will generally determine the character of every case that can arise."

We have set out earlier the general announced purposes of the wheat marketing allocation program for the 1964–65 marketing year. These are consistent with an exercise of the commerce power. Nothing in the legislative history of the Act indicates that the purpose of the legislation was in any way related to the raising of revenue. As the Supreme Court said in Board of Trustees, etc. v. United States, supra, note 21: "The purpose to regulate commerce permeates the entire congressional plan." All indications are that the purpose was to induce producers to comply with crop controls, and to regulate the price of wheat reaching both domestic and foreign markets. It has long since been established that the commerce power will support federal regulation of crops and prices; and whether this is done directly as under former programs, or indirectly through the issuing and buying and selling of marketing certificates is a matter for the discretion of Congress.

Certainly if the record in any way indicated that substantial amounts of revenue had been generated by the sale of export certificates, we would hesitate before deeming the program an exercise of the commerce power. Pace v. Burgess, supra, teaches us to look at things rather than names. But the "thing" of the export marketing certificate program is that funds raised by the sale of export certificates are used by CCC to help defray the cost of purchases from producers, and that in the 1964–65 marketing year, CCC paid out to producers substantially more than it took in from exporters.

Looking at things instead of names from another point of view, we see that appellant was forced to purchase export certificates only because he did not agree to cooperate with the Secretary's production controls. Had he cooperated with the Secretary, he would have received free export certificates for 45 per cent of the projected yield from his approved acreage, and there is nothing in the record indicating that in these circumstances he would have been required to purchase any export certificates for the shipment involved here. This approach shows that appellant was in effect penalized for his failure to cooperate with the regulation of production on his farm. The fact that the program was denominated "voluntary" should make no difference. Other circuits have approved such impositions as incidents of regulation, even where the production or marketing penalized was not forbidden. And such penalties have been upheld against charges that they amounted to a tax on exports.

We hold that appellant has not been forced to pay a tax or duty in the constitutional sense, and that the export marketing certificate program is a valid exercise of the federal government's power to regulate commerce.

Affirmed.

Note

See Annotation, What Amounts to Prohibited Federal Tax or Duty on Exports Within Article I, Section 9, Clause 5, of Federal Constitution, 3 A.L.R. Fed. 550 (1970). For a view that all export controls are unconstitutional, see Note, Constitutionality of Export Controls, 76 Yale L.J. 200 (1966). See also United States v. Hvoslef, 237 U.S. 1, 35 S.Ct. 459, 59 L.Ed. 813 (1914), which did not directly face the question of export controls, but which did identify as unconstitutional, stamp taxes or fees for export licenses, saying at 237 U.S. at 13, 35 S.Ct. at 463: "This constitutional freedom, however, plainly involves more than mere exemption from taxes or duties which are laid specifically upon the goods themselves. If it meant no more than that, the obstructions to exportation which it was the purpose to prevent could readily be set up by legislation nominally conforming to the constitutional restriction but in effect overriding it."

(B) UNITED STATES EXPORT CONTROLS [1]

(1) Overview of the Export Administration Act

The United States has a comprehensive system of export controls, based on the Export Administration Act (EAA) of 1979, as amended in 1985 (see Documentary Supplement).[2] The Act, which is scheduled to expire on September 30, 1989, authorizes the control of exports in certain circumstances for reasons of national security, foreign policy and short supplies. In this subsection, we will outline the general provisions of U.S. law applicable to exports and the rules applicable to short supply controls. We will then look at presidential authority to control exports under other laws and at the problem of hazardous exports. In Chapter 13, we will examine the specific rules applicable to national security and foreign policy controls, focusing on such questions as the effectiveness of those controls and their extraterritorial application.

The EAA sets out an extensive list of congressional findings and declarations of policies in its first two sections. Basically, the thrust of those sections seems to be that export controls should be used sparingly so as not to harm U.S. businesses and only where necessary for reasons of national security, foreign policy or short supplies. However, a review of these two sections also leaves one with a sense of confusion as to the extent that Congress really favors or disfavors the use of export controls. This confusion is probably an accurate reflection of congressional attitudes. There are

---

1. The focus here is exclusively on United States law as an example of export controls. For discussion of other national mechanisms for export control, see Baker & Bohlig, The Control of Exports, 1 Intl. Lawyer 163 (1967); Matsushita, Export Control and Export Cartels in Japan, 20 Harv.Intl.L.J. 103 (1979).

For a history of U.S. export controls, see Berman & Garson, United States Export Controls—Past, Present, and Future, 67 Colum.L. Rev. 791 (1967).

2. 50 U.S.C.A.App. §§ 2401–2420.

some Congressmen who seem in principle to favor controls for national security reasons but who bow to business and agricultural interests when specific instances of use of national security controls are at issue. Other Congressmen seem less supportive of controls based on national security grounds but support controls imposed to express U.S. opposition to particular policies of other governments. These and other conflicting viewpoints have often in recent years left Congress unable to legislate on the subject of export controls, with the result that several times in the last 10 years, the basic U.S. export control legislation has lapsed and the President has had to operate the export control system on the basis of other legislation, which raises the issues discussed in subsection (B)(3) below.

In substantive terms, the broad outlines of the EAA are simple enough. The President is given the power to "prohibit or curtail the export of any goods subject to the jurisdiction of the United States or exported by any person subject to the jurisdiction of the United States" for reasons of national security, foreign policy or short supplies.[3] The statute itself, however, is incredibly complex, reflecting (i) congressional mistrust of the Executive Branch of the type that led to the detailed antidumping and countervailing duty laws discussed in Chapter 10 supra and (ii) many special provisions applicable only to specific products or exporters of specific products. The complexity is heightened by numerous requirements for reports to Congress, frequent reviews of the need for controls and consultations with private groups. As in the import restraint laws, many strict deadlines for executive action are established.

The Department of Commerce has primary responsibility for the administration of the EAA, and it has issued extensive regulations based on the Act.[4] Until 1985, the regulations were administered by the International Trade Administration, but the 1985 amendments provided for a new Under Secretary of Commerce and two Assistant Secretaries to administer the EAA, so the current administrators will likely be given a new name.

The regulations adopted to implement the EAA provide that essentially all exports from the United States are subject to control and may only be made pursuant to a valid license. In practice, most exports to most countries may be made pursuant to a general license, which is not really a license at all but rather a regulation authorizing exports without specific authorization. There is a not insignificant number of commodities that require a validated license, which is issued to a specific exporter for a specific transaction or group of transactions. These commodities are those controlled for national security, foreign policy or short supply purposes and the precise licensing requirement and the likelihood of approval depend on the commodity involved and the country to which it is being exported. For example, at the moment, almost all exports to North Korea, Kampuchea, Vietnam and Cuba are subject to a validated license requirement and the U.S. policy is to deny all license applications.[5] As countries are considered to be more

---

3. See 50 U.S.C.A.App. §§ 2404(a), 2405(a), 2406(a). In the case of national security controls, the authorization to control extends to technology, as well as goods. 50 U.S.C.A.App. § 2404(a). In the case of foreign policy con-

trols, it extends to technology or other information. 50 U.S.C.A.App. § 2405(a).

4. 15 CFR Pts. 368–99 (1985).

5. 15 CFR § 385.1 (1985).

friendly toward the United States, the number of commodities controlled decreases and the likelihood of approval increases.

The EAA provides that applications must be processed within specified time limits, which were generally shortened by one-third by the 1985 amendments.[6] The EAA specifies that within 10 days of the filing of an application, it must be acknowledged in writing and the applicant advised as to the procedures that will be followed. If an application is not referred to another agency for its recommendation, the application must be accepted or rejected within 60 days of filing. If another agency is involved up to 60 additional days are allowed, the limit being extendible in the event of a determination by the Secretary of Commerce that the application is of exceptional importance and complexity. If these deadlines are exceeded by more than 20 days, a court order directing compliance may be sought. Otherwise, there is only the most limited judicial review of actions taken under the EAA, as Congress has explicitly provided that the rulemaking, adjudicatory and judicial review provisions of the Administrative Procedure Act do not apply, except that the rules on adjudication apply to the imposition of civil sanctions.[7]

Violations of the EAA are generally punishable by fine (up to $50,000) and imprisonment (up to five years),[8] but if the violation is willful and with knowledge that the exports will be used for the benefit of a country subject to national security or foreign policy controls, the maximum fine is the greater of five times the value of the exports or $1,000,000 ($250,000 for individuals) and up to ten years imprisonment.[9] The EAA also provides for civil penalties. Fines of up to $10,000 ($100,000 in national security control cases) are authorized.[10] In addition, the EAA authorizes the suspension of export and import privileges of violators, i.e. a U.S. company could be barred from exporting or importing goods, while a foreign company would be prohibited from receiving U.S. exports or exporting goods to the United States. These are potentially very heavy penalties, at least for multinational enterprises and companies active in international trade. A review of the Federal Register suggests that two dozen or so companies a year are denied export privileges (see Section 13.3 supra).[11]

Notes and Questions

(1) The frustration of Congress in attempting to control presidential discretion in respect of the imposition of export controls was eloquently expressed by Congressman Bonker in his statement excerpted in Section 3.4(A)(1) supra. It should be reread at this point.

(2) Why do you think that Congress did not provide the kind of judicial review under the Export Administration Act that it did the same year in respect of antidumping and countervailing duty actions? Do you think Congress will continue to follow this policy?

6. 50 U.S.C.A.App. § 2409.

7. 50 U.S.C.A.App. § 2412.

8. 50 U.S.C.A.App. § 2410(a).

9. 50 U.S.C.A.App. § 2410(b).

10. 50 U.S.C.A.App. § 2410(c).

11. 50 U.S.C.A.App. § 2410(c) (exports); 19 U.S.C.A. § 233 (imports).

(3) If the Secretary of Commerce has almost unreviewable discretion to deny licenses, why has Congress gone into so much detail as to how quickly license applications are to be processed?

(4) Not all export controls are based on the Export Administration Act. According to the most recent Commerce Department regulations,[12] the State Department regulates the export of arms on the Munitions List, the Drug Enforcement Administration of the Justice Department regulates the export of certain drugs, the Nuclear Regulatory Commission regulates the export of nuclear equipment and materials, the U.S. Maritime Administration regulates the export of certain vessels, the Department of Energy regulates the export of natural gas and electric power, the Department of Agriculture regulates the export of tobacco seeds and plants and the Department of the Interior regulates the export of endangered fish and wildlife and migratory birds (including products containing parts thereof).

(2) Short Supply Controls

The Act authorizes the President to control exports "to protect the domestic economy from the excessive drain of scarce materials and to reduce the serious inflationary impact of foreign demand." [13]   The President is directed to allocate a portion of the exports on a basis other than the historical pattern of exports and in allocating exports he is to consider the extent to which a country engages in equitable trade relations with respect to United States goods and treats the United States equitably in respect of items in short supply.   At the moment, the United States imposes export controls to conserve short supplies only in respect of certain petroleum products and western red cedar.[14]   These controls are largely mandated by statute,[15] although in the past the powers under similar provisions have been used by the President to restrain exports of other commodities in short supply.   This was particularly true in the early 1970's, as described in the following Note.

NOTE, ADMINISTRATIVE SURVEY: OCTOBER 1972 to SEPTEMBER 1973

(1974)[16]

B.   SHORT-SUPPLY CONTROLS

In response to both domestic inflation and the unprecedented foreign demand for certain products, a number of short-supply export controls and licensing procedures were initiated during the second quarter of 1973.

On May 22, 1973, the Department of Commerce began to monitor the foreign demand for, and actual export of, ferrous scrap. Weekly reports were required to be submitted by June 1973 to reflect both future orders for exports and actual exports of 500 or more short tons of ferrous scrap. On July 2, 1973, at the urging of domestic steel and foundry companies, the

---

12. 15 CFR § 370.10 (1985).

13. 50 U.S.C.A.App. §§ 2406, 2402(2)(C).

14. See generally, 15 CFR Pt. 377 (1985).

15. See 50 U.S.C.A.App. § 2406.

16. 6 Law & Poly.Intl.Bus. 727, 743. Reprinted by permission of Law & Policy in International Business.

Department of Commerce subjected exports of ferrous scrap to a validated-license control for all destinations except Canada. No licenses were issued for exports against orders of 500 or more short tons accepted after July 1, 1973, or orders that called for exports after July 31, 1973. Applications to export less than 500 short tons, however, were not automatically denied, but were considered regardless of the date on which such orders were accepted. The Office of Export Control announced additional changes in ferrous-scrap licensing on July 27, 1973, extending the validity of licenses until August 30, 1973, and creating a licensing system for August exports. On August 24th, licensing procedures were extended for September 1973, and a prohibition of the evasionary tactics of splitting orders was implemented. Controls on ferrous scrap were eased on September 12th, however, when it announced that there would be a discontinuance of export licensing for orders of less than 500 short tons during September.

On June 13th, 1973, the Commerce Department instituted a weekly surveillance system to monitor exports and anticipated exports of certain grains, oilseeds, and oilseed products in order amounts of $250 or more. Certain types of barley, corn, cottonseeds and cottonseed products, grain sorghums, oats, rice, rye, soybeans and soybean products, and wheat were placed under monitoring procedures. The system culminated on June 27th with a revision of the Commodity Control List. Because of the shortage of domestic supplies and an abnormal foreign demand for soybeans, an embargo was placed on the export of cottonseed, soybeans, and related products. The OEC also warned of the possibility of restrictions on the export of corn.

On July 2, 1973, a validated-export-licensing system replaced the June 27th embargo. Any exporter holding an outstanding contract for the delivery to a foreign firm of either soybeans or soybean oil-cakes and meal that was accepted on or before June 13th, and that called for delivery during the crop year, was eligible to file an export-license application for those goods that had not yet been shipped. The OEC was authorized to issue a license, after appropriate verification, for export of 50 percent of the soybeans and 37 per cent of soybean oilcakes and meal. Licenses filed for cottonseed could be issued for 100 percent of the unshipped balance of the contract.

As a result of the U.S. controls imposed on cottonseed and soybeans, foreign demand shifted to other sources of high-protein feeds, which necessitated further U.S. action to control commodities such as cottonseed oil, soybean oil, and substitutes for them, as well as the raw materials for the substitutes. Thus, on July 5, 1973, after approval by the Secretary of Agriculture, validated-export licenses were imposed on 41 additional agricultural commodities including animal fats, edible oils, livestock protein feed, and soybean oil-cake and meal.

The licensing procedure for soybean oil-cake and meal created a threat of spoilage for portions of the commodity that were already in transit. To remedy this situation, the OEC, in conjunction with the Export Control Design Committee, permitted the licensing of soybean oil-cake and meal that was either en route to port or in port and earmarked for loading on an exporting vessel when the validated-licensing requirement was imposed.

On August 1, 1973, a more liberal licensing policy was announced for shipment of soybean exports during September on the basis of 100 percent of the unfilled balance of orders accepted by the exporter on or before June 13th and previously reported to the Commerce Department.

After review of the supply and demand situation for September, there occurred a further liberalization of export restrictions on all the agricultural commodities subject to validated licensing. Effective September 8th, applications for export contracts consummated after that date for all agricultural commodities subject to controls were licensed for 100 percent of the quantity specified in the contract. Licenses that were to be issued against such applications were to expire on October 15, 1973.

The remaining controls on these agricultural commodities were removed on October 1, 1973, as a result of the excellent harvest prospects of all commodities for the new crop year. Although licenses were no longer required for the export of this group of commodities, the monitoring system continued in full force.

Question

Are U.S. short supply rules consistent with Articles XI and XIII of GATT?

(3) Presidential Authority to Control Exports

As noted above, Congress has had difficulty agreeing on the terms of the various export control acts. Since it has enacted them for only short periods, they have on occasion expired without Congress extending them or passing a new act. When this happens, what power does the President have to continue the controls or to impose new ones? To the extent that the President has such power, what is its source? Recall our discussion of presidential power in Chapter 3 supra. Do you think that congressional failures to extend export control legislation occur in part because Congress believes that the President has the power to impose such controls if it fails to act?

An example of congressional failure to keep export controls in place occurred when the 1979 Act expired on October 15, 1983. Congress did not agree to extend it until December 5, 1983, and then only for a short period, and the Act expired again in March 1984. The 1985 amendments extending the Act for four years were not passed until July 1985. Consequently, the President acted both in October 1983 and March 1984 to keep the regulations in place.

CONTINUATION OF EXPORT CONTROL REGULATIONS
Executive Order 12470 of March 30, 1984 [17]

By the authority vested in me as President by the Constitution and laws of the United States of America, including section 203 of the International Emergency Economic Powers Act (50 U.S.C. 1702) (hereinafter referred to as "the Act"), and 22 U.S.C. 287c,

17. 49 Fed.Reg. 13099 (1984). The 1984 Order was extended in March 1985. 50 Fed. Reg. 12513 (1985). The 1983 Order is at 48 Fed.Reg. 48215 (1983).

I, RONALD REAGAN, President of the United States of America, find that the unrestricted access of foreign parties to United States commercial goods, technology, and technical data and the existence of certain boycott practices of foreign nations constitute, in light of the expiration of the Export Administration Act of 1979, an unusual and extraordinary threat to the national security, foreign policy and economy of the United States and hereby declare a national economic emergency to deal with that threat.

Accordingly, in order (a) to exercise the necessary vigilance over exports from the standpoint of their significance to the national security of the United States; (b) to further significantly the foreign policy of the United States, including its policy with respect to cooperation by United States persons with certain foreign boycott activities, and to fulfill its international responsibilities; and (c) to protect the domestic economy from the excessive drain of scarce materials and reduce the serious economic impact of foreign demand, it is hereby ordered as follows:

Section 1. Notwithstanding the expiration of the Export Administration Act of 1979, as amended (50 U.S.C.App. 2401 *et seq.*), the provisions of that Act, the provisions for administration of that Act and the delegations of authority set forth in Executive Order No. 12002 of July 7, 1977 and Executive Order No. 12214 of May 2, 1980, shall, to the extent permitted by law, be incorporated in this Order and shall continue in full force and effect.

Sec. 2. All rules and regulations issued or continued in effect by the Secretary of Commerce under the authority of the Export Administration Act of 1979, as amended, including those published in Title 15, Chapter III, Subchapter C, of the Code of Federal Regulations, Parts 368 to 399 inclusive, and all orders, regulations, licenses and other forms of administrative action issued, taken or continued in effect pursuant thereto, shall, until amended or revoked by the Secretary of Commerce, remain in full force and effect, the same as if issued or taken pursuant to this Order, except that the provisions of sections 203(b)(2) and 206 of the Act (50 U.S.C. 1702(b)(2) and 1705) shall control over any inconsistent provisions in the regulations with respect to, respectively, certain donations to relieve human suffering and civil and criminal penalties for violations subject to this Order. Nothing in this section shall affect the continued applicability of administrative sanctions provided for by the regulations described above.

* * *

Sec. 4. This Order shall be effective as of midnight between March 30 and March 31, 1984 and shall remain in effect until terminated. It is my intention to terminate this Order upon the enactment into law of a bill reauthorizing the authorities contained in the Export Administration Act.

Ronald Reagan

THE WHITE HOUSE,
March 30, 1984.

A similar mechanism was used to continue export controls in 1976 when a previous version of the 1979 Act expired. Its use gave rise to litigation over the legality of the extension solely on presidential authority.

UNITED STATES v. SPAWR OPTICAL RESEARCH, INC.

United States Court of Appeals, Ninth Circuit, 1982.
685 F.2d 1076, cert. denied, 461 U.S. 905, 103 S.Ct. 1875, 76 L.Ed.2d 807 (1983).

CHOY, CIRCUIT JUDGE:

Walter and Frances Spawr and their family-owned corporation, Spawr Optical Research, Inc. (the Spawrs), appeal their convictions resulting from their unlicensed export of laser mirrors destined for the Soviet Union. Their principal challenge is to the Government's reliance on allegedly defunct export regulations that they were convicted of violating. * * *

I. BACKGROUND

In 1969, Frances and Walter Spawr formed Spawr Optical Research, Inc., as a means of exploiting Walter's skills as an optics expert. * * *

As the Spawrs began to explore international markets in 1974, they established a business arrangement with Wolfgang Weber, a West German national, calling for Weber to promote and distribute Spawr mirrors in Central and Eastern Europe, including the Communist Block nations. Weber, who was named an unindicted coconspirator with the Spawrs, arranged and facilitated the two orders of laser mirrors which underlie the Spawrs' convictions.

In October 1975, Spawr provided Weber with sample laser mirrors to exhibit at a trade show in Moscow. The laser mirrors attracted considerable interest and in January 1976 Weber obtained the Spawrs' authorization to accept an order for mirrors from a purchasing agency of the Soviet Government. When Weber visited California in late spring of 1976, the Spawrs provided him with some of the mirrors for the order. In July, the Spawrs shipped the balance of the order to Weber in West Germany. Weber then forwarded the entire order to Moscow. In the shipping documents accompanying the mirrors, Frances listed the value of each mirror at $500. The Spawrs never attempted to obtain a validated export license for the mirrors exported for this first order.

In April 1976, Weber notified Spawr that he had received a second Soviet order for Spawr mirrors. Walter told Weber that he thought it might be better to ask for an export license for at least a part of this order. Weber then provided Walter with an end-user statement. On May 4, 1976, Walter filed an application with the Commerce Department for a validated export license for some of the mirrors by the Soviets. The Commerce Department denied the application on October 7, 1976 pursuant to Executive Order 11940 and existing export regulations, because the mirrors were found to have "significant strategic applications" posing a potential threat to national security. Weber sent a letter cancelling the second Soviet order on November 3, 1976 after Spawr informed him that the application had been denied. In February 1977, however, Spawr shipped mirrors to a freight forwarder in Switzerland. Weber then relabeled the boxes containing the mirrors and shipped them to Moscow. The shipping documents accompanying the mirrors again stated that the value of each mirror did not exceed $500.

II. THE VALIDITY OF THE EXPORT REGULATIONS

In light of the pending expiration of the Export Administration Act of 1969 (EAA), President Gerald Ford issued Executive Order No. 11940 on September 30, 1976 to maintain the EAA regulations forbidding the shipment of specified strategic items to certain foreign countries. He acted pursuant to § 5(b) of the Trading with the Enemy Act (TWEA), 50 U.S.C. app. §§ 1–44. When the Order was issued and while it remained in effect, the TWEA empowered the President, during a presidentially-declared national emergency, to "regulate, * * * prevent or prohibit * * * any exportation of * * * or transactions involving any property in which a foreign country * * * has any interest." Id. at § 5(b)(1)(B).*5 Rather than declare a new national emergency to support the Executive Order, President Ford relied on the continued existence of national emergencies declared in 1950 by President Truman relating to the Korean War and in 1971 by President Nixon concerning an international monetary crisis. See Exec. Order No. 11940, 3 C.F.R. 150 (1976 compilation), reprinted in 50 U.S.C. app. § 2403 (1976).

The laser mirrors for the first Russian order were exported before the EAA expired on October 1, 1976, and the Spawrs do not dispute the Government's authority to prosecute them for exporting mirrors to fill the first Soviet order. The Spawrs exported laser mirrors for the second Soviet Order, however, after the EAA had expired and before it was reenacted on June 22, 1977, when the sole basis for the regulations was the Executive Order. The Spawrs assert that the Order did not preserve the export regulations and, therefore, the Government lacked authority to prosecute them for their exporting mirrors for the second Soviet orders because: (1) there was no genuine national emergency, (2) the regulations were not rationally related to any emergency then in existence, and (3) the lapse of the EAA shows that Congress intended to terminate the regulations.

Former section 5(b) of the TWEA delegated to the President broad and extensive powers; "it could not have been otherwise if the President were to have, within constitutional boundaries, the flexibility required to meet problems surrounding a national emergency with the success desired by Congress." United States v. Yoshida International, Inc., 526 F.2d 560, 573 (Cust. & Pat.App.1975) (footnote omitted). Wary of impairing the flexibility necessary to such a broad delegation, courts have not normally reviewed "the essentially political questions surrounding the declaration or continuance of a national emergency" under former § 5(b). Id. at 579.*8 The

* 5. Section 5(b) was later amended to eliminate all reference to "national emergency." See Act of Dec. 28, 1977, Pub.L.No. 95–223, §§ 101(a), 102, 103(b), 91 Stat. 1625, 1626 (1977) (codified at 50 U.S.C. app. § 5(b) (Supp. III 1979).

* 8. Since the 1975 decision of the Court of Custom and Patent Appeals in Yoshida, Congress has eliminated all references to a national emergency in § 5(b), see supra note 5, and has established procedures for declaring and terminating a national emergency. See The National Emergencies Act, Pub.L. 94–412, 90 Stat. 1255 (1976), codified at 50 U.S.C. § 1601–41 (1976). We need not decide how these changes might affect the reviewability of the above issues.

statute contained no standards by which to determine whether a national emergency existed or continued; in fact, Congress had delegated to the President the authority to define all of the terms in that subsection of the TWEA including "national emergency," as long as the definitions were consistent with the purposes of the TWEA. 50 U.S.C. app. § 5(b)(3). In the absence of a compelling reason to address the difficult questions concerning the declaration and duration of a national emergency under former § 5(b), we decline to do so.

Although we will not address these essentially-political questions, we are free to review whether the actions taken pursuant to a national emergency comport with the power delegated by Congress. See *Yoshida,* 526 F.2d at 579.*10 The standard proffered by the Spawrs is that the President's action must be rationally related to the national emergencies invoked. Assuming, without deciding, that the Spawrs are correct, we believe that there is a rational relationship.

One source invoked by President Ford was Presidential Proclamation No. 2914. It declared a national emergency based in part on events which "imperil the efforts of this country and those of the United Nations to prevent aggression and armed conflict." 3 C.F.R. 99, 100 (1949–53 compilation). President Ford's effort to limit the exportation of strategic items clearly had a rational relationship to the prevention of aggression and armed conflict.

The Spawrs' final argument, that Congress intended to terminate these export regulations by allowing the EAA to lapse, is rebutted by presidential and congressional actions taken concerning the EAA. The EAA had previously lapsed three times. In each instance, the President used an executive order virtually identical to Executive Order No. 11940 to maintain the export regulations. All three orders relied upon the same unrevoked declarations of national emergencies and upon § 5(b) of the TWEA.

Congress not only tolerated this practice, it expressed approval of the President's reliance on the TWEA to maintain the export regulations. In passing the 1977 amendments to the EAA, Congress again conferred on the President the rule-making authority necessary to maintain the regulations. The legislative history of the 1977 amendments indicates that the reenactment of § 5(b) "reflected concern for preserving existing regulation imposed under emergency authority, including * * * the transaction control regulations, which prohibit U.S. persons from participating in shipping strategic goods to * * * the Soviet Union." S.Rep. No. 466, 95th Cong., 1st Sess. 3, *reprinted in* 1977 U.S.Code Cong. & Ad.News 4540, 4542.

Moreover, the EAA apparently was allowed to lapse only because Congress could not resolve questions relating to the antiboycott provisions. *See* Arab Boycott Hearings on S. 69 and S. 92, Before the Subcommittee on International Finance of the Senate Committee on Banking, Housing and

---

* **10.** As noted previously, the express delegation in § 5(b) to the President was broad and enabled him to regulate, prevent or prohibit the exportation of *any* property to *any* foreign country. The unambiguous wording of the statute clearly shows that the Presi- dent's actions were in accordance with the power Congress delegated. Cf. United States v. Yoshida International, Inc., 526 F.2d 560, 573 (Cust. & Pat.App.1975) (that President can regulate imports is incontestable under language of § 5(b)).

Urban Affairs, 95th Congress, 1st Sess. 1 (Senator Stevenson) (1977). The Spawrs have offered no evidence that Congress intended to dismantle the export controls.

In conclusion, even under the demanding scrutiny the Spawrs argue is appropriate because of the criminal nature of this case, it is unmistakable that Congress intended to permit the President to use the TWEA to employ the same regulatory tools during a national emergency as it had employed under the EAA. We, therefore, conclude that the President had the authority during the nine-month lapse in the EAA to maintain the export regulations. * * *

Affirmed.

Notes and Questions

(1) As Judge Choy noted, Congress revised the Trading With the Enemy Act in 1977. It also adopted the International Economic Emergency Powers Act (IEEPA) at the same time. Presidential extensions of export controls since that time have been pursuant to IEEPA, which was discussed in Section 3.4(B)(1) supra. Is there any reason why a challenge would come out differently under IEEPA than *Spawr* did?

(2) In 1984, could the President have used his authority under IEEPA to establish an export control system different from and/or contrary to the 1979 Export Administration Act? What if the Act had not lapsed? If so, which system of controls would prevail? Would courts be more likely to intervene in this sort of conflict than in a case challenging the President's extension of a congressional act?

(4) Exportation of Hazardous Products

In recent years, much attention has been focused on the question of whether the United States should restrict the export of goods from the United States in cases where those goods could not be sold in the United States.[18] The EAA does not mandate such controls, although the 1985 amendments provide: "It is the policy of the United States to control export of goods and substances banned or severely restricted for use in the United States in order to foster public health and safety and to prevent injury to the United States as well as to the credibility of the United States as a responsible trading partner." [19] At this writing, the United States has not yet acted under this provision, and as we will see in Chapter 13, it may not be likely to do so because Congress, in its attempt to reduce the use of export controls for foreign policy purposes, has imposed so many requirements and conditions that the Act may not be suitable for imposing these kinds of

18. See generally Street, U.S. Exports Banned for Domestic Use But Exported to Third World Countries, 6 Intl.Trade L.J. 95 (1981); Comment, State Responsibility and Hazardous Products Exports, 13 Cal.Western Intl.L.J. 116 (1983); Comment, United States Export of Products Banned for Domestic Use, 20 Harv.Intl.L.J. 331 (1979); Note, Hazardous Exports from a Human Rights Perspective, 14 Sw.U.L.Rev. 81 (1983).

19. 50 U.S.C.A. App. § 2402(13). In 1981, President Carter established detailed rules concerning the manner in which the United States would inform foreign governments that products banned in the United States were being exported to their countries. 46 Fed.Reg. 4659 (1981). The rules were withdrawn a month later by President Reagan. 46 Fed. Reg. 12943 (1981).

controls. Moreover, in general, the specific U.S. statutes that regulate hazardous products either do not regulate the export of such products or regulate products intended for export much less stringently than they do products intended for domestic use. For example, the Toxic Substances Control Act does not restrict export of substances controlled under the Act so long as manufacture and exportation of such substances has not been determined to present an unreasonable risk of injury to health within the United States or to the environment of the United States. The Act does require that notice of exportation be given to the U.S. authorities, who are to forward specified information about the substance to the foreign government involved.[20]

As a result of these differences in the scope of regulation, products not allowed to be sold in the United States often may be legally exported. Should this be permitted? It can be argued that it is not improper because of the concept of national sovereignty. If the nation to which a product is to be exported does not feel its use should be banned, what gives the U.S. government the right to keep the citizens of the other nation from buying that product? Arguably, the decision is one for their government to make taking local conditions and attitudes into account. On the other hand, most nations do not have the sophisticated testing and evaluation capabilities of the United States. This argument suggests, of course, that different standards may be appropriate depending on the sophistication level of the importing country. Establishment of different levels would involve many administrative and diplomatic problems. If U.S. standards are not to be applied across the board, it would be necessary to consider how dangerous the product is, including the degree and certainty of the danger. Consider, in this regard, the recent attempt to organize a boycott of Nestle Co. because of its sale abroad of infant formula mix. There was no claim the product itself was dangerous. The fear was that improper use such as mixing it too thin or using contaminated water to prepare it would cause harm to the infants so fed. Is this a proper case for export controls? Are these concerns met by a requirement such as mentioned above that a foreign government be notified in the event a product not able to be sold in the United States is exported to it?

Exports are not, of course, the only problem. If it is agreed that hazardous exports should be controlled, should such controls extend to licensing agreements related to the product in question? Should the United States attempt in general to control the manufacture of such products outside the United States by U.S.-based or controlled corporations? Does the United States have the authority to do so? Without such additional controls as these, would controls on exports be meaningless?

---

20. 15 U.S.C.A. § 2611. See also 7 U.S.C.A. § 136o(a) (pesticides—exemption and notification provision); 15 U.S.C.A. § 1202 (flammable fabrics—exemption and notification provision); 15 U.S.C.A. § 1273(d) (hazardous substances—exemption and notification provision); 15 U.S.C.A. § 2067 (1982) (consumer products—exemption and notification provision).

Chapter 13

TRADE CONTROLS FOR NATIONAL SECURITY AND POLITICAL PURPOSES

SECTION 13.1 INTRODUCTION: HISTORICAL BACKGROUND

A classic exception to liberal trade policies and rules is the so-called national security exception. It is generally accepted that the benefits normally associated with free markets, such as efficient allocation of resources, do not outweigh the imperative need to ensure national survival. Thus, if a nation's defense and security depend, or are believed to depend, on the existence of industries such as shipbuilding or steelmaking, those industries are likely to be maintained regardless of cost or any other economic considerations. The issue of national security being so important, it has always seemed inevitable that a national security exception would apply to international trade rules. The problem with a national security exception in international agreements, however, is that it is virtually impossible to define its limits. Almost every sector of economic endeavor can and does argue that it is necessary for national security, from shoes to watches, radios to beef production.

The basic justification for the national security exception is that it is necessary to provide for national defense by ensuring production of goods essential for defense. That is not, however, the only reason that the exception exists. Nations often wish to use trade controls for political purposes that may have only a tangential relationship to national security. For example, a country may dislike the discriminatory racial policies of another government and therefore exercise controls over trade with that government. Countries may choose to refrain from granting MFN status to other countries, because those countries are viewed as unfriendly or because to grant such status would be politically unpopular and therefore risk the survival of elected officials in their positions. For whatever the reasons, the facts of international economic life are that nations will pursue political goals with economic means.

911

The materials in this chapter review the GATT rules applicable to the use of trade controls for national security and political purposes and then analyze the U.S. statutes that authorize such use. These statutes can only be understood in light of the relative extensive and very controversial use made by the United States of such controls during the period from 1980 to 1982. The two most controversial U.S. actions were taken to protest certain activities of the Soviet Union.[1] For example, following the December 1979 Soviet invasion of Afghanistan, President Carter took action to limit exports of grains and fertilizers to the Soviet Union, to tighten already existing restrictions on exports of high technology goods and to cause a U.S.-led boycott of the 1980 Summer Olympic Games that were held in Moscow. President Reagan lifted the grain and fertilizer export restrictions in April 1981, but following the declaration of martial law in Poland in late 1981, he imposed certain trade-related sanctions against Poland and the Soviet Union. The sanctions imposed against the Soviet Union included a further tightening of the restrictions on exports of high technology goods, and, in particular, certain equipment necessary for construction of a gas pipeline from central Russia to Europe that the United States opposed because of fears that it would make U.S. allies in Europe too dependent on the Soviet Union for energy supplies. The restrictions were extended in June 1982 to apply to equipment produced by overseas subsidiaries and foreign licensees of U.S. companies. The controversy surrounding the imposition of these controls centered (i) on their perceived ineffectiveness in changing Soviet policy, which in the view of U.S. farmers and businessmen whose exports were curtailed meant that their financial sacrifices were totally unjustified, and (ii) on their extraterritorial application, which was vehemently protested by many U.S. allies, particularly in Europe. In the sections that follow we will treat separately these two major issues.

Of course, the United States is not the only nation to impose trade controls for national security or foreign policy purposes, and before turning to the issues raised above, it is instructive to consider a brief historical overview of the use of such controls.

GARY CLYDE HUFBAUER & JEFFREY J. SCHOTT, ECONOMIC SANCTIONS RECONSIDERED

4–7 (1985)[2]

In the period following World War II, other foreign policy motives became increasingly common, but sanctions were still deployed to force a target country to withdraw its troops from border skirmishes, to abandon plans of territorial acquisition, or to desist from other military adventures. In most instances in the postwar period where economic pressure was brought to bear against the exercise of military power, the United States played the role of international policeman. For example, the United States was able to coerce the Netherlands into backing away from its military

1. These controls and the facts surrounding their imposition are reviewed in detail in Moyer & Mabry, Export Controls As Instruments of Foreign Policy: The History, Legal Issues, and Policy Lessons of Three Recent Cases, 15 Law & Poly.Intl.Bus. 1–172 (1983).

2. © 1985, Institute for International Economics. Reproduced by permission.

efforts in 1948–49 to forestall the Indonesian federation; in 1956, the United States pressed the French and British into leaving the Suez; and in the early 1960s, the United States persuaded Egypt to withdraw its troops from Yemen and the Congo by withholding development and PL 480 food aid.

More recent attempts have not been as successful. Turkish troops continue to be stationed in Cyprus over a decade after the invasion and in spite of US economic pressure in the mid-1970s. The grain and Olympic boycott of the USSR did not discourage the Soviet occupation of Afghanistan. Indeed, major powers have never been able to deter the military adventures of other major powers simply through the use of economic sanctions.

Closely related to military adventure cases are the episodes where sanctions are imposed to impair the economic capability of the target country, thereby limiting its potential for military activity. This was an important rationale for the broad-based multilateral controls on strategic trade that the United States instituted against the USSR and China in the late 1940s, and was cited by US officials in defense of recent sanctions against the USSR following the invasion of Afghanistan and the crisis in Poland. It is doubtful whether these cases have yielded positive results, not least because it is difficult to hamper the military capabilities of a major power with marginal degrees of economic deprivation.

*   *   *

Sanctions have also been deployed in pursuit of a number of other foreign policy goals. Especially noteworthy is the frequent resort to sanctions to help destabilize foreign governments, usually in the context of a foreign policy dispute involving other issues. Destabilization episodes have often found a superpower pitted against a smaller country. The United States has engaged in destabilization efforts 14 times, often against neighboring countries in the hemisphere such as Cuba, the Dominican Republic, Nicaragua, Brazil, and Chile. Sanctions contributed at least in part to the overthrow of Trujillo in 1961, Goulart in 1964, and Allende in 1973; on the other hand, Castro's Cuba and the Sandinistas in Nicaragua have not succumbed to US pressure, in large measure due to compensating aid from the USSR.

The USSR has also picked on its neighbors, though less successfully. Every time the USSR used sanctions in an effort to topple a government of the socialist bloc, it failed (Yugoslavia in 1948, China in 1960, and Albania in 1961); the only success story came when the USSR coerced Finland into adopting a more pliant attitude toward Soviet policies during the "Nightfrost Crisis" of 1958. Finally, the United Kingdom also has participated in the destabilization game through the use of economic sanctions to topple hostile or repressive regimes in areas where Britain once exercised colonial influence—Iran in 1951–53, Rhodesia in 1965–79, and Uganda in 1972–79.

Since the early 1960s, sanctions have been deployed in support of numerous other foreign policy goals, most of them relatively modest compared to the pursuit of war, peace, and political destabilization. For example, sanctions have been used on behalf of efforts to protect human rights, to halt nuclear proliferation, to settle expropriation claims, and to combat international terrorism. Here again, the United States has played the dominant role as guardian of its version of global morality.

Following a series of congressionally inspired initiatives beginning in 1973, human rights became a "cause célèbre" of the Carter administration. In the early phase, country-specific riders were attached to military aid bills requiring the Nixon and Ford administrations to deny or reduce assistance to countries found abusing human rights. In the later phase, President Carter adopted the congressional mandate as his own guiding light. Eventually, many countries in Latin America and elsewhere became targets of US sanctions.

Sanctions were also frequently used, by both the United States and Canada, to enforce compliance with nuclear nonproliferation safeguards. In 1974, Canada acted to prevent Pakistan from acquiring nuclear explosive capability, and tried to control the reprocessing of spent fuel in both India and Pakistan to guard against weapons production. The United States joined the Canadians in applying financial pressure on South Korea to forestall its purchase of a nuclear reprocessing plant. Subsequently, the United States imposed sanctions on shipments of nuclear fuel and technology to South Africa, Taiwan, Brazil, Argentina, India, and Pakistan in similar attempts to secure adequate multilateral surveillance of nuclear facilities.

Since World War II, the United States has used sanctions nine times in its efforts to negotiate compensation for property expropriated by foreign governments. In almost all the cases, the United States hoped to go beyond the claims issue and resolve conflicting political philosophies. This was true the first time the US pressured Iran—seeking the overthrow of the Mussadiq regime—and was behind US efforts to undermine Castro in Cuba, Goulart in Brazil, and Allende in Chile.

Antiterrorism has been another of the modest (but important) policy goals sought by the United States through the imposition of economic sanctions. A wave of international plane hijackings in the 1960s and 1970s, and the massacre of Israeli athletes at the Munich Olympics in 1972, focused world attention on terrorism. The hijacking problem was greatly reduced through international hijacking agreements—including one signed in 1973 by the United States and Cuba. Lethal terrorist raids, often funded by radical, oil-rich countries, have proven much harder to control. In 1980, following a congressional directive, the US State Department branded four countries—Libya, Syria, Iraq, and South Yemen—as international outlaws because of their support of terrorist activities. The United States soon imposed sanctions on Libya and Iraq in an attempt to limit their ability as suppliers of military equipment to terrorist groups.

This brief historical review illustrates the important role that economic sanctions have played since World War I in the conduct of US foreign policy. Of the 103 cases documented in table 1.1, the United States, either alone or in concert with its allies, has deployed sanctions 68 times. Other significant users have been the United Kingdom (21 instances, often in cooperation with the League of Nations and the United Nations); the Soviet Union (10 uses, usually against recalcitrant satellites); and the Arab League and its members (4 uses of its new-found oil muscle).

This overview also demonstrates that sanctions have been deployed more frequently with each passing decade. * * * The summary in table 1.3 indicates that the quinquennial level of new episodes has increased from under 5 in the pre-1945 period to approximately 10 to 15 in the post-1960 period.

SECTION 13.2 INTERNATIONAL RULES AND NATIONAL SECURITY AND POLITICAL CONTROLS ON TRADE

We will distinguish trade controls imposed for national security purposes and those imposed for political purposes. Although such a distinction may be rather artificial in some cases, it is explicitly made in U.S. law, while the basic GATT provision in principle deals only with national security controls.

(A) THE GATT EXCEPTION FOR NATIONAL SECURITY TRADE CONTROLS

GATT Article XXI contains a general exception to all GATT obligations for certain measures taken by a member "necessary for the protection of its essential security interests." Although in principle limited to the three specified situations listed in Article XXI(b), the exception is broad enough to be subject to abuse.[1] In addition, at the time a country becomes a GATT Contracting Party, Article XXXV of GATT permits that country or any other Contracting Party to refuse to apply GATT as between designated countries. This authority can be used to prevent GATT trade rules applying for any reasons—political, national security or otherwise.[2]

The question of the scope of Article XXI has only infrequently arisen in GATT. Czechoslovakia complained against the United States in 1949, arguing that the U.S. export controls preventing certain exports to Czechoslovakia were a violation of U.S. GATT obligations. The Czechoslovakian complaint was rejected by the GATT Contracting Parties. During the discussion it was contended that:

> every country must have the last resort on questions relating to its own security. On the other hand, the CONTRACTING PARTIES should be cautious not to take any step which might have the effect of undermining the General Agreement.[3]

As a result of congressional action, the United States suspended MFN treatment in 1951 towards Communist countries, including Czechoslovakia.[4] Again, the United States-Czechoslovakia relationship was brought to GATT, and the GATT Contracting Parties finally ruled that these two governments "shall be free to suspend, each with respect to the other, the obligations of the General Agreement on Tariffs and Trade."[5] No explicit reference was

1. See generally J. Jackson, World Trade and the Law of GATT 748–52 (1969).

2. Id., at 100–102.

3. Id., at 749; GATT Doc. CP.3/SR. 22, at 7 (1949).

4. 65 Stat. 73, § 5 (1951).

5. J. Jackson, note 1 supra, at 749–50; GATT, BISD Vol. II, 36 (1952).

made in this declaration to any clause of GATT that might authorize this action, although it might be termed a "waiver." Other comparably ambiguous cases have included a Peruvian prohibition of Czechoslovakian imports, ultimately lifted after consultation, and a Ghanaian ban on Portuguese products, exercising Article XXXV of GATT.[6] Article XXXV has been invoked in a number of other situations, of course.[7]

More recently, the issue of the scope of the national security exception has come before GATT as a result of Nicaragua's protest of U.S. controls on trade between the United States and Nicaragua. For example, in 1983, when the United States cut Nicaragua's sugar import quota from 58,000 to 6,000 short tons, the GATT Council unanimously approved a panel report concluding that the U.S. action violated Article XIII:2 because the United States did not hold negotiations with Nicaragua.[8] The United States did not press an argument that its actions were justified under Article XXI, and it did not attempt to block a decision by the Council on the Nicaraguan complaint. Nonetheless, the United States did not change its policy as a result of the GATT decision.

Indeed, in 1985, President Reagan, prohibited all trade between the United States and Nicaragua.[9] Nicaragua again raised objections in GATT. This time the United States explicitly took the position that its actions were imposed for national security reasons pursuant to Article XXI of GATT and that, in the reported words of the U.S. ambassador to GATT, "The GATT is not an appropriate forum for debating political and security issues." According to the U.S. ambassador, the United States "sees no basis for GATT Contracting Parties to question, approve, or disapprove the judgment of each Contracting Party as to what is necessary to protect its national security interests." Reportedly, the U.S. position was supported by Australia, Canada and most European countries, as well as the EC, whose ambassador stated, "while we do not wish to pass judgment before the Council, it is not the role of GATT to resolve disputes in the field of national security." Nicaragua argued that the United States could not credibly claim that Nicaragua was a threat to U.S. security. The United States ultimately did not block the creation of a panel to consider the dispute.[10]

(B) THE USE OF ECONOMIC SANCTIONS FOR POLITICAL PURPOSES UNDER INTERNATIONAL LAW

GATT does not specifically authorize the use of trade controls for political purposes, except that in Article XXI(c) there is an exemption from

6. J. Jackson, note 1 supra, at 750–51; see GATT Doc. SR. 9/27, at 10 (1955), but see also GATT Doc. L/2844 (1967), wherein Peru announced that it had abrogated, as of August 1, 1967, its decree of March 11, 1953, which restricted trade with countries having centrally planned economies. GATT Doc. SR. 19/12, at 196 (1961).

7. See note 2 supra, and Section 5.4(I)(2) below.

8. GATT, 31st Supp. BISD 67 (1985).

9. Executive Order No. 12513, 50 Fed.Reg. 18629 (1985). The controls are contained in 31 CFR Pt. 540.

10. 2 BNA Intl. Trade Rptr. 765 (1985); 3 BNA Intl. Trade Rptr. 380 (1986).

GATT obligations in respect of actions taken by a Contracting Party "in pursuance of its obligations under the United Nations Charter for the maintenance of international peace and security."

The United Nations Charter empowers the Security Council to impose economic and military sanctions upon nations which threaten world peace. A prerequisite to the imposition of such sanctions is a Security Council determination of the existence of "any threat to the peace, breach of the peace, or act of aggression." [11] Once such a determination is made, recourse may be had to either Article 41 or Article 42 of the Charter.

Article 41 provides in a general way for taking measures "not involving the use of armed force." Economic and diplomatic sanctions are suggested, along with interruption of communications. Article 42 permits military action should the Council "consider that measures provided for in Article 41 would be inadequate or have proved to be inadequate." Once the Security Council has made an Article 39 determination and has decided upon sanctions, it may invoke Article 25 of the Charter, which binds member nations "to accept and carry out the decisions of the Security Council."

A Security Council resolution calling for broad-based economic sanctions to be applied against a country has been adopted only once. That instance involved a call for economic sanctions to be imposed on Rhodesia, as described in Section 13.7 infra.[12] In addition, the Security Council has adopted resolutions calling for more limited sanctions to be applied to the Republic of South Africa to protest its policy of apartheid. For example, in 1977 it called for an arms embargo to be imposed on South Africa and in 1985 it called for the adoption of such measures as suspension of new investment, prohibition of the sale of South African gold coins, suspension of guaranteed export loans, prohibition of new contracts in the nuclear field and prohibition of all sales of computer equipment that might be used by

---

11. United Nations Charter arts. 25, 39, 41, 42:

Art. 25. The Members of the United Nations agree to accept and carry out the decisions of the Security Council in accordance with the present Charter.

* * *

Art. 39. The Security Council shall determine the existence of any threat to the peace, breach of the peace, or act of aggression and shall make recommendations, or decide what measures shall be taken in accordance with Articles 41 and 42, to maintain or restore international peace and security.

* * *

Art. 41. The Security Council may decide what measures not involving the use of armed force are to be employed to give effect to its decisions, and it may call upon the Members of the United Nations to apply such measures. These may include complete or partial interruption of economic relations and of rail, sea, air, postal, telegraphic, radio, and other means of communication, and the severance of diplomatic relations.

Art. 42. Should the Security Council consider that measures provided for in Article 41 would be inadequate or have proved to be inadequate, it may take such action by air, sea, or land forces as may be necessary to maintain or restore international peace and security. Such action may include demonstrations, blockade, and other operations by air, sea, or land forces of Members of the United Nations.

12. S.C.Res. 232, U.N.Doc. S/Res/232 (1966); 30 U.N. SCOR, Spec.Supp. No. 2, Vol. II, at 100; U.N.Doc. S/11594/Rev. 1 (1975). See also McDougall & Riesman, Rhodesia and the United Nations: The Lawfulness of International Concern, 62 Am.J.Intl.L. 1 (1968).

South African army or police units.[13]   The United States has implemented both of these resolutions.[14]

The U.N. General Assembly has called upon the Security Council to impose broader economic sanctions on South Africa, but the Security Council has not yet done so.[15]

Questions

(1) Suppose that imports of watches increase to the point that they threaten to eliminate all U.S. watch production. Could the United States impose import restrictions on watch imports under GATT Article XXI? What if a similar situation existed for bicycles? Shoes? Cotton? Computers? Steel? Foodstuffs? Is there any limiting principle to the national security exception? After all, don't armies need watches and shoes and food and just about everything imaginable at one time or another?

(2) Review GATT Article XXI(b). Can you formulate more precisely defined and limited rules as to when the national security exception may be used? What assumptions must be made for such a formulation?

(3) Should GATT or a successor institution contain an explicit "political escape clause" to allow any country to "opt out" of trading relationships with any other country on political grounds (much as Article XXXV of GATT now allows such an option at the time a country becomes a member of GATT)?

(4) Do the GATT responses to the U.S.—Czechoslovakia and U.S.—Nicaragua cases essentially create a political purposes exception to GATT?

SECTION 13.3 U.S. TRADE CONTROLS FOR NATIONAL SECURITY PURPOSES [1]

In this section, we look first at the requirements under the Export Administration Act (EAA) for imposition of export controls for national security purposes and consider the methods by which the United States coordinates the imposition of such controls with its military allies. Second, we examine the U.S. legal requirements for the imposition of import controls for national security purposes.

(A) NATIONAL SECURITY CONTROLS UNDER THE EAA

As outlined in Section 12.3(B) supra, the United States controls exports under the Export Administration Act of 1979 (the "EAA") for reasons of

13. S.C.Res. 569, U.N.Doc. S/Res/569 (1985); S.C.Res. 418, U.N.Doc. S/Res/417 (1977).

14. Executive Order No. 12532, 50 Fed. Reg. 36861 (1985); 15 CFR § 385.4(a) (1985).

15. See, e.g., G.A.Res. 35/227, U.N.Doc. A/Res/35/227 (1981).

1. In addition to materials cited elsewhere in this chapter, see R. Lillich (ed.), Economic Coercion and the New International Economic Order (1976); M. Czinkota (ed.), Export Controls: Building Reasonable Commercial Ties with Political Adversaries (1984). For a de-

tailed evaluation of U.S. economic sanctions imposed in the Iranian hostage situation, to protest the Soviet invasion of Afghanistan and to protest the imposition of martial law in Poland, see Moyer & Mabry, Export Controls as Instruments of Foreign Policy: The History, Legal Issues, and Policy Lessons of Three Recent Cases, 15 Law & Poly.Intl.Bus. 1 (1983). For a discussion of the U.S. embargo of Cuba, the Arab Boycott of Israel and the global sanctions against Rhodesia, see D. Losman, International Economic Sanctions: The Cases of Cuba, Israel, and Rhodesia (1979).

national security, foreign policy and short supply. The EAA, as amended in 1985, provides that [2]

> in order to carry out the policy set out in section 3(2)(A) of this Act, [i.e. "to use export controls only after consideration of the impact on the economy of the United States and only to the extent necessary ＊ ＊ ＊ to restrict the export of goods and technology which would make a significant contribution to the military potential of any other country or combination of countries which would prove detrimental to the United States"], the President may ＊ ＊ ＊ prohibit or curtail the export of any goods or technology subject to the jurisdiction of the United States or exported by any person subject to the jurisdiction of the United States.

As explained in Section 12.3(B) supra, U.S. export controls are implemented by licensing requirements applicable to a list of specified products and destinations. Particularly in recent years and in respect of the controls imposed on exports to the Soviet Union in connection with its actions in Afghanistan and Poland, many congressmen have felt that the Executive Branch, under the influence of the Defense Department, has been imposing validated licensing requirements on the export of many products that do not need to be controlled for national security reasons, particularly items that incorporate technology that has ceased to be sensitive. As a consequence, many provisions of the EAA, as amended in 1985, are designed to limit the use of such controls. For example, the list of products subject to control for national security reasons is to be reevaluated annually by the Executive Branch, certain exports to certain U.S. military allies (the so-called COCOM countries discussed below) are not to be subjected to controls and the use of validated licenses authorizing multiple exports (instead of the traditional practice of requiring a license for each individual export) is to be encouraged.[3]

The principal statutory limitation on the use of controls for national security purposes concerns the question of whether the controlled goods are available from other sources. If goods are available in fact in sufficient quantity and comparable quality so that the Secretary of Commerce determines that a validated license requirement would be "ineffective" in achieving the purposes of controls (as quoted above), such a license may not be required (or even if required in general, must be approved in a specific case), unless the President determines that the absence of controls would be detrimental to U.S. national security.[4] In the event the President so determines, he is required to enter into negotiations with other governments with a view toward eliminating the availability of the goods. If such negotiations do not eliminate the foreign availability within six months, no validated license may be required, except that this six-month period may be extended by twelve months if the President certifies to Congress that the required negotiations are proceeding and that the lack of export controls would be detrimental to U.S. national security.[5] Despite the detail of these provisions, which are reminiscent of the detailed time limits imposed in import relief cases, the Executive Branch's discretion is very broad, especial-

2. 50 U.S.C.A.App. § 2404(a).

3. See 50 U.S.C.A. App. §§ 2404(c), (d), (e).

4. See 50 U.S.C.A. App. § 2404(f).

5. Id.

ly given the absence in general of judicial review of its actions. If the Secretary of Commerce determines initially that there is no foreign availability, or studies the question for an extended period, there is little than a putative exporter can do except complain to its congressman. Although the EAA establishes a system of technical advisory committees that have the power to decide that an item is available in foreign markets, the committees consist in part of government representatives and may be effectively overruled by the Secretary.[6]

The EAA does, however, effectively require prompt action on license applications, particularly in respect of exports to COCOM countries,[7] and despite broad discretion in the Executive Branch, the congressional intent that unnecessary controls are to be avoided is crystal clear. A feeling that such intent is being ignored could conceivably lead to tighter restrictions on the use of such controls, as has happened in the case of controls for political purposes. The conference committee report on the 1985 amendments made this clear: [8]

> The review by the conferees of the implementation of the Act during the last session of the 98th Congress revealed instances in which the competitiveness of U.S. exporters has been hampered by the inefficiency of the agencies with regulatory and enforcement authority over exports. Specifically, the conferees are aware that the application of the export administration regulations in some cases is inconsistent and irrational, and that some U.S. exporters and foreign customers are not accorded the fair and equal treatment on a day-to-day basis to which they are entitled.

> These problems are not specifically addressed in the conference substitute, in the belief that it is the express policy of the United States that these controls be administered fairly. The two committees of jurisdiction intend, however, to monitor closely the administrative practices in the future and, if necessary, to consider remedial legislation.

To be effective national security controls must prevent export of controlled items after they have been exported from the United States and must be imposed by U.S. allies that produce similar items. The control of reexports raises the question of the extraterritorial effect of controls, which also arises under foreign policy controls and which is discussed separately in Section 13.5 below. The problem of coordinating U.S. allies necessitates a discussion of COCOM.

CECIL HUNT, MULTILATERAL COOPERATION IN EXPORT CONTROLS—THE ROLE OF COCOM

(1983) [9]

"CoCom" stands for Coordinating Committee, the grey and uninformative name for an intergovernmental apparatus that has operated for over thirty years to control "strategic" trade from West to East.

---

6. 50 U.S.C.A. App. § 2404(h).

7. 50 U.S.C.A. App. § 2409(o).

8. H.Conf.Rep. No. 180, 99th Cong., 1st Sess. 56 (1985).

9. 14 U. Toledo L.Rev. 1285, 1285–89, 1291–92, 1294. Reprinted by permission of the University of Toledo Law Review.

The fifteen participants in CoCom are the NATO countries (less Iceland and Spain) and Japan.

CoCom is an informal cooperative arrangement through which the United States and its allies seek to coordinate the national controls they apply to the export of strategic goods and technology to the Communist world. The details of the founding of CoCom are obscured by the official secrecy that surrounded its establishment and that continues to apply to much of its work. *   *   *

The system of export controls which the United States had instituted for defense purposes during World War II was continued during the immediate post-war period, primarily to deal with shortages at home and abroad. The advent of the Cold War turned U.S. attention to the need for controls to deal with the perceived security threat posed by the Soviet bloc. This strategic trade concern became the primary focus of the Export Control Act of 1949. Even before the enactment of that legislation, the United States had entered into discussions with its key European allies concerning a coordinated embargo policy toward the Soviet bloc.

Embargo lists were developed and a body known as the Consultative Group was set up to supervise the lists. The initial Consultative Group was composed of export control officials from the United Kingdom, France, Italy, the Netherlands, Belgium, Luxembourg and the United States. These officials were joined by representatives from Norway, Denmark, Canada and West Germany in 1950, Portugal in 1952, and Japan, Greece and Turkey in 1953. In addition to the policy level Consultative Group, the Coordinating Committee (CoCom) was established as a group of specialized representatives, resident in Paris, to carry out the embargo policy on a day-to-day basis. Within a few years, the Consultative Group ceased to meet and the entire multilateral apparatus became known as CoCom. Policy guidance has been provided *ad hoc* through instructions from governments to their CoCom representatives and through equally *ad hoc* consultations among the governments concerned with particular matters relating to CoCom. A more structured recent development has been the convening of "high-level" meetings at which political level representatives of the CoCom countries have met to discuss basic issues of CoCom policy and practice.

CoCom exists as an informal and voluntary arrangement. It is not based on any treaty or other agreement that obligates the participants internationally. The members retain the right to act independently in accord with their own legal, administrative and policy situations. Agreements must be reached unanimously, but the final decision in matters before CoCom rests with each country.

CoCom's structure is such that it cannot properly be termed an "organization." CoCom acts only through the member governments. CoCom has a small permanent staff performing secretariat functions. Notwithstanding this legal and organizational insubstantiality (some would say because of it), CoCom has continued as an influential trade control mechanism for nearly thirty-five years, and the participating governments have shown significant respect for the discipline inherent in this unusual "gentlemen's agreement."

The accomplishment of the CoCom objective of parallel administration of these security-related export controls involves four interrelated aspects: agreement on strategic criteria for controls; formulation of detailed lists of embargoed items; evaluation of individual cases for possible exception from the embargo; and, coordination of efforts to assure enforcement of the embargo.

EMBARGO POLICY

The fundamental objective of CoCom controls is to restrict the exports of goods and technology which would make a significant contribution to the military potential of proscribed destination countries (principally the Warsaw Pact countries and China) and thus have an adverse effect on the security of member states. The term commonly used to describe the object of CoCom controls is "strategic" goods and technology. Not only does this terminology admit of widely varied interpretations and applications, but the adverse security effects aspect of the fundamental control objective will reflect changing facts and perceptions as to the power and intentions of the countries to which the embargo is directed.   *   *   *

CoCom coordinates national controls through three embargo lists and an exceptions procedure. The three lists are: the International Atomic Energy List, the International Munitions List and the International List. The International List contains dual-use items not included in the other two lists.

The secrecy surrounding CoCom activities is an obstacle to discovering the precise terms of CoCom control policy formulations and the positions urged by governments in the formation of the control consensus. Much can be inferred, however, from the control lists themselves. Although the CoCom lists are not public, their content is necessarily reflected to a great extent in the national lists of the member states which are published to guide exporters and administrators of the controls. The United States Commodity Control List (CCL) has in recent years added a notation distinguishing between multilaterally and unilaterally controlled items.

*   *   *

The basic purpose of the exceptions procedure in CoCom is to permit a specific export of an item to a controlled destination if the security risk of the transaction is acceptable. Such a determination can be based upon a verifiable dedication of the item to civilian use, or upon a judgment that no strategically significant transfer of technology will occur through access to embargoed equipment. The determination to issue a validated license may also be based upon a combination of these factors and a variety of political, economic, and military concerns.

When a U.S. exporter submits an application to the Department of Commerce for a validated license to export to a controlled destination, the exporter is to be informed within ten days if the application must be submitted to a "multilateral review process", i.e., to CoCom.

The application will first be evaluated within the U.S. government. If the decision is that the export should be licensed and it is not covered by the national discretion category, the case will be submitted to CoCom with the United States requesting an exception from the embargo and citing the circumstances believed to warrant an exception. CoCom procedures call for a decision on an exception request eighteen days after it has been submitted, with an automatic two-week rescheduling in the absence of a decision. Further weekly extensions are granted at the discretion of the requesting member. Approval of an exception request requires the unanimous agreement of the member countries represented at the CoCom meeting at which the request is considered. As indicated in the scene sketched at the outset, CoCom meets every Tuesday to act on such requests.

How numerous are exception requests and what is their usual fate? A 1978 report to the Congress stated that about one thousand exception cases valued at about $200 million were being submitted to CoCom annually and that the U.S. submits about half of these cases. Two to four percent of the requests were disapproved in CoCom, three to five percent withdrawn and many were revised to take into account changes recommended during the CoCom review process. During the 1970's the value of CoCom exception cases was running at a rate of less than one percent of total exports from CoCom countries to controlled destinations.

*   *   *

CoCom's limited functions as a *coordinating* mechanism should again be stressed. Cocom does not perform an investigative or police function and there is no CoCom "law" to enforce. CoCom does have a subcommittee which develops coordinated procedures to deter violations and which exchanges information on national enforcement.

The principal enforcement safeguard that is harmonized and coordinated through CoCom is the Import Certificate/Delivery Verification (IC/DV) system. This is an export documentation system designed to prevent exports between CoCom members from being diverted to a controlled destination. In the controlled transactions to which this system is applied, the exporter is required to obtain from the importer a statement, certified by the importer's government, assuring that the importer intends to receive the goods and that they will not be reexported without approval from the importer's governmental authorities. The importer may further be required to have his government certify a delivery verification to confirm entry of the goods. By conditioning export license issuance on the exporter's agreement to obtain the IC/DV documents, the exporting country knows that the importing country will be in a better position under its own procedures to detect and prevent diversion.

Notes and Questions

(1) Some COCOM countries impose export controls without a clear statutory basis. As noted in the case of Japan, see Section 4.3 supra, there was one court ruling some years ago that suggested that such controls were not authorized. Japan nonetheless continues to participate in COCOM.

(2) The United States has put considerable pressure on certain countries, such as Austria and Spain, to adopt export controls sufficient to control reexport of U.S. goods and technology. It essentially threatened to block U.S. exports of controlled goods to those countries if they did not implement controls. Such

pressures led Spain to join COCOM and Austria to adopt export control legislation.[10]

(3) As corporate counsel, what problems do you think might arise as a result of your company's submission of detailed information about its export transactions and products to the U.S. Commerce Department to obtain a license or to COCOM to obtain an exception? To what extent does U.S. law deal with these problems?

(B) NATIONAL SECURITY CONTROLS UNDER SECTION 232

Section 232 of the Trade Expansion Act of 1962 [11] provides that the President shall not reduce duties or eliminate other import restrictions if such action would threaten to impair national security. In addition, it establishes a procedure by which any interested party can ask that an investigation be conducted to determine if imports of any article into the United States are threatening to impair the national security. Although the wording of Section 232 suggests that it could have broad application, it has essentially been used only to control imports of petroleum products. The details of the various controls that were applied to petroleum imports, which ranged from voluntary quotas to mandatory quotas to licensing requirements (with or without fees), are much too complicated to discuss here,

---

10. See N.Y. Times (natl. ed.), Dec. 5, 1985, at 32 (Spain); id., Jan. 2, 1985, at 21 (Austria).

11. **Sec. 232.**

(a) No action shall be taken pursuant to section 201(a) or pursuant to section 350 of the Tariff Act of 1930 to decrease or eliminate the duty or other import restriction on any article if the President determines that such reduction or elimination would threaten to impair the national security.

(b) Upon request of the head of any department or agency, upon application of an interested party, or upon his own motion, the Director of the Office of Emergency Planning (hereinafter in this section referred to as the "Director") shall immediately make an appropriate investigation, in the course of which he shall seek information and advice from other appropriate departments and agencies, to determine the effects on the national security of imports of the article which is the subject of such request, application, or motion. If, as a result of such investigation, the Director is of the opinion that the said article is being imported into the United States in such quantities or under such circumstances as to threaten to impair the national security, he shall promptly so advise the President, and, unless the President determines that the article is not being imported into the United States in such quantities or under such circumstances as to threaten to impair the national security as set forth in this section, he shall take such action, and for such time, as he deems necessary to adjust the imports of such article and its derivatives so that such imports will not so threaten to impair the national security.

(c) For the purposes of this section, the Director and the President shall, in the light of the requirements of national security and without excluding other relevant factors, give consideration to domestic production needed for projected national defense requirements, the capacity of domestic industries to meet such requirements, existing and anticipated availabilities of the human resources, products, raw materials, and other supplies and services essential to the national defense, the requirements of growth of such industries and such supplies and services including the investment, exploration, and development necessary to assure such growth, and the importation of goods in terms of their quantities, availabilities, character, and use as those affect such industries and the capacity of the United States to meet national security requirements. In the administration of this section, the Director and the President shall further recognize the close relation of the economic welfare of the Nation to our national security, and shall take into consideration the impact of foreign competition on the economic welfare of individual domestic industries; and any substantial unemployment, decrease in revenues of government, loss of skills or investment, or other serious effects resulting from the displacement of any domestic products by excessive imports shall be considered, without excluding other factors, in determining whether such weakening of our internal economy may impair the national security.

* * *

although it is worth noting that they have at times been very controversial.[12] Suffice it to say that in December 1983, President Reagan revoked the oft-amended 1959 proclamation establishing the petroleum controls, except to provide for monitoring of petroleum imports and to exclude crude oil produced in Libya from the United States because imports of such oil would be inimical to U.S. national security.[13]

Except for petroleum products, Section 232 investigations, which are conducted by the International Trade Administration (ITA) of the Commerce Department, have been rare, numbering perhaps a little more than one dozen since the 1962 Act was adopted. Under its rules, to determine the effect of imports on national security, the ITA considers such factors as the domestic production needed for projected national defense requirements and the capacity of domestic producers to meet those requirements. The ITA also considers the effect of imports on the domestic economy in general in recognition of "the close relationship between the strength of our national economy and the capacity of the United States to meet national security requirements." [14] Among the industries that have unsuccessfully sought relief under Section 232 in the decade ending in 1985 were makers of bolts and screws, glass-lined chemical processing equipment and machine tools, as well as producers of various ferroalloys.

An example of the analysis applied by the ITA is given in the most recent bolt and screw investigation, where the ITA summarized its conclusions as follows: [15]

> The report shows that there would be a shortfall in domestic fastener supplies to meet scenario-based requirements. Domestic producers of the industrial fasteners under investigation can, in surge and conflict years, meet only the defense requirements for these products. Imports can help us reduce the shortfall in requirements for civilian production. The analysis has shown that most of our foreign sources are politically reliable, due to their stable pro-U.S. governments; and that their geographic locations, in light of projected shipping losses under the scenario, make them reliable in practice, as well. While it is true that the domestic industry has declined, general economic conditions contributed greatly, and import penetration alone is not causal to its reduced capacity.

Can this conclusion be reconciled with the conclusion that oil imports from Libya would be inimical to our national security?

SECTION 13.4　U.S. TRADE CONTROLS FOR FOREIGN POLICY PURPOSES

The United States frequently imposes export and import restrictions for foreign policy purposes.[1] Controls on exports for foreign policy purposes are

---

12. See, e.g., Pub.L. No. 96–264, § 2, 94 Stat. 439 (1980) (mandating elimination of import fee imposed by the President).

13. Presidential Proclamation No. 5141, 48 Fed.Reg. 56929 (1983).

14. 15 CFR § 359.4(b) (1985). The ITA rules are set out in 15 CFR Pt. 359 (1985).

15. Investigation of Imports of Bolts, Nuts and Large Screws of Iron or Steel, 48 Fed.Reg. 8842, 8844–45 (1983).

1. In addition to controls specifically mentioned elsewhere in this chapter, the United States has in recent years imposed sanctions, inter alia, on Uganda for human rights violations and on Argentina in connection with its

explicitly authorized by the Export Administration Act, although they are often imposed as part of a general ban on imports and exports from countries of which the United States disapproves. These broader bans have usually been imposed pursuant to the President's emergency powers under the Trading With the Enemy Act (TWEA) and the International Emergency Economic Powers Act (IEEPA), discussed in Section 3.4 supra, and will not be treated separately here. As has been mentioned previously, most trade with Cuba, Cambodia, Iran, Vietnam, Korea and Nicaragua is prohibited and limited restrictions apply on trade with South Africa.[2] These restrictions have at least in part been based on the TWEA and IEEPA.

The Export Administration Act (EAA) also provides for export controls to be imposed, on a year-to-year basis, to curtail or prohibit the exportation of any goods, technology or other information subject to the jurisdiction of the United States or exported by any person subject to the jurisdiction of the United States to the extent such controls are necessary to further significantly the foreign policy of the United States or to fulfill international obligations of the United States.[3]

The EAA authorizes such controls only if the President determines, *inter alia,* that (1) the controls are likely to achieve their purpose (in light of possible alternative sources of supply) and that such purpose cannot be otherwise achieved; (2) the negative effect of the controls on the export performance of the United States, on the international reputation of the United States as a supplier of goods and technology and on individual U.S. companies, their employees and communities does not exceed the benefits to U.S. foreign policy objectives and (3) the United States can effectively enforce the controls.[4] In addition, the EAA mandates prior consultation with and submission of a detailed report to Congress and consultation where possible with industry and U.S. allies.[5] Prior to the 1985 amendments to the EAA, the consultation and reporting requirements were less detailed and phrased in more discretionary terms. This section of the EAA also contains provisions on foreign availability similar to those discussed in Section 13.3 in respect of national security controls.[6]

One of the more controversial issues involved in the application of export controls concerns the so-called "contract sanctity" issue: Should existing contracts be exempted from controls? This had not been done in the case of the controls imposed to protest Soviet actions in Afghanistan and Poland. U.S. business interests claimed that forcing the cancellation of contracts gave the United States a bad reputation as an international supplier. Underlying those claims, of course, was the belief that the U.S.

war with Great Britain over the Falkland Islands (Malvinas). At present, controls are imposed on certain exports to Syria, Yemen, Iran and Libya because of their support of international terrorism. See 15 CFR § 385.4 (1985). U.S. treatment of imports from the Communist bloc nations, which generally do not receive most-favored-nation treatment, are detailed in Chapter 21 supra.

2. See 31 CFR §§ 500.201 (Cambodia, North Korea, Vietnam), 515.201 (Cuba),

535.201 (Iran), 540.204–05 (Nicaragua) (1985); Executive Order No. 12532, 50 Fed.Reg. 36861 (1985) (South Africa); 15 CFR § 385 (1985).

3. 50 U.S.C.A.App. § 2405(a).

4. 50 U.S.C.A.App. § 2405(b).

5. 50 U.S.C.A.App. §§ 2405(c), (d), (f).

6. 50 U.S.C.A.App. § 2405(h).

controls were ineffective anyway because the embargoed goods were readily available elsewhere, often from European and Japanese competitors of U.S. business. The 1985 amendments to the EAA were responsive to these claims and provided that controls for foreign policy purposes cannot be applied to exports made pursuant to pre-existing contracts or validated licenses unless the President determines and certifies to Congress, inter alia, that "a breach of the peace poses a serious and direct threat to the strategic interest of the United States" and that an export prohibition would be instrumental in remedying the situation posed by the threat.[7]

As noted above, President Carter restricted certain U.S. agricultural exports to the Soviet Union in 1980 in protest of its occupation of Afghanistan.[8] This action was deeply opposed by many U.S. farming interests, and in the 1985 amendments to the EAA, Congress provided that in imposing controls for foreign policy or short supply reasons or to discourage international terrorism or export cartels, the President is authorized to impose export controls on agricultural commodities for more than 60 days only if Congress affirmatively approves the controls.[9]

Notes and Questions

(1) The foregoing discussion makes clear that the President has more discretion to impose export controls under the EAA for national security reasons than for foreign policy reasons. How would you explain the distinction between the two? In the Afghanistan case, President Carter justified his actions on both the national security and the foreign policy grounds.[10] Does this option effectively negate congressional efforts to restrict use of export controls for foreign policy purposes more strictly than their use for national security reasons? The reader should consider what exactly are the different degrees of restriction in light of the materials in this section and Section 13.3 supra. In light of such differences, how significant is the fact that the distinction between foreign policy and national security justifications is so blurred?

(2) In Sections 3.4(B)(1) and 12.3(B)(3) supra, we discussed the emergency powers of the President. In 1985, while the EAA had lapsed, President Reagan relied on the International Emergency Economic Powers Act (IEEPA) to impose extensive controls on trade and other economic relations with Nicaragua.[11] Could IEEPA be used in lieu of following the prescribed procedures under the EAA to impose today the sort of controls that President Carter imposed on trade with the Soviet Union in 1980? Review the statement by Congressman Bonker in Section 3.4(B)(1) supra.

(3) Recall that the EAA deals only with exports. To impose an embargo on all trade with a country (exports and imports), it is necessary to rely on some other authority such as the International Emergency Economic Powers Act

7. 50 U.S.C.A.App. § 2405(m).

8. See Section 13.1 supra.

9. 50 U.S.C.A.App. § 2406(g). In addition, in 1981 Congress provided that if national security or foreign policy controls were invoked to halt agricultural exports to a country where (i) all exports to such country were not so controlled and (ii) U.S. agricultural exports the preceding year to such country exceeded three percent of total U.S. agricultural exports, then the producers of the exports in question would be entitled to special compensation. 7 U.S.C.A. § 1736j.

10. See 45 Fed.Reg. 1883 (1980).

11. Executive Order No. 12513, 50 Fed. Reg. 18629 (1985).

(IEEPA) to block imports. Would this fact affect the way a court would view the use of IEEPA to impose export controls?

(4) In light of the materials in this chapter, in Section 3.4(B)(1) supra and in Chapter 12 supra, what would you say are the effective legal limits on the President's authority to impose trade restraints on imports or exports?

(5) Summarize the legal limits on the President's authority to use trade controls (import or export) for the purpose of applying pressure to a foreign nation for political or humanitarian goals. Consider, for example, (i) a desire by the United States to apply pressure to a country to encourage it to cease using torture on its own citizens, and (ii) a desire to apply pressure to encourage a nation to vote for or against a proposal at the United Nations.

SECTION 13.5 THE EXTRATERRITORIAL APPLICATION OF TRADE CONTROLS

The EAA authorizes controls to be imposed on any goods, technology or persons subject to U.S. jurisdiction. In implementing controls, the United States has taken a very broad and controversial view of what is subject to U.S. jurisdiction. In reading the following materials, the reader should consider what limits international law places on the extraterritorial application of export controls and whether the United States exceeded those limits when it imposed the controls described below on exports and reexports to the Soviet Union.

NOTE, EXTRATERRITORIAL APPLICATION OF THE EXPORT ADMINISTRATION ACT OF 1979 UNDER INTERNATIONAL AND AMERICAN LAW

(1983) [1]

Section six of the Export Administration Act of 1979 (EAA) authorizes the President to "prohibit or curtail the exportation of any goods, technology, or other information subject to the jurisdiction of the United States or exported by any person subject to the jurisdiction of the United States, to the extent necessary to further significantly the foreign policy of the United States. * * *" Pursuant to this authorization, on June 18, 1982, President Reagan announced that, as an intensified response to the continued repression in Poland, he was extending and expanding export controls on oil and gas equipment destined for the Soviet Union. The expanded controls sought to regulate not only exports from American corporations but also goods produced by the overseas subsidiaries of American corporations. Furthermore, the export controls purported to control the exports of foreign corporations that had received specified American goods or were producing these goods under licensing agreements with the American companies. This action marked the first extraterritorial application of the EAA to foreign subsidiaries and licensees.

1. 81 Mich.L.Rev. 1308, 1308–09, 1318–21. Reprinted by permission of the Michigan Law Review Association. See also Conference on Extraterritoriality for the Businessman and the Practicing Lawyer, 15 Law & Poly. Intl. Bus. 1095–1222 (1983) (with extensive bibliography); Thompson, United States Jurisdiction over Foreign Subsidiaries: Corporate and International Law Aspects, 15 Law & Poly. Intl. Bus. 319 (1983).

*   *   *

The most fundamental precept of international law—indeed, "the basic constitutional doctrine of the law of nations"—recognizes the sovereign and equal status of the nations comprising the international community. As a function of this status, nations are generally considered to possess rights of independence, territorial supremacy, and personal supremacy. Territorial supremacy is a state's power to "exercise supreme authority over all persons and things" within its territory; personal supremacy is the state's power "to exercise supreme authority over its citizens at home and abroad."

As a corollary to territorial supremacy, each state has jurisdiction over acts committed within its territory and over the permanent population living therein. This "territorial principle" provides that a state has absolute dominion and control over all individuals and property within its borders, including an unchallenged right to regulate corporations within its territory. As the United States Supreme Court declared at an early date: "The jurisdiction of a nation within its own territory is necessarily exclusive and absolute. It is susceptible to no limitation not imposed by itself. Any restriction upon it *   *   * from an external source, would imply a diminution of its sovereignty *   *   *." *69

Territorial jurisdiction is closely related to the concepts of territorial integrity and nonintervention. While territorial jurisdiction gives the state the *right* to prescribe or enforce a rule of law within its territory, the latter concepts impose a *duty* on other states to refrain generally from any act that infringes on the territorial supremacy of a state, including any action that interferes with the domestic relations or international intercourse of another nation. A state's attempts to enforce its laws extraterritorially may violate this duty, and give rise to a cause of action for the states adversely affected.

Although a state's right to territorial jurisdiction is frequently phrased in exclusive terms, some exceptions have evolved and are now generally accepted in international law. But as assertions of extraterritorial jurisdiction typically risk interference with the territorial integrity of other nations—and at the same time provide a precedent for such nations to engage in similar interference—the evolution of these exceptions has provoked serious controversy, and the accepted scope of the exceptions remains rather limited. Customary practice among states confirms the need for limiting principles to preserve the core notion of territorial jurisdiction: even those states taking the most expansionist view of extraterritorial jurisdiction have generally recognized these concerns.

The extraterritorial application of the EAA calls into question the scope of these exceptions. As this application involves foreign subsidiaries and licensees acting within the territory of other sovereign nations, it may impermissibly intrude on the right of territorial jurisdiction and violate the United States' duty to respect the territorial integrity of these nations. For example, in the Soviet pipeline case the United States sought to interfere with the domestic relations and international intercourse of the EEC countries by attempting to enforce export controls and curtail export activities

* **69.** Schooner Exchange v. McFadden, 11 U.S. (7 Cranch) 116, 136 (1812).

that were legal in the EEC countries. The remainder of this section considers whether such interference is sustainable under three principles of extraterritorial jurisdiction: the nationality principle, the objective territorial principle, and the protective principle.

EUROPEAN COMMUNITIES, COMMENTS ON THE U.S. REGULATIONS CONCERNING TRADE WITH THE U.S.S.R.[2]

A. Generally Accepted Bases of Jurisdiction in International Law

4. The U.S. measures as they apply in the present case are unacceptable under international law because of their extra-territorial aspects. They seek to regulate companies not of U.S. nationality in respect of their conduct outside the United States and particularly the handling of property and technical data of these companies not within the United States.

They seek to impose on non-U.S. companies the restriction of U.S. law by threatening them with discriminatory sanctions in the field of trade which are inconsistent with the normal commercial practice established between the U.S. and the E.C.

In this way the Amendments of June 22, 1982, run counter to the two generally accepted bases of jurisdiction in international law; the territoriality and the nationality principles.

5. The *territoriality principle* (i.e. the notion that a state should restrict its rule-making in principle to persons and goods within its territory and that an organization like the European Community should restrict the applicability of its rules to the territory to which the Treaty setting it up applies) is a fundamental notion of international law, in particular insofar as it concerns the regulation of the social and economic activity in a state. The principle that each state—and *mutatis mutandis* the Community insofar as powers have been transferred to it—has the right freely to organize and develop its social and economic system has been confirmed many times in international fora. The American measures clearly infringe the principle of territoriality, since they purport to regulate the activities of companies in the E.C., not under the territorial competence of the U.S.

6. The *nationality principle* (i.e. the prescription of rules for nationals, wherever they are) cannot serve as a basis for the extension of U.S. jurisdiction resulting from the Amendments, i.e. (i) over companies incorporated in E.C. Member States on the basis of some corporate link (parent-subsidiary) or personal link (e.g. shareholding) to the U.S.; (ii) over companies incorporated in E.C. Member States, either because they have a tie to a U.S.-incorporated company, subsidiary or other "U.S. controlled" company through a licensing agreement, royalty payments, or payment of other compensation, or because they have bought certain goods originating in the U.S.

2. This memorandum was submitted by the EC to the U.S. government. It is reproduced in 21 Intl. Legal Materials 891, 893–99 (1982).

7. *ad (i)* The Amendments in two places purport to subject to U.S. jurisdiction companies, wherever organized or doing business, which are subsidiaries of U.S. companies or under the control of U.S. citizens, U.S. residents or even persons actually within the U.S. This implies that the United States is seeking to impose its corporate nationality on companies of which the great majority are incorporated and have their registered office elsewhere, notably in E.C. Member States.

Such action is not in conformity with recognized principles of international law. In the Barcelona Traction Case, the International Court of Justice declared that two traditional criteria for determining the nationality of companies; i.e. the place of incorporation and the place of the registered office of the company concerned, had been "confirmed by long practice and by numerous international instruments". The Court also scrutinized other tests of corporate nationality, but concluded that these had not found general acceptance. The Court consequently placed primary emphasis on the traditional place of incorporation and the registered office in deciding the case in point. This decision was taken within the framework of the doctrine of diplomatic protection, but reflects a general principle of international law.

8. *ad (ii)* The notion inherent in the subjection to U.S. jurisdiction of companies with no tie to the U.S. whatsoever, except for a technological link to a U.S. company, or through possession of U.S. origin goods, can only be that this technology or such goods should somehow be considered as unalterably "American" (even though many of the patents involved are registered in the Member States of the European Community). This seems the only possible explanation for the U.S. Regulations given the fact that national security is not at stake here (see below under B).

Goods and technology do not have any nationality and there are no known rules under international law for using goods or technology situated abroad as a basis of establishing jurisdiction over the persons controlling them. Several Court cases confirm that U.S. jurisdiction does not follow U.S. origin goods once they have been discharged in the territory of another country.

9. The Amendments of 22 June 1982, therefore, cannot be justified under the nationality principle, because they ignore the two traditional criteria for determining the nationality of companies reconfirmed by the International Court of Justice and because they purport to give some notion of "nationality" to goods and technologies so as to establish jurisdiction over persons handling them.

The purported direct extension of U.S. jurisdiction to non-U.S. incorporated companies not using U.S. origin technology or components is *a fortiori* objectionable to the E.C., because neither of these (in themselves invalid) justifications could apply.

10. The last mentioned case exemplifies to what extent the wholesale infringement of the nationality principle exacerbates the infringement of the

territoriality principle.* Thus even E.C. incorporated companies in the example mentioned above according to the Amendments would have to ask special written permission not of the E.C., but of the U.S. authorities in order to obtain permission to export goods produced in the E.C. and based on E.C. technology from the territory to which the E.C. Treaties apply to the U.S.S.R. The practical impact of the Amendments to the Export Administration Regulations is that E.C. companies are pressed into service to carry out U.S. trade policy towards the U.S.S.R., even though these companies are incorporated and have their registered office within the Community which has its own trade policy towards the U.S.S.R.

The public policy ("ordre public") of the European Community and of its Member States is thus purportedly replaced by U.S. public policy which European companies are forced to carry out within the E.C., if they are not to lose export privileges in the U.S. or to face other sanctions. This is an unacceptable interference in the affairs of the European Community.

11. Furthermore, it is reprehensible that present U.S. Regulations encourage non-US companies to submit "voluntarily" to this kind of mobilization for U.S. purposes.

Even when submission to a foreign boycott is entirely voluntary, such submission *within* the U.S. has been considered to be undesirable and contrary to U.S. public policy. By the same token it must have been evident to the U.S. Government that the statutory encouragement of voluntary submission to U.S. public policy in trade matters *within* the E.C. is strongly condemned by the European Community. Private agreements should not be used in this way as instruments of foreign policy. If a Government in law and in fact systematically encourages the inclusion of such submission clauses in private contracts the freedom of contract is misused in order to circumvent the limits imposed on national jurisdiction by international law.

It is self-evident, moreover, that the existence of such submission clauses in certain private contracts cannot serve as a basis for U.S. regulatory jurisdiction which can properly be exercised solely in conformity with international law. Nor can a company prevent a state from objecting to any infringement which might occur of the jurisdiction of the state to which it belongs.

B. Other Bases of Jurisdiction

12. There are two other bases of jurisdiction which might be invoked by the U.S. Government, but which have found less than general acceptance under international law. These are:

(a) the protective principle (para. 33 of the 2nd Restatement), which would give a State jurisdiction to proscribe acts done outside its territory but threatening its security or the operation of its governmental functions, if such acts are generally recognized as crimes by States with reasonably developed legal systems;

---

* The application of the nationality principle would imply *ipso facto* some overlapping with the application of the territoriality principle and this is acceptable under international law, in some instances, but we are not in such a situation in this case.

(b) the so-called "effects doctrine", under which conduct occurring outside the territory but causing direct, foreseeable and substantial effects—which are also constituent elements of a crime or tort—within the territory may be proscribed (para. 18 of the 2nd Restatement).

13. However, it is clear *ab initio* that the extension of U.S. jurisdiction implicit in the Amendments cannot be based on the principles mentioned under 12(a) or (b).

The "protective principle" has not been invoked by the U.S. Government, since the Amendments are based on Section 6 (Foreign Policy Controls) and not on Section 5 (National Security Controls) of the Export Administration Act. The U.S. Government itself, therefore, has not sought to base the Amendments on considerations of national security.

The "effects doctrine" is not applicable. It cannot conceivably be argued that exports from the European Community to the U.S.S.R. for the Siberian gas pipeline have within the U.S.A. direct, foreseeable and substantial effects which are not merely undesirable, but which constitute an element of a crime or tort proscribed by U.S. law. It is more than likely that they have no direct effects on U.S. trade.

14. For the reasons expounded above, it is clear that the U.S. measures of June 22, 1982 do not find a valid basis in any of the generally recognized—or even the more controversial—principles of international law governing state jurisdiction to prescribe rules. As a matter of fact the measures by their extra-territorial character simultaneously infringe the territoriality and nationality principles of jurisdiction and are therefore unlawful under international law.

III. The Amendments Under U.S. Law

A. U.S. Reactions to Measures Similar to the June 22 Amendments

15. If a foreign country were to take measures like the June 22 Amendments, it is doubtful whether they would be in conformity with U.S. law and they would therefore probably not be recognized and enforced by U.S. courts.

The kind of mobilization of E.C. companies for U.S. purposes to which the Community objects was subject to strong American reactions and legislative counter-measures, when U.S. companies were similarly mobilized for the foreign policy purposes of other states.

The anti-foreign-boycott provisions of Section 8 of the Export Administration Act are testimony to that [see Section 13.8 infra]. In the same way as the U.S. could not accept that its companies were turned into instruments of the foreign policy of other nations, the E.C. cannot accept that its companies must follow another trade policy than its own within its own territorial jurisdiction.

It is noteworthy that the anti-boycott provisions of the Export Administration Act can be invoked in response to a boycott that takes a less direct form than the June 22 Amendments, namely a boycott which merely tries to dissuade persons from dealing with a third country by refusing to trade with such persons. An export restriction patterned on the June 22 Amendments, in contrast, would directly prohibit a person from dealing with a particular country under the threat of government-imposed penalties. Therefore, the latest Amendments would appear to be even more far-reaching than a boycott which might give rise to the application of the anti-boycott provisions.

16. Even if for some reason the foreign boycott provisions of the Export Administration Act were not considered applicable, a foreign country imposing such restrictions as those imposed by the June 22 Amendments would probably be viewed by U.S. Courts as attempting to extend its laws beyond its territory without sufficient nexus with the U.S. entity to justify such an extension. This certainly would be the case with respect to a mere licensee of a foreign concern.

If a foreign government complained that a U.S. licensee of a foreign company was not complying with that foreign government's export restrictions prohibiting such exports, a U.S. federal court would decline jurisdiction, because U.S. Courts will not enforce foreign penal statutes.

If the observance of a foreign export control by a U.S. subsidiary or licensee were to become an issue in litigation between the latter and its foreign parent company or licensor, a federal or state court would probably not refuse jurisdiction, but would decline to enforce the export restrictions of the foreign country on the grounds that it would be contrary to the strong public policy of the forum and not in the interest of the United States to do so.

This being the reaction of the U.S. legislator and judiciary to foreign measures comparable to its own measures of June 22, the U.S. Government should not have inflicted these measures on the E.C. companies concerned in the virtual knowledge that these measures would be regarded as unlawful and ineffective by public authorities in the E.C.

AMERICAN LAW INSTITUTE, RESTATEMENT OF THE LAW: FOREIGN RELATIONS LAW OF THE UNITED STATES (REVISED)

(Tentative Draft No. 7, 1986; id. No. 6—Vol. 1, 1985)[3]

§ 402. Bases of Jurisdiction to Prescribe

Subject to § 403, a state has jurisdiction to prescribe law with respect to

(1)(a) conduct a substantial part of which takes place within its territory;

(b) the status of persons, or interests in things, present within its territory;

(c) conduct outside its territory which has or is intended to have substantial effect within its territory;

3. Copyright 1985/1986 by the American Law Institute. Reprinted with the permission of the American Law Institute.

(2) the activities, status, interests or relations of its nationals outside as well as within its territory; or

(3) certain conduct outside its territory by persons not its nationals which is directed against the security of the state or a limited class of other state interests.

§ 403. Limitations on Jurisdiction to Prescribe

(1) Even when one of the bases for jurisdiction under § 402 is present, a state may not exercise jurisdiction to prescribe law with respect to the activities, relations, status, or interests of persons or things having connections with another state or states when the exercise of such jurisdiction is unreasonable.

(2) Whether the exercise of jurisdiction is reasonable or unreasonable is judged by evaluating all the relevant factors, including, where appropriate,

(a) the extent to which the activity (i) takes place within the regulating state, or (ii) has substantial, direct, and foreseeable effect upon or in the regulating state;

(b) the connections, such as nationality, residence, or economic activity, between the regulating state and the persons principally responsible for the activity to be regulated, or between that state and those whom the law or regulation is designed to protect;

(c) the character of the activity to be regulated, the importance of regulation to the regulating state, the extent to which other states regulate such activities, and the degree to which the desirability of such regulation is generally accepted;

(d) the existence of justified expectations that might be protected or hurt by the regulation in question;

(e) the importance of the regulation in question to the international political, legal or economic system;

(f) the extent to which such regulation is consistent with the traditions of the international system;

(g) the extent to which another state may have an interest in regulating the activity; and

(h) the likelihood of conflict with regulation by other states.

(3) When more than one state has a reasonable basis for exercising jurisdiction over a person or activity, but the prescriptions by two or more states are in conflict, each state has an obligation to evaluate its own as well as the other state's interest in exercising jurisdiction in light of all the relevant factors, including those set out in Subsection (2); and should defer to the other state if that state's interest is clearly greater.

§ 414. Jurisdiction With Respect to Activities of Foreign Branches and Subsidiaries

(1) Subject to §§ 403 and 436, a state may exercise limited jurisdiction with respect to activities of foreign branches of corporations organized under its laws.

(2) A state may not ordinarily exercise jurisdiction with respect to activities of corporations organized under the laws of a foreign state on the basis that they are owned or controlled by nationals of the state exercising jurisdiction. However, subject to §§ 403 and 436, it may not be unreasonable for a state to exercise limited jurisdiction with respect to activities of foreign entities

(a) by direction to the parent corporation in respect of such matters as uniform accounting, disclosure to investors, or preparation of consolidated tax returns of multinational enterprises; or

(b) by direction to the parent or the subsidiary in other exceptional cases, depending on all relevant factors, including:

(i) whether the regulation is essential to implementation of a program to further a major, urgent national interest of the state exercising jurisdiction;

(ii) whether the national program of which the regulation is a part cannot be carried out effectively unless it is applied also to foreign subsidiaries;

(iii) whether the regulation is in potential or actual conflict with the law or policy of the state where the subsidiary is established; and

(c) in the exceptional cases referred to in paragraph (b), the burden of establishing reasonableness is heavier when the direction is issued to the foreign subsidiary than when issued to the parent corporation.

Notes and Questions

(1) Despite the controversy generated by the U.S. export controls described in the EC memorandum, Congress did not act to cut back the authority of the President to impose such controls when it extended the Export Administration Act in 1985.

(2) In light of the foregoing materials, did the United States violate international law in imposing controls on the exports of foreign-based subsidiaries and licensees of U.S. companies?

(3) The provisions of the original Restatement differed from those of the proposed Revised Restatement. For example, the original Restatement, in the case where two states had jurisdiction to prescribe and enforce rules of law and the result was that a person was subject to conflicting rules, provided that "each state is required by international law to consider, in good faith, moderating the exercise of its enforcement jurisdiction [in light of listed factors]." Restatement of the Law (Second), Foreign Relations Law of the United States § 40. How does the Revised Restatement modify this rule?

The proposed Revised Restatement provisions on extraterritoriality are controversial. The American Law Institute was scheduled to give it final approval in 1985, but following requests for postponement of a final decision, made by U.S. government agencies and the American Bar Association, final approval did not occur until 1986.

(4) How much guidance do the provisions of Section 403 of the Revised Restatement actually provide? Given the provisions of Section 403, how easy will it be to predict whether a court in a given case will determine that an extraterritorial measure is reasonable? See Comment, Extraterritorial Applica-

tion of U.S. Law: The Case of Export Controls, 132 U.Pa.L.Rev. 355, 377–80 (1984). Problems concerning the extraterritorial application of U.S. antitrust laws have raised questions as to how courts should decide whether to apply those laws in cases involving a substantial foreign element. Some courts have applied the sort of balancing test suggested by the proposed Revised Restatement, while others have indicated that such a test is not useful. Two contrasting views on this question in the context of applying U.S. antitrust laws are set out in Section 18.3(C) and could be profitably read at this time.

(5) One of the most difficult questions raised by the extraterritorial application of export controls is faced by the foreign company that will violate U.S. law if it performs its export contract and may violate the contract without a legally justifiable excuse if it does not. Indeed, in the case of the 1982 controls applied to exports related to the construction of the Russian gas pipeline, several European governments ordered their nationals to disregard the U.S. controls and to perform their contracts, and a number of European companies did so. Their actions resulted in Commerce Department decisions suspending their right to export and receive exports from the United States.[4] As noted in Section 12.3(B) (1) supra, as a result of the 1985 amendments, a person who violates any U.S. national security export control or (in certain circumstances) any regulation issued under COCOM may be denied the right to import goods and technology into the United States and to receive U.S. exports. Given the size of the U.S. market, this power could probably be used very effectively to coerce foreign companies into following U.S.-imposed export controls.

(6) The gas pipeline cases were not the first time the problem of extraterritorial application of U.S. controls caused problems for European based subsidiaries of U.S. companies. For example, U.S. controls on trade with China led to the following case in the 1960's:[5]

In December 1964 Fruehauf-France, S.A., a French Company in which the Fruehauf Corporation (United States) held a two-thirds stock interest, signed a contract with Automobiles Berliet, S.A., another French company, for delivery of 60 "Fruehauf" vans, valued at 1,785,310 francs, for eventual delivery to the People's Republic of China. The first deliveries were to be made in February 1965. In January 1965 the U.S. Treasury Department issued an order directing the Fruehauf Corporation to suspend execution of the contract as violating the U.S. Transaction Control Regulations.

When Fruehauf-France approached Automobiles Berliet about rescinding the contract, Berliet refused. Fearing that failure to perform the contract would weaken the company's position to obtain future contracts from its largest customer (Berliet) and subject the company to suit for damages, the French minority directors on February 15, 1965, instituted a proceeding against the Fruehauf Corporation and the American directors before the Tribunal of Commerce of Corbeil Essonnes. On February 16 the President of the Tribunal appointed a temporary administrator to head Fruehauf-France, S.A., for three months and to execute the contract.

---

4. See, e.g., 47 Fed.Reg. 38169 (Creusot-Loire S.A.), 38170 (Dresser (France) S.A.) (1982). The sanctions were revoked when the United States and its European allies reached an accord of sorts on how to deal with East-West trade issues. See 47 Fed.Reg. 52489 (1982).

5. Fruehauf Corporation v. Massardy. Court of Appeals of Paris, 14th Chamber, De-

cision of May 22, 1965. American Society of International Law, Internal Legal Materials 476 (May 1966). Reprinted by permission of the American Society of International Law. For a similar case involving the pipeline controls, see Compagnie Europeenne des Petroles S.A. v. Sensor Nederland B.V., 22 Intl. Legal Materials 66 (1982).

The Fruehauf Corporation appealed to the Court of Appeals of Paris. The Court of Appeals in a decision of May 22, 1965, affirmed the order of February 16, 1965, appointing an administrator for three months to execute the contract with Berliet. Among the considerations cited by the Court of Appeals in its decision were:

> The evidence demonstrates, without serious question, not only the clear and present interest Fruehauf-France, S.A. has in the execution of a contract made with its principal customer, Berliet, S.A., which accounts for about 40 per cent of its exports, but above all the catastrophic results which would have been produced, on the eve of delivery date, and which would be felt even today, if the contract had been breached, because the buyer would be in a position to demand of its seller all commercial damages resulting therefrom, valued at more than five million francs, following upon the break-off of its dealings with China.
>
> *   *   * these damages, which Fruehauf Corporation or Fruehauf-International [the United States parent companies] did not indicate any intention of assuming, would be of such an order as to ruin the financial equilibrium and the moral credit of Fruehauf-France, S.A. and provoke its disappearance and the unemployment of more than 600 workers; *   *   * in order to name a temporary administrator the judge-referee must take into account the interests of the company rather than the personal interests of any shareholders even if they be the majority.

In commenting on the *Fruehauf* case, William Laurence Craig writing in "Application of the Trading with the Enemy Act to Foreign Corporations Owned by Americans: Reflections on Fruehauf v. Massardy," [6] 83 Harvard Law Review, 579 at 595, said:

> French laws thus may require actions in France that are inconsistent with the United States regulation. The Treasury Department—which, like other governmental agencies, would probably not admit to the existence of legal principles restraining the exercise of concurrent jurisdiction—appears to have adopted the policy that foreign legislation shall not be allowed to predominate over United States embargo legislation despite the dilemma in which the regulated enterprise may be placed. This suggests that the "moderation" called for in the exercise of concurrent jurisdiction may not be applied unless there is an actual and not only a potential, litigation abroad requiring conflicting action.
>
> *   *   *
>
> The possibility of retaliation is not the only factor which might influence the United States to release its jurisdictional claim over American corporations abroad. There is also the legitimacy of host country objections. Capital-importing nations have compelling reasons to require foreign corporate investors to abide by their laws and policies without regard to the policies of the capital-exporting state. Public uproar and diplomatic protest could be expected to ensue if Péchiney, a French subsidiary in the State of Washington, were ordered by the French government to cancel a contract for the delivery of aluminum to Israel, resulting in the shut-down of a plant

and the laying-off of workers. Yet even such a bizarre occurrence would not stir up as much emotion as can be aroused in a capital-importing country in which entire sectors of the economy are under foreign, often American, control. In the long run, it is to the benefit of the capital-exporting country that its capital be welcomed and that its subsidiaries be treated as citizens of the host country. To be treated as such, they must act as good citizens, and United States regulations frequently make this difficult.

*   *   *

A third, and probably the best, solution would be an extension of the "Cuban exemption," under which foreign subsidiaries owned or controlled by Americans are now exempted from the embargo on trade in goods with Cuba provided that no American participates in the transaction. This exemption was designed to alleviate hostility abroad to the Cuban embargo, but by a strained interpretation of participation the Treasury Department has continued to threaten legal action when American directors sit on the board of a controlled foreign company engaged in Cuban trade.

See also Comment, Western European Sovereignty and American Export and Trade Controls, 9 Colum.J.Transnat'l L. 109 (1970).

(7) What actions might the EC or its member states take to discourage U.S. use of extraterritorial trade control measures besides issuing directives to ignore the measures? Assuming the U.S. companies involved had European operations or connections of some sort, could statutes be fashioned that would penalize U.S. companies that complied or tried to cause compliance with the U.S. controls? For possible ideas along this line, see Section 18.3(C) infra (blocking statutes).

(8) Does GATT address the issue of extraterritorial trade control measures? Suppose a U.S. ally helps the United States enforce U.S. national security export controls by prohibiting the reexport from its territory of items subject to U.S. controls. Does GATT require the ally to justify its action in reference to its own national security or is it enough that a U.S. national security interest is involved?

SECTION 13.6 THE EFFECTIVENESS OF TRADE CONTROLS IMPOSED FOR NATIONAL SECURITY OR FOREIGN POLICY PURPOSES

Measuring the effectiveness of trade controls is very difficult. By necessity, a subjective judgment must be made as to the degree of effectiveness and that is very difficult to do. This is especially true if a significant factor in the decision to impose controls was simply to register a protest or to attempt to deter similar future actions by others. Moreover, even ineffective controls may have seemed at the time they were imposed to be the only viable alternative in a situation in which it was deemed that some action was mandatory. Nonetheless, attempts have been made to measure effectiveness of trade controls and the following summarizes the conclusions of one such study of 103 cases between 1914 and 1983. The authors also offer their views on rules to follow to increase the likelihood of successful application of sanctions.

GARY CLYDE HUFBAUER & JEFFREY J. SCHOTT, ECONOMIC SANCTIONS RECONSIDERED

79–92 (1985) [1]

A number of lessons can be abstracted from the sanctions episodes of the past seventy years. In this concluding chapter, we first assess the overall effectiveness of sanctions, based on the experience of 103 cases. We then group the lessons learned into a list of propositions—nine commandments— to guide governments in the use of economic sanctions.

First a word of caution. Forecasting the outcome of statecraft, like forecasting the stock market, is hazardous business. Idiosyncratic influences are often at play. Human personalities and plain luck may well determine the outcome of a sanctions episode. These simple truths are underscored by appendix A, which presents our multiple regression analysis. In this analysis, success scores were related to the variables catalogued in Chapters 3 and 4. As one might expect from a diverse collection of 103 cases, the statistical results are not always clearcut. Much depends on the personalities of national leaders, the kaleidoscope of contemporaneous world events, and other factors which are not captured by our variables. Hence our summary assessments and nine commandments must be read as general indicators, not infallible guideposts, in the fine art of statecraft.

ARE SANCTIONS EFFECTIVE?

Policymakers need to take a close look at the cost and effectiveness of sanctions when designing foreign policy strategy. In most cases, sanctions do not contribute very much to the achievement of foreign policy goals; however, in some instances—particularly situations involving small target countries and modest policy goals—sanctions have helped alter foreign behavior. Table 5.1 summarizes the score card. * * *

Table 5.1   Success by type of policy goal

Policy goal	Success cases	Failure cases	Success ratio (percentage of total)
Modest policy changes	18	26	41
Destabilization	10	9	53
Disruption of military adventures	6	12	33
Military impairment	2	8	20
Other major policy changes	3	14	18
Totals [a]	39	69	36

a. The figures include five instances of cases included under two different policy goals: * * * Since these cases are generally failures, double counting them adds a small negative bias to the success ratio.

Perhaps surprisingly, sanctions have been "successful"—by our definition—in 36 percent of the cases overall. However, the success rate impor-

1. © 1985, Institute for International Economics. Reproduced by permission.

tantly depends on the type of goal sought. Episodes involving destabilization succeed in half the cases, (usually against target countries that are small and shaky), while modest goals are attained in just over 40 percent of the cases. But attempts to disrupt military adventures, to impair a foreign adversary's military potential, or otherwise to change its policies in a major way, generally fail. Our multiple regression analysis indicates that, all other things equal, the success scores on average were 1.0 index points higher for destabilization and modest goal cases than for other categories.

Success has proven more elusive in recent years than in earlier decades. This point is made in table 5.2 [omitted]. Taking the pre-1973 period as a whole, not quite half of the episodes succeeded. In the period 1973–84, the success rate was just over a quarter. The difference seems to reflect much poorer results in episodes entailing modest policy goals. While the number of these episodes ballooned, the success rate dropped markedly between the two periods, from 75 percent to 28 percent. The impression conveyed by table 5.2 is confirmed by our multiple regression analysis. The time trend is negative: with all other things equal, an episode launched in 1984 would, on average, have a success score 0.05 index points lower than the same episode launched just a year earlier. Put another way, over a 20-year period, the representative success score dropped by 1.0 index points ($0.05 \times 20 = 1.0$).

With the frequent use of economic sanctions (particularly by the US) to achieve modest goals, target countries may have become more immune to their impact. This immunity may derive from two factors: first, latter-day target countries are less dependent on trade with sender countries; and second, more nations are willing and able to play Sir Galahad to target countries. Ties between target and sender countries have become more remote: the average trade linkage fell from 26 percent to 15 percent in recent cases compared to the pre-1973 period. Many of the failures in recent years are connected with the widespread use of sanctions by the United States in support of human rights and nuclear nonproliferation campaigns against countries as remote as Pakistan and Argentina. Moreover, the growth in global economic interdependence and the East-West confrontation have made it easier for target countries to find alternate suppliers, markets, and financial backers to replace goods embargoed or funds withheld by the sender country. For these reasons, we conclude that sanctions are a decreasingly useful policy instrument.

NINE COMMANDMENTS

From the summary in table 5.1, it is clear that sanctions occasionally bear fruit, but only when planted in the right soil and nurtured in the proper way. Nine propositions are offered for the statesman who would act as a careful gardener.

I. "Don't Bite Off More Than You Can Chew"

Sanctions cannot move mountains nor can they force strong target countries into making fundamental changes. Countries often have inflated expectations of what sanctions can accomplish. This is especially true of the US today and the UK in an earlier era. At most, there is a weak correlation between economic deprivation and political willingness to change. The *economic* impact of sanctions may be pronounced, both on the sender and the target country, but other factors in the situational context almost always overshadow the impact of sanctions in determining the *political* outcome.

* * * Excluding the two world wars and the two civil wars, we have found only one case (Arab League v. US and Netherlands) where economic coercion was effective in changing major domestic policies. In this case, the Arab oil embargo helped accomplish two of its four objectives: it caused a significant shift, namely a more pro-Arab slant, in European and Japanese policies toward the Palestinian question; and it supported OPEC's decision to boost the world price of oil to OPEC's enormous economic benefit. But the embargo failed to get Israel to retreat behind its pre-1967 frontiers, and it failed to persuade the US to abandon its pro-Israel policy stance. * * *

To justify even a remote hope for success in military impairment and major change cases, sender countries would have to form a near monopoly over trading relations with the target country. This obvious precept, learned in the first and second world wars, was forgotten in the case of UN sanctions against South Africa and turned on its head in the recent case of US sanctions to block construction of the Soviet-European gas pipeline.

II. "The Weakest Go to The Wall"

Summing up all cases in the five groups, there seems to be a direct correlation between the political and economic health of the target country and its susceptibility to economic pressure. Our multiple regression analysis indicates that sanctions imposed on a "strong and stable" country on average are characterized by a success score that is 2.8 index points lower than sanctions imposed on a "distressed" country.

* * *

III. "Attack Your Allies, Not Your Adversaries"

Economic sanctions seem most effective when aimed against erstwhile friends and close trading partners. By contrast, sanctions directed against target countries that have long been adversaries of the sender country, or against targets that have little trade with the sender country, are generally less successful. * * *

The higher compliance with sanctions by allies and trading partners reflects their willingness to bend on specific issues in deference to an overall relationship with the sender country. Such considerations may not be decisive in the calculus of an antagonistic target country, or a target country that has little economic contact with the sender.

* * *

IV. "If It Were Done, When 'Tis Done, Then 'Twere Well It Were Done Quickly"

A heavy, slow hand invites both evasion and the mobilization of domestic opinion in the target country. Sanctions imposed slowly or incrementally may simply strengthen the target government at home as it mobilizes the forces of nationalism. Moreover, such measures are likely to be undercut over time either by the sender's own firms or by foreign competitors. Sanctions generally are regarded as a short-term policy, with the anticipation that normal commercial relations will be reestablished after the resolution of the crisis. This explains why, even though popular opinion in the sender country may welcome the introduction of sanctions, public support for sanctions often dissipates over time.

* * *

V. "In for a Penny, in for a Pound"

Cases that inflict heavy costs on the target country are generally successful. As shown in table 5.7, the average cost for all success cases was over 2 percent of GNP; by contrast, failed episodes barely dented the economy of the target country, averaging well under 1 percent of GNP.

* * *

VI. "It You Need to Ask the Price, You Can't Afford the Yacht"

The more it costs a sender country to impose sanctions, the less likely it is that the sanctions will succeed.

* * *

The results suggest that sender governments should design sanctions so as not to impose unduly concentrated costs on particular domestic groups. One example of actions to avoid is the retroactive application of sanctions to cancel existing contracts. Such actions not only leave the affected firms "high and dry" with unsold inventories and excess capacity, but they also sour chances of competing for future business. If the sender government believes that retroactive application is essential to the success of an episode, then it might do well to compensate affected domestic firms.

Sanctions episodes that are least costly to the sender are often those that make use of financial leverage—manipulating aid flows, denying official credits, or, at the extreme, freezing assets—rather than trade controls. The multiple regression analysis suggests that financial controls are marginally more successful than export controls, but that import controls are the most successful of all types.

VII. "More Is Less"

Economic sanctions are often deployed in conjunction with other measures directed against the target: covert action, quasi-military measures, or regular military operations. * * * On balance, there is little evidence that covert and military actions, when used in parallel with economic sanctions, tip the scales in favor of success. * * *

VIII. "Too Many Cooks Spoil the Broth"

The greater the number of countries needed to implement the denial measures, the less likely sanctions will be effective. Contrary to conventional wisdom, multilateral sanctions are not frequently associated with success.

In a sense, the importance of international cooperation is over-played. Basically, a country looks to its allies for help because its goals are ambitious; in cases involving more modest goals, such cooperation is not needed. * * *

Without significant cooperation from its allies, a sender country stands little chance of achieving success in cases involving "high" policy goals. However, international cooperation does not guarantee success even in these cases, as evidenced from the long history of the US and COCOM strategic controls against the USSR and COMECON, and the Arab League's futile boycott of Israel.

* * *

To be sure, international cooperation serves three useful functions: it increases the moral suasion of the sanction; it helps isolate the target country from the global community; and it preempts foreign backlash, thus minimizing corrosive friction within the alliance. These observations, together with our statistical analysis, suggest that forced international "cooperation" brought about by the heavy hand of extraterritorial controls will seldom yield desirable results. Sanctions should be either deployed unilaterally—because the impact on one's allies is slight—or they should be designed in cooperation with one's allies in order to reduce backlash and evasion.

* * *

IX. *"Look Before You Leap"*

The sender government should think through its means and objectives *before* taking a final decision to deploy sanctions. Leaders in the sender country should be confident that their goals are within their grasp, that they can impose sufficient economic pain to command the attention of the target country, that their efforts will not simply prompt offsetting policies by other major powers, and that the sanctions chosen will not impose insupportable costs on their domestic constituents and foreign allies. These conditions will arise on only infrequent occasions, and even then the odds of success are not great. The prudent leader will weigh carefully the costs and benefits of economic sanctions before resorting to their use in foreign policy ventures.

SECTION 13.7 A CASE STUDY: UNITED NATIONS SANCTIONS AGAINST RHODESIA

In recent years, there has been considerable pressure placed on the U.S. and other governments to impose economic sanctions on South Africa in an effort to convince it to abandon its system of apartheid.[1] In September 1985, the United States imposed limited economic sanctions,[2] a move joined by some other countries.[3] It is too early to gauge the effect of the sanctions, but it does bring to mind a prior attempt by a more united world community to use broader economic sanctions to bring down the white minority government of Rhodesia.[4]

1. See Davis, Cason & Hovey, Economic Disengagement and South Africa: The Effectiveness and Feasibility of Implementing Sanctions and Disinvestment, 15 Law & Poly. Intl.Bus. 529 (1983); Hearings on Economic Sanctions and Their Potential Impact on U.S. Corporate Involvement in South Africa Before the Subcomm. on Africa of the House Comm. on Foreign Affairs, 99th Cong., 1st Sess. (1985).

2. Executive Order 12532 of September 9, 1985, 50 Fed.Reg. 36861 (1985).

3. See 24 Intl. Legal Materials 1464 (1985).

4. See McDougall & Riesman, Rhodesia and the United Nations: The Lawfulness of International Concern, 62 Am.J.Intl.L. 1 (1968); R. Zacklin, The United Nations and Rhodesia: A Study in International Law (1974).

NOTE, INTERNATIONAL SANCTIONS—UNITED NATIONS SECURITY COUNCIL RESOLUTION—ECONOMIC SANCTIONS AGAINST SOUTHERN RHODESIA

(1974) [5]

Rhodesia's 1965 unilateral declaration of independence (UDI) from the British Commonwealth became the catalyst for an unprecedented invocation of mandatory non-military sanctions by the United Nations. The history leading up to the 1965 UDI began in the 1890's when the British South Africa Company of Cecil Rhodes, assisted by regular British troops, conquered the tribal territories of Mashonaland and Matabeleland. An influx of European colonists followed, and when the British formally annexed the area in 1923 these settlers were granted internal control over the area. Alarmed by African nationalist movements in Northern Rhodesia and Nyasaland in the late 1940's, the white Europeans in the south persuaded Britain to establish the Federation of Rhodesia and Nyasaland in 1953. The white minority dominated this federation until its dissolution in 1963. During this period, the white minority established a policy of segregation and political and economic discrimination against all non-Europeans. Because of this apartheid practice, the U.N. as early as 1962 took note of the white government's contravention of the customary international law against racial discrimination and the resulting volatile situation in Rhodesia.

When in 1964 Britain permitted the two northern territories (now Zambia and Malawi) to proceed towards independence under an African majority rule, the white minority in the south attempted to retain its dominant position there by seeking Southern Rhodesia's independence from Britain. Britain refused to grant independence until the apartheid practices of the white minority had been replaced by five principles for equalitarian reform. Negotiations between the British and the Ian Smith regime on the issue of independence proved futile and on November 11, 1965, Ian Smith unilaterally declared his government's independent status.

International reactions to the secessionist regime were swift and abrupt. On the same day as the Rhodesian UDI, the General Assembly issued a condemnation of "the unilateral declaration of independence by the racialist minority in Southern Rhodesia," and called the situation to the attention of the Security Council. The following day, the Security Council paralleled the General Assembly's action by condemning "the usurpation of power by a racist settler minority," and called upon all member states not to recognize the illegal regime. On November 20, 1965, the Council called upon all states "to refrain from any action which would assist and encourage the illegal regime and, in particular, to desist from providing it with arms, equipment and military material, and to do their utmost in order to break all economic relations with Southern Rhodesia, including an embargo on oil and petroleum products." The action taken outside of the U.N. also was substantial. Within the three-month period following the UDI, Great Britain enacted a

5. 14 Va.J.Intl.L. 319, 320. Reprinted by permission of the Virginia Journal of International Law.

series of economic restraints aimed at limiting Southern Rhodesia's trade with the Commonwealth countries. The Organization of African Unity (OAU) in December, 1965, announced a comprehensive economic boycott of Rhodesian exports. In March, 1965, the United States prohibited unlicensed exports to Southern Rhodesia.

Attempts by South Africa and Portugal to break the oil embargo in early April, 1966, prompted the Security Council to initiate further action. Deciding that the situation constituted a threat to world peace, the Security Council invoked Article 39 of the Charter and authorized Britain to use force if necessary to intercept ships believed to be carrying oil eventually bound for Southern Rhodesia. On December 16, 1966, following another collapse of negotiations between Britain and Southern Rhodesia, the Council ordered an unprecedented mandatory embargo of arms, oil, and motor vehicles to Rhodesia and a boycott of major Rhodesian exports.

The execution of five blacks in Salisbury in March, 1968, precipitated renewed demands for more stringent measures against the Smith regime. After lengthy discussions, the Security Council unanimously adopted a British-proposed resolution which, in addition to extending the previous sanctions to cover all Southern Rhodesian goods, established a Security Council Sanctions Committee. The purpose of the Committee is to examine the Secretary-General's reports on sanction implementation and to investigate any trading activities which appear to be in violation of the sanction provisions.

Resumption of negotiations between Britain and Rhodesia occurred in October, 1968, aboard the HMS *Fearless,* but they proved nugatory. Meanwhile, the Rhodesian government had issued proposals for a new constitution, and had stated its intention to become a republic. A June, 1969 referendum held in Rhodesia confirmed a majority support for these measures, and official proclamation of the Republic came on March 2, 1970. As anticipated, these acts exacerbated tensions at the United Nations. African states participating on the Security Council found a resolution proposed by Britain to be inadequate and countered with a resolution calling for the use of force. This measure was vetoed,*[37] but a compromise resolution was adopted on March 18, 1970. In addition to reaffirming the prior mandatory sanctions and calling upon members to take more stringent measures to make these sanctions effective, the resolution called upon the states to sever diplomatic-consular relations with and to impose a communications ban against Rhodesia. As a result of this resolution, eight countries—including the United States—closed their consular offices in Salisbury.

Security Council resolutions subsequent to March 18, 1970, primarily have been aimed at the effective enforcement of the U.N. action against Rhodesia. Concerned by the findings in the third annual report of the Security Council Sanctions Committee that the sanctions had not been fully effective, the Security Council on November 17, 1970, adopted a resolution deploring the actions of those members who had given assistance in any form to the Smith regime and urging all members to comply with past

* 37. The vetoes were cast by Britain and the United States.

decisions of the Council. The adoption by the United States in 1971 of the Byrd Amendment, which allows chrome and other "strategic and critical" materials to be imported from Rhodesia, prompted the Security Council on February 28, 1972 and July 28, 1972 to adopt resolutions reaffirming its imposition of the sanctions against Rhodesia and urging all members to comply with the sanctions.

SEVENTH REPORT OF THE SECURITY COUNCIL COMMITTEE ESTABLISHED IN PURSUANCE OF RESOLUTION 253 (1968) CONCERNING THE QUESTION OF SOUTHERN RHODESIA

U.N. Doc. S/11594/Add. 3

Southern Rhodesian exports: 1965–1973
(in millions of US dollars)

	1965	1966	1967	1968	1969	1970	1971	1972	1973
Domestic exports (excluding gold)	399	238	238	234	297	346	379	474	640
To reporting countries	343	181	96	68	48	50	48	60	63
To S. Africa Customs Union	41	60	80	80	85	95	90	100	103
To non-reporting countries	15	—	—	—	—	—	—	—	—
To world markets via indirect trade	—	–3	62	86	164	201	241	314	474
Re-exports	43	24	17	12	10	8	9	9	12

Table 4

Southern Rhodesian imports: 1965–1973
(in millions of US dollars)

	1965	1966	1967	1968	1969	1970	1971	1972	1973
Imports	334	236	262	290	278	329	395	404	480
From reporting countries	253	79	63	44	15	16	18	19	16
From S. Africa Customs Union	78	110	135	150	155	160	170	165	180
Unspecified origin . .	3	—	—	—	—	—	—	—	—
Unaccounted for . . .	—	47	64	96	108	153	207	220	284

KAPUNGU, THE UNITED NATIONS AND ECONOMIC SANCTIONS AGAINST RHODESIA

128 (1973) [6]

In no way can the Rhodesian rebellion be said to have been weakened by economic sanctions. In fact, economic sanctions have welded together the Rhodesian conservative elements in support of the survival of the regime. A number of those Europeans who were opposed to a UDI and remained opposed to it after the Rhodesian regime had proved that it was the *de facto* government have left Rhodesia. Those who remained in Rhodesia and tried to organize themselves into the Center Party were repudiated by the Europe-

6. Reprinted by permission of the publisher from The United Nations and Economic Sanctions Against Rhodesia by Leonard T. Kapungu (Lexington Books, Lexington, Mass. D.C. Heath and Company, 1973).

an electorate in the elections of April 10, 1970. All the sixteen European candidates of the party were defeated. When the Anglo-Rhodesian Proposed Settlement of 1971 was announced, the Center Party eagerly supported it only to be repudiated also by the Africans who rejected the Settlement.

But if the economic effects of the sanctions against Rhodesia are projected into the future, a different political goal than that which Britain had sought to achieve might be attained. Rhodesia, faced with a stagnant economy, is failing to provide employment or to keep in school a growing number of the African population. At the same time, Rhodesia must continue to fight against nationalist guerillas. Rhodesia allocates an unrevealed substantial part of its budget for its military operations against the nationalist guerillas. If, at a point in the future, the nationalist guerillas should be able to launch effective operations in Rhodesia, can the regime, faced with economic stagnation, be able to continue spending large sums of its budget fighting the guerillas? Furthermore, since economic stagnation has led to increased African unemployment, creating a social problem which could in the future turn out into political unrest, can the regime, at that point in time, be in a position to maintain large security forces to deal with African political unrest as well as the nationalist guerillas? This is assuming that the application of economic sanctions is continued and that Rhodesia, as a result, continues to face economic stagnation. During the riots of January and February 1972 the regime ran short of security forces to quell the riots all over the country. It had to recall from the Zambezi Valley some of its military units which were keeping vigilance on the infiltration of the guerillas through the Rhodesian northern borders. If the Zimbabwe political groups in exile had mounted coordinated military operations in Rhodesia simultaneously with the riots, the Rhodesian regime might have been faced with an untenable situation.

NOTE, THE RHODESIAN CHROME STATUTE: THE CONGRESSIONAL RESPONSE TO UNITED NATIONS ECONOMIC SANCTIONS AGAINST SOUTHERN RHODESIA

(1972) [7]

Sanctions have had an economic impact even though they have not eradicated Rhodesian trade. The United Nations must have anticipated enforcement problems, but the objective of the sanctions may be achieved without total compliance. The intent behind the sanctions is not to punish for past conduct but to influence and change future policy. Broader compliance will accomplish this result sooner, but recent negotiations between Southern Rhodesia and Great Britain about the status of the African population [*183] indicate that the goal is realistic. Any determination that

7. 58 Va.L.Rev. 511, 543.

* 183. In November 1971 British Foreign Secretary Sir Alec Douglas-Home and Southern Rhodesian Prime Minister Ian Smith reached a tentative settlement of Rhodesia's rebellion against Britain. Mr. Smith made limited constitutional concessions which would supposedly have insured black majority rule sometime during the next century. See Washington Post, Dec. 1, 1971, § A, at 32, col. 1. According to one observer, the reason for the Smith régime's concessions was the crisis in foreign currency reserves created by sanctions. N.Y. Times, Jan. 22, 1972, at 3, col. 2.

economic sanctions have failed is premature and probably wrong. And one thing is clear: American non-compliance *will* promote failure.

Notes and Questions

(1) In 1979, Rhodesia returned to its status of a British colony. It thereafter became independent under the name of Zimbabwe in 1980 and is now ruled by an African government.

(2) The United States initially complied with the U.N. resolution calling for imposition of economic sanctions. In 1971, however, Congress adopted and the President signed the so-called Byrd Amendment, which was the subject of litigation in Diggs v. Shultz, 470 F.2d 461 (D.C.Cir.1972), cert. denied, 411 U.S. 931, 93 S.Ct. 1897, 36 L.Ed.2d 390 (1972). In that case, the court described the facts surrounding the amendment as follows:

> In 1966 the Security Council of the United Nations, with the affirmative vote of the United States, adopted Resolution 232 directing that all member states impose an embargo on trade with Southern Rhodesia—a step which was reaffirmed and enlarged in 1968. In compliance with this resolution, the President of the United States issued Executive Orders 11322 and 11419, 22 U.S.C. § 287c, establishing criminal sanctions for violation of the embargo. In 1971, however, Congress adopted the so-called Byrd Amendment to the Strategic and Critical Materials Stock Piling Act, 50 U.S.C. § 98–98h, which provides in part:

> > Sec. 10. Notwithstanding any other provision of law * * * the President may not prohibit or regulate the importation into the United States of any material determined to be strategic and critical pursuant to the provisions of this Act, if such material is the product of any foreign country or area not listed as a Communist-dominated country or area * * * for so long as the importation into the United States of material of that kind which is the product of such Communist-dominated countries or areas is not prohibited by any provision of law.

> Since Southern Rhodesia is not a Communist-controlled country, and inasmuch as the United States imports from Communist countries substantial quantities of metallurgical chromite and other materials available from Rhodesia, the Byrd Amendment contemplated the resumption of trade by this country with Southern Rhodesia. By direction of the President, the Office of Foreign Assets Control issued to the corporate appellees in this case a General License authorizing the importation of various materials from Southern Rhodesia, and they began importation.

> Alleging that the Byrd Amendment did not and could not authorize issuance of such a license contrary to this country's treaty obligations, appellants sought to enjoin further importation, to require official seizure, and to restrain use, of materials already imported under the General License, and to declare the General License null and void.

The agreement will not become effective unless a British commission headed by Lord Pearce determines that the proposal is acceptable to a majority of the Southern Rhodesian people. Thus far the response of the Africans who make up 95 percent of the total population has not been favorable to the plan. In response Prime Minister Smith has warned, "If the present generation of Africans are [sic] so stupid as to reject this offer of advancement for their people, they will bear the curses of their children forever." Id. at 3, col. 1.

After concluding that the plaintiffs had standing, the court ruled on the merits as follows:

The District Court, in its comments to the effect that non-justiciability would necessitate dismissal of the complaint even if standing be found, reasoned as follows: It is settled constitutional doctrine that Congress may nullify, in whole or in part, a treaty commitment. Congress, by the Byrd Amendment in 1971, acted to abrogate one aspect of our treaty obligations under the U.N. Charter, that is to say, our continued participation in the economic sanctions taken against Southern Rhodesia. The considerations underlying that step by Congress present issues of political policy which courts do not inquire into. Thus, appellants' quarrel is with Congress, and it is a cause which can be pursued only at the polls and not in the courts.

In this court appellants do not seriously contest the first of these propositions, namely, the constitutional power of Congress to set treaty obligations at naught.[*4] They seek, rather, to show that, in the Byrd Amendment, Congress did not really intend to compel the Executive to end United States observance of the Security Council's sanctions, and that, therefore, it is the Executive which is, without the essential shield of Congressional dispensation, violating a treaty engagement of this country. Appellants point out in this regard that the Byrd Amendment does not in terms require importation from Southern Rhodesia, but leaves open two alternative courses of action. The statute says the President may not ban importation from Rhodesia of materials classified as critical and stategic unless importation from Communist countries is also prohibited. Instead of permitting resumption of trade with Rhodesia, the President, so it is said, could (1) have banned importation of these materials from Communist nations as well as from Rhodesia, or (2) have taken steps to have these materials declassified, thereby taking them in either case out of the scope of the Byrd Amendment.

Citing the canon of construction that a statute should, if possible, be construed in a manner consistent with treaty obligations, appellants argue that the Byrd Amendment, although discretionary on its face, should be construed to compel the President to take one or the other of these two steps as a means of escape from the necessity of breaching the U.N. Charter. But these alternatives raise questions of foreign policy and national defense as sensitive as those involved in the decision to honor or abrogate our treaty obligations.[*5] To attempt to decide whether the President chose properly

*4. * * * Although appellants concede that Congress has the power to override treaty obligations (Appellants' Br. at 23), they contend that our commitment to the U.N. has more force than an ordinary treaty. Appellants argue on the basis of their interpretation of the U.N. Charter that Congress could override Resolution 232 only by withdrawing from the U.N. entirely. There is, however, no evidence that this country's membership in that organization was intended to be on the all-or-nothing basis suggested by appellants.

*5. Russia supplied 60 per cent of our metallurgical chromite in 1970 while the embargo was being observed by the United States, S.Rep. No. 92–359, 92d Cong., 1st Sess., 121

(1971), and a decision to discontinue importation would be a serious step in a very delicate area. Similarly, the decision to remove certain materials from the critical and strategic list should be done in a manner consistent with the objectives of that act. 50 U.S.C. § 98. Appellants' view would require reclassification of materials without regard to whether they continue to be critical to national defense. Appellants argue that the apparent surplus in the stockpile indicates the materials are no longer critical. This confuses two distinct functions under the act. One is classification of materials as strategic or critical in order to encourage their development in this country and to avoid dangerous

among the three alternatives confronting him "would be, not to decide a judicial controversy, but to assume a position of authority over the governmental acts of another and coequal department, an authority which plainly we do not possess." Frothingham v. Mellon, 262 U.S. 447, 489, 43 S.Ct. 597, 601, 67 L.Ed. 1078 (1923).

We think that there can be no blinking the purpose and effect of the Byrd Amendment. It was to detach this country from the U.N. boycott of Southern Rhodesia in blatant disregard of our treaty undertakings. The legislative record shows that no member of Congress voting on the measure was under any doubt about what was involved then; and no amount of statutory interpretation now can make the Byrd Amendment other than what it was as presented to the Congress, namely, a measure which would make—and was intended to make—the United States a certain treaty violator. The so-called options given to the President are, in reality, not options at all. In any event, they are in neither case alternatives which are appropriately to be forced upon him by a court.

Under our constitutional scheme, Congress can denounce treaties if it sees fit to do so, and there is nothing the other branches of government can do about it. We consider that this is precisely what Congress has done in this case; and therefore the District Court was correct to the extent that it found the complaint to state no tenable claim in law.

The Byrd Amendment was repealed in 1977. Pub.L. No. 95–12, 91 Stat. 22 (1977).

(3) Would you conclude that the sanctions against Rhodesia were effective or ineffective?

(4) Is it sensible to place great stress on the question of effectiveness? If a government wishes to show its support of certain principles, such as basic human rights, why should it not use trade controls to do so? Does the fact that speaking out against a foreign government's policies is by itself unlikely to change them mean that it should not be done?

SECTION 13.8 FOREIGN USE OF TRADE CONTROLS: U.S. ANTIBOYCOTT RULES [1]

Section 8 of the Export Administration Act (EAA) regulates compliance by U.S. persons with a boycott by foreign countries against a country that is friendly to the United States and that is not the object of a boycott pursuant to U.S. law or regulation.[2] Essentially, the purpose of the provision, which was first adopted in 1977, is to make it unlawful for U.S. companies to participate in the Arab boycott of Israel. That boycott, which is followed to varying degrees by the various Arab countries, calls for a ban on imports from and exports to Israel. In addition, it provides for a so-called secondary

dependency upon other nations. The other is the acquisition of certain quantities of these materials to be stockpiled for use in an emergency. A surplus in the stock pile at a given moment does not mean that it is no longer necessary to be concerned about the dependency of this country on outside sources for the materials in question.

1. See generally K. Teslik, Congress, the Executive Branch, and Special Interests: The American Response to the Arab Boycott of Israel (1982).

2. 50 U.S.C.A.App. § 2407.

boycott of Israel, pursuant to which firms that do business with Israel or have certain other relations with it are blacklisted and unable to do business in the Arab world. The U.S. antiboycott rules usually do not, as a practical matter, prevent U.S. businesses from doing business with Arab countries or complying with the terms of the primary Arab boycott, i.e. that part of the boycott prohibiting the importation into Arab countries of Israeli origin goods. They do serve, however, to discourage U.S. businesses from complying too readily with the secondary boycott. As such, the rules seem to have been largely accepted by all concerned, although U.S. business interests cite them as an impediment that costs them business vis-à-vis European and Japanese competitors who do not have to worry about such rules.[3] Moreover, the complexity of the rules creates a trap for the unwary, as the distinction between what is permitted and what is prohibited by the EAA may often seem virtually indistinguishable to the untrained eye.[4] For example, it is permissible to agree to certify that the goods to be supplied to an Arab country are of U.S., Canadian or whatever origin, but not that the goods are not of Israeli origin.[5]

Section 8 of the EAA applies only to U.S. persons (broadly defined to include controlled foreign subsidiaries) and only with respect to activities in the interstate or foreign commerce of the United States.[6] Obviously, many activities of U.S. controlled subsidiaries would not involve the foreign commerce of the United States. The EAA provides that U.S. persons should not engage in any boycott-related activities listed in Section 8(a)(1), except to the extent permitted by Section 8(a)(2). In addition, the law requires extensive reporting of requests to support boycotts.

Different antiboycott rules are found in the Internal Revenue Code. These provisions, added by the Tax Reform Act of 1976, require U.S. taxpayers to report operations in, with or related to a boycotting country or national thereof and participation in the boycott, including receipt of requests to participate. Participation may lead to a loss of tax benefits.[7]

3. K. Teslik, note 1 supra, at 234–35.

4. The regulations are set out at 15 CFR Pt. 369 (1985).

5. 50 U.S.C.A.App. § 2407(a)(2)(B); 15 C.F.R. § 369.3(b) (1985).

6. 50 U.S.C.A.App. § 2407(a)(1).

7. Tax Reform Act of 1976, Pub.L. No. 94–455, § 1061–64, 90 Stat. 1520 (adding 26 U.S.

C.A. §§ 908, 952(a), 995(b)(1)(F)(ii) and 999). The Treasury Department issued Guidelines explaining the scope of the statute on several occasions between 1976 and 1978. See 1976–2 C.B. 628, 1977–1 C.B. 529, 1977–2 C.B. 505, 1978–1 C.B. 521. See generally Kaplan, Income Taxes and the Arab Boycott, 32 Tax Lawyer 313 (1979).

Chapter 14

INTERNATIONAL TRADE IN AGRICULTURAL AND OTHER COMMODITIES

SECTION 14.1 INTRODUCTION

The subject of this chapter is less one of law and rules, and more one of perplexing political, social, and economic factors. Although one cannot conclude generally that there are no rules governing international trade in commodities, such rules as do exist tend often to be ignored or to be very "primitive," in the sense of being either ambiguous or minimal in their impact. For a lawyer, then, the subject has less to do with professional skills than many other subjects of international trade policy. Nevertheless, the subject is very important. General problems of world food supply, and related problems of population growth and control, may be among the most important issues of international relations, directly affecting the prospects of peace in the longer term. The growing aspirations of developing countries, many of whom are major exporters of commodities, to change their condition of poverty also impose some important constraints on international relations, both economic and political.

The problems of agricultural and other commodities, however, are not only the problems of developing countries. It is often forgotten that developed or industrialized countries are among the major producers and exporters of many commodities—the United States, for instance, in recent years has typically exported about one-half of its wheat and soybean production, and over one-quarter of its corn production.[1] As such, the United States is a major factor in the world trade of these products. Indeed, it has been said that programs to increase the price of raw materials could well benefit industrialized countries to the detriment of developing countries (who often are major importers of food, oil, and other commodities).[2]

---

1. See Lesher, Perspectives from the U.S. Department of Agriculture: Agricultural Exports and Trade Policy, in Trade Policy Perspectives: Setting the Stage for 1985 Agricultural Legislation, at 7, 8, Senate Comm. on Agriculture, Nutrition and Forestry, 98th Cong., 2d Sess. (Comm. Print 98–263, 1984).

2. N.Y. Times, July 19, 1976, at 29, 31, col. 2.

Furthermore, even if it were not for the relations between developed and developing countries, there would be severe difficulties between the industrialized countries as to agricultural commodities. Many of the major trade controversies between the United States and the EC, and the United States and Japan or Canada, have concerned agricultural products such as meat, poultry, cheese and cotton.[3] The developed countries often have political systems that give great weight to agricultural producers, and this political force often manifests itself in governmental programs designed to protect domestic agriculture producers from foreign agricultural imports and to promote exports. Some of these considerations are ably described by Gerard Curzon, in his book, Multilateral Commercial Diplomacy: The General Agreement on Tariffs and Trade and Its Impact on National Commercial Policies and Techniques (1965): [4]

> [T]he protectionism which remained [in Europe] once foreign exchange controls were removed was of a dual nature. On the one hand there was the desire in a number of industrial countries, notably Germany, Switzerland, Belgium, Holland and the Scandinavian countries to maintain a peasant class for meta-economic reasons, what has been described as "die Erhaltung und Wiederbefestigung des Bauerntums und der bäuerlichen Landwirtschaft in ihrer subtilen und dem Bauernfremden schwer zu beschreibenden ökonomischsozial-geistigen Gesamtstruktun *1 ".

> In these countries the peasantry represents a sociologically necessary element which serves not simply to produce essential food supplies in emergencies or to provide the towns with new blood but whose existence embodies a traditional mode of life to which many people living in town and countryside are strongly attached. For the maintenance of this peasantry they are prepared to make considerable sacrifices which are reflected in the prices they pay for their food. The population of these countries, and this was clearly demonstrated in the Swiss referendum of 1951, is prepared to accept protection if it is essential to the survival of the peasant class. It is probably no accident that in a country like Britain, where the peasant no longer exists, agricultural protection is at its lowest.

In addition, a "national security" argument, or at least a "national independence" argument, must be recognized in connection with the trade policies relating to foodstuffs.[5] A nation which cannot feed its own population must rely upon imports and therefore is vulnerable to potential export controls of those countries supplying them.

In this chapter, we cannot discuss in depth the many perplexing problems related to international trade in commodities. We will, however, outline the applicable GATT provisions and give an overview of the policies and practices now in effect and of the major issues that may be the subject of negotiations in the near future.

3. See, e.g., Sections 6.3(C) and 10.5(C) ("Chicken War"), 10.3(B) (EC wheat and pasta subsidies), 5.6(D) (U.S. import restrictions on cheese) supra.

4. Reprinted by permission of the author.

* 1. W. Röpke, Die Gesellschaftskrise der Gegenwart, Zurich, 1942, p. 317. Translation: "the maintenance and strengthening of the peasantry and of peasant agriculture in its subtle and to the townsman almost incomprehensible economic, social and spiritual structure."

5. Riesenfeld, Common Market for Agricultural Products and Common Agricultural Policy in the European Economic Community, 1965 Ill.L.F. 658.

SECTION 14.2　AGRICULTURAL PRODUCTS AND INTERNATIONAL TRADE RULES

(A)　GATT AND AGRICULTURE

(1) The Rules and Their Application

KENNETH W. DAM, THE GATT: LAW AND INTERNATIONAL ECONOMIC ORGANIZATION 257

(1970) [1]

It would be difficult to conclude that the GATT's record in the sphere of temperate agricultural commodities is other than one of failure. Not only is effective protection in all likelihood higher on average than in any other sector of the international economy, but there are many indications that the rate of effective protection is increasing. Domestic prices exceed import prices by as much as 100 percent in some products and in some countries.

If the only thing at stake were high tariffs, one's judgment could be more generous. After all, one can argue from the text of the General Agreement that the GATT merely provides the facilities for negotiations looking toward the reduction of tariffs and that there is nothing in the General Agreement requiring contracting parties to reduce tariffs. Unfortunately for the prestige of the GATT, however, the most important restrictions on international trade in temperate agricultural commodities are nontariff barriers, and a large proportion of these are maintained in blatant violation of the General Agreement. This continued violation of the terms of the General Agreement by a substantial number of contracting parties has become such a way of life that little embarrassment seems to be felt by national representatives and no effort is made to suggest dates on which violations might be terminated.

Some of the reasons for this state of affairs were mentioned in the quotation from Professor Curzon's work in the previous section.

On their surface, the GATT rules for agricultural trade are basically the same as the rules for any other kind of trade.[2] As Curzon has indicated, because the United States and the United Kingdom were the major negotiating partners in the 1947 preparatory sessions for GATT, and because these two countries were oriented towards free trade policies in agriculture, it was

---

1. Reprinted by permission of the University of Chicago Press. © 1970 by the University of Chicago.

2. See generally J. Jackson, World Trade and the Law of GATT, chs. 25, 27 (1969). In addition to the materials cited or quoted in the text of this section, the reader may find the following references useful in further research on this subject: G. Curzon, Multilateral Commercial Diplomacy ch. 7 (1965); Malm-

gren & Schlecty, Rationalizing World Agricultural Trade, 4 J. World Trade L. 515 (1976); A. Kruse-Rodenacker, Organization of World Markets for Agricultural Commodities: A Joint Action Programme for Developed and Developing Countries, E.E.C. (Brussels, Etudes: Serie Agriculture No. 15, 1964); Schmittken, Reflections on Trade and Agriculture, 9 Atl. Community Q. 362 (1971).

natural for them to think that the general liberal trade rules of GATT should apply to agricultural goods also. In the GATT agreement, therefore, agricultural goods are segregated from the general applicability of rules in only three places. In Article XI, generally prohibiting the use of quantitative restrictions, there is an elaborately crafted exception for agricultural or fishery products, when quotas are necessary for the enforcement of governmental measures to restrict production of like domestic products and an exception on the use of export prohibitions where they are necessary to relieve critical shortages of foodstuffs. In Article XVI (and in the recently negotiated Subsidies Code), the rules relating to the use of export subsidies are different for "primary" products and non-primary products.[3] Finally, in Article XX (concerning general exceptions to GATT), there is an exception allowing export restrictions of "domestic materials necessary to ensure essential quantities of such materials to a domestic processing industry." Tariffs on agricultural products, like those on industrial products are negotiable and can be bound in the tariff schedules. In contrast to tariff concessions on industrial products, however, those on agricultural products, are neither as numerous nor as meaningful. Agricultural trade is restricted by a plethora of nontariff barriers, which are much more important than tariffs.[4]

Although the exception in GATT Article XI for domestic agricultural surplus programs was largely tailored to then existing U.S. domestic agricultural legislation, it was only a few years later that the United States found its agricultural program coming into conflict with GATT. A 1948 congressional amendment to section 22 of the Agricultural Adjustment Act established new quotas for importation of agricultural goods into the United States,[5] but contained a clause preventing enforcement of the statute in contravention of GATT or other similar agreements. In 1950 Congress mandated that no new international agreement should thereafter be entered into which did not permit enforcement of the statute.[6] In 1951, however, Congress added a section to another Act which required import quotas on fats, oils and certain dairy products in contravention of GATT.[7] Action taken under this statute provoked the Netherlands to complain to GATT and, under Article XXIII, a compensatory withdrawal of concessions to the United States by the Netherlands resulted. Finally, also in 1951, Congress again amended section 22 of the Agricultural Adjustment Act,[8] this time specifying that "no trade agreement or other international agreement heretofore or hereafter entered into by the United States shall be applied in a manner inconsistent with the requirements of this section." Since the measure was later in time than the GATT agreement, it prevailed under

3. See Section 10.3(B) supra.

4. For general studies of barriers to trade in agriculture, see U.S. Intl. Trade Commn., World Trade Flows in Major Agricultural Products (ITC Pub. No. 1684, 1985); J. Hillman, Nontariff Agricultural Trade Barriers (1978).

5. 62 Stat. 1248 (1948); Jackson, The General Agreement on Tariffs and Trade in United States Domestic Law, 66 Mich.L.Rev. 249,

266 (1967). For an analysis of Section 22 and its use, see Zedalis, Agricultural Trade and Section 22, 31 Drake L.Rev. 587 (1981).

6. 64 Stat. 261 (1950); Jackson, note 5 supra, at 266.

7. 65 Stat. 131, 132 (1951); Jackson, note 5 supra, at 267.

8. 65 Stat. 75 (1951); Jackson, note 5 supra, at 268.

United States law, and any action by the United States under that law would constitute a breach of GATT. Consequently, the United States, at the 1954–55 review session, applied to GATT for a waiver. Recognizing political reality, the other GATT members granted the following waiver to the United States:

WAIVER GRANTED TO THE UNITED STATES IN CONNECTION WITH IMPORT RESTRICTIONS IMPOSED UNDER SECTION 22 OF THE UNITED STATES AGRICULTURAL ADJUSTMENT ACT (OF 1933), AS AMENDED

Decision of 5 March 1955 [9]

*   *   *

THE CONTRACTING PARTIES

Decide, pursuant to paragraph 5(*a*) of Article XXV of the General Agreement and in consideration of the assurances recorded above, that subject to the conditions and procedures set out hereunder the obligations of the United States under the provisions of Articles II and XI of the General Agreement are waived to the extent necessary to prevent a conflict with such provisions of the General Agreement in the case of action required to be taken by the Government of the United States under Section 22. The text of Section 22 is annexed to this Decision,

Declare that this Decision shall not preclude the right of affected contracting parties to have recourse to the appropriate provisions of Article XXIII, and

Declare, further, that in deciding as aforesaid, they regret that circumstances make it necessary for the United States to continue to apply import restrictions which, in certain cases, adversely affect the trade of a number of contracting parties, impair concessions granted by the United States and thus impede the attainment of the objectives of the General Agreement.

Conditions and Procedures

1. Upon request of any contracting party which considers that its interests are seriously prejudiced by reason of any import restriction imposed under Section 22, whether or not covered by this Decision, the United States will promptly undertake a review to determine whether there has been a change in circumstances which would require such restrictions to be modified or terminated. In the event the review shows such a change, the United States will institute an investigation in the manner provided by Section 22.

2. Should the President of the United States acting in pursuance of Section 22 cause an investigation to be made to determine whether any existing import restriction should be modified, terminated or extended, or whether restrictions should be imposed on the import of any additional product, the United States will notify the CONTRACTING PARTIES and, in accordance with Article XXII of the General Agreement, accord to any contracting party which considers that its interests would be prejudiced the

---

9. GATT, 3d Supp. BISD 32 (1955).

fullest notice and opportunity, consistent with the legislative requirements of the United States, for representations and consultation.

3.   The United States will give due consideration to any representations submitted to it including:

(*a*) When investigating whether any existing import restriction should be modified, terminated or extended, representations that a greater volume of imports than is permitted under the import restriction would not have the effects required to be corrected by Section 22, including representations that the volume of imports that would have entered in the absence of governmental agricultural programmes would not have such effects;

(*b*) When investigating with respect to import restrictions on additional products representations with regard to:

(i) the effects of imports of any product upon any programme or operation undertaken by the United States Department of Agriculture or any agency under its direction, or upon the domestic production of any agricultural commodity or product thereof for which such a programme or operation is undertaken, including representations that the volume of imports which would have entered in the absence of governmental agricultural programmes will not have the effects required to be corrected by Section 22;

(ii) the representative period to be used for the determination of any quota;

(*c*) Representations by any contracting party that the portion of a total quota allotted or proposed to be allotted to it is inequitable because of circumstances that operated to reduce imports from that contracting party of the product concerned during the past representative period on which such import quota is based.

4.   As soon as the President has made his decision following any investigation the United States will notify the CONTRACTING PARTIES and those contracting parties which have made representations or entered into consultations.   If the Decision imposes restrictions on additional products or extends or intensifies existing restrictions the notification by the United States will include particulars of such restrictions and the reasons for them (regardless of whether the restriction is consistent with the General Agreement).   At the time of such notification the provisions of the General Agreement are waived to the extent necessary to permit such restrictions to be applied under the General Agreement, subject to the review herein provided and, as declared above, without prejudice to the right of the affected contracting parties to have recourse to the appropriate provisions of Article XXIII.

5.   The United States will remove or relax each restriction permitted under this waiver as soon as it finds that the circumstances requiring such restriction no longer exist or have changed so as no longer to require its imposition in its existing form.

6.   The CONTRACTING PARTIES will make an annual review of any action taken by the United States under this Decision.   For each such review the United States will furnish a report to the CONTRACTING PARTIES showing any modification or removal of restrictions effected since the previ-

ous report, the restrictions in effect under Section 22 and the reasons why such restrictions (regardless of whether covered by this waiver) continue to be applied and any steps it has taken with a view to a solution of the problem of surpluses of agricultural commodities.

Notes and Questions

(1) As can be seen, the waiver requires the United States to make regular reports. Each year GATT holds a review of the United States' waiver and actions thereunder, and the unfairness of the waiver and its long duration are pointed out.[10] The United States typically argues, however, that it has exercised its rights under the waiver with considerable reserve and, in a recent report, it noted that it was restraining imports under the waiver of only the following commodities: cotton and cotton waste, peanuts and certain dairy products.[11]

The continuing existence of the waiver, nevertheless, poses a number of questions, in particular concerning the nature and extent of the waiver power discussed in Chapter 5 of this book. Moreover, it establishes an undesirable precedent in that the major trading member of GATT is allowed to escape from its GATT obligations on an important sector of its economy, making it more difficult to constrain similar actions by other nations, with or without the benefit of a waiver.

(2) As a matter of policy, should the United States undertake to negotiate the elimination of its waiver? Is it entitled to receive a "quid pro quo" from other major trading partners for giving up its waiver?

(3) A number of GATT members have maintained quotas on agricultural products which are probably inconsistent with GATT obligations.[12] A major complaint in GATT against German agricultural quotas occurred in the late 1950's, and although Germany argued that its quotas were permitted under the "grandfather clause" of the protocol of accession, most contracting parties concluded otherwise on the grounds that the German marketing law involved did not impose a mandatory requirement. After elaborate discussion, a waiver was granted in May, 1959, which authorized temporary import quotas on certain agricultural products and provided a schedule under which the quotas would be terminated.[13] Nevertheless, the waiver itself recognized that some products would likely continue to be restricted.

(4) As described in Section 6.3(C) supra, the United States still treasures its unrequited "grain rights" derived from the withdrawal of tariff bindings on grain by members of the Common Market. Both in the formation of the original EEC with six members, and at the times of its enlargement, bindings on grain which benefitted the United States exports of grains were withdrawn so that the Common Agricultural Policy could be put in its place. Despite its attempts to negotiate "compensation" for those withdrawals, the United States claims that it has not yet received such compensation.[14]

10. GATT, 31st Supp. BISD 198 (1985); GATT, 30th Supp. BISD 221, 222 (1984).

11. See, e.g., GATT, 30th Supp. BISD 221, 224 (1984).

12. K. Dam, The GATT: Law and International Economic Organization 150, 231–32, 257–66 (1970); G. Curzon, note 2 supra, at 130–31, 179–80, 202–05.

13. GATT, 8th Supp. BISD 31–58, 160–63 (1960); GATT, 7th Supp. BISD 99–107 (1959).

14. This controversy has arisen most recently with respect to Spain and Portugal. The U.S. has threatened significant retaliation against EC exports if it is not compensated for its lost agricultural exports. See BNA, 3 Intl.Trade Rptr. 426 (1986).

(2) The Multilateral Trade Negotiations and Agricultural Products

Negotiations on agricultural products were an important element in the Tokyo Round negotiations. Indeed, a basic dispute between the United States and the European Community on how talks on agricultural products should be structured essentially stalled progress in all areas of negotiation for several years.

GATT, THE TOKYO ROUND OF MULTILATERAL TRADE NEGOTIATIONS: REPORT BY THE DIRECTOR–GENERAL OF GATT

18–20 (1979)

When the GATT rules were originally drafted in the 1940s, they were intended to apply to trade in agricultural and industrial products alike. Things have worked out differently however. Agriculture has been virtually excluded from the broad sweep of trade liberalization and insulated from the normal disciplines of market forces and international competition.

Agricultural problems were prominent in the Kennedy Round but the results were minimal compared with the objectives that were set.

For agricultural exporters a significant enlargement of agricultural markets as a result of the Tokyo Round was an essential requirement. Such countries had a strong political commitment to negotiate and achieve results on agriculture.

The variety and complexity of the protective measures used in agriculture made the negotiation of balanced reductions particularly difficult. If the underlying problems were essentially technical, ways could be found of overcoming them by the adoption of appropriate negotiating techniques. It is, however, the fundamental political and social factors governing the protection of farmers, and the link between production policies and measures at the frontier, that give rise to the basic problems.

* * *

[The U.S.–EC dispute centered] on whether agricultural and industrial products should be taken together and treated similarly—for example, in such fields as tariffs, non-tariff measures and standards—or whether all matters relating to agricultural products should be handled separately by whatever body was set up to deal with agriculture. This was to lead to endless debate later on the question of competence and on where and how negotiations on agriculture should be conducted.

The differences in approach between, among others, the United States and the European Economic Community were fundamental. The United States wanted the negotiations to lead to the liberalization of agricultural trade and increased access to foreign markets for products of which they were efficient producers.

The European Economic Community, on the other hand, sought the stabilization of agricultural trade through commodity arrangements, a sufficiently high income level for its farmers, and the preservation of an effective Common Agricultural Policy.

These differences of substance had as a corollary and consequence a divergence of view on how to negotiate—in other words what procedures to follow in the negotiations.

The United States considered that the same treatment and solutions should be applied to agricultural and industrial products alike, be it in the area of tariffs, subsidies and countervailing duties, or elsewhere, although it conceded that there might be instances where special characteristics in agricultural trade might justify exceptional treatment.

For the European Economic Community, agriculture had unique characteristics, sharply distinguishing it from the industrial sector; agriculture should be dealt with separately. In the view of the Community, solutions should often take the form of "managed markets" with all that implied in terms of international agreements on prices, stockpiling procedures, "phasing" of exports, consultations and so on. As regards tariffs in particular, these could not be considered in isolation from what should be done about minimum prices, maximum prices, stockpiling, subsidies, international supply commitments, etc.

Note

The U.S. position on how to conduct negotiations on agricultural issues was not easily arrived at. There was considerable concern among certain U.S. groups, especially the dairy industry, that concessions would be made adversely affecting them in order to gain benefits for other sectors of the U.S. economy. The problems faced by the United States were outlined in an Executive Branch report, intended to be confidential but leaked to the public, as follows: [15]

Nevertheless, neither Japan nor the [European] Community, we are sure, will consider the balance in this commodities sector or in agricultural as a whole reciprocal. Our agricultural exports to Western Europe amounted to $2.2 billion in calendar year 1969, for example, whereas our imports of agricultural commodities amounted to only $.9 billion. Similarly our exports to Japan amounted to $.9 billion, whereas our imports of agricultural products from them amounted only to $40 million. * * *

We will be able to negotiate in agriculture only in the context of a very broad negotiation. What is needed in our view is a negotiation of sufficient scope and magnitude to warrant the overriding by presidents and heads of states of the objections of their agriculture and finance ministers and to provide members of legislatures with the rationale for overcoming the protectionist pressures of their constituencies. In our judgment, a negotiation of proper magnitude would be one involving both money and trade. We do not think that a negotiation involving trade only is adequate.

The negotiating tactics suggested by the Flanigan Report, namely, to obtain some market access abroad for agricultural products by furnishing market access in the United States to industrial products, and to trade United States market access for European dairy products in exchange for European market access for exports of United States grain and meat, became a controversial topic in the consideration of the Trade Act of 1974 (see particularly section 104 on sector

15. Flanigan Report on Agricultural Trade Policy, 119 Cong.Rec. 12029, 12040 (April 12, 1973).

negotiating requirements). In a hearing on these requirements, Mr. Bell, a high official of the Department of Agriculture, said: [16]

> And this leads us to the reason why we have concern about the sector-by-sector negotiations. If you look at our trade barriers on agricultural commodities coming into the United States, you see they are very low. Our duties are only in the vicinity of 5 to 10 percent on most of the agricultural imports, and we have very few nontariff trade barriers. In fact, about the only one that we have left today is the import quotas on dairy products, which is used to support the price support system for milk.
>
> * * *
>
> If we are going to be put into a position of having to negotiate only on a sector-by-sector basis, we feel that there can be very little to come out of any trade negotiation for agriculture because we have very little to give.

The Senate Finance Committee Report on the Trade Act of 1974 explained a earlier version of section 104 of the Trade Act as follows: [17]

> * * * The intent of the Committee is that both industry or agricultural trade barriers be eliminated, harmonized, or reduced. The Committee believes that barriers to U.S. agricultural exports cannot be ignored in this negotiation as was the case, in large measure, in the Kennedy Round. Thus, the words "to the maximum extent feasible, the elimination or reduction of agricultural trade barriers shall be undertaken in conjunction with the elimination, harmonization, or reduction of industrial trade barriers and distortions," is intended to mean that agriculture shall be included in this negotiation. It is not a directive for cross-sectorial trade-offs between agriculture and industry. * * * "

(3) The Results of the Multilateral Trade Negotiations

Although considerable time and effort was devoted to negotiations on agricultural issues in the Tokyo Round, progress on many issues was not great. In addition to the Subsidies Code, which introduced the changes in the rules applicable to export subsidies on primary products discussed in Section 10.3(B) supra, there were negotiations on three other side agreements dealing with agricultural products in the Tokyo Round. Two side agreements—one on bovine meat,[18] one on dairy products [19]—were reached, while negotiations for an agreement on wheat were unsuccessful.[20] Generally speaking, the meat and dairy agreements provide for exchange of information between the parties and establish administration committees. The committees may consider disputes between signatories, but do not have the authority to take binding decisions. The dairy agreement also establishes minimum export prices for various milk products. The United States withdrew from the dairy agreement in 1985 in protest of EC sales of butter at prices below those minimum prices.[21]

16. Executive Hearing on Sector Negotiations before the Senate Comm. on Finance, 93d Cong., 2d Sess. 11 (1974).

17. S.Rep. No. 93–1298, 93d Cong., 2d Sess. 79 (1974).

18. GATT, 26th Supp. BISD 84 (1980).

19. GATT, 26th Supp. BISD 91 (1980).

20. GATT, The Tokyo Round of Multilateral Trade Negotiations: Report by the Director General of GATT 25–26 (1979).

21. 1 BNA Intl. Trade Rptr. 770 (1984); 2 BNA Intl. Trade Rptr. 16 (1985).

The concessions given and received by the United States in the Tokyo Round can be summarized as follows:

SENATE REPORT NO. 96–249
96th Cong., 1st Sess. 211–13 (1979)

The trade concessions received by the United States under the MTN are difficult to determine with precision although various estimates place the expected increase in U.S. agricultural exports at around $500 million. This figure relates to 1976 exports worth about $2.4 billion. The total value of U.S. agricultural exports covered by concessions received is nearly $4 billion, but many concessions are designed to protect our markets more than to expand them. The administration has argued that, in spite of the modesty of the concessions, the agreement will not only increase trade but also stem the rise of protectionism which would be very harmful to agriculture.

* * *

Concessions From Japan. The trade negotiations with Japan were carried out in a strained atmosphere. As in the case of most agricultural negotiations, the discussions were carried out bilaterally and then added to the total package when completed.

The U.S. negotiators and the Agricultural Technical Advisory Committees were impatient with Japan's unwillingness to allow freer trade and its insistence on protecting its agricultural system for reasons of national security and self-sufficiency.

The United States insisted that additional agricultural exports were needed to help reduce the trade imbalance between the two countries, but the Japanese responded they were already heavily dependent on the United States for food imports. The Japanese also pointed out that the United States had established an embargo on soybean exports in 1973; therefore, they could not afford to become even more dependent on the United States for food imports.

In addition, several of the most important U.S. requests—especially beef and citrus products—related to extremely sensitive and heavily protected Japanese industries.

After extensive negotiations, the Japanese finally agreed to expand their imports of 150 agricultural products. High quality beef, orange and grapefruit juices, and oranges represented the main increases. The quota increases for these commodities do not represent a change in the Japanese import system. The Japanese also agreed to fix or bind the existing duty on soybeans, which is zero. The zero binding on soybeans is an insurance policy to meet possible future competition. It is estimated that the concessions from Japan could approach $200 million in increased trade when fully implemented.

Concessions From the EEC. The European Economic Community's Common Agricultural Policy has created serious concern among U.S. agricultural producers because of its restrictions on trade and its subsidization of exports to third-country markets. The United States does not have a trade imbalance with the European Community, and, therefore, the atmosphere of the EC negotiations was less strained than those with Japan. In addition, the United States was faced with having to grant agricultural concessions to the EC.

The major concessions granted by the European Community were in the area of high quality beef, poultry, rice, tobacco, and speciality products. These concessions are expected to be worth over $150 million annually when fully implemented.

Concessions From Mexico and Other Countries. The trade negotiations with Mexico became involved with other issues, such as the migration of illegal aliens to the United States, the possible sale of petroleum to the United States, and the sale of Mexican winter vegetables to the United States. Nonetheless, the Mexican Government has made a tentative offer to allow unlimited imports of soybean meal, a concession which is expected to be worth $55 million in additional trade.

Concessions were received from other countries on a variety of commodities such as almonds, canned peaches and fruit cocktail, rice, vegetable protein concentrates and isolates, raisins, prunes, and certain fresh fruit.

Trade Concessions Granted by the United States. Concessions were offered by the United States on approximately $2.6 billion of agricultural imports. These concessions by the United States are expected to increase annual agricultural imports by about $156 million annually by 1987.

Most of the increase in agricultural imports is accounted for by the expanded cheese import quotas. This increase has been estimated, based on 1976 statistics, at approximately $120 million.

Since the progress on agricultural issues in the Tokyo Round can be considered to have been modest, it is expected that these issues will arise again in the next round of negotiations. A GATT Committee on Trade in Agriculture was established in 1982 and is now preparing for such negotiations.[22]

(B) UNITED STATES LAW

A list of the imports quotas currently applied by the United States is set out in Section 6.4 supra. Many of the products subject to quotas are agricultural products: cotton, peanuts, dairy, sugar. In addition, as noted in Section 3.4 supra, quotas may be imposed on meat imports if certain import limits are exceeded. As noted in Chapter 12 (and cited in the last extract by the Japanese as a reason to avoid depending on U.S. agricultural exports), the United States has also on occasion controlled the export of agricultural goods in short supply so as to avoid inflation in the United States.

In addition to direct controls limiting agricultural imports and exports, the United States has a number of programs designed to promote agricultural exports. These programs include provision of export credits to help finance such exports and of food assistance under the so-called P.L. 480

---

22. See GATT, 30th Supp. BISD 100 (1984) (Report of Committee on Trade in Agriculture).

program, which, *inter alia,* authorizes the sale of agricultural commodities by the United States for dollars on very favorable credit terms (or for foreign currencies in certain limited cases), the barter of agricultural commodities for strategic materials and grant of food for famine relief. In fiscal year 1985, $1.9 billion was expected to be spent on these programs.[23]

It is claimed that "[a]t some time, nearly every country in the world has received P.L. 480 food under one type of program or another." Between 1954 and 1969, India received $4.3 billion in goods under the Act. Other major participants have included Pakistan, Yugoslavia, Egypt, the Republic of Korea, Brazil and Spain, with receipts from $1.3 billion to $618 million. The leading export commodity under P.L. 480 has been wheat, other major exports have included feedgrains, rice, cotton oilseeds and dairy products.[24]

Recently, in an effort to regain export markets for U.S. agricultural products that allegedly have been lost to subsidized EC exports, the United States has threatened to use export subsidies of its own. As of October 1985, the United States had offered to subsidize U.S. grain exports to Algeria and Egypt by providing a free bonus of U.S. grain, which would have the effect of lowering the average cost of sales to those countries.[25] Immediately following the announcement of an actual contract with Egypt, the EC retaliated with higher export subsidies on EC sales to Egypt, Algeria, Tunisia and Syria.[26]

(C) THE EC'S COMMON AGRICULTURAL POLICY

The operation of the EC's Common Agricultural Policy has been controversial, as was seen in the subsidy cases discussed in Section 10.3(B) supra. The policy has been described in general terms elsewhere; the following extract explains its operation in more detail.

JOHN F. HUDSON, THE EUROPEAN COMMUNITY'S COMMON AGRICULTURAL POLICY

(1984)[27]

The foremost example in the Western world of a managed market approach to farm support is the Common Agricultural Policy of the European Community.

* * *

The central feature of the European Community is the customs union, or common market, created by removing all duties and restrictions on trade between the member countries, and adopting a common tariff for imports from the rest of the world. The Common Agricultural Policy is a unified price support policy devised to deal with the problems caused for agricultur-

---

23. Hearings on International Trade Distortions Harming U.S. Agricultural Exports before the Senate Comm. on Foreign Relations, 98th Cong., 2d Sess. 113–14 (1984).

24. Goolsby, Kruer & Santmyer, P.L. 480 Concessional Sales 6 (U.S.D.A. Foreign Agricultural Economic Report No. 65, 1970).

25. See 2 BNA Intl. Trade Rptr. 978 (1985).

26. Europe, Agence Internationale D'Informationa Pour La Presse, September 20, 1985, at 10 (No. 4166 n.s.).

27. From Trade Policy Perspectives: Setting the Stage for 1985 Agricultural Legislation, Senate Comm. on Agriculture, Nutrition and Forestry, 98th Cong., 2d Sess. 323, 323–28 (Comm.Print 98–263, 1984).

al support programs when the customs union was applied to agricultural products.

* * *

The Common Agricultural Policy today is expanded and refined over what it was when the first regulations were issued in 1962. The basic concepts remain the same, however. Farm income is supported by managing the internal market price level. There are few serious restraints on production. Variable import levies assure that imports will always be priced higher than the domestic product. Export subsidies are available for products in surplus. This system, which varies from product to product, applies to more than 90 percent of EC production by value. Variable levies protect more than 70 percent of production including (with variations) grains, rice, olive oil, sugar, beef, pork, poultry, eggs and dairy products. No support prices are set for poultry and eggs; prices for these products are maintained solely by the import levy and export subsidy system. There is limited support for pork, and in the case of beef, price support purchases are phased out at predetermined price levels. In a few cases it was decided not to make the consumer pay the full cost of support through the market price; instead the market price is pegged a bit lower and the difference made up by a direct subsidy. This procedure applies to durum wheat and EC grown oil seeds.

Where support prices apply, they are maintained by government purchases, much as in the dairy program in the United States. The EC does not use price support loans. Member government agencies are the immediate owners of the stocks they purchase, and may dispose of them within certain guidelines, the usual procedure for disposing of government stocks is to tender them for export with a subsidy. For a number of products the EC does offer subsidies for private storage. These, however, are not designed to build up farmer owned reserves, but rather to permit a more orderly management of government stocks or, in the case of commodities (especially pork) where there is not an intervention program, to help support prices during periods of excessive supplies.

While variable levies apply to the products listed above, administration of the levy system is not uniform. The tightest control is maintained over the grain market, where levies are set daily according to a complicated formula which relates price quotations at various points outside the EC, for different grades and types, to a calculated equivalent at Rotterdam for each EC grain of a specified grade and type. The lowest calculated price is then deducted from an EC "threshold price," which in turn is set higher than the intervention price support level. The levy so determined is applied to all shipments of the grain in question, regardless of the actual price or grade.

* * *

The EC also uses minimum import prices or "reference" prices for a number of other products, especially in the horticultural sector, as a basis for levying additional charges on imports offered at less than that price. These charges may not apply to all shipments or all countries. They are used for a number of the most important fruits and vegetables, for wine and for fish.

Import licenses are required in nearly every situation where variable levies are used. The licenses provide a means of monitoring import levels, and more importantly licenses usually specify the amount of the levy to be applied. The levy can by this means be fixed in advance of importation and provide a means of hedging against future price changes.

Perhaps one of the more interesting features of the levy system results from the fact that the agricultural products to which it applies are often raw materials for the manufacture of processed foods, and some industrial products. Consequently there is a large range of processed products which are subject to the levies as well as import duties. The levies are fixed in proportion to the amount of agricultural raw material assumed used in the product. For example, a cake mix will be subject to an import duty as a processed product and subject also to a levy in proportion to the amount of flour, eggs, milk and sugar it contains. These import charges, of course, add to the cost of the processed food and make it difficult for the manufacturer to remain competitive on export markets. Hence the EC is obligated also to extend export subsidies to these processed goods. In one or two cases the EC gives a production subsidy to the manufacturer instead. The most significant examples are subsidies for the manufacture of starch and beer. The starch subsidy also provides a degree of support to the potato market which is not otherwise covered by the Common Agricultural Policy.

The fixing of export subsidies also varies in administration. In most cases the EC Commission publishes subsidy rates which may be obtained simply by applying for an export license valid for a specified period of time. The export of government stocks, however, is done by tender, and such exports can often be significant in volume. Subsidy rates are set by the European Commission on the basis of periodic meetings with market experts from member governments who have determined where the best marketing opportunities lie. The subsidy rates, therefore, reflect the amount of money necessary to assure the sale of EC products in individual markets in competition with other countries. Rates will vary from week to week or even more frequently and by destination.

* * *

In summary, the EC has relied almost exclusively on price policies and subsidies to guarantee a satisfactory level of farm income. Disincentives to production have been introduced for certain products—for example, subsidies for the slaughter of dairy cows, quotas on the quantity of sugar production eligible for full price support and recently quotas on milk deliveries to dairies. These measures, however, have not resulted in a significant decrease in production although the recent dairy quotas appear to be more effective than previous attempts to control production. The common pricing and production policies for sugar, for example, were introduced in 1967 when the EC was a major net importer of sugar. Today the EC produces nearly 50 percent more sugar than it consumes. In fact, the European Community is now not only the world's largest exporter of sugar but also the largest exporter of dairy products, pork, eggs, broilers, wheat flour and last year the third largest exporter of beef and veal. Based on 1985 forecasts, however, the EC will move to the number one position in beef exports also. For all of these except dairy products and pork, the EC was a major net importer in the 1960's.

As phenomenal as this growth has been, it has not been successful in increasing farm income at a pace equal to growth in nonfarm income. * * * The issue, therefore, of greatest concern to EC policy makers is how to meet the cost of the program—a program still based on an open-ended commitment by the government to buy any quantity offered to it and to export all surpluses produced.

EC programs for agriculture in 1984 are budgeted at $13.4 billion, of which $8.1 billion is for intervention costs (primarily government purchasing) and $5.3 billion for export subsidies. Because of the unrestrained growth in EC production and the effectiveness of import protection, levies on imports now generate relatively much less revenue. Meanwhile the cost of intervention and export subsidies has sharply increased. For example, in 1967 when the European Community was only six countries, the total cost of EC support programs was only $1.3 billion, of which $900 million was for export subsidies. Receipts from import levies covered 45 percent of the total. The 1984 budget for the current programs for 10 countries totalled $13.4 billion, as indicated above. Levies were sufficient to fund only 12 percent of these agricultural programs.

Notes and Questions

(1) There have been a number of disputes in GATT over the issue of whether the operation of the EC Common Agricultural Policy violates (i) the GATT ban on export subsidies for non-primary products (e.g. pasta) or (ii) the GATT requirement that export subsidies for primary products (e.g. wheat flour) not be used to increase traditional market shares. See Section 10.3(B) supra for a discussion of these issues.

(2) Can the present GATT rules for international trade in general be sensibly applied to agricultural products if U.S. and EC farm programs continue in effect?

(3) Given the present and past agricultural policies of the United States and the EC, what modifications do you think would be desirable to the GATT rules now applicable to international trade in agriculture?

(4) Should changes in current GATT rules be negotiated separately or as part of a broader discussion of GATT issues, such as tariff reductions, use of safeguards and expansion of GATT to cover services?

(5) Should GATT treat specifically the problem of national desires to be self sufficient in the production of major agricultural products? If so, how?

(6) Should GATT treat specifically the problem of disposal of government-owned farm surpluses on world markets? If so, how?

(D) JAPAN'S AGRICULTURAL POLICIES

MTN STUDIES: THE RESULTS FOR U.S. AGRICULTURE

(1979) [28]

Japan is the largest single-country importer of U.S. agricultural products. * * * One-third of U.S. exports to Japan have been agricultural products in recent years.

28. From a report prepared by Schnittker Associates for the Congressional Research Service at the request of the Subcommittee on International Trade of the Senate Committee

* * *

Japan was only about 50 percent self-sufficient in food energy in 1978, but it was 80 percent self-sufficient in food energy in 1955. * * *

* * * Policies adopted in 1975, partly as a result of the agricultural product shortages in 1973–75 [29], have the objective of protecting the present degree of self-sufficiency in Japan, if possible. * * *

Whether or not these objectives can be attained is another matter. The important point is that Japan has undertaken policies to interrupt the rapid and fairly steady decline of self-sufficiency that has been underway for some 25 years. These policies are inherently trade restrictive, although they may seem justified by Japan's objectives.

RELATIVE IMPORTANCE OF VARIOUS FOODS IN JAPAN

Cereals, especially rice, remain the principal food of the Japanese people, who consumed 268 lbs. per capita in 1975. Cereal consumption per capita in Japan was roughly twice as high as in the United States.

Meat consumption has risen rapidly during the last 20 years, but at 37 lbs. per capita, it was only 25 percent of the U.S. level in 1975. Dairy product consumption has also been rising rapidly. At 115 lbs. per capita in 1975, it was 35 percent of the U.S. consumption level.

Fish consumption, at 77 lbs. per capita, represents a major part of the Japanese protein supply, and is 6.5 times as large as U.S. per capita fish consumption. * * *

AGRICULTURAL POLICIES

Grains. Agricultural policies affecting grain production in Japan are important principally for their direct effect upon wheat imports and their indirect effect upon feed grain and soybean imports.

Japan protects its rice growers, historically the most important agricultural group in the country, by means of a government purchase program at a level about four times the level of world prices for rice. To put it even more graphically, Japanese farmers receive nearly four times as much for a ton of rice as American farmers receive. * * *

The purpose of the high support price is to protect the incomes of Japanese rice producers and to respond to the strong political power of rural people in Japan. Because of high prices, and because the Japanese people are slowly reducing their consumption of rice in favor of wheat, Japan has produced a surplus of rice in a number of recent years. This further inhibits the importation of wheat and other food products.

[The report found that Japanese wheat support prices were four times the world price, that soybean prices were close to world market prices and that dairy price support levels were twice the U.S. levels.]

on Finance, at 220–26 (96th Cong., 1st Sess. 220–26 (Comm.Print 96–11, 1979)).

29. U.S. controls on soybean exports to Japan and other nations are described in Section 12.3(B)(2) supra.

SUMMARY

It is apparent that Japan maintains a high level of support and protection of its agricultural sector. Without support levels, Japanese farmers would produce less of many products and Japanese consumers would consume larger quantities. Trade would expand as a result of both factors. Japan's agricultural policies are thus seriously "trade restrictive."

The effects of the high support prices and the relatively high retail food prices in Japan are probably greater in limiting consumption than in expanding production. Japan, unlike Europe, has very limited resources for the expansion of agricultural production. Even at higher price support levels, production increases would be negligible. Consumption, however, could be reduced materially by higher retail food prices.

Questions

(1) Review the questions at the end of the preceding subsection about U.S. and EC agricultural policies. How would your answers change, if at all, in light of the foregoing description of Japanese agricultural policies?

(2) Are their fundamental differences between the agricultural problems faced by the United States and the EC and those faced by Japan? What implications do you think any such differences might have for the next round of trade negotiations?

SECTION 14.3   COMMODITIES AND COMMODITY AGREEMENTS[1]

For many years, there has been a continuing controversy over what should be the appropriate policy for international regulation of trade in commodities such as metals, grains, coffee, etc. One viewpoint is that such trade should be as free from governmental interference (national or international) as possible, so that the free market can have its beneficial influence in encouraging supply to meet demand. Another view, however, is that the market does not do well in influencing supply and demand for basic commodities, because of the time it takes to react to market signals (e.g., lead time to add new supply), the insufficiency of information, or other reasons. As a result, prices tend to fluctuate greatly, and this leads some to conclude that

---

1. For a collection of commodity agreements and information about them, see C. Johnston, Law and Policy of Intergovernmental Primary Commodity Agreements (2 vols. Oceana looseleaf). For works on commodity agreements in general, see F. Gordon-Ashworth, International Commodity Control: A Contemporary History and Appraisal (1984); E. Ernst, International Commodity Agreements: The System of Controlling the International Commodity Market (1982); K. Kahn, The Law and Organization of International Commodity Agreements (1982). See also U.S. Intl. Trade Commn., The Concepts and Principles Which Should Underlie the Formation of an International Commodity Code (ITC Pub. No. 729, 1975); General Accounting Office, U.S. Actions Needed to Cope with Commodity Shortages: A Report to Congress, in Hearing on Growth and Its Implications for the Future before the House Comm. on Merchant Marine and Fisheries, 94th Cong., 1st Sess. 140–425 (1975); Fawcett, Function of Law in International Commodity Agreements, 44 Brit.Y.B. Intl.L. 157 (1970); Mikesell, Commodity Agreements and Aid to Developing Countries, 28 Law & Contemp.Prob. 294 (1963); Schmidt, The Case Against Commodity Agreements, 28 Law & Contemp.Prob. 313 (1963); H. Johnson, Economic Policies Toward Less Developed Countries, Brookings Inst'n (1967).

it would be better to regulate trade in these commodities. In the light of current world economic and political pressures, there is renewed debate about the advisability of the market regulatory devices for a variety of commodities. We cannot here examine these arguments in detail—economists have commented extensively upon them. However, from the lawyer's viewpoint it is useful to treat three subjects briefly: 1) the state of current general rules relating to commodity trade; 2) an overview of commodity agreements; and 3) some problems with producer alliance agreements (such as the oil cartel: OPEC—the Organization of Petroleum Exporting Countries.)

(A) INTERNATIONAL RULES ON COMMODITY TRADE: GATT AND UNCTAD

GATT has even less to say about commodity trade than about export controls (see Chapter 12). Theoretically, the GATT rules all apply to raw materials and agricultural commodities just as they do to industrialized goods, unless there is a specific exception. A few specific exceptions exist for agricultural goods; subsidy rules apply to "primary goods" differently than they apply to non-primary goods; and waivers add to these exceptions.[2]

But the GATT Agreement recognizes the possibility of special regulatory systems for various commodities. Article XX(h) excepts from GATT obligations generally, measures:

> (h) undertaken in pursuance of obligations under any intergovernmental commodity agreement which conforms to criteria submitted to the CONTRACTING PARTIES and not disapproved by them or which is itself so submitted and not so disapproved;

In the 1948 proposed ITO Charter[3] (which never came into effect), an entire chapter was devoted to the subject of Commodity Agreements, setting forth procedures by which a member country could initiate a study of a commodity or call for a conference to develop an agreement on the commodity. Various sections set forth principles which any such agreement should follow. For example, Article 63 specified:

Article 63

Additional Principles governing Commodity Control Agreements

The Members shall observe the following principles governing the conclusion and operation of commodity control agreements, in addition to those stated in Article 60:

(a) Such agreements shall be designed to assure the availability of supplies adequate at all times for world demand at prices which are in

---

2. See Section 14.2(A)(1) supra; Section 10.3(B) supra; and Section 5 supra; see also J. Jackson, World Trade and the Law of GATT §§ 13.4, 15.7–.8 (1969); K. Dam, The GATT: Law and International Economic Organization 258–62 (1970); G. Curzon, Multilateral Commercial Diplomacy 130–31 (1965).

3. United Nations Conference on Trade and Employment, Final Act and Related Documents, Havana, Cuba, U.N.Doc. ICITO/1/4 (1948). For further information on the ITO Charter, see W. Diebold, The End of ITO (Princeton Essays in Int'l Finance No. 16, 1952); R. Gardner, Sterling-Dollar Diplomacy chs. 6, 17 (rev. ed. 1969); C. Wilcox, A Charter for World Trade, (1949); W. Brown, The United States and the Restoration of World Trade 391–557, Brookings Inst'n (1950).

keeping with the provisions of Article 57(c), and, when practicable, shall provide for measures designed to expand world consumption of the commodity.

(*b*) Under such agreements, participating countries which are mainly interested in imports of the commodity concerned shall, in decisions on substantive matters, have together a number of votes equal to that of those mainly interested in obtaining export markets for the commodity. Any participating country, which is interested in the commodity but which does not fall precisely under either of the above classes, shall have an appropriate voice within such classes.

(*c*) Such agreements shall make appropriate provision to afford increasing opportunities for satisfying national consumption and world market requirements from sources from which such requirements can be supplied in the most effective and economic manner, due regard being had to the need for preventing serious economic and social dislocation and to the position of producing areas suffering from abnormal disabilities.

(*d*) Participating countries shall formulate and adopt programmes of internal economic adjustment believed to be adequate to ensure as much progress as practicable within the duration of the agreement towards solution of the commodity problem involved.

It was agreed in the ITO Charter, however, that "commodity control agreements may be entered into only when a finding has been made * * *" that a "burdensome surplus" or "widespread unemployment or underemployment in connection with a primary commodity" exists, and government action is necessary to correct such conditions.[4]

A 1947 United Nations Economic and Social Council (ECOSOC) meeting established an "Interim Coordinating Committee for International Commodity Arrangements" (ICCICA), to facilitate intergovernmental consultation and, at the same time, urged that the principles developed for drafts of the ITO Charter be "a general guide" to consultation or action.[5] GATT originally contained a clause urging conformity to the principles of the ECOSOC resolution, but after the ITO failed to become effective, this clause was dropped from the GATT.[6] However, an "interpretative note" to GATT Annex I, Ad Article XX, was added:

Sub-paragraph (h).

The exception provided for in this sub-paragraph extends to any commodity agreement which conforms to the principles approved by the Economic and Social Council in its resolution 30 (IV) of 28 March 1947.

Although the GATT Article XX exception arguably embodies the ITO commodity chapter through the ECOSOC resolution,[7] it is probably fair to say that this is a "dead-letter" provision. ICCICA has functioned from time

---

4. Final Act, note 3 supra, Art. 62.

5. 4 U.N. ECOSOC Res. 30, U.N. Doc. E/ 437, at 3–4 (1947); see also U.N.Doc. E/403.

6. J. Jackson, note 2 supra, at 723.

7. Id.

to time, and GATT also has attempted to develop further general principles for commodity agreements, but has been unable to do so.[8]

(B) COMMODITY AGREEMENTS

In recent years, international rules and negotiations in respect of commodity agreements have taken place largely under a framework provided by the United Nations Conference on Trade and Development (UNCTAD), which first met in 1964. Following a brief outline of the issues and economic problems faced by UNCTAD in devising a commodity control program, we will consider the development of its Integrated Commodity Program.

MEIER, UNCTAD PROPOSALS FOR INTERNATIONAL ECONOMIC REFORM

(1967) [9]

International commodity agreements can take a variety of forms, but essentially they involve (either separately or in combination) the operation of a system of export quotas (as in the coffee agreement), an international buffer stock which operates within a range of prices (as in the tin agreement), or a multilateral long-term contract which stipulates a minimum price at which importing countries agree to buy specified quantities and a maximum price at which producing countries agree to export a stated amount (as originally in the wheat agreement).

The general purpose of international commodity agreements is "stabilization"; however, the concept of "stabilization" is ambiguous. "Stabilization" may refer to the international price of an export commodity, to producers' money income or real income, to export earnings, or to the purchasing power of primary-product exports over imports. An inescapable difficulty of a commodity-control scheme is that in stabilizing one of these variables (for instance, price), it may at the same time destabilize another variable (for instance, export earnings).

However, it is apparent from the emphasis that UNCTAD gives to the attainment of "equitable and remunerative prices" that the main objective is not simply to obtain stable export prices but to use commodity-control arrangements as instruments for increasing export prices. In drawing an analogy to the protection afforded by domestic price-support programs to agricultural producers in the developed countries, the less developed countries are clearly seeking similar protection for their primary-product producers through international price-support plans, with the hope of raising the level of their export earnings and the purchasing power of their exports in terms of industrial imports. But, while under a domestic price-support program the domestic consumers are in effect being taxed to support domestic producers, an international commodity agreement would in effect tax the consumers in the importing country for the benefit of the exporting country and thus would be a means of transferring resources from the advanced importing country to the less developed exporting country. In-

---

8. Id., at 727.

9. 19 Stan.L.Rev. 1173, 1195–96. Reprinted by permission of the Board of Trustees of the Leland Stanford Junior University.

deed, the distinctive feature of an international commodity agreement is precisely that it might raise the long-term trend of the developing country's export prices, improve its terms of trade, and thereby have the quality of giving aid to the exporting country.

If, in contrast, the objective were to offset only the domestic effects of instability in export prices, the developing country could simply utilize national policy measures—for example, marketing boards or variable export duties—without the need for an international agreement. For purposes of pure stabilization, internal policies may be used to break the link between export earnings and the level of domestic spending. A marketing board could limit the impact of export fluctuations on the domestic economy by paying a price to the producer that differs from the price which the board receives when it sells in the export market. And export duties could be set on a sliding scale so that they are higher when the export price is high and lower when the export price is low. More effective monetary and fiscal measures could also reduce instability.

It is one thing to evaluate a commodity agreement as a technique for offsetting the range of fluctuation in export prices around a long-run average trend; it is quite a different matter to view it as a means of raising the price above what is justified by the average trend in supply and demand conditions. While an international commodity agreement appeals to the less developed countries because of its potential use as a form of aid, it is highly questionable whether in practice such use would even be feasible, let alone desirable.

KABIR–UR–RAHMAN KAHN, THE LAW AND ORGANISATION OF INTERNATIONAL COMMODITY AGREEMENTS

74–75, 249–51 (1982) [10]

The development of an international policy since the first session of the United Nations Conference on Trade and Development (UNCTAD) has been swift and wide-ranging. The positive role of international commodity agreements is now recognised. International trade is declared to be 'one of the most important factors in economic development'. UNCTAD recognises that 'commodity agreements serve to secure over-all stabilisation in primary commodity markets'; and stresses the 'special role they should perform in stimulating economic development of the developing countries'. The objective of the international commodity agreement is recognisedly to 'stimulate the dynamic and steady growth and secure reasonable predictability in the real export earnings of developing countries so as to provide them with expanding resources for their economic and social development, while taking into account the interests of consumers in importing countries'. These provisions have been reiterated in UNCTAD and elsewhere. The Charter of Economic Rights and Duties, for example, affirms that 'all states have the right to associate in organisation of primary commodity producers to develop their national economies'.

10. Reprinted by permission of Martinus Nijhoff Publishers, The Hague.

The General Assembly of the United Nations in its special session for the first time devoted study to the problems of raw materials and development declared that a new international economic order (NIEO) should be founded on full respect for, among others, the principles of

(j) Just and equitable relationship between prices of raw materials, primary commodities, manufactured and semi-manufactured goods exported by developing countries and the prices of raw materials, primary commodities, manufactured capital goods and equipment imported by them with the aim of bringing about sustained improvement in their unsatisfactory terms of trade and the expansion of world economy; * * *

(t) Facilitating the role which producers' associations may play within the framework of international co-operation and in pursuance of their aims, inter alia, of assisting in the promotion of sustained growth of world economy and accelerating the development of developing countries.

The idea of linking the prices of primary commodities and that of related raw materials and manufactured goods is similar to that advocated in relation to wheat by the United States earlier in the League phase.

The General Assembly also declares that all efforts should be made to 'facilitate the functioning and to further aims of producers' associations, including their joint marketing arrangements, orderly commodity trading improvement in the export income of producing countries and in their terms of trade, and sustained growth of the world economy for the benefit of all'. It also called for the preparation of an overall integrated programme setting out guidelines and taking into account the current work in the field, for a comprehensive range of commodities for export of interest to developing countries.

UNCTAD, in pursuance of that request, approved an Integrated Programme for Commodities.*[118] The programme covers at present eighteen commodities, and specifies a multidimensional approach to the commodity problems, including the establishment of a common fund. This approach comprises supply management, access to market and development measures. A framework for co-ordinated negotiation on the specified commodities is given.

* * *

The Integrated Programme for Commodities (IPC) is the most recent step towards international measures relating to the commodities. It seeks to provide, inter alia, increased and stable export earnings to developing countries. In its rationale and scope the IPC differs from the Havana principles which, until UNCTAD I in 1964, were the prime regulators of international commodity agreements. The Havana concept of commodity regulation recognised the need for an international commodity agreement in an extreme situation of 'burdensome surplus' of a commodity and heavy unemployment in a commodity industry which could not be dealt with by normal market forces within a reasonable time.

The IPC moved away from this concept, and is firmly based on the UNCTAD principles first declared in 1964. These reiterate that internation-

* 118. For the text of the IPC, see UN Conference on Trade and Development   (UNCTAD) Conf.Res. 93 (IU) of 30 May 1976. * * *

al trade is 'one of the most important factors in economic development', and recognise that 'commodity agreements serve to secure overall stabilisation in primary commodity markets'. International measures on commodities are now sought not only to deal with emergency situations mentioned in the Havana Charter, but also for providing stable means of securing economic and social well-being in developing countries. The apparent advance that the IPC has made is in its 'integrated' approach to the attainment of declared objectives.

There are three main elements in the IPC: it covers a wide range of commodities on which international measures are considered necessary; the recognized measures are broad in scope, extending to supply management (the traditional field of an international commodity agreement), finance, trade, transport etc; lastly, the IPC provides a framework for co-ordinated negotiations and for an institutionalised initiative to facilitate these negotiations.

The criterion for inclusion of a commodity in the IPC is that it should be 'of export interest to developing countries'. This is somewhat vague, because every commodity which is exported by a country is of 'export interest' to that country. From the antecedents of Resolution 93 (IV) it is evident that this phrase means the commodities on which developing countries lean heavily for their export earnings, and which are prone to economic instability in the world market, with the concomitant result of a decline in real export earnings of those countries. The eighteen 'Nairobi' commodities fall into three categories: first, food commodities comprise bananas, cocoa, coffee, sugar, meat, tea, vegetable oils (including olive oil). The second is the agricultural raw materials and comprises cotton and cotton yarns, hard fibres and hard fibre products, jute and jute products, rubber and timber. The third category includes minerals, namely, bauxite, copper, iron ore, manganese, phosphate and tin. Other commodities may be added.

* * *

The IPC provides machinery for securing a consensus of international measures before convening a negotiating conference. The Secretary-General of UNCTAD is authorized to convene, in consultation with the international organisations concerned, preparatory meetings 'for international negotiations on individual products'. The term 'international negotiations' is used here in its wider sense to mean an exchange of views among interested parties to determine future paths of action, but it has to be differentiated from the conclusion of a treaty, for which special negotiating conferences are to be convened 'as and when required'. Because the main assignment of the preparatory meetings is to discuss and propose appropriate measures and prepare a draft for international arrangements, the term 'negotiation' used in relation to preparatory meetings refers to the pre-conference stage. An Ad Hoc Intergovernmental Committee is also established for inter alia coordinating the work of preparatory meetings. The IPC reiterates certain rules for conducting these negotiations. The principle of commodity-by-commodity negotiation is maintained; negotiations or renegotiations on commodities already regulated by international commodity agreements are to be conducted in accordance with the respective 'established procedures for the purpose of concluding international arrangements', that is on the basis of the initiative and proposals emanating from the appropriate commodity councils.

Commodity organisations are based on institutionalised polarization between producing and consuming members. * * *

The negotiations under the IPC relate firstly to the establishment of a common fund and secondly to the adoption of measures on the IPC commodities.

Note

The Common Fund [11] is designed to play two roles: to help finance buffer stocks set up pursuant to international commodity agreements and to help support other activities related to commodities, including development measures. The resources of the Fund would be divided between these two functions. The former function would be financed largely by subscriptions by members of the Fund plus contributions from associated international commodity organizations and borrowings; while the latter would depend heavily on voluntary contribution. Almost two-thirds of the subscriptions would be from the western industrialized countries, who would receive only about 40% of the voting power in the Fund. This would constitute blocking power since Fund decisions would require a vote of at least two-thirds of those voting. The Fund has not yet come into existence as the agreement establishing it has yet to be ratified by many countries, including the United States (whose share of the subscriptions is about 15%). To come into effect, inter alia, the Fund agreement must be ratified by 90 countries representing two-thirds of the total subscription amount provided for.

The second aspect of the IPC, the negotiation of international commodity agreements for the 18 specified commodities, has proceeded in the absence of an effective agreement on the Common Fund.[12] An IMF Study has examined the operation of a number of these agreements and concluded:

MARKETS TEST COMMODITY AGREEMENTS' ABILITY TO MEET OBJECTIVES OF PRICE STABILIZATION
IMF Survey, Dec. 10, 1984, at 370

Through market-intervention provisions designed to dampen excessive price fluctuations, international commodity agreements play a role in determining market prices of a number of primary commodities. Their objective of price stabilization has taken on added importance in recent years in the face of adverse commodity market conditions and the heavy external indebtedness of commodity exporting developing countries.

---

11. UNCTAD/TD/IPC/CF/CONF/24, 29 July 1980.

12. For developments on individual agreements, see C. Johnston, supra note 1 and the Journal of World Trade Law (JWTL), where new international commodity agreements are typically noted. See, e.g., Wassermann, UNCTAD: International Agreement on Jute and Jute Products, 1982, 18 JWTL 173 (1984); Wassermann, UNCTAD: International Tropical Timber Agreement, 18 JWTL 89 (1984); Stubbs, The International Natural Rubber Agreement, 18 JWTL 16 (1984); Smith, Prospects for a New International Sugar Agreement, 17 JWTL 308 (1983); Wassermann, UNCTAD: International Jute Agreement, 17 JWTL 65 (1983); Wassermann, UNCTAD: Proposals on Commodity Issues, 17 JWTL 266 (1983).

Five international commodity agreements with market-intervention provisions are currently in operation: the International Sugar Agreement 1977, the International Natural Rubber Agreement 1979, the Sixth International Tin Agreement (1981), the International Cocoa Agreement 1980, and the International Coffee Agreement 1983. During 1978–81, the five commodities covered by these agreements accounted for about 35 percent of the earnings of the non-oil developing countries from non-oil primary commodity exports.

To date, the agreements on rubber, tin, and coffee have achieved their price objectives to varying degrees and at varying costs.[13] The cocoa agreement, however, has been much less successful in meeting its stated price objectives, while the sugar agreement succeeded in its early years, but has been unsuccessful since 1982 in keeping prices above the established "floor" level.

Sugar Agreement. The 1977 Sugar Agreement initially covered 1978–82, but was extended to cover 1983–84. When the Agreement became operational in January 1978, the price of sugar on the free market was below the lower limit of the initial price range of 11 to 21 U.S. cents a pound. Consequently, all of the Agreement's provisions became operative, including the obligation of exporting countries to adhere to export quotas in the form of "basic export tonnages" (BETs) and to accumulate "special stocks." The [International Monetary] Fund approved the Sugar Agreement for buffer stock financing in December 1977, and six Fund members were granted financial assistance totaling SDR 74 million shortly thereafter.

Sugar prices rose gradually at first, as the control measures took effect, but rose rapidly in 1980, partly in response to a small Cuban crop. In February 1980, prices rose above the upper limit of the price range, thus triggering a removal of all supply restrictions, including the release of the special stocks accumulated.

In May 1981, when the price of sugar on the free market fell below 16 U.S. cents a pound, the revised lower intervention point was reached, and export quotas were reimposed. The BETs were reduced in stages as the price of sugar fell below the levels specified for quota adjustments. The BETs were reduced to 85 percent of their initial levels when prices dropped below 13.5 U.S. cents, the revised floor price. In addition, exporting members were again required to accumulate stocks. The price decline was temporarily halted and there were some signs of recovery, but the price never remained above 13.5 U.S. cents for more than a few days.

Sugar prices began to decline again in March 1982. As the BETs for 1983 and 1984 were frozen at their 1982 levels, arrangements were made to speed the accumulation of special stocks and to provide for voluntary "additional" stocks. During 1982–84, seven Fund members were provided buffer stock financing of SDR 128 million. Despite these various measures, prices failed to rise to the lower limit of the price range (13.5 U.S. cents), remaining well below 10 U.S. cents except during July-September 1983. Following the failure in June 1984 of a negotiating conference to agree on provisions for a new agreement, the average price of sugar in the free market fell to 4 U.S. cents a pound in August-September 1984, the lowest

13. The tin agreement later collapsed.

level since 1971. Only very small increases were recorded in the price of sugar in the free market during October-November 1984.

The accumulation of stocks in the early years of the Sugar Agreement and their release in 1980 appear to have dampened price fluctuations in that period. But the Agreement failed to prevent prices from remaining below the floor level from 1982 to 1984. Key problems include the nonparticipation of the European Community, which has been the largest sugar exporter in the free market since 1977, and the introduction in the United States in May 1982 of an import quota system as part of a domestic price-support program. Another problem has been the design of the Agreement itself; its formula for calculating BETs is based on retrospective trade averages that have had the effect of inflating export quotas in years when the demand for sugar from members of the Agreement is falling.

Rubber Agreement. The 1979 Natural Rubber Agreement took effect in October 1980 and is set to expire in October 1985, unless it is extended for an additional two years. Preparations for negotiations on an agreement to succeed the current one have already begun.

When the 1979 Agreement entered into force the market-indicator price was above the intervention range of the Agreement. In October 1981, however, the indicator price fell below the lower intervention price of 179 Malaysian/Singapore cents a kilogram—the price at which the buffer stock manager "may buy" rubber. Between November 1981 and January 1983, the buffer stock manager, intervening in the market in all but two months, purchased 270,000 tons of natural rubber, about one half of the maximum capacity of 550,000 tons provided for in the Agreement. In May 1982, the market-indicator price, averaged over a six-month period, fell below the "trigger action" price of 168 Malaysian/Singapore cents—the price at which the buffer stock manager "must buy" rubber. In response, the International Natural Rubber Council revised the reference price and the upper and lower intervention and trigger action prices downward by 1 percent. The Fund, which approved the Natural Rubber Agreement for support under the buffer stock financing facility in November 1982, provided SDR 132 million to five exporting members of the Agreement.

Beginning in February 1983, rubber prices began to rise sharply and the market-indicator price rose well into the nonintervention zone. In June-July 1983, and again in January-February 1984, the market-indicator price rose above the upper intervention price of 239 Malaysian/Singapore cents a kilogram. However, as the penetration of the "may sell" sector of the intervention range was only temporary, no sales were made from the buffer stock, and in April 1984 the market-indicator price fell back well into the nonintervention zone. From June to November 1984, the indicator price was once again approaching the lower intervention price at which the buffer stock manager "may buy."

The Natural Rubber Agreement appears to have achieved its price objectives. The accumulation of stocks during November 1981-January 1983 was sufficient to prevent the market-indicator price from falling below the lower trigger action price. These purchases coincided with a period of much-reduced demand for natural rubber owing to the world recession. Although none of the accumulated stocks was sold during the subsequent recovery, one half of the capacity of the buffer stock as provided in the

Agreement remains to be filled if necessary. The procedure for compulsory "call-ups" of funds from both exporting and importing members to finance buffer stock purchases has not posed any major problems. In June and July 1984, the International Natural Rubber Council refunded surplus cash to its members, although given the current price weakness, further call-ups are possible before the Agreement ends.

———

As noted earlier, one goal that international commodities agreements may seek is stabilization of export earnings. Since 1975, the EC arrangements with various African, Caribbean and Pacific nations (ACP nations) under the Lomé conventions (see Section 7.3(B) supra) have included provisions designed to help achieve such stability. The working of Lomé I is described in the following excerpt:

GERRIT FABER, THE ECONOMICS OF STABEX

(1984) [14]

Stabex was hailed as a major innovation of the association policy of the European Communities (EC) when the first Lomé Convention was concluded in 1975.

* * *

Stabex is directed at the stabilization of export earnings from individual products (raw materials and products in a first stage of processing). All products are agricultural commodities, except iron ore.

* * *

Export earnings from exporting to the EC only are stabilized in principle. * * * Two thresholds have to be crossed in order [for an ACP nation] to receive a [payment from the EC]. First there is a "dependency threshold": the export earnings of the product for which a transfer is requested has in principle to account for at least 7.5 per cent of total export earnings of the country concerned in the year prior to the year for which a transfer is claimed. This percentage has been fixed at 5 per cent for sisal and 2.5 per cent for the least developed, land-locked and insular ACP states.[*8] Second is the "fluctuation threshold": the export earnings of the product concerned have to be on a level that is 7.5 per cent or more below a reference level. This percentage is again 2.5 for the least developed, land-locked and insular ACP states.[*9] The reference level is the average of the earnings of the previous four years. The difference between reference level and actual earnings constitutes the basis for the transfer. It is obvious that the calculation of the reference level is of crucial importance. The advantage of the method used is its relative simplicity. But the method does not take into account the development of the price level of the ACP countries' imports. Constant nominal export earnings result in a decrease of real export earnings if import prices are increasing. There is no right on Stabex transfers in

14. 18 J. World Trade L. 52. Reprinted by permission of the Journal of World Trade Law.

*8. These percentages are 6.5, 5 and 2 respectively in Lomé II.

*9. These percentages are 6.5 and 2 respectively in Lomé II.

these cases, as Stabex is not an instrument of indexation. This may result in the situation that a country experiences a gradual decrease of real export earnings without, however, crossing the fluctuation threshold. A lower fluctuation threshold could solve this problem partially.

The actual transfer is not necessarily equal to the difference between actual earnings and reference level. The transfer base will be reduced if the decline of export earnings is the consequence of a trade policy that has adversely affected exports to the Community or if trade flows have changed significantly. Reductions have been applied to cases in which the share of the EC in total exports of the product concerned decreased or in which there was an increase of domestic consumption in the ACP country. Reductions are fixed after consultations have taken place between the Commission and the ACP state concerned. This may affect the automatic character of Stabex as these consultations may develop into negotiations. The same may happen when the Commission and the ACP country use different statistical sources. Statistical data may differ significantly from source to source. The Commission and the ACP country have to come to terms on one set of data which the Commission needs to calculate the transfers.

Transfers are free of interest. Least developed countries receive nonrepayable transfers, while the other countries have to refund as far as the reference level of unit value of the product concerned is below the actual unit value in a certain year and if the quantity exported to the EC is equal to or exceeds the reference quantity (art. 21).

The ACP country concerned receives the transfer in hard currency and may use the money as it sees fit. The country is obligated to report annually on the use of the transfer to the Commission.

* * *

From the above it can be concluded that Stabex does not operate well as an instrument of macroeconomic stabilization because the system frequently improves the balance of payments and public revenues when they have not suffered from a fall in export earnings. At the same time, Stabex is not capable—at a microeconomic level—of giving producers a warranted, reasonable compensation for decreasing export incomes, because public authorities may put transfers to other uses. The rules of Stabex are responsible for this twofold negative judgement. It has been tried to establish Stabex as a hybrid of macro-and microeconomic stabilization elements. By this endeavour to unite both aspects, a system has been created that does not work well from either point of view. To link ends and means of Stabex in a more adequate way, one has to choose between a micro- or a macroeconomic setup. In 1973 the Commission proposed to establish Stabex in a more microeconomic way. These proposals have not been put into practice insofar as the ACP states are allowed to spend transfers as they wish, which makes Stabex an inadequate microeconomic instrument of stabilization. Apparently, the direct link between transfer and stricken sector is unacceptable to the ACP countries. An obvious reason for this stand is that the ACP states view this link as an interference in their internal affairs. Additionally, the link is undesirable because it may conflict with the domestic development policy. Finally, producers do not bear the entire burden of a decrease of export earnings if marketing boards, public companies or domestic stabilization funds shield producers from the world market. Consequently, a macroeconomic structure of Stabex is to be preferred.

Stabex should eliminate the adverse effects of a fall in export earnings on the balance of payments and public revenues. To this end, the product-by-product approach could be abandoned which would necessitate transfers in cases of decreases of total export incomes only. This would have the advantage that Stabex would cover a much larger flow of trade. The risks to be covered would also expand significantly. This explains the Community's wish to maintain the product-by-product approach. If this approach is not abandoned, Stabex has to be supplied with the constraint that a transfer will be made available only as far as total export earnings (all products and all destinations) have decreased, in which case adverse macroeconomic effects really have taken place.

Questions

(1) Do you think that UNCTAD should sponsor organizations or agreements that do more than stabilize commodity prices? What problems might arise if it attempts to sponsor developmental aid programs or programs to increase the general level of commodity prices?

(2) What voting arrangements do you think are appropriate for an international financial organization, such as the Common Fund? To what extent should voting depend on capital contributions? On share of world trade in a particular product? On other considerations? Is the principle of equality of voting between exporters and importers desirable? Workable?

(3) Should the United States, alone or with others, adopt a Stabex-type program for developing countries? What might be the advantages or disadvantages of such a program vis-à-vis the more traditional price stabilization programs?

SECTION 14.4 CARTELS AND PRODUCER ALLIANCES

Intimately related to the problems of regulating international trade in commodities by agreement, are the problems that arise when producers of a particular commodity or product themselves attempt to regulate international trade therein without the participation of importing countries. The principal example of such an attempt in recent years has been the Organization of Petroleum Exporting Countries (OPEC).

FIONA GORDON–ASHWORTH, INTERNATIONAL COMMODITY CONTROL: A CONTEMPORARY HISTORY AND APPRAISAL

250–54 (1984) [15]

Early attempts to coordinate the policies of countries (as opposed to corporations) producing oil began in the mid-1940s with the establishment of

15. © 1984 F. Gordon-Ashworth and reprinted here and elsewhere in this section by permission of St. Martin's Press Inc.

the Arab League. Iraq and Saudi Arabia signed an agreement for cooperation on oil matters and in 1959 called an Arab Petroleum Conference in Cairo under the sponsorship of the Arab League. In 1960, when the US imposed a mandatory import quota system, many of the independent oil companies, shut off from the US market, cut posted prices of Middle Eastern oil with a view to improving their profit margins. These cuts, which meant an aggregate loss of US $231 million for Kuwait, Iran, Iraq and Saudi Arabia, encouraged the establishment of OPEC in the same year, with those four countries and Venezuela as founder members. The aim of OPEC was to restore prices to the level prevailing before the reduction and OPEC's founder members held 67 per cent of world oil reserves and accounted for about 38 per cent of world oil production and nearly 90 per cent of internationally traded oil. (By 1973, OPEC included amongst its members Qatar (1961), Indonesia and Libya (1962), Abu Dhabi (1967), Algeria (1969), Nigeria (1971) and Ecuador and Gabon (1973)).

In its first ten years, OPEC's main actions were defensive and centred on attempting to prevent a further erosion in posted prices. In 1964, agreement was also reached with the major oil companies to change the method by which oil company profits were calculated, the net effect of which was to lead to some increase in the revenues of oil-producing countries. By 1968, OPEC was also urging its members to undertake the production and processing of crude oil themselves and to revoke the traditional export licenses granted to foreign firms, a system which had itself replaced long-term concessions from the late 1940s. In the same year, a second association of oil-exporting countries, the Organization of Arab Petroleum Exporting Countries (OAPEC), was established following the 1967 Arab-Israeli War. Its main purpose was to create an effective instrument of political rather than economic policy although OAPEC members were required to respect OPEC resolutions even if they were not OPEC members.

On balance, the defensive period of OPEC's operations to 1970 did not achieve the success that had been envisaged in respect of its pricing objectives. In 1970, for example, the real price of oil was 47 per cent below the 1955 level. However, in the 1960s the coordinated action of OPEC not only prevented any further cuts in posted prices but also separated the payment of royalties from taxes and restored to the producer control of unexploited territories.

D. CONTROLS AFTER 1970

The 1970s, in contrast, heralded two dramatic rises in oil prices, the first from 1971 to 1974 and the second from 1979 to 1981 (Figure 14:1). The first rise was triggered by Libya, a relatively new oil exporter supplying about a quarter of Western Europe's oil, which in 1970, under the revolutionary government of Qadaffi, demanded and achieved a 13 per cent rise in prices. In conditions of short supplies and strong demand, Libya's move was followed by several other countries, including Iraq, Iran and Kuwait, and at its twenty-first conference in December 1970, OPEC advocated formally higher posted prices and higher minimum rates of taxation on oil company profits. Members resolved to undertake 'concerted and simultaneous action' in pursuit of these goals.

The gradual upward trend in prices continued between 1971 and 1973 accompanied by nationalisation measures in Libya, Iraq and Algeria and moves in Iran and Saudi Arabia to increase their equity stakes in oil production. It was not until October 1973, however, following the move in the market price of oil above the posted price (for the first time in OPEC's history) and the outbreak of the fourth Arab-Israeli War, that OPEC members decided to raise prices—to $5.12 a barrel—and to restrict output. This was accompanied by the imposition by some countries of an embargo on oil shipments to the US. A combination of continued supply shortages and speculative buying then enabled OPEC, led by Iran, to push the posted price further to $11.65 per barrel. At the beginning of 1974, in the words of Sampson,

> The Western nations * * * found themselves, to their bewilderment, confronted with a cartel, not of companies, but of sovereign states.

In order to control over 80 per cent of oil exports and 45 per cent of global production, OPEC had to obtain the cooperation of twelve producers. As Brown has noted, however, the ability of OPEC to quadruple royalties in 1973 did not lie only in the concentration of supply but also in the inelasticity of demand, the limited possibilities for substitution and the lack of organised response from consumers. It is also important to note that the gains made were far less spectacular than they appeared at first since for a number of years prior to 1971 the tax and royalty per barrel for oil exporters had remained unchanged and oil prices had declined in real terms.

Nevertheless, the implications of the oil price hike, as outlined in Chapter 1, were far-reaching. Oil-exporting countries emerged as a new category in international trade, with additional earnings of $60 billion a year, more than six times concessional flows from developed to developing countries in 1973 and more than three times global financial flows between the two groups. This represented one of the largest and most rapid shifts in world income, equal in magnitude to two per cent of world GNP. A second result was that oil price rises added to existing inflationary pressures and invoked a restrictive policy response from major industrialised countries. Thirdly, the rise in oil prices generated a strong ripple effect, both in terms of strong speculative movements in the prices of other primary commodities and in terms of the difficult environment it created for the negotiation of international commodity agreements.

In these circumstances, and after a four year period in which the price of crude oil remained comparatively steady in nominal terms—although falling by almost twenty per cent in real terms—the second oil price surge, which took place towards the end of 1978, was viewed by many as a second oil crisis. Although the revolution in Iran and the consequent reduction in Iranian output provided a trigger mechanism, the sharp rises in the official Middle East price—from US $13.5 per barrel in the first quarter of 1979 to US $34 in the fourth quarter of 1981—were associated with an increased speculative demand for inventories. Bi-lateral sales between consumer and producer governments doubled in two years and the spot market, formerly the locus only of marginal sales, became a more important avenue for transactions.

By the beginning of 1983, however, this situation had altered markedly: with a glut in world oil supplies and slack world demand, relations within OPEC came under increasing strain. On the one hand, producers found difficulty in agreeing on the allocation of individual quotas to achieve a targeted output of 17.5 million barrels a day. On the other, divisions existed on the appropriate differentials to be charged over the official reference price of $34 per barrel for some premium grades of crude oil. With a cut in prices triggered by the British National Oil Corporation in February, it appeared to some commentators that OPEC had lost, at least for the time being, its ability to determine world oil prices.

The potential impact of the apparent reverse in OPEC's fortunes was considered to be as far-reaching as its rise to power. Concern was expressed, for example, that if oil prices fell substantially, the strain placed on heavily indebted oil-producing countries, such as Mexico, Venezuela, and Nigeria, would pose a serious problem for the world banking system, which had expanded rapidly partly on the basis of the re-cycling of petro-currency flows. The uncertainty created was also felt as an important influence in the foreign exchange markets. Thus, from its role as a model for developing country producers of primary commodities, OPEC had by 1983 substantially diminished in stature.

E. CONCLUSION

The case of oil suggests that raw material cartels may vary substantially in terms of participation (corporate in the pre-War period and governmental afterwards), in objectives (market division, the prevention of price falls, price stabilisation, the raising of prices, increasing national control, nationalisation and so on) and in methodology (the exchange of information, measures concerning royalties and production restraints). Oil represented a special case, however, as a leading and strategic world commodity and OPEC, similarly, must be viewed as an extraordinary example of cartelisation. Although OPEC's control over prices was weakened by divisions between members, the emergence of important non-member producers and some structural shifts away from oil as a result of conservation and substitution, particularly in the late 1970s, its impact on the world oil import bill, nevertheless, was substantial, especially between 1973 and 1974. The countries mostly seriously affected by OPEC's activities were the lowest income developing countries with little or no oil of their own.

In general, producer cartels, have not been very successful.

FIONA GORDON–ASHWORTH, INTERNATIONAL COMMODITY CONTROL: A CONTEMPORARY HISTORY AND APPRAISAL
Supra, at 266–67

The examples of cartelisation examined in this chapter do not suggest that such arrangements were more successful than international commodity agreements in meeting their objectives. For those with pricing provisions, OPEC probably came closest to doing so, followed by the short-lived Uranium

Cartel of the early 1970s, although in both instances the results were not sustained and unforeseen repercussions such as substitution and over-production were also experienced.   In contrast, neither the mercury nor the copper cartels met with long-term success in their repeated attempts to raise prices before and after the Second World War; and the IBA [bauxite] cartel announced a minimum price to the US market only in 1977 when prices had already risen above the level set.

Slightly more success was achieved by cartels than by their international commodity agreement equivalents in respect of their broader structural goals.   The action of OPEC, for example, substantially increased the control of producers over royalty levels.   And the existence of OPEC and the IBA probably encouraged producers in their endeavours to increase national control over production.   However, such actions were not without their costs.   In the case of bauxite, for example, the increased royalties achieved in Jamaica probably encouraged the diversion of corporate investment elsewhere;   and the greater insecurity of oil supplies and higher oil prices were instrumental in encouraging consumers to investigate alternative sources of energy, particularly after 1979.   In addition, although producers increased their influence over the supplies of oil, copper and bauxite in the 1970s, multi-national companies remained for each of these three commodities the decisive influence in terms of marketing and distribution.

It seems fair to conclude that cartelisation or uni-lateral producer action were only realistic alternatives to international commodity agreements when the commodity in question was subject to several important conditions such as a relative high concentration of supply and relative inelasticity of demand—conditions which help to explain why minerals rather than agricultural commodities provided the outstanding examples of cartelisation. Even in cases when these conditions were met, the lack of consultative framework in general and the absence of consumer participation in particular may have limited the sustainability of such arrangements, particularly when policy goals were altered and allegiances wavered.   Cartels, in sum, offered few instant cures to the problems facing the producers of primary commodities.   Like international commodity agreements, they were forced to work within the constraints of prevailing market conditions.

Notes

(1) In December 1985, the OPEC nations announced that they would no longer restrain their production of oil or set minimum prices for oil. The effect that the OPEC action will have for the future of oil prices is not clear as of this writing (December 1985).   Some believe that it could lead to a price war that would cause both OPEC and non-OPEC producers to attempt to establish a new system of production restraints and price minimums.

(2) In 1978 a U.S. labor union, the International Association of Machinists and Aerospace Workers, sued OPEC and its member nations, alleging that their price-setting activities violated U.S. antitrust laws.   International Association of Machinists and Aerospace Workers (IAM) v. Organization of the Petroleum Exporting Countries (OPEC), 649 F.2d 1354 (9th Cir.1981), cert. denied, 454 U.S.

1163, 102 S.Ct. 1036, 71 L.Ed.2d 319 (1982). The suit was dismissed on the following grounds (649 F.2d at 1361–62):

> The act of state doctrine is applicable in this case. The courts should not enter at the will of litigants into a delicate area of foreign policy which the executive and legislative branches have chosen to approach with restraint. The issue of whether the FSIA [Foreign Sovereign Immunities Act and its commercial activities exception] allows jurisdiction in this case need not be decided, since a judicial remedy is inappropriate regardless of whether jurisdiction exists.

The court also noted that in light of the application of the act of state doctrine, it was inappropriate to consider whether U.S. antitrust laws should be applied to activities occuring outside the United States. The extraterritorial application of the U.S. antitrust laws is discussed in more detail in Section 18.3 infra.

Chapter 15

INTERNATIONAL TRADE IN SERVICES

SECTION 15.1 INTRODUCTION

In recent years, governments and international trade specialists have been giving increasing attention to trade in services.[1] Indeed, one of the major issues to be faced in structuring the new round of trade negotiations is whether, to what extent and how those negotiations should deal with international trade in services. The United States has been the prime proponent of negotiating in respect of trade in services at the new round, a stance in the main supported by the EC and Japan, but opposed by a number of major developing countries, such as India and Brazil (see Section 5.5 supra).

This interest in services is new. Historically, economists and trade theorists have been principally concerned with the production and exchange of goods. The service sector of an economy, usually referred to as the "tertiary sector" (after agriculture and manufacturing), was considered "unproductive" by economists as widely divergent as Adam Smith and Karl Marx.[2] Indeed, many people still picture the service sector as a labor-intensive, low-paying, low-technology area of the economy. But in recent years, many western economists have heralded the coming of the "post-industrial economy," characterized by the rapid growth of service industries, many of which depend on (or develop) advanced technology and highly skilled, high-paid workers. Increased attention to the production of services has revealed the importance that this "invisible" sector has had all along, both as an adjunct to the production of goods and in its own right.

In this chapter, we will first trace briefly the growth in the importance of the service sector—both in the economies of developed countries and in

---

1. For a recent bibliography of works relevant to the issues discussed in this chapter, see R. Krommenacker, World-Traded Services: The Challenge for the Eighties 207–21 (1984). In addition to the materials cited elsewhere in this chapter, see Symposium: Trade in Services, 19 J. World Trade L. 219 (1985); Hultman, International Banking and U.S. Commercial Policy, 19 J. World Trade L. 219 (1985); Cohen & Morante, Elimination of Nontariff Barriers to Trade in Services: Recommendations for Future Negotiations, 13 Law & Poly.Intl.Bus. 495 (1981).

2. R. Krommenacker, note 1 supra, at vii, 3–4.

world trade. In Section 15.2, we look briefly at U.S. legal rules relevant to international trade in services, and in Section 15.3, we consider how GATT or another organization might regulate international trade in services, which in the view of the United States is one of the most significant trade issues of the 1980's. Finally, in Sections 15.4 and 15.5, we consider two important service industries: insurance, which has figured prominently in discussions on international trade in services, and legal services, which are, of course, of great interest to many users of this book.

In reviewing the following introductory materials on the importance of services and the gains to be had in trading services, the reader should keep a number of questions in mind. First, although it is clear that many services are "tradable" in the international sense, many are not. Obviously trade-related services, such as shipping and insurance, are generally tradable. In contrast, haircuts and "fast food" cannot be exported; the producer and the consumer must be face to face. There are, of course, gradations. Hairstyling and fast food restaurant management techniques may be tradable. Do the following materials give sufficient consideration to these differences?

A second, and related, question arises from the fact that although services constitute a large component of national economies, trade in services has been relatively minor compared to trade in goods. Given the fact that services often need to be rendered on the spot, are the gains to be had in internationalizing the provision of services more likely to come from liberalizing barriers to trade in services or from increased freedom for nationals of one country to invest and provide services in another country?

Finally, data on existing service trade is not thought to be very accurate. There is a large error component in balance of payments statistics that is thought to represent in part trade in services, but that is not certain. Is it a wise policy to embark upon negotiations on trade in services without more complete data?

WILLIAM E. BROCK, A SIMPLE PLAN FOR NEGOTIATING ON TRADE IN SERVICES

(1982) [3]

"GROWTH OF TRADE IN SERVICES"

World trade in services is in the vicinity of $400 billion or about one fifth of world trade in goods. Its volume doubled between 1960 and 1970 and again between 1970 and 1975. According to estimates of the Organisation for Economic Cooperation and Development (OECD), trade in services among its twenty four member countries rose from $85 billion to $300 billion over the past decade. In the United States alone, the value of service exports increased to $42 billion in 1981, reflecting an increase of about 300 per cent since 1970. Similar trends are noticeable in other OECD countries. Over

3. 5 The World Economy 229, 232–33 (1982). Reprinted by permission of The World Economy.

the coming decade the growth of trade in services is expected to exceed the growth of trade in goods.

A number of studies suggest that these numbers significantly under-state the true value of service exports. One source, for example, estimated that American exports of services were in excess of $60 billion in 1980, as compared with the $35 billion recorded in official data. It is likely that official data in other countries also seriously under-state the true value of internationally-traded services. The reason for this is that services are not as easily measured as goods as they cross international borders and few governments have developed the comprehensive data-collection systems re-quired to obtain more accurate figures.

The growth of trade in services is the result of a number of trends.

First, it reflects an underlying shift in employment from manufacturing to services in most OECD countries. In the United States, according to Department of Labor statistics, 72 per cent of the non-agricultural working population was engaged in service activities in 1981, up from 68 per cent in 1971 and from 63 per cent in 1961. Similar trends are occurring in other countries. For example, in Japan, the percentage of the labour force employed in services increased from 37 per cent in 1960 to 49 per cent in 1980; in the Republic of Korea during the same time period the percentage increased from 25 to 37 per cent. In fact, in 1980 more than half the work force in twelve middle-income developing countries was employed in services; and in 21 additional middle-income developing countries at least one third of the work force was employed in services, according to World Bank statistics.

Another development has been a trend towards greater specialisation in services. The gains in productivity made possible by greater specialisation and economies of scale have persuaded many manufacturing enterprises to pull together internal service activities into separate profit centres. These new profit centres have found it advantageous to market their services outside the company both at home and abroad.

Many service industries also have become more international in scope as the economic advantages of specialisation and greater economies of scale have become apparent at an international level.

Technological advances in telecommunications and data processing have greatly facilitated 'internationalisation' as numbers, texts and pictures have come to be transmittable almost instantly to any place in the world. An engineer can work on drawings that are needed thousands of miles away. An energy expert can tap data stored on the other side of the world. Funds can be transferred electronically from one end of the United States to the other. And books and newspapers can be offset in type from either the editorial office or the printing plant. These possibilities for trade in infor-mation-dependent services have come as a tremendous boon to the telecom-munication services and have also led to increased trade in insurance, banking, accounting, management consulting, executive placement as well as other service industries.

Trade in services provides the same mutual economic gains made possible by trade in goods. It permits international specialisation on the basis of comparative advantage. It increases the efficiency of domestic industries through increased competition. And it enriches consumer choice by widening the range of available services.

As key manufacturing industries grow more and more automated, the creation of new jobs in services will be an increasingly important economic-policy objective for governments. And trade in services obviously enlarges the scope for new jobs in these service industries.

In sum, there are tremendous new opportunities for expanding trade in services, opportunities that could impart new growth impulses to the sluggish economies of the industrialised world. But it will only be possible to obtain these benefits if an international effort is made to prevent new barriers to trade in services from stifling growth in this area.

H. PETER GRAY, A NEGOTIATING STRATEGY FOR TRADE IN SERVICES

(1983) [4]

1. ESTABLISHING THE EXISTENCE OF GAINS FROM TRADE IN SERVICES

Gains from international trade in a product will exist when countries have different comparative (opportunity) costs of production of the same good and the difference in costs exceeds any costs of transportation. If product-specific human capital and proprietary knowhow are considered as arguments in the production functions, a sufficient argument for the existence of gains from trade is that the costs of human capital and proprietary knowledge used in the preparation of individual services vary in the two countries. For services for which location-specific attributes are dominant, differences in particular natural resource endowments may also be sufficient to establish the existence of gains from trade.

The argument for the existence of gains from trade in services is essentially the same as that for tangible commodities. It may vary in intensity since the existence of non-competitive imports in services due to the non-availability of product-requisite inputs seems improbable. Nearly all nations are capable of producing a full range of services at some cost. Since non-competitive imports are likely to provide the most significant *per* unit gain from trade, international trade in services may seem to be less important than trade in tangible goods.

However, two other kinds of gains from trade than those normally countenanced by the traditional analysis may prove more important for services. Traditional analysis is concerned with gains deriving from the reallocation of production. Trade in services may well generate more important gains by virtue of the effect on the kind (quality) of service supplied and on the inherent efficiency of the domestic industry—through innovation and input reduction.

In the absence of international trade and competition in services, domestic industries may fail to innovate at the rate achieved in foreign countries.

---

4. 17 J. World Trade L. 377, 378–79. Reprinted by permission of the Journal of World Trade Law.

So-called product technology may develop spontaneously in more competitive foreign industries and, in the absence of the competitive stimulus of international trade, a national services industry may fail to adopt such innovations. Alternatively, a local industry may not achieve peak efficiency without the stimulus of foreign competition. * * * These possibilities de-emphasize the importance of allocative gains and, echoing Adam Smith, attribute much of gains from trade to improved industrial efficiency deriving from the degree of competition. These aspects of the benefits of international trade in services are likely to be particularly important.

Note

Not everyone agrees with the arguments advanced in the two principal extracts in this subsection. For example, it has been noted that according to IMF statistics, trade in services did not grow as fast as trade in goods during the 1970 to 1982 period, which may in part be due to the fact that less than eight percent of services are traded. Moreover, not all economists are confident that the traditional theory of comparative advantage applies to trade in services.[5]

SECTION 15.2   U.S. LAW AND
TRADE IN SERVICES

As noted above, the United States has been the prime exponent of including services in the new round of trade negotiations. This is largely due to a belief that the United States has a comparative advantage in many services and that it would be in the U.S. interest to liberalize trade in services. However, the U.S. initiative to include services in the new trade round negotiations is only one aspect of the U.S. drive to liberalize world trade in services.

Section 301 of the Trade Act of 1974 (see Documentary Supplement), which was analyzed in Section 10.5 supra, initially provided a means for the U.S. President to retaliate against countries that, inter alia, maintained unjustifiable or unreasonable import restrictions that burdened, restricted or discriminated against U.S. commerce.[1] It was unclear whether services were covered by Section 301. That ambiguity was clarified in 1979, when Section 301 was extensively revised. A provision was added at that time that defined the term "commerce" to include "services associated with international trade, whether or not such services are related to specific products."[2] In 1984, Section 301 was further amended to specify that the concept of services includes transfers of information.[3] This change was made by the International Trade and Investment Act, which was title III of the 1984 Trade and Tariff Act. The International Trade and Investment Act contains many provisions dealing with trade in services and foreign investment, particularly in respect of requiring reports and information gathering

5. See, e.g., Gibbs, Continuing the International Debate on Services, 19 J.World Trade L. 199, 209–10 (1985).

1. Pub.L. No. 93–618, § 301, 88 Stat. 2041 (1974).

2. Pub.L. No. 96–39, § 901, 93 Stat. 295 (1979).

3. Pub.L. No. 98–573, § 304(f)(1), 98 Stat. 3005 (1984), codified at 19 U.S.C.A. § 2411(e) (1).

activities on the part of the Executive Branch.[4] The Act also establishes the liberalization of international trade in services as a principal U.S. objective in trade negotiations.[5]

As a result of the various amendments to Section 301, it now seems to be suitable for use by the Executive Branch or U.S. service industries to initiate complaints about foreign restrictions of their activities. If the President accepts the complaint as justified, it provides for an extensive selection of countermeasures that the President could impose in an attempt to cause the foreign government to remove the restriction in question. Thus, even in the absence of an agreement to discuss trade in services in the next trade round, or in the absence of a meaningful agreement coming out of such discussions, U.S. law has given the President considerable authority to force U.S. trading partners to liberalize their rules on trade in services. As noted in Section 10.5 supra, Section 301 complaints by private parties have often involved services and it was used in 1985 by the U.S. Trade Representative to initiate a complaint in respect of South Korea's restrictions on foreign insurance companies (see Section 15.4 infra). As was noted in Section 10.5, Section 301 has served as a useful tool in a number of other cases to obtain liberalization of restrictions applicable to U.S. companies through negotiation. The future may see much more extensive use of Section 301 in this area.

SECTION 15.3 NEGOTIATING RULES ON INTERNATIONAL TRADE IN SERVICES

As noted at the outset of this chapter, one of the key issues to be faced in the new round of trade negotiations is whether, to what extent and how trade in services should be a subject of negotiations in the GATT framework. In this section, we look first at how GATT now treats services and then consider the questions of (1) whether GATT or some other organization would be the most appropriate forum for negotiating an international agreement on trade in services, (2) what sort of restrictions on trade in services and other issues would have to be treated in such an agreement and (3) how those issues might be resolved in such an agreement.

(A) GATT'S PRESENT TREATMENT OF SERVICES

Although a few miscellaneous provisions of GATT deal with services, GATT is basically concerned with goods. However, issues concerning trade in services are not new to GATT.[1] The never-ratified Havana Charter of the International Trade Organization (ITO), discussed in Section 5.4 supra, provided in Article 53:

> The Members recognize that certain services, such as transportation, telecommunications, insurance and the commercial services of banks, are substantial elements of international trade and that any restrictive business

4. Pub.L. No. 98–573, title III, 98 Stat. 3000 (1984).

5. Pub.L. No. 98–573, § 305(a)(1), 98 Stat. 3006 (1984), codified at 19 U.S.C.A. § 2114a(a) (Trade Act of 1974, § 104A).

1. See R. Krommenacker, World-Traded Services: The Challenge for the Eighties 141– 56 (1983) for a discussion of GATT's past consideration of issues related to services.

practices by enterprises engaged in these activities in international trade may have harmful effects * * *.

Article 54 went on to require members to consult with and give "sympathetic consideration" to complaints about such practices. If the affected members were unable to resolve their differences, the ITO was authorized to refer the matter to the appropriate international organization dealing with the service in question or, if none existed, to make recommendations for and promote an international agreement to resolve the problems raised. No provision comparable to Article 53 is contained in GATT. During the 1950's, GATT considered the problem of restrictions on the business of issuing transport insurance, which restrictions were found to have at least some adverse effect on international trade. A U.S. proposal to eliminate such restrictions was not adopted, and ultimately, the only action taken was the adoption in 1959 of a recommendation that in the formulation of national policies in respect of such insurance, the Contracting Parties should avoid measures that would have a restrictive effect on international trade.[2]

In the Tokyo Round, a number of the side agreements dealt directly or indirectly with services. For example, the Subsidies Code defines as subsidies the provision of certain services, such as transportation or insurance, at subsidized rates,[3] and the Customs Valuation Agreement excludes certain services (e.g., erection of machinery after importation) from consideration in the valuation process, although it provides for some other services to be considered (such as design work in some circumstances).[4] More specifically, the Agreement on Government Procurement applies to services incidental to the supply of products and provides that the signatories shall give early consideration to extending the agreement to cover services contracts,[5] and the Agreement on Trade in Civil Aircraft explicitly covers certain services, such as repairs.[6]

A number of other proposals relating to services were reportedly made in the bilateral offer and request procedures, but few requests were honored.[7] Thus, GATT at present does not regulate trade in services in any significant manner. In response to a 1982 U.S. proposal that GATT consider negotiation of an agreement on trade in services as part of its work program, GATT asked the Contracting Parties to provide information on trade in services and barriers thereto,[8] and as noted elsewhere, the next round of GATT negotiations will probably include discussions of trade in services.

2. GATT, 8th Supp. BISD 26 (1960). See generally J. Jackson, World Trade and the Law of GATT 529–31 (1969).

3. See Annex to Agreement on Interpretation and Application of Articles VI, XVI and XXIII, in GATT, 26th Supp. BISD 56, 80 (1980).

4. See Art. VIII and Annex—Note to Art. 1 in the Agreement on Implementation of Article VII, in GATT, 26th Supp. BISD 116, 123, 135 (1980).

5. Agreement on Government Procurement, Arts. I(1)(a) & IX(6), in GATT, 26th Supp. BISD 33, 34, 54 (1980).

6. Agreement on Trade in Civil Aircraft, Art. 2, in GATT, 26th Supp. BISD 162, 164 (1980).

7. R. Krommenacker, note 1 supra, at 154–56.

8. GATT Ministerial Declaration of November 29, 1982, in GATT, 29th Supp. BISD 9, 21–22 (1983).

(B) THE FORUM FOR NEGOTIATIONS ON INTERNATIONAL TRADE IN SERVICES

In any discussion of the appropriate forum for negotiating agreements on services, one issue must be faced at the outset: Should there be one forum aiming at a comprehensive agreement on international trade in services or should the negotiations be conducted on an industry by industry basis? Assuming that the preference is to have one forum negotiate a global agreement, it is necessary to decide which forum would be best. Three fora are typically suggested: GATT, the OECD and UNCTAD. Obviously, the choice of the OECD would effectively rule out the participation of the developing world, although it might well be more likely that negotiations among the limited membership of the OECD would be most likely to result in a meaningful agreement. The following two excerpts consider the appropriateness of these various fora.

MURRAY GIBBS, CONTINUING THE INTERNATIONAL DEBATE ON SERVICES

(1985) [9]

While this is only a hypothetical issue at present, the concerns regarding the effect of an attempt to include services in GATT on the overall structure of rights and obligations of the General Agreement must be recalled. The GATT/MTN system consists of a careful balance of concessions with respect to customs duties constructed over almost forty years in the course of seven multilateral rounds of trade negotiations and various accession negotiations, and it is difficult to foresee how commitments relating essentially to national policies with respect to the treatment of foreign enterprises and persons could be easily incorporated into such a framework. For example, would contracting parties which refuse to extend national treatment to foreign banks risk retaliation in the form of the withdrawal of tariff concessions on bananas or orange juice? Such an approach opens a virtual Pandora's Box of coercion and retaliation, as the other side of the coin would be to penalize foreign-owned firms in retaliation for trade measures (e.g. countervailing duties), imposed by the home country. In addition, the fact that services are produced and consumed simultaneously introduces a serious conceptual problem with respect to the "country of origin" of services, as all that can be identified is the entity (eg. TNC) [transnational corporation] supplying, whose nationality may not always be easy to establish and could quickly change with corporate takeovers. Considerable imagination would be required to fit such "trade" within the GATT system of reciprocal concessions.

* * *

The expression "international debate on services", which has been used throughout this article, may have been somewhat misleading. What has been taking place is that a few countries, and international organizations, with varying degrees of caution and originality, have presented selected facts

---

9. 19 J. World Trade L. 199, 214–18. Reprinted by permission of the Journal of World Trade Law.

and ideas with respect to trade in services and services and development. Most governments have had little to say, at least not in multilateral fora. To effectively take part in such international discussions on services, countries would seem to require a "service policy", in the same way in which a trade policy is a prerequisite for participation in international discussions and negotiations on trade issues. The formulation of a trade policy requires an understanding of the interrelationships of a variety of external and domestic factors, and the economic effects of increased trade (whether imports or exports) on the domestic economy, on the balance-of-payments situation and an assessment of the country's competitiveness in foreign markets and its ability to protect and improve access to these markets. It does not seem that many countries have acquired sufficient understanding of the services sectors to enable them to formulate an analogous services policy of comparable coherence. The work of international organizations should appropriately be directed towards assisting countries in obtaining the factual and methodological basis for achieving this understanding.

* * *

If it is determined that serious insufficiencies exist in the supply of vital services the question arises of what to do about it. The solution may rest in obtaining the services in one form or another from abroad (i.e. through "trade" or "investment"), the other of stimulating domestic production, the final decision might involve a combination of the two. However, a variety of considerations relating to issues such as the development of indigenous technologies, national sovereignty and international vulnerability, and the trade-offs between long-term development and short-term gains would have to be taken into account. Results which may seem consistent with a developed country's social and economic objectives may be seen as having less relevance and a negative effect in the context of a developing economy. In a developing economy considerations such as employment, foreign exchange or income redistribution may be paramount.

The decisions implied above could not be based on an analysis confined to the domestic economy without a clear idea of the external implications, such as the balance-of-payments effects, as well as other considerations relating to a greater foreign participation in the service sector. Such an assessment, however, would necessitate an improved understanding of the mechanisms of trade or international transactions in services; as trade in different sectors takes place in different forms, with differing implications in terms of a foreign presence in the domestic market (i.e. investment), immigration related issues, independence of local subsidiaries of TNCs, transfer of technology, etc. The links between trade in goods and services requires particular attention, especially given the higher service content in technologically advanced goods. The key role of data and information services as a "service to the service industry" should be given particular attention.

A coherent services policy would also have to be drawn up in the context of a greater understanding of the role of services in the international adjustment process. The relationship between the shift to service sector in the major industrialized countries and external factors must be studied in greater detail to determine whether such a shift is based on factors relating to international competition or to purely domestic considerations. What is the effect of these tendencies on the demand for the goods and services produced in developing countries? How will they affect the trade and economic policies of the major trading countries in the future?

Is the existence of a strong domestic service sector essential for maintaining productivity and an international competitive position in both goods and services?

The preceding paragraphs have suggested a few of the questions which the international community might wish to address in continuing the international debate and acquiring a more comprehensive understanding of service issues. UNCTAD with its universal membership, interdisciplinary and development-oriented character would seem to have a heavy responsibility in this respect.

JEFFREY J. SCHOTT, PROTECTIONIST THREAT TO TRADE AND INVESTMENT IN SERVICES
(1982) [10]

In spite of constant prodding by the United States, most OECD member countries have not been enthusiastic in support of efforts in the OECD related to the liberalisation of trade in services. Work has been allowed to proceed, but only grudgingly. The language of the 1982 OECD ministerial *communiqué* attests to this tepid attitude: "Ministers . . . decided to encourage the competent committees to progress as soon as possible in their analytical and fact-finding work." This is hardly a rousing call to action.

Moreover, the agreements that have been reached in the OECD—in particular, the Code of Liberalisation of Capital Movements and the Code of Liberalisation of Current Invisible Operations—have been noted more for their reservations and derogations than for their obligations to liberalise transactions in the services sector. The discipline of these OECD codes has been quite weak, although attempts are being made to shore up the invisibles code in the area of insurance. In a similar way, a 1976 OECD declaration that sets out an obligation to provide national treatment to foreign companies already established in the country suffers from two major weaknesses: first, it does not deal with barriers to entry and, second, it is not legally binding on OECD countries.

This last point underscores one of the basic problems with OECD agreements: for the most part, they consist of hortatory provisions of what countries should do rather than commitments by countries of what they will do. The OECD is a valuable *consultative* forum for the developed countries. But it is not an effective negotiating body.

The other key problem with the OECD is its limited membership. Without the participation of developing countries, it is hard to put together a clear picture of the global service-trade problems and what can be done about them. Many of the restrictions in the inventory compiled by the

10. 6 The World Economy 195, 212–13.
Reprinted by permission of The World Economy.

Office of the United States Trade Representative, in the Executive Office of the President, are imposed by developing countries; rules on the liberalisation of these measures will either have to take into account the particular reasons why they are maintained or provide for special exemptions from the general discipline for developing countries. In this regard, one argument that is often raised for advancing work in services in the OECD before entering into negotiations in the framework of the GATT is to coordinate the position of developed countries on this very question of special rules for developing countries. Such an 'us-against-them' approach has not been successful in the past and is unlikely to be helpful in talks on trade in services in the future. One need only look at the OECD experience on the government-procurement code and OECD preparations for UNCTAD meetings to judge the value of 'coordinated' OECD positions in international trade negotiations.

By contrast, the GATT is a better forum for talks on trade in services, for it is the only international body that seriously negotiates binding agreements. It is the only place where both developed and developing countries feel they can do business with each other.

Questions

(1) Do you think it would be preferable to negotiate an international agreement on trade in services under the auspices of GATT, the OECD, UNCTAD or some other organization?

(2) Does it necessarily follow that if only developed countries will initially subscribe to an agreement, only developed countries should be involved in its negotiation?

(C) CURRENT RESTRICTIONS ON TRADE IN SERVICES

In considering how international trade in services could be liberalized by international agreement, it is useful to consider both the types of current restrictions applicable to trade in services, and the effect of nontrade restrictions, such as those on investment or immigration, that directly or indirectly affect trade in services. The following excerpts treat these issues.

MICHAEL A. SAMUELS, CHAMBER OF COMMERCE OF THE UNITED STATES

(1982) [11]

American service industries are encountering growing barriers both in developing and industrial countries. In spite of the diversity of the service sector, many of the obstacles faced are common and, in many cases identical—whether services are supplied through trade or through local establishment of subsidiaries, branches, etc. Furthermore, barriers are looming over some of the new, heretofore unrestricted and high potential service activities, such as information transmittal, electronic communication, and transportation data flows. Also, in certain service areas where international

11. Statement on The Trade in Services Act of 1982, in Hearings on Trade in Services before the Subcomm. on Intl. Trade of the Senate Comm. on Finance, 97th Cong., 2d Sess. 136–37 (1982).

arrangements once protected international commerce, for example, in the acquisition and protection of industrial property rights, the traditional protections are being eroded and ignored.

Major types of barriers to trade in services, both barriers to "international trade" and to "establishment" can be grouped as follows:

Interference with access to market. The provision of a service may be blocked by a country prohibiting across-the-border importation of a service and/or by denying the foreign service enterprise the right of establishment. Other less blatant protectionist practices—for example, discriminatory licensing and registry of foreign service firms—can have the same effect of blocking market access.

Interference with transactions and financial structure. Regulatory practices can be used to slow or block international transactions by foreign service firms. Discriminatory taxation or tariffs may create barriers. Issuance of foreign exchange can be denied both to service firms and to clients purchasing a service. Unreasonable discriminatory requirements may be applied to capital structure, ownership and financial management of establishments.

Interference with access to production inputs. Foreign service firms may be denied access to necessary equipment; visa restriction may limit access to foreign personnel or access to producer services sourced outside the importing economy may be denied. Or, access may be restricted by local content requirements, performance requirements, or employment quotas. Proprietary information, industrial property rights, processes, or know-how used by a firm may not be protected.

Interference with marketing. Sales by foreign service enterprises may be subject to quotas or restrictions which limit their range of commercial activity. Technical or other standards may be used to block foreign services sales. Marketing practices by foreign service firms may be curtailed or prohibited. Government procurement opportunities may be denied. Contract arrangements with local customers may be unenforceable. Monopolistic arrangements by local private sector companies may, with official cognizance, close a service market to foreign competitors or official policies may also restrict sales to national or other selected companies.

Trade-distorting government behavior. The provision of most services is heavily regulated and this offers great opportunity for interference with the trade of foreign service companies through discriminatory, protectionist behavior by regulators. Protectionist regulatory behavior may be formal, based upon law or written regulation, or it may be achieved indirectly through pettifogging, delay or other arbitrary practices by officials. Also, government-controlled services or government facilities that are made available to local competitors may be denied to foreign firms or made available on less favorable terms. Subsidization of national service firms can skew competition in domestic markets and in third country markets. Such subsidization may make it possible for the national firm to offer its services at prices that would otherwise be uneconomic and to sustain the operating loss for indefinite periods of time.

RAYMOND J. KROMMENACKER, WORLD–TRADED SERVICES: THE CHALLENGE FOR THE EIGHTIES

41–42 (1983) [12]

In most instances, government intervention in restricting the flow of world-traded services is motivated by the same factors that are present in its intervention in goods trade. First, the employment argument justifies restrictions by maintaining the level of employment or minimizing the pressures toward unemployment. This argument appears to be a major factor behind government intervention, even if it is not listed openly by the authorities. Restrictions for employment are spread throughout the service sectors.

Second, the monetary and balance-of-payments control argument provides economic justification for restricting services. This argument is also used for justifying the limitation or prohibition of foreign investment. In insurance, for example, it is often argued by developing countries that foreign companies reinsure a higher percentage of their business abroad than do national companies, thus utilizing valuable foreign exchange. Analogous arguments are made for banking and other foreign services companies, such as construction/engineering, computers, and communications, which unnecessarily use foreign exchange to purchase technical, managerial, and other services from their parent firms.

Third, the infant-industry argument states that small industries do not have the experience or economies of scale to compete with large established firms. Thus if they are to expand enough to become competitive, they must be protected in their home markets through high tariffs or some other form of protection that restricts foreign competition. This argument is widely used by developing countries to justify protecting their merchant marine, insurance business, as well as other services. In the case of developed countries, although the infant-industry argument is not used to defend protection against foreign penetration in well-established traditional service industries, it is used to limit foreign penetration of new service sectors such as telematics.

Fourth, the argument of protecting domestic consumers from risk is defended by public administrators against foreign bankers and insurers, who are told that the financial sector must be highly regulated to protect consumers and the general public. Similar arguments are used to control franchising or leasing facilities and the activities of professionals such as doctors, lawyers, accountants, and engineers. Consumers can be either private or legal persons, firms, or state-trading enterprises that the public administration seeks to protect through the mandatory surveillance of all or part of imports at the place of expedition.

Fifth, the national security argument asserts that a nation must control a specific service industry on national security grounds. Limitations on foreign participation in communications exist in many developed countries. Cabotage laws restrict coastal shipping to national vessels. In developing countries, the justification is that certain service industries should be domestically owned and controlled. In other words, foreign competition should not be allowed to dominate vital national industries.

Sixth, the cultural and social sensitivities' argument will be invoked more and more frequently in connection with the foreseeable growing impact of television satellites. This argument—which is the only one of the six that is noticeably more important for services than for goods—is often used to impose restrictions on international activities of motion pictures and television programs. Several countries have extended this argument to the activities of the advertising industry because of its relationship to the media.

U.S. NATIONAL STUDY ON TRADE IN SERVICES, A SUBMISSION BY THE UNITED STATES GOVERNMENT TO THE GENERAL AGREEMENT ON TARIFFS AND TRADE
37–39 (1982)

CONCEPTUAL ISSUES RELATED TO TRADE IN SERVICES

In examining issues surrounding services and trade in services, a number of generic issues common to many service sectors call for specific attention. Discussion of these issues may help conceptualize general principles, rules and procedures as they relate to trade in services.

Three questions regarding generic issues are considered in this section. First, how should competition between private service firms and public service monopolies be managed? This problem arises much more in services than in goods because many countries provide services through public monopolies in order to regulate service industries. Second, to what extent can trade in services and investment in services be distinguished and how important is it to be able to make that distinction clear? The answer to this question is significant as service firms may find it necessary to establish operations (i.e. invest) in the countries to which they export. In order to properly manage issues that affect service exports, countries must determine whether they should be dealt with as investment or trade problems. Third, to what extent is it necessary for countries to allow the movement of labor in order to make it possible for service companies to export? Because services are closely linked to people and the knowledge and experience they possess and because countries are sensitive to the movement of people across their borders, appropriate, balanced treatment of conflicting goals concerning immigration, employment, and trade in services is desirable.

A. *Competition Between Private Firms and Government Monopolies*

Many important service industries are highly regulated by national governments because the services they supply are perceived as vital to national sovereignty, well-being, and security. Indeed, many countries provide such critical services through government-owned or controlled monopolies. * * *

There are three main issues concerning competition between public and private service firms. The first concerns competition between public service monopolies and private service firms outside the national borders of the country involved. Problems arise, in particular, in transborder services between one country and another. The monopoly position at home inevitably gives public service monopolies an unequal advantage vis-a-vis private competitors from other countries in transborder services such as aviation and telecommunications. The monopolies can use their dominant position in their home market to disadvantage their foreign private competitors. Also, the allocation of rates or fees for international services are frequently established through negotiations between domestic and foreign carriers. Where this results in a negotiation between a monopoly on one side and competing foreign firms on the other side, questions can arise concerning the equity of the outcome.

Another type of issue concerns the supply of services by a public service monopoly to foreign firms. In some cases, domestic monopolies have charged foreign firms higher fees for services rendered, or have provided foreign firms a lower quality service than that provided domestic firms. These types of issues become particularly acute when the domestic monopoly also happens to be a competitor. For example, a national airline which owns the ground servicing monopoly can put competing foreign airlines at a distinct disadvantage through a variety of discriminatory practices.

A third type of issue concerns competition between public service monopolies and private foreign firms in service activities outside the scope of the domestic monopoly. There has been a growing tendency to allow public service monopolies to compete with other firms in providing services not covered by the monopoly. In such competition, the public service monopolies can use their inherent power to disadvantage foreign private competition.

In each of these areas, the issue is whether monopolies should be required to adopt an arms-length relationship between its monopoly activities and its activities as a competitor internationally, as a competitor domestically in other services, and as a supplier of services.

B. Distinguishing Trade in Services From Investment in Services

Governments have traditionally separated trade issues from investment issues, developing separate disciplines in each area. Trade rules, covering "the right to sell" abroad, have tended to be more comprehensive than investment rules. If countries are to embark on the formulation of rules for trade in services, they must know whether this can be done in a meaningful way without dealing with the more sensitive issue of investment in services.

In order to separate trade and investment issues, countries must be capable of distinguishing between the services, or the component of services, which is traded (i.e., produced abroad) and the services, or the component of a service which can only be produced locally. Thus, for example, data processing services provided by a foreign computer center through long-distance communication links is clearly trade. Data processing services provided locally by a foreign-owned computer processing facility is an investment activity.

An important issue with respect to the distinction between trade and investment concerns the distribution system. Under traditional trade concepts the question of access to the distribution system or to service/maintenance facilities is a trade issue, while ownership of the distribution system is an investment issue. Under the principles of the GATT, a product which has overcome the legitimate barriers at the border is entitled to full national treatment, i.e., there is an obligation to treat a foreign producer in the same manner as a domestic producer. Thus, a foreign producer is entitled to the same access to the domestic distribution system as a domestic producer. For example, a foreign manufacturer of autos, who has paid the tariff at the border, is entitled to have the same access to the domestic distribution system as a domestic manufacturer.

The existing GATT approach to the distribution system could be applied to trade in services. Thus, access to a local distribution system would be treated as a trade issue, while ownership of the distribution system would be treated as an investment issue. Access to the distribution system would include the right of a foreign supplier of services to negotiate a contract with local businesses to provide distribution or servicing facilities. Thus, for example, if the national treatment principle were adopted for trade in services, a foreign insurance company that was able to overcome the agreed restrictions at the border, would have a right to sign a contract with local insurance brokers or claims adjusters to sell their policies and to handle claims.

A somewhat different issue arises with respect to some service industries, such as insurance, over the matter of establishment. In a number of countries, domestic regulatory authorities require insurance companies to fully establish themselves legally before they are given a right to sell insurance to local residents. Establishment, in this case, is a requirement imposed in order to protect domestic policyholders; it is no different from any other regulatory requirement imposed by governments for the protection of local citizens, such as health, safety or environmental regulations. Under current trade rules covering trade in goods, the national treatment principle ensures that foreign producers of goods receive the same treatment under domestic regulations as domestic producers. If the national treatment principle were adopted for trade in services, a domestic regulation requiring legal establishment for insurance companies should be treated in the same way as any other domestic regulation. In other words, foreign insurance companies granted access to the local market under trade rules, would have a right to establish themselves legally under the national treatment principle.

A still different issue arises in the context of professional services, in particular professional services that require a local presence. The sale of professional services which are to be provided locally is not a trade issue as such, while the sale of professional services produced outside the importing country is clearly a trade issue. Thus, the purchase of engineering services produced outside the importing country by a foreign engineering firm would clearly be a trade issue. The establishment of a local engineering practice by a foreign engineer would not be a trade issue. Locally delivered professional services, however, could have a trade component as well as a non-trade component and trade rules would apply to the traded component. A fully accredited local engineer could, for example, establish a contractual relationship with a foreign engineering firm whereby that engineering firm would agree to provide certain engineering drawings or technical information. The drawings or information provided by the foreign engineering firm would clearly be trade. Or if the issue is put the other way, foreign suppliers of services given access to the local market under trade rules would have the right to contract with fully accredited local professionals to deliver the service. In other words, local professionals, as local businessmen, could have the right under trade rules to buy expertise, support services from a foreign firm. Issues concerning a foreign-owned professional practice or the admission of foreign professionals to a domestic practice would not be covered by international trade rules.

While it is important for trade negotiating purposes to make a distinction between trade issues and investment issues, this does not imply that investment barriers are irrelevant to trade. Indeed, in many cases, the ability to invest in elements of the distribution system or in local enterprises can substantially enhance a firm's ability to export its services. In order to exploit these trade opportunities, parallel efforts need to be pursued in other fora to reduce foreign investment barriers. The OECD Code of Liberalization of Capital Movements, one such parallel effort, has expanded investment opportunities among developed countries. Furthermore, the Code is about to be amended to include those aspects of the right of establishment most closely related to direct investment. Another effort has been the negotiation of Bilateral Investment Treaties, particularly with developing countries. These treaties cover many areas of services; though here too, efforts will need to be undertaken to improve coverage.

C. IMMIGRATION, LABOR AND TRADE IN SERVICES

The ability of a company to conduct service business internationally depends, in many instances, on the ability of salesmen or professionals with specific skills to move across national borders. This is the case for trade in services, as it has been the case for trade in goods.

International trade depends on some movement of people. Those engaged in international sales and financing of goods frequently travel abroad to market their products, to locate sources of supply and to arrange transactions. Trade in services may depend even more heavily on the movement of people than trade in merchandise. Service professionals may have special expertise that is not available locally. For example, services industries have complained that foreign personnel that are needed to set up data processing systems, to audit financial records, to train or supervise workers and to transmit or use other special knowledge, skills, expertise or talent required for commercial activities are frequently unavailable.

These industries have expressed concern about personnel-type and professional-practice problems that exist in banking, insurance, law, engineering and construction, hotels/motels, telecommunications, data processing, accounting, advertising, franchising and health care. Among the complaints listed are work permit requirements for professional and technical personnel; minimum percentages of local nationals to be employed; hiring restrictions or quotas; citizenship or licensing requirements for foreign engineers, lawyers and other professionals.

* * *

Immigration laws that restrict the availability of many types of workers exist in many countries including the United States. * * *

The United States feels that it is unlikely that a general approach to visa or professional practice problems would be either feasible or desirable over the foreseeable future. Few, if any, countries are likely to be willing to open their borders to face international movement of people in a general way. Thus, while governments are willing to accommodate individual salesmen or professionals and while mechanisms have been developed through bilateral agreements to establish appropriate ground rules, no government has been willing to undertake generalized obligations vis-a-vis the world as a whole. This reluctance is due to a variety of political, social and cultural concerns which dominate national policymaking in this area, and which inevitably override trade concerns.

The United States does not believe that it would be useful or appropriate to negotiate immigration problems in a trade forum such as GATT nor does it believe that immigration rules should be subordinated to trade rules. Efforts to deal with disputes over the legitimacy of the rules governing the movement of labor should be dealt with under existing consular mechanisms.

(D) A PROPOSAL FOR A GENERAL AGREEMENT ON SERVICES

RAYMOND J. KROMMENACKER, WORLD–TRADED
SERVICES: THE CHALLENGE
FOR THE EIGHTIES

(1984) [13]

A General Agreement on services should theoretically provide for the basic GATT concepts as well as for new rules governing investments. The proposed General Agreement on services limits itself to a mechanism governing only trade in services. Such a "bottom-up" approach is suggested because it would provide a more effective way to get at a number of the real issues for many world-traded services in a less confrontational and charged atmosphere, with less likelihood of failure. Adequate links would ensure that the General Agreement on services embodies the principles, rules, and procedures of the enlarged nontariff measures agreements to world-traded services. This most promising approach would help in dealing with specific nontariff measures already legally covered by existing provisions. Finally, the major benefit of such an approach is that it would satisfy the need to

13. Copyright © 1984 Artech House, Inc., 610 Washington St., Dedham, MA 02026. Reprinted with permission from World-Traded Services: The Challenge for the Eighties by Raymond J. Krommenacker, pages 167–70. Dr. Krommenacker is a GATT counselor.

work toward general rules, as opposed to industry-specific rules, to govern world-traded services.

BASIC OBJECTIVES, PRINCIPLES, AND PROCEDURES

Basic Objectives. The trading nations would recognize that their relation in the field of trade and economic endeavor should be conducted with a view to raising standards of living, ensuring full employment, ensuring a large and steadily growing volume of real income and effective demand, developing the full use of the resources of the world, and expanding the production and exchange of goods and services. The trading nations would express their desire to contribute to these objectives by entering into reciprocal and mutually advantageous arrangements directed to the substantial reduction of barriers to trade and to the elimination of discriminatory treatment in international commerce.

PRINCIPLES

Most-Favored-Nation Principles

The most-favored-nation (MFN) principle would provide that any advantage, favor, privilege, or immunity granted by any contracting party should be accorded immediately and unconditionally to the world-traded services originating in or destined for the territories of all other contracting parties. The MFN principle would require any world-traded-services originating in any other country to be subject to equal treatment by the recipient nation as the one that is granted to the most favored nation.

National Treatment Principle

The national-treatment (NT) principle would mean that imported services would be accorded the same treatment as services of local origin with respect to matters under government control, such as taxation and regulation. If each signatory nation were to eliminate all distinctions between foreign services and domestic services, world-traded services would be liberalized and each country would retain control over those service industries that it feels should be regulated. A situation of reciprocity would thus amount to each government's treating foreign services on a basis no less favorable than that given to domestic firms.

More Favorable Treatment to Developing Countries

It may be necessary for developing countries not to apply the most-favored-nation principle as well as the national-treatment principle, to respond to their development, financial, and trade needs. The specific provisions of the differential and more favorable treatment, reciprocity, and fuller participation of developing countries, as agreed by GATT on 28 November 1979, would apply.

Procedures for Allowing National Preference on a Temporary Basis. The application of the MFN and NT principles to world-traded services requires a system that treats equally all foreign service industries while conceding a degree of national preference in certain strictly defined conditions. For traded goods, the method of preference is the tariff. Given the intangible nature of most of world-traded services and the fact that some service industries do not involve across-the-border trade, it is apparent that an import tax at the border—i.e., a tariff on world-traded services—is impracticable. Procedures for allowing a degree of national preference could not be based on tariff flexibility. Consequently, three types of instruments should be permitted for protection.

First, parties to the General Agreement on services should be allowed to apply temporary restrictions to the importation of world-traded services for balance-of-payments purposes. Parties would take these restrictions in accordance with the GATT declaration on trade measures taken for balance-of-payments purposes adopted on 28 November 1979. Second, a safeguard clause should also be included to permit injured countries to suspend their obligations under the MFN and NT clauses. A practical difficulty could be the drafting of such a safeguard clause to find agreed criteria for determining the conditions of application of the clause. Third, specific provisions should also take care of the special exceptions necessary for consumer, environmental, and security interests.

The General Agreement on World-Traded Services Linked with Enlarged Nontariff Measures Agreements and Sector Agreements. For the settlement of specific disputes relating to the maintenance of the nontariff measures in the field of subsidies, dumping, government procurement, customs valuation, and standards, recourse would be made to the existing nontariff measures agreements whose coverage would have been enlarged to include world-traded services. The question arises whether reference should also be made in the General Agreement on services to sectorial agreements dealing with trade barriers in specific service industries. If so, the General Agreement on services would represent the angular stone of an array of sectorial agreements, adapting its principles and procedures. These sectorial agreements could cover the following four areas of interest to a great number of trading-nations: (1) telecommunications, data processing, and information services, (2) insurance and reinsurance, (3) engineering, construction, and related consultancy services, and (4) motion pictures.

Benefits and Disadvantages. A General Agreement on services, which would establish for the first time an agreed international framework of rights and obligations in the area of world-traded services, would be a significant first step toward reducing protection to domestic services and suppliers, toward eliminating discrimination among foreign world-traded services and suppliers, toward providing transparency, and toward establishing international procedures on consultations, surveillance, and dispute settlement. The General Agreement on services would constitute a reference agreement in the context of the liberalization of world-traded services. Once agreed on, its basic objectives, principles, and procedures could be embodied in sectorial agreements where particular problems have to be considered on a general-rule basis as opposed to industry-specific basis.

Notes and Questions

(1) Is it practical to think in terms of one general agreement covering services (as GATT does trade)? Are the types of services too diverse for similar treatment (e.g., banking, insurance, legal services, etc.)? Even if theoretically

possible and desirable, would negotiations on such an agreement have a realistic chance of success? Would negotiations on a sector-by-sector basis be more likely to be successful? In the absence of a general agreement, do you think sector-by-sector agreements would be so diverse in their principles as to be undesirable in any event?

(2) Do you agree with Krommenacker that the GATT principles of most-favored-nation treatment and national treatment would be appropriately applied to trade in services?

(3) Although not all trade in services is subject to customs duties, services are sold and therefore could be subject to sales taxes. Would it be desirable to restrict a nation's right to protect its service industries to the levying of higher sales taxes on foreign-origin services? See Maffucci, Liberalization of International Trade in the Service Sector: Threshold Problems and a Proposed Framework under the GATT, 5 Fordham Intl.L.J. 371, 392–403 (1982). Could a sales tax be set so as to duplicate the degree of protection afforded by current non-tariff barriers? What problems might arise in defining foreign-origin services?

(4) To what extent is progress in liberalizing trade in services limited if concurrent liberalization in foreign investment and immigration does not occur? To what extent will increased trade in services occur if such liberalization does not occur?

(5) As suggested by the Gibbs article in subsection (B), the developing countries are particularly leary of liberalizing trade in services because of the dominant role that multinational enterprises play in international trade in services. As we will see in Chapter 17 infra, the developing countries have been active in attempting to regulate the activities of multinationals and may view negotiations on trade in services as undermining their efforts at such regulation.

SECTION 15.4   A CASE STUDY: INSURANCE

Insurance is one of the most important internationally traded services. It became of particular interest in 1985, when the Reagan Administration initiated a Section 301 action (see Section 10.5 supra) in respect of South Korea's restrictions on insurance services provided by U.S. companies.[1] The following catalog of restrictions is also of interest because it demonstrates the incredible range of restrictions that affect trade in services, from direct prohibitions to discriminatory policies in trade association memberships.

In studying the following extract, the reader should consider, inter alia, the following questions: (1) Should an international agreement applicable to trade in insurance be limited to the insurance sector or part of a broader agreement on trade in services? Why? (2) Should such an agreement distinguish between insurance related to international transactions and domestic transactions? If so, where should the line be drawn? (3) How should an agreement deal with the problem of establishing adequate financial reserves for insurance companies? In that regard, should there be a requirement that insurance companies, to avail themselves of the agreement's benefits, must invest a portion of their reserves in each country where they do business? Or are there other ways to assure access to such reserves in disputes over claims? (4) To what extent are the restrictions on

---

1. 50 Fed.Reg. 37609 (1985).

insurance related to general restrictions on foreign exchange and investment? Could an agreement on trade in services approximately cover these matters? How?

U.S. NATIONAL STUDY ON TRADE IN SERVICES, A SUBMISSION BY THE UNITED STATES GOVERNMENT TO THE GENERAL AGREEMENT ON TARIFFS AND TRADE
141–46 (1982)

Insurance is one of the most important international service industries. It represents the acceptance of a relatively large risk by the insurer in return for relatively small payment. By insuring a large number of similar risks, the insurer can calculate the likely claims that will be paid, and the required premium for each risk that will be necessary to meet those claims. Risks come in many different sizes and forms. No individual country has the insurance capacity necessary to efficiently cover all of the risks present in that country. This is the fundamental basis for the internationalization of insurance. While these principles have always applied, the economic development of modern societies has resulted in a radical increase in individual risks which must utilize international insurance capacity. Nuclear power plants and large off-shore oil and gas drilling complexes are just two examples of risks that have emerged in recent years that require extraordinary insurance capacity to provide the necessary security.

Some classes of insurance are inherently "international": (1) transport insurance, including marine and aviation; (2) bonding and insurance related to the provision, installation and performance of goods in international trade; (3) insurance of large risks associated with natural catastrophes and large industrial facilities; and (4) reinsurance. The many other classes of insurance which are less directly "international" in nature offer, however, commercial opportunities which should be accessible to foreign insurers or intermediaries which desire to enter the market.

In addition to underwriting risks, the industry provides a wide range of services to help control these risks such as loss control, inspection and actuarial services and to minimize the cost of losses including loss control, rehabilitation, and recovery, salvage and subrogation services. The industry also provides a range of savings and investment programs. Brokerage and agency services serve insurance consumers by efficiently allocating risks among underwriters.

International insurance has grown and diversified as an essential part of the expansion of trade, worldwide industrialization, technological progress and economic development. Worldwide insurance premium value (excluding the Communist Bloc) totaled $450 billion in 1981, of which approximately 42 percent is attributable to life and 58 percent to nonlife business. This business was transacted by approximately 10,000 domestic companies and 3,000 branch offices abroad. About 95 percent of worldwide premium was produced by the OECD nations. The 5 percent of world premium attributable to nonindustrial countries has doubled since 1950. Overall, the growth of insurance has exceeded the pace of global economic development.

Insurers conduct business in foreign markets through branch offices, local subsidiaries, joint ventures, brokers and independent agents. In addition, insurers may conduct "home-foreign" insurance, i.e. insurance written in the home country of the company on risks located abroad. Each of the different forms of operations has advantages and disadvantages. Generally, insurance can be provided most efficiently when the insurer has the freedom to choose its method of operation based on its own assessment of how it can best serve the market rather than on government strictures on form of operation.

It is generally accepted that some control or regulation of insurance is necessary to protect against financially unsound operations and to ensure fairness of contract terms and performance. The degree and nature of such regulation varies among countries according to the composition, regional organization and operation of the market, differing perceptions of the need for protection of various types of insurers, and differing national attitudes toward governmental intervention in the economy and public administration in general.

The need for reasonable regulation and regulatory practices is not questioned. However, there are a wide variety of nontariff measures in law, regulation and administrative practice which discriminate against foreign insurance, insurers, reinsurers and intermediaries which have a protectionist or unnecessary "chilling" effect upon international trade in insurance. A wide variety of barriers exist which unreasonably restrict international commerce in insurance. Because of this, insurers find it increasingly difficult to gain access to foreign markets, to operate to full capacity in such markets or to enjoy competitive opportunity equivalent to that of domestic insurers. The discussion below examines the main types of obstacles to insurance services, the impact of these obstacles and suggests various means by which these problems can be pursued internationally.

BARRIERS TO TRADE IN INSURANCE

Barriers may be grouped into three general categories as they relate to: (1) access to market and establishment; (2) transactions and financial operations; and (3) equivalent competitive position. (Restrictions on reinsurance and transportation insurance are described separately.)

a. Restrictions on Access to Market and Establishment.

Denial of Market Access: Some governments do not allow any foreign participation in their insurance market, substantially restrict it, or are in the process of eliminating foreign participation. The most prevalent restriction on insurance placement requires that a particular line of insurance be purchased within the domestic market. In more severe cases, which are not uncommon, a prospective buyer must not only purchase locally, but with locally owned insurance firms or a state insurance agency (thereby excluding foreign admitted insurers). Regulations which restrict insurance placement involve many lines of general and life insurance.

Government Policies which Discourage Nationals from Purchasing Insurance From Foreign Entities: While "technically" permitting foreign insurers to compete, many governments carry out policies which effectively discourage nationals from placing insurance with foreign firms. A common restriction of this type is the assessment of a tax on insurance placed outside the local market (and in some cases with foreign-admitted insurers). Similarly, some governments discourage insurance placement with foreign entities by not allowing domestic policy-holders to charge premiums paid to foreign insurers as tax deductible business expenses (although such concessions exist for premiums paid to domestic insurers), or by treating claims received on insurance policies placed outside the local markets as income and thus subject to tax.

Another method is the prohibition or restriction on the placement of insurance through foreign intermediaries (brokers and agents). Such restrictions are commonly employed in markets which also limit the operations of foreign insurers. Typically in such a market, local companies operate only through paid staff agents. Accounts are coinsured or reinsured with other local companies. Thus foreign companies are effectively frozen out of participation in the market through local entities. By prohibiting or restricting foreign intermediaries, the market can be almost completely closed to foreign competition.

Arbitrary and Discriminatory Licensing Procedures: Licensing is the primary means used by governments to regulate insurers. Before an insurance company can operate within a market, it must obtain a license for each line of insurance it desires to sell. Arbitrary and discriminatory licensing procedures have been vigorously applied by some governments as a means of denying foreign participation (or additional foreign participation) in the market, either totally or with respect to certain lines of insurance. Such practices often discourage foreign firms from applying for licenses.

Characteristics of such discrimination vary but may include: (1) denial of a license to a qualified foreign branch or subsidiary; (2) grant of a license for only limited classes of business, in particular, classes deemed unprofitable or undesirable by local insurers; (3) absence of adequate written regulations or regulatory procedures, leaving extensive opportunity to use administrative discretion for protectionist purposes in considering licensing requests; (4) difficulty in obtaining an explanation as to the reasons an application to obtain a license has been denied; (5) lack of an administrative appeal process in cases of licensing requests being denied; (6) extensive delays in processing an application to obtain a license; and (7) failing to process an application to obtain a license.

Discrimination Against Foreign Branch Operations: Branch offices have traditionally been the predominant mode of operations for insurance companies in foreign markets. In recent years, some governments have moved to forbid and/or eliminate foreign branches by prohibiting any further establishment of branch operations and requiring the local incorporation of existing branches. Other forms of discrimination may include delays in granting licenses for branch operations, and blatantly discriminatory taxation of branches vis-a-vis local corporations, and arbitrary restrictions on the freedom of foreign branches to offer new products.

Forced Localization: In most instances, mandatory local incorporation is accompanied by national majority ownership requirements. Governments can also force localization through discriminatory regulatory policies (e.g., taxes, capital requirements) which make it impossible to stay in business in branch form. If a government has prohibited further foreign investment in insurance, it can, over the long run, force divestment of foreign holdings even without officially requiring it. One way is to raise capital requirements—requirements foreign insurers cannot comply with because additional investment is prohibited. To meet such capital requirements, a foreign investor must attract national investors and in the process dilute his percentage of ownership.

b. Restrictions on Transactions and Financial Operations.

Restrictions on Remittances: A common practice in a number of insurance markets is a system of exchange control which unreasonably restricts the remittance of funds by insurers, intermediaries or the insured. These practices may take the form of denial of foreign exchange needed; procedural and processing delays in obtaining permission from local authorities to carry out the transfer; or prohibition upon payments of component parts of an insurance transaction.

Discriminatory Deposit or Capital Requirements Placed on Foreign-Admitted Insurers: It is an accepted regulatory policy to require that insurance companies operating in a market meet and maintain a minimum deposit requirement. In a number of markets, however, the amount of the deposit, the form, or the manner in which it is held, is more stringent on the foreign company than on the domestic company. Foreign-admitted insurers may also be subject to higher requirements than domestic firms and more stringent solvency criteria.

Discriminatory Taxation of Foreign-Admitted Insurers: In a number of countries, various taxes, including income and premium taxes, fall more heavily on foreign-admitted insurers than on local insurance companies. In the case of income tax, foreign-admitted insurers may be required to pay a higher level of tax or have their taxes computed on a different, more costly, basis than local companies. Other discriminatory forms of taxation may include taxes on premiums paid to foreign insurers or taxation of indemnity payments as income from abroad. The higher taxes can have substantial impact on relative prices for insurance coverage, making the foreign insurer uncompetitive.

c. Restrictions on Competitive Equality.

Discrimination in Government Procurement: A number of governments require that the insurance procured by government departments, local authorities, state corporations, other government related organizations and government contractors be placed only with local insurance companies owned by local citizens.

Exclusion of Foreign-Admitted Insurers: From Trade Associations: In many countries, trade associations provide a critical link to local regulators and market information. The exclusion of foreign companies from participation in such associations places them at a severe disadvantage vis-a-vis domestic firms. Membership in such associations also may give added prestige or credibility to the insurance company.

Restrictions on the Employment of Non-Nationals: To be competitive, it is necessary that a foreign insurance company have management, professional, and technical expertise adequate to relate local needs to its worldwide experience and accumulated insurance know-how. This is an important and often essential dimension of competition with local firms which often have superior personal contacts, market relationships, etc. Thus, it is often necessary to complement local management and technical personnel with personnel from elsewhere within a firm or from its home office. Restrictions or unreasonable delays in obtaining work permits often act as barriers to the provision of efficient insurance services.

d. Restrictions on Reinsurance and Transportation Insurance.

Reinsurance: Restrictions on reinsurance placement may take many forms. Most common are compulsory internal cessions of reinsurance transactions. In some instances, governments require a fixed percentage of all reinsurance to be ceded to private companies within the local market. In other instances, reinsurance must first be offered to local companies before it can be placed outside. Some countries have established national or regional reinsurance institutions and require that all or part of reinsurance cessions made by companies be placed with the designated reinsurance entity. Other factors which may inhibit placement of reinsurance abroad include disallowance of credit for solvency computation purposes of reinsurance placed with a non-admitted insurer, and restrictions on the remittance of funds overseas.

Transportation Insurance: Some countries have applied restrictions specifically to transport insurance. These restrictive practices range from requiring that all imports, and, in some cases, all exports be insured within the domestic market, to financial incentives (usually tax or foreign exchange regulations) which benefit the domestic market.

* * *

POSSIBLE STRATEGIES FOR RESOLVING PROBLEMS

The proliferation of impediments to international insurance operations makes it essential to counter current protectionist trends and remove some of the uncertainty insurers face when seeking to expand overseas. A strategy for liberalizing insurance trade must recognize the special nature of insurance and the concomitant requirement for some level of government intervention. Insurance is essentially a contract for payment in the future. Generally, its fiduciary character makes it a legitimate subject of government regulation to guarantee performance. However, such regulation should be reasonable and not be used to protect domestic markets from foreign competition. Elements of specific concern to the insurance industry that should be considered in a multilateral understanding include the following:

MARKET ACCESS

The thrust of efforts internationally should be to obtain, perhaps through an agreement on insurance, acceptance of the principle of the right of access to domestic markets, subject to adherence to legitimate local regulatory requirements. "Access" would mean basically the right to sell policies within the guidelines established earlier in this study dealing with trade and investment. A multilateral arrangement might commit governments to establish guidelines that ensure fair and equitable access to local markets, taking into account the sovereignty of domestic regulatory procedures. Once access is gained, national treatment would be the operative principle.

REINSURANCE AND TRANSPORT INSURANCE

Although reinsurance and transport insurance could be included in a broader insurance code, it may be possible to negotiate some form of multilateral understanding in these sectors that would reflect their inherently international character. Transport insurance is, by nature, international business, covering the movement of imports and exports. The basic concept underlying reinsurance is the spread of large risks among companies and geographically. The objective of a multilateral understanding should be open competition and complete freedom of choice for the placement of reinsurance and the purchase of transport insurance. It might also be desirable to include special provisions to take into account the protection of "infant" insurance industries in certain countries, and to allow some method of graduation as local companies develop expertise and markets. In addition, provisions might be included that would subject state-owned or controlled insurance organizations to the same competitive pressures as market-oriented firms.

INVISIBLES AND ESTABLISHMENT

The insurance sector shares many of the same problems related to establishment in foreign countries as other business sectors. The objective for work in this area would be to allow the greatest freedom possible to respond to market forces without government-induced distortions. Although each government has the right to determine the conditions under which foreign firms will be permitted entry, national treatment would govern once establishment is attained. The current effort in the OECD to revise the insurance Annex of the Code of Current Invisibles Operations illustrates some of the establishment issues of particular concern to insurers:

- freedom of choice to operate in the form in which they wish to be established (subsidiary, branch or agency);

- transparency with respect to authorization procedures, market needs tests, and the cause for refusal of authorization; and

- deadlines for action on applications for authorization.

In addition, the OECD Code of Liberalization of Capital Movements, as it relates to right of establishment, may provide a basis for further work on that issue with respect to insurance and other services. Any discussion should consider the specific ideas being generated by the OECD Insurance Committee, which has examined difficulties in performing insurance business abroad in a thorough and systematic manner.

REGULATION

Another area where international efforts would be beneficial is the regulatory area. Government regulations on insurance have the purpose of affecting the quality, performance and safety of insurance services. These regulations are similar to government-mandated standards for the characteristics of a product. There already exists an international agreement concerning product standards, the GATT Standards Code, whose purpose is to ensure that signatory governments do not prepare, adopt or apply standards in a manner that would create obstacles to trade. It might be possible to build on this concept for insurance regulations and incorporate provisions for national treatment (or competitive equality), transparency, notification and surveillance, and dispute settlement.

The concept of national treatment, as employed in FCN treaties and the OECD Declaration on International Investment of 1976, means that foreign insurance companies, for example, are allowed to compete on essentially equal terms with domestic insurers in the host country, even if some specific regulations or requirements applied to foreign insurers differ from those affecting domestic insurers. National treatment in this sense is not necessarily the same as assuring competitive equality.

Equality of competitive opportunity focuses on the opportunity provided by rules and regulations, rather than the equality of the rules themselves. Sometimes laws and regulations applied equally to foreign and domestic companies may have a differentially adverse impact on foreign companies due to the nature of their operations. (For example, uniform controls on foreign exchange may be more burdensome for foreign insurers.) Government policy should seek de facto national treatment, not simply de jure national treatment.

A multilateral understanding should also require an adequate degree of transparency of regulations and their application. For example, insurers would be able to find out who applies insurance laws and regulations, and their criteria for making decisions. Officials would be available to answer the questions of foreign insurers and help them understand the domestic insurance regulatory system. Copies of relevant laws and regulations should be easily available.

With regard to notification and surveillance and dispute settlement, countries could set up an internal process for monitoring the complaints of foreign insurers. They might, for example, agree to notify other signatories before introducing new regulations or changing old ones, and give the other parties a chance to comment on the proposals. The dispute settlement mechanism of such an arrangement might begin with bilateral consultation between the parties involved. If bilateral discussions do not result in resolution of the dispute, discussions and appropriate actions might be taken by a broader group of countries that have accepted the provisions of the understanding.

SECTION 15.5 INTERNATIONAL LEGAL SERVICES [1]

U.S. NATIONAL STUDY ON TRADE IN SERVICES, A SUBMISSION BY THE UNITED STATES GOVERNMENT TO THE GENERAL AGREEMENT ON TARIFFS AND TRADE

148 (1982)

The demand for international legal services has grown considerably over the past three decades due to increased international business transactions and the greater interdependence of the world economy. As a result, foreign lawyers have sought to establish themselves in major cities throughout the world. Law firms maintain offices in foreign countries primarily to provide host country clients with advice on laws and regulations concerning the law firms' home country. They also oversee legal matters of home country clients involved in business transactions in the host country. This is often done in association with a local law firm.

Provisions of legal services in foreign countries, however, have not always been possible, or attainable without great difficulty. Governments have legitimate interest in strictly regulating who may provide legal services and in determining their qualifications, but may also carry a bias against foreigners.

IMPEDIMENTS TO TRADE IN LEGAL SERVICES

Impediments to trade in legal services occur in the following areas:

a. Denial of Access to Market. Foreign law firms wishing to establish an office to provide international legal services are often unable to do so in many countries. The fundamental obstacle to establishment is that foreign lawyers are subject to exactly the same regulations and qualifications as nationals involved in domestic legal practice. Most problems in this regard center around admission to the bar. In most countries, admission to the local bar is required in order to use the title of lawyer and to engage in law practice. The most direct obstacle to local bar admission is the requirement of citizenship. In most countries, one cannot take the bar examination without being a citizen.

Some countries do provide to foreign lawyers the opportunity to be "legal advisers". Legal advisers, while not being able to represent clients in court proceedings, can engage in direct legal consultation. The legal adviser status would, in fact, satisfy the needs of most foreign lawyers who are only seeking to provide direct legal consultation. However, the requirements for legal adviser in most nations are very difficult to meet. They often require considerable local education or training.

b. Restrictions on Entering into Partnership with Local Attorneys. Some countries prohibit local lawyers from partnership or associations with

---

1. See generally Issues of Transnational Legal Practice, 7 Mich.Y.B.Intl. Legal Studies (1985); S. Cone, The Regulation of Foreign Lawyers (3d ed. 1984); D. Campbell (ed.), Transnational Legal Practice (1982); Kosugi, Regulation of Practice by Foreign Lawyers, 27 Am.J.Comp.L. 678 (1979).

foreign lawyers. In other countries, associations are permitted, but only with the foreign lawyer in a subservient role. Local attorneys are not normally permitted to work for, or under, foreign attorneys, nor are foreign lawyers allowed to become partners in local firms.

———

Various bar associations, including the American Bar Association and the Association of the Bar of the City of New York, have expended considerable efforts to cause the relaxation of foreign rules hindering the practice of U.S. lawyers abroad. In part because of the particular interest of New York City law firms in such practice, and the need to show that the United States allowed what it was asking other nations to allow, New York State has liberalized its rules on the admission to the bar of non-U.S. citizens and foreign-trained lawyers. For example, to accommodate the desire of foreign lawyers to give legal advice in New York on matters involving their national law, the status of legal counsellor was created.[2]

2. N.Y.Ct.App.R. 521.

Chapter 16

INTERNATIONAL REGULATION OF NATIONAL CONTROLS ON INTERNATIONAL INVESTMENT

SECTION 16.1 INTRODUCTION

(A) INTRODUCTION TO CHAPTERS 16–19 [1]

Thus far, the focus of this book has been on the interrelationship of international agreements and institutions and national measures and institutions that promote, inhibit or prohibit international trade in goods. A discussion of international trade relations would not be complete, however, without examining more closely national and international measures that regulate the persons engaged in producing and selling the goods that are traded. Clearly, the pattern of international trade will be influenced by national decisions that promote, inhibit or otherwise regulate the establishment in a particular country of sales agencies, distributorships, servicing centers or production facilities associated with or owned by enterprises engaged in international trade. In addition, trade flows will be affected by national decisions on how to tax activities related to international trade, by national rules on what constitutes acceptable business practice—such as rules banning anticompetitive behavior and by national laws on the protection of intellectual property created abroad and owned by foreigners.

The potential impact on trade flows of such regulations is easy to see. For example, if a U.S. exporter opens a manufacturing plant outside the United States, it may no longer export the particular product produced to the country where the plant is located. Indeed, it may instead begin to import that product into the United States. On the other hand, if the plant produces only components of a product, it may be that the U.S. company will simply import the components into the United States, assemble the product in the United States and then sell or export it as before. However, if the foreign plant represents only one of several stages of manufacture, the U.S.

---

1. In addition to the materials cited in this chapter and Chapter 17, see generally G. Schwartzenberger, Foreign Investment and International Law (1969) (extensive bibliography).

company may export other components to the foreign plant and then import the still unfinished product back into the United States for completion. As a consequence, an investment in a plant abroad may have a multitude of effects. Traditional trade flows may be eliminated, or they may remain at the same level but flow differently or the flows may increase. In particular, if a company is able to produce its product more efficiently as the result of using a foreign plant, it may be able to lower the price and increase total sales of its product. National rules regulating investments in manufacturing plants would obviously impinge on a decision to open such a plant. Such rules could operate to encourage such investment—for example, by restricting sales agencies or distributorships, thus encouraging local production facilities or by providing incentives to promote such investments. On the other hand, national rules may discourage such investments by requiring that local residents be allowed to participate in the investment or by imposing other conditions on the making of such investments that a potential investor might find burdensome.

In the next four chapters, we consider the issues raised by national laws regulating international investment, multinational enterprises, restrictive business practices and taxation. Because of the limited nature of our discussion, we will limit our examination of national regulation to a brief review of the controls typically applied and will focus on existing and proposed international standards and agreements restricting national regulation. Some of the issues that we will consider are raised in the problem set out below. In addition, the problem suggests how the international trading rules discussed in Part II are related to the issues we consider in the next four chapters.

In studying the next chapters, the reader should focus, in particular, on how the national controls described affect trade flows, and thereby impact upon trade agreements reached in GATT, and on what the most desirable and practical form of international regulation of a particular subject would be: multilateral convention, "side" agreement to GATT, a network of bilateral agreements or nonmandatory codes. The various non-GATT related groups that are likely candidates for providing a forum for negotiations on many of these topics are described in Sections 2.1 and particularly 5.3(B) supra.

Problem

United Japan (UJ) has developed an advanced model personal computer (PC), which it wishes to sell in the U.S. market. A dozen U.S. companies dominate the U.S. market. While the capital investment needed to build a plant to produce PCs is moderate, considerable resources for research and development are necessary to keep abreast of technological changes. Moreover, for success in marketing it is necessary to have (or have access to) an extensive distribution and service network, and to sell a PC that is able to use the most popular software.

(1) United Japan would prefer to make the key components of its PC in Japan. This would enable it to monitor quality control most effectively, and while it would require an expansion of its Japanese facilities, UJ understands

that it could obtain "cheap" credit and certain tax incentives for expanding its production facilities from local authorities and from the national government to the extent that it equips the plant with modern robots and that it could write-off immediately against profits most of its startup costs. Exporting the key components from Japan would also enable UJ to take advantage of government export credits. UJ is less concerned about where the PC is assembled. It would prefer to have sufficient control over distribution and, particularly, servicing so as to foster an image of a high quality product and to maintain high quality standards. Given UJ's preferences, what alternatives are available to it in determining how to market its PC in the United States? What trade-related issues should be considered? (In particular, consider customs law issues, the availability of subsidies for investment, the existence of Buy-American laws, the possible reaction of U.S. manufacturers and the remedies available to them, the applicable tax laws, etc.) In light of your analysis of these issues, would you recommend any particular changes in UJ's plans? How would your answers probably differ if the target market was a developing country?

(2) United Japan believes that its home market is relatively secure because of the specialized software it has developed to appeal specifically to Japanese consumers. As a consequence, it believes it can sell its PC in Japan for a higher price than in the United States. Indeed, it may need to do so to finance its expansion into the U.S. market. How should this fact affect its manufacturing and marketing strategy?

(3) United Japan has had preliminary contact with a significant U.S. manufacturer of PCs. The U.S. manufacturer has an excellent distribution and servicing network. Its own principal product is less sophisticated than the UJ PC so it is interested in expanding the scope of its product line. Among the possibilities being considered by the two companies are a joint venture company that would market (and perhaps assemble) the UJ PC in the United States. The parties have considered a 10 year venture, renewable by agreement, and intend to agree not to compete with the joint venture in North America or Europe, where the joint venture hopes to market the UJ PC. What practical and legal problems may arise in connection with such a venture? You should consider, in addition to the issues discussed in the prior questions, such issues as whether and how such a venture could be structured to meet UJ's desire for control (keeping in mind that the U.S. company views itself as an equal partner) and the legality and practicality of the type of restrictions on competition and marketing that the companies want to impose. The organizational form of the joint venture should also be considered, as well as tax consequences of choosing one form over another.

(4) One of United Japan's principal concerns is that whatever operation is established it should remain sufficiently "Japanese" so as to help maintain the PC's image as a quality product and to ease supervision of U.S. activities from Tokyo. How does this desire restrict the choice of strategies that would be available to UJ? How might U.S. law restrict the ability of UJ to keep the operation a "Japanese" operation?

(5) If UJ sold a mass-produced, low-priced item whose appeal did not greatly depend on quality, what additional options might be available to UJ for commercializing its product in the United States?

(B) INTRODUCTION TO CHAPTER 16

In recent decades, there has been a substantial increase in the value of investments located in one country, but owned by nationals or corporations based in another country. The existence of and continued possibility of making such investments, which we will call "international investments," has a number of important consequences for international trade. First, in the case of certain goods and many services, it may be necessary as a practical matter to invest in a country before it is feasible to sell the goods or services there. This is, of course, true particularly of goods that need frequent maintenance and servicing by the seller and of services that must be rendered "on the spot." Second, the existence of investments in plants located in several countries that are owned by one entity—often referred to as a multinational enterprise (MNE)—may result in considerable trade between the members of the commonly controlled group. Indeed, it is estimated that a significant percentage of international trade takes place between components of MNEs. Third, the existence of MNEs can have important effects on international trade relations. When the principles of comparative advantage suggest that production should be shifted from one country to another, the shift occurs much more easily between the components of a single enterprise than when the shift requires that one enterprise go out of business. Moreover, in periods of international friction over trade matters, it may be very useful for exporters to defuse tensions by reducing their exports through investing in the importing country and performing some operations there.

For these trade-related reasons, as well as others, national controls on foreign investment have long been a concern in international relations. These controls take numerous forms, but they can be usefully categorized and studied as follows: First, there are direct controls on the making of investments—some countries prohibit virtually all foreign investment, others prohibit all foreign investment in certain sectors of the economy, others restrict foreign investment in amount or by requiring local partners to be given a substantial minority or controlling interest in the investment. Second, there are rules that govern the investor's financial relationship with the investment. In particular, these rules may specify the circumstances under which (i) payments may be made to the investor for goods sold or services provided to the investment and (ii) earnings from the investment, as well as the initial investment itself, may be paid to the investor. Third, there are limitations placed on the business activities of the investor and the investment. These restrictions may be imposed because international investments are often viewed with considerable suspicion by so-called host countries. From the perspective of the host country, decisions about investments controlled by foreign interests are made by persons with no special interest in the well being of the host country, even though their decisions may have serious consequences for the host country, for example, on employment levels and transfers of technology. These suspicions were heightened in recent years as scandals involving bribery by multinational enterprises came to light. As a consequence, there have been many national and multinational efforts to regulate the operation of multinationals enterprises generally by specifying the sorts of conduct that are deemed acceptable.

Finally, there is an issue that has frequently arisen when governments have changed—to what extent can the above rules be changed after the investment is made? In particular, if a government decides to nationalize the investment—to expropriate it—what compensation is due to the investor?

In this chapter, after reviewing materials on the recent history of international investment and the relationship between trade and investment, we consider the types of national regulation that impinge on international investments, many of which have been discussed in other sections. In this connection, we examine the use of bilateral investment treaties to regulate these matters. We then turn to attempts at multilateral regulation of international investment—particularly whether GATT should include such rules. Finally, we consider the international law principles relating to expropriation and alternatives to investment such as distribution and licensing agreements. In Chapter 17, we focus on multilateral efforts to control the behavior of MNEs.

(C) A HISTORICAL OVERVIEW OF INTERNATIONAL INVESTMENT

The following two studies published by the OECD outline the historical development of international investment. The reader should consider whether the fact that the form of international investment may be changing should affect bilateral and multilateral efforts to develop international rules regarding national controls on international investment.

OECD, INTERNATIONAL INVESTMENT AND MULTINATIONAL ENTERPRISES: RECENT INTERNATIONAL DIRECT INVESTMENT TRENDS

5–8, 11 (1981)[2]

[F]oreign investments have played an important role in the international economy since the latter part of the XIXth century. The majority of the earlier investments were in the form of portfolio investments in fix[ed]-interest loans and securities. The United Kingdom was the most important creditor nation, investing abroad up to 7 per cent of its GNP in the years preceding World War I. However, a few companies undertook direct investment and thereby established foreign productive operations during that period. The 1920s witnessed an increasing role of the United States as a source of foreign investment; and, in parallel, the rate of direct investment expanded to account for 25 per cent of total overseas lending. In the 1930s direct investment, especially from the United States to Europe, continued to grow but only slowly, while portfolio investment suffered the most from the severely depressed levels of economic activity. The economic climate for international investment improved dramatically after the Second World War and produced an upsurge of private investment, the majority of which was direct rather than portfolio capital. This was in particular the case for

2. Reprinted by permission of the Organization for Economic Cooperation and Development.

United States direct investment in Europe, as United States firms gradually moved in, in order to retain the markets they had established through trade in the immediate post-war period. International direct investment continued to expand in the 1950s, but the flows involved were not as important as those which were to develop in the 1960s, for in the earlier decade foreign investment activities were still hampered by remaining barriers to capital flows, including the non-convertibility of major currencies, which during the latter years of the 1950s were gradually reduced, particularly among the OECD member countries.

The period ranging from the early sixties to the mid-seventies witnessed a rapid development of international direct investment both in absolute terms and relative to the growth of other economic aggregates such as visible trade, domestic investment and GNP. The United States remained the dominant country of origin, although some European countries began to be more active as exporters of direct investment. International direct investment was heavily oriented towards developing sources of primary products and oil at the outset of the period. Later, an upsurge of direct investment in manufacturing developed in the OECD area due to a number of factors, including, in particular, the need for large firms to protect their markets developed through international trade but threatened, inter alia, by tariff cuts among members of custom unions and the growth of domestic firms in these markets.

*   *   *

Looking at some further indications of the growing economic importance of multinational enterprise activities, the order of magnitude of international production by United States-based multinationals, i.e. the production by branches and subsidiaries abroad, was roughly estimated to be some three times the value of United States exports in 1960; and by 1971 this ratio had increased to four times United States exports. In 1960 the same ratio of international production to exports was at a low level for both Germany and Japan but subsequently rose rapidly, reaching a value of approximately 2.5 by 1971.

The volume of intra-company trade which passed national frontiers also rose notably. There are few reliable figures on this, but as regards the United States it was estimated that, by the mid-1970s, imports by United States-based multinationals from their majority-owned foreign affiliates were close to 30 per cent of total United States imports. An analysis of the importance of intra-group trade in total international trade concluded that the percentages of the total due to intra-group trade were 22 per cent in 1966 and 25 per cent in 1970, excluding trade with centrally-planned economies.

If one looks at the activities of multinational enterprises from the side of the host countries, by the mid-to-late 1970s they occupied a significant share of total industrial activity. Thus, the share of foreign-controlled local enterprises in employment was reported to be above 15 per cent in the Federal Republic of Germany, Australia, Austria, Canada, France and Italy, while their share in manufacturing sales exceeded 20 per cent and sometimes even 30 per cent in many OECD countries. The relative weight of multinational enterprise affiliates was considerably greater than these averages in some sectors such as oil, electronics, chemicals and the automotive industries.

* * *

The period since the mid-seventies stands in quite sharp contrast with the period which preceded it in a number of important respects. At the overall level, the previously rapid and steady rise in direct investment flows has given way to a more moderate rate of growth. * * * At one and the same time a cause and a result of this break, the geographical and sectoral distributions of direct investment flows have changed. Technological and market factors and, to some extent also, home and, especially, host country policies have also contributed to this result.

CHARLES OMAN, NEW FORMS OF INTERNATIONAL INVESTMENT IN DEVELOPING COUNTRIES

11–12 (OECD Development Centre Studies, 1984) [3]

The 1970s witnessed a continued rapid expansion of international investment in developing countries. What is less certain is the significance of the growing diversity of forms which such investment has taken since the late 1960s/early 1970s. On the one hand there can be little doubt * * * that the amount of foreign direct investment (FDI) in developing countries has continued to grow. But it is equally clear that over the last decade or so not only has the flow of financial capital grown more rapidly than that of FDI, but also a variety of *new forms* of international investment has come to play an increasingly important role in the North-South context.

The term "new forms of investment" used in this study may be defined, generically, as international investments in which foreign investors do not hold a controlling interest via equity participation, that is, as investments in which foreign-held equity does not constitute majority ownership. More specifically, new forms of investment refer to:

    (a) joint international business ventures in which foreign-held equity does not exceed 50 per cent;

    (b) various international contractual arrangements which involve at least an element of investment from the foreign firm's viewpoint but which may involve no equity participation by that firm whatsoever, as is frequently the case with licensing agreements, management, service and production-sharing contracts, and occasionally with sub-contracting and turnkey operations.

The new forms of investment may be thought of as constituting a grey area between the "classic" international activities of firms, namely wholly/majority-owned foreign direct investment and exports. The new forms are rather heterogeneous, and can perhaps be defined most simply by distinguishing them from what they are not. They are not investments in majority-or wholly foreign-owned subsidiaries—which we refer to as the traditional form of foreign direct investment—nor are they bank lending or

---

3. Reprinted by permission of the Organization for Economic Cooperation and Development.

other purely financial operations, although these may be used to finance new forms of investment. * * *

In Chapter 2 we present three working hypotheses regarding overall trends in the use of new forms of investment and traditional FDI in the North-South context. One is that traditional FDI is becoming obsolete and is being replaced or superseded by new forms of investment; we argue that FDI data do not sustain this "obsolescence-of-FDI" hypothesis. A second hypothesis is that during the 1980s FDI may gain renewed importance in relation to international borrowing and "indebted industrialisation" in a number of developing countries, including many of the heavy borrowers of the 1970s. A third hypothesis is that there is emerging a new division of risks and responsibilities among the three principal sets of actors involved in international investment in developing countries—host-country élites, multinational firms and international lending organisations—such that the new forms of investment will continue to gain importance, if not actually supersede traditional FDI, in the North-South context over the coming years.

Chapter 3 summarises trends in the use of new forms of investment on a sectoral basis. It is in the extractive industries of petroleum and metals mining that one finds the strongest empirical support for both the first and third hypotheses. Evidence from the manufacturing industries is less clear-cut, both on the extent to which the new forms may be superseding traditional FDI, and the extent to which a new division of risks and responsibilities among the three major actors is superseding the traditional FDI "package" supplied and owned by multinational firms. Although it is clear that globally the new forms have gained increasing importance in manufacturing industries over the last ten to fifteen years, what stands out is the wide variation among host countries both as regards the importance of certain new forms relative to others, and as regards the importance of the new forms as a group relative both to traditional FDI and to gross industrial capital formation.

(D) THE INTERRELATIONSHIP BETWEEN INTERNATIONAL TRADE AND INVESTMENT

RACHEL McCULLOCH & ROBERT F. OWEN, LINKING NEGOTIATIONS ON TRADE AND FOREIGN DIRECT INVESTMENT

(1983) [4]

National policies toward foreign direct investment constitute an important class of nontariff trade distortions. Surprisingly, although the Tokyo Round of multilateral trade negotiations focused its efforts on nontariff barriers, the trade-distorting effects of policies toward foreign direct investment were largely ignored.

* * *

4. © 1983, Massachusetts Institute of Technology. Reprinted by permission of the publisher MIT Press, from C. Kindleberger & D. Audretsch (eds.), The Multinational Corporation in the 1980s 334, at 334, 343–46.

* * * Mutual gains from trade reflect an appropriate international division of labor, with production processes located according to comparative advantage. In recent decades, however, multinational corporations have become a primary vehicle for the "internationalization of production." Responding to differentials in cost and profitability world-wide, MNCs break down into many separate steps production processes that begin with extraction of raw materials and end with distribution and service of final products; each step in the complex operation is moved to the location most advantageous to the firm. The significance of multinational activities for international trade flows is obvious from available data. In the case of the United States, for example, approximately half of total exports involve multinational corporations, while a quarter consist of intra-corporate transactions and are thus potentially affected by MNC transfer-pricing policies.

TRADE BARRIERS AND FOREIGN DIRECT INVESTMENT

In a world without trade barriers or other distortions, the process of internationalization would imply not only that each good is produced at the location offering lowest cost, but that each step in its production is located so as to minimize overall cost of serving a particular market. Of course, under real-world conditions, production cost differentials reflecting comparative advantage are just one of several important factors determining the location of economic activity. Location decisions are also influenced by tariffs, quantitative trade restrictions, taxes, and subsidies, as well as by national policies toward foreign investment. Thus, changes in trade barriers may have important implications for direct investment decisions. Conversely, the efficiency and distributive effects of trade barriers depend crucially upon the extent of induced capital flows, so that policies toward foreign investment may have an important although indirect influence on the consequences of protection and the gains from trade liberalization.

Ultimately, the impact of tariffs and nontariff barriers, including restrictions on foreign direct investment, depends crucially on the degree to which foreign investment and trade are substitutes or complements. Initial evidence from research on the role of tariff levels in explaining the distribution of foreign investment across manufacturing industries in Australia, Canada, and Europe established the role of high tariffs or other barriers to trade as investment incentives for MNCs seeking to sell in the protected market. Likewise, the role of protection in attracting foreign investments to developing nations has been well documented in the literature evaluating import-substituting industrialization policies. However, several recent studies for Canada have found little support for the substitutability hypothesis, so that the overall evidence on this issue appears to be inconclusive.

Although the relationship between trade barriers and foreign investment has been used mainly as a way to explain differences in the extent of MNC activity across industries within a country, the same logic suggests that *discriminatory* trade barriers may promote investment flows between particular countries. Selective trade restrictions used by the United States to slow down the growth of its imports from Japan and certain other nations have undoubtedly contributed to the rapid growth of Japanese foreign investment in the United States, especially by firms that have already incurred substantial costs in developing a US market for their products. For similar reasons, Japanese firms may have accelerated their foreign investments in Asian developing countries not affected by voluntary export restraints and orderly marketing agreements on trade with the United States, resulting in faster relocation of production than would have occurred on the basis of changing relative costs alone.

*   *   *

TRADE BARRIERS AND THE COMPETITIVENESS OF MNCS

Because a key difference between MNCs and domestic firms is the degree of internationalization of production, changes in trade barriers will have important effects on their relative competitiveness. General reductions in trade barriers, such as those negotiated in the Kennedy and Tokyo Rounds, may increase incentives for foreign investment *globally* by allowing MNCs greater latitude for internationalization of production according to comparative advantage. Trade liberalization tends to increase the advantage of international firms over domestic ones, as MNCs are better able to capture the potential efficiency gains from reduced barriers, especially in the short term. If effective protection rates fall, domestic firms encounter increased foreign competition, whereas MNCs have the ability to serve an established domestic market by imports. Moreover, in light of their substantially higher import propensities, foreign subsidiaries are likely to enjoy greater cost reductions than domestic firms as a result of across-the-board tariff reductions. Thus, for a country like Canada, with a large existing *stock* of foreign investment, participation in the multilateral trade negotiations may have actually improved the competitive position of foreign subsidiaries and exacerbated the foreign domination of industry, notwithstanding the role played by protection in attracting the foreign capital in the first place.

A further consequence of the MNCs' "international technology" is that scale economies in any particular stage of production can have important implications for the effects of trade policy on investment patterns and of investment policy on trade patterns. Multilateral trade liberalization should promote investments to centralize production activities subject to important scale economies. Moreover, in the presence of scale economies, trade barriers, investment incentives, and/or export performance requirements can lead to a reversal of the pattern of trade that would be implied by comparative advantage alone. In the case of export performance requirements, the subsidiary once established may exceed the minimum level set by the host country—so that the requirement appears, misleadingly, to be redundant. In fact, the requirement in this instance may have played an important role in determining the size of the production subsidiary established in the host country; once the fixed costs have been committed, the higher export level is determined by the firm's own profit calculations.

Note

A GATT Panel considered the effect of restrictions on international investment on trade flows in the Canadian Foreign Investment Review Act case, discussed in Section 8.2(C) supra.

SECTION 16.2 NATIONAL CONTROLS ON INTERNATIONAL INVESTMENT

(A) AN OVERVIEW OF NATIONAL CONTROLS

There are a wide variety of controls imposed by nations on investments from abroad. Indeed, there are far too many controls to discuss them in detail here, but we will try to give an overview of the more common types of controls. Controls range from a complete prohibition on investments by foreigners—either in certain sensitive areas of the economy or in general—to more or less detailed regulation of the conditions under which an investment is permitted.

The rules on international investments in the United States are typical of a nation with an advanced developed economy. Although there are generally applicable reporting requirements for significant international investments,[1] the United States by and large does not regulate such investments. However, there is regulation of investments in a few areas of the economy where it is thought that foreign ownership would be undesirable for national security or other reasons. For example, foreign ownership of U.S. nuclear facilities, U.S. communications facilities (radio, television), U.S. registered commercial aircraft and vessels engaged in the coastal trade is strictly limited.[2] Restrictions on foreign investment are also found in some states.[3] These sorts of minor restrictions are not uncommon in developed countries.[4] In addition, foreign investment in developed countries is often controlled indirectly in that certain activities are state monopolies or are restricted to holders of a special license, which in practice may be more easily obtained by nationals. More significant controls may be imposed from time to time. A prime example is Canada where the Foreign Investment Review Act, discussed in Section 8.2(C) supra, was enacted, at least in part, to limit the influence of U.S. corporations and nationals in the Canadian economy. Another example is Japan. Although the rather strict post-war controls of international investment have been liberalized, there is still considerable discretion residing in the Japanese authorities to restrict and regulate such investments.[5]

Among developing countries, controls on international investment are much more pervasive.[6] Two types of controls are particularly common.

1. See, e.g., 15 CFR Pt. 806 (1985); 31 CFR Pt. 129 (1985).

2. See 42 U.S.C.A. §§ 2131, 2133(d), 2134(d) (nuclear); 46 U.S.C.A. § 883 (coastal trade); 47 U.S.C.A. § 310 (radio and TV); 49 U.S.C.A. § 140(b) (commercial aircraft).

3. See, e.g., Iowa Code Ann. § 567.3 (Supp. 1985) (farmland).

4. The OECD publishes from time to time studies on controls applicable to international investment in its member countries. See, e.g., OECD, Controls and Impediments Affecting Inward Direct Investment in OECD Member Countries (1982).

5. See Section 4.3 supra.

6. For a recent study summarizing some of the restrictions applied to international investment in several major developing countries, see IMF Research Dept., Foreign Private Investment in Developing Countries (Occasional Paper No. 33, 1985). The International Center for Settlement of Investment Disputes publishes a collection of investment laws of many countries. ICSID, Investment Laws of the World (Oceana looseleaf). Several of the international accounting firms publish information about doing business in the many countries where they operate. This information is typically updated regularly.

First, in many such countries, a foreign investor must have a local partner, who is required to have a specified ownership percentage in the investment. The specified percentage is often 50% or more. This requirement that local investors be involved is often reinforced by requirements that local personnel be used to the extent feasible. A second type of control takes the form of performance requirements that condition the approval of the investment on a commitment by the investor that the investment will result in the achievement of certain export goals, will not require significant importation of goods, and/or will introduce advanced technology to the country. If a proposed investment meets such requirements, it may be eligible for special government subsidies. These two types of controls may be interrelated—a higher level of foreign control may be allowed in the case of an investment to produce goods for export.

The U.S. Department of Commerce estimated in 1977 that of foreign-based affiliates of U.S.-based MNEs, 14% were subject to performance requirements (typically requirements on use of local labor, but also including export requirements (2%), maximum import levels (3%) and minimum local input levels (3%)). Additionally, 26% of such affiliates received investment incentives, typically subsidies, tariff concessions or tax concessions.[7]

Once an international investment is made, the foreign investor will be very concerned with its ability to realize a return on its investment. In most developed countries, there are no significant controls on the remission of profits from the country where the investment is located to the investor's country, nor are there restrictions on repatriation of the capital originally invested. As discussed in Section 11.3 supra, the OECD has adopted codes on the liberalization of such payments. However, it is not at all uncommon in developing countries to find controls on all payments by a subsidiary to its foreign parent, encompassing remission of dividends and repatriation of capital, but also including payments for management and other services, and the payments that are allowed may be conditioned on the achievement of a certain level of export earnings by the investment. Generally, developing countries are not under any sort of international obligation to liberalize these controls. As noted in Chapter 11, the IMF Agreement does not obligate a country to do so.

(B) BILATERAL INVESTMENT TREATIES

As major sources of international investment, the United States and other developed countries have been particularly interested in reducing restrictions on investment and in recent years have attempted to negotiate bilateral agreements on investment with less developed countries.[8] As part

7. U.S. Dept. of Commerce, Office of Intl. Investment, The Use of Investment Incentives and Performance Requirements by Foreign Governments (1981).

8. See generally Pattison, The United States-Egypt Bilateral Investment Treaty: A Prototype for Future Negotiations, 16 Cornell Intl.L.J. 305 (1983); Bergman, Bilateral Investment Protection Treaties: An Examination of the Evolution and Significance of the U.S. Prototype Treaty, 16 N.Y.U.J.Intl.L. & Pol. 1 (1983); Comment, The BIT Won't Bite: The American Bilateral Investment Treaty Program, 33 Am.U.L.Rev. 931 (1984) (critical of the program because Prototype is less favorable to developing countries than the treaties typically entered into by European countries); Recent Development, Developing a Model Bilateral Investment Treaty, 15 Law & Poly.Intl.Bus. 273 (1983).

of its effort to do so, the United States has developed a model bilateral investment treaty (the "Prototype"). A close examination of this agreement is quite instructive. It gives a fairly clear indication of the issues that the United States considers to be most important and how the United States believes they should be treated.

TREATY BETWEEN THE UNITED STATES OF AMERICA AND _____ CONCERNING THE RECIPROCAL ENCOURAGEMENT AND PROTECTION OF INVESTMENT
(Revised Feb. 24, 1984)

* * *

Article I

1. For the purposes of this Treaty,

(a) "company of a Party" means any kind of corporation, company, association, or other organization, legally constituted under the laws and regulations of a Party or a political subdivision thereof whether or not organized for pecuniary gain, or privately or governmentally owned;

(b) "investment" means every kind of investment in the territory of one Party owned or controlled, directly or indirectly by nationals or companies of the other Party, such as equity, debt, and service and investment contracts; and includes:

(i) tangible and intangible property, including rights, such as mortgages, liens and pledges;

(ii) a company or shares of stock or other interests in a company or interest in the assets thereof;

(iii) a claim to money or a claim to performance having economic value, and associated with an investment;

(iv) intellectual and industrial property rights, including rights with respect to copyrights, patents, trademarks, trade names, industrial designs, trade secrets and know-how, and goodwill;

(v) any right conferred by law or contract, and licenses and permits issued pursuant to law;

(c) "national" of a Party means a natural person who is a national of a Party under its applicable law;

(d) "return" means an amount derived from or associated with an investment, including profit; dividend; interest; capital gain; royalty payment; management, technical assistance or other fee; or returns in kind;

(e) "associated activities" include the organization, control, operation, maintenance and disposition of companies, branches, agencies, offices, factories or other facilities for the conduct of business; the making, performance and enforcement of contracts; the acquisition, use, protection and disposition of property of all kinds including intellectual and industrial property rights; and the borrowing of funds, the purchase and issuance of equity shares, and the purchase of foreign exchange for imports.

2. Each Party reserves the right to deny to any company the advantages of this Treaty if nationals of any third country control such company and, in the case of a company of the other Party, that company has no substantial business activities in the territory of the other Party or is controlled by nationals of a third country with which the denying Party does not maintain normal economic relations.

3. Any alteration of the form in which assets are invested or reinvested shall not affect their character as investment.

Article II

1. Each Party shall permit and treat investment, and activities associated therewith, on a basis no less favorable than that accorded in like situations to investment or associated activities of its own nationals or companies, or of nationals or companies of any third country, whichever is the most favorable, subject to the right of each Party to make or maintain exceptions falling within one of the sectors or matters listed in the Annex to this Treaty. Each Party agrees to notify the other Party before or on the date of entry into force of this Treaty of all such laws and regulations of which it is aware concerning the sectors or matters listed in the Annex. Moreover, each Party agrees to notify the other of any future exception with respect to the sectors or matters listed in the Annex, and to limit such exceptions to a minimum. Any future exception by either Party shall not apply to investment existing in that sector or matter at the time the exception becomes effective. The treatment accorded pursuant to any exceptions shall not be less favorable than that accorded in like situations to investments and associated activities of nationals or companies of any third country, except with respect to ownership of real property. Rights to engage in mining on the public domain shall be dependent on reciprocity.

2. Investments shall at all times be accorded fair and equitable treatment, shall enjoy full protection and security and shall in no case be accorded treatment less than that required by international law. Neither Party shall in any way impair by arbitrary and discriminatory measures the management, operation, maintenance, use, enjoyment, acquisition, expansion, or disposal of investments. Each Party shall observe any obligation it may have entered into with regard to investments.

3. Subject to the laws relating to the entry and sojourn of aliens, nationals of either Party shall be permitted to enter and to remain in the territory of the other Party for the purpose of establishing, developing, administering or advising on the operation of an investment to which they, or a company of the first Party that employs them, have committed or are in the process of committing a substantial amount of capital or other resources.

4. Companies which are legally constituted under the applicable laws or regulations of one Party, and which are investments, shall be permitted to engage top managerial personnel of their choice, regardless of nationality.

5. Neither Party shall impose performance requirements as a condition of establishment, expansion or maintenance of investments, which require or enforce commitments to export goods produced, or which specify that goods

or services must be purchased locally, or which impose any other similar requirements.

6. Each Party shall provide effective means of asserting claims and enforcing rights with respect to investment agreements, investment authorizations and properties.

7. Each Party shall make public all laws, regulations, administrative practices and procedures, and adjudicatory decisions that pertain to or affect investments.

8. The treatment accorded by the United States of America to investments and associated activities under the provisions of this Article shall in any State, Territory or possession of the United States of America be the treatment accorded therein to companies legally constituted under the laws and regulations of other States, Territories or possessions of the United States of America.

Article III

[Compensation for Expropriation]

[*See Section 16.4*]

Article IV

1. Each Party shall permit all transfers related to an investment to be made freely and without delay into and out of its territory. Such transfers include: (a) returns; (b) compensation pursuant to Article III; (c) payments arising out of an investment dispute; (d) payments made under a contract, including amortization of principal and accrued interest payments made pursuant to a loan agreement; (e) proceeds from the sale or liquidation of all or any part of an investment; and (f) additional contributions to capital for the maintenance or development of an investment.

2. Except as provided in Article III paragraph 1, transfers shall be made in a freely convertible currency at the prevailing market rate of exchange on the date of transfer with respect to spot transactions in the currency to be transferred.

[Articles VI and VII of the Prototype contain detailed provisions for the resolution of disputes between the government parties to the treaty and between nationals of one party and the other party. In both instances, binding arbitration is provided for.]

Article X

1. This Treaty shall not preclude the application by either Party of measures necessary in its jurisdiction for the maintenance of public order, the fulfillment of its obligations with respect to the maintenance or restoration of international peace or security, or the protection of its own essential security interests.

*   *   *

Annex

Consistent with Article II paragraph 1, each Party reserves the right to maintain limited exceptions in the sectors or matters it has indicated below: The United States of America

Air transportation; ocean and coastal shipping; banking; insurance; government grants; government insurance and loan programs; energy and power production; custom house brokers; ownership of real estate; ownership and operation of broadcast or common carrier radio and television stations; ownership of shares in the Communications Satellite Corporation; the provision of common carrier telephone and telegraph services; the provision of submarine cable services; use of land and natural resources.

Notes and Questions

(1) Although the United States had negotiated a number of bilateral investment treaties that are more or less based on the Prototype (or one of its earlier versions), as of December 1985, none of them had been submitted to the U.S. Senate for approval. U.S. activity in this field has lagged behind that of Japan and a number of European countries, who have in the past established broader networks of such treaties.[9] The United States, of course, has a large network of FCN treaties, discussed in Section 5.2(D) supra. These treaties often deal with investment issues in general terms, but they are not considered to deal adequately with investment issues because they are often outdated and typically do not give detailed treatment to many of the important problems that the United States believes should be considered today in regulating international investment.

(2) U.S. officials have expressed the hope that negotiation of a network of bilateral investment treaties could lead ultimately to a multilateral agreement on investment containing provisions similar to the Prototype.[10] The United States, however, is not depending solely upon its efforts to enter into bilateral agreements or upon the possibility of a multilateral agreement on investment to advance its goal of a more favorable climate for international investment. Section 301 of the Trade Act of 1974, which was discussed generally in Section 10.5 supra and in respect of its application to services in Section 15.2 supra, is also relevant to questions of international investment. As amended in 1984, Section 301 authorizes the President to retaliate against a foreign country that acts unjustifiably, unreasonably or discriminatorily to burden or restrict U.S. commerce. The term commerce is defined to include "foreign direct investment by United States persons with implications for trade in goods or services." [11] Unreasonable acts are defined to include those that deny "fair and equitable— (A) market opportunities; (B) opportunities for the establishment of an enterprise; or (C) provision of adequate and effective protection of intellectual property rights." [12] Thus, if a country should maintain restrictions on U.S. investment in its territory and not negotiate some sort of agreement with the

---

9. A list of bilateral investment treaties as of October 1, 1982, appears in 21 Intl. Legal Materials 1208 (1982).

10. Recent Development, note 8 supra, at 274.

11. 19 U.S.C.A. § 2411(e)(1).

12. 19 U.S.C.A. § 2411(e)(3).

United States limiting those restrictions, the President has authority to act so as to try and force such country to change its policies. Indeed, in 1985, the U.S. Trade Representative initiated Section 301 proceedings in respect of Brazil's restrictions on foreign investment in its informatics industry, and in respect of Korea's allegedly inadequate protection of U.S. intellectual property rights.[13] At this writing, the result of these cases and the extent to which Section 301 will be used in similar cases is not known. In addition, Section 307 of the 1984 Trade and Tariff Act authorizes the U.S. Trade Representative to negotiate to remove export performance requirements imposed by other nations and to impose import restrictions on the goods subject to such requirements to offset adverse impacts on the United States. In 1986, the Trade Representative invoked this section in respect of Taiwanese export performance requirements for automobiles.[14]

(3) The countries with whom the United States has negotiated bilateral investment agreements have not accepted the U.S. proposals without change. For example, in the case of Egypt, the exclusions from the national treatment coverage of the treaty on the Egyptian side include "commercial activity such as distribution, wholesaling, retailing, import and export activities." To what extent does this constitute a significant gap in the treaty's coverage? In particular, how significant of an impact could this be expected to have on U.S. investors who might be interested in investing in Egypt? The Egyptian treaty does not include the language of Article II(2) of the Prototype that prohibits a party from impairing the "use" and "enjoyment" of the investment by "arbitrary and discriminatory measures." Does this mean that investments made in Egypt may be worthless or not made at all because of discriminatory treatment occurring after the investment is made? To what extent would Article II(1), which does appear in the Egyptian treaty in a revised form, affect your answer to this question?

(4) The heart of the Prototype is Article II. Many of its provisions are designed to limit imposition of restrictions or conditions on investments that are commonly used by developing countries. Can you think of others that might be included? Note the broad definition of "investment" in the Prototype, and the list of associated activities. Of particular importance is the inclusion of such associated activities as service contracts and contracts for transfer of technology. To what extent does (or should) a bilateral investment treaty restrict the ability of the host country to regulate the prices paid by the investment for services and technology transfers? Are these provisions consistent with the apparent thrust of the current and proposed multilateral codes on these subjects discussed in Chapter 17?

(5) Article II(4) of the Prototype provides that a company organized under the laws of one party, and which is an investment, shall be permitted to engage "top management personnel of their choice." How should this provision of the Prototype be interpreted in light of the employment discrimination laws of the United States? What percentage of an organization's total employment or what type of position constitutes "top managerial personnel?" Under the Prototype and U.S. domestic law, could a foreign investor impose a requirement that all management personnel must be fluent in the language of the foreign investor?

13. 50 Fed.Reg. 37608 (1985) (Brazil); 50 Fed.Reg. 45883 (1985) (Korea).

14. 3 BNA Intl. Trade Rptr. 427 (1986).

Would it matter how fluency was measured and whether a significant number of potential workers in the United States could meet the fluency test?

In Sumitomo Shoji America, Inc. v. Avagliano, 457 U.S. 176, 102 S.Ct. 2374, 72 L.Ed.2d 765 (1982), the U.S. Supreme Court considered whether Article VIII(1) of the U.S.-Japan Treaty of Friendship, Commerce and Navigation provided a defense to an allegation of employment discrimination in violation of U.S. law. Article VIII provides that "1. Nationals and companies of either Party shall be permitted to engage, within the territories of the other Party, * * * executive personnel * * * and other specialists of their choice." The Supreme Court essentially ducked the issue and held that as a U.S. corporation, Sumitomo Shoji America, Inc. could not avail itself of the treaty's provisions—thus leaving open the question of whether a non-U.S. entity operating in the United States, for example, as a branch of its foreign parent, could rely on the treaty as a defense to a charge of discrimination. The U.S. Courts of Appeals have split on that issue.[15] Would this issue arise under the Prototype?

(6) Article XI(1) provides that in respect of tax policies, "each Party should strive to accord fairness and equity in the treatment of investments of nationals and companies of the other Party." However, Article XI(2) limits the application of the treaty to only a very few taxation matters (those related to expropriation, Article IV transfers, agreements between a government and an investor). How significant do you think this limitation is? We will consider problems of taxation in Chapter 19.

SECTION 16.3 INTERNATIONAL REGULATION OF NATIONAL CONTROLS ON INTERNATIONAL INVESTMENT

Despite the interrelationship of international trade and investment, GATT does not directly deal with investment issues, and although the proposed Havana Charter did include two articles concerning investment, it did not impose any significant restrictions on national regulation of international investment.[1] Until recently, the only multilateral standards applicable to national regulation were embodied in the OECD's code calling for the liberalization of capital movements and current transactions, which were discussed in Section 11.3 supra. These codes, of course, provided little real regulation of national controls on international investment. They were limited in application to OECD members, limited in scope and subject to numerous reservations. In the last decade there has been much more interest in adopting international rules regarding regulation of international investment, and there has been some controversy over the form such regulation should take. As noted earlier, the United States would like an agreement with concrete rules on international investment, such as those contained in the Prototype discussed in Section 16.2 supra, to be negotiated under GATT auspices. Given the divergent views of the developed and developing countries on the relevant issues, such negotiations would probably be very difficult. Thus far, creation of international rules in this area

---

15. Compare Avaglino v. Sumitomo Shoji America, Inc., 638 F.2d 552 (2d Cir.1981) (reversed on other grounds, as noted above) with Spiess v. C. Itoh & Co., 643 F.2d 353 (5th Cir. 1981), vacated for reconsideration, 457 U.S. 1128, 102 S.Ct. 2951, 73 L.Ed.2d 1344 (1982).

1. ITO Charter, arts. 11, 12.

has been largely limited to a nonbinding OECD Declaration on International Investment and several related OECD Decisions. In considering the OECD actions and the discussion of the prospects for an international agreement set out below, the reader should consider whether a binding international agreement is realistically possible and whether nonbinding codes of conduct serve any useful purpose. The effect of such codes is examined in more detail in Section 17.2 infra.

THE GOVERNMENTS OF THE OECD MEMBER COUNTRIES, DECLARATION ON INTERNATIONAL INVESTMENT AND MULTINATIONAL ENTERPRISES

(1976) [2]

CONSIDERING

- that international investment has assumed increased importance in the world economy and has considerably contributed to the development of their countries;

- that multinational enterprises play an important role in this investment process;

- that co-operation by Member countries can improve the foreign investment climate, encourage the positive contribution which multinational enterprises can make to economic and social progress, and minimise and resolve difficulties which may arise from their various operations;

- that, while continuing endeavours within the OECD may lead to further international arrangements and agreements in this field, it seems appropriate at this stage to intensify their co-operation and consultation on issues relating to international investment and multinational enterprises through interrelated instruments each of which deals with a different aspect of the matter and together constitute a framework within which the OECD will consider these issues:

DECLARE:

Guidelines for Multinational Enterprises
I. [See Section 17.3 infra.]

National Treatment
II. 1. that Member countries should, consistent with their needs to maintain public order, to protect their essential security interests and to fulfil commitments relating to international peace and secur-

---

2. Reprinted by permission of the OECD. The Declaration was reviewed in 1979 and 1984. The version in the text reflects those reviews. See OECD, International Investment and Multinational Enterprises—Review of the 1976 Declaration and Decisions (1979); OECD, International Investment and Multinational Enterprises—The 1984 Review of the 1976 Declaration and Decisions (1984). For commentary on the OECD Decisions relating to investment, see Lévy, The OECD Declaration on International Investment and Multinational Enterprise, in S. Rubin & G. Hufbauer (eds.), Emerging Standards of International Trade and Investment: Multinational Codes and Corporate Conduct 47 (1983).

ity, accord to enterprises operating in their territories and owned or controlled directly or indirectly by nationals of another Member country (hereinafter referred to as "Foreign-Controlled Enterprises") treatment under their laws, regulations and administrative practices, consistent with international law and no less favourable than that accorded in like situations to domestic enterprises (hereinafter referred to as "National Treatment");

2. that Member countries will consider applying "National Treatment" in respect of countries other than Member countries;

3. that Member countries will endeavour to ensure that their territorial subdivisions apply "National Treatment";

4. that this Declaration does not deal with the right of Member countries to regulate the entry of foreign investment or the conditions of establishment of foreign enterprises;

International Investment Incentives and Disincentives

III. 1. that they recognise the need to strengthen their co-operation in the field of international direct investment;

2. that they thus recognise the need to give due weight to the interests of Member countries affected by specific laws, regulations and administrative practices in this field (hereinafter called "measures") providing official incentives and disincentives to international direct investment;

3. that Member countries will endeavour to make such measures as transparent as possible, so that their importance and purpose can be ascertained and that information on them can be readily available;

Consultation Procedures

IV. that they are prepared to consult one another on the above matters in conformity with the Decisions of the Council relating to Inter-Governmental Consultation Procedures on the Guidelines for Multinational Enterprises, on National Treatment and on International Investment Incentives and Disincentives.

The OECD Decisions are worded in general terms and apply only to its members, most of whom do not have extensive controls on international investment. There is some doubt as to the feasibility of negotiations among developed and developing countries an international agreement containing more detailed limitations on national regulation of international investment.

Certainly, the wide disparity of views on appropriate standards would make such negotiations exceedingly difficult.

RACHEL McCULLOGH & ROBERT F. OWEN, LINKING NEGOTIATIONS ON TRADE AND FOREIGN DIRECT INVESTMENT

(1983)[3]

INVESTMENT ISSUES AND THE GATT

The logic of the Tokyo Round seems to apply in the case of policies toward foreign direct investment. However, host countries have increasingly assumed the right to regulate new foreign investment. Although somewhat more controversial, many nations have also sought to alter the terms of established foreign investment, i.e., to change the rules of the game once appreciable sunk costs are involved. Thus, unlike international negotiations on trade liberalization, where there is considerable agreement regarding relatively neutral rules and disagreement is focused more on the specific applications of these rules, the underlying principles of international negotiations on investment are themselves likely to be controversial, with host and home countries pursuing antithetical objectives. Furthermore, the potential division between host and home countries corresponds roughly to the division between developing and developed countries. This suggests both that the United States, by far the world's most important home country in absolute terms, plays an asymmetrical role in international negotiations relating to investment and that the most important potential gains may involve countries which are simultaneously important home and host countries of multinationals, in particular, the United States and certain other industrial nations.

* * *

A more basic issue is that as with other governmental policies affecting trade, GATT success in limiting trade-distorting practices in the investment area ultimately depends upon the willingness of its members to surrender national sovereignty in a politically sensitive area. Despite the successful efforts of the Tokyo Round in negotiating the new codes on nontariff barriers, the degree to which members are willing *in practice* to accept limits on their domestic options in order to promote collective goals remains in doubt. To extend the GATT's fragile achievements in this difficult area to a set of issues as sensitive and politically explosive as host-country regulation of foreign direct investment could be premature and counterproductive.

A related consideration is that any GATT-sponsored effort to limit host-country prerogatives on efficiency grounds might well be interpreted as further evidence that the GATT remains primarily a rich man's club dedicated to preservation of the status quo in the world economy. Given present North-South differences on foreign investment issues and the role of the United States in the dispute currently before the GATT, initiatives to extend the GATT mandate to include host-country investment regulation (or

3. © 1983, Massachusetts Institute of Technology. Reprinted by permission of the publisher, MIT Press, from C. Kindleberger & D. Audretsch (eds.), The Multinational Corporations in the 1980s, at 334, 348–50.

even just trade-related investment performance requirements) have the potential of reversing the modest progress made in the Tokyo Round toward bringing less-developed countries into fuller participation in the GATT.

Notes and Questions

(1) If an agreement on international investment is negotiated as part of GATT, what implications would the 1979 GATT Decision on Differential and More Favourable Treatment of Developing Countries have on any obligations agreed upon?

(2) Would the existence of extensive networks of U.S., European and Japanese bilateral investment treaties, which are roughly similar but by no means identical, make negotiation of an international agreement easier or more difficult? Or does the answer depend less on the extent of such networks and more on whether and on what terms several key developing countries, such as India and Brazil, are willing to enter such agreements?

(3) To what extent do you think that a binding agreement on the conduct of multinational enterprises, such as one of those outlined in Chapter 17 infra, would affect negotiations of restrictions on national investment controls of the sort outlined in this chapter?

(4) All things considered, do you think that the United States would be better advised to pursue an agreement on international investment in the GATT framework, in another international body or on a bilateral basis?

SECTION 16.4 INTERNATIONAL LAW AND EXPROPRIATION

One of the more controversial issues in international law concerns (i) whether there are limits on the rights of nations to expropriate or nationalize property owned by aliens and (ii) the extent to which, and the terms under which, compensation must be paid if property is expropriated. Here we briefly outline the contrasting positions taken on these issues. Much more detailed consideration of this topic is typically found in the basic casebooks and texts on international law.[1]

1. I. Brownlie, Principles of Public International Law 531–45 (3d ed. 1979); H. Steiner & D. Vagts, Transnational Legal Problems: Materials and Text 479–561 (3d ed. 1986); L. Henkin, R. Pugh, O. Schachter & H. Smit, International Law: Cases and Material ch. 11 (1980). See generally R. Lillich, The Valuation of Nationalized Property in International Law (1976); C. Lipson, Standing Guard: Protecting Foreign Capital in the 19th & 20th Centuries (1985); Dolzer, New Foundations of the Law of Expropriation of Alien Property, 75 Am.J.Intl.L. 553 (1981); Fales, A Comparison for Nationalization of Alien Property with Standards of Compensation Under United States Domestic Law, 5 N.W.J.Intl.L. & Bus. 871 (1983–1984); Koven, Expropriation and the "Jurisprudence" of OPIC, 22 Harv.Intl. L.J. 269 (1981); Muller, Compensation for Nationalization: A North-South Dialogue, 19 Colum.J.Transnatl.L. 35 (1981).

AMERICAN LAW INSTITUTE, RESTATEMENT OF THE LAW: FOREIGN RELATIONS LAW OF THE UNITED STATES (REVISED)

(Tentative Draft No. 7, 1986)[2]

§ 712. Economic Injury to Nationals of Other States

A state is responsible under international law for injury resulting from:

(1) a taking by the state of the property of a national of another state that is (a) not for a public purpose, or (b) discriminatory, or (c) not accompanied by provision for just compensation; for compensation to be just under this Subsection, it must, in the absence of exceptional circumstances, be in an amount equivalent to the value of the property taken, be paid at the time of taking, or within a reasonable time thereafter with interest from the date of taking, and in a form economically usable by the foreign national;

(2) a repudiation or breach by the state of a contract with a national of another state

(a) where the repudiation or breach is (i) discriminatory; or (ii) motivated by other non-commercial considerations and compensatory damages are not paid; or

(b) where the foreign national is not given an adequate forum to determine his claim of breach or is not compensated for any breach determined to have occurred;

(3) other arbitrary or discriminatory acts or omissions by the state that impair property or other economic interests of a national of another state.

TREATY BETWEEN THE UNITED STATES OF AMERICA AND _____ CONCERNING THE RECIPROCAL ENCOURAGEMENT AND PROTECTION OF INVESTMENT (Revised—Feb. 24, 1984)

ARTICLE III

1. Investments shall not be expropriated or nationalized either directly or indirectly through measures tantamount to expropriation or nationalization ("expropriation") except for a public purpose; in a non-discriminatory manner; upon payment of prompt, adequate and effective compensation; and in accordance with due process of law and the general principles of treatment provided for in Article II(2). Compensation shall be equivalent to the fair market value of the expropriated investment immediately before the expropriatory action was taken or became known; include interest at a commercially reasonable rate from the date of expropriation; be paid without delay; be fully realizable; and be freely transferable at the prevailing market rate of exchange on the date of expropriation.

2. A national or company of either Party that asserts that all or part of its investment has been expropriated shall have a right to prompt review by

the appropriate judicial or administrative authorities of the other Party to determine whether any such expropriation has occurred and, if so, whether such expropriation, and any compensation therefor, conforms to the principles of international law.

3. Nationals or companies of either Party whose investments suffer losses in the territory of the other Party owing to war or other armed conflict, revolution, state of national emergency, insurrection, civil disturbance or other similar events shall be accorded treatment by such other Party no less favorable than that accorded to its own nationals or companies or to nationals or companies of any third country, whichever is the most favorable treatment, as regards any measures it adopts in relation to such losses.

There are differences between the Revised Restatement and the Prototype. Note that the Prototype requires "prompt, adequate and effective compensation," while the Revised Restatement does not use these terms. The Second Restatement does use them [3] and it is unclear to what extent the revision intends to change the meaning of the original.[4] The revision seems to focus more on whether compensation is just.[5] In any event, it is a matter of some controversy whether the U.S. view now or ever reflected international law.[6] Certainly the U.S. view of the law is quite different than that held by some developing countries. Their view is represented in number of United Nations actions.[7]

DECLARATION ON THE ESTABLISHMENT OF A NEW ECONOMIC ORDER

(1974) [8]

* * *

4. The new international economic order should be founded on full respect for the following principles:

* * *

(e) Full permanent sovereignty of every State over its natural resources and all economic activities. In order to safeguard these resources, each State is entitled to exercise effective control over them and their exploitation with means suitable to its own situation, including the right to nationaliza-

3. American Law Institute, Restatement of the Law (Second): Foreign Relations Law of the United States §§ 185–90 (1965).

4. Comment *b* to Section 712 of the Revised Restatement states that Section 712 is essentially takes the same substantive position as the Second Restatement.

5. See Robinson, Expropriation in the Restatement (Revised), 78 Am.J.Intl.L. 176 (1984); Schachter, Compensation for Expropriation, 78 Am.J.Intl.L. 121 (1984); Mendelson, Compensation for Expropriation: The Case Law, 79 Am.J.Intl.L. 414 (1985); Schachter, Compensation Cases—Leading and Misleading, 79 Am.J.Intl.L. 420 (1985).

6. See Comment *c* to Section 712.

7. In addition to the materials quoted in the text, see U.N. General Assembly Resolution 1803 (XVII) on Permanent Sovereignty over Natural Resources, G.A. Res. 1803, 17 GAOR, Supp. 17 (A/5217) and 15 (1962); UNCTAD Trade and Development Board, Resolution 88 (XII), 12 U.N. TDOR, Supp. 1 at 1, U.N. Doc. TD/B/423 (1972).

8. G.A. Res. 3201 (S–VI), Sixth Spec.Sess. GAOR, Supp. 1 (A/4559) (1979). See Chapter 20 infra for more on the New International Economic Order.

tion or transfer of ownership to its nationals, this right being an expression of the full permanent sovereignty of the State. No State may be subjected to economic, political or any other type of coercion to prevent the free and full exercise of this inalienable right.

CHARTER OF ECONOMIC RIGHTS AND DUTIES OF STATES
(1974) [9]

CHAP. II, ART. 1, PARA. 2

Each State has the right:

(a) To regulate and exercise authority over foreign investment within its national jurisdiction in accordance with its laws and regulations and in conformity with its national objectives and priorities. No State shall be compelled to grant preferential treatment to foreign investment;

(b) To regulate and supervise the activities of transnational corporations within its national jurisdiction and take measures to ensure that such activities comply with its laws, rules and regulations and conform with its economic and social policies. Transnational corporations shall not intervene in the internal affairs of a host State. Every State should, with full regard for its sovereign rights, co-operate with other States in the exercise of the right set forth in this subparagraph;

(c) To nationalize, expropriate or transfer ownership of foreign property, in which case appropriate compensation should be paid by the State adopting such measures, taking into account its relevant laws and regulations and all circumstances that the State considers pertinent. In any case where the question of compensation gives rise to a controversy, it shall be settled under the domestic law of the nationalizing State and by its tribunals, unless it is freely and mutually agreed by all States concerned that other peaceful means be sought on the basis of the sovereign equality of States and in accordance with the principle of free choice of means.

Notes and Questions

(1) One interesting issue in public international law today is the extent to which declarations or resolutions of U.N. bodies constitute international law or create customary international law. For a more extensive consideration of this and related issues in this book, see Sections 5.2(A) supra and 17.2 infra.

(2) Compare the requirements of Article III(1) of the Prototype with paragraph 2(c) of the Charter of Economic Rights and Duties of States. What are the basic differences in these two approaches to expropriation? If you were charged with mediating an international dispute on this subject, how would you attempt to reconcile the two approaches?

(3) To what extent does the U.N. Resolution on the New Economic Order provide different standards in the case of expropriation of natural resources? Is there any justification for treating natural resources differently?

9. G.A. Res. 3281 (XXIX), 29 GAOR, Supp. 30 (A/9030) (1974).

(4) Notice the breadth of the definition of "expropriation" in the Prototype. Would it call for compensation even if the measures complained of applied generally to foreign- and locally owned business alike? On a broader level, should foreign investors ever enjoy greater protections than those afforded by a country to its own nationals? The problem of defining when property has been expropriated is a difficult one. Many types of governmental action affect the value of property, but may not be considered sufficiently serious to amount to a "taking" of the property. There is, of course, much literature on this issue as it arises under U.S. constitutional law. See J. Nowak, R. Rotunda & J. Young, Constitutional Law 483–93 (2d ed. 1983). For a discussion of the international law aspects of this question, see Dolzer, Indirect Expropriation of Alien Property, 1 ICSID-Foreign Investment L.Rev. (1986).

(5) To protect international investment by its citizens, governments have established agencies to insure against political risks, such as expropriation. For example, in the United States, such insurance is provided by the Overseas Private Investment Corporation (OPIC).[10] In an effort to discourage expropriation of U.S. interests, Congress adopted the so-called Hickenlooper Amendment in 1962. 22 U.S.C.A. 2370(e)(1). The Amendment provides for termination of U.S. foreign assistance in event of expropriation of U.S. interests without meaningful compensation. It has rarely been invoked.

(6) As noted in Section 2.3 supra, the World Bank sponsored International Center for Settlement of Investment Disputes provides an arbitration procedure for resolution of investment disputes between individuals of one party and the government of another party. In 1985, the World Bank announced that it would establish the Multilateral Investment Guarantee Agency, which would have the function of issuing guarantees for investments against noncommercial risks in an effort to stimulate capital flows to developing member countries. It is anticipated that the agency will start operations in 1986, assuming a minimum of five capital exporting states and 15 capital importing states have ratified the convention establishing the agency and sufficient subscriptions have been received.[11]

(7) Even if it is accepted that an unlawful expropriation has occurred, the investor may have difficulty in obtaining compensation. The expropriating state is unlikely to offer a forum for making or enforcing claims against it. Pursuing a claim in another country, such as the investor's home country, may also be difficult, especially if a court declines to adjudicate the claim because of the doctrines of sovereign immunity or act of state. In the United States, the latter doctrine was considered to be a bar to such an action by the U.S. Supreme Court in 1964 in Banco Nacional de Cuba v. Sabbatino, 376 U.S. 398, 84 S.Ct. 923, 11 L.Ed.2d 804 (1964). Later in 1964, Congress acted to attempt to override the doctrine. See 22 U.S.C.A. § 2370(e)(2). As to the problem of sovereign immunity, the Foreign Sovereign Immunities Act of 1976, 28 U.S.C.A. § 1602 et seq., provides that a foreign state is not immune from the jurisdiction of U.S. courts in a case where property has been taken in violation of international law and that property or any property exchanged for that property is present in the United States in connection with a commercial activity carried on in the United States by the foreign state or one of its agencies or instrumentalities or such

10. See 22 U.S.C.A. § 2191 et seq.

11. The Convention Establishing the Multilateral Investment Guarantee Agency is set out in 24 Intl. Legal Materials 688 (1985).

property is owned or operated by an agency or instrumentality of the foreign state and that agency or instrumentality is engaged in commercial activity in the United States. Thus, as a practical matter, a U.S. national with a claim against a foreign sovereign based on an allegedly illegal expropriation will probably have some difficulty obtaining a favorable judgment on the claim.

SECTION 16.5 ALTERNATIVES TO INVESTMENT: AGENTS, DISTRIBUTORS AND LICENSING

It is not necessary to invest in a country to do business there. Indeed, for a smaller company or one selling a specialized product to a limited market, making a direct investment in a foreign country often is not a realistic alternative. Moreover, even a larger multinational enterprise may choose not to invest in particular countries, either because of the limited market or because of restrictions placed on foreign investments such as were described in Section 16.2 supra. If companies do not wish to invest directly, there are a number of alternatives that permit them to commercialize their products in another country. The simplest is simply to send catalogs or salesmen to likely customers. The difficulty with this approach is that it may be difficult for the catalogs or salesmen to do an effective selling job if they do not use the native language and do not emphasize particular local business needs. To avoid such problems, companies often enter into some sort of contractual relations with an entity in the local country in order to commercialize their products. The three most common types of agreement are agency, distributorship and licensing.

Agency and distributorship agreements are probably the two most common forms of selling arrangements used by foreign companies to sell into local markets through local entities. The essential difference between the two is that an agent essentially collects orders and forwards them to the seller for acceptance or rejection, while the distributor buys for his own account and then resells the goods. The agent never actually owns the goods and is not directly involved in the sale between the foreign seller and local buyer. The agent is compensated typically by the seller, who pays a commission that is often a percentage of the purchase price of the goods sold. On the other hand, the foreign seller is typically not part of the contract between the distributor and the local buyer and the distributor's compensation is not paid by the seller, but rather is the difference between the price that the distributor pays the seller and the price it charges the buyer for the goods.

Although the categorization of selling arrangements as being either agency or distribution arrangements is typical, it is of course possible and not uncommon for a specific agreement between two parties to have elements of both types of agreement. It is beyond the scope of this book to go into a detailed analysis of the two types of agreements and their advantages and disadvantages, but a few general comments may be in order.[1] First,

---

1. For more detailed consideration of agencies and distributorships, see Rigaud, Agency, in III Int.Ency.Comp.L. ch. 29 (1973); U.S. Dept. of Commerce, Intl.Trade Admin., Foreign Business Practices: Materials on Practical Aspects of Exporting, International Licensing and Investment (1982).

whenever a seller depends on an independent entity for sales, there is a question of whether the customers are really those of the seller or those of the person who makes the actual sale. In an agency relationship, the customers are more aware of the actual seller since they have direct contractual dealings with it, while in the case of a distributor that is not the case. Thus, it may be argued that in the event of a change in the selling arrangements, the seller is more likely to retain customers if it has sold through an agency relationship than if it has used a distributor. Second, an offsetting consideration is that in an agency relationship the seller must worry about having a direct relationship with the buyer—it will be necessary to check the buyer's credit, there may be contract disputes that end up in a foreign court, etc. With the distributor as an independent, intermediate party these problems may be avoided. Of course, in many cases there may be no real choice of the form of selling arrangements. In some instances it may be possible to sell a product only if the prospective customer has a wide variety of models to choose from, is able to receive immediate delivery and can be provided with competent servicing. The typical agent is not going to be able or willing to perform these services. A distributor, on the other hand, who is an independent contractor, probably will be willing to do so. An agency arrangement is better suited to products that can be supplied from the seller's plant and do not require extensive servicing later.

The basic agreement between an agent or distributor and the foreign seller is essentially contractual and the same sort of considerations that were raised in Chapter 2 concerning simple sales transactions are relevant. Care must be taken to spell out the financial arrangements between the parties and to specify whether the rights granted to the agent or distributor are exclusive (an issue of considerable importance and one that may raise antitrust law considerations, particularly in the EC). Liabilities for breach of warranties or other product liability claims need to be considered as well. The Agreement should also choose an applicable law and method and place of settling disputes. Finally, but of no less importance, it is necessary to be aware of rules existing in many countries that provide special compensation to an agent or distributor in the event that the agency or distributorship is terminated. The precise content and coverage of such rules varies from country to country, but it is not uncommon to find that an agent (and sometimes, but probably less often, a distributor) will be entitled to some sort of termination payment based on its income from the agency or distributorship, the extent of its investment therein and the length of the relationship. In some cases, local courts may hold that these rules cannot be limited by contract.[2]

A different method of commercializing a product in a foreign country is to enter into a licensing arrangement with an entity located in such country pursuant to which the foreign entity is given certain technical information and assistance that will enable it to produce the product in that country. In return, the foreign entity agrees to pay royalties to the licensor. Licensing is often a very attractive alternative. It requires little investment by the

2. See generally Sales, Termination of Sales Agents and Distributors in France, 17 Intl.Law. 741 (1983); Simons, Termination of Sales Agents and Distributors in Belgium, 17 Intl.Law. 752 (1983).

licensor, yet may lead to a considerable stream of royalty payments if the licensee is successful. There are of course dangers. At the end of the license, the licensee may become a competitor of the licensor if it has been successful. On the other hand, the licensee may make such an inferior product that it will destroy the reputation of the licensor in the market in question. Thus, it is necessary to exercise some care in selecting a licensee and to maintain amicable relations with it.

We cannot in this limited space analyze the various legal problems that arise in licensing in any detail, but the following comments suggest some of the more serious ones.[3] At the outset, it is necessary to consider the scope of the license, i.e. in what territory it will apply and whether or not it is exclusive. Second, it is necessary to consider how to treat improvements made by either party—does the licensee automatically receive them without a greater royalty payment, does the licensor obtain rights to improvements made by the licensee, at what cost and for what territories? Third, in some countries it may be appropriate to obtain the licensee's agreement that it will not contest the validity of any licensed patents. Fourth, it is necessary to specify who has rights to what on termination of the agreement. Finally, as in other cases, careful consideration must be given to choosing the applicable law and the form and location of dispute settlement.

The discussion of topics commonly covered in licensing agreements raises one additional and often very difficult issue. Licensing agreements, by their very nature, raise problems under antitrust laws, particularly in respect of division of markets or allocation of customers and of agreements not to contest the validity of patents. Such problems may be of particular concern and require advice from an expert in both the United States and the EC.[4]

One final aspect of licensing deserves mention. Less developed countries are often very concerned about promoting the transfer of technology from more advanced countries. As a consequence, such countries often have laws and rules that regulate such transactions. In particular, these rules may be enforced through the requirement of approval for payment of royalties, a type of payment that is likely to be subject to exchange controls. In addition, some developing countries do not protect intellectual property rights, such as patents, as fully as is customary in developed countries. As noted earlier, the United States has sought to cause some developing countries to broaden the scope of protection that they grant.[5] Some of the concerns of the less developed countries will be discussed in Chapter 17 infra where we discuss UNCTAD's proposed Code on Transfer of Technology.

3. For more detailed consideration of licensing problems, see, e.g., G. Pollzien & E. Langen, International Licensing Agreements (2d ed. 1973).

4. See generally P. Areeda & D. Turner, IV Antitrust Law §§ 704–09 (1978); B. Hawk, United States, Common Market and International Antitrust: A Comparative Guide ch. 11 (2d ed. 1985).

5. See, e.g., 50 Fed.Reg. 45883 (1985) (Section 301 proceeding initiated against Korea in respect of its allegedly inadequate protection of U.S. intellectual property rights).

Chapter 17

MULTINATIONAL ENTERPRISES

SECTION 17.1 INTRODUCTION [1]

An explosive expansion in the volume and extent of international investment has occurred in recent years, a fact that was documented in Chapter 16. As noted there, much of this investment has been made by multinational enterprises (MNEs), i.e. by enterprises operating in several countries. The activities of such an enterprise outside of its home country, in so-called host countries, are often quite substantial and therefore of considerable importance both to the economic success of the enterprise and the well being of the host country. Unfortunately, decisions that promote the economic success of the enterprise may not necessarily be in the best interest of any particular host country. A multinational enterprise will typically want to make its investment and operating decisions on the basis of their effect on the enterprise as a whole, without reference to possible adverse effects occurring in some of the local economies where it operates (except, of course, to the extent those adverse effects impinge on the MNE itself). Moreover, unlike a local enterprise, which is likely to be controlled by persons who live in the local community and who therefore will be aware of and may be directly affected by decisions made in respect of their enterprise, the decision-makers in an MNE may be largely unaware, unaffected and unconcerned by such local effects. Not surprisingly, this state of affairs may not be at all acceptable to a host country. It may simply be unwilling to accept that an MNE should be permitted to take actions that have an adverse economic or other effect on the host country without some sort of consultation with or regulation by it. Views of the resulting conflict of interests between MNEs and host countries have ranged from suggestions

---

1. In addition to the materials cited in this chapter and Chapter 16, see generally J. Kline, International Codes and Multinational Business: Setting Guidelines for International Business Operations (1985); C. Kindleberger, Multinational Excursions (1984); S. Rubin & G. Hufbauer (eds.), Emerging Standards of International Trade and Investment (1984); J. Robinson, Multinationals and Political Control (1983); W. Goldberg (ed.), Governments and Multinationals: The Policy of Control versus Autonomy (1983); Symposium: Codes of Conduct for Transnational Corporations, 30 Am.U.L.Rev. 903 (1981); R. Grosse, Foreign Investment Codes and the Location of Direct Investment (1980); W. Feld, Multinational Corporations and U.N. Politics: The Quest for Codes of Conduct (1980); C. Bergsten, T. Horst & T. Moran, American Multinationals and American Interests (1978); K. Simmonds, Multinational Corporations Law (Oceana looseleaf).

in the early 1970's that the very existence of national sovereignty was threatened by MNEs to suggestions a decade and a half later that the number of proposed and existing regulations applicable to MNEs was so great and their provisions sufficiently inconsistent that a plausible argument could be made that the tide had turned and that MNEs were in danger of being overregulated.[2]

We are interested in MNEs mainly because of their importance to the international economy, particularly with respect to their creation and direction of international trade flows and their role in the process of structural adjustment. However, to understand the genesis of many of the proposals to regulate MNE conduct, it is important to have some historical background concerning the behavior of MNEs in the recent past. Much of the controversy surrounding MNE activities in the 1960s and 1970s concerned their involvement in political activities and their improper payments to government officials. For example, the International Telephone and Telegraph Corporation (ITT) was alleged to have participated in the political affairs of Chile in an attempt to prevent the election of and later to promote the ouster of the Allende government in the early 1970's [3] and a number of U.S. corporations were involved in controversies concerning their payments to foreign government officials allegedly made for the purpose of obtaining or retaining business in the countries in question.[4] The latter events resulted in the adoption in the United States of the Foreign Corrupt Practices Act, which makes it a crime under U.S. law for U.S. companies or persons to make certain payments to foreign government officials or foreign politicians.[5] (As noted at the end of this chapter, U.S. efforts to promote multinational rules banning such payments, so as to avoid prejudicing U.S. companies in markets where such payments are common, have so far been largely unsuccessful.)

We have briefly considered elsewhere how activities of MNEs may affect international trade and the problems of structural adjustment (see Sections 16.1 and 9.6(B) supra). As noted earlier, the investment decisions of MNEs (i.e., where to locate production facilities) can have a significant effect on trade patterns. Likewise, the ability of MNEs to shift production activities from one country to another can effectively implement structural adjustments that a purely local enterprise would never undertake. Such adjustments may, of course, be very controversial in the country from which production is transferred. As we consider the proposals to regulate MNEs in this chapter, it is important not to consider only the host country viewpoint; a pertinent question should always be: How does a proposed regulation affect the basic free trade principles of GATT?

2. See, e.g., R. Vernon, Sovereignty at Bay: The Multinational Spread of U.S. Enterprises (1971).

3. See Hearings on Multinational Corporations and U.S. Foreign Policy Before the Senate Committee on Foreign Relations, 93d Cong., 1st Sess. (1973).

4. Hearings to Consider Allegations that Lockheed Aircraft Corp. Made Bribes, etc. to Officials of Foreign Governments Before the Senate Committee on Banking, Housing and Urban Affairs, 94th Cong., 1st Sess. (1975).

5. Pub.L. No. 95–213, §§ 103–04, 91 Stat. 1494 (1977) (codified at 15 U.S.C.A. §§ 78dd–1, 78dd–2).

In this chapter, we consider how codes of conduct for MNEs should be established. In particular, we focus on the question of the form that such codes should take, e.g., whether they should be voluntary or mandatory. We then examine one of the more important codes—the 1976 OECD Guidelines for Multinational Enterprise—and how it has operated in practice. We will also catalog a number of other codes, both proposed and in place.

SECTION 17.2   CODES OF CONDUCT FOR MULTINATIONAL ENTERPRISE: THE PHILOSOPHICAL PROBLEMS

In response to the perceived need to control the conduct of MNEs, a number of international organizations have adopted or are in the process of adopting codes of conduct to be applicable to MNEs. Such organizations include the International Chamber of Commerce, the OECD, the International Labor Organization, the United Nations Economic and Social Council and UNCTAD. The process of drafting and adopting such codes presents a number of fundamental problems, including the following: What topics are appropriately addressed in such codes and what issues need to be considered by the drafters of codes? Should the codes be implemented as treaties in which nations undertake to adopt certain rules of conduct for MNEs into law? Or is it sufficient for the codes to be "voluntary" guidelines, subscribed to by nations, but understood to apply to MNEs? What, if anything, is the effect of a voluntary guideline? If codes conflict, are some entitled to more deference than others? Beyond these philosophical issues is the question of what substantive rules a code should contain. In this section, we consider the philosophical issues and in Section 17.3 we consider the substantive provisions of one of the first, and probably the most important, codes to have been adopted to date—the OECD Guidelines for Multinational Enterprises.

JOHN H. JACKSON, TRANSNATIONAL ENTERPRISES & INTERNATIONAL CODES OF CONDUCT

(1980)[1]

Although the issues encountered in the various code drafting exercises are not always the same, there do seem to arise in a number of these efforts certain major general problems. * * *

(1) IMPLEMENTATION AND ADOPTION

The question of how to adopt or implement the code arises in a number of the yet uncompleted code drafting efforts, and has had to be faced in connection with those codes already approved. It seems clear in these debates over implementation that participants' views of the substance of the proposed rules greatly affect their views about implementation. Potential alternatives range from the promulgation of a code as merely a "morally persuasive" set of principles, to a set of legally binding rules established in domestic or international law. Yet, as has been so ably pointed out, no one

---

1. Speech to International Bar Association meeting in Berlin, August 27, 1980.

should be fooled by the seeming informality of a "voluntary" code or set of guidelines. Even these can have considerable impact, attract the sanction at least of public opinion, and influence national or international courts or other government officials.

Formal legal adoption of a code, such as through a binding treaty, may in fact prove politically impossible to accomplish; thus the attraction of less formal means. But carefully crafted informal institutions of "surveillance" can often make the voluntary code as effective as that which is legally binding. The risk is that the informality of proposed implementation may induce some to-be-affected parties to relax their attention to the code formulating process. The reception by the arbitrator in the 1977 Texaco (TOPCO)-Libyan oil case of certain language of a U.N. General Assembly Resolution demonstrates the impact that non-legally binding international consensus documents can have in some circumstances.

(2) SCOPE OF A CODE'S REACH

What type of enterprises should be covered by a proposed code of conduct? Considerable attention has been devoted to this issue, particularly regarding enterprises owned by a government. Those who urge that coverage include all types of enterprises, government owned or not, domestic host country corporations as well as foreign corporations, have on their side the arguments of equal treatment and reciprocity. On the other hand, some of the goals sought to be achieved by a code * * * could lead one to a contrary conclusion.

(3) INTERNATIONAL LAW PRINCIPLES, NATIONAL TREATMENT, AND EXPROPRIATION COMPENSATION

This issue could be called "linking." The basic goal of some code formulators is that if a code contains rules obligating foreign TNE's [Transnational Enterprises] operating in a host country, that the host country should reciprocate by undertaking obligations also. The two prime candidates for such reciprocal obligations seem to be national treatment, and the rule of prompt, adequate and effective compensation for expropriation of private property. Reciprocity encourages the idea that code proponents not be allowed to obtain something for nothing, that is, that reciprocal obligations encourage a sense of responsibility. Likewise, the proponents of reciprocity may in fact be uninterested in a code which one-sidedly obligates only the TNE, and see in the code effort an opportunity to promote other rules long-desired by them. On the other hand, it isn't logically necessary that linkage occur. A code might enhance certain goals, such as predictability, or evening out the competitive environment for TNE's even if no "linkage" occurs. Some who make linkage a sine quo non may simply recognize that the proposed reciprocal rules are so unacceptable that imposing them as a condition is a way to defeat the code proposal generally.

(4) NEW RULES, AMENDMENTS, AND CODE EVOLUTION

One troublesome aspect of many code endeavors is the lack of adequate and effective means to change the code rules when they become outmoded or are shown to be defective. The GATT experience is testimony to what happens when an amendment or new rule procedures turns out to be basically unworkable—some GATT rules have become painfully out of date, but the amending procedure has basically been unworkable. One possible advantage of a voluntary code or guideline approach, of course, is to avoid the rigidities which a legal rule might have. But even voluntary rules can become outdated. Indeed because they were drafted as voluntary, the draftsmen often overlook the need for including in them a system for keeping the rules fresh and up to date.

To launch a set of rules for TNE behavior at a time of great controversy over many fundamental issues about the purpose and proper function of TNE's is particularly risky unless effective review and revision is built in. Some codes purport to have procedures, but if change requires "unanimity" or "consensus" those procedures could become as unusable as those of the GATT. Once fixed, the code words become very hard to revise. Perhaps a term of years should be specified in each code, after which any governmental party could, on due notice, declare itself no longer bound by the code (as a way to bring pressure for the revision of the rules). When a set of rules loses its consensus support, it also tends to lose effectiveness or compliance. In such a case the rules can become traps for the unwary or inexperienced, engendering conflict, and promoting instability.

HANS W. BAADE, THE LEGAL EFFECTS OF CODES OF CONDUCT FOR MULTINATIONAL ENTERPRISES

(1980)[2]

Conventions embodying definite legal obligations of the contracting states are—at least *inter partes* and if compatible with *ius cogens*—hierarchically the top layer of "hard" international law. The major codes of conduct for MNEs currently in existence or close to the point of formal adoption do not belong to that category. It is readily apparent that this is due not to any intrinsic defects of the international "legislative" process, but to a deliberate choice of the states concerned in the international norm-creating process, influenced in good part by considerations just mentioned. For as shown by a comparison of the instruments adopted with the norm-creating powers of the international organizations involved, at least the codes of conduct extant today have quite uniformly failed to make full use of these powers.

*   *   *

Similarly, the Principles Concerning Multinational Enterprises and Social Policy adopted by the ILO in 1977 are not embodied in a Recommendation of the General Conference (which would have automatically entailed reporting obligations based on treaty commitments already in effect) but by a Declaration of the Governing Body—an instrument not contemplated in the Constitution of the ILO. The OECD Guidelines, finally, were adopted without formal use of the OECD Council, which could have promulgated a Decision legally binding upon the member states or issued a formal Recommendation of the Organisation. Additionally, they expressly state, in so many words, that their observance is "voluntary and not legally enforceable."

2. From N. Horn (ed.), Legal Problems of Codes of Conduct for Multinational Enter- prises 5–8, 37–38 (1980). Reprinted by permission of the editor.

There is, thus, a marked tendency on the part of the major state actors in the international norm-creating process to make less than full use even of the extant "legislative" competences of international organizations in connection with the regulation of the conduct of MNEs. This leads to the conclusion that at least for some time to come, codes of conduct for MNEs will not be adopted in the form of a multilateral convention or as normative acts of international organizations, i.e., essentially as multilateral conventions once removed. This does not, however, preclude the possibility of the substantive contents of such codes, or of parts thereof, rising to the quality of "hard" international law at a somewhat less august hierarchical rank.

The primary "lesser" normative level of potential significance here is, of course, customary international law. (The next-lower level, "general principles of law recognized by civilized nations," is of limited intrinsic utility for present purposes, and in any event, of doubtful normative quality.*[20]) Customary international law is authoritatively defined, in the Statute of the International Court of Justice, as "international custom, as evidence of general practice accepted as law." It has been clear at least since "Sputnik," and was confirmed in the *North Sea Continental Shelf Cases,* that the time element involved in the transformation of state practice into international custom is not necessarily a major factor. Not so, however, with the *opinio necessitatis iuris,* i.e., the acceptance of that practice as required by law.

* * *

Each of the seven chapters of the OECD Guidelines starts with the words, "Enterprises should." With "transnational corporations" substituted, the vast majority of the provisions of the current UN draft are similarly addressed to MNEs directly, without the intermediaries of their home and host countries. MNEs are, however, neither states nor public international organizations, and thus neither general 'natural' nor 'artificial' subjects of international law as presently defined. Even if their procedural role in follow-up proceedings should, in analogy to human-rights complaint mechanisms, suffice to confer upon them "partial" or *ad hoc* international subjectivity, they would still lack at least one of the essential attributes of full international personality. This is the power to participate directly in the international norm-creating process. It follows that the practice of MNEs in response to codes of conduct or guidelines, quite irrespective of its motivations, cannot supply the element of *opinio necessitatis iuris* that remains an indispensable prerequisite for the development of customary international law.

* * *

Five major conclusions emerge from the present study. First, the codes, guidelines, and other declarations concerning the conduct of MNEs that are extant today or at advanced stages of elaboration are not "instant international law" in the sense that they are transformed into customary interna-

---

* **20.** Because of the hierarchical interrelationship of the sources of international law and the basic presumption of the absence of restraints on sovereign states, general principles of law cannot prevail over contrary custom. For more detail, see Baade, "Foreign and International Law in Domestic Tribunals," 18 Va.J.Int'l L. 619, 633–34 note 79 (1979).

tional law through the mere act of being adopted. Secondly, however, these instruments are not inherently incapable of rising to that level through state practice, especially through host and home country participation in intergovernmental follow-up proceedings. Thirdly, self-descriptive clauses, declarations, and reservations specifying that compliance with such codes, guidelines, or declarations on the part of MNEs is voluntary and/or not legally enforceable do not shield MNEs from the domestic enforcement of the substantive contents of these instruments or from their transformation into treaties or customary international law.

Fourth, and most importantly, codes, guidelines, and other intergovernmental declarations concerning MNE conduct are declarations of international policy which, by virtue of the anti-inconsistency rule (frequently reenforced by the principle of estoppel) "legitimize" the transformation of their substantive contents into domestic law at the option of the declarant states. Fifth, these instruments also have legal effects as agreed-on data and criteria of international public policy and legal terminology. Their application by domestic courts so as to refuse recognition to transactions in violation of their substantive contents is legitimate, although not as yet required. Furthermore, their provisions are relevant to the interpretation of prior instruments in force between the parties, including treaty clauses of a general or potentially ambiguous nature.

In analytical terms, intergovernmental codes, guidelines, and declarations are multilateral declarations affecting the rights and obligations of the declarant states *inter sese* by virtue of the anti-inconsistency rule and/or the principle of estoppel, both of which are ultimately derived from the ground rule of good faith. These declarations affect the contents of customary international law because practice in conformity with them is legitimate state practice which defines, or refines, international-law rules on the protection of foreign investment. That alone is insufficient, however, for the transformation of the prescriptions contained in these instruments into rules of customary international law imposing affirmative duties of enforcement upon the declarant states. This can be achieved only through the transformation of the substantive contents of codes, guidelines, and other instruments concerning MNE conduct into international law by treaty or by state practice reflecting the requisite *opinio necessitatis iuris* as regards that particular obligation.

NORBERT HORN, NORMATIVE PROBLEMS OF A NEW INTERNATIONAL ECONOMIC ORDER

(1982) [3]

* * * There has been a fundamental change in the process of international rule-making.

Formerly, comparative legal scholarship, in long and slow deliberations and discussions, paved the way for internationally unified law. Such was the case in the drafting of the Hague Convention on the Law of Sales. In

---

3. 16 J. World Trade L. 338, 346–51. Reprinted by permission of the Journal of World Trade Law.

public international law, similarly, a *communis opinio* slowly emerged from legal scholarship and books of authority. Now, international institutions and agencies, inter-governmental committees and conferences have taken over to a large extent. The process of rule-making has been considerably expanded and accelerated, and has become subject to direct political influence. There are various reasons for this change: an increased need for international rules and regulations as tools of international politics and, finally, Parkinson's law: bureaucracy, at some point, begins to reproduce itself. The more this process of accelerated rule-making continues, the more legal scholarship is called upon to provide its advice, its methods and its capacity to analyse complex problems and harmonize opposing interests.

Soft Law and the Confusion of Normative Categories

In the NIEO [4] rule-making process, two contradictory tendencies can be observed. One is to avoid a formal law-making procedure, the other is to make rules and establish regulations which have the effects and binding force of law. The reason for avoiding formal law-making procedures is simple: in international law, there is a long lag until a convention or treaty is negotiated, consented to by all concerned, and then formally accepted. In the preparation of codes of conduct, there seems to be a preference for the promulgation of non-binding rules which might later be made the subject of a formal convention. The OECD Declaration and Guidelines for Multinational Enterprises of 1976 can serve as a model; these guidelines are expressly declared to be "voluntary and not legally enforceable". In contrast, however, there are deliberations to establish international control mechanisms and follow-up procedures for the international codes and guidelines allowing for enforcement.

A confusion of normative categories can be observed in this process. It is a specific characteristic of European legal history developed from Roman law, that the legal system is viewed as clearly distinct from other systems of social rules such as ethics, social behaviour, or political goals and programmes. Certainly, legal norms have some connections with these other systems. But the process of law-making invariably involves an isolation of the newly-drafted legal norm from the ethical values and political goals which preceded the law-making process.

If there is no formal law-making procedure, this differentiation of legal norms from ethical values and political principles and goals is not achieved. If any institution promulgates a text which is not formally law, the result is a mixture of ethical values, political norms and claims which looks a little bit like law. This mixture is a characteristic of the UN resolutions of NIEO. These resolutions admittedly are not sources of international law. Besides, their wording and formulation meet the technical requirements of legal norms only to a limited extent. On the other hand, these resolutions are made by a great number of member states of the UN with the intention to create a legal effect sooner or later. These considerations apply equally to the forthcoming international codes of conduct. A somewhat perplexed or

4. New International Economic Order. See Section 20.4 infra.

concerned science of public international law has termed these texts "soft law."

"The law is public if it is anything," said Allen. We may add: the law must be distinguishable from other sorts of principles, rules and declarations. This problem traditionally has been more crucial in public international law than in other areas of the law. Nevertheless, in the interest of the rule of law in international economic co-operation, there is an urgent need to end the confusion of normative categories. Here again, legal science must lend its services. A solution is certainly not to be found in any simple principle such as: all NIEO principles or declarations are or should be law or are not or should not be law. Such statements would be rather unrealistic in the current international scene. The contribution of legal science should be rather to help to clarify the distinction between the different normative categories and should define their possible connections.

We should briefly describe the two main questions involved: First, how can an international consensus be reached on the ethical values and standards involved? Secondly, how can these values and standards be transformed into law?

*   *   *

On the level of modern international commerce and economic cooperation, it should be even less difficult to find a consensus on common legal concepts, avoiding most differences in cultural traditions. There is an additional advantage in creating this consensus through the activity of international institutions and conferences. Here, it is not a question of the reception of an already existing foreign law, but the question is rather to find a new consensus of newly formulated rules. The verdict of "cultural imperialism" is easily avoided this way. We should not forget, however, that international rule-making meets tremendous difficulties in those areas where cultural differences have a direct impact on legal evaluations. This is the case, for example, in the area of corrupt practices.

The other successful approach to reach international consensus on ethical values and political concepts is to confine any discussion strictly to those questions directly relevant for technical rule-making. Today, this method is mainly adopted in the business of NIEO rule-making and other discussions on international economic law. We will give a few examples. It might be difficult to reach an international consensus as to the function of private ownership in an economic system; it seems to be less difficult, on the other hand, simply to define relations between supplying and acquiring parties concerning industrial property rights in the UNCTAD Code on Transfer of Technology, or to agree on a certain protection for private investment as in the Treaty of Lomé II. A global concept on the role of multinational enterprises is hard to define; it is more easy to define certain obligations in industrial and social relations in the ILO Declaration. Fairness in international commerce can hardly be fostered through global accusations or admonitions but can certainly be promoted through a definition of contractual obligations in sales contracts, such as is contained in the UNCITRAL Convention.

In this way, the implied ethical and political values and principles are not directly addressed. These ethical and political values and principles may find their way indirectly into the future world economic order. Indeed, it can be expected that some of the basic values of the law of a democratic and liberal industrialized society will survive in this international order to the extent that the indispensable market mechanisms survive.

THE LAW TRANSFORMATION PROCESS

The separation of rules from their underlying ethical and political values and principles, as employed in the process of negotiating the codes of conduct, is a typical criterion for the law-making process, as we observed. On the other hand, we have seen that the codes of conduct will probably stop half-way before becoming international law, as did the UN resolutions on NIEO. But there remains the question of how and under what conditions these texts may have legal effects or may be transformed, partly or completely into law. Such a transformation into law is desired by developing countries and feared by others who would not subscribe to all political claims or legal consequences contained in the texts.

One question is to what extent the texts or parts thereof may become customary public international law. In international commerce or other areas of international economic co-operation between private parties, the question is how far the values and principles spelt out in these texts will influence international commercial arbitration or national courts in their interpretation of municipal law. In this respect, the texts partly may serve as elements of an international *ordre public*. Moreover, the texts may serve as models for national legislation.

These questions cannot be discussed here in detail. We can only identify the transformation problem and ask whether the uncertain normative nature of the texts of NIEO will have beneficial or negative effects for international economic co-operation. One beneficial effect may be that the texts help to establish some general guidance in the legal practice of international commercial transactions and economic co-operation, to create common standards and uniform patterns as well as guidance, through what one may term international *ordre public*. International economic co-operation needs a certain degree of uniformity.

On the other hand, the uncertain and hybrid normative nature of the NIEO texts means that there will be a slow and gradual transformation process into law, led by national legislators, national courts, commercial arbitration and practicing lawyers drafting international contracts. In this process, those rules and principles must be spelt out which deserve and obtain international recognition as common rules with a legal effect. Legal science must help to overcome the confusion as to the normative categories. Peaceful international economic co-operation and commerce can work for the welfare of nations only under one essential and basic prerequisite: the rule of law.

Notes and Questions

(1) Some of the issues raised in the foregoing extracts—particularly those dealing with the nature and creation of customary international law—were

treated in more general terms in Section 5.2(A) supra and should be reviewed in considering the materials of this chapter.

(2) It seems clear that over time rules of customary international law may result from the current code drafting activities. Based on the foregoing excerpts is it possible to hazard an answer to the question of what minimum requirements would have to be met for that to occur?

(3) If MNEs are going to be the subjects of these codes, to what extent should they be permitted to participate formally in the drafting and adoption process?

(4) As noted above, some codes seem to have no mechanisms for adjusting to changes in economic and other conditions over time. Is there a possibility in such cases that the standards adopted today will be locked in forever, even though different (and likely stricter) standards would probably be adopted if the code had been considered a few years later? If this possibility exists, does this suggest that opponents of the codes may attempt to agree now on "watered-down" versions in hopes of avoiding stricter standards later?

(5) What is the effect of compliance with a code? In particular, to what extent should an MNE be able to defend its actions against criticism by a government or others, in judicial proceedings or otherwise, on the grounds that those actions were in compliance with a code? What difference does it make whether or not the government subscribes to the code?

(6) What problems do you think would arise if government-owned enterprises were subjected to the various MNE codes?

SECTION 17.3   THE 1976 OECD GUIDELINES FOR MULTINATIONAL ENTERPRISES

The 1976 OECD Guidelines for Multinational Enterprises are subscribed to by the member states of the OECD. Since most MNEs are based in those countries and since most investment by MNEs is located in those countries, the Guidelines are of considerable importance. Their significance is further heightened, at least for the present, by the fact that although other codes of similar breadth have been proposed and are now the subject of negotiations, no other code of comparable scope has yet been agreed to by a significant number of major nations. Moreover, although it is certainly true that the interests of the OECD member states, even in their role as host countries, are not the same as the interests of less developed countries, the Guidelines were written from the perspective of both home and host countries. As such, in reviewing the Guidelines the reader should consider why each particular topic was selected for treatment by the Guidelines, i.e. what is it about the nature of MNEs that would potentially cause problems concerning that topic? This exercise is particularly useful because the Guidelines deal with most of the significant issues raised by MNEs, albeit from a perspective more concerned with the problems of MNEs in advanced industrial economies. Following the Guidelines, a series of notes highlights some of these problems.

OECD, GUIDELINES FOR MULTINATIONAL ENTERPRISES

(1976) [1]

GENERAL POLICIES

Enterprises should

1. take fully into account established general policy objectives of the Member countries in which they operate;

2. in particular, give due consideration to those countries' aims and priorities with regard to economic and social progress, including industrial and regional development, the protection of the environment and consumer interests, the creation of employment opportunities, the promotion of innovation and the transfer of technology;

3. while observing their legal obligations concerning information, supply their entities with supplementary information the latter may need in order to meet requests by the authorities of the countries in which those entities are located for information relevant to the activities of those entities, taking into account legitimate requirements of business confidentiality;

4. favour close co-operation with the local community and business interests;

5. allow their component entities freedom to develop their activities and to exploit their competitive advantage in domestic and foreign markets, consistent with the need for specialisation and sound commercial practice;

6. when filling responsible posts in each country of operation, take due account of individual qualifications without discrimination as to nationality, subject to particular national requirements in this respect;

7. not render—and they should not be solicited or expected to render— any bribe or other improper benefit, direct or indirect, to any public servant or holder of public office;

8. unless legally permissible, not make contributions to candidates for public office or to political parties or other political organisations;

9. abstain from any improper involvement in local political activities.

DISCLOSURE OF INFORMATION

Enterprises should, having due regard to their nature and relative size in the economic context of their operations and to requirements of business confidentiality and to cost, publish in a form suited to improve public understanding a sufficient body of factual information on the structure, activities and policies of the enterprise as a whole, as a supplement, in so far as necessary for this purpose, to information to be disclosed under the

1. Reprinted by permission of the OECD. OECD, International Investment and Multinational Enterprises (rev. ed. (1979)), as amended, OECD, International Investment and Multinational Enterprises: The 1984 Review of the 1976 Declaration and Decisions 9 (1984). For an early analysis of the Guidelines, see P. Coolidge, G. Spina & D. Wallace (eds.), The OECD Guidelines for Multinational Enterprises: A Business Appraisal (1977).

national law of the individual countries in which they operate. To this end, they should publish within reasonable time limits, on a regular basis, but at least annually, financial statements and other pertinent information relating to the enterprise as a whole, comprising in particular:

   (i) the structure of the enterprise, showing the name and location of the parent company, its main affiliates, its percentage ownership, direct and indirect, in these affiliates, including shareholdings between them;

   (ii) the geographical areas where operations are carried out and the principal activities carried on therein by the parent company and the main affiliates;

   (iii) the operating results and sales by geographical area and the sales in the major lines of business for the enterprise as a whole;

   (iv) significant new capital investment by geographical area and, as far as practicable, by major lines of business for the enterprise as a whole;

   (v) a statement of the sources and uses of funds by the enterprise as a whole;

   (vi) the average number of employees in each geographical area;

   (vii) research and development expenditure for the enterprise as a whole;

   (viii) the policies followed in respect of intra-group pricing;

   (ix) the accounting policies, including those on consolidation, observed in compiling the published information.

COMPETITION

Enterprises should, while conforming to official competition rules and established policies of the countries in which they operate.

   1. refrain from actions which would adversely affect competition in the relevant market by abusing a dominant position of market power, by means of, for example,

   (a) anti-competitive acquisitions,

   (b) predatory behaviour toward competitors,

   (c) unreasonable refusal to deal,

   (d) anti-competitive abuse of industrial property rights,

   (e) discriminatory (i.e. unreasonably differentiated) pricing and using such pricing transactions between affiliated enterprises as a means of affecting adversely competition outside these enterprises;

   2. allow purchasers, distributors and licensees freedom to resell, export, purchase and develop their operations consistent with law, trade conditions, the need for specialisation and sound commercial practice;

   3. refrain from participating in or otherwise purposely strengthening the restrictive effects of international or domestic cartels or restric-

tive agreements which adversely affect or eliminate competition and which are not generally or specifically accepted under applicable national or international legislation;

4. be ready to consult and co-operate, including the provision of information, with competent authorities of countries whose interests are directly affected in regard to competition issues or investigations. Provision of information should be in accordance with safeguards normally applicable in this field.

FINANCING

Enterprises should, in managing the financial and commercial operations of their activities, and especially their liquid foreign assets and liabilities, take into consideration the established objectives of the countries in which they operate regarding balance of payments and credit policies.

TAXATION

Enterprises should

1. upon request of the taxation authorities of the countries in which they operate, provide, in accordance with the safeguards and relevant procedures of the national laws of these countries, the information necessary to determine correctly the taxes to be assessed in connection with their operations, including relevant information concerning their operations in other countries;

2. refrain from making use of the particular facilities available to them, such as transfer pricing which does not conform to an arm's length standard, for modifying in ways contrary to national laws the tax base on which members of the group are assessed.

EMPLOYMENT AND INDUSTRIAL RELATIONS

Enterprises should, within the framework of law, regulations and prevailing labour relations and employment practices, in each of the countries in which they operate,

1. respect the right of their employees to be represented by trade unions and other bona fide organisations of employees, and engage in constructive negotiations, either individually or through employers' associations, with such employee organisations with a view to reaching agreements on employment conditions, which should include provisions for dealing with disputes arising over the interpretation of such agreements, and for ensuring mutually respected rights and responsibilities;

2. *(a)* provide such facilities to representatives of the employees as may be necessary to assist in the development of effective collective agreements,

   (b) provide to representatives of employees information which is needed for meaningful negotiations on conditions of employment;

3. provide to representatives of employees where this accords with local law and practice, information which enables them to obtain a

true and fair view of the performance of the entity or, where appropriate, the enterprise as a whole;

4. observe standards of employment and industrial relations not less favourable than those observed by comparable employers in the host country;

5. in their operations, to the greatest extent practicable, utilise, train and prepare for upgrading members of the local labour force in co-operation with representatives of their employees and, where appropriate, the relevant governmental authorities;

6. in considering changes in their operations which would have major effects upon the livelihood of their employees, in particular in the case of the closure of an entity envoluing collective lay-offs or dismissals, provide reasonable notice of such changes to representatives of their employees, and where appropriate to the relevant governmental authorities, and co-operate with the employee representatives and appropriate governmental authorities so as to mitigate to the maximum extent practicable adverse effects;

7. implement their employment policies including hiring, discharge, pay, promotion and training without discrimination unless selectivity in respect of employee characteristics is in furtherance of established governmental policies which specifically promote greater equality of employment opportunity;

8. in the context of bona fide negotiations with representatives of employees on conditions of employment, or while employees are exercising a right to organise, not threaten to utilise a capacity to transfer the whole or part of an operating unit from the country concerned nor transfer employees from the enterprises' component entities in other countries in order to influence unfairly those negotiations or to hinder the exercise of a right to organise;

9. enable authorised representatives of their employees to conduct negotiations on collective bargaining or labour management relations issues with representatives of management who are authorised to take decisions on the matters under negotiation.

SCIENCE AND TECHNOLOGY

Enterprises should

1. endeavour to ensure that their activities fit satisfactorily into the scientific and technological policies and plans of the countries in which they operate, and contribute to the development of national scientific and technological capacities, including as far as appropriate the establishment and improvement in host countries of their capacity to innovate;

2. to the fullest extent practicable, adopt in the course of their business activities practices which permit the rapid diffusion of technologies with due regard to the protection of industrial and intellectual property rights;

3.   when granting licences for the use of industrial property rights or when otherwise transferring technology do so on reasonable terms and conditions.

Notes and Questions

(1) The introductory comments to the Guidelines provide that they are "recommendations jointly addressed by Member countries to multinational enterprises operating in their territories." They go on to state explicitly: "Observance of the guidelines is voluntary and not legally enforceable." The introductory comments also note, however, that each country "has the right to prescribe the conditions under which multinational enterprises operate within its national jurisdiction." In light of the *Badger* case described below and the materials in Section 17.2 supra, the reader should consider: How "voluntary" are the Guidelines?

(2) In a separate Decision adopted at the time the Guidelines were issued, the OECD set up a Committee on International Investment and Multinational Enterprise. The Committee is to exchange views on the application of the Guidelines and to be responsible for their "clarification." Although the Committee is not authorized to "reach conclusions" on the conduct of an individual company, it does consider interpretative issues arising out of concrete factual situations. See Second Revised Decision of the Council on the Guidelines for Multinational Enterprises, in OECD, International Investment and Multinational Enterprises: The 1984 Review of the 1976 Declaration and Decisions (1984).

The so-called *Badger* case, described in the following extract, has probably been the best known case to come before the Committee.

JOHN ROBINSON, MULTINATIONALS AND POLITICAL CONTROL
125–28 (1983) [2]

The first case submitted to the OECD's IME Committee immediately raised the Guidelines from the level of an arcane bureaucratic exercise to the first rank of political and economic reality. Concerning the Badger Co., a wholly-owned Belgian subsidiary of American multinational Raytheon, this case was brought not just by TUAC on behalf of the unions involved but also by the Belgian government in the shape of Minister Mark Eyskens, then Secretary of State for the Regional Economy, and since Belgian Prime Minister.

The situation was triggered when in late 1976 it became clear that the central management of Raytheon was actively considering the closedown of Badger in the absence of a prospective buyer for its unprofitable Belgian subsidiary—which management claimed had in any case been only kept alive by transfer to it of work and orders from other of Raytheon's European subsidiaries. By early February 1977, closure was effected and by the time of the 30 March session of OECD government officials, the following state of affairs had been reached, according to Minister Eyskens' letter to the IME Committee:

> compulsory winding-up of Badger (Belgium) has been ordered and it has not paid its creditors. The compensation owed to members of staff in the case of the closure of an enterprise amounts, according to Belgian law, which makes

---

2. © John Robinson 1983 and reprinted by permission of St. Martin's Press Inc. The author discusses other issues considered by the Committee at 122–40.

no distinction here between national and foreign enterprises, to BF 250 million (6.5 million dollars) (compensation for dismissal + additional compensation for workers in the case of the closure of an enterprise). The parent company has refused to intervene to settle the liabilities of its subsidiary not covered by the available assets.

At stake in the Badger case, then, were a variety of issues of seminal interest, including in particular: the application of the Guidelines in bringing about actual changes in corporate behaviour; the issue of parent company responsibility over a foreign subsidiary limited in liability, the question of the notice to workers and public authorities to be given by a company envisaging shutdown and lay-offs and the compatibility of this practice with national laws.

In summary these issues were resolved or debated along the following lines:

—*the Guidelines and individual MNCs:* as laid down in the 1976 decision of the OECD Council, the IME Committee 'shall not reach conclusions on the conduct of individual enterprises', a point eagerly made by the 30 March 1977 meeting of the Committee. However, there can be no doubt that the Guidelines were used successfully to exert pressure on Raytheon's central management to change its initial position, and in this the use of the Guidelines was not restricted to the forum of the IME Committee. Strong bilateral representations were made by the Belgian government to the American State Department, to say nothing of parallel interventions between Brussels and respectively the Netherlands and Britain where two other subsidiaries of Raytheon were located. Set against the background of these intergovernmental contracts, continued union pressure and IME Committee debate, Raytheon finally agreed a settlement with the Belgian government in April 1977. The Badger case thus contains an important lesson for the future. While there is no question of the OECD governments constituting a court to sit in judgment over individual multinationals, the Guidelines themselves can clearly be used as a strong basis for high-level political and economic leverage outside the formal context of the IME Committee. This lesson was to be reinforced in the Hertz case.

—*parental responsibility over a foreign wholly-owned subsidiary:* this in many senses is the key issue of the Badger case, since the extent to which Raytheon was to be considered responsible for the activities (or the cessation of those activities) of a subsidiary raised the central question of the legal status of corporate groups, and got the IME Committee willy-nilly into a debate directly associated with this question. Is a parent company liable, beyond its equity stake, for a subsidiary's obligations to its local environment? Considered 'crucial' by government representatives, this issue was given in-depth debate by them in late 1977 when the Badger case continued to smoulder. The confidential report of the Lévy subcommittee of the IME Committee said:

> It was generally recognized that there was no absolute, unqualified principle of responsibility on the part of the parent company. On the other hand, it was also generally recognized that in some circumstances, which would have to be defined pragmatically, some degree of responsibility on the part of the parent company did exist as a complement to the existing legal provisions. * * * It was suggested that consideration be given to the idea that the responsibility of the parent company might be based on the notion of some behaviour on its part which would

lead to its having a responsibility in certain situations. Lastly, it was also suggested that the IME Committee should examine the actual situation as it existed in each Member country as regards the responsibility of parent companies with respect to their subsidiary companies located within the country.

(All of which have proved grist to the mill of EEC company lawyers who are now actively preparing such an initiative on multinational group law.) The report by Mr. Levy was in fact in response to the Belgian government memo on Badger which, invoking the introduction to the OECD Guidelines in support of its case, stated baldly that 'a parent company is obliged to help its subsidiaries to fulfil their obligations'. In actual fact, section 8 of the introduction to the Guidelines is provocatively evasive when it states:

> the guidelines are addressed to the various entities within the multinational enterprise (parent companies and/or local entities) according to the actual distribution of responsibilities among them on the understanding that they will co-operate and provide assistance to one another as necessary to facilitate observation of the guidelines. The word 'enterprise' as used in these guidelines refers to the various entities in accordance with their responsibilities.

—*company dealings with workers and governments:* the Belgian government referring to section 7 of the introduction to the Guidelines, had made much of the need for Badger to meet its obligation under Belgian law. Section 7 states:

> Every State has the right to prescribe the conditions under which multinational enterprises operate within its national jurisdiction, subject to international law and to the international agreements to which it has subscribed. The entities of a multinational enterprise located in various countries are subject to the laws of these countries.

This, together with section 8 of the introduction (see above) was the basis for the Belgian government's contention that Raytheon should be liable for Badger (Belgium's) debts and severance indemnities for its workforce. However, in the view of other OECD governments, 'it would seem to be interpreting the guidelines too broadly' to say on the basis of the Guidelines that 'parent company should be liable for debts of subsidiaries even if the latter has been declared bankrupt unless the law provides for such responsibility'. As against this, said the OECD Committee: 'it must be recognised that section 6 of the Section on Employment and Industrial Relations places termination claims in an exceptional position by virtue of the parent company's responsibility for the livelihood of the employees of its subsidiary when deciding to close down the operations which lead to the collective lay-off or dismissal of labour employed by a subsidiary'. Section 6 of the Guidelines section on Employment and Industrial Relations states:

> in considering changes in their operations which would have major effects upon the livelihood of their employees, in particular in the case of the closure of an entity involving collective lay-offs or dismissals, enterprises should provide reasonable notice of such changes to representatives of their employees, and where appropriate to the relevant governmental authorities, and co-operate with the employee representatives and appropriate governmental authorities so as to mitigate to the maximum extent practicable adverse effects.

So despite the strictures put by the IME Committee on an interpretation of the Guidelines which would offend accepted wisdom on parent company responsibility, 'the Guidelines may, and sometimes do, put obligations on multinational enterprises going beyond what it required from them by law'. More ominous still for MNCs is the assertion made in the closed-door intergovernmental discussion of the Badger case that the Guidelines, while not legally binding, may become *de facto* part of customary international law: *'in the course of time, sections of the Guidelines, although voluntary in their origin and not being sanctioned by law, may pass, by virtue of their general acceptance and frequent application, into the general corpus of customary international law, even for those international enterprises that have never explicitly accepted them'.* So is 'soft law politically hardened.'

In light of the result of the Badger case, is it correct to view the Guidelines as voluntary? Does the Badger case suggest that the decision to close a plant is limited by the Guidelines, or is it really only about the responsibility of a parent company for the debts of its wholly-owned subsidiaries? Consider your answer further when you read the following note.

(3) Probably the most controversial provisions of the Guidelines are those that impinge on an MNE's right to operate on a global basis and make decisions regarding components of the MNE without regard to local effects. In recent years, the need for structural adjustment has caused many MNEs to rationalize production. A particularly difficult issue has been the extent to which the General Policies expressed in the Guidelines should or do already purport to limit an MNE's freedom to do so. The Committee explained these issues as follows in 1984:

REPORT BY THE COMMITTEE ON INTERNATIONAL INVESTMENT AND MULTINATIONAL ENTERPRISE

(1984) [3]

2. STRUCTURAL ADJUSTMENT AND MULTINATIONAL ENTERPRISES

46. In recent years, a number of issues that have come up in discussion in the Committee in relation to the Guidelines have centered on the relevance of the Guidelines in instances where multinational enterprises undertake substantial reorganisation of their activities following changes in technology and market conditions and prospects. Structural adjustments of this kind are a permanent feature of the life of enterprises. But it does seem that the long period of industrial recession in OECD countries, characterised by a relatively low level of investment, a high rate of bankruptcy of firms and the major growth of unemployment under conditions of the growing competitive power of some developing countries, major technological developments, declining tariffs and changing trade barriers, and redirections of Member government policies has imposed upon many multinational groups hard decisions regarding their business strategies and their geographical implantation. The Guidelines address many of the issues relating to multinational enterprise responses to structural challenges which can be a source of concern of governments and in this respect it

3. Reprinted by permission of the Organization for Economic Cooperation and Development. OECD, note 1 supra, at 18, 32–35.

is clear that the Guidelines should be applied by enterprises in a way that will contribute to increasing the benefits and decreasing the costs of adjustments. The Committee recognised that further analysis of this phenomenon, particularly as concerns strategies which have become evident more recently, should be carried out in order, inter alia, to ensure that the solutions proposed by the Guidelines when restructuring takes place are still workable and satisfactory. A major study of the structural adjustment strategies of multinational enterprises was undertaken and the issue was discussed several times with representatives of BIAC and TUAC. The main results of this study and its implications are found below.

47. Structural adjustment is neither a new nor necessarily a problematical phenomenon, as many of the experiences of the fifties and sixties illustrate. It is also a process which may take the form of a series of relatively minor steps, rather than a major upheaval in the life of an enterprise. Structural adjustment may nevertheless be seen to present a particular issue today because the coincidence of a number of major structural changes in the seventies, and the slowness to realise their secular rather than cyclical nature, has resulted in serious structural imbalances in some industrial and geographical areas, creating major pressures for change, often of an abrupt and lumpy nature. In this respect, there is a broad consensus in the OECD area for the adoption of positive adjustment policies aimed at promoting and managing structural change by enhancing the flexibility of the market mechanism to foster the changes required by new patterns of demand and supply while recognising that government measures aimed at bringing about positive structural adjustment under socially acceptable conditions and at a speed which is politically feasible may be fully legitimate in specific cases.

48. The reactions of enterprises to adjustment pressures may take many forms, and the Committee's study has found, in general, few major differences in the strategies and reactions of multinational vis-à-vis domestic enterprises, as both groups are subject to relatively similar sets of pressures. The available evidence suggests that, broadly speaking, multinational enterprises have made a positive contribution to structural adjustment because they have often been able to adjust more flexibly, sometimes even in anticipation of adjustment pressures due to their managerial, financial and technology position, before problems grow acute. Their employment performance has been at least equal to, and in some cases superior to, domestic firms. Nor do they, from the evidence collected by the Committee, resort more to the closure of an entity, in comparison to their domestic counterparts. Despite these broad similarities, however, there are a number of areas where the actions of some multinational enterprises may differ from domestic firms, stemming in particular from features unique to multinationals, such as their internationality, operations across national boundaries, unity of purpose and pursuit of global strategies. Differences of degree, for example, concerning technology, marketing or managerial or financial resources also exist.

49. Such differences can have implications for the nature of decision making inside a group of related enterprises or for the implementation of strategic decisions implying structural adjustment. It is understandable, in this connection, that a number of issues and concerns should have been raised in areas covered by the Guidelines, for example in the chapters on General Policies, Disclosure of Information, Employment and Industrial Relations and Science

and Technology. For example, there may be considerable political sensitivity at the national level if restructuring decisions by multinational enterprises leading to plant closures or substantial layoffs are taken at head offices, outside the jurisdiction of the country concerned. When major restructuring activities are carried out across national boundaries the Guidelines, for example paragraph 2 of the General Policies chapter, which requests enterprises to give due consideration to the aims and priorities with regard to economic and social progress of the Member countries in which they operate, may provide guidance to multinational enterprises as to how they should take into account the interests of the countries in which they operate. In this respect paragraph 8 of the Introduction to the Guidelines, which states, inter alia, that the Guidelines are addressed to the various entities within the multinational enterprise according to the actual distribution of responsibilities among them on the understanding that they will cooperate and provide assistance to one another as necessary to facilitate observance of the Guidelines, is also relevant.

50. In discussing the issues and concerns raised in connection with the adjustment strategies of multinational enterprises, the Committee noted a relatively recent aspect of these strategies, concerning the still recent advent of technologies permitting rapid collection and treatment of information on the performance of the group as a whole. These technologies may facilitate some multinationals to adopt a more centralised decision-making structure while, for others, they may permit greater decentralisation. Many feel that the latter is to be encouraged to minimise and to equitably distribute the costs, and maximise the benefits, of adjustment.

51. In those cases where multinational enterprises are pursuing more centralised control of their activities as a whole, it can easily be understood that this leads to concern that the degree of autonomy of subsidiary entities is being reduced excessively, thus possibly rendering the latter less responsive to local conditions. The desirability of having subsidiaries develop freely their activities or exploit competitive advantages in domestic and foreign markets, consistent with the need for specialisation and sound commercial practice, is addressed by paragraph 5 of the Guideline on General Policies. The Guideline does not call for the freezing of the existing structures of multinational enterprises, nor do they infringe on the freedom of these enterprises to take decisions to divest in the furtherance of global strategies judged to be in the best interests of the firm as a whole. But paragraph 5 (together with paragraph 4 of the General Policies chapter of the Guidelines) is to be understood as recommending that enterprises should favour, to the extent possible, integration of the component entities of a multinational enterprise into the economic context of the countries in which they operate, and give to these entities sufficient responsibilities and resources to enable them to maintain and develop their competitive potential, giving due concern to the interests of the enterprise as a whole as well as the situation of any of its entities. These considerations may allow entities greater opportunities for competitive structural adjustment, as opposed to contraction, when realistic choices exist, and to engage in adjustments that may be important for some governments such as developing and utilising economic local sources of supply, upgrading natural resources before export and allowing local equity participation.

52. Structural adaptation may involve decisions which have major effects on the livelihood of employees, such as closure or transfer of an entity or part

thereof, the reorganisation or concentration of activities, and the introduction of new technologies. In cooperation between management and labour for the purpose of mitigating to the maximum extent practicable the adverse effects on labour of such decisions, some governments and some trade union representatives have reported instances where they feel that the provision of information on such decisions on an adequate and timely basis has not been forthcoming. Employees and their representatives may require particular information including, for example and in specific situations, information on the allocation of markets and production between entities, in order for them to assess the position of their entity in a wider context. A further area where concerns have been raised by employees and their representatives is that of access to management representatives with sufficient authority to take any decisions which might be called for in the circumstances. The specific concerns in the field of co-operation between management and labour relating to changes in operations which would have major effects on the livelihood of employees are addressed by paragraph 6 of the Employment and Industrial Relations Guidelines. The special character of multinational enterprises is also recognised in this regard, as in other matters related to the Guidelines, in paragraph 8 of the introduction to the Guidelines, which states that "Guidelines are addressed to the various entities within the multinational enterprise (parent companies and/or local entities) according to the actual distribution of responsibilities among them on the understanding that they will co-operate and provide assistance to one another as necessary to facilitate observance of the Guidelines." The Committee has provided a clarification to paragraph 9 of the Employment and Industrial Relations Guideline regarding different ways in which, when negotiations or collective bargaining or labour management relations issues are concerned, firms can ensure that management representatives who participate in such negotiations "are authorised to take decisions on the matters under negotiation." Regarding paragraph 6, which states that, in considering changes in their operations, enterprises should "provide reasonable notice of such changes" and "co-operate with the employee representatives and appropriate governmental authorities so as to mitigate to the maximum extent practicable adverse effects", the Committee has indicated, by means of a clarification, its opinion that it would be in conformity with the intention of paragraph 6 of the Employment and Industrial Relations Guideline if representatives of management participating in the process of co-operation addressed in this paragraph had sufficient authority to co-operate in good faith and consistent with paragraph 8 of the introduction to the Guidelines, to take the decisions that might be called for as required by the circumstances.

How would you characterize the limitations that are placed on an MNE by the Guidelines in respect of restructuring through closing unprofitable operations? Exactly how far should an MNE have to go to try to make one of its units economically viable? What should an MNE do if it believes that efforts to make one lagging unit viable may jeopardize the health of other units? To the extent that limitations are placed on the actions of MNEs, to what extent do you think similar sorts of requirements apply to domestically owned companies? If they do not, can a difference in treatment between MNEs and domestic companies be justified? In this regard, it should be noted that the introductory comments to the Guidelines state that "The guidelines are not aimed at introducing differences of treatment between multinational and domestic enterprises; wherever relevant they reflect good practice for all." Query: When, if ever, are the Guidelines "relevant" to domestic enterprise?

(4) The question of how much information must be disclosed to employees of an MNE, both about the individual unit concerned and the entity as a whole, is a matter of some controversy. A number of European countries, such as Belgium, the Netherlands and Germany have various laws requiring provision of information to workers, or, even, in the case of Germany, worker participation on supervisory boards of corporations of certain size.[4] Attempts to standardize practice in the EC on such topics have generated much controversy. The so-called Fifth Directive on company law harmonization—which originally would have provided for worker representation on the boards of certain large corporations and as now proposed would provide more flexibility in the way in which employees participation or consultation could be structured—has not yet been adopted, although it was proposed in 1972.[5] A more recent proposal for a directive on provision of information to and required consultations with workers, the so-called Vreedling directive (named after the member of the Commission who sponsored it) has generated even more controversy and, although it has been revised to meet the objections of some, has also not been adopted.[6] The controversy over the issues discussed in this Note is instructive for it underscores the fact—sometimes forgotten—that regulation of MNEs is not an issue solely of interest to the developing countries. Indeed, issues concerning MNEs provoke considerable controversy in many advanced industrialized countries.

(5) The Guidelines' provisions on taxation are not extensive, but they highlight one of the most significant governmental concerns about MNEs. As noted before, MNEs engage in a significant amount of intra enterprise trade. As a consequence, by setting relatively high or low prices for transfers between its various units, an MNE can determine which of these units will be relatively profitable or unprofitable. Since the principal taxes on corporations are levied on corporate income, an MNE may be able to reduce its tax burden significantly by adjusting its transfer prices. The Guidelines call upon MNEs to refrain from doing this, at least to the extent that the resultant prices cannot be justified as arm's length prices. We will consider this issue again in Chapter 19 infra. The problem of transfer prices is of relevance to other issues as well. For example, in a country with exchange controls, purchases of raw materials may be approved routinely, while there may be restrictions on repatriation of earnings or capital to a foreign investor. Such exchange control restrictions could be effectively circumvented by an MNE if it were to charge excessive raw materials prices to its local subsidiary.

(6) The Guidelines' treatment of science and technology issues also highlights another major concern about MNE behavior. Developing countries in particular (but other countries as well) are concerned about improving the state of technology used in their economies. An MNE has considerable control over the extent and the terms pursuant to which technology is transferred from the parent company to various subsidiaries. It is sometimes argued that MNEs tend to focus their research and development activities in home country facilities and

---

4. See generally Kolvenbach, The Evolving Concept of European Labor Relations Legislation, 3 Nw.J.Intl.L. & Bus. 535 (1981).

5. The current proposal is set out in [1983] Eur.Comm.O.J. No. C 240/2. See E. Stein, P. Hay, M. Waelbroeck & J. Weiler, European

Community Law and Institutions in Perspective: Text, Cases and Readings 182–84 (1985 Supp.).

6. The current proposal is set out in [1983] Eur.Comm.O.J. No. C 217/3. See E. Stein et al., note 5 supra, at 372–75.

transfer technology to subsidiaries only for excessive payments. The Guidelines call upon MNEs to ensure that their activities in this regard "fit" into the policies of the countries in which they operate. The concern of developing countries in respect of these issues has led to efforts by UNCTAD to draft an International Code of Conduct on the Transfer of Technology. The aim of the developing countries in urging the creation of a code such as this is to speed the unfettered transfer of technology to such countries. A number of major issues concerning the code have not yet been resolved, including the precise practices to be banned and the coverage of the code (e.g., should it apply to transfers made within a single firm, or only to transfers between unrelated parties).[7]

Note on Existing and Proposed Codes of Conduct [8]

We cannot hope in this short chapter to consider in any detail the many existing and proposed codes of conduct for MNEs. The following list is, however, an effort to call the reader's attention to the more significant codes and their general coverage.

International Chamber of Commerce, Guidelines for International Investment (1972). The Guidelines are not meant to be a code of conduct, but express the ICC's view on issues later dealt with in the OECD Guidelines.

International Labor Organization, Tripartite Declaration of Principles Concerning Multinational Enterprises and Social Policy (1977).[9] The Declaration is mainly concerned with employment related issues and is considered by the OECD Committee to be consistent with the Guidelines.

UNCTAD, Set of Multilaterally Agreed Equitable Principles and Rules for the Control of Restrictive Business Practices (1980).[10] The Principles are aimed at controlling restrictive business practices affecting international trade and the economic development of developing countries. See Chapter 18 infra.

UNCTAD, Proposed Code of Conduct on the Transfer of Technology. The proposed code is concerned with the liberalization of transfer of technology to developing countries.[11]

United Nations, Economic and Social Council, Commission on Transnational Corporations, Proposed Code of Conduct for Transnational Corporations. The proposed code is concerned with corporate activities in general and the rights of countries to regulate them.[12]

---

7. See generally Roffe, Transfer of Technology: UNCTAD's Draft International Code of Conduct, 19 Intl.Law. 689 (1985).

8. A particularly rich source of materials on codes of conduct, including an introductory survey by Hans Baade and a bibliography is N. Horn (ed.), Legal Problems of Codes of Conduct for Multinational Enterprises (1980). Other useful sources, in addition to works cited elsewhere in this chapter, include Wallace, International Codes and Guidelines for Multinational Enterprises: Update and Selected Issues, 17 Intl.Law. 435 (1983); Grosse,

Codes of Conduct for Multinational Enterprises, 16 J. World Trade L. 414 (1982); Bobrow & Kudrle, MNE Disclosure Alternatives and their Consequences, 18 J. World Trade L. 437 (1984).

9. 17 Intl.Legal Materials 423 (1978).

10. 19 Intl.Legal Materials 813 (1980).

11. See Roffe, note 7 supra.

12. 23 Intl.Legal Materials 626 (1984). For a report on outstanding issues see id. at 602.

United Nations Economic and Social Council, International Agreement on Illicit Payments.[13] The draft agreement has not been acted upon by the General Assembly.

13. 18 Intl.Legal Materials 1025 (1979).

Chapter 18

RESTRICTIVE BUSINESS PRACTICES AND INTERNATIONAL ECONOMIC RELATIONS

SECTION 18.1 INTRODUCTION [1]

With the passage of the Sherman Act in 1890, the United States became the first country to attempt general statutory control of the power wielded by large business enterprises. Since World War II, most of the world's developed countries and many developing nations have enacted laws of one sort or another to control restrictive or anti-competitive business practices. In addition to these national laws, the EC has its own supranational antitrust provisions—generally referred to as competition rules—modelled on the Sherman Act and effective in its member states. The growing interdependence of the developed nations' economies, the increase in the size and reach of multinational enterprises (MNEs) and the developing nations' concern with the power that the MNEs have over their economies, all have raised doubts as to whether existing national or regional controls adequately regulate restrictive business practices and as to whether such practices are appropriately the subject of control only by uncoordinated national laws. Particularly in respect of international transactions affecting more than one country, it has been argued that it may be necessary to establish international standards and, as a consequence, various international organizations have examined these problems and in some cases have acted to establish standards.

This chapter will address a number of problems raised by the existence and regulation of restrictive business practices. We consider first the close

---

1. In addition to the materials cited elsewhere in this chapter, the following sources may prove helpful to the interested student: B. Hawk, United States, Common Market and International Antitrust: A Comparative Guide (2d ed.1985); ABA Antitrust Section, Antitrust Law Developments (2d ed.1984); S. Oppenheim, G. Weston & J. McCarthy, Federal Antitrust Laws: Cases, Text and Commen- tary ch. 15 (4th ed.1981); O. Schachter & R. Hellawell (eds.), Competition in International Business (1981); J. Atwood & K. Brewster, Antitrust and American Business Abroad (2d ed.1981); W. Fugate, Foreign Commerce and the Antitrust Laws (3d ed.1982); Symposium: Current Antitrust Law and United States International Trade Practices, 15 Vand.J.Transnatl.L. 667 (1982).

relationship between trade and competition (antitrust) policies. Indeed, in reviewing the material in Section 18.2, the reader should ask whether the interrelationship is so great that the rules applicable to trade should be required to be taken into account in applying competition rules and vice versa.

In this brief overview of the interrelationship of competition policies and international economic relations, we cannot hope to sketch the substance of national antitrust laws except with a broad brush. Nonetheless, in Section 18.3, we briefly outline the U.S. rules and consider examples of their application to international transactions of the type considered in this book. We then turn to the most controversial issue arising out of the application of national laws on restrictive business practices to international transactions: the question of extraterritorial enforcement of such laws. The issues here are similar to those we have seen elsewhere, particularly in respect of export controls (see Section 13.5 supra). However, extraterritorial application of antitrust laws is of special interest because of the various countermeasures that nations have taken to deter attempts to exercise extraterritorial jurisdiction.

SECTION 18.2   THE RELATIONSHIP OF COMPETITION AND TRADE POLICIES

The Sherman Act is the cornerstone of U.S. antitrust law, and the model for many other countries' statutes. In discussing the principles underlying the Act, the Supreme Court has said: [1]

> The Sherman Act was designed to be a comprehensive charter of economic liberty aimed at preserving free and unfettered competition as the rule of trade. It rests on the premise that the unrestrained interaction of competitive forces will yield the best allocation of our economic resources, the lowest prices, the highest quality and the greatest material progress, while at the same time providing an environment conducive to the preservation of our democratic political and social institutions. But even were that premise open to question, the policy unequivocally laid down by the Act is competition.

The fact that antitrust laws are aimed at promoting free competition suggests their importance to international trade. If private parties are permitted to interfere with free market forces and to restrain trade between countries, e.g., by entering into anticompetitive price-fixing or market-sharing agreements, they may effectively replace the government-imposed barriers to trade that GATT is supposed to limit. Conversely, to the extent GATT allows departures from the free trade norm, e.g., by allowing inefficient producers to be protected from the rigors of competition, GATT may contribute to thwarting the policies of antitrust laws.

---

1. Northern Pacific Railway Co. v. United States, 356 U.S. 1, 4, 78 S.Ct. 514, 517, 2 L.Ed. 2d 545, 549 (1958).

OECD, COMPETITION AND TRADE POLICIES: THEIR INTERACTION

87, 112–13 (1984)[2]

* * * [R]estrictive business practices can have significant effects on the competitive functioning of international markets and are thus of concern to trade policy. It is similarly the case that trade policy measures that result in barriers to international trade can have important detrimental effects on domestic market structures by diminishing competition. For example, a trade policy that permits domestic firms to co-ordinate their exports in a cartel-like manner may weaken competition to the extent that export co-ordination also facilitates co-ordination of domestic sales. On the other hand, trade policy that permits a free flow of imports is likely to cause domestic markets to behave more competitively. Thus, trade policy can either significantly promote or substantially impede the economic goals of competition policy. With national economies being increasingly linked and interdependent, trade liberalisation policies maintain a climate conducive to the effective functioning of competition in national and international markets.

* * *

* * * [T]rade policy measures exercise a significant impact on competition and on markets. This is also the case with the enforcement of laws relating to unfair trade practices. While designed to adjust competitive disequilibria brought about by unfair and injurious import pricing practices, the enforcement of these laws can, in certain circumstances, restrict competition in domestic markets by raising entry barriers to foreign competitors. In this respect, two fundamental concerns arise for competition policy. The first is whether private firms abuse unfair trade laws by bringing actions to gain leverage over foreign competitors and either control or exclude their presence in domestic markets. Second, the question arises whether the effects on competition of proceedings under laws relating to unfair trade practices are adequately considered, in particular in the measurement of injury to domestic industry and in the level of relief granted. * * *

There are certain common elements in competition policy and laws relating to unfair trade practices. Both share the common objective of seeking to remove artificial distortions in markets. But differences emerge in the nature of the interests they seek to protect and in the ways in which standards are applied. The principal goal in competition policy is to preserve and maintain competitive domestic market structures and the efficient allocation of resources by prohibiting practices that restrain competition or impose barriers to new entrants. Emphasis is placed on market performance, costs and scale economies. The principal concern is to protect competition, and not competitors. Competition policy does not seek to protect inefficient competitors against lower prices that are achieved through efficiency, economies of scale, cheap labour or technological expertise, so long as

---

2. Reprinted by permission of the Organization for Economic Cooperation and Development. See also Goldsweig, Enborg & Walton, The Impact of United States Antitrust Law on the Balance of Trade, 15 Vanderbilt J.Transnatl.L. 751 (1982).

the advantage is fairly attained. Nor, in most countries, does competition policy allow a departure from competitive principles for firms buffeted by recessionary conditions, shrinking markets or technological obsolescence.

Laws relating to unfair trade practices, in contrast, aim to protect domestic industry from unfair import pressures causing injury to domestic competitors. Thus, the basic issue in the application of these trade laws is generally the legitimacy or illegitimacy of various competitive advantages which foreign producers enjoy over domestic firms and the resultant harm to domestic industry. Under these laws, the effect of the practices on competition in the market and the ultimate effect on consumers are not at issue, nor are they elements of the offence, except insofar as they relate to the causation of harm to the domestic industry. These differences in comparison with competition policy can be partly explained by the divergent concepts upon which rules of international trade are based and the different interests considered in formulating and applying trade policies.

Notes and Questions

(1) The economic analysis of tariffs in Chapter 1 demonstrates that government interference in the marketplace through artificially raising a price by imposing a tariff is inefficient. The same analysis applies in the case of private parties raising a price by agreement between themselves. The incentive for such agreements can easily be seen. As the analysis of Chapter 1 showed, the increased prices resulting from interference with market prices may mean increased profits for the sellers of the particular product. Thus, those sellers, absent legal constraints, may be eager to obtain those increased profits. Antitrust laws exist to prevent them from doing so.

(2) National antitrust laws sometimes do not concern themselves with, or often even explicitly permit, anticompetitive behavior in international markets. Among the competition policies noted by the OECD study that affect international trade are (A) laws authorizing export cartels, which may restrict international trade by causing excessively high export prices or trade-inhibiting market allocation, (B) laws authorizing import cartels, which may allow private parties to control prices and quantities as if they had the power to impose tariffs and quotas, (C) policies that fail to control the practices of trading companies, which means the prices and quantities of significant numbers of imported and exported products in some countries are determined by a small number of private companies and (D) policies that allow multinational enterprises to allocate functions among various components and to set transfer prices that do not reflect market prices. Should GATT concern itself with the existence of such practices? Are there meaningful differences between the effects on international trade of a state-owned trading company with exclusive trading rights (the activities of which would be subject to some controls under GATT, see Section 21.2 infra) and a private firm or group of firms that enjoys an effective monopoly?

(3) As stated in the OECD study, exceptions to general free trade policies that are designed to prevent unfair trade practices often operate not to protect competition per se, but rather to protect individual competitors. An example is the protection afforded in escape clause proceedings, such as those discussed in Chapter 9 supra. Should more consideration be given by competition authorities

to trade policy issues and vice versa? The OECD study suggests that the answer is clearly yes. The difficult question then becomes how much consideration should be given? For example, should escape clause relief, or antidumping or antisubsidy relief, be conditioned upon a requirement that there will be no adverse competitive effects? Or would such a finding preclude relief in most cases and thereby effectively repeal those statutes? Is there a more acceptable intermediate position?

(4) Antitrust authorities typically try to discourage mergers that significantly increase market concentration, i.e., the extent to which a few firms have a large share of the market. One controversial issue in analyzing market concentration and the effect of mergers is the extent to which the possibility or existence of international trade flows should be considered. In its 1984 Merger Guidelines, the U.S. Department of Justice explained its treatment of import competition in analyzing the competitive impacts of mergers as follows: [3]

> Actual import sales, shipment data, or capacity in some cases may tend to overstate the relative competitive significance of foreign firms. This will be the case, for example, if foreign firms are subject to quotas (imposed either by the United States or by their own country) that effectively limit the volume of their imports into this country. Foreign firms that are subject to such quotas generally cannot increase imports into the United States in response to a domestic price increase. In cases of restraints that limit imports to some percentage of the total amount of the product sold in the United States (i.e., percentage quotas), a domestic price increase that reduces domestic consumption would actually reduce the volume of imports into the United States. Thus, actual import sales and shipment data will tend to overstate the competitive significance of firms in countries subject to binding quotas. Less significant, but still important factors, such as other types of trade restraints and changes in exchange rates, also may cause actual import sales and shipment data to overstate the future competitive significance of foreign firms. To the extent that the relative competitive significance of imports is overstated by the current market shares of foreign firms, the relative competitive significance of domestic firms concomitantly will be understated.

These factors seem to suggest that the Justice Department would give import competition only limited consideration in merger cases. For example, in 1984, the Justice Department initially announced that it would oppose the merger of LTV Corporation and Republic Steel Corporation, the third largest and fourth largest U.S. steelmakers, a position that in part led United States Steel Corporation, the largest U.S. steelmaker, and National Steel Corporation to call off merger plans. Because of the precarious state of the U.S. steel industry, largely blamed upon import competition (see Section 9.6(B) supra), there was considerable criticism of this position, including that of other government agencies.[4] The Justice Department did not oppose a subsequent merger proposal between Republic and LTV that provided for divestment of certain mills.[5] In 1986, the Reagan administration proposed that merger restrictions be relaxed in the case of industries injured by imports, as determined in an escape clause proceeding.[6]

3. U.S. Dept. of Justice, Merger Guidelines ¶ 3.23 (1984). See also Report of the President's Commission on Industrial Competitiveness, Global Competition: The New Reality 188–93 (Vol. II 1985).

4. 9 BNA ITIM 673, 756, 757 (1984).

5. 9 BNA ITIM 812 (1984).

6. 3 BNA Intl.Trade Rptr. 268 (1986).

If potential or actual import competition is given prominent consideration in analyzing mergers, what does that imply for the degree of concentration among national firms in national economies? Are these effects desirable or not? Given that a domestic industry may succeed in obtaining political support to reduce imports, is it unrealistic to rely upon imports as a restraining force on the behavior of domestic firms? Or will a failure to consider imports lead to disallowance of mergers necessary to maintain the competitiveness of domestic industry?

SECTION 18.3 APPLICATION OF NATIONAL ANTITRUST LAWS TO INTERNATIONAL TRANSACTIONS

(A) U.S. ANTITRUST LAWS AND INTERNATIONAL TRANSACTIONS

U.S. DEPT. OF JUSTICE, ANTITRUST GUIDELINES FOR INTERNATIONAL OPERATIONS
(1977)

The U.S. antitrust laws are the foundation of our broad national commitment to competition based on efficiency—to providing consumers with goods at the lowest price that efficient business operation can justify, and to allowing enterprises to compete on the basis of their own merit. The most relevant provisions are still Sections 1 and 2 of the Sherman Act, enacted in 1890. Section 1 bars "every contract, combination * * *, or conspiracy, in restraint of trade or commerce among the several States, or with foreign nations * * *." Section 2 makes it a violation of law to "monopolize, or attempt to monopolize, or combine or conspire with any other person or persons, to monopolize any part of the trade or commerce among the several States, or with foreign nations * * *." Certain types of agreements are regarded as illegal per se—including, most notably, agreements among competitors to fix prices at which their offerings are sold, or to allocate territories or customers in order to avoid competing with each other. This is done because experience generally has established that such agreements' "pernicious effect on competition and lack of any redeeming virtue" makes an "elaborate inquiry as to the precise harm [that individual restraints] have caused or the business excuse for their use" generally not worth the effort.

Most other restraints are tested by a full factual inquiry as to whether they will have any significantly adverse effect on competition, what the justification for them is, and whether that justification could be achieved in a less anticompetitive way. This test is the so-called "rule of reason" first enunciated by the Supreme Court in 1911. The rule of reason may have a somewhat broader application to international transactions where it is found that (1) experience with adverse effects on competition is much more limited than in the domestic market, or (2) there are some special justifications not normally found in the domestic market. Either circumstance could justify a fuller factual inquiry. We emphasize, however, that the normal per se rules will be applied fully to basic horizontal restraints designed to affect U.S. market prices or conditions or to divide the U.S. market from other markets.

* * *

A special antitrust exemption is provided under the Webb-Pomerene Act for acts of a collective export association of American producers, provided that the association does not (i) artificially or intentionally restrain U.S. domestic trade or affect U.S. domestic prices, or (ii) restrain the export trade of any U.S. competitor of the association.

* * *

PART II. ILLUSTRATIVE CASES

These selected cases illustrate how U.S. antitrust enforcement is likely to apply in some representative fact situations.

* * *

Case E: Manufacturing Joint Venture and Know-how License

Hot Chip, Inc. is the third largest U.S. manufacturer of certain key transistor parts. It has about 22 percent of the domestic market. It has been unsuccessful in its attempts to market its transistor parts in Japan, one of the world's most important markets for the product. In order to surmount this difficulty, it has entered into a joint venture with Japan Manufacturing (JM), one of Japan's largest industrial combines. They will form a manufacturing joint venture, JZC, using Hot Chip know-how to produce completed transistors. Hot Chip will have 49 percent of the stock and half of the Board of Directors. JM will be responsible for the day-to-day operation of JZC. JM has not been in this particular field, but does manufacture a great deal of electronic equipment. Accordingly, the joint venture company will be operating on know-how licensed by Hot Chip.

Hot Chip is very concerned because JZC will have lower manufacturing costs than it has in the United States, and JM and JZC may be sources of disruption to Hot Chip's existing marketing arrangements in Australia, New Zealand, the Philippines, Europe, and the United States. Accordingly, Hot Chip has inserted into the agreement with JM a condition that neither JZC nor JM will export the transistors to the United States or other designated markets.

Discussion

The mere creation of this joint venture does not appear to violate U.S. antitrust law. The joint venture does not appear to eliminate any direct competition. Hot Chip and JM are not direct competitors in the relevant U.S. market because JM was not producing the product.

The joint venture by itself does not appear to be any part of a broader arrangement to divide world markets between JM and Hot Chip, nor does it seem in any way to prevent JM from selling *other* products in the United States. It is, on its face, supported by a legitimate factual basis, established by Hot Chip's difficulty in exporting to Japan.

However, JM might be a potential entrant into the U.S. market by virtue of its size and experience in closely related electronic products. Thus, the joint venture might eliminate potential competition, which stems from the possibility that JM would develop the relevant transistor and then directly compete with Hot Chip in the United States. If Hot Chip's leading position in the concentrated U.S. market gives it a substantial degree of market power—the ability to control competitive parameters such as pricing in its market—fear of entry by a firm in the wings of the market may be a significant constraint on its abuse of that power. Therefore, elimination of one of a small group of potential entrants could possibly give rise to an antitrust violation under Clayton Act § 7 if the jurisdictional requirements of Section 7 are satisfied. This, however, is not clear from these facts, and further inquiry would be necessary along the lines suggested above in connection with Case B [omitted]. Whether JM was capable of developing the product and entering the U.S. market would be significant in determining whether the joint venture would substantially lessen competition. The fact that JM does not now make the product anywhere does reduce its significance as a potential entrant vis-a-vis any capable foreign firms that do make it, for it introduces another level of uncertainty into the possibility that it would enter.

The more manifest problem is with the collateral restraints imposed by the venture. The limitations on export by JZC and JM constitute a territorial allocation agreement, and this would be a matter of antitrust concern, at least as to exports back to the U.S. market.

The mere existence of a technology-sharing agreement between two firms is not by itself an antitrust defense to a charge that the firms have entered into a larger agreement with the purpose or effect of restraining competition. The courts generally will permit a moderate competitive restraint if the defendants can show that the main purpose of the agreement between the parties is some legitimate business objective (such as the transfer of technology), and the restraint is "ancillary" to that main purpose—that is, the restraint is reasonably necessary if the main purpose is to be achieved. This involves a balancing of the anticompetitive effects of the restraint (to be proved by the government or other antitrust plaintiff) against the business considerations which are alleged to justify the arrangement (to be proved by the defendant).

In this case, the Department would be likely to challenge the open-ended restraint on selling transistors into the United States.

The agreement permanently precludes JZC and JM from exporting the relevant products to the United States. This exclusion probably is of substantial competitive significance because Hot Chip is a leading firm in the concentrated domestic market for the products associated with the license, and it is predicated on the fact that JZC will have lower manufacturing costs than Hot Chip. Such potential "disruption" from cost-cutting entrants is something which the antitrust laws are designed to preserve.

On the other hand, the antitrust laws permit reasonable ancillary restraints, as noted above. In order to establish that their territorial restraint is reasonably ancillary to their joint venture and licensing agreement, Hot Chip and JM must prove that the know-how being transferred is of substantial value, and that the territorial restraint is no greater in scope or duration than is necessary to prevent frustration of the underlying contract. One measure for insuring that the restraint is truly no longer in duration than necessary, is to limit an ancillary territorial restraint of this type to no longer than the time it would take for JM to develop equivalent know-how itself (the "reverse engineering" period). Where the restraint exceeds the reverse engineering period, a defendant must be prepared to bear the burden of proving the necessity of the restraint. The permanent restraint in this case would seem virtually impossible to justify. Where technology is changing as rapidly as it is in Hot Chip's field, only a short-term restriction would seem appropriate. JM's status as a very substantial firm which manufactures products technologically similar to those affected by the know-how license would be highly relevant to the determination of how much time it would require to develop equivalent know-how itself.

* * *

Case N: Government-Imposed Restraint

A, a corporation organized under the laws of Country X, is a wholly-owned subsidiary of AUSA, a U.S. company. A manufactures and sells 25 percent of the widget market in Country X. Two of the other widget suppliers, B and C, are entirely locally owned and together account for about 20 percent of the market in X. The fourth supplier, D, is a majority-owned subsidiary of a manufacturer located in the Federal Republic of Germany, and accounts for about 30 percent of the market. The remaining 25 percent of the X market is accounted for by imports from U.S., Japanese and Swiss manufacturers.

B and C find the widget market in X unprofitable. The government of X asks A, B, C and D to form an advisory council to advise it on how to strengthen the local widget manufacturing industry. A joins B, C and D in advising the X government that the market in X is not large enough to sustain four local manufacturers plus substantial imports; and A, B, C and D suggest either a tariff increase or an embargo for a specified period. This action, if taken, would affect exports by a second U.S. manufacturer presently accounting for about six percent of the market in X. Officers of AUSA are advised of this action of A.

Discussion

The key restraint on U.S. export competition has been imposed by the government of X. A government imposition of protectionist tariffs and quotas is normally considered a sovereign function of the state within its own territory and therefore exempt from U.S. antitrust enforcement under the act of state doctrine, discussed above in the Introduction, pp. 7–8, and Case L at pp. 54–55 [omitted].

In 1961 the Supreme Court enunciated another exemption to antitrust prohibitions, holding that "the Sherman Act does not prohibit two or more persons from associating together in an attempt to persuade the legislature or the executive to take particular action with respect to a law that would produce a restraint or monopoly." This has become known as the *Noerr-Pennington* doctrine. There is an exception to this rule when the collective activity, ostensibly intended to get the government to impose a restraint, is in fact a "sham" which conceals a direct restraint by the parties, such as a misuse of administrative procedures. There is another exception where private parties, at least in the regulatory context, collectively lie to the government and thereby cause it to impose a restraint. A similar exception might exist for conspiracy with a licensing authority, or bribery. None of these possible exceptions seems applicable here.

The only question here, therefore, is whether the *Noerr-Pennington* doctrine applies to efforts to cause a foreign government to impose restraints on U.S. commerce. While the *Noerr* case turns in part on U.S. domestic constitutional considerations, the Department does not consider it to be limited to the domestic area. The Supreme Court's discussion in Continental Ore Co. v. Union Carbide & Carbon Corp., implies as much. The Court there distinguished *Noerr*—not on the ground that a foreign government was involved—but rather on the ground that the private party was directly restraining commerce itself.

Accordingly, we conclude that A's activity, joining B, C, and D in the making of a recommendation that the government of X exclude another U.S. competitor, does not violate U.S. antitrust law. The fact that this activity occurred in the context of an advisory council appointed by the government of X reinforces this conclusion, but the result would be the same even if A, B, C and D had jointly initiated the idea in an informal way. Under *Noerr-Pennington*, the collective exercise of the right of political expression is protected, even where its goal is highly anticompetitive.

Notes and Questions

(1) The Department of Justice announced in early 1986 that it intended to update the foregoing guidelines. Nonetheless in light of the current guidelines, what antitrust law considerations would affect your analysis of the problem set out in Section 16.1 supra?

(2) Is it appropriate to allow foreign entities to engage in otherwise forbidden activities simply because they have obtained the approval of their government? To what extent will this rule enable foreign governments to prevent the effective application of U.S. antitrust laws?

(3) The focus of U.S. antitrust laws is on the effect that an activity has in the United States. As a consequence, there has been less concern with activities that only have an effect outside the United States. For example, the Webb-Pomerene Act has long exempted certain export cartels from the application of U.S. antitrust laws.[1] In 1982, Congress adopted two acts that emphasized a lesser U.S. concern in the case of exports. The Foreign Trade Antitrust Improvements Act essentially provided that the Sherman Act does not apply to foreign commerce unless there is a direct, substantial and reasonably foreseeable effect on U.S. trade and commerce or on a U.S. person engaged in foreign commerce.[2] Congress also adopted the Export Trading Company Act in 1982.[3] This Act expanded the exemption contained in the Webb-Pomerene Act to

1. 15 U.S.C.A. §§ 61–66.

2. Pub.L. No. 97–290, tit. IV, 96 Stat. 1246 (1982), codified at 15 U.S.C.A. §§ 6a, 45(a)(3).

3. Pub.L. No. 97–290, 96 Stat. 1233 (1982); codified at 15 U.S.C.A. §§ 4001–21. Rules im-

plementing the Act are found at 15 CFR Pt. 325 (1985). See Note, The Export Trading Company Act of 1982: Theory and Application, 14 Ga.J.Intl. & Comp.L. 525 (1984).

include export trading companies that had received government certification. The Act was designed to promote exports by small and medium-sized businesses through export trading companies. Congress apparently felt that such exports were not occurring to the extent they might otherwise occur because of uncertainty over whether and the extent to which U.S. antitrust laws would limit the activities of export trading companies. The Act aims to solve this problem by allowing an export trading company to obtain prior approval of its activities from the Department of Commerce. The basic requirements for certification are that the proposed activities (a) not substantially lessen competition in the United States nor substantially restrain the export trade of a competitor of the applicant, (b) not unreasonably affect U.S. prices of the export product and (c) not constitute unfair methods of competition vis a vis the applicant's competitors. The Secretary of Commerce issues the certification only with the concurrence of the Attorney General. The usefulness of this procedure was called into question in early 1986 when a decision to grant a certificate was overturned in a lawsuit filed by competitors of the certificate recipients. Horizons Intl., Inc. v. Baldridge, 624 F.Supp. 1560, 3 BNA Intl.Trade Rptr. 101 (E.D.Pa.1986).

(B) FOREIGN ANTITRUST LAWS [4]

JAMES A. RAHL, INTERNATIONAL APPLICATION OF AMERICAN ANTITRUST LAWS: ISSUES AND PROPOSALS

(1980) [5]

One hears with amazing frequency that antitrust laws reflect techniques of the 19th Century and should be abolished or greatly curtailed. As a description of domestic law this claim is uninformed, and is outlandish in light of recent actions in many parts of the world. Antitrust policy has been growing recently by leaps and bounds in the free world, and almost every judgment about international policy in this area must take account of this.

Since World War II, over 20 nations comprising most of the developed countries have enacted laws to control restrictive trade practices, cartels, and abuses of dominant power. In the midst of the current objections by the United Kingdom to some American antitrust actions affecting British firms, one might miss the fact that that nation, beginning in 1948, has adopted eight major antitrust statutes, including the Competition Act of 1980 sponsored by the Thatcher Government now in power. Together, these laws give the United Kingdom a system of antitrust measures which are almost as comprehensive as the American laws, although the remedies are not always as strict.

4. See generally OECD, Guide to Legislation on Restrictive Business Practices (looseleaf); OECD, Annual Reports on Competition Policy in OECD Member Countries; D. Gijlstra, Competition Law in Western Europe and the USA (Kluwer looseleaf); B. Hawk, United States, Common Market and International Antitrust: A Comparative Guide (2d ed. 1985); Grendell, The Antitrust Legislation of the U.S., the European Economic Community, Germany and Japan, 29 Intl. & Comp.L.Q. 64 (1980).

5. 2 Nw.J.Intl.L.Bus. 336, 355–57. Reprinted by special permission of the Northwestern Journal of International Law and Business, © by Northwestern University School of Law, Vol. 2, No. 2.

West Germany has a fairly strong antitrust law, adopted in 1956, that has recently been amended to increase controls over mergers, along with continued strict treatment of cartels and other restrictive arrangements. France also has a substantial set of laws, which have recently been strengthened. Although enforcement and interpretation of the French laws tend to be lenient, they are still of major significance. Even Japan has a broad antitrust law, although for years it was given only mild enforcement and in the foreign trade area it was relatively ineffective. There are signs worth studying that Japanese antitrust is becoming more significant, however. Smaller developed nations in Europe, as well as Canada, have antitrust laws which are less strict either in substance or as a practical matter than those already mentioned, but which nonetheless represent increasing reliance upon a policy favoring more competition. Many developing countries have recently adopted such laws as well.

Rivaling the U.S. antitrust laws in importance are those of the European Economic Community (EEC), presently comprising nine member nations including all the major powers of Western Europe, i.e., France, Italy, the United Kingdom and West Germany, along with Belgium, Denmark, Ireland, Luxemburg and the Netherlands. Launched in 1957 by the Rome Treaty, the EEC has major antitrust provisions modeled largely after the Sherman Antitrust Act and serving as one of the cornerstones of development of the Common Market. These laws substantially prohibit both horizontal and vertical agreements in restraint of trade, subject to certain exemptions, and single-firm abuses of dominant market positions anywhere in the area of the Common Market are also prohibited if interstate commerce is affected. The laws have been implemented by regulations, and numerous enforcement actions and court decisions have established them as a major matter to be reckoned with by all who do business in the Common Market.

These laws are overlaid on the national laws of the member states of the European Communities in much the same way that American federal antitrust laws operate with reference to state laws in this country. Thus, Common Market antitrust law is part of the governing law of each member nation, is binding on its citizens, is enforcible in its courts, and is supreme over national law in cases of inconsistency. In considering what is the antitrust policy of Italy, which has no national antitrust statute, and the United Kingdom, which has several laws, for example, one must remember that both have the same supra-national (Community) antitrust law, which provides a uniform antitrust policy for a great many major transactions.

Inevitably, this large and growing number of national and regional antitrust laws occasionally overlap. Enforcement of given laws often affects business activity outside the jurisdiction of the particular nation. Conversely, international business activities invariably affect more than one nation, and where antitrust problems arise, more than one set of laws becomes involved. Both cooperation and conflict are possible in these circumstances. Within the Organization for Economic Cooperation and Development, of which the United States is a member, a procedure has been adopted to encourage consultation and cooperation among the nations in such cases. OECD has also adopted guidelines for multinational enterprises, which include provisions on avoidance of restrictive practices and abuse of dominant power. In addition, the United States has bilateral agreements for consultation with Canada, and West Germany, and an informal working relationship with the European Communities.

(C) EXTRATERRITORIAL ENFORCEMENT OF ANTITRUST LAWS [6]

(1) Conflicts of Jurisdiction: U.S. Law

TIMBERLANE LUMBER CO. v. BANK OF AMERICA, N.T. & S.A.

United States Court of Appeals, Ninth Circuit, 1976.
549 F.2d 597.

CHOY, JUDGE:

The basic allegation of the Timberlane plaintiffs is that officials of the Bank of America and others located in both the United States and Honduras conspired to prevent Timberlane, through its Honduras subsidiaries, from milling lumber in Honduras and exporting it to the United States, thus maintaining control of the Honduran lumber export business in the hands of a few select individuals financed and controlled by the Bank. The intent and result of the conspiracy, they contend, was to interfere with the exportation to the United States, including Puerto Rico, of Honduran lumber for sale or use there by the plaintiffs, thus directly and substantially affecting the foreign commerce of the United States.

* * *

There is no doubt that American antitrust laws extend over some conduct in other nations.

* * *

The act may encompass the foreign activities of aliens as well as American citizens.

That American law covers some conduct beyond this nation's borders does not mean that it embraces all, however. Extraterritorial application is understandably a matter of concern for the other countries involved. Those nations have sometimes resented and protested, as excessive intrusions into their own spheres, broad assertions of authority by American courts. * * * [I]t is evident that at some point the interests of the United States

---

6. See generally the materials cited in Section 13.5 supra; Hood, The Extraterritorial Application of United States Antitrust Law: A Selective Bibliography, 15 Vanderbilt J. of Transnatl.L. 765 (1982); J. Lacey, Act of State and Extraterritorial Reach: Problems of Law and Policy (1983); D. Rosenthal & W. Knighton, National Laws and International Commerce: The Problem of Extraterritoriality (1982); A. Lowe, Extraterritorial Jurisdiction: An Annotated Collection of Legal Materials (1983); Meessen, Antitrust Jurisdiction Under Customary International Law, 78 Am.J.Intl.L.

783 (1985); Baxter, Standards for Application of United States Antitrust Law in an International Environment, 1982 B.Y.U.L.Rev. 841; Davidow, Extraterritorial Antitrust and the Concept of Comity, 15 J. World Trade L. 500 (1981). On issues of extraterritoriality outside the antitrust field, see Blakesley, United States Jurisdiction Over Extraterritorial Crime, 73 J.Crim.L. & Criminology 1109 (1982); Johnson, Application of Federal Securities Laws to International Securities Transactions, 45 Alb.L.Rev. 890 (1981).

are too weak and the foreign harmony incentive for restraint too strong to justify an extraterritorial assertion of jurisdiction.

What that point is or how it is determined is not defined by international law. Nor does the Sherman Act limit itself. In the domestic field the Sherman Act extends to the full reach of the commerce power. To define it somewhat more modestly in the foreign commerce area courts have generally, and logically, fallen back on a narrower construction of congressional intent, such as expressed in Judge Learned Hand's oft-cited opinion in *Alcoa*, 148 F.2d at 443:

> [T]he only question open is whether Congress intended to impose the liability and whether our own Constitution permitted it to do so: as a court of the United States we cannot look beyond our own law. Nevertheless, it is quite true that we are not to read general words, such as those in this Act, without regard to the limitations customarily observed by nations upon the exercise of their powers; limitations which generally correspond to those fixed by the "Conflict of Laws." We should not impute to Congress an intent to punish all whom its courts can catch, for conduct which has no consequences within the United States.

It is the effect on American foreign commerce which is usually cited to support extraterritorial jurisdiction. *Alcoa* set the course, when Judge Hand declared, *id.:*

> [I]t is settled law * * * that any state may impose liabilities, even upon persons not within its allegiance, for conduct outside its borders that has consequences within its borders which the state reprehends; and these liabilities other states will ordinarily recognize.

Despite its description as "settled law," *Alcoa's* assertion has been roundly disputed by many foreign commentators as being in conflict with international law, comity, and good judgment. Nonetheless, American courts have firmly concluded that there is some extraterritorial jurisdiction under the Sherman Act.

Even among American courts and commentators, however, there is no consensus on how far the jurisdiction should extend.

* * *

The effects test by itself is incomplete because it fails to consider other nations' interests. Nor does it expressly take into account the full nature of the relationship between the actors and this country. Whether the alleged offender is an American citizen, for instance, may make a big difference; applying American laws to American citizens raises fewer problems than application to foreigners.

* * *

A tripartite analysis seems to be indicated. As acknowledged above, the antitrust laws require in the first instance that there be *some* effect—actual or intended—on American foreign commerce before the federal courts may legitimately exercise subject matter jurisdiction under those statutes. Second, a greater showing of burden or restraint may be necessary to demonstrate that the effect is sufficiently large to present a cognizable injury to the plaintiffs and, therefore, a civil *violation* of the antitrust laws. Third, there is the additional question which is unique to the international setting of whether the interests of, and links to, the United States—including the magnitude of the effect on American foreign commerce—are sufficiently strong, vis-à-vis those of other nations, to justify an assertion of extraterritorial authority.

It is this final issue which is both obscured by undue reliance on the "substantiality" test and complicated to resolve. An effect on United States commerce, although necessary to the exercise of jurisdiction under the antitrust laws, is alone not a sufficient basis on which to determine whether American authority *should* be asserted in a given case as a matter of international comity and fairness. In some cases, the application of the direct and substantial test in the international context might open the door too widely by sanctioning jurisdiction over an action when these considerations would indicate dismissal. At other times, it may fail in the other direction, dismissing a case for which comity and fairness do not require forebearance, thus closing the jurisdictional door too tightly—for the Sherman Act does reach some restraints which do not have both a direct and substantial effect on the foreign commerce of the United States. A more comprehensive inquiry is necessary. We believe that the field of conflict of laws presents the proper approach, as was suggested, if not specifically employed, in *Alcoa* in expressing the basic limitation on application of American laws:

> [W]e are not to read general words, such as those in this Act, without regard to the limitations customarily observed by nations upon the exercise of their powers; limitations which generally correspond to those fixed by the "Conflict of Laws."

148 F.2d at 443. The same idea is reflected in Restatement (Second) of Foreign Relations Law of the United States § 40:

> Where two states have jurisdiction to prescribe and enforce rules of law and the rules they may prescribe require inconsistent conduct upon the part of a person, each state is required by international law to consider, in good faith, moderating the exercise of its enforcement jurisdiction * * *.

The act of state doctrine discussed earlier demonstrates that the judiciary is sometimes cognizant of the possible foreign implications of its action. Similar awareness should be extended to the general problems of extraterritoriality. Such acuity is especially required in private suits, like this one, for in these cases there is no opportunity for the executive branch to weigh the foreign relations impact, nor any statement implicit in the filing of the suit that that consideration has been outweighed.

What we prefer is an evaluation and balancing of the relevant considerations in each case—in the words of Kingman Brewster, a "jurisdictional rule of reason." * * *

The elements to be weighed include the degree of conflict with foreign law or policy, the nationality or allegiance of the parties and the locations or principal places of business of corporations, the extent to which enforcement by either state can be expected to achieve compliance, the relative significance of effects on the United States as compared with those elsewhere, the extent to which there is explicit purpose to harm or affect American commerce, the foreseeability of such effect, and the relative importance to the violations charged of conduct within the United States as compared with conduct abroad. A court evaluating these factors should identify the potential degree of conflict if American authority is asserted. A difference in law or policy is one likely sore spot, though one which may not always be present. Nationality is another; though foreign governments may have some concern for the treatment of American citizens and business residing there, they primarily care about their own nationals. Having assessed the conflict, the court should then determine whether in the face of it the contacts and interests of the United States are sufficient to support the exercise of extraterritorial jurisdiction.

* * *

The comity question is more complicated. From Timberlane's complaint it is evident that there are grounds for concern as to at least a few of the defendants, for some are identified as foreign citizens: Laureano Gutierrez Falla, Michael Casanova and the Casanova firms, of Honduras, and Patrick Byrne, of Canada. Moreover, it is clear that most of the activity took place in Honduras, though the conspiracy may have been directed from San Francisco, and that the most direct economic effect was probably on Honduras. However, there has been no indication of any conflict with the law or policy of the Honduran government, nor any comprehensive analysis of the relative connections and interests of Honduras and the United States. Under these circumstances, the dismissal by the district court cannot be sustained on jurisdictional grounds.

LAKER AIRWAYS LTD. v. SABENA, BELGIAN WORLD AIRLINES

United States Court of Appeals, District of Columbia Circuit, 1984.
731 F.2d 909.

WILKEY, JUDGE:

[This appeal involved an antitrust action brought in the United States by Laker Airways, an airline known for its low transatlantic fares, charging that a number of other transatlantic airlines had successfully conspired to drive it out of business. The British defendants—British Airways and British Caledonian Airways—obtained an injunction in an English court ordering Laker not to proceed against them. Sabena and KLM, the Dutch national airline, were not beneficiaries of that injunction, and Laker had obtained a U.S. court order, the subject of this appeal, enjoining Sabena and KLM from seeking in a foreign action to prevent adjudication of Laker's claim in the U.S. proceedings. In the course of deciding to uphold the order of the district court (with Judge Starr dissenting), the court of appeals had occasion to discuss the role of a court in trying to balance the apparently irreconcilable interests of two nations, each claiming jurisdiction in a matter.]

E. JUDICIAL RECONCILIATION OF CONFLICTING ASSERTIONS OF JURISDICTION

We recognize that the district court's injunction, precipitated as it was by preemptive interim injunctions in the High Court of Justice, unfortunately will not resolve the deadlock currently facing the parties to this litigation.

We have searched for some satisfactory avenue, open to an American court, which would permit the frictionless vindication of the interests of both Britain and the United States. However, there is none, for the British legislation defines the British interest solely in terms of preventing realization of United States interests. The laws are therefore contradictory and mutually inconsistent.

* * *

The suggestion has been made that this court should engage in some form of interest balancing, permitting only a "reasonable" assertion of prescriptive jurisdiction to be implemented. However, this approach is unsuitable when courts are forced to choose between a domestic law which is designed to protect domestic interests, and a foreign law which is calculated to thwart the implementation of the domestic law in order to protect foreign interests allegedly threatened by the objectives of the domestic law. Interest balancing in this context is hobbled by two primary problems: (1) there are substantial limitations on the court's ability to conduct a neutral balancing of the competing interests, and (2) the adoption of interest balancing is unlikely to achieve its goal of promoting international comity.

a. Defects in the Balancing Process

Most proposals for interest balancing consist of a long list of national contacts to be evaluated and weighed against those of the foreign country. These interests may be relevant to the desirability of allocating jurisdiction to a particular national forum. However, their usefulness breaks down when a court is faced with the task of selecting one forum's prescriptive jurisdiction over that of another.

Many of the contacts to be balanced are already evaluated when assessing the existence of a sufficient basis for exercising prescriptive jurisdiction. Other factors, such as "the extent to which another state may have an interest in regulating the activity," and "the likelihood of conflict with regulation by other states" are essentially neutral in deciding between competing assertions of jurisdiction. Pursuing these inquiries only leads to the obvious conclusion that jurisdiction could be exercised or that there is a conflict, but does not suggest the best avenue of conflict resolution. These types of factors are not useful in resolving the controversy.

Those contacts which do purport to provide a basis for distinguishing between competing bases of jurisdiction, and which are thus crucial to the balancing process, generally incorporate purely political factors which the court is neither qualified to evaluate comparatively nor capable of properly balancing. One such proposed consideration is "the degree to which the *desirability of such regulation* [of restrictive practices] is *generally accepted.*" We doubt whether the legitimacy of an exercise of jurisdiction should be measured by the substantive content of the prescribed law. Moreover, although more and more states are following the United States in regulating restrictive practices, and even exercising jurisdiction based on effects within territory, *the differing English and American assessment of the desirability of antitrust law is at the core of the conflict. An English or American court cannot refuse to enforce a law its political branches have already determined is desirable and necessary.*

The court is also handicapped in any evaluation of "the existence of *justified* expectations that might be protected or hurt by the regulation in question." In this litigation, whether the reliance of Laker and its creditors on United States anti-trust laws is justified depends upon whether one accepts the desirability of United States anti-trust law. Whether the defendants could justifiably have relied on the inapplicability of United States law to their conduct alleged to have caused substantial effects in the United States is based on the same impermissible inquiry. The desirability of applying ambiguous legislation to a particular transaction may imply the presence or absence of legislative intent. However, once a decision is made that the political branches intended to rely on a legitimate base of prescriptive jurisdiction to regulate activities affecting foreign commerce within the domestic forum, the desirability of the law is no longer an issue for the courts.

The "importance of regulation to the regulating state" is another factor on which the court cannot rely to choose between two competing, mutually inconsistent legislative policies. We are in no position to adjudicate the relative importance of anti-trust regulation or nonregulation to the United States and the United Kingdom. It is the crucial importance of these policies which has created the conflict. A proclamation by judicial fiat that one interest is less "important" than the other will not erase a real conflict.

Given the inherent limitations of the Judiciary, which must weigh these issues in the limited context of adversarial litigation, we seriously doubt whether we could adequately chart the competing problems and priorities that inevitably define the scope of any nation's interest in a legislated remedy. This court is ill-equipped to "balance the vital national interests of the United States and the [United Kingdom] to determine which interests predominate." When one state exercises its jurisdiction and another, in protection of its own interests, attempts to quash the first exercise of jurisdiction "it is simply impossible to judicially 'balance' these totally contradictory and mutually negating actions."

* * *

b. *Promotion of International Comity*

We might be more willing to tackle the problems associated with the balancing of competing, mutually inconsistent national interests if we could be assured that our efforts would strengthen the bonds of international comity. However, the usefulness and wisdom of interest balancing to assess the most "reasonable" exercise of prescriptive jurisdiction has not been affirmatively demonstrated. This approach has not gained more than a temporary foothold in domestic law. Courts are increasingly refusing to adopt the approach. Scholarly criticism has intensified. Additionally, there is no evidence that interest balancing represents a rule of international law. Thus, there is no mandatory rule requiring its adoption here, since Congress cannot be said to have implicitly legislated subject to these international constraints.

If promotion of international comity is measured by the number of times United States jurisdiction has been declined under the "reasonableness" interest balancing approach, then it has been a failure. Implementation of this analysis has not resulted in a significant number of conflict resolutions favoring a foreign jurisdiction. A pragmatic assessment of those decisions adopting an interest balancing approach indicates *none where United States jurisdiction was declined* when there was more than a *de minimis* United States interest. Most cases in which use of the process was advocated arose before a direct conflict occurred when the balancing could be employed without impairing the court's jurisdiction to determine jurisdiction. When push comes to shove, the domestic forum is rarely unseated.

Despite the real obligation of courts to apply international law and foster comity, domestic courts do not sit as internationally constituted tribunals. Domestic courts are created by national constitutions and statutes to enforce primarily national laws. The courts of most developed countries follow international law only to the extent it is not overridden by national law. Thus, courts inherently find it difficult neutrally to balance competing foreign interests. When there is any doubt, national interests will tend to be favored over foreign interests. This partially explains why there have been few times when courts have found foreign interests to prevail.

The inherent noncorrelation between the interest balancing formula and the economic realities of modern commerce is an additional reason which may underlie the reluctance of most courts to strike a balance in favor of nonapplication of domestic law. An assertion of prescriptive jurisdiction should ultimately be based on shared assessments that jurisdiction is reasonable. Thus, international law prohibits the assertion of prescriptive jurisdiction unsupported by reasonable links between the forum and the controversy.

However, it does not necessarily follow, as the use of interest balancing as a method of choosing between competing jurisdictions assumes, that there is a line of reasonableness which separates jurisdiction to prescribe into neatly adjoining compartments of national jurisdiction. There is no principle of international law which abolishes concurrent jurisdiction. Since prescriptive jurisdiction is based on well recognized state contacts with controversies, the reality of our interlocked international economic network guarantees that overlapping, concurrent jurisdiction will often be present. There is, therefore, no rule of international law holding that a "more reasonable" assertion of jurisdiction mandatorily displaces a "less reasonable" assertion of jurisdiction as long as both are, in fact, consistent with the limitations on jurisdiction imposed by international law. That is the situation faced in this case: the territoriality and nationality bases of jurisdiction of the United Kingdom and the United States are both unimpeached.

* * * [T]he problems associated with overlapping bases of national taxation in international law are directly addressed by numerous bilateral and multilateral treaties rather than a judicially developed rule of exclusive jurisdiction grounded in a prioritization of the relative reasonableness of links between the state and the taxed entity. Because we see no neutral principles on which to distinguish judicially the reasonableness of the concurrent, mutually inconsistent exercises of jurisdiction in this case, we decline to adopt such a rule here.

* * *

Although, in the interest of amicable relations, we might be tempted to defuse unilaterally the confrontation by jettisoning our jurisdiction, we could not, for this is not our proper judicial role. The problem in this case is essentially a political one, arising from the vast difference in the political-economic theories of the two governments which has existed for many years. Both nations have jurisdiction to prescribe and adjudicate. Both have asserted that jurisdiction. However, this conflict alone does not place the court in a position to initiate a political compromise based on its decision that United States laws should not be enforced when a foreign jurisdiction, contrary to the domestic court's statutory duty, attempts to eradicate the domestic jurisdiction. Judges are not politicians. The courts are not organs of political compromise. It is impossible in this case, with all the good will manifested by the English Justices and ourselves, to negotiate an extraordinarily long arms-length agreement on the respective impact of our countries' policies regulating anti-competitive business practices.

Notes and Questions

(1) On remand in the *Timberlane* case, the District Court ultimately dismissed the action because analysis of most of the factors considered relevant by the Court of Appeals (potential for conflict with foreign law, effect on U.S. foreign commerce, location of conduct, intent to harm U.S. commerce, foreseeability of anticompetitive consequences) did not support accepting jurisdiction. 574 F.Supp. 1453, affirmed, 749 F.2d 1378 (9th Cir.1984), cert. denied, ____ U.S. ____, 105 S.Ct. 3514, 87 L.Ed.2d 643 (1985).

(2) The House of Lords eventually overturned the injunction that the British defendants in the *Laker* case had obtained in England. British Airways Board v. Laker Airways Ltd., [1985] A.C. 58. The House of Lords did, however, uphold blocking orders issued by the British government pursuant to the Protection of Trading Interests Act. That act and the blocking orders are discussed in the next subsection.

(3) Is the *Timberlane* decision consistent with the principles of the proposed Revised Restatement, discussed in Section 13.5 supra? Is the *Laker* decision consistent with them? Which of the two courts has the more persuasive argument? Should different principles apply in analyzing extraterritoriality issues in antitrust cases than in the export control cases discussed in Section 13.5? Are the bases for jurisdiction the same?

(4) Legislation proposed in 1986 by the Reagan Administration would require U.S. courts to consider an exclusive list of factors in deciding whether to apply U.S. antitrust laws. Among the factors to be considered would be the relative significance to the alleged violation of the U.S. conduct compared to the foreign conduct, the nationality of the parties, the degree of conflict with foreign law and the relative significance and foreseeability of the effects of the conduct on the United States and foreign nations.[7] In light of the *Laker* case, do you think such legislation will be helpful?

(5) As noted in the Rahl article, the United States has occasionally entered into bilateral agreements in respect of antitrust matters. For example, in 1984

7. 3 BNA Intl.Trade Rptr. 268 (1986).

the United States and Canada entered into a memorandum of understanding providing for notification and consultation whenever one nation's antitrust enforcement efforts may affect the national interests of the other.[8] The United States also has agreements with Australia [9] and West Germany.[10]

(2) Conflicts of Jurisdiction: Blocking Statutes [11]

The assertion by the United States of extraterritorial jurisdiction in respect of antitrust and securities law and export controls, U.S. attempts to investigate alleged violations thereof by ordering production or disclosure of documents and other evidence located outside the United States, and the Sherman Act provision allowing actual damages to be trebled in antitrust cases, have all greatly annoyed many countries. In recent years, some of these countries have retaliated by adopting legislation designed to counteract the effect of U.S. claims of extraterritorial jurisdiction and to forbid cooperation with U.S. authorities enforcing such claims. Perhaps the best known of these statutes is the British Protection of Trading Interests Act, adopted in 1980.[12]

PROTECTION OF TRADING INTERESTS ACT 1980

1.—(1) If it appears to the Secretary of State—

(*a*) that measures have been or are proposed to be taken by or under the law of any overseas country for regulating or controlling international trade; and

(*b*) that those measures, in so far as they apply or would apply to things done or to be done outside the territorial jurisdiction of that country by persons carrying on business in the United Kingdom, are damaging or threaten to damage the trading interests of the United Kingdom,

the Secretary of State may by order direct that this section shall apply to those measures either generally or in their application to such cases as may be specified in the order.

---

8. 9 BNA ITIM 799 (1984).

9. Agreement relating to cooperation on antitrust matters, entered into force June 29, 1982, TIAS 10365.

10. Agreement relating to mutual cooperation regarding restrictive business practices, entered into force September 11, 1976, 27 UST 1956; TIAS 8291.

11. See generally Blythe, Extraterritorial Impact of the Anti-trust Laws: Protecting British Trading Interests, 31 Am.J.Comp.L. 99 (1983); Lowe, Blocking Extraterritorial Jurisdiction: The British Protection of Trading Interests Act, 1980, 75 Am.J.Intl.L. 257 (1981); Note, Shortening the Long Arm of American Antitrust Jurisdiction: Extraterritoriality and the Foreign Blocking Statutes, 28 Loyola L.Rev. 213 (1982); Note, Power to Reverse Foreign Judgments: The British Clawback

Statute under International Law, 81 Colum.L. Rev. 1097 (1981); Rosen, The Protection of Trading Interests Act, 15 Intl.Law. 213 (1981).

12. For an extensive discussion of blocking statutes in the United Kingdom, Canada, Australia, South Africa, the Netherlands and France, see Note, Shortening the Long Arm, note 11 supra. The Note includes a chart citing (or indicating the absence of) judgment blocking, clawback and discovery blocking laws in 19 countries. According to the author, most of the countries surveyed had discovery blocking provisions of one sort or another, while clawback and judgment blocking provisions were not so common. See also Pettit & Styles, International Response to the Extraterritorial Application of United States Antitrust Laws, 37 Bus.Law. 697 (1982).

(2) The Secretary of State may by order make provision for requiring, or enabling the Secretary of State to require, a person in the United Kingdom who carries on business there to give notice to the Secretary of State of any requirement or prohibition imposed or threatened to be imposed on that person pursuant to any measures in so far as this section applies to them by virtue of an order under subsection (1) above.

(3) The Secretary of State may give to any person in the United Kingdom who carries on business there such directions for prohibiting compliance with any such requirement or prohibition as aforesaid as he considers appropriate for avoiding damage to the trading interests of the United Kingdom.

*   *   *

2.—(1) If it appears to the Secretary of State—

(*a*) that a requirement has been or may be imposed on a person or persons in the United Kingdom to produce to any court, tribunal or authority of an overseas country any commercial document which is not within the territorial jurisdiction of that country or to furnish any commercial information to any such court, tribunal or authority; or

(*b*) that any such authority has imposed or may impose a requirement on a person or persons in the United Kingdom to publish any such document or information,

the Secretary of State may, if it appears to him that the requirement is inadmissible by virtue of subsection (2) or (3) below, give directions for prohibiting compliance with the requirement.

(2) A requirement such as is mentioned in subsection (1)(*a*) or (*b*) above is inadmissible—

(*a*) if it infringes the jurisdiction of the United Kingdom or is otherwise prejudicial to the sovereignty of the United Kingdom; or

*   *   *

[(3)] (*b*) if it requires a person to state what documents relevant to any such proceedings are or have been in his possession, custody or power or to produce for the purposes of any such proceedings any documents other than particular documents specified in the requirement.

*   *   *

4. A court in the United Kingdom shall not make an order under section 2 of the Evidence (Proceedings in Other Jurisdictions) Act 1975 for giving effect to a request issued by or on behalf of a court or tribunal of an overseas country if it is shown that the request infringes the jurisdiction of the United Kingdom or is otherwise prejudicial to the sovereignty of the United Kingdom; and a certificate signed by or on behalf of the Secretary of State to the effect that it infringes that jurisdiction or is so prejudicial shall be conclusive evidence of that fact.

5.—(1) A judgment to which this section applies shall not be registered under Part II of the Administration of Justice Act 1920 or Part I of the Foreign Judgments (Reciprocal Enforcement) Act 1933 and no court in the

United Kingdom shall entertain proceedings at common law for the recovery of any sum payable under such a judgment.

(2) This section applies to any judgment given by a court of an overseas country, being—

(*a*) a judgment for multiple damages within the meaning of subsection (3) below;

(*b*) a judgment based on a provision or rule of law specified or described in an order under subsection (4) below and given after the coming into force of the order; or

(*c*) a judgment on a claim for contribution in respect of damages awarded by a judgment falling within paragraph (*a*) or (*b*) above.

(3) In subsection (2)(*a*) above a judgment for multiple damages means a judgment for an amount arrived at by doubling, trebling or otherwise multiplying a sum assessed as compensation for the loss or damage sustained by the person in whose favour the judgment is given.

(4) The Secretary of State may for the purposes of subsection (2)(*b*) above make an order in respect of any provision or rule of law which appears to him to be concerned with the prohibition or regulation of agreements, arrangements or practices designed to restrain, distort or restrict competition in the carrying on of business of any description or to be otherwise concerned with the promotion of such competition as aforesaid.

* * *

6.—(1) This section applies where a court of an overseas country has given a judgment for multiple damages within the meaning of section 5(3) above against—

(*a*) a citizen of the United Kingdom and Colonies; or

(*b*) a body corporate incorporated in the United Kingdom or in a territory outside the United Kingdom for whose international relations Her Majesty's Government in the United Kingdom are responsible; or

(*c*) a person carrying on business in the United Kingdom,

(in this section referred to as a "qualifying defendant") and an amount on account of the damages has been paid by the qualifying defendant either to the party in whose favour the judgment was given or to another party who is entitled as against the qualifying defendant to contribution in respect of the damages.

(2) Subject to subsections (3) and (4) below, the qualifying defendant shall be entitled to recover from the party in whose favour the judgment was given so much of the amount referred to in subsection (1) above as exceeds the part attributable to compensation; and that part shall be taken to be such part of the amount as bears to the whole of it the same proportion as the sum assessed by the court that gave the judgment as compensation for the loss or damage sustained by that party bears to the whole of the damages awarded to that party.

(3) Subsection (2) above does not apply where the qualifying defendant is an individual who was ordinarily resident in the overseas country at the

time when the proceedings in which the judgment was given were instituted or a body corporate which had its principal place of business there at that time.

(4) Subsection (2) above does not apply where the qualifying defendant carried on business in the overseas country and the proceedings in which the judgment was given were concerned with activities exclusively carried on in that country.

Notes and Questions

(1) The blocking orders issued in the *Laker* litigation provided, inter alia,

Except with the consent of the Secretary of State no person or persons in the United Kingdom shall comply, or cause or permit compliance, whether by themselves, their officers, servants or agents, with any requirement to produce or furnish to the United States' Department of Justice, the grand jury or the District Court any document in the United Kingdom or any commercial information which relates to the said Department of Justice investigation or the grand jury or District Court proceedings.

British Airways Board v. Laker Airlines Ltd., [1985] A.C. 58, 91.

(2) Section 6 of the Act is known as the "clawback" provision. It is obviously aimed at the treble damages provision of the Sherman Act, which allows private parties to recover three times their actual damages. The clawback provision would allow the persons specified in the Act to recover from a successful plaintiff in a U.S. treble damage action, any amount paid in excess of actual damages. The clawback provision essentially permits a British court to reverse a satisfied foreign judgment. British and U.S. courts have generally hesitated to take such action unless the foreign action involved a serious procedural defect, a lack of jurisdiction or offended domestic public policy. The clawback provisions of the Protection of Trading Interests Act do not seem to be based on these grounds. While one general concern of the Act is extraterritorial exercise of jurisdiction, the application of the clawback provision is not strictly limited to such cases (see Section 6(4)). While provisions for treble damages are not common, they are quite similar (except in being awarded automatically) to punitive damages, so it is difficult to say they offend public policy. Is there any other justification of the Act—one that has traditionally been used to reverse a satisfied foreign judgment? If not, could it be argued that the Act violates international law?

(3) The actual effect of the clawback provision is difficult to assess. It would be useful to a party only to the extent that the person to whom the party had paid treble damages had assets subject to British jurisdiction. This would, of course, include many multinational enterprises, but perhaps not many potential claimants under U.S. law.

SECTION 18.4 INTERNATIONAL EFFORTS TO CONTROL RESTRICTIVE BUSINESS PRACTICES

Throughout the period since the end of World War II, efforts have been made to achieve an international agreement on the control of restrictive business practices—a sort of international law of antitrust or competition.[1] The proposed International Trade Organization's charter contained nine articles dealing with restrictive business practices, but none of them were carried over into GATT. Interest in reaching some sort of agreement in GATT did not die. Proposals were made for GATT action in both 1954 and in 1956. In 1956, the matter was referred to the GATT Intersessional Committee, which commissioned a study of existing intergovernmental agreements in this area. Later, in 1959 the Contracting Parties appointed a group of experts to recommend whether, to what extent and how GATT should undertake to deal with restrictive business practices. In the end, however, no agreement could be reached on how GATT could regulate such practices, without structural change. The group concluded:[2]

> it would be unrealistic to recommend at present a multilateral agreement for the control of international restrictive business practices. The necessary consensus among countries upon which such an agreement could be based did not yet exist, and countries did not yet have sufficient experience of action in this field to devise an effective control procedure.

In the meantime, other international bodies were also trying to establish agreement on controlling restrictive business practices. For example, the Economic and Social Council of the United Nations considered such practices in the 1950's. The OECD has been active in collecting information about national laws controlling such practices and in encouraging governments to notify each other and consult in instances where application of the law of one jurisdiction could impact the interests of another.[3] In 1976, of course, the OECD adopted guidelines for multinational enterprises, which included rules on competition practices (see Section 17.3 supra).

So far, the most detailed internationally agreed statement on restrictive business practices has been that adopted by the United Nations. The initial consideration of the issue occurred under the auspices of UNCTAD in the 1970's. In 1979 and 1980 the United Nations Conference on Restrictive Business Practices met and adopted a code of conduct that was later adopted by the United Nations General Assembly as a resolution. The important parts of the so-called agreed principles and rules are set forth below.

THE SET OF MULTILATERALLY AGREED EQUITABLE PRINCIPLES AND RULES FOR THE CONTROL OF RESTRICTIVE BUSINESS PRACTICES

U.N.Doc. TD/RBP/10 (1980)

For the purpose of this Set of Multilaterally Agreed Equitable Principles and Rules:

1. See generally J. Jackson, World Trade and the Law of GATT 522–29 (1969): Brusick, UN Control of Restrictive Business Practices, 17 J. World Trade L. 337 (1983); Miller & Davidow, Antitrust at the U.N.: A Tale of Two Codes, 18 Stan.J.Intl.L. 347 (1982); Recent Development, The Set of Multilaterally Agreed Equitable Principles and Rules for the Control of Restrictive Business Practices, 13 Law & Poly.Intl.Bus. 313 (1981).

2. GATT, 9th Supp. BISD 171 (1961). See also GATT, Restrictive Business Practices (1959).

3. See OECD, Competition Law Enforcement: International Co-operation in the Collection of Information (1984).

(i) *Definitions*

1. "Restrictive business practices" means acts or behaviour of enterprises which, through an abuse or acquisition and abuse of a dominant position of market power, limit access to markets or otherwise unduly restrain competition, having or being likely to have adverse effects on international trade, particularly that of developing countries, and on the economic development of these countries, or which through formal, informal, written or unwritten agreements or arrangements among enterprises, have the same impact.

2. "Dominant position of market power" refers to a situation where an enterprise, either by itself or acting together with a few other enterprises, is in a position to control the relevant market for a particular good or service or group of goods or services.

3. "Enterprises" means firms, partnerships, corporations, companies, other associations, natural or juridical persons, or any combination thereof, irrespective of the mode of creation or control or ownership, private or State, which are engaged in commercial activities, and includes their branches, subsidiaries, affiliates, or other entities directly or indirectly controlled by them.

(ii) *Scope of Application*

* * *

9. The Set of Principles and Rules shall not apply to intergovernmental agreements, nor to restrictive business practices directly caused by such agreements.

* * *

C. MULTILATERALLY AGREED EQUITABLE PRINCIPLES FOR THE CONTROL OF RESTRICTIVE BUSINESS PRACTICES

In line with the objectives set forth, the following principles are to apply:

(i) *General Principles*

1. Appropriate action should be taken in a mutually reinforcing manner at national, regional and international levels to eliminate, or effectively deal with, restrictive business practices, including those of transnational corporations, adversely affecting international trade, particularly that of developing countries and the economic development of these countries.

(ii) *Relevant Factors in the Application of the Set of Principles and Rules*

6. In order to ensure the fair and equitable application of the Set of Principles and Rules, States, while bearing in mind the need to ensure the comprehensive application of the Set of Principles and Rules, should take due account of the extent to which the conduct of enterprises, whether or not created or controlled by States, is accepted under applicable legislation or regulations, bearing in mind that such laws and regulations should be clearly defined and publicly and readily available, or is required by States.

(iii) *Preferential or Differential Treatment for Developing Countries*

7. In order to ensure the equitable application of the Set of Principles and Rules, States, particularly developed countries, should take into account

in their control of restrictive business practices the development, financial and trade needs of developing countries, in particular of the least developed countries, for the purposes especially of developing countries in:

(*a*) Promoting the establishment or development of domestic industries and the economic development of other sectors of the economy, and

(*b*) Encouraging their economic development through regional or global arrangements among developing countries.

D. PRINCIPLES AND RULES FOR ENTERPRISES, INCLUDING TRANSNATIONAL CORPORATIONS

1.   Enterprises should conform to the restrictive business practices laws, and the provisions concerning restrictive business practices in other laws, of the countries in which they operate, and, in the event of proceedings under these laws, should be subject to the competence of the courts and relevant administrative bodies therein.

2.   Enterprises should consult and co-operate with competent authorities of countries directly affected in controlling restrictive business practices adversely affecting the interests of those countries. In this regard, enterprises should also provide information, in particular details of restrictive arrangements, required for this purpose, including that which may be located in foreign countries, to the extent that in the latter event such production or disclosure is not prevented by applicable law or established public policy. Whenever the provision of information is on a voluntary basis, its provision should be in accordance with safeguards normally applicable in this field.

3.   Enterprises, except when dealing with each other in the context of an economic entity wherein they are under common control, including through ownership, or otherwise not able to act independently of each other, engaged on the market in rival or potentially rival activities, should refrain from practices such as the following when, through formal, informal, written or unwritten agreements or arrangements, they limit access to markets or otherwise unduly restrain competition, having or being likely to have adverse effects on international trade, particularly that of developing countries, and on the economic development of these countries:

(*a*) Agreements fixing prices, including as to exports and imports;

(*b*) Collusive tendering;

(*c*) Market or customer allocation arrangements;

(*d*) Allocation by quota as to sales and production;

(*e*) Collective action to enforce arrangements, e.g. by concerted refusals to deal;

(*f*) Concerted refusal of supplies to potential importers;

(*g*) Collective denial of access to an arrangement, or association, which is crucial to competition.

4.   Enterprises should refrain from the following acts or behaviour in a relevant market when, through an abuse or acquisition and abuse of a dominant position of market power, they limit access to markets or other-

wise unduly restrain competition, having or being likely to have adverse effects on international trade, particularly that of developing countries, and on the economic development of these countries:

(*a*) Predatory behaviour towards competitors, such as using below-cost pricing to eliminate competitors;

(*b*) Discriminatory (i.e. unjustifiably differentiated) pricing or terms or conditions in the supply or purchase of goods or services, including by means of the use of pricing policies in transactions between affiliated enterprises which overcharge or undercharge for goods or services purchased or supplied as compared with prices for similar or comparable transactions outside the affiliated enterprises;

(*c*) Mergers, takeovers, joint ventures or other acquisitions of control, whether of a horizontal, vertical or a conglomerate nature;

(*d*) Fixing the prices at which goods exported can be resold in importing countries;

(*e*) Restrictions on the importation of goods which have been legitimately marked abroad with a trademark identical with or similar to the trademark protected as to identical or similar goods in the importing country where the trademarks in question are of the same origin, i.e. belong to the same owner or are used by enterprises between which there is economic, organizational, managerial or legal interdependence and where the purpose of such restrictions is to maintain artificially high prices;

(*f*) When not for ensuring the achievement of legitimate business purposes, such as quality, safety, adequate distribution or service:

(i)   Partial or complete refusals to deal on the enterprise's customary commercial terms;

(ii) Making the supply of particular goods or services dependent upon the acceptance of restrictions on the distribution or manufacture of competing or other goods;

(iii) Imposing restrictions concerning where, or to whom, or in what form or quantities, goods supplied or other goods may be resold or exported;

(iv) Making the supply of particular goods or services dependent upon the purchase of other goods or services from the supplier or his designee.

Notes and Questions

(1) Since the principles and rules are embodied only in a resolution of the U.N. General Assembly, they are not considered to be binding. See Section 17.2 supra for a general discussion of the binding nature of codes of conduct.

(2) Are there significant differences in substance between the principles and rules and the provisions on competition of the OECD Guidelines for Multinational Enterprise, which are set out in Section 17.3 supra?

(3) To what extent do the principles and rules apply to transactions between components of a multinational enterprise?

(4) To what extent do the principles and rules provide for differential treatment of developing countries?

(5) To what extent can a government act, unilaterally or through an agreement with another government, to exempt activities from the coverage of the principles and rules?

Chapter 19

TAXATION AND INTERNATIONAL COMMERCE

SECTION 19.1   INTRODUCTION [1]

In this chapter we examine the problems involved in taxing entities involved in international commerce. As we have seen elsewhere, taxation policies may have significant effects on international trade and investment. They are a major motivating factor in the location of international investment, which indirectly has a significant effect on trade flows (see Chapter 16 supra). Moreover, decisions to tax or not, or to allow deductions, credits and the like or not, are similar to decisions to grant or withhold subsidies. There is little difference between a government grant to an entity and the adoption of rules absolving the entity from taxes normally payable by those in its position. Thus, as we have seen, certain tax practices are regulated by GATT rules, particularly those concerning subsidies. For example, we saw in Section 10.3(E) supra that border tax adjustments, including VAT refunds on exports are explicitly permitted by GATT, while other tax practices have been found to violate GATT rules, such as those practices involved in the DISC and related cases, discussed in Section 10.3(B) supra. In addition, although a comprehensive treatment of the tax/subsidy issue at the Tokyo Round was not possible, the illustrative list of export subsidies annexed to the Subsidies Code specifies in some detail when certain tax practices constitute export subsidies.[2]

Our focus in this chapter is largely on other tax issues. We review in Section 19.2 the wide variance in tax burdens among countries, reflecting, among other things, different views of the extent to which government has a useful role to play in the national economy. We also consider variances in the types of taxes imposed to raise government revenues and the extent to

1. It is beyond the scope of this chapter to treat international tax law in any detail. For general works on the subject, the reader is directed to R. Rhoades & M. Langer, Income Taxation of Foreign Related Transactions (4 vols. looseleaf); J. Bischel, Fundamentals of International Taxation (2d ed. 1985); P. Postlewaite, International Corporate Taxation (1985); P. McDaniel & H. Ault, Introduction to United States International Taxation (2d ed. 1981); E. Owens, International Aspects of U.S. Income Taxation (3 vols. 1980); W. Gifford, International Tax Planning (2d ed. 1979); J. Chown, Taxation and Multinational Enterprise (1974).

2. GATT, 26th Supp. BISD 56, 80 (1980).

which such differences in tax burdens and usage affect the location and the general "competitiveness" of industry.

Generally speaking, corporate income taxes are of the greatest interest to entities engaged in international trade, and a number of very difficult issues are raised by such taxes. There are almost no limits imposed by international law on national powers to tax, and as we will see, different nations have different philosophies of taxation. Consequently, entities like multinational enterprises that are potentially subject to tax in more than one jurisdiction are very concerned with the possibility of so-called double taxation, i.e. the imposition of taxes on the same income by two countries. At the same time, however, such entities may be able to avail themselves of techniques to increase their income subject to tax in low-tax countries and decrease their income subject to tax in high-tax countries. The desire of high-tax countries to avoid such revenue losses may lead to rules that exacerbate the problem of double taxation. As we see in our consideration of corporate taxation in Section 19.3, problems of double taxation are to a large extent dealt with in bilateral treaties. However, the lack of uniformity in such treaties has led to the phenomenon of "tax havens"—jurisdictions with low tax rates and favorable networks of tax treaties.

In federal systems, one of the more difficult issues that must be faced is to define the limitations on the taxing powers of the lower governmental jurisdictions. This is a particular problem in the United States because state taxation may have effects on foreign commerce, an area of federal concern. We thus conclude in Section 19.4 with an examination of one of the most controversial issues in international taxation: the appropriateness of the so-called global unitary tax system used by a handful of U.S. states.

One of the themes of this chapter will be to examine the efforts at multilateral coordination of taxing multinational enterprises. Obviously, differing revenue needs of governments will preclude uniform rates and different traditions may preclude any standardization of taxing practices. The reader should thus consider the extent to which multilateral coordination or cooperation is possible given these and other differences between countries.

SECTION 19.2   COMPARATIVE TAX BURDENS AND THEIR EFFECT ON INTERNATIONAL TRADE AND INVESTMENT

Comparing the tax burdens of different countries is difficult. It is not clear that countries collect and report data in the same way. Moreover, it can be argued that any consideration of tax burden should consider the extent to which the taxpayer receives government benefits and the extent to which the taxpayer on whom the tax is imposed is able to shift its burden to others. Nonetheless, determining who benefits from many government programs is very difficult, as is determining the amount of the benefit received, especially since many beneficiaries may themselves not want the benefit, but would rather pay lower taxes and decide themselves how to spend their income. As to tax shifting, it is true that the question of who bears the incidence of a tax is an important one, but unfortunately economists are not in general agreement on how to measure it. Even given these measurement difficulties, it remains instructive to consider the tax burdens of the leading industrial countries as they are typically calculated.

1983 Tax Revenues as a Percentage of Gross Domestic Product

Country	Total Tax Revenue	Personal Income Taxes	Employees' Social Security Taxes	Employers' Social Security Taxes	Corporate Income Taxes	Taxes on Goods and Services
Australia	30	13	0	0	0	10
Canada	33	12	2	3	4	11
France	45	6	5	13	20	13
Germany	37	11	6	7	13	10
Japan	28	7	3	4	8	4
Netherlands	47	10	9	8	21	11
Sweden	51	20	0	13	14	12
Switzerland	32	11	3	3	10	6
United Kingdom	38	10	3	3	7	11
United States	29	11	3	5	8	5

[Source: OECD, Revenue Statistics of OECD Member Countries 1965–84]

As the foregoing table indicates, there is a considerable variation in the taxation policies of the major industrialized nations. Among the more noticeable differences is the much greater reliance by countries other than the United States and Japan on indirect taxes, (taxes on goods and services), such as value added taxes. The fact that value added taxes are permitted to be refunded on export by GATT rules, while no such adjustment is permitted for direct taxes, is sometimes claimed to be an impediment to exports from countries like the United States, which does not have a value added tax. The arguments on this issue were set out in Section 10.3(E) supra.

It is difficult to draw precise conclusions on how differences in tax burdens and taxation policies affect international investment and trade, but it seems clear that different tax burdens, both overall and as allocated among economic sectors, will affect a nation's ability to compete in producing tradable goods and as a result will make the nation more or less attractive as a site for investment. The following excerpt indicates one view of how the U.S. tax system affects U.S. competitiveness.

GLOBAL COMPETITION: THE NEW REALITY: THE REPORT OF THE PRESIDENT'S COMMISSION ON INDUSTRIAL COMPETITIVENESS

120–25 (Vol. II, 1985)

* * * [V]ariations in [the U.S.] tax system depress and distort investment at least as much as the overall level of capital taxation (which seems roughly comparable to that of other nations). One witness, Professor Mervyn King, recently completed a detailed study of taxation of income from capital in the United States, Germany, Sweden, and the United Kingdom * * *. King found that the United States had the highest tax rate on manufacturing, as well as a very wide disparity in rates, depending on type of asset, industry, source of finance, and type of investor. He stated * * *: "It is the variation of tax rates between industries and firms which seems more significant than the level of the average marginal effective tax rate in the economy as a whole."

TYPES OF TAX-INDUCED DISTORTION

Both of these taxes [corporate and individual income] would be far less damaging to competitiveness if the tax system were less distortive; in other words, more neutral. Seven aspects of neutrality appear relevant to competitiveness:

(1) Investment versus consumption. The current system is biased against investment by requiring cost recovery over a period of years and taxing income from some investments at extremely high marginal rates (over 100 percent, according to King). This contributes to the relatively low rate of capital formation in the United States compared to other countries.

(2) Saving versus borrowing. The system encourages borrowing by allowing full deductibility of interest for consumer and business debt and imposes unequal and often high tax rates on different forms of saving. This may help explain why United States personal savings rates are lower than those in other countries (although a host of nontax reasons are also important).

(3) Depreciable versus nondepreciable assets. There is a wide divergence of rates affecting different assets, depending on what tax credits and deductions they qualify for. This steers investment toward assets that may not contribute as much to competitiveness and raises the cost of capital for investments in nonfavored assets.

(4) Long- versus short-term investments. The lack of inflation adjustments for depreciation, interest, and capital gains discriminates against long-term investment, particularly in inflationary periods. This also can discourage investments most needed to improve competitiveness.

(5) High- versus low-risk investments. Incomplete loss offsets, limitations on incentive stock options, and nonindexed capital gains taxation are among the provisions that impede risk-taking, ventures, and startups and that direct capital flows toward safer investments and established but possibly less competitive businesses.

(6) Corporate versus noncorporate investments. Individuals must pay personal income tax on corporate dividends and capital gains, even though both are the result of profits that have already been taxed at the corporate level. These provisions drive up the cost of corporate capital, especially when firms must compete for funds against investments such as municipal bonds that are free of corporate and individual tax.

(7) Work versus leisure. High marginal rates on labor income or on employers for compensation push up labor costs. Although this problem is beyond the scope of the Committee's work, two related issues are pertinent. Excessive taxation of labor income can distort

the choice for producers of how much labor and capital to use in production. Also, neither income nor payroll taxes distinguish the capital and labor portions of self-employment income; thus, they can add to the total tax burden on entrepreneurs.

AGGREGATE IMPACT

Many of the present distortions were enacted for valid public purposes, and the tax system will always be used to serve some objectives other than raising revenue (such as income redistribution). However, the many special provisions in effect now exact a high cost in reduced competitiveness.

Charles Hulten of The Urban Institute summed up the effects of tax-caused misallocations. * * * Hulten states:

This variegated system of taxation . . . has diverted investment from the business sector to tax-favored alternatives in the real estate and State and local government sectors. Within the business sector, investment has been steered toward industries that make more intensive use of depreciable assets and away from high technology industries where technical knowledge is the most important asset. The U.S. tax code has thus operated as a de facto industrial policy that has penalized the activities that many observers consider the leading edge of economic growth.

Four general aspects of the U.S. income tax system contribute to misallocation of capital among competing uses. First, corporate equity income is taxed twice while income from owner-occupied housing and municipal bonds is excluded from income taxation. Second, arbitrary capital cost recovery schemes and tax credits are used in place of neutral depreciation methods. Third, the tax system is not indexed for inflation; and fourth, gains and losses are treated asymmetrically.

Hulten also found that high-technology manufacturing industries have a higher tax burden than "smokestack" or other manufacturing industries, and King found that the manufacturing sector as a whole was taxed substantially more heavily than others (an effective marginal rate, counting corporate and individual provisions, in 1982 of 46.4 percent versus 30.5 percent for commerce and 11.4 percent for other industries). Both of these findings appear ominous for competitiveness. Numerous other studies also blame lack of neutrality in tax law for causing much of the misallocation, short supply, or high cost of capital.

EFFECTS OF RECENT LEGISLATION

The Economic Recovery Tax Act of 1981 altered many of these distortions, but it did not eliminate any. The act brought down marginal personal rates substantially and introduced partial indexing, effective in 1985. It greatly speeded up cost recovery on equipment and structures and increased or initiated tax credits for investment in equipment, rehabilitated structures, and research and development. It introduced or expanded assorted individual savings provisions.

The 1982 and 1984 tax bills have undone many of the tax reductions enacted in 1981. Whereas business tax cuts amounted to only one-fifth of the tax relief included in the 1981 act, businesses paid the majority of the increases enacted in 1982 and 1984, leaving them with a relatively small net tax cut from the three laws combined. Given these legislated increases, plus the growth of profits due to the recovery, it should not be surprising that the corporate income tax was the fastest growing category of tax receipts in fiscal year 1984, and that the tax is projected to keep growing relative to GNP and to other taxes in the next few years. (Nevertheless, the corporate income tax is projected to remain a smaller share of total receipts than in past decades.)

In short, distortions caused by the tax system remain serious, even though some have been lessened.

Notes and Questions

(1) In addition to an effect on the general competitiveness of an economy, the way in which a tax system operates will have an effect on investment decisions. Obviously, if the goal is to produce goods for export, it will be more attractive to invest in a country with a tax system that promotes the competitiveness of its economy. The importance of tax policies to international investors can also be seen in the popularity of so-called tax havens, which we examine in the next section.

(2) As this is written, there are proposals under consideration in the U.S. Congress to revamp significantly the U.S. tax system. It is unclear whether such proposals will be adopted and, if so, what changes in the present system will in fact be made. Assuming changes are made, the reader should consider to what extent the concerns of the President's Commission were dealt with. In doing so, it is appropriate to consider how international competitiveness should rank as a factor in determining tax policy. For example, how should considerations of equity or progressivity be weighed in comparison to considerations of international competitiveness?

(3) The overall level of taxation is an important determinant of the extent of a government's role in its national economy. Can a decision that the government's role should be substantial, which means that overall tax rates will be relatively high and that accordingly the economy may suffer some loss of international competitiveness, be reconciled with an open international trading system? Put another way, would achievement of an open international trading system inevitably require relative uniformity in the extent of a government's role in its economy? If so, does this suggest a difficulty in ever achieving such a trading system? In this regard, it is instructive that although the Treaty of Rome makes some provision for harmonization of indirect taxes, and although it is thought that it will be necessary to attempt to harmonize direct taxes to some extent as economic integration progresses, progress in the EC toward tax harmonization has been relatively slow.[1]

1. See generally Tugendhat, The State of Tax Harmonization in the European Community, Intertax 6 (1983/1); Easson, Tax Harmonisation in the EEC: The Commission's Programme, 1981 Brit.Tax.Rev. 329 (1981).

SECTION 19.3   TAXATION OF MULTI- NATIONAL ENTERPRISES

(A) INTRODUCTION: INTERNATIONAL LAW LIMITATIONS ON NATIONAL TAXATION POWERS

There are few limitations imposed by international law on the right of nations to tax. The three commonly recognized restrictions are (1) limitations on the power to tax foreign diplomats, (2) the rule against arbitrary extraterritorial taxation and (3) the rule prohibiting one government from acting in the territory of another.[1] The first limitation is not of great importance and the third is essentially a restatement of one of the general rules of international law related to the concept of national sovereignty, a concept that we have discussed in the context of extraterritorial application of trade and antitrust laws (see Sections 13.5 and 18.3(C) supra).

The rule against arbitrary extraterritorial taxation is limited in scope. It seems clear that a nation may tax its own citizens wherever they live. The burden imposed may be limited by national law, but not by international law. Moreover, it is clear that a nation may tax residents, again without limitation once the existence of residency is established. How to define residency can be a difficult question. An overbroad definition might raise problems under international law if its effect were to subject an alien to arbitrary taxation, but it seems clear that international law does not require the use of a particularly restrictive definition of residency. Finally, even with respect to nonresident aliens, international law recognizes a nation's right to tax provided that some territorial connection is established. Such a link could be established if the income to be taxed arose in a nation or if the property to be taxed was located there.

In Burnet v. Brooks, 288 U.S. 378, 53 S.Ct. 457, 77 L.Ed. 844 (1933), the U.S. Supreme Court upheld the imposition of federal estate tax on the estate of a British subject who was a resident of Cuba. The taxes were imposed in respect of cash and securities owned by the decedent that were located in New York City. The Court concluded that Congress had intended to tax the estate in the given factual situation. As to the question of whether the United States could properly levy a tax on such property, the Court stated (288 U.S. at 396, 399):

> As a nation vested with all attributes of sovereignty, the United States is vested with all the powers of government necessary to maintain an effective control of international relations. * * * So far as our relation to other nations is concerned, and apart from any self-imposed constitutional restriction, we cannot fail to regard the property in question as being within the jurisdiction of the United States,—that is, it was property with the reach of the power which the United States by virtue of its sovereignty could exercise as against other nations and their subjects without violating any established principle of international law.

* * *

1. See generally Rädler, Basic Origins of International Double Taxation and Measures for Its Avoidance, in E. Owens, International Aspects of U.S. Income Taxation 59 (1980).

As jurisdiction may exist in more than one government, that is, jurisdiction based upon distinct grounds—the citizenship of the owner, his domicile, the source of income, the situs of the property—efforts have been made to preclude multiple taxation through the negotiation of appropriate international conventions. These endeavors, however, have proceeded upon express or implied recognition, and not in denial, of the sovereign taxing powers as exerted by governments in the exercise of jurisdiction upon any of these grounds. * * *

The outer limits of national taxing power are difficult to define with any clarity. Presumably an exercise of taxing power could be so arbitrary, in the sense that the taxed person had no relationship at all with the taxing country, that the taxed person's country would protest the tax on that person's behalf. Such cases are not likely to occur often, however, because it is not likely that the taxing country will be in a position to collect the tax, unless the person or the person's property has some relationship to the taxing country.

(B) U.S. TAXATION OF INTERNATIONAL TRADE AND INVESTMENT

While we cannot hope in this brief chapter to give even an overview of international taxation, the following excerpt summarizes a number of the basic principles applied by the United States.

PAUL R. McDANIEL & HUGH J. AULT, INTRODUCTION TO UNITED STATES INTERNATIONAL TAXATION

38–40 (2d ed. 1981)[2]

* * * [T]he literal scope of the United States income tax on *individuals* is to tax all individuals in the world on their worldwide income! However, subsequent provisions make it clear that the assertion of worldwide taxing jurisdiction is only meant to include individuals who are U.S. citizens or residents. For these taxpayers, U.S. taxing jurisdiction is based on their personal relationship or status with respect to the U.S.; the geographic source of their income is irrelevant. * * *

The remaining class of potential taxpayers, nonresident aliens and foreign trusts and estates, are also subject to U.S. tax. For such taxpayers, however, the U.S. tax jurisdiction is based on the *geographic source* of the taxpayer's income. These taxpayers are in general only subject to tax on income from sources within the U.S. Their business income from U.S. sources is taxed in much the same way as that of a U.S. citizen or resident, while their investment income is subject to a special set of tax rules.

As respects *corporations*, the assertion of U.S. worldwide tax jurisdiction is based solely on the place of incorporation. A corporation incorporated in the U.S. is subject to tax on its worldwide income just as are U.S. citizens and residents. Correspondingly, a corporation incorporated under the laws of some other country is treated for U.S. tax purposes as a foreign corpora-

2. Reprinted by permission of Kluwer, Deventer, The Netherlands.

tion. Foreign corporations, like nonresident alien individuals, are subject to U.S. tax on the basis of the *U.S. source* of their income.

While the U.S. asserts taxing jurisdiction over the foreign income of its citizens and residents, it alleviates the so-called "international double taxation", which may arise when another country also attempts to tax a portion of that income, through a foreign tax credit. The credit is available to U.S. citizens and residents and domestic corporations who pay taxes on foreign income to other countries. In addition, an indirect credit is provided to U.S. domestic corporations which receive dividend income from foreign corporations in which they own at least 10% of the voting stock.

The U.S. in some situations also looks to the nationality or residence of a foreign corporation's shareholders in determining the appropriate pattern of taxation. In the case of *controlled foreign corporations* (that is a foreign corporation more than 50 percent of whose voting stock is owned by U.S. individuals or corporations), the normal U.S. jurisdictional rules, which would allow deferral of U.S. tax on the foreign income earned by a foreign corporation until its distribution to its U.S. shareholders, are modified for certain types of undistributed income of the foreign corporation. In such cases, the U.S. shareholders of the "controlled foreign corporation" are subject to tax on their allocable share of the described income, even though it is not distributed as a dividend to the U.S. shareholders. Special treatment is also provided for "foreign personal holding companies", again with the object of currently taxing to the U.S. shareholders the undistributed taxable income of the foreign corporation.

A number of provisions are intended to prevent avoidance of U.S. tax jurisdiction, for example, section 482 (dealing with allocation of income and deductions among enterprises controlled or owned by the same interests in order clearly to reflect income) and section 367 (requiring the approval of the Secretary of the Treasury or his delegate when a U.S. person enters into a tax-free organization, reorganization or liquidation involving a foreign corporation).

The U.S. has entered into a number of bilateral tax treaties which modify the above general pattern of United States income taxation of international transactions.

Notes

(1) As noted in the DISC cases discussed in Section 10.3(B) supra, many countries choose to tax only residents of their territory, as opposed to all of their citizens. Under such a system, a nonresident citizen with foreign-source income would not be subject to tax in his native land. To prevent tax avoidance by corporations under such a system, the residence of a corporation is often determined by its actual seat of operations, as opposed to its place of incorporation.

(2) An example of the extent to which the United States attempts to tax income is U.S. taxation of income "effectively connected" with U.S. business activities. Typically investment income paid to a foreign entity may be subject to withholding tax under U.S. law, but the foreign recipient is not considered to be otherwise subject to U.S. tax. The provisions for taxation of effectively-

connected income change this rule in some circumstances. The report of the House of Representatives on the provisions gives a number of interpretative illustrations.[3] For example, if a foreign corporation had an importing and selling branch in the United States that required large dollar balances that it invested in Treasury securities, the income on the securities would be considered to be effectively connected with its U.S. business activities and subject to tax, regardless of where the securities were physically located. Interest income on the branch's delinquent accounts would also be subject to U.S. tax under this provision. A different example would be the case of a foreign manufacturer with a U.S. plant and investments in the securities of U.S. corporations unconnected with such plant. The income on such securities would not be considered effectively connected to its U.S. business activities. The focus of the provision seems to be to tax income on securities that are used or held for use of the U.S. business.

The drafters of the American Law Institute's Federal Income Tax Project note that the U.S. provision indicates a congressional desire to tax income with an "economic genesis" in the United States and that such a desire is consistent with international law. They propose, however, that the effectively-connected rule be applicable only when the income is connected with the conduct of a trade or business in the United States through a fixed place of business.[4]

(C) TAXATION OF MULTINATIONAL ENTERPRISES: AN OVERVIEW OF CURRENT PRACTICE

The preceding section makes clear that nations have broad powers to tax and that the person or property legally subject to such powers may be taxed by different nations in respect of the same income or property. This problem of double taxation is particularly serious in respect of income taxes applicable to multinational enterprises (MNEs) because by their very nature they are likely to be subject to taxation in more than one jurisdiction—a fact that will require the respective taxing authorities to determine what income of the MNE should be subject to tax and what allowance, if any, should be made because the income may have been taxed in another jurisdiction. The following excerpt describes some of the problems arising in taxing MNEs.

CARL S. SHOUP, TAXATION OF MULTINATIONAL CORPORATIONS

(1974)[5]

In the multinational setting, tax problems turn out to be concerned almost entirely with income tax and particularly corporation income tax.

* * *

* * * [T]he taxation of corporate income varies intricately from one country to another. The differences lie not only in the levels of the tax rates. They are found also in definitions of taxable profits, net royalties, interest, and other taxable items, and above all in the allocation of a firm's

---

3. H.Rep. No. 1450, 89th Cong., 2d Sess. 60 (1966).

4. American Law Institute, Federal Income Tax Project 1–13 (Tentative Draft No. 13, 1984).

5. From United Nations Dept. of Econ. & Soc. Affairs, The Impact of Multinational Corporations on Development and on International Relations, Technical Papers: Taxation 3–9, U.N.Pub. No. ST/ESA/11.

world-wide income among the taxing jurisdictions in which it does business, receives income, or engages in some other taxable activity. Home countries differ in the degree to which they make allowance for host country taxes. A separately incorporated foreign subsidiary is often, but not always, treated differently from a foreign branch of the home country corporation. A depressingly large number of possible different tax outcomes is therefore faced by any one multinational corporation. From a government's point of view there are a depressingly large number of more or less legal patterns from which a multinational corporation can choose, to try to minimize its world-wide tax bill.

Differences in the rates of tax on corporate profits are perhaps not so great as the layman might expect, though still large enough to cause trouble. In most countries, developed and developing, the rate of corporate income tax stipulated in the tax law seems to fall within a range of 35 to 50 per cent. The dispersion of rates, however, is somewhat greater among the developing countries than among the developed. A zero tax rate for the first few years of a new corporation's life is common in developing countries, for approved or "pioneer" industries. This is the so-called "tax holiday." The existence of only a few countries with very low corporate rates is enough to threaten the revenue of other countries, not to mention the influence of certain taxing jurisdictions that offer themselves as tax havens.

These differences in corporate income tax rates are sometimes exacerbated and sometimes softened by differences in rates of withholding taxes on dividends, interest, and other remittances by a subsidiary to a parent company elsewhere. They are termed "withholding" taxes because, although legally imposed on the recipient abroad, they are collected from the domestic corporation (the payor) by requiring it to withhold the tax when paying dividends, interest, and the like. The host country is of course unable to reach the foreign recipient directly, in contrast to the recipient who resides within its borders.

What is fast becoming more serious than differences in tax rates, however, is the proliferation of gaps and overlappings in definitions of taxable net profit. One country may allow a 100 per cent depreciation deduction for the cost of machinery and equipment in the year of purchase, while another country requires the depreciation to be spread more or less evenly over the years of useful life of the asset. Some countries grant an investment credit for purchase of machinery and certain other capital equipment, say 7 per cent of the cost, to be deducted directly from the tax otherwise due. The valuation of inventories is another source of considerable difference, quite important when the specific commodity prices rise or fall. The balance sheet method of computing a firm's net income, found in many European countries, is somewhat different in its approach, though not markedly different in end results, from the profit and loss account method (income method) used in, for example, the United Kingdom and the United States of America.

IV.   ALLOCATION OF NET INCOME AMONG
COUNTRIES: TRANSFER PRICING

Even if taxable net income were similarly defined in all countries, there would remain the problem of how to allocate a given firm's worldwide profit among the countries in which it operates.   Every country claims the right to tax net income that arises within its borders, including income that flows abroad.   Some countries * * * claim more.   The chances for double taxation are obvious.

One of the most troublesome aspects of this allocation problem is that of transfer pricing, sometimes referred to as clearing prices.   Parent company P in a capital-exporting country, E, sells semi-finished goods that it has manufactured in E to its wholly-owned subsidiary, S, in capital-importing country I.   The subsidiary S adds further processing and sells the finished product in I.   The two countries' tax authorities, if they had access to all the relevant data in the books of both P and S, might conceivably agree on a figure for the consolidated profit of the two companies.   But they might disagree appreciably on how much of the profit arose in E, and how much in I.   They would therefore differ on how much of the total profit should be taxable to P, to yield revenue to E's treasury, and how much should be taxable to S, to swell I's revenues.

*   *   *

On the other hand, P and S may deliberately set transfer prices at unreasonable levels, high or low, to evade tax in some country, at the expense, perhaps, of paying more tax in another country.   If the tax rate in I is low, that country is the preferred one for tax purposes, with some exceptions (e.g., if the parent is operating at a loss in E).   If the sale of goods or services is from P to S, and if I has the lower tax rate, transfer prices will tend to be set unreasonably low, to allocate as much profit as possible to I.   Conversely, if the sale is from S to P, perhaps raw materials extracted in I, the transfer price will tend to be set unreasonably high.

Even if the tax rates in E and I are the same, P and S may tend to set the transfer prices at unreasonable levels, if the two countries differ in the degree to which they enforce their tax laws.   *   *   *

Even if the tax rates and degrees of enforcement are the same in the two countries, P and S may employ unrealistic transfer prices.   Their motives may have nothing to do with income tax.   Perhaps they are trying to avoid exchange controls, to minimize customs duties, or to reward executives in one of the countries under a profit-sharing plan.

———

The foregoing suggests three particular problems of taxing MNEs: The need to consider double taxation problems, the ability of MNEs to manipulate their taxable income through use of transfer prices and the use of so-called tax havens.   We examine each of these subjects in the next three subsections.

(D) AVOIDANCE OF DOUBLE TAXATION

There are essentially two ways to avoid double taxation. One of the two nations with jurisdiction may recognize the fact that the other has imposed a tax when it imposes its own tax, e.g., by allowing the tax paid to the other nation to be taken as a credit against such tax. Or the two nations may by agreement or otherwise decide how their respective jurisdictions should be exercised.

(1) *Unilateral Methods*

JOHN I. FORRY & PERRY A. LERNER, TAXING MULTINATIONAL ENTERPRISES: BASIC ISSUES OF INTERNATIONAL INCOME TAX HARMONIZATION

(1976) [6]

One basic unilateral approach to international tax harmonization is to grant a deduction from worldwide income or a credit against the home country tax on foreign source income for foreign taxes paid on such income by the multinational enterprise. A deduction provides only partial harmonization, since the home country tax is reduced by only a portion of the foreign taxes. In the case of the foreign tax credit, if the foreign tax rate is lower than the home country rate, only the excess of the home country tax over the foreign tax on the foreign income is payable to the home country. If the foreign tax rate is higher, the home country foregoes tax on the income. However, the credit generally is limited to the amount of home country tax on the foreign income with respect to which the foreign taxes are paid, so the credit does not affect home country tax on domestic income. The home country may require the income and credit limitation of each foreign country to be calculated separately, or may permit high and low taxes of various foreign countries to be combined and so averaged over all foreign source income. The home country may also permit excess foreign tax to be carried over for possible credit in a prior or subsequent year.

Certain countries grant a credit only for foreign taxes imposed directly on the enterprise, such as taxes on foreign branch operations and withholding taxes on investment income. Other countries such as the United States also allow an indirect credit for taxes paid by a substantially owned foreign corporation to the extent the previously taxed profits are distributed in the form of dividends to the parent corporation. The effect of the foreign tax credit, together with possible carryovers of excess credits to other years, is to subject the enterprise's foreign source income to total income taxes at least equal to the home country tax rate on domestic source income. Accordingly a tax incentive in favor of foreign over domestic investment is avoided.

6. 10 Intl. Law. 623, 628. Reprinted by permission of the American Bar Association.

(2) Bilateral Treaties on Avoidance of Double Taxation

The United States is a party to about 50 bilateral treaties on the avoidance of double taxation.[7] To understand how these treaties operate in depth, it would obviously be necessary to understand the underlying tax code provisions that would otherwise be applicable. That is beyond the scope of this book, but it is possible, by looking at model treaties, to obtain an overview of how such treaties typically work with respect to income earned by different components of multinational enterprises. In considering the U.S. model treaty, the reader should ask why the activities listed in Article 5 as not constituting a permanent establishment were selected? Where does the line seem to lie between activities constituting a permanent establishment and those that do not? How does the model handle the problem of related enterprises? To what extent would the taxing authorities of the two parties have to coordinate their investigations and treatment of multinational enterprises or other associated enterprises? To what extent is the taxing authority of one party limited by unilateral decisions of the other?

UNITED STATES DRAFT MODEL INCOME TAX TREATY OF JUNE 16, 1981 [8]

Article 5

Permanent Establishment

1. For the purposes of this Convention, the term "permanent establishment" means a fixed place of business through which the business of an enterprise is wholly or partly carried on.

* * *

4. Notwithstanding the preceding provisions of this Article, the term "permanent establishment" shall be deemed not to include

(a) the use of facilities solely for the purpose of storage, display, or delivery of goods or merchandise belonging to the enterprise;

(b) the maintenance of a stock of goods or merchandise belonging to the enterprise solely for the purpose of storage, display, or delivery;

(c) the maintenance of a stock of goods or merchandise belonging to the enterprise solely for the purpose of processing by another enterprise;

(d) the maintenance of a fixed place of business solely for the purpose of purchasing goods or merchandise, or of collecting information, for the enterprise;

(e) the maintenance of a fixed place of business solely for the purpose of carrying on, for the enterprise, any other activity of a preparatory or auxiliary character;

(f) the maintenance of a fixed place of business solely for any combination of the activities mentioned in subparagraphs (a) to (e).

---

7. See Burke, Report on Proposed United States Model Income Tax Treaty, 23 Harv. Intl.L.J. 219, 220 (1983).

8. The Model can be found in Commerce Clearing House, Tax Treaties ¶ 158.

5. Notwithstanding the provisions of paragraphs 1 and 2, where a person—other than an agent of an independent status to whom paragraph 6 applies—is acting on behalf of an enterprise and has and habitually exercises in a Contracting State an authority to conclude contracts in the name of the enterprise, that enterprise shall be deemed to have a permanent establishment in that State in respect of any activities which that person undertakes for the enterprise, unless the activities of such person are limited to those mentioned in paragraph 4 which, if exercised though a fixed place of business, would not make this fixed place of business a permanent establishment under the provisions of that paragraph.

6. An enterprise shall not be deemed to have a permanent establishment in a Contracting State merely because it carries on business in that State through a broker, general commission agent, or any other agent of an independent status, provided that such persons are acting in the ordinary course of their business.

7. The fact that a company which is a resident of a Contracting State controls or is controlled by a company which is a resident of the other Contracting State, or which carries on business in that other State (whether through a permanent establishment or otherwise), shall not of itself constitute either company a permanent establishment of the other.

* * *

Article 7

Business Profits

1. The business profits of an enterprise of a Contracting State shall be taxable only in that State unless the enterprise carries on business in the other Contracting State through a permanent establishment situated therein. If the enterprise carries on business as aforesaid, the business profits of the enterprise may be taxed in the other State but only so much of them as is attributable to that permanent establishment.

2. Subject to the provisions of paragraph 3, where an enterprise of a Contracting State carries on business in the other Contracting State through a permanent establishment situated therein, there shall in each Contracting State be attributed to that permanent establishment the business profits which it might be expected to make if it were a distinct and independent enterprise engaged in the same or similar activities under the same or similar conditions.

3. In determining the business profits of a permanent establishment, there shall be allowed as deductions expenses which are incurred for the purposes of the permanent establishment, including a reasonable allocation of executive and general administrative expenses, research and development expenses, interest, and other expenses incurred for the purposes of the enterprise as a whole (or the part thereof which includes the permanent establishment), whether incurred in the State in which the permanent establishment is situated or elsewhere.

4.   No business profits shall be attributed to a permanent establishment by reason of the mere purchase by that permanent establishment of goods or merchandise for the enterprise.

* * *

Article 9

Associated Enterprises

1.   Where

(a) an enterprise of a Contracting State participates directly or indirectly in the management, control or capital of an enterprise of the other Contracting State; or

(b) the same persons participate directly or indirectly in the management, control, or capital of an enterprise of a Contracting State and an enterprise of the other Contracting State, and in either case conditions are made or imposed between the two enterprises in their commercial or financial relations which differ from those which would be made between independent enterprises, then any profits which, but for those conditions would have accrued to one of the enterprises, but by reason of those conditions have not so accrued, may be included in the profits of that enterprise and taxed accordingly.

2.   Where a Contracting State includes in the profits of an enterprise of that State, and taxes accordingly, profits on which an enterprise of the other Contracting State has been charged to tax in that other State, and the profits so included are profits which would have accrued to the enterprise of the first-mentioned State if the conditions made between the two enterprises had been those which would have been made between independent enterprises, then that other State shall make an appropriate adjustment to the amount of the tax charged therein on those profits.   In determining such adjustment, due regard shall be paid to the other provisions of this Convention and the competent authorities of the Contracting States shall if necessary consult each other.

3.   The provisions of paragraph 1 shall not limit any provisions of the law of either Contracting State which permit the distribution, apportionment, or allocation of income, deductions, credits, or allowances between persons, whether or not residents of a Contracting State, owned or controlled directly or indirectly by the same interests when necessary in order to prevent evasion of taxes or clearly to reflect the income of any of such persons.

* * *

Article 11

Interest

1.   Interest derived and beneficially owned by a resident of a Contracting State shall be taxable only in that State.

2.   The term "interest" as used in this Convention means income from debt-claims of every kind, whether or not secured by mortgage, and whether

or not carrying a right to participate in the debtor's profits, and in particular, income from government securities, and income from bonds or debentures, including premiums or prizes attaching to such securities, bonds, or debentures. Penalty charges for late payment shall not be regarded as interest for the purposes of the Convention.

3. The provisions of paragraph 1 shall not apply if the beneficial owner of the interest, being a resident of a Contracting State, carries on business in the other Contracting State, in which the interest arises, through a permanent establishment situated therein, or performs in that other State independent personal services from a fixed base situated therein, and the interest is attributable to such permanent establishment or fixed base. In such case the provisions of Article 7 (Business Profits) or Article 14 (Independent Personal Services), as the case may be, shall apply.

4. Interest shall be deemed to arise in a Contracting State when the payer is that State itself or a political subdivision, local authority, or resident of that State. Where, however, the person paying the interest, whether he is a resident of a Contracting State or not, has in a Contracting State a permanent establishment or a fixed base in connection with which the indebtedness on which the interest is paid was incurred, and such interest is borne by such permanent establishment or fixed base, then such interest shall be deemed to arise in the State in which the permanent establishment or fixed base is situated.

5. Where, by reason of a special relationship between the payer and the beneficial owner or between both of them and some other person, the amount of the interest, having regard to the debt-claim for which it is paid, exceeds the amount which would have been agreed upon by the payer and the beneficial owner in the absence of such relationship, the provisions of this Article shall apply only to the last-mentioned amount. In such case the excess part of the payments shall remain taxable according to the laws of each Contracting State, due regard being had to the other provisions of the Convention.

6. A Contracting State may not impose any tax on interest paid by a resident of the other Contracting State, except insofar as

(a) the interest is paid to a resident of the first-mentioned State;

(b) the interest is attributable to a permanent establishment or a fixed base situated in the first-mentioned State; or

(c) the interest arises in the first-mentioned State and is not paid to a resident of the other State.

The U.S. model is not the only model treaty in this area. The OECD has developed one as well,[9] and the United Nations has drafted another that is designed primarily for use between a developed and developing country.[10]

9. Id., ¶ 151. OECD, Model Double Taxation Convention on Income and Capital (1977).

10. Commerce Clearing House, Tax Treaties ¶ 171. UN Pub. No. ST/ESA/102 (1980). See S. Surrey, United Nations Model Convention for Tax Treaties Between Developed and Developing Countries: A Description and Analysis (Harvard Law School International Tax Program/International Bureau of Fiscal

The salient differences between the U.S. and OECD models are set out in the following:

STATEMENT OF H. DAVID ROSENBLOOM, INTERNATIONAL TAX COUNSEL, DEPARTMENT OF THE TREASURY

(1981) [11]

The point of reference for all United States income tax treaty negotiations undertaken today is the U.S. model income tax treaty, which follows the OECD model in most important respects. * * *

The most important differences between the U.S. model and that of the OECD are as follows.

Citizenship Basis Taxation. The OECD model applies only to states which tax globally on the basis of domicile or residence. We, of course, tax on a citizenship basis in addition to a residence basis. We regard it as appropriate to attempt to relieve double taxation which occurs when a nonresident U.S. citizen is taxed on a source basis by a treaty partner. In addition, the U.S. model contains a "saving" clause permitting taxation of U.S. citizens (including former citizens) as if no treaty were in effect. Since this rule is overbroad in certain respects, it is necessary to accompany the saving clause with specific exceptions.

Coverage of State and Local Taxes. Under the U.S. model, state and local taxes are not covered, except for the nondiscrimination article. The OECD model provides for general coverage of the taxes of a political subdivision or local authority.

Corporate Residence. The United States treats place of incorporation as the test of corporate residence, and the U.S. model reflects this statutory rule. Some other countries use a "managed and controlled" test. The OECD model provides that when a corporation is, under the domestic law of the contracting states, deemed a resident of each state, its residence is determined by the place where its "effective management" is situated. The U.S. model resolves such cases on the basis of place of incorporation.

* * *

Non-discrimination. The U.S. model covers discrimination against nonresidents but provides that, in effect, nonresident aliens will not be entitled to net basis taxation in the United States. In addition, the model provides a relatively detailed rule governing the allowance of indirect expenses as deductions in the source state. In these respects the U.S. model extends principles found in the OECD model. On the other hand, the U.S. model—unlike the OECD model—provides no protection against discrimination by the source state for corporations not having a permanent establishment in that state.

Documentation: Selected Monographs on Taxation, 1980).

11. Hearings on Income Tax Treaties Before the Subcomm. on Oversight of the House Comm. on Ways and Means, 96th Cong., 2d Sess. 61, 70–73 (1980) (reprinted in 19 Colum. J.Transnatl.L. 359 (1981)).

Mutual Agreement. The U.S. model provides for no time limit on the period in which a case can be presented to the competent authority, and spells out in detail some of the actions which are permissible for the competent authority to take. We think it helpful to provide as much guidance to the competent authority as possible. Many countries, which have more flexible competent authority mechanisms than the United States, do not perceive the need for such rules, which are not found in the OECD model.

Exchange of Information and Administrative Assistance. The U.S. model provision on exchange of information is broader than that of the OECD. It expressly requires a state of which information is requested to take depositions, and engage in other specified information-gathering activities, on behalf of the requesting state. The U.S. model is intended to produce information in a form that will be usable in U.S. courts. It also contains a provision requiring the residence state to collect taxes on behalf of the source state for the purpose of ensuring that relief granted by the source state does not inure to the benefit of persons not entitled to such relief. This feature is aimed at combatting the use of nominees to secure unintended advantages under a treaty.

(E) TRANSFER PRICING

As has been discussed elsewhere in this section, multinational enterprises have considerable opportunity to determine the net profits of their various components by setting relatively high or low prices for transfers of materials and services among them. The OECD Guidelines for Multinational Enterprises (see generally Section 17.3 supra) provide that MNEs should "refrain from making use of the particular facilities available to them, such as transfer pricing which does not conform to an arm's length standard, for modifying in ways contrary to national laws the tax base on which members of the group are assessed." There is general international agreement on the principle that arm's length prices should normally be used. In addition to the Guidelines, the principle is found in the OECD model treaty on avoidance of double taxation, as well as in the U.S. model set out above. It is, however, a principle that is often difficult to apply. Moreover, as we see in Section 19.4 infra, it is a principle that is rejected by a number of states in the United States.

In considering the following extract, and the previous materials on corporate taxation in this section, readers should consider how rules on transfer pricing and corporate taxation would affect their answers to the questions raised by the problem in Section 16.1 supra.

OECD, TRANSFER PRICING AND MULTI-NATIONAL ENTERPRISES

13–15 (1979) [12]

THE ARM'S LENGTH PRINCIPLE

Comparable Uncontrolled Prices

11.   Making a judgment whether a particular transfer price conforms to the arm's length principle would ideally require direct reference to prices in comparable transactions between enterprises independent of each other or between the group and unrelated parties.   This method is frequently referred to as the "comparable uncontrolled price" method and in principle it is the most appropriate to use and in theory the easiest.   In practice, however, it often happens that such evidence is not available or it is impracticable to collect it together or there is argument about whether the prices quoted are comparable or not.   Other methods may therefore need to be used to obtain an arm's length price.

Cost Plus and Resale Methods

12.   There will be many cases where no useful evidence of uncontrolled transactions will be available because, for example, the goods or services etc. which are supplied are so special to the group that there is no open market in them and they are not supplied to independent enterprises.   This may be particularly the case for example for semi-finished products or in relation to transfers of technology.   In other cases the transactions within the group may not be satisfactorily comparable with those between the group and independent third parties, for example because they take place at a different stage in the chain of production or distribution or because the independent third party is too small a customer to claim the discounts for volume which an entity within the group might be big enough to achieve if it were independent.   In such circumstances it will often be necessary, in order to establish an arm's length price, to use either the cost plus method or the resale method, the cost plus method starting from the cost of providing the goods or services etc. and adding whatever cost and profit mark-up is appropriate and the resale price method starting from the final selling price and subtracting the cost and an appropriate profit mark-up.

Other Methods

13.   The complexities of real life business situations may put many conceptual and practical difficulties in the way of the application of the methods referred to above.   A mixture of these methods, or other methods still, may sometimes therefore have to be used.   Any method which is used will involve problems of judgment and the evaluation of evidence and it has to be recognised that the object of using it is to produce a figure which is acceptable for practical purposes.   Experience shows that the difficulties can in general be satisfactorily dealt with and acceptable prices agreed.

12.   Reprinted by permission of the Organization for Economic Cooperation and Development.

The So-called "Global" Methods

14. Proposals for radical reformulations of the approach to intragroup transfer pricing which would move away from the arm's length approach towards so-called global or direct methods of profit allocation, or towards fixing transfer prices by reference to predetermined formulae for allocating profits between affiliates, are not endorsed in this report. The use of such alternatives to the arm's length principle is incompatible in fact with Articles 7 and 9 of the OECD Model Double Taxation Convention. Such methods would necessarily be arbitrary, tending to disregard market conditions as well as the particular circumstances of the individual enterprises and tending to ignore the management's own allocation of resources, thus producing an allocation of profits which may bear no sound relationship to the economic facts and inherently running the risk of allocating profits to an entity which is in truth making losses (or possibly the contrary). A number of such methods are sometimes advocated, allocating profits in some cases in proportion to the respective costs of the associated enterprises, sometimes in proportion to their respective turnovers or to their respective labour forces, or by some formula taking account of several such criteria. They are all however to some degree arbitrary. For example, it does not follow that profit is uniformly related to cost at all stages in an integrated production and marketing process. Indeed the problem of allocating costs could well be no easier than in using the cost plus method to arrive at an arm's length price. Nor does it follow that labour costs are the same for the same labour in different countries, or that profits are necessarily related to any simple combination of such factors. To allocate profits by such methods in a way which reduced the arbitrariness of the results to a negligible degree would necessitate a complex analysis of the different functions of the various associated enterprises and a sophisticated weighing up of the different risks and profit opportunities in the various different stages of manufacturing, transportation, marketing and so on. Nor would the information necessary for such an assessment be readily available or, in many cases, available at all. The need would be for full information about the total activities of the whole MNE. While the widest range of such information may be available to the tax authorities in the country of the parent company in a group even those tax authorities will be limited to some extent in the information which they can compile. The tax authorities of the country in which a subsidiary is situated will on the other hand be in no position to acquire even this amount of information without imposing on the MNE itself a possibly intolerable administrative burden, or a similar burden on the tax authorities of the parent company's country if they seek to get the information by way of exchange of information provisions under double taxation agreements. Nor can it be generally assumed that the tax authorities of the country of the subsidiary should in any case be entitled to quite such a wide range of information about the group's worldwide activities. In practice moreover the information may simply not be available to those authorities. Even if the information were available, however, the varied activities of any MNE and the varied circumstances and situations in which they are carried on must make it impracticable for the tax authorities of the country in which one subsidiary is situated to judge in any satisfactory manner the profitabili-

ty of any of the other parts of the group situated elsewhere. Moreover, problems would still arise in the comparison of figures produced in different countries by different accounting methods and different legal requirements. Another major disadvantage of any attempt to use such global methods of profit allocation as an alternative to the arm's length principle is that their unco-ordinated use by the tax authorities of several countries would involve the danger that, overall, the MNE affected would suffer double taxation of its profits. This is not to say, however, that in seeking to arrive at the arm's length price in a range of transactions, some regard to the total profits of the relevant MNE may not be helpful, as a check on the assessment of the arm's length price or in specific bilateral situations where other methods give rise to serious difficulties and the two countries concerned are able to adopt a common approach and the necessary information can be made available.

(F) TAX HAVENS AND TREATY SHOPPING [13]

STATEMENT OF H. DAVID ROSENBLOOM, INTERNATIONAL TAX COUNSEL, DEPARTMENT OF THE TREASURY

Supra, at 75–76

Third Country Use. Most United States treaties allow benefits in the nature of reductions in source basis taxation to corporations organized in the treaty partner, regardless of whether the owners of the corporation are residents of, or are in any other way connected with, that country. Any treaty conceivably can, therefore, be used to effect an overall change in the incidence of United States taxation of U.S. source income, by the simple formation of a "holding company" qualifying for treaty benefits. If a person, for instance, holds equity securities subject to our 30 percent withholding tax on dividends, he can normally reduce that tax by organizing a corporation in a country with which we have a treaty reducing the rate to 15 percent.

In practice, however, this kind of "third country use" of tax treaties does not routinely arise, because it is ordinarily not cost-free to make investments through a holding company specially organized in a treaty partner. Most treaty partners of the United States will tax income received by the corporation, which ordinarily will eliminate any advantage from the reduction of the U.S. rate at source. To the extent the investor will be subject to withholding tax on payments from the corporation, or to the extent he is not able to claim complete relief in his home country for a dividend from a foreign corporation, the additional tax burden will often exceed the benefits achieved under the treaty with the United States.

This protection of the treaty process depends, however, on the existence of normal taxing provisions in the law of the treaty partner. Some of our treaty partners have special provisions granting privileges to holding companies, which result in reduced taxation of the holding company or reduced taxation on the payment of income from the treaty country to a third

---

13. See generally Richard Gordon, Tax Havens and Their Use by United States Taxpayers—An Overview, A Report to the Commissioner of Internal Revenue, the Assistant Attorney General (Tax Division) and the Assistant Secretary of the Treasury (Tax Policy), Pub.No. 1150 (1981).

country. Sometimes this occurs for reasons of domestic policy, but sometimes the treaty partner has deliberately enacted provisions with the aim of attracting "offshore" business, with an eye to the revenues that can be collected from licensing fees or those taxes which are imposed; and to the service industry that can be built up around an "offshore" financing business.

In addition, treaties can be used to channel benefits to "third country" beneficiaries through the use of "conduit" companies. This practice depends upon an exemption from source basis taxation of payments from that country, and an hospitable attitude toward "offshore" business. The conduit company earns income in the United States which is subject, under the treaty, to reduced U.S. tax; the income is then siphoned off as payments deductible from the base subject to tax in the treaty partner, to the person who is the real investor.

These "treaty shopping" practices are objectionable for a number of reasons, which I have previously described to this Subcommittee. The practices cause unintended revenue loss, not contemplated by the treaty "bargain". They may undermine the willingness of third countries to enter into treaty negotiations with us. And, perhaps most seriously, such practices are contrary to the spirit of international double tax treaties, and enhance opportunities for international tax evasion. Double tax treaties are founded on the principle of allocating taxing rights based on "economic allegiance"; treaty shopping accords a revenue power to a third country, the "base country", which has little or no claim to such allegiance. In addition, since most "base countries" have local law provisions which ensure confidentiality of the identity of the ultimate investor, the conclusion is inescapable that the practices are employed to a large extent by persons evading taxes in their home country.

Within the last two years we have initiated negotiations aimed at modifying three treaties which we believe present treaty shopping problems—with Switzerland, the Netherlands Antilles, and the British Virgin Islands. Our objective in these negotiations, generally, is to secure new provisions that will eliminate or materially reduce the potential for abuse.

Note

The United States has in recent years taken a harder line towards the use of tax havens and treaty shopping. For example, it cancelled the tax treaty provisions applicable to the British Virgin Islands and several other Caribbean nations, and it is in the process of negotiating new treaties with these nations that limit the possibility of treaty abuse.[14] The United States is also renegotiating the treaty provisions applicable to the Netherlands Antilles. In addition, the elimination in 1984 of the 30% withholding tax on "portfolio interest" paid to foreign persons by U.S. entities, has reduced the attractiveness of using a Netherlands Antilles finance subsidiary to sell bonds to European and other foreign investors.[15]

14. See, e.g., 2 BNA Intl. Trade Rptr. 246 (1985) (new tax treaty with Barbados).

15. See generally Segal & Davis, Repeal of the 30% Withholding Tax on Portfolio Interest, 11 Intl. Tax J. 125 (1985).

SECTION 19.4 U.S. STATE TAXATION OF INTERNATIONAL TRADE AND INVESTMENT

Taxation of multijurisdictional entities by state governments in the United States raises a number of difficult issues. First, as we saw in Barnet v. Brooks, discussed in Section 19.3 supra, the U.S. Constitution limits state power to tax enterprises engaged in interstate activities. Second, as we saw in Section 3.6 supra, the Constitution also limits state power to regulate foreign commerce by taxing it or otherwise. In this section, we examine the general constitutional limitations on state taxing power, with particular reference to how they apply to so-called unitary taxation—the taxation of a multijurisdictional entity's income on the basis of a particular allocation formula. Both of these issues, as well as a useful summary of the relevant constitutional principles, are set out in the following case. Before reading it, however, the student should review Japan Line, Ltd. v. County of Los Angeles, in Section 3.6(C) supra, and the OECD report on transfer pricing in the previous subsection. That report's rejection of formula taxation is aimed at unitary taxation.

CONTAINER CORPORATION OF AMERICA v. FRANCHISE TAX BOARD

United States Supreme Court, 1983.
463 U.S. 159, 103 S.Ct. 2933, 77 L.Ed.2d 545.

JUSTICE BRENNAN delivered the opinion of the Court.

This is another appeal claiming that the application of a State taxing scheme violates the Due Process and Commerce Clauses of the Federal Constitution. California imposes a corporate franchise tax geared to income. In common with a large number of other States, it employs the "unitary business" principle and formula apportionment in applying that tax to corporations doing business both inside and outside the State. Appellant is a Delaware corporation headquartered in Illinois and doing business in California and elsewhere. It also has a number of overseas subsidiaries incorporated in the countries in which they operate. * * *

Various aspects of state tax systems based on the "unitary business" principle and formula apportionment have provoked repeated constitutional litigation in this Court. See, e.g., ASARCO, Inc. v. Idaho State Tax Comm'n, 458 U.S. ___, 102 S.Ct. 3103, 73 L.Ed.2d 787 (1982); F.W. Woolworth Co. v. Taxation and Revenue Dept., 458 U.S. ___, 102 S.Ct. 3128, 73 L.Ed.2d 819 (1982); Exxon Corp. v. Wisconsin Dept. of Revenue, 447 U.S. 207, 100 S.Ct. 2109, 65 L.Ed.2d 66 (1980); Mobil Oil Corp. v. Commissioner of Taxes, 445 U.S. 425, 100 S.Ct. 1223, 63 L.Ed.2d 510 (1980); Moorman Mfg. Co. v. Bair, 437 U.S. 267, 98 S.Ct. 2340, 57 L.Ed.2d 197 (1978); General Motors Corp. v. Washington, 377 U.S. 436, 84 S.Ct. 1564, 12 L.Ed.2d 430 (1964); Butler Bros. v. McColgan, 315 U.S. 501, 62 S.Ct. 701, 86 L.Ed. 991 (1942); Bass, Ratcliff & Gretton, Ltd. v. State Tax Comm'n, 266 U.S. 271, 45 S.Ct. 82, 69 L.Ed. 282

(1924); Underwood Typewriter Co. v. Chamberlain, 254 U.S. 113, 41 S.Ct. 45, 65 L.Ed. 165 (1920).

Under both the Due Process and the Commerce Clauses of the Constitution, a state may not, when imposing an income-based tax, "tax value earned outside its borders." In the case of a more-or-less integrated business enterprise operating in more than one State, however, arriving at precise territorial allocations of "value" is often an elusive goal, both in theory and in practice. For this reason and others, we have long held that the Constitution imposes no single formula on the States, and that the taxpayer has the "distinct burden of showing by 'clear and cogent evidence' that [the state tax] results in extraterritorial values being taxed. * * *"

One way of deriving locally taxable income is on the basis of formal geographical or transactional accounting. The problem with this method is that formal accounting is subject to manipulation and imprecision, and often ignores or captures inadequately the many subtle and largely unquantifiable transfers of value that take place among the components of a single enterprise. The unitary business/formula apportionment method is a very different approach to the problem of taxing businesses operating in more than one jurisdiction. It rejects geographical or transactional accounting, and instead calculates the local tax base by first defining the scope of the "unitary business" of which the taxed enterprise's activities in the taxing jurisdiction form one part, and then apportioning the total income of that "unitary business" between the taxing jurisdiction and the rest of the world on the basis of a formula taking into account objective measures of the corporation's activities within and without the jurisdiction. This Court long ago upheld the constitutionality of the unitary business/formula apportionment method, although subject to certain constraints. The method has now gained wide acceptance, and is in one of its forms the basis for the Uniform Division of Income for Tax Purposes Act (Uniform Act), which has at last count been substantially adopted by 23 States, including California.

* * *

The Due Process and Commerce Clauses of the Constitution do not allow a State to tax income arising out of interstate activities—even on a proportional basis—unless there is a " 'minimal connection' or 'nexus' between the interstate activities and the taxing State, and 'a rational relationship between the income attributed to the State and the intrastate values of the enterprise.' " At the very least, this set of principles imposes the obvious and largely self-executing limitation that a State not tax a purported "unitary business" unless at least some part of it is conducted in the State. It also requires that there be some bond of ownership or control uniting the purported "unitary business."

In addition, the principles we have quoted require that the out-of-State activities of the purported "unitary business" be related in some concrete way to the in-State activities. The functional meaning of this requirement is that there be some sharing or exchange of value not capable of precise identification or measurement—beyond the mere flow of funds arising out of a passive investment or a distinct business operation—which renders formula apportionment a reasonable method of taxation.

[The Court then noted that it had upheld application of a state tax based on unitary principles where there was "a vertically integrated business whose various components (manufacturing, sales, etc.) operated in different States," a "vertically integrated business operating across national boundaries," and a "series of similar enterprises operating separately in various jurisdictions but linked by common management or operational resources that produced economies of scale and transfers of value."]

The California statute at issue in this case, and the Uniform Act from which most of its relevant provisions are derived, tracks in large part the principles we have just discussed. In particular, the statute distinguishes between the "business income" of a multi-jurisdictional enterprise, which is apportioned by formula, and its "non-business" income, which is not. Although the statute does not explicitly require that income from distinct business enterprises be apportioned separately, this requirement antedated adoption of the Uniform Act, and has not been abandoned.

A final point that needs to be made about the unitary business concept is that it is not, so to speak, unitary: there are variations on the theme, and any number of them are logically consistent with the underlying principles motivating the approach. For example, a State might decide to respect formal corporate lines and treat the ownership of a corporate subsidiary as *per se* a passive investment. * * * [S]uch a *per se* rule is not constitutionally required.

* * *

(2)

Having determined that a certain set of activities constitute a "unitary business," a State must then apply a formula apportioning the income of that business within and without the State. Such an apportionment formula must, under both the Due Process and Commerce Clauses, be fair. The first, and again obvious, component of fairness in an apportionment formula is what might be called internal consistency—that is the formula must be such that, if applied by every jurisdiction, it would result in no more than all of the unitary business's income being taxed. The second and more difficult requirement is what might be called external consistency—the factor or factors used in the apportionment formula must actually reflect a reasonable sense of how income is generated.

California and the other States that have adopted the Uniform Act use a formula—commonly called the "three-factor" formula—which is based, in equal parts, on the proportion of a unitary business's total payroll, property, and sales which are located in the taxing State. We approved the three-factor formula in Butler Bros. v. McCoglan, supra. Indeed, not only has the three-factor formula met our approval, but it has become, for reasons we discuss in more detail infra, something of a benchmark against which other apportionment formulas are judged.

Besides being fair, an apportionment formula must, under the Commerce Clause, also not result in discrimination against interstate or foreign commerce. Aside from forbidding the obvious types of discrimination against interstate or foreign commerce, this principle might have been construed to require that a state apportionment formula not differ so substantially from methods of allocation used by other jurisdictions in which the taxpayer is subject to taxation so as to produce double taxation of the same income, and a resultant tax burden higher than the taxpayer would incur if its business were limited to any one jurisdiction. At least in the interstate commerce context, however, the anti-discrimination principle has not in practice required much in addition to the requirement of fair apportionment. In Moorman Mfg. Co. v. Bair, in particular, we explained that eliminating all overlapping taxation would require this Court to establish not only a single constitutionally mandated method of taxation, but also rules regarding the application of that method in particular cases. Because that task was thought to be essentially legislative, we declined to undertake it, and held that a fairly apportioned tax would not be found invalid simply because it differed from the prevailing approach adopted by the States. As we discuss infra, however, a more searching inquiry is necessary when we are confronted with the possibility of international double taxation.

[Container Corporation had some 20 foreign subsidiaries, in which it had interests ranging from two-thirds to complete share ownership. The subsidiaries were generally individually integrated producers of paper products. Their purchases from the U.S. parent accounted for less than one percent of their total purchases. The U.S. parent did exercise general supervision over the operation of the subsidiaries, although it was not active in day-to-day management. The parent did, however, hold or guarantee about one-half of the subsidiaries long-term debt, provided technical advice and provided assistance in acquiring equipment.

[The Court noted that the burden was on the taxpayer to establish that it did not have a unitary business and it concluded that it should not overturn the decision of the California Supreme Court that the taxpayer had not met that burden. The state court had stressed the fact that major decisions were subject to review by the parent and that the parent gave directions to the subsidiaries for compliance with the parent's standards of professionalism, profitability and ethical practices as major factors in its decision that the business was a unitary one.

[The Supreme Court refused to require that there be a substantial flow of goods between components of a unitary business because of its rule that the required flow is of "value." It reiterated one of its prior statements that "a relevant question in the unitary business inquiry is whether 'contributions to income [of the subsidiaries] result[ed] from functional integration, centralization of management, and economies of scale.' "

[The Court also found that the three-factor test for apportionment— payroll, property and sales—was fair.]

For the reasons we have just outlined, we conclude that California's application of the unitary business principle to appellant and its foreign subsidiaries was proper, and that its use of the standard three-factor formula to apportion the income of that unitary business was fair. This proper and fair method of taxation happens, however, to be quite different from the method employed both by the Federal Government in taxing appellant's business, and by each of the relevant foreign jurisdictions in taxing the business of appellant's subsidiaries. Each of these other taxing jurisdictions has adopted a qualified separate accounting approach—often referred to as the "arm's-length" approach—to the taxation of related corporations. Under the arm's-length approach, every corporation, even if closely tied to other corporations, is treated for most—but decidedly not all—purposes as if it were an independent entity dealing at arm's length with its affiliated corporations, and subject to taxation only by the jurisdictions in which it operates and only for the income it realizes on its own books.

If the unitary business consisting of appellant and its subsidiaries were entirely domestic, the fact that different jurisdictions applied different methods of taxation to it would probably make little constitutional difference. * * * Given that it is international, however, we must subject this case to the additional scrutiny required by the Foreign Commerce Clause. The case most relevant to our inquiry is *Japan Line*.

* * *

This case is similar to *Japan Line* in a number of important respects. First, the tax imposed here, like the tax imposed in *Japan Line*, has resulted in actual double taxation, in the sense that some of the income taxed without apportionment by foreign nations as attributable to appellant's foreign subsidiaries was also taxed by California as attributable to the State's share of the total income of the unitary business of which those subsidiaries are a part. Second, that double taxation stems from a serious divergence in the taxing schemes adopted by California and the foreign taxing authorities. Third, the taxing method adopted by those foreign taxing authorities is consistent with accepted international practice. Finally, our own Federal Government, to the degree it has spoken, seems to prefer the taxing method adopted by the international community to the taxing method adopted by California.

Nevertheless, there are also a number of ways in which this case is clearly distinguishable from *Japan Line*. First, it involves a tax on income rather than a tax on property. We distinguished property from income taxation in *Mobil Oil Corp.*, 445 U.S., at 444–446, 100 S.Ct., at 1235–1236, and *Exxon Corp.*, 447 U.S., at 228–229, 100 S.Ct., at 2122–2123, suggesting that "[t]he reasons for allocation to a single situs that often apply in the case of property taxation carry little force" in the case of income taxation. Second, the double taxation in this case, although real, is not the "inevitabl[e]" result of the California taxing scheme. In *Japan Line*, we relied strongly on the fact that one taxing jurisdiction claimed the right to tax a given value in full, and another taxing jurisdiction claimed the right to tax the same entity in part—a combination resulting necessarily in double taxation. Here, by contrast, we are faced with two distinct methods of allocating the income of a multi-national enterprise. The "arm's-length" approach divides the pie on the basis of formal accounting principles. The formula apportionment method divides the same pie on the basis of a mathematical generalization. Whether the combination of the two methods results in the same income being taxed twice or in some portion of income not being taxed at all is dependent solely on the facts of the individual case. The third difference between this case and *Japan Line* is that the tax here falls, not on the foreign owners of an instrumentality of foreign commerce, but on a corporation domiciled and headquartered in the United States. We specifically left open in *Japan Line* the application of that case to "domestically owned instrumentalities engaged in foreign commerce," and—to the extent that corporations can be analogized to cargo containers in the first place—this case falls clearly within that reservation.

* * *

In *Japan Line,* we said that "[e]ven a slight overlapping of tax—a problem that might be deemed *de minimis* in a domestic context—assumes importance when sensitive matters of foreign relations and national sovereignty are concerned." If we were to take that statement as an absolute prohibition on state-induced double taxation in the international context, then our analysis here would be at an end. But, in fact, such an absolute rule is no more appropriate here than it was in *Japan Line* itself, where we relied on much more than the mere fact of double taxation to strike down the state tax at issue. Although double taxation in the foreign commerce context deserves to receive close scrutiny, that scrutiny must take into account the context in which the double taxation takes place and the alternatives reasonably available to the taxing State.

In *Japan Line,* the taxing State could entirely eliminate one important source of double taxation simply by adhering to one bright-line rule: do not tax, to any extent whatsoever, cargo containers "that are owned, based, and registered abroad and that are used exclusively in international commerce * * *." 441 U.S., at 444, 99 S.Ct., at 1819. To require that the State adhere to this rule was by no means unfair, because the rule did no more than reflect consistent international practice and express federal policy. In this case, California could try to avoid double taxation simply by not taxing appellant's income at all, even though a good deal of it is plainly domestic. But no party has suggested such a rule, and its obvious unfairness requires no elaboration. Or California could try to avoid double taxation by adopting some version of the "arm's-length" approach. That course, however, would not by any means guarantee an end to double taxation.

* * * [E]ven though most nations have adopted the arm's-length approach in its general outlines, the precise rules under which they reallocate income among affiliated corporations often differ substantially, and whenever that difference exists, the possibility of double taxation also exists. Thus, even if California were to adopt some version of the arm's-length approach, it could not eliminate the risk of double taxation of corporations subject to its franchise tax, and might in some cases end up subjecting those corporations to more serious double taxation than would occur under formula apportionment.

That California would have trouble avoiding double taxation even if it adopted the arm's-length approach is, we think, a product of the difference between a tax on income and a tax on tangible property. Allocating income among various taxing jurisdictions bears some resemblance, as we have emphasized throughout this opinion, to slicing a shadow. In the absence of a central coordinating authority, absolute consistency, even among taxing authorities whose basic approach to the task is quite similar, may just be too much to ask. If California's method of formula apportionment "inevitably" led to double taxation, that might be reason enough to render it suspect. But since it does not, it would be perverse, simply for the sake of avoiding double taxation, to require California to give up one allocation method that sometimes results in double taxation in favor of another allocation method that also sometimes results in double taxation.

* * *

We come finally to the second inquiry suggested by *Japan Line*— whether California's decision to adopt formula apportionment in the international context was impermissible because it "may impair federal uniformity in an area where federal uniformity is essential," and "prevents the Federal Government from 'speaking with one voice' in international trade." * * * Thus, a state tax at variance with federal policy will violate the "one voice" standard if it *either* implicates foreign policy issues which must be left to the Federal Government *or* violates a clear federal directive.

* * *

When we turn to specific indications of congressional intent, appellant's position fares no better. First, there is no claim here that the federal tax statutes themselves provide the necessary pre-emptive force. Second, although the United States is a party to a great number of tax treaties that require the Federal Government to adopt some form of arm's-length analysis in taxing the domestic income of multi-national enterprises, that requirement is generally waived with respect to the taxes imposed by each of the contracting nations on its own domestic corporations. This fact, if nothing else, confirms our view that such taxation is in reality of local rather than international concern. Third, none of the tax treaties into which the United States has entered covers the taxing activities of sub-national governmental units such as States, and the Senate has on at least one occasion, in considering a proposed treaty, attached a reservation declining to gives its consent to a provision in the treaty that would have extended the restriction against apportionment taxation to the States. Finally, it remains true, as we said in *Mobil,* that "Congress has long debated, but has not enacted, legislation designed to regulate state taxation of income."

* * *

[JUSTICE STEVENS took no part in the consideration or argument of the case. JUSTICE POWELL dissented in an opinion joined by THE CHIEF JUSTICE and JUSTICE O'CONNOR.]

GEORGE H. WEISSMAN, UNITARY TAXATION: ITS HISTORY AND RECENT SUPREME COURT TREATMENT

(1983) [1]

The unitary tax is perhaps the most controversial of all revenue raising measures presently employed by states in this nation. The unitary method or formula apportionment,[*1] which is currently used by forty-five states and the District of Columbia to tax multistate and multinational corporations,

---

1. 48 Albany L.Rev. 48, 48, 50–56. Reprinted by permission of Albany Law Review.

* 1. The formula apportionment or unitary method of taxation is an attempt by the tax-

has incurred severe criticism in both the national and international economic and legal arenas. The uproar caused by world-wide combined reporting, now being employed by twelve states, has brought forth legislation in Congress and the topic has become the subject of debate in treaty discussions between the United States and its allies.

* * *

I. TAXING CORPORATE INCOME

Presently, two diametrically opposed methods exist among states for attributing corporate income between parent and related subsidiary corporations. The first method is commonly referred to as separate accounting, geographical accounting, or the separate entity theory. The second method of taxing corporate income is referred to as the unitary method, combined reporting, or formula apportionment. Neither separate accounting nor combined reporting are without shortfalls.

A. *Separate Accounting*

The separate accounting method assumes that each commonly controlled entity carries out its business with the same type of tax related conduct as would any independent corporation. A taxing jurisdiction which uses this method views all transactions between affiliated corporations as if the companies were unrelated and always dealing at arm's length. All transactions, independent or intercompany, are treated as taxable events with the taxing jurisdiction viewing intercompany transactions as arm's length transactions. Separate accounting can be used effectively by a state tax administrator when the income producing activity of an entity within a state can be distinguished from the income producing activity outside the state.

Possibly the greatest defect of separate accounting when used to divide the income of a unitary business is that it completely rejects the economic interdependencies and the positive effects that horizontal and vertical integration have on corporate purchasing, marketing, and selling. * * * To believe that multinational corporations do not maintain an advantage over independent corporations operating within a similar business sphere is to ignore the economic and political strength of the multinational giants. By attempting to treat those businesses which are in fact unitary as independent entities, separate accounting "operates in a universe of pretense; as in Alice in Wonderland, it turns reality into fancy and then pretends it's in the real world."

A second problem inherent in the separate accounting method is determining what constitutes an arm's length transaction, especially when intercompany transfers are involved. There are two methods available for such determinations, transfer price review and profit splitting, and neither is foolproof. Applying transfer price review to a large, vertically integrated corporation may require the "wisdom of a Solomon" in determining a fair,

ing state to ensure that the income of a business conducted partly within and partly without the taxing state shall be determined and apportioned in the same manner regardless of whether the business is conducted by one corporation or by two or more related corporations. This is accomplished by an apportionment formula which utilizes three factors: property, payroll, and sales. * * *

arm's length price. In many instances insufficient data exists to apply imputed prices to transfers among affiliated corporations, especially those entities which are essentially monopolies or oligopolies. The profit splitting method, by contrast, requires that a comparison be made between all similar businesses and products. Depending on the product, its cost and its quality, an attempt must be made to impute a profit margin which can be compared to a similar product. In many cases, however, there are more dissimilarities existing between products than similarities, and rarely are two transactions in fact identical. This only compounds the difficulties inherent in separate accounting.

Another important deficiency of separate accounting is its cost to both the state and the taxpayer. One writer noted that to properly follow "the myriad of transfers which take place daily, monthly, yearly, would require an army of agents greater than the total number of agents employed by all the states and the federal government combined." Moreover, for the taxpayer to properly use separate accounting would require it to maintain books detailing all operations and transactions on a state by state basis.

These defects in the separate entity approach explain the reluctance on the part of state tax administrators to rely upon this method of accounting for determining the tax liability of a unitary business. A substantial risk of income shifting exists not only within the United States, as corporations attempt to place income producing activities in states with lower tax rates, but may also occur in the international arena, as corporations use transfer pricing to avoid the effects of disparities in tax rates between nations, while at the same time gaining favorable tax treatment.

B. Combined Reporting

The unitary method ignores the legal existence of one corporation or several affiliated entities constituting a unitary enterprise and begins with the economic reality that the whole exceeds the sum of its parts. To determine tax liability the taxing jurisdiction looks not at a corporation's in-state earnings, but rather compares the total value of a corporation's in-state and out-of-state sales, payroll, and property with the total value of the corporation's in-state sales, payroll, and property. This percentage is then applied to combined business income to ascertain income attributable to the states.

Unfortunately, combined reporting or formula apportionment does not provide the panacea for all the ills inherent in separate accounting. When states extend the unitary concept to include foreign corporations, this approach, known as worldwide combined reporting, creates a number of deficiencies which could severely affect this nations economic relations with its international trading partners.

A major dilemma confronting states that use worldwide combined reporting is that the United States Government and the Internal Revenue Service rely on separate accounting as a means to apportion the business income of multistate and multinational corporations. Section 482 of the Internal Revenue Code and the regulations promulgated pursuant to the Code make it clear that commonly controlled entities are to be treated as if they were separate entities for the purpose of determining taxable income from intercompany transactions.   *   *   *

The use of separate accounting found in section 482 is claimed to be the accepted international apportionment method. Most nations apportion income between taxing jurisdictions using arm's length transactions as the basis. Consequently, use of worldwide combined reporting by states could have a destructive effect on some of this nation's most revered alliances. Almost every major trading partner of the United States has cried foul to signify their displeasure with states that employ worldwide combined reporting. Also inherent in the use of combined reporting to determine the tax liability of multinational corporations is the distinct possibility of double taxation.

The last valid objection to worldwide combined reporting is that this method tends to distort the amount of income attributable to a state. Formula apportionment is based on the premise that a dollar, whether earned from wages, spent on property, or used to purchase an item, produces the same amount of income in all jurisdictions. Within the United States, this premise generally holds true; however, when compared with the worldwide operations of a multinational corporation, this is rarely the case. The payroll and property factors used in formula apportionment tend to be significantly different between the United States and most foreign countries. The values of these formula factors are generally lower in foreign countries than in this country and will attribute more income to the location where the factors are highest. A similar inequitable result may occur if two members of a unitary group are combined and one entity is labor intensive while the second is capital intensive. Finally, fluctuations of foreign exchange rates may exacerbate the difficulty in apportioning income.

Notes And Questions

(1) The extent to which the Supreme Court will review the decisions of state taxing authorities is not clear. The *Container Corporation* case suggests that the Court will tend to defer to state allocation decisions, although only one year earlier in 1982 it seemed to suggest that it might interfere with state authorities more frequently. After the 1982 cases, which seemed to indicate a reversal of judicial deference enunciated in 1980, a leading scholar in this area wrote: [2]

The Court's opinions in *ASARCO* [*2] and *Woolworth* [*3] picked up where its opinions in *Mobil* [*4] and *Exxon* [*5] left off. Yet the direction taken by these more recent decisions veers sharply from the course ostensibly set by their predecessors.

*   *   *

2. Hellerstein, State Income Taxation of Multijurisdictional Corporations, Part II: Reflections on *ASARCO* and *Woolworth*, 81 Mich.L.Rev. 157, 157, 188–89 (1983). Reprinted by permission of the Michigan Law Review Association.

[*2.] ASARCO Inc. v. Idaho State Tax Comm'n., 458 U.S. 307, 102 S.Ct. 3103, 73 L.Ed.2d 787 (1982).

[*3.] F. W. Woolworth Co. v. Taxation and Revenue Dept., 458 U.S. 354, 102 S.Ct. 3128, 73 L.Ed.2d 819 (1982).

[*4.] Mobil Oil Corp. v. Commissioner of Taxes, 445 U.S. 425, 100 S.Ct. 1223, 63 L.Ed.2d 510 (1980).

[*5.] Exxon Corp. v. Department of Revenue, 447 U.S. 207, 100 S.Ct. 2109, 65 L.Ed.2d 66 (1980).

[The earlier] themes—wide latitude for the states in dividing the income of a multijurisdictional enterprise, self restraint by the Court in overseeing state initiatives for dealing with this task, and deference to Congress as the appropriate body for drawing definitive guidelines in this domain—firmly underpinned the Court's decisions two years later in *Mobil* and *Exxon*. In the course of its opinions in these cases, the Court stressed the freedom the states enjoyed in apportioning a multijurisdictional corporation's income "in order to obtain a 'rough approximation' of the corporate income that is 'reasonably related to the activities conducted within the taxing State' "; it emphasized that its own role was confined to assuring that the corporation's tax liability was not "out of all appropriate proportion to the business transacted by the [taxpayer] in th[e] State"; and it adverted to the preemptive role that Congress might play in providing uniform rules governing division of income among the states.

As the preceding discussion has indicated, the Court's opinions in *ASARCO* and *Woolworth* reflect a strikingly different judicial perspective on state division-of-income issues. No longer are we told that the essential question is whether the state's apportionment formula has produced a "grossly distorted result" or one "out of all appropriate proportion to the business transacted * * * in th[e] State." Instead of a detached judicial tolerance for inferences a state is "entitled" to draw from the record, we find the Court immersing itself in the factual details of the state administrative proceedings and rejecting state court inferences with which it disagrees.

(2) Do you agree with the arguments used by Justice Brennan to distinguish the *Japan Line* case?

(3) The *Container Corporation* case involved a U.S.-based multinational. Would the result be the same if a foreign-based multinational were involved?

(4) In such an event, it might be difficult for the foreign company to argue its position since it would only be a *shareholder* of the subsidiary on which the tax was imposed.[3] Justice Powell's dissent stresses the fact that the California system leads to higher taxes in a state with higher wages and property values (e.g. California) than the international standard of arm's length transfer pricing would. In the case of Container Corporation, for example, its Latin American operations accounted for 27% of its income under arm's length transfer pricing, but only 6% of its wages, 14% of its sales and 20% of its property, or about 13% of its income under the California formula, an amount less than one-half that under the usual international standard. Given the almost inevitable tendency for the allocation formula to increase income attributable to the United States, at least in the present state of the world economy, there is considerable opposition to the California tax among U.S. trading partners, a fact noted in Justice Powell's dissent.

(5) The United States government did not submit an amicus brief in the *Container Corporation* case, although it had opposed California type taxation in another case then pending before the Court. In late 1985, the Reagan Administration indicated that it favored congressional action that would prohibit state taxation of profits earned outside the United States. The action was taken in

---

3. Compare Section 16.2(B), Note 5 (U.S. subsidiary of Japanese company not allowed to invoke U.S.-Japan FCN Treaty); Note, Standing Under Commercial Treaties: Foreign Holding Companies and the Unitary Tax, 97 Harv.L.Rev. 1894 (1984).

part to forestall retaliatory action by U.S. trading partners angered by California's application of its tax.[4]

(6) Because of the controversy surrounding the taxation of foreign income, a number of states have repealed laws similar to California's in recent years. As this is written, only six states—California, Alaska, Idaho, Montana, New Hampshire and North Dakota—maintain global or worldwide unitary tax systems. The repeals in other states have come about in part because of business pressure, which has led to increased investment in states not using such a system. In particular, Oregon has reportedly benefitted from investments by companies unwilling to subject themselves to the California system. Recall the problem presented in Section 16.1 supra. How would the existence of a tax system like California's affect your advice?

4. 2 BNA Intl. Trade Rptr. 1453, 1502 (1985).

*

Part IV

MANAGING WORLD ECONOMIC INTERDEPENDENCE

Chapter 20

DEVELOPING COUNTRIES AND THE GATT SYSTEM

SECTION 20.1   INTRODUCTION

One of the more difficult problems that has faced the international trading system as embodied in GATT is how developing countries should be integrated into that system. Although a large number of developing countries are Contracting Parties to GATT and others apply GATT on a de facto basis (see Section 5.4(I) supra), they in general have not been happy with the way they are treated in GATT. Of course, there are great differences among the countries commonly referred to as developing countries—they include the poorest of the poor nations as well as the so-called newly industrialized countries, they include dictatorships and democracies, state-run economies and free-market economies and they vary politically from one end of the spectrum to the other. There are nonetheless many issues on which the developing countries seem to take a common position and they often refer to themselves as part of the same group, so despite the differences it is justifiable to treat them together in this chapter.

The dissatisfaction of the developing world with GATT has a number of causes. There has been a perception among the developing countries that GATT is a club for the rich nations, and that although it purports to operate on a one-country/one-vote principle, in fact it is an organization where the views of only a very few major developed countries count. More significantly, there is a feeling among them that some of the fundamental principles of GATT are unsuited for trade involving developing countries. For example, the most-favored-nation rule is one of the underlying principles of GATT. Yet developing countries believe that to develop economically, i.e. to become more than economically disadvantaged suppliers of raw materials to the developed world, they must receive special assistance. One form of such assistance, in their view, should be favored treatment in trade matters, even if such treatment is feasible only if it is limited to them and thereby violates the MFN principle.

The developing countries have had more specific complaints as well. In order to develop economically, they perceive a need to have export industries, both to provide jobs and export earnings that can finance internal development. As to the type of exports needed, they believe that they must reduce their dependence on the production of one or two raw materials and expand their manufacturing capabilities. As we saw in Section 14.3 supra, exporting commodities is often a risky and unpredictable business because of the wide swings in prices that occur. Such swings mean that commodity exports are not a steady source of export earnings, and therefore cannot be relied upon to finance development or even to service development loans. Thus, developing countries view the development of manufacturing industries as critical to their future. Unfortunately, an underdeveloped economy is often unable to support an efficient manufacturing facility unless a significant proportion of its production can be exported. The belief that export industries are a key to development is supported by the fact that the most recent notable economic successes in the developing world have occurred in countries that have experienced significant growth in their export sectors.

The developing countries believe, however, that GATT rules, as now enforced, hinder their ability to expand exports. In their view, either by design or as a result of indifference, while raw materials are typically subject to low tariff rates in the developed countries, considerably higher tariffs are often applicable to the simpler manufactured goods that are of interest to developing countries, such as textiles and clothing. In contrast, much lower tariff rates are typically applied to sophisticated manufactured products. To developing countries, this suggests that the developed countries want them to remain suppliers of raw materials and not to develop and to become competitive in manufactured goods on world markets. They find further support for their beliefs in the fact that the types of goods they are interested in exporting are often subject to nontariff barriers that are not regulated effectively by GATT. Thus, to the extent that GATT has failed to remedy these problems, and thereby failed to ensure access of developing country products to developed country markets, the developing countries have viewed GATT as a stumbling block on their path to improving the lot of their people.

As a consequence, for many years, the developing countries have been pressing for special treatment in GATT and have attempted to create new rules, not related to GATT, to embody their concept of how the world economy should operate. In this chapter, we look at the responses that have been made to the developing country demands. In particular, we examine the special provisions of GATT and the Tokyo Round agreements that provide for special treatment for developing countries and then turn to the most ambitious scheme adopted by the developed countries to promote trade with developing countries—the Generalized System of Preferences, with particular attention to U.S. implementation of that system. We then consider the efforts of the developing countries to reorder legal thinking in respect of the international economic system by pressing for the acceptance of a new international economic order. We conclude with a brief discussion of how the massive debts of developing countries affect the world trading system.

SECTION 20.2   GATT RULES AND DEVELOPING COUNTRIES

The debate over whether developing countries should receive special treatment in GATT is not new.   In the negotiations on the ITO, the developing countries tried to obtain rules more favorable to them.   However, as one of the authors of this book has concluded: [1]

> The issues at Geneva in 1947 did not, viewed from the perspective of the present day, seem to be free trade versus protectionism, or internationalism versus national sovereignty.   Each of the groups in the debate desired international control of some things and not of others.   Both sides desired to use certain types of trade protective measures but wanted to limit or restrict others.   The controversy seemed to be over *which* trade restrictions would be subjected to international control and which not.   From the point of view of the less-developed country, the wealthy countries wanted freedom to use those restrictions that only they were most able to use effectively while banning those restrictions that less-developed countries felt they were most able to use.

Although the developing countries were largely unsuccessful in their early efforts to obtain special treatment, they have continued to press their case.

GATT has not been oblivious of developing country complaints and they have been studied by GATT committees of experts on more than one occasion.   For example, in 1958, the so-called Haberler Report concluded that the developed countries should lower their barriers to exports of primary products from developing countries.[2]   As we saw in Chapter 14, the GATT rules apply to agriculture, but are largely ignored in practice.   Since 1958, the desire of developing countries has been to expand their manufactured exports, particularly of simpler goods such as textiles and clothing.   In 1984, a GATT-sponsored group of experts noted the adverse effect that nontariff barriers were having on developing country exports and called for their reduction.[3]   Nonetheless, as we have seen in Chapters 9 and 14, GATT has not been very successful in reducing the barriers to trade that developing countries have complained about, but it has responded more favorably to claims that they are deserving of special, differential treatment under GATT rules.

In this section, we examine the rules of GATT and the provisions of the Tokyo Round Agreements that explicitly provide for differential treatment of developing countries as opposed to other members of GATT.   In the following section, we consider the action of the GATT Contracting Parties in authorizing the Generalized System of Preferences.   As noted in the introduction, there may be other rules or practices in GATT that in fact discriminate against (or perhaps favor) developing countries even though they are facially nondiscriminatory.

---

1.   J. Jackson, World Trade and the Law of GATT 637–38 (1969).

2.   GATT, Trends in International Trade (1958).

3.   GATT, Trade Policies for A Better Future (1985) (Report of Eminent Persons on Problems Facing the International Trading System).

In the GATT agreement there are only two provisions which explicitly allow differential treatment for developing countries—and in both cases the objective of the provision is to give more favorable treatment to developing countries.[4] These provisions are Article XVIII, and Part IV of GATT comprising Articles XXXVI through XXXVIII, discussed below. Other articles of GATT, however, distinguish between primary and non-primary goods, and thus may have an impact on the trade of developing countries that differs from that on the trade of developed countries. Several clauses of GATT in operation benefit the developing countries. For example, they have benefited from waivers granted under the authority of Article XXV. Article II requires GATT members to limit tariffs to the "bindings" listed in the schedule of that member, but many developing countries, as noted in Section 5.4 supra, have very short schedules or no schedule at all—and thus are relatively free to use any level of tariffs for any imported goods, as they desire. Furthermore, there is an important exception to GATT rules for countries with balance of payments difficulties. Many developing countries have chronic balance of payments difficulties and therefore have constant access to the privileges of these "BOP" exceptions. In addition, it is probably true that in recent years there has been a tendency in GATT to overlook trade policy actions of developing countries which are "technically" inconsistent with GATT obligations.

(A) GATT ARTICLE XVIII

Article XVIII was the original article of GATT designed to grant certain privileges to developing countries. Although amended in 1955, it has not often been formally invoked.

The reader will note, in examining Article XVIII, that it first establishes criteria describing those nations entitled to utilize its provisions, and then basically grants four types of privileges:

Part A: The right to renegotiate tariff bindings so as to raise tariffs on products it desires to produce, thus enabling protection of so-called infant industries (see Section 1.3 supra);

Part B: The privilege to use quantitative restrictions when in balance-of-payments difficulties (with criteria and actions permitted being slightly different from the general BOP clauses of GATT Article XII);

Part C: A privilege to use any measure necessary to promote a *particular* industry;

Part D: Under this part, certain countries with economies in process of development, but not falling within the criteria of low living standards, can apply for permission to deviate from GATT rules so as to establish a particular industry.

What nations are eligible? Interpretative notes in the GATT agreement state:[5]

1. When they consider whether the economy of a contracting party "can only support low standards of living," the CONTRACTING PARTIES

---

4. See generally, J. Jackson, note 1 supra, ch. 25.

5. GATT, Annex I, Notes and Supplementary Provisions (Ad Article XVIII, paragraphs 1 and 4).

shall take into consideration the normal position of that economy and shall not base their determination on exceptional circumstances such as those which may result from the temporary existence of exceptionally favourable conditions for the staple export product or products of such contracting party.

2.   The phrase "in the early stages of development" is not meant to apply only to contracting parties which have just started their economic development, but also to contracting parties the economies of which are undergoing a process of industrialization to correct an excessive dependence on primary production.

A 1958 panel report which judged Ceylon (now Sri Lanka) qualified noted:[6]

(1) Its economy could support only low standards of living:

The gross national product *per caput* for Ceylon in 1955 is estimated at $128; although this figure is higher than the gross national product *per caput* of countries such as Burma and India, it is lower than the corresponding figure for Greece, Cuba and the Dominican Republic and very substantially below the figure of industrialized countries in Western Europe.

(2) It was in the early stages of development:

[T]he Panel has taken as a general indication the share of manufacturing, mining and construction in the gross national product; in the case of Ceylon, this share (including mining which is a primary industry) is about 10 per cent, a figure lower than that of Burma and Greece and very substantially smaller than that of industrial countries.

Questions

(1) Would an oil exporting country such as Saudi Arabia or Iran, if it were a GATT member, be entitled to the Article XVIII exceptions?

(2) Could a GATT member eligible for Article XVIII treatment prohibit all imports of a luxury good (perfume from Paris or transistor radios from Japan) on the grounds that such imports were a low priority use of scarce foreign exchange?

(3) Could a GATT member which was accumulating reserves of foreign exchange through excellent export sales of one primary product (e.g., bauxite or coffee beans) invoke Article XVIII to prohibit imports of processed products depending on that primary good (e.g., aluminum products or powdered instant coffee) so as to develop an indigenous processing industry for such goods?

(4) As in (3), could such a country limit or prohibit *exports* under Article XVIII so as to favor its domestic processing industry?

6. See Report of the Panel on Article XVIII Applications by Ceylon (Sri Lanka), GATT Doc. L/751 of 27 Nov. 1957, GATT, 6th Supp. BISD 14, 112 (1958) and Notifications by Ceylon (Sri Lanka) under Article XVIII(C): Report to the CONTRACTING PARTIES, GATT Doc. L/932 of 22 Nov. 1958, GATT, 7th Supp. BISD 75 (1959). See also the Bangkok Agreement, First Agreement on Trade Negotiation Among Developing Member Countries of the Economic and Social Commission for Asia and the Pacific, signed July 31, 1975 by Bangladesh, India, Laos, Philippines, Republic of Korea, Sri Lanka and Thailand. GATT Document L/4418 of 2 November 1976.

(B) PART IV OF GATT

Following the 1958 Haberler Report referred to above, and as a result of developing country initiatives in the early and mid-1960's, Articles XXXVI, XXXVII and XXXVIII were added to GATT as Part IV.[7] These articles are devoted solely to the problems of developing countries. Although it has been suggested that they are primarily "hortatory" in wording, and so without direct legal implications, Article XXXVIII, paragraphs 1(b) and 1(c), arguably may have direct legal impact. In addition, some procedural obligations are spelled out by the new clauses.

Problems

(1) Is section 106 of the United States Trade Act of 1974 compatible with U.S. obligations under Article XXXVI, paragraph 8?

(2) Does Article XXXVII, paragraph 1(b) amount to a "standstill" pledge by developed countries against new trade barriers? For example, could the EC or the United States consistent with Article XXXVII, paragraph 1(b):

    (a) Raise a tariff on a particular developing country product pursuant to an escape clause action?

    (b) Introduce an antidumping or countervailing duty against a product from a developing country?

    (c) Negotiate a voluntary restraint agreement on a product which a developing country exports?

    (d) Establish a tariff surcharge for balance of payments reasons without exempting developing countries from its operation?

    (e) In each case above, does it matter whether a Parliament or Congress causes the result by passage of a new law, or whether the Executive causes the result utilizing existing Executive powers?

(3) Part IV was added to GATT by a "Protocol Amending the General Agreement on Tariffs and Trade to Introduce a Part IV on Trade and Development," dated February 8, 1965, and entered into force June 27, 1966.[8] This protocol was accepted for the United States by the Executive Branch as an "executive agreement." It has not been submitted to Congress for approval. Furthermore, it has never been "proclaimed" by the President. In light of the materials in Chapter 3, would you say that acceptance of these clauses as an executive agreement was within the President's

    (a) inherent "foreign affairs" power?

    (b) authority under the Trading with the Enemy Act?

    (c) authority under Section 201(a) of the Trade Expansion Act of 1962 [9] which was in force at that time and read:

7. See GATT Docs. L/2281 of 26 Oct. 1964, and L/2297 of 17 Nov. 1964; GATT, 12th Supp. BISD (1964) and GATT, 13th Supp. BISD (1965); J. Jackson, note 1 supra, ch. 25. See also the annual reports of the participating countries (e.g. 3d annual report in 1976).

8. Protocol Amending the GATT to Introduce a Part IV on Trade and Development, and to Amend Annex I. Done at Geneva, Feb. 8, 1965; entered into force for the United States on June 27, 1966; 17 UST 1977; TIAS No. 6139; 572 UNTS 320.

9. Trade Expansion Act of 1962, 76 Stat. 872; 22 U.S.C. §§ 1801–1991, approved Oct. 11, 1962; as amended, 77 Stat. 379, approved Dec. 16, 1963.

Sec. 201. Basic Authority for Trade Agreements

(a) Whenever the President determines that any existing duties or other import restrictions of any foreign country or the United States are unduly burdening and restricting the foreign trade of the United States and that any of the purposes stated in section 102 will be promoted thereby, the President may—

(1) after June 30, 1962, and before July 1, 1967, enter into trade agreements with foreign countries or instrumentalities thereof; and

(2) proclaim such modification or continuance of any existing duty or other import restriction, such continuance of existing duty-free or excise treatment, or such additional import restrictions, as he determines to be required or appropriate to carry out any such trade agreement.

(C) THE TOKYO ROUND AND DEVELOPING COUNTRIES

Only a few years after the addition of Part IV to GATT, the Kennedy Round of tariff negotiations was concluded. The developing countries were generally very dissatisfied with the results of that negotiation. Little was done with respect to nontariff barriers that they had complained about and the tariff cuts were mainly on goods that held little interest for them. Although the Generalized System of Preferences, described in the next section, was implemented in the period between the Kennedy and Tokyo Rounds, the developing countries entered the Tokyo Round with the hope that at last their concerns would receive serious attention. We have already viewed the results of the tariff reductions and the extent that those reductions affected products of interest to developing countries. (See Section 5.5(B) supra.) The following is a more general comment on the Tokyo Round from the developing country viewpoint.

UNCTAD, REPORT BY THE SECRETARY–GENERAL OF UNCTAD: ASSESSMENT OF THE RESULTS OF THE MULTILATERAL TRADE NEGOTIATIONS

(1982) [10]

9. Since the conclusion of the Kennedy Round in 1967, the developing countries have pressed in GATT and in UNCTAD for improvement in access for their exports to the markets of the developed countries through the liberalization of tariff and non-tariff barriers. Hence, although not involved in the decision to initiate the negotiations, the developing countries agreed to participate in the MTN with high expectations that those negotiations would enable them finally to realize substantial benefits for their international trade.

10. As set out in paragraph 2 of the Tokyo Declaration, the overall aim of the MTN was to

achieve the expansion and ever greater liberalization of world trade and improvement in standard of living and welfare of the people of the world

10. TD/B/778/Rev. 1, at 5–9.

. . . through the progressive dismantling of obstacles to trade and the improvement of the international framework for the conduct of world trade.

11. Specifically for the developing countries, the aim of the negotiations was to

secure additional benefits for the international trade of developing countries so as to achieve a substantial increase in their foreign exchange earnings, the diversification of their exports, the acceleration of the rate of growth of their trade, taking into account their development needs, an improvement in the possibilities for these countries to participate in the expansion of world trade and a better balance as between developed and developing countries in the sharing of the advantages resulting from this expansion, through, in the largest possible measure, a substantial improvement in the conditions of access for the products of interest to the developing countries and, wherever appropriate, measures designed to attain stable, equitable and remunerative prices for primary products.

12. In pursuance of the above objectives, the Declaration provided that

co-ordinated efforts shall be made to solve in an equitable way the trade problems of all participating countries, taking into account the specific trade problems of the developing countries.

13. The Tokyo Declaration set out principles governing treatment of developing countries in the trade negotiations. These concern, among others, non-reciprocity in favour of the developing countries, the need for special measures, the importance of the application of differential measures and the particular situation and problems of the least developed among the developing countries. The stated principles set out in paragraph 5 of the Declaration include the following:

(*a*) Negotiations shall be conducted on the basis of the principles of mutual advantage, mutual commitment and overall reciprocity, while observing the MFN clause, and consistently with the provisions of the General Agreement relating to such negotiations;

(*b*) Participants shall jointly endeavour in the negotiations to achieve, by appropriate methods, an overall balance of advantage at the highest possible level;

(*c*) Developed countries do not expect reciprocity for commitments made by them in the negotiations to reduce or remove tariff and other barriers to the trade of developing countries, i.e. the developed countries do not expect the developing countries, in the course of the trade negotiations, to make contributions that are inconsistent with their individual development, or with their financial and trade needs;

(*d*) The need is recognized for special measures to be taken in the negotiations to assist the developing countries in their efforts to increase their export earnings and promote their economic development and, where appropriate, for priority attention to be given to products or areas of interest to developing countries;

(*e*) The importance of maintaining and improving the GSP is recognized;

(*f*) The importance is recognized of applying differential measures to developing countries in ways that will provide special and more favourable treatment for them in areas of the negotiations where that is feasible and appropriate.

14.   Furthermore, the Ministers recognized that the particular situation and problems of the least developed among the developing countries should be given special attention, and stressed the need to ensure that those countries received special treatment in the context of any general or specific measures taken in favour of the developing countries during the negotiations.

*   *   *

*   *   * [I]n the context of the benchmarks mentioned in paragraph 5 above, namely, the extent to which the aims and objectives of the MTN for the developing countries have been achieved, the overall results of the trade negotiations would appear to be modest and wanting in many specific respects. Thus there remains a wide gap between the objective originally set out and the achievements finally arrived at. The proposals by developing countries for the application in concrete terms of differential and more favourable treatment in the various codes or agreements have not been fully realized. While general provisions are included in many of these instruments, concrete and specific measures for their application are somewhat vague, lacking or inadequate. The tariff reductions resulting from the MTN will erode the preference margins that developing countries currently enjoy in many products of export interest to these countries, thus reducing whatever tariff advantages they now have. Also, many products of export interest to developing countries not enjoying preferences have been excepted from the tariff cuts. The failure to reach agreement on safeguards, an area of crucial importance for the developing countries, leaves an element of uncertainty hanging over the results of the negotiations. The institutionalization of the concept of conditionality and graduation have far-reaching consequences for these countries and could lead to arbitrary discriminatory treatment of developing countries. Moreover, a number of general and other issues remain ambiguous and unresolved, causing uncertainty for developing countries, including those that are parties to the General Agreement.

22.   More than the presence or absence of special provisions for differential and more favourable treatment in the various MTN instruments, or the extent to which greater or lesser tariff reductions were achieved on specific products, the most important result of the MTN, especially from the point of view of developing countries, would seem to have been the major restructuring of the legal system for world trade relations as embodied in the General Agreement on Tariffs and Trade. The re-emergence of the "conditional MFN" principle, which plagued international trade relations in the past, the formation of an inner GATT or several GATTs, comprising those countries in a position to participate in and conform their legislation to the various agreements, the likelihood that in future the main problems arising in world trade will be resolved in closed groups, to which the majority of UNCTAD members will have no right of access, cannot but have serious

implications. In particular, developing countries may face considerable difficulties, for various reasons, including technical reasons, in deriving effective benefits from the new GATT/MTN system.

23. The spokesman for the developing countries at the thirty-fifth session of the Contracting Parties to the General Agreement on Tariffs and Trade succinctly summarized the final outcome of the MTN, saying that "it was difficult for the developing countries to determine what additional benefits were obtained in the negotiations, since the results did not correspond to their aspirations as expressed in the Tokyo Declaration."

* * *

27. The Tokyo Declaration contained provisions that reflected the specific objectives of the developing countries with respect to tariffs, including the GSP. In the context of its overall aim of securing additional benefits for the international trade of developing countries, the Tokyo Declaration recognized, *inter alia,* the importance of maintaining and improving the GSP as well as of applying differential measures to developing countries in ways that would provide special and more favourable treatment for them including, in particular, the least developed countries. Those general provisions were further elaborated to reflect the specific interests of the developing countries in Conference resolution 91 (IV).

28. The outcome of the Tokyo Round in respect of tariffs appears to fall far short of those objectives and the specific expectations of the developing countries. The results of the negotiations indicate that the expressed goal of maintaining and improving the GSP has not been met and that, by contrast, there has been a general, across-the-board, erosion of GSP margins and a consequent reduction of effective GSP product coverage, less-than-average MFN tariff cuts on products not covered by the GSP, and important exceptions from the application of the tariff-cutting formula on non-GSP products of particular export interest to the developing countries.

29. Imports by EEC, Japan and the United States of America of both agricultural and industrial GSP-covered products from beneficiaries of their preferential schemes amounted to $19.4 billion in 1976. The pre-MTN trade-weighted average preferential margin of 9.2 per cent was to decline to 6.7 per cent in the post-MTN period, representing a 27.2 per cent erosion of preferential margins. By contrast, the average MFN tariff cut on imports of non-GSP products, valued at $15.8 billion, was to amount to 22.4 per cent owing to the decline in pre-MTN average tariffs of 17.4 per cent to 13.5 per cent in the post-MTN period.

30. A further indication of the shortcomings of the MTN in maintaining the scope of the GSP is the effective loss of preferential advantages on imports, valued at $509 million. This has occurred either as a result of the elimination of GSP margins through MFN tariff reductions or by the granting of duty-free treatment to GSP-covered products on a MFN basis.

31. Imports of all types of products valued at $7.4 billion from beneficiaries were excepted from the MTN tariff cuts. About one half of these exceptions, or $3.7 billion, can be construed as positive from the point of view of developing countries since they applied to GSP-covered products, and thereby preserved existing average GSP margins of 11.4 per cent. The

remaining MTN exceptions, valued at $3.7 billion, were on products of important export interest to developing countries. Their relative importance is reflected in the high trade-weighted average MFN rate of 27.5 per cent, which will be maintained in the post-MTN period. Thus the dual goal of developing countries, namely, to maintain existing GSP margins to the maximum extent and to seek deeper than average cuts on non-GSP products of export interest to them in order to compensate for GSP losses, does not appear to have been achieved.

32. In sum, these findings indicate that in respect of developing countries the tariff-cutting exercise has fallen short of fulfilling the objectives of the Tokyo Declaration. There has been in varying degrees an across-the-board erosion of GSP margins, offset only slightly by exceptions on GSP-covered products. However, the effects of these exceptions have been diluted by the loss of GSP advantages owing to the elimination of preferential margins. Finally the hoped-for deep tariff cuts on products not covered by the GSP has fallen short of compensating for the erosion of GSP margins owing to the MTN exemptions of other important products not covered by the GSP. It also appears that certain special measures regarding tariffs on behalf of the least developed countries will have only a marginal impact on the trade of those countries.

33. Further analyses of a more dynamic nature concerning the "net" outcome of the MTN for the developing countries support the above conclusions. It is estimated that that the losses in potential trade expansion resulting from the erosion of the GSP amount to $1.7 billion and are offset by only $0.6 billion through the potential trade expansion resulting from MFN tariff cuts on products not covered by the GSP, thus generating a net loss of over $1 billion of potential trade expansion by the developing countries as a result of the MTN tariff cuts. Thus the analyses on both a static and on a more dynamic basis lead to the conclusion that the expectations and objectives of the developing countries regarding tariffs, as expressed in the Tokyo Declaration, various United Nations resolutions and elsewhere, have not been fully realized. Part two of this report contains a detailed quantitative analysis of all aspects of the MTN as they relate to tariffs.

––––––––

The developing countries were particularly upset that an agreement on safeguards was not reached (see Section 9.6 supra). Their position in the negotiations had been that

> all safeguard measures should be applied on a global basis without discrimination as between sources of imports, that imports of special interest to developing countries should be excluded from such measures and that those measures should not be applied to developing countries that were small suppliers of the product or new entrants to the market. Moreover, strictly defined conditions of market injury should accompany safeguard action, which should be time-bound and accompanied by adjustment measures.[11]

11. Id. at 31.

It cannot be said, however, that the developing countries obtained nothing of significance in the Tokyo Round. As noted above in this subsection, and as mentioned elsewhere, many of the side agreements concluded in the Tokyo Round contained special provisions applicable only to developing countries, generally designed to make their adherence easier by imposing less strict obligations of compliance upon them. A prime example was the Subsidies Code, discussed in Section 10.3(B) supra, which explicitly recognized in Article 14 (see Documentary Supplement) that subsidies were an integral part of economic development programs and provided that the ban on export subsidies in respect of nonprimary products would not apply to developing countries with the same rigor that it applied in general.[12]

Moreover, the developing countries obtained the adoption by the Contracting Parties of an explicit recognition of the principle that developing countries should receive differential and more favorable treatment in GATT under certain circumstances.

GATT CONTRACTING PARTIES
Decision of November 28, 1979

DIFFERENTIAL AND MORE FAVOURABLE TREATMENT, RECIPROCITY AND FULLER PARTICIPATION OF DEVELOPING COUNTRIES [13]

Following negotiations within the framework of the Multilateral Trade Negotiations, the Contracting Parties *decide* as follows:

1. Notwithstanding the provisions of Article I of the General Agreement, contracting parties may accord differential and more favourable treatment to developing countries, without according such treatment to other contracting parties.

2. The provisions of paragraph 1 apply to the following:

(*a*) Preferential tariff treatment accorded by developed contracting parties to products originating in developing countries in accordance with the Generalized System of Preferences,

(*b*) Differential and more favourable treatment with respect to the provisions of the General Agreement concerning non-tariff measures governed by the provisions of instruments multilaterally negotiated under the auspices of the GATT;

(*c*) Regional or global arrangements entered into amongst less-developed contracting parties for the mutual reduction or elimination of tariffs and, in accordance with criteria or conditions which may be

12. Other Tokyo Round Agreements with special provisions for developing countries include Article III of the Government Procurement Code, GATT, 26th Supp. BISD 33, 35 (1980) (see Section 8.4 supra); Part III of the Customs Valuation Code and the Protocol thereto, id. at 116, 130 and at 151 (see Section 6.2(D) supra); Article 13 of the Antidumping Code, id. at 171, 184 (see Section 10.2(B) supra); Article 12 of the Agreement on Technical Barriers to Trade, id. at 8, 20 (see Section 8.5 supra).

13. GATT, 26th Supp. BISD 203 (1980). See generally Yusuf, "Differential and More Favorable Treatment": The GATT Enabling Clause, 14 J. World Trade L. 488 (1980); Balassa, The Tokyo Round and the Developing Countries, 14 J. World Trade L. 93 (1980); Meier, The Tokyo Round of Multilateral Trade Negotiations and the Developing Countries, 13 Cornell Intl.L.J. 249 (1980).

prescribed by the Contracting Parties, for the mutual reduction or elimination of non-tariff measures, on products imported from one another;

(d) Special treatment of the least developed among the developing countries in the context of any general or specific measures in favour of developing countries.

3. Any differential and more favourable treatment provided under this clause:

(a) shall be designed to facilitate and promote the trade of developing countries and not to raise barriers to or create undue difficulties for the trade of any other contracting parties;

(b) shall not constitute an impediment to the reduction or elimination of tariffs and other restrictions to trade on a most-favoured-nation basis;

(c) shall in the case of such treatment accorded by developed contracting parties to developing countries be designed and, if necessary, modified, to respond positively to the development, financial and trade needs of developing countries.

4. Any contracting party taking action to introduce an arrangement pursuant to paragraphs 1, 2 and 3 above or subsequently taking action to introduce modification or withdrawal of the differential and more favourable treatment so provided shall:

(a) notify the Contracting Parties and furnish them with all the information they may deem appropriate relating to such action;

(b) afford adequate opportunity for prompt consultations at the request of any interested contracting party with respect to any difficulty or matter that may arise. The Contracting Parties shall, if requested to do so by such contracting party, consult with all contracting parties concerned with respect to the matter with a view to reaching solutions satisfactory to all such contracting parties.

5. The developed countries do not expect reciprocity for commitments made by them in trade negotiations to reduce or remove tariffs and other barriers to the trade of developing countries, i.e., the developed countries do not expect the developing countries, in the course of trade negotiations, to make contributions which are inconsistent with their individual development, financial and trade needs. Developed contracting parties shall therefore not seek, neither shall less-developed contracting parties be required to make, concessions that are inconsistent with the latters' development, financial and trade needs.

6. Having regard to the special economic difficulties and the particular development, financial and trade needs of the least-developed countries, the developed countries shall exercise the utmost restraint in seeking any concessions or contributions for commitments made by them to reduce or remove tariffs and other barriers to the trade of such countries, and the least-developed countries shall not be expected to make concessions or contributions that are inconsistent with the recognition of their particular situation and problems.

7. The concessions and contributions made and the obligations assumed by developed and less-developed contracting parties under the provisions of the General Agreement should promote the basic objectives of the Agreement, including those embodied in the Preamble and in Article XXXVI. Less-developed contracting parties expect that their capacity to make contributions or negotiated concessions or take other mutually agreed action under the provisions and procedures of the General Agreement would improve with the progressive development of their economies and improvement in their trade situation and they would accordingly expect to participate more fully in the framework of rights and obligations under the General Agreement.

8. Particular account shall be taken of the serious difficulty of the least-developed countries in making concessions and contributions in view of their special economic situation and their development, financial and trade needs.

9. The contracting parties will collaborate in arrangements for review of the operation of these provisions, bearing in mind the need for individual and joint efforts by contracting parties to meet the development needs of developing countries and the objectives of the General Agreement.

UNCTAD, REPORT BY THE SECRETARY–GENERAL OF UNCTAD: ASSESSMENT OF THE RESULTS OF THE MULTILATERAL TRADE NEGOTIATIONS

Supra, at 29

176. This decision embodies the first and fourth topics of the framework agenda, which are linked in a single text containing the provision referred to as the "enabling clause." The key provisions of the clause allow countries parties to the General Agreement to accord differential and more favourable treatment to developing countries without according such treatment to other countries, notwithstanding the MFN provisions of article I of the General Agreement. The enabling clause imposes no obligation on developed countries to accord differential treatment to developing countries. As its name implies, it merely "enables" Contracting Parties to accord differential and more favourable treatment to developing countries, in four specific areas: (a) preferential tariff rates accorded by developed to developing countries under the GSP; (b) differential and more favourable treatment for developing countries under agreements concerning non-tariff measures negotiated multilaterally in GATT; (c) regional or global arrangements among developing countries for the mutual reduction or removal of tariffs, and—subject to whatever conditions may be prescribed by the Contracting Parties—of non-tariff measures; (d) special treatment for least developed countries, which remains undefined.

177. A footnote to paragraph 1 of the decision states that it will remain open to the Contracting Parties to consider on an *ad hoc* basis, under the provisions of the General Agreement for joint action, any proposal for differential treatment in other areas. Therefore any other proposals for differential treatment outside the scope of paragraph 1 (i.e. granted on a bilateral or regional basis) should be considered by the Contracting Parties

under a procedure identical with that of obtaining a waiver under article XXV of the General Agreement, which does not involve any improvement over the pre-MTN legal situation as far as those "other proposals" are concerned.

178. The "enabling clause" is counterbalanced by the "graduation" clause in paragraph 7 of the decision. The graduation clause restates the non-reciprocity principle of article XXXVI, paragraph 8, of the General Agreement, but goes on to provide that the developing countries would accept greater obligations under the GATT as their economic situation improves, i.e. "that their capacity to make contributions or negotiated concessions . . . would improve with the progressive development of their economies . . . and they would accordingly expect to participate more fully in the framework of rights and obligations under the General Agreement." It is also stated that differential treatment should be modified as the development, financial and trade needs of developing countries change.

179. It may be noted that the results achieved in this area of the negotiations are more a matter of form than of substance. On the one hand, the enabling clause introduces in the GATT legal system differential treatment in four areas where the developing countries already enjoyed it on a *de facto* basis (and to some extent on a legal basis). On the other hand, the clause limits any further enlargement of the scope of differential treatment within the GATT structure by making it subject to approval by the Contracting Parties to the General Agreement. Furthermore, the decision introduces the graduation principle, which, although vaguely worded, establishes a legal precedent within the GATT system by requiring the developing countries to accept greater obligations as their economic situation improves. This concept could have far-reaching consequences for the future world trading system if its implementation were to allow developed countries to discriminate among developing countries in a unilateral and arbitrary manner.

Notes and Questions

(1) To what extent does the granting of special treatment to developing countries undermine the basic GATT principle of most-favored-nation treatment? In considering your answer, you should review the materials in Chapter 7 above.

(2) Do you agree with the UNCTAD Report that developing countries should be disappointed with the results of the Tokyo Round?

(3) Should there be a "graduation" principle applied to developing countries, such as that contained in paragraph 7 of the Declaration?

(4) Given the diversity of economic development in the developing countries, should those countries be subdivided according to their level of development, with the more advanced countries being entitled to fewer special privileges than the least developed developing countries? How many subdivisions should there be? What becomes of the most-favored-nation principle if this is done? If it is not done, consider whether the whole GSP scheme may be jeopardized? In this

connection, see the recent amendments to the U.S. GSP scheme described later in this section.

(D) THE POSITION OF DEVELOPING COUNTRIES IN GATT

As noted in Section 5.6 supra, the developing countries have long expressed dissatisfaction with the GATT dispute resolution system. In 1962, Uruguay brought a series of complaints in GATT against 15 of the leading developed countries, alleging that hundreds of practices by those countries had restricted Uruguayan export opportunities and thereby had generally nullified and impaired benefits accruing to Uruguay. Uruguay did not play an active role in prosecuting its complaint, however, despite the conclusion by the panel set up to investigate the complaints that

> [W]hile it is not precluded that a *prima facie* case of nullification and impairment could arise even if there is no infringement of GATT provisions, it would be incumbent on the country invoking Article XXIII to demonstrate the grounds and reasons for its invocation. Detailed submissions on the part of that contracting party on these points were therefore essential for a judgment to be made under this Article.[14]

Ultimately the panel essentially only called for the removal of measures that several of the accused countries admitted were maintained in violation of GATT rules.[15] The complaint was viewed more as an attempt to call attention to the problems of developing countries in general, than as an attempt to obtain special relief for Uruguay. Nonetheless, it indicated the basic problems that small countries have in trying to invoke the GATT dispute settlement process. To establish a complaint may require extensive investigation of trade flows and to prevail in GATT may require extensive lobbying of other GATT members. Although developing countries may be better off with GATT than without it in the sense that GATT does establish rules that developed countries may hesitate to ignore completely, it is nonetheless true that the process of dispute settlement in GATT is in part a negotiation process and smaller countries may be less able to participate effectively in it. One result of the Uruguayan complaint was the establishment of special dispute settlement procedures for use by developing countries, described in Section 5.6 supra, which continue to exist.[16]

A recent example demonstrates that the problems of the developing countries remain. In 1983, Nicaragua initiated a complaint against the United States, in which Nicaragua alleged that the U.S. decision to reduce the amount of Nicaraguan sugar allowed to be imported into the United States under the U.S. sugar quota system violated GATT rules on the administration of quotas. Although a GATT panel sided with Nicaragua, the United States indicated that it did not intend to change its practice.[17] Although Nicaragua may thus be entitled to some sort of compensation from

---

14. GATT, 11th Supp. BISD 95, 100 (1963).

15. See GATT, 11th Supp. BISD 95–147 (1963).

16. See Understanding Regarding Notification, Consultation, Dispute Settlement and Surveillance par. 7, GATT, 26th Supp. BISD 210, 211 (1980). But see A. Yusuf, Legal As-

pects of Trade Preferences for Developing States: A Study of the Influence of Development Needs on the Evolution of International Law 73–76 (1982).

17. See Section 13.2(A) supra for a more detailed discussion of the U.S.–Nicaragua incident.

the United States, the usual way of obtaining such compensation would have Nicaragua impose restrictions on imports from the United States, an action that would probably have no noticeable impact on the United States and might even be contrary to Nicaragua's best interests. While the GATT system may work when the United States and the EC have a dispute and threaten each other with meaningful retaliatory measures, such threats are not likely to be taken seriously when made by a developing country. As such, because of their limited resources to devote to litigating trade disputes and their limited ability to retaliate against developed countries, developing countries may not be able to obtain meaningful redress in the GATT dispute settlement system.

SECTION 20.3   THE GENERALIZED SYSTEM OF PREFERENCES (GSP) [1]

(A)   INTRODUCTION

OECD, REPORT BY THE SECRETARY–GENERAL, THE GENERALISED SYSTEM OF PREFERENCES: REVIEW OF THE FIRST DECADE

9–12, 90–91 (1983) [2]

At the first session of the United Nations Conference on Trade and Development (UNCTAD I) in 1964, a report was presented by Raul Prebisch, first Secretary-General of UNCTAD, which brought international attention to focus on the idea that preferential tariff rates in the markets of developed countries could provide impetus for the industrial development of the Third World. The thesis of Prebisch was that the promotion of developing countries' exports of manufactured products could help free those countries from heavy dependence on trade in primary products, whose slow long-term growth and marked price instability contributed to chronic trade deficits. By adopting a deliberate policy of export-oriented industrialisation, developing countries could benefit not only from employment and production creation but also from greater export earning potential, based on products for which demand was strong. To attain these goals, however, only the markets of the industrialised countries appeared large enough to provide the desired growth stimulus.

The solution proposed was the creation of a system of generalised, non-reciprocal preferences, under which the developed countries would lower the customs duties they assessed on goods imported from developing countries. Through this approach, producers in the latter countries would benefit from a price advantage over other foreign producers, whose goods would continue to attract duty at the normal rates. At the same time, developing country producers would be able to compete on more equal terms with domestic producers in importing countries. The basic economic justification for such a system of tariff preferences was seen as an extension of the infant industry

---

1. In addition to the materials quoted or cited elsewhere in this section, see generally UNCTAD, Operation and Effects of the Generalized System of Preferences, UN Doc. TD/B/ C.5/79 (1981) (sixth review of GSP by UNCTAD).

2. Reprinted by permission of the OECD.

argument, assisting developing countries to overcome difficulties in export markets arising from high initial costs.

Some experience already existed in operating more limited preferential systems between developed and developing regions. These had been created in the past principally between certain industrial countries and their colonies, for example in the framework of the Commonwealth or between France and her colonies. The principle of these preferential regimes was continued in the Yaoundé Convention, first signed in 1963 by the European Economic Community and a group of 18 former colonies in Africa.

It was not possible to reach agreement at UNCTAD I on the creation of a new system of generalised tariff preferences for all developing countries and with the participation of all industrialised countries. Some OECD countries had difficulty accepting the principle of such action; at the very least, it would raise a number of new technical problems. It was therefore agreed to continue to study the issue in appropriate international bodies.

During the next few years discussions continued in bodies set up under UNCTAD. At the same time a detailed consideration of the issue was undertaken in OECD, in the course of which there emerged a broad measure of agreement among developed countries on general principles and elements for a system of preferences in favour of developing countries. This work provided the basis for the adoption of Resolution 21(II) at the second session of UNCTAD in 1968, which recognised "the unanimous agreement in favour of the early establishment of a mutually acceptable system of generalised, non-reciprocal and non-discriminatory preferences". The objectives of the system would be: (a) to increase developing countries' export earnings; (b) to promote their industrialisation; and (c) to accelerate their rates of economic growth.

Following the adoption of this resolution, intensive work continued in OECD and in the newly created Special Committee on Preferences of UNCTAD. It became increasingly apparent that it would be very difficult to create one unified system under which identical concessions would be granted across-the-board by all developed countries, because of the differences in these countries' economic structures and systems of tariff protection. The GSP thus came to be understood as a system composed of individual national schemes each based on common goals and principles and aiming to provide developing countries with broadly equivalent opportunities for expanded export growth. At the same time, each developed country would be free to determine the exact nature of the preferential concessions it would include in its national scheme.

The legal basis for the system was laid in June 1971 when the Contracting Parties to the General Agreement on Tariffs and Trade (GATT) approved a waiver to Article I of the General Agreement, which requires that trade policy measures be applied without discrimination to all contracting parties ("most-favoured-nation treatment"). Under the waiver, developed contracting parties were permitted to accord more favourable tariff treatment to products imported from developing countries than to similar products imported from developed countries, for a period of 10 years.

Following the approval of this waiver, the GSP fell quickly into place, with the first scheme of generalised preferences being implemented by the European Economic Community on 1st July, 1971. Over the following months most of the other developed countries put their own schemes into effect. Australia had established a system of tariff preferences for developing countries as early as 1966, which it expanded and brought under the GATT GSP waiver at the beginning of 1974. The GSP itself became complete on 1st January, 1976, when the scheme of the United States became operational. Since the accession of Greece to the European Communities in 1981, twenty OECD countries accord preferences under the GSP to developing countries (Australia, Austria, Canada, Finland, Japan, New Zealand, Norway, Sweden, Switzerland, the United States and the EEC: Belgium, Denmark, France, Federal Republic of Germany, Greece, Ireland, Italy, Luxembourg, the Netherlands and the United Kingdom).

In the early 1970s most of the countries of Eastern Europe also expressed their intention to take measures to further the objectives of Resolution 21(II). Tariff preferences were subsequently announced by those East European countries with customs tariffs (Bulgaria, Czechoslovakia, Hungary, Poland and the USSR). The German Democratic Republic, which does not have a customs tariff, undertook to apply other economic and foreign trade measures of a preferential nature. It is not clear what role such measures can play in state trading countries; however it is beyond the scope of the present report to examine or assess the measures taken by the East European countries.

From the beginning, the OECD preference schemes represented a delicate compromise between the developing countries' desire to have the fewest possible obstacles to market access and the fear in the industrialised countries that a general tariff "disarmament" would create serious disruptions. Initially, the developed countries considered that their preference schemes represented the maximum concession they could give in this field and they consequently looked forward to a period of stability in the operation of the system. Most of the schemes were established for a period of 10 years, although a few schemes had no time-limit. However, the beneficiary developing countries continued to press for a broader system corresponding more to their original demands, in terms of product and country coverage and depth of preferential tariff reduction. As time passed, the preference-giving countries came to accept that the system should evolve and be improved. As a result, the GSP has in fact continued to change and develop throughout its first decade of operation, despite the domestic economic difficulties experienced in the preference-giving countries during this period and the political pressures which these difficulties have on occasion aroused.

As each of the schemes originally implemented by OECD countries had distinct characteristics, the improvements and changes made to each scheme have been neither the same nor systematically co-ordinated. Some schemes have been reviewed and modified annually, while others have been modified as the occasion arose. In some cases these changes have added to the apparent complexity of the schemes, even though their aim was generally to expand the benefits accorded. The numerous changes to the schemes, accompanied by the strong growth of preferential imports from developing countries, underscore the dynamic nature of the GSP. These two broad aspects of the operation of the system have been the subject of continuing consultations and discussions in UNCTAD and in OECD since the implementation of the schemes.

It has proved difficult to assess the actual effects of the GSP, due to the unavailability of relevant statistics in certain cases and the problem of isolating the GSP from other factors influencing the rapid overall growth of developing countries' exports since the early 1970s. Some of these growth factors are outside the realm of trade policy; others are directly related to the elements of such policy. In this latter category, some measures are *relatively favourable* for developing countries: for example, the duty-free treatment which is already applicable at MFN levels to a fairly high proportion of developing countries' exports to OECD countries (about 42 per cent in 1980). This reflects the fact that primary commodities, which continue to make up a large part of developing countries' exports, are often exempt from duty in developed countries. In addition, the latter countries are committed under Part IV of the GATT to give special attention to the interests of developing countries in the formulation of trade policy. On the other hand, some aspects of the industrialised countries' trade policies may seem *relatively disadvantageous* for many developing countries, such as the trade restrictions which exist in the field of textiles and clothing and the tariff escalation which may still be observed in some cases, particularly with respect to more processed goods not covered by preferential arrangements. It is against the background of such policy factors, both favourable and unfavourable for developing countries, that the GSP must be seen. (The same is true for preferential arrangements other than the GSP which are available for some developing countries, as discussed at the end of this report.)

In the context of the developed countries' overall trade policies toward developing countries it appears nevertheless that the GSP has been playing an important role in contributing to freer market access and to trade expansion. During the 1970s the developing countries as a group were the most dynamic participants in world trade, increasing their shares in both world exports and world imports. From 1976 to 1980 OECD imports from developing countries grew at an average annual rate of 21 per cent, compared with 19.6 per cent growth for OECD imports from all sources. The positive influence of the GSP on the evolution of imports from developing countries can be seen from the fact that imports benefiting from GSP treatment grew over the period at an average rate of nearly 27 per cent per year.

This is not to say, however, that the system has completely fulfilled its original goals. In 1980 UNCTAD undertook a general review of the GSP, as had been foreseen, to determine whether the system should be continued, modified or ended after the initial period of operation. At the conclusion of this exercise the Special Committee on Preferences agreed in its Resolution 6(IX) that the objectives of the GSP as set out in Conference Resolution 21(II) had not been fully achieved and that the system should be continued beyond its initial period. Accordingly, in 1981 as the schemes originally limited in time began to expire, they have been renewed for a second period of 10 years.

Table II. Major GSP Beneficiaries in 1980

(Values of GSP imports in millions of US dollars)

TEN LARGEST BENEFICIARIES	11 OECD schemes together	AUSTRALIA (FY)	AUSTRIA	CANADA	FINLAND	JAPAN (FY)	NEW ZEALAND * (FY)	NORWAY	SWEDEN	SWITZERLAND	UNITED STATES	EEC
1. South Korea	3 328.0	129.7	45.7	167.4	15.2	1 204.2	27.0	17.2	53.9	36.7	775.7	855.3
2. Taiwan	3 086.4	254.0	31.7	—	—	933.3	32.1	—	—	—	1 835.4	—
3. Hong Kong	2 454.7	171.1	44.9	159.4	—	118.7	52.7	—	64.7	55.2	803.5	984.5
4. Brazil	1 706.6	58.9	16.2	52.1	5.0	214.0	6.0	6.1	39.0	41.7	441.7	825.6
5. India	1 271.8	64.2	7.5	21.9	2.2	142.5	12.8	4.6	13.3	43.0	139.1	817.6
6. Singapore	1 207.6	167.0	1.2	99.3	1.8	204.7	17.3	5.5	8.7	11.0	300.5	390.6
7. China	1 066.4	135.6	4.8	20.8	3.3	385.1	33.7	7.1	26.0	17.5	—	432.4
8. Yugoslavia	1 040.7	5.6	63.0	17.3	9.7	16.7	0.9	7.2	34.5	59.1	176.8	649.9
9. Mexico	943.0	6.9	1.0	28.4	1.6	113.2	0.9	0.8	13.6	34.2	509.1	233.4
10. Philippines	930.0	44.4	5.0	22.8	4.5	347.1	2.2	2.1	8.0	7.3	135.8	350.8
Total of above	17 034.9	1 037.4	221.0	589.4	43.3	3 679.5	185.6	50.6	261.7	305.7	5 117.6	5 540.1
This group as a % of total GSP benefits accorded	66.1%	62.3%	63.7%	78.5%	51.1%	73.8%	83.9%	76.4%	78.6%	45.2%	69.9%	59.3%

Notes: FY = fiscal year 1980–81

— = not a beneficiary

* Figures for New Zealand represent imports covered by the GSP; imports accorded GSP treatment may have been slightly lower.

(B) GATT AND THE GSP

GENERALIZED SYSTEM OF PREFERENCES
GATT Decision of 25 June 1971.
GATT Doc. (L/3545) [3]

The CONTRACTING PARTIES to the General Agreement on Tariffs and Trade,

DECIDE

(a) That without prejudice to any other Article of the General Agreement, the provisions of Article I shall be waived for a period of ten years to the extent necessary to permit developed contracting parties, subject to the procedures set out hereunder, to accord preferential tariff treatment to products originating in developing countries and territories with a view to extending to such countries and territories generally the preferential tariff treatment referred to in the Preamble to this Decision, without according such treatment to like products of other contracting parties.

Provided that any such preferential tariff arrangements shall be designed to facilitate trade from developing countries and territories and not to raise barriers to the trade of other contracting parties;

(b) That they will, without duplicating the work of other international organizations, keep under review the operation of this Decision and decide, before its expiry and in the light of the considerations outlined in the Preamble, whether the Decision should be renewed and if so, what its terms should be;

(c) That any contracting party which introduces a preferential tariff arrangement under the terms of the present Decision or later modifies such arrangement, shall notify the CONTRACTING PARTIES and furnish them with all useful information relating to the actions taken pursuant to the present Decision;

(d) That such contracting party shall afford adequate opportunity for consultations at the request of any other contracting party which considers that any benefit accruing to it under the General Agreement may be or is being impaired unduly as a result of the preferential arrangement;

(e) That any contracting party which considers that the arrangement or its later extension is not consistent with the present Decision or that any benefit accruing to it under the General Agreement may be or is being impaired unduly as a result of the arrangement or its subsequent extension and that consultations have proved unsatisfactory, may bring the matter before the CONTRACTING PARTIES which will examine it promptly and will formulate any recommendations that they judge appropriate.

The Tokyo Declaration quoted in Section 20.2 is generally viewed as legitimizing GSP arrangements indefinitely.

3. GATT, 18th Supp. BISD 24 (1972).

(C) THE UNITED STATES AND THE GSP

The U.S. GSP scheme was authorized by Title V of the Trade Act of 1974. The provisions of Title V, as originally passed and as amended in 1984, are very detailed, reflecting congressional desires to exclude certain categories of countries and products from the scheme and to afford protection to U.S. industry in certain cases.

The U.S. GSP scheme is potentially applicable to most developing countries. The statutory scheme grants broad discretionary authority to the President to designate countries as beneficiaries.[4] It does, however, direct the President to take a number of factors into account. Some of these factors are simple enough: Has the country in question expressed a desire to be a GSP beneficiary? Is it truly a developing country? Do other major developed countries grant it GSP status? Other factors are more trade related: Has the country assured the United States of equitable and reasonable access to its markets and commodity resources? Has it assured the United States that it will refrain from engaging in unreasonable export practices? Does the country provide adequate and effective protection of intellectual property rights? Has the country taken action to reduce trade distorting investment policies and to reduce barriers to trade in services?

Even if the President is disposed to grant GSP status, there are certain countries that Congress has excluded from receiving GSP status: Communist countries (except in certain instances), OPEC members and certain other export cartel members, countries that expropriate U.S. property without compensation, countries that fail to take adequate steps to control illegal drug traffic, countries that fail to recognize arbitral awards in favor of U.S. citizens, countries that aid and abet international terrorism, and, since 1984, countries that do not afford internationally recognized worker rights to workers in the country.[5] In general, the President has the power to designate a country as a GSP beneficiary despite the exclusion provisions if he determines that to do so would be in the national economic interest of the United States.

The 1974 Act provided that certain articles would not be eligible for GSP treatment: Textiles and apparel articles subject to textile agreements, watches, import-sensitive electronic articles, import-sensitive steel articles, certain footwear articles, import-sensitive glass products. In 1984, the list was modified to provide for exclusion of footwear, handbags, luggage, flat goods, work gloves and leather wearing apparel.[6] These articles are produced by the industries that most frequently seem to complain of import competition. As to articles that are not automatically excluded, the President has fairly broad discretion in selecting which articles to accord GSP treatment.[7]

4. Section 502(a); 19 U.S.C.A. § 2462(a).

5. Section 502(b); 19 U.S.C.A. § 2462(b). The statute also excludes by name the following countries: Australia, Austria, Canada, Czechoslovakia, EC member states, Finland, East Germany, Iceland, Japan, Monaco, New Zealand, Norway, Poland, South Africa, Swe-

den, Switzerland and the Soviet Union. Countries that give preferences to products from developed countries other than the United States are also excluded.

6. Section 503(c); 19 U.S.C.A. § 2463(c).

7. Section 503(a); 19 U.S.C.A. § 2463(a).

In addition to providing for the exclusion of certain articles, the Act provides for the exclusion of otherwise eligible articles if they are exported from certain countries (the "competitive need" exclusion).[8] Essentially this provision is intended to prevent a GSP beneficiary from becoming a significant supplier, in percentage or dollar terms, of the U.S. market. The theory is that if the specified thresholds are exceeded, the country in question has demonstrated its ability to compete in the United States without special treatment and that the GSP scheme should thereafter restrict that country's exports so as to allow other GSP beneficiaries to have a better chance to compete for the market in question. Under the 1974 Act the thresholds were set at 50% or more of the total value, or $25 million (in 1974 dollars), of U.S. imports of the article during the latest calendar year. By 1984, the dollar limit was $57 million current dollars.

At the time of the 1984 renewal, protectionist pressures in Congress were strong, and additional limitations were placed on GSP eligibility. These are described in the House Report as follows:

HOUSE REPORT NO. 98–1090
98th Cong., 2d Sess. 2–3, 17–21 (1984)

IMPORTS UNDER THE GSP PROGRAM

Although the value of U.S. imports receiving GSP duty-free treatment has grown from $3.2 billion in 1976 to $10.8 billion in 1983, imports receiving GSP duty-free treatment constitute only 4 percent of total U.S. imports. GSP duty-free imports constitute only about 11 percent of total U.S. imports of all products from GSP beneficiary countries. Further, the $10.8 billion imports entering duty-free under GSP in 1983 constituted only 15 percent of total U.S. imports of GSP-eligible products from all sources. Sixty-eight percent of total imports of these products entered from non-beneficiary countries subject to duty.

GSP imports have not resulted in significant increases in the overall import share of the U.S. market. GSP imports averaged only 0.5 percent or less of total U.S. consumption during the 1978–1981 period, as reported by the International Trade Commission (ITC). In only 12 of 650 sectors have GSP imports resulted in significant increases in import penetration. In many areas, increased GSP imports appear to be at the expense of imports from developed countries.

As of 1983, a greater volume of potential GSP-eligible imports were denied than were granted duty-free treatment. Of the $11.9 billion imports of GSP-eligible articles denied duty-free treatment, imports of $10.7 billion were articles from particular countries exceeding the statutory "competitive need" ceilings. The remaining imports of $1.2 billion were excluded as a result of discretionary "graduation" under an administrative procedure of the Office of the U.S. Trade Representative (USTR) based upon (1) the country's general level of development; (2) the country's competitiveness in the particular product; and (3) overall U.S. economic interests, including domestic import sensitivity.

8. Section 504; 19 U.S.C.A. § 2464.

The Committee is concerned, however, that a relatively few advanced developing countries receive most of the GSP benefits, despite the growth of their imports excluded from eligibility annually under the "competitive need" limits and discretionary graduation of competitive articles. The three leading beneficiary countries (Taiwan, Korea, and Hong Kong) receive 52 percent of total benefits. Taiwan and Korea's share has actually increased somewhat since 1976. The leading seven beneficiary countries (including Mexico, Brazil, Singapore, and Israel) account for nearly 75 percent of total GSP imports. The least developed countries receive less than one percent of total GSP benefits. Developed countries and advanced developing countries, rather than other developing countries, usually gain import share following exclusion of competitive products from GSP eligibility.

* * *

Discretionary graduation is designed to promote the continued graduation of the more advanced developing countries from GSP benefits in products where they have demonstrated competitiveness. In addition, discretionary graduation is intended to promote a shift of benefits to the less advanced and less competitive developing countries.

The following table demonstrates the effect on GSP duty-free import coverage of product exclusions from particular countries under the competitive need ceilings and discretionary graduation:

Product Graduation Under The GSP

[Dollar amounts in millions]

Year	Discretionary graduation	Competitive need exclusions	Total exclusions	GSP-free imports	Ratio of exclusion to GSP imports (percent)
1980	$ 443	$5,600	$6,043	$7,328	0.82
1981	651	6,782	7,433	8,395	.89
1982	900	7,108	8,008	8,426	.95
1983	1,211	10,661	11,872	10,765	1.11

Note: Data shown for graduation and competitive need exclusions pertain to actions implemented in March of the following year.

* * *

Section 5(b) of the bill, as amended, would retain the basic competitive need standards currently provided for in section 504(c)(1), but would make substantial changes in their application to particular countries in order to encourage a more equitable distribution of GSP benefits among countries based upon their relative development level and competitiveness in particular products. First, subsection (b) amends section 504(c) by adding a new paragraph (2) to require a general review by the President on all GSP-eligible articles based on the country and product eligibility considerations of sections 501 or 502(c). This review, which is distinct from the annual product reviews that will continue as under existing law, must be completed not later than January 4, 1986 and periodically thereafter. The general review will seek to identify articles in which a BDC [Beneficiary Developing Country] has demonstrated, compared to other BDCs, that it has achieved sufficient competitiveness in a particular product so that it is appropriate to trigger faster graduation from benefits.

The following factors in section 501 or 502(c), as amended by the bill, would govern the President's determinations in the general product review:

(1) the effect such action will have on furthering the economic development of developing countries through the expansion of their exports;

(2) whether or not the other major developed countries are extending generalized preferential tariff treatment to such product or products;

(3) the anticipated impact of such action on United States producers of like or competitive products;

(4) the extent of BDC's competitiveness with respect to eligible articles;

(5) an expression of the country's desire for GSP treatment;

(6) the economic developmental level of individual BDCs;

(7) the extent to which the BDC has assured the United States it will provide equitable and reasonable access to the markets and basic commodity resources of such country;

(8) the extent to which U.S. intellectual property rights are recognized;

(9) the extent to which the country has taken action to reduce or eliminate barriers to trade and services; and

(10) the extent to which the country has taken steps to afford internationally recognized rights to its workers.

On the basis of this review of product competitiveness and the additional new statutory standards pertaining to a country's relative development level, the President will be authorized to make "cutbacks" in the competitive need limits as described below. These reductions, which are mandatory for some countries and discretionary for others, would result in lower dollar and percentage competitive need limits.

At the same time, in order to promote further the goal of promoting important U.S. trade interests, paragraph (6) amends section 504(c) to allow the President to waive the application of competitive need limits as described below. For some countries this waiver authority would only allow restoration of benefits which have been reduced by procedures described above and would not permit waiver beyond the competitive need limits in present law. For others, it provides the latitude to waive competitive need limits and expand GSP benefits on a product-by-product basis. These waivers can be made if the following circumstances are met:

(1) the President receives the advice of the ITC on whether any U.S. industry is likely to be adversely affected by the proposed waiver;

(2) the President determines, based on the ITC advice and the considerations described in section 501 and 502(c) as amended, that the waiver is in the U.S. national economic interest; and

(3) he publishes this determination in the Federal Register.

The purpose of granting the President this waiver authority is to provide him additional tools to achieve U.S. trade interests with BDCs, such as greater market access for U.S. exports, greater discipline in protecting intellectual property rights, and improvements in workers rights. However, in order to prevent abuse of this discretionary waiver authority and to insure that GSP benefits are dispersed among BDCs which truly need them, several restrictions on the President's waiver authority are included. The bill as amended provides varying degrees of cutback and waiver authority of three different groupings of countries.

None of these changes would go into effect before January 3, 1986. This one-year period from date of enactment of the bill will give the President the opportunity to conduct the initial general product review required under section 504(c)(2) as amended, and to discuss with individual BDCs the potential application of the new designation criteria under section 502(b) and (c). This period is also necessary for adjustment by BDCs and the trading public.

Per Capita GNP Below $5,000 and GSP Share Below 10 Percent. For any country which had a per capita income of less than $5,000 and accounted for less than 10 percent of total U.S. GSP duty-free imports in the preceding calendar year, the President may effectively reduce the competitive need limits by one-half for any article from such country which he determines to meet the test under the general product review of "sufficient degree of competitiveness". This would be accomplished by changing the base year for adjusting the dollar limit in sections 504(c)(1)(A) from "1974" to "1984", thus reducing the absolute amount from the present $57 million to $25 million, and by reducing the percentage limit in section 504(c)(1)(B) from 50 percent to 25 percent. Any such article from such country for which imports into the United States in any calendar year exceed $25 million (indexed annually to changes in the U.S. GNP) or exceed 25 percent of total U.S. imports of the article, would be ineligible for GSP duty-free treatment in subsequent years unless imports fall below these new competitive need limits for two consecutive years.

The President may waive the competitive need limits on any article, except that the total dollar value of all waivers for such countries for any calendar year may not exceed 25 percent of the total value of GSP duty-free imports from all BDCs in the previous calendar year. Only those waivers on articles from countries with a per capita GNP of below $5,000 and which accounted for less than 10 percent of duty-free GSP imports will be assessed against this 25 percent total waiver authority, and such waivers shall only be counted to the extent they exceed the present competitive need limitations on such articles under section 504(c)(1) (i.e., $57 million/50 percent). Waivers under the de minimis and "no U.S. production" criteria in section 504(d) shall not be included in this calculation.

Each such waiver must be based on the national economic interest determination by the President required in new paragraph (5) of section 504(c). This determination must be based on ITC advice, and consideration of the factors in section 501 and 502(c), including efforts by the country to protect intellectual property rights, reduce trade barriers and trade distorting practices, and recognize workers rights.

Per Capita GNP $5,000 or More or GSP Share of 10 Percent or More. For any country which the President has determined either had a per capita GNP of $5,000 or more or accounted for more than ten percent of total GSP duty-free imports in the preceding calendar year, the competitive need limits applicable to that country must be cut in half for all of its GSP-eligible products (i.e., to the 1974 level of $25 million and from 50 percent to 25 percent as described above).

The President may waive this cutback in competitive need limits for any article from such a country, after taking into account the ITC advice and making the national interest determination under new section 504(c)(5) as described above, and restore the present limits (i.e., up to $57 million/50 percent). However, under no circumstances may the competitive need limits for any article be increased beyond the levels now authorized under section 504(c)(1).

Per Capita GNP $9,000 or More. Finally, if a country reaches a level of $9,000 per capita GNP [$8,500 as enacted] in any calendar year (none have currently attained this level), all of that country's products would be graduated from receiving any GSP benefits over a two-year period under new paragraph (4) of section 504(c). The competitive need limits on those products subject to the present limits (i.e., $57 million/50 percent) during the calendar year when the $9,000 GNP level is attained, would be cut in half (i.e., $25 million/25 percent) for two years and then completely removed from GSP eligibility. Articles which had been subject to the reduced ($25 million/25 percent) limits during the year in which the $9,000 level was reached would remain eligible for GSP benefits at these competitive need limits for one year, and then would be ineligible for GSP benefits in the following year. Thus after a two-year period, the country would be completely graduated and none of its articles would be eligible for GSP benefits. The President would have no waiver authority for these countries.

It is the Committee's belief that countries which reach a per capita GNP level of $9,000 should be considered to be developed countries for purposes of the GSP program and therefore no longer in need of the benefits of preferential duty-free treatment.

Notes and Questions

(1) The GSP statute is instructive because of the insights it lends to analyzing the relationship of the President and Congress in foreign affairs. As the quoted congressional report makes clear, Congress has taken a substantial interest in the operation of the GSP system and has placed many limitations on the President's freedom of action. For example, Congress ignored warnings by the Executive Branch that excluding all OPEC members from participation in the GSP program was undesirable because it would seriously damage U.S. relations with certain poorer members of OPEC such as Ecuador and Indonesia.

(2) In addition, the statute indicates Congress' penchant, at least where U.S. industry may be protected as opposed to injured, for using trade legislation to attempt to accomplish numerous other U.S. foreign policy goals such as discour-

aging export cartels, expropriation and terrorism and encouraging protection of workers' rights. Is this appropriate, given the nature of GSP legislation? What about those provisions of the U.S. statute that suggest GSP status may be affected by a country's position on protection of intellectual property rights or trade in services?

(3) A key issue in GSP schemes is how to define the origin of goods. If strict definitions are not used, the goal of promoting development may be undermined by exporters performing only minor finishing activities in the developing country. Rules of origin are analyzed in Section 6.2(E) supra.

(4) Given the sensitivity of developing countries to the graduation concept, how do you expect that the provisions of the U.S. statute on graduation will affect U.S. relations with developing countries? To what extent does the U.S. statute suggest that the United States is unwilling to see developing countries achieve their development potential?

(5) To the extent that the recent U.S. amendments will have the effect of cutting exports from developing countries, what implications do you think that such action will have for the ability of those countries to purchase U.S. exports and to repay loans from U.S. banks?

SECTION 20.4 INITIATIVES FOR A "NEW INTERNATIONAL ECONOMIC ORDER" (NIEO)

CHARTER OF ECONOMIC RIGHTS AND DUTIES OF STATES [1]

On April 19, 1972, President Echeverria of Mexico proposed to the Third United Nations Conference on Trade and Development that a Charter of Economic Rights and Duties of States should be drafted in order to protect the economic rights of all countries, especially the developing countries. On May 18, 1972, UNCTAD (III) voted to establish a Working Group to draw up such a Charter.[2] Although the United States abstained, it did consent to participate on the Working Group. The original intent was to create a document that would be binding upon the signatories and become a part of international law. Given the lukewarm reception the proposal received from most developed countries, however, political reality eventually dictated that this would not be possible.

Many of the countries that refused to accept the Charter did so partly because of its failure to contain either a commitment to follow international law or an acknowledgement of the relevance of international law.[3] With

1. The text of the charter is found in Report of the Second Committee, U.N. Doc. A/9946, 28 (Dec. 9, 1974) and U.N. Doc. A/RES/3281 (XXIX) (Jan. 15, 1975); see also 14 Intl. Leg. Matls. 251; Brower & Tepe, The Charter of Economic Rights and Duties of States: A Reflection or Rejection of International Law?, 9 Intl.Law. 295 (1975); Note, Charter of Economic Rights and Duties of States: A Solution to the Development Aid Problem?, 4 Georgia J. Intl. & Comp.L. 441 (1974). Compilations of references made to the Charter may be found in U.N. Docs. A/C.2/300 (Nov. 3, 1975); A/

C.2/300/Add. 1 (Nov. 6, 1975); A/C.2/300/Add. 2 (Nov. 18, 1975).

2. UNCTAD Res. 45 (III), U.N. Doc. TD/180.

3. Eighteen different amendments were offered by various combinations of a total of fourteen developed countries in an effort to conform the Charter to their understanding of international law. All failed adoption. See Brower & Tepe, note 1 supra, at 303–04. For the amendments, see U.N. Doc. A/9946, 14–19

regard to expropriation, a topic discussed in Section 16.5 supra, the Charter calls for questions of compensation to be "settled under the domestic law of the nationalizing state and its tribunals," unless otherwise agreed by the states concerned. While the Charter affirms that "[n]o State shall be compelled to grant preferential treatment to foreign investment," it fails to disavow discriminatory treatment of aliens. The Charter proclaims "full, permanent sovereignty," without any suggestion of the inviolability of contracts. An amendment to Article 2, which would have required States to exercise good faith in fulfillment of their international obligations, was defeated.[4]

A second contested area concerned the legitimacy of cartels. The Charter states that all States have the right to associate in organizations of primary commodity procedures to further their national interests. "Correspondingly all States have the duty to respect that right by refraining from applying economic and political measures that would limit it."[5]

The developed countries also unsuccessfully opposed Article 28 which imposes a duty on all States to adjust the prices of the exports of developing countries in relation to those of their imports.

Article 16 calls for restitution to be made for the economic and social costs of "colonialism, *apartheid*, racial discrimination, neocolonialism and all forms of foreign aggression, occupation and domination." It also provides that States shall not encourage investments that inhibit "the liberation of a territory occupied by force." This Article was opposed by the developed countries as irrelevant and not in accord with international law. An attempt to delete Article 15 calling for disarmament, on grounds of irrelevance, also failed.[6] The United Nations General Assembly adopted the resolution incorporating the "Charter" on December 12, 1974, by a roll-call vote of 120 to 6, with 10 abstentions. Voting against were the United States, Belgium, Denmark, the Federal Republic of Germany, Luxembourg, and the United Kingdom. Abstaining were: Austria, Canada, France, Ireland, Israel, Italy, Japan, the Netherlands, Norway, and Spain.[7]

EMILIO O. RABASA, SECRETARY OF FOREIGN RELATIONS OF MEXICO, THE CHARTER OF ECONOMIC RIGHTS AND DUTIES OF STATES

(1974)[8]

On the one hand, the transformation of the world into a "global village" has resulted in a change in the attitude of the underdeveloped countries

(1974). Votes on the amendments are shown at 22–23.

4. See Brower & Tepe, note 1 supra, at 305–06; Art. 2(1) of U.N. Doc. A/9946 (1974) at 16 and 22.

5. Art. 5 of the Charter.

6. For an analysis of the Charter provisions and proposed amendments, see generally Brower & Tepe, note 1 supra, at 303–18, and U.N. Doc. A/9946 (1974).

7. U.N. Doc. A/RES/3281 (XXIX).

8. Address to a joint meeting of the Section on International Law of the American Bar Association and the American Society of International Law in Washington, D.C., April 26, 1974, American Society of International Law, Proceedings of the 68th Annual Meeting 302, 303–305 (1975).

This and other excerpts from this publication in this chapter are reprinted by permis-

which have decided not to continue to play a passive role, but to be active participants in the changing of those structures that hinder their well-being. On the other hand, the interdependence of all the components of the global economic system demands a modification of the international structures that condition their behavior. Thus the elaboration of global strategies that take into consideration the domestic as well as the international aspects of the problem is based not solely on moral considerations but on the conviction that all countries should accept the principle of shared common responsibility and join in efforts to create world prosperity.

There exists, and will continue to exist, a close relationship between the problems of peace, security, and development. Real peace cannot be attained if we do not understand that it is intimately related with these other two elements. It is thus necessary to accept a new rational attitude of conciliation and cooperation that will suppress sterile confrontations by establishing a set of rules of authentic international solidarity.

* * *

In the United States, legislative measures, such as the Social Security Act of 1935, the National Labor Relations Act of the same year, the Fair Labor Standards Act of 1938, the Employment Act of 1946, the Economic Opportunity Act of 1964 and many others, have served within the domestic frontiers as a fundamental support for the proper development of the masses. Why not then transfer the philosophy that has been the basis for this new process to the international field? An equitable distribution of resources, investments, and incomes between individuals, regions, and economic sectors are principles commonly accepted at a national level. In the final analysis—and justly so—the supremacy of social needs and values over parochial interests has been recognized. This has been inevitably imposed as a result of the growing interdependence that characterizes modern times. The ascendancy that the Western political tradition has given to government by law, and in particular the peculiar character of the Anglo-Saxon legal tradition that allows for social change within frameworks of great flexibility without any loss of continuity, have eased the incorporation in legislative ordinances of the demands generated by the social structure.

A brief review of the stages that international law has followed in its historical development allows us to appreciate the fact that up to the first decade of the present century, the main concern in this field was to regulate political relations among states. The international legal norms became efficient means to legitimize economic and political domination exercised over other parts of the planet. International law was then conceived from a colonialist point of view.

Basically after World War II, as a consequence of the hardening of ever-present international economic problems and, in particular, after the emergence during the first years of the decade of the 60's of a considerable number of countries to independence, a great transforming tendency was initiated that tended to incorporate social legislation into the field of international relations. The demands of the developing countries were

sion of the American Society of International Law.

increasingly accepted and this was reflected in the creation of several organizations and, particularly, in the launching of the First and Second Development Decades by the United Nations. Notwithstanding, the achievements obtained with these programs have been almost nil, or, to say the least, very modest. That is why it is so necessary to endow an increasingly integrated global society with a set of rules that regulates fundamental activities within the framework of healthy development strategies. We must transform the philosophy of social well-being into a global concept. That is one of the main objectives of the Charter of Economic Rights and Duties.

When we contemplate the trends toward economic inequality, the ever-growing gap that separates the poor countries from the rich, and the lack of equilibrium between man and his environment, it is obvious that parallel to all the tendencies towards integration and interdependence are powerful forces in existence that, if not properly checked, would lead to the disintegration of the world community. The greatest menace to peace that we face nowadays is the increasing tension and the very noticeable separation between the industrialized countries and those which are underdeveloped.

* * *

Let us subject the fundamental economic elements for the future of world development to the rule of law. Let us clarify and ordain concepts. Let us codify norms and create an authentic body of rules that will allow the international community to settle disputes and control abuses.

Law represents a force in itself that can become a basic source of innovation for society. All members of the legal profession have the duty of stressing the value of law to the global community.

STEPHEN M. SCHWEBEL, STATE DEPARTMENT COUNSELOR ON INTERNATIONAL LAW, ENTENTE CORDIALE? DIVERGENCE AND ACCOMMODATION: APPROACHES TO MULTILATERAL ISSUES

(1974) [9]

Our view is that any Charter which will attract the consensus of UNCTAD and of the General Assembly of the United Nations must be balanced between the interests of the developing and the developed countries—not a subtle point, but an important one. If the Charter turns out to be simply a statement of the alleged rights of the developing countries and the alleged duties of the developed, it will be a kind of bill of particulars, if not an indictment, which will have no more impact on international economic affairs, not to speak of international law, than a number of self-serving calls which developing countries have issued in the past in UNCTAD and elsewhere.

* * *

Divergence is further illustrated by another proposal of Mexico that:

9. Remarks in Panel Discussion, April 26, 1974, American Society of International Law, Proceedings of the 68th Annual Meeting 209, 210 and 212 (1975).

Every State has the right to regulate and control transnational enterprises within its national jurisdiction. The State whose nationals or registered transnational corporations invest in other States must ensure that such investors comply fully with the laws, rules and regulations of the State in whose territory the investment is made.

While it may be readily agreed that a state has the right to regulate a transnational enterprise within its jurisdiction, provided that such regulation is nondiscriminatory and otherwise in accordance with international law, a proposal that the state of domicile must ensure that its transnational companies comply fully with whatever laws, rules, and regulations other states adopt applicable to such companies is quite a proposal. Again, it is hard to regard such a proposal as a basis for consensus between the developed and the developing worlds.

Note

Since the adoption of the Charter, there has been considerable controversy over its legal standing.[10] The developed countries take the position in general that the Charter is not a binding legal document and that would seem to be consistent with the rules on the creation of international law that we examined in Section 5.1 supra.

The debate over the Charter's legal effect sometimes obscures the important effect it has had on the way developing countries are viewed by the rest of the world. The Charter has been one of a number of efforts that developing countries have made to urge adoption of their views by the international community. As we have seen throughout this book, and in particularly in this chapter, the developing countries have been active in making their views known on the various issues facing the international trading system, through the United Nations, UNCTAD and other bodies. Their success has been considerable in the view of some. They have basically established the principle that developing countries are entitled to more favorable treatment than developed countries, despite the fact that that principle goes against one of the foundations of GATT—the most-favored-nation rule. Of course, as we saw in Section 20.2(C) supra, the developing countries are not satisfied with the progress they have made, but it is undeniable that they have made progress. Perhaps most importantly, the developing world has been effective in making its views on issues well known and causing the developed countries to negotiate on numerous issues—from the law of the sea to the economic rights of nations to the obligations of multinational enterprises. Indeed, in some endeavors, the leading oar has been taken by the developing countries in trade matters, in particular the effort to stabilize commodity prices through the Integrated Commodity Program that we discussed in Section 14.3 supra.

Thus, although the Charter has not caused the revolutionary change in thinking that its proponents wished, and although not all demands of developing countries have been met, it has been one important means of bringing developing country concerns to the attention of the developed world.

10. See, e.g., G. Varges, The New International Economic Order Legal Debate (1983); K. Hossain (ed.), Legal Aspects of the New International Economic Order (1980).

SECTION 20.5 DEVELOPING COUNTRIES AND THE INTERNATIONAL DEBT CRISIS

One of the more significant international problems as this book was prepared was the so-called international debt crisis. In the early 1980s, a large number of developing countries and entities located therein found themselves unable to pay back or even to pay interest on loans owed to international lenders. Among the countries that found themselves in this position were not only a number of very poor countries, but some of the leading nations of the developing world—Mexico, Brazil, Argentina and Chile to name a few. The causes and effects of this crisis were numerous and to some extent controversial. For our purposes, we consider only a number of trade-related issues.

While some of the proceeds of the loans made to these countries may well have been diverted to private ends or squandered, many of the loans were used for industrial development. While it was thought that the exports of the borrowers, both traditional and those made possible through the industrial development resulting from the loans, would enable the interest and principal on the loans to be paid back when due, a number of factors made this impossible. First, the significant increase in the cost of oil meant that those many borrowers who were not self sufficient in energy had to spend considerable amounts of their foreign exchange simply to maintain their current energy usage. Second, because of recessions in the developed world, the market for developing country products did not expand as rapidly as anticipated. Moreover, as a result of protectionist pressures caused by the recessions, restrictions on imports from developing countries became more common. Thus, the export earnings necessary to generate the foreign exchange needed to meet loan payments were not available.

While the developing countries have had some success in restructuring their loans, i.e. delaying repayment, and in obtaining limited new loans, the problem remains very serious. Indeed, some smaller countries have simply stopped making payments. Because of the huge amount of money involved, a default by the major borrowers could have serious repercussions on the domestic banking systems of a number of developed countries. The major international banks have, as a result, been very eager to avoid major defaults. As noted in Chapter 11 supra, the International Monetary Fund has also been involved in attempts to solve the debt crisis. As noted there, the IMF typically assists a country only if certain corrective measures are taken. Thus, as a condition of IMF loans, as well as a condition to the international banks' agreement to restructure loans, the borrower countries involved have been required to implement various austerity measures, designed in particular to reduce imports and inflation. It is too soon to tell if these austerity measures will measurably improve the situation. One effect of such measures is clear, however. Exports by the developed countries to the debtor countries have fallen off. For example, U.S. exports to Latin America fell approximately 40% from 1981 to 1983.[1] This, of course,

---

1. Statistical Abstract of the United States 816 (1985).

has worsened the U.S. balance of payments and harmed U.S. export industries.

The interrelationship of the debt problem, the problem of developing country access to developed country markets and preferences for developing countries was recently commented upon by a group of GATT experts:

GATT, TRADE POLICIES FOR A BETTER FUTURE
(Report of Eminent Persons on Problems Facing the International Trading System)
(1985)

A number of developing countries have built up huge and almost unmanageable debts—partly through their own errors, partly as a result of the oil price shocks of the 1970s, partly because private banks were too eager to lend recycled OPEC surpluses, and partly because anticipated export earnings never materialized owing to recession, deteriorating terms of trade and protectionism.

The burden of high real interest rates and principal repayments has forced these nations to cut back on imports, causing both immediate hardships and long-term reductions in their productive capacity. The consequences have been felt in other countries, which have lost exports and hundreds of thousands of jobs through the contraction of demand in the indebted countries. (Much the same happened in Europe in the 1930s because of World War I debts and reparations.) International cooperation in meeting the debt problem has bought time. A more lasting solution must enable the debtor countries to regain the capacity to service their debts while allowing their economies to expand at a healthy rate. More open markets and expanding trade are central requirements for any lasting solution.

The debt crisis has taught one important lesson, at great cost: developing and developed countries are all in the same boat. Both sides have suffered from the problem, even if not comparably. Both will gain when the crisis is mastered.

* * *

Developing countries receive special treatment in the GATT rules. But such special treatment is of limited value. Far greater emphasis should be placed on permitting and encouraging developing countries to take advantage of their competitive strengths and on integrating them more fully into the trading system, with all the appropriate rights and responsibilities that this entails. Additional help should be given to the least-developed countries of Africa and elsewhere in developing their trade. Removal of obstacles to their agricultural exports should be a primary target.

Most preferential tariff schemes in favour of developing countries are of very limited value. Developing countries have allowed themselves to be distracted by the idea of preferences, seeing them as a means of offsetting handicaps created by trade restrictions and distortions in developed country markets. They have done so at the cost of overlooking their fundamental interest in a non-discriminatory trading system. Developed countries have used preferences as an easy substitute for action in more essential areas.

Preferences may have value as a form of encouragement to infant industries, but developing countries should not depend on them indefinitely. The more advanced developing countries should also be expected to contribute market opportunities.

There is still room for further most-favoured-nation reductions in developed-country tariffs. In particular these tariffs now discourage developing countries from exporting semi-finished and finished products. The worldwide tendency toward "tariff escalation", whereby import duties are higher on semi-finished products than on raw materials, and higher still on finished products, gives high protection for processing activities (often of the order of 100 per cent or more of the value added). This greatly handicaps many developing countries, as well as more advanced countries largely dependent on their natural resources, by discouraging resource-based industries such as metal refining and fabricating, and plywood and furniture manufacture.

The debt problems of developing countries provide an important reason for removing trade barriers against their exports and, even more, for making the trading system more stable and predictable. In no circumstances, however, should these problems be used as an excuse for introducing new discrimination into the international trading system.

Problems of human and material infrastructure, rather than of trade, dominate the economic situation of most African and other least-developed countries. However, trade policy, and especially production and export subsidies in other countries, should at least be prevented from hampering exports of primary commodities and other products from the least-developed countries. Preferences find their strongest justification when given to the least-developed countries. In general, it should be remembered that even if actions taken now have little immediate effect on exports of the least-developed countries, they will help to open up longer-term market opportunities, and thus to attract and induce export-oriented investment. Generally speaking, greater and assured access to export markets will encourage all developing countries to be more ready to accept foreign investment.

We see little basis for negotiations organized on "North-South" lines. The major problems of the trading system today are global: to put them into North-South terms is to oversimplify them. Moreover, the trade patterns and concerns of developing countries are just as varied as those of developed countries. Multilateral negotiations on market access, and on the improvement of particular trading rules, are likely to involve coalitions of interest that will vary according to the products and issues under discussion, and will only occasionally be clearly North-South in character. Individual developing countries will also have specific trade interests to pursue in negotiations. Since their own economies would benefit if they reduced their trade barriers, they would be well advised to turn such reductions to further advantage by obtaining, in exchange, improvements in access for their exports to the developed-country markets, and indeed to the markets of other developing countries.

Chapter 21

NONMARKET ECONOMIES, STATE TRADING AND INTERNATIONAL ECONOMIC REGULATION

SECTION 21.1 TRADE BETWEEN MARKET AND NONMARKET ECONOMIES

(A) INTRODUCTION [1]

The term "nonmarket economy" is commonly used to describe countries where goods and resources are allocated by government planning agencies rather than by prices freely set in a market. Thus, people and not markets balance supply and demand. In general, the Communist bloc countries are viewed as having nonmarket economies, while the developed Western countries are viewed as having market economies. This categorization is not as precise as might be desired. For example, some members of the Communist bloc, in particular Hungary and China, have recently instituted new economic rules that permit market forces to play a role in some sectors of their economies.[2] On the other hand, the governments of some Western countries exercise such extensive direct control over certain economic sectors, e.g., through government ownership of companies, that market forces are of arguably little importance in those sectors.[3] This definitional difficulty is exacerbated when developing countries are considered since government control of at least some economic sectors is a common feature of many of their economies.[4]

A common feature of a nonmarket economy is the existence of government controlled entities through which all international trade in particular goods must be channelled. These entities, commonly called "state trading agencies" or "state trading monopolies," are also found in Western countries.

---

1. See generally T. Hoya, East West Trade—Comecon Law—American Soviet Trade (1984); D. Loeber, East West Trade (3 vols. 1976–77).

2. See Section 10.2(C)(2) supra (Hungary).

3. In the EC for example, the EC Commission exercises considerable control over the output and pricing decisions of steel companies. See Commission of the European Communities, Eighteenth Annual Report of the Activities of the Community 99–102 (1985).

4. See Section 4.5 supra.

For example, in many European countries government monopolies have existed for various products, such as tobacco and salt. These monopolies were considered to be sufficiently serious barriers to free trade within the EC that they were significantly limited under the Treaty of Rome.[5] Another common example can be found in respect of exports of agricultural products. Such exports, particularly if significant to the national economy, are often controlled by marketing boards with exclusive marketing rights. For example, in Canada, sales of grain abroad are the exclusive prerogative of the Canadian Wheat Board.[6]

The GATT trading system is based on principles of free trade in free markets. The GATT rules make sense in that context. As we demonstrate below, they make much less sense in the case of trade involving nonmarket economies or state trading monopolies. This problem was of course recognized at the time GATT was drafted. Unfortunately, the only treatment of the problem was in Article XVII, which deals with state trading monopolies. As we will see, that treatment was not completely satisfactory for application to isolated instances of such monopolies in market economies, let alone for dealing with nonmarket economies in general.

After a brief introduction in the next subsection to the structure in which international trade is typically conducted in a nonmarket economy, we consider in Section 21.2 how nonmarket economies and state trading monopolies fit into the GATT system. As has already been suggested, the simple answer is that they do not. Nonetheless, they must somehow be accommodated, and we examine how GATT has attempted to do that. We then analyze U.S. laws specifically aimed at the principal nonmarket economies, i.e. the Communist bloc. Finally, we consider the problem of countertrade—the exchange of goods not for money, but for other goods. Although becoming a common feature of international trade involving all countries, we deal with it here because it was first utilized significantly by nonmarket economies.

(B) THE STRUCTURE OF INTERNATIONAL TRADE IN NONMARKET ECONOMIES

The organization of international trade varies in detail from one nonmarket economy to another and varies over time within such an economy. There are nonetheless basic structural features that are common to most nonmarket economies and that are found most notably in the Soviet Union. The following excerpt summarizes the Soviet foreign trading system and discusses a number of legal issues that arise in contracting with an entity in a nonmarket economy, including in particular the problem of dispute settlement. The reader should also review the materials in Section 4.4 supra concerning COMECON, the Council for Mutual Economic Assistance—sometimes referred to as the East European Common Market.

5. Article 37 of the Treaty of Rome provides: "Member States shall progressively adjust any State monopolies of a commercial character so as to ensure that * * * no discrimination regarding the conditions under which goods are procured and marketed exists between nationals of Member States." See generally Commission of the European Communities, note 3 supra, at 116–17.

6. Canadian Wheat Board Act, 1935, Revised Statutes of Canada, c. C–12 (1970).

HAROLD J. BERMAN & GEORGE L. BUSTIN, THE SOVIET SYSTEM OF FOREIGN TRADE

(1975) [7]

Foreign trade is designated by the Soviet Constitution, by Soviet legislation, and by Soviet writers as a "state monopoly." Although many other branches of the Soviet economy are also within the exclusive competence of state agencies, the distinctive phrase "state monopoly" is used only to refer to foreign trade. The reasons are partly historical; foreign trade was declared to be a state monopoly as early as April 1918—it was one of the first of the "commanding heights" of the economy to be taken into the hands of the state after the Bolshevik Revolution. The phrase "state monopoly" also reflects the fact that the planning, administration, and conduct of foreign trade are and always have been much more highly centralized than the planning, administration, and conduct of most other major branches of the Soviet planned economy.

The planning—as distinct from administration and conduct—of Soviet foreign trade is part of the task of overall national economic planning assigned to the State Planning Committee of the USSR Council of Ministers. In addition, Soviet foreign trade policy, being linked with general foreign policy, must be worked out in conjunction with the USSR Ministry of Foreign Affairs. Behind these and other *governmental* planning and policy agencies responsible for foreign trade stand *party* agencies responsible for foreign trade within the Central Committee of the Communist Party of the Soviet Union, headed by the Politburo.

Within this broader framework of planning and policy the chief responsibility for administering and conducting Soviet foreign trade rests with the USSR Ministry of Foreign Trade and its subordinate Trade Representations and Foreign Trade Organizations (FTOs). Since the late 1950s, however, various other branches of the USSR Council of Ministers—State Committees and Ministries—have also been assigned tasks in the area of foreign trade. Of these the most important is the State Committee on Foreign Economic Relations, formed in 1957, which is in charge of certain aspects of trade with, and aid to, other socialist countries and developing non-socialist countries. Also the State Committee on Science and Technology, formed in 1961, plays an important intermediary role in the acquisition for the Soviet Union of foreign technology and know-how.

* * *

I. THE ADMINISTRATION AND CONDUCT OF SOVIET FOREIGN TRADE

A. *The Ministry of Foreign Trade and Its Subordinates*

Under the USSR Constitution, the Ministry of Foreign Trade is an all-union ministry with a permanent seat on the USSR Council of Ministers. It is charged with the following principal tasks: (a) helping to prepare export and import plans, (b) helping to draft and negotiate trade agreements with

---

7. From R. Starr (ed.), Business Transactions with the U.S.S.R., ch. 2. Reprinted by permission of the American Bar Association.

See also J. Quigley, The Soviet Foreign Trade Monopoly: Institutions and Laws (1974).

foreign governments, (c) directing the export and import activities of Trade Representations of the USSR situated abroad and of the All-Union Foreign Trade Organizations situated in the Soviet Union, (d) issuing licenses for export, import and transit of goods, (e) elaborating customs policy and administering the customs regulations issued by it under that policy, and (f) generally formulating and administering rules for import and export of goods.

*   *   *

Foreign Trade Organizations. By far the most active, or at least the most visible, of the instrumentalities of the Soviet foreign trade monopoly are the FTOs, of which there were 61 early in 1974.[8] These *   *   * are legal entities (*Iuridicheskie litsa*, "juridicial persons"). Each may acquire property rights and duties in its own name and may sue and be sued. Each is responsible for debts out of those of its assets which are within its power of free disposition. It receives a charter which enumerates its powers and declares the amount of its chartered capital. It operates on the basis of "economic accountability" (*Khozraschot*), that is, roughly, on the basis of profit and loss, like most state production or supply enterprises in the Soviet Union, with which, indeed, the FTO may make binding contracts. The pursuit of profits by FTOs, as by Soviet state enterprises generally, is encouraged by a system of incentives in which a percentage of the annual net profit of the FTO is retained by it for allocation to special "funds" from which bonuses are paid and certain other benefits obtained.

Thus the Soviet state—i.e., the treasury or fisc—is not liable under Soviet law for the obligations of the FTO, nor is the FTO liable for the obligations of the Soviet state or of any state organization other than itself.

The separate identity of the FTO is reinforced by the specificity of its functions. Each is given the exclusive right—and duty—to engage in foreign trade transactions or services of a specific character, defined in terms either of product or of geographic market or of type of service. For example, all Soviet exports of lumber and of lumber products, such as cellulose and paper, are transacted by the All-Union Export-Import Organization Eksportles. (*Les* means "lumber.") Similarly, all exports and imports of oil (*neft*) and oil products are within the charter competence of Soiuznefteksport. Vostokintorg, on the other hand, handles export and import transactions with the Mongolian People's Republic, Afghanistan, Iran, Turkey, and the Arab Republic of Yemen in a wide variety of goods ranging from rolled steel and cement to citrus fruits and almonds. Other FTOs provide insurance (Ingosstrakh), or carriage of goods by sea (Sovfrakht), or tourist services (Intourist), or technical assistance of various kinds.

*   *   *

[The authors, Professor Berman and Mr. Bustin, then proceed to examine "legal problems arising from the Soviet system of administration and conduct of foreign trade," which include questions such as the following:

8. In 1984, sixty-four FTOs were listed in Businessman's Moscow 84, a publication of the advertising FTO.

(1) The nonliability of the Soviet state for obligations incurred by the Soviet foreign trade organizations.

(2) Problems arising from substantive norms of Soviet contract law, particularly:

(a) Formal governmental requirements of Soviet foreign trade contracts;

(b) Strict doctrine of ultra vires in Soviet law;

(c) More extensive use of penalty clauses;

(d) Stronger insistence on performance guarantees or warranties;

(e) A narrow doctrine of force majeure, rather than broader frustration of purpose and impossibility doctrines.]

C. THE IMPARTIALITY OF SOVIET FOREIGN TRADE ARBITRATION

The FTAC was established in 1932 to serve at least two purposes of the Soviet state as its trade relations with capitalist countries began to expand in the early 1930s. First, it was intended to provide the means for avoiding the submission of disputes involving Soviet FTOs to hostile bourgeois courts for judgment under an ideologically unacceptable foreign law. Recognizing that foreigners could not easily be brought within the jurisdiction of the regular Soviet courts, and further that those courts lacked expertise in resolving foreign trade disputes, the Soviet policymakers wisely placed their hopes in an arbitral body to whose jurisdiction foreigners might be persuaded to accede voluntarily. The second purpose of establishing the Commission—assuming its first purpose could be accomplished—was to enhance the international reputation of Soviet commercial and legal institutions and concepts as well as to accommodate those institutions and concepts to international standards.

In the course of more than 40 years, the FTAC has undoubtedly succeeded in the fulfillment of these aims. A very large number, and apparently a very large proportion, of disputes arising between Soviet FTOs and their foreign trading partners have been resolved by it. This is due partly, but by no means solely, to the fact that the FTOs have generally pressed for a clause submitting disputes to its jurisdiction. In fact, they do not invariably insist on such a clause—contrary to the assertions of some writers; many of their contracts provide for arbitration in other countries, and some contain no arbitration clause whatsoever. Moreover, where non-Soviet parties do accept Moscow arbitration, it is due in part to the fact that after some years of only begrudging acceptance by the international trading community, the FTAC has gained a reputation for a high degree of professional competence and of fairness. Sheer bargaining power of Soviet FTOs could hardly have saved it from desuetude if its reputation were otherwise.

There is nothing in the rules of procedure of the FTAC to put its impartiality in doubt.

*   *   *

* * * As we indicated earlier, Soviet FTOs have often accepted third-country arbitration, and there is good evidence that, during the last year or so, they have been far more flexible in this regard (at least in their

negotiations with American traders) than in the past. This Soviet behavior may derive from a provision which the US government wrung from the Soviet government in the 1972 US–USSR Trade Agreement, to the effect that both governments would "encourage" their traders to agree to arbitration in a third country under the rules of the United Nations Economic Commission for Europe. Presumably, a word of encouragement from the Soviet government to one of its FTOs would be sufficient. However, it would be premature to conclude that American traders need no longer seriously contemplate the prospect of arbitration in Moscow, Soviet trade negotiators may always offer concessions in other terms (including price) in exchange for the convenience of arbitration in the home forum. Moreover, the same article of the 1972 Agreement cited earlier goes on to provide that "[s]uch (natural and legal) persons (of the United States) and (foreign trade) organizations (of the USSR), however, may decide upon any other form of arbitration which they mutually prefer and agree best suits their particular needs"—a clause which the Soviet government wrung out of the United States. A number of recent contracts in Soviet-American trade have, in fact, included terms specifying arbitration at the Moscow Commission, and in simple transactions for the purchase and sale of goods such terms may continue to be the rule. Moreover, most Soviet-American trade in the first two years since the signing of the Trade Agreement has consisted of US exports to the Soviet Union; when Soviet exports to the United States increase in volume, it may well be that Soviet parties will be in a stronger position to bargain for Moscow arbitration.

SECTION 21.2 GATT AND NONMARKET ECONOMIES: THE PROBLEM OF INTERFACE

(A) AN OVERVIEW OF THE INTERFACE PROBLEM [1]

A basic structural assumption of GATT is an international, free market system for trading. Many of the GATT rules make sense only in the context of such a market system, since they restrict the types of regulations which governments can impose on international traders, but do not purport to regulate the traders themselves. This makes the problem of integrating nonmarket systems into GATT very difficult.

This problem can be seen in a number of different contexts. For example, how can the rules against dumping be applied to exports from a nonmarket economy when there is no freely determined price in that economy to which the export price can be compared? How can the rules against subsidies be applied when government control so permeates an economy that either everything or nothing can be considered a subsidy? These last two questions were explored in Sections 10.2(C)(2)(c) and 10.3(C)(2)(d) supra. The problem as to what constitutes a subsidy in a nonmarket economy is particularly difficult and the Subsidies Code explicitly provides

---

1. See generally D. Wallace, G. Spina, R. Rawson & B. McGill (eds.), Interface One (1980).

in Article 15:1 that antidumping rules may be applied in lieu of the antisubsidy rules. But as noted in the Interpretative Notes to Article VI of the GATT Agreement, there are problems calculating dumping margins in the case of state trading countries. U.S. legislators have proposed that a new rule is needed to deal with unfair trade practices by nonmarket economies. One such proposal would subject imports from nonmarket economies to offsetting duties if they are made at prices below the average prices charged by the most suitable U.S. producer or market economy foreign exporter.[2]

There are, however, more fundamental problems to be faced in integrating nonmarket economies into the GATT trading system. How can the rule against use of quantitative restrictions be applied to a nonmarket economy where a government agency determines import and export levels in advance? Even more basic, how can negotiations over tariff levels—the essential subject matter of GATT negotiations—be meaningful if import levels are determined not by tariffs, but rather by economic plans? The following hypothetical situation illustrates this problem.

Let us assume that country M, a market economy country, and country S, a socialist or nonmarket economy country, are both members of GATT. GATT limits the use of quantitative restrictions on the importation of goods, and provides for negotiation leading to "tariff bindings" restricting the level of tariffs which a country can impose on its imports from GATT member countries. Suppose countries M and S have negotiated between themselves and M has promised to bind its tariff on bicycles and widgets at no more than 10%. Suppose S has agreed to bind its tariffs on automobiles and gadgets at no more than 8% and 12%, respectively. In the case of M, private traders will go into the international market and buy goods for the importation into M, with the confidence that they will be able to import without incurring more than a 10% tariff charge. They can price their goods accordingly and proceed to import goods. If the tariff has been higher previously, the lower price due to the tariff binding should cause an increase in imports.

In the case of S, however, importing is accomplished only through a state trading monopoly, which is regulated by the government and pursues its import plans according to the economic plan of the country (and other foreign policy considerations). Consequently, the state trading monopoly can decide, as a matter of enterprise decision, to import no more than a given quantity of automobiles or gadgets, and could conceivably decide to import those only from country A or B, rather than M. The fact that the tariff on automobiles and gadgets had been lowered would not necessarily result in an increase of imports. Consequently, M can argue that it has not received reciprocity for its trade concessions given to S in the previous negotiations. S can sell more goods to M, through M's private traders; but M cannot sell more goods to S, because S's state trading agency has simply decided not to purchase more goods.

In an oversimplified form, this hypothetical situation illustrates the major problem of establishing trade relations between Communist or

---

2. See, e.g., S. 1351, 98th Cong., 1st Sess. (1983).

nonmarket economies on the one hand, and the industrialized free market economies on the other.

After considering the terms of Article XVII—the only GATT provision dealing with nonmarket economies, we will examine how GATT has in fact dealt with the interface problem in admitting several East European countries to membership.

(B) THE GATT RULES AND STATE TRADING [3]

The principal obligations of GATT concerning state trading enterprises are those contained in Article XVII. In addition, Article II, paragraph 4, contains an obligation relating to import monopolies. Article XVII applies to "state enterprises" and enterprises that have "exclusive or special privileges." Apart from a provision requiring notification to GATT of products which are covered by such enterprises, the obligations of Article XVII have not generally been considered to be very stringent. A modified or relaxed form of the "Most-Favored-Nation" obligation seems to be the general thrust of Article XVII, as one reads the text. Several GATT reports have elaborated possible interpretations of Article XVII.

The scope of paragraph 1(a) has been most often discussed in GATT in connection with the obligation of paragraph 4(a) of Article XVII, to notify products imported or exported by enterprises covered in paragraph 1(a). In a 1959 report [4] adopted by the CONTRACTING PARTIES, a panel constituted to review notifications of state trading measures drew some interpretative conclusions, as follows:

> (a) [N]ot only State enterprises are covered by the provisions of Article XVII, but all enterprises which enjoy "exclusive or special privileges";
>
> (b) [M]arketing boards engaged directly or indirectly in purchasing or selling are enterprises in the sense of Article XVII paragraphs 1(a) and 1(b), but the activities of marketing boards which do not purchase or sell must be in accordance with the other provisions of GATT. * * *

In a 1960 report,[5] this GATT panel further discussed the meaning of "enterprise" within Article XVII, paragraph 1(a), as follows:

> 21. In this phrase the Panel did not use the word "enterprise" to mean any instrumentality of government. There would be nothing gained in extending the scope of the notification provisions of Article XVII to cover governmental measures that are covered by other articles of the General Agreement. The term "enterprise" was used to refer either to an instrumentality of government which has the power to buy or sell, or to a nongovernmental body with such power and to which the government has granted exclusive or special privileges.

3. See generally J. Jackson, World Trade and the Law of GATT ch. 14 (1969); M. Kostecki, East-West Trade and the GATT System (1978); Ianni, The International Treatment of State Trading, 16 J. World Trade L. 480 (1982).

4. Notifications of State-Trading Enterprises, Report adopted on 13 May, 1959 (GATT Doc.L/970), GATT, 8th Supp. BISD 142–43 (1960).

5. Notifications of State-Trading Enterprises, Final Report adopted on 24 May, 1960 (GATT Doc.L./1146), GATT, 9th Supp. BISD 179, 183–84 (1961).

(What Enterprises are Affected?)

The activities of a marketing board or any enterprise defined in paragraph 1(a) of Article XVII should be notified where that body has the ability to influence the level or direction of imports or exports by its buying or selling.

22.   It is clear from the interpretative note to paragraph 1 of Article XVII that the activities of a marketing board or any enterprise covered by paragraph 1(a) of the Article and not covered by paragraph 21 of this report would not be notifiable solely by virtue of a power to influence exports or imports by the exercise of overt licensing powers; where such measures are taken they would be subject to other Articles of the General Agreement.

23.   Where, however, an enterprise is granted exclusive or special privileges, exports or imports carried out pursuant to those privileges should be notified even if the enterprise is not itself the exporter or importer.

As to the substance of the obligation imposed upon the state enterprises,[6]

> The preparatory work reflects that the words "general principles of nondiscriminatory treatment" were inserted in Article XVII, paragraph 1(a), at Geneva (1947) in order to allay the doubt that " 'commercial principles' [in Article XVII, paragraph 1(b)] meant that exactly the same price would have to exist in different markets." Thus it appears that what is meant by "nondiscriminatory treatment" is a Most-Favored-Nation principle tempered by "commercial considerations," such as those listed in Article XVII, paragraph 1(b). The obligation in this paragraph also requires that adequate opportunity be granted to the other contracting parties' enterprises to compete "in accordance with customary business practice," which the draftsmen understood was "intended to cover business practices customary in the respective line of trade."

One of the authors has argued elsewhere that the preparatory work for the drafting of GATT seems to limit the notion of Article XVII to an "MFN" nondiscriminatory treatment obligation, and it was not intended for this article to also require "a national treatment standard." Thus, the enterprise is entitled to discriminate between domestic and foreign products in its purchases or its sales, as long as it does so on an "MFN" basis. An explicit exception for "tied loans" is covered in an interpretative note.[7] Another interpretative note, however, explicitly provides that the term "quantitative restrictions," which restrictions are prohibited or governed by Articles XI through XIV and Article XVIII of GATT, was meant to include restrictions "made effective through state trading operations." [8]

This clause in Article II, paragraph 4 of GATT, relating to import monopolies, adds another obligation. If the tariff binding exists in the schedule of a country, it may not evade that binding through the use of an import monopoly. But the interpretative problems are considerable.

6.   J. Jackson, note 3 supra, at 346.

7.   General Agreement on Tariffs and Trade (GATT), Annex I, Notes and Supplementary Provisions, Ad. Article XVII, para. 1(b).

8.   General Agreement on Tariffs and Trade (GATT), Annex I, Notes and Supplementary Provisions, Ad. Articles XI, XII, XIII, XIV and XVIII; see J. Jackson, note 3 supra, at 348.

There are, moreover, a number of exceptions to the state trading obligations of GATT.

(C) NONMARKET ECONOMIES IN GATT

The problems of integrating a nonmarket economy into the GATT system perplexed the drafters of GATT and the ITO Charter. The provisions now in GATT do not go as far toward attempting to resolve these problems as did the ITO Charter, which provided, inter alia, for the encouragement of negotiations on binding the "mark up" or difference between the purchase price paid by a state trading agency and the price charged by that agency on its resale. Such a binding would have the effect of limiting the extent to which a state trading agency could utilize domestic pricing policies to discourage purchases of the imported product. It did not, of course, deal with the problem that the state trading agency might simply decline to purchase the product.

GATT first had to face the problem of integrating nonmarket economies in the 1960's when Poland applied for membership. Poland was admitted and more recently Romania and Hungary have become members of GATT.[9] (Cuba and Czechoslovakia, each of which is a nonmarket economy, became members of GATT when they were market economies.) Yugoslavia is also a member, but has a sufficiently market-oriented economy that its membership was not thought to raise the problems encountered when the other East European countries applied for membership.[10] Although until recently the Soviet Union had expressed no interest in GATT membership, China has given some indications that it may be interested in joining GATT. Indeed, it is a party to the Multifiber Arrangement sponsored by GATT.[11] The prospect of Chinese or Russian membership raises the problems of interface to a vastly greater degree than did membership for Poland, Romania and Hungary. The volume of trade involving China, not only now but especially in the future, would be of a completely different order of magnitude. Moreover, China's level of development is currently much below that of the Soviet Union and the East European GATT members. Thus, membership for China presents the dual problem of integrating into GATT a large state-trading and developing country.

In reviewing GATT's handling of the admission of the East European countries, as described in the following materials, the reader should consider whether the accommodations reached would work in the case of China or the Soviet Union. The three countries discussed include the most market oriented East European country (Hungary), one of the poorest East European countries (Romania) and one of perhaps the more typical state trading countries (Poland).

9. See Protocol for the Accession of Poland, GATT, 15th Supp. BISD 46 (1968); Protocol for the Accession of Romania, GATT, 18th Supp. BISD 5 (1972); Protocol for the Accession of Hungary, GATT, 19th Supp. BISD 5 (1974).

10. J. Jackson, note 3 supra, at 363.

11. See U.S. Dept. of State, Treaties in Force (1985).

M.M. KOSTECKI, EAST–WEST TRADE AND
THE GATT SYSTEM
91–98 (1978) [12]

The GATT * * * was drafted for market economies, controlling their trade essentially by means of price-mechanism devices, and resorting to state trading only occasionally. Its provisions could therefore be expected to apply only with difficulty to Eastern European state-trading economies controlling their trade by means of plan targets, especially in view of the GATT principles of non-discrimination and reciprocity and to the GATT rules on integration.

*   *   *

Basically, the problem of finding a reciprocity formula for trade with the target-protected economies could have been approached in two ways: exchange of tariff reduction by the tariff-protected economy for import expansion on the part of the target-protected economy; or explicit provision for exchange of tariff reduction for a commitment to reduce level of protection.

The first solution had proved to be realistic in the past. The earliest examples of this type of reciprocity arrangement were the bilateral trade agreements concluded by Soviet Russia with some market economies in the 1920s. The reciprocity formula provided for tariff concessions by the Western governments in exchange for import commitments from the target-protected economy. These arrangements were usually supplemented by safeguard clauses that provided for a right to suspend application of the tariff reduction if the target-protected economy failed to make the purchases envisaged.

*   *   *

Poland's participation in the GATT provided the first occasion where a multilateral reciprocity formula for trade relations with a target-protected economy could be used. Initially, Poland desired a reciprocity formula based on her import commitment in respect to certain goods. Two main proposals were discussed.

The first proposal provided for the establishment of a Polish import commitment through negotiations on an item-by-item basis. The Polish Government suggested that the initial negotiated import level should be established through a representative period approach. Its partners, however, were assured that the approach did not exclude the possibility of establishing new import rights to the Polish market. In the Polish view, allocation of the imports by country should either take place during negotiations or be regulated by some scheme like tenders. The suggestion was rightly refused on the grounds that it conflicted with the GATT principle of non-discrimination, banning country-specific direct trade control. Instead, it was decided that any interested enterprise from the GATT countries might compete for the Polish market; it would then be up to the Polish import unit

12. © M.M. Kostecki and the Trade Policy Research Centre 1978 and reprinted by permission of St. Martin's Press Inc.

to choose the most advantageous offer according to normal commercial practice.

The suggested formula relied thus on item-by-item concessions. * * *

The second formula suggested for Poland's participation in the Kennedy Round provided that:

> Increased export earnings obtained by Poland as a result of tariff cuts or elimination of other barriers to her exports to the contracting parties will be used to increase her imports from the contracting parties in proportions and on the conditions to be agreed upon.

It was supposed to be achieved by the intermediary of a 'special fund' consisting of savings from import duties which would be used for additional imports. The exact proportion of these savings, which should be reflected in increased imports to Poland, would be subject to negotiations. Poland was also expected to agree with interested members of the GATT to include certain categories of goods in its import plans or to secure for certain imports a percentage increase higher than that for average Polish imports.

Thus the project provided mainly for exchange of linear concessions with item-by-item bargaining reserved for exceptional cases. To this extent the suggested formula was in conformity with that of the Kennedy Round negotiations. The proposal strongly emphasized the balance-of-trade criterion for reciprocity and to a country like Poland, under continuous balance-of-payments pressure, this was of no minor importance.

The formula finally agreed upon for Poland in the GATT, provided that, in return for tariff reductions by the GATT partners, the Polish Government would undertake to:

> increase the total value of its imports from the territories of contracting parties by not less than 7 per cent per annum.

* * *

The Polish reciprocity arrangement, however, suffers from some important weaknesses. First of all, the formula does not pay enough attention to the balance-of-trade criterion of reciprocity. It does not establish any direct link between export and import performance to the disadvantage of Poland which suffers from permanent balance-of-payment pressure. Secondly, the Polish import commitment is to be evaluated on the basis of current dollar prices. No inflation clause or provision permitting adjustments for the fall of the dollar *vis-à-vis* other currencies are included in the Polish-GATT arrangement. This is a serious omission which also works to the disadvantage of Poland's GATT partners and may considerably limit the effectiveness of Polish concessions. Finally, the global character of the Polish commitment, and especially the lack of explicit recommendations for negotiation on specific import targets, did not seem an appropriate framework in which to determine Western market openings for Polish exports. * * *

Poland's 7 per cent annual commitment was replaced three years later by a compound commitment. It provided essentially for the same average rate of import increase per annum, but it was to be calculated over a longer range of time. This rendered the Polish cooperation with the GATT much more flexible—since a shortfall of Poland's imports in one year could be offset by a satisfactory import performance in another year and an average of 7 per cent import increase could be maintained.

* * *

Though at the time of its accession to the GATT, Romania—like Poland—was a target-protected economy, it decidedly opposed any type of arrangement based on an obligation to increase imports from the GATT countries.

Romania was a low-income economy. It was thought that this should be kept in mind in negotiations on the reciprocity formula with GATT members. The GATT should not expect the less-developed countries to make contributions that were inconsistent with their development needs.

* * *

The final text of the arrangement provided that, in exchange for better access to the GATT markets, Romania firmly intends:

> to increase its imports from the contracting parties as a whole at a rate not smaller than the growth of total Romanian imports provided for in its Five-Year Plan.

* * *

The Romanian arrangement also distinguishes between imports from the contracting parties and total Romanian imports. It seems to aim at assuring the GATT countries of, what could be called, a "fair share" of total Romanian imports. From the economic perspective the "fair share" approach is not fully understandable in the context of GATT principles. It is hardly possible to relate it to the GATT concept of nondiscrimination or to the provisions on regional integration. "Fair share" in import expansion says nothing about non-discrimination, or protection—and non-discrimination and protection are what the GATT is about.

* * *

Hungary considered its customs tariffs a main protective element and desired to accede to the GATT on this basis. Therefore, the function and effects of the Hungarian tariffs and the applicability of the GATT traditional reciprocity formula became the main objects of examination during negotiations with Hungary.

The Hungarian tariff approach met with scepticism from some GATT countries (especially the European Community members, Canada, the United Kingdom and Sweden). They noted that the effectiveness of the Hungarian tariff could be weakened by quotas, operation of monopolies on the domestic markets and restrictions on free price formation in Hungary. It was thus put forward that a quantitative import commitment along the lines of the Polish solution was required to assure reciprocity at least during an initial period. If the Hungarian tariff proved effective, a quantitative commitment would then be replaced by a tariff arrangement.

The Hungarian Government contended on its part that it did not dispose of any direct means to guarantee the value of overall imports from the GATT countries, since no import targets were maintained for trade with the market economies. Besides, it noted that most GATT countries combined tariffs with other instruments of trade control and that this did not prevent them from agreeing on the exchange of tariff concessions.

* * *

Thus the GATT countries accepted the tariff approach as valid for Hungary and concurred that reciprocity could be reached on the basis of a symmetric reciprocity formula as traditionally adopted in the negotiations of tariff-protected members of the GATT. In this respect Hungary followed the Yugoslav example of participation in the General Agreement.

Notes and Questions

(1) The issue of access by GATT members to the "markets" of nonmarket economies has a converse. To what extent will the nonmarket economies enjoy access to the markets of other GATT members? As we will see in the next section, the United States has been slow to grant most-favored-nation treatment to Communist countries. As for the EC, it continues to maintain an extensive quota system regulating imports from those countries.[13] This problem continues to fester, as is indicated in the regular reviews held in respect of the accession of these countries.

(2) In addition to the question of access to East European markets in general, which is treated in the Kostecki excerpt, there is the question of whether that access will be accorded on the same terms as access is given to trade with other members of COMECON, as would normally be required by GATT's MFN requirements. Because of the difficult political issues raised by this question, it was largely not treated in the protocols of accession of the three countries discussed above, although the Romanian "fair share" commitment does address the question to some extent. The Hungarian protocol rather vaguely provided that Hungary's relations with other COMECON members should not detrimentally affect the interests of other GATT members.

(3) Each of the three protocols of accession provided for regular reviews of their implementation. These reviews have in particular considered the problems of market access, in both directions.[14]

(4) Which of the arrangements described above is most consistent with GATT principles? Which would you suggest as the best basis for negotiating Chinese accession to GATT? Why?

SECTION 21.3   THE UNITED STATES AND COMMUNIST COUNTRIES

United States controls on exports to Communist countries were analyzed in Chapters 12 and 13 supra. In this section, we consider U.S. treatment of imports from Communist countries. In general, the United States has not extended most-favored-nation treatment to imports from most Communist countries[1] and they are not eligible to participate in the U.S. Generalized

---

13. See [1985] Eur.Comm.O.J. No. C 196.

14. See, e.g., GATT, 24th Supp. BISD 139 (1979) (Poland); GATT, 30th Supp. BISD 194 (1984) (Romania); GATT, 31st Supp. BISD 180 (1985) (Hungary).

1. The following Communist countries do not benefit from U.S. most-favored-nation

treatment: Afghanistan, Albania, Bulgaria, Cuba, Czechoslovakia, Estonia, German Democratic Republic and East Berlin, Indochina (any part of Cambodia, Laos, or Vietnam which may be under Communist domination or control), Korea (any part of which may be under Communist domination or control),

System of Preferences program.[2] This means that imports from those countries are subject to the high duties established in the Smoot-Hawley Tariff Act of 1930. To a large degree this situation is the result of congressional mandate. In this section, we describe briefly the history and current status of legislation on these subjects.

The United States extended most-favored-treatment to the Soviet Union in 1937.[3] However, in 1951 Congress directed that MFN treatment be withdrawn from all countries controlled or dominated by the World Communist movement.[4] Yugoslavia was not so considered. In 1960, as a part of a settlement of various differences with Poland, the President extended MFN treatment to Poland, finding that Poland was not Soviet dominated.[5] Thereafter, in 1962, Congress passed legislation requiring the denial of MFN treatment to all countries dominated or controlled by communism.[6] A short time later in 1963 Congress provided that MFN treatment did not have to be withdrawn from Yugoslavia or Poland.[7] Then in 1972, the United States entered into a trade agreement with the Soviet Union, which provided that Soviet exports to the United States were to receive MFN treatment.[8] It was understood that implementation of that part of the trade agreement would require congressional action. The President proposed approval of the MFN agreement as part of the general trade bill introduced in 1973, which eventually was adopted as the Trade Act of 1974. The provisions dealing with MFN and Communist countries were the most controversial in the proposed legislation. The controversy centered on the extent to which the United States should use the prospect of granting MFN treatment to the Soviet Union as a lever to extract Soviet policy changes in other areas, and, in particular, the expansion of emigration opportunities for Soviet citizens.

The following materials describe the background of the controversy and provisions of the Trade Act that were affected by it.

NOTE, AN INTERIM ANALYSIS OF THE EFFECTS OF THE JACKSON–VANIK AMENDMENT ON TRADE AND HUMAN RIGHTS: THE ROMANIAN EXAMPLE

(1976) [9]

Following the May 1972 summit meeting in Moscow, President Nixon announced that the United States would soon begin negotiations with the

Kurile Islands, Latvia, Lithuania, Outer Mongolia, Polish People's Republic, Southern Sakhalin, Tanna Tuva and the Union of Soviet Socialist Republics and the area in East Prussia under its provisional administration. Headnote 3(d), Tariff Schedules of the United States Annotated (1985).

2. Trade Act of 1974, Section 502(b)(1); 19 U.S.C.A. § 2462(b)(1).

3. Presidential Proclamation, 50 Stat. 1619 (1937).

4. Pub.L. No. 49, ch. 139, § 5, 65 Stat. 73 (1951).

5. 25 Fed.Reg. 12501 (1960).

6. Trade Expansion Act of 1962, Pub.L. No. 87–794, § 231, 76 Stat. 876 (1962).

7. Pub.L. No. 88–205, § 402, 77 Stat. 390 (1963).

8. U.S.–U.S.S.R. Agreement Regarding Trade, with annexes and exchange of letters; signed at Washington, 18 Oct. 1972. For reasons made clear in the text of this section, this agreement failed to enter into force.

9. 8 Law & Poly. Intl. Bus. 193, 195–219. Reprinted by permission of Journal of Law and Policy in International Business.

U.S.S.R. on a reciprocal trade agreement which was to include MFN treatment. Shortly thereafter, the U.S.S.R. imposed a tax of from $5,000 to $30,000 on persons wishing to emigrate as compensation for their "free education" from the State. This and other Soviet emigration policies were perceived as being directed at Russian Jews, and resulted in an organized campaign of retaliation by the American Jewish community. A loosely-knit coalition, led by Senators Jackson, Jacob Javits, Abraham Ribicoff, and Representative Vanik, and strongly supported by the National Conference on Soviet Jewry, initially conceived the idea of linking trade to emigration.

On September 26, 1972, Senator Jackson announced the amendment proposal at a Washington, D.C., meeting of Jewish leaders: "The time has come to place our highest human values ahead of the trade dollar." By combining intense Jewish constituent and congressional staff pressure on his colleagues, Jackson formally introduced his amendment to the Senate on October 4, 1972, with 72 senators listed as co-sponsors. He justified the internal intervention in Soviet affairs with a moral appeal, quoting Alexander Solzhenitsyn: "There are no internal affairs left on our crowded Earth." Congressman Vanik, Jackson's chief ally in the House, utilized the same tactics and had enlisted 259 co-sponsors by the time he formally introduced the amendment to the House on February 7, 1973.

* * *

Jewish leaders also produced evidence of over 100 years of U.S. intervention in the internal affairs of other countries on behalf of humanitarian causes. Particularly relevant was the abrogation, in 1913, of an 80-year-old Soviet-U.S. commercial treaty by the State Department after it had become clear that Congress was about to repeal it. The cause of the legislature's concern was the Czarist government's barbaric treatment of its Jewish minority. Publication of these abuses led to a massive popular movement for repeal of the treaty, culminating in a vote of 301 to 1 in the House of Representatives to repeal the treaty. Then, as now, the State Department led the fight against abrogation, arguing that "quiet and persistent endeavor" would be more effective than trade sanctions in changing Czarist policy, that U.S. commercial and industrial interests would be harmed, and that the United States had no right to intervene in the internal affairs of other countries. However, after the lopsided vote in the House, with Senate passage certain, the State Department quietly abrogated the treaty. Thus, the amendment supporters contended that similar restrictions on trade with Communist countries was in the best tradition of unqualified support for human rights in all countries.

[When the Act was passed with the linkage in it, U.S.S.R. representatives announced that the 1972 US-USSR trade agreement was at an end because the Act contradicted the commitments of the agreement.[10]]

* * * Soviet Foreign Trade Minister Nikolai Patolichev * * * announced on July 10, 1975, that the congressional emigration conditions "have nothing to do with trade and the economy [but] relate wholly to the internal competence of the U.S.S.R. It was entirely natural that the Soviet

10. 72 Dept. State Bull. 139–40 (1975).

Union felt itself unable to base its trading and economic dealings with the U.S.A. on legislation of this kind." Patolichev continued that limitations on trade are damaging only the United States itself, noting that while Congress debated the granting of $300 million in credits to the U.S.S.R., the Soviet Union received $7 billion in credit from other capitalist countries. Trade with Western Europe and Japan in general commodities is a clearly available alternative to the Soviet Union.

––––––

The Trade Act as passed tied the President's power to enter into commercial agreements with a Communist country and to grant MFN treatment to such country to the emigration rules of that country. The Act also provided, however, that the President could waive the free-emigration rule in certain circumstances. To prevent presidential misuse of the waiver power, the Act provided an elaborate process through which Congress had the right to review individual waivers granted by the President, as well as the right to review whether the waiver power should be continued at all. Although some of the congressional veto rights contained in the Act probably did not survive the *Chadha* decision, discussed in Section 3.2(C)(2) supra, a brief description of them is useful to indicate the extent of congressional concern in respect of this issue.

BACKGROUND MATERIALS RELATING TO UNITED STATES–ROMANIAN TRADE AND THE EXTENSION OF THE PRESIDENT'S POWER TO WAIVE SECTION 402 OF THE TRADE ACT OF 1974 [11]

Subsections 402(a) and (b) of the Trade Act prohibit the granting of MFN treatment, the extension of government credits, or the negotiation of a commercial agreement with any non-market economy country not now receiving MFN, if such country:

(1) denies its citizens the right or opportunity to emigrate;

(2) imposes more than a nominal tax on emigration; or

(3) imposes more than a nominal charge on any citizen who wants to emigrate to the country of his choice.

Section 402(c)(1) of the Trade Act authorizes the President to waive the requirements of section 402(a) and (b) until July 3, 1976, for any communist country if he reports to the Congress that:

(1) he has determined that the waiver for that country would substantially promote the objectives of freedom of emigration; and

(2) he has received assurances that the emigration practices of that country would henceforth lead substantially to the achievement of the objectives of freedom of emigration.

The first period for congressional review of the President's waiver authority has now begun. In recommending the extension for another 12 months of MFN treatment to Romania, the President has determined that

11. Senate Comm. on Finance, 94th Cong., 2d Sess. 1–3 (1976).

the continuation of his waiver authority promotes the objective of freedom of emigration. * * * The Trade Act establishes an elaborate timetable under which the extension of the President's waiver authority can be reviewed. * * *

Further extensions of the waiver authority may be recommended by the President for successive 12-month periods. In such event, either House of Congress will have a 60-day period following the end of the previous extension (July 3) in which to veto the extension. If neither House has vetoed the extension by the end of that period, it will be extended automatically until the following July 3.

Procedures for Review of the Waiver Provisions of Section 402 of the Trade Act

Beginning with the date of enactment of the Trade Act, January 3, 1975, the President was given authority to waive the requirements of section 402 until July 3, 1976, 18 months, for any country after receiving assurances that the emigration practices of that country will lead substantially to the achievement of the objectives of section 402.

Eighteen months after the date of enactment of the Act, the waiver authority may be renewed upon the adoption of a concurrent resolution extending the authority for one year. If an extension is desired, a request shall be made by the President no later than 30 days prior to expiration of the 18-month period, or June 3, 1976.

* * *

The waiver may be further extended by Executive order at one-year intervals upon a Presidential determination and report to Congress that such extension will substantially promote the objectives of Section 402, provided that neither House of Congress (within 60 calendar days of the issuance of the Executive Order) adopts a resolution of disapproval of the extension.

The statutory language permits the concurrent resolution or the simple resolution of disapproval to exclude one or more countries from the extensions of the waiver authority. Resolutions may be amended to include or exclude any particular country.

Any extension of waiver authority will not apply to any country which has been excluded in a concurrent resolution or in a resolution of either House.

Notes

(1) The meaning of the term "free emigration" as used in the Act is specified in an exchange of letters between Senator Jackson and Secretary of State Kissinger: [12]

October 18, 1974.

DEAR SENATOR JACKSON: I am writing to you, as the sponsor of the Jackson Amendment, in regard to the Trade Bill (H.R. 10710) which is currently

12. S.Rep.No. 93–1298, 93d Cong., 2d Sess. (1974).

before the Senate and in whose early passage the administration is deeply interested. As you know, Title IV of that bill, as it emerged from the House, is not acceptable to the administration. At the same time, the administration respects the objectives with regard to emigration from the U.S.S.R. that are sought by means of the stipulations in Title IV, even if it cannot accept the means employed. It respects in particular your own leadership in this field.

To advance the purposes we share both with regard to passage of the trade bill and to emigration from the U.S.S.R., and on the basis of discussions that have been conducted with Soviet representatives, I should like on behalf of the administration to inform you that we have been assured that the following criteria and practices will henceforth govern emigration from the U.S.S.R.

First, punitive actions against individuals seeking to emigrate from the U.S.S.R. would be violations of Soviet laws and regulations and will therefore not be permitted by the government of the U.S.S.R. In particular, this applies to various kinds of intimidation or reprisal, such as, for example, the firing of a person from his job, his demotion to tasks beneath his professional qualifications and his subjection to public or other kinds of recrimination.

Second, no unreasonable or unlawful impediments will be placed in the way of persons desiring to make application for emigration, such as interference with travel or communications necessary to complete an application, the withholding of necessary documentation and other obstacles including kinds frequently employed in the past.

Third, applications for emigration will be processed in order of receipt, including those previously filed, and on a nondiscriminatory basis as regards the place of residence, race, religion, national origin and professional status of the applicant. Concerning professional status, we are informed that there are limitations on emigration under Soviet law in the case of individuals holding certain security clearances, but that such individuals who desire to emigrate will be informed of the date on which they may expect to become eligible for emigration.

Fourth, hardship cases will be processed sympathetically and expeditiously; persons imprisoned who, prior to imprisonment expressed an interest in emigrating, will be given prompt consideration for emigration upon their release; and sympathetic consideration may be given to the early release of such persons.

Fifth, the collection of the so-called emigration tax on emigrants which was suspended last year will remain suspended.

Sixth, with respect to all the foregoing points, we will be in a position to bring to the attention of the Soviet leadership indications that we may have that these criteria and practices are not being applied. Our representations, which would include but not necessarily be limited to the precise matters enumerated in the foregoing points, will receive sympathetic consideration and response.

Finally, it will be our assumption that with the application of the criteria, practices, and procedures set forth in this letter, the rate of emigration from the U.S.S.R. would begin to rise promptly from the 1973 level and would continue to rise to correspond to the number of applicants.

I understand that you and your associates have, in addition, certain understandings incorporated in a letter dated today respecting the foregoing criteria and practices which will henceforth govern emigration from the U.S.S.R. which you wish the President to accept as appropriate guidelines to determine whether the purposes sought through Title IV of the trade bill and further specified in our exchange of correspondence in regard to the emigration practices of non-market economy countries are being fulfilled. You have submitted this letter to me and I wish to advise you on behalf of the President that the understandings in your letter will be among the considerations to be applied by the President in exercising the authority provided for in Sec. 402 of Title IV of the trade bill.

I believe that the contents of this letter represent a good basis, consistent with our shared purposes, for proceeding with an acceptable formulation of Title IV of the trade bill, including procedures for periodic review, so that normal trading relations may go forward for the mutual benefit of the U.S. and the U.S.S.R.

Best regards,
HENRY A. KISSINGER

October 18, 1974.

DEAR MR. SECRETARY: Thank you for your letter of Oct. 18 which I have now had an opportunity to review. Subject to the further understandings and interpretations outlined in this letter, I agree that we have achieved a suitable basis upon which to modify Title IV by incorporating within it a provision that would enable the President to waive subsections designated (a) and (b) in Sec. 402 of Title IV as passed by the House in circumstances that would substantially promote the objectives of Title IV.

It is our understanding that the punitive actions, intimidation or reprisals that will not be permitted by the government of the U.S.S.R. include the use of punitive conscription against persons seeking to emigrate, or members of their families; and the bringing of criminal actions against persons in circumstances that suggest a relationship between their desire to emigrate and the criminal prosecution against them.

Second, we understand that among the unreasonable impediments that will no longer be placed in the way of persons seeking to emigrate is the requirement that adult applicants receive the permission of their parents or other relatives.

Third, we understand that the special regulations to be applied to persons who have had access to genuinely sensitive classified information will not constitute an unreasonable impediment to emigration. In this connection we would expect such persons to become eligible for emigration within three years of the date on which they last were exposed to sensitive and classified information.

Fourth, we understand that the actual number of emigrants would rise promptly from the 1973 level and would continue to rise to correspond to the number of applicants, and may therefore exceed 60,000 per annum. We would consider a benchmark—a minimum standard of initial compliance—to be the issuance of visas at the rate of 60,000 per annum; and we understand that the President proposes to use the same benchmark as the minimum standard of initial compliance. Until such time as the actual number of emigrants corresponds to the number of applicants the benchmark figure will not include categories of persons whose emigration has been the subject of discussion between Soviet officials and other European governments.

In agreeing to provide discretionary authority to waive the provisions of subsections designated (a) and (b) in Sec. 402 of Title IV as passed by the House, we share your anticipation of good faith in the implementation of the assurances contained in your letter of Oct. 18 and the understandings conveyed by this letter. In particular, with respect to paragraphs three and four of your letter we wish it to be understood that the enumeration of types of punitive action and unreasonable impediments is not and cannot be considered comprehensive or complete and that nothing in this exchange of correspondence shall be construed as permitting types of punitive action or unreasonable impediments not enumerated therein.

Finally, in order adequately to verify compliance with the standard set forth in these letters, we understand that communication by telephone, telegraph and post will be permitted.

Sincerely yours,
HENRY M. JACKSON

(2) After the passage of the Act, the Soviet Government indicated, as it had previously warned, that it "cannot accept a trading relationship based on the legislation recently enacted in this country." The United States Government statement,[13] of which "the Soviet Government is aware. * * *" continued with the following language:

It [the Soviet Government] considers this legislation as contravening both the 1972 Trade Agreement, which had called for an unconditional elimination of discriminatory trade restrictions, and the principle of noninterference in domestic affairs. The Soviet Government states that it does not intend to accept a trade status that is discriminatory and subject to political conditions and, accordingly, that it will not put into force the 1972 Trade Agreement. Finally, the Soviet Government informed us that if statements were made by the United States, in the terms required by the Trade Act, concerning assurances by the Soviet Government regarding matters it considers within its domestic jurisdiction, such statements would be repudiated by the Soviet Government.

In view of these developments, we [the United States Government] have concluded that the 1972 Trade Agreement cannot be brought into force at this time and that the President will therefore not take the steps required for this purpose by the Trade Act. The President does not plan at this time to exercise the waiver authority.

(3) Pursuant to the authority in Sections 404 and 405 of the Trade Act of 1974, the United States has entered into trade agreements with Hungary, Romania and China and currently accords those countries MFN treatment.[14] Congress in each case approved the waiver of Section 402,[15] and the President has annually determined that the use of the Section 402 waiver authority is

13. Statement of Secretary of State Kissinger at news conference of Jan. 14, 1975, reported in 72 Dept. State Bull. 139 (Feb. 3, 1975).

14. Presidential Proclamation No. 4369, 40 Fed.Reg. 18389 (1975) (Romania); Presidential Proclamation No. 4560, 43 Fed.Reg. 15125 (1978) (Hungary); Presidential Proclamation No. 4697, 44 Fed.Reg. 61161 (1979) (China).

See generally Lansing & Rose, The Granting and Suspension of Most-Favored-Nation Status for Nonmarket Economy States: Policy and Consequences, 25 Harv.Intl.L.J. 329 (1984).

15. S.Con.Res. 35, 94th Cong., 1st Sess. (1975) (Romania); H.R.Con.Res. 555, 95th Cong., 2d Sess. (1978) (Hungary); H.R.Con.Res. 204, 96th Cong., 2d Sess. (1980) (China).

appropriate in these three particular cases.[16] MFN treatment for Poland was suspended in 1982, as part of the U.S. protest of the Polish government's attempt to dissolve the "Solidarity" labor union.[17]

(4) Imports from Communist countries may be subjected to trade restraints as a result of proceedings under the Section 406 of the Trade Act of 1974, which provides protection for domestic industry from market disruption by imports from any country dominated or controlled by communism. Market disruption is defined to exist when there are rapidly increasing imports that are a significant cause of material injury to domestic industry. Relief under Section 406 has not often been granted, but it is thought to be obtainable more easily than under the regular escape clause proceedings. See Section 9.2(C)(4) supra.

Questions

(1) Why is MFN treatment important? Without MFN treatment, what chance do Soviet exports have in the United States market?

(2) In the broadest perspective of world affairs, including not only economic objectives but attention to appropriate objectives concerning human liberties, was the congressional "Jackson-Vanik amendment" to the Trade Act of 1974 a wise measure?

(3) When is it good policy to link economic measures to political goals in international affairs?

(4) Examine closely Section 402 of the Trade Act of 1974 (in the Documentary Supplement). Are the letters of Secretary Kissinger and Senator Jackson consistent with those provisions?

(5) If you were advising a business client about the long term stability of trade relations between the United States and Romania, what would you advise?

SECTION 21.4 COUNTERTRADE

POMPILIU VERZARIU, INTERNATIONAL COUNTERTRADE: A GUIDE FOR MANAGERS AND EXECUTIVES

8–15 (U.S. Dept. Commerce 1984)[1]

II. FORMS OF COUNTERTRADE

In its simplest sense, countertrade involves the linked trade obligations of two enterprises in two countries, as stipulated in their import and export contracts. Such obligations may be encouraged or mandated by government policies (e.g., Norway's tying offshore oil concessions to contributions to the development of the Norwegian industry). They could be on a "best effort" basis (e.g., as in some West European countries); involve only government procurement (e.g., as in Indonesia); be required for specific industrial sectors

---

16. See, e.g., Determination of President, 48 Fed.Reg. 26585 (1983); 2 BNA Intl. Trade Rptr. 790 (1985).

17. Presidential Proclamation No. 4991, 47 Fed.Reg. 49005 (1982).

1. See generally L. Welt, Trade Without Money: Barter and Countertrade (1984);

Lochner, Countertrade and International Barter, 19 Intl. Law. 725 (1985); McVey, Countertrade: Commercial Practices, Legal Issues and Policy Dilemmas, 16 Law & Poly. Intl. Bus. 1 (1984); Griffin, Antitrust Law Issues in Countertrade, 17 J. World Trade L. 236 (1983).

(e.g., as in Mexico); or be required for all foreign trade transactions (e.g., as in Romania).

In a broader sense, countertrade arrangements include government-to-government bilateral agreements transferring reciprocal market access privileges (beyond tariff treatment agreements) between two nations. These agreements, in the form of bilateral clearing agreements, trade protocols, or trade investment treaties, may stipulate or facilitate exchanges of goods between two countries under preferential terms. They are intended to integrate economies of particular countries, recognize special relations existing among politically allied nations, or reflect trading interests for scarce raw material resources.

* * *

Offsets. Government acquisitions involving military and major civil procurements (e.g., commercial aircraft, telecommunication systems) are often tied to requirements by the importing country for domestic content, inclusive of coproduction involving transfers of sensitive processes and advanced technology manufacturing; investments; as well as to long-term countertrade commitments for local goods and services. The range of these requirements is known as "offsets." Countertrade, local subcontracting and investment requirements are known as indirect offsets. Coproduction requirements based on production technology transfers to the importing country are known as direct offsets. Such practices have been used by importing governments as a tool of industrial development, domestic employment, as well as a means to finance payment balances. In the past, most offsets were requested by industrialized countries. Specifically, coproduction began in the early 1960's in Europe and Japan and, by value, has represented a major portion of offset packages. Now the developed nations are joined in similar demands by a growing number of developing countries, most of which have limited industrial and technological bases which would allow coproduction arrangements. For these countries, countertrade will provide the major vehicle for fulfilling offset obligations assumed by Western suppliers.

Barter. A classical barter arrangement involves the direct exchange of goods between two trading parties. No cash changes hands for the reciprocal exports which have counterbalancing values and which are usually governed by a single contract. Because of the limited flexibility of this type of arrangement, barter agreements are rare in international trade. They may find application in the trade between countries under government-to-government agreements which often are dictated for reasons of national interest (e.g., the Bangladesh-arrangements with the People's Republic of China and several other communist countries, or the recent U.S.-Jamaican transactions involving the exchange of U.S. government-owned dairy products for Jamaican bauxite destined for the U.S. national strategic stockpile).

Commodity traders may also swap deliveries of equivalent products to each other's clients around the world in order to save on transportation costs. On occasion a Western supplier may agree to accept barter for a portion of its exports, when Western export credits are not available to finance trade with the customer (e.g., the arrangement between General Electric and Romania for the sale of steam turbines). * * *

Direct and Indirect Compensation. Under these types of arrangements the value of a supplier's exports are partially or fully counterbalanced by imports from the client's country, normally under parallel contracts providing for separate cash settlements for each leg of the transaction. The contractual separation between the two contracts provides for flexibility in financing, guarantee coverages, maturity of payments, and deliveries. It also facilitates the transfer of the offsetting marketing obligation from the primary exporter to third parties designated by him. The proportion of the original export which is offset by counterdeliveries is known as the "countertrade ratio."

In "direct compensation" arrangements (also known as buybacks) the counterdeliveries are related to, or result from, the original export. Examples are capital projects, such as turnkey production facilities or production sharing ventures related to the extraction and processing of minerals, which benefit from Western-supplied technology, capital, and equipment, and for which the Western contractor obliges himself to market a portion of the project's output. Because of the current moratorium in financing new production capacity in many areas of the world, the growth of direct compensation arrangements in developing countries lies now in upgrading and modernizing existing manufacturing facilities. * * *

In "indirect compensation" arrangements (also known as counterpurchases), counterdeliveries may involve such products as manufactures, components, raw materials, foodstuffs, and machinery, which are not related to the primary export for which they constitute repayments. For example, government procurements in Indonesia require counterpurchases of domestic agricultural goods, foodstuffs, manufactures, and raw materials. Iraq, Qatar, and Libya have provided petroleum as payment to foreign suppliers of capital projects. The communist countries have exported large quantities of industrial products under indirect compensation arrangements. On some occasions, anticipatory purchases by Western exporters have been contractually qualified for credit to be applied against later sales by the exporter or his designated parties. This form of reverse countertrade is known in Europe as "junktim."

Counterpurchases under indirect compensation arrangements also figure prominently in agreements involving the sale of military equipment or other technology-intensive high dollar-value government procurements (offset arrangements). Offset arrangements involve a "direct offset" commitment by the exporter, which comprises advanced technology coproduction in the buyer's country (inclusive of assembly, processing, manufacture, and technology transfers). "Indirect offsets" relate to counterpurchases of goods to be exported from the buyer's country, subcontracting and investments. Because indirect offsets under indirect compensation arrangements involve substantial dollar values, they tie down significant production and shares in the importer's country for many years. This is particularly so in countries with a limited coproduction capability which necessitates substantial indirect offset commitments by the supplier. * * *

Officially-Sponsored Bilateral Trade Arrangements. Government-to-government bilateral trade and payment agreements under clearing arrangements have gradually been decreasing in number over the last decade, although additional government-sponsored commercial bilateral arrangements or protocols which involve full settlements in currency have been signed since the late 1970s. Under the latter agreements, for example, Japan has committed itself to build industrial complexes in the Middle East and Mexico in exchange for petroleum deliveries and is trading industrial goods for deliveries of petroleum and coal from the People's Republic of China under a 13-year agreement (1978–1990). France, Canada, and Italy have also signed commercial agreements involving technical assistance and exports of their goods for petroleum deliveries from Mexico and Venezuela.

Under a bilateral clearing arrangement, two nations with foreign exchange controls and shortages of foreign currency agree officially to exchange goods over a specified period of time (usually 1 year). Exporters in each country are paid by the respective central banks in domestic currencies. The volume of the goods is specified in the agreement and their value is denominated in artificial accounting units (e.g., clearing dollar, Swiss franc, rupee). The agreement requires that all trade exchanges stop beyond a maximum specified trade imbalance or "swing" which usually is set at about 30 percent of yearly volume of trade in the bilateral clearing accounts. Such an imbalance, until removed, represents an interest-free credit by the country with the trade surplus to the other country.

Trade imbalances at the end of the contractual period have to be settled in cash in the specified currency, or converted into cash by "switching" the rights to the trade imbalance to interested third parties at discounted prices.

The third party, usually a financial institution or bank will, through a series of complex international transactions involving other middlemen, convert the clearing imbalance into hard currency. Clearing agreements between communist countries and developing countries have been used on occasion by Western exporters to trade with either the developing or the communist country. * * *

Another type of government-sponsored countertrade agreement is known as an "evidence account." Evidence accounts are umbrella trade agreements between a Western exporter and a government entity in the developing country (e.g., an industrial ministry, a provincial authority), which are designed to facilitate trade flows when countertrade is a requirement, and when the existing trade turnover between the two parties is significant and expected to increase.

Under this type of an agreement, two-way trade turnover between the Western signatory, other parties designated by him, and the commercial organizations under the jurisdiction of the developing country signatory, must be partially or fully balanced over a specified period of time (typically 1 to 3 years). Unlike in clearing agreements, individual import/export transactions are settled by the trading parties through cash. Financial settlements occur through banks designated by the signatories to the agreement. The banks also monitor trade flows and ensure that cumulative payment turnovers at the end of the specified period balance according to the terms of the agreement. Trade under evidence accounts is rare in international commerce and has been occasionally practiced in trade with centrally-planned economies. Several such accounts have been signed by Western exporters with communist countries and with the People's Republic of China, where the U.S. firm, General Motors, has signed several such agreements with Chinese industrial ministries, and the British trading house, Bowater, has an agreement with Guangdong province.

Special Practices. As marketing of counterdeliveries, especially those originating in developing countries, becomes increasingly costly, Western exporters may find it necessary to resort to alternate approaches to satisfy their countertrade commitments. For example, such initiatives as promotion of tourism within the customer's country, training of his work force, use of his transportation services, contracting with his construction crews abroad, or cooperating with his firms in engineering projects in third countries may qualify for countertrade credit, as may the creation of local employment through investments in labor-intensive projects in his country.

To compensate for hard currency credit constraints affecting exports to many developing countries, Western exporters also are being compelled to devise creative ways which can reduce the need for such credits. Examples of approaches are the partial procurement of supplies and services in soft currency countries, acceptance of partial payments in soft currencies (which may then be used to defray local costs incurred by the Western exporter, or for local reinvestments, or be transferred to third parties), or in clearing currencies. Such expedient but costly approaches lend themselves to the larger dollar volume transactions, where the benefits to the Western exporter include incremental exports and maintenance of production and employment levels.

Notes and Questions

(1) Countertrade arrangements can be very complicated. Consider how you would diagram the flow of goods and other consideration that would occur under the standard countertrade arrangements that are described in the foregoing excerpt. What sort of agreements would be needed to implement the arrangements? What key issues would have to be covered in those agreements?

(2) There is some controversy over the extent that countertrade is practiced. In a 1985 study, the OECD estimated that countertrade encompassed 4.8% of world trade, a figure in between GATT's estimate of 8% and the IMF's estimate of 1%. The OECD study indicates, however, that the number of countries using countertrade has increased sharply in recent years, from 15 in 1972 (principally the Communist bloc) to 27 in 1979 and to 67 in 1983. Indeed, if the use of countertrade in connection with sales of military equipment is considered, the number rises to 88.

(3) A number of questions can be raised about the compatability of countertrade with GATT.[2] For example, normally an exporter manufactures its products using whatever inputs it wishes and sells the product for cash, which it is normally free to spend as it wishes. It may decide to buy certain goods, but it buys goods of its choice and such goods may or may not be imported from the

2. See generally Gadbaw, The Implications of Countertrade Under the General Agreement on Tariffs and Trade, 5 J.Comp.Bus. & Cap.Mkt.L. 355 (1983); Baker & Cunningham, Countertrade and Trade Law, 5 J.Comp.Bus. & Cap.Mkt.L. 376 (1983).

country purchasing its exports. With countertrade the exporter may be forced to use certain inputs (perhaps made in the country to which it is exporting) and may be forced to take goods instead of currency as payment from the importing country. This can have a number of effects. The exporter will not purchase inputs it otherwise would have purchased, thereby distorting normal trade patterns. If the exporter uses the goods it receives in payment in lieu of purchasing them from a third country, there has been another diversion of trade. If the exporter resells the goods in its country, it may displace goods normally imported from a third country.

Are these trade diversions violations of GATT? Does it matter whether the countertrade arrangement was required or sponsored by a government as opposed to negotiated between private parties? Could a countertrade arrangement required by a government constitute an impairment and nullification of benefits under GATT Article XXIII in the case of the country who is adversely affected by it? Consider the analysis used in the Canadian Foreign Investment Review Act case discussed in Section 8.2(C) supra, in which the panel discussed a requirement that investors purchase goods locally in lieu of imports.

(4) A number of other GATT provisions could arguably be violated by countertrade arrangements. For example, could government involvement in arranging the export of a product pursuant to a countertrade arrangement violate the GATT Subsidies Code's ban on export subsidies? What if the export consisted of surplus agricultural products acquired by the government as part of its farm price support program?[3] If a country generally requires importers to enter into countertrade agreements, but does not do so in respect of certain countries, has it violated the most-favored-nation requirement of Article I? If imports into a country are allowed only if made pursuant to a countertrade agreement, has that country imposed a quantitative restriction (i.e. a zero quota) in violation of Article XI? On the other hand, could it be argued that countertrade arrangements are used to remedy balance of payment difficulties and therefore cannot violate GATT because they are exempt from the general application of GATT rules? See Articles XII and XIII. Do the special rules applicable to developing countries, see Chapter 20 supra, have the effect of exempting their use of countertrade agreements from any otherwise applicable GATT requirements?[4]

(5) Countertrade poses obvious problems for the entity that is required to use inputs it does not want or to accept in payment for its exports goods that it does not want. How will it dispose of the goods? Usually, of course, the goods will be of some value to someone, but by definition that someone could have acquired the goods directly and did not. Thus, it is quite possible that the goods will have to be sold at a discount. This raises the possibility that disposition of the goods may violate the antidumping rules discussed in Section 10.2 supra. Indeed, if the volume of goods is large, it may lead domestic industry to seek relief in an escape clause proceeding (see Chapter 9 supra) or, if a Communist

---

3. The United States has bartered surplus butter for bauxite from Jamaica. See Note, Bauxite for Butter: The U.S.-Jamaican Agreement and the Future of Barter in U.S. Trade Policy, 16 Law & Poly.Intl.Bus. 239 (1984). The Export Administration Amendments Act of 1985, in title II, explicitly authorizes the President to barter stocks of agricultural com- modities for petroleum and other materials vital to the national interest. Pub.L. No. 99–64, § 203, 99 Stat. 158 (1985).

4. See generally Liebman, Comment: GATT and Countertrade Requirements, 18 J. World Trade L. 252 (1984).

country is involved, pursuant to Section 406 under the 1974 Trade Act (see Section 9.2(C) supra). One such example concerned anhydrous ammonia obtained pursuant to a countertrade arrangement from the Soviet Union and imported into the United States. As discussed in Section 9.2(C) supra, no relief was ultimately obtained.[5]

(6) There are a number of advantages to countertrade arrangements. Probably the most important is that they allow countries with balance of payments problems to conserve scarce foreign exchange. On balance, however, countertrade is usually thought to be undesirable. The 1985 OECD study concluded that countertrade was undesirable because it may lead to fraudulent transactions (particularly in respect of valuing goods received for customs or other purposes); it destabilizes markets for raw materials (particularly oil, coffee and cocoa); it encourages inefficient transactions and thereby slows the adjustment process that trade flows should encourage and it often leads to problems in respect of quality and servicing in the case of industrial goods. Do you think these criticisms seem to be valid? Can you think of counterarguments or reasons why countertrade may be beneficial?

5. Potter, East-West Countertrade: Economic Injury and Dependence Under U.S. Trade Law, 13 Law & Poly.Intl.Bus. 413 (1981).

Chapter 22

INTERDEPENDENCE AND THE INDUSTRIAL MARKET ECONOMIES

SECTION 22.1 THE PROBLEMS OF INTERDEPENDENCE

In the previous two chapters, we have examined the special problems that arise in connection with the rules of international trade as applied to nations which do not easily fit the model of a market oriented economic system for which the GATT and other rules have been written. But even as to nations which do fit that model, particularly the western industrial democracies, a number of very difficult problems have been growing in importance in recent years, partly as a consequence of greater economic interdependence.

Nations such as Japan, the United States and the United Kingdom have economic systems that are relatively similar, at least in comparison to those of nonmarket economies or developing country economies. Nevertheless the shrinking world is posing a number of difficult questions to the leaders of these relatively similar countries as to economic relations among them. This shrinking world has been caused by remarkably easier transportation (shoes and even heavy machinery are often shipped by air!) and communications (where transactions are often completed by pressing a few computer keys).

In Chapter 10 we explored a "variable cost" hypothetical to illustrate how trade between rather similar economies could still create problems that might be deemed unfair by industries and workers. In that chapter also, we noticed the extraordinary difficulty of defining "subsidy" for purposes of applying international rules and national countervailing duty laws. Even fairly minimal differences between nations as to the amount of government ownership of industrial sectors can create stresses and strains in an interdependent and free trading environment.

Each of the "big three" international traders—Japan, the United States and the EC—has certain societal characteristics which make the other two sometimes feel aggrieved. As to Japan, there is much spoken and written about "cultural barriers to trade". It is sometimes suggested that there is a national "buy Japanese" ethic, and that certain Japanese consumer preferences or bureaucratic governmental attitudes tend to restrict imports. As to the United States, many nations argue that its legal and governmental system, with its highly legalistic (and costly) procedures as well as the uncertainty and risks resulting from the constant battles between the Executive and Congress, amount to nontariff barriers to trade. As to the EC, it is sometimes said that there is a natural proclivity towards protection against imports influenced by certain member states, which have a long tradition of government involvement in business, and an "inner group" mentality of businessmen that is reminiscent of the guilds of the middle ages. In addition it is observed that the EC is going through a very significant constitutional evolution which may influence its leaders to look inward, trying to keep out external pressures so as to preserve as much room for maneuver for the internal compromises that may be necessary to hold the EC together in the face of certain strong centrifugal forces.

In the sections of this chapter that follow, we look at several problems concerning the economic relations between industrial market economies. These have been increasingly perplexing in recent years, and do not fit very well into any of the various traditional subjects of international trade law and regulation. In the next chapter (which is the last of this book), we then look at some broad basic themes of our subject and point to some tentative conclusions about them.

SECTION 22.2 TARGETING AND INDUSTRIAL POLICY

Particularly in the United States, there has been growing concern about the competitive impact on U.S. industries of imports which appear to be beneficiaries of a certain type of foreign government policy, sometimes called "targeting." This word is used to describe conscious government intervention in a market economy to influence its direction and allocation of resources. It is said that foreign governments are able explicitly or implicitly to direct greater capital investment to certain favored sectors, such as computers, while at the same time "tilting" their regulatory mechanisms (including those restraining imports) to assist the favored sectors. Some practices, when fairly explicit and obviously tied to the favored sectors, such as direct financial grants, or low-interest rate loans, can be attacked by an importing country under various existing GATT rules such as those on subsidies or countervailing duties. However, some of the practices do not seem to be covered by existing rules. The materials which follow illustrate the dilemma of this subject matter. How intrusive should the international trade rules be upon national government policies? On the other hand, should importing nations simply sit back and watch some of their domestic business sectors decline or expire because of imports which have benefited from certain targeting practices?

HOUSE REPORT NO. 98–725

98th Cong., 2d Sess. 25–29 (1984)

[I]ntervention by governments in the marketplace to enhance the competitive performance of particular industries has increased and the form of subsidy practices has proliferated far beyond the imagination of the original drafters of the term "bounty or grant" in U.S. law or in the GATT. The Committee is very concerned about the distortions of trade patterns caused by subsidies and their impact on the competitiveness of domestic industries. Stronger disciplines are necessary to discourage the use of injurious subsidies, otherwise, in the longer run, they threaten the operation of market forces and the viability of domestic economies as governments are forced to misallocate resources by matching foreign subsidy levels. A remedy should be available to restore "a level playing field" for U.S. industries in international trade competition with respect to current forms of subsidy practices.

* * *

EXPLANATION OF PROVISION

Section 771(5)(B)(i), as added by section 105(a)(1) of the bill, defines the term "export targeting subsidy" as "any government plan or scheme consisting of coordinated actions, whether carried out severally or jointly or in combination with any other subsidy under subparagraph (A), that are bestowed on a specific enterprise, industry, or group thereof, * * * the effect of which is to assist the beneficiary to become more competitive in the export of any class or kind of merchandise."

In addition to export or domestic subsidy practices covered under present law, export targeting actions under subparagraph (B)(i) would include, but not be limited to, the following practices:

(1) The exercise of government control over banks and other financial institutions that requires diversion of private capital on preferential terms to specific beneficiaries or into specific sectors. Provision of government loans on preferential terms, as opposed to diversion of private capital, is defined as a subsidy under present law.

(2) Extensive government involvement in promoting or encouraging anticompetitive behavior among specific beneficiaries, including:

(a) Assistance in planning and establishing joint ventures which have an anticompetitive export effect;

(b) Relaxation of antitrust rules normally applied to industries to assure the development of anticompetitive export cartels;

(c) Assistance in planning or coordinating joint research and development among selected beneficiaries to promote export competitiveness; and

(d) Regulations concerning the division of markets or allocation of products among selected beneficiaries.

(3) Special protection of the home market that permits the development of competitive exports in a specific sector or product.

(4) Special restrictions on technology transfer or government procurement that limit competition in a specific sector or industry and thereby promote export competitiveness.

(5) The use of investment restrictions, including domestic content and export performance requirements, that limit competition in a specific sector or industry and thereby promote export competitiveness.

Section 771(5)(B)(ii), added by section 105(a)(1), specifies that in determining the level of an export targeting subsidy, the administering authority must use a method of calculation which, in its judgment and to the extent possible, reflects the full benefit of the subsidy to the beneficiary over the period during which the subsidy has an effect, rather than the cash cost of the subsidy to the government.

REASONS FOR CHANGE

The inclusion of export targeting as defined in new section 771(5)(B)(i) as a subsidy within the scope of the countervailing duty law reflects the growing recognition in the United States that foreign industrial targeting practices can have an injurious impact upon the viability and competitiveness of U.S. industries. Basically, the provision applies to situations where the foreign government has sought to develop a particular industry by creating a relatively risk free environment to provide a competitive advantage the industry would not otherwise have under normal market conditions. This advantage is typically achieved through a combination of practices such as directing private capital as well as government financial resources to the particular industry on a preferential basis, establishing an industry cartel, providing preferential sourcing of government procurement, closing the home market to foreign competition or investment during the establishment and development of the industry, then perhaps subsidizing export sales. Targeting is different from other potentially trade distorting practices in that it involves a combination of actions, any one of which may have a marginal impact on the industry's competitiveness, but which taken together artifically create a comparative advantage for the selected industry.

At the same time, the provision is not directed in any way against foreign industrial policies per se, which are solely a matter of internal government choice. Rather, it applies only when those targeting practices have the effect of increasing the export competitiveness of a particular industry in a manner that is injurious to U.S. producers. If such policies cause harm to U.S. industries, they become an appropriate matter for remedy under U.S. trade laws.

The inclusion of export targeting practices as subsidies subject to the countervailing duty law if they meet the conditions specified in the bill is not intended to prejudice the seeking of relief under other existing trade remedy laws as appropriate in the particular circumstances of each case. Rather, the countervailing duty law will provide an alternative avenue of relief from practices which have an injurious effect on domestic industries similar to more traditional forms of subsidies.

Implementation of the exporting targeting subsidy provisions would require a three-step determination by the Department of Commerce. First, there must be a government scheme or plan involving coordinated actions. Information obtained by the ITC and provided the Department of Commerce under the targeting subsidy monitoring program established under section 201 of H.R. 4784 is intended to assist the Department in making this determination in a timely manner. A positive determination would require that the targeting policy actually involve definite actions, not merely advice or a "vision" by the government. The actions also must not be isolated or uncoordinated; rather, they must be integrated into a reasonably coherent plan or scheme. While a showing of specific intent is unworkable given the unlikelihood of available evidence, the "plan or scheme" requirement is designed to ensure that the law deals with purposeful targeting and not with discrete forms of government activity.

Second, the Department must determine that targeting practices are involved. Current countervailing duty law specifically addresses only those subsidies which involve a cash transfer to the particular industry from the government treasury, such as grants, loans, or certain tax benefits. The inclusion of actions such as those listed under section 771(5)(B)(i) as added by the bill supplements these more traditional forms of subsidies with practices which, when part of a government plan or scheme, have a subsidizing effect similar to financial assistance in assisting a specific enterprise or industry to become more export competitive. Export targeting subsidies may include forms of cash assistance covered by present countervailing duty law. However, the provision is directed primarily to the more sophisticated, less direct techniques of subsidizing which governments have resorted to as more traditional export subsidy practices are prohibited under international rules. The listing of targeting practices under subparagraph (B)(i) is purely illustrative and not exhaustive since it is not possible to anticipate the full scope of actions that governments may utilize to achieve the same results.

Third, the Department of Commerce must determine that the export targeting subsidy has the effect of assisting a discrete class of companies or industries to become more competitive in their export activities. The provision does not require a showing that the intent or purpose of the export targeting subsidy is to improve the competitiveness of a foreign industry in the U.S. market. A determination of motivation would be extremely difficult to make and subject to judicial challenge that would reduce the prospects for timely relief. Rather, the *effect* of the government plan or scheme must be to promote export competitiveness in a manner that is injurious to U.S. industry.

As in the case of export and domestic subsidies covered by present law, the types of actions envisioned as export targeting subsidies would not be countervailable unless they were bestowed upon a specific enterprise or industry or group thereof. Such practices which are generally available to industries within the country would not be covered within the definition of export targeting subsidies under subparagraph (B)(i).

Finally, no countervailing duty would be imposed on export targeting subsidies unless the ITC determines that the subsidized imports of the merchandise cause or threaten material injury to the U.S. industry, except in cases where the injury test does not apply to the country involved under present law. While individual targeting actions may have only a marginal impact, their cumulative effect may create an export competitive advantage which is injurious to the U.S. industry.

In determining the value of a targeting subsidy, section 771(5)(B)(ii) would require the Department of Commerce to use a method of calculation which reflects as accurately as possible the full benefits of the subsidy to the beneficiary enterprise or industry over the period during which the subsidy has an effect, rather than solely the cash cost of the subsidy to the government. This method is necessary for making a realistic assessment of the actual subsidy level in targeting cases, since many of the practices may not involve a simple cash transfer and their cumulative benefit may be greater than the current monetary value of an individual practice. For example, closing the home market to foreign competition or suspending antitrust laws may yield profits from higher prices and economies of scale that confer substantial competitive advantages to an industry that would not be offset under the current method of assessing benefits and would neither deter the foreign practices nor remedy the injury to U.S. industry. Depending on the circumstances of the particular case, the assessment of the full benefit of the subsidy could include the effect of subsidies which were bestowed prior to the period of importation but which are still having an effect on the imports of the particular merchandise.

Concerns have been expressed that certain U.S. Government practices (for example, investment tax credits; "spillover" benefits of defense and space research and development programs to the computer, commercial aviation, and spacecraft industries; financing of agricultural price supports; and measures to promote formation of export trading companies) may become subject to mirror legislation in foreign countries imposing countervailing duties against U.S. exports. It is highly questionable however, that such practices would constitute targeting as defined in subparagraph (B)(i), which would require a government plan or scheme consisting of coordinated actions assisting a specific industry to become export competitive in a manner which is injurious to foreign producers. The effect of such practices on sales in third country markets is not within the scope of the injury test as defined in present law or in the bill.

Questions

(1) Are you as sanguine as the House Report that retaliation against the United States is unlikely? Consider that any foreign legislation would be tailored to apply to U.S. practices, just as the above proposal seems clearly tailored to apply to alleged Japanese practices.

(2) Is there really anything wrong with targeting as described in the foregoing report? Should national or international rules constrain a national government's attempt to direct its economy to advance in certain chosen sectors? Is this too much of an intrusion on national sovereignty?

(3) Once targeting has occurred, and an industry is established or greatly expanded because of it, will it help or hurt world welfare for foreign governments to restrain imports from that industry?

UNITED STATES INTERNATIONAL TRADE COMMISSION, FOREIGN INDUSTRIAL TARGETING AND ITS EFFECTS ON U.S. INDUSTRIES

40, 48, 17 (1985) [1]

[This two-volume report gives extensive details on various practices of foreign governments which could be called targeting. The following are just a few selected examples:]

Brazil:

Government Purchasing. Government purchasing is used to increase the share of domestic value added in selected product areas, as well as to encourage majority Brazilian ownership in certain sectors of the economy. Because of the size of the State-owned enterprises, the practice of making Government purchases contingent upon fulfilling local-content and ownership criteria can have a significant effect in certain targeted sectors.

Directing Investors. In most industrial sectors, foreign investment does not require prior government approval. Nonetheless, the Government maintains some control over foreign investment by awarding investment incentives. These investment incentives include exemption from import duties, exemption from certain value-added taxes, depreciation for income tax purposes at three times the normal rates, and subsidized Government financing.

Because local firms receive investment incentives from the Government and because the currency has been historically overvalued, foreign investment incentives are needed to help attract capital from overseas. Through its incentive system, the government is able to influence the size, location, and nature of the foreign investment. The Brazilian Government prefers joint ventures with Brazilian majority ownership and investments that use current technology, increase Brazil's exports, and create employment in the less developed regions of the country. The Government also prefers equity investments over loans.

Another major source of Government control comes from requiring that capital investments be registered for remitting profits. Unless a foreign investment is registered, the investor cannot legally repatriate profits or remit dividends, although the investor may still receive the investment's return if it is kept in Brazil.

Mexico:

One of the most important lending programs is article 94 of the banking law under which 25 percent of commercial bank reserves must be loaned to specific industrial sectors at rates stipulated by the central bank. Another important aspect of government control over credit allocation is the magnitude of lending by official banking institutions, referred to as development banks. Development banks accounted for 50 percent of total banking system

---

1. USITC Inv. No. 332–162, Report to the
Subcomm. on Trade of the House Comm. on
Ways and Means (1985).

assets, and for about 45 percent of total bank lending in 1983. Development banks lend most heavily to the agriculture and infrastructure sectors.

Canada:

The targeting that takes place is more prevalent in declining industries. For example, Canada has a program designed to revitalize the textiles, clothing, and footwear industries. This revitalization program is supposed to last only from 1981 to 1986, and its overall budget is less than $350 million. The program is supported by Canadian home-market protection of textiles and footwear.

A source of potential targeting is the large number of publicly owned enterprises and the regulation of foreign investment. Not only does the Canadian Government own a number of public utilities, but it also owns other companies in aerospace, petroleum and natural gas, steel, pulp and paper.

LYNN G. KAMARCK, AN EXAMINATION OF FOREIGN INDUSTRIAL TARGETING PRACTICES AND THEIR RELATIONSHIP TO INTERNATIONAL AGREEMENTS AND U.S. TRADE LAWS

(1985) [2]

The term "industrial targeting" cannot be easily defined. The term has been used to describe a variety of practices. For example, the House Committee on Ways and Means listed the following specific policies as frequently mentioned elements of industrial targeting: (1) government financial support shared by a group of companies; (2) government-sponsored or government-conducted research and development projects to assist a selected group of companies; (3) industry rationalization programs; (4) suspension of antitrust rules on industrial policy grounds; (5) manipulation of capital markets by government or government-backed entities to benefit certain sectors; (6) administrative guidance to divide markets or allocate products among competing domestic companies; (7) government control of technology transfer; (8) government restrictions on foreign investment in order to limit and control competition within certain sectors; (9) government procurement policies designed to assure demand for certain products; and (10) import protection policies.

* * *

Any distinction between acceptable targeting practices and unacceptable ones must take into account the fact that the U.S. Government has a considerable number of programs which could be construed as industrial targeting and there is growing pressure for the United States to develop even more of an industrial targeting policy.

The number of industrial targeting programs by the United States may be as great, if not greater, than that of Japan, or the other industrialized nations. For example, a recent Commerce Department study noted that in

---

2. From J. Jackson, R. Cunningham & C. Fontaine (eds.), International Trade Policy: The Lawyer's Perspective, at 15–5 to –18, 15– 38 to –39. Reprinted by permission of the American Bar Association.

absolute terms, the United States supports more research and development ("R & D") than Japan, West Germany or France. The U.S. Government also manipulates capital markets through its Eximbank programs and, in the Export Trading Company Act, has relaxed the application of its antitrust laws. Other U.S. measures which affect the structure of the national economy are farm policies, subsidies for shipping and shipbuilding, depletion allowances for extractive industries, and the "Buy American" laws.

The United States cannot take a strong stand against industrial targeting without considering the effects of such a stance on its own programs and the resulting political repercussions.

* * *

§ 15.05 Relationship of Targeting Practices and International Trade Agreements

As noted earlier, government intervention in the form of industrial targeting is inconsistent with traditional trade theory based on competitive models of global commerce. There is, however, nothing in the General Agreement on Tariffs and Trade (GATT) or any of the agreements entered into under the auspices of the GATT that prohibits a country from developing an industrial targeting policy as such. The only types of industrial targeting practices which are specifically addressed by any international agreements are certain types of subsidies which are prohibited by the Subsidies Code negotiated in the Tokyo Round of the multilateral trade negotiations.

The GATT may, however, reach industrial targeting practices where the effects of those policies are to "nullify or impair" obligations assumed, or the benefits to other contracting parties under the GATT. Such practices may be held to violate GATT Article XXIII.

Similarly, the Subsidies Code was drafted so as to provide a code signatory with a remedy against subsidies causing (a) serious prejudice, (b) nullification or impairment, or (c) injury to the interests of that signatory, even though the subsidy practice might not, itself, be prohibited.

The Subsidies Code also sets forth what adverse effects may be required to meet this standard—

(a) the effects of the subsidized imports in the domestic market of the importing signatory, or

(b) the effects of the subsidy in displacing or impeding the imports of like products into the market of the subsidizing country, or

(c) the effects of the subsidized exports in displacing the exports of like products of another signatory from a third country market.

Thus, the GATT and the Subsidies Code provide a means to address industrial targeting practices that, while technically not prohibited, may have a severe impact on international trade.

It is doubtful that a more specific multilateral consensus on what are acceptable and unacceptable industrial targeting practices could realistically be achieved. Generally these are seen as primarily matters of domestic economic policy. Each country wants to preserve the flexibility to mold its own industrial policies, including targeting policies, as the need arises.

Certainly, it would be extremely difficult to distinguish acceptable targeting programs from unacceptable ones on the basis of "legitimate" domestic economic justification for a program. Even if it were possible to make such distinctions, the United States might be unwilling to accept the ·impact of foreign targeting practices that are based on legitimate domestic policy grounds. For example, there was significant economic justification for many of Japan's industrial targeting practices when these were initially instituted, as Japan's industrial base had been largely destroyed in World War II and it was necessary for Japan to reindustrialize as soon as possible. Indeed, there are many who contend that there has been significant economic justification for most of Japan's industrial targeting practices.

Thus, there are very few industrial targeting practices that could be considered per se intolerable in international trade terms. A practice which may be designed for legitimate internal economic purposes, like a domestic subsidy, becomes intolerable to American interests when it begins to have an impact on U.S. markets or third-country markets in which American industry competes. This "relativity" of the offensiveness of a targeting practice makes it extremely difficult to reach any kind of comprehensive multilateral consensus defining appropriate and inappropriate targeting practices in any way other than their impact on international trade or degree of economic distortion.

* * *

§ 15.08 Conclusion

Many forms of industrial targeting practices can be addressed by existing U.S. trade laws. As noted, however, there are a number of respects in which these laws are inadequate and various amendments may be helpful.

* * * It would be a mistake to expand the category of foreign actions which are deemed to be "unfair" as this would generate international trade tensions and cut off U.S. policy options.

Of the "fair" trade statutes, Section 301 does, in theory, address many forms of industrial targeting practices. Because of the degree of Presidential discretion involved, and the lack of investigative procedures or mechanisms for negotiation, it is doubtful that Section 301 will, in fact, be an effective tool against industrial targeting.

Thus, Section 201 is probably the most useful mechanism to address those forms of industrial targeting practices not covered by the countervailing duty law. Under Section 201, it is unnecessary to show that the nations or foreign manufacturers against which relief is sought have engaged in unfair trade practices—rather the focus is simply on whether the domestic industry has been harmed by imports.

SECTION 22.3 THE HOUDAILLE CASE

Closely related to targeting concepts was an ingenuous complaint brought to the U.S. Government against practices of Japan which allegedly favored Japan's machine tool industry and its exports. The complaint, which we referred to briefly in Section 10.4(D) supra, was based on Section 103 of the Revenue Act of 1971, an obscure provision of the U.S. Internal Revenue Code dealing with business income taxes, which provides that the President may deny investment tax credit benefits in respect of purchases of imported capital goods which have benefited from certain foreign government practices. The language of the section reads: [1]

If, * * * the President determines that a foreign country—

> (i) maintains nontariff trade restrictions including variable import fees, which substantially burden United States Commerce in a manner inconsistent with provisions of trade agreements, or

> (ii) engages in discriminatory or other acts (including tolerance of international cartels) or policies unjustifiably restricting United States commerce,

he may provide by Executive order for the application of subparagraph (A) to any article or class of articles manufactured or produced in such foreign country for such period as may be provided by Executive order.

Subparagraph A referenced above states: "Property shall not be treated as section 38 property" if it was produced outside the United States. Section 38 property qualifies for the investment tax credit.

This section had not been invoked before 1982, when attorneys for Houdaille (pronounced Hoo-die) Industries, Inc., a machine tool manufacturer headquartered in Florida, filed with the U.S. government a large document in which they argued that the criteria of Section 103 had been fulfilled and that therefore the President should deny investment tax credits to U.S. purchasers of machine tools imported from Japan. Portions of the petition follow.

HOUDAILLE INDUSTRIES, INC., PETITION TO THE PRESIDENT OF THE UNITED STATES

1–2, 47–52 (1982) [2]

In only a few years a Japanese machine-tool cartel has taken away a major share of the United States market for these machines—nearly 50 percent in the case of NC [numerically controlled] machining centers and nearly 40 percent in the case of NC punching machines—from American manufacturers and their workers. The petitioner Houdaille Industries, Inc., (hereinafter "Houdaille"), has uncovered conclusive evidence that the Japanese Government instigated the formation of this cartel and continues to shield its members from competition by sanctioning market allocation and other anticompetitive agreements and practices. This is exactly the situation for which Congress provided a remedy in Section 103 of the Revenue Act

---

1. 26 U.S.C.A. §§ 38, 46–48 (1982).

2. The petition is reproduced in W. Hancock (ed.), Guide to Antidumping and Countervailing Duties and Other Unfair Import Laws 645 (looseleaf). See generally Copaken, The Houdaille Petition: A New Weapon Against Unfair Industry Targeting Practices, 17 Geo.

Wash.J.Intl.L. & Econ. (1983); Macrory & Juster, Section 103 of the Revenue Act of 1971 and the Houdaille Case: A New Trade Remedy, 9 N.Car.J.Intl.L. & Comm.Reg. 413 (1984); Dumas, Suspending the Investment Tax Credit: The "Tolerance of International Cartels" Standard, 17 Cornell Intl.L.J. 161 (1984).

of 1971. Section 103 delegates to the President authority to suspend eligibility of foreign-made products for the investment tax credit when he determines that a foreign government has unjustifiably restricted United States commerce by its "tolerance of international cartels."

The Government of Japan has unjustifiably restricted United States commerce by acts and policies that go well beyond tolerance of international cartels. By encouraging, nurturing, guiding and protecting its machine-tool cartel, the Japanese Government has put United States manufacturers at a severe competitive disadvantage both in Japan and in the most important market in the world—the United States. In 1975 the Japanese machine-tool cartel accounted for only 3.7 percent of the U.S. market in NC machining centers. By the first nine months of 1981 this market share had grown to 50.1 percent.

In the same brief period the Japanese cartel's share of the U.S. market in NC punching machines jumped from 4.7 percent to 37.6 percent. At this rate Japan would completely displace American companies from the U.S. markets in NC machining centers by late 1983 and NC punching machines by the end of 1984.

* * *

A. OVERVIEW

Beginning in the mid-1950's the Japanese Government engaged in a well-coordinated effort to concentrate its highly fragmented domestic machine-tool industry into a cartelized oligopoly composed of highly successful manufacturers. To this end, the Government directed companies to stop manufacturing those machine tools for which they had secured only small market shares, and nurtured and supported the firms that survived in these particular product lines. It encouraged them to exploit fully the economies of scale and opportunity for specialization created by such governmental intervention and urged them to engage in joint anticompetitive conduct. When the Japanese machine-tool industry responded by forming a cartel, the Government of Japan shielded it from both outside competition and the operation of Japan's Anti-Monopoly Law.

Once cartelization had been achieved, the Government of Japan induced its machine-tool cartel to shift its focus to the higher-value-added NC end of the machine-tool product line.

This historic undertaking had the ambitious goal of capturing a major share of the main export markets, especially the United States—the largest market in the world for these high-technology products.

The anticompetitive activities of the Japanese machine-tool cartel—tolerated, promoted, and, in effect, mandated by the Japanese Government—included sharing of detailed pricing information, allocation of product markets, and joint development of products and production policy. Further, the Government of Japan actually deputized the private machine-tool cartel to carry out governmental responsibilities in managing and policing the Government's price-fixing scheme. Moreover, the Japanese Government sustained the cartel by means of significant tax benefits, concessionary loans, grants for research and development and other promotional activities, and by funnelling to it off-budget funds generated from lucrative import rights and from wagering on bicycle and motorbike races.

The current penetration of the United States market in NC machining centers and NC punching machines achieved by the Japanese cartel can be explained only in part by past Japanese Government policies. The Government of Japan continues to tolerate and encourage the anticompetitive activities of its machine-tool cartel, including conduct that, under certain circumstances, would be considered *per se* violative of U.S. antitrust law, and to assist the cartel with extensive tax concessions and grants, concessionary loans, and off-budget funds. Indeed, Japanese penetration of the U.S. market in NC machining centers and NC punching machines continues and this growing dominance is the product of both the present and past acts and policies of the Japanese Government.

———

On April 26, 1983, the U.S. Administration turned down the request of Houdaille, but only after almost a year of intense internal U.S. government debate, and a heated debate in the press and elsewhere about the case. Some of the flavor of this debate can be seen from the following press excerpt:

STUART AUERBACH, TRADE BATTLE WITH JAPAN SHOWS POLICY CONFUSION

(1983) [3]

On the night of April 15, members of President Reagan's Cabinet, weary after 2½ hours of often fractious debate over a trade problem that had wide ramifications for relations with Japan, left the White House pledged to keep secret the details of their meeting.

But within minutes, a Japanese Embassy trade specialist, Kazuniko Otsuka, had cut through the secrecy to learn that the Cabinet members were unable to resolve their differences, and was told that the issue would be thrown into Reagan's lap a week later on April 22. Otsuka immediately flashed the news to his superiors in Tokyo.

In a controversy involving the future of the American machine tool industry, Otsuka's early warning triggered an intensive, high-level Japanese lobbying effort that involved two personal messages from Prime Minister Yashuiro Nakasone. Those messages eventually persuaded Reagan to side with the Japanese without hearing the debate of his Cabinet.

"I was told that at the [April 22] meeting President Reagan made it clear the request from Nakasone was first and foremost on his mind," said Richard Copaken, the Covington & Burling attorney who pressed the case alleging unfair trading practices by Japan in the machine tool industry on behalf of his client, Houdaille Industries Inc. of Fort Lauderdale.

3. Washington Post, August 15, 1983, at 1, col. A4. Reprinted by permission of the Washington Post.

"The president succumbed to lobbying pressure from Japan," added Houdaille's president, Phillip A. O'Reilly.

At the meeting, a surprised Commerce Secretary Malcolm Baldrige, who had supported the Houdaille complaint, reportedly told Reagan, "Mr. President, you are being naive" in placing so much weight on the Nakasone messages, according to a high administration official. The Cabinet discussion that Reagan never heard involved a set of laboriously hammered-out "agreed facts" concluding that Japan had protected, nurtured and subsidized its machine tool industry in a way that gave it a trade advantage over U.S. companies and allowed it to capture more than half of the United States machine tool market.

Furthermore, the Cabinet officials had agreed that the facts justified Reagan's authorizing of unfair-trade charges against the Japanese, although there was a group of self-described "white-hat" pure free traders who, on ideological grounds, vehemently opposed taking action.

The trade case was watched closely at the time for signs that the White House was shaping a unified policy with Japan.

———

Various other press articles reported that the case split the U.S. administration,[4] attracted strong support in the Senate,[5] and argued the merits, in one case under a headline that said "Playing Games with Protectionism".[6]

On the question of whether Section 103 was intended to be applicable in cases like Houdaille, i.e. cases complaining about unfair imports, as opposed to cases complaining about unfair practices hindering U.S. exports, two authors concluded that [7]

> * * * an examination of the express language of congressional reports and statements accompanying the enactment of Section 103, as well as similar reports relating to Section 252(b) of the Trade Expansion Act of 1962 (from which the language of Section 103 was borrowed), clearly indicates that Congress intended Section 103 to apply only to actions of foreign governments which unjustifiably restrict U.S. exports; Congress did not contemplate that the statute would be used to retaliate against activities designed to promote imports to the United States.

SECTION 22.4 LEVELS OF BARRIERS TO TRADE: A TAXONOMIC NOTE [1]

As we have seen in previous chapters, there are a myriad of barriers to trade. The ingenuity of man will always invent new ones, and the process of trying to overcome such newly-invented trade obstacles is perpetual. No one should have the notion that, in a short-term surge of international cooperation and negotiation, a mechanism can be put in place, which then will operate by itself. The mechanism will always require tinkering, and indeed the processes of that tinkering (new rule formulation, dispute settlement) are

4. Wall St. J., Mar. 29, 1983, at 1.

5. Wall St. J., Jan. 13, 1983, at 34.

6. N.Y. Times, Nov. 8, 1982, at 22.

7. Macrory & Juster, note 2 supra, at 425.

1. ©1986 by John H. Jackson. Adapted from a manuscript for a forthcoming book.

perhaps the essence of that mechanism and need considerable attention. Part of the problem is that as barriers explicitly addressed by GATT and the rules of international trade are disciplined, it becomes more apparent that other types of barriers also have a serious effect on trade impeding the realization of the goals of trade liberalization.

Obstacles to international flows can be analyzed on at least four different levels. Approaches to these obstacles for the purposes of disciplining them or understanding them, may differ, depending in which category or level the obstacle falls. In some cases international discipline may be so intrusive upon national sovereignty and culture that it would not be deemed appropriate. In such a case other measures to maximize the various (sometimes conflicting) goals of the international economic system may be called for. We return to this issue in the last section of the next chapter.

Level 1: Governmental explicit obstacles to imported goods.

This category includes various traditional, well-known trade barriers, such as tariffs and quantitative restrictions. The category can be further subdivided for analytical purposes into the following:

a. Practices which are contrary to the GATT obligations: (quantitative restrictions, tariffs above binding levels, etc.).

b. Practices not contrary to GATT obligations, but amounting to nullification or impairment under Article XXIII of GATT. This might include certain domestic subsidies, for example.

c. Practices that are neither of the above, but pose questions of fairness. These are the GATT "loophole" matters, i.e., government obstacles to imports or benefits to exports which are not adequately covered by GATT rules. Examples would include the state trading monopoly, the problem of monopoly practices, various voluntary export restraints, and government procurement practices. In some of these cases, however, "nullification or impairment" could be found under GATT clauses.

The GATT's system of consultation and dispute settlement can be used to obtain progress in dismantling some of the barriers listed under (a) and (b). The practices listed under (c) are much more difficult. In some cases these may be brought under existing rules by interpretation of those rules. In other cases new rules are needed. The difficulty of amending GATT and the frequent lack of political will to create new rules make it hard to create new rules, however. The Tokyo Round made some progress, but the subject of subsidies is a particularly difficult one, and the Tokyo Round code on this subject has many weaknesses.

Level 2: Government internal practices or regulations which have protective effects.

These often violate GATT national treatment rules (Article III) and can be considered in conjunction with them. They can be further subdivided as follows:

a. Regulations which discriminate on their face against imports. (These would almost certainly be a violation of Article III of GATT, see Chapter 8.) An example would be a regulation that required a higher standard of safety for imports, or limited the number of retail outlets which would be allowed to sell imports.

b. Regulations which are nondiscriminatory on their face, but which grant considerable government discretion, and the application of these regulations or the exercise of government discretion can be shown to discriminate against imports. An example would be a government requirement that importers be licensed, or goods be inspected and tested, and an administrative practice (sometimes not easily discovered) which in effect discriminated against imports (by delay, or inaction, or refusal of licenses).

c. Regulations which on their face and as applied by government officials are apparently nondiscriminatory, but which because of the particular background facts or circumstances operate to discriminate unnecessarily against imports. Prime example: the wine gallon-proof gallon practice in the United States prior to the Tokyo Round (see Chapter 8). Another example would be licensing rules that required applicants be experienced in the domestic market, when only firms handling domestic products had such experience.

In each of the above, it should be recognized that there is often a valid domestic governmental purpose (such as consumer health or protection) being addressed by the government regulation. The problem is balancing the application of governmental measures for a legitimate purpose, against the requirements of the international trading system to minimize obstacles to imports.

A second problem is eliminating those practices which have no utility for a valid governmental purpose and which are merely disguised import barriers. These are difficult cases to discover and to research. Several Tokyo Round codes are designed to deal with some of these problems, particularly the "Standards Code." One question is whether these codes can be effective enough or whether something more is needed.

Level 3: Problems which arise due to the economic structure of the importing country.

A number of problems have been noticed in connection with the freer flow of trade in today's interdependent world, which can probably be traced to differences of economic structure between the countries which are trading with each other, or to the nature or structure of the economic system of an importing country. This is a category which may include totally nongovernmental measures or institutions, such as the structure of corporations. On the other hand, the structure may be related to governmental measures, and to government policies which have been undertaken, perhaps consciously to influence that structure.

The category can be further subdivided as follows:

a. Government induced or connected structural problems. Prime examples would be governmental allocation of credit, or investment capital; government "industrial policy"; and at least some forms of administrative guidance.

b. Structural practices that are not primarily governmentally induced or designed. The structure of industry, as well as the structure of other domestic economic institutions (e.g., the distribution system), sometimes are such that they may, unintentionally (or otherwise), pose obstacles to the importation of goods or promote the exportation of goods. For example, the ratio of debt to equity of an enterprise (as mentioned in Chapter 10), as well as the concept of tenure for workers, can have an influence on the short-term marginal variable costs of an enterprise, which in times of slack demand can have a strong influence on competitiveness of an enterprise.

These problems are almost totally untouched by the GATT system, except peripherally by certain rules that affect (inadequately and bluntly) the consequences of structural differences (such as rules on subsidies or anti-dumping). These problems (and those of Level 4 discussed below) also raise some of the most difficult and fundamental questions of how far should the international system go in asking nations to change their economic and social structures.

Level 4: Business practice—custom—culture (nongovernmental).

This is a category that can comprise a number of different kinds of subtle obstacles to trade, but which also poses some of the most difficult conceptual problems as to whether governments, or at least an international government institution, should try to do anything to minimize or remove these obstacles.

This category can be further subdivided as follows:

a. Governmentally-induced practices. Even though an obstacle to trade, such as a refusal to purchase foreign goods by a private firm, may apparently be the result of private decisions, such decisions may in fact have been subtly or otherwise induced by governments by "administrative guidance," by the "telephone call from the Ministry," or by other measures. GATT does not have much to say about these measures, yet they could very well be insidious, and perhaps should be the subject of future negotiations.

b. Restrictive business practices of private enterprises (raising anti-trust and monopoly questions). A number of private enterprise practices pose substantial obstacles to international trade, but are not the "fault" of governments. These could include concerted refusals to purchase, or a variety of exclusive dealing arrangements which make it very difficult for a new or foreign entrepreneur to "break into" established business channels. As we have seen, although the ill-fated ITO charter would have covered such practices, GATT does not.

c. Business practice and structure. Businessmen in a particular society often develop certain habits and preferences for the way they deal. For example, it is said in Japan that businessmen prefer to have long-term relationships with each other, and there is a certain moral code of responsibility involved in these relationships that differs substantially from Western, or at least U.S., notions of contract law. In some cases, this relationship may be based simply on close friendship, or several generations of constant dealing. In other cases, the structure of this relationship may be related to the problems just mentioned above under (b), which can be traced to restrictive business practices of a variety of kinds (such as exclusive dealing within a "group" of enterprises).

    d.   "Cultural barriers" and consumer preferences. Consumers in each society, including consumers of intermediate goods (parts) often develop a series of cultural preferences. They may like certain colors; dislike certain brand names; be influenced by a certain kind of advertising; prefer to deal with small shop owners in the neighborhood; prefer to have long-established distributor relationships; be willing to pay a premium for certain quality or specialty goods; prefer job security over higher pay; recognize that certain kinds of economic structures may have some noneconomic purposes such as providing employment for disadvantaged groups; etc. To a certain extent these preferences are not properly the subject matter of government attention, but instead require marketing expertise on the part of the particular companies who wish to penetrate the market.

Again, the practices in this category are almost untouched by the GATT system. Except for those in (a) above, they involve exceptionally delicate questions of how far to force conformity on the world's trading nations.

Chapter 23

PERSPECTIVES AND CONCLUSIONS

SECTION 23.1 REFLECTING ON THE PROBLEMS EXAMINED IN THIS BOOK

There is no dearth of perplexing issues presented in this book. The underlying economic policies involved are themselves intricate, subject to challenge, and often undergoing reappraisal. In a world of dramatically reduced transportation and communication costs, coupled with government tendencies to influence market structures and mechanisms, do the traditional economic theories of comparative advantage really work? To what extent can political leaders and practitioners afford to ignore these economic policies? Why do governments seem to opt often for third or even fourth best measures?

But our concern, as lawyers or prospective lawyers, must also be directed to the jurisprudential and governmental questions of how to make the world system work so as to promote the appropriate economic policies. In this book we have faced dozens of difficult conceptual problems related to this broad theme. Is a rule system really appropriate for this endeavor? Are the international institutions adequate to cope with the problems of the next decades or the next century? Are national institutions adequate? Does the U.S. Constitutional system penalize the United States in the context of today's interdependent world and the many international negotiations which occur in it? Do the constitutional and other legal constraints on policy makers nudge them into inferior policy choices? Or do these choices merely reflect compromises with alternative and competing policy goals (such as those mentioned in Section 23.2 below)?

Is the asymmetry of economic power an advantage for the world or does it prevent necessary progress? How can developing countries, nonmarket economies, or the giant combination of both—China—be integrated into the system so as to complement the underlying policies of that system? A further detailed inventory of the many problems and issues would take considerably more space.

In this chapter we first look at a pervasive theme of considerable interest to thoughtful legal practitioners—the role of rules. Then in a final section we suggest (albeit very briefly) some more fundamental perspectives and tentative conclusions. These the reader can take as sort of "hypotheses" for his or her own further thinking, in the light of later experience or observation.

SECTION 23.2 LEGAL RULES OR GOVERNMENT DISCRETION—WHICH MODEL IS BEST?

(A) INTRODUCTION

One of the recurring themes of international trade diplomacy and policy is the question of the role of "rule" or "law." To greatly oversimplify the issue, one can observe a sort of dichotomy between a goal of developing and implementing rules of national economic behavior, and a goal of keeping as much freedom or discretion for national political leaders as possible. A great deal has been written on this theme in the broader context of international affairs. Much has also been written on this theme in the particular context of international trade and economic relations. In many of the chapters of this book we have had occasion to refer both to writings of this type, and to particular problems or issues which concern this issue. In some of the published writings about trade policy generally, one can sometimes observe ambivalence and indeed even contradiction within the same work!

In this section we would like explicitly to address this issue of "rule" versus "government discretion." In doing this we will avoid repeating materials on this subject found elsewhere in this book, but we will refer to them as needed.

There are several dimensions to this issue, three of which we will take up in separate parts of this section. First, we turn to the question of the "legalistic" U.S. system, sometimes alleged to be itself a nontariff barrier because of its costs. Second, we briefly overview some issues of judicial review in the U.S. system. The key question here, addressed also in Chapter 3, is what is the appropriate role of the courts in reviewing and supervising administrative agencies in the United States? Third, and finally, we turn to the international dimension of this problem. To what extent should the international economic regulatory system—the Bretton Woods System—rely on a rule structure with implementing mechanisms such as dispute settlement procedures and retaliation?

(B) THE UNITED STATES AND LEGAL PROCEDURES: COSTS AND BENEFITS APPRAISED

JOHN H. JACKSON, PERSPECTIVES ON THE JURISPRUDENCE OF INTERNATIONAL TRADE: COSTS AND BENEFITS OF LEGAL PROCEDURES IN THE UNITED STATES

(1984)[1]

Both in the United States and abroad the U.S. legal system has been strongly criticized for its handling of international trade regulation. Some of this criticism parallels general statements made about the United States as a litigious society, with too many lawyers and too much attention to "legalism." Despite their serious data faults and some serious misconceptions about comparing the role of a lawyer in the United States to false counterparts in other countries, I feel that it is worthwhile to examine these criticisms more systematically.

* * *

Having given due obeisance to substantive policy, most of the remaining policies that I will mention could be categorized as "procedural." These are the policies that underlie the way that institutions and procedures have been shaped within the United States. Unfortunately, many of these policies are overlooked by important critics of the system. Perhaps it will be easiest for the reader if I enumerate them briefly:

(1) The procedure should maximize the opportunity of government officials to receive all relevant information, arguments, and perspectives. Thus, a procedure that allows all interested parties to present evidence and arguments would enhance the realization of this goal.

(2) The procedure should prevent corruption and ethical *mala fides*, even when the latter fall short of corruption and illegal activity. Another way to express this is that an important policy goal of the procedure is to prevent "back room political deals" that favor special or particular interests while defeating broader policy objectives of the U.S. government.

(3) The procedure should enhance the perception of all parties who will be affected by a decision that they have had their chance to present information and arguments, i.e., that they have had their "day in court." This is an important policy objective, particularly for democratic societies; affected parties must have some confidence in the decision-making process, even when the decision goes against them.

(4) The procedure should be perceived by the citizens at large as fair and tending to maximize the chances for a correct decision. A sense of fairness will include a desire that even weaker interests in a society be treated fairly, i.e., that the ability to get a favorable decision will not depend only on money, political power, status, or other elements deemed unfair.

(5) The procedure should be reasonably efficient, that is, it should allow reasonably quick government decisions and minimize the cost both to government and to private parties of arriving at those decisions. It is this

1. 82 Mich.L.Rev. 1570, 1570, 1574–76, 1578–82, 1587. Reprinted by permission of the Michigan Law Review Association.

policy goal that is most questioned by the criticisms of the American "legalistic" procedures.

(6) The procedure should tend to maximize the likelihood that a decision will be made on a general national basis (or international basis), not catering particularly to special interests. In other words, the procedure should be designed so that government officials can realistically be assisted in "fending off" special interests that conflict with the general good of the nation.

(7) The procedure must fit into the overall constitutional system of the society concerned and be consistent with policy goals underpinning that constitutional system. For the United States, as stated above, an important policy underpinning the Constitution is the prevention of power monopolies within our society. The system of checks and balances thus creates a constant tension between various branches of the government, which may often appear messy, costly, and inefficient, but which is based on fundamental constitutional principles.

(8) Predictability and stability of decisions are important values. Predictability of decisions, whether based on precedent, statutory formulas, or something else, enables private parties and their counselors (lawyers, economists, and politicians) to calculate generally the potential or lack of potential for a favorable decision under each of a variety of different regulatory schemes. The greater the predictability, the more likely that cases will be brought only if they have a good chance to succeed. The private lawyer often experiences the situation wherein he counsels clients in the privacy of his office in such a way that the client will use her best judgment to decide not to bring a case.

I make no claim that the list of policy objectives enumerated above is exhaustive; I am certain that others can be considered. Likewise, as stated earlier, the policy goals mentioned tend to be related to national procedures rather than to international procedures. However, many of these goals also apply, sometimes with modified weight, to international institutions and procedures.

IV. COSTS OF THE U.S. SYSTEM—QUANTIFIABLE AND NON-QUANTIFIABLE

I want to turn now to an attempt to appraise the costs to U.S. society of the U.S. government system of regulating imports. Again, I am only looking at the import side (export regulations could be taken up separately). Furthermore, I am attempting to evaluate the costs of the "legalistic system." There are certain costs that would be incurred no matter what type of import regulation system a government operated, whether it was a system of broad government discretion or a more legalistic system with hearings, statutory criteria, and judicial review.

[See chart on page 1228]

* * *

4. Combining the Various Figures

One can easily see that the figures under the three parts above would total approximately $238 million for 1983. To give due allowance to the imprecision of the estimates, we can expand that figure and say that the probability is very high that the total is less than $250 million.

With what can we compare this figure? One obvious comparison is the total value of imports during the year, which for 1983 is estimated to be $254 billion. The result is that the cost of the U.S. import regulation system is 0.0009, or approximately 1/10th of 1 percent of the total annual value of imports. One could conclude that this figure is reasonably insignificant, if it were considered as a sort of "transaction cost" for a regulatory system that had other benefits. It is perhaps not entirely fair, however, to measure or evaluate the cost of the system by dividing those quantifiable costs by the total value of imports. A better cost-benefit approach would be to look at the regulatory system's welfare benefit to society, and I return to that question in the next section of this article. It should also be recognized that this aggregate approach does not answer all relevant questions. For example, the distribution of costs can vary enormously, and may in fact be very unfair (imposing, for example, substantial burdens on certain sectors of the economy, and few burdens on other sectors). Finally, we must remember that there are a number of nonquantifiable costs that need to be weighed in the balance.

B. Nonquantifiable Costs of the Import Regulatory System

To focus only on the quantifiable dollar costs of the system would be a major mistake. Some of the most important costs may in fact be nonquantifiable. A few of these should be mentioned.

1. Foreign Policy Rigidity

A system that depends on statutory criteria and procedures, allows citizen access, and establishes predictability, will inherently diminish the discretion and flexibility of government officials. Indeed, that is exactly what it is designed to do. However, certain types of foreign policy activities may be inhibited by such a system. Secret negotiations are much more difficult and quick decisions are sometimes almost impossible under a "legalistic" system. Indeed, as was demonstrated in the recent countervailing duty case concerning Chinese textiles, as well as in certain portions of the 1982 carbon steel countervailing duty cases, a "legalistic system" tends to give citizen complainants a considerable amount of control over their cases, which in turn risks giving those particular citizens undue advantage to the detriment of broader U.S. foreign policy considerations.

2. Manipulation or Harassment

The legalistic type of system that exists in the United States also lends itself to some abuse by special interests that manipulate the system for their own advantage in ways not necessarily contemplated by the Congress when it enacted the relevant statutes. For example, a complainant may be tempted to initiate a proceeding knowing that the procedure will present considerable opportunity to create mischief and difficulty for U.S. foreign policy while the real motive for using the procedure is to negotiate with the government towards some solution that is not contemplated within the statutory or regulatory procedure set up by Congress. A complainant may really desire certain tax benefits or cartel-like quotas dividing up the U.S. market and ensuring domestic interests of a certain portion of that market. It may bring a trade proceeding that contemplates relief through imposition of a certain amount of tariff-like duties at the border solely to try to get the U.S. government to negotiate in a way that would achieve the complainant's true objective of quota-like restraints. In addition, it has been alleged in some commentary and by some foreign observers that the U.S. system tends to result in "multiple harassment," by which domestic industry complainants can bring one procedure after another even though they know that they probably will not succeed in such procedures. The running battle of domestic television interests against imported television sets is often cited as one instance of multiple harassment. The mere institution of such procedures creates considerable uncertainty in the market for the imports and creates costs for the importing firms concerned. Both factors tend to reduce the importation of such challenged goods initially and to increase importers' general costs of penetrating the U.S. market, with attendant effects upon their later price structure and competitiveness in the U.S. market. Although appraisal of the "multiple harassment" charge is not easy, there appear to be few instances in which it can actually be established that such action has occurred. Even the threat of such activity, however, may itself be somewhat inhibiting to foreign exporters who are eyeing the potential of the U.S. market.

3. Wrong Law Rigidity

One of the results of the U.S. "legalistic" system of regulating imports is that criteria tend to be embodied in statutes enacted by Congress and then become very hard to change. Because Congress distrusts executive discretion, it tends to establish rather elaborate detail in statutory criteria. But on some occasions the statutory formulas prove later to be inappropriate from a policy or economic point of view. Or an international proceeding will find that the U.S. law violates U.S. international obligations. In these cases it has proved very difficult to get the Congress to change the law, because a variety of special interests tend to be able to block such change. Consequently, the result is that the system has a certain amount of "wrong law rigidity" built into it.

4. Special Interest Influence on the Formulation of the Statutory Criteria

The processes by which the Congress writes the statutory criteria and formulates the law are reasonably well known. The system sometimes lends itself to manipulation by special economic interests in the United States that can foresee the results of certain statutory wordings on their potential cases in the future. Thus, an important economic sector can sometimes influence the Congress in developing criteria that will later prove to be very beneficial to it in particular cases, even though such criteria may not be in the overall best interests of the United States. In this respect, however, the process is no different from that of any domestic subject matter. It is perhaps a price one pays for an open democratic system.

5. *Big Cases Mishandled*

One of the allegations often made is that the United States' elaborately legalistic system of import regulation may operate with reasonable satisfaction only as to the little cases that are generally unimportant in themselves. But when it comes to very big cases that have a broad influence in major sectors of the economy (such as autos, textiles, agriculture, and steel), it is said that the system breaks down and in fact returns, by one subterfuge or another, to a "non-rule system" of extensive executive discretion and "back-room bargaining."

6. *The Dilemma of a Legalistic System*

As one can begin to surmise from analyzing these various costs, both quantifiable and nonquantifiable, there is to a certain extent a dilemma involved in designing any institutional system for regulating imports. The dilemma is not unique to this subject and is involved in a number of other areas of governmental endeavor also. This dilemma is that the more one maximizes the goals of a legalistic system (predictability, transparency and elimination of corruption and political back-room deals), the more one sacrifices other desirable goals such as flexibility and the ability of government officials to make determinations in the broad national interest as opposed to catering to specific special interests.

V. THE BENEFITS OF THE SYSTEM

The benefits of the legalistic system may be considerable, but they are perhaps harder to appraise. I will discuss them under two categories.

A. *Procedural Benefits of the System*

Apart from costs and delays, the legalistic system responds well to many of the goals and objectives set out in section III above. Clearly, the more extensive and detailed are the statutory criteria, the public proceedings, the opportunity for judicial review and the like, the more likely that the system will be predictable, corruption-proof and devoid of back-room political deals. An exception to this might be the "big case" question: If the system becomes too rigid, the big cases—those involving considerable political power—will tend to make "end runs" around the system, and thus will not be channeled by the rules and will perhaps be even more vulnerable to flexible executive official discretion than would be the case if the formal procedures were less rigid and could better accommodate the big cases.

B. *Substantive Benefits*

One of the critical questions, and perhaps the most critical question, is whether this legalistic system, given its costs, in fact provides a substantial measure of benefits (benefits that exceed the costs) to the general welfare of the United States. Here it is necessary to indulge in some assumptions, and to recognize that conclusions are only tentative, in the form of hypotheses that need further testing.

The basic assumption that may be required to justify the legalistic system is that it in fact allows a higher degree of liberal trade access for imports into the U.S. economy. This assumption itself is premised on the assumption that such trade liberalization provides a benefit to the U.S. economy. Most economists believe that trade liberalization does provide such a benefit, and my colleagues at the University of Michigan Department of Economics, Alan Deardorff and Robert Stern, have used their very large international trade model to compute some of the welfare benefits of liberal trade. For example, they conclude that a fifty percent reduction across the board in pre-Tokyo Round tariff levels (from an average of about eight percent to half that), would result in an additional welfare benefit to the U.S. economy of approximately one billion dollars. There is some indication by them and others that this welfare benefit amount is understated, but we can accept it provisionally, for purposes of comparison.

If we can believe (and although it is essentially a "judgment call" many people do believe it) that the U.S. legalistic system—cumbersome, rigid, and costly as it is—in fact provides for an economy more open to imports than virtually any other major industrial economy in the world, then we could count this as a benefit. But measuring that benefit is obviously very difficult. We are measuring it against an unknown—namely, what would be the degree of import restraint in the U.S. economy if the U.S. system were not so legalistic and were more "discretion prone." Morici and Megna of the National Planning Association have tried to evaluate the current costs of all the various nontariff barriers in the United States, and they arrived at an amount of less than one percent tariff equivalent. The current import restraints, they report, are fairly modest in comparison with those of other economies, so one might well imagine that the tariff equivalent of import restraints unfettered by a legalistic system might be considerably more restrictive. Another way to say it is that overall import restraint tariff equivalents could increase by fifty percent over pre-Tokyo Round U.S. tariff levels (in the Deardorff-Stern model). Thus the Deardorff-Stern welfare benefit amount of about one billion dollars might be one "ballpark" measure of the more quantifiable of the economic benefits of the trade regulatory system. This compares quite favorably to the quantifiable costs mentioned above (and in Appendix B), although this comparison depends on much-hedged assumptions.

One must not forget, however, that there are also a number of non-quantifiable benefits to the system—greater confidence of the citizenry in the operation of its government in this subject matter, the business planning advantage of a higher degree of stability in governmental actions, reduction of corruption, etc.

*   *   *

Appendix B
Cost Estimates of U.S. Import Regulation

Millions of Dollars

1. U.S. Government Costs—Estimates* Name of Agency	Budget 1982	1983	Annual Estimate
International Trade Commission	17.6	19.8	20
Intl. Trade Admin. (Commerce, Import reg.)	8.1	N/A	10
Office of U.S. Trade Representative	9.2	10.5	11
Bureau of Econ. & Bus. Affairs, Dept. State	N/A	2.23	2.5
Annual Total	34.9	32.53	43.5

2. Private Costs: Extra-Firm (Attys. etc.)** Type of Action	Approx.*** No. per Yr.	Total Cost (Mil.)
Escape Clause (201–203)	9	$ 4.125
Anti-dumping: New	50	$23.750
AD—annual reviews	109	$13.625
Countervailing Duty—New	40	$16.300
CV—annual reviews	81	$10.125
Section 337	40	$28.000
Section 301	6	$ 1.050
TOTAL	335	$96.975

3. Private Costs: Intra-Firm $96.975
    (Guess based on extra-firm costs)

4. OVERALL TOTAL ANNUAL ESTIMATE OF COSTS $237.450
   TOTAL VALUE OF IMPORTS—1983 ($ Billion)   254
   COSTS AS A PERCENT OF IMPORTS   0.0935%
   COSTS AS A FRACTION OF IMPORTS   0.000935

NOTES: * Amounts are overstated since little attempt has been made to disaggregate for various functions within a unit. On the other hand, as explained in the text, agencies with a very small amount of activities in this area are omitted.

      ** Estimates of total costs are not simply a multiple of cases times average costs per case, but involve estimates of the number of cases which are appealed, go on for further procedures (injury test), etc.

      *** Based largely on 1983 filings, with averages of prior years used to estimate an annual number if 1983 figures seemed unrepresentative.

THOMAS R. HOWELL & ALAN WILLIAM WOLFF, THE ROLE OF TRADE LAW IN THE MAKING OF TRADE POLICY

(1985) [2]

Innate hostility to centralized economic authority has been one of the basic organizing principles of American democracy. To be sure, we have always recognized the need for some form of government oversight of commercial activity. Entrepreneurs need a stable business environment—some guarantee that their investments will not be wiped out by "domestic violence and the depredations which the democratic spirit is apt to make on property." The need to protect property rights has been met largely through the establishment of an independent judiciary to ensure the sanctity of contracts and settle private disputes impartially, based on mutually agreed principles and procedures, and whose decisions are for the most part, accepted by all parties.

This sytem has worked so well for the U.S. domestic economy for a period of nearly two centuries that its basic features have been incorporated as guiding principles in the formulation of international economic policy. As the nation has grown, economic conflicts between private interests have generally proven capable of resolution through the judicial system. While the state and federal courts may not have always dispensed justice in such disputes with perfect understanding of the economic effects of their decisions, they have functioned with sufficient even-handedness to permit a capitalist economy to flourish and grow.

The propensity to regulate economic behavior, if at all, through adjudication, was manifested in the reforms adopted to curb the growing power and abuses of big business in the years between the Civil War and the Depression. Our response to the growth of trusts and holding companies with power to control entire industries was not nationalization of these industries, but, rather, the passage of antitrust laws prohibiting a wide range of activities deemed to be "anticompetitive" or "unfair"—enforceable in the federal courts or before a quasi-judicial Federal Trade Commission. These laws were designed to preserve a competitive environment by defining rules of conduct and vesting adjudicative tribunals with the authority to resolve complaints that those rules were being violated.

From this experience America has inherited certain values with respect to commercial and industrial activity. It has little tradition, prior to this century, of comprehensive government involvement in promoting or planning the growth of particular industrial sectors. Despite the exceptional treatment granted defense-related industries, agriculture, and housing, the limited experience with more pervasive government regulation of industries—notably public utilities and the railroads—has, if anything, simply reinforced the view that increasing government intervention leads to inefficiency, protection of the industry by government regulators, and loss of

---

2. From J. Jackson, R. Cunningham & C. Fontheim (eds.), International Trade Policy: The Lawyer's Perspective, at 3–10 to –13, 3–21 to –24. Reprinted by permission of the American Bar Association.

competitiveness. This experience has reinforced a general consensus that the government's proper role should be confined to that of an arbiter. Thus did Herbert Hoover articulate this abiding view of the proper role of government in the Presidential campaign of 1928:

> It is as if we set a race. We, through free and universal education provide the training for the runners; we give to them an equal start; we provide in the government the umpire of the fairness of the race. The winner is he who shows the most conscientious training, the greatest ability, and the greatest character.

This spirit, quite naturally, has been extended to U.S. trade laws—several of which, in their original versions, were enacted during the same era (the latter nineteenth and early twentieth century) that produced our first antitrust laws.

As in our domestic laws governing commercial behavior, a fundamental purpose of the trade laws is to provide equity. "Unfair" conduct is defined with as much precision as possible, and a carefully prescribed set of procedures is established for gathering evidence, presenting opposing views, and appealing adverse determinations. Decisions are, for the most part, based on the evidence of record rather than political pressure. While foreigners frequently complain of the multiplicity of overlapping U.S. trade remedies, upon participation in an antidumping or countervailing duty action they cannot fail to be impressed by the fairness, thoroughness, and impartiality with which such cases are tried and decided, in contrast to the procedures under less legalistic systems.

At the same time, however, the operation of the trade laws has often diverted attention from and undermined the ability of the United States to respond effectively to broad problems of international competition. The precise definition of specific types of actionable conduct requires a petitioning industry to fit its problem into the parameters of the statutes. This cannot always be done satisfactorily—in part because many of the problems which U.S. industries confront today are far more complex than those contemplated by the framers of the trade laws—but also because many of the more serious problems in international trade do not readily lend themselves to an adjudicative resolution.

With the reduction of tariff and nontariff barriers at the border to the extent that they are no longer a decisive influence on trade in most sectors, national economies of significantly different structure are now in direct competition. Our trade competitors include, for example, not only the dynamic capitalist economies of East Asia, but a variety of developing and Soviet bloc nations where state involvement in the economy is pervasive. In some cases systemic differences bestow clear natural trade advantages on foreign producers—not necessarily flowing from superior efficiency or productivity—which have enabled them to prevail in competition with U.S. industries.

The American response to such developments has been hamstrung by the intellectual framework within which we have traditionally approached trade issues. Thus, when a foreign industry prevails over an American industry, trade policy makers most frequently ask whether the foreign industry has benefited from an "unfair" advantage—more specifically, some advantage that can be fit within the carefully-drawn legal requirements established by U.S. trade remedies. Not surprisingly, in many cases, the trade laws offer no solution, or only a partial solution.

* * *

§ 3.06 Conclusion

The application of U.S. trade remedies—whether the narrow, specialized laws such as antidumping or the broader discretionary statutes such as Section 301—produces results that bear little more than a random relationship to the long run international competitiveness of American industries. The specialized remedies can be triggered by any industry that invokes them. The discretionary remedies are available to those industries which have been seriously injured (in the case of the import relief provisions) and possess the political muscle, good timing, and sheer luck needed to secure relief. In neither case, however, can any government action be said to bear more than a coincidental relationship to the overall competitive posture of U.S. industries in international trade.

One is forced to conclude that to a degree unmatched in other nations, trade law is not merely an important aspect of U.S. trade policy—it actually *is* trade policy. The trade laws dictate how trade officials spend a large amount of their time—in effect responding to complaints generated by producers of plant hangers, fishing rods, strontium carbonate, circulating pumps, potato starch, ear tags, latchet hook kits, golf carts, and a staggering variety of other commodities that bears tribute, if nothing else, to the diversity of the American industrial and agricultural economy. Trade officials' commitment to deal with these matters tends to obscure the question of what they would do if they sat down and attempted to identify those trade concerns which were most important from the standpoint of long range national interest.

Most fundamentally the U.S. trade policy system suffers from a lack of clear national priorities with respect to the application of trade remedies. The system expends the largest part of governmental resources to provide equity. The actions taken, however, may be of little long-run significance to the country as a whole or to the industry immediately concerned. The concept of national economic interest does not play an identifiable role. Under such circumstances, the provision of equity permits the avoidance of making more substantive choices. Not only has a more active role by the government not been sought, but the whole history of Congressional enactments of trade remedy legislation provides a record of a progressive narrowing of the scope for Executive discretion.

A related problem is the severe compartmentalization which results from an adjudicatory approach to trade problems. Each case is considered separately from all other cases and resolved outside of any larger context. Trade officials do not have the mandate, the inclination or, in many cases, the research capabilities, to recognize or act upon the interrelationships between their cases and any overall concerns over U.S. international competitiveness.

The systematic designation by our government of certain manufacturing industries for special treatment (e.g., preferential loans, tax breaks, subsidized research and development) would represent something of a departure from our political traditions. However, the establishment of a more direct relationship between our system of trade laws and our own economic self-interest should not require nearly so major a change. Modifications in the laws themselves—together with some institutional reforms—could be implemented which would add a needed measure of coherence to the application of U.S. trade remedies without sacrificing a significant degree of the equity which our traditions have led us to value.

Institutionally, one of the primary obstacles to a better coordinated application of trade remedies is the current separation of the responsibility for trade policy formation and negotiations—vested in the Office of U.S. Trade Representative—from that of trade law implementation, which rests with the Department of Commerce and the International Trade Commission. This separation of functions, which was implemented pursuant to President Carter's Reorganization Plan No. 3 of 1979, was designed in part to insulate the application of trade remedies from political pressure, but it has also served to limit the flexibility to provide effective relief. Consolidation of trade policy formation, trade negotiation and trade law enforcement functions within a single agency—whether it be a new Department of Trade and Industry, as proposed by the Reagan administration, or USTR, the Commerce Department, or some other entity, would seem to be a desirable and perhaps essential first step. This entity should receive a legislative mandate to establish national priorities with respect to trade issues—in consultation with Congress and private sector trading interests—and to exercise its authority over trade law enforcement in a manner consistent with those priorities.

The establishment of trade priorities would not mean denial of relief, where it should appropriately be granted, to various small U.S. industries under the antidumping, countervailing duty, and other trade laws. These remedies would remain available to any petitioner who could come forth and make the requisite showing under the statutory standards. Rather, the setting of priorities would mean the identification, by a governmental authority—in consultation with private sector advisers and the Congress—of certain trade sectors and trade problems vital to our long-term national economic interests, where the coordinated application of the trade laws could further those interests.

For example, the filing of dozens of steel cases over the last few years would indicate a fundamental disequilibrium in the conditions of competition in this sector that calls for a less reactive and *ad hoc* decision-making process. A thorough review of public policy options—including trade policy and the possible application of trade remedies—is required. It need not be concluded that such an approach would lead to greater protection. Quite the reverse, with appropriate domestic adjustment measures and international accords on trading practices in this sector, a comprehensive approach to the problems of the steel industry might well be less disruptive of trade and of shorter duration than a succession of disconnected, *ad hoc* relief measures undertaken in reaction to the immediate pressure of events.

As a practical matter, trade cases will persist in a sector as long as there is a shortfall in U.S. competitiveness or the conditions of competition are distinctly unequal, in particular due to foreign government intervention. Attempting to deal with these broad industrial problems through discrete trade actions can only lead to a deterioration in international trade relations as well as the erosion of domestic political support for full U.S. participation in the international trading system.

The establishment of certain trade policy priorities and the integration of the multiplicity of individual trade actions into a coherent larger whole would require a more active government policymaking role in trade than that to which Americans are accustomed. At the same time, the alternative—continued reliance on *ad hoc* policy decisions heavily shaped by random events—will come under progressively greater criticism as the U.S. economy is subject to more direct competition from abroad. Under such circumstances, Congress will likely attempt to legislate its own solutions. The choice, in other words, may not be between a continued *ad hoc* system on the one hand, and a more active, pro-competitiveness national trade policy on the other but between a more active policy and a succession of Congressional enactments providing specific responses, often protectionist, for those industries which possess the political influence to secure such relief.

(C) JUDICIAL REVIEW AND UNITED STATES TRADE LAWS

One of the more important issues of the U.S. governmental system is the question of the appropriate role for the courts. This issue arises in many areas of U.S. law, but it has some additional layers of perplexity in the context of U.S. international trade laws, for two reasons: First, it is part of the general question of whether courts should interfere with activities of the President or Congress relating to foreign affairs, a question we examined in Chapter 3. Second, Congress has specified varying statutory formulae for judicial review of international trade actions of administrative agencies, a situation made more complex by the courts, who have adopted varying review standards depending on the question before them.

In the Trade Agreements Act of 1979, for example, there are two different standards of judicial review applicable to countervailing or antidumping duty determinations. For administrative determinations not to commence an antidumping or countervailing duty investigation, the standard of review applied by the Court of International Trade (CIT) is whether the determination was "arbitrary" or "capricious."[3] On the other hand, for a variety of final administrative determinations in connection with a formal investigation, the standard of review is whether the determination is supported by "substantial evidence."[4]

While judges and scholars have attempted to distinguish the two standards, in practice courts probably exercise considerable discretion in interpreting their powers of review. Indeed, one commentator has asserted that

3. 19 U.S.C.A. § 1516a(b)(1)(A).   **4.** 19 U.S.C.A. § 1516a(b)(1)(B).

the courts ultimately apply a single standard of reasonableness in reviewing questions outside their special competence.[5] However, the legislative history of the 1979 Act states that the arbitrary-capricious standard requires only "a rational basis in fact for the determination."[6] The substantial evidence standard, in contrast, requires the court to reverse the determination if, after review of the complete record, it decides that a "reasonable mind" could not have made the determination.[7]

In Section 3.5(C)(2) supra, we reviewed some of the other international trade statutes and how administrative action taken pursuant to them is reviewed by the courts. The material in that section, which could be profitably reviewed at this time, demonstrated that there are even more gradations of review than called for by the 1979 Act.

Since 1979, there has been considerably more judicial review of administrative actions relating to trade. Arguably this is exactly what Congress intended. Suspicious of administration handling of these endeavors, particularly in the antidumping and countervailing duty areas, Congress limited executive branch discretion. Through the Customs Courts Act of 1980,[8] Congress clarified and expanded the jurisdiction of the courts over Executive Branch actions in international trade. In 1979, Congress also provided private parties with increased access to the courts by expanding the definition of "interested party," i.e. one who can seek court review.[9] It is currently estimated that almost 80% of antidumping and countervailing duty cases are appealed to the CIT.

When we step back from the various types of trade actions to try to ascertain a broader picture, we view a very confusing scene. In certain kinds of cases, the courts have been very deferential to administrative agencies. For example, in a case brought by a textile importers' association to challenge the U.S. program of bilateral agreements to restrain textile imports, the association argued that the agency involved had exceeded its statutory powers and abused its discretion in unilaterally setting textile quotas. The Court of Appeals for the Federal Circuit upheld the agency's action, stating:[10]

> [L]egislation conferring upon the President discretion to regulate foreign commerce invokes, and is reinforced and augmented by, the President's constitutional power to oversee the political side of foreign affairs. * * * In the area of international trade, "intimately involved in foreign affairs," "congressional authorizations of presidential power should be given a broad construction and not [be] 'hemmed in' or 'cabined, cribbed, confined' by anxious judicial blinders."

5. K. Davis, Administrative Law Treatise § 29.1 (1984).

6. S.Rep. No. 96–249, 96th Cong., 2d Sess. 252 (1979).

7. Consolidated Edison Co. v. N.L.R.B., 305 U.S. 197, 229, 59 S.Ct. 206, 217, 83 L.Ed.2d 126, 140 (1938).

8. Pub.L. No. 96–417, 94 Stat. 1727 (1980).

9. Trade Agreements Act of 1979, § 101 (codified at 19 U.S.C.A. § 1677(9)).

10. American Assn. of Exporters and Importers—Textile and Apparel Group v. United States, 751 F.2d 1239, 1248 (Fed.Cir.1985), quoting Florsheim Shoe Co. v. United States, 744 F.2d 787, 793 (Fed.Cir.1984), quoting South Puerto Rico Sugar Co. Trading Corp. v. United States, 334 F.2d 622, 632 (Ct.Cl.1964).

The court continued: [11]

> "Once it is determined, as we have just done, that the President's exercise of this authority * * * was within his constitutionally delegated power, there is no further role for the CIT or for this court. * * * The President's findings of fact and the motivations for his actions are not subject to review."

On the other hand, the CIT digs very deeply into the substance of the cases in reviewing countervailing and antidumping duty actions. In many cases, the CIT seems almost to try the case de novo, as indeed the law seemed to provide prior to 1979.[12] To confuse the scene further, the Court of Appeals for the Federal Circuit seems not to hesitate to overrule the CIT.

Thus, in the United States, the problem of the complexity and cost of the legalistic system is further complicated by the wide variance in the scope of review that the court system may give to Executive action. This means, of course, that as to some matters, the U.S. system may be less rule governed and more discretionary than it would first appear.

(D) INTERNATIONAL DISPUTE SETTLEMENT—RULE OR NEGO-TIATION? POWER OR PRINCIPLE?

JOHN H. JACKSON, PERSPECTIVES ON THE JURISPRU-DENCE OF INTERNATIONAL TRADE: COSTS AND BENE-FITS OF LEGAL PROCEDURES IN THE UNITED STATES

Supra, at 1571–72

I. RULE ORIENTATION VERSUS POWER ORIENTATION FOR THE
PROCEDURES OF INTERNATIONAL ECONOMIC RELATIONS

I have written elsewhere about the distinction between "power-oriented" and "rule-oriented" diplomacy. Roughly categorizing diplomatic techniques into these two groups is an oversimplification, of course, but it is a useful one in describing a certain difference in technique and spirit that is involved in international discourse. Particularly when it comes to international affairs, these distinctions can have considerable importance.

Power-oriented techniques suggest a diplomat asserting, subtly or otherwise, the power of the nation he or she represents. Often diplomats of the more powerful nations prefer negotiation as a method of settling matters because they can bring to bear that power to win advantage in the particular negotiation. The "bargaining chips" involved could be promised aid, trade concessions, movement of an aircraft carrier, influence on exchange rates, and the like.

A rule-oriented approach, by way of contrast, would be designed to help institutions which would insure the highest possible degree of adherence and conformity to a set of rules. The rules themselves would be formulated in advance and would presumably make broad policy sense for the benefit of the world and the parties concerned. Of course, the process of formulating the rules will involve, to a certain extent, power-oriented techniques.

---

11. 751 F.2d at 1248, quoting Florsheim Shoe Co. v. United States, 744 F.2d 787, 795–96 (Fed.Cir.1984).

12. See 28 U.S.C.A. §§ 2631–39 (1976), amended by the Customs Courts Act of 1980, Pub.L. No. 96–417, 94 Stat. 1727 (1980).

In negotiations for the settlement of disputes between countries, both techniques will be used in varying degrees. If a power orientation prevails, however, the dispute is likely to be settled more from the point of view of which party has the greater power. By contrast, if a rule-oriented approach prevails, the negotiation would resolve the dispute by reference to what the participants expect an international body would conclude about the application of preexisting international obligations.

Although to a large extent all government activity involves a mixture of these two techniques, and indeed to a large degree the history of civilization may be described as a gradual evolution from a power-oriented approach towards a rule-oriented approach, nevertheless the present state of international affairs tips the scales heavily in favor of the power orientation. Yet a strong argument can be made that the same evolution must occur in international affairs and that, as to international economic affairs particularly, there are strong arguments for pursuing evenhandedly, and with a fixed direction, progress in international procedures towards a rule-oriented approach. Several advantages accrue generally to international affairs through a rule-oriented approach, such as: (1) less reliance on raw power and the temptation to exercise it; (2) fairer treatment of the smaller countries, or at least a perception of greater fairness; and (3) the development of agreed procedures to achieve the necessary compromises. In economic affairs there are additional reasons for a rule-oriented approach.

Economic affairs tend (at least in peace time) to affect more citizens directly than do political and military affairs. As the world becomes more economically interdependent, private citizens increasingly find their jobs, their businesses, and their quality of life affected, if not controlled, by forces from outside their country's boundaries. Thus, they are more affected by the international economic negotiations pursued by their own country on their behalf. A rule-oriented approach allows citizens a greater opportunity to give their "input" into the processes, and also allows decentralized decision makers (such as entrepreneurs in market-oriented economies) a greater opportunity to plan and to base action on more predictable and stable governmental policies.

JOHN H. JACKSON, JEAN–VICTOR LOUIS & MITSUO MATSUSHITA, IMPLEMENTING THE TOKYO ROUND: NATIONAL CONSTITUTIONS AND INTERNATIONAL ECONOMIC RULES

207–09 (1984) [10]

Much has been written in recent decades about the tendency of international law to accept individuals as well as national states as its proper subjects. Without trying to get into the somewhat theoretical questions involved in those writings, we would like simply to point out that it has now become established that it is possible to design procedures under which private citizens or firms have some sort of direct access (usually limited) to international bodies for the purpose of asserting their rights. The two prime

10. Reprinted by permission of the authors.

examples that come to mind are the European Convention on Human Rights and the International Convention for the Settlement of Investment Disputes (ICSID). Under the former, an individual citizen can go to an international body with a complaint against his own government, on the grounds that it has violated its obligations under the international convention in a way that has directly affected him. The international procedures then call for a commission to look into the complaint and possibly to help mediate a solution between the citizen and his government. Where the commission feels it is justified, it may bring the complaint to a court—the European Court on Human Rights. That court then has the authority to rule on whether the state concerned has violated its obligations under the European Convention. Only states that have explicitly accepted this fairly far-reaching procedure under the appropriate convention can be brought into these procedures by their own citizens.

Likewise, the ICSID, set up under the auspices of the World Bank, provides a mechanism by which governments who have accepted the ICSID in advance can subsequently provide in any contract with a foreign private firm or citizen that disputes about the contract will be referred to an arbitration process set up by ICSID.

There are some interesting potentials in these precedents for the GATT and the international economic system, although they will probably not be readily accepted by the governments that participate in the GATT. But governments and business firms do desire greater predictability of national government economic actions in an increasingly interdependent world, and do desire greater balance and equality in actual implementation of negotiated international rules on economic matters. Those factors could lead governments to be willing to accept some sort of a mechanism by which individual citizens or firms could appeal directly to an international body like the GATT to determine whether a government obligated under the GATT or one of its codes has taken an action that is inconsistent with its international obligations.

Several particulars are likely to be necessary in any such procedure. First, a requirement that national internal administration and judicial remedies be exhausted before an international body is consulted seems appropriate. Second, some sort of a filter would probably be needed, much as is the case currently with the European procedure for human rights. Thus, some international body, such as a GATT unit, could be charged with initially receiving complaints from private citizens or firms and making a preliminary investigation to see whether they have any merit. This would prevent spurious complaints from getting very far. Third, it is likely that at the outset, any procedure of this type would have to accommodate itself to the lack of effective sanctions. It is doubtful that states would soon be willing to accept such a procedure if truly effective sanctions could be applied. However, that does not make such a procedure useless. The fact that there could be a reliable third-party determination on the facts and the application of the law (the international obligation) would itself be salutary. To a certain extent, the mere fact of findings by an international panel, when such findings are made public, is a sort of sanction that many governments try to avoid.

Clearly, the typical governmental reluctance to relinquish any power or to constrain its field of discretion would discourage a move in the direction of the procedures described. On the other hand, it should be recognized that there are some advantages for governments in such a procedure. For one thing, if it were carefully designed and became reliable, governments might well find that the procedure would tend to deemphasize and depoliticize many relatively minor trade or economic complaints that now exist between nations. For example, let us assume that Mr. A, a citizen in country A finds that his exports to country B are being restrained improperly by country B, inconsistent with country B's international obligations. Under the current procedure, Mr. A must go to his own national government and get it to take up his matter with the foreign government. Thus, his case has immediately been raised to a diplomatic level. That quite often means, by the nature of things, that it has been raised to a fairly high level of official attention and consequently of public perception. On the other hand, if an appropriate international procedure existed, when Mr. A came to his government to complain about country B, country A officials could refer Mr. A to that procedure and encourage him to use it, without taking any stand on the matter. It is quite possible that the issue could then be handled more expeditiously and routinely. The case would continue to be Mr. A's case, and not become country A's case. The issue would be Mr. A versus country B, instead of Mr. A and country A versus country B.

It is the view of at least one of the authors of this book that in all probability, early versions of such a procedure would have to allow the individual governments to exercise some kind of right of veto over their own citizens' attempts to invoke the process. However, this right could be accorded to national governments as a way to make them more comfortable with experimenting with the procedure, and could be designed to gradually die out (at least for all but the most exceptional cases).

PHILLIP R. TRIMBLE, INTERNATIONAL TRADE AND THE "RULE OF LAW"

(1985) [11]

A. OBJECTIONS TO THE SUPERCOURT

1. Impracticability

It seems inconceivable that a President (Republican or Democrat) or the Congress would go along with the proposal. In the United States a distrust of international supervision is deeply embedded in our political tradition and has been repeatedly demonstrated in this century. The Senate frustrated a variety of attempts to conclude arbitration treaties by Presidents Cleveland, McKinley, Roosevelt and Taft. It then repudiated the League of Nations, and for twelve years stalled consideration of U.S. participation in the World Court before finally rejecting it in 1935. When the Senate eventually

---

11. 83 Mich.L.Rev. 1016, 1026 (book review of J. Jackson, J.-V. Louis & M. Matsushita, note 10 supra). Reprinted by permission of the Michigan Law Review Association.

consented to the jurisdiction of the International Court of Justice in 1945, it did so only with a reservation that essentially negated the effect of ratification. More recently, the prospect of international supervision has led the Senate to refuse to consider the Human Rights Conventions. President Carter did not even submit to the Senate the Optional Protocol to the International Covenant on Civil and Political Rights, which would have subjected the United States to international supervision.

These are not isolated acts. They reflect a deep and enduring American attitude toward law-making authority removed from representative control. The authors clearly share my skepticism on this score, citing "the typical government reluctance to relinquish any power or to constrain its field of discretion" (p. 209). I think, however, that the causes of this reluctance are deeper than the egos of bureaucrats and politicians. They are expressed in basic national political philosophy. Even the active involvement of the United States in world affairs, and the dramatically increased national interdependence of the international economy, will alter this attitude only slowly, if at all. In the next section, I will explain why I think that this attitude should not be changed.

2. Political Philosophy

My objection is more than a prediction that Congress will reject the scheme. In reaching the conclusion that a supercourt should not be accepted, I start with the assumption that any exercise of authority by a government should be explained by a coherent theory of power that is acceptable to the relevant political community. Accordingly, I look to American political philosophy and tradition in order to test the novel supranational authority proposed by the authors. In this regard the proposal does not pass muster.

The kind of international law making envisioned by the authors cannot easily be reconciled with American political tradition. For over 200 years the theory and rhetoric used to justify law making in the United States has exalted limited and representative government resting on the "consent of the governed." Authority is said to be delegated to a federal government of limited powers, with law making concentrated in politically accountable branches of government that are responsive to the interests of their constituencies. It is true that we entrust wide law-making power to unelected judges, but they are products of the domestic political system and in fact are responsive to political changes in society. Judges read the newspapers and follow the election returns.

* * *

3. The Undesirable Effects of Emphasizing Economic over Political Values

* * *

In the specific context of the GATT, the question comes down to who will be primarily in charge of trade policy—elected officials and political branch bureaucrats, who are responsive to the constituencies of their districts and agencies, or private litigants and international judges, who are responsive to a body of rules. In favoring the former I simply doubt that rules can be drafted with sufficient prescience, or that they can be changed quickly enough, to respond to the legitimate needs of domestic constituencies. Free trade is an important goal, but it is not the only one, and I doubt our capacity to create institutions that will respond the way we expect representative government to respond. Some observers may think that the executive branch has not been sufficiently responsive to domestic interests, and others may believe that special interests have too much influence. I trust the political process to reach a fair balance. In my view the value of representative government outweighs the value of free trade.

As I noted at the outset, however, the legalists have scored some victories in their quest for the "rule of law." Fortunately their momentum has been blunted. While the "commercial activity" doctrine permits lawsuits against foreign governments, the courts have apparently reacted by expanding the act of state doctrine. And although the political question doctrine may be in general retreat domestically, it still seems vibrant in the foreign affairs field. American judges have been conspicuously cautious in applying rules to unfamiliar areas involving foreign relations. Their example suggests further caution before accepting the legalist line.

4. The Undesirability of a Strict "Rule of Law" in International Trade

My fourth point focuses specifically on the debate over how best to understand the GATT's contribution to the "rule of law." I agree with the authors that governments will be reluctant to accept their proposal. One reason is that many GATT obligations are intentionally general or vague, concealing important differences of opinion. The Subsidies Code is a good example. Judicial interpretation would disrupt the appearance of agreement by applying the language of a convention in unambiguous concrete ways. It could also inhibit the successful negotiation of future agreements. Although one may object that such agreements are undesirable anyway, I would respond that vague agreements are frequently important politically. Indeed, vague agreements may be the only agreements possible. Even if an agreement does not reflect a "genuine meeting of the minds," it may temporarily defuse conflicts, make other agreements possible, or help hold the jerry-rigged system together for another few years during which the conditions for real agreement may improve.

Judicial clarification is inconsistent with this approach. Here too I side with the pragmatists and see a major value of the GATT in its ambiguous, flexible and "nonlegal" approach. In view of the GATT's success, the proponents of radical change bear a heavy burden of persuasion to justify abandonment of the GATT's self-conscious accommodation to political reality.

5. Adverse Effects on Free Trade

Finally, it is not clear that international litigation to enforce rules will even serve to promote an open trading system. In theory it may sound desirable. U.S. exporters could strike down Japanese quotas maintained in violation of article XI of the GATT. A German exporter of specialty steel could sue to force U.S. revocation of escape clause relief recently granted to the specialty steel industry. There is no problem for free trade as long as the suit is brought against an inefficient producer hiding behind an illegal practice.

On the other hand, suits by competitors to enforce rules against "unfair" actions (like subsidies) are just as likely. Thus, the threatened U.S. steel industry could sue to halt illegal Brazilian subsidies. Such litigation may simply lead the defendant government to do whatever is necessary to stop the lawsuit, and not necessarily to change its practices to conform to the rules. Even if one believes the classic argument that subsidization (or dumping) is unfair, and therefore ought to be eliminated, the range of opinion among nations about subsidies and dumping is so wide, and the practices subject to attack so entrenched, that it seems extremely doubtful that litigation to resolve the differences of opinion would be tolerated. The result of domestic litigation by the steel industry has been the effective cartelization of world steel trade through "voluntary" restraint agreements. The likely result of establishing a supercourt would simply be more "voluntary" agreements, serving protectionist rather than free trade objectives. The "high degree of legalization" of the U.S. system applauded by the book under review has itself been seen by some observers as a nontariff barrier.

SECTION 23.3   MANAGING ECONOMIC INTERDEPENDENCE [1]

What then can we conclude overall from the materials in this book? One approach is to recognize that the problem of international economics today is largely a problem of "managing" interdependence. The Bretton Wood System and its evolution has been so successful that it has created a host of new problems. When economic transactions so easily transit national borders, tensions occur merely because of the differences between economic institutions as well as cultures. In addition, the freedom of border "transit" sometimes allows unscrupulous entrepreneurs to manipulate it in such a way as to evade national government regulation. Even morally sensitive entrepreneurs find their effective power enhanced when they can move activity quickly from one nation to another. Governments, to the contrary, find themselves increasingly frustrated by effective evasion of their regulatory powers. Furthermore, governments themselves find that actions of other governments cause them great difficulties.

Several government responses are observed. One set of responses governments pursue is to join other governments in an attempt to create an international regulatory system to help ameliorate the "free-for-all" aspects of potential beggar-thy-neighbor policies, or to provide a unified posture to confront the less public spirited entrepreneurs. Another set of responses governments pursue is to develop internal policies designed to enable their nations to cope better with the challenges of the world economy. Thus, governments adopt "industrial policies," such as measures to enhance "competitiveness," measures (usually at the border) to offset foreign government

---

1. ©1986 by John H. Jackson. Adapted from a manuscript for a forthcoming book.

or private actions deemed potentially damaging, or reciprocal responses of various kinds.

In considering any of these responses, however, governments participating in the "Bretton Woods System" confront international as well as national sets of rules, procedures and principles that may narrowly constrain their options.

These problems lead policy leaders to search for "principles of management" which can provide the basic conceptual framework for taking action to overcome them. In searching for these principles, three basic goals of international economic relations in the world today must be considered. To a certain extent these goals conflict with each other, and this is what causes some of the difficulties which the world seems to be encountering. To develop actions and institutions which can manage international economic interdependence requires balancing these goals, in an attempt to maximize them and to reconcile them whenever possible.

These goals include:

First, there is the central goal to liberalize the barriers to transactions which cross national borders, in order to obtain the benefits which economics and personal anecdotal experience teaches us come from the theories of comparative advantage, economies of scale and enhanced competition.

Second, there is a goal to cause the least amount of interference to national sovereignties and national preferences. In order to obtain the advantages of the first goal, it has been found necessary to have some international discipline upon actions of governments and other national institutions in matters which affect international trade or other transborder economic transactions. But doing this, of course, infringes on the freedom of action of national governments and other national power centers. Governments are less free today than before to impose barriers on imports, even when those imports are harming various domestic constituencies. Governments are also less free today to determine independently their own fiscal or monetary policy, or even the structure of their tax laws applicable to broadcasting.

We have recognized that some national goals and aspirations are an essential part of individual national cultures or governmental systems. It is not obvious that national governments or national non-governmental institutions should always be required to relinquish their ability to influence events or institutions in a way that suits the national culture. This is an issue that could be called the true "international federalism issue" (in contrast to the question of imposing an overriding international government). It is the subtle question (often discussed within the United States) as to what level of government is best suited to make certain categories of decisions for its constituency. Consequently, in constructing international institutions designed to provided the legal and disciplinary framework for transborder economic transactions, policy-makers must recognize that complete centralization or internationalization of all aspects of economic life is not a desirable objective. How far to go is a perplexing question.

Third, and perhaps most important, is the goal of "maintaining the peace," or, to state this goal in the context of economic relations, the goal of minimizing economic conflict among nations. Economic conflict can very easily be caused by some of the problems of interdependence that have not been managed well. In the past it has been recognized that such economic conflict can contribute to or lead to severely damaging consequences for the world, including war. But even without the threat of such doomsday scenarios, an important objective of managing international economic interdependence is to minimize the kinds of rancor and friction that we sometimes see in current trade relations (such as between the United States, the EC and Japan). Minimization of such tensions should prevent trade or economic friction from getting out of hand, but it should also occur so as to minimize the risk of political reactions to international trade liberalizations, which could result in reactionary governmental actions which could greatly diminish the attainability of the first goal (trade liberalization).

What, then, are some of the possible "principles of management for interdependence?" Four such principles can be mentioned here but we make no claim that these exhaust the possibilities.

The Harmonization Principle

One approach to managing international economic interdependence is "harmonization." This is the process by which various countries try to develop some uniformity among themselves in their government and non-government economic structures, rules and practices. For example, the development of a uniform set of standards for automobile pollution devices would fall in this category. Those areas in the world which have proceeded far along the scale of economic integration, such as the United States or the EC, find it necessary to introduce a high degree of harmonization. Free flow of goods across borders leads almost inevitably to the necessity of free flow of other activities, such as laborers, investment, etc. This leads in turn to the need to coordinate, and probably ultimately to harmonize, such activities previously thought to be at the core of national sovereignty, such as tax laws, monetary and fiscal policies, accreditation of professions, patent laws, product liability laws and the flow of information.

Yet harmonization does the most injury to the second goal discussed above. At some point, to require different cultural groups, and different nations, to engage in a locked-step process of uniformity that is implied by ultimate harmonization, seems to defeat some of the very values of life (perhaps non-economic values) which are desired by citizens.

The Interface Principle

A slightly different concept for management of international economic interdependence is a principle which we have elsewhere labeled the "interface" principle. The terminology comes from those situations where you have two different systems and the desire to have those two systems work together in some way. It is often necessary, in such a circumstance, to have an "interface" mechanism or program, designed to provide the necessary communication between the two mechanisms, and to allow them to work together despite their mechanical or logical differences. Similarly, when two economies work together, such a mechanism is needed.

Reciprocity

The concept of reciprocity has been an enormously significant political motivating force during the last century of international trade policy. Yet the concept is very ambiguous. There are at least four different kinds of reciprocity in connection with international trade policy. Indeed, the concept of reciprocity is found in a number of different international relations endeavors, and may appeal to some sort of basic aspect of human nature.

Reciprocity No. 1: Conditional MFN—The idea of conditional MFN, as we saw in Chapter 7, was that when two countries bargained for favorable treatment as to trade, and came to an agreement based on what they deemed to be reciprocally equivalent concessions, those concessions would be granted to other nations in the world only when such other nations came forward with "payment" in the form of reciprocally equivalent concessions on their own part. This was deemed necessary to avoid the "third party free rider" problem. Nevertheless, the conditional MFN policy proved very cumbersome, and was abandoned by many countries prior to World War I.

Reciprocity No. 2: Unconditional MFN: The Traditional GATT Reciprocity—Under this principle, tariff reduction concessions are made universal through the unconditional MFN clause. That is, they are extended to all other countries to whom the MFN obligation is owed, by bilateral or multilateral agreement, regardless of whether those other countries reciprocated with equivalent concessions. (Again we refer to Chapter 7.) In circumstances where bilateral negotiations for such trade concessions prevailed, this unconditional MFN concept proved to be inhibiting for the advancement of further trade liberalization, because countries refused to go very far with tariff reductions, since they knew that there would be certain third party free riders also receiving the benefits. One of the purposes of making trade negotiations multilateral, as they were developed in the negotiations of 1946–1947 leading to the formulation of GATT, was to encourage deeper tariff cuts by multilateralizing the negotiating process.

Often, however, it is not clear how reciprocity should be measured, nor is it clear that reciprocity can be supported very strongly with economic policy arguments. Nevertheless, reciprocity remains a powerful political motivating force. Politicians find it easy to persuade constituents and parliaments that trade barriers should be reduced as a way to obtain equivalent reductions on the part of other countries. The "bargaining" notion has been very influential.

Reciprocity No. 3: Sector Harmonization—Although not always termed "reciprocity," this concept has an objective which can be characterized broadly as similar to ideas of reciprocity. This objective is to provide, at least as among major industrial nations, for equivalent competitive or commercial opportunities for products from each country to be introduced into the other participating countries, within an appropriate product sector. The basic idea appears to have sound economic principles behind it—that in a modern interdependent world, enterprises should be competing against other enterprises in the same product area, regardless of national boundaries. Thus, auto companies should compete against auto companies, and each enterprise should have approximately the same advantages and disadvantages for such competition, so that principles of competition and allocation of goods by market forces create the greatest amount of efficiency. The concept is very difficult to implement, however. Instead of measuring reciprocity from the point of view of previous barriers, it measures reciprocity with respect to the status of barriers after the results of the negotiation have been implemented. Therefore some countries are likely to be asked to give up more in the way of current concessions than other countries, and this is very hard to negotiate, unless certain cross-sectoral "swaps" are possible.

Reciprocity No. 4—In recent years, especially in the United States, there has been much talk about another "reciprocity" concept. Certain proposals for legislation speak about "commercial opportunities substantially equivalent to those afforded by the United States." There are a number of possible dimensions to this concept. First of all, it may go beyond merely governmental obstacles to trade, and include such things as economic structures (such as the distribution system, or consumer habits and preferences). Secondly, this concept is usually designed to address bilateral relationships, and that an overall multilateral "equivalent opportunity" is not what is contemplated. Thirdly, it is not clear how the equivalent opportunities would be related to the product sectors. In this dimension of the problem, equivalent opportunities could be measured at one end of the scale on a completely "global" basis, that is, all trade between two countries. On the other end of the scale, it might be addressed purely to a specific product (which seems absurd in economic terms). In between, it could be addressing appropriate "product sectors," defined as broadly as "agriculture" or "industrial," or subdivided into sectors such as "steel," "dairy," "automobiles," or even further subdivided. Finally, there is considerable difficulty as to how to measure equivalent opportunity. To tie this reciprocity concept merely to a trade deficit between two countries would seem highly inappropriate, and also could subject trade to a great deal of uncertainty since exchange rate shifts and other forces in international economics can cause a deficit to become a positive balance or to fluctuate, without regard to the status of particular trade obstacles in a sector. Likewise, why focus on a particular sector if in other sectors trade balances are positive?

Another way to examine this would be to confine attention to various governmental barriers or governmentally-induced barriers. Even in this case, it would be hard to measure "equivalent opportunity." It would probably require an attempt to reduce various nontariff barriers to a "tariff equivalent," but conceptually this is very difficult to do, as economists can testify. Another possibility is to compare trade penetration to that which occurs in other nations. But this may overlook important international economic factors that affect trade, including distance, relative isolation from certain markets, and comparative advantage of competing foreign domestic industry.

Exchange Rates

A final "managing principle" for world economic interdependence is the exchange rate system. At least where exchange rates are free to float and respond to market forces, economists argue that exchange rates will shift on the basis of various economic forces, including changes in the balances of trade between two countries, so that the new exchange rates will themselves affect the trade flow and adjust it. What is key, in this viewpoint, is the overall balance of payments of the country, not that particular portion of the balance of payments that is directed to trade. Furthermore, multilateral balance with the rest of the world, and not any particular bilateral balance, is the important fact. In a multilateral trading world, where Country A exports to Country B which exports to Country C, which in turn exports back to Country A, many countries may have bilateral imbalances, but all countries may at the same time have an overall multilateral balance in their total trade. Furthermore, some countries (such as the United States) export services to such an extent that the positive service balance partly makes up for the deficit on trade in goods. Finally, there are various investment flows, both short-term and long-term, that have impacts on this process. In theory, we are told, if the exchange rate is allowed to fluctuate reasonably freely, there is a self-correcting aspect of international trade and financial flows which should result over time in equilibrium between each nation and the rest of the world.

In practice, we know that there is reason to be concerned that this process is not working in a completely satisfactory manner. An important part of managing international economic interdependence, is to try to develop a better understanding of the workings of the exchange rate process and its impact on trade and transborder economic transactions. It should also be noted, that the question of trade barriers affects the operation of the exchange rate system. If important sectors of the economy are essentially insulated from foreign import competition, then the effect on trade of a change in the exchange rate will be considerably less than it perhaps should be for optimal efficiency of the exchange rate in redressing important disequilibrium in the world economic system. Thus we can see that the problems are enormous, and the available tools for dealing with them relatively restricted. In fact, responses to complicated problems in the context of government goals which are sometimes mutually competing or contradictory, almost always involve much compromise and a lack of "tidyness." It would be surprising if the subject of international economic relations were different. The various approaches mentioned above do not necessarily exhaust all possibilities. But whether that is so or not, it is most likely that whatever strategy is chosen for managing such relations will undoubtedly utilize not just one approach, but a shifting mix of all of the above. The post World War II period has been remarkably successful in preventing major catastrophes of world economic or political affairs, despite a number of institutional weaknesses which we have noted elsewhere in this book. Let us hope that the next 40 years (at least) will witness as much success.

Index

References are to Pages. See also Table of Cases, Table of Statutes, and Table of International Agreements.

†